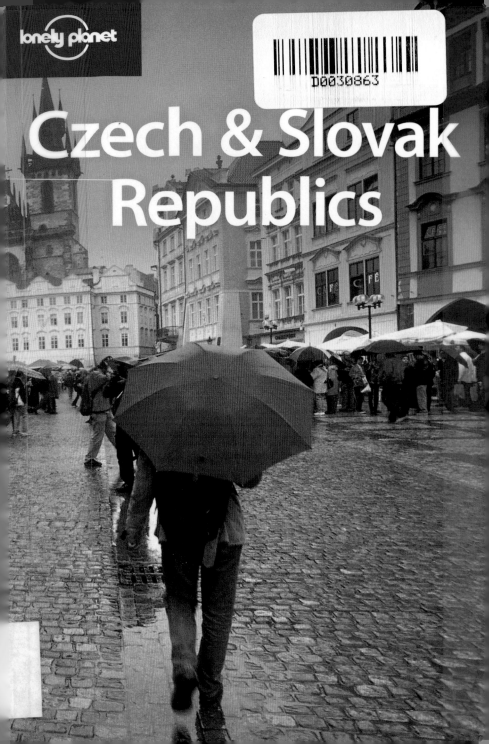

lonely planet

Czech & Slovak Republics

HOW TO USE THIS BOOK

Sleeping and Eating reviews are listed in budget order.
For d...

EXCHANGE RATES

Prices in this guide are quoted in Czech crowns (Koruna
česká; Kč) and Slovak crowns (Slovenská koruna; Sk)
unless otherwise stated.
1 Koruna česká (Kč) = 100 haléřů (h); 1 Slovenská koruna
(Sk) = 100 halierov (h)
For current exchange rates see www.xe.com.

		Czech Republic	Slovak Republic
	A$1	28Kč	38Sk
Euro zone	€1	28Kč	38Sk
Japan	¥100	16Kč	25Sk
New Zealand	NZ$1	14Kč	19Sk
UK	UK£1	42Kč	
USA	US$1		29Sk

PRICE RANGES

	Sleeping	Eating
Budget	<600Kč/1000Sk	<150Kč/Sk
Midrange	600Kč/1600Sk to 2000Kč/2700Sk	150-300Kč/Sk
Top end	>2000Kč/2700Sk	>300Kč/Sk

Prices in this book are for a double in high season and include
bathroom. Exceptions are noted in specific listings.

BUSINESS HOURS

Banks & post offices	8.30am-4.30pm Mon-Fri
	...m-10.30pm
	...m Mon-Fri, ...on or 1pm Sat
	...m Mon-Fri, ...Sat & Sun
	...stings.

... for the Czech Republic.

Bratislava area code	☎ 02
Czech Republic country code	☎ 420
Directory assistance	☎ 1181
International access code	☎ 00
Slovakia country code	☎ 421
Emergency	☎ 112

PHRASES

Czech terms appear first, followed by Slovak terms.

Hello.	*Ahoj/Dobrý deň.*
Goodbye.	*Na shledanou/Do videnia.*
Thank you.	*Děkuji/Ďakujem.*
Cheers!	*Na zdraví!/Na zdravie!*
I (don't) understand.	*(Ne)rozumím/(Ne)rozumiem.*
How much is it?	*Kolik to stojí?/Koľko to stojí?*

CONVERSIONS

1in = 2.54cm
1cm = 0.39in
1m = 3.3ft = 1.1yd
1ft = 0.3m
1km = 0.62 miles
1 mile = 1.6km

1kg = 2.2lb
1lb = 0.45kg
1g = 0.04oz
1oz = 28g

1 imperial gallon = 4.55L
1L = 0.26 US gallons
1 US gallon = 3.8L
1L = 0.22 imperial gallons

ISBN 978-1-74104-300-6

USA $22.99
UK £14.99

Published April 2007
5th Edition
First Published February 1995

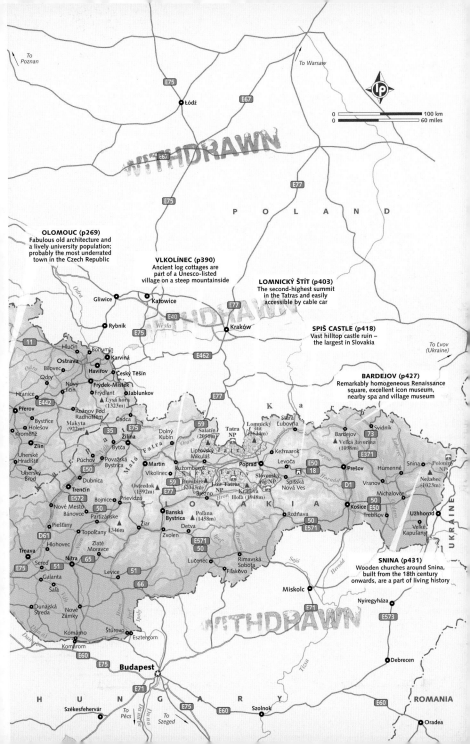

To Poznan

To Warsaw

E75

Łódź

E67

100 km
60 miles

WITHDRAWN

E67

E77

E75

P O L A N D

OLOMOUC (p269)
Fabulous old architecture and
a lively university population;
probably the most underrated
town in the Czech Republic

VLKOLÍNEC (p390)
Ancient log cottages are
part of a Unesco-listed
village on a steep mountainside

LOMNICKÝ ŠTÍT (p403)
The second-highest summit
in the Tatras and easily
accessible by cable car

WITHDRAWN

Odra

Gliwice

Katowice

E77

E40

Rybnik

E75

Wisła

Kraków

E462

SPIŠ CASTLE (p418)
Vast hilltop castle ruin –
the largest in Slovakia

To Lvov
(Ukraine)

11

Hlučín

Bohumín

Ostrava

Havířov

Karviná

Český Těšín

BARDEJOV (p427)
Remarkably homogeneous Renaissance
square, excellent icon museum,
nearby spa and village museum

Odra

Bílovec

Odry

Nový
Jičín

Frýdek-Místek

Jablunkov

E77

Hranice

E442

Frýdlant

Lysá hora
(1323m)

K

a

Přerov

Rožnov Pod
Radhoštěm

Stará
Ľubovňa

Svidník

Bystřice

Makyta
(922m)

Cadca

Dolný
Kubín

Salatín
(2050m)

59

Lomnický
štít
(2634m)

Bardejov

73

Holešov

35

Žilina

Tatra
NP

Velká Javorina
(1098m)

E371

Kroměříž

Zlín

Bytča

Orava

Liptovský
Mikuláš

Kežmarok

Snina

Polonin
NP

Uherské
Hradiště

Púchov

Považská
Bystrica

Martin

Ružomberok

Poprad

Levoča

E50

Prešov

Humenné

Uherský
Brod

Dubnica

Vlkolínec

59

Low Tatras NP

Slovenský
raj NP

18

Nežabec
(1023m)

E50

Trenčín

E572

Bojnice

Ostredok
(1592m)

E77

Ďumbier
(2043m)

Kráľova
hoľa

Spišská
Nová Ves

D1

Vranov

Nové Mesto
Bánovce

Prievidza

Brezno

Kráľova
Hoľa (1948m)

Michalovce

Partizánske

50

S L O V A K I A

Rožňava

Košice

E50

Užhorod

Piešťany

346m

Banská
Bystrica

Poľana
(1458m)

E571

Trebišov

Veľké
Kapušany

D61

Topoľčany

Žiar

Detva

Hlohovec

Zlaté
Moravce

Zvolen

E571

Trnava

Nitra

51

Sereď

51

Levice

Galanta

Šaľa

66

Lučenec

Rimavská
Sobota

Fiľakovo

Sajó

U K R A I N E

Hernád

SNINA (p431)
Wooden churches around Snina,
built from the 18th century
onwards, are a part of living history

E75

Dunajská
Streda

Nové
Zámky

Miskolc

Nyíregyháza

E573

Komárno

Danube

Šťúrovo

Esztergom

E71

Tisza

Komárom

E60

E75

Budapest

E71

Debrecen

H U N G A R Y

ROMANIA

Székesfehérvár

To Pécs

To Szeged

E75

E60

Szolnok

E60

Oradea

Destination
Czech & Slovak Republics

What comes to mind when you think of the Czech and Slovak Republics? If you envisage the mystical Gothic buildings of Prague's historic centre, you're not alone. The Czech capital justifiably attracts millions of visitors each year, but the republics have more to offer than that. In two compact countries you can climb eerie sandstone rock formations, hike alpine slopes, enjoy what some argue to be the world's best beer, soak in a hot-spring spa, watch swordplay by firelight at a medieval castle, and down a shot of *slivovitz* (plum brandy, aka firewater) with the locals.

By all means, explore Prague (did you know the city's cubist architecture is found nowhere else in the world?), but then go beyond. If it's beer you're after, most any town will do, but the kings are Plzeň (for Pilsner Urquell) and České Budějovice (for Budvar), both in Bohemia. Seeking natural beauty? The 2600m High Tatra mountain range in Slovakia is packed with incredible vistas and ultramarine lakes, and smaller ranges abound throughout the country. History-hunters should look into the hundreds of castles – from elaborate sgraffito palaces to stony medieval ruins – that dot the Czech and Slovak landscapes, some of the finest being in Central Bohemia.

Want to meet the locals? You can dance with the younger crowd at discos in Prague, Bratislava and Ostrava. Though generous and warm-spirited, people in the cities can be slightly reserved, so get out to the villages of Moravia and Central and East Slovakia to learn the true meaning of hospitality. The best time to visit is during the colourful summer festivals, replete with sausages, spirits and folk dancing, but no matter when or where you go, a little exploring beyond the capitals of the Czech and Slovak Republics will reap great rewards. Don't forget to drink a toast for us – *Nazdraví!*

GLENN BEANLAND

Towns & Villages

Grab a just reward for pounding the
cobblestones in Prague (p134)

JULIET COOMBE

LISA DUNFORD

Meet the residents of folksy
Vlkolínec (p390) in Central
Slovakia – all 35 of them

Page 4: Climb the multihued
round tower of Krumlov chateau
(p172) in South Bohemia

WITOLD SKRYPCZAK

Marvel at the Renaissance perfection of Telč (p313) in South Moravia

WITOLD SKRYPCZAK

Explore the fine balance between virtue and vice in the West Bohemian spa town of Mariánské Lázně (p206), with its 39 therapeutic springs and a robust array of good restaurants and cosy bars

Join the gawkers around the astronomical clock in Olomouc (p269), North Moravia

It's easy to see why Malá Strana (p93) in Prague is a sought-after film location

Castles & Peaks

Succumb to the fairy-tale good looks of Karlštejn castle (p148) in Central Bohemia

RICHARD NEBESKÝ

NEIL WILSON

Discover World Heritage–listed Spiš castle (p418), one of East Slovakia's true wonders

Teeter on the Slovak–Polish border in Tatra National Park, High Tatras (p394), Slovakia

MARK DAFFEY

Contents

Regional Map Contents

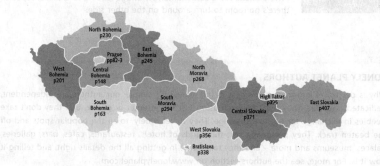

The Authors

LISA DUNFORD

A fascination with the Czech–Slovak region has gripped Lisa since childhood, probably because her grandfather came from the Carpathian mountains. She studied junior year in Budapest and arrived in Bratislava, Slovakia, after graduation. Various projects led to a job with the embassy at the US Agency for International Development. While living in Slovakia, Lisa danced with the country as it became an independent nation, learned the language and made lifelong friends. Lisa, her husband and their dog now live on a riverfront in southeast Texas, but assignments and personal travel take her back to Slovakia often. It still feels like going home.

My Favourite Trip

The first night in Bratislava I'd drink Frankovka modra red wine at a café with friends to stay up late and ward off jet lag. It never really works, so a few slow-paced days wandering the city's historical centre (p344) would follow. I'd then fly to Košice and drive to Tatranská Lomnica (p403) in the High Tatras. No, better yet, maybe this is the trip where I'll have time to rent a log cabin for a week outside Slovenský raj National Park (p420), where I can hike past waterfalls and go horseback riding. I'd time it so I could spend the last weekend at the European Folk Craft Market in Kežmarok (p414) or the Východná Folk Festival (p390) before flying back to Bratislava. Sorry, Prague – I'm a Slovakia kind of gal.

BRETT ATKINSON

Brett's first experiences of Eastern Europe were Bulgaria and Yugoslavia, when the Iron Curtain was still pulled tightly shut. He has since returned to write about Hungary's communist legacy, island-hopped in Croatia and honeymooned in Sarajevo. During eight weeks' research in the Czech Republic, he furthered his hobby of beer appreciation, especially while watching Friday night ice hockey at the local *pivnice* (pub). When he's not travelling for Lonely Planet, Brett lives in Auckland, New Zealand. He advises never to drive a Škoda Fabia across a narrow bridge leading to a castle, especially if there's no room to turn around on the other side.

LONELY PLANET AUTHORS

Why is our travel information the best in the world? It's simple: our authors are independent, dedicated travellers. They don't research using just the internet or phone, and they don't take freebies in exchange for positive coverage. They travel widely, to all the popular spots and off the beaten track. They personally visit thousands of hotels, restaurants, cafés, bars, galleries, palaces, museums and more – and they take pride in getting all the details right, and telling it how it is. For more, see the authors section on www.lonelyplanet.com.

NEIL WILSON

Neil first shuffled round a Czech castle wearing cotton overshoes and gripping an *anglický* (English) text, back in 1995, and soon became fascinated by the country's combination of deep history, weird scenery and off-the-wall humour. He has returned regularly for a fix of the world's finest beers and the opportunity to hike yet another obscure trail. A full-time freelance writer since 1988, Neil has travelled in five continents and written about 45 travel and walking guides for various publishers. In recent years he has been working on Lonely Planet guides to Prague, Eastern Europe and the Czech & Slovak Republics. He is based in Edinburgh, Scotland.

Getting Started

In many ways the Czech and Slovak Republics are a traveller's dream destination: the distances aren't immense, and both natural and manmade beauty abounds. The streets of Prague and the trails of the High Tatras are well trod. And it doesn't take too long to get off the beaten path and find a medieval gem in the form of an old town, or a deserted hiking path.

Though lodging prices are rising, you can still plan an itinerary to suit any budget – from student dorm with sandwiches to go, to top end with trendy dining.

You may want to plan and book ahead if: (1) you're going to the mountains in peak winter/summer seasons; (2) you want to rent a holiday *chata* (mountain hut or cabin) or apartment; (3) you're visiting Prague from June to August; or (4) you're flying between towns. In the smallest, most easterly village, tourism drops way off during low season; small guesthouse owners may not be on site full time, so booking ahead means you can set a time to meet. Otherwise, a few nights mulling over what you'd like to see (and the transport required to get there) will make your travels more fluid by the time you hit the road.

Note: in this book where you see two italicised words separated by a slash (/), this indicates the Czech and Slovak terms, respectively.

WHEN TO GO

For the majority of Czech and Slovak destinations, the best time to visit is in May or September, when the weather is mild and the crowds fewer. A large percentage of museums, galleries, castles and the like are open only during high season (May to September). April and October are chillier but you'll benefit from smaller crowds and cheaper rooms. In winter you'll likely get to see it all under a blanket of snow; camping grounds are closed, as are attractions in the smaller towns. High in the mountains, November to March is an additional high season.

Most Czechs and Slovaks, like residents of the rest of Europe, take their holidays in July and August, then again over the Easter and Christmas/New Year holiday periods. Accommodation facilities are often booked; crowds, particularly in Prague and the mountain resort areas, can be unbearable; and prices spike to their highest. On the other hand, most festivals take place during the summer months and the supply of cheap sleeps in university towns increases as student dorms are thrown open to visitors.

The seasons are distinct. Summer (June to August) receives the highest temperatures and heaviest rainfall. The cold, bitter winter months of December, January and February often see temperatures reaching as low as -5°C in the cities and -10°C to -15°C in the mountainous areas (-30°C at higher altitudes). Tailor-made for skiing and other winter pursuits, the mountains receive about 130 days of snow a year, but other areas get coverage as well.

See Climate Charts (p439) for average temperatures and precipitation.

DON'T LEAVE HOME WITHOUT...

- Health insurance – it's technically required for all visitors (p465)
- Insect repellent – for hiking and camping (p467)
- A little language – knowing a few key phrases goes a long way (p469)
- Thirst – there's really great Czech beer (p68) and Slovak wine (p68) to be had

TOP TENS

Must-See Films
For more information see p44.

- *Štěstí* (Something Like Happiness, 2005) directed by Bohdon Sláma
- *Kolya* (1996) directed by Jan Svěrák
- *Vesničko má středisková* (My Sweet Little Village, 1985) directed by Jiří Menzel
- *Sedím na konári a je mi dobre* (I'm Sitting on a Branch and I'm Fine, 1989) directed by Juraj Jakubisko
- *Smrt si říká Engelchen* (Death Calls Itself Engelchen, 1963) directed by Ján Kádár
- *Žert* (The Joke, 1970) directed by Jaromil Jireš
- *Všetko, čo mám rád* (Everything I Like, 1992) directed by Martin Sulík
- *Obchod na korze* (The Shop on Main Street, 1965) directed by Ján Kadár & Elmar Klos
- *Swimming Pool* (2001) directed by Boris von Sychowski
- *Markéta Lazarová* (1967) directed by František Vláčil

Top Reads
Immersing yourself in a good novel is the perfect way to get a sense of people and place. The following translated page-turners have won critical acclaim in the Czech and Slovak Republics and abroad. For more information see p47.

- *The Book of Laughter & Forgetting* by Milan Kundera
- *Metamorphosis* by Franz Kafka
- *Closely Watched Trains* by Bohumil Hrabal
- *Babička* by Božena Němcová
- *The Amazing Adventures of Kavalier & Clay* by Michael Chabon
- *The Unbearable Lightness of Being* by Milan Kundera
- *Year of the Frog* by Martin Šimečka
- *Bringing up Girls in Bohemia* by Michal Viewegh
- *Summer Meditations* by Václav Havel
- *Utz* by Bruce Chatwin

Our Favourite Festivals
The following list represents our Top 10, but numerous other festivals and events take place year-round. For those on an international scale see p443. Individual town celebrations are covered throughout the book in the relevant destination chapters.

- Prague Spring (Prague), May (p122)
- International Festival of Spirits and Ghosts (Bojnice), May (p380)
- Ride of the Kings Festival (Vlčnov), May (p328)
- International Folk Festival (Strážnice), June (p326)
- Východná Folk Festival (Východná), June/July (p390)
- Open-Air Cinema Festival (Prague), June to September (p122)
- Karlovy Vary Film Festival (Karlovy Vary), July (p215)
- European Folk Craft Market (Kežmarok), July (p414)
- Salamander Festival (Banská Štiavnica), September (p375)
- Bratislava Jazz Days (Bratislava), September (p347)

Spring (late March to May) brings changeable, rainy weather and sometimes flooding. Autumn is also variable but temperatures can be as high as 20°C in September.

COSTS & MONEY

By European standards, the Czech and Slovak Republics are fairly reasonable. Food, transport and sights are still a bargain; accommodation less so. Consumables like cosmetics remain relatively inexpensive, but clothing, CDs and electronics are on a par with European prices. A surprise cost in both countries is having to fork out as much as 100Kč/Sk to take a camera or video into museums, castles and caves.

How much you spend will depend on how you travel. If you're a budget backpacker who likes to stretch your koruna as far as it will go, 800Kč/Sk will get you from one place to another, a bed in a dorm, entry to a museum or castle, two cheap meals a day and three or four beers a night. Those who like a little more comfort can expect to pay around 2300Kč/Sk per day for a *pension* or hotel, train trip between cities, lunch and dinner at a decent restaurant (including coffee and/or wine) and entry to a couple of big-ticket attractions. If money is no object, 6000Kč/Sk is sufficient to cover all your needs, including a night in a top hotel and car hire for the day. Prague, however, is another story: whack on another third to the prices mentioned.

INTERNET RESOURCES

Bratislava Guide (www.bratislavaguide.com) Loads of in-town listings.
Czech Republic (www.czech.cz) Informative official site with all the practicalities.
Czech Tourism (www.czechtourism.com) Get to know the Czech Republic.
Lonely Planet (www.lonelyplanet.com) Supposedly a fantastic site for travellers, but we're a bit dubious.
Prague TV (www.prague.tv) Insider's perspective on the city.
Slovak Tourist Board (www.slovakiatourism.sk) Good theme-related pages (hiking, spas, caves, castles).
Slovakia Document Store (www.panorama.sk) Buy books, travel info and maps of Slovakia before you leave home.

HOW MUCH?

Night in a dorm
350Kč/300Sk

Average double room in a
pension 1500Kč/Sk

Pork and potatoes
130Kč/Sk

Shot of *slivovitz* (plum
brandy) 35Kč/45Sk

Postcard 9Kč/6Sk

**LONELY PLANET
INDEX**

1L petrol 40Kč/44Sk

1L bottled water
30Kč/40Sk

Beer – glass of Budvar
draught 30Kč/35Sk

Souvenir T-shirt
300Kč/250Sk

Street snack – ice cream
8Kč/6Sk

Itineraries
CLASSIC ROUTES

PRAGUE TO SOUTH BOHEMIA
10 days

Take your time in **Prague** (p79); get up early to see Charles bridge without the mobs, buy an architectural walking map and follow the architectural style of your choice, and by all means make enough time to stop in as many summer beer gardens as suit you. Three nights is the minimum, but spend five so you can go on day trips. In **Kutná Hora** (p156), for example, you can see the soaring cathedral of St Barbara and the creepy art (made out of 40,000 skeletons) at Sedlec ossuary. The next morning decide between the photogenic clusters of turrets at **Karlštejn castle** (p148) or the medieval-cum-neo-Gothic **Konopiště chateau** (p152), a grand hunting lodge of sorts. Or you might opt to do a day trip to the evocative, heart-rending **Terezín** (p231), a transit camp for European Jews during the Holocaust that is known for the art made by its youth.

On day six, take the train to **Plzeň** (p219) for the night; there you can tour the brewery where Pilsner Urquell is made and visit the brewery museum. From there, you might as well make this a beer-flavoured tour and stop for one night in **České Budějovice** (p164), the home of the Budvar brewery. The next day, it's an easy 50-minute ride to the Unesco-recognised beauty of **Český Krumlov** (p170). Spend one day wandering around in awe of the Renaissance and baroque buildings, and a second taking a float down the Vltava river before heading back up to Prague.

This 10-day, 600km route radiates from Prague before following the beer trail from Plzeň to South Bohemia.

ALL OF CZECHIA
Three to four weeks

Start by following the 10-day itinerary from Prague to South Bohemia (p17), adding a couple of days if you want to do all the day trips from Prague, or if you want to add a trip to a West Bohemian spa town like **Karlovy Vary** (p211) or **Mariánské Lázně** (p206) before Plzeň.

> This 1040km, one-month route circumnavigates the Czech Republic, from Prague to the spa towns of West Bohemia, then south and east to the gentle hills of South Moravia, then north to Bohemia's rock towns.

From Český Krumlov, transfer in České Budějovice to **Telč** (p313), where you can relive the Renaissance. Stroll over the narrow bridges spanning ancient fish ponds and tour the ornate chateau before settling into a sidewalk café for the evening. Move on to **Brno** (p295), the country's second city, for a night before heading to **Mikulov** (p321), another baroque and Renaissance beauty with an ancient synagogue. Here you're in the heart of South Moravian wine country. Do stop at a local winery, or rent a bicycle and spend a couple of days exploring a few wineries in the surrounding hills.

Afterwards, move on to **Olomouc** (p269), which has a great old town and a large student population that makes the eating and drinking fun. This is one of the best value towns in the Czech Republic, so spend a night or two. Then peek at the Renaissance façades of **Pardubice** (p249) and, overnight, among the architectural mix that is **Hradec Králové** (p245) before going to see one of the rock towns. Choose from the sandstone shapes and spires in the **Adršpach-Teplice Rocks** (p260), probably the most dramatic, or those in **Český ráj** (p255), which are slightly easier to access. After you're done hiking (or rock climbing), it's back to the capital and your transport home – if you can bear to leave.

SLOVAK & CZECH REPUBLICS   One month

Two days can easily be spent on the old-town streets of **Bratislava** (p337), stopping in cafés and taking time to seek out the views from atop the old castle or the communist-era New bridge. Then take a day trip to **Devín castle** (p353), where among the restoration and the ruins you can trace the development of Slovakia's medieval fortifications. The castle in **Trenčín** (p363), where you're off to next, is a lot more complete, romantic, embellished – you pick the adjective. Make sure you track down the chocolate shop while in town a night or two. **Žilina** (p376), a university town with reasonable restaurants, isn't anything special, but you have to transfer here to get to the **Malá Fatra National Park** (p380), which is. Spend a couple of days hiking the mountain tops, aided by an excellent system of trails and chairlifts.

Continue on to the **High Tatras** (p394) for higher altitude hiking and splendid vistas of rocky mountain peaks. Spend at least two nights, maybe three, or if you prefer steep trails and waterfalls to mountain peaks, head south to **Slovenský raj** (p420) to hike. Then from gateway city **Poprad** (p398), take an overnight train to **Prague** (p79); three days is enough to see the sights and get sick of the crowds. Afterwards head for one of the spa towns, **Karlovy Vary** (p211) or **Mariánské Lázně** (p206), for a night's rest, and **Plzeň** (p219) for some golden elixir (ie beer).

From there, it's on to **České Budějovice** (p164), the home of the Budvar brewery, and the Unesco-recognised beauty of **Český Krumlov** (p170) for two days before heading to Renaissance **Telč** (p313). It's up to you whether you head back to Bratislava or Prague from there.

Take in the highlights of the Slovak and Czech Republics; from Bratislava to the High Tatras, then Prague to South Bohemia, you'll cover about 1550km if you make it a round trip.

ROADS LESS TRAVELLED

LESSER KNOWN SLOVAKIA   Two weeks

The obvious starting point is **Bratislava** (p337); spend a couple of days wandering the old town and sampling the restaurants and bars. Then get off the beaten track by taking a day trip to the **Small Carpathians** (p356), where you can tour Červený Kameň, a 16th-century fortress and falconry yard, or taste wine and buy ceramics in Modra. The next day take the bus to **Banská Štiavnica** (p374), a steep little town that looks much like it did in the 15th century when it was a mining centre. It's a pleasant place to spend a night. Transfer to **Banská Bystrica** (p371), a bigger city, where you can learn about Slovakia's involvement in World War I and II at the nation's most high-tech museum.

Ride the twisted hillside roads to get to the **Low Tatras** (p388) and spend a day or two hiking in Demänova valley, or hook up with a paragliding outfitter in **Liptovský Mikuláš** (p389). Don't pass up the opportunity to eat in a *salaš* (rustic restaurant specialising in sheep's cheese).

Next it's on to the walled city of **Levoča** (p416), where the Church of St James is treasured for Master Pavol's Gothic altar. The ruins of **Spiš castle** (p418), about 15km east, deserve a day, too. Last stop is **Bardejov** (p427), a Gothic-Renaissance marvel. Tour the icon museum before going to nearby spa town **Bardejovské Kúpele** (p429), where you can sign up for a treatment and tour the *skanzen* (open-air museum) to get a feel for village life. Make your way down to **Košice** (p408) and from there you can get a bus, train or plane back to Bratislava.

Going from Bratislava to middle Slovakia, up to the Low Tatra mountains, through the Spiš region and down to Košice will take you about two weeks and cover 700km.

TAILORED TRIPS

WORLD HERITAGE SITES

The historic centre of **Prague** (p79) must be on everyone's list, but Unesco has also recognised the historic centres of **Český Krumlov** (p170) and **Telč** (p313). **Kutná Hora** (p156) is noted for the Gothic cathedral of St Barbara and the creepy bone art at **Sedlec**. In **Brno**, contemporary Villa Tugendhat (p302) was one of the first open-plan homes ever, and the church of St John of Nepomuk (p313) in **Žďár nad Sázavou** was constructed in a star shape. Also in Moravia, Holy Trinity column (p271) in **Olomouc** is a baroque medley of gold and grey.

Several Czech castles have made the list: the baroque chateau at **Kroměříž** (p332), the Renaissance castle at **Litomyšl** (p254) and the **Lednice-Valtice Cultural Landscape** (p323), a compendium of castles and grounds. **Holašovice** (p169) is a fine example of a baroque village, and the Jewish quarter and St Procopius' basilica in **Třebíč** (p316) remind us of the coexistence of Jewish and Christian cultures in the Middle Ages.

In Slovakia, the mountainside village of **Vlkolínec** (p390) is on the World Heritage List for the age and homogeneity of its log dwellings; the mining town of **Banská Štiavnica** (p374) for its uniform Renaissance architecture. The sprawling ruins of **Spiš castle** (p418) epitomise a medieval castle, and **Bardejov** (p427) is a supreme example of a fortified medieval town. The **caves of Slovak Karst** (p424) are recognised by Unesco, along with the adjacent Aggletek Karst in Hungary.

CLASSIC CASTLES

Prague castle (p87) is in the record books as the world's largest ancient castle, but it's more like a city than a fortified dwelling. Close by, **Karlštejn castle** (p148), with its stunning exteriors (and immense crowds), and **Konopiště chateau** (p152) are stand-alone wonders. The nature around **Křivoklát castle** (p151), which once belonged to the Přemysl Dynasty, is part of the attraction.

On the romantic side: lovely **Rožmberk castle** (p181) is said to be haunted by a pining White Lady; the intricate sgraffito design of **Litomyšl chateau** (p254) may be too prissy for some.

In Slovakia, **Bojnice castle** (p379) is by far the most ornate and Disneyesque (it hosts the fabulous Festival of Spirits and Ghosts for a week in May), but **Orava castle** (p386) comes a close second. Both are fairly complete, as is **Trenčín castle** (p363). Less perfect, and more evocative in some ways, are the partial ruins of **Ľubovňa castle** (p415) and **Devín castle** (p353). **Spiš castle** (p418) is the granddaddy of them all, spreading across four hectares. The view from below is one of the most photographed in Slovakia.

Castles are generally open from May to September; to see the interior you'll probably have to take a native-language tour, so ask for the written English narrative (*anglický* text).

FOLK LIFE & ART

The colourful local folk culture has been preserved in Moravia and central and East Slovakia. The best place to see it is at a *skansen/skanzen*, an open-air museum where folk-furnished regional buildings have been collected for you to tour. The best ones even have an operating pub – a village staple. Costumed dancers and musicians perform at summer weekend programmes at the museums.

The **Moravské Slovácko region** (p325) is filled with villages that still have a strong folk flavour; Strážnice (p326), for example, has a *skansen* and hosts the country's biggest folk festival. In North Moravia, walk among beehives carved with faces straight to the *hospoda* (pub) at the **Wallachian open-air museum** (p289).

In central Slovakia, a few villages stand out as living examples of folk vernacular. The dark log cabins with white geometric designs in **Čičmany** (p379) are highly photogenic (one is a museum). Up in the mountains, the log houses in Unesco-listed **Vlkolínec** (p390) are mostly plastered, some painted in pastels.

Slovakia has several open-air museums, including the **Museum of the Slovak Village** (p384) in Martin, the country's largest. The dark log homes of **Orava Village Museum** (p387) are arranged along a creek, true to the layout of a proper mountain village. Thousands of people gather in late June at the *skanzen* of the **Museum of Ukrainian-Rusyn culture** (p433) in Svidník for the annual folk festival.

SPA LIFE

Once considered purely medicinal, spas in the Czech and Slovak Republics these days are focusing more on relaxation treatments that might interest a short-stay traveller.

Františkovy Lázně (p201) is the prototypical quiet, leafy spa town, where after you soak, you stroll. There's a bit more life to **Mariánské Lázně** (p206), West Bohemia's prettiest spa town, which has all the requisite treatments and drinking cures plus sights and history. **Karlovy Vary** (p211) is bigger still and attracts a larger number of international visitors. If you ignore the communist development, you can still see the 19th-century spa complex at the heart of **Teplice** (p236). Less frequented and lower key is the spa at **Luhačovice** (p331) in Moravia.

Piešťany (p360) is Slovakia's biggest spa town, a complex of neoclassical and modern communist buildings that contain pools, baths and treatment rooms for its signature mud wraps. **Bardejovské Kúpele** (p429) is a spa town with some romantic old villas set in a forest. The drinking cure is big there. For your soaking pleasure there are several outdoor and indoor pools at **Bešeňová Thermal Park** (p390), and the pools at Aphrodite in **Rajecké Teplice** (p378) look like surreal Roman baths. Though water parks at heart, **Aqua Park Tatralandia** (p389), in the Low Tatras, and **Aqua City** (p399) in Poprad do use natural thermal springs and both have spa and sauna zones.

Snapshot

Parliamentary elections in June 2006 brought changes to the leadership of both the Czech and Slovak Republics. The left-of-centre parties won a few seats more than the right-of-centre ones in the Czech Republic, but when the Green party went with the more conservative coalition (so as not to be lumped with the communist party), the process was thrown into a stalemate. Months went by without an agreement or a prime minister until September 2006 when Mirek Topolánek of the Civic Democrats (ODS) assumed leadership. He stepped down one month later when his party failed to garner the necessary vote of confidence in the lower house. Negotiations began again, the power vacuum continued and many called for a new general election. At the time of writing, the government was undecided.

In Slovakia, elections brought to power parties that have at times been antireform. The coalition is headed by Prime Minister Robert Fico of Smer, a left-wing party, but also includes Vladimir Mečiar's isolationist Movement for a Democratic Slovakia (HZDS); see p31. It's feared the nationalist tendencies of the coalition could stunt economic growth if it repeals the business deals and market reforms started by PM Mikuláš Dzurinda's previous government. Indeed, Fico used a technicality to nix the already agreed-to sale of Bratislava's airport to a consortium that included the owners of the Vienna airport. It's now unclear who will pay for needed airport upgrades. Despite contradictory statements early on, however, Fico promised to keep Slovakia on fiscal track to adopt the euro by 2009.

Though both the Czech and Slovak Republics joined the European Union (EU) in 2004, the subject of the euro still remains a hot topic. The ramifications are endless. Every new thought on monetary issues is now scrutinised in light of whether it will adversely affect the republics' readiness to adopt the euro. Currently the Slovaks are aiming for 2009, and the Czechs 2010, but that's likely to change.

Visas are another EU-related issue that comes up a lot. Though the immigration policies of both states were good enough to qualify them for EU membership, they weren't in line enough for membership of the Schengen agreement, which allows member states to eliminate internal EU borders. For the time being, you still have to go through (now somewhat nominal) checkpoints to get into the bordering countries of Austria, Germany, Hungary and Poland. The Czech and Slovak Republics have been hoping for Schengen inclusion by the original October 2007 target, but at the time of writing that deadline had been pushed back at least a year by the European Commission. In the meantime, for those that need them, a visa for the Czech and Slovak Republics is not good in other EU states, and vice versa. For more information see p450.

While EU inclusion is, for the most part, seen as a step towards higher living standards and a brighter future for subsequent generations, especially by the younger generation, many are still sceptical. They see bitter irony in the fact that they paid for border crossings to be erected between the republics in 1993, only to be negotiating to tear them down a little more than 10 years later. There are also concerns about the possibility of EU nationals taking advantage of comparatively low land prices and buying up prime real estate.

So far most financial indicators suggest positive change. Foreign investment has been pouring in, with auto manufacturers investing in both countries. GDP (gross domestic product) growth is up since EU induction and

FAST FACTS

Population Czech Republic/Slovakia: 10,249,034/5,384,822

GDP growth: 5%/5.5%

Inflation: 2.8%/3.3%

Unemployment: 8.3%/18.2%

Average monthly wage: 18,903Kč/17,274Sk

Area: 78,869 sq km/49,034 sq km

Total combined railway system: 13,130km

Per capita annual beer consumption: 157L/89L

there's been no massive wave of private land sales. In general, families are doing OK, if not great. Most city dwellers have at least one car, and eating out every once in a while is a possibility. In the villages, both cars and restaurants are usually beyond reach. Prices for everyday items like food and dry goods have risen since 2004, while wages have only crept forward. The fear is that once the republics adopt the euro, the cost of consumables will rise even higher. This may explain the large number of communist officials elected in 2006 – it's not unusual to hear the older generation waxing nostalgic about the days when everyone had a state-subsidised job.

The discrimination against minorities, primarily the Roma people, which caused major headaches in the lead-up to EU entry hasn't died down much. A recent sensational court case garnering international attention suggested that in the 1990s doctors in East Slovakia may have performed sterilisation treatments on Roma women without adequately informing them. Today, the governments and Non-Governmental Organisations (NGOs) are funnelling money into support programmes to promote Roma language, culture, education, housing and social welfare, and recent human rights reports have sighted progress. But advocates say more can be done. In one suburb of the East Slovak town Prešov, 1700 people live in just 174 public-funded apartments. (For more on the Roma minority see p35.)

Outside the Czech and Slovak borders, EU nations expressed concerns that Roma immigrants would flood into cities like London. (And it would be fair to say some Czechs and Slovaks hoped large numbers of the Roma would emigrate.) Though some families set off, reports are that many have already returned to their home towns and villages. The final results of this (and other EU-related issues) are yet to be seen. Time will tell if the Czechs and Slovaks adopt the euro by 2010, and if the people end up viewing it as a positive or negative.

History

Did you know the Czech and the Slovak Republics were united under one flag for a grand total of about 88 years in all their history? That the Great Moravian Empire initially didn't include Prague? That Bratislava was officially called Pressburg (German) or Pozony (Hungarian) until 1919? Despite the disparate histories of the Czech, Moravian, Slovak and Ruthenian (more about that to come) people, they did share a united government for a time; they all have a common Slavic language base, and they all have a history of foreign domination.

Slap-bang in the middle of Europe, the current territory of the Czech Republic was controlled by the Holy Roman Empire, invaded by the Hapsburgs – then the Nazis, then the Soviets – and finally conquered by tour groups; a few Czechs even see the republic's membership of the EU as just another occupation. The territory of Slovakia came under the rule of the Magyars (you and I know them as Hungarians) for more than 1000 years, before being subsumed into a Czechoslovakia that was far from a 50–50 partnership. Oh, and there were all those years of communist rule…

WAY BACK WHEN

Celtic tribes settled in these parts in the 5th century BC. They didn't stay long, but they did leave a few artefacts behind, as well as the name Bohemia. The Latin term for the Czech Lands, Boiohaemum, comes from the name of a Celtic tribe; at least that's what Roman reports said. The Roman Empire didn't actually push into the Moravian, let alone the Czech Lands. The furthest north the Romans had an established garrison was at Trenčín in West Slovakia, where you can still see some of their graffiti (p364).

Slav tribes started migrating into the area during the late 5th and early 6th centuries AD; they were the first agriculturists on the scene. By 833 the initial territory of Veľká Moravia (Great Moravian Empire) included Moravia and a good chunk of Slovakia. Though short-lived, the Veľká Moravia was an extremely influential enterprise; it served as the historical precedent used to justify the creation of Czechoslovakia after WWI, and had an impact on all of Eastern Christianity (which would become the Orthodox Church).

Moravian Prince Rastislav (846–870) invited missionaries to visit the empire and was most taken with Christians (and later saints) Cyril and Metoděj (Methodius). Cyril and Metoděj showed up in the 860s and created the first Slavic translation of biblical text (in Old Church Slavonic, still used in some churches to date). To do so, they had to invent the Glagolitic alphabet, which was the precursor to the Cyrillic alphabet of today. Czechs and Slovaks are rightly proud of the saints, whose names you'll see on churches, streets and statues across both republics.

By 894 Veľká Moravia had grown to include Prague and Bohemia, Silesia and parts of modern-day Hungary; however, fighting over succession weakened the empire and Moravian troops lost to the Magyars in 907. Slovakia gradually came under the complete control of the Hungarians. Prior to this, up north, members of the first Czech dynasty, the Přemysls, threw up a couple of huts on a hill in what was to become Prague around 870 and

The *Historical Atlas of Central Europe*, by Paul Robert Magocsi, illustrates the complicated comings and goings of the region's conquerors.

833	907
Veľká Moravia (the Great Moravian Empire) takes shape	The break-up of the Great Moravian Empire; beginning of Hungarian rule in Slovakia

WHAT'S IN A NAME?

Which is correct, the Czech Republic or Czechia? Slovakia or the Slovak Republic? Most English-speakers still call the Czech Republic by that name, but some, particularly in Europe, use Czechia. There is no precedent for the use of Czechia in English, and this book doesn't use it. Surprisingly, not even in Czech is there a single word that describes the joint Czech and Moravian lands.

The situation in Slovakia is, thankfully, easier. Both Slovak Republic (Slovenská republika) and Slovakia (Slovensko) are used interchangeably in the country and abroad – although the former is a little more official – and we've done the same.

called it Pražský hrad. After the collapse of Moravian rule, the Bohemian rulers annexed Moravia.

And then came the conquerors: German King Otto I took control of Bohemia and Moravia and made them part of the Holy Roman Empire in 950. The Přemysls – including Václav, or Good 'King' Wenceslas – ruled on behalf of the Germans until 1212. The Přemysl family dynasty ruled Czech lands on behalf of the Germans for several subsequent centuries. Perhaps the most famous member of the clan was Saint Wenceslas, aka the Good 'King' (really a duke). In 1306 the last of the Přemysl line died heirless.

After a bit of manoeuvring, the royal family of Luxembourg stepped in to rule. Theirs was the line that produced Holy Roman Emperor Karel (Charles) IV (r 1316–78), who made Prague the centre of the Holy Roman Empire. He did a nice renovation job on the city, too: all that Gothic splendour you see can be attributed to him. Karel's son, the mercurial Václav IV, gave Bohemia its patron saint when he tortured Jan of Nepomuk to death over a bureaucratic dispute with Jan's boss, the archbishop.

Under Hungarian rule, Slovakia prospered for a time. In the 13th century, mining (silver, copper and gold) centres such as Banská Štiavnica were booming; in fact, the look of that town today dates to this period. Saxon German craftsmen also settled in East Slovakia during the 13th century, creating a unique Germano-Slovak style and a lot of great art in what came to be known as the Spiš region.

THOSE HUSSITES

A century before Martin Luther nailed his demands to a church door, the Czechs were agitating for church reform. Jan Hus (1372–1415), a fan of English theologian John Wycliffe, led a movement that espoused – among other things – giving services in Czech rather than Latin, letting the congregation taste the sacramental wine as well as the host (the Hussites' symbol was the chalice), and ending the selling of indulgences (really church wealth in general). When he was burned for heresy in 1415, Hus' martyrdom sparked a religious, nationalist and class-based rebellion in Bohemia. It'd be hard to overestimate the influence Jan Hus has had on the Czech nationalist spirit up to the present day.

After Hus' death, his followers moved swiftly from rhetoric to warfare: on 30 July 1419, Hussite preacher Želivský delivered a blood-stirring sermon at St Mary of the Snows in Prague, then led the congregation to the New Town Hall to confront the Catholic burghers. Militant Hussite Jan Žižka led a charge up the stairs and seven councillors were thrown out the windows

General Jan Žižka continued to successfully command the Hussite armies for years after he'd been blinded in battle.

1415	1419
Czech church reformer Jan Hus burned at the stake	Catholic councillors are thrown from the New Town Hall window by Hussites intent on taking Prague

onto the spears of the mob below. After four months of church burning and street battles, the Hussites held Prague and Holy Roman Emperor Sigismund had retreated to Moravia.

The pope told Sigismund to take Prague back, but the Catholic attack in 1420 was defeated by the forces of ferocious, farm-implement-wielding commander Žižka. Vitkov Hill, where the battle took place, is now called Žižkov Hill and is topped by a massive equestrian statue of the general; see p116. The Hussites also managed to make inroads into West Slovakia, until their defeat at the Battle of Lipany in 1434. Hussite influence in general did not disappear (there are still churches) but, for the most part, the real power in Bohemia came to lie with the Protestant Utraquist nobles, the so-called Bohemian Estates.

AUSTRIANS, HUNGARIANS RULE

In 1526, Hungary suffered a major defeat by Ottoman Turks at Mohács in West Hungary. The capital of the Kingdom of Hungary was relocated from Budapest to Bratislava, Slovakia, in 1536 and Budapest fell under Turkish control for 150 years.

The Austrian Hapsburgs, already Holy Roman emperors and rulers of the Czech Lands, thereby added the Hungarian crown to their list of titles. Though the Hapsburgs defeated the Turks in 1683 (practically at the gates of Vienna), St Martin's Cathedral in Bratislava would be the coronation place of Hungarian kings and queens until 1830.

The brief, failed Hungarian War of Independence (1703–11) against the Hapsburgs was lead by Transylvanian prince Ferenc Rákóczi II, headquartered in Košice, Slovakia.

It wasn't until the second half of the 18th century that Empress Maria Theresa and Emperor Joseph II made life easier for Slovaks through educational and labour reforms, including basic schooling for all children. (They also commissioned a lot of the fancy buildings you see in Bratislava's old town.)

For the Czechs the year 1526 was also important; it was when the Czech kingdom came under the control of the Catholic Austrian Hapsburgs. In the latter half of the century, Prague became the seat of their empire, which lifted the country's fortunes.

On 23 May 1618, the Bohemian Estates, angry that the Hapsburgs had failed to deliver on promised religious tolerance, threw two Hapsburg government agents from a Prague Castle window (see the boxed text, p28). The squabble escalated into the Catholic–Protestant Thirty Years' War, which was to devastate much of Central Europe and shatter Bohemia's economy.

The Czechs lost their rights and property, and almost their national identity, through forced Catholicisation and Germanisation. Saxons occupied Prague and much of Bohemia in 1631 and 1632; Swedes also seized large parts of the kingdom. By 1648 the population of the Czech Lands had been reduced by up to 40% in many areas.

The Hapsburgs eventually moved their throne back to Vienna, and with the passing of time, the Hapsburg line softened; serfdom was abolished between 1781 and 1785, and religious freedom was allowed. By the 19th century, educational reforms by Empress Maria Theresa meant that even the poor had access to schooling; a vocal middle class was emerging.

A History of Slovakia: The Struggle for Survival by Stanislav Kirshbaum, updated in 2005, is one of the most comprehensive works on Slovak History.

1536	1781–85
Royalty moves Hungarian capital to Bratislava, Slovakia, after Turks threaten Budapest.	Serfdom abolished in the Czech Lands

DEFENESTRATION

Defenestration (the act of throwing someone out of a window) is an extreme form of political dissent, but it's a method that's been used more than once in Prague. In addition to the unlucky Catholics whom the Hussites tossed out the window in 1419, there was a second rebellious window event in 1618. This time it was when Hapsburg-backed Catholic clergy tried to reclaim land under Imperial order; members of the Czech Estates argued that it was not church land and convicted two government officials, sentencing them to be thrown from the high castle windows. They landed on a pile of manure (some say this was divine intervention) and escaped serious injury.

Possibly a third, and even more sinister defenestration occurred in 1948. Foreign Minister Jan Masaryk was found on the ground in front of the Czechoslovak Ministry of Foreign Affairs on 10 March. It was ruled a suicide at the time, but a 2004 report concluded that he was murdered by communist opponents.

NATIONAL AWAKENING

During the Industrial Revolution economic and industrial reforms forced Czech labourers into the bigger towns, where they soon overwhelmed the German minorities. Political activity was banned under the Hapsburgs, so the new nationalist movement was linguistic: Josef Jungmann, Josef Dobrovský and František Palacký, the author of the *History of the Czech Nation*, all worked on regenerating the Czech language and stirred nationalistic feelings.

A similar national cultural awakening took place on intellectual levels in Slovakia. One of its early leaders was a Catholic priest named Anton Bernolák, who published the first Slovak grammar book, taking baby steps towards codifying a national language. Until this time there had been no unified written Slovak language; dialects used in the regions were distinct. Ľudovít Štúr, a major figure in the Slovak cultural renaissance, continued the process in the 1840s. His inspirational efforts would make nationalist ideas more accessible to the mass of Slovak people.

By 1848 revolutions were widespread in Europe. The Austrian Hapsburgs faced rebellion on many fronts. Hungary revolted against the Austrians, but many in Slovakia sided with the Hapsburgs. The rebellion in Bohemia was the first the Hapsburgs crushed; the Hungarians were defeated shortly after.

A gradual awakening of a Slovak national consciousness continued, with the small Central Slovakian town of Martin at the epicentre. It was there that the cultural and educational foundation for the promotion of all things Slovak, the Matica slovenská (still active today), was formed.

Despite putting down the rebellions, things were not completely hunky-dory within the Austrian Empire. After losing a war with Prussia in 1867, the Austrians were forced to rule with the Hungarians in a 'dual monarchy'. Under the new Austro-Hungarian Empire, the Hungarians pursued a policy of Magyarisation, which meant only Hungarian was to be taught in school and used in businesses across all lands, including Slovakia.

Jaroslav Hašek's iconic satire, *Good Soldier Švejk*, reveals the Czech state of mind during WWI.

A NEW NATION

During WWI, Czechs and Slovaks had little interest in fighting for the empire, and a large number defected to fight against the Germans and Austrians. Meanwhile, politicians of both Czech and Slovak nationality began

1848	28 October 1918
Slovak nationalists stand with Austrians against the Hungarians; serfdom abolished in Slovakia	First Czechoslovak Republic becomes a nation

to argue the case for independence; US president Woodrow Wilson, a big proponent of linguistic self-determination and keen to establish stronger ties with Europe, was all for it. The Pittsburgh Agreement was signed by representatives of Czech, Slovak and Rusyn organisations in America, proposing the creation of a Czechoslovak State that included all three ethnolinguistic regions. Ruthenia, or Podkarpaska Rus, was the Carpathian region to the east of Slovakia that was historically part of the Kingdom of Hungary, but the majority of residents were an east Slavic people called the Rusyn. For more, see the boxed text, p434.

On 28 October 1918 the new Czechoslovak Republic was declared with Prague as its capital and Tomáš Garrigue Masaryk its first president; his son Jan Masaryk would also become a politician, and a victim of defenestration. Industry boomed in the Czech Lands, and the new republic set about industrialising Slovakia, a traditionally agrarian-based country. Czechs were happy, Slovaks mildly content, Rusyns felt left out, and Germans were downright miserable. By the mid-1930s, many of Bohemia's three million German speakers wanted to be part of a greater Germany.

The first president of the first Czechoslovak Republic, Tomáš Masaryk, began his working life as a blacksmith.

WWII

Germans in the Sudetenland (an area running the length of the border between Germany/Poland and Bohemia/Moravia, encircling what is now the Czech Republic on the west, north and south) had been discriminated against by Czechs and wanted out, so when Hitler demanded the Sudetenland in 1938, the Czechs prepared for war. The British and French governments pressed the Czechoslovak president, Edvard Beneš, to give up these lands for the sake of European peace. In October 1938, under the infamous Munich Agreement between the Germans, French, British and Italians (the Czechs were notably absent), the Nazis occupied the Sudetenland. The Poles took part of Silesia in North Moravia and the Hungarians seized Ruthenia and southern areas of Slovakia (about 22% of the Slovak territory). On 15 March 1939 Germany occupied all of Bohemia and Moravia, pronouncing the whole region a 'protectorate'.

The rapid changes meant the countries' buildings suffered little damage during the war. However, the Czech intelligentsia and 80,000 Jews died at the hands of the Nazis. When Czech paratroopers assassinated the Nazi governor in 1942, the entire town of Lidice was wiped off the map in revenge. A peaceful park stands there today as a memorial.

I Never Saw Another Butterfly..., edited by Hana Volaková, is a moving collection of children's words and drawings made inside the Terezín concentration camp.

Meanwhile, the day before the German occupation, Slovakia was declared a separate, independent state (read 'Nazi puppet'). The government of the new state was headed by Jozef Tiso, leader of the nationalist Hlinka Slovak National People's Party that had been seeking autonomy from the Czechs. Tiso immediately banned all opposition political parties and instituted censorship along Nazi lines.

The Slovak government promulgated its own 'Jewish Code'. More than 73,000 Jews were deported from Slovakia to the Nazi extermination camps. Roma (Gypsies) were also targets of the Nazi regime: the number of deaths during the war is not known, but estimates go as high as 300,000.

The Nazi state did not enjoy popular support in Slovakia. In August 1944 units of the Slovak army and thousands of poorly armed partisans took up arms in the Slovak National Uprising (Slovenské národné povstanie; SNP)

1938	1939
Western powers hand the Sudetenland to Hitler at the Munich Agreement	An independent but fascist state declared in Slovakia

based around Banská Bystrica; a great museum there fills in the details. It was quashed after two months by 35,000 German troops, apparently invited by Tiso. This short, ill-fated uprising is today remembered in monuments and street names all over Slovakia.

Czech fighter pilots are credited with downing 56 German planes as a part of the British Royal Air Force during the Battle of Britain in WWII.

On 5 May 1945 as the Red Army approached from the east, Prague rose against the German forces. US troops had reached Plzeň, but held back in deference to their Soviet allies. The Czechs, assisted by Russian renegades, granted the Germans free passage out of Prague provided they left the city intact; the Germans began pulling out on 8 May. Most of Prague was thus liberated before Soviet forces arrived the following day.

COMMUNISM

At the end of the war, Czechoslovakia was reconstituted minus Ruthenia, which went to the USSR. Population 'exchanges' ensued – Germans were forced out of Czech Lands, Hungarians out of Slovakia. In the 1946 elections the communists became the largest party, forming a coalition government. In February 1948 the communists staged a coup d'état with the backing of the USSR. A new constitution established the Communist Party's dominance, and government was organised along Soviet lines. Thousands of non-communists fled the country. Although the communists represented both Czech and Slovak communities, the party was based in Prague and dominated by Czechs. Slovak interests and representation were largely forgotten in the halls of power right up until the fall of the communist regime. Centuries-old buildings were ploughed under in the Slovak capital in the name of progress.

Alexander Dubček, the Communist Party boss known for his compassionate leadership, was conceived in Chicago, USA, although he was born in the Slovak village of Uhrovec.

The 1950s was an era of harsh repression and decline as communist economic policies nearly bankrupted the country. Many people were imprisoned for real or imagined dissident views, and hundreds were executed or died in labour camps. As the 1960s rolled along and the rest of the world was all about peace and love, the Czechoslovak Communist Party started to let its hair down. Reformist general secretary Alexander Dubček, a Slovak, took over in January 1968 and the party started talking about 'socialism with a human face'. The April 1968 'Action Programme' of reform filled hearts with hope, and there was an outpouring of literature, art and political expression, which came to be known as the 'Prague Spring'.

Just when Czechoslovaks thought it safe to express themselves, more than 200,000 Soviet and Warsaw Pact troops rolled into Prague on the night of 20 August 1968, killing 58 people. Dubček was replaced by the orthodox Dr Gustav Husák and exiled to Krasňany, a village close to Bratislava, to work as a mechanic. Around 14,000 Communist Party functionaries, and 500,000 members who refused to renounce their belief in reform, were expelled from the party. Many educated professionals including teachers and doctors were forbidden to work in their field. Totalitarian rule was re-established, and dissidents routinely imprisoned. But this didn't stop Czech and Slovak authors from writing; they just went underground.

The Unbearable Lightness of Being, by Milan Kundera, has sections on the Prague Spring that are an easy-to-read, emotive look at this turbulent time.

In 1977 the trial of a Czech rock group, the Plastic People of the Universe, inspired a group of 243 writers, artists and intellectuals, including the future president of the Czech Republic, Václav Havel, to sign a public demand for basic human rights known as the Charter '77. This became a focus for opponents of the regime.

1944	1945
Partisans take up arms in the short-lived Slovak National Uprising against the Nazis	Czechoslovakia reunited; Ruthenian lands ceded to USSR

PLAYWRIGHT, POLITICIAN, PRESIDENT

The Czech Republic's first president, Václav Havel, is a rarity in the world of politics – a playwright, a poet and former dissident. Born on 5 October 1936 in Prague, Havel was supposed to be a laboratory technician, but couldn't resist the stage. His first play, *Zahradní slavnost* (The Garden Party), premiered at divadlo na Zábradlí in 1963. Its theme was, of course, the oppressive political system in Czechoslovakia.

Despite four spells in jail, Havel kept writing; his works were published by *samizdat* (underground) presses and in the West. Two of his better-known works are *Dopisy Olze* (Letters to Olga; 1983) a compilation of 144 letters he sent to his former wife from prison, and the play *Largo Desolato* (1984).

On 29 December 1989 he was elected president of Czechoslovakia. The obligations of the presidential office took him away from writing, but in 1991 he did manage to publish *Letní přemítání* (Summer Meditations). It's a great read for insight into the man's philosophy of leadership, reflections on his career and his hopes for the future.

After retiring from office in 2003, Havel suffered recurrent bouts of pneumonia. He also suffered some tarnishing of his saintly reputation – even a poet can't run a country without getting his hands dirty occasionally. He celebrated his 70th birthday during a teaching residency at Columbia University in the US during the autumn of 2006. Many of his plays and speeches have been translated and all of those referred to are available in English.

THE VELVET REVOLUTION & DIVORCE

Even as Soviet Premier Gorbachov embraced *perestroika* and *glasnost*, and when the Berlin Wall was breached on 9 November 1989, the Czechoslovak Communist Party refused to bend. However, on 17 November 1989 things changed. Prague's communist youth movement organised an officially sanctioned demonstration in memory of nine students executed by the Nazis in 1939. A peaceful crowd of 50,000 was cornered in Národní třída in Prague; some 500 were beaten by the police and about 100 were arrested. It is suggested now that the whole thing was precipitated by reformist party members to trigger a revolution. In Slovakia, public protests in Nám SNP in Bratislava were more peaceful, but still pronounced.

The following days saw constant demonstrations by students, artists and writers, and in the end by most of the populace. Though news of the uprising was officially kept from many Czechoslovaks, demonstrations spread throughout the country, culminating in a rally of 750,000 people on Letná Hill in Prague. Leading dissidents, with Václav Havel at the forefront, formed the Anti-Communist Civic Forum that negotiated for the government's resignation on 3 December. A Government of National Understanding was formed, with the communists as minority members. Havel was elected president of the republic by the federal assembly on 29 December 1989, and Alexander Dubček was elected speaker of the national assembly.

There were no shots fired in the 'Velvet Revolution' (Sametová revoluce); the downside of the nonviolent transformation being that ex-communists were free to reintegrate themselves into government and buy up privatised properties. There was no political tradition in the country, and so there was no party system and little precedent to go on. Tensions increased between Czech and Slovak political figureheads and some of them started agitating for independence.

20 August 1968	**17 November 1989**
Soviet tanks roll in, crushing the Prague Spring	The Velvet Revolution overturns communist rule

INDEPENDENCE DAY *Lisa Dunford*

A bottle rocket zoomed across the tightly packed crowd, whistling shrilly as it passed. I watched as it landed on the end of a young girl's hand-crocheted scarf, which caught fire. She shrieked and threw the scarf to the ground. At first no-one moved; then an old man with a grey, stubbly beard and a rumpled overcoat came forward and stomped out the small flames. Everyone around laughed. I turned back to see a policeman lighting a sparkler for a *babka* ('little grandmother').

This New Year's Eve in Bratislava was special: at 12.01am on 1 January 1993, Slovakia would become an independent nation. The night was painfully cold. Even with long underwear, two pairs of socks, jeans, two shirts and a sweater underneath my trench coat, I still hurt. I saw the man next to me take a swig of something out of a bottle. Why hadn't I thought of that? Centuries-old buildings with ornate façades, grey and sagging from years of coal-fire heating and pollution, stared down at us.

At 9pm we'd walked to within 15m of the stage on Nám SNP, the same square where protestors had gathered during the Velvet Revolution in 1989. More and more bodies pressed in as midnight approached. The newspapers would later say that more than 200,000 turned out to celebrate a new capital, a new country, a new life, a new year. Not everyone who usually celebrated New Year's on the square was there though; some stayed home to mourn the loss of Czechoslovakia.

There was no violence, no revolution. This split came to be called the Velvet Divorce, and like many divorces, it just happened. Few claimed to want it. Public opinion polls did not support it. Calls for a national referendum went unheeded. But in the end, too many hateful things had been said, and both sides agreed it would be best to part. Slovakia had never before been a self-ruling nation, unless you count the 18 months during WWII when it was a Nazi protectorate. For the past 67 years Bratislava had played second fiddle to the central government of Prague. Now, for better or worse, it would get to stand alone.

Months of bickering about how to divide the assets were yet to come. The new Slovak Republic would end up with no aeroplanes of its own. Prague would put out new money so fast it would catch Bratislava off guard (the parties had agreed to wait a year). But New Year's Eve traditionally is a time for jubilation, a time of pure promise. I doubt anyone that night discussed economic feasibility.

A few minutes before the hour, Vladimír Mečiar, a thick man in a black suit, took the stage. The soon-to-be prime minister was reported to be popular with the people, a charismatic, if somewhat heavy-handed, parliamentary leader who had pushed for independence. I couldn't say I'd met anyone who liked him in the three months I'd lived in Slovakia, though.

Mečiar shouted into the microphone; I didn't understand all the words, but I knew the sentiment. He spoke about the future, about triumph. At midnight, Mečiar declared Slovakia a nation and the audience erupted. A teenage boy hoisted aloft by the crowd frantically waved the Slovak flag before falling back. The old woman with the sparklers held her daughter and cried. The man who put out the fire popped a champagne cork, sending an arc of sticky liquid cascading down. Firecrackers roared in every direction. And then as a waltz blared from the loudspeakers, the crowd fell silent and we swayed together.

No guns were fired. No soldiers died. The split just happened. And the people danced.

In the June 1992 elections, the right-of-centre Civic Democratic Party (Občanská demokratická strana; ODS) led by Václav Klaus took a slim victory in the Czech Republic. Coming to power in Slovakia was the left-leaning nationalist Movement for a Democratic Slovakia (HZDS), headed by the controversial Vladimír Mečiar, a firm believer in Slovak independence and slow economic reform. In 1991 the former boxer Mečiar had been dismissed by the Slovak National Council from his post as prime minister because of both his autocratic temperament and revelations of involvement with the former secret police.

Mečiar held negotiations with Klaus, as neither could form a stable government. Despite numerous efforts, the two leaders could not reach a compromise. The incompatibility of Klaus and Mečiar became apparent and they decided (or perhaps one persuaded the other?) that splitting the country was the best solution. Many people on both sides, including President Havel, repeatedly called for a national referendum, but even a petition signed by a million Czechoslovaks was not enough for the federal parliament to agree on how to arrange it. On 1 January 1993 Czechoslovakia ceased to exist for the second time in the 20th century. For a first-hand account of the experience in Bratislava, see the boxed text, opposite.

Prague became capital of the new Czech Republic, and Havel was elected its first president. Thanks to Klaus' economic policies, booming tourism and a solid industrial base, the Czech Republic started strongly. Unemployment was negligible, shops were full and many cities were getting face-lifts; by 2003 Prague had the highest standard of living in Eastern Europe. However, capitalism also meant a shortage of affordable housing, rising crime and a deteriorating health system.

In 2003, after two terms as president, Havel was replaced by former prime minister Klaus. It took three elections for Czechs to settle on the new president, and the uncharismatic Klaus is far from the popular leader Havel was. While Klaus stood for a free-market economy and ever-increasing privatisation, the prime minister in 2003, Vladimír Špidla, was much more left-leaning. The Czech Republic became a member of NATO in 1999 and in May 2004 joined the EU.

Slovakia's transition from communism to capitalism was not so smooth. As the first prime minister of the Slovak Republic, Mečiar cancelled the sale of state-owned enterprises, halted Slovakia's privatisation scheme and threatened independent radio stations and newspapers with legal action if they dared criticise the government. The international community was none too pleased.

In part due to this international pressure, the elections of 1998 ousted Mečiar and ushered in Mikuláš Dzurinda, leader of the right-leaning Slovak Democratic Coalition (SDK). Dzurinda changed the course of recent Slovak history by launching a policy of economic and social reform that got Slovakia into NATO and the EU alongside the Czech Republic and other new members in May 2004.

Both nations are now on the road to euro conversion by 2009. Summer 2006 parliamentary elections seem to indicate changes to come, but the history of conquerors is at an end and independence reigns – for now anyway. To read more on the current political climate, see p23.

Český Sen (Czech Dream), a 2004 documentary, follows a hoax launch of a new Czech department store. It's a wry observation of the expectations of a market-oriented Czech society.

Pluto lost its status as a planet at the annual meeting of the International Astronomical Union held in Prague in August 2006.

2007	2009
Czech and Slovak Republics aim to meet Schengen requirements and eliminate internal EU borders	Goal for Czech and Slovak Republics' adoption of the euro as national currency

The Culture

THE NATIONAL PSYCHE

To equate the Czechs with big-city slickers and the Slovaks with their country cousins may sound trite, but there's some truth to it. On the whole, the Czechs are slightly more cosmopolitan and progressive, the Slovaks more traditional and religious. The grey years of communism are far enough behind that many young locals wouldn't recognise a picture of Stalin. Youthful optimism for an EU-accepted future pervades, tempered with the older generation's stoic reserve.

There's no denying German culture has had something of an influence on the Czech Lands. Here there tends to be more of a businesslike determinism, especially in Prague. That's not to say the people don't enjoy their *pivo* (beer). Strike up a conversation with the locals in a busy pub and you're likely to run into some definite opinions about politics and history – symptomatic of their intellectual streak combined with a long national history. Slovaks tend to be strongly family oriented and perhaps slightly more gregarious and less concerned about work. A friend described the difference this way: if a Czech and a Slovak family each had the same amount of money for a vacation at the Croatian seashore, the Czechs would drive, plan out and pack all their own food, rent a place where they could cook, and stay for 10 days. The Slovaks would fly, get a hotel room, throw a big party, spend all their money in the first weekend and have to go home early.

Most of the younger generations in both countries speak at least some English. Pensioners can still be a little surly on the surface (why don't people on buses ever smile?), but ask about their country, or show a little language knowledge, and the shell cracks to reveal generosity and warmth. Both nations share a deep poetic sense and a talent for literature that comes out colourfully in everyday conversation – even in English.

LIFESTYLE

Though less so in the capitals, family is still at the centre of most lives here. Because of economic realities, young adults often live with their parents in the family flat until they marry. Getting around without a car used to be quite common, but that's changed, and usually a town-living family will have at least one. In the villages, bicycles are still the way to go.

Czechs tend to have a slightly higher standard of living; dining out, especially in Prague, is commonplace. Going out to dinner is not a regular event for most older Slovaks, and the young people just frequent the cafés, nursing drinks for hours on end. Large groups of relatives and friends get together for name days, weddings, any communal event. Weekends are usually spent walking in nature whenever possible.

While things are moving towards a more American model of work (you hardly ever see a bottle of brandy brought out for morning meetings any more), both Czechs and Slovaks go to work early (many before 7am), leave early (by 4.30pm) and take long lunches and breaks. Maternity leave is extremely generous (six months paid at 90%, with up to three years off allowed). Paternity leave as such doesn't yet exist. For the most part, both incomes are necessary and mothers usually work. Divorce and remarriage are not uncommon.

Both the Czechs and Slovaks are united in their distrust of minorities in general and the Roma people (see opposite) in particular.

The A to Z of all things Czech is at your fingertips in *From Good King Wenceslas to the Good Soldier Šejk* by Andrew Roberts.

DID YOU KNOW?

Before 1848, high schools in Bohemia used German, not Czech, as the language of instruction.

The word for 'gay' in Czech and Slovak (*teplouš/teplý*) also means warm or hot. Many a novice speaker has erroneously come out of the closet on a sunny day!

ECONOMY

The post-2004 EU membership years have been a time of economic boom for both nations. Gross domestic product (GDP) growth in the Czech Republic jumped from 1.5% to 4.6% in 2005; Slovakia's was up from 4% to 5.5%. EU involvement has helped with everything, from the production of shiny new tourist brochures, to improved roads for those tourists, so enticed, to travel on.

In the past few years, Peugot-Citröen, Volkswagen and Kia auto manufacturers have built plants in Slovakia. In the Czech Republic, auto parts manufacturing is also big (many are then shipped off for assembly). Steel, refining and other heavy industries still play a key role in the Slovak economy, while tourism and service industries play an increasing role in the Czech Republic.

DID YOU KNOW?

Czech and Slovak jokes about misers are generally aimed at the Dutch.

POPULATION

The Czech Republic is a homogenous place: of the approximately 10.2 million people living there, a little more than 94% identify themselves as ethnic Czechs. Slovaks make up 1.9%, Poles 0.5%, Germans 0.4%, Roma 0.1%, and the rest 'other'. (Activists claim the Roma figure is closer to 2%.) About 20% of those living in Moravia identify themselves as ethnic Moravians rather than Czechs. Population density is 130 people per square kilometre – a little more than half that in the UK (246). The average life span is 72 years for men and 78.5 years for women. A little more than a quarter of the population lives in the major cities, more than a tenth in Prague.

Almost 86% of Slovakia's 5.35 million people class themselves as ethnic Slovaks. The largest minority, the Hungarians, comprises around 11% of the population; they live mostly in southern and southeastern Slovakia. Czechs account for 1.2% of the population. Officially, the Roma people make up about 1.8% of the population, the vast majority living in East Slovakia. (Civil rights groups say the correct figure is closer to 4%.) The average life span is 69.9 years for men and 77.2 years for women. Population density is 111 people per square kilometre. Seven per cent of the population lives in Bratislava.

Božena Němcová is loved as much for her ground-breaking views on women's rights as her literature. Some scholars see her main work, *Babička*, as a commentary on the existential struggles of women.

Roma

The Roma people *(Romové/Romská kommunita)*, sometimes called Romany, are the most conspicuous minority in both nations. (Note: the term 'gypsies' *(cikáni/cigány)* is considered derogatory.) Roma tribes migrated to Europe from India and by the 16th century had spread into Central Europe. Roma numbers are hard to pin down in both republics. Officially, the populations are around 11,800 in the Czech Republic and 90,000 in Slovakia, but advocacy groups claim the actual populations could be closer to 200,000 and 400,000, respectively. The largest concentration of Roma people is in East Slovakia.

The majority of Czechs hold a low opinion of the Roma and are not shy about saying so, blaming them for crimes, taking advantage of the social welfare system etc. Most Slovaks share this opinion, if not a more virulent version of it. (They call anything dirty and disagreeable 'gypsy business'.) In the late '90s, Slovak parliament members would deride the Roma people from the podium.

Fourteen female voices are heard in *Povidky: Short Stories by Czech Women*, edited by Nancy Hawkins. What may be most remarkable is that Hawkins includes the writing of Roma women.

To qualify for EU membership, the government had to clean up its stance towards minorities, especially the Roma. A Ministry of Minority Affairs was created in Slovakia, and housing and other programmes got under way; a Commission on Romany Affairs was created in Prague. Both nations were welcomed into the EU in 2004 and the world is still watching.

As of late, more services for the Roma people are being offered in the Czech Republic: a computer learning centre recently opened in Prague, and the police force is actively recruiting more Roma candidates. But the future is uncertain in Slovakia, where the Slovak National Party (SNS) became part of the ruling coalition in June 2006. Racism is still institutionalised in Slovak villages: in one, the town government built a wall to separate the main township and the Roma settlement; in another village, the Roma were banned from a local swimming pool. Even in the Czech Republic there are still issues: the city of Brno, for example, recently refused to sponsor an exhibit on the extermination of the Roma during the Holocaust.

Tragically, sporadic violence against the Roma people also happens, but as a traveller you're unlikely to encounter it. If you are dark skinned, you might get a few sideways glances, but that's about it. On the other side of the coin, it would be difficult to deny that pickpocketing schemes targeting tourists often originate from Roma individuals.

The Roma culture has long been famous for its musical ability. For information on authentic Romany music see p51.

SPORT

Ice hockey is by far the most popular sport. Football (soccer) comes second, but everything else is very much an also-ran. Slovaks especially love the outdoors and hiking, but playing at spectator sports besides hockey or football is not really that big a deal.

Ice Hockey

The rivalry between the Czech and Slovak Republics in ice hockey is hot enough to melt the rink, but the Czechs usually come out ahead. Both countries have world-class players in the North American leagues. Most of the world's hockey pucks are made at Gulfex in the Czech Republic and Vergum in Slovakia. During the national and international playoffs, you can't escape hockey – it's on most every TV set in most every bar and restaurant in both republics. During the 2004–05 National Hockey League (NHL) lockout in North America, 51 players returned home to play in the Czech and Slovak leagues.

The Czech national ice hockey team is a world powerhouse. They took gold at the 1998 Winter Olympics in Nagano and again at the World Championships in 1999, 2000, 2001 and 2005. At the 2006 Winter Olympics in Torino, the Czechs beat the Russians to take the bronze medal.

Although only eight Czech players were selected for the NHL draft in 2006, there is still a number of famous players shooting it out on North American ice. Jaromir Jagr (New York Rangers), one of the top NHL players, is probably the most well known. He has set numerous goal-scoring records and played on the last two Czech Olympic medal–winning teams. Dominik Hašek (Detroit Red Wings), the 'Dominator', is the oldest active goalie in the NHL and has several Stanley Cups 'under his stick'. Patrik Elias (New Jersey Devils), a goal-scoring left wing, is one to watch.

Ice hockey in Slovakia has a long history; the first puck was placed on Slovak ice just after WWI. Although the Slovak national team brought home the bronze at the 2003 World Championships, Slovakia was knocked out of the Olympics medal race during the quarterfinals in Torino in 2006 – by the Czech Republic. The announcement that Slovakia will host the 2011 World Championships (and Bratislava will get a new multibillion-koruna hockey stadium) surely perked up the fans. Marián Hossa (Atlanta Thrashers), right wing, is one of the most well known Slovak players in the NHL.

There are rinks all over both republics where local games can be seen, but the major stadiums are in Prague, Bratislava and Košice. The season runs from September to April. HC Sparta Praha (2006 Czech national champions)

Romea (www.romea.cz) is a good source of news and information about the Roma communities in both countries.

DID YOU KNOW?

The heaviest train ever pulled by a man – 20 freight cars loaded with metal (total weight 1000 tonnes) – was moved by Juraj Barbaric in Košice, Slovakia. He dragged it for 4.5m.

For the history of Slovakia's triumphs in the sporting arena, see www .sportslovakia.sk.

and HC Slavia Praha are the two Prague teams. HC Slovan and HC Košice play in Bratislava, but neither were contenders in the 2006 playoffs.

As with football, women's hockey attracts very little interest in either republic.

Football

The Czech Republic national football team is currently ranked 10th in the world. They made the first round of the World Cup finals in 2006 and generally acquit themselves quite well. Czech footballers are even more loved at a local level. Most years, the top teams are from Prague: AC Sparta Praha and SK Slavia Praha. Bohemia, a lesser Prague team, has a kangaroo as its mascot – go figure! The soccer season runs from September to December and March to June. Games are usually held on Sunday afternoon and are televised. Watching football in a pub full of Czech partisans is a real experience.

The Slovak national team has yet to make its mark on the international stage, not having qualified for the World Cup or European championships, but it does have a long tradition of local league teams. SK Slovan Bratislava is the country's most famous and successful team. The Union of European Football Associations (UEFA) Cup normally sports two or three Slovak teams each year.

There are also women's leagues, but attendance figures are abysmal.

Tennis

The Czech Republic has produced more than its share of international tennis stars, including Ivan Lendl, Martina Navrátilová and Jana Novotná. However, within the country, tennis has nothing like the following of hockey or football. Radek Stepanek, who made it to the quarterfinals at Wimbledon in 2006, has been ranked as high as eighth in world standings. Up-and-comer Lukáš Dlouhý made it to the third round in the 2006 French Open. Nicole Vaidišová and Tomas Berdych are names to watch.

Slovakia has produced the occasional top player. Martina Hingis spent her formative years in Košice before moving to Switzerland. After fighting back from injuries, she is currently ranked 12th, but she has been ranked as high as first in the world. She has won nine Grand Slam titles in various opens. Local sweetheart Daniela Hantuchová has had quite some success in mixed doubles, most recently at the 2005 US Open.

Other Sports

Prague's mayor, Pavel Bém, has been pushing his city as potential host of the 2020 Olympic Games. Public response has been mixed; there was even talk of a national referendum on the issue. However, they still have time, as bids won't be finalised until 2010.

Canoeing and kayaking have been gaining in popularity over the past few years in both republics, mainly as a result of international success, including eight individual Slovak medals at the 2004 Olympics. The ICF Canoe Kayak Slalom Racing World Championships was held in Prague in 2006 and the sponsoring country did quite well, with five kayaking medals overall.

In 2005, Banská Bystrica, Slovakia, held the World Mountain Bike Orienteering Championships, a testimony to the nation's hilliness.

MEDIA

In the Czech Republic the majority of media emanates from Prague. Well, sort of. Though produced in the capital city, most of the daily newspapers are owned by foreign firms. The daily broadsheet *Mlada Fronta Dnes* (owned by Mediaprint-Kappa; German) and the tabloid *Blesk* (owned by Ringier;

Swiss) garner the largest market share. International ownership of radio outlets is not uncommon either. Public radio has about a third of the market; the classical music station Frekvence 1 is owned by the French. The nation has 72 regional broadcasts.

Czech TV has four stations: two analog variety and two digital sports. TV Nova, the biggest commercial station, was the first to operate after the former Soviet bloc crumbled, and Prima TV began broadcasting in 1997.

The Slovak media have not always been known for their independence from politics. That said, there are 13 dailies to choose from (and more evening papers), so the full range of opinions should certainly have a forum. The largest publisher is Ringier (Swiss); its daily, *Nový Čas*, is the most popular.

The country's most popular TV station, Markíza, is privately owned by Pavol Rusko, a Berlusconi-type media magnate in miniature. Slovak TV has two national stations (which often air dubbed American series) and there's a second, smaller, private station, Joj. Slovakia has 30 radio stations broadcasting.

<aside>While Michael Chabon isn't Czech, his story of a Prague Jew who leaves his home and family at the beginning of WWII, *The Amazing Adventures of Kavalier & Clay*, has some grim insights and gorgeous evocations of Prague's Jewish quarter.</aside>

RELIGION

Despite the Czech Republic's Hussite history (see p26), these days the country seems to be phenomenally uninterested in God. About 60% of Czech citizens call themselves agnostic. Roman Catholic believers make up 26% (mostly in Moravia), and Hussites less than 2%.

The first Christian church in Slovakia was founded at Nitra way back in 833. Despite communist suppression, the faith has really held on. More than 60% of the population claims Roman Catholic affiliation, another 6% are Lutheran, 4% are Greek Catholic and 2% are Calvinist. Churches fill to overflowing on Sunday. The late Pope John Paul II visited the country three times, so if that rate of visits continues, Benedict XVI should be arriving any day now.

Jews came to what is now the Czech Republic in the 11th century (they were among Prague's first inhabitants) and to Slovakia in the 13th century. When Czechoslovakia was founded in 1918, Jews comprised about 4% of the population. At the outbreak of WWII the Jewish population in Czechoslovakia was around 122,000; at least 70% were deported and killed. Many who did survive subsequently immigrated to Israel. In 2006 the Jewish population in Prague numbered around 1600, the total in the country being a few thousand. About 2300 Jews are registered in the Slovak Republic. Though some old synagogues have been restored and are used as concert halls and the like, many more, especially in Slovakia, are in sad decay.

ARTS
Architecture

<aside>Track down info on even the most obscure castles in Slovakia at www.castles.sk and in the Czech Republic at www.zamky-hrady.cz.</aside>

Clearly the Gothic playground, Prague is what first springs to mind when you mention architecture in the two republics, but there are also Art Nouveau flights of fancy, indigenous wooden churches, grand castles and a style unique to the Czech Republic: cubism.

CASTLE ROCK

Castles from the 12th century onwards dot hilltop outcrops in both republics. Many rocky ruins of medieval fortifications remain today. Dated to 1209, Spiš Castle (p418) in East Slovakia is the grandest and most photogenic relic. Threats came and went, later-style buildings were added and the battlements bulked up. Central Bohemia's Křivoklát Castle (p151) is one of the oldest in that region, but there are dozens more in the republics. For more information see the destination chapters and the Classic Castles itinerary (p21).

GOTHIC TO RENAISSANCE

Prague is a gallery of Gothic architecture. In the 14th century, King Karel (Charles) IV sponsored a massive Gothic building campaign, under the guidance of his chief architect, Peter Parler. There are Gothic buildings all over town, but the most famous extant works are Charles bridge (p100) and St Vitus cathedral (p89). The style was employed from about the 13th to the 16th century, with earlier incarnations being simpler, and later ones more ornate. Look for stained glass, pointed arches, external flying buttresses, spires and gargoyles. The diamond vaulting you see in ceilings all over Prague (and the rest of the country) is also a product of the era. The cathedral of St Barbara (p157) in Kutna Horá, Central Bohemia, is one of the finest Gothic shrines anywhere, says Unesco.

Most of the Gothic grandiosity that remains in Slovakia is ecclesiastical. The examples are relatively fewer and farther between. First prize would go to either the massive Cathedral of St Elizabeth (p408) in Košice or the majestic Church of St James (p416) in Levoča.

Many of the originally Gothic burghers' houses on old Slovak town squares were remade with Renaissance façades when that Italian-influenced style arrived in the 16th century. Bardejov (p427) is a shining, uniform example that has been recognised by Unesco; Levoča (p416) comes a close second. Renaissance style characteristics include symmetry, elaborate gables and exterior walls covered in sgraffito (mural technique whereby the top layer of plaster is scraped away or incised to reveal the layer beneath; painting is done on top). Sgraffito was popular in palaces as well as town houses, so you can find examples everywhere.

In the Czech Republic, the Summer Palace (p89) at Prague Castle took the city by Renaissance storm, spawning a host of imitations. Czech designs often featured legendary or historical scenes. In the provinces, Telč (p313) is another Unesco-noted town full of Renaissance regalia, and the chateau (p254) in Litomyšl is a knockout.

BAROQUE & ROCOCO

When the Catholics thrashed the Hussites in the 1620 Battle of the White Mountain (following a couple of hundred years of sporadic street battles that demolished large parts of Prague), the Jesuits sponsored lavish baroque (17th to 18th century) rebuilding throughout Prague. Germanic landowners took a fancy to the style and it spread to the rest of the country. Look for curved walls, domes, gilding and elaborate, emotional sculpture – indoors and out – all across the nation.

The best-known practitioners of baroque architecture were the unstoppable Bavarian father-and-son team of Kristof and Kilian Ignatz Dientzenhofer, whose obsession with gold-plating can be seen all over Prague, but especially at St Nicholas church (p102). The church of Mary Magdalene (p214) in Karlovy Vary is another good example.

The baroque style, with a Viennese twist, was also appreciated by wealthy Slovak aristocrats and merchants of the 17th century. A fine example of early works is the University church of St John the Baptist (p358) in Trnava. The rococo (a lighter, more flowery outgrowth of baroque) influence of Austrian empress Maria Theresa in the 18th century can be seen in the swags and other plasterwork ornamentation of town buildings, especially in Bratislava's old town (p342).

VILLAGE VERNACULAR

Numerous villages in Slovakia are photogenic folk art in themselves. Vernacular architecture – typically log or wood structures, occasionally plastered over –

DID YOU KNOW?

Prague's Hradčany Castle, which covers 7.83 hectares, is in the *Guinness Book of World Records* as the largest ancient castle.

can be downright decorative. Examples from the 18th century are usually the oldest you'll see. In Čičmany (p379) white geometric patterns painted on dark logs create a graphic picture. The pastel plaster homes of Vlkolínec (p390) are on Unesco's World Heritage List.

You can find some of the best village architecture in a *skansen/skanzen* (open-air village museum), where houses, churches, barns and other buildings have been collected. The better ones are an attempt to show whole communities. Inside the buildings you'll find typical furniture, linen, clothing, utensils, tools and decorations. For more information see the Folk Life & Art itinerary, p22.

WOODEN CHURCHES

Dark wooden shingles cover onion-domed roofs, and brilliant icon screens decorate the interiors: East Slovakia is dotted with picturesque wooden churches, largely made without nails. These houses of worship from the 18th to the early 20th century belong primarily to the Greek Catholic and Orthodox faiths. Parts of the Sariš region and the Eastern Borderlands were home to the Rusyn minority usually associated with these churches. See the East Slovakia chapter for more information about wooden churches around Bardejov (p430) and Snina (p432).

ART NOUVEAU

Curvaceous shapes, recurrent undulations, natural flow…the organic elements of early-20th-century Art Nouveau certainly seemed to be a reaction to uptight Victorianism. The art of Art Nouveau is in the details, so get your camera and telephoto lens ready and be prepared to look up, down and every way. The theory of Art Nouveau was there should be no line drawn between art and everyday life, so everything down to the doorknobs was designed in style.

The Czech Republic, then part of the Austro–Hungarian Empire, embraced Art Nouveau with open arms. You can see good examples scattered throughout the country, including in Karlovy Vary (p211) in West Bohemia, but the largest concentration is in Prague. The extraordinary Municipal house (p103) in Prague is a showcase of arches and sculpture, wrought iron and stained glass; this is the Art Nouveau design not to miss! Wander around the streets of the city's Nové Město district (p105) and you can't help but notice the elaborate, whimsical façades and mosaic elements. Also look for the graphic flourishes on smaller façades, like that of the 1906 Hotel Evropa on Wenceslas Square (p107). Pragotur (p121) leads Art Nouveau–oriented walking tours of the capital.

One of the leading Czech architects of the period was Jan Kotěra, a professor at Charles University, who designed the Art Nouveau East Bohemia regional museum (p247) in Hradec Králové. Moravian designer Alfons Mucha, who specialised in Art Nouveau (p42), was one of the most influential visual artists of the period.

Examples of Art Nouveau are scattered throughout Slovakia. In Bratislava you should seek out the fanciful Blue Church (p344) designed by Hungarian architect János Ödön Lechner. Hotel Slávia (1902) in Košice (p410) has an exquisite Art Nouveau mosaic façade and café, but the rooms aren't particularly period.

CUBISM

Prague is one of the few cities in the world where you can see cubist architecture – a simple, nonconfrontational style that's extremely functional. For more information see What's in the Box? (opposite).

The vivid village photos in *Folk Treasury of Slovakia*, by Vladimir Barta, are enough to make you want to go and visit a *skanzen* today.

WHAT'S IN THE BOX?

A handful of Czech architect-artists belonged to an early-20th-century avant-garde modernist group with French influence (cubism in art took shape in France). They broke out of the box in about 1911 and *voilà!* an indigenous Czech architecture materialised. Actually, it might be fairer to call cubist architecture Pragocentric; although there are a few examples in Brno (p295) in South Moravia, the vast majority of these angular gems are in the capital city.

The theory was that a simple cube is the most basic of shapes and therefore the use of geometric forms is tantamount to boiling things down to their essential elements. Czech cubists got downright playful with the idea, creating hexagonal windows, zigzag fences, a lamppost made of dodecahedrons (20-sided 3D shapes – really, look it up). Many of the shapes were almost crystalline. The main proponents of this architecture (which some link to a search for a Czech national identity within the Austro–Hungarian Empire) were Josef Chochol and Josef Gočár.

Probably the most well-known example is Gočár's chart-topping house of the black Madonna (p103), which contains the museum of Czech cubism – three floors full of geometric dynamism. The museum shop, Kubista (p140), sells an illustrated map (190Kč) of cubist architectural sights around town. Vyšehrad (p110) should be a definite stop on your tour. Even Kafka's grave (p117) in the local cemetery is crystal shaped. When you're tired of walking, head to the cubist-style pub, U Neklana (p132), to refresh.

You won't find infinite examples, though. In the end, Czech cubism didn't compute for the masses, and the last buildings were constructed by 1919.

COMMUNIST REALISM?

The communist era basically dotted the landscape and cities with eyesores. The building material of choice was concrete. Vast, truly ugly *panelák* (concrete apartment buildings made with prefabricated panels) popped up on the outskirts of cities in both nations, especially during the 1960s and '70s. Slovakia was particularly hard hit. The communist era left some monumentally odd structures, such as the New bridge (p347) and Radio building (p347) in Bratislava.

MODERN DAY

Restoration is the biggest architectural movement these days; nothing particularly interesting is being done with new buildings. The one exception is Prague's most idiosyncratic and appealing newer building, Vlado Milunć and Frank Gehry's Dancing building (p110) – an exercise in fluid unconventionality.

Visual Arts

GOTHIC TO BAROQUE

During the Middle Ages, the style of a painting or sculpture generally followed the architectural style of the building in which it was housed, so you'll find Romanesque paintings in Romanesque churches, for instance. However, the Czechs took the Gothic template and gave it their own Bohemian twist; medieval art from this region seems brighter, more humorous and more personal than much of the dour work produced in Italy. Some of the best is contained in the National Gallery's exhibits in the convent of St Agnes (p104) in Prague. Also look there for the late-14th-century Třeboň Altar panels and the Master Theodoric panels originally in Karlštejn castle (p148) in Central Bohemia.

Slovakia's premier artist lived way back in the 15th century: Master Pavol was a woodcarver and painter extraordinaire. His impressive Gothic art (and that of his students) decorates numerous churches in the Spiš region in East Slovakia and the High Tatras, including St George Church (p399) in Poprad.

By far the most celebrated of his works is the Gothic altar in the Church of St James (p416) in Levoča; the 16m-high structure has several painted panels and sculptures depicting scenes and figures from the life of Christ.

The Counter-Reformation brought a wave of religious sculpture into both republics, including hundreds of plague columns dedicated to the Virgin Mary or the Holy Trinity, carved to give thanks for deliverance from the Black Death in the 1700s. You can't miss these ornate baroque monuments covered with gilding and sculptures; they're usually found at the centre of a main town square. Holy Trinity column (p271) in Olomouc, North Moravia, is on Unesco's World Heritage List.

DID YOU KNOW?

The rebuilding of the Globe Theatre in London in the 1990s was based on a series of engravings done by a Czech artist from 1607 to 1677 for English King Charles II.

ICONS

The Greek Catholic and Orthodox wooden churches of East Slovakia have their own interesting art: icons. These stylised representations of the saints and Jesus were used as a gateway to worship. Extant examples date back to the 15th century, but those from the 18th are much more common. You could spend days, even weeks, going from church to church, looking at the iconostases (icon-covered screens set before the altar with doors for the priest and the holy liturgy), but the finest works have been gathered for safekeeping in the Icon Exposition (p428) in Bardejov.

NATIONAL REVIVAL

From the late 18th to the 20th century, the Czech National Revival spurred an interest in Czech themes and representations of everyday life. The biggest name from this period is Josef Mánes; some of his work can be seen in the Centre for Modern & Contemporary Art (p113) in Prague, which is an excellent place for all kinds of post-18th-century Czech painting.

Mikuláš Aleš is regarded as one of the best artists of folk and national themes. You can see three of his murals near náměstí Republiky (p220) in Plzeň, West Bohemia. There are more of his murals in the towns of South Bohemia, including Mirotice, where his home has been turned into a small museum (p189).

Sculptors like Josef Myslbek immortalised legendary Czechs: his equestrian statue of St Wenceslas (p108) is a popular meeting place in Prague's Wenceslas Square. Bohumil Kafka's muscular 1941 statue of Jan Žižka (p114) – again, in Prague – was at the tail end of this Czech-pride movement.

The Slovak National Revival also created a crop of painters eager to do justice to the new movement. The most well-known 20th-century painter who specialised in Slovak themes was Martin Benka. In addition to his pastoral paintings in the Slovak National Gallery (p344), there's the Martin Benka museum (p384) in Martin. Miloš Bazovský also used folk themes and village life in his sometimes abstract work, and he too has his own museum: the Gallery Bazovský (p364) in Trenčín.

ART NOUVEAU

Want to know more about Alfons Mucha? Head to www.muchafoundation.org.

While Alfons Mucha's mystic Art Nouveau posters are known worldwide, not many people think of him as a Czech artist born in Moravia. That's how he thought of himself, though. While he predominantly lived in Paris and was associated with the French Art Nouveau movement, Mucha's heart remained Slavic to the core. He often claimed his famous Art Nouveau illustrations were based on Czech folk art themes. His more serious paintings revisit the themes of Slavic suffering, courage and crossnational brotherhood.

You can see the most outstanding of his non–Art Nouveau works – a series of 20 large canvases called *Slav Epic* – in the Mucha gallery (p310) in Moravský Krumlov. For more on this colossal work see Epic Art, opposite.

You can check out Mucha's Art Nouveau decoration work at the Municipal house (p103) in Prague. His design and print work can be seen all over the Czech Republic, but there are good collections in Prague at the museum of Decorative Arts (p97) and the Mucha museum (p105).

AVANT-GARDE

In the early 20th century Prague became a major European centre for avant-garde art, which included movements like cubism and surrealism. The Mánes gallery (p110) in Prague was established as the counterculture to the Academy of the Arts; it still shows provocative exhibits.

Leading cubist painters included Josef Čapek and Emil Filla. Surrealists included Zdenek Rykr, Josef Šíma and Jindřich Štýrský.

Between the two World Wars, functionalism evolved and flourished within a group called Devětsil, led by Karel Teige, who worked in all kinds of media.

The lines between the artistic disciplines were blurred at the time, so in addition to looking for progressive works at the Centre for Modern & Contemporary Art (p113), check out the museum of Decorative Arts (p97) and the museum of Czech cubism (p103), all in Prague.

Illustrator Josef Váchal produced some stunning surrealist design work. The home of one of his biggest collectors has been turned into Portmoneum (p254), virtually a Váchal museum, in East Bohemia.

Mikuláš Galanda was a big Slovak name from the avant-garde movements of the 1930s, and Peter Matejka managed to capture sensualism and surrealism on canvas. The works of both are in the collection of the Slovak National Gallery (p344).

EPIC ART

Hear the name Alfons Mucha (1869–1930) and you probably think Art Nouveau. After all, it's the fanciful posters and illustrations he did in France and the USA that made him famous. But this Moravian-born boy remembered his homeland. In 1910 he moved to Prague and turned his attention to Pan-Slavism and his *Slovanská epopej* (Slav Epic). He envisioned the work taking five or six years but it ultimately took 18. During all that time, his backer, American plumbing magnate Charles Crane, kept forking out the dough. (Crane was known for investing his money to foster revolution around the world; apparently Slav nationalism fit his criteria.)

The results were, um, epic. Twenty canvases measuring up to 6m by 8m were donated to the city of Prague in 1928, with mixed success. Critics thought Mucha's 19th-century style was outdated, and after all the years he'd lived abroad, they considered him a Frenchman. The few canvases that were shown in Chicago and New York received much more acclaim there. No permanent hall was provided for Mucha's monumental art in Prague. Instead, after a temporary exhibit, in 1939 it was rolled up and put in storage. The canvases weren't to be shown as a set again until they were installed in 1967 in the castle in Moravský Krumlov, where they are now part of the Mucha gallery (p310). Not for long, though. More than 150 million crowns has been allocated for the building of a hall to house the *Slav Epic* in Prague. A modernist structure has been designed and a site in Stromovka Park chosen.

The intricate paintings allegorically appeal to Slavic unity and reproach foreign oppression, many with an overtly Christian perspective (no wonder the communists hid them away). Ten of the works have Czech themes (of which six relate to Jan Hus and the Hussite Wars) and 10 relate to events and themes in larger Slavdom, like *Praise of the Slavonic Liturgy*. The *Apotheosis of the Slavs,* representing Slavic peoples worldwide, is one of the most striking. An Art Nouveau poster commemorating the gift of the paintings (1928), also entitled *Slav Epic,* was perhaps more famous than the paintings at the time. It's expected that by 2010 the greatest Czech nationalist painting will finally be moved home to be displayed in the city the artist intended.

SOCIALIST REALISM

Communism pretty much pushed real art underground. Socialist realism was the only form of art officially tolerated. Look for statues of happy peasants and smiling soldiers holding flags patriotically aloft. Though many of the public statues have been removed, you can still find them on the main squares of smaller, modern, industrialised towns, or hidden off the main squares. (Write and tell us which you think are the best. The one on the square in Michalovce (p431), East Slovakia, is especially cheery.) Otherwise, the museum of communism in Prague (p107) is the place to go to see institutionalised art.

To look through the history of famous Moser glass, go to www .moser-glass.com.

CONTEMPORARY

Sculptor David Černý spent much of the late communist and early postcommunist era in serious play. His major works include the *Miminka* sculpture – giant babies clambering all over the TV Tower (p117) in Žižkov, Prague. In recent years, sculptor Pavel Opočenský, once a member of Charter 77 (a group that strove for artistic freedom during the communist era), is perhaps known as much for his passion for underage girls as for his abstract, geometric works. To see what's new and current in Prague, go to the Centre for Modern & Contemporary Art (p113) and the Mánes gallery (p110).

Photographer Karol Plicka (1894–1987) was born in Vienna and spent some time in Prague, but most of his career was spent in Slovakia. In his lifetime he created an impressive portfolio of Czechoslovak images, many in villages. The small Karol Plicka museum (p386) is hidden in a little town in the Veľká Fatra mountains in Central Slovakia, but his books are available everywhere.

To see the latest in Slovak art, head to the Danubiana – Meulensteen art museum (p354) outside Bratislava and the Milan Dobeš museum (p345) in Bratislava.

FOLK ART

Both republics have a deep and enduring tradition of turning everyday objects into art. Tools, utensils, musical instruments, linen, furniture and even entire buildings may be decorated with elaborate folk designs. Of the two nations, Slovakia is the more traditional and therefore the more folksy. Just about every town museum has a display of local folk art. The Ethnographic museum (p384) in Martin, Central Slovakia, has the most impressive collection, even if they could do a more dynamic job of presenting the material. Úľuv ('www .uluv.sk), the national cooperative of *ludové umelec* (folk art, literally art 'of the people'), sponsors festivals and has stores in addition to a training studio. Items to look for include reverse glass folk paintings, embroidered folk dress, ceramics from Modra (p356) in the Small Carpathians, and Hrnčiar pottery from near Michalovce (p431) in the Eastern Borderlands.

The slender novel *Utz* by British writer Bruce Chatwin looks back on the life of a Prague ceramics collector, recently deceased, and is a sharp and charming insight into Czech life. Chatwin died in 1989 and *Utz* was his last work.

Czech and Slovak *skanseny/skanzeny* (open-air village museums) serve as repositories for home crafts. For more information see the Folk Life & Art itinerary, p22. Another place to see traditional crafts is at folk festivals and markets held around the countries, the biggest craft market being in Kežmarok (p412) in Slovakia. In the Czech Republic, the Moravské Slovácko region (p325) in South Moravia contains the country's most fascinating pocket of traditional culture and festivals.

Cinema

A strong artistic sense, a moody rawness, a willingness to deal with the grit of everyday life, characters who regularly ask ineffable questions...these are the qualities that have attracted audiences to Czech and Slovak cinema. The

---

CRYSTAL MADE CLEAR

Glass-making goes way back in the Czech Republic; beads dated to the Bronze Age have been found in excavations. Medieval glass-makers created 'forest glass' using the abundant wood and sand quartz in Bohemia. The impurities produced gave the glass a green tint. It's thought the intricate cut glass associated with Bohemian crystal came to be in the court of King Ruldolf II, during the late 1500s, where engraving techniques were perfected. The composition of Czech crystal makes it particularly well suited to cutting (to be considered crystal, glass must have at least 24% lead, which makes it softer, and engraving easier).

In subsequent centuries the process was refined and gradually artisans learned how to take elements out to create clear crystal (or add them to give colour; cobalt, for example, turns the glass deep blue). In the 18th century Czech crystal was huge all across Europe, but the discovery of English crystal in the 19th century led to a decline. Still, the crystal industry has persevered.

Perhaps the most well-known glass-maker today is Moser (p212) in Karlovy Vary, West Bohemia. Moser crystal is not highly engraved; instead the glass-makers use translucent colour and gold enamel to great effect on simple, elegant shapes. There is a more traditional cut glass–making centre in North Bohemia, near Nový Bor (p242).

Glass-makers also create handblown ornaments and figurines. Here are some you might see, along with their traditional symbolic meanings:

- stars and moon – being close to heaven; blessing
- swan – gracefulness
- owl – wisdom
- birds – joy and cheerfulness

Czechoslovak film industry was never a powerhouse; not all that many films were made annually, and today only the Czech movie industry really remains. But what was made did garner international attention from the start.

In 1921, *Jánošík*, a US–Czechoslovak collaboration about the legendary 17th-century Slovak 'Robin Hood', came out in two versions: a domestic version showing his execution, and an American one where the hero escaped and lived happily ever after. However, it wasn't until the legendary Barrandov Studios in Prague (the biggest in the Czech Republic today) opened in 1930 that Czechoslovak film-making really took off. Notoriety ensued almost immediately. *Extaze* (Ecstasy), directed by Gustaf Machatý in 1932, was the first film ever to show full frontal nudity. (The pope objected to its screening at the 1934 Venice Film Festival.) Revealing all was one Hedwig Kiesler, who went on to Hollywood fame as Hedy Lamarr. Another early Czech director, Hugo Haas, filmed an excellent adaptation of Karel Čapek's anti-Nazi, science fiction novel, *Bílá smrt* (White Death, 1937), before finding fame in Hollywood.

Few films were made by Slovak directors before WWII, but cinematography saw a real evolution after the war, typified by the light-hearted and ever popular *Cathy* (1949) by Ján Kádar. In 1953, Koliba, Slovakia's film studio, opened in Bratislava, creating a backbone for Slovak cinema for years to come.

A NEW WAVE

The new wave *(nová vlna)* of artsy avant-garde productions washed ashore in the mid-1960s. Among the earliest and best were *Černý Petr* (Black Peter, 1963; the US version was called *Peter & Paula*) and *Lásky jedné plavovlásky* (Loves of a Blonde, 1965) by Miloš Forman. Slovak director Ján Kádar forged ahead with *Smrt si říká Engelchen* (Death Calls Itself Engelchen, 1963) and teamed up with Elmar Klos to produce *Obchod na korze* (The Shop on Main

Street, 1965), which won an Academy Award for best foreign film. It's a moving film depicting the life of Jews in Slovakia under Nazi occupation. In 1967, Czech director Jiří Menzel garnered the same honour with *Ostře sledované vlaky* (Closely Watched Trains), based on Bohumil Hrabal's eponymous book about growing up during WWII. František Vláčil's *Markéta Lazarová* (1967), a medieval epic of paganism versus Christianity on a personal level, usually tops polls ranking the best Czech films of all time.

Czech Film Center (www .filmcenter.cz) has the lowdown on film festivals and current Czech productions.

It was a busy, successful period, but just a few short years later the Soviet invasion stopped the flow abruptly. Many young directors of the time escaped censorship because they were among the first graduates of the Academy of Film during communist rule and were therefore assumed to be ideologically 'clean'. Some took a hiatus; some left the country. Forman became a successful Hollywood director with films like *One Flew Over the Cuckoo's Nest*, *Amadeus* (filmed in Prague) and *The People vs Larry Flint*.

Films critical of the postinvasion regime were made during 1969 and 1970 but were promptly banned from public screening. The most outstanding of those from Czech directors were the morbid *Spalovač mrtvol* (The Cremator of Corpses), directed by Juraj Herz, and the gloomy *Ucho* (The Ear), directed by Karel Kachyňa. *Žert* (The Joke, 1970), directed by Jaromil Jireš, is a film version of Milan Kundera's eponymous book. The gritty and powerful documentaries by Slovak film-makers Dušan Hanák and Dušan Dušek were banned during the communist years but their popularity remained strong.

Probably the best among the films of the next two communist decades was the comedy *Vesničko má středisková* (My Sweet Little Village, 1985) directed by Jiří Menzel – a subtle look at the workings and failings of socialism in a village cooperative. One of Slovakia's best-loved directors is Juraj Jakubisko; his *Sedím na konári a je mi dobre* (I'm Sitting on a Branch and I'm Fine, 1989) is an excellent but bizarre tale of life in Slovakia after WWII involving stolen gold, murder, bad luck and tree climbing.

One of the greatest Czech exports is the animated work of Jan Švankmajer; his creepy *Alice* (1988) is a masterpiece. *The Cabinet of Jan Švankmajer* (1984) is a tribute to the film-maker by underground American animators the Quay Brothers.

You can read snippets of Czech and Slovak authors in translation at http:// centomag.org/ceslit/.

THE '90S TO TODAY

Director Jan Svěrák and his screenwriting brother Zdeněk are among the biggest names of modern Czech cinema. Their 1994 hit, *Akumulátor,* was the most expensive Czech film produced at the time. In 1996 it was surpassed at the box office by the internationally acclaimed *Kolja* (Kolya), another of Svěrák's works, which managed to score the two big film prizes of 1997: best foreign film at both the Cannes Film Festival and the US Academy Awards. It's a slightly sugary story about a confirmed Czech bachelor saddled with a small Russian child on the eve of the Velvet Revolution. *Samotáři* (Loners, 2000), by director David Ondříček, centres on a group of people trying to find love in the 1990s.

Martin Sulík is one of Slovakia's most prominent current directors, winning an Oscar nomination for *Všetko, čo mám rád* (Everything I Like, 1992) and international acclaim for *Krajinka* (The Landscape, 2000). Lack of funding and the subsequent closing of the Koliba movie studios in 2000 meant moving production to Prague for more recent titles like *Sluneční stát* (City of the Sun, 2005). *Kruté Radosti* (Cruel Joys, 2003), directed by Juraj Nvota, is a comedy of unwanted family reunions and love set in small-town Slovakia c 1993.

In 2005 Czech writer-director Bohdon Sláma came out with a real winner in *Stestí* (Something Like Happiness), a black comedy about young people trying to make their way during economic hardship. (Part of it is set in one of the ugly concrete *panelák* buildings of the communist era.) Sláma won various awards and showings at international film festivals for *Stestí*, which is a follow-up to his acclaimed *Divoké vcely* (Wild Bees, 2001).

Copies of Czech and Slovak films can be tough to track down abroad. The newer and award-winning titles are easier to find, often available with English subtitles. It's not a piece of pie in the films' countries of origin, either. Only a handful of Czech- and Slovak-language movies are box-office successes at home. Most Czech and Slovak cinemas screen Hollywood movies either dubbed *(dabovat)* or subtitled *(pod titul* or *titulký)* in the local language. Art-house cinemas in Prague (p138) are the most reliable places to catch the most recent indigenous films. Charlie Centrum (p351) in Bratislava occasionally has special showings of classic Slovak films.

ON LOCATION

Spooky Orava Castle (p386) in Central Slovakia appeared in the seminal vampire chiller, *Nosferatu,* way back in 1922. And with the republics' romantic old-town streets, hilltop fortresses and stunning scenery, it's not really surprising that both are still players in the movie biz. Because Prague has studio production capabilities, most of the international films are made there.

Prague itself has starred in numerous movies, including *Amadeus,* Barbara Streisand's *Yentl,* Tom Cruise's *Mission Impossible,* the *Bourne Identity* with Matt Damon, and the 2006 remake of the *Pink Panther* with Steve Martin, to name only a few. And the country's exposure goes beyond the capital. The 2005 blockbuster, *Chronicles of Narnia,* was filmed in part among the sandstone formations of the Adršpach Rocks (p261) in East Bohemia.

Behind Enemy Lines (2001) used Bratislava's old-town streets as a substitute for Vienna. Not all the coverage of Slovakia has been positive in recent times. For example, in the 2004 movie *Eurotrip,* the characters make a brief appearance in the capital, which is portrayed as a trash-strewn hellhole. But the movie the Slovak Tourist Board wishes had never been made is *Hostel* (2005). In this horror film presented by Quentin Tarantino and directed by Eli Roth, two young travellers are lured to a hostel in Slovakia where they get mixed up with gorgeous, easy women, human trafficking and murder. (Incidentally, the whole movie was shot in the Czech Republic – mostly Prague.) Incensed that their country was portrayed as a dangerous and licentious place, Slovak image-makers extended a formal invitation to the director to tour the country himself. He hasn't yet shown, but *Hostel II* is already in the works.

Literature

CZECH

The Czech authors you're likely to have heard of are Franz Kafka, whose bleakly paranoid works were made just before WWII, and Milan Kundera, an expatriate Czech living in Paris who hit the big time in the 1980s with *The Unbearable Lightness of Being.* With icons like these, it's no wonder most people think of Czech writers as dark, mystical, otherworldly, philosophical and obsessed with sex. Oppression and the legacy of history have long been Czech literary themes. The majority of the books mentioned below can be found in English translation.

Though he wrote in German, Franz Kafka, with a circle of other German-speaking Jewish writers in Prague, played a major role in the literary scene at the beginning of the 20th century. The hopelessness and sense of the absurd that pervade his writing have come to define existentialism. Kafka only published short stories during his lifetime; his novels were incomplete when he died and were arranged by a friend, Max Brod, afterwards. You probably know his novella, *Metamorphosis,* in which a man turns into a bug, but other works include *The Trial, In the Penal Colony* and *Amerika.*

The 1960s liberalisation of socialism (prior to 1968) encouraged a resurgence in Czech literature. The main topic for writers like Josef Škvorecký *(The Cowards)* and Milan Kundera *(The Joke)* was communist oppression; both became known in translation. Kundera's commercially huge success, *The Unbearable Lightness of Being,* was made into a movie. Bohumil Hrabal wrote down-to-earth novels about the way people lived, as in *Ostře sledované vlaky* (Closely Watched Trains) about coming of age during WWII. After the crushing of the Prague Spring in 1968 (see Communism, Less Then More, p30), some writers fled; others stayed and wrote for the *samizdat* (underground) press, as did playwright and future president Vaclav Havel.

The frustration of Czech scholars unearthing their own history under domination existed even in the 19th century, when František Palacký wrote a seminal history of Bohemia and Moravia in Czech that pretty much classified history according to whether the Germans or Slavs were in control during a given period. Romantic views of traditional Slav life took hold about this time. Karel Hynek Mácha wrote probably the most famous Czech poem, *Máj* (May), which tells a tragic tale of love, betrayal and death, though it's known more for the romantic imagery of nature. (Mácha died at the age of 26, fighting a fire a few days before his scheduled wedding.) One of the nation's most beloved novels is Božena Němcová's *Babička,* a story of village life ('little grandma' comes to live with her daughter and grandchildren) that illustrates Czech customs and an affection for the native language. Czech history was a great source of inspiration for world-renowned poet and essayist Jan Neruda, whose short stories in *Povídky Malostranské* (Tales of the Malá Strana) are a satirical look at Prague's bourgeois in 1878.

After WWI, Jaroslav Hašek devoted himself to taking the piss out of the Hapsburg empire and its minions; itinerant and impoverished, he wrote *The Good Soldier Švejk,* a rambling, hysterical study of a Czech soldier during WWI (it's 'laugh out loud in public places' kind of stuff). In the years between the two World Wars, Karel Čapek was probably the best-known author; his science fiction works included *Rossum's Universal Robots.*

Most recently, there hasn't been a whole lot of Czech literature translated into English. Jáchym Topol, a rock lyricist from a dissident family, won several awards for his novel, *Sestra* (translated as *Silver City Sister*). The book is a dark and complicated romp through postcommunist Prague. Michal Viewegh's *Bringing Up Girls in Bohemia* is a satirical look at teen angst and a great snapshot of modern life in Prague. Czech native Iva Pekarkova's novels span the globe, from Prague to New York to Nigeria. Names to watch include Emil Hakl (Prague based) and Jaroslav Rudiš, whose graphic novels have garnered local praise.

SLOVAK

In Slovakia, too, literature – poetry and poets especially – played a big part in the national history, and vice versa. Unfortunately not very much has been translated, so unless otherwise noted, the texts mentioned below are not in English.

There was no such thing as a Slovak literary language until 1790, when Anton Bernolák published his *Slovak Grammar,* followed in 1827 by a Slovak dictionary – early cornerstones in the gathering Slovak National Revival. The 19th-century nationalist, linguist and poet Ľudovít Štúr took Bernolák's work one step further in 1845 by creating a grammar based on central Slovak dialects – a basis for the language still used today.

The Book of Laughter & Forgetting by Milan Kundera is one of the author's less well-known but better books, mingling bites of philosophy with sex and humour to result in a very entertaining and thought-provoking package.

DID YOU KNOW?

The word 'robot' entered the English language because of Karel Čapek's play, *Rossum's Universal Robots.* (*Robota* means 'labour', as in hard work, in Czech.)

Year of the Frog by Martin Šimečka is the story of a young intellectual living in Bratislava during the communist era, who can work only menial jobs because he is barred from college as a result of his family's antigovernment attitudes.

It's not surprising that writers of this era produced romantic fiction with a 'folk' flavour. The towering figure of the time was the Pan-Slavic poet and hero of the 1848 revolution, Janko Kráľ, who wrote in the new language and barely escaped execution by the Hungarians. (Well-known poet Jozef Šafarík wrote mostly in Czech.)

Slovakia's best-loved poet at the turn of the 20th century was Pavol O Hviezdoslav, who was also a main proponent of the Slovak language. He published some 15 volumes of verse in his lifetime. His anti-WWI *Krvave Sonety* (Bloody Sonnets) won him a nomination for the Nobel Peace Prize. His works have been translated into several foreign languages, including English.

Post-WWI Slovak literary giants included Petr Jilemnický, whose immense leftist and visionary *Kronika* (Chronicle) describes the Slovak National Uprising (SNP), and Dominik Tatrka, who wrote in surrealist prose. Today, Michal Hvorecký is one of the most celebrated young writers. His cyberpunk novels have been translated into German, Czech and Slovenian. Not much Slovak writing has been translated into English.

In Search of Homo Sapiens: Twenty Five Contemporary Slovak Short Stories, edited by Paul Hudik and published in 2002, is one of the few places you can read writing out of modern Slovakia.

Music
ROCK & POP

Rock was banned by the communist authorities because of its Western 'corrupting influence'. Pop music was allowed, but mainly harmless local clones of Western groups like ABBA. Rock found fans among political dissidents like Václav Havel but remained an underground movement, with a handful of bands playing to small audiences in obscure pubs and country houses. Raids and arrests were common. Czech band Plastic People of the Universe gained international fame when they were imprisoned in 1976 as the result of a trial intended to discourage underground music. The tactic was successful only temporarily and by the mid-1980s there was a lively underground scene.

Today, some of these bands, such as Plastic People and Tony Ducháček & Garage, have re-formed and are worth seeing live, as their music is very Czech. Veterans of the scene, Support Lesbians was once a hard rock outfit but these days is producing catchy dance pop. Bands with a harder edge include intellectual punk Už Jsme Doma and indie Freak Parade.

The Slovak scene is not as heavily into punk and rock as the Czech (DJ'ed dance music is quite popular here now), nor does it have as long a history. Marián Varga and the Collegium Consortium were the progressive rock legends that played from the 1970s to 1990s. Now Varga is on his own, riffing instrumental on classical themes and appearing as a guest with other bands. Richard Muller and Paľo Habera are pop classics. Elán is another well-known pop band that's been around for years.

Slovak bands to listen out for today include No Name (pop/rock), IMT Smile (pop/rock with jazz influences) and Polemic (ska). Also listen out for individual singers Zuzana Smatanová and Jana Kirshner, who've had platinum success.

Tom Stoppard's 2006 play, *Rock 'n' Roll*, tells a love story set amidst Prague's underground dissident artistic movement of the 1960s and '70s. It features songs of the Plastic People of the Universe.

JAZZ, BLUES & FUNK

After WWII, Czechoslovak musicians were at the forefront of European jazz, but this came to an end with the 1948 communist putsch. Restrictions were gradually lifted in the 1960s. One of the top Czech bands was the SH Quintet, though it played for only three years at Prague's Reduta Jazz Club (p137), the first Czech professional jazz club. Another group was the Junior Trio, with Jan Hamr and the brothers Miroslav and Allan Vitouš, who all escaped to the USA after 1968. Jan Hamr (keyboards) became prominent in

1970s American jazz rock as Jan Hammer and received a Grammy for the *Hawaii Five-O* theme. Miroslav Vitouš (bass) also rose to fame in several American jazz rock groups.

Flautist and composer Jiří Stivín sprang onto the jazz scene in the 1970s and produced two excellent albums with the band System Tandem. Still today he's an original, though his last album was classical. Another longtime jazzman is pianist Milan Svoboda, who also composes scores. Stan Wolarz is Scottish but has been pounding out the blues for 10 years in Prague. Open Sextet has three Czech and three Slovak members and plays original contemporary jazz around both countries. Band 123 belts out a healthy mix of jazz, blues and funk.

For more information about jazz in the Czech Republic, go to www .jazzport.cz.

Jazz is a mainstay of the tourist entertainment scene in Prague and there are clubs on what seems like every corner. But a lot of what plays is stale, because there are fresh tourist faces to hear it nightly. One of the newer restaurant clubs, Dinitz Café (p137), has a good reputation for fresher jazz, blues and funk. There are small clubs in cities nationwide and several jazz festivals, including ones in Karlovy Vary (p215) and Český Krumlov (p174).

Peter Lipa *is* jazz in Slovakia. For 25 years this singer has been organising the international Bratislava Jazz Days festival (p347). In the '80s he was consistently ranked among the top performers in Europe; in the '90s he had his own club. Today you can hear his eclectic repertoire (classical jazz to Latin and funk) at venues around the country.

Good jazz bands first appeared in the 1960s, among them the Traditional Club Bratislava, Combo 4, Bratislava Jazz Quartet and Medik Quintet. Dodo Šošoka is a living jazz legend, having played drums and percussion around the country and internationally for almost 40 years. Born in Slovakia, jazz trumpeter Laco Déczi now lives in the USA and has put out some 50 records, most with the band Celela NY.

On the funkier side, Slovakia has an active blues scene. Silvia Josifovska is a young jazz and blues singer with a big sound. Boboš Procházka is known for his soulful blues harmonica playing with band Frozen Dozen. The newest name to listen for is Juraj Haruštiak and his BluesBanda.

To learn more about classical music and current musicians in the Czech Republic, go to www .musica.cz.

You'll see plenty of 'jazz cafés' throughout Slovakia, but quite often their live concerts are infrequent. The Jazz Café (p351) in Bratislava is one you can count on; Art Jazz Gallery (p362) in Piešťany is good, too.

CLASSICAL

A flowering of Czech music took place in the mid-19th century. Bedřich Smetana, the first great Czech composer and an icon of Czech pride, created a national style by incorporating folk songs and dances into his classical compositions. His best-known pieces are the operas *Prodaná Nevěsta* (The Bartered Bride) and *Dalibor a Libuše,* and the symphonic poem cycle *Má vlast* (My Country). Prague Spring (p122), the country's biggest festival, is dedicated to Smetana and begins with a parade from his grave to Smetana Hall, where *Má vlast* is performed.

Antonín Dvořák is perhaps everyone's favourite Czech composer. Among his best-known works are his symphony *From the New World* (composed in the USA while lecturing there for four years), his *Slavonic Dances* of 1878 and 1881, the operas *The Devil & Kate* and *Rusalka,* and his religious masterpiece *Stabat Mater.*

Well-known early-20th-century composers such as Zdeněk Fibich, Josef Suk and Bohuslav Martinů also became famous outside their country. Some of the most recent composers are Jan Novák, with his best-known work being the sonata *Chorea Vernales,* and Svatopluk Havelka, whose first symphony, *Pěna* (1965), is still his most notable.

During the 18th century the likes of Haydn, Mozart, Schubert and Beethoven graced the courts of the Hungarian nobility in Bratislava. Of the Slovak composers, the most prominent at the time were Juraj Jozef Zlatník and Anton Zimmermann, a cathedral organist who composed cantatas, symphonies, concertos and chamber music. Another contemporary was Georg Druschetzky, known for his solo, orchestral and chamber pieces.

Slovaks began to redefine their folk song heritage in the 19th century and Slovak composers of the time often used traditional folk motifs in their classical compositions. Only Ján Levoslav Bella and Mikulás Schneider-Trnavský, however, achieved any substantial fame. Among Bella's best works are the opera *Kovář Wieland* and the symphonic poem *Fate & Dreams*.

Alexander Moyzes created probably the best Slovak compositions of the mid-20th century. One of Moyzes' students, Dezider Kardoš, has written the country's most innovative post-WWII music, especially his second symphony, *Hero's Ballad,* and *Concerto for Orchestra*.

The four main cities of Prague, Brno, Bratislava and Košice all have city orchestras that stage classical music regularly (usually September through to May), but smaller towns like Karlovy Vary also either have orchestras or occasional performances.

FOLK MUSIC

Traditional folk music, especially in Slovakia and Moravia, is well preserved by regional dance and song ensembles that play at festivals or community centres. These well-loved songs once helped conserve the native languages in villages dominated by Austrian or Hungarian rulers. Today, folk lyrics and rhythms are taken to new heights by performers who use them as a starting point on the journey to a new musical genre.

The original musical instruments were flutes or pipes, like the *fujara* (2m-long flute) and *koncovka* (strident shepherd's flute), drums and cimbalom (copper-stringed dulcimer of Middle Eastern origin that stands on four legs and is played by striking the strings with two mallets). Bagpipes *(dudy/gajdy)* were also popular. You'll likely still see the cimbalom today, accompanied by fiddle, bass, clarinet and sometimes trumpet or accordion. There are almost always dancers in regional costume, and a lot of skirt-twirling and foot-stamping to go with the music. Don't be surprised if you hear a high-pitched squeal intermittently throughout a song; it's not one dancer treading on another, but a sign of joy and enthusiasm.

In the modernised folk genre, Slovak artist Zuzana Mojžišová demands to be heard. Her eclectic, jazzy, almost Indian sound stems from original folk songs. Hrdza, a folk rock band from Prešov, uses lyrics from the national poet Janko Kráľ. Czech artist Ivana Bittová is doing earthy things with voice and sound, as an outshoot from Romany folk music (see below).

Folk ensembles keep the more traditional versions of folk music alive. You can see them perform at regional festivals, especially those in the Moravské Slovácko Region of South Moravia and in Central and Eastern Slovakia. Two of the biggest are the International Folk Festival (p326) in Strážnice and the Východná Folk Festival (p390) below the Tatras mountains in Slovakia.

Seeing musical theatre staged by folk ensembles is another way to experience the colour, showmanship and elaborate costumes of this style of music and dance. Look for performances of *Janošík* (about the Slovak Robin Hood) and *Hra a Svadba* (Play and Marriage) by folk ensemble Lúčnica.

ROMANY MUSIC

Despite hardship, the Roma people have maintained a strong musical tradition through the centuries. Traditional Romany music sung at home was often

Radio Prague (www .radio.cz) is an excellent online source of cultural news from the Czech Republic.

DID YOU KNOW?

Flamenco music from Spain and Rom pop from the Czech Republic are both music styles with Roma roots.

in the form of a long, slow lament, though dance songs did exist. For years, all anybody outside the community heard was the schmaltzy 'gypsy' music – essentially Hungarian dance tunes (csardas) accompanied by violin and cimbalom – first at wedding parties and then in restaurants, where you can still hear it today. Thankfully there are moves afoot to conserve and record more traditional songs. (For more information see Ancient Rhythms, opposite.)

Latcho Drom (1994) is a French art film that follows the Roma people out of India, through Slovakia and into Western Europe, led by their music, which is mesmerising.

The biggest name in Rom pop, a genre inspired by French group the Gypsy Kings, is Vera Bila. She was born in Slovakia and grew up in a village in the Czech Republic, where she still resides. Vera and her big voice have appeared worldwide, in New York, Paris and Singapore. Ida Kelarova is a teacher of Roma songs and a popular music artist with the band Roma Rats. In 2005 and 2006 she hosted a Roma music workshop; the resulting CD, Gypsy Music Festival 2005, is one to look for. Another Rom pop band is Gulo čar, from Brno.

Iva Bittová comes from Romany roots in Slovakia (and she lives in Brno) but her music defies classification. Her haunting violin and vocals have been likened to avant-garde art and an abstraction. Whatever you call it, her alternative music springs from the same sources as folk music variations.

A good place to experience the exuberance of Romany music is at a performance of the Romathan theatre group (p411) in Košice. You might also hear more traditional Roma folk bands at large music and folk festivals, such as the Východná Folk Festival (p390) in Central Slovakia and the Bazant Pohoda Festival (p365) in Trenčín, West Slovakia.

Theatre
MARIONETTE & PUPPET THEATRE

Marionette plays have been popular since the 16th century, and puppet plays since before then. Even under communism, puppet and marionette theatre was officially approved of and popular. A legendary figure in the 18th and early 19th century was Matěj Kopecký (1775–1847), who performed original pieces. The famous Czech composer Bedřich Smetana also wrote plays for marionettes.

DID YOU KNOW?

Mahen's theatre in Brno, South Moravia, was the world's first electrified theatre (1882). Thomas Edison himself helped install the lighting.

After a lull, marionette theatre for adults was revived in the 20th century. Josef Skupa's legendary puppets, Špejbl & Hurvínek, still perform in Prague; replicas of the little chaps can be seen in tourist shops all over the country. The National marionette theatre (p139) in Prague is the place to see shows for adults.

In Bratislava, the State Puppet Theatre (p346) was founded in 1957. Today its shows are aimed at children as young as three. Many more theatres around both countries cater to this younger set.

BLACK-LIGHT & LATERNA MAGIKA

Anything avant-garde is bound to find a home in the city that invented cubist architecture. Black-light theatre was part of the avant-garde movement of the 1950s in France, catching on in Prague during subsequent decades.

The technique, first used by the ancient Chinese to entertain emperors, takes advantage of the imperfection of our eyesight. Our eyes have difficulty distinguishing black against black, so if a man dressed in black is inside a black box, holding a puppet painted with yellow phosphorescent paint, when a fluorescent light is turned on, the puppet appears to float.

In today's black-light theatre, technical tricks are mixed with mime, dance, puppetry and the absurd. These days, you can barely move in the Golden City without stumbling over a black-light theatre. It's touristy but it's pretty particular to Prague.

ANCIENT RHYTHMS

Making an ethnolinguistic recording of traditional Romany songs in Slovakia is a revolutionary idea, given the pervasiveness of negative Roma stereotypes in the country. But ethnographer Jana Belišová and her team, which included Zuzana Mojžišová (a writer and adoptive mother of a Roma son), set out to see if they could do it. The result was spontaneous recordings, new connections, a book and now several CDs. In 2005, *Phurikane gilá: Ancient Roma Songs* came out in English translation; the book and companion CD chronicle the team's experiences. The other CDs are *Karačoňa* (contains Romany Christmas music) and *Hoj na nej* (has upbeat dance compositions). Following are Zuzana's answers to some questions we asked:

■ *How would you define the difference between 'gypsy' music played at restaurants and traditional, authentic Romany music?*
'Those two types of music could be totally different (eg have a different repertoire) or they could be an identical song. It's the performance in the bar versus at home that is so different that we may talk about other types of work. In front of an audience it's done for effect, to be pleasing; they ['gypsy' musicians] play what is expected by the audience. Roma people at home sing for personal pleasure, personal need, for sorrow or joy. The song is the way to express emotions, to share them. They really can do it more truly, more essentially, than we do.'

■ *What role does Rom pop play in the Romany music culture?*
'A big one. Rom pop is a kind of murder of authentic Roma music. It's a natural progression, which happened a long time ago in other cultures; it can't be stopped. But it's very important to make records written and recorded in the way of original songs, tunes, words – to help them survive.'

■ *Of the Romany musicians and groups performing in the Czech and Slovak Republics today, which ones are truest to the authentic sound, in your opinion?*
'I don't dare to answer in...[terms of the] whole range, because I don't know all Romany groups. There are some who came in a blaze of glory in the media; mostly those left the authentic sound. These on CD are authentic: Radišagos from Prakovce, Siblings from Markušovce, Sol.'

■ *What projects are you working on next?*
'Jana Belišová is trying to find enough money to record and print our CD and book of children's Roma songs. Dana Rusnoková, the photographer in our book, is finishing a documentary about a Roma family in Rudňany. I'm writing my dissertation about European movies in which Roma people take part and about those that take place in a Roma *osada* (settlement) with the main protagonist a Roma man.'

Laterna magika (magic lantern) is the other interesting form of Prague theatre that survived the communist censors and continues today. In 1958, director Alfréd Radok and stage designer Josef Svoboda used projected images as part of their programmes that showed at the Czech booth at the World Expo that year.

Today, the theatre performances tell a story with the use of projected images, opera, dance, some black-light techniques and occasionally live animals, but no words. This mixed-media approach is a sellout. For more information see p139.

DRAMA

Drama, historical plays and fairy tales contributed to the Czech National Revival, with the first professional companies appearing in Prague and Brno. Major 19th-century playwrights were often those who, like Ján Kolár, were also active in writing novels. In 1883 the National theatre (p138) opened in Prague, cementing the Czech language's place on the stage.

In the early years of the first Czechoslovak Republic the leading lights among playwrights were the novelist Karel Čapek and the brilliant František Langer. During the communist era classical theatre was of a high quality, but the modern scene was stifled. Some excellent plays, including those by Václav Havel, went unperformed locally because of their antigovernment viewpoint, but appeared in the West. In the mid-1960s, free expression was explored in Prague's divadlo na Zábradlí (theatre on the Balustrade) with works by Ladislav Fialka, Havel, Milan Uhde and comedy duo Jiří Suchý and Jiří Šlitr. Suchý is still performing today and has a successful show.

Environment

THE LAND

Czech Republic

The 78,864 sq km of the Czech Republic, squeezed between Germany, Austria, Slovakia and Poland, is made up of Bohemia in the west and Moravia in the east.

Roughly speaking, Bohemia is a 500m-high plateau surrounded by low mountains, forming a basin drained by the Labe (upper Elbe) river and its tributary, the Vltava (Moldau), the republic's longest river at 430km. Along the German border are the Šumava mountains in the southwest, and the Bohemian Forest in the west. At the eastern Polish border rises the impressive Krkonoše mountain range, which contains the republic's highest peak, Sněžka (1602m). East Bohemia, in the northeastern corner of the country, is home to the striking 'rock towns' of Český ráj and Adršpach-Teplice Rocks. The biggest lake in the republic, the 4870-hectare Lake Lipno, is in South Bohemia.

Moravia is mostly lowlands, drained by the river Morava flowing south to the Danube, and bordered by the Odra (Oder) river, which rounds the eastern end of the Sudeten Range into Poland. While Moravia is generally flat, it does have a few mountains, namely the White Carpathians and Javorníky in the east, and Beskydy and Jeseníky in the north. The 120-sq-km Moravian Karst, north of Brno, features limestone caves and subterranean lakes.

There are more than 1500 sandstone spires that average 15m in height in the Adršpach-Teplice Rocks area.

Slovakia

The Slovak Republic is hill country; almost 80% of Slovakia's 49,035 sq km is more than 750m above sea level. Bordered by Austria, Hungary, Ukraine, Poland and the Czech Republic, it sits on the western end of the great Carpathian mountain chain that arcs up through Romania and western Ukraine.

Much of Slovakia is steep, forested mountains, which is probably its most endearing feature. Most well known are two parallel branches of the western Carpathians: the High Tatras, rising to about 2500m and spilling over into Poland, and the Low Tatras, reaching about 2000m in Central and East Slovakia. The republic's highest peak, the 2654m Gerlachovský štít, is in the High Tatras. Outdoor enthusiasts also frequent two subsidiary ranges of the Tatras: the Malá Fatra and Veľká Fatra. Slovakia faces the Czech Republic across the modest White Carpathians.

At the eastern end of the Low Tatras is the Slovenský raj region, which is riddled with gorges and mountain streams. Several thousand limestone caves dot the Slovak Karst in the south.

The main exception to all this high relief is the southwestern lowland region outside Bratislava around the Danube river, which is also Slovakia's main agricultural area. The river and its two tributaries form much of the area's boundary with Hungary, and the Váh, Slovakia's longest river at 433km, joins the Danube here. Slovakia's largest natural lake is the 218-hectare Veľké Hincovo in the High Tatras.

The Jasov Cave in the southern part of East Slovakia bears graffiti scrawled by Czech Hussites in 1452.

Birds of the Czech Republic, by Joseph Kren, details 394 friendly fliers to look for while you're out and about.

WILDLIFE

Even though there is a plethora of plant and animal life in the Czech and Slovak Republics, wildlife-watching is not a huge tourist draw-card. This is due mainly to the republics' natural features: densely forested hills provide perfect cover for many species and the steep alpine mountains in Slovakia don't make life easy for amateur animal-spotters. Nevertheless, the **Slovak Wildlife Society** (☎ 044-5293752; www.slovakwildlife.org) occasionally organises wildlife-watching walks in the Tatras.

Animals

For more on the endangered great bustard, or dropie, in Slovakia, go to www.dropy.sk.

Slovakia's most diverse wildlife area is the High Tatras – home to brown bears, wolves, lynxes and other wildcats, marmots, otters, eagles and mink. Most of these animals are protected from hunting in national parks. One animal protected even outside parks is the chamois, a mountain antelope, which was for a time near extinction but is now making a comeback. Deer, pheasants, partridges, ducks, wild geese, storks, grouse, eagles and vultures can be seen throughout the countryside. Europe's heaviest bird, the great bustard (or dropie), makes a home on the Danube flood plains.

The most common types of wildlife in the Czech mountains are marmots (giant ground squirrels), otters, martens (weasel-like carnivores) and mink. In the woods and fields there are pheasants, partridges, deer, ducks and wild geese. Rarer animals are lynxes, eagles, vultures, ospreys (large, long-winged hawks), storks, bustards and grouse. Very occasionally, wolves and brown bears wander across the Carpathian mountains into eastern Moravia.

You might see a less frequently spotted eagle in the High Tatras; otherwise, the flood plains of the Danube river in West Slovakia are an excellent region for bird-watching, particularly during the migration periods of spring and autumn.

The smallest mammal in Slovakia, the lesser shrew, is an average of 5cm long. There's a 2000Sk fine for killing one.

As for animal dangers, there's not much to speak of; Slovakia witnesses the occasional bear attack, but that's about it. Bears, wolves and lynxes roam the bigger national parks and protected areas in Slovakia, but a pile of excrement is the closest you'll likely come to them.

Plants

Despite centuries of clear-felling for cultivation, forests – mainly oak, beech and spruce – still cover about one-third of the Czech Republic. Dwarf pine is common near the tree line (1400m). Above it there is little but grasses, shrubs and lichens.

Most remaining virgin forest is in inaccessible mountain areas. Over half of the high-altitude forest in North Bohemia – especially in the Krušné hory, Jizerské hory and Krkonoše mountains – has been killed or blighted by acid rain from unregulated industrial development.

Forests still cover 41% of Slovakia, including 70 fragments of virgin forest, despite centuries of deforestation. Low-lying areas (up to 800m) are populated by oak and beech, midrange (700m to 1500m) with fir and spruce, and upper alpine areas (above 1500m) are dotted with dwarf pine. A devastating windstorm whisked through the Tatra National Park in 2004, uprooting huge swaths of midrange trees wholesale. Parts of the once heavily forested High Tatras resorts are barren. The last storm of this magnitude hit in the 1920s, so it'll be another 80 years or so until trees reach prestorm levels.

The bilingual pictorial *Slovak National Parks (Slovenské Národné Parky)*, by Vladimir Barta, is a stunning look at Slovakia's natural assets.

NATIONAL PARKS

Though national and local authorities have set aside numerous national parks and protected landscape areas, the emphasis is on visitor use as well as species protection.

National parks and protected areas make up approximately 16% of the Czech Republic and 23% of Slovakia. Their diverse landscapes and easy accessibility make them popular with both locals and tourists. Out of the four national parks in the Czech Republic, Šumava and Krkonoše win the popularity race hands down: both are well-known winter ski resorts and

CZECH REPUBLIC NATIONAL PARKS & NOTABLE PROTECTED LANDSCAPES

Park	Features	Activities	Best time to visit	Page
Šumava National Park (685 sq km)	gentle rolling hills and pristine forest; lynxes, deer, grouse	hiking, cycling, skiing	year-round	p179
Krkonoše National Park (363 sq km)	rounded, alpine mountains; boar, deer, badgers, foxes, martens, buzzards, hawks, eagles	hiking, skiing	year-round	p262
Czech Switzerland National Park (117 sq km)	sandstone rocks and rich forest	hiking, cycling, rock climbing	May-Sep	p240
Podyjí National Park (63 sq km)	river valleys and gentle pastures; otters, bats, fire salamanders, buzzards, eagles owls	hiking, cycling	May-Sep	p320
Bohemian Paradise Protected Landscape Region (92 sq km)	sandstone rock formations and wetlands	hiking, rock climbing	May-Sep	p255
Adršpach-Teplice Rocks Protected Landscape Region (20 sq km)	mesmerising sandstone pinnacles and caves	hiking, rock climbing	May-Sep	p260

SLOVAKIA NATIONAL PARKS & NOTABLE PROTECTED LANDSCAPES

Park	Features	Activities	Best time to visit	Page
Tatra National Park (795 sq km)	pristine mountains; deer, boar, foxes, lynxes, otters, golden eagles	hiking, cycling, skiing, rock climbing	year-round	p396
Pieniny National Park (21 sq km)	steep gorge and gentle river; lynxes, otters, black storks, owls, woodpeckers	hiking, cycling, rafting	May-Sep	p414
Low Tatras National Park (810 sq km)	dense forest and alpine meadows; brown bears, wolves, deer, foxes, golden eagles	hiking, cycling, skiing, rock climbing	year-round	p388
Slovenský raj National Park (197 sq km)	waterfalls and stunning gorges; brown bears, wolves, lynxes, martens, golden eagles, deer, chamois	hiking, cycling, caving	May-Sep	p420
Malá Fatra National Park (226 sq km)	steep alpine pastures; golden eagles, deer, bears	hiking, cycling, skiing	year-round	p380
Poloniny National Park (668 sq km)	dense forest, rugged hills and mountain meadows; wolves, lynxes, wildcats, golden eagles	hiking, cycling	May-Sep	p432
Velká Fatra National Park (403 sq km)	subalpine meadows and grassy uplands; brown bears, lynxes, boar, deer, golden eagles	hiking, cycling, skiing	year-round	p386
Slovak Karst National Park (440 sq km)	gentle hills and a plethora of caves; brown bears, wolves, lynxes, deer, otters, bats, common vipers	hiking, cycling, caving	May-Sep	p424
Murán Plain National Park (219 sq km)	dense woodlands, deep chasms and unexplored caves; brown bears, wolves, lynxes, deer	hiking, cycling	May-Sep	p424

summer hiking areas. Of the seven national parks in Slovakia, the High Tatras and the Slovenský raj are the most frequented. For more information about activities in the parks see p60.

ENVIRONMENTAL ISSUES
Czech Republic

Single-minded industrial development policies during successive communist governments caused environmental havoc for decades in both republics. In the 18 years since the Velvet Revolution, policies have changed significantly; standards were increased again to meet EU regulations for 2004 membership.

In the Czech Republic improvements have been significant in several areas. In the 1980s the biggest problem was the sulphur content in the brown coal used as fuel by industries. Resulting sulphur dioxide emissions caused acid rain that decimated forests, especially in Northern Bohemia, in an area adjacent to Austria and Germany that was called the 'Black Triangle'. A reported 71% of Czech forests were affected. Stricter laws post-1989 and replanted forests have gone a long way to cleaning up this problem. About half the rivers in the country are now safe enough to swim in and fish are slowly coming back to rivers, like the Labe that in 2006 recorded the first salmon seen there since 1954.

The biggest issue today is the increase in the number of cars (four times as many in Prague as prerevolution). The Czech Republic has the highest rate of greenhouse emissions of any EU member state. But in other areas the World Economic Forum rated the state fourth best in environmental management in 2005, and the government seems committed to cleaning up past messes. The Spolana plant outside Prague, a site that contaminated local water when floods hit in 2002, is being completely dug up. It should be 'decontaminated' by 2008.

Temelín, one of two nuclear plants in the Czech Republic (the other is in Dukovany), came on line in 2000. Protests from neighbouring Austria (just 50km away) haven't died down much (some groups tried to block the Czech Republic's entry into the EU because of it). A small (3 cu metres) radioactive water leak in 2004 was contained and didn't threaten any populations, but it reignited critics' fire.

Private involvement in environmental projects is adding to environmental progress. Groups include the **Friends of Nature Society** (www.novyprales.cz), which bought a 7-hectare site in North Bohemia and plans to reforest it and return it to indigenous vegetation.

Slovakia

Compared with the Czech Republic, more agrarian Slovakia has not been as badly damaged by industrial pollution; overall, its rivers and forests are in far better shape than the Czech Republic's. That said, the Slovak government's progress in addressing environmental issues has been slower than its northern neighbour. In a 2005 study the European Environmental Agency reported improvements in emissions and waste disposal (Slovakia is on target to reach the 8% reduction of greenhouse gases required by the Kyoto agreement). But following environmental nitrate guidelines is still completely voluntary for the nation's farmers.

As of late the government's attitude towards environmental concerns has also come into question. Critics fear that the separate €25 million environmental fund, created in 2006, is a ploy to eliminate the transparency required by law in other environmental agencies. On a smaller scale, local officials in Bratislava took a lot of heat in 2005 for tearing out many of the old-growth trees in the town's main square, Hlavné nám.

Margin notes:

Monitor Czech air and water quality online at www.chmi.cz.

Check out what the Agency for Nature Conservation and Landscape Protection is doing in the Czech Republic at www.nature.cz.

In terms of power usage, residents have, for the most part, turned to natural gas as the domestic heating source of choice, but as prices rise, brown coal again becomes attractive.

The Slovak Republic has two nuclear power plants that produce approximately 55% of Slovak power. Despite upgraded safety equipment, one of the units (two reactors) at the older plant, Jaslovské Bohunice (c 1980), is scheduled to be decommissioned in 2008 as part of the agreement for EU accession. The second plant came online at Mochovce in the late 1990s and was purchased by Italian energy company Enel in 2006, along with the majority of Slovak electric interests. There's been much talk of completing construction of two more nuclear units already planned at Mochovce.

The Gabčíkovo hydroelectric project, on the Danube west of Komárno, was not part of the Enel sale. Despite original controversy when Hungary pulled out of the project in 1989, the dam produces enough power to cover the needs of every home in Slovakia. Some believe it exacerbates the damage caused by annual floods, but studies are inconclusive. Events like **Danube Day** (www.danubeday.sk, in Slovak), which occurs every June, aim at raising awareness and money for river restoration. Groups such as the **Organisation for Forest and Wildlife Protection** (Lesoochranárske zoskupenie; www.wolf.sk, in Slovak) are involved in increasing forestland and tree planting in national parks (you can buy your own tree to be planted).

Outdoor Activities

As soon as the first shoots of spring poke through the earth, people in both republics take to the trails. Though the most rugged mountains are in Slovakia, there are undulating hills in both countries just waiting to be walked. You can hike up steep gorges past waterfalls, climb sandstone formations or stroll along gentle nature trails. There are rivers to float down and cycle paths to zip along. Then, just as the last of the autumn rays dip below the horizon, skiers and snowboarders come out to carve up the slopes.

HIKING

From scrambling up ladders to meandering across meadows, you can find the hike you are looking for in the Slovak and Czech Republics. Want to go for two hours or two weeks? With a network of some 48,000km well-marked and very well-connected trails for *turistika* (hiking), it's your choice. The colour-coded paths are clearly marked (about every 300m), and are visible on the great hiking maps available. (For more on maps see opposite.) Red trails are usually the main connecting paths between points of interest. The first trail in the area was established near Banská Štiavnica in 1874; today they are mostly maintained by the volunteers of the **Czech Hiking Club** (Klub českých turistů; ☎ 235 514 529; www.klubturistu.cz in Czech) and **Slovak Hiking Club** (Klub slovenských turistov; ☎ 02-4924 9223; www.kst.sk in Slovak).

Many trailheads link up with train station bus stops or train stations, making access to starting and finishing points straightforward. *Chaty* (mountain huts), which can be anything from basic shelter to a *horský hotel* (mountain hotel), are situated along many of the primary trails. Note that camping is restricted to designated camping sites and open fires are prohibited everywhere.

For more on exploring the mountains of Bohemia and Moravia, take a look at www.czech-mountains.com.

Walks

Slovakia has more rugged and unspoilt mountain scenery than its neighbour, the superlative of which is the High Tatras (p394). In this compact mountain range, you'll find the tallest peaks out of both countries (above 2600m) and plenty of alpine hiking, including the Tatranská magistrála (65km), a four-day trek along the southern flank of the High Tatras between Podbanske and Tatranská Lomnica. Its southwestern neighbour, the Low Tatras around Demänova valley (p391), is no less impressive; its 80km ridge through forested slopes and bare mountain passes is well suited for backpacking trips. Otherwise, some may prefer the pleasant, lower Malá Fatra range and Vratná valley (p382), with great access and much more greenery.

Slovenský raj National Park (p420) may not be easy to get to, but the hike to stunning gorges cut by waterfalls is worth it. Make sure you're in shape and not afraid of heights; many of the trails require use of precipitous ladders anchored into sheer cliff-face. The trails through the undulating forests of remote Polonini National Park (p432), on the far east Ukrainian border, are the least accessed and most peaceful in the nation.

The main long-distance route across Slovakia is the red, 762km-long Cesta hrdinov SNP (Path of the Heroes of the Slovak National Uprising), which takes about four weeks all told. Part of it is included in the European E8 long-distance path. To start the Slovakia section of the E8 in Bratislava, head up to the TV tower on Koliba (p345); you will eventually cross the Small Carpathians, the Low Tatras and Slovenský raj before turning north toward Dukla Pass, where the E8 crosses into Poland. The **Footpath-Marking Club of Slovakia** (Klub značkarov Slovenska; www.kst.kst.sk/znackari) has a full itinerary on its website.

The Czech Republic's landscapes may not be as dramatic as Slovakia's, but they still have much to offer. The gentle hills of Šumava (p178) have the best and longest hikes, some through virgin forest. It's possible to trek the length of the range from Nová Pec, at the northern tip of Lake Lipno, up to Nýrsko, southwest of Klatovy (about 120km).

Rugged sandstone formations studded with pine trees are the defining features of a Czech skalní město (rock town). You can find plenty of hiking in and among the rocks in Český ráj (p255) and the Sandstone Rocks of Labe (p240). The Adršpach-Teplice Rocks (p260), one of the most impressive, was a location for the filming of *The Chronicles of Narnia*.

The lightly forested Krkonoše mountains (p262) contain the country's highest peaks (around 1600m) and the 17km-long Czech–Polish Friendship Trail, following a border ridge from Špindlerova Bouda to Pomezní Boudy. It's part of the European E3 walking path that skirts along the northern boundaries of both Czech and Slovakia.

It's possible to circumnavigate the entire Czech Republic by bicycle, a distance of some 1780km.

Equipment

Backpacks, hiking boots and other camping gear are easy to find in sports shops near parks and outdoor recreation areas, as well as at large Tesco outlets, but campers who are particular about certain high-quality brands should bring gear with them. Mountain weather is incredibly changeable here – even in summer freak snowstorms are possible – and warm, water-resistant clothing is essential.

Information

The best hiking maps are generally from **VKÚ** (www.vku.sk) and **Kartografie Praha** (www.kartografie.cz). Look for VKÚ's *edice Klub Českých turistů* series (1:50,000) and Kartografie Praha's *soubor turistických map* series (usually at 1:100,000) for the Czech Republic; and VKÚ's *turistická mapa* series (1:25,000 or 1:50,000). *Knapsacked Travel in Slovakia*, by **Dajama** (www.dajama.sk), is a series of detailed hiking books, in English and German, on the popular walking areas in Slovakia.

Both maps and books are generally available in bookshops throughout the republics as well as at chain department stores.

CYCLING

One of the best ways to enjoy the Czech and Slovak Republics is from the saddle of a bike. There are over 60 clearly marked cycle paths (*cyklotrasy*) across the length and breadth of both republics. The Czech Republic is far more organised in providing multilingual information and having plentiful rental outlets. Though mountain biking in Slovakia is quite popular it is actually fairly difficult to find bike rental in Slovak towns. You usually only find bike rental at hotels in resort areas.

If you're not willing to go it alone, but would still like to cycle through the republics, there are several tour outfitters who would be happy to assist. **Top Bicycle** (☎ 519 513 745; www.topbicycle.com; Nám 24/27, Mikulov), based in South Moravia, runs bike tours in both the Czech and Slovak Republics. They will also transport bikes to you from almost anywhere in either country, for €0.80 per km plus rental. **Cycle Tours Slovakia** (☎ 0904042833; www.cycle-sk.com) has classic, all-inclusive Slovakia cycling itineraries, as well as self-guided tours where they plan it out, but you get there on your own. A part of the proceeds goes to environmental stewardship.

The Danube Cycleway, by John Higginson, maps the riverfront route from Germany through Slovakia into Hungary.

Paths

The natural areas mentioned in Hiking (p60) also have mountain-biking paths. The flat, popular Danube cycle way (200km) in Slovakia may suit some cyclists better; it follows the banks of the Danube through gentle countryside from Bratislava to Komárno. Or, if you have 20 days to spare, you can start in Donaueschingen, Germany, pass through Slovakia and end in Budapest. Another well-marked trail leads from Piešťany to Žilina (250km) along the Váh river.

Cycling is growing as a hobby in and around Prague (p117), where there are 60km of traffic-free cycle paths. You can cycle from Prague all the way to Vienna on the Greenways trail (456km), which passes through Jindřichův Hradec and Znojmo.

South Bohemia is an excellent region for cycling; highlights include the 240km Šumavská magistrála trail in the Šumava foothills (p178). A special bus transports cyclists and their bikes in the region. (For more on cycling in South Bohemia see p164.)

The South Moravian Borderlands (p317), especially the Unesco World Heritage area surrounding Lednice and Valtice, is a good place for cycling, too.

Cycle paths also link up with the Europewide network of trails, **Euro Velo** (www.eurovelo.org). Three trails pass through the Czech Republic: route N4 runs west to east via Prague and Brno, N7 north to south through Prague and onto Berlin, and N9 north to south via Olomouc and Brno to either Vienna or Poland. In Slovakia, the N6 hugs the Danube banks on its way to the Black Sea.

Equipment

A mountain bike or touring bike with at least 18 gears is a good choice, since both republics are hilly. There are cycle shops and repair centres in large towns, but for rural riding you should carry all essential spare parts. Security – a lock and chain for the frame and both wheels – is essential, as bikes are popular targets for theft. Children up to 15 years of age are required to wear helmets. See p458 for information on renting and buying bikes.

Information

Cycle paths are marked on hiking maps. Regional cycling maps (*cykloturistická mapa*; 1:75,000 to 1:100,000), published by **SHOCart** (www.shocart.cz) and **VKÚ** (www.vku.sk), are available in many bookshops, and often come with a handy booklet in English and German. VKÚ also produces the *Cykloturistický atlas Slovenska* (1:100000) for Slovakia.

Czech Tourism (www.czechtourism.sk) publishes a special cycling brochure titled *Cycling – Free and Easy*, in English and German, which gives details of long-distance and regional cycle routes.

Getting Around

Away from cycle tracks, stick to minor roads where possible. Motorists tend to give cyclists a wide berth, though narrow country roads are still potentially dangerous, especially at night. Like in any big city, cycling in Prague is more of an adrenaline rush than fun.

You can take your bike on the train quite safely. The charge is usually 60% of your own fare. Present your ticket at the railway luggage office and fill out a tag, to be attached to the bike, with your name, address, departure station and destination. If time is short, take your bike directly to the freight carriage and the conductor will load it for a small fee.

Bicycles can be transported on buses at the discretion of the driver.

Everything you ever wanted to know about skiing in Slovakia is at www.ski.sk.

Prepare to ride the rapids in the Czech Republic at www.raft.cz.

CONSIDERATIONS FOR RESPONSIBLE HIKING

The popularity of hiking is placing great pressure on wilderness areas. Please consider the following tips when hiking and help preserve the ecology and beauty of the Czech and Slovak Republics.

Rubbish

Carry out all your rubbish. If you've carried it in you can carry it out. Don't overlook those easily forgotten items, such as silver paper, orange peel, cigarette butts and plastic wrappers. Empty packaging weighs very little anyway and should be stored in a dedicated rubbish bag. Make an effort to carry out rubbish left by others.

Never bury your rubbish: digging disturbs soil and ground cover and encourages erosion. Buried rubbish will more than likely be dug up by animals, who may be injured or poisoned by it. If animals don't get to the rubbish it will probably take years to decompose, especially at high altitudes.

Minimise the waste you must carry out by taking minimal packaging and no more than you'll need. Take reusable containers or stuff sacks (sacks or bags you can stuff a lot of gear into).

Don't rely on bought water in plastic bottles. Disposal of these bottles is creating a major problem, particularly in developing countries. Use iodine drops or purification tablets instead.

Human Waste Disposal

Many think our ability to rationalise separates us from the animal kingdom – we beg to differ. It's our ability to use a toilet; where there is one, please use it.

Contamination of water sources by human faeces can lead to the transmission of hepatitis, typhoid and intestinal parasites, such as *Giardia lamblia*, amoebae and roundworms. It can cause severe health risks not only to members of your party, but also to local residents and wildlife.

If there is no toilet, bury your waste. Dig a small hole 15cm deep and at least 100m from any watercourse. Consider carrying a lightweight trowel for this purpose. Cover the waste with soil and a rock. Use toilet paper sparingly and bury it with the waste. In snow, dig down to the soil otherwise your waste will be exposed when the snow melts.

Ensure that these guidelines are applied to a portable toilet tent if one is being used by a large hiking party. Encourage all party members to use the site.

Erosion

Hillsides and mountain slopes (especially high altitude) are prone to erosion, so stick to existing tracks and avoid shortcuts that bypass a switchback. If you blaze a trail down a slope, it will become a watercourse with the next heavy rainfall and eventually cause soil loss and deep scarring.

If a well-used track passes through a mud patch, walk through the mud; walking around the edge will increase the size of the patch.

Don't remove plant life; it keeps topsoil in place. Picking wildflowers is illegal in the republics.

Wildlife Conservation

Do not engage in or encourage hunting. It is illegal in all parks and reserves.

Don't buy items made from endangered species.

Don't assume animals in huts to be introduced vermin and attempt to exterminate them. In wild places they are likely to be protected native animals.

Don't encourage the presence of wildlife by leaving food scraps behind you. Do not feed the wildlife as this can lead to their dependence on trekker hand-outs, unbalanced populations and diseases such as 'lumpy jaw' (a fungal disease).

Park Regulations

Take note of and observe any rules and regulations particular to the reserve that you are visiting. Generally speaking, neither free camping nor open fires are allowed in parks in the Czech and Slovak Republics.

ROCK CLIMBING & MOUNTAINEERING

With all those rock towns in the Czech Republic, it comes as no surprise that rock climbing is big here. The majority of climbing options in the Czech Republic are concentrated in North and East Bohemia, especially the Sandstone Rocks of Labe (p240) and the Adršpach-Teplice Rocks (p260). The rock in both places is a fairly soft sandstone, which has eroded into a spectacular profusion of pinnacles, towers, walls and arêtes (a sharp ridge separating two valleys), with many routes of a high standard. The more modest Český ráj (p255) also attracts wannabe spidermen and women.

> The fastest running river in Slovakia is the Poprad in the High Tatras. It drops 1567m in just 107km before it merges with the Dunajec.

The High Tatras (p394) in Slovakia have summer mountaineering routes on a near-alpine scale (the main summits rise to 2600m) and serious winter climbing. To go off trail, you have to have a guide: contact the **Mountain Guides Society Office** (☎ 052-442 2066; www.tatraguide.sk; Starý Smokovec 38, Stary Smokovec).

Tourist offices in these regions have details of mountaineering clubs, otherwise contact the **Czech Mountaineering Union** (Český horolezecký svaz; Map p92; ☎ 233 017 347; www.horosvaz.cz; Strahov Stadium, Zátopkova 100, Strahov) or the **Slovak Mountaineering Union** (Slovenský horolezecký spolok; ☎ 02-4924 9628; www.james.sk in Slovak; Junácka 6, Bratislava).

There isn't a lot of information available in English, but the websites www.adrex.cz and www.lezec.cz have some on climbing in the Czech Republic and www.tatry.sk has info on climbing in the High Tatras, Slovakia.

SKIING & SNOWBOARDING

The Alps it ain't, but skiing and snowboarding in the Czech and Slovak Republics is plentiful, popular and cheap; a ski pass at the top resorts will cost at most €25 per day, the less-frequented ski resorts can be half that price. The downhill ski areas are typically compact and crowded during school holidays. Rental equipment is decent, but skiers who are particular about certain brands should bring their own. The season lasts from late December to early April.

The best ski area is at Jasná (p392) in Slovakia's Low Tatras, where there are a dozen linked runs and chairlifts. Other good spots in Slovakia include the Štrbské Pleso and Skalnaté Pleso resorts of the High Tatras (p403) and the Vrátná valley (p382) in the Malá Fatra mountains. In the Czech Republic, the Krkonoše mountains (p262) have the best downhill skiing, at the resorts of Pec pod Sněžkou, Špindlerův Mlýn and Harrachov.

VKÚ (www.vku.sk) publishes ski-touring maps (*lyžiarska a turistická mapa*) that mark downhill runs, cross-country trails, chairlifts and areas of avalanche danger. Their blue covers distinguish them from the green hiking maps.

WATER SPORTS

Canoeing and kayaking are very popular in both countries, which have produced several world- and Olympic-champion paddlers. However, there are more opportunities for you to participate in these sports in the Czech

---

KNOWING THE ROPES

Though the same rules of responsible rock climbing apply in both republics, there are some extra things you need to know:

- Magnesium chalk is prohibited; it damages rocks.
- Rocks must be completely dry, or climbing is prohibited.
- If birds are nesting in the rocks, climbing is prohibited (areas are signposted).
- No metal hooks or nuts can be used on climbing ropes.

Republic than in Slovakia. The top canoe-touring rivers include the scenic Sázava (p153), which stretches from West Moravia into Central Bohemia; the equally popular upper reaches of the Vltava (p173) in South Bohemia; and the Berounka (p150) in Central and West Bohemia. In Slovakia there's the upper Váh, which can be accessed in the Low Tatras near Liptovský Mikuláš (p388). For more turbulent white-water rafting, head to the manmade rapids at Čunovo, (p354) outside Bratislava.

Flat-bottom boat trips are a tranquil way to spend a few hours. The Dunajec gorge (p414) in East Slovakia, is perhaps the most scenic, but there are also trips on the Váh river (p378) in Central Slovakia, and at the Kamenice gorge (p241) in North Bohemia.

CAVING

Both republics are honeycombed with dramatic caves, the best of which are in the Moravian Karst area (p306), north of Brno, and the Slovak Karst (p423), in East Slovakia (which includes one of the largest caves in central Europe). Another fine cave system is beneath the Demänova valley (p391) in Central Slovakia. In general, caving here is not about donning a hard hat mounted with a torch and scrambling around in a dark place on your hands and knees. It's about a gentle, albeit cold, stroll through underground caverns on a tour guide's leash.

OTHER ACTIVITIES

If you'd prefer a bird's-eye view of the republics, there are a couple of options open to you. The Low Tatras in Slovakia and the Krkonoše mountains in the Czech Republic are centres for paragliding and scenic flights. Contact **Mutton Sport Services** (☎ 0907481311; www.mutton.sk; Ul 1 mája 25, Liptovský Mikuláš) for the former, and the **Yellow Point Adventure** (☎ 499 433 505; www.yellow-point.cz; Svatopetrská 278, Špindlerův Mlýn) for the latter. For paragliding links in both republics, go to www.paragliding.net.

Food & Drink

Roast pork and dumplings vs fried pork and potatoes; on the surface Czech and Slovak cuisines aren't all that different. Both are solidly Central European, with shared influences from time spent as part of the Austrian empire (fried meat schnitzels is very popular). It's in the subtleties of preparation and in the secondary influences that differences exist. Northern Bohemia is big on roast meat. Slovakia's cuisine is slightly more spiced up, influenced by Hungarian traditions, and has a strong rural tradition and love for simple staples that hark back to shepherding camps. For the most part, the cuisines are national, with little regional variation. Although what they prepare may be similar, cooks in Moravia are considered the best in both countries.

The Best of Czech Cooking by Peter Trnka has been expanded to cover even more pork dishes.

Breakfast is usually a quick meal of bread and jam, sometimes augmented by cold meats and cheeses and/or yogurt. The main, hot meat-and-potatoes meal in both republics has traditionally been lunch, but the growing influence of Western business practices means the lunch break is becoming shorter and a sandwich at the desk more common. Dinner is usually a lighter version of lunch. 'Chinese' dishes – stir fries modified for local ingredients – have made inroads into home cooking and sometimes appear on the evening table.

Note: in this book where you see two italicised words separated by a slash (/), this indicates the Czech and Slovak terms, respectively.

STAPLES & SPECIALITIES

The solid heart of Czech cooking is roast pork with dumplings and sauerkraut. The *houskové knedlíky* (bread dumplings) are what Czech food is all about. Fluffy, light and soft, they are made from flour, yeast, egg yolk and milk, mixed with pieces of baguette. The mixture is raised like bread dough then boiled in hot water and sliced. These disklike pieces are served with anything that has a sauce or meat juice. They are best used for sopping up *svíčková* (roast beef served in a sour cream sauce and spices, best topped with tart cranberries). Much heavier than the bread version, *bramborové knedlíky* (potato dumplings) are made from shredded, boiled potato mixed with flour and egg yolk.

Zelí/kyslá kapusta (sauerkraut) is a usual accompaniment to roast meat dishes, but cabbage steamed with onions, apple, salt and caraway (it should be crunchy, not like English boiled cabbage) is an option. *Bramborový salát* (potato salad) is also served as a side dish and used as the base spread for most *chlebíčky* (Czech open sandwiches). Any Czech will tell you the most important thing when making potato salad (boiled potatoes mixed with carrots, onions, celeriac, mayonnaise, yogurt, pickles, ham, salami, eggs, cheese and parsley) is to let it sit for a day.

The hotel where the Czech 2006 World Cup football team stayed in Germany hired a Czech chef for the restaurant, specifically so the team could have knedlíky (dumplings) nightly.

Slovakia's 'national dish', *bryndžové halušky,* was a staple in shepherding camps in Central Slovakia and is still served at home. *Gnocchi*-like dumplings made from potato batter are dropped into boiling water and served topped with soft sheep's cheese (sometimes mixed with sour cream) and bits of bacon fat. Even the most progressive menus can have *halušky* hiding on them, however, the dish is almost never as good out (where dumplings are usually made ahead) as at someone's house. Try it at a more expensive place, where they're less likely to skimp on the toppings. Some restaurants get fancy, adding sausage to the dumplings (*fumánsky halušky*) or making the dough with spinach (*špenatovy halušky*). *Strapačky* is *halušky* mixed with warm sauerkraut.

Bryndža, a slightly sharp, spreadable sheep's cheese, is all but a national institution in Slovakia, especially in mountain regions such as the Low Tatras. You can have it as an appetiser served with bread and onions, or on top of

TRAVEL YOUR TASTEBUDS

Lard spread on bread with onions *(chleb/chlieb s masťou a cibuľou)*, anyone? Czechs and Slovaks have a fondness for animal products that might generally fall under the 'miscellaneous' category. The adventurous should try *kolínko* (braised pork knuckles), a specialty, or *drštková/držková* (sliced tripe soup), which actually has a calamarilike texture.

pirohy (moon-shaped dumpling pockets, like Polish *pierogies*) in addition to *halušky*. A particular treat is having it on top of fried potato pancakes, or in a thick soup called *demikat*. The freshest *bryndža* to be had is at a *salaš* (rustic sheep-dairy restaurant).

While pork is usually roasted in the Czech lands, *bračove rezeň* (pork cutlet) in Slovakia is almost always fried, in egg-and-flour batter, potato batter or breadcrumbs. It's also stuffed with all kinds of things, like ham and cheese (à la cordon bleu), before being dipped in hot oil, or occasionally served 'natural' without a coating. Stews and sautés are quite common. *Diabolské soté* (devil's sauté – mixed pork and semihot peppers) comes stuffed in a potato pancake *(v zemiakovej placke)*. Side dishes are extra and usually include fried, baked or boiled potatoes.

Traditionally, soups like *cesnaková* (garlic; creamy or clear, with croutons and cheese) and *kapustnica* (cabbage; with a paprika and pork base) started most meals at home. They are still on menus in both republics (portions are generally large and well worth trying) but the tradition is dying out at home.

The cheapest meal on the menu in either republic is usually *guláš* (goulash – cubes of beef or pork mixed with an equal quantity of sliced onions, fried with paprika then stewed with stock and tomatoes). The best *guláš* is three days old (though EU regulations now prohibit serving warm, cooked food that's been standing for more than three hours) and each fresh batch should be seasoned with a spoonful of the last batch.

For dessert, try *palačinky/palacinky* (crepes) stuffed with jam, chocolate or fruit. *Ovocné knedličky* (fruit dumplings) are ball-like dumplings filled with fruit and coated with crushed poppy seeds or breadcrumbs and melted butter, sometimes accompanied by fruit purée and ice cream.

Snacks sold at food stands or from the 'with your beer' section of the menu include: *klobásy* (sausages) served with mustard and a slice of rye bread; *párky* (frankfurters); *langoše* (fried dough coated with various savoury toppings); and *bagety* (sandwiches made on baguettes, usually pretty light on meat). 'Beer cheese' (cheese marinated in garlic, spices and oil; mainly available in the Czech Republic) is a great accompaniment to a cold lager.

Slovak Cooking, by Jozef Rybár, is one of the few Slovak cookbooks available in English today. Too bad it doesn't have the Slovak food name translations.

DRINKS
Nonalcoholic Drinks

Bottled water is cheap and easy to get. Fizzy Mattoni is from the springs of Karlovy Vary. The Czech Republic's own 'energy drink' goes by the attention-grabbing name of Semtex (yes, it's named after the plastic explosive).

In Slovakia, the popular brand of mineral water is Bon Aqua, and the nonalcoholic drink that wins the popularity race hands-down is Vinea, a fizzy white grape juice produced by wine maker Vinarsky Zavod Pezinok.

Káva (basic coffee) is most likely to be *presso* (espresso) these days, so you needn't forego your cappuccino. Instant is usually served in homes. A range of *čaj* (tea) is available at all restaurants. Coffee and tea *bez kofein* (without caffeine) is not easy to find.

Alcoholic Drinks

BEER

Did you know *pivo* is a synonym for 'Czech Republic'? Seriously, the Czech people are happy to tell you they consume more beer per capita (at least 157L, though some claim it's 161) than any other nation. There's even a consumption counter at http://prague.tv/toys/beer/. Slovaks consume a measly 89L per capita of beer, but they do have a few tasty local options; try full-bodied Zlatý Bažant or dark, sweet Martiner.

If you just order a *pivo* you'll get a lager; dark beers are called *černý*. Draught beer comes in *malé* (small, 300mL) or *veľké* (large, 500mL). The number of degrees on a beer (10, 11 or 12) is not an indicator of alcohol content but of the amount of malt extract used; it has to do with the strength of its taste. Most beers are between 3% and 6% alcohol. You can return glass bottles to a point of purchase for a refund.

Visit www.brandchannel .com for a rundown on the Budvar/Anheuser-Busch Budweiser dispute (see Which Bud's for You?).

WINE

Slovaks produce and consume more *víno* (wine) per capita than the Czechs in both the *červené* and *bílé/biele* (red and white) varieties. Their wine history dates back to the 7th century BC when Celtic tribes, under the watchful Romans, planted grapevines in the hills north of Bratislava. Today, wine production is still concentrated in the Small Carpathians, around the villages of Modra and Pezinok. Though the quality may not reach snobbish standards, the varieties are eminently drinkable (read good and cheap) table wines.

BOHEMIAN BREWS

Rumour has it that Czech beer leads to a longer life, doesn't negatively affect your body shape, can cure menopause, and is so pure that it's impossible to get a hangover from drinking it. (While we can't comment on the first three, Lonely Planet authors have done thorough research disproving that last claim.) Whether or not it has healing properties, Czech beer is universally recognised as one of the world's best. The Czech Beer & Malt Association even filed for protected status of the classification 'Czech beer' with the EU. (You know, like Parma ham, or French champagne.)

Beer history in Bohemia dates back at least to the 850s, when growing hops is first mentioned in chronicles, but residents may have discovered they had ideal conditions for growing hops before that. The first larger-scale brewery was built in 1118 and beer was exported to Bavaria. In the late 13th century, Good 'King' Wenceslas granted the city of Plzeň, West Bohemia, the right to brew beer. Fast-forward to 1974 when future president Václav Havel wrote the play *Audience*, about a brewery worker in the employment of a diabolical brew master, and you'll get some idea of the influence of beer on the local psyche.

Including microbreweries, there are more than 100 beer makers in the Czech Republic. Don't get us to arguing about which is the best. You know the big guys: Prazdroj brewery (Pilsner Urquell, Gambrinus and Primus) in Plzeň (p222), and Budvar (aka Budweiser – the one in the big fight with American brewer Anheuser-Busch) in České Budějovice (p166). Both give brewery tours.

Really, you can't go wrong with any local brew: as the Czechs say, *Kde se pivo vari, tam se dobre dari* (Where beer is made, life is good). Here are a few names to look for that you may not have heard of:

- Ježek (Hedgehog; www.pivovar-jihlava.cz; South Moravia) – nine brews of varying intensity.

- Eggenberg (www.eggenberg.cz; South Bohemia) – a lager, a porter and Dia (a sugar-free beer).

- Černá Hora (Black Mountain; www.pivovarch.cz; South Moravia) – operating since 1530; its Kvasar (Light) is flavoured with honey.

- Svijany (www.pivovarsvijany.cz; East Bohemia) – a dark beer that has won honours, but the wheat beer isn't bad too.

The dry reds, like Frankovka and Kláštorné, are especially worth looking for. Names of makers to watch for are Masaryk and Matyšák. Slovak Tokaj, a white dessert wine from the southeast, is trying to give the more famous Hungarian version a run for its money (though it falls short).

You can taste and buy Small Carpathian wine at several wine shops in Bratislava (p352), and wine bars and shops in Modra (p356). One weekend in November, Small Carpathian vintners throw open their doors for Open Cellar Day (see boxed text, p357). You can winery-hop to your heart's content for one set price that includes a souvenir glass but not transportation.

In the Czech Republic wine is only big in Moravia. White wines are markedly better than reds. Good semidry whites are Tramín and Rulandské bílé. (Czechs tend to prefer sweetish whites.) In southeast Moravia people still gather at *vinné sklípky* (semi-underground family-run wine cellars) for a tipple and a song. You can find one in the towns of the South Moravian Borderlands (p317), which also have salons where you can taste Moravian vintages.

In both nations, a popular wine cooler and budget stretcher is a *střik* (half wine, half soda) with ice. A popular winter drink is *svařené víno/varené víno* (hot spiced wine). At the end of summer, shops and bars start selling *burčak/burčiak*, the fermented juice of the first grapes. It's a fizzy, tart sensation that tastes deceptively nonalcoholic but rapidly produces giggling and a serious need to sit down.

> According to *My Sweet Little Village* (1985), directed by Jiří Menzel, the perfect temperature for beer can be achieved by putting the beer on the seventh step down into the cellar.

SPIRITS

Slivovitz is a fiery, potent plum brandy said to have originated in Moravia, where the best brands, like Jelínek, still come from. (See the boxed text, p70.) If you have a sweet tooth, try *griotka* (cherry liqueur). *Meruňkovice* is a brandy made from apricots, *borovička* from juniper berries. Czechs love the unique herbal spirit Becherovka, from the spa town of Karlovy Vary (p211); it tastes like cinnamon or cloves and is said to aid digestion. The Slovak version is Demänovka. Another popular bitter spirit is Fernet; the 'stock' version tastes like medicine, but try the citrus version with tonic water. Locally made vodka and rum (actually vodka with rum flavouring) is sold by the (incredibly cheap) shot from all kinds of outlets, including bakeries and sausage stands. For some warming grog, try rum with hot water and lemon.

> A grant from the Czech Ministry of Agriculture financed research in 2006 into creating an 'antimenopausal beer' (2% alcohol, with added phytoestrogens) that may ease annoying symptoms.

CELEBRATIONS

In Slovakia, name days (the saint's day associated with your name) are more celebrated than birthdays. The person celebrating their name day provides open sandwiches and drinks; people even bring elaborate spreads into the office.

At Easter, traditional foods like Easter egg bread are part of large communal meals. Christmas means carp, and rubber tanks full of live fish pop up on the pedestrian town squares a few days before 24 December. People take them home and let them live in the bathtub until Christmas Eve dinner.

WHERE TO EAT & DRINK

There isn't necessarily a difference between a *restaurace, kavárna/kaviareň* (café) or *vinárna* (wine bar, usually a cellar restaurant); all three may serve food and alcohol. Though a wine cellar might be a little more casual than a restaurant, in general what matters more on the fanciness scale is the price category.

In Prague, and to a lesser extent Bratislava, there is some really fine upscale dining. It may be obvious, but midrange places will have better cuts of meat and more elaborate décor than budget ones. You'll find international cuisines galore in the capitals, but as you get to smaller towns, pizza places and Chinese restaurants are usually as exotic as it gets.

> Find your saint's name day at www.slovensko .com/about/calendar and then make sure to throw your friends a party!

Self-service cafeterias (*samoobsluha, jedáleň* or *bufet*) are great places for a decent meal at unbeatable prices (as little as 80Kč/Sk for a soup and main). They serve hot meals like goulash and cutlets but also usually have soup and sandwiches. Self-service places generally cater to workers, so they close early and aren't always open on weekends. A *bageteria* is a simpler establishment, with made-to-order baguettes and sandwiches. Look for food stands near train and bus stations selling anything from sausages to sandwiches to gyros. You can buy fruit and vegetables at the local *tržiště/tržnica* (market).

Koliba are Slovak-style rustic country restaurants found across both republics. Typically, you walk into a log- or wood-panelled room where folk art and farm implements hang on the wall, and aromatic wood smoke drifts from the open fire where spit-roast chicken and other barbecue specialties are sometimes cooked. The Slovak *salaš* (literally 'sheep dairy', or shepherd encampment) has come to mean a rural country restaurant where sheep's products and traditional home cooking are the specialties. The accoutrements are similar to a *koliba*, minus the barbecue. A *salaš* is the place to have the freshest *bryndžové halušky*.

A *pivnice/pivnica* is a pub without food. A *hospoda/hostinec* is a pub or beer hall that serves basic meals. They're usually pretty smoky places where diners pull up a chair at the nearest communal table. Women sitting alone may feel uncomfortable in this male-dominated arena. If the name of a place includes the word 'pub' (in English) it's usually slightly more upscale, with food and a mixed-gender crowd. A traditional *krčma* was the village tavern, but the word is used for pub-restaurants nowadays.

For coffee, a streetside table at a *kavárna/kaviareň* is the place to be; they often also have food and adult beverages. Hanging out at a café is usual evening entertainment. If 'café' is spelled out in English/French in the name of a place, it's likely to be more bar and restaurant than coffee house. A *cukrárná/cukareň* (pastry shop café) is like a French patisserie, serving cakes, *koláče* (pastries), coffees and ice cream. For tea, find a *čajovna* (teahouse), where Eastern influences are evident; they're often smoke free.

Check out menus for restaurants in Slovakia online at www.menu.sk, and for the Czech Republic at www.czrb.cz.

MORAVIAN MOONSHINE *Neil Wilson*

Bohemia is famous for its beer and Slovakia for its wine, but in the wooded hills of Wallachia along the Moravian–Slovakian border it's *slivovitz* that puts a warm glow in the belly. Beware – this potent plum brandy (50% alcohol by volume) is strong enough to fell an ox. Local custom says that when you take the top off a bottle of *slivovitz*, you shouldn't put it back until the bottle is empty – by which time you will be fluent in Czech and Slovak, and mysteriously able to sing all the words to Wallachian folk songs.

Common or garden variety *slivovitz* is crystal clear and is traditionally drunk straight from shot glasses. If your palate is more accustomed to fine malt whiskies, the flavour can be – how shall we put this? – a little industrial. However, there is also *zlatá slivovitz* (golden *slivovitz*), which has been infused with oak shavings, and *slivovitz sudová* (*slivovitz* from the barrel), which has been aged in oak barrels. These are golden in colour and have a much mellower flavour.

Slivovitz distilling became a Moravian cottage industry in 1835, when the Hapsburg Empire relaxed the excise laws. Each farm had its own pot still, and the *slivovitz* season was a much-anticipated part of the agricultural calendar. Although it has been produced commercially for 150 years, locals still insist that the best *slivovitz* is *domácí* (homemade – now illegal).

The biggest brand in the business is R Jelínek, based in Vizovice (p331) in South Moravia. (It recently launched a plum-flavoured vodka, too.) The smooth, distinctive *slivovitz* produced by Žufánek, a small family firm in the Zlínsko region (established only in 2000), has in recent years become one of Prague's trendiest tipples. You can find it behind the bar at the Palác Akropolis (p137), Chateau L'Enfer Rouge (p135), Velryba (p135) and Klub Újezd (p134), among others.

CZECH & SLOVAK REPUBLICS' TOP FIVE

Here are the authors' top picks for restaurants in their regions:

- Kampa Park (Prague, p130) – awesome views of Charles bridge.
- V Zátiší (Prague, p131) – crisp roast duckling with herb-infused dumplings.
- Hanácacká Hospoda (Olomouc, p273) – rare Moravian cuisine.
- Spišsky Salaš (Spiš, p419) – rustic fun, great lamb dishes.
- Zbojnícka Koliba (High Tatras, p404) – folk music and spit-roast chicken on the fire.

Most restaurants are honest, though it pays to watch out for mistakes in the bill. Prague is a different matter (see the boxed text, p135, for ways to cope with restaurants there). Tipping is the same in restaurants and pubs, ie 5% to 10%. Locals usually round the bill up to the next 10Kč/Sk. Tip at the higher end of the scale if you're in a top-end establishment. In a pub with communal tables, always ask if a chair is free before sitting down: *Je tu volno?*

Quick Eats

A *bufet* or *bageteria* is the usual place to grab a quick meal. Bakeries and supermarkets sell savoury and sweet pastries for a quick snack. In bigger towns, at most transportation stations and near the base of ski and hiking trails, food stands can provide you with a hot or cold meal and a beer; hygiene is generally pretty good. Supermarket delis have good spreads, meats and bread rolls.

VEGETARIANS & VEGANS

Outside of Prague and Bratislava, where there are dedicated restaurants, it's slim pickings for vegetarians; vegans will find eating out next to impossible. There are a few standard meatless dishes *(bezmasá jídla/bezmäsité jedlá)*, but watch out for that category on the menu, as dishes like *bryndzové halušky* are usually listed there (guess those chunks of bacon fat on top don't count!). Don't assume that if something sounds vegetarian, it is (for example, most vegetable soup is made from beef stock); ask first.

The most common meatless meal is *smažený sýr/vprmážaný syr* (fried cheese) but you may also find risotto with vegetables, or pasta. In most cities there's at least one pizzeria and sometimes Chinese food, offering more vegetarian options. Fresh fruit and vegetables, grains and other ingredients are easy to obtain at most *potraviny* (supermarkets).

The Czech equivalent for the saying 'No pain, no gain' is *'Bez práce nejesou koláče'* (Without work, you can't eat pastries).

EATING WITH KIDS

Children are generally welcome in eating establishments. Pubs that serve food are in a 'restaurant' class, so there's no age minimum. Children's menus are more common in the Czech Republic than in Slovakia, but you may be able to ask the staff for smaller portions, or order for yourself and get an extra plate to share. See p438 for more information on travelling with children.

HABITS & CUSTOMS

If you're invited to someone's house for a meal, bring some flowers or a bottle of wine, and when you get there ask if you should take your shoes off (most Czechs and Slovaks switch to slippers inside the house).

Whether you're drinking in a bar or with a meal, you should always toast with the first drink (it's terrible manners not to). Clink glasses and say *'na zdraví!/na zdravie!'* (to your health). Before eating, you should wish your compatriots *'dobrou chuť/dobrú chuť'* (good appetite).

EAT YOUR WORDS

For more information on how to pronounce Czech and Slovak words, see the Language chapter (p469).

Useful Phrases

Can you recommend a restaurant?

Můžete doporučit restauraci?   moo·zhe·te *do*·po·ru·chit *res*·tow·ruh·tsi

Môžete mi odporučiť reštauráciu?   mwo·zhe·tye mi *od*·po·ru·chit' *resh*·tow·ra·tsi·yu

We have a reservation.

Máme rezervace/rezerváciu.   ma·me re·zer·vuh·tse/re·zer·va·tsi·yu

I'd like ..., please.

Chtěl/Chtěla bych ..., prosím. (m/f)   khtyel/*khtye*·luh bikh ... *pro*·seem

Chcel/Chcela by som ..., prosím. (m/f)   khtsel/*khtse*·luh bi som ... *pro*·seem

   a table for (five)

    stůl pro (pět)   stool pro (pyet)

    stôl pre (päť)   stwol pre (pet')

   the nonsmoking section

    nekuřáckou místnost   ne·ku·rzhats·koh *meest*·nost

    nefajčiarsku časť   nye·fai·chyuhr·sku chuhst'

   the smoking section

    kuřáckou místnost   ku·rzhats·koh *meest*·nost

    fajčiarsku časť   fai·chyuhr·sku chuhst'

What's the local speciality?

Co je místní specialita?   tso ye *meest*·nyee spe·tsi·uh·li·tuh

Čo je miestna špecialita?   cho ye *myest*·nuh shpe·tsyuh·li·tuh

What would you recommend?

Co by ste doporučil/doporučila? (m/f)   tso bi ste do·po·ru·chil/do·po·ru·chi·luh

Čo by ste mi odporučili?   cho bi stye mi od·po·ru·chi·li

Bon appétit.

Dobrou chuť/Dobrú chuť.   do·broh khut'/do·broo khut'

Cheers!

Na zdraví!   nuh zdruh·vee

Na zdravie!   nuh zdruh·vye

Some more ..., please.

Ještě ..., prosím./Ešte ..., prosím.   yesh·tye/esh·tye ... *pro*·seem

   mineral/bottled water

    minerálka   mi·ne·ral·kuh

   sparkling/still water

    bublinkové/bez bubliniek   bu·blin·ko·ve/bez bu·bli·nyek

   a bottle/glass of beer

    fláša/pohár piva   flyuh·shuh/po·har pi·vuh

   a bottle/glass of ... wine

    láhev/sklenička ... vína   la·hef/skle·nyich·kuh ... vee·nuh

    fláša/pohár ... vína   flyuh·shuh/po·har ... vee·nuh

   red/sparkling/white

    červeného/šumivého/   cher·ve·nair·ho/shu·mi·vair·ho/

    bílého   bee·lair·ho

    červeného/šumivého/bieleho   cher·ve·nair·ho/shu·mi·vair·ho/bye·le·ho

I'd like (the) ..., please.

Chtěl/Chtěla bych ..., prosím. (m/f)   khtyel/*khtye*·luh bikh ... *pro*·seem

Prosím si ...   pro·seem si ...

menu
jídelníček   yee·del·nyee·chek
jedálny lístok   ye·dal·ni *lees*·tok
bill
účet   oo·chet
účet   oo·chet

I'm a vegetarian.
Jsem/Som vegetarián/ka. (m/f)   ysem/som ve·ge·tuh·ri·yan/·ka

I don't eat ...
Nejím .../Nejem ...   ne·yeem .../nye·yem ...
  meat
  maso/mäso   ma·so/me·so
  chicken
  kuře/kuracinu   ku·rzhe/ku·ruh·tsi·nu
  fish
  rybu   ri·bu
  ham
  šunku   shun ku

I'm allergic to ...
Mám alergii na ...   mam uh·ler·gi·yi nuh ...
Som alergický/   som uh·ler·gits·kee/
  alergická na ... (m/f)   uh·ler·gits·ka nuh ...
  nuts
  ořechy   o·rzhe·khi
  orechy   o·re·khi
  seafood
  plody moře   plo·di mo·rzhe
  dary mora   duh·ri mo·ruh

Food Glossary
SOUPS (POLÉVKA/POLIEVKA)

bramborová/	bruhm·bo·ro·va/	potato
zemiaková	ze·mi·yuh·ko·va	
dršťková/držková	drshtʼ·ko·va/drzh·ko·va	sliced tripe
fazulová	fuh·zo·lo·va	bean soup with pork
houbová/hríbová	hoh·bo·va/hree·bo·va	mushroom
hrachová	hruh·kho·va	pea soup with bacon
kapustnica	kuh·pust·ni·tsuh	cabbage with pork
slepačí vývar	sle·puh·chee vee·vuhr	chicken bouillon
zeleninová	ze·le·nyi·no·va	vegetable

COLD STARTERS (STUDENÉ PŘEDKRMY/STUDENÉ PREDJEDLÁ)

chlebíčky	khle·beech·ki	open sandwiches on French bread, with cold meat, eggs, cheese, potato, ham or peas
Pražská šunka s okurkou/	pruhzh·ska shun·kuh s o·kur·koh/	Prague ham with gherkins
uhorkou	u·hor·koh	
ruské vejce/vajcia	rus·kair vey·tse/vay·tsi·ya	hard-boiled egg, potato and salami, with mayonnaise
sýrový nářez/	see·ro·vee na·rzhez/	cheeseboard
syrový tanier	si·ro·vee tuh·ni·yer	

MAIN DISHES (HLAVNÍ JÍDLA/HLAVNÉ JEDLÁ)

Mains are usually divided into *hotová jídla/hotová jedlá* (ready to serve) and *jídla na objedna/jedlá na objednávku* (prepared as they're ordered).

dušená roštěnka/	du·she·na *rosh*·tyen·kuh/	braised beef slices in
dusené hovädzie	du·se·nair ho·ved·zye	sauce
hovězí guláš/	ho·vye·zee/	beef goulash
hovädzí guláš	ho·ved·zee *gu*·lash	
karbanátky/karbonátky	*kar*·ba·nat·ki/*kar*·bo·nat·ki	hamburger with
		breadcrumbs, egg,
		a sliced roll and onion
kuře na paprice/	*ku*·rzhe nuh *puh*·pri·tse/	chicken boiled in spicy
kurací paprikáš	*ku*·ruh·tsee *puh*·pri·kash	paprika cream sauce
plněná paprika/plnená paprika	*pl*·nye·na *puh*·pri·kuh	capsicum stuffed with
		minced meat and rice,
		served with tomato sauce
rizoto	*ri*·zo·to	risotto, usually mixed
		with meat or veggies
segedínsky guláš	se·ge·dyeens·ki *gu*·lash	goulash with meat and
		sauerkraut in a creamy
		paprika sauce
svíčková na smetaně/	sveech·ko·va nuh *sme*·ta·nye/	roast beef with a sour
sviečková na smotane	svi·ech·ko·va nuh *smo*·ta·nye	cream sauce and spices
telecí pečeně/	te·le·tsee pe·che·nye/	roast veal
teľacie pečené	tye·lya·tsi·e pe·che·nair	
vepřová pečeně/	vep·rzho·va pe·che·nye/	roast pork
bravčové pečené	brav·cho·vair pe·che·nair	with caraway seeds
víděvský řízek/	vee·dyev·skee rzhee·zek/	fried pork or veal steak,
výprážaný rezeň	vee·pra·zhuh·nee re·zen'	aka wiener schnitzel

MEATLESS DISHES (BEZMASÁ JÍDLA/BEZMÄSITÉ JEDLÁ)

míchaná vejce/	mee·khuh·na *vey*·tse/	scrambled eggs
praženica	pruh·zhe·nyi·tsuh	
omeleta se sýrem/	o·me·le·tuh se *see*·rem/	cheese omelette
omeleta so syrom	o·me·le·tuh zo *si*·rom	
smažené žampiony/	smuh·zhe·nair zhuhm·pi·yaw·ni/	fried mushrooms with
vyprážané šampióny	vi·pra·zhuh·nair *shuhm*·pi·yaw·ni	potatoes
smažený sýr/	smuh·zhe·nee seer/	fried cheese
vyprážaný syr	vi·pra·zhuh·nee sir	

SIDE DISHES (PŘÍLOHY/PRÍLOHA)

bramborový salát/t	bruhm·bo·ro·vee suh·lat/	potato salad
zemiakový šalá	ze·mi·a·ko·vee shuh·lat	
hranolky	hruh·nol·ki	french fries
krokety	kro·ke·ti	deep-fried mashed potato
		(croquettes)
opékané brambory/	o·pair·kuh·nair *bruhm*·bo·ri/	fried/roast potatoes
opekané zemiaky	o·pe·kuh·nair ze·mi·a·ki	
tatarská omáčka/	tuh·tuhrs·ka o·mach·kuh/	creamy tartar sauce
tatárska omáčka	tuh·tars·kuh o·mach·kuh	

SALADS (SALÁT/ŠALÁTKY)

hlavkový/hlávkový	hlaf·ko·vee/hlav·ko·vee	lettuce
míchaný/miešaný	mee·khuh·nee/mye·shuh·nee	mixed cabbage or lettuce
		with tomatoes
okurkový/uhorkový	o·kur·ko·vee/u·hor·ko·vee	cucumber

| rajský/paradajkový | rais·kee/puh·ruh·dai·ko·vee | tomato and onion |
| šopský/balkánsky | shop·skee/buhl·kan·ski | lettuce, tomato, onion and cheese |

DESSERTS & SWEETS

jablečný štrúdl/ jablková štrudľa	yuh·blech·nee shtroodl/ yuh·bl·ko·va shtrood·lyuh	apple strudel
koláč	ko·lach	sweet filled pastries
makový	muh·ko·vee	poppy seed
ovocné knedlíky	o·vots·nair kned·lee·ki	fruit dumplings
palačinky/palacinky	puh·luh·chin·ki/puh·luh·tsin·ki	pancakes
zmrzlina	zmrz·li·nuh	ice cream

English-Czech/Slovak Glossary

MEAT & FISH

beef	hovězí (maso)/ hovädzie (mäso)	ho·vye·zee (muh·so)/ ho·ve·dzi·ye me·so
beef steak	biftek	bif·tek
carp	kapr/kapor	kuh·pr/kuh·por
chicken	kuře/kura	ku·rzhe/ku·ruh
cutlet, chop	kotleta/ rebierko (karé)	kot·le·tuh/ re·byer·ko (kuh·rair)
duck	kachna/ kačica	kuhkh·nuh/ kuh·chi·tsuh
fish	ryba	ri·buh
goose	husa/hus	hu·suh/hus
ham	šunka	shun·kuh
hamburger	hamburger	ham·bur·ger
lamb	jehně or jehněčí (maso)/ jahňa or jahňacie (mäso)	yeh·nye/ yeh·nye·chee (muh·so)/ yuh·hnyuh/ yuh·hnya·tsi·ye (me·so)
liver	játra/pečeň	yat·ruh/pe·chen'
meat	maso/mäso	muh·so/me·so
sirloin	svíčkova/sviečková	sveech·ko·va/svyech·ko·va
trout	pstruh	pstrooh
turkey	krůta/ morčacie (mäso)	kroo·tuh/ mor·cha·tsi·ye (me·so)
veal	telecí (maso)/ teľacie mäso	te·le·tsee (muh·so)/ tye·lyuh·tsi·ye me·so
venison	jelení (maso)/ jelenie	ye·le·nyee (muh·so)/ ye·le·ni·ye

FRUIT & VEGETABLES

apricot	meruňka/marhuľa	me·run'·kuh/muhr·hu·lyuh
beans	fazolové lusky/ fazuľa	fuh·zo·lo·vair lus·ki/ fuh·zu·lyuh
capsicum	paprika	puh·pri·kuh
carrot	mrkev/mrkva	mr·kev/mrk·vuh
cauliflower	květák/karfiol	kvye·tak/kuhr·fi·yol
cucumber/pickle	okurka/uhorka	o·kur·kuh/u·hor·kuh
fruit	ovoce/ovocie	o·vo·tse/o·vo·tsi·ye
garlic	česnek/cesnak	ches·nek/tses·nuhk
horseradish	křen/chren	krzhen/khren
lemon	citrón	tsi·trawn

mushrooms	houby/hríby	hoh·bi/hree·bi
onion	cibule/cibuľa	tsi·bu·le/tsi·bu·lyuh
peas	hrášek/hrášok	hra·shek/hra·shok
pickled cabbage	sterilizované zelí/ sterilizovaná kapusta	ste·ri·li·zo·vuh·nair ze·lee/ ste·ri·li·zo·vuh·na kuh·pus·tuh
plum	švestka/slivka	shvest·kuh/sliv·kuh
potato	brambor/zemiak	bruhm·bor/ze·myuhk
raspberries	maliny	muh·li·ni
sauerkraut	zelí/kyslá kapusta	ze·lee/kis·la kuh·pus·tuh
spinach	špenát	shpe·nat
strawberries	jahody	yuh·ho·di
tomato	rajče/paradajka	rai·che/pa·ruh·duhy·kuh
vegetables	zelenina	ze·le·nyi·nuh

OTHER ITEMS

black pepper	pepř/čierne korenie	pe·przh/chyer·ne ko·re·ni·ye
bread	chléb/chlieb	khlairb/khli·yeb
butter	máslo/maslo	mas·lo/muhs·lo
cheese	sýr/syr	seer/sir
chocolate	čokoláda	cho·ko·la·duh
coffee	káva	ka·vuh
cottage cheese	tvaroh	tvuh·rawkh
cream	smetana/smotana	sme·tuh·nuh/smo·tuh·nuh
eggs	vejce/vajcia	vey·tse/vuhy·tsya
honey	med	med
jam	džem	dzhem
mustard	hořčice/horčica	horzh·chi·tse/hor·chi·tsuh
salt	sůl/soľ	sool/sol
sugar	cukr/cukor	tsu·kr/tsu·kor

COOKING TERMS

boiled	vařený/varený	vuh·rzhe·nee/vuh·re·nee
broiled	roštěná (na roštu)/ roštenka (na ražni)	rosh·tye·na (nuh rosh·tu)/ rosh·tyen·kuh (nuh ruhzh·nyi)
fresh	čerstvý	cherst·vee
fried	smažený/ vyprážaný	smuh·zhe·nee/ vi·pra·zhuh·nee
grilled/ on the spit	grilovaný/ na rošte	gri·lo·vuh·nee/ nuh rosh·tye
homemade	domácí/domáci	do·ma·tsee/do·ma·tsi
roasted or baked	pečený	pe·che·nee
smoked	uzený/údený	u·ze·nee/oo·dye·nee
steamed	dušený/dusený	du·she·nee/du·se·nee
sweet	sladký	sluhd·kee

UTENSILS

ashtray	popelník/popolník	po·pel·nyeek/po·pol·nyeek
cup	šálek/šálka	sha·lek/shal·kuh
fork	vidlička	vid·lich·kuh
glass	sklenice/pohár	skle·nyi·tse/po·har
knife	nůž/nôž	noozh/nwozh
plate	talíř/tanier	tuh·leezh/tuh·ni·yer
spoon	lžíce/lyžica	lzhi·tse/li·zhi·tsuh

Czech Republic

CZECH REPUBLIC

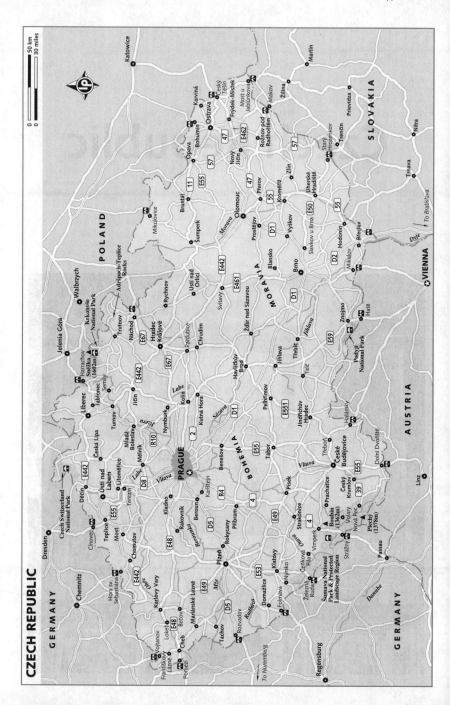

Prague

Magic, golden, mystical Prague, Queen of Music, City of a Thousand Spires, famed for Kafka, the Velvet Revolution, and the world's finest beers. The locals call her *matička Praha*, Little Mother Prague, the cradle of Czech culture and one of Europe's most fascinating cities. The tourist brochures go into overload when describing the Czech capital, but the city lives up to the hype – the city centre is a smorgasbord of stunning architecture, from Gothic, Renaissance and baroque to neoclassical, Art Nouveau and cubist. There's a maze of medieval lanes to explore, riverside parks for picnics, lively bars and beer gardens, jazz clubs, rock venues, museums and art galleries galore.

There's also no denying that the charm can occasionally be obscured by an overcrowding of tourists, congested traffic and tacky commercialism. So don't be angry with yourself if Prague leaves you a bit cold at first. Packed in among thousands of other visitors, trying like crazy to see the city in three days, worrying about getting ripped off; it's no wonder you think the city is overrated. Relax. It takes some time and searching to discover those magical moments when Prague reveals its full beauty – mist floating over the Charles bridge at dawn; the castle silhouetted against a stormy sky; finding yourself alone on the rain-washed cobblestones of a back-street alley, with piano music tumbling from an upstairs window.

Prague is an unmissable stop on any visit to the Czech and Slovak Republics. Beware, though – it is a city that gets under your skin, and many people stay longer than they intended. As Kafka once wrote, 'this little mother has claws'.

HIGHLIGHTS

- Wandering through the grounds of **Prague castle** (p87) in the early morning, before the crowds arrive
- Admiring the overblown magnificence of the **church of St Nicholas** (p94) in Malá Strana
- Enjoying a peaceful picnic on the battlements of historic **Vyšehrad fortress** (p110)
- Seeing as many as possible of **David Černý**'s (p121) endlessly amusing public sculptures
- Sitting with a cold beer in **Letná beer garden** (p136) after a long day of pounding the cobblestones

Letná Beer Garden
★

Prague Castle
★

Church of
St Nicholas
★

David Černý's
Sculptures
★

★ Vyšehrad Fortress

- POPULATION: 1,184,000

PRAGUE

HISTORY

Crossing the Charles bridge may be the quintessential Prague experience for today's visitors, but crossing the river was also the reason for the city's existence – it grew up next to a shallow spot in the Vltava river, a ford where people and animals could wade across (the spot now occupied by the Charles bridge).

Guarded by fortified hilltops on either bank – now Prague castle and Vyšehrad – the settlement developed into a busy trading centre and later a royal seat. But the growing town really came of age in the 14th century, when the Bohemian King Karel (Charles) IV became Holy Roman Emperor. Karel, still revered as the father of the Czech nation, made his home town capital of the empire, and funded a building boom that saw the creation of Charles University, the Charles bridge and St Vitus cathedral. Adding the New Town to the freshly Gothicised city saw Prague become one of the biggest cities in Europe.

In the following century Prague was the focus of religious conflict that would eventually see the whole continent plunged into war. Radicalised by the sermons of proto-Protestant reformer Jan Hus, who was burned at the stake in 1415, the population rebelled against the Roman Catholic elite, and nobles tossed several Catholic councillors out of a window in the New town hall (p110) – an act that became known as the First Defenestration of Prague. A year later, in 1420, Hussite forces led by General Jan Žižka successfully defended the city against a Catholic crusade at the Battle of Vítkov (now Žižkov) Hill (p116).

The Catholic Hapsburg dynasty took power in 1526. Later that century Prague became the seat of the Hapsburg Empire and, under Emperor Rudolf II, a focal point for European art and science. But in 1618 religious squabbling began anew when representatives of the city's Protestant nobles threw two Hapsburg councillors out a window of Prague castle (Old Royal palace; p89) – the Second Defenestration of Prague – sparking Europe's Thirty Years' War. Prague's Protestants lost early on in the piece: in 1620 the Hapsburgs routed them at the Battle of White Mountain (Bílá hora), just west of the city, and they sat out the rest of the war they'd started until 1648, when Swedish troops seized Hradčany and Malá Strana.

Eventually, the Hapsburgs moved their imperial seat back to Vienna, reducing Prague to a provincial town. A devastating fire in 1689 led to a spate of rebuilding, mostly in the baroque style that symbolised the power and wealth of the resurgent Roman Catholic church, and in 1784 the four towns of Prague – Staré Město (Old Town), Nové Město (New Town), Malá Strana (Lesser Quarter) and Hradčany (Castle District) – officially became one city.

In the 19th century Prague became the centre of the so-called Czech National Revival as Czechs struggled to keep their native culture alive under the German-dominated Hapsburg Empire. The movement found its initial expression not in politics – political activity was forbidden by the Hapsburgs – but in Czech-language journalism, literature and drama. A distinctive architecture also took form; Prague landmarks of this period include the National theatre (p109) and the National museum (p107).

As WWI drew to a close Czechoslovakia declared its independence, with Allied support, on 28 October 1918. Prague became the capital, and the popular Tomáš Garrigue Masaryk, a writer and political philosopher, became the republic's first president. Several days after the announcement, the country's new government had to ask Prague's citizens to please stop partying and do a little work, or the fresh-minted country's economy would collapse. But their new-found independence was short-lived.

On 15 March 1939 Nazi Germany occupied all of Bohemia and Moravia, declaring the region a 'protectorate' with Prague as its capital. The city suffered little physical damage during the war; however, its people – particularly the Jewish community – suffered a great deal. The Nazi Governor of Czechoslovakia, Reichsprotektor Reinhard Heydrich, was assassinated in Prague by British-trained Czech paratroopers in 1942; in a lather of revenge the Nazis executed hundreds of innocent Czech villagers (see the church of SS Cyril and Methodius, p110, and Lidice, p154) and a large number of Prague's intellectuals, pretty much wiping out the Czech resistance. But there were enough left in Prague to rise up against the Nazi occupiers – who were already militarily on the back foot – on 8 May 1945, driving them out one day before the Soviets marched in. Most of Prague was thus liberated by its own residents before Soviet forces arrived the following day. Liberation Day is now celebrated on 8 May; under communism it was 9 May.

After the communist coup of February 1948, proclaimed from the balcony of the Kinský palace (p102), economic and social policies almost bankrupted the country and crushed all dissent, sending Prague into a slow decline. Many people were imprisoned. Hundreds were executed and thousands died in labour camps, often for little more than a belief in democracy.

In 1968, under the leadership of Alexander Dubček, the party introduced reforms to ease censorship and increase democratic freedoms; the resultant flowering of artistic and intellectual activity was known as the Prague Spring. The Soviet Union, unimpressed by the direction Czechoslovakia was taking, sent in the tanks (supported by Warsaw Pact troops) on the night of 20–21 August. Fifty-eight Praguers died.

The extraordinary Velvet Revolution was set in motion on 17 November 1989, when marchers in Prague commemorating the execution of nine students by the Nazis 50 years earlier were beaten up by baton-wielding police. The communist government was brought down within a fortnight. On 1 January 1993, by agreement between the elected Czech and Slovak leaders, Czechoslovakia ceased to exist and Prague became the capital of the new Czech Republic.

Prague was ideally positioned to take advantage of the change – with its gorgeous pristine architecture, delicious beer and Eastern bloc prices, Western tourists found the city irresistible. Tourist income, combined with relentlessly capitalist economic policies, made Prague one of the wealthiest cities in Eastern Europe within a few years. The combination of picturesque streets, skilled workers and cut-rate costs also made the city a top location for international filmmaking.

PRAGUE IN...

Two days

Walk across **Charles bridge** (p100) in the early-morning light and head up to the **castle** (p87) before the crowds arrive. Take a tram to Staré Město and have a traditional Czech lunch at **U Pinkasů** (p130), then look around the **Prague city museum** (p105). Enjoy an evening of classical music at Malá Strana's **church of St Nicholas** (p94), then have dinner and a drink at **Hergetova Cihelna** (p129). Start your second morning with a tour of the **Municipal house** (p103), then head over to Josefov for a day at the **Jewish museum** (p96). Taste the new Prague at hip restaurant **Hot** (p132), then wander through Staré Město's **Old Town square** (p96) after dark to one of the area's many bars.

Four days

Follow the two-day itinerary above, then spend a relaxed day at **Vyšehrad** (p110). Head to the river and rent a **pedal boat** (p117) to watch the sun set, then treat yourself to a fancy dinner at **V Zátiší** (p131). On day four spend the morning seeing the **museum of Decorative Arts** (p97) and the exhibition of medieval Bohemian art at the **convent of St Agnes** (p104); after lunch take in the **museum of communism** (p107). Have dinner at **Kampa Park** (p130), with its awesome views of the river and Charles bridge.

One week

Spread the four-day itinerary over five days and give yourself time to sit around in some parks; **Kampa** (p95), **Wallenstein garden** (p94) and the **Palace gardens below Prague castle** (p94) all have their charms. On day six head out to Žižkov to see the **graves of Jan Palach and Franz Kafka** (p117), the **TV tower** (p117) and the tiny, uncrowded **Jewish cemetery** (p117) below it. Beer break! Stop off at Riegrovy Sady's **Park Café** (p136) for a sausage and cleansing pilsner, then hike up Žižkov Hill to see the **Jan Žižka statue** (p116). Spend the evening at **Futurum's** (p137) '80s and '90s party or hear some jazz at **Agharta Jazz Centrum** (p137). Grab some fried cheese and a beer in **Wenceslas square** (p107) on your way home. By day seven you should be exhausted! Take the funicular railway up to **Petřín** (p96). Revisit anything you really need to see again, and top it all off with a few shots of *slivovitz* (plum brandy) at **Palírna Igor Sevčík** (p135).

PRAGUE

GREATER PRAGUE

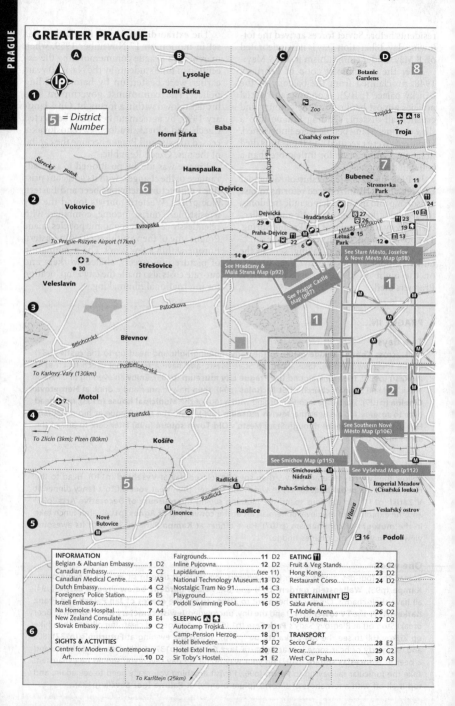

5 = District Number

Lysolaje

Dolní Šárka

Botanic Gardens

Zoo

Trojská

Troja

17 18

Horní Šárka   Baba

Císařský ostrov

Šárecký potok

Jug patyzáno

Hanspaulka

Bubeneč   11

Stromovka Park

6   Dejvice

7

Vokovice

Dejvická   4

Hradčanská

Evropská

To Prague-Ruzyně Airport (17km)

Dejvická
29   M
Praha-Dejvice   22   2
9   6   Letná Park

27
26
15   12   19

M   10
24
23

Milady Horákové

See Staré Město, Josefov & Nové Město Map (p98)

14

Střešovice

3
30

See Hradčany & Malá Strana Map (p92)

See Prague Castle Map (p87)

1

1

Veleslavín

Patočkova

Bělohorská   Břevnov

M

Podbělohorská

To Karlovy Vary (130km)

M

2

Motol   Plzeňská

7

See Southern Nové Město Map (p106)

To Zličín (3km); Plzeň (80km)

Košíře

M

Radlická

See Smíchov Map (p115)

Smíchovské Nádraží   M   See Vyšehrad Map (p112)

Radlická   Praha-Smíchov

Imperial Meadow (Císařská louka)

5

Radlice

Veslařský ostrov

Jinonice

Vltava

Nové Butovice   M

16   Podolí

To Karlštejn (25km)

INFORMATION
Belgian & Albanian Embassy.......1 D2
Canadian Embassy.....................2 C2
Canadian Medical Centre............3 A3
Dutch Embassy..........................4 C2
Foreigners' Police Station...........5 E5
Israeli Embassy..........................6 C2
Na Homolce Hospital.................7 A4
New Zealand Consulate..............8 E4
Slovak Embassy.........................9 C2

SIGHTS & ACTIVITIES
Centre for Modern & Contemporary
    Art..................................10 D2

Fairgrounds............................11 D2
Inline Pujcovna.......................12 D2
Lapidárium.........................(see 11)
National Technology Museum...13 D2
Nostalgic Tram No 91.............14 C3
Playground.............................15 D2
Podolí Swimming Pool.............16 D5

SLEEPING
Autocamp Trojská....................17 D1
Camp-Pension Herzog..............18 D1
Hotel Belvedere......................19 D2
Hotel Extol Inn........................20 E2
Sir Toby's Hostel.....................21 E2

EATING
Fruit & Veg Stands...................22 C2
Hong Kong.............................23 D2
Restaurant Corso.....................24 D2

ENTERTAINMENT
Sazka Arena............................25 G2
T-Mobile Arena.......................26 D2
Toyota Arena..........................27 D2

TRANSPORT
Secco Car................................28 E2
Vecar......................................29 C2
West Car Praha........................30 A3

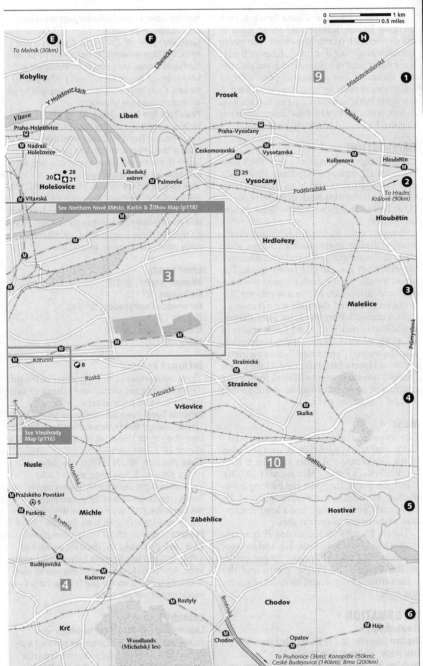

In August 2002 the Vltava flooded, submerging Karlín, Kampa and other parts of the city beneath its muddy waters. The metro system was almost destroyed, Charles bridge was under threat of collapse and many galleries and museums lost substantial parts of their collections as cellar archives were inundated. A few years later, however, the city was back on its feet, protected by new flood defence barriers that can be erected in a matter of hours.

ORIENTATION

Central Prague nestles in a bend of the Vltava river, which separates Hradčany (the medieval castle district) and Malá Strana (Little Quarter) on the west bank from Staré Město (Old Town) and Nové Město (New Town) on the east.

Prague castle, visible from almost everywhere in the city, overlooks Malá Strana, while the twin Gothic spires of Týn church dominate the wide open space of Old Town square. The broad avenue of Wenceslas square stretches southeast from Staré Město towards the National museum and the main train station.

You can walk from the main train station, Praha-hlávní nádraží, to Old Town square in 10 to 15 minutes. From Praha-Holešovice, take the metro (10 minutes). There's a metro station at Florenc bus station too – take Line B (yellow) two stops west to Můstek for the city centre. For more information about getting around Prague see p143.

Maps

City maps are available at newsagents, bookshops and travel agencies. A detailed plan of the city centre and inner suburbs is Kartografie Praha's *Praha – plán města* (1:10,000). It includes public transport and parking information, an index, a metro map, plans of the castle and Charles bridge, and a brief description of the major historical sites.

Lonely Planet's plastic-coated *Prague* city map is handy and hard-wearing, and has sections covering central Prague, Prague castle, greater Prague, the Prague metro and the region around Prague, and an index of streets and sights.

INFORMATION
Bookshops

Big Ben (Map p98; ☎ 224 826 565; Malá Štupartská 5, Staré Město; ☯ 9am-6.30pm Mon-Fri, 10am-5pm Sat, noon-5pm Sun) Small but well-stocked English-language

bookshop. There are also English-language newspapers and magazines at the counter.

Globe (Map p106; ☎ 224 934 203; Pštrossova 6, Nové Město; ☯ 10am-midnight) The best selection of second-hand books in town, and a comfortable atmosphere in which to browse through them. There's a coffee shop out the back, a wide range of international newspapers for sale and internet access (see following).

Palác Knih Neo Luxor (Map p106; ☎ 221 111 336; Václavské nám 41; ☯ 8am-8pm Mon-Fri, 9am-7pm Sat, 10am-7pm Sun) They're not kidding when they call this a palace of books. Head downstairs for a great selection of English-language novels and an internet café; maps and guidebooks are on the ground floor.

Shakespeare & Sons Vinohrady (Map p116; ☎ 271 740 839; Krymská 12; ☯ 10am-7pm) Malá Strana (Map p92; ☎ 257 531 894; U Lužickéo semináře 10; ☯ 11am-7pm) More than a second-hand bookshop, the Vinohrady outlet is a congenial literary hangout with a café that hosts poetry readings, author events and live jazz.

Emergency

All emergencies (☎ 112)
Ambulance (☎ 155)
Automobile Emergencies (☎ 1240)
Fire (☎ 150)
Municipal Police (☎ 156)
Police (☎ 158)

Internet Access

There are internet cafés everywhere in Prague. The following are particularly cheap or central, or have additional services.

Bohemia Bagel (www.bohemiabagel.cz; per min 1.50Kč; ☯ 7am-midnight Mon-Fri, 8am-midnight Sat & Sun) Staré Město (Map p98; ☎ 224 812 560; Masná 2) Malá Strana (Map p92; ☎ 257 310 694; Újezd 18)

Globe (Map p106; ☎ 224 934 203; www.globebookstore.cz; Pštrossova 6, Nové Město; per min 1.50Kč; ☯ 10am-midnight) One of the first internet cafés in Prague. Laptop connections available, same price.

net k@fe (Map p118; Na poříčí 8; Nové Město; per min 1Kč; ☯ 9am-11pm) Cheapest in the city centre.

Pl@neta (Map p118; ☎ 267 311 182; www.planeta .cz, in Czech; Vinohradská 102, Vinohrady; per min 0.40-0.80Kč; ☯ 8am-11pm) Good luck finding cheaper internet access. Pl@neta also has computers loaded with Microsoft Office – if you need to work on your CV or use Outlook – or you can connect your own laptop.

Laundry

Laundryland (☎ 777 333 466 for delivery; www .laundryland.cz for pick-up locations; per load wash & dry approx 120Kč) Nové Město (Map p106; 1st fl, Černá růže shopping mall, off Na příkopě; ☯ 9am-8pm Mon-Fri,

---

PRAGUE CARD

The Prague Card is a combined public transport pass and admission card that is valid for one year (the transport ticket is valid only for three consecutive days, allowing unlimited travel on the metro, trams and buses). It provides free entry to more than a dozen city sights, including the Military museum, the Vyšehrad casemates, and discounted fees (from 10% to 50%) at a couple of dozen more, including Troja chateau, the TV tower and a range of guided walks. However, it does not include major attractions such as Prague castle, the church of St Nicholas in Malá Strana and the Jewish museum.

It costs 860Kč (or €30 if bought via the internet), and can be purchased from the EuroAgentur desk at Prague Airport, the **Prague Card Change Office** (Map p98; Vodičkova 34, Nové Město) and online at www.praguecard.info.

9am-7pm Sat, 11am-7pm Sun, closed 1.15-2pm); Žižkov (Map p118; down steps beside Táboritská 3; 8am-10pm, closed 1.15-2pm); Vinohrady (Map p116; Londýnská 71; 8am-10pm, closed 1.15-2pm) The bar downstairs opens at 4pm.

Prague Cyber Laundromat (Map p116; ☎ 222 510 180; Korunní 14, Vinohrady; per load wash & dry approx 130Kč; 8am-8pm, until 9pm in summer) Internet café, graffiti wall and children's play area.

Left Luggage

There are left luggage services at the main train station (Hlavní nádraži; p142) and Florenc bus station (p141).

Media

The weekly English-language *Prague Post* (50Kč; www.praguepost.com) is fairly meagre reading, but its 'Night & Day' lift-out is an invaluable entertainment and dining resource.

The BBC World Service broadcasts in English and Czech on 101.1FM.

The city's best alternative music station is Radio 1 (91.9MHz FM), though good things are also being said about the newest kid on the block, commercial-free Radio Wave (100.7MHz FM).

Czech-language TV runs plenty of American sitcoms and films in the evening, but they're all dubbed: surrealists may get a kick out of watching *Friends* and *Baywatch* in Czech.

Medical Services

American Dental Associates (Map p118; ☎ 221 181 121; www.americandental.cz; 2nd fl Atrium, Stará Celnice Bldg, V celnici 4; Nové Město) Entirely English-speaking.

Canadian Medical Care (Map pp82-3; ☎ 235 360 133, after hrs 724 300 301; Veleslavínská 1, Veleslavín; 8am-6pm Mon, Wed & Fri, 8am-8pm Tue & Thu) A pricey but professional private clinic with English-speaking

doctors; an initial consultation will cost from US$50 to US$200. It's near the seventh stop – Nádraží Veleslavín – on tram 20 or 26 from Dejvická metro.

Lékárna U sv Ludmily (Map p116; ☎ 222 513 396; Belgická 37, Vinohrady; 24hr) This pharmacy is right by náměstí Míru metro.

Na Homolce Hospital (Map pp82-3; ☎ 257 271 111; www.homolka.cz; 5th fl, Foreign Pavilion, Roentgenova 2, Motol) The best hospital in Prague, with English, French, German and Spanish spoken. Take bus 167 from Anděl metro station.

Policlinic at Národní (Poliklinika na Národní; Map p98; ☎ 222 075 120, 24hr emergencies 720 427 634; www.poliklinika.narodni.cz; Národní 9, Staré Město; 8.30am-5pm Mon-Fri) A central clinic with English-, German-, French- and Russian-speaking staff. Expect to pay around 800Kč to 1200Kč for an initial consultation.

Money

Try to avoid the many private exchange booths (*směnárna*) in central Prague – they lure tourists in with attractive-looking exchange rates which turn out to be 'sell' rates (if you want to change foreign currency into Czech crowns, the 'buy' rate applies). There may also be an even worse rate for transactions under a certain amount, typically around €500. Check the small print carefully, and ask exactly how much you will get before parting with any money.

The main Czech banks – Komerční banka, Česká spořitelna, Československá obchodní banka (ČSOB) and Živnostenská banka – are the best places to change cash. They charge 2% commission with a 50Kč minimum (but always check, as commissions can vary from branch to branch). They will also provide a cash advance on Visa or MasterCard without commission. Using your debit card in the city's ubiquitous ATMs will get you the best rate of all.

American Express (Map p106; ☎ 234 711 711; Wenceslas Sq 56, Nové Město; ☺ 8am-10pm daily)
Travelex (Map p106; ☎ 224 946 066; Národní třída 28, Nové Město; ☺ 9am-1.30pm & 2-6.30pm daily)

Post

The main **post office** (Map p106; ☎ 221 131 111; www .cpost.cz; Jindřišská 14, Nové Město; ☺ closed midnight-2am) is just off Wenceslas square. There's an information desk just inside the main hall to the left.

The main post office uses an automatic queuing system. Take a ticket from one of the machines in the entrance corridors – press button No 1 for stamps, letters and parcels, or No 4 for Express Mail Service (EMS), and take a ticket. Then watch the display boards in the main hall – when your ticket number appears (flashing) – go to the desk number shown.

Most of the city's other post offices open from 8am to 6pm or 7pm Monday to Friday, and until noon Saturday.

Tourist Information

The **Prague Information Service** (Pražská Informační Služba, PIS; ☎ 124 44; www.prague-info.cz) Staré Město (Map p98; Old town hall, Staroměstské náměstí 5; ☺ 9am-7pm Mon-Fri, 9am-6pm Sat & Sun Apr-Oct; 9am-6pm Mon-Fri, 9am-5pm Sat & Sun Nov-Mar) main train station (Praha hlavní nádraží; Map p118; Wilsonova 2, Nové Město; ☺ 9am-7pm Mon-Fri, 9am-6pm Sat & Sun Apr-Oct; 9am-6pm Mon-Fri, 9am-5pm Sat & Sun Nov-Mar) Malá Strana bridge tower (Map p92; Charles bridge; ☺ 10am-6pm Apr-Oct) is a municipal agency that has Prague well covered, with good maps and detailed brochures (including accommodation, historical monuments and monthly entertainment), all free. All offices have Ticketpro's concert tickets and AVE's accommodation services.

Czech Tourism (Map p116; ☎ 221 580 111; www.czech tourism.com; Vinohradská 46, Vinohrady; ☺ 8:30am-noon & 1-4pm) Has information about sights, museums and festivals for the entire Czech Republic.

Travel Agencies

Čedok (Map p106; ☎ 221 447 242; www.cedok.cz; Na příkopě 18, Nové Město; ☺ 9am-7pm Mon-Fri, 9am-1pm Sat) Tour operator and travel agency. Also does accommodation bookings, excursions, concert and theatre tickets, car rental and money exchange. There are several other branches around town and at the airport.

GTS International (Map p106; ☎ 222 211 204; www .gtsint.cz; Ve Smečkách 33, Nové Město; ☺ 9am-7pm Mon-Fri, 10am-4pm Sat) Issues student cards, bus, train and air tickets.

DANGERS & ANNOYANCES

Although Prague is considered as safe as any European capital, the huge influx of money to the city has spawned an epidemic of petty crime.

Where tourists are concerned, this mainly means pickpockets. The prime trouble spots requiring vigilence are Prague castle (especially during the changing of the guard), Charles bridge, Old Town square (in the crowd watching the Astronomical clock), the entrance to the Old Jewish cemetery, Wenceslas square, the main train station, in the metro (watch your backpack on the escalators) and on trams (notably on the crowded Nos 9, 22 and 23).

There's no need to be paranoid, but keep valuables well out of reach, and be alert in crowds and on public transport. A classic ruse involves someone asking directions and thrusting a map under your nose, or a woman with a baby hassling you for money – anything to distract your attention – while accomplices delve into your bags and pockets.

Don't hand over money or passports to anyone stopping you on the street and claiming to be a plain-clothes police officer – insist on going back to the police station.

Avoid the park in front of Prague's main train station after dark, and be aware that the area around the intersection of Wenceslas square and Na příkopě is effectively a red-light district at night. The city has developed a burgeoning sex industry, with strip clubs, brothels and street workers all in evidence.

If you hail a taxi on the street, it's almost inevitable they'll rip you off. Public transport here is excellent, even at 3am, but if you must catch a taxi, call one of the companies listed in Getting Around (p146) rather than flagging a cab.

If you have lost your passport, wallet, or other valuables, report the loss to the **Foreigners Police Station** (Map pp82-3; Sdružení 1, Pankrac; ☺ 7.30-11.30am & 12.15-3pm Mon, Tue & Thu, 8am-12.15pm & 1-5pm Wed).

If your passport, wallet or other valuables have been stolen, obtain a police report and crime number from the **State Police Station** (Map p92; Vlašská 3, Malá Strana; ☺ 24hrs); you will need this to make an insurance claim. Unless you speak Czech, forget about telephoning the police, as you will rarely get through to an English speaker. You can apply to your embassy for a replacement passport.

PRAGUE

SIGHTS

For visitors from outside Europe, wandering through the ancient, winding streets of central Prague is enough of an experience to count as a sight in its own right.

Budget some time just to lose yourself in this medieval maze (let's face it, it'll happen to you whether you plan it or not) – if you spend all your time with your nose buried in a map, you'll miss some of the best spontaneous moments the city has to offer.

The most popular sights are in Staré Město (Old Town), Hradčany (the castle district) and Malá Strana (the Lesser Quarter). Nové Město (the New Town) is also packed with interesting things, including the city's best Art Nouveau architecture.

You should try to get beyond the city's centre for at least half a day; historic Vyšehrad, the birthplace of Prague, is worth a visit, while the inner suburbs of working-class Holešovice and Smíchov, genteel Vinohrady or grungy, youthful Žižkov will give you an insight into what regular Praguers get up to while the rest of us are watching the Astronomical clock.

Prague Castle

Prague castle (Map p87) – Pražský hrad, or just *hrad* to Czechs, and almost a small town in itself – is Prague's most popular attraction. According to *Guinness World Records,* it's the largest ancient castle in the world – 570m long, an average of 128m wide and covering a total area bigger than seven football fields.

Its history dates to the 9th century when Prince Bořivoj founded a fortified settlement here. It grew haphazardly as successive rulers made additions, creating an eclectic mix of architectural styles. The castle has always been the seat of Czech rulers and the official residence of the head of state, although the Czech Republic's first president, Václav Havel, chose to live in his own house on the outskirts of the city.

Prague castle has seen four major reconstructions, from that of Prince Soběslav in the 12th century to a classical face-lift under Empress Maria Theresa (r 1740–80). In the 1920s President Masaryk hired a Slovene architect, Jože Plečník, to renovate the castle; his changes created some of the castle's most memorable features, and made the complex more tourist-friendly.

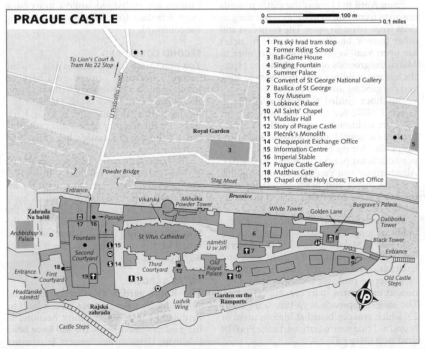

PRAGUE CASTLE

0 ———————————— 100 m
0 ———————————— 0.1 miles

1 Pražský hrad tram stop
2 Former Riding School
3 Ball-Game House
4 Singing Fountain
5 Summer Palace
6 Convent of St George National Gallery
7 Basilica of St George
8 Toy Museum
9 Lobkovic Palace
10 All Saints' Chapel
11 Vladislav Hall
12 Story of Prague Castle
13 Plečník's Monolith
14 Chequepoint Exchange Office
15 Information Centre
16 Imperial Stable
17 Prague Castle Gallery
18 Matthias Gate
19 Chapel of the Holy Cross; Ticket Office

PRAGUE CASTLE TICKETS

Ticket A (adult/concession/family 350/175/520Kč) Includes St Vitus cathedral, Great tower, Old Royal palace, Story of Prague castle, basilica of St George, Powder tower, Golden lane and Daliborka.

Ticket B (adult/concession/family 220/110/330Kč) Includes St Vitus cathedral, Great tower, Old Royal palace, Golden lane and Daliborka.

Ticket C (adult/family 50/100Kč) Admission to Golden lane and Daliborka only.

Ticket D (adult/concession/family 50/25/100Kč) Admission to basilica of St George only.

Ticket E (adult/concession/family 50/25/100Kč) Admission to Powder tower only.

Ticket F (adult/concession/family 100/50/150Kc/v) Admission to convent of St George only.

ORIENTATION & INFORMATION

Entry is free to the castle courtyards and gardens, and to the nave of St Vitus cathedral. There are six different tickets (valid for two days), which allow entry to various combinations of sights (see boxed text above); you can buy tickets at the **information centre** (Map p87; ☎ 224 373 368, 224 372 434; www.hrad.cz; ⏰ 9am-5pm Apr-Oct, to 4pm Nov-Mar) in the Third Courtyard (opposite the main entrance to St Vitus cathedral), or from ticket offices at the entrance to each of the main sights (St Vitus cathedral, Old Royal palace and basilica of St George).

From April to October the castle grounds are open from 5am to midnight, and the gardens from 10am to 6pm. The cathedral and other historic buildings accessible by ticket are open 9am to 5pm. From November to March the grounds open from 6am to 11pm, the historic buildings open from 9am to 4pm, and the gardens are closed.

One-hour guided tours are available in Czech (200Kč for up to five people, plus 40Kč per additional person), and in English, French, German, Italian, Russian and Spanish (450Kč for up to five people, plus 90Kč per additional person) Tuesday to Sunday. Alternatively you can rent an audio-guide (cassette player and headphones) for two/three hours for 145/180Kč. Ask at the information centre.

Most approaches to the castle require some uphill walking. The usual ones are from the tram stop in Malostranské náměstí, up Nerudova and Ke Hradu to the main gate; and from Malostranská metro station, up the old castle steps – probably the least pleasant option, as the narrow stairs are often crowded. The easiest approach is to take tram 22 or 23, which you can board at Malostranská or Národní Třída metro stations, to the Pražský hrad stop (Map p87).

FIRST COURTYARD

The castle's main gate, **Matthias gate**, is flanked by huge, baroque statues of **battling Titans** (1767–70), which dwarf the castle guards who stand beneath them. After the fall of communism in 1989, then-president Václav Havel hired his old pal Theodor Pistek, the Czech costume designer on the film *Amadeus* (1984), to replace their communist-era khaki uniforms with the stylish pale-blue kit they now wear.

The **changing of the guard** takes place every hour on the hour, however the longest and most impressive display is at noon, when banners are exchanged while a brass band plays a fanfare from windows overlooking the courtyard.

SECOND COURTYARD

You pass through the Matthias gate into the Second Courtyard, centred on a baroque fountain and a 17th-century well with beautiful Renaissance lattice work. On the right, the **chapel of the Holy Cross** (kaple sv Kříže; 1763) was once the treasury of St Vitus cathedral; today it houses the castle's box office and souvenir shop.

The **Prague castle gallery** (adult/concession 100/50Kč; ⏰ 10am-6pm) features 17th- and 18th-century European and Czech art. Opposite is the **Imperial stable** (Císařská konírna), which hosts temporary art exhibits. Past the gallery, the 1540 **Powder bridge** (Prašný most) crosses the **Stag moat** (Jelení příkop), where deer were raised for the royal table, and leads into the Royal garden.

ROYAL GARDEN

The Royal garden (Královská zahrada) started life as a Renaissance garden built by Ferdinand I in 1534. The most beautiful of the garden's buildings is the **Ball-Game house** (Míčovna; 1569), a masterpiece of Renaissance sgraffito, and where the Hapsburgs once played a primitive version of badminton. To the east is the **Summer palace** (Letohrádek; 1538–60), or Belvedere, the most authentic Italian Renaissance building outside Italy, and to the west the **former riding school** (jízdárna; 1695). All three are used as venues for temporary exhibitions of modern art.

ST VITUS CATHEDRAL

As you pass through the passage on the eastern side of the Second Courtyard, the huge western façade of St Vitus cathedral (chrám sv Víta) soars directly above you. Occupying the site of a Romanesque rotunda built by Duke Václav in 929, it's the largest church in the country.

You enter the cathedral through the western door; everything between here and the crossing was built during the late 19th and early 20th centuries. Inside, the nave is flooded with colour from beautiful **stained-glass windows** created by eminent Czech artists of the early 20th century – note the one by Art Nouveau artist Alfons Mucha (third chapel on the northern side), depicting the lives of SS Cyril & Methodius (1909).

Just to the right of the south transept is the entrance to the 96m-tall **Great tower** (☺ last entry 4.15pm Apr-Oct, closed during bad weather). You can climb the 297 slightly claustrophobic steps to the top for excellent views, and you also get a close look at the clockworks.

You'll need your castle admission ticket (A or B) to enter the eastern end of the cathedral, whose graceful late-Gothic vaulting dates from the 14th century. In the centre lies the ornate **Royal mausoleum** (1571–89) with its cold marble effigies of Ferdinand I, his wife Anna Jagellonská and son Maximilián II. At the far end is the spectacular, baroque silver **tomb of St John of Nepomuk**, its draped canopy supported by chubby, silver angels (the tomb contains two tons of silver in all).

The biggest and most beautiful of the cathedral's numerous side chapels is the **chapel of St Wenceslas**. Its walls are adorned with gilded panels containing polished slabs of semiprecious stones. Early 16th-century wall paintings depict scenes from the life of the Czechs' patron saint, while even older frescoes show scenes from the life of Christ. On the southern side of the chapel, a small door – locked with seven locks – hides a staircase leading to the Coronation Chamber above

the Zlatá brána, where the Czech **crown jewels** are kept.

Stairs lead down to the crypt, where you can see the remains of earlier churches that stood on the site of the cathedral, including an 11th-century Romanesque basilica. Beyond, you can crowd around the entrance to the **Royal crypt** to see the marble sarcophagi (dating only from the 1930s), which contain the remains of Czech rulers, including Charles IV, Wenceslas IV, George of Poděbrady (Jiří z Poděbrad) and Rudolf II.

THIRD COURTYARD

South of the cathedral is the Third Courtyard, which contains a granite **monolith** (1928) dedicated to the victims of WWI, designed by Jože Plečník, and a copy of a 14th-century bronze **statue of St George** slaying the dragon; the original statue is in the convent of St George.

The southern doorway of the cathedral is known as the **Golden gate** (Zlatá brána), an elegant, triple-arched Gothic porch designed by Petr Parler. Above it is a **mosaic of the Last Judgment** (1370–71) – on the left, the godly rise from their tombs and are raised to heaven by angels; on the right, sinners are cast down to hell by demons. In the centre, Christ reigns in glory, with six Czech saints – Procopius, Sigismund, Vitus, Wenceslas, Ludmila and Adalbert – below. Beneath them, on either side of the central arch, Charles IV and his wife kneel in prayer.

The **Old Royal palace** (Starý Královský palác; admission incl in ticket A or B) is one of the oldest parts of the castle. At its heart is the Vladislav hall (Vladislavský sál), famous for its beautiful, late-Gothic vaulted roof – with its rough wooden floors and vast, rustic spaces it feels more medieval than anywhere else in the castle, and may make you want to slug from a tankard and gnaw on a hapless animal's roasted limb. It was used for banquets, councils and coronations and, during bad weather, jousting: hence the sloping Riders' Staircase leading in from the northern side. In one corner of the hall is the entrance to the **Ludvík wing** where, on 23 May 1618, Bohemian nobles threw two Catholic councillors from the window. They survived, as their fall was broken by the dung-filled moat, but this so-called Second Defenestration of Prague sparked off the Thirty Years' War.

Housed in the Gothic vaults beneath the Old Royal palace is an exhibition called the

PRAGUE

Story of Prague castle (☎ 224 373 102; www.pribeh -hradu.cz; admission incl in ticket A, or adult/concession 140/50Kč; ☺ 9am-5pm), a huge and impressive collection of artefacts that is the most interesting exhibit in the entire castle. It traces 1000 years of the castle's history, from the building of the first wooden palisade to the present day, illustrated by large models of the castle at various stages in its development. Precious items on display include the helmet and chain mail worn by St Wenceslas, illuminated manuscripts and the Bohemian crown jewels. Anyone with a serious interest in Prague castle should visit here first, as orientation.

ST GEORGE SQUARE

St George square (náměstí U sv Jiří) is the plaza behind the cathedral, and the heart of Prague castle. The very plain-looking **convent of St George** (klášter sv Jiří; admission incl in ticket F) was Bohemia's first convent, established in 973 by Boleslav II. It's now a branch of the National gallery, with an excellent collection of Renaissance and baroque art.

The **basilica of St George** (bazilika sv Jiří; admission incl in ticket D or A) is the striking brick-red façade adjoining the convent, established in the 10th century. It's the best-preserved Romanesque structure in the Czech Republic, though most of what you see is from an 1887–1908 reconstruction. The Přemysl princes are buried here. On the left wall is a hole that enabled the nuns from the convent next door to communicate with the outside world.

POWDER TOWER

A passage to the north of St Vitus cathedral leads to the **Powder tower** (Mihulka; admission incl in ticket E), built at the end of the 15th century as part of the castle's defences. Later it became the workshop of the cannon- and bell-maker Tomáš Jaroš, who cast the bells for St Vitus cathedral. Alchemists employed by Rudolf II also worked here. Today the first floor houses a rather dull exhibition of 17th- and 18th-century weaponry.

GEORGE ST

Off George St (Jiřská), along the northern wall of the castle, is **Golden lane** (Zlatá ulička; admission incl in ticket A, B or C), also known as Goldsmiths' lane (Zlatnická ulička). Its tiny, colourful cottages were built in the 16th century for the sharpshooters of the castle guard, and later used by goldsmiths. In the 18th and 19th centuries they were occupied by squatters, and later by artists like Kafka (who stayed at No 22 in 1916–17) and the Nobel-laureate poet Jaroslav Seifert. These days, the houses are souvenir shops and the street is crammed with tour groups trying to get into them.

At the western end of the lane is the **White tower** (Bílá věž), touted as a prison where failed Irish alchemist Edward Kelley was locked up by Rudolf II – in reality, Kelley's prison sentences, for killing someone in a duel, were served outside the capital. At the eastern end is the **Daliborka tower**, which got its name from the knight Dalibor of Kozojed, who played the violin when he was imprisoned here in 1498: Smetana based his opera *Dalibor* (1868) on the tale.

Just inside the eastern gate is the **Lobkowicz palace** (Lobkovický palác; adult/concession 20/10Kč; ☺ 9am-5pm Tue-Sun). Built in the 1570s this aristocratic palace now houses a branch of the National museum, with a good collection on Czech history from prehistoric times until 1848. Exhibits include the sword of executioner Jan Mydlář (who lopped off the heads of 27 rebellious Protestant nobles in Old Town square in 1621) and some of the oldest marionettes in the Czech Republic, but to be honest this is a place for history buffs only.

Opposite Lobkowicz palace is the Burgrave's palace (Purkrabství) and its **toy museum** (adult/child 50/30Kč; ☺ 9.30am-5.30pm), allegedly the world's second largest, with tons of Barbies and toys going back to Greek antiquity. Sadly, it's frustrating for kids as most displays are hands-off.

Hradčany

The lanes and stairways of Hradčany, which stretches west from the castle to Strahov monastery, are an ideal place to wander – most of this area around the west gate of Prague castle is residential, with just a few strips of shops, pubs and restaurants. Before it became a borough of Prague in 1598, Hradčany was almost levelled by Hussites and fire – in the 17th century palaces were built on the ruins.

HRADČANY SQUARE

Hradčany square (Hradčanské náměstí; Map p92), the square outside the western entrance to the castle, has kept its shape since the Middle Ages. At its centre is a **plague column** by Ferdinand Brokoff (1726), and at its south edge stands the bronze figure of **Tomáš Masaryk**, the first president of Czechoslovakia.

On the north side of the square is the rococo **Archbishop's palace** (Arcibiskupský palác), bought and remodelled by Archbishop Antonín Bruse of Mohelnic in 1562, and the seat of archbishops ever since. Its wonderful interior is only open on the day before Good Friday; chances are you won't have time to wait around that long.

Opposite stands the Renaissance **Schwarzenberg palace** (Schwarzenberský palác), acquired by the powerful Schwarzenberg family in 1719, with a striking black-and-white sgraffito façade. Due to reopen in November 2007, it will house the National gallery's Old Masters collection.

Diagonally behind the Archbishop's palace is the 1707 baroque **Sternberg palace** (Šternberský palác), home to the **National gallery** (☎ 220 514 599; adult/child 150/70Kč; ⏰ 10am-6pm Tue-Sun) and its splendid collection of 14th- to 18th-century European art. Fans of medieval altarpieces will be in heaven; there's also a number of Rubens, a Dürer, some Rembrandts and Breughels, and a large collection of Bohemian miniatures. It's worth a trip to the back of the first floor to see van Heemskerck's *The Tearful Bride*, who seems to have stepped right out of a drag-queen show.

LORETA SQUARE

From Hradčanské náměstí it's a short walk to Loreta square (Loretánské náměstí, Map p92), created early in the 18th century when the **Černín palace** (Černínský palác, Map p92) was built. This palace today houses the foreign ministry, but during the Nazi occupation it was SS Headquarters. In 1948 the foreign minister Jan Masaryk, son of the founding president of Czechoslovakia, fell to his death from one of the top-floor windows. Did he fall, or was he pushed?

The square's main attraction is the **Loreta** (Map p92; ☎ 224 510 789; Loretánské náměstí 7; adult/child 80/60Kč; ⏰ 9am-12.15pm & 1-4.30pm), an extraordinary baroque place of pilgrimage founded by Benigna Kateřina Lobkowicz in 1626. The centrepiece of the Loreta is a replica of the Virgin's house, the **Santa casa**. Its interior has a naive charm, despite the opulence of its silver altar.

Across from it is the decidedly un-naive **church of the Nativity of Our Lord** (Map p92; kostel Narození Páně), built in 1737 by Kristof

Dientzenhofer. This church features two skeletons, of Spanish saints Felicissima and Marcia, dressed in nobles' clothing with wax masks over their skulls. The **chapel of Our Lady of Sorrows** (kaple Panny Marie Bolestné) features a crucified bearded lady, St Starosta. She was the daughter of a Portuguese king who promised her to the king of Sicily against her wishes. After a night of tearful prayers she awoke with a beard, the wedding was called off, and her loving father had her crucified. She was later made patron saint of the needy and godforsaken.

Loreta's most eye-popping attraction is the **treasury** (1st floor). It's been ransacked several times over the centuries, but some amazing items remain. Most over-the-top is the 90cm-tall **Prague sun** (Pražské slunce), made of solid silver and gold and studded with 6222 diamonds. Try not to get confused when you see the boxes asking for donations.

In addition, above the Loreta's entrance are 27 bells made in Amsterdam in the 17th century; they play *We Greet Thee a Thousand Times*.

STRAHOV MONASTERY

At the far end of Hradčany, Strahov monastery (Strahovský klášter; Map p92) is an enclosed oasis, a quiet escape from the castle-going crowds. Founded in 1140 by Vladislav II for the Premonstratensians. The present monastery buildings, completed in the 17th and 18th centuries, functioned until the communist government closed them down and imprisoned most of the monks, who returned in 1990; these days you can once again see robed figures striding across courtyards and slipping into cloisters.

The centrepiece of the courtyard is the stocky **church of the Assumption of Our Lady** (kostel Nanebevzetí Panny Marie; Map p92), whose green domes you can see from everywhere else in Prague. Built in 1143, the church is filled with baroque gilt; Mozart allegedly played the organ here on one visit.

But what the tour groups come to see is the **Strahov library** (Strahovská knihovna; www.strahovmonastery.cz; adult/child 80/50Kč; ⏰ 9am-noon & 1-5pm), the largest monastic library in the Czech Republic. The stunning interior of the two-storey-high **Philosophy hall** (Filozofický sál; 1780–97) was built to fit around carved and gilded, floor-to-ceiling walnut shelving that was rescued from another monastery in South

HRADČANY & MALÁ STRANA

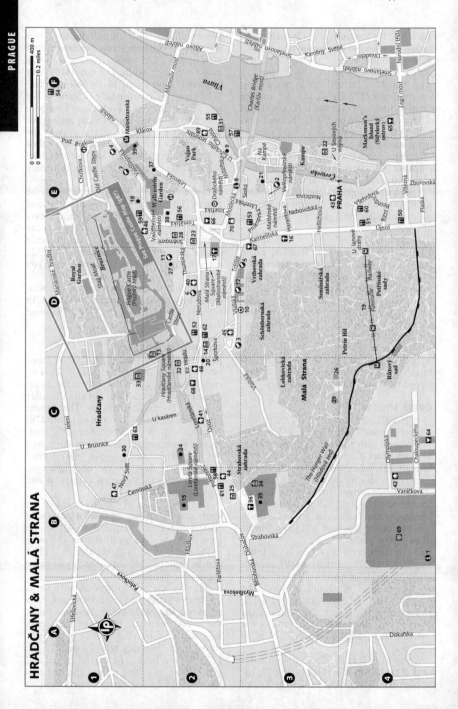

Bohemia. The lobby outside the hall contains an 18th-century Cabinet of Curiosities, displaying the grotesquely shrivelled remains of sharks, skates, turtles and other sea creatures; these flayed and splayed corpses were prepared by sailors, who flogged them to credulous landlubbers as 'sea monsters'.

A corridor leads to the older but even more beautiful **Theology hall** (Teologiský sál; 1679). On a stand outside the hall door is a facsimile of the library's most prized possession, the **Strahov Evangeliary**, a 9th-century codex in a gem-studded 12th-century binding. A nearby bookcase houses the **Xyloteka** (1825), a set of book-like boxes, each one bound in the wood and bark of the tree it describes, with samples of leaves, roots, flowers and fruits inside.

In the connecting corridor, look out for the two long, brown, leathery things beside the model ship and narwhal tusk – if you ask, the prudish attendant will tell you they're preserved elephants' trunks, but they're actually whales' penises.

Tucked behind the library and largely ignored, the **Strahov gallery** (Strahovská obrazárna; adult/child 50/20Kč; ☻ 9am-noon & 1-5pm Tue-Sun) contains a fabulous collection of Bohemian Gothic, baroque, rococo and Romantic artworks. Some of the medieval works are extraordinary – don't miss the very modern-looking 14th-century Jihlava Crucifix.

The 'write your name on a grain of rice' movement may have undermined the respectability of miniature artists, but Siberian technician Anatoly Konyenko will restore your faith with his **Miniature museum** (muzeum Miniatur; Map p92; ☎ 233 352 371; www.muzeumminiatur .com; Strahovské Nádvoří 11; adult/child 50/30Kč; ☻ 10am-5pm). Konyenko used to manufacture tools for eye microsurgery, but these days he'd rather spend seven-and-a-half years crafting a pair of gold horseshoes for a flea. See those, plus the world's smallest book and strangely beautiful silhouettes of cars on the leg of a mosquito. Weird.

Malá Strana

Malá Strana (Little Quarter) lies between Prague castle and the Vltava river. Most tourists climb up to the castle along the Royal Way, on Mostecká and Nerudova streets, but the narrow side streets of this baroque district also have plenty of interest. Almost too picturesque for its own good, Malá Strana is now much in demand as a film location.

Malá Strana started out as a market settlement in the 8th or 9th century, and was almost destroyed on two separate occasions: during battles between the Hussites and the Prague castle garrison in 1419, and then in the Great Fire of 1541. Following this massive devastation, Renaissance buildings and palaces replaced the destroyed houses, followed by the 17th- and 18th-century baroque churches and palaces that give Malá Strana much of its charm.

NERUDA STREET

Neruda Street (Nerudova Ulice, Map p92), part of the Royal Way, is an architectural delight. Most of its Renaissance façades have been 'baroquefied'; many still have their original shutter-like doors, and are adorned with emblems of some kind. No 47 is the **house of two suns** (dům U dvou slunců, Map p92), an early baroque building where the Czech poet Jan Neruda lived from 1845 to 1891, while No 12 is the **house of the three fiddles** (dům U tří houslíček, Map p92), which once belonged to a family of violin makers.

On the corner with Janský vršek is **Bretfeld palace** (Map p92), which Josef of Bretfeld made a centre for social gatherings starting in 1765; among his guests were Mozart and Casanova.

MALÁ STRANA SQUARE

Malá Strana square (Malostranské náměstí, Map p92) is really two squares, with the church of St Nicholas – Malá Strana's primary landmark – between them. It has been the hub of Malá Strana since the 10th century.

Malostranská beseda, at No 21, was once the **Old town hall**, where in 1575 the non-Catholic nobles wrote the 'Czech Confession' (České konfese), a pioneering demand for religious tolerance eventually passed into law by Rudolf II in 1609. In practice the demands were not fully met, and the nobles eventually got angry enough to fling two Hapsburg councillors out of a castle window (see Ludvík wing, p89).

In a city of butt-kicking churches, the **church of St Nicholas** (kostel sv Mikuláše; www.psalterium.cz; adult/concession 60/30Kč; 9am-5pm Mar-Oct, 9am-4pm Nov-Feb) – not to be confused with the other church of St Nicholas on Old Town square – has to be the best of all; the huge green dome is a Prague landmark. Baroque star designer Kristof Dientzenhofer pulled out all the stops on this one, and when he died his son Kilian picked up where he left off.

No matter how many baroque churches you've peered into over the last few days, this one will take your breath away. The ceiling fresco *Apotheosis of St Nicholas* (1770) by Johann Kracker – is the largest in Europe; clever trompe l'oeil technique makes the painting merge almost seamlessly with the architecture. Take the stairs up to the gallery for a closer look at the ceiling, and a balustrade scarred with the scratchings of bored 19th-century tourists and wannabe Franz Kafkas.

NORTHERN MALÁ STRANA

The castle steps (zámecké schody, Map p92) were originally the main route to the castle, and lead down into Thunovská street. Around the corner at Sněmovní is the **Parliament house** (Sněmovna, Map p92), the seat of the lower house of parliament. Historically it was also the seat of the national assembly, which on 14 November 1918 deposed the Hapsburgs from the Bohemian throne.

On Valdštejnské náměstí is the first of the monumental baroque structures built by Albrecht of Wallenstein, general of the Hapsburg armies in the 17th century. The **Wallenstein palace** (Valdštejnský palác, Map p92), built between 1623 and 1629, displaced 23 houses, a brickworks and three gardens. It's now occupied by the Senate of the Czech Republic.

Beside the palace is the huge, geometrically designed **Wallenstein garden** (Valdštejnská zahrada; Map p92; 10am-6pm Apr-Oct). Its finest feature is the huge loggia decorated with scenes from the Trojan Wars, flanked to one side by a fake **stalactite grotto** full of hidden animals and grotesque faces. The **bronze statues** of Greek gods lining the avenue opposite the loggia are copies – the originals were carted away by marauding Swedes in 1648 and now stand outside the royal palace of Drottningholm near Stockholm. At the eastern end of the garden, the **Wallenstein riding school** (Valdštejnská jízdárna, Map p92) is home to changing exhibitions of modern art.

Across Valdštejnská street, the immaculately kept terraces of the **Palace gardens beneath Prague castle** (Palácové zahrady pod Pražským hradem; Map p92; 257 010 401; Valdštejnksé nám 3; adult/child 79/49Kč; 10am-9pm Jun & Jul, 10am-8pm Aug, 10am-7pm May & Sep, 10am-6pm Apr & Oct) rise steeply up to the castle. These beautiful terraced gardens on the steep southern slope of the castle hill date from the 17th and 18th centuries, when they were created for the owners of the adjoining palaces. They were restored in the 1990s and contain a Renaissance loggia with frescoes of Pompeii, espaliered vines, soft patches of lawn, fruit orchards, herb gardens, statuary and lots of steep stairs. There's another entrance/ exit at the top, near the eastern end of the castle grounds.

HERGETOVA CÍHELNA

On the bank of the river lies the Hergetova Cíhelna, a restored brickworks complex that now houses a restaurant (p129), café and a couple of museums. In the courtyard is one of David Černý's more controversial artworks, called **Piss** – an animated bronze sculpture of two men pissing in a puddle (whose irregular outline, you'll notice, is actually the map outline of the Czech Republic) and spelling out famous quotations from Czech literature with their pee (the sculpture is computer controlled).

Across the courtyard is the **Franz Kafka museum** (muzeum Franzy Kafky; Map p92; ☎ 257 535 507; www.kafkamuseum.cz; Hergetova Cíhelná, Cihelná 2b; adult/child 120/60Kč; ⊙ 10am-6pm), a much-hyped exhibition on the life and work of Prague's most famous literary son. It explores the intimate relationship between the writer and the city that shaped him through the use of original letters, photographs, quotations, period newspapers and publications, and video and sound installations.

The **Prague jewellery collection** (Pražský kabinet šperku; Map p92; ☎ 221 451 333; Cihelná 2b; adult/child 60/50Kč; ⊙ 10am-6pm), next door to the Franz Kafka museum, provides a showcase for some of the finest items of jewellery in the collection of the museum of Decorative Arts. There are exquisite Art Nouveau and Art Deco designs, as well as several pieces by Tiffany and Fabergé.

SOUTHERN MALÁ STRANA

The **church of Our Lady Victorious** (kostel Panny Marie Vítězné, Map p92) in Karmelitská, built in 1613, has on its central altar a 47cm-tall waxwork figure of the baby Jesus brought from Spain in 1628.

Known as the **Infant Jesus of Prague** (Pražské Jezulátko), the figure is said to have protected Prague from the plague and from the destruc-tion of the Thirty Years' War. It is visited by a steady stream of pilgrims.

It was traditional to dress the figure in beautiful robes, and over the years various benefactors donated richly embroidered dresses. Today the Infant's wardrobe consists of more than 70 costumes donated from all over the world; at the back of the church is a **museum** (admission by donation; ⊙ 10am-5.30pm Mon-Sat & 1-5pm Sun, closed 25 Dec & Easter Mon) displaying a selection of the frocks used to dress the Infant.

A short way south lies the French embassy, and opposite it is the **John Lennon Wall**. After his murder in 1980, Lennon became a pacifist hero for many young Czechs An image of Lennon was painted on the wall (there is a niche that looks like a tombstone), along with political graffiti. Despite repeated coats of whitewash, the secret police never managed to keep it clean for long. Today it's home to lightweight graffiti of the 'Wendy & Michele wuz 'ere' variety, plus the odd incitement to give peace a chance. Graffiti is encouraged here. Why not bring some paint and lift the tone a bit?

A footbridge leads east from the Lennon Wall to **Kampa**, an 'island' created by the Čertovka (Devil's Stream), and the most peaceful and picturesque part of Malá Strana. In the 13th century the town's first mill, the Sovovský mlýn (now Kampa museum), was built on the island, and other mills followed. The southern part of Kampa is a park, ideal for summertime naps, Frisbee and picnics – local hippies love the place.

Housed in a renovated mill building, **Kampa museum** (muzeum Kampa; Map p92; ☎ 257 286 147; www .museumkampa.cz; U Sovovský mlýnů 2; adult/child 120/60Kč; ⊙ 10am-6pm) is devoted to 20th-century and contemporary art from Central Europe. The highlights are extensive collections of bronzes by cubist sculptor Otto Gutfreund, and paintings by František Kupka, a pioneer of abstract art.

Across Legii most, **Marksmen's island** (Střelecký ostrov) has a small sandy beach at its northern end. Lounge about with a beer from Letní bar (p136) or take a paddle in the Vltava if you dare.

PETŘÍN

One of the largest green spaces in Prague, 318m Petřín hill is great for cool, quiet walks and outstanding views of the city. Once upon a time there were also vineyards, and a quarry from which most of Prague's Romanesque and Gothic buildings were assembled.

Petřín is easily accessible from Hradčany and Strahov, or you can ride the **funicular railway** (Map p92) from Újezd (at U lanové dráhy). It runs every 10 to 20 minutes from 9.15am to 8.45pm, for the same price as a tram ride (and you can use city transit tickets).

North of the summit terminus is the **Petřín tower** (Petřínská rozhledna; Map p92; adult/child 50/40Kč; ☼ 10am-10pm May, 10am-8pm Jun-Aug, 10am-7pm Apr & Sep, 10am-6pm Oct, 10am-5pm Sat & Sun Nov-Mar), a 60m Eiffel Tower lookalike built in 1891 for the Prague Exposition. Those who don't think climbing 299 steps is an act of lunacy will enjoy the best views of Prague and surrounds from the top. On the way to the tower you pass through the **Hunger wall** (Hladová zeď), built in the 1360s by the city's poor in return for food – another of Karel IV's bright ideas. Stations of the Cross – small markers depicting the stages of Jesus' journey from conviction to crucifixion – run along the wall, part of the way down to Malá Strana.

Below the tower is the **mirror maze** (bludiště; Map p92; adult/child 40/30Kč; ☼ 10am-10pm May, 10am-8pm Jun-Aug, 10am-7pm Apr & Sep, 10am-6pm Oct, 10am-5pm Sat & Sun Nov-Mar), also built for the 1891 Exposition and later moved here. It's a damn fine laugh.

Staré Město & Josefov

The Old Town – Staré Město in Czech – has been Prague's working heart ever since it was honoured with a town charter by Wenceslas I in 1231, and given the beginnings of a fortification. The town walls are long gone, but their line can still be traced along the streets Národní třída, Na příkopě and Revoluční, and the main gate – the Powder gate – still survives.

To ease the devastation of frequent flooding by the Vltava River, the level of the town was gradually raised, beginning in the 13th century, with new construction simply rising on top of older foundations (many of Staré Město's buildings have Gothic interiors and Romanesque cellars). A huge fire in 1689 contributed to an orgy of rebuilding during the Catholic Counter-Reformation of the 17th and 18th centuries, giving the formerly Gothic district a heavily baroque face.

At the centre of everything is Old Town square, one of Europe's biggest and most beautiful urban spaces. If the maze of nar-row streets around the square can be said to have a 'main drag' it's the so-called Royal Way (Královská cesta), the ancient coronation route to Prague castle, running from the Powder gate along Celetná to Old Town square and Malé náměstí, then along Karlova and across Charles bridge.

JOSEFOV

The slice of Staré Město within Kaprova, Dlouhá and Kozí streets contains the remains of the once-thriving mini-town of Josefov, Prague's former Jewish ghetto: half a dozen old synagogues, the town hall, a ceremonial hall and the cluttered and picturesque Old Jewish cemetery. In an act of grotesque irony, the Nazis preserved these places as part of a planned 'museum of an extinct race'. Instead they have survived as a memorial to seven centuries of oppression.

As well as being a repository of ancient Jewish buildings, modern Josefov – particularly along Pařížská, Kozí and V kolkovně – is a neighbourhood of hip sidewalk cafés, international designer boutiques and drop-dead-cool cocktail bars. Paris Ave (Pařížská třída), built at the time the ghetto was cleared, is lined with courtly four- and five-storey Art Nouveau apartment blocks adorned with stained glass and sculptural flourishes – just off the strip, Maiselova 21 is particularly stunning.

JEWISH MUSEUM

The **Jewish museum** (Židovské muzeum; ☎ 222 317 191; www.jewishmuseum.cz; ☼ 9am-6pm Sun-Fri Apr-Oct, 9am-4.30pm Sun-Fri Nov-Mar, closed on Jewish hols), as the area's attractions are collectively known, takes in: the cemetery, ceremonial hall, gallery Roberta Guttmanna, and Spanish, Maisel, Pinkas, Klaus and Old-New synagogues. The Old-New synagogue is still used for religious services; the others have been converted to exhibition halls holding what is probably the world's biggest collection of sacred Jewish artefacts, many of them saved from demolished Bohemian and Moravian synagogues.

You have the choice of paying to see all of them (adult/child 500/340Kč) or splitting the museum in two – the Old-New synagogue alone (200/140Kč), and everything else (300/200Kč). All tickets include the gallery. You can buy tickets at Pinkas synagogue, the Spanish synagogue and the Ceremonial hall.

If you don't think you'll make it around all the locations, start with the cemetery, follow it up with the excellent exhibition at the Maisel synagogue and then see the exhibition's continuation in the gorgeous Spanish synagogue.

Old-New Synagogue

Completed about 1270, the **Old-New synagogue** (Staronová synagóga; Map p98; ☾ 9.30am-5pm Sun-Thu, 9am-4pm Fri) is one of Prague's earliest Gothic buildings and Europe's oldest 'working' synagogue – it hosts weekly Orthodox ceremonies. The oxymoronic name caught on because this is one of two synagogues built in the 13th century, at a time when Prague already had one old synagogue – of the two new ones, this one is slightly older. Around the central chamber are an entry hall, a winter prayer hall and the room from which women watch the men-only services (it's at the back, through the vents in the wall). The interior, with a pulpit surrounded by a 15th-century wrought-iron grille, looks much as it would have 500 years ago. The 17th-century scriptures on the walls were recovered from beneath a later 'restoration'. On the eastern wall is the Holy Ark that holds the Torah scrolls, hidden by a wall hanging. Rumour has it the steep roof hides the slumbering mythical golem, a giant Jewish superhero made of mud from the Vltava and brought to life by supernatural means.

Old Jewish Cemetery

Founded in the early 15th century, the Old Jewish cemetery (Starý židovský hřbitov, Map p98) is Europe's oldest surviving Jewish cemetery (it was closed in 1787). Some 12,000 toppling, faded stones lean up against one another, but beneath them are perhaps 100,000 graves, piled in layers. The oldest standing stone (now replaced by a replica) dates from 1439. The most prominent graves, marked by pairs of marble tablets with a 'roof' between them, are near the main gate. They include those of Mordechai Maisel and Rabbi Löw. You'll see pebbles and notes (prayers) balanced on many of the stones along the edges of the path – these are left as a mark of respect. There's also a Braille trail around the cemetery. Since the cemetery was closed, burials have taken place at the Jewish cemetery in Žižkov.

The ancient cemetery – you enter via the Pinkas synagogue – is certainly picturesque and can be quite eerie. However, this is also one of the most popular sights in Prague, and if you're hoping to have a moment of

quiet contemplation you'll probably be disappointed (try either of the Žižkov cemeteries for a more solitary experience).

Other Jewish Museum Sights

Opposite the Old-New synagogue is the elegant 16th-century **High synagogue** (Vysoká synagóga, Map p98) and the **Jewish town hall** (Židovská radnice, Map p98), both closed to the public.

By the cemetery exit, the **Klaus synagogue** (Klausová synagóga, Map p98), a 1694 baroque building, holds exhibits relating to Jewish ceremonies for birth, worship and holy days. In the **Ceremonial hall** (Obřadní síň, Map p98), built in 1906 on the other side of the cemetery exit, you'll see exhibits on Jewish rituals for illness and death – if you're particularly interested in the importance of the cemetery, you may choose to visit this exhibition first.

The handsome **Pinkas synagogue** (Pinkasova synagóga, Map p98) was built in 1535 and used for worship until 1941. After WWII it was converted into a moving memorial, with the names, birth dates and dates of disappearance of the 77,297 Bohemian and Moravian victims of the Nazis inscribed across wall after wall (at one point the communist regime removed them, but they've since been reinscribed). It also has a collection of paintings and drawings by children held in the Terezín concentration camp (p231) during WWII.

The neo-Gothic **Maisel synagogue** (Maiselova synagóga, Map p98) hosts the pre-1780 part of the museum's exhibit on the history of Jews in Bohemia and Moravia. The quantity and quality of artefacts is astounding, and the text accompanying them is excellent. The exhibition continues up to the present day (taking in the Nazi occupation) at the **Spanish synagogue** (Španělská synagóga, Map p98), though your eyes may be drawn away from the exhibits to the building's beautiful Moorish interior.

Gallery Roberta Guttmanna (Map p98; ☎ 224 819 456; U Staré Školy 1; adult/child 30/15Kč; ☾ 9am-6pm Sun-Fri Apr-Oct, 9am-4.30pm Sun-Fri Nov-Mar), behind the Spanish synagogue, hosts rotating exhibits of Jewish artists' work – the ticket price is included in your Jewish museum ticket, or you can visit individually.

MUSEUM OF DECORATIVE ARTS

One of those museums where every little item is just begging to be stroked, the **museum of**

PRAGUE

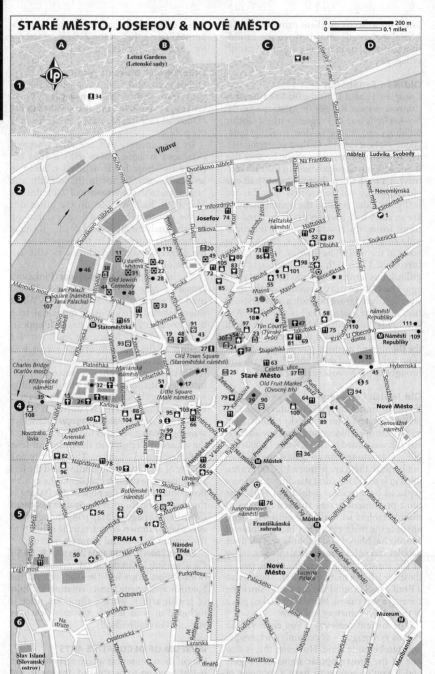

STARÉ MĚSTO, JOSEFOV & NOVÉ MĚSTO

Decorative Arts (Umělecko-průmyslové muzeum; Map p98; ☎ 251 093 111; www.upm.cz, in Czech; 17.listopadu 2; permanent collection adult/child 80/40Kč, temporary exhibitions 80/40Kč, combined 120/60Kč; ⊙ 10am-6pm Tue-Sun) arose as part of a European movement to encourage a return to the aesthetic values that had been sacrificed to the Industrial Revolution.

One of Prague's highlights, the museum's collections include jewellery, furniture, clocks, ceramics, glass, textiles and graphic arts. There are glass cases full of 1940s frocks, walls of Art Nouveau poster art, beautifully illuminated ancient religious texts, pocket watches in the shape of leering skulls and the rococo grandfather of all grandfather clocks. Even the museum building, built in 1898, is gorgeous. The collection on display is only a fraction of what the museum owns; other bits appear now and then in temporary exhibitions.

The little gift shop here has some sublime pieces of ceramic, glass and jewellery design, and there's an excellent café too. If you want a peek into the Old Jewish cemetery without braving the crowds, head for the museum's toilets where the landing window provides a good view.

RUDOLFINUM

Presiding over Jan Palach square (náměstí Jana Palacha) is the Rudolfinum (Map p98), home of the Czech Philharmonic (see Entertainment, p138). This and the National theatre, both designed by the architects Josef Schulz and Josef Zítek, are considered Prague's finest neo-Renaissance buildings. Completed in 1884, the Rudolfinum served between the wars as the seat of the Czechoslovak parliament. Across the road, on the philosophy faculty building, where student martyr Jan Palach (p117) once studied, is a memorial sculpture incorporating his death mask.

CHARLES BRIDGE

Part of Karel IV's Gothic building frenzy, Charles bridge (Karlův most, Map p98) was constructed to replace the earlier Judith bridge (named after Vladislav I's queen), which had been irreparably damaged by ice. Designed by Peter Parler, it was completed in about 1400, though it was known simply as Kamenný most (Stone bridge) until the 19th century. Despite occasional flood damage, it withstood wheeled traffic for 600 years without a shudder – thanks, legend says, to eggs mixed into the mortar – until it was made pedestrian-only after WWII. During the floods of 2002, cranes stood watch over the bridge, pulling large pieces of detritus out of the water so the pillars would not be damaged.

Many of the statues were later additions, put up to promote their particular ecclesiastical orders. These days the most popular is that of the country's patron saint, John of Nepomuk, who was thrown off the bridge by Wenceslas IV in 1393 for refusing to divulge the queen's confessions. It's said that if you rub the plaque at the statue's base, you'll one day return to Prague. Most of the statues are copies – the originals are preserved in Vyšehrad's casemates (p111) and the Lapidárium (p113).

Strolling across the bridge is everybody's favourite Prague pastime. If you come in the early morning you might have the place to yourself, but by 11am you might as well be in the front row of a Linkin Park concert for all the room you'll have to yourself. On a warm evening, even with the throng, it's a pretty romantic place.

In summer you can climb up into the old **bridge towers** (adult/child 40/30Kč, child under 10 free; ⌚ 10am-6pm Apr-Nov) at either end for an even better view.

Gangs of pickpockets work the bridge day and night, so watch your valuables.

OLD TOWN SQUARE

The huge Old Town square (Staroměstské náměstí, also called Staromák for short, Map p98) has been Prague's principal public square since the 10th century, and was its main marketplace until the beginning of the 20th century. These days it's a seething mass of humanity, as tourists nudge one another for space in front of the Astronomical clock, peer bemusedly at maps or try to find a place to sit down for a minute without forking over half their budget. Regular Praguers also use the square as the site for art and sporting events, and on days when something's going on here you can't move for people. Despite all

---

MENDELSSOHN IS ON THE ROOF

The roof of the Rudolfinum – a complex of concert halls and offices built in the late 19th century – is decorated with statues of famous composers. It housed the German administration during WWII, when the Nazi authorities ordered that the statue of Felix Mendelssohn – who was Jewish – be removed.

In *Mendelssohn Is on the Roof*, a darkly comic novella about life in wartime Prague, the Jewish writer Jiří Weil weaves a wryly amusing story around this true-life event. The two Czech labourers given the task of removing the statue can't tell which of the two dozen or so figures is Mendelssohn – they all look the same, as far as they can tell. Their Czech boss, remembering his lectures in 'racial science', tells them that Jews have big noses. 'Whichever one has the biggest conk, that's the Jew.'

So the workmen single out the statue with the biggest nose – 'Look! That one over there with the beret. None of the others has a nose like his' – sling a noose around its neck, and start to haul it over. As their boss walks across to check on their progress, he gapes in horror as they start to topple the figure of the only composer on the roof that he does recognise – Richard Wagner.

this, it remains an awe-inspiring assemblage of architecture and history – late at night, in particular, it's incredibly atmospheric. Stand still for a moment, take a deep breath, and really look around you.

Ladislav Šaloun's brooding Art Nouveau sculpture of **Jan Hus** dominates the square. It was unveiled on 6 July 1915, the 500th anniversary of the death of Hus at the stake.

OLD TOWN HALL

Founded in 1338, Staré Město's ancient **town hall** (Staroměstská radnice; Map p98; adult/child 50/40Kč; separate ticket for tower; 11am-6pm Mon, 9am-6pm Tue-Sun Apr-Oct; 9am-5pm Tue-Sat, 11am-5pm Sun Nov-Mar) looks like a row of private buildings with a tower at the end. And that's what it is – the skint medieval town council bought it from previous owners one house at a time whenever funds were available. You can visit selected rooms in the town hall, including the Gothic chapel and the clock's interior workings.

The sgraffito-covered building at the corner, called **dům U minuty**, was one of Franz Kafka's childhood homes. A Gothic chapel and a neo-Gothic north wing were destroyed by the retreating Nazis in 1945, on the day before the Soviet army marched into Prague. The chapel has been laboriously reconstructed.

A plaque on the tower's eastern face contains a roll-call of the 27 Czech Protestant nobles beheaded in 1621 after the Battle of Bílá Hora (White Mountain); crosses on the ground mark the spot where the deed was done.

It's *de rigueur* to wait for the hourly show by the hall's slightly overrated **Astronomical clock** (see following) – you can't really see what's going on if you're standing at an angle, but to get a spot in front you'll need to arrive half an hour early. The 60m **tower** (admission 50Kč; same hrs as town hall) is the only one in Prague with a lift all the way to the top – perhaps more interesting than watching the clock is nipping up here to watch the people watching the clock.

ASTRONOMICAL CLOCK

The Old town hall tower was given a clock in 1410 by the master clockmaker Mikuláš of Kadaně; this was improved in 1490 by one Master Hanuš, producing the mechanical marvel, the Astronomical clock (Map p98) you see today. Legend has it that Hanuš was afterwards blinded so he could not duplicate

the work elsewhere, and in revenge crawled up into the clock and disabled it. (Documents from the time suggest that he carried on as clock master for years, unblinded, although the clock apparently didn't work properly until it was repaired in about 1570.)

Four figures beside the clock represent the deepest civic anxieties of 15th-century Praguers: Vanity (with a mirror), Greed (with his money bag; originally a Jewish moneylender, cosmetically altered after WWII), Death, and Pagan Invasion (represented by a Turk). The four figures below these are the Chronicler, Angel, Astronomer and Philosopher.

On the hour, Death rings a bell and inverts his hourglass, and the 12 Apostles parade past the windows above the clock, nodding to the crowd. On the left side are Paul (with a sword and a book), Thomas (lance), Jude (book), Simon (saw), Bartholomew (book) and Barnabas (parchment); on the right side are Peter (with a key), Matthew (axe), John (snake), Andrew (cross), Philip (cross) and James (mallet). At the end, a cock crows and the hour is rung.

On the upper face, the disc in the middle of the fixed part depicts the world known at the time – with Prague at the centre, of course. The gold sun traces a circle through the blue zone of day, the brown zone of dusk (Crepusculum in Latin) in the west (Occasus), the black disc of night, and dawn (Aurora) in the east (Ortus). From this the hours of sunrise and sunset can be read. The curved lines with black Arabic numerals are part of an astrological 'star clock'.

The sun-arm points to the hour (without any daylight-saving time adjustment) on the Roman-numeral ring; the top XII is noon and the bottom XII is midnight. The outer ring, with Gothic numerals, reads traditional 24-hour Bohemian time, counted from sunset; the number 24 is always opposite the sunset hour on the fixed (inner) face.

The moon, with its phases shown, also traces a path through the zones of day and night, riding on the offset moving ring. On the ring you can also read which houses of the zodiac the sun and moon are in. The hand with a little star at the end of it indicates sidereal (stellar) time.

The calendar-wheel beneath all this astronomical wizardry, with 12 seasonal scenes celebrating rural Bohemian life, is a duplicate of one painted in 1866 by the Czech Revivalist

Josef Mánes. You can have a close look at the beautiful original in the Prague city museum (p105). Most of the dates around the calendar-wheel are marked with the names of their associated saints; 6 July honours Jan Hus.

ST NICHOLAS CHURCH

The baroque wedding cake in the northwestern corner of the square is **St Nicholas church** (kostel sv Mikuláše; Map p98; admission free; noon-4pm Mon, 10am-4pm Tue-Sat, noon-3pm Sun), built in the 1730s by Kilian Dientzenhofer. This is now a Hussite church, though its Protestant inhabitants have held onto the gilt extravagances of the Catholic Counter-Reformation.

Franz Kafka was born just next door, though the building was later demolished. The building that replaced it is now a privately run and pretty dull **Franz Kafka exhibition** (Map p98; U Radnice 5; admission 40Kč; 10am-6pm Tue-Fri, 10am-5pm Sat).

KINSKÝ PALACE

Fronting the late-baroque **Kinský palace** (Goltz-Kinský palace or palác Kinských; Map p98; 224 301 003; 12 Staroměstské náměstí; adult/child 100/50Kč; 10am-5.30pm) is probably the city's finest rococo façade, completed in 1765 by the very productive Kilian Dientzenhofer. In 1948 Klement Gottwald proclaimed communist rule in Czechoslovakia from the building's balcony. These days it's a branch of the National gallery, showing temporary exhibitions.

HOUSE AT THE STONE BELL

The 14th-century Gothic **house at the stone bell** (dům u kamenného zvonu; Map p98; 13 Staroměstské náměstí; adult/child 90/50Kč; 10am-6pm Tue-Sun), named after the house sign at the corner of the building, houses two restored Gothic chapels. It is now a branch of the Prague city gallery, with changing modern-art exhibits.

CHURCH OF OUR LADY BEFORE TÝN

The spiky-topped church of Our Lady before Týn (kostel Panny Marie před Týnem, Map p98), or 'Týn church', is early Gothic, though it takes some imagination to visualise the original in its entirety because it's strangely hidden behind the contemporaneous four-storey Týn School. Inside it's smothered in heavy baroque, but you'll be lucky to get a decent look – the glassed-in vestibule at the church's entrance is always crammed full of visitors. The church actually looks best from

a distance – in our opinion, the best view is from Letná beer garden (p136).

The Danish astronomer Tycho Brahe, one of Rudolf II's most illustrious 'consultants' (who died in 1601 of a burst bladder – he was too polite to leave the table during a royal function), is buried near the chancel.

TÝN COURT

The Týn church's name comes from the medieval courtyard that lies behind it, the Týn court (Týnský dvůr). Originally constructed to house visiting foreign merchants, this atmospheric cobbled square and the tiny lanes around it are now home to shops and restaurants.

Just outside the courtyard, in the restored Renaissance **house at the golden ring** (dům U zlatého prstenu; Map p98; 224 828 245; Týnská 6/630; adult/child 60/40Kč; 10am-6pm Tue-Sun), is another branch of the Prague city gallery, with a fine collection of 20th-century Czech art.

ST JAMES CHURCH

The long, tall Gothic **St James church** (kostel sv Jakuba; Map p98; Malá Štupartská), behind the Týnský dvůr, began life in the 14th century as a Minorite monastery church. It had a beautiful baroque face-lift in the early 18th century. Pride of place goes to the over-the-top tomb of Count Jan Vratislav of Mitrovice, an 18th-century lord chancellor of Bohemia, on the northern aisle.

Hanging to the left of the main door (on the inside, as you face the door) is a shrivelled human arm. In about 1400 a thief apparently tried to steal the jewels off the statue of the Virgin. Legend says the Virgin grabbed his wrist in such an iron grip that his arm had to be lopped off. (The truth may not be far behind: the church was a favourite of the guild of butchers, who may have administered their own justice.)

It's well worth a visit to enjoy St James' splendid pipe organ and famous acoustics – check the notice board outside.

KLEMENTINUM

To boost the power of the Roman Catholic Church in Bohemia, the Hapsburg emperor Ferdinand I invited the Jesuits to Prague in 1556. They selected one of the city's choicest pieces of real estate and in 1587 set to work on the **church of the Holy Saviour** (kostel Nejsvětějšího Spasitele, Map p98), Prague's flagship of the Counter-Reformation and the Jesuit's original church. The western façade faces Charles bridge, its sooty stone saints glaring down at the traffic jam of trams and tourists on Křižovnické náměstí.

After gradually buying up most of the adjacent neighbourhood, the Jesuits started building their college, the Klementinum, in 1653. By the time of its completion a century later it was the largest building in the city after Prague castle. When the Jesuits fell out with the pope in 1773, it became part of Charles University.

The Klementinum is a vast complex of beautiful baroque and rococo halls, now occupied by the Czech National Library. Most of it is closed to the public, but you can visit the baroque **library hall & astronomical tower** (Map p98; ☎ 221 663 111; adult/child 100/30Kč; ♥ 2-7pm Mon-Fri, 10am-7pm Sat & Sun) on a guided tour. Gates on Křižovnická, Karlova and Seminářská allow free access to the Klementinum's courtyards, which offer a less crowded alternative to Karlova if you're walking to or from Charles bridge.

A popular concert venue (programme and tickets are available at most ticket agencies) is the Klementinum's **chapel of Mirrors** (Zrcadlová kaple, Map p98). Dating from the 1720s, the interior is an ornate confection of gilded stucco, marbled columns, fancy frescoes and ceiling mirrors – think baroque on steroids.

There are two other interesting churches. The **church of St Clement** (kostel sv Klimenta; Map p98; ♥ services 8.30am & 10am Sun), lavishly redecorated in the baroque style from 1711 to 1715 to plans by Kilian Dientzenhofer, is now a Greek Catholic chapel. Conservatively dressed visitors are welcome to attend the services. And then there's the elliptical **Italian chapel of the Assumption of the Virgin Mary** (Vlašská kaple Nanebevzetí Panny Marie, Map p98), built in 1600 for the Italian artisans who worked on the Klementinum (it's still technically the property of the Italian government).

LITTLE SQUARE

Little square (Malé náměstí, Map p98) is surrounded by several fine, baroque and neo-Renaissance exteriors decorating some of Staré Město's oldest structures. Have a gander at the **VJ Rott building** (Map p98) at No 3, decorated with wall paintings by Mikuláš Aleš, and now housing four floors of crystal, garnet and jewellery shops. This square is a

good place to stand at five minutes to the hour, when you can watch panicked tourists sprint through on their way to catch the Astronomical clock show.

CELETNÁ STREET

Pedestrianised Celetná, leading from the Powder gate to Old Town square, is an open-air museum of pastel-painted baroque façades covering Gothic frames resting on Romanesque foundations, deliberately buried to raise Staré Město above the Vltava River's floods. But the most interesting building dates only from 1912 – Josef Gočár's delightful **house of the black Madonna**. Prague's first and finest example of cubist architecture still looks modern and dynamic, and now houses the **museum of Czech cubism** (muzeum Českého kubismu; ☎ 224 301 003; Ovocný trh 19; adult/child 100/50Kč; ♥ 10am-6pm Tue-Sun), three floors of cubist paintings and sculpture, as well as furniture, ceramics and glassware in cubist designs.

The eastern end of Celetná is guarded by the gloomy 65m-tall **Powder gate** (Prašná brána; Map p98; adult/child 30/40Kč; ♥ 10am-6pm May-Oct), begun in 1475 during the reign of King Vladislav II Jagiello but never finished. Used to store gunpowder in the 18th century, it was refurbished in the 19th century and the steeple and decorations were added. There are great views from the top, and there's an exhibit about Prague's medieval towers.

MUNICIPAL HOUSE

Don't even consider missing the **Municipal house** (Obecní dům; Map p98; ☎ 222 002 101; www.obecni-dum.cz; náměstí Republiky 5; guided tours 150Kč; ♥ bldg 7.30am-11pm, information centre 10am-6pm), Prague's most exuberant and sensual building, with an unrivalled Art Nouveau interior and a façade that looks like a Victorian Easter egg. Bring your smelling salts – the sheer relentlessness of the decoration may make you woozy.

The complex was built between 1906 and 1912 in an attempt to one-up German architectural developments. Thirty of the leading artists of the day worked together to make this the architectural climax of the Czech National Revival.

The mosaic above the entrance, *Homage to Prague*, is set between sculptures representing the oppression and rebirth of the Czech people. You pass beneath a wrought-iron and stained-glass canopy into an interior that is Art Nouveau down to the doorknobs.

To go upstairs, you have to join a guided tour, which is well worth the price. You'll see half a dozen over-the-top salons, including the incredible **Lord Mayor's hall**, done up entirely by Art Nouveau superstar Alfons Mucha, who didn't let a single fitting escape his attention. Also here is the **Smetana hall**, Prague's biggest concert hall, and a **gallery** (admission 100Kč) with temporary art exhibits.

Pivotal events that took place here include the proclamation of an independent Czechoslovak Republic on 28 October 1918, and meetings between Civic Forum and the Jakeš regime in November 1989. The Prague Spring music festival always opens on 12 May, the anniversary of Smetana's death, with a procession from Vyšehrad to Municipal house, and a gala performance of his symphonic cycle *Má vlast* (My Country) in Smetana hall.

NA PŘÍKOPĚ

Na příkopě (p98) means 'on the moat'; with Národní třída, 28.října and Revoluční this street marks the moat (filled in at the end of the 18th century) that ran along the Old Town walls.

This was the haunt of Prague's German café society in the 19th century. Today it is the main upmarket shopping precinct (along with Národní), lined with banks, bookshops, tourist cafés and shopping malls.

Na příkopě continues southwest across the foot of Wenceslas square as 28.října (28 October; Czechoslovak Independence Day). Here Na můstku (On the Little bridge) runs northwest where a footbridge once crossed the moat – you can see an arch of it, on the left just past the ticket machines in the underground entrance to Můstek metro station.

KAROLINUM

Charles University – central Europe's oldest university, founded by Karel IV in 1348 – originally set up shop here at the Karolinum (Map p98) at Železná 9. With Protestantism and Czech nationalism on the rise, the reformist preacher Jan Hus became rector in 1402. On 18 January 1409, in an effort to increase his voting bloc in manoeuvrings to regain the crown of Holy Roman Emperor, Václav IV slashed the voting rights of the university's German students and lecturers. The 'Decree of Kutná Hora', as it was known, meant thousands of Germans left Bohemia in disgust, and the previously world-beating

university, known as the Karolinum, became considerably more parochial.

Charles University now has faculties all over Prague, and the original building is used only for some medical faculty offices, the University Club and occasional academic ceremonies. Its finest room is the high-ceilinged assembly hall upstairs.

Among pre-university Gothic traces is the **chapel of SS Cosmas & Damian**, with its extraordinary oriel protruding from the southern wall. Built around 1370, it was renovated in 1881 by Josef Mocker.

ESTATES THEATRE

Beside the Karolinum is the **Estates theatre** (Stavovské divadlo; Map p98; Železná 11), Prague's oldest theatre and finest neoclassical building. Opened in 1783 as the Nostitz theatre (after founder Count Anton von Nostitz-Rieneck), it was patronised by upper-class German Praguers. It was later named after the local nobility, the Estates. In summer it hosts performances of Mozart's *Don Giovanni*, which premiered here in 1787 with the maestro himself conducting.

CONVENT OF ST AGNES

In the northeast corner of Staré Město is the former **convent of St Agnes** (klášter sv Anežky; Map p98; ☎ 224 810 628; www.ngprague.cz; U milosrdných 17; adult/child 100/50Kč; ⏰ 10am-6pm Tue-Sun), Prague's oldest surviving Gothic buildings. In 1234 the Franciscan Order of the Poor Clares was founded by the Přemysl king Václav I, who made his sister Anežka (Agnes) its first abbess; since 1989 she's been St Agnes.

The complex consists of the cloister, a sanctuary and a church in French Gothic style. In the **chapel of the Virgin Mary** (kaple Panny Marie) are the graves of St Agnes and Václav I's queen Cunegund. Alongside is the smaller **church of St Francis** (kostel sv Františka), where Václav I is buried in the chancel.

The first floor rooms now hold the National gallery's collection of **medieval Bohemian art**, a brilliantly curated exhibition of extraordinary, glowing works, including some of Master Theodoricus' paintings from Karlštejn castle (p148), the beautiful three-piece Třeboň altarpiece and the terrifically ungloomy work of the Master of Sorrows from Žebrák.

BETHLEHEM CHAPEL

The **Bethlehem chapel** (Betlémská kaple; Map p98; Betlémské náměstí 3; adult/child 40/20Kč; ⏰ 9am-6.30pm

Tue-Sun Apr-Oct, to 5.30pm Nov-Mar) is one of Prague's most important churches, the true birthplace of the Hussite cause (though what you see is largely a reconstruction).

In 1391, Reformist Praguers won permission to build a church where services could be held in Czech instead of Latin, and proceeded to construct the biggest chapel Bohemia had ever seen, able to hold 3000 worshippers. Architecturally it was a radical departure, with a simple square hall focused on the pulpit rather than the altar. Jan Hus preached here from 1402 to 1412, marking the emergence of the Reform movement from the sanctuary of the Karolinum (where he was rector).

In the 18th century the chapel was torn down. Remnants were discovered around 1920, and from 1948 to 1954 – because Hussitism had official blessing as an ancient form of communism – the whole thing was painstakingly reconstructed in its original form, based on old drawings, descriptions, and traces of the original work. It's now a national cultural monument.

Only the southern wall of the chapel is brand new. You can still see some original parts in the eastern wall: the pulpit door, several windows and the door to the preacher's quarters. These quarters, including the rooms used by Hus and others, are also original; they are now used for exhibits. The wall paintings are modern and are based on old Hussite tracts. The interior well predates the chapel.

The chapel has an English text available at the door. Every year on the night of 5 July, the eve of Hus' burning at the stake in 1415, a commemorative celebration is held here, with speeches and bell ringing.

Nové Město

Although it's called New Town, this crescent-shaped district to the east and south of Staré Město was only new when it was founded by Charles IV in 1348. It extends eastwards from Revoluční and Na příkopě to Wilsonova and the main railway line, and south from Národní třída to Vyšehrad.

Most of Nové Město's outer fortifications were demolished in 1875 – a section of wall still survives in the south, facing Vyšehrad – but the original street plan of the area has been essentially preserved, with three large market squares that once provided the district's commercial focus – Senovážné náměstí (Hay Market), Wenceslas square (Václavské náměstí;

originally called Koňský trh, or Horse Market) and Karlovo náměstí (Charles square; originally called Dobytčí trh, or Cattle Market).

Though originally medieval, most of the surviving buildings in this area are from the 19th and early 20th centuries, many of them among the city's finest. Many blocks are honeycombed with pedestrian-only passages and lined with shops, cafés and theatres.

PRAGUE CITY MUSEUM

Tucked in a bit of wasteland near the Florenc metro station, the excellent **Prague city museum** (muzeum hlavního města Prahy; Map p118; ☎ 224 816 773; www.muzeumprahy.cz; Na poříčí 52; adult/child 80/30Kč; 1st Thu of each month 1Kč; ☺ 9am-6pm Tue-Sun, to 8pm 1st Thu of each month) displays the rich pickings of Prague's florid pre-19th century history. Brutal Hussite 'beating weapons' (what good Protestant doesn't need one?), elaborate ancient door furniture and some choice medieval and Renaissance carvings are excellent appetisers for the main attraction, Antonín Langweil's incredible scale model of Prague c 1830: the poor hobbyist (who died without the recognition he so richly deserved) even included teeny tiny frescoes and broken windows. Don't miss the ceilings of the museum's upstairs galleries (one gallery hosts rotating contemporary exhibitions).

AROUND JINDŘIŠSKÁ ULICE

Squarely at the end of Jindřišská is the **Jindřišská tower** (Jindřišská věž, Map p106), a former watchtower or bell tower built in the 15th century. Now renovated and re-opened as a tourist attraction, it's complete with exhibition space, shop, café and restaurant, and a lookout gallery on the 10th floor.

Around the corner is the 1906 **Jubilee synagogue** (Jubilejní synagóga; Map p106; Jeruzalémská 7; admission 30Kč; ☺ 1-5pm Sun-Fri, closed Jewish holidays), or the Great (Velká) synagogue. Note the names of donors on the colourful, stained-glass windows, and the grand organ above the entrance.

The **Mucha museum** (Map p106; ☎ 221 451 333; www.mucha.cz; Panská 7; adult/child 120/60Kč; ☺ 10am-6pm) features the sensuous Art Nouveau works of Alfons Mucha, as well as sketches, photographs and other memorabilia. Because the exhibit focuses on his prints without much consideration of his work in object design, it gets a bit samey. There's also an interesting video on his life (available in English or Czech) and a substantial gift shop.

PRAGUE

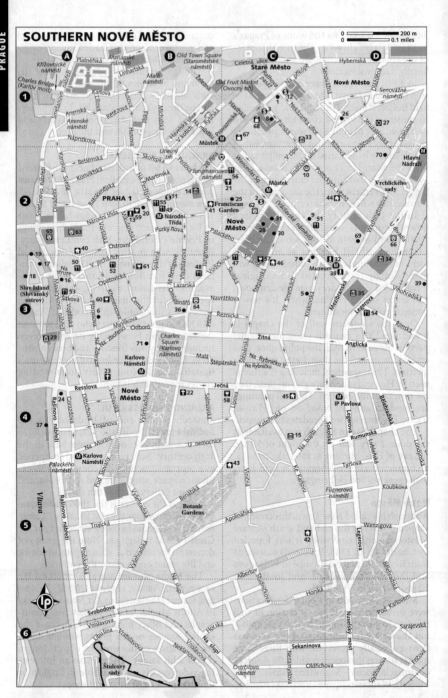

SOUTHERN NOVÉ MĚSTO

NATIONAL MUSEUM

Taxidermophiles rejoice! The **National museum** (Map p106; ☎ 224 497 111; www.nm.cz; Václavské náměstí 68; adult/child 100/50Kč, free 1st Mon of month; ⊙ 10am-6pm May-Sep, 9am-5pm Oct-Apr, closed 1st Tue of month) scoffs at multimedia and modern theories of materials' interpretation. The museum does the classics – rocks, dead animals, bones – and does them well. Among the more interesting of the exhibits (very few have English labels, but a multilanguage audio tour is available for 200Kč) is a large collection of stuffed anteaters, pangolins and aardvarks, the corpse of an extinct thylacine, a cross-section of a domestic cat and – for those who don't care for roadkill – a display of Czech printed works.

Looming above Wenceslas square, the neo-Renaissance building was designed in the 1880s by Josef Schulz as an architectural symbol of the Czech National Revival. The interior of the museum is quite overwhelming, with its grand stairwell and pantheon gallery. The upstairs murals feature a boys' own interpretation of Czech legends and history by František Ženíšek and Václav Brožík, and pink-bottomed cherubs by Vojtěch Hynais.

MUSEUM OF COMMUNISM

It would be difficult to think of a more ironic site for the **museum of communism** (Map p106; ☎ 224 212 966; www.muzeumkomunismu.cz; Na příkopě 10; admission 180Kč; ⊙ 9am-9pm) – in an 18th-century aristocrat's palace, stuck between a casino on one side and a McDonald's burger restaurant on the other. It devotes itself to presenting the corruption, empty shops, oppression, fear and double-speak of life in socialist Czechoslovakia. It's a bit one-sided, and more than a little text-heavy, but definitely worth a visit. Make sure to watch the video about protests leading up to the Velvet Revolution: you'll never think of it as a pushover again.

WENCESLAS SQUARE

A horse market in medieval times, Wenceslas square (Václavské náměstí, also called Václavák, Map p106) got its present name during the nationalist upheavals of the mid-19th century, and since then it's been the favourite spot for anyone trying to make their mark on Czech history. A giant Mass was held in the square during the revolutionary upheavals of 1848, and in 1918 the creation of the new Czechoslovak Republic was celebrated here.

ON THE KAFKA TRAIL

Prague seemingly can't get enough of its favourite literary son, and luckily for tourist operators, the itinerant Kafka lived in a multitude of different houses and worked in buildings all over the city. Get a feeling for what it was like being Franz by wandering around some of the spots he favoured in 1913, the year he turned 30.

In that year, Franz was living with his mother and father and his youngest sister, Ottla, aged 21, in a top floor flat in the **Oppelt building** (Map p98) at the northern end of Old Town square, across Pařížská from St Nicholas church. All three of Franz's sisters died in the ghettos or camps in WWII. Franz's domineering father was a wholesale haberdasher with a store on the ground floor of the **Kinský palace** (p102).

Since 1908 Franz had been working at the Workers Accident Insurance for the Kingdom of Bohemia at Na poříčí 7, Nové Město; the cream building now houses a hotel, the Mercure. It's rumoured that while working at this job, Franz came up with the bright idea that on sites where workers might get hit on the head, they should wear hard hats.

At this time he wrote in his diary, 'From 8 until 2 or 2.30 office, until 3 or 3.30 dinner, after that sleep in bed…until 7.30, then 10 minutes exercise, naked, with open window, then an hour taking a walk…then evening meal with the family…then at 10.30 sit down to write and remain there as long as strength, desire, and happiness permit until 1, 2, 3 o'clock, once even until 6 in the morning'.

The writing at this time would have included letters to Felice Bauer, the first of five women he fell in love with, wrote copious letters to, and never married. His *Meditations,* a collection of some early short stories, had just been published, and he was working on *Amerika.*

When he wasn't writing, Franz wasn't above a little idle fun. In his diary he wrote, 'Went to the cinema. Wept. Matchless entertainment': the cinema would probably have been in the **Estates theatre** (p104).

On Tuesday evenings the radical chic of Prague met at the salon of Berta Fanta at her apartment on the first floor at the **house of the Unicorn** (Map p98; Staroměstské náměstí 17). There is now a plaque on the wall, commemorating Einstein playing his violin at these salon meetings. Franz and his friend and biographer Max Brod also went to fortnightly meetings at **Cafe Louvre** (Map p106; Národní Trida 20, Nové Město) to debate philosophy and to read from their work. At the **Cafe Savoy** (Map p115; Vítezná 5, Malá Strana) Franz met and became friends with the Yiddish theatre troupe actor, Isaac Lowy, sparking a hitherto dormant interest in his own Jewishness.

In this café society Franz revealed himself, to Brod at least, as 'one of the most amusing of men' who 'liked a good hearty laugh, and knew how to make his friends laugh too'. Whether Franz, a vegetarian who drank no alcohol, became addicted to coffee is not known.

Fancy a full Kafka pilgrimage? See Marilyn Bender's paper, 'Franz Kafka's Prague: a literary walking tour' (www.nysoclib.org/travels/kafka.html), and visit the new Franz Kafka museum (p95).

Following the 17 November 1989 beating of students on Národní třída, thousands gathered here in anger, night after night. A week later, in a stunning mirror-image of Klement Gottwald's 1948 proclamation of communist rule from the balcony of the Kinský palace in the Old Town square, Alexander Dubček and Václav Havel stepped onto the balcony of the **Melantrich building** to a thunderous and tearful ovation, and proclaimed the end of communism in Czechoslovakia.

At the top of the square is Josef Myslbek's muscular equestrian **St Wenceslas statue** (sv Václav, Map p106), the 10th-century pacifist Duke of Bohemia. Flanked by other patron saints of Bohemia he has been plastered over

with posters and bunting at every single one of the square's historical moments. If you've got a date with a Praguer, chances are they'll want to meet you under the horse's tail.

The square has become a monument to consumerism, a gaudy gallery of cafés, shops, moneychangers, cabbies and pricey hotels. If you like Times Square or Leicester Square, this is your kind of place.

LUCERNA PASSAGE

The most elegant and convoluted of Nové Město's many arcades, or *pasáží,* Lucerna passage (Map p106) runs beneath the Lucerna palace between Štěpánská and Vodičkova streets. The arcade was designed by Václav

---

THE MISSING DICTATOR

If you stand on Old Town square (Map p98) and look north along the arrow-straight avenue of Pařížská you will see, on a huge terrace at the far side of Bohemia bridge (Čechův most), a giant metronome. If the monumental setting seems out of scale that's because the terrace was designed to accommodate the world's biggest statue of Stalin. Unveiled in 1955 – two years after Stalin's death – the 30m-high, 14,000-tonne colossus showed Uncle Joe at the head of two lines of communist heroes, Czech on one side, Soviet on the other. Cynical Praguers used to constant food shortages quickly nicknamed it 'fronta na maso' ('the meat queue').

The monument was dynamited in 1962, in deference to Krushcev's attempt to airbrush Stalin out of history. The demolition crew were instructed: 'It must go quickly, there mustn't be much of a bang, and it should be seen by as few people as possible'. The museum of communism (p107) has a superb photo of the monument – and of its destruction.

Havel, the ex-president's grandfather, so it's no surprise Havel chose to walk through this *pasáž* on his way to proclaim the end of communism. The Lucerna complex includes theatres, a cinema, shops, a rock-music club and cafés. In the marbled atrium hangs artist David Černý's sculpture *Horse*, a wryly amusing counterpart to the equestrian statue of St Wenceslas (opposite) in Wenceslas square.

CHURCH OF OUR LADY OF THE SNOWS

If you haven't had enough medieval architecture in Staré Město, head for the Gothic church of Our Lady of the Snows (kostel Panny Marie Sněžné, Map p106) at the bottom end of Wenceslas square. Karel IV began its construction in the 14th century, but only the chancel was ever completed, which is why it looks taller than it is long. Karel had intended it to be the grandest church in Prague – the nave is higher than that of St Vitus and the altar, an extravagance of black and gold, is the city's tallest. It was a Hussite stronghold, echoing to the sermons of Jan Želivský – these days it has a strict 'no talking' rule.

While you're here, rest your feet in the **Franciscan garden** (Františkánská zahrada; Map p106; ✿ 7am-10pm Apr-Sep, 7am-8pm Oct, 8am-7pm Nov-Mar), formerly part of a monastery and now a peaceful, rigorously groomed park where office workers scoff a quick sandwich and read the paper.

ALONG NÁRODNÍ TŘÍDA

Národní třída (National Ave) is central Prague's 'high street', a row of midrange shops and grand government buildings whose stateliness is somewhat obscured by rushing traffic.

At Národní 40, fronting Jungmannovo náměstí, is an imitation Venetian palace known as the **Adria palace** (Map p106); you'll

have seen a lot of heavily decorated buildings in Prague, but this one takes the cake. Beneath it is the Adria theatre, original home of Laterna Magika and meeting place of Civic Forum in the heady days of the Velvet Revolution.

Along the street, inside the arcade near No 16, is a bronze **17.11.89 memorial** (Map p106) on the wall with a cluster of hands making the peace sign and the date '17.11.89', in memory of the students clubbed in the street by police on that date.

Across the road at No 7 is the fine Art Nouveau façade (by architect Osvald Polívka) of the **Viola building** (Map p98), former home of the Prague Insurance Company, with the huge letters 'PRAHA' around five circular windows.

On the southern side at No 4, looking like it has been built out of old TV screens, is **Nová scéna** (Map p106), the 1983 'New National theatre' building, home of Laterna Magika (see Theatre p139). Finally, facing the Vltava across Smetanovo nábřeží is the **National theatre** (Národní divadlo; Map p106), the neo-Renaissance flagship of the Czech National Revival, funded entirely by private donations. Architect Josef Zítek's masterpiece burned down within weeks of its 1881 opening, but, incredibly, was funded again and restored in less than two years. You have to attend a performance to get inside.

Across from the theatre is the **Kavárna Slavia** (Map p98) café, once the haunt of theatre and literary types but now largely living on its past glory. The river views are still just as lovely, though.

MASARYK EMBANKMENT

Masaryk Embankment (Masarykovo nábřeží) sports a series of stunning **Art Nouveau buildings**

(Map p106). At No 32 is the duck-egg green Goethe Institut (the German Cultural Institute), once the East German embassy, while No 26 is a beautiful apartment building with owls perched in the decorative foliage that twines around the door, and dogs peeking from the balconies on the 5th floor.

Opposite this is **Slav island** (Slovanský ostrov), a sleepy sandbank with river views and gardens, named after Slav conventions held here since 1848. Around the northern tip of the island there are three little boat-hire places. In the middle of the island is a 19th-century meeting hall, and at the southern end is **Šítkovská věž**, a 15th-century water tower (once part of a mill) with an 18th-century onion-dome roof, and a children's playground featuring arcane playthings seemingly sourced from Soviet-era torture manuals.

Beneath the tower is the **Mánes gallery** (Map p106; ☎ 224 931 410; Masarykovo nábřeží; adult/child 40/20Kč; ☉ 10am-6pm Tue-Sun), established in the 1920s by a group of artists headed by painter Josef Mánes as an alternative to the Czech Academy of Arts; it's still a great place to find out what's happening right now in Czech art. The building itself, designed by Oskar Novotný, is considered a masterpiece of Functionalist architecture.

CHARLES SQUARE

At over seven hectares, Charles square (Karlovo náměstí) is Prague's biggest square – actually it's more of a park. Presiding over it is the baroque 1678 **church of St Ignatius of Loyola** (kostel sv Ignáce, Map p106), designed by Carlo Lurago for the Jesuits. Inside see the 'Mary in a rock garden', diorama-style Chapel of Our Lady of Lourdes.

The square's historical focus is the **New town hall** (Novoměstská radnice, Map p106) at the northern end, built when the 'New Town' was new. From its windows several of Sigismund's Catholic councillors were flung to their deaths in 1419 by followers of the Hussite preacher Jan Želivský. 'Defenestration' (the act of throwing someone out of a window) got its meaning, Czechs got a new political tactic, and the Hussite Wars were off to a flying start. The **tower** (admission 30Kč; ☉ 10am-6pm Tue-Sun May-Sep) was added 35 years later.

CHURCH OF SS CYRIL & METHODIUS

In 1942 seven Czech paratroopers who were involved in the assassination of Reichspro-tektor Reinhardt Heydrich hid in the crypt of the **church of SS Cyril & Methodius** (kostel sv Cyril a Metoděj; Map p106; ☎ 224 920 686; Resslova 9; adult/child 50/20Kč; ☉ 10am-5pm Tue-Sun May-Sep, to 4pm Oct-Apr) for three weeks after the killing, until their hiding place was betrayed by the Czech traitor Karel Čurda. The Germans besieged the church, first attempting to smoke out the paratroopers and then flooding the church using fire hoses. Three paratroopers were killed in the ensuing fight; the other four took their own lives rather than surrender. The crypt now houses a moving memorial, where you can still see bullet marks and shrapnel scars on the walls – on the Resslova side of the church the narrow gap in the wall of the crypt is still pitted with bullet marks – and signs of the paratroopers' last desperate efforts to dig an escape tunnel to the sewer under the street.

DANCING BUILDING

If you've taken a boat on the river you've no doubt wondered what's up with that entirely modern, curvy building with the ball on its head. Emerging from between its Art Nouveau neighbours, the joyfully daring **Dancing building** (Tančící dům; Map p106; Rašínovo nábřeží 80) was designed by Czech Vlado Milunč and American Frank Gehry, who originally called it the 'Fred and Ginger building'. Completed in 1996, it's an excellent addition to the ageing skyline.

DVOŘÁK MUSEUM

One of the city's finest baroque houses is the Vila Amerika, a 1720, French-style summer-house, again designed by Kilian Dientzenhofer, and now home to the **Antonín Dvořák museum** (muzeum Antonína Dvořáka; Map p106; ☎ 224 918 013; Ke Karlovu 20; adult/child 50/25Kč; ☉ 10am-1.30pm & 2-5pm Tue-Sun Apr-Sep, from 9.30am Oct-Mar). If you have more than a passing interest in the composer, you might enjoy browsing the exhibits while listening to his work. It's a great place to buy a Dvořák CD, as the staff at the store give excellent advice.

Vyšehrad

Vyšehrad (High Castle, Map p112) is regarded as Prague's mythical birthplace. According to legend the wise chieftain Krok built a castle here in the 7th century. Libuše, the cleverest of his three daughters, prophesised that a great city would rise here. Taking as her king a ploughman named Přemysl, she founded the city of Prague and the Přemysl dynasty.

Archaeologists know that various early Slavonic tribes set up camp at Vyšehrad, a crag above the Vltava River south of the Nusle Valley. Vyšehrad may in fact have been permanently settled as early as the 9th century, and Boleslav II (r 972–99) may have lived here for a time. There was a fortified town by the mid-11th century. Vratislav II (r 1061–92) moved his court here from Hradčany, beefing up the walls and adding a castle, the basilica of St Lawrence, church of SS Peter & Paul and the rotunda of St Martin. His successors stayed until 1140, when Vladislav II returned to Hradčany.

Vyšehrad then faded until Charles IV, aware of its symbolic importance, repaired the walls and joined them to those of his new town, Nové Město. He built a small palace, and decreed that the coronations of Bohemian kings should begin with a procession from here to Hradčany.

Nearly everything on the hilltop was wiped out during the Hussite Wars. The hill remained a ruin – except for a township of artisans and traders – until after the Thirty Years' War, when Leopold I refortified it.

The Czech National Revival generated new interest in Vyšehrad as a symbol of Czech history. Painters painted it, poets sang about the old days, Smetana set his opera *Libuše* here. Many fortifications were dismantled in 1866 and the parish graveyard was converted into a national memorial cemetery.

Vyšehrad retains a place in Czech hearts and is a popular destination for weekend family outings. Since the 1920s the old fortress has been a quiet park, with splendid panoramas of the Vltava Valley. Take along a picnic and find a quiet spot among the trees, or on the battlements with a view over the river.

VYŠEHRAD CITADEL

Most visitors enter Vyšehrad through the **Tábor gate** (Táborská brána, Map p112), where they find a sign with extensive rules about ways in which they may and may not use the grass. Inside are the scant remnants of the Gothic Peak gate (Špička brána) – a fragment of arch that is now part of the **information centre** (Map p112; ☎ 241 410 348; www.praha-vysehrad.cz; admission free; ☻ 9.30am-6.30pm), and all that remains of Charles IV's 14th-century fortifications. Beyond that lies the grand, 17th-century **Leopold**

gate (Leopoldova brána), the most elegant of the fortress gates.

Vratislav II's little **rotunda of St Martin** (rotunda sv Martina) is Prague's oldest surviving building. In the 18th century it was used as a powder magazine. The door and frescoes date from a renovation made about 1880.

If you enjoy making pilgrimages to the graves of your heroes, then the **Vyšehrad cemetery** (Vyšehradský hřbitov; Map p112; ☻ 8am-5pm Nov-Feb, 8am-6pm Mar-Apr & Oct, 8am-7pm May-Sep) is your one-stop Czech shop. Composers Smetana and Dvořák, writers Karel Čapek, Jan Neruda and Božena Němcová, painter Alfons Mucha and sculptors Josef Myslbek and Bohumil Kafka are all here. A directory of big names is at the entrance. In between the stars, the graves of the lesser known are a real showcase of headstone design. The Prague Spring music festival (p122) kicks off every 12 May, the anniversary of Smetana's death, with a procession from his grave to the Municipal house.

Vratislav II's **church of SS Peter & Paul** (kostel sv Petra a Pavla; Map p112; adult/child 20/10Kč; ☻ 9am-noon & 1-5pm Mon, Wed & Sat, 9am-noon Fri, 11am-noon & 1-5pm Sun, closed Tue & Thu) has been built and rebuilt over the centuries, culminating in a neo-Gothic makeover by Josef Mocker in the 1880s. The towers were added in 1903; the beautiful Art Nouveau frescoes inside – very unusual in this baroque-obsessed city – were painted in the 1920s, largely by František and Marie Urban. Each chapel has an English label explaining its story and artist.

Beside the church are the **Vyšehrad gardens** (Vyšehradské sady, Map p112), with four statues by Josef Myslbek, based on Czech legends of mythological Vyšehrad. Libuše and Přemysl are in the northwestern corner; in the southeast are Šárka and Ctirad. From May to August, open-air concerts are held here at 2.30pm on Sunday, with anything from jazz to oompah and chamber music.

Within the Vyšehrad's ramparts there are many vaulted **casemates**. At the 1842 **Brick gate** (Cihelná brána), 30Kč will buy you a guided tour through several of these chambers, now used as a historical exhibit and for storing four of Charles bridge's original baroque statues (other originals are at the Lapidárium, p113).

If you want to see the ruined foundations of the 11th-century Romanesque **St Lawrence basilica** (bazilika sv Vavřince; Map p112; admission 10Kč; ☻ 11am-6pm), ask for the key in the snack bar by the Old

PRAGUE

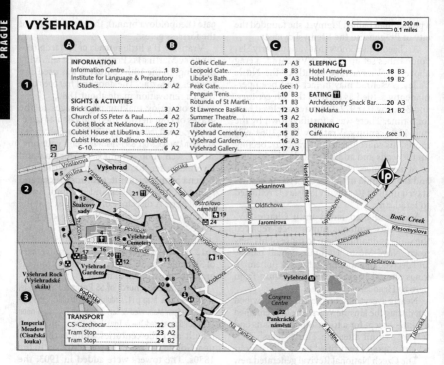

VYŠEHRAD

0 —————— 200 m
0 —————— 0.1 miles

INFORMATION			Gothic Cellar...................7 A3		SLEEPING	
Information Centre...................1 B3			Leopold Gate...................8 B3		Hotel Amadeus...................18 B3	
Institute for Language & Preparatory			Libuše's Bath...................9 A3		Hotel Union...................19 B2	
Studies...................2 A2			Peak Gate...................(see 1)			
			Penguin Tenis...................10 B3		EATING	
SIGHTS & ACTIVITIES			Rotunda of St Martin...................11 B3		Archdeaconry Snack Bar......20 B3	
Brick Gate...................3 A2			St Lawrence Basilica...................12 A3		U Neklana...................21 B2	
Church of SS Peter & Paul...........4 A2			Summer Theatre...................13 A2			
Cubist Block at Neklanova......(see 21)			Tábor Gate...................14 B3		DRINKING	
Cubist House at Libušina 3..........5 A2			Vyšehrad Cemetery...................15 B2		Café...................(see 1)	
Cubist Houses at Rašinovo Nábřeží			Vyšehrad Gardens...................16 A3			
6-10...................6 A2			Vyšehrad Gallery...................17 A3			

TRANSPORT		
CS-Czechocar...................22 C3		
Tram Stop...................23 A2		
Tram Stop...................24 B2		

Archdeaconry. In front of the southwestern bastion are the foundations of a small **palace** built by Charles IV, and its restored **Gothic cellar** (Gotický sklep; Map p112; adult/child 30/20Kč; 9.30am-6pm Apr-Oct, to 5pm Nov-Mar) that houses an exhibition dedicated to the history of Vyšehrad. It is packed with archaeological finds and religious relics associated with life on the fortress from 3800 BC until the present day.

Perched on the bastion is the **Vyšehrad gallery** (galérie Vyšehrad; Map p112; 241 410 348; www .praha-vysehrad.cz; admission 10Kč; 9.30am-5.30pm Tue-Sun), which holds temporary exhibitions and often sells the artworks at very reasonable prices. Below the bastion are some ruined guard towers poetically named **Libuše's Bath** (Map p112).

In the northwest corner is an open-air **Summer theatre** (Letní scéna; Map p112; admission 35Kč; 5pm Thu) where you can catch a concert or cultural show.

There are a few spots to eat around the complex, though a picnic lunch is definitely a good option. You can grab a sausage with bread or a marinated cheese and a beer at the Archdeaconry snack bar.

The simplest way to get to Vyšehrad is by metro. Exit Vyšehrad metro station on the Hajé-bound side, towards the Congress Centre – you'll see brown tourist signs directing you to 'Vyšehrad', where you enter through the Tabor gate. There's more climbing if you walk up from tram 7, 18 or 24 on Na slupi (from Karlovo nám metro), through the Brick gate. A quicker, steeper route is up the long stairs from tram 3, 7, 16 or 17 on the riverside drive – the stairs come out by the Vyšehrad cemetery.

CUBIST ARCHITECTURE

If you've taken the trouble to come out to Vyšehrad, don't miss a clutch of Prague's famous cubist buildings in the streets north of the Brick gate. Cubist architecture, with its eye-catching use of elementary geometric forms, is more or less unique to the Czech Republic, particularly Prague.

One dramatic villa, designed by Josef Chochol, the dean of Czech cubist architects, is at **Rašínovo nábřeží 6-10** (Map p112), just before the street tunnels beneath Vyšehrad rock. Others by Chochol are a very well-preserved freestanding house at **Libušina 3** (Map p112) and the clean lines of an apartment block at **Neklanova 30** – look for the U Neklana restaurant (p132). All date from around 1913.

Holešovice

With its wide, leafy streets, grimy buildings and an air of just going about its daily business, Holešovice (Map pp82–3) is a real contrast to central Prague. Up-and-coming in the late 1990s, Holešovice apparently called a halt to development before the malls and multiplexes started moving in – consequently, you'll find a few good modern restaurants, bars and cafés, plenty of old *hospodas* (pubs) and an easily accessible atmosphere of 'so this is what Prague is *really* like'.

This patch of the city in the Vltava's 'big bend' sprang from two old settlements – the farming hamlet of Holešovice and the fishing village of Bubny. Both remained small until industry arrived in the mid-19th century. When the Hlávkův bridge was built in 1868, linking the area to Nové Město, the population swelled. A horse-drawn tram, a river port and the exhibition grounds of Výstaviště followed, and the area became a part of Prague in 1884.

VÝSTAVIŠTĚ

This vast exhibition area of these **fairgrounds** (Map pp82–3) are home to the popular **St Matthew Fair** (Matějská pouť), held annually in February and March when it's full of rides, candy-floss, and half of Prague having fun. Some of the buildings went up in 1891 for the Jubilee Exposition, including the Prague Pavilion (Pavilón hlavního města Prahy), which houses the Lapidárium and the palace of Industry (Průmuslový palác).

It's a popular weekend destination, a great spot for a sausage, a beer and some *dechovka* (Bohemian brass-band music). The whole complex is closed on Monday during the day. **Křižík fountain** (Křižíkova fontána; ☎ 220 103 280; www .krizikovafontana.cz; admission 200Kč; ☾ 8, 9, 10 & 11pm Mar-Oct) performs computer-controlled acts of water gymnastics to music – expect treats like the soundtrack from *Jurassic Park* or *Pearl Harbor*, or you might get a bit of Smetana or Dvořák (the *Prague Post* has weekly details of the programme).

While the gullible saps are marvelling at the replica statues on the Charles bridge, you could be at the **Lapidárium** (Map pp82–3; ☎ 233 375

636; adult/child 20/10Kč; ☾ noon-6pm Tue-Fri, 10am-6pm Sat & Sun) checking out the real thing. This is a repository of some 400 sculptures from the 11th to the 19th centuries, removed from Prague's streets and buildings to save them from demolition or pollution.

Get to the Fairgrounds on tram 12, 15 or 17 from nádraží Holešovice metro station and get off at the Výstaviště stop.

STROMOVKA PARK

West of the Fairgrounds, this is Prague's largest park. In the Middle Ages it was a royal hunting preserve, and is referred to as Royal Deer Park (Královská obora). Rudolf II had rare trees planted and several lakes dug (fed from the Vltava by a still-functioning canal). You can get here across the Vltava via Císařský ostrov.

CENTRE FOR MODERN & CONTEMPORARY ART

The National gallery's massive **Centre for Modern & Contemporary Art** (Map pp82–3; ☎ 824 301 003; Dukelských hrdinů 47; adult/child from 100/50Kč for any 1 fl to 250/120Kč for all 4 fls; ☾ 10am-6pm Tue-Sun) has seemingly collected every work of modern Czech art, plus a fair swathe of other big names from the rest of Europe. If you don't have the time or money to see the full collection (it would take a whole day to see it properly), you can choose to do the gallery a floor at a time. Highlights include Czech cubists, Art Nouveau, Mánes' portraits and Mařák's landscapes, social realism and Karel Pauzer's grotesque *Dog Family*. Your ticket lasts a whole day, and you can go in and out as much as you want. Take tram 12, 15 or 17 west from Nádraží Holešovice metro station, two stops to Veletržní.

NATIONAL TECHNOLOGY MUSEUM

For hands-on fun, visit the **National technology museum** (Národní technické muzeum; Map pp82–3; ☎ 220 399 111; Kostelní 42; adult/child 70/30Kč; ☾ 9am-5pm Tue-Fri, 10am-6pm Sat & Sun). The giant main hall is full of old trains, planes and automobiles, including 1920s and '30s Škodas. There are also some great old motorbikes and bicycles. You can take a tour down a mineshaft, or learn about photography, astronomy or timepieces. From the Vltavská metro station, take tram 1 or 25 three stops to Letenské náměstí and walk down Nad štolou and Muzejní streets.

LETNÁ

Letná is a vast park between Hradčany and Holešovice, where Přemysl Otakar II held his coronation celebrations in 1261. Today it's given over to playgrounds, tennis courts, meandering paths packed with inline skaters, and an outdoor **beer garden** (p136) with postcard-perfect views of the city and the Vltava bridges.

The present layout dates from the early 1950s when a 30m, 14,000-tonne statue of Stalin, the biggest monument in the Eastern bloc, was erected by the Czechoslovak Communist Party, only to be blown up in 1962 when Kruschev took over (see The Missing Dictator, p109). Today, in its place, stands a peculiar giant **metronome** – if you stand in Old Town square facing up Pařížvská you can see it ticking out time against the sky. The terraced area around the metronome is a wonderland of rail slides and 50/50s, adored by local skateboarders.

Letná used to be the site of May Day military parades, similar to those in Moscow. In late 1989, some 750,000 people demonstrated here in support of what became known as the Velvet Revolution. In 1990 Pope John Paul II gave an open-air Mass here to more than one million people, most of whom were probably looking for the beer garden.

Smíchov

In Smíchov, Prague changes before your very eyes with the speed of time-lapse photography. Ten years ago tourists might have crossed over to this dirty, rough neighbourhood to get a taste of the real Prague; these days 'real' equals shopping malls, multiplexes, trendy bars and construction, construction, construction. Tourist attractions are few and far between, which means the beautiful, grubby baroque and Art Nouveau buildings are uncluttered with souvenir stores. The swarming, shopping masses clot around Anděl metro station; the northern end of Smíchov is a happening enclave of sushi restaurants and modern theatre. Head to the southern end to get the old-school version; the rail yards, old pubs and Staropramen brewery (just follow your nose) still have the air of 1838 Smíchov, when the suburb became Prague's industrial quarter.

MOZART MUSEUM AT BERTRAMKA

You'll need more than a passing interest in Wolfgang Amadeus to get the most out of this **museum** (Map p115; ☎ 257 317 465; www.bertramka

.cz; Mozartova 169; adult/child 110/30Kč, concerts 390-450Kč; ⊗ 9.30am-6pm Apr-Oct, to 5pm Nov-Mar), where they're keen to remind you that Prague liked Mozart before anyone else. Mozart finished *Don Giovanni* while staying here. The museum has a couple of instruments the master may once have played, and lots of information about local musicians with whom Mozart was involved. Regular concerts are held in the salon, and in the garden (April to October only). Take tram 4, 6, 9, 12 or 14 from the Anděl metro station.

Vinohrady

The suburb of Vinohrady lies southeast of the National museum and main train station. The name refers to vineyards that grew here centuries ago; even as recently as 200 years ago there was little urbanisation. Now the tree-lined streets are peppered with little cafés and bars, and the buildings have all had a good scrubbing and a fresh coat of paint – it's one of the prettiest of Prague's inner suburbs. There's not a lot to see here, but walking the Parisian-style streets from náměstí Míru to Havlíčkovy sady is a very pleasant way to spend a few hours.

PEACE SQUARE

Vinohrady's physical and commercial heart is Peace square (náměstí Míru, Map p116), dominated by the brick, neo-Gothic **St Ludmilla church** (kostel sv Ludmily) – the church steps are a popular meeting spot. Right behind it at No 9 is the neo-Renaissance **National house** (Národní dům), with exhibitions and concert halls. On the northern side of the square is the 1909 **Vinohrady theatre** (divadlo na Vinohradech), a popular drama venue.

CHURCH OF THE MOST SACRED HEART OF OUR LORD

With its perforated brickwork, stocky, looming clock tower and ultrasimple interior, this is probably Prague's most original church, its brawny charm reminiscent of a solid, rough factory worker downing his first beer of the afternoon. The **church** (kostel Nejsvětějšího Srdce Páně; Map p118; náměstí Jiřího z Poděbrad) was built in 1932 by Slovenian Josef Plečnik (who made the eyebrow-raising modern additions to Prague castle).

Žižkov

Named after the Hussite hero and formidable military commander Jan Žižka, who whipped Holy Roman Emperor Sigismund and his

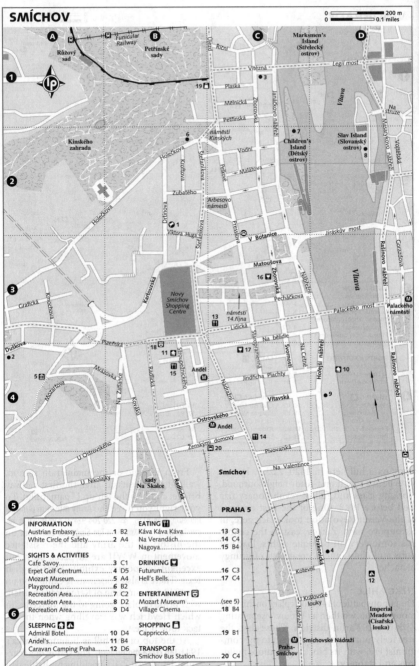

SMÍCHOV

INFORMATION	
Austrian Embassy	1 B2
White Circle of Safety	2 A4

SIGHTS & ACTIVITIES	
Cafe Savoy	3 C1
Erpet Golf Centrum	4 D5
Mozart Museum	5 A4
Playground	6 B2
Recreation Area	7 C2
Recreation Area	8 D2
Recreation Area	9 D4

SLEEPING	
Admirál Botel	10 D4
Andel's	11 B4
Caravan Camping Praha	12 D6

EATING	
Káva Káva Káva	13 C3
Na Verandách	14 C4
Nagoya	15 B4

DRINKING	
Futurum	16 C3
Hell's Bells	17 C4

ENTERTAINMENT	
Mozart Museum	(see 5)
Village Cinema	18 B4

SHOPPING	
Cappriccio	19 B1

TRANSPORT	
Smíchov Bus Station	20 C4

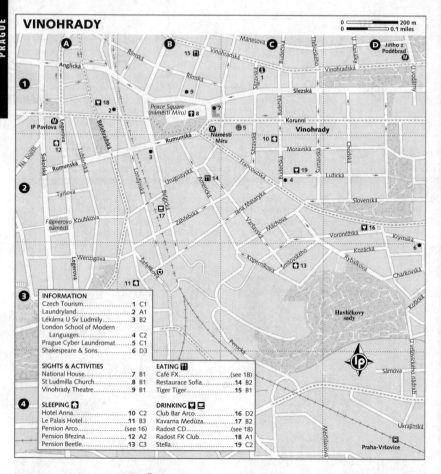

VINOHRADY

army on a hill here in 1420, Žižkov has always been a rough-and-ready neighbourhood, working-class and full of revolutionary fizz well before 1948. One of the first protests of the Velvet Revolution took place here, in Škroupovo nám. Žižkov, east of the centre, has some very un-baroque sights, loads of pubs and clubs, and a great deal of grungy panache.

ŽIŽKOV HILL

The famous battle of 1420 took place on this long mound – known then as Vitkov – separating Žižkov and Karlín districts. These days the area feels more like a monument to the communist era, with its blocky, grandiose buildings and statuary.

From Florenc or the main train station, walk along Husitská; after the first railway bridge, climb to the left up U památníku. To your right you'll see the **Army museum** (Armádní muzeum; Map p118; ☎ 220 204 924; U památníku 2; admission free; ☑ 10am-6pm Tue-Sun); its exhibits on the history of the army and the resistance movement in WWII are in Czech only, but excellent temporary exhibits have English texts. There is also a fascinating exhibition on the 1942 assassination of Reinhard Heydrich, with pride of place going to the Mercedes in which Heydrich was travelling when the attack took place.

At the top of the hill is Bohumil Kafka's 1941 **Jan Žižka monument**. The statue of a fearsome, bandaged Žižka wielding his battle flail from atop a vein-popping horse must have given Kafka some terrifying nightmares during its design.

Behind Žižka, the over-the-top **National memorial** (Národní památník, Map p118) was completed around 1930 as a memorial to the Czechoslovak 'unknown soldier', but later hijacked as a mausoleum for communist leader Klement Gottwald (the embalming didn't take, and when old Klement started rotting the memorial was closed and he was buried elsewhere). The outside of the memorial is covered in bas-reliefs glorifying the worker and soldier, but you can only visit the inside on the first Saturday of the month at 2pm: call **Prague Information Service** (☎ 222 781 676) to find out more.

TV TOWER

Prague's tallest landmark (and depending on your tastes, either its ugliest or its most futuristic) is the 216m-tall **TV tower** (Televizní věž; Map p118; ☎ 267 005 778; www.tower.cz, in Czech; Mahlerovy sady 1; adult/child 150/30Kč; ✆ 10am-11pm), erected between 1985 and 1992. It's worth getting up close to this '80s vision of the future for a good look at the faces of David Černý's bizarre sculptural installation (giant babies), *Miminka*. While the outside of the tower is one of the city's highlights, the inside is a wash-out. Views through the grubby windows are bigger but not necessarily better than those from St Vitus cathedral or Petřín tower.

The foundations of the TV tower were excavated in an old **Jewish cemetery** (admission 20Kč; ✆ 9am-1pm Tue & Thu), which operated between the closing of Josefov, at a time of plague outbreak, and the opening of the cemetery near Želivského metro, in 1890. It's estimated that 40,000 people have been crowded into this tiny yard.

OLŠANY CEMETERY & JAN PALACH'S GRAVE

A world away from the insanity of Old Town square, the inhabitants of the **Olšany cemetery** (Olšanské hřbitovy; Map p118; ☎ 267 310 652; Vinohradská 2807; admission free; ✆ 8am-7pm May-Sep, 8am-6pm Mar-Apr & Oct, 8am-5pm Nov-Feb) rest in some serious peace. This cool, green graveyard overgrown with ivy is Prague's main burial place, founded in 1680 during a plague epidemic.

To find Jan Palach's grave, the student who set himself on fire in January 1969 in protest at the Soviet invasion, enter the main gate and

turn right – it's about 50m along on the left of the path. For nearly 20 years Palach's body was moved around by the government to stop his grave becoming a protest site. It's worth visiting the museum of communism (p107) first to find out more about him.

JEWISH CEMETERY & FRANZ KAFKA'S GRAVE

Franz Kafka is buried in this **cemetery** (Židovské hřbitovy; Map p118; admission free; ✆ 9am-5pm Sun-Thu & 9am-2pm Fri Apr-Oct, 9am-4pm Sun-Thu & 9am-2pm Fri Nov-Mar, closed on Jewish hols), which opened around 1890 when the previous Jewish cemetery – now at the foot of the TV tower – was closed. To find Kafka's grave, follow the main avenue east (signposted), turn right at row 21, then left at the wall; it's at the end of the 'block'. Fans make a pilgrimage on 3 June, the anniversary of his death.

The entrance is beside Želivského metro station; men should cover their heads (yarmulkes are available at the gate). Last admission is 30 minutes before closing.

ACTIVITIES

Prague has lots of free **recreation areas**. The one on Children's Island (Dětský ostrov; Map p115), just south of Most Legii (access is from Janáčkovo nábřeži), has a playground, skate park, soccer pitch, concrete table-tennis tables and a strange combination boules/tenpin bowling game. It's open from 9am to 8pm daily from April to October and 10am to 6pm the rest of the year. The one in Smíchov (Map p115; Hořejší nábřeží) has a skate park, a basketball hoop, a small soccer pitch and a good kids' playground.

The city has about 180km of signposted **cycle routes**, about 60km of which are traffic-free (see http://doprava.praha-mesto.cz for an interactive map, in Czech only), and the popularity of cycling is steadily increasing. Stromovka Park and Troja are good places for pedalling. See p143 for details of bike hire places.

Inline skaters and **skateboarders** should head to Letná (Map pp82–3). The paths here are a very popular after-work in-line skating area. You can rent inline skates from **Inline Půjčovna** (Inline Skate Rental; Map pp82-3; ☎ 739 046 040; Nad štolou 1, Holešovice; ✆ noon-10pm Mon-Fri, 10am-10pm Sat & Sun); they speak a bit of English.

You can rent a **rowing boat** (from 60Kč per hour per person) or **pedal boat** (80Kč) from

PRAGUE

NORTHERN NOVÉ MĚSTO, KARLÍN & ŽIŽKOV

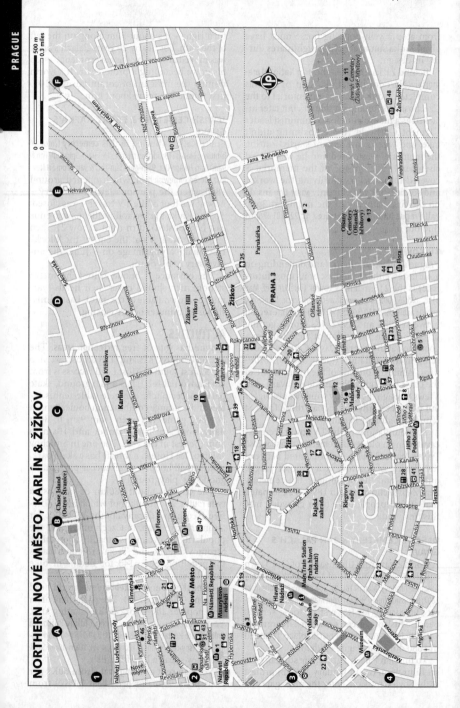

the northern end of Slav Island (Slovanský ostrov, Map p106). The rental spots are generally open from 10am to 8pm in summer, and close when the weather gets bad. Only one (Slovanka, on the western side of Slav Island) rents a pedal boat shaped like a swan – you'll pay 100Kč per person for the privilege of floating around in this beauty. None of the boats can be taken beyond the upstream and downstream weirs. All the boat rental spots sell beer, of course.

For outdoor swimming head to the **Podolí Swimming Pool** (Plavecký stadión Podolí; Map pp82-3; ☎ 241 433 952; Podolská 74, Podolí; admission 80/125Kč per 1½/3hr, child under 13 half-price; ☼ 6am-9.45pm) south of Vyšehrad. This huge complex has Olympic-sized pools, both indoor and outdoor, with plenty of sunbathing space (best to bring flip-flops for the grotty showers, though). To get there, take tram 3, 16, 17 or 21 to the Kublov stop, from where it's a further five-minute walk.

In winter, an **ice-skating** rink is set up at the feet of Jan Hus in the Old Town square – little kids and silly adults will enjoy being guided around the rink by university students dressed as princesses and jesters.

Those who can't bear a day without a session on the treadmill should try the centrally located **Fitness Týn** (Map p98; ☎ 224 808 295; Týnská 21, Staré Město; casual workout 95Kč; ☼ 7am-9pm Mon-Fri, 10am-8pm Sat & Sun) gym, which also has aerobics (80Kč) and spinning (110Kč) classes. Most

of the top-end hotels have gyms that can be used on a casual basis, but it will cost you at least 500Kč.

Prague's Range Rover drivers love **Erpet Golf Centrum** (Map p115; ☎ 257 321 229; www.erpet. cz, in Czech; Strakonická 2860/4, Smíchov; ☼ 8am-9pm). A one-day pass giving entry to the outdoor pool and sunbathing area per adult/concession costs 600/300Kč. Tennis court hire starts at 200Kč per hour, squash is from 150Kč, and the golf-driving range costs 100Kč an hour. Erpet also has a sauna, Jacuzzi and offers massage.

Clay tennis courts in the Vyšehrad historic grounds are managed by **Penguin Tenis** (Map p112; ☎ 241 407 619; Vyšehrad complex, Vyšehrad). Call for rates and reservations.

WALKING TOUR – WENCESLAS SQUARE

> **Distance:** 1.5km
> **Duration:** 30 minutes

Start at the steps in front of the neo-Renaissance **National museum** (1; p107), which dominates the upper end of Wenceslas square. From the steps you have a grand view down the square, a focal point of Czech history since the 19th century. At the foot of the steps is a pavement memorial to student martyr Jan Palach (p117).

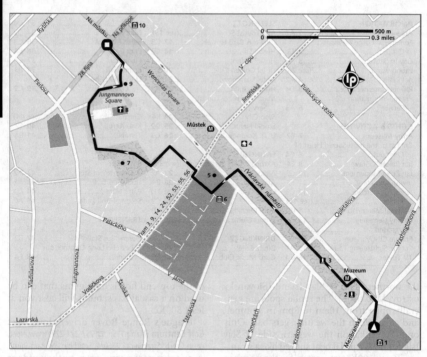

Cross the busy traffic artery of Mezibranská to Prague's famous equestrian **statue of St Wenceslas** (**2**; p108), the 10th-century 'Good King Wenceslas' of Christmas carol fame. Below the statue is a modest **memorial (3)** to those who died for their resistance to communism.

Wander down the middle of the square, admiring the grand buildings on either side. The finest is the 1906 **Grand Hotel Evropa (4)** at No 25, about halfway down on the right, which is Art Nouveau inside and out; have a peep at the French restaurant at the rear of the ground floor, and at the 2nd-floor atrium. Across the street at No 36 is the **Melantrich building (5)**, from whose balcony the death of Czech communism was pronounced by Alexander Dubček and Václav Havel on 24 November 1989 (it now houses a Marks & Spencer store).

Turn left into Pasáž Rokoko, a shopping arcade directly across the street from the Grand Hotel Evropa. It leads to the central atrium of the **Lucerna palace (6**; p108), dominated by David Černý's *Horse,* an ironic twist on the St Wenceslas statue in the square outside (it helps to know that the first prime minister of the Czech Republic was also a Václav).

Turn right beneath the dead horse (you'll see when you get here), and follow the passage to Vodičkova. Bear right across the street and enter the Světozor arcade. Up ahead you'll see a stained-glass window dating from the late 1940s – it's actually an advertisement for Tesla Radio, an old Czech electronics company.

At the far end of the Světozor arcade, turn left into the **Franciscan garden (7**; p109), a hidden oasis of peace and greenery. Make your way to the far northern corner of the garden, diagonally opposite to where you came in, and you'll find an exit to Jungmannovo square. Go past the arch leading to the **church of Our Lady of the Snows (8**; p109) and turn right.

Keep to the right of the Lancôme shop, and you will come to what must be the only **cubist lamppost (9)** in the entire world, dating from 1915. Turn left here and then duck right through the short Lindt arcade which returns you to Wenceslas square.

PRAGUE FOR CHILDREN

Prague probably isn't the most exciting destination for kids – baroque architecture, castles without armour or crossbows, churches, and museums of Jewish history don't generally get the youngsters all fired up. However, there are a few sights around town that kids might enjoy. **Petřín** (p95) has a mirror maze that has the kids cracking up, a playground and a replica Eiffel Tower. The **National technology museum** (p113) has plenty of hands-on entertainment, while the **National museum** (p107) is good for those who like stuffed animals and skeletons. There's a big **toy museum** (p90) and the very medieval **Old Royal palace** (p89) at the castle.

Prague has lots of good **playgrounds** – there are several on islands in the Vltava, one in the Kinský gardens in Malá Strana, a huge one in Letná, one beneath the Charles bridge on Kampa island in Malá Strana and one near the river in Smíchov. Many kids enjoy renting a boat (p117) on the river. If your kids have skateboards or inline skates with them, take them to Letná (p114). **Minor theatre** (p139) hosts traditional marionette shows for kids.

If you'd rather leave the kids behind while you hit the town, most top-end and many midrange hotels have baby-sitting services – call ahead to see whether yours does. Alternatively, **Prague Information Service** (Pražská Informační Služba, PIS; ☎ 124 44; www.prague-info.cz) usually has a list of baby-sitting *(hlídaní dětí)* agencies; rates are generally around 120Kč per hour. **Prague Family** (☎ 224 224 044; www.praguefamily.cz) is an agency that can provide English-speaking baby-sitters.

QUIRKY PRAGUE

Sculptor David Černý, a big success in the USA, has made a huge effort to make Prague a more interesting, less precious place. Many of his efforts have been thwarted – the giant statue of a naked, masturbating man intended for the roof of the National theatre was somehow never approved – while others, like his *Pink Tank* (p122), a revolutionary nose-thumbing piece, have been removed, but several of his works are on public display.

The TV tower (p117) in Žižkov crawls with the giant babies of *Miminka;* the Lucerna Passage (p108) is home to *Horse*, his interpretation of Wenceslas square's equestrian statue; while his *Hanging Around* (Map p98) caused complaints to the police after it was installed on the roof of a house in Husova street, Staré Město. There's also *Piss*, in the courtyard of Hergetova Cíhelna (p95), and *Quo Vadis* (Map p92), his famous sculpture of a Trabant car on legs in the garden of the German Embassy (go past the embassy, left through a playground, and along the lane at the back of the building). You can find out more, including plans for the future, at www.davidcerny.cz.

TOURS

Thanks to its excellent public transport system, Prague is very easy to get around, and if you already know a bit about the city a tour is probably a waste of time and money – a ride on tram 22 from Peace square (p114) in Vinohrady to the castle provides a good sightseeing trip for only 20Kč, and without the annoying commentary.

George's Guided Walks (☎ 607 820 158; www.praguemaster.com; per 2 persons 1500Kč, per additional person 300Kč) Lots of travellers have recommended George, whose intimate, personalised tours include a four-hour History Walk (if you have been to Prague before, he'll take you off the beaten track), a two-hour Iron Curtain Walk, and a five-hour pub crawl, including dinner in a Czech pub. George will meet you at your hotel, or anywhere else that's convenient.

Martin Tour (Map p106; ☎ 224 212 473; www.martintour.cz; Štepanska 61, Nové Město) Bus tours with headphone commentary (which means you can't ask questions) of Prague sights (two hours 350Kč), river cruises, trips to Terezín, Karlovy Vary, Karlštejn, Konopište, Kutná Hora, Český Krumlov and Dresden. Some tours involve walking; commentary tends to gloss over the interesting details. Pick-up Staroměstské nám.

Nostalgic Tram 91 (Map pp82-3; ☎ 233 343 349; www.dpp.cz; Public Transport museum; Patočkova 4, Střešovice; adult/child 25/10Kč; ⏲ departs hourly noon-6pm Sat, Sun & hols Apr–mid-Nov) Vintage tram cars dating from 1908 to 1924 trundle back and forth along a special sightseeing route, starting at the Public Transport museum and stopping at Prague castle, Malostranské náměstí, National theatre, Wenceslas square, náměstí Republiky and Štefánikův most, terminating at Výstaviště. You can get on and off at any stop, and buy tickets on board; ordinary public transport tickets and passes cannot be used on this line.

Pragotur (Map p98; ☎ 236 002 562; guides.pis@volny.cz; Old town hall, Staroměstské nám, Staré Město) The Prague Tourist Board's guide service, provides tailor-made walking tours from 600Kč per person for three hours. Tours include architecture, history, Art Nouveau and Jewish culture.

Prague Passenger Shipping (Pražská paroplavební společnost, PPS; ☎ 224 930 017; www.paroplavba.cz; Rašínovo nábřeží 2, Nové Město) From April to October PPS runs cruise boats along the Vltava, departing from the central quay on Rašínovo nábřeží (Map p106). A one-hour

---

THE PINK TANK

Náměstí Kinských, at the northern edge of Smíchov (Map p115), was until 1989 known as náměstí Sovětských tankistů (Soviet tank crews square), named in memory of the Soviet soldiers who 'liberated' Prague on 9 May 1945. For many years a Soviet T-34 tank – allegedly the first to enter the city – squatted menacingly atop a pedestal here (in fact it was a later Soviet 'gift').

In 1991 artist David Černý decided that the tank was an inappropriate monument, considering that Czechoslovakia had hardly been 'liberated' by the Soviet regime, and painted it bright pink. The authorities had it painted green again, and charged Černý with a crime against the state. This infuriated many parliamentarians, 12 of whom re-painted the tank pink themselves. Their parliamentary immunity saved them from arrest and secured Černý's release.

After complaints from the Soviet Union the pink tank was removed. Its former setting is now occupied by a circular fountain surrounded by park benches; the vast granite slab in the centre is split by a jagged fracture, perhaps symbolic of a break with the past. The tank still exists, and is still pink – it's at the Military museum in Lešany, near Týnec nad Sázavou, 30km south of Prague. For more on Černý see Quirky Prague, p121.

---

jaunt goes from the National theatre to Vyšehrad, departing at 11am, 2pm, 4pm, 5pm and 6pm from April to September (170Kč); a 1¼-hour trip to Troja (near the zoo; 100/190Kč one way/return) departs at 8.30am on weekdays in May and June only, and at 9.30am, 12.30pm and 3.30pm daily May to August and at weekends and holidays September and October. At 9am on Saturday and Sunday from May to August, a boat goes 37km south (upstream) through wild, green landscape to the Slapy Dam at Třebenice (300Kč return), arriving back in the city at 6.30pm.

Praha Bike (Map p98; ☎ 732 388 880; www .prahabike.cz; Dlouhá 24, Staré Město; 2hr-tour 420Kč; ☯ 9am-7pm) Take a two-hour guided cycling tour through the city, or an easy evening pedal through the parks. Tours depart from the Praha Bike office at 2.30pm from mid-March to October, and also at 11.30am and 5.30pm from May to mid-September. Trips outside the city can also be arranged. Helmets and locks are provided, and bikes are also available for private rental (p143).

Silver Line through Golden Prague This self-guided walking tour designed by the Prague Information Service (PIS; p86) takes in 38 sights in Staré Město, Malá Strana, Hradčany and Nové Město. The comprehensive guide booklet is available at PIS.

Wittmann Tours (Map p118; ☎ 222 252 472; www .wittmann-tours.com; Mánesova 8, Vinohrady; adult/ student 630/500Kč; ☯ tours begin 10.30am & 2pm Sun-Fri May-Oct, 10.30am Apr, Nov & Dec) This outfit's three-hour walking tour of Josefov starts from the square in front of the Hotel Inter-Continental on Pařížská. Wittmann also runs seven-hour day trips to North Bohemia's Terezín (p231) for adults/students costing 1150/1000Kč.

FESTIVALS & EVENTS

Throughout summer, Prague can barely move for festivals. Keep an eye on *Houser*, the *Prague Post* and posters to see what's

happening while you're in town. Updates on festivals can be found at www.prague-info.cz and www.prague.tv. Some regularly scheduled events include the following:

Open-Air Cinema Festival (☎ 266 712 746; www .strelak.cz, in Czech) From June till mid-September, films are shown outdoors on Marksmen's Island (Střelecký Ostrov) – screenings include English-language films, German and French art-house classics, recent releases and Czech favourites.

Prague Spring (Pražské Jaro; ☎ 227 059 234; www .festival.cz; Rudolfinum Box Office, náměstí Jana Palacha, Staré Město) Prague's biggest festival drawcard begins on 12 May with a procession from Smetana's grave at Vyšehrad to the Municipal house, and a performance of *Má vlast*. The festival of classical music continues until 2 June. The cheapest tickets are available from the box office, open from 10am to 6pm Monday to Friday from April to 12 May, and until 5pm during the festival. For a guaranteed seat, though, you will have to book by mid-March.

Vinobraní From 1 August, you'll see signs popping up around the city advertising *burčák*: it's slightly fermented grape juice, the first product of the wine harvest. Prague toasts *burčák* for a few days in late September at náměstí Míru in Vinohrady, traditionally a wine-growing area.

SLEEPING

There are hundreds of hotels in Prague, but the incredible demand for beds means this is one of Europe's more expensive places to stay. During high season it pays to book ahead; see p436.

Staré Město, Nové Město and Malá Strana – the tourist centres – have the greatest variety and charge the most. Vinohrady has a lot of midrange, smaller hotels, and is a very pleasant place to stay, within easy reach of the centre and with lots of restaurants and bars. Žižkov has hostels and budget hotels, as well as a few midrange options, and is popular with younger travellers – it's a bit grungy, and has tons of bars and clubs. Holešovice and Vyšehrad are both good options for midrange hotels within easy reach of the centre, though there's less going on in these suburbs than in Vinohrady.

Camping is prohibited on public land and most campgrounds are on the outskirts of Prague – we've listed some of those that are in closer.

In summer, many schools and universities convert themselves to hostels – look for big, yellow 'Travellers Hostel' banners. We've generally only listed year-round hostels.

Touts swarm on the arrival platforms of the main and Holešovice train stations offering private rooms. Check the location and availability of transport: some are right out in the suburbs. Prices start around 500Kč per person

if you're sharing entrance and bathroom with the family. If you want to organise a private room ahead of time, some accommodation agencies handle them.

Apartments are an increasingly popular option. If you're staying more than a week, they can be very good value, particularly as you can cook meals at home. We've listed agencies that handle apartments.

Accommodation Agencies

Agencies are a good option for private rooms or apartments, or if you show up in high season and can't find a bed. If you're booking a hotel it's cheaper to do so direct.

Alfa Tourist Service (Map p118; ☎ 224 230 037; www.alfatourist.cz; Opletalova 38, Nové Město; ⏰ 9am-5pm Mon-Fri) Accommodation in student hostels, *pensions*, hotels and private rooms.

Apartments.cz (Map p106; ☎ 224 990 900; www.apartments.cz; Ostrovní 7, Nové Město; ⏰ 9am-5pm

---

GAY & LESBIAN PRAGUE

For a city where it seems like every third person is making out in public, Prague is notable for the lack of gay affection displayed on its streets. While there are no laws against homosexuality in the Czech Republic – the age of consent is 15, the same as for straights – public opinion seems to be lagging behind legislation.

Amigo magazine's website (www.amigo.cz/en) has English-language listings. Tourist services, accommodation, listings and a bulletin board can be found at www.praguegaycity.com. Gay Iniciativa (http://gay.iniciativa.cz in Czech) is a gay and lesbian support service. Probably the most comprehensive information source is Gay Guide Prague (www.gayguide.net/europe/czech/prague), with online forums, events, accommodation, tours, newsletters and support groups.

Gay-owned accommodation includes **Pension Arco** (p128) and **Studio Henri** (Map p118; ☎ 271 773 837; www.studiohenri.cz; Jeseniova 52, Žižkov; d from 3000Kč; **P** ☒ ☒), a four-person apartment with a whirlpool.

Bars & Clubs

The gay scene in Prague changes fast – check out one of the listings services mentioned earlier before you head out.

Club Bar Arco (Map p116; ☎ 271 740 734; Voroněžská 24/172, Vinohrady; ⏰ 8am-midnight) A quiet little spot in genteel Vinohrady, popular with older men. There's also accommodation (see Pension Arco above) and an internet café.

Friends (Map p98; ☎ 224 211 920; Bartolomějská 11; ⏰ 8pm-6am) This welcoming music and video bar has excellent coffee and wine, and DJs after 10pm on Friday and Saturday.

Piano Bar (Map p118; ☎ 222 727 496; Milešovská 10, Žižkov; ⏰ 5pm-midnight) A stalwart of the Prague gay scene, frequented mainly by locals, this is a homely little cellar bar cluttered with junk and bric-a-brac.

Stella (Map p116; ☎ 224 257 869; Lužická 10, Vinohrady; ⏰ 8pm-5am) Probably the most popular gay bar in town, Stella is intimate and candlelit. You have to ring the doorbell to get in.

Termix (Map p118; ☎ 222 710 462; www.club-termix.cz; Třebízského 4a, Vinohrady; admission free; ⏰ 8pm-5am Wed-Sun) One of Prague's most popular gay and lesbian dance clubs, with a young crowd that contains as many tourists as locals. The smallish dance floor fills up fast during Thursday's techno party, when you'll probably have to queue to get in.

Mon-Fri) Long-established specialist in holiday apartments near the city centre.

AVE (☎ 251 551 011; www.avetravel.cz) Walk-in booking offices at the main train station, Holešovice train station and the airport; efficient and helpful, with hostel, *pension* and hotel rooms and a few private rooms. The branch at the main train station specialises in finding last-minute accommodation.

Happy House Rentals (Map p106; ☎ 224 946 890; www.happyhouserentals.com; Jungmannova 30, Nové Město; ☉ 9am-5pm Mon-Fri) One of Prague's friendliest, most helpful agencies, Happy House rents out apartments and rooms all over the city in all price ranges.

Maja Rentals (☎ 224 911 850; www.majarentals.com; ☉ 11am-8pm) Good value short- and long-term apartment rentals in the centre and suburbs. No office, call the phone number or use the website to make inquiries.

Mary's Travel & Tourist Service (Map p118; ☎ 222 253 510; www.marys.cz; Italska 31, Vinohrady; ☉ 9am-9pm) Friendly and efficient agency offering private rooms, hostels, *pensions*, apartments and hotels in all price ranges in Prague and surrounding area.

Stop City (Map p118; ☎ 222 521 233; www.stopcity .com; Vinohradská 24, Vinohrady; ☉ 10am-9pm daily Apr-Oct, 10am-8pm Mon-Sat Nov-Mar) Specialising in apartments, private rooms and *pension* accommodation in the city centre, Vinohrady and Žižkov areas.

Hradčany & Malá Strana
BUDGET
Hostel ESTEC (Map p92; ☎ 257 210 410; estec@jrc.cz; blok 2, Vaníčkova 5, Strahov; s/d 360/720Kč; ☉ year-round) The best of several Strahov student dormitories offering traveller accommodation, ESTEC is a good deal cheerier than its neighbours. Take bus 143, 149 or 217 from Dejvická metro to Kolej Strahov.

Hostel Sokol (Map p92; ☎ 257 007 397; hostel@sokol-cos .cz; 3rd fl, Hellichova 1; dm 350Kč; ☉ year-round; ☒) Sokol is accessed via a courtyard from Všehrdova 42 (take the metro to Malostranská and then tram 12, 22 or 23 two stops south). While the location and price are choice, the dorms are ultrabasic and can be crowded.

MIDRANGE
Castle Steps (Map p92; ☎ 257 532 921; www.castlesteps .com; Nerudova 10; r €37-78, apt €62-168) The name applies to a range of suites and apartments spread across three buildings on Nerudova street and one a little further uphill on Úvoz. Management is laid-back, helpful, gay-friendly, and decidedly informal – don't expect porters and room service! (There are no lifts either.) The apartments sleep from two to eight, and

offer remarkable value in a great location; all have been beautifully renovated and are furnished with antiques and pot plants. The reception office is at Nerudova 10 (ring the buzzer on the street, and wait for someone to come down and meet you).

Hotel Sax (Map p92; ☎ 257 531 268; www.sax.cz; Jánský vršek 328/3; s/d 4100/4400Kč; ℗ ☒ ⌨) In a quiet, atmospheric corner of Malá Strana, eclectically furnished Hotel Sax has huge baths, big flat-screen TVs, primary-coloured leather couches, striking abstract photography and some of the chintziest bedrooms in Prague. It's very reasonably priced for the area and has a great ambience.

TOP END
Romantik Hotel U Raka (Map p92; ☎ 220 511 100; www.romantikhotels.com; Černínská 10; s/d from €160/180; ℗ ☒ ☒) Totally secluded but within an easy walk of Strahov and the castle, this tiny six-room hotel in an 18th-century wooden house with its own walled garden is the epitome of privacy. The owners have managed to blend 18th-century atmosphere with entirely modern fittings – each room is unique. Be sure to book at least a few months in advance.

Hotel U Zlaté Studně (Map p92; ☎ 257 011 213; www.zlatastudna.cz; U Zlaté studně 4; d from €200, ste from €250; ⌨) 'At the Golden Well' is one of Malá Strana's hidden secrets, tucked away at the end of a cobbled cul-de-sac – a Renaissance house that once belonged to Emperor Rudolf II, with an unbeatable location perched on the southern slope of the castle hill. The rooms are quiet and spacious, with polished wood floors, reproduction period furniture, and blue and white bathrooms with underfloor heating and whirlpool baths; many have views over the palace gardens below.

Hotel Questenberk (Map p92; ☎ 220 407 600; www .questenberk.cz; Úvoz 15/155; s/d €160/200; ℗ ☒ ☒ ⌨) Once Strahov Monastery's hospital building, this hotel has lots of character and is on a quiet street close to the castle. The rooms are sunny and furnished with old-fashioned opulence, though the atmosphere is more modern than medieval. There's an internet connection in every room if you have your own laptop.

Other recommendations:

U Páva (Map p92; ☎ 257 533 360; www.romantic hotels.cz; U lužického semináře 32; s/d from 5700/6200Kč; ℗ ☒ ⌨) Gothic detailing and heavy, dark furniture throughout, some rooms have stained glass and magical views of the castle.

Hotel U krále Karla (Map p92; ☎ 257 532 869; www.romantichotels.cz; Úvoz 4; s/d from 5000/5500Kč; Ⓟ ✖) You can't get closer to the castle than this hotel, right at the base of the walls. Rooms are spacious and the atmosphere fairy-tale.

Domus Henrici (Map p92; ☎ 220 511 369; www .domus-henrici.cz; Loretánská 11; s/d from €155/170; 💻) Stylish rooms with polished wood floors, large bathrooms, comfy beds and fluffy bathrobes. Service is impeccable, and there's a sunny outdoor terrace with gorgeous views over the city.

Staré Město & Josefov
BUDGET

Hostel Týn (Map p98; ☎ 224 808 333; www.tyn.prague -hostels.cz; Týnská 19; dm 400Kč, s & d 1200Kč; ✖) This spic-and-span little hostel is the most central budget accommodation in Prague, a couple of minutes' walk from Old Town square. The rooms themselves are basic and unadorned and all have shared bathrooms, but they're spotlessly clean and comfortable.

Hostel Dlouhá (Map p98; ☎ 224 826 662; www.travellers .cz; Dlouhá 33; dm/s/d/tr 380/1120/1300/1500Kč; Ⓟ 💻) The only Travellers' Hostel that is open year-round (if you're visiting in summer, you can book one of four other centrally located hostels by calling Dlouhá). The main dorm is a bit dark and grim, but smaller dorms are bright and clean if a little cramped (each bed has its own reading lamp, a nice touch). There's also a bar with pizza and a jukebox.

Pension Unitas (Map p98; ☎ 224 211 020; www.unitas .cz; Bartolomějská 9; dm per person 350-510Kč, s/d 1280/1580Kč; ✖) Set in a former convent that was once used as a prison, the rooms here are quiet (but cramped), and have shared bathrooms. Václav Havel was held here for a day, and if it's available you can stay in the very cell (No P6). If all this seems a bit too grim, the larger '*pension*' rooms on the ground floor and first floor provide more comfort, with brightly painted walls, flowery curtains, pot plants and prints.

MIDRANGE

Hotel Antik (Map p98; ☎ 222 322 288; www.hotelantik .cz; Dlouhá 22; s/d 3590/3990Kč) As the name suggests, this place has an antique shop on the ground floor and various pieces scattered elsewhere throughout the building, which is right in the heart of the Old Town. The cosy rooms have been thoroughly modernised and are perfectly comfortable, though a little lacking in character – ask for one with a balcony overlooking the garden out back.

Pension U Medvídků (Map p98; ☎ 224 211 916; www .umedvidku.cz; Na Perštýně 7; s/d from 2300/3500Kč) Cosy and centrally located, 'At the Little Bear' is a traditional beer hall and *pension* on the southern edge of the Old Town, about 10 minutes' walk from Old Town square. Some of the first-floor rooms have Renaissance painted wooden ceilings, and a few are almost big enough to be called a suite – No 33 is the best in the house, spacious and atmospheric, with a big pine bed and huge exposed roof beams.

Hotel Cloister Inn (Map p98; ☎ 224 211 020; www .cloister-inn.com; Konviktská 14; s/d €122/130; Ⓟ ✖ 💻) The Cloister Inn's refurbished convent rooms were once part of the still-operational St Bartholomew church. While some architectural touches remain from the convent, they're a little overwhelmed by the hotel's resolutely modern décor and warm, brown and yellow colour scheme. The rooms are comfortable and spotlessly clean, with great power showers.

Other recommendations:

Hotel Černý Slon (Map p98; ☎ 222 321 521; www .hotelcernyslon.cz; Týnská ulička 1; s/d 3200/3900Kč) Set in a lovely historic building barely 30 paces from Old Town square, with smallish but comfortable rooms, a Gothic-vaulted dining room and a tiny courtyard garden.

Hotel U Klenotníka (Map p98; ☎ 224 211 699; www.uklenotnika.cz; Rytířská 3; s/d 2500/3800Kč; ✖) This friendly central hotel has 10 plain-but-comfy rooms decorated with unique art and a stylish little restaurant adorned with surreal painted glass.

Pension U Lilie (Map p98; ☎ 222 220 432; www .pensionulilie.cz; Liliová 15; s/d 2000/3050Kč) This plain but pleasant *pension* is right in the heart of things.

Hotel Mejstřik (Map p98; ☎ 224 800 055; www .hotelmejstrik.cz; Jakubská 5; s/d €178/203; Ⓟ 💻) This small boutique hotel in a reasonably quiet back street has striking Art Deco furnishings and a garden, just around the corner from the Municipal house.

TOP END

Hotel Josef (Map p98; ☎ 221 700 111; www.hoteljosef .cz; Rybná 20; s/d from €149/173; Ⓟ ✖ 💻) The Josef is one of Prague's most stylish contemporary hotels. From the stark, white, minimalist lobby – with its glass spiral staircase – to the designer bedrooms, where lines are kept clean and simple with plenty of white and subtle neutral tones in the bed linen and furniture. The glass-walled en suites are especially attractive, boasting extra-large 'rainfall' shower-heads and modish glass bowl basins.

Northern Nové Město

BUDGET

Hostel Jednota (Map p118; ☎ 224 230 038; www.alfa
tourist.cz/ejednota.html; Opletalova 38; dm/s/d incl breakfast 385/650/940Kč) Don't be put off by the glum
Soviet-style lobby: the rooms at Jednota are
bright, airy, well laid-out for maximum privacy and thoroughly 21st century. There are
cooking facilities and a bar, and the hostel is
close to the main train station.

MIDRANGE

Hotel Harmony (Map p118; ☎ 222 319 807; www.hotel
harmony.cz; Na poříčí 31; s/d 2900/3900Kč; ✗) The
rooms here are sparklingly clean, simple and
comfortable and the staff business-like and
friendly: it's good value for money, and only a
short walk from the Old Town. Three-person
suites go for 4200Kč.

TOP END

Hotel Yasmin (Map p118; ☎ 234 100 100; www.hotel
-yasmin.cz; Politických věžňů 12; d from €260; ✗) This boutique hotel a block east of Wenceslas square is
very cutting-edge. The public areas are covered
in jasmine blossom motifs and decorated with
birch twig arrangements and chrome balls. The
spacious bedrooms have a neutral palette of
white, beige and tan, the clean lines set off by
plants, flowers or a curved edge here and there.
The bathrooms are in black tile and chrome.

Southern Nové Město & Vyšehrad

BUDGET

Miss Sophie's (Map p106; ☎ 296 303 530; www.miss
-sophies.com; Melounova 3; dm 440Kč, s/d from 1500/1700Kč,
apt from 21,000Kč; ✗ 💻) This hostel in a converted apartment building on the southern
edge of the New Town offers a touch of contemporary style, with oak-veneer floors and
stark, minimalist décor. There is a very cool
lounge in the basement, with red-brick vaults
and black leather sofas, and reception (open
24 hours) is staffed by a young, multilingual
crew who are always eager to help.

Hostel U Melounu (Map p106; ☎ 224 918 322; www
.hostelumelounu.cz; Ke Karlovu 7; dm 390Kč, s/d from
700/1000Kč; P 💻) One of the prettier hostels
in town, U Melounu is in a historic building on a quiet back street, a short walk from
Vinohrady's restaurants and bars, and there's
the added attraction of a peaceful, sunny garden complete with barbecue. It's about a 10-
minute walk south of IP Pavlova metro, or
take bus 504 or 505 down Sokolská.

MIDRANGE

Hotel 16 U sv Kateřiny (Map p106; ☎ 224 920 636; www
.hotel16.cz; Kateřinská 16; s/d from 2800/3500Kč; P ✗ 💻)
Near the Botanic gardens and about 10 min-
utes' walk from Karlovo nám metro station,
this friendly boutique hotel is quiet, clean and
comfortable. The rooms vary in size and are
simply but smartly furnished; the best ones are
those at the back with views onto the peaceful
terraced garden.

Hotel Amadeus (Map p112; ☎ 224 937 572; www
.dhotels.cz; Slavojova 8; s/d/ste 3050/3250/4750Kč;
P ✗ 💻) This good-value hotel is located
on a quiet street below the Vyšehrad citadel.
Rooms in the front block are spacious and
elegant, decorated in shades of pale yellow,
dark blue and tan; those at the back are a
little more cramped, but overlook a peaceful
courtyard. The city centre is just 10 minutes
away by tram.

Hotel Union (Map p112; ☎ 261 214 812; www.hotel
union.cz; Ostrčilovo náměstí 4; s/d from €98/120; P ✗)
The Union is a grand old hotel that dates
from 1906; it is still family-run, and the staff
take great pride in looking after their guests
properly. Comfortably renovated, with a few
period touches left intact, the bedrooms are
plain but pleasant, and the double glazing
helps to cut down on street noise; ask for one
of the deluxe corner rooms, which are huge
and have bay windows with a view of either
Vyšehrad or the distant castle

TOP END

Radisson SAS Alcron Hotel (Map p106; ☎ 222 820 000;
www.radissonsas.com; Štěpánská 40; d from €200; P 💻)
The five-star Radisson is the modern reincar-
nation of the 1930s Alcron Hotel, and has long
been favoured by celebrities and diplomats.
Much of the original Art Deco marble-and-
glass fittings have been preserved, and the 211
rooms have been tastefully renovated with
pleasant soft furnishings, retro prints and chic
marble bathrooms.

Holešovice

BUDGET

Sir Toby's Hostel (Map pp82-3; ☎ 283 870 635; www
.sirtobys.com; Dělnická 24, Holešovice; dm 340-400Kč, s/d
1000/1350Kč; P ✗ 💻) Set in a quiet, nicely
refurbished apartment building with spacious kitchen and common room, and run
by friendly, cheerful staff, Sir Toby's is only
10 minutes north of the city centre by tram.
The dorms have between four and eight

bunks, and there's a communal kitchen for self-caterers to do their thing, a lounge and a relaxing little garden where you can sit back and chat.

Hotel Extol Inn (Map pp82-3; ☎ 220 876 541; www .extolinn.cz; Přístavní 2, Holešovice; s/d from 790/1350Kč; **P** ⊠) The bright and modern Extol Inn provides budget accommodation within easy reach of the city centre. The cheapest rooms (on the upper floors) are basic, no-frills affairs with shared bathrooms; these are often occupied by large groups of school children, so if you value your peace and quiet it might be worth paying a bit extra for the more expensive three-star rooms (doubles from 2260Kč) which have private bathroom, TV, minibar and free use of the hotel sauna and spa.

MIDRANGE

Hotel Belvedere (Map pp82-3; ☎ 220 106 111; www .europehotels.cz; Milady Horákové 19, Holešovice; s/d from €95/128; **P** ⊠ ✖) The Belvedere is an old communist-era hotel that has been completely refurbished, and now provides good-value accommodation within easy reach of the city centre. The standard rooms are nothing special, but they're comfortable and spotlessly clean. The 'executive' rooms (doubles €147) on the 2nd floor are much more spacious, with sound-proofed windows, smart crimson drapes and bedspreads, and huge, white, marble-lined bathrooms.

Smíchov
BUDGET

Caravan Camping Praha (Map p115; ☎ 257 317 555; www.caravancamping.cz; Císařská louka 162; per person 95Kč, plus per tent/car 90/90Kč; ☺ year-round; **P**) At the tip of quiet Císařská louka island, this narrow strip of grass has fine views across to Vyšehrad. The camp site has a restaurant (open in summer) and a shop. From Smíchovské nádraží metro and train station, take tram 12 two stops south to Lihovar, cross the freeway and walk down the sliproad by the petrol station – it's about a 10-minute walk.

MIDRANGE

Admirál Botel (Map p115; ☎ 257 321 302; www.admiral -botel.cz; Hořejší nábřeží 57; s/d 2980/3130Kč, ste 5400Kč; **P**) This floating hotel – a permanently moored riverboat – has compact, well-designed cabins: simple, compact and functional rather than luxurious, with tiny en-suite shower

rooms; those facing the river have an attractive outlook, and you can feed the swans from your window.

TOP END

Andel's (Map p115; ☎ 296 889 688; www.andelshotel .com; Stroupežnického 21; s/d from €235/255; **P** ⊠ 🖵) Nowhere sums up new Smíchov quite like Andel's. This sleek designer hotel, all stark contemporary-style in beige, black and red, has floor-to-ceiling windows, DVD and CD players, internet access, and modern abstract art in every room, while the bathrooms are a wonderland of polished chrome and frosted glass. Superior 'club rooms', come with pleasurable perks such as bathrobes and slippers, newspapers delivered to your room and free room-service breakfast.

Troja

Troja is out by the zoo, across the Vltava northwest of Holešovice; take bus 112 from Nádraží Holešovice metro station.

BUDGET

Autocamp Trojská (Map pp82-3; ☎ 283 850 487; www .autocamp-trojska.cz; Trojská 157; site per person 100Kč, plus per tent/car 150/90Kč; ☺ year-round) The most comfortable and secure of half a dozen camp sites in this quiet northern suburb, Trojská offers a garden bar and restaurant, a laundry and an on-site shop. Get off the bus at the Kazanka stop.

Camp-Pension Herzog (Map pp82-3; ☎ 283 850 472; www.campherzog.cz; Trojská 161; per person 80Kč, plus per tent 60-150Kč, per car 80Kč; ☺ year-round) Another of the Troja camp sites, Herzog is set in an orchard, and has cooking and washing facilities, a fridge and freezer, and free hot showers. Get off the bus at the Čechova škola stop.

Žižkov
BUDGET

Hostel Elf (Map p118; ☎ 222 540 963; www.hostelelf .com; Husitská 11; dm 320-360Kč, s/d 1000/1200Kč; 🖵) Friendly, bright and cheerful, Hostel Elf has lots of nooks and crannies where you can spend some quiet time, as well as a convivial terrace bar and lounge room. Nine-bed dorms are comfortable and well laid-out. Some doubles have their own bathrooms, but even the shared bathrooms allow a lot of privacy.

Clown & Bard Hostel (Map p118; ☎ 222 716 453; www.clownandbard.com; Bořivojova 102; dm 300-380Kč, d 1000Kč, apt 2400Kč; **P** 🖵) You're guaranteed a party in Clown & Bard's 36-bed dorm – if you want things quieter, pay a little more for the five- to seven-person rooms, or one of the six-person self-catering flats in the attic. The party crowd gravitates towards the thumping basement bar which stays open till midnight and features regular live acts and DJ nights.

MIDRANGE

Hotel Golden City (Map p118; ☎ 222 711 008; www.golden city.cz; Táboritská 3; s/d/tr 1900/2700/2900Kč; P ☒ ☐) The Golden City is a converted 19th-century apartment block with crisp, clean, no-frills rooms, good buffet breakfasts and friendly, helpful staff. The main train station is just two tram stops away, and Wenceslas square is four stops.

Hotel U Tří Korunek (Map p118; ☎ 222 781 112; www .3korunky.cz; Cimburkova 28; s/d from 2480/3380Kč; P) Spread across three buildings in a peaceful corner of Žižkov, the 'Three Crowns' has 78 comfortable, spotless rooms; most are spacious, with room for a table and a couple of armchairs, but it's worth shelling out for one of the 'superior' rooms (300Kč extra), which are rather more stylish, with wood veneer floors, designer furniture, flat-screen TVs and huge walk-in showers.

Vinohrady

BUDGET

Pension Arco (Map p116; ☎ 271 742 908; www.arco -guesthouse.cz; Voroněžská 21; d/apt from 1200/1900Kč; ☐) The Arco is a gay-owned *pension* and café-bar offering clean and comfortably furnished *pension* rooms, as well as several two- to four-person apartments in nearby buildings. The apartments are good value – bright and clean with laminate floors and Ikea furniture, and close to a tram line that will take you all the way to the castle. Vino-hrady's restaurants, pubs and clubs are just a few blocks away.

Pension Beetle (Map p116; ☎ 222 515 093; www .beetle-tour.cz; Šmilovského 10; d from 1800Kč; ste from 3200Kč) The Beetle occupies a lovely 1910 apart-ment building in a leafy back street, far from the tourist throng. The cheaper rooms are plain but functional, while the larger rooms and 'suites' (like two-room apartments) are more stylishly decorated and furnished with antique and stripped-pine furniture, and are equipped with bedside lamps, minibar, table and chairs.

MIDRANGE

Pension Březina (Map p116; ☎ 296 188 888; www.brezina .cz; Legerova 41; s/d 2000/2200Kč; P ☐) Set in a con-verted apartment block that retains traces of its Art Nouveau heritage, this attractive *pen-sion* boasts rooms that are spacious, comfort-able and neatly laid out. Try to get a room at the back as the street out front can be noisy.

Hotel Anna (Map p116; ☎ 222 513 111; www.hotel anna.cz; Budečská 17; s/d from €70/90, d from €100) This late 19th-century building retains many of its Art Nouveau period features. The bedrooms are bright and cheerful, with floral bedspreads and arty black-and-white photos of Prague buildings on the walls. There are two small suites on the top floor, one of which has a great view towards the castle.

TOP END

Le Palais Hotel (Map p116; ☎ 234 634 111; www.palais hotel.cz; U Zvonařky 1; s/d €335/370, ste from €680; ☒ P ☐) Housed in a gorgeous belle époque building dating from the end of the 19th cen-tury, this luxury hotel has been beautifully restored, complete with original floor mosaics, period fireplaces, marble staircases, wrought-iron balustrades, frescoes, painted ceilings and delicate stucco-work. The bedrooms are decorated in warm shades of yellow, pink and ochre, while the various suites – some located in the corner tower, some with a south-facing balcony – make the most of the hotel's superb location perched on top of a bluff with views of Vyšehrad fortress.

EATING

Fifteen years ago, Prague's eateries offered little more than pork and dumplings and deep-fried cheese. These days, if you can imagine eating it, some entrepreneurial Pra-guer is cooking it. Italian, French, Indian, Moroccan, Lebanese, Thai, Greek, Chinese and Icelandic are all on offer, as is the sort of fusion food filling plates in San Fran-cisco, Sydney and London. Vegetarian food is widely available, though finding anything vegan is difficult.

However, don't let this kaleidoscope of cuisines blind you to the pleasures of good old-fashioned Czech grub. The city's many pubs dish up tasty traditional dishes, often at very low prices, and a lot of the more up-market restaurants offer gourmet versions of classic Bohemian dishes such as pork knuckle or roast duck.

Prices soar as you approach Old Town square and Malostranské náměstí, but it's only rarely that quality soars as well. You can still find plenty of good, reasonably priced food in side streets near even the biggest tourist centres. Restaurants are generally open by 10am or 11am, and close at 11pm or midnight.

Hradčany
BUDGET
Saté (Map p92; ☎ 220 514 552; Pohořelec 3; mains 80–125Kč; ◷ 11am-10pm) Saté is one of Prague's longest-serving Asian restaurants, a no-frills place just five minutes' walk west of the castle serving inexpensive Indonesian and Malaysian dishes such as *nasi goreng* (fried rice with veggies, prawns and egg), beef *rendang* (coconut-based curry), Javanese beefsteak and a string of tasty vegetarian dishes.

Malý Buddha (Map p92; ☎ 220 513 894; Úvoz 46; mains 60–120Kč; ◷ noon-10.30pm Tue-Sun; ✗) Like stepping into a Saigon temple, Malý Buddha is all tinkling music, oriental knick-knacks and an atmosphere of enforced peace. The food is mostly Vietnamese influenced, with lots of vegetarian offerings and an interesting selection of 'healing' wines, though it doesn't mention which is recommended for cobblestone-inflicted blisters.

TOP END
U Zlaté Hrušky (Map p92; ☎ 220 514 778; Nový svět 3; mains 600–800Kč; ◷ 11.30am-3pm & 6.30pm-midnight) 'At The Golden Pear' is a cosy, wood-panelled gourmet's corner, serving beautifully prepared Czech fish, fowl and game dishes. It's frequented as much by locals as by tourists and visiting dignitaries (the Czech foreign ministry is just up the road). In summer you can opt for a table in its leafy *zahradní restaurace* (garden restaurant) across the street.

Malá Strana
BUDGET
Hostinec U Tří Zlatých Trojek (Map p92; ☎ 257 534 377; Tomášská 6; mains 100–160Kč; ◷ 11am-midnight) Hidden among the overpriced tourist traps of Malá Strana is this traditional pub, serving good, solid, Prague pub grub at surprisingly low prices.

Restaurace Bar Bar (Map p92; ☎ 257 312 246; Všehrdova 17; mains 90–155Kč; ◷ noon-midnight Sun-Thu, noon-2am Fri & Sat) A cosy cellar bar decked with posters and works by local artists, Bar Bar serves up Slovak *halušky* (cheese dumplings

with bacon), giant salads and a zillion kinds of tasty crepes, ranging from savoury pancakes stuffed with smoked bacon, sauerkraut and cheese to sweet ones filled with ice cream, walnuts and maple syrup.

Bohemia Bagel (Map p92; ☎ 257 310 831; Újezd 18; snacks 90–270Kč; ◷ 7am-midnight Mon-Fri, 8am-midnight Sat & Sun) A backpackers' favourite, Bohemia Bagel serves up bagels, quiches, soups, salads and all-you-can-drink soft drinks and coffee, as well as internet access. There's another branch (Map p98; Masná 2, Staré Město) that is also an internet café.

MIDRANGE
Cantina (Map p92; ☎ 257 317 173; Újezd 38; mains 120–300Kč; ◷ noon-midnight) This homely hacienda serves up the most authentic margaritas in Prague. The menu is as good as Tex-Mex gets in this town, with big portions of burrito, *chimichanga, quesadilla* and fajitas with both meat and vegetarian fillings.

Hergetova Cihelna (Map p92; ☎ 257 535 534; Cihelná 2b; mains 225–550Kč; ◷ 9-2am) This converted brickworks enjoys one of Prague's hottest locations with a riverside terrace offering sweeping views of Charles bridge and the Old Town waterfront. The menu is as sweeping as the view – choose from tempura-fried tuna, chicken fajitas, Czech dishes, burgers and stirfries, washed down with a bottle of local wine (the Sonberg Rýnský Ryzlink is an excellent Moravian white).

El Centro (Map p92; ☎ 257 533 343; Maltézské náměstí 9; mains 150–375Kč; tapas 80–200Kč; ◷ noon-midnight) Bright colours, chunky wooden furniture and Spanish-speaking staff lend an authentic air to this classic tapas bar. Nibble on snackettes of chorizo, calamari and *gambas pil-pil* (prawns in garlic) over a bottle of Rioja, or splash out on a full meal of steak, grilled chicken or paella washed down with a jug of sangria.

Cowboys (Map p92; ☎ 296 826 107; Nerudova 40; mains 200–500Kč; ◷ noon-2am) This sophisticated steakhouse and cocktail bar inhabits a stylishly up-lit cavern of red-brick vaults with so-tacky-they're-cool cow-hide patterned banquettes and efficient staff sporting jeans, cowboy hats and smiles the size of Texas. The menu offers meltingly tender steaks and burgers, but also caters for vegetarians, and there's an outdoor terrace for those long, sunny, summer afternoons.

U Sedmi Švábů (Map p92; ☎ 257 531 455; Jánský vršek 14; mains 180–350Kč; ◷ 11am-11pm) This rather silly –

PRAGUE

the name means 'At the Seven Cockroaches' – but also rather charming medieval-themed restaurant serves meaty Czech platters (with a few vegetarian alternatives) in an authentic, electricity-free atmosphere – all the illumination is provided by candles. There's an all-you-can-eat-and-drink deal for 1555Kč.

TOP END

Kampa Park (Map p92; ☎ 257 532 685; Na Kampě 8a; mains 600-800Kč; ⏱ 11.30-1am) Kampa Park was a pioneer of Prague's fine-dining scene, opened back in 1994. Since then it has attracted celebrity visitors like moths around a flame – Mick Jagger, Johnny Depp, Lauren Bacall, Robbie Williams, and Bill and Hilary Clinton have all over-tipped the staff here. The cuisine is as famous as the clientele, from the grilled octopus with roasted broccoli, raisins and capers, to the filet mignon with glazed sweetbread and *chanterelles*. There's a stylish dining room and roof terrace, but for a really romantic dinner, reserve a candlelit table on the cobble-stoned terrace, draped in fairy lights, right beside the river, with the lights of Charles bridge glittering on the water.

Josefov

BUDGET

Pivnice U Milosrdných (Map p98; ☎ 222 327 673; Milosrdných & Kozí; mains 80-120Kč; ⏱ 10am-10pm Mon-Fri, 11am-10pm Sat) Solidly typical Czech pub, always packed – particularly at lunchtime – with office workers and elderly locals, this *pivnice* serves all the Czech favourites, including a hearty goulash with bacon dumplings.

TOP END

Bodeguita del Medio (Map p98; ☎ 224 813 922; Kaprova 5; mains 300-550Kč; ⏱ 10am-2am) This outpost of the famous Havana cocktail-bar-and-restaurant chain brings a whiff of Hemingway to the Old Town streets, with its chunky wooden tables, ceiling fans and cigars. The seafood is excellent, especially the zingy *gambas Punta Arenas* (prawns with chilli, lime and ginger), the cappuccinos are froth-topped caffeine bombs, and the pavement tables catch the sun at lunchtime…perfecto.

King Solomon (Map p98; ☎ 224 818 752; Široká 8; set menu 550Kč; ⏱ noon-11pm Sun-Thu, noon-sundown Fri, closed Sat) The most kosher restaurant in town, King Solomon serves carefully prepared meals in a lovely glassed conservatory. While the restaurant is closed to walk-in traffic on

Shabbat, you can call ahead for meals at that time. A catering service can deliver kosher meals to your hotel.

Staré Město

BUDGET

Beas Vegetarian Dhaba (Map p98; ☎ 603 035 727; Týnská 19; mains 80-100Kč; ⏱ 10am-8pm Mon-Sat, 10am-6pm Sun) Tucked away in a courtyard off Týnská, this friendly and informal little restaurant offers vegetarian curries (cooked by chefs from Northern India) served with rice, salad, chutneys and raita; an extra 20Kč gets you a drink and dessert. It's tasty, good value, and a great place to meet Czechs of an alternative bent.

Giallo Rossa (Map p98; ☎ 604 898 989; Jakubská 1; pizzas 70-130Kč; ⏱ 10am-midnight) Half of Prague seems to be lining up at the takeaway counter here come lunchtime. Huge pizza slices go for 70Kč. If you'd rather sit down, there's a restaurant by the storefront; there's internet access upstairs.

Au Gourmand (Map p98; ☎ 222 329 060; Dlouhá 10; snacks 60-120Kč; ⏱ 7am-7pm Mon-Fri, 8.30am-7pm Sat, 9am-7pm Sun) Au Gourmand is a French-style patisserie and café gaily decked out in colourful 19th-century tiles and wrought-iron furniture. It offers baguettes, pastries and a joyously bewildering array of cakes, and its caffè latte is among the best in town.

Country Life (Map p98; ☎ 224 213 336; Melantrichova 15; mains 75-150Kč; ⏱ 8.30am-7pm Mon-Thu, 8.30am-6pm Fri, 11am-6pm Sun) Prague's best health-food shop and vegetarian salad-and-sandwich bar has vegetarian pizza and goulash too. Food is sold by weight, and you should be able to fill up for under 80Kč. The original Old Town branch has sit-down service at the back, while the other branch (opposite), in Nové Město, is cafeteria style. Both get densely crowded at lunch time, so go early or get a takeaway.

U Pinkasů (Map p98; ☎ 221 111 150; Jungmannova nám 16, Nové Město; mains 100-200Kč; ⏱ 11am-11pm) If you do some sort of complicated equation matching cost against quality, this has to be the best Czech food in Prague. You'll eat every scrap of dumpling on your plate, and wish you had one more to sop up that last bit of goulash. The roast pork and sauerkraut is excellent, and the service is friendly and professional. There's a small garden out the back, under the walls of the church of Our Lady of the Snows, and a basement pub that stays open until 4am.

MIDRANGE

Red, Hot & Blues (Map p98; ☎ 222 314 639; Jakubská 12; mains 180-480Kč; ☺ 9am-11pm) This long-established New Orleans–style restaurant pulls in the crowds with great nachos, burgers, burritos and shrimp creole, plus some wicked desserts. It also serves a range of Western breakfasts, including pancakes and maple syrup, and a full British fry-up; the 'Home Run Special' (bacon, eggs, hash browns, pancakes and toast) will soak up the heaviest hangover, and lay a firm foundation for further debauchery.

Ambiente Pasta Fresca (Map p98; ☎ 224 230 244; Celetná 11; mains 180-350Kč; ☺ 11am-midnight) Slick styling and service with a smile complement an extensive menu at this busy Italian restaurant. Choose from dishes such as melt-in-the-mouth carpaccio of beef, piquant spaghetti aglio-olio with chilli and crisp pancetta, and rich creamy risotto with porcini, along with a wide range of Italian and Czech wines.

Orange Moon (Map p98; ☎ 222 325 119; Rámová 5; mains 165-230Kč; ☺ 11.30am-11.30pm) Buddhist statues, oriental carved-wood panels, paper lanterns and warm, sunny colours make for a welcoming combination at this popular Asian restaurant. The menu is mostly Thai, with authentically spicy *tom yum kai* (hot and sour chicken broth) laden with smouldering chillies, crispy *pow pyet* (spring rolls) and fragrant *kaeng phed kai* (chicken in red curry).

Kolkovna (Map p98; ☎ 224 819 701; V Kolkovně 8; mains 160-400Kč; ☺ 9am-midnight) Owned and operated by the Pilsner Urquell brewery, Kolkovna is a stylish, modern take on the traditional Prague beer hall, with décor by top Czech designers and posh (but hearty) versions of classic Czech dishes, such as goulash, roast duck and roast pork, including the Czech favourite pork and dumplings (the dish of the day is only 95Kč).

Dahab (Map p98; ☎ 224 827 375; Rybná 28; mains 200-400Kč; ☺ noon-1am) Dahab is a dimly lit North African *souq* scattered with oriental rugs and cushions where you can lounge on a divan and sip Moroccan mint tea to an oriental-jazz-ragga soundtrack. The menu ranges from baklava and other sweet snacks to more substantial couscous, *tajine* (meat and vegetable stew), lamb and chicken dishes, and there are teas from India, China and Turkey. Or you can just kick back with a hookah (hubble-bubble pipe); 175Kč gets you a chunk of perfumed baccy that'll last around 45 minutes.

TOP END

U Zavoje (Map p98; ☎ 226 006 120; Havelská 25; mains 350-500Kč; ☺ 11am-midnight) This gourmet complex, set in a beautiful old passageway between Havelská and Kožná streets, includes a wine bar, restaurant, coffee house and deli, all dedicated to fine food and French and Czech wines. The menu concentrates on fresh seasonal produce, while the wine list makes a good starting point for learning about Moravian wines.

V Zátiší (Map p98; ☎ 222 221 155; Liliová 1; mains 500-800Kč; ☺ noon-3pm & 5.30-11pm) One of Prague's best restaurants, famed for the quality of its cuisine. There are two dining rooms, one classically decorated in shades of ochre, with wrought-iron chairs and lamp fittings, the other more modern. Of the dozen or so main courses on offer, four are seafood and three are vegetarian; there are also gourmet versions of traditional Czech dishes – the crispy roast duckling with red cabbage and herb dumplings is superb.

Nové Město

BUDGET

The sausage stands lining the sides of Wenceslas square will rustle you up a hot dog or *smažený syr* (fried cheese) for 25Kč; wash it down with a shot of vodka or rum for 15Kč, or beer in a plastic cup for 20Kč (also useful for obliterating the memory of that mysterious chunk you found in your sausage).

Country Life (Map p106; ☎ 224 247 280; Jungmannova 1; mains 75-150Kč; ☺ 9.30am-6.30pm Mon-Thu, 9am-6pm Fri) Country Life is a cafeteria-style health-food restaurant with all-vegan food and buffet service. Load up your plate and pay by weight. That's right – you weigh in at the till. There are only four tables at this branch, which caters mainly to the takeaway trade, so if you want to increase your chances of getting a seat, head for the branch in Staré Město (opposite).

Pizzeria Kmotra (Map p106; ☎ 224 915 809; V jirchářích 12; pizzas 85-130Kč; ☺ 11am-midnight) One of Prague's oldest and best pizzerias, 'The Godmother' can rustle up more than two dozen varieties, from Margherita to Marinara, cooked in a genuine, wood-fired pizza oven. Sit beside the bar upstairs, or head down to the basement where you can watch the chef slinging pizza dough in the open kitchen. It gets busy after 8pm, so try to snag a table before then.

PRAGUE

Branický Sklípek (U Purkmistra; Map p106; ☎ 224 237 103; Vodičkova 2; mains 70–270Kč; ⏰ 9am–11pm Mon–Fri, 11am–11pm Sat & Sun) This is one of the few rough-and-ready, old-fashioned beer halls left in central Prague, serving meaty, good-value Czech dishes washed down with cheap beer. Menus and staff are Czech only, which puts off most tourists, but persevere – this is the real deal.

MIDRANGE

Albio (Map p118; ☎ 222 325 414; Truhlářská 18; mains 100–260Kč; ⏰ 11am–10pm) This family-friendly wholefood restaurant is as bright and fresh as an Alpine morning, decked out in blonde wood and rustic timber. It sources all its food from local organic farmers and serves fish, vegetarian and vegan dishes, and there are organic wines and unpasteurised beer so you can work up a wholesome hangover.

Dinitz Café (Map p118; ☎ 222 313 308; Na poříčí 12; mains 200–400Kč; ⏰ 9am–3am) This cool, Art Deco coffee house harks back to the sophisticated café society of the 1920s, with fine food and drink served from breakfast till 2am, and live music every night from 9pm. The menu focuses on fresh food, simply prepared – don't miss the city's finest fish and chips, fried in crisp beer-and-parsley batter with crunchy, golden fries and delicious herb aioli.

Siam Orchid (Map p118; ☎ 222 319 410; Na poříčí 21; mains 160–280Kč; ⏰ 10am–10pm) This tiny restaurant, tucked away beside a Thai massage studio, offers some of the city's most authentic Thai cuisine. From the crisp, grease-free *po-pia thot* (spring rolls with pork and black mushrooms) and succulent *kai sa-te* (chicken satay) to the fiery *kaeng khiao wan kai* (chicken in green curry with basil), pretty much everything on the menu is a delight.

Taj Mahal (Map p106; ☎ 224 225 566; Škrétova 10; mains 200–300Kč; ⏰ noon–11pm Mon–Fri, 1–11pm Sat & Sun) The Taj Mahal is one of the city's best Indian restaurants, complete with live sitar-twanging in the evenings. There are separate smoking and nonsmoking dining rooms, and though the food is delicious, the atmosphere can occasionally be a little formal and restrained.

Dynamo (Map p106; ☎ 224 932 020; Pštrossova 29; mains 125–280Kč; ⏰ 11.30am–midnight) Don't be put off by the funky font, spearmint-green décor or look-at-me light fittings – there's more to Dynamo than hipster flash. The cook here has some bright ideas, and throws together unusually fresh ingredients in all kinds of inter-esting ways. The menu includes baked salmon wrapped in parma ham with honey-mustard sauce, the chicken Caesar salad is delicious and the staff are friendly and unpretentious. It's a great place for a girls' night out.

TOP END

Hot (Map p106; ☎ 222 247 240; Václavské náměstí 45; mains 360–650Kč; ⏰ 7am–1am) Set in an old Art Deco space that has been stylishly transformed with the use of stainless steel, polished marble and leather, this place has a great location – halfway up Wenceslas square. And the food is top-notch – an inventive mix of Asian and European dishes (the honey and soy glazed salmon with wasabi mayonnaise is superb). If only the staff could stop checking themselves in the mirror long enough to take your order…

Suterén (Map p106; ☎ 224 933 657; Masarykovo nábřeží 26; mains 350–500Kč; ⏰ 11.30am–midnight Mon–Sat) 'The Basement' is a beautiful cellar space, where modern detailing complements the old red-brick and wooden beams perfectly – cream linen chairs set at gleaming black tables with a single deep-pink rose in the middle of each one. The menu leans towards seafood, beef and game, and the signature dishes take their inspiration from cocktails – the 'salmon mojito', for example, has the fish marinated in rum and lime juice, served with tart lime jam and sweet rum and mint sauce.

Vyšehrad

U Neklana (Map p112; ☎ 224 916 057; Neklanova 30; mains 100–200Kč; ⏰ 11am–midnight) U Neklana is a welcoming local pub nestled in the corner of one of Prague's coolest apartment buildings, a cubist classic dating from 1915. Decked out in the cheerful red colours of the Budvar brewery, it dishes up hearty Czech fare such as potato and mushroom soup served in a scooped-out loaf of rye bread (the menu is in English and German as well as Czech), and there's a hits-of-the-80s jukebox providing a suitably retro soundtrack.

Holešovice

MIDRANGE

Hong Kong (Map pp82–3; ☎ 233 376 209; Letenské náměstí 5; mains 150–300Kč; ⏰ 10.30am–11pm) The impressively gaudy décor and mostly Cantonese menu smack of authenticity, with favourites such as dim sum, soy sauce duck and salt-and-pepper shrimp, and more adventurous options such as 'cold sliced pork tongue with soy sauce', 'chicken with strange tastes' and 'chicken with five smells'.

Restaurant Corso (Map pp82-3; ☎ 220 806 541; Dukelských hrdinů 48; mains 125-350Kč; 🕙 10am-10pm) The Corso has 'interesting' décor – something like a cross between abstract Asian design and Art Deco on acid – but serves traditional Czech cuisine, steaks and pasta dishes, including delicious cream of onion soup and home-made apple strudel. The great-value three-course set lunch (300Kč) includes a beer and a Becherovka.

TOP END
Hanavský Pavilón (Map p92; ☎ 253 323 641; Letenské sady; mains 600-900Kč; 🕙 11am-1am, terrace till 11pm) Tuxedoed waiters glide between linen-topped tables at this overpriced but gorgeous restaurant. Originally built for the 1891 Prague Exposition, the pavilion still has some of the best views in town. It also has some hysterical dinner music – the resident Hammond organ maestro is a whiz.

Smíchov
BUDGET
Káva Káva Káva (Map p115; ☎ 257 314 277; Lidická 42; mains 70-120Kč; 🕙 7am-10pm) This popular internet café offers an extensive menu – you can snack on salads, sandwiches, quiches or nachos, or tuck into more substantial chicken gyros, Mexican chilli or home-made soup of the day. There's free wi-fi access too (provided you spend at least 50Kč).

MIDRANGE
Na Verandách (Map p115; ☎ 257 191 200; Nádražní 84; mains 100-200Kč; 🕙 11am-midnight) Bustling green-aproned waiters bearing trays of foaming Staropramen dodge among crowds of local drinkers, business people and tourists in this big, brassy, modern bar and restaurant. It's part of the Staropramen Brewery, so there's no shortage of quality beer (there are seven varieties on tap) to wash down the traditional Czech pub grub.

TOP END
Nagoya (Map p115; ☎ 251 511 724; Stroupežnického 21; mains 150-400Kč; 🕙 6-11pm Mon-Sat) Nagoya is one of the few truly authentic Japanese restaurants in Prague. It has crisp, minimalist décor with paper screens, globe lampshades and bamboo plants; most of the seating is at ordinary

tables, but there are also some low tables with tatami mats if you want to take off your shoes and get the genuine Japanese dining experience. The menu ticks all the usual boxes – sushi, sashimi, teriyaki, yakitori, tempura, miso soup – but also includes *sakana*, small savoury snacks a bit like Japanese tapas, great if you want to try a range of flavours.

Vinohrady
BUDGET
Restaurace Sofia (Map p116; ☎ 603 298 865; Americká 28; mains 60-180Kč; 🕙 noon-11pm) If you're not going to make it to Bulgaria on this trip, don't fret: Restaurace Sofia whips up Bulgarian classics like buttered tripe, beef tongue fried in butter, mixed grill and *musaka* (Bulgarian for 'moussaka'). If you like this sort of thing, you'll love it – if you don't, at least it will revive your enthusiasm for goulash.

MIDRANGE
Café FX (Map p116; ☎ 224 254 776; Bělehradská 120; mains 100-200Kč; 🕙 11.30am-2am) FX offers some of the best food in Prague in its price range – and it's all veggie. This hippy-chic restaurant at the entrance to the nightclub Radost FX comes up with imaginative dishes ranging from spinach ravioli stuffed with hazelnut pesto and cheese, to sage and mushroom 'meatballs' with mashed potatoes and creamy mushroom sauce.

Ambiente (Map p118; ☎ 222 727 851; Mánesova 59; mains 200-400Kč; 🕙 11am-midnight Mon-Fri, noon-midnight Sat & Sun) 'Ambiente' means atmosphere, and the warm yellow walls, bottle-green banquettes, bamboo and basketwork chairs and rich mahogany woodwork make for a relaxing one in this popular Vinohrady restaurant – a pioneer of Prague's new wave of welcoming, well-run, service-with-a-smile eateries. The American-themed menu offers a huge range of salads (including Caesar, goat's cheese, roast veggies, avocado), tasty pasta dishes, barbecue ribs, fajitas, steaks and chicken wings, and there are excellent house wines for around 90Kč a glass.

Tiger Tiger (Map p116; ☎ 222 512 048; Anny Letenské 5; mains 190-280Kč; 🕙 11.30am-11pm Mon-Fri, 5-11pm Sat & Sun) Tiger Tiger has a dapper little dining room dressed in cheerful yellow with smart navy upholstery, a restrained and elegant setting for some of the city's best Thai cuisine. Authentic specialities include *tom yam kung* (hot and sour prawn soup), *som tam* (spicy carrot salad) and *kaeng ped gai* (chicken in red curry sauce).

Wings Club (Map p118; ☎ 222 713 151; Lucemburská 11; mains 130-300Kč; ⏰ 11.30am-11pm) Wings Club is half restaurant, half museum, filled with fascinating memorabilia of WWII Czech aviation ranging from photographs and uniforms to a gleaming, full-sized propeller mounted on one wall. The menu is solid, good-quality Czech pub grub, from smoked pork with sauerkraut and dumplings to pork kebabs marinated in mustard.

Žižkov

BUDGET

Akropolis Café-Restaurant (Map p118; ☎ 296 330 990; Kubelíkova 27; mains 80-180Kč; ⏰ 11.30-1am Mon-Sat) A Žižkov institution, this eccentric café sports a décor of marble panels, quirky metalwork light fittings and weird fishtank installations designed by local artist František Skála. The menu has a good selection of vegetarian dishes, from nachos to gnocchi, plus great garlic soup, searingly hot buffalo wings and steak tartare. Kids are welcome – you'll find toys and colouring books (though it can get a bit smoky).

MIDRANGE

Mailsi (Map p118; ☎ 060 346 6626; Lipanská 1; mains 160-425Kč; ⏰ noon-3pm & 6-11pm) Mailsi was Prague's first Pakistani restaurant, and is still one of the city's best for authentic curry cuisine. The outside is inconspicuous, and it's only the *qawwali* music that guides you into the attractively decorated green and terracotta dining room with its tropical fishtank. Service is courteous, the food delicious and prices modest for a specialty restaurant – though helpings are often small.

Self-Catering

There are corner stores (*potraviny*) and supermarkets everywhere. The five million people shopping in **Tesco** (Map p106; Národní třída 26; ⏰ 8am-9pm Mon-Fri, 9am-8pm Sat, 10am-8pm Sun) all at the same time all seem to have left their manners at the door, but this supermarket has just about everything you'll need.

If you don't need to buy everything in one place, fruit and vegetable stores (*ovoce-zelelina*) have better and cheaper produce than the supermarkets, though the selection is smaller and the opening hours shorter. Delis (*lahůdky*) sell all kinds of cold meats and cheeses, as well as great little Czech open

sandwiches (*chlebíčky*) with ham, egg or salami, which go for less than 20Kč each.

There aren't many open-air produce markets in the city. The biggest one near the centre is the **daily market** (Map p98; Havelská), south of Old Town square, but you have to wade through a lot of souvenirs to get to the food. There's also a daily market (Map p106) behind Tesco, and a selection of **fruit and veg stands** (Map pp82-3; Václavkova) in Dejvice, near Hradčanská metro.

Note that some perishable supermarket food items bear a date of manufacture (*datum výroby*) plus a 'consume-within…' (*spotřebujte do…*) period, whereas others, such as long-life milk, will have a stated minimum-shelf-life (*minimální trvanlivost*) date (after which freshness of the product is not guaranteed).

DRINKING

Once the preserve of traditional Czech *pivnice* (beer halls) and *kavárny* (cafés), Prague is now awash with stylish cocktail bars, arty pubs and pretty much any variation on the drinking theme you can think of. Traditional pubs are generally open from 11am to 11pm, while bars tend to be open noon to 1am during the week; they may stay open until 4am or 5am on weekends. Fancy cocktail bars are concentrated in the centre and Vinohrady; grungy student bars are out in Žižkov; traditional Czech pubs are everywhere.

Hradčany & Malá Strana

U Zavěšeného Kafe (The Hanging Coffee; Map p92; ☎ 605 294 595; Úvoz 6; ⏰ 11am-midnight) This is a superb little drinking den barely five minutes' walk from the castle. Head for the cosy, wood-panelled back room, quirkily decorated with weird art and mechanical curiosities (all for sale), and an ancient jukebox crammed with Beatles, Stones and Czech rock. Foaming Gambrinus is only 20Kč a half-litre, and the coffee is damn fine too.

Klub Újezd (Map p92; ☎ 257 316 537; Újezd 18; ⏰ 2pm-4am) Klub Újezd is one of Prague's many 'alternative' bars, spread over three floors (DJs in the cellar, and a café upstairs) and filled with a fascinating collection of hand-made furniture and fittings, original art and weird wrought-iron sculptures.

Josefov

Ocean Drive (Map p98; ☎ 224 819 089; V Kolkovně 7; ⏰ 7pm-2am) A 1930s American-style bar, with

FUNNY, I DON'T REMEMBER ORDERING THAT

Keep in mind that nothing comes for free in Prague's more touristy restaurants – if the waiter offers you fries with that, and you accept, you'll be charged for them. Bread, mayonnaise, mustard, vegetables…everything has a price tag. Many restaurants also have a cover charge (couvert) which every diner must pay regardless of what they eat and even if they eat nothing. It's not a scam, it's just the way things are done.

If the menu has no prices, ask for them. Don't be intimidated by the language barrier; know exactly what you're ordering. If something's not available and the waiter suggests an alternative, ask for the price. Immediately return anything you didn't order and don't want, such as bread, butter or side dishes; don't just leave them to one side or, chances are, they'll appear on your bill.

Art Deco imagery, lots of dark, polished wood, and a glittering array of glasses and liqueur bottles, Ocean Drive is typical of Prague's new wave of sophisticated cocktail bars. Have more than a couple of the expertly mixed cocktails and you may be wondering whether you got on the plane to Miami by accident.

Palírna Igor Sevčík (Map p98; ☎ 222 319 097; Rámová 3; ☒ 8am-10pm Mon-Fri, 10am-10pm Sat & Sun) If you're keen to try *slivovitz* (plum brandy), there's no better place to start than this funky café-cum-wine bar. A temple to the fiery spirit, it stocks more than a dozen varieties, as well as *jablkovice* (apple brandy), *hruškovice* (pear brandy), *meruňkovice* (apricot brandy) and a range of Moravian wines.

Staré Město

U Zlatého Tygra (At the Golden Tiger; Map p98; ☎ 222 221 111; Husova 17; ☒ 3-11pm) This is one of the few old-town drinking holes that has hung on to its soul – and its low prices (26Kč per 0.5L of Pilsner Urquell), considering its location. It was novelist Bohumil Hrabal's favourite hostelry – there are photos of him on the walls – and the place that Václav Havel took then fellow president Bill Clinton in 1994 to show him a real Czech pub.

Chateau L'Enfer Rouge (Map p98; ☎ 222 316 328; Jakubská 2; ☒ noon-3am Mon-Thu, noon-4am Fri, 4pm-4am Sat & Sun) When this raucous place gets fired up you can barely hear yourself think, but who needs thinking anyway? Bar service is fast and friendly, there are all kinds of bizarre happenings going on outside the bathroom and it's often so crowded you'll be drinking on the pavement (if the bouncers let you). Embrace your inner lad and enjoy.

Blatouch (Map p98; ☎ 222 328 643; Vězeňská 4; ☒ 11am-1am Mon-Thu, 11am-3am Fri, 2pm-3am Sat, 1pm-midnight Sun) Blatouch is a pleasantly relaxed literary hangout, with a long, narrow bar lined

with antique bookcases and Edward Hopper prints, and a tiny garden courtyard at the back. It serves coffee, tea and snacks as well as alcoholic drinks – the perfect place to read the papers over an afternoon glass of wine.

Kozička (Map p98; ☎ 224 818 308; Kozí 1; ☒ noon-4am Mon-Fri, 6pm-4am Sat, 6-3pm Sun) The 'Little Goat' is a buzzing, red-brick basement bar decorated with cute steel goat sculptures, serving Krušovice on tap at 35Kč for 0.5L (though watch out, the bar tenders will sling you a 1L glass if they think you're a tourist). It fills up later in the evening with a mostly Czech crowd, and is a very civilised setting for a late-night session.

Nové Město

Pivovarský Dům (Map p106; ☎ 296 216 666; Lípová 15) While the tourists flock to U Fleků (following), locals gather here to sample the classic Czech lager (in light, dark and mixed varieties; 33Kč per 0.5L) that is brewed on the premises, as well as wheat beer and a range of flavoured beers (including coffee, banana and cherry, 33Kč per 0.3L). The pub itself is a pleasant place to linger, decked out with polished copper vats and brewing implements and smelling faintly of malt and hops.

U Fleků (Map p106; ☎ 224 934 019; Křemencová 11; ☒ 9am-11pm) A festive warren of drinking and dining rooms, U Fleků is a Prague institution, though usually clogged with tour groups high on oompah music and the tavern's home-brewed, 13° black beer (59Kč for 0.4L), known as Flek. Purists grumble but go along anyway because the beer is good, though tourist prices have nudged out many locals.

Velryba (Map p98; ☎ 224 912 484; Opatovická 24) The 'Whale' is an arty café-bar – usually quiet enough to have a real conversation – with vegetarian-friendly snacks, a smoky back room and a basement art gallery. A clientele of Czech

---

BEER GARDENS

On a hot summer day, what could be finer than sitting outdoors with a chilled glass of Bohemia's finest, admiring a view over river or city. Many of Prague's pubs have small beer gardens or courtyards, but the following summer-only spots are truly out in the open air. Opening times are weather-dependent, but typically noon to midnight April to September; expect to pay around 25Kč a half-litre for beer.

Letná beer garden (Map pp82–3; Letná gardens, Bubeneč) This slew of rickety benches and tables spread along a dusty scarp beneath the trees at the eastern end of Letná Park enjoys one of the city's most stunning views, looking across the river to the spires of Staré Město, and southwest to Malá Strana. Gambrinus on tap.

Letní bar (Map p92; Střelecký ostrov, Malá Strana) Basically a shack serving Budvar in plastic cups, this is the place to pick up a beer before hitting the little 'beach' at the northern end of the island, or settling in for a starlit screening at the Open-Air Cinema Festival (p122).

Park Café (Map p118; Riegrovy sady, Vinohrady) Perched on top of precipitous Riegrovy Park, this bustling beer garden has awesome night-time views of the castle, a big screen showing sport and the opportunity to play table football and table hockey with half of Prague. Pilsner Urquell and Gambrinus.

---

students, local office workers and foreign backpackers attracted by the low prices keep the place jumping.

Jáma (Map p98; ☎ 224 222 383; V jámě 7) The Hollow is a popular American expat bar and restaurant, with a leafy little beer garden out back shaded by lime and walnut trees. The clientele is a mix of expats, tourists and young Praguers, and there's Pilsner Urquell, Gambrinus and Velkopopovický Kozel on draught. The food menu includes good burgers, steaks, ribs and chicken wings.

Vinohrady & Žižkov

Kavárna Medúza (Map p116; ☎ 222 515 107; Belgická 17; ⏰ 10am-1am Mon-Fri, noon-1am Sat & Sun) The perfect Prague coffee house, Medúza is an oasis of old, worn furniture, dark wood, creaking armchairs and local artworks, with an antique sugar bowl on every table and an atmosphere that invites you to sink into a novel or indulge in a conversation on the nature of self.

Hapu (Map p118; ☎ 222 720 158; Orlická 8, Žižkov; ⏰ 6pm-2am) Low-ceilinged, dimly lit and immensely cool, Hapu is almost in Vinohrady – geographically and socially on the opposite side of Žižkov from U Vystřeleného oka (following). It's a tiny, smoky cocktail lounge with shabby-chic décor and expert staff who really know how to mix a mean cocktail – not only that, but every drop of fruit juice is freshly squeezed.

U Vystřeleného Oka (Map p118; ☎ 226 278 714; U Božích bojovníků 3; ⏰ 4.30pm-1am Mon-Sat) You've got to love a pub that has vinyl pads on the wall

above the gents' urinals to rest your forehead on. 'The Shot-Out Eye' (the name pays homage to the one-eyed Hussite hero atop the hill behind the pub) is a bohemian (with a small 'b') hostelry with a raucous beer garden whose cheap food and beer pulls in a typically heterogeneous Žižkov crowd, ranging from art students and writers to lost backpackers and tattooed bikers.

Clubs

Prague's club scene is nothing to rave about. With few exceptions, the city's dance clubs cater to crowds of partying teenagers and tourists weaned on MTV Europe – if you want to dance to anything other than '80s hits or happy house, you'll have to look long and hard. Prague's main strengths are its alternative music clubs, DJ bars and 'experimental' venues such as Palác Akropolis and the Roxy.

Refreshingly, dress codes don't seem to have reached Prague yet, and it's unlikely you'll be knocked back anywhere unless you're stark naked. Check www.prague.tv, www.techno .cz/party, www.badpoint.com or www.hip -hop.cz for up-to-date club listings.

Roxy (Map p98; ☎ 224 826 296; www.roxy.cz; Dlouhá 33, Staré Město; cover 100-250Kč Fri & Sat; ⏰ 7pm-midnight Mon-Thu, 7pm-6am Fri & Sat) Set in the ramshackle shell of an Art Deco cinema, the Roxy nurtures the more independent and innovative end of Prague's club spectrum – this is the place to check out the Czech Republic's top DJs. On the first floor is NoD, an 'experimental space' that stages drama, dance, performance art, cinema and live music.

Palác Akropolis (Map p118; ☎ 296 330 911; www .palacakropolis.cz; Kubelíkova 27, Žižkov; cover free-30Kč; ☾ club 7pm-5am) The Akropolis is a Prague institution, a labyrinthine, sticky-floored shrine to alternative music and drama. Its various performance spaces host a smorgasbord of musical and cultural events. DJs do their stuff in the Theatre Bar (Divadelní Bar) and Small Hall (Malá Scéna), spinning everything from house to hip hop, reggae to breakbeat.

Radost FX Club (Map p116; ☎ 224 254 776; www .radostfx.cz; Bělehradská 120, Vinohrady; cover 100-250Kč; ☾ 10pm-6am) Though not quite as hot as it once was, Prague's slickest, shiniest and most self-assured club is still capable of pulling in the crowds, especially for its Thursday hip hop night, FXbounce (www.fxbounce .com). The place has a chilled out, bohemian atmosphere, with Moroccan-boudoir-meets-Moulin-Rouge décor, and there's an excellent lounge-cum-vegetarian restaurant that keeps serving into the small hours.

Other recommendations:

Futurum (Map p115; ☎ 257 328 571; www.musicbar.cz; Zborovská 7, Smíchov; cover 100Kč; ☾ 9pm-3am) Regular Friday and Saturday night '80s and 90s Video Party', with local DJs blasting out everything from REM and Nirvana to Bon Jovi and Village People, complete with cringe-worthy videos. Occasional live bands.

Matrix Klub (Map p118; ☎ 608 333 198; www .matrixklub.cz; Koněvova 12, Žižkov; ☾ 8pm-4.30am Tue-Sat) DJs, parties and occasional live shows. Take bus 133 or 207 from Florenc metro, or night bus 504 from IP Pavlova metro.

Sedm Vlků (Map p118; ☎ 222 711 725; www.sedm vlku.cz; Vlkova 7, Žižkov; ☾ 5pm-3am Mon-Sat) A cool, art-studenty café-bar and club – down in the darkened cellar, DJs pump out techno, breakbeat, drum 'n' bass and ragga from 9pm on Friday and Saturday nights.

Jazz & Blues

Prague has a lot of places claiming to be jazz bars; like marionettes and tiny glass bottles, jazz has become a mainstay of the tourist industry. But most of what you'll hear is actually blues or very tame jazz. Most of the clubs listed have good jazz CD stores on the premises. Cover charges are around 200Kč unless otherwise stated. The *Prague Post* 'Night & Day' lift-out has listings of who's playing when.

Agharta Jazz Centrum (Map p98; ☎ 222 211 275; www.agharta.cz; Železná 16, Staré Město; ☾ 7pm-1am, music 9pm-midnight) A typical jazz cellar with red-brick

vaults and a cosy bar and café, this place also has a music shop (open 7pm to midnight), which sells CDs, T-shirts and coffee mugs. As well as hosting local musicians, the centre occasionally stages gigs by leading international artists.

U Malého Glena (Map p92; ☎ 257 531 717; www.maly glen.cz; Karmelitská 23, Malá Strana; ☾ 10am-2am, music from 9.30pm Sun-Thu, from 10pm Fri & Sat) 'Little Glen's' is a lively American-owned bar and restaurant where hard-swinging local jazz or blues bands play in the stone-vaulted cellar every night. There are regular jam sessions where amateurs are welcome (as long as you're good!). It's a small venue, so get here early.

Reduta Jazz Club (Map p106; ☎ 224 933 487; www .redutajazzclub.cz; Národní třída 20, Nové Město; cover 300Kč; ☾ 9pm-3am) The Reduta is Prague's oldest jazz club, founded in 1958. It has an intimate setting, with smartly dressed patrons squeezing into tiered seats and lounges to soak up the big-band, swing and Dixieland atmosphere.

Dinitz Café (Map p118; ☎ 222 313 308; www.dinitz.cz; Na poříčí 12, Nové Město; admission free Sat-Thu, 150Kč Fri; ☾ 9am-3am, music 9pm-midnight) Dinitz is a relatively new bar and restaurant (see p132) that has swiftly gained a reputation for excellent live jazz, blues, Latin and funk, including a regular Tuesday night session by Prague blues legend Stan the Man.

Rock & Other Music

While Prague was once a thriving live-music scene, the influx of hotels and affluent apartment buyers into the centre of town has meant a tightening of noise restrictions and the death of many live venues. These days you often have to head out to the 'burbs for live music, or make do with cover bands and revival acts tailored for the tourist market.

Guru Music Club (Map p118; ☎ 222 783 463; www .guruclub.cz, in Czech; Rokycanova 29, Žižkov; cover charge 30Kč; ☾ 11am-5am) This independent club – a café-bar decked out in red brick and aging sofas – takes rock seriously, with hardcore, grunge, 'trashcore', 'pig beat' and open mikes almost every night of the week. DJs fill the gaps.

Malostranská beseda (Map p92; ☎ 257 532 092; Malostranské náměstí 21, Malá Strana; cover 50-120Kč; ☾ bar 5pm-1am, music from 8.30pm) Malá Strana's former town hall now houses a large café-bar that hosts anything from hard rock to bluegrass via jazz and folk, playing to a young and mostly Czech crowd. It packs out early, particularly on weekends.

Klub 007 Strahov (Map p92; ☎ 257 211 439; www .klub007strahov.cz; Block 7, Chaloupeckého 7, Strahov; cover 50-250Kč; ☽ 7pm-1am Sun-Thu, 7pm-2am Fri & Sat) One of several grungy student clubs in the basements of the big dormitory blocks in Strahov, the legendary 007 has been around since 1987 and is famed for its devotion to hardcore, punk, ska, ragga, jungle, ambient and other alternative sounds. On Saturday nights it hosts a regular hip-hop party.

Other recommendations:

Hells' Bells (Map p115; ☎ 257 320 436; www .hellsbells.cz; Na Bělidle 27/302, Smíchov; ☽ 3pm-3am Mon-Fri, 5pm-3am Sat, 5pm-midnight Sun) Hells' Bells has live metal on the weekends and head-banging ambience during the week.

Rock Café (Map p106; ☎ 224 914 416; www.rockcafe .cz; Národní třída 20, Nové Město; ☽ 10am-2.30am Mon-Fri, 5pm-2.30am Sat, 5pm-1am Sun, music from 7.30pm) A stripped-down venue for DJs and live rock. Mainly features tribute bands.

ENTERTAINMENT

For reviews, an up-to-the-minute directory of venues and day-by-day listings, consult the 'Night & Day' section of the *Prague Post*. Look out for *Provokátor* (www.provokator .org), a free monthly magazine dedicated to art, music, culture and politics; the website has listings of upcoming cultural events. You can pick up the print magazine in clubs, cafés, art-house cinemas and backpacker hostels.

There are ticket consolidators on nearly every street corner in Staré and Nové Městos. They're convenient and they usually take credit cards, but you'll pay around 10% markup over buying direct from the venue. Ask if there are discounts for students, seniors or the disabled. **Bohemia Ticket International** (BTI; Map p98; ☎ 224 227 832; www.ticketsbti.cz; Na příkopě 16, Nové Město; ☽ 10am-7pm Mon-Fri, to 5pm Sat, to 3pm Sun) and **Ticketpro** (Map p106; ☎ 296 333 333; www.ticketpro .cz; pasáž Lucerna, Štěpánská 61, Nové Město; ☽ 9am-1pm & 1.30-5.30pm Mon-Fri) cover most venues and events – the addresses given here are head offices, but you can find outlets all over town or order on the web.

Cinema

There's been a multiplex building boom in Prague in recent years, and you'll have no problem finding a first-run Hollywood movie in English with Czech subtitles. The big operators have squeezed out a lot of the smaller cinemas,

so seeing art-house has become more difficult. Admission is from around 90Kč to 160Kč.

The closest multiplexes to the centre are:

Cinema City (Map p118; ☎ 255 742 021; www .cinemacity.cz, in Czech; Palác Flóra Shopping Centre, cnr Vinohradská & Jičínská, Žižkov)

Palace Cinemas (Map p98; ☎ 257 181 212; www .palacecinemas.cz; Slovanský dům, Na Přikopě 22, Nové Město)

Village Cinemas (Map p115; ☎ 251 115 111; www .villagecinemas.cz; Nový Smíchov Shopping Centre, Radlická 1E, Smíchov)

The city's many art-house cinemas include:

Kino Aero (Map p118; ☎ 271 771 349; www.kinoaero .cz; Biskupcova 31, Žižkov)

Kino Perštýn (Map p98; ☎ 221 668 559; Na Perštýně 6, Staré Město)

Kino Světozor (Map p106; ☎ 224 946 824; www.kino svetozor.cz; Vodičkova 41, Nové Město)

Classical Music, Opera & Ballet

There are around half a dozen concerts of one kind or another almost every day in summer. For information on current performances, ask at the Prague Information Service (PIS; p86), one of the ticket consolidators or check the 'Day & Night' section of the *Prague Post*.

The following are some major venues:

Mozart museum (Map p115; ☎ 257 316 753; www .bertramka.cz; Mozartova 169, Smíchov) Hosts afternoon and evening garden concerts of music by Mozart and other composers (see p114).

Municipal house (Obecní dům; Map p98; ☎ 222 002 101; www.obecni-dum.cz; náměstí Republiky 5, Staré Město) Classical concerts in the Smetana Hall, one of Prague's most stunning venues. The box office is open 10am to 6pm daily.

National theatre (Národní divadlo; Map p106; ☎ 224 913 437; Národní 2, Nové Město) Mainly opera, ballet and high-brow theatre. The box office is next door at Nová Scéna, and is open from 10am to 6pm. There is wheelchair access.

Rudolfinum (Map p98; ☎ 224 893 111; www.ceskafil harmonie.cz; Alšovo nábřeží 12, Staré Město) Home of the Czech Philharmonic. The box office is open from 10am to 6pm Monday to Friday, and for one hour before performances; there is wheelchair access.

Prague State opera house (Státní opera Praha; Map p106; ☎ 224 227 266; www.opera.cz; Legerova 75, Nové Město) Opera and ballet performances. The box office is on U Divadla, open from 10am to 5.30pm daily (closed from noon to 1pm Saturday and Sunday).

Estates theatre (Map p98; ☎ 224 215 001; Ovocný trh 1, Staré Město) Hosts *Don Giovanni* by **Opera Mozart** (☎ 271 741 403; www.mozart-praha.cz) at 8pm every night during summer: anyone who's been to a high-school production of *Godspell* will be familiar with the production values. Other opera and classical productions year-round.

Daily chamber concerts, solo performances and organ recitals in the city's various churches are good value at 350Kč to 500Kč. There are several cathedrals and churches frequently used as concert venues; full details are available from PIS (p86).

Sport

FOOTBALL (SOCCER)

SK Slavia Praha and AC Sparta Praha are leading teams in the national league. Matches are mostly played on Wednesday, Saturday and Sunday afternoons. The season runs from August to December and March to June. Tickets cost from 50Kč to 250Kč and you can usually pick up a ticket at the stadium just before the game.

Slavia play at the **Evžena Rošického stadium** (Map p92; ☎ 257 213 290; Diskařská 100, Strahov) – take the 176 bus from Karlovo nám metro. Sparta's home ground is the **Toyota arena** (Map pp82-3; ☎ 220 57 03 23; Milady Horákové 98, Bubeneč), opposite Letná Park, and is very convenient to the beer garden for post-game drinks; take tram 1, 8, 25 or 26 one stop east from Hradčanská metro.

When the Czech Republic is playing international matches, a big screen is set up in Old Town square and the place is packed with yelling, flag-waving fans.

ICE HOCKEY

HC Sparta Praha and HC Slavia Praha are Prague's two big teams. The season runs from September to early April, and tickets cost 40Kč to 160Kč.

Sparta's home rink is the **T-Mobile arena** (Map pp82-3; Za elektrárnou 419, Výstaviště, Holešovice) next to the Výstaviště exhibition grounds; take tram 5, 12, 14, 15 or 17 to the Výstaviště stop. Slavia plays at the giant **Sazka arena** (Map pp82-3; ☎ 266 212 111; Ocelařská 2, Vysočany) next to the Českomoravská metro station.

Theatre

Prague has no shortage of theatre shows, though most serious drama is in Czech. English-language theatre is dominated by black-light theatre, where live or animated actors in phosphorescent costumes do their thing on a stage lit by ultraviolet lights.

Laterna Magika (Magic Lantern; Map p106; ☎ 224 931 482; www.laterna.cz; Nová Scéna, Národní třída 4, Nové Město; tickets 680Kč; ☉ box office 10am-8pm Mon-Sat) Prague's most famous theatre happening, an imaginative blend of live dance, opera, music and projected images, continues to pull in the crowds despite being founded in 1958. Even if it's 'sold out', you can often bag a leftover seat at the box office on the day before a performance, or a no-show seat half-an-hour before the show starts.

National marionette theatre (Národní divadlo marionet; Map p98; ☎ 224 819 322; www.mozart.cz; Puppet Kingdom, Žatecká 1; adult/child 490/390Kč; ☉ box office 10am-8pm) It might sound silly, watching life-size marionettes perform Mozart's *Don Giovanni*, but it's one of the longest-running shows in town so they must be doing something right.

Other venues:

Estates theatre (Stavovské divadlo; Map p98; ☎ 224 215 001; Ovocný trh 1, Staré Město) Some plays include simultaneous translation on headphones.

Image theatre (Map p98; ☎ 222 314 448; Classic Club, Pařížská 4; tickets 400Kč; ☉ box office 9am-8pm) Mime and black-light theatre.

Minor theatre (divadlo Minor; Map p106; ☎ 222 231 351; Vodičkova 6, Nové Město; ☉ box office 10am-1.30pm & 2.30-8pm Mon-Fri, 11am-6pm Sat & Sun) Children's puppet theatre has shows at 9.30am on most weekdays; wheelchair access.

SHOPPING

The city centre's single biggest – and most exhausting – retail zone is around Wenceslas square (Václavské náměstí), its pavements jammed with browsing visitors and locals making beelines for their favourite stores. You can find pretty much everything here, from high fashion and music megastores to run-of-the-mill department stores and gigantic book emporia. Many of the more interesting shops are hidden away in arcades and passages, such as the Lucerna Passage (p108).

The other main shopping drag intersects with the lower end of Wenceslas square, comprising Na příkopě, 28.října and Národní třída (Map p98). Most of the big stores and malls are concentrated on Na příkopě.

In Staré Město, the elegant avenue of Pařížská (Map p98) is lined with international designer boutiques, including Dior, Boss, Armani and Louis Vuitton, while the winding lanes between the Old Town square and Charles bridge are thronged with tacky souvenir shops flaunting puppets, Russian dolls and 'Czech This Out' T-shirts.

In recent years many new shops have opened up outside the centre, notably in Vinohrady (Map p98), which is good for antiques and designer furniture, Smíchov (Map p98), dominated by the huge Nový Smíchov mall, and in the suburb of Zličín on the far western edge of the city, which has a vast shopping centre anchored around Tesco and Ikea.

Antiques & Bric-a-Brac

Art Deco galerie (Map p98; ☎ 224 223 076; Michalská 21, Staré Město; ☽ 2-7pm Mon-Fri) All kinds of gorgeousness, mostly Art Deco, fill this well-ordered and very reasonably priced store. A great selection of glassware, clocks, china, jewellery and dresses, with many things under 600Kč.

Brí á Brac (Map p98; ☎ 224 815 763; Týnská 7, Staré Město; ☽ 10am-6pm) An Aladdin's cave of old household items and trophies and toys and cigar boxes and typewriters and stringed instruments and… Despite the junky look of this place, the knick-knacks are surprisingly expensive.

Eduard Čapek (Map p98; Dlouhá 32, Staré Město; ☽ 10am-6pm Mon-Fri) You may not need a door knob, rusty bed springs or a cracked teapot, but drop in anyway at the old hardware/homeware shop founded before WWI and doing a roaring trade ever since. Promotional badges from Czech companies start at 10Kč.

Ceramics, Glass & Crystal

Tupesy Lidová Keramika (Map p98; ☎ 224 210 728; Havelská 21, Staré Město; ☽ 10am-6pm) This place stocks a selection of charming ceramic household goods featuring naive floral designs from Southern Moravia.

Moser (Map p106; ☎ 224 211 293; Na příkopě 12, Nové Město; ☽ 10am-8pm Mon-Fri, 10am-7pm Sat & Sun) Prague's most prestigious glassmaker has been around since 1857. You may not be able to afford any of the gorgeous fripperies on display, but treat the place like a museum and visit anyway.

Balnys Spa (Map p98; ☎ 222 222 123; Náprstkova 4, Staré Město; ☽ 10am-6pm Mon-Fri) Modern glass featuring semiprecious stones that are quite unlike what you'll find at most souvenir shops

in town. This store also stocks original black-and-white photos and pen-and-ink drawings of Prague.

Kubista (Map p98; ☎ 224 236 378; Ovocný trh 19; ☽ 10am-6pm) Kubista specialises in limited-edition reproductions of distinctive cubist furniture and ceramics, and designs by masters of the form such as Josef Gočár and Pavel Janák. It also has a few original pieces for serious collectors with serious cash to spend.

Rott Crystal (Map p98; ☎ 224 229 529; Malé náměstí 3, Staré Město; ☽ 10am-8pm) Housed in a beautifully restored neo-Renaissance building – originally an ironmongers' – with 1890s wall paintings on the façade, Rott now has four floors of glassware, jewellery and ceramics, but it's best known for its stock of fine-quality Bohemian and imported crystal.

Clothing & Jewellery

Second Hand Land (Map p118; ☎ 241 711 995; Hybernská 5, Nové Město; ☽ 9am-6pm Mon-Fri, 10am-2pm Sat) When the kids have dirtied everything they own, when you absolutely must have a T-shirt featuring some form of Czech logo, or if you just feel like stocking up on frocks without spending three weeks' beer money, head to Second Hand Land.

Granát Turnov (Map p98; ☎ 222 315 612; Dlouhá 28-30, Staré Město) One of the biggest manufacturers and stockists of silver and gold garnet jewellery in Prague. The semiprecious Czech garnet – usually a dark red stone – is supposed to replace sadness with joy: its effectiveness probably depends on who's doing the buying.

TEG (Map p98; ☎ 222 327 358; V kolkovně 6, Staré Město; ☽ 10am-7pm Mon-Fri, 10am-5pm Sat) TEG (Timoure et Group) is the design team created by Alexandra Pavalová and Ivana Šafránková, two of Prague's most respected fashion designers. This boutique showcases their quarterly collections, which feature a sharp, imaginative look that adds zest and sophistication to everyday, wearable clothes.

Helena Fejková gallery (Map p106; ☎ 224 211 514; 1st fl, Lucerna Passage, Štěpánská 61, Nové Město; ☽ 10am-7pm Mon-Fri, 10am-3pm Sat) Kit yourself out in the latest Czech fashions at this chic boutique, which stocks contemporary men's and women's fashion and accessories by Prague designer Helena Fejková and other local designers.

Gifts & Souvenirs

Manufaktura Malá Strana (Map p92; ☎ 257 533 678; Mostecká 17); Staré Město (**Map p98**; Melnatrichova 17); Staré

Město (Map p98; Karlova 26) There are Manufakturas all over town, mostly in Staré Město and Malá Strana. All feature quality traditional handcrafts – the bulk of their stock is wooden toys, but they also have ceramics, textiles, soaps, candles and knick-knacks.

Fun Explosive (Map p98; ☎ 224 236 369; Jilská 14, Staré Město; ⊗ 10am-7pm) You'll have seen Fun Explosive's bright, cartoony T-shirts in stores all over town, but this is the mother lode. T-shirts, mugs, calendars, posters, original art and other assorted bits and bobs.

Music
If it's jazz you're after, most jazz clubs (p137) sell excellent selections of CDs, and knowledgeable staff can provide good advice.

Bontonland (Map p106; ☎ 224 473 080; Václavské náměstí, Nové Město; ⊗ 9am-8pm Mon-Sat, 10am-7pm Sun) Prague's music megastore, in the basement of the Koruna palace, stocks classical, jazz, folk, soundtracks, rock, metal, Czech pop compilations and a limited selection of vinyl. Bontonland also has an internet and Playstation café, DVDs, books, T-shirts and tickets for shows.

Radost CD (Map p116; ☎ 224 252 741; Bělehradská 120, Vinohrady; ⊗ 10am-9pm Mon-Fri, 11am-7pm Sat, 1-7pm Sun) A great selection of hip-hop, dance, reggae, jazz, rock classics and independent artists – finally get a copy of that Kool Keith or White Stripes album that's come out since you've been on the road.

Trio (Map p98; ☎ 222 322 583; Franz Kafka nám 3, Staré Město; ⊗ 10am-7pm Mon-Fri, 10am-6pm Sat & Sun) A great little shop specialising in classical CDs. It also has collections of Jewish music and Czech and Slovak folk.

Cappriccio (Map p115; ☎ 257 320 165; Újezd 15, Smíchov; ⊗ 10am-6pm Mon-Fri) Pick up the score for *Don Giovanni* or *From the New World* at this eclectic sheet music shop. Those who don't play an instrument might enjoy the books of country music favourites; after all, who wouldn't want to learn *Rhinestone Cowboy* in Czech?

Sporting Goods
Hudy Sport (Map p118; ☎ 224 813 010; Havlíčkova 11, Nové Město; ⊗ 9am-7.30pm Mon-Fri, 10am-6pm Sat, 1-4pm Sun) A huge outdoor shop with all the latest in fleece, Goretex, backpacks, rock-climbing gear, skis, stoves, shoes, sleeping bags and accessories. Six other Hudys are scattered around the city.

Giga (Map p98; Mýslbek Shopping Centre, Na přikopě, Nové Mesto; ⊗ 9.30am-7.30pm) Balls, boots, flippers, sports bras and no end of Nike and Puma street wear – Giga has three floors of sportswear and equipment.

GETTING THERE & AWAY
Air
Prague-Ruzyně Airport (☎ 220 113 314; www.csl.cz) is 17km west of the city centre. There are two international terminals – Terminal North 2 is for flights to/from Schengen Agreement countries (most EU nations, plus Switzerland, Iceland and Norway), and Terminal North 1 is for flights to/from non-Schengen countries (including the UK, Ireland and non-European destinations).

In both terminals the arrival hall and departure hall are next to each other, on the same level. The arrival halls have exchange counters, ATMs, accommodation and car-hire agencies, public-transport information desks, taxi services and 24-hour left-luggage counters. The departure halls have restaurants and bars, information offices, airline offices, an exchange counter and travel agencies. Once you're through security, there are shops, restaurants, bars and internet access (including wi-fi).

The national carrier, **Czech Airlines** (ČSA; Map p98; ☎ 239 007 007; www.csa.cz; V celnici 5, Nové Město), has several flights a day to Brno and Ostrava and numerous international connections. For more on getting to Prague from abroad, see p452.

Bus
INTERNATIONAL
Nearly all international buses leave from the **Florenc bus station** (ÚAN Praha Florenc; Map p118; ☎ 12 999; www.jizdnirady.cz; Křižíkova 4, Karlín), outside Florenc metro station. At least one of the four ticket windows (AMS) sells both domestic and international tickets; try ticket window No 5. Overall it is much simpler to book through a good travel agency; see p86.

DOMESTIC
All long-distance domestic buses and many regional services (such as those for excursions around Prague) depart from Florenc station (see International, earlier). Some regional buses depart from stands near most metro stations Anděl, Dejvická, Černý Most, Hradčanská, Nádraží Holešovice, Radlická, Roztyly, Smíchovské Nádraží, Zličín and Želivského.

Agencies don't book seats on domestic buses, but they can tell you which stand is best for a particular trip or whether you should take the train instead; you can get information at Florenc's **information desk** (☎ 900 144 444; ☯ 6am) or use the touch-screen computer; if you get no joy there, try the friendly Tourbus travel agency in a corridor off the main hall. You can find online bus timetables at www .jizdnirady.cz.

Long-distance domestic tickets are sold from AMS counters: Nos 11 to 13 at Florenc; short-haul tickets are sold on the bus. Since ticketing is computerised at most major bus stations, you can book ahead from 10 days to 30 minutes prior to your departure.

There are generally more departures in the morning. Buses, especially if full, sometimes leave a few minutes early, so be there about 10 minutes before departure time. Many services don't operate on weekends, so trains are a better bet then.

Florenc has a **left-luggage office** (úschovna zavazadel; ☯ 5am-11pm).

Car & Motorcycle

For information on car rental, documents, road rules and fuel, see p459.

Train

INTERNATIONAL

Most international trains arrive at the main station, Praha hlavní nádraží (Map p118), which is three blocks northeast of Wenceslas square. International trains between Berlin and Budapest often stop at Praha-Holešovice (metro nádraží Holešovice; Map pp82–3) on the northern side of the city.

At the main train station, you can get information on international train services at the ČD info centre at the south end of the main concourse, and from ticket windows Nos 2 to 8 (usually only one of these windows – look for a sign advertising information in English). Full printed timetables are displayed on level 3; timetable information is also available online at www.idos.cz.

You can buy international train tickets in advance from train stations, **ČD Travel** (Map p98; ☎ 972 233 930; V Celnici 6, Nové Město) and Čedok travel agencies.

DOMESTIC

Most domestic trains arrive at the main station, Praha hlavní nádraží, or at Masarykovo

nádraží, two blocks to the north. Other stations where you might end up include Praha-Holešovice (next to metro station Nádraží Holešovice) and Praha-Smíchov (adjacent to metro Smíchovské nádraží).

Domestic and Slovakian destinations served by fast/express train from the main station include:

Benešov (64Kč, 1¼hr, 49km)
Brno (294Kč, 3½hr, 257km)
České Budějovice (204Kč, 2½hr, 169km)
Cheb via Plzeň (250Kč, 3½hr, 220km)
Karlovy Vary (274Kč, 4hr, 236km)
Košice (990Kč, 10hr, 700km)
Mariánské Lázně (224Kč, 3hr, 190km)
Plzeň (140Kč, 1¾hr, 114km)
Tábor (130Kč, 1½hr, 103km)

Trains going to Bratislava (500Kč, 4¼ hours, 398km) may leave from either Hlavní nádraží or Praha Holešovice. For more on getting to Prague by train from across Europe, see Transport, p456.

At the main station, you can buy domestic tickets (*vnitrostátní jízdenky*) at the odd-numbered ticket windows (marked with an A) to the left of the departures board on the main concourse; for international advance reservations (*mezinárodní rezervace*) go to windows 2 to 8 (marked B), and for international tickets (*mezinárodní jízdenky*) go to windows 12 to 24 (marked C) to the right.

MAIN TRAIN STATION

On arriving at Praha hlavní nádraží, the underpass from the platforms leads you to level 3 of the four-level station complex; turn left here to find the AVE (p124) accommodation agency.

Continue down a short flight of stairs to level 2, the main concourse, where you'll find the helpful **PIS Tourist Information Booth** (☯ 9am-7pm Mon-Fri, 9am-5pm Sat & Sun) beside the metro entrance at the southern (left) end.

Ramps to either side of the ticket counters in the main concourse lead down to level 1, which has a **left-luggage office** (úschovna; 15Kč or 30Kč per bag per day; ☯ 24 hours) and luggage lockers (60Kč; they accept 5, 10 and 20Kč coins).

There are four metro station entrances in the concourse – the two nearer the stairs from level 3 lead to the northbound platform (direction Ladví), the two nearer the exits are southbound (direction Haje). Public transport tickets and information are available at the

DPP booths beside the southbound metro entrances. There are taxi ranks at either end of the concourse. To find the nearest tram stop (tram Nos 5, 9 and 26) exit the main concourse and turn right; the stop is at the far end of the park.

The big display board on the main concourse lists departures with columns marked *druh vlaku* (type of train – EC, IC etc), *číslo vlaku* (train number), *cílová stanice* (final destination), *směr* (via), *odjezd* (departure time) and *našt* (platform number). To make sure you're on the correct train, makes sure its number (displayed on a panel on the side of the coach) matches the train number of the service you want.

Try not to arrive in the middle of the night – the station closes from 12.40am to 3.40am, and the surrounding area is a magnet for pickpockets and drunks.

Note – Praha hlavní nádraží is set to undergo a major redevelopment between 2006 and 2009; during this period the layout of the station may be changed.

GETTING AROUND
To/From the Airport

To get into town, buy a ticket from the public transport (Dopravní podnik; DPP) desk in arrivals and take bus 119 (20Kč, 20 minutes, every 15 minutes) to the end of the line (Dejvická), then continue by metro into the city centre (another 10 minutes; no new ticket needed). Note that you'll also need a half-fare (10Kč) ticket for your backpack or suitcase (if it's larger than 25cm x 45cm x 70cm).

Alternatively, take a **Cedaz minibus** (☎ 220 114 296; www.cedaz.cz) from just outside arrivals – buy your ticket from the driver (90Kč, 20 minutes, every 30 minutes between 5.30am and 9.30pm). There are city stops near metro Dejvická and at the Czech Airlines office close to náměstí Republiky. You can also get a Cedaz minibus right to the door of your hotel or any other address (480Kč for one to four people, 960Kč for five to eight) – book and pay at the Cedaz desk in the arrivals hall.

Airport Cars (☎ 220 113 892) taxi service, whose prices are regulated by the airport administration, charges 650Kč (20% discount for the return trip) into the centre of Prague (a regular taxi fare *from* central Prague should be about 450Kč). Drivers usually speak some English and accept Visa credit cards.

Bicycle

Prague is not the best city for getting around by bike. Traffic is heavy, exhaust fumes can be choking, tram tracks can be dangerous and there are few dedicated bicycle lanes.

Bikes must be equipped with a bell, mudguards, a white reflector and white light up front, a red reflector and flashing red light at the rear, and reflectors on pedals – if not, you can be fined up to 1000Kč. Cyclists up to the age of 15 must wear helmets.

If you're aged at least 12 you can take your bicycle on the metro, but you must place it near the last door of the rear carriage, and only two bikes are allowed. Bikes are not permitted if the carriage is full, or if there's already a pram in the carriage.

Bicycle Hire

Praha Bike (Map p98; ☎ 732 388 880; www.praha bike.cz; Dlouhá 24, Staré Město; 4hr 360Kč, 8hr 500Kč; ⊙ 9am-7pm mid-Mar–mid-Nov) Good, new bikes with lock, helmet and map, plus free luggage storage. Also offers student discounts and group bike tours; see p122.

City Bike (Map p98; ☎ 776 180 284; www.citybike -prague.com; Královodvorská 5, Staré Město; ⊙ 9am-7pm Apr-Oct) Rental includes helmet, padlock and map; two hours costs 280/340Kč for a cruiser/mountain bike.

Car & Motorcycle

Driving in Prague is no fun, especially in the narrow, winding streets of the city centre. Trying to find your way around – or to park legally – while coping with trams, buses, other drivers, cyclists and pedestrians, can make you wish you'd left the car at home.

Try not to arrive or leave on a Friday or Sunday afternoon or evening, when half the population seems to be heading to and from their weekend cottages.

Central Prague has many pedestrian-only streets. They are marked with 'Pěší zóna' (Pedestrian Zone) signs, and only service vehicles and taxis are allowed in these areas.

CAR RENTAL

The main international car-hire chains all have airport pick-up points as well as city centre offices. Rates per day/week begin at 1900/10,700Kč for a Škoda Fabia, including unlimited mileage, collision-damage waiver and value-added tax (VAT, or DPH in Czech). There's a 400Kč surcharge to pick up your vehicle from the airport, but delivery to hotels in central Prague is free.

Small local companies such as Secco, Vecar and West Car Praha offer much better rates, but are less likely to have fluent, English-speaking staff – it's often easier to book by email than by phone. Typical rates for a Škoda Fabia are around 800Kč a day, including unlimited mileage, collision-damage waiver and VAT.

A-Rent Car/Thrifty (Map p106; ☎ 224 233 265; www .arentcar.cz; Washingtonova 9, Nové Město)

Avis (Map p118; ☎ 221 851 225; www.avis.com; Klimentská 46, Nové Město)

CS-Czechocar (Map p112; ☎ 261 222 079; www .czechocar.cz; Congress Centre, 5.května 65, Vyšehrad)

Europcar (Map p98; ☎ 224 810 515; www.europcar.cz; Pařížská 28, Staré Město)

Hertz (Map p106; ☎ 225 345 000; www.hertz.cz; Karlovo náměstí 15, Nové Město)

Secco Car (Map pp82–3; ☎ 220 802 361; www.secco car.cz; Přístavní 39, Holešovice)

Vecar (Map pp82–3; ☎ 224 314 361; www.vecar.cz; Svatovítská 7, Dejvice)

West Car Praha (Map pp82–3; ☎ 235 365 307; www .westcarpraha.cz, in Czech; Veleslavínská 17, Veleslavín)

EMERGENCIES

For emergency service, the Czech automobile and motorcycle club **ÚAMK** (Automoto-klub; ☎ 1230) has 'Yellow Angels' (*Žlutý andělé*) that provide 24-hour nationwide assistance.

Another outfit offering round-the-clock repair services nationwide is **Autoklub Bohemia Assistance** (ABA; Map p106; ☎ 26 14 91, 222 241 257; Opletalova 29, Nové Město; ✆ 8am-noon & 12.30-4.30pm Mon-Fri), which also has a Prague information centre.

PARKING

Meter time limits range from two to 24 hours at 30Kč to 40Kč per hour. Parking in one-way streets is normally only allowed on the right-hand side. Traffic inspectors are always keen to hand out fines, clamp wheels or tow away vehicles.

There are several car parks at the edges of Staré Město and around the outer city near metro stations. Most are marked on city maps.

Public Transport

Prague has an excellent integrated public transport system that combines metro, tram and bus. It's operated by **Dopravní podnik hlavního město Prahy** (DPP; ☎ 296 191 817; www.dpp .cz), which has information desks at Ruzyně airport (7am to 10pm) and in four metro stations – Muzeum (7am to 9pm), Můstek, Anděl and Nádraží Holešovice (all 7am to 6pm) – where you can get tickets, directions, a multilingual transport system map, a map of night services (*noční provoz*) and a detailed English-language guide to the whole system.

On metro trains and newer trams and buses, an electronic display shows the route number and the name of the next stop, and a recorded voice announces each station or stop. As the train, tram or bus pulls away, the announcer says '*Příští stanice…*' (The next station is…) or '*Příští zastávka…*' (The next stop is…), perhaps noting that it's a *přestupní stanice* (transfer station). At metro stations, signs point you towards the *výstup* (exit) or to a *přestup* (transfer to another line).

The metro operates from 5am to midnight. After the metro closes, night trams (Nos 51 to 58) and buses (Nos 501 to 512) still rumble across the city about every 40 minutes through the night. If you're planning a late evening, find out if one of these services passes near where you're staying.

TICKETS

You need to buy a ticket before you board a bus, tram or metro. Tickets are sold from machines at metro stations and major tram stops, at newsstands, Trafiky snack shops, PNS newspaper kiosks, hotels, PIS tourist information offices (p86), all metro station ticket offices and DPP information offices.

A transfer ticket (*jízdenka*) valid on tram, metro, bus and the Petřín funicular (p96) per adult/child aged six to 15 years costs 20/10Kč; kids under six ride free. You'll also need a 10Kč ticket for each large suitcase or backpack (larger than 25cm x 45cm x 70cm). Validate (punch) your ticket by sticking it in the little yellow machine in the metro station lobby or on the bus or tram the first time you board; this stamps the time and date on it. Once validated, transfer tickets remain valid for 75 minutes if stamped between 5am and 8pm on weekdays, and for 90 minutes at all other times. Within this time period you can make unlimited transfers between all types of public transport (you don't need to punch the ticket again).

There's also a short-hop ticket (adult/child 14/7Kč), valid for 20 minutes on buses and trams, or for up to five metro station. No transfers are allowed with these (except

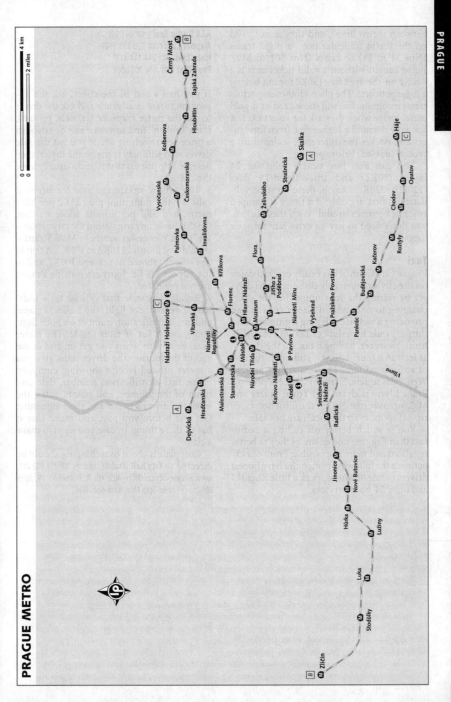

PRAGUE METRO

0 ———— 4 km
0 ———— 2 miles

Černý Most Ⓑ
Rajská Zahrada
Hloubětín
Kolbenova
Vysočanská
Českomoravská
Palmovka
Invalidovna
Křižíkova
Florenc
Nádraží Holešovice Ⓒ
Vltavská
Náměstí Republiky
Staroměstská
Dejvická Ⓐ
Hradčanská
Malostranská
Můstek
Národní Třída
Muzeum
Hlavní Nádraží
Jiřího z Poděbrad
Náměstí Míru
Flora
Želivského
Strašnická
Skalka Ⓐ
Háje Ⓒ
Opatov
Chodov
Roztyly
Kačerov
Budějovická
Pankrác
Pražského Povstání
Vyšehrad
IP Pavlova
Karlovo Náměstí
Anděl
Smíchovské Nádraží
Radlická
Jinonice
Nové Butovice
Hůrka
Lužiny
Luka
Stodůlky
Zličín Ⓑ

VLTAVA

between metro lines), and they're not valid on the Petřín funicular nor on night trams (Nos 51 to 58) or buses (Nos 501 to 512). Being caught without a valid ticket entails a 400Kč on-the-spot fine (50Kč for not having a luggage ticket). The plain-clothes inspectors travel incognito, but will show a red-and-gold metal badge when they ask for your ticket. A few may demand a higher fine from foreigners and pocket the difference, so insist on a receipt *(doklad)* before paying.

You can also buy tickets valid for 24 hours (80Kč) and three/seven/15 days (220/280/320Kč). Again, these must be validated on first use only; if a ticket is stamped twice, it becomes invalid. With these tickets, you don't need to pay an extra fare for your luggage.

Taxi

Prague City Council has finally cracked down on the city's notoriously dishonest taxi drivers by raising the maximum fine for overcharging to one million Czech crowns and providing a website detailing legitimate fares (http://panda.hyperlink.cz/taxitext/etaxiweb. htm). However, hailing a taxi on the street – at least in a tourist zone – still holds the risk of an inflated fare. The taxi stands around Wenceslas square, Národní třída, Na příkopě, Praha hlavní nádraží, Old Town square and Malostranské náměstí are the most notorious rip-off spots; even the locals are not safe.

You're much better off calling a radio-taxi than flagging one down, as they're better regulated and more responsible. From our experience the following companies have honest drivers (some of whom speak a little English) and offer 24-hour services.

AAA Radio Taxi (☎ 14 014)
Airport Cars (☎ 220 113 892)
Halo Taxi (☎ 244 114 411)
ProfiTaxi (☎ 844 700 800)

If you hail a taxi in the street, ask the approximate fare in advance and ask the driver to use the meter *(zapněte taximetr, prosím)*. If it's 'broken', find someone else or establish a price before setting off. If you get the rare driver who willingly turns on the meter, they deserve a tip just for that (Czechs usually leave the change).

The official maximum rate for licensed cabs is 34Kč minimum plus 25Kč per kilometre, and 5Kč per minute while waiting. On this basis, any trip within the city centre – say, from Wenceslas square to Malá Strana – should cost around 110Kč to 170Kč. A trip to the suburbs should not exceed 300Kč, and to the airport 450Kč. Journeys outside Prague are not regulated.

Regulations state that official taxis must have a yellow roof light, the business name and taxi identification number on both front doors, and a list of fares inside. The meter must be at zero when you get in, and at the end of the journey the driver must give you a meter-printed receipt showing: company name, taxi identification number, date and times of the journey, end points, rates, the total, the driver's name and their signature. Get one before you pay, and make sure it has all these things in case you want to make a claim.

Complaints about overcharging should be directed to **City hall** (Pražské radnice; ☎ 236 002 269; www.prague-city.cz; Office 405, 4th fl, Platnéřská 19, Staré Město; ☾ noon-5pm Mon, 8am-6pm Wed).

Central Bohemia

Beyond the serried apartment blocks of Prague's outer suburbs, the city gives way to the surprisingly green hinterland of Central Bohemia, a region of rolling hills, rich farmland and thick forests dotted with castles, chateaux and picturesque towns. Rural and rustic, yet within easy reach of the capital, for centuries it has provided an escape for generations of city dwellers, from the aristocrats and kings who built their country retreats here, to the modern-day Praguers who head out on weekends to hike, bike and canoe on its network of trails and rivers.

Most of Central Bohemia can be easily explored on day trips from Prague, from the medieval silver-mining town of Kutná Hora to the fairy-tale castles of Karlštejn and Křivoklát, and the fascinating excesses of Konopiště. The downside of such convenience is the crowds that throng to these places on summer weekends, but you can avoid them by visiting in winter – Karlštejn under snow is a magical sight – or on weekdays, or better still by staying overnight. As the tour coaches and caravans roll out at nightfall, many of the towns and villages belong once again to the locals and an overnight stay will immerse you in the region's blissful serenity – Central Bohemia's true, although sometimes elusive, highlight.

HIGHLIGHTS

- Be dazzled by Kutná Hora's beautiful **cathedral of St Barbara** (p157)
- Admire the art of bone-arranging in ghoulish **Sedlec ossuary** (p159) in Kutná Hora
- Check out the region's best castles at **Karlštejn** (p148) and **Konopiště** (p152)
- Take in the views and sample the wines in **Mělník** (p154)
- Get off the beaten track and explore the beautiful back roads of **Kokořínsko** (p156)

★ Kokořínsko
★ Mělník

★ Karlštejn   Cathedral of St Barbara & Sedlec Ossuary

★ Konopiště

Castles & Chateaux

Central Bohemia is castle country, with more than half a dozen castles and chateaux you can visit. The two most popular, Karlštejn and Konopiště, are busy on summer weekends.

Tours

If you're short on time or want a guided tour, Prague-based tour companies have a range of all-day excursions from the capital during summer. Tour operators include:

Martin Tour (Map p106; ☎ 224 212 473; www.martin tour.cz; Štepanská 61, Nové Město, Prague) Tours, available in 25 languages and using headphones rather than guides, include Konopiště (850Kč, five hours) Karlštejn (950Kč, five hours) and Kutná Hora (850Kč, five hours).

Prague Sightseeing Tours (Map p118; ☎ 224 314 661; www.pstours.cz; Klimentská 52, Nové Město, Prague) Tours include Konopiště (890Kč, four hours), Karlštejn (960Kč, 4½ hours) and Kutná Hora (980Kč, five hours).

KARLŠTEJN

pop 800

Karlštejn castle is in such good shape these days it wouldn't look out of place on Disney's Main St. The crowds come in theme-park proportions as well (it's best to book ahead if you want to be sure of a guided tour), but the peaceful surrounding countryside offers views of Karlštejn's stunning exterior that rival anything you'll see on the inside.

Orientation & Information

From the train station it's a 500m walk to Karlštejn village (turn left out of the station, cross the river and turn right), and then another 800m uphill to the castle through a gamut of souvenir stalls selling everything from giant rubber spiders to African wood-carvings. If you don't want to walk, you can take a taxi (110Kč per person) or a horse-drawn coach (150Kč per person); both depart from the car park (70Kč per day for a car). Private vehicles are not allowed to drive up to the castle.

There's an information office, public toilets, telephones and an ATM at the car park.

Sights & Activities

Karlštejn castle (☎ 274 008 154; www.hradkarlstejn.cz; Tour I adult/concession 220/120Kč, Tour II 300/100Kč; 9am-6pm Tue-Sun Jul & Aug; 9am-5pm May, Jun & Sep; 9am-4pm

Apr & Oct; 9am-3pm Nov-Mar) was born of a grand pedigree, starting life in 1348 as a hideaway for the crown jewels and the treasury of the Holy Roman Emperor, Charles IV. Run by an appointed burgrave, the castle was surrounded by a network of land-owning knight vassals, who came to the castle's aid whenever enemies moved against it.

Karlštejn again sheltered the Bohemian and Imperial crown jewels during the Hussite Wars, but it fell into disrepair as its defences became outmoded. Considerable restoration work, not least by Josef Mocker in the late 19th century, has returned the castle to its former glory.

Perched high on a crag that overlooks the Berounka river, and sporting a spotless paint job, this cluster of turrets, high parapets and looming towers is as immaculately maintained as it is powerfully evocative. Rightly one of the top attractions of the Czech Republic, its only drawback is its overwhelming popularity: in the summer months it is literally mobbed with visitors, ice-cream vendors and souvenir stalls.

There are two guided tours through the castle. Tour I (50 minutes) passes through the Knight's hall, still daubed with the coats of arms and names of the knight vassals, Charles IV's bedchamber, the Audience hall and the Jewel house, which includes treasures from the chapel of the Holy Cross and a replica of the St Wenceslas crown.

Tour II (70 minutes) must be booked in advance and takes in the Great tower, the highest point of the castle, which includes a museum on Mocker's restoration work, the Marian tower and the exquisite chapel of the Holy Cross with its decorative ceiling.

You can avoid some of the crowds on the way uphill by taking the alternative walking route – turn left just past Pension Restaurant U Janů, and follow this sideroad for 10 minutes or so. About 50m before you reach Pension pod Dračí Skálou, cross the little footbridge on the right and follow the footpath uphill through the woods to reach the castle entrance.

A red-marked hiking trail leads 7km from Karlštejn village via Mořinka (not Mořina) village to the **Karlík valley** (Karlícké údolí), a nature reserve where a yellow-marked trail leads north to the remains of Charles IV's **Karlík castle**, abandoned in the 15th century. Karlík village, 1km down the valley, has a

12th-century rotunda. A road and a green-marked trail run 1.5km southeast from there to Dobřichovice, on the Prague–Beroun train line.

You can also hike 14km from Karlštejn to Beroun (p150 for details).

Sleeping & Eating
Autokemp Karlštejn (☎ 311 681 263; tent per person 60Kč; ✆ Mar-Sep; **P**) On the northern side of the river, 500m west of the bridge, this has a top location and staff can help organise a canoe for a paddle on the river.

Penzión Slon (☎ 311 681 550; www.penzionslon.cz; s/d 800/1200Kč; mains 80-130Kč; **P**) Away from the crowds, on the opposite side of the railway tracks from the village (follow the elephant signs), the 'Elephant Pension' offers brightly decorated en suite rooms, and a restaurant with Czech home cooking.

Pension & Restaurant U Janů (☎ 311 681 210; info@ujanu.cz; d/apt 1000/1200Kč) Located on the road up to the castle, this atmospheric place has a decent dollop of authentic charm. There are three apartments and one double room. The restaurant is good (mains 70Kč to 160Kč), with a menu that includes the Slovak speciality, *halušky* (cheesy dumplings with bacon bits), but the staff could have been friendlier.

Penzión U královny Dagmar (☎ 311 681 378; www .penziondagmara.cz; d/t/apt 1150/1350/1550Kč) Close to the castle and a rung up the price ladder, this slick place has all the creature comforts and a top-notch eatery, with mains from 80Kč to 200Kč.

Getting There & Away
Trains to Beroun from Prague's hlavní nádraží (main station) and Praha-Smíchovské stations stop at Karlštejn (46Kč, 45 minutes, hourly). The last train back to Prague doesn't leave until 9.57pm.

BEROUN
pop 17,600
The town was established at a ford on the Berounka river, on the road between Prague and Plzeň, and was subject to flooding during 2002.

Newly restored, the spick-and-span Beroun makes an attractive base for exploring Křivoklát, Karlštejn, the Koněprusy caves and the surrounding hiking trails, or as the starting point for a canoe trip on the Berounka river.

CENTRAL BOHEMIA

Orientation & Information

The town's main square, Husovo náměstí, is 500m north of the train station; go under the underpass, across the stream, and keep going in a straight line till you reach the square. From the bus station, 250m east of the square, take the footbridge across the river, bear right and cross another footbridge, then keep heading straight.

ČSOB (Husovo náměstí 38) Has a currency exchange and ATM.

Tourist information office (☎ 311 654 321; mic@muberoun.cz; Husovo náměstí 69; ⊗ 8am-12.30pm & 1-6pm Mon-Fri, 8am-noon Sat Jun-Aug; 8am-12.30pm & 1-4.30pm Mon-Fri Sep-May) On the southeastern corner of the square.

Sights & Activities

Beroun's recent makeover has made the most of its expansive town square, the old town gates and the 14th-century walls, making it a pleasant place for a leisurely stroll. You can climb to the top of the **Plzeň gate tower** (adult/concession 20/10Kč; ⊗ 9am-noon Wed & Sat) at the west end of the square for a fine view over the town.

The wooded hill to the west of the old town is home to the **Medvědarium** (admission free; ⊗ dawn to dusk), an enclosure inhabited by three brown bears, relatives of the bears at Český Krumlov (p172).

From Beroun train station you can hike a red-marked trail east for 6km to the **monastery of St John Under the Rock** (klášter sv Jan pod Skálou), situated in a spectacular limestone gorge. The baroque Benedictine monastery was allegedly once an StB (secret police) training camp. From here, you can continue 1.5km north on a blue-marked trail to Vráž, where you can catch a train or bus back to Beroun or to Prague. Alternatively, you can continue on the red trail for another 8km to Karlštejn. Allow five hours from Beroun to Karlštejn.

The Berounka river is popular for **canoeing**, and the trip downstream from Beroun to Radotín is a leisurely 32km paddle that can be spread over a weekend, with a visit to Karlštejn castle thrown in.

BiSport (☎ 317 701 460; www.bisport.cz; Janečka 511, Týnec nad Sázavou) can arrange equipment hire and transport for around 600Kč for a two-person canoe for the weekend, though you'll need to pay extra for a night camping or in a *pension*.

Sleeping

Autocamp Na Hrázi (☎ 311 623 294; Vančurova 1126; tent per person 60Kč; P) The nearest camp site is 800m northeast of the town square and across the river.

Penzion Berona (☎ 311 626 184; www.berona.cz; Havlíčkova 116; s/d 500/1000Kč, apt 2500Kč) This brand new *pension* is on a quiet street just a block south of the town square, and has bright, modern rooms with shared bathrooms. There's also a family apartment for four, on the second floor.

Hotel Parkan (☎ 311 624 372; rtot@iol.cz; Horno-hradebni 162; s/d incl breakfast 1200/1600Kč; P) Set into the old town walls in a pedestrianised alleyway near the Plzeň gate tower, this family-friendly *pension* has spacious en suite rooms and a pleasantly old-fashioned atmosphere.

Eating

Pizzeria alla Madonna (☎ 311 610 066; Husovo náměstí 75; mains 75-165Kč; ⊗ 11am-11pm) A classic pizzeria with pine tables, wrought-iron chairs and rag-rolled ochre walls, this lively little place sports an English-language menu. Choose from a range of pizzas, pasta dishes, lasagne and steaks, washed down with Pilsner Urquell or Stella Artois.

Restaurace Na Baště (☎ 311 623 364; Hornohradební 98; mains 90-150Kč; ⊗ 11am-11pm Mon-Sat) Just across from the Hotel Parkan, this rustic little pub-restaurant (the dining room is upstairs) has decent Czech grub – from garlic soup to goulash – and Pilsner Urquell on tap.

Getting There & Away

From Prague it's a beautiful train ride along the Berounka river to Beroun (46Kč to 64Kč, 40 to 60 minutes). Trains depart at least hourly from Prague's hlavní nádraží (main station), calling at Praha-Smíchov station where you can also board.

KONĚPRUSY CAVES

Human bones, the remains of a woolly rhino and a forge for counterfeiting coins are some of the oddities to be found in the guts of these impressive 600m-deep limestone **caves** (Koněpruské jeskyně; ☎ 311 622 405; adult/concession 80/40Kč; ⊗ 8am-5pm Jul & Aug, to 4pm Apr-Jun & Sep, 8.30am-3pm Oct).

Take a jumper: it's a constant, chilly 10°C, and you'll be down there for 45 to 60 minutes. There's no food to speak of except a snack bar at the caves.

The caves lie 6km south of Beroun. Buses run to the caves from Beroun's bus station (17Kč, 20 minutes) at 9.25am, 12.20pm and 2.20pm on weekdays, and from the train station (11Kč, 15 minutes) at 9.30am, 11am and 1.40pm on Saturdays and Sundays. It's worth checking these times with the Beroun tourist office before you go.

KŘIVOKLÁT

pop 650

Křivoklát is a drowsy village beside the Rakovnický potok river. The main attraction is Křivoklát castle, but half the pleasure of visiting lies simply in getting there – by train up the scenic Berounka valley.

The valley is dotted with holiday bungalows and hemmed in by limestone bluffs, and the surrounding forests are included in the Křivoklátsko Protected Landscape Region, a Unesco 'biosphere preservation' area.

Visit on a weekday and you'll escape the crowds associated with places like Karlštejn.

Orientation

From the train station, turn right as you exit the train (in the direction of Beroun) and follow a footpath that leads to the main road in the centre of the village. From here, the **tourist information centre** (☎ 313 558 263; 🕙 9am-4pm Jul & Aug) is a few metres to your right, while the castle is 500m uphill along the road opposite you, to the left of the post office.

Sights & Activities

KŘIVOKLÁT CASTLE

With origins stretching back to the 12th century, **Křivoklát castle** (☎ 313 558 120; www.krivoklat .cz; 🕙 9am-noon & 1-5pm Tue-Sun May-Aug, to 4pm Apr & Sep, to 3pm Oct, 9am-noon & 1-3pm Sat & Sun Nov & Dec) is one of Bohemia's oldest fortresses.

Once a celebrated hunting lodge, it has survived several fires and seemingly endless renovations as a prettified chateau reflecting the whimsy of 19th-century Romanticism.

There are two guided tours. **Tour I** (adult/ concession 80/40Kč, with English-language guide 150/80Kč) takes 70 minutes and visits the castle's interiors, including the chapel, one of the Czech Republic's finest, with its unaltered late-Gothic décor full of intricate polychrome carvings and an altar decorated with angels carrying instruments of torture – a legacy of the castle's 16th-century role as a political prison (the prison and torture cham-

bers are directly beneath the chapel). The Knights' hall features a permanent collection of late-Gothic religious sculpture and painted panels, while the 25m-long King's hall is the second-biggest Gothic hall in the country, after the Vladislav hall in Prague castle (p87). There is also a library of 52,000 volumes.

Tour II (adult/concession 40/20Kč, with English-speaking guide 80/40Kč; 🕙 Apr-Oct) visits the castle fortifications, including a strenuous climb to the top of the impressive donjon, the massive round tower that dominates the complex.

HIKING

If you have the gear and an extra day or two, consider hiking the 18km trail (marked red) southwest up the Berounka valley to Skryje. It starts on the western side of Rakovnický potok tributary near the train stop.

Sleeping & Eating

There are **camping grounds** about 2km south of Křivoklát at Višnová, and across the river at Branov (cross at Roztoky).

Hotel Roztoky (☎ 313 558 931; www.hotelroztoky.cz; Roztoky u Křivoklátu 14, Roztoky; r per person 260-450Kč; 🅿) Plain but pleasant, with recently redecorated rooms kitted out with Ikea furniture, this family-run place has a decent restaurant and beer hall, and is 1km south of Křivoklát in the village of Roztoky.

Pension restaurace U Jelena (☎ 313 558 529; www .u-jelena.cz; Hradní 53; d/tr/q 1000/1500/2000Kč; 🕙 11am-10pm; 🅿) Located down the hill from Křivoklát castle, 'The Stag' is an attractive, modern *pension* with rustic, hunting-lodge décor. It has a good restaurant with an outdoor terrace and barbecue overlooking the Rakovnický potok river. Main dishes range in price from 75Kč to 250Kč.

Getting There & Away

Křivoklát is 24km northwest of Beroun. If arriving by car, park in the official car park beside the petrol station on the way from Beroun; from here a path leads over a footbridge to the castle.

There are plenty of trains from Prague to Beroun (see opposite). The key is making sure there's a good connection from there; there are only two direct trains a day between Prague and Křivoklát (98Kč, 1½ to two hours). From Beroun there are nine trains a day to Křivoklát (40Kč, 40 minutes).

PRŮHONICE

As landscaped parks go, **Průhonice** (admission free; ☯ 8am-7pm Apr-Oct, to 5pm Nov-Mar), on the south-eastern fringes of Prague, has long been one of Europe's finest. Now a state botanical preserve, it is a green oasis of exotic gardens, colourful flowerbeds, sweet-smelling woodland and artificial lakes. In May, thousands of rhododendron bushes provide a spectacular display of pink, red and yellow blooms.

The **chateau**, once the property of Count Arnošt Emmanuel Sylva-Taroucca, is now occupied by the Botanical Institute of the Czech Academy of Sciences and is closed to the public. Nearby is the little **church of the Nativity of Our Lady** (kostel Narození Panny Marie), which was consecrated in 1187. Some of its Gothic frescoes, dating from 1330, are still visible. This too is closed, unless you attend the 5pm Sunday mass.

On weekends Průhonice is packed with day-tripping Czech families, but on a weekday morning you could have the place to yourself.

Getting There & Away

Take bus 325 or 363 from Prague's Opatov metro station, on the C line (14Kč, 15 minutes, every 15 to 20 minutes).

KONOPIŠTĚ

Archduke Franz Ferdinand d'Este, heir to the Austro-Hungarian throne, is most famous for being dead – it was his assassination in Sarajevo on 14 June 1914 that sparked WWI. But during his lifetime the archduke was an enigmatic figure who avoided the intrigues of the Vienna court, and for the last 20 years of his life hid away in Konopiště, which he gradually converted into his ideal country retreat.

Sights

Originally dating from 1300, **Konopiště chateau** (☎ 317 721 366; Benešov; Tour I or II adult/child 180/100Kč, Tour III 300/200Kč; ☯ 9am-5pm Tue-Sun May-Aug; to 4pm Tue-Fri, to 5pm Sat & Sun Sep; to 3pm Tue-Fri, to 4pm Sat & Sun Apr & Oct; to 3pm Sat & Sun Nov; closed 12.30-1pm year-round) is a testament to the archduke's twin obsessions – hunting and St George. Having renovated the massive Gothic and Renaissance building in the 1890s, and installed all the latest technology – including electricity, central heating, flush toilets, showers and a luxurious water-powered lift – Franz Ferdi-

nand proceeded to decorate his home with his hunting trophies.

It seems that Franz Ferdinand shot anything that moved, from elephants and tigers to foxes and hares. His game books record that he shot about 300,000 creatures during his lifetime, including innocuous birds such as spoonbills, cormorants and great-crested grebes. About 100,000 of his victims adorn the walls, each meticulously marked with the date and place where it met its end – the crowded Trophy corridor (on Tours I and III) sprouts a forest of mounted animal heads, while the Chamois room (on Tour III only), with its serried ranks of chamois antlers and a 'chandelier' fashioned from a stuffed condor, is a truly bizarre sight.

There are three guided tours available in English. Tour III is the most interesting, visiting the private apartments used by the archduke and his family, which have remained entirely unchanged since the state took possession of the chateau in 1921. At the end you can see the death masks of the archduke and his wife, as well as the blood-stained clothing they were wearing at the time of assassination. (The assassin, Gavrilo Princip, a Bosnian Serb, was imprisoned at Terezín; p231.) Tour I visits the castle's guest rooms and the Trophy corridor, while Tour II takes in the Great armoury, one of the largest and most impressive collections in Europe, and the chapel.

The archduke's collection of art and artefacts relating to St George is no less impressive (not to say obsessive), amounting to 3750 items ranging from tiny images on silver rings to wooden effigies more than 2m tall, many of which are on show in the **St George museum** (muzeum sv Jiří; adult/child 25/10Kč; ☯ same as chateau) beneath the terrace at the front of the castle.

Sleeping & Eating

KONOPIŠTĚ

Hotel Nová Myslivna (☎ 317 722 496; www.hotel myslivna.zde.cz; d/t 550/825Kč; ☐) The sweeping angular roof of this chalet-style hotel clashes somewhat with the softer lines of the castle, but its location beside the Konopiště chateau car park is unbeatable.

BENEŠOV

Hotel Pošta (☎ 317 721 071; hotel-posta@quick.cz; Tyršova 162; s/d incl breakfast 360/720Kč; ☐) There's more than a hint of 1970s communist-era atmosphere (lots of brown and beige décor) in this once-grand hotel just off the town square. But hey, the price is right.

Hotel Atlas (☎ 317 724 771; www.hotel-atlas.cz; Tyršova 2063; s/d 742/864Kč) This business hotel is plain and functional, but the rooms are spotless and comfortable, and it is bang on the main street in Benešov.

Hotel Benica (☎ 317 725 611; www.benica.cz; Ke Stadionu 2045; s/d 950/1700Kč; P ⊡ ☎) Located beside the main E55 highway on the southern outskirts of neighbouring Benešov, the Benica is a bright, modern motel with a decent restaurant specialising in wood-fired pizzas.

Hostinec U zlaté hvězdy (☎ 317 723 921; Masarykovo náměstí 2; mains 80-150Kč; ☀ 11am-11pm) Enjoy Bohemian pub grub at this snug central *pivnice* (beer hall).

Getting There & Away

Konopiště is 50km south of Prague, near the town of Benešov. There are frequent direct trains from Prague's hlavní nádraží to Benešov u Prahy (64Kč, 1¼ hours, hourly). Most trains to and from Tábor and České Budějovice also stop here.

There are buses from Prague's Roztyly metro station to Benešov (37Kč, 40 minutes, twice hourly) – their final destination is usually Pelhřimov or Jihlava. There are also buses to Benešov from Prague's Florenc bus station (44Kč, 40 minutes, eight daily).

The castle is 2km west of Benešov train and bus stations, which are next to each other. Local bus 2 (7Kč, six minutes, hourly) runs from a stop on Dukelská, 400m north of the train station (turn left out of the station, take the first right on Tyršova then the first left) to the castle car park. Otherwise it's a 30-minute walk. Turn left out of the train station, go left across the bridge over the railway, and follow Konopišťská west for 2km. Drivers can go straight down Konopišťská from the bridge.

SÁZAVA
pop 3800

The massive **Sázava monastery** (Sázavský klášter; ☎ 327 321 177; adult/concession 30/15Kč; ☀ 9am-noon & 1-6pm Tue-Sun May-Aug, to 5pm Tue-Sun Sep, to 4pm Sat & Sun Apr & Oct) was founded in the 11th century as a centre of Orthodox Christianity; it was the first place in Bohemia to conduct services in Old Church Slavonic, though the brethren were booted out of Bohemia a few decades later. Rebuilt in the 13th century and defaced by a heavy-handed baroque renova-

tion, it served as a private chateau in the 19th century.

Star of the show is the monastery's **Gothic chapter hall**, rediscovered under whitewash and masonry during excavations in the 1940s, and restored in the 1970s. All the baroque renovations were meticulously scraped away to reveal the original Gothic chamber, complete with fragmentary frescoes.

These ancient elements are really the only reason to drop by on your way to or from Český Šternberk.

While the compulsory tours are in Czech, English-language text is available.

Trains from Čerčany to Český Šternberk (see below) stop at Sázava Černé Budy (34Kč, 40 minutes, six daily). Go behind the station, cross the tracks, descend the hill, cross the Sázava river and make for the monastery church steeple. It's an 800m-walk – a sign by the station that puts it at 4.5km presumably predates the bridge over the river.

ČESKÝ ŠTERNBERK
pop 100

The crumbling grey hulk of 13th-century **Šternberk castle** (☎ 317 855 101; adult/concession 70/40Kč, in English 130/80Kč; ☀ 9am-6pm Tue-Sun Jun-Aug, to 5pm Tue-Sun May & Sep, to 5pm Sat & Sun Apr & Oct) looms above the village of Český Šternberk, hidden away among humpbacked hills and thick pine forest to the southeast of Prague. It succumbed to heavy baroque remodelling in the 17th and 18th centuries, but traces of its darker Gothic personality remain,

---

CANOEING THE SÁZAVA

The Sázava river, which flows from South Moravia to join the Vltava just south of Prague, is one of the country's most popular canoeing rivers. It passes close by Český Šternberk and Sázava, and you can arrange canoeing and rafting trips lasting from one to nine days through **BiSport** (☎ 317 701 460; www.bisport.cz; Janečka 511, Týnec nad Sázavou). Hire of a two-person, plastic touring canoe costs 330/980Kč for one/five days, plus 2700Kč a day for a guide/instructor. A trip from Český Šternberk down to Týnec nad Sázavou (72km), where the best rapids are, takes four days. The going is fairly easy, with nothing graded higher than WW 1–2.

CENTRAL BOHEMIA

lending it all the brooding grandeur of vampire mythology. The scenery on the train journey up the Sázava river valley – deep woods, steep contours and limestone crags – is itself worth the ride.

The castle's interior is bit of a let down after the imposing façade. The rather slow 50-minute tour reveals an Italian baroque renovation, very heavy on the stucco. Highlights include the rococo St Sebastian chapel (kaple sv Šebastiána) and the Yellow room, with sweeping vistas over the countryside. From here you can see the trees marking out a 17th-century French-style park across the river, the only part of a planned Šternberk chateau that was completed before the money ran out.

You can eat at the rustic *vinoteka* (wine shop) below the castle, and there are a couple of unremarkable *pension*s in the village.

Trains between Prague and Benešov (see p153) call at Čerčany, where you change trains for Český Šternberk (get off at Český Šternberk zastávka, one stop after the main Český Šternberk station – it's much closer to the castle). There are around six trains a day between Čerčany and Český Šternberk (46Kč, one to 1½ hours).

LIDICE

When British-trained Czechoslovak paratroops assassinated Reichsprotektor Reinhard Heydrich – the Nazi governor of Bohemia and Moravia – in Prague on 27 May 1942 (see p110), the Nazis took a savage revenge. The Gestapo suspected a link between the assassination and a family living in the village of Lidice (they had a son serving in the Czechoslovak army in Britain), and on 10 June 1942 the Nazis proceeded to erase the village from the face of the earth. All 173 men were rounded up and shot, and all the women were shipped to the Ravensbrück concentration camp. Of 105 children, 82 were gassed in the extermination camp in Chelmno, Poland, and six died in a children's home; only 17 survived, having been farmed out to German foster families or children's homes. The village was systematically burned and bulldozed so that no trace of it remained.

The atrocity electrified the world and triggered a campaign to preserve the village's memory. Ironically, instead of wiping Lidice from the face of the earth, the Nazis' act of vengeance inspired nations around the world to rename towns, suburbs, streets and squares in its honour, from Lidice, Illinois (USA); and Barrio Lidice in Caracas, Venezuela; to Lidice Ave in Tabor, South Dakota (USA); and the Lidice Memorial Rose Garden in Hackney, London (UK).

The village's former site is now occupied by peaceful parkland, eloquent in its silence, fringed with rose gardens and dotted with memorials. The most moving of these is the **children's monument**, a huddled crowd of bronze figures representing the 82 village children who were murdered at Chelmno.

Between the bus stop and the car park is **Lidice museum** (muzeum Lidice; ☎ 312 253 088; www .lidice-memorial.cz; adult/concession 80/40Kč; ◷ 9am-6pm Apr-Sep, 9am-5pm Oct & Mar, 9am-4pm Nov-Feb), which commemorates the village with photographs, artefacts and multimedia displays, and also screens chilling SS film footage of Lidice's destruction.

Lidice is 18km northwest of Prague. Buses from Prague to Lidice (21Kč, 30 minutes, hourly) depart from the bus stop on Evropska, opposite the Hotel Diplomat, just west of Dejvická metro station. *Přímý spoj* (direct services) to Kladno don't stop at Lidice, but anything going via Buštěhrad does.

MĚLNÍK
pop 19,000

The old town of Mělník sits perched atop a rocky promontory overlooking the confluence of the Labe and Vltava rivers, with its Renaissance chateau gazing out across the flatlands of Central Bohemia. It's the focus of Bohemia's modest wine-growing region, and provides the opportunity to indulge in a spot of wine-tasting bacchanalia far from the bustle of Prague.

Staunchly Hussite in its sympathies, the town was flattened by Swedish troops in the Thirty Years' War, but the defensive castle was rebuilt as a prettier, less threatening chateau in the late 17th century, and the old town retains a strong historical identity. Modernity has caught up with the town, bringing a clutch of factories to its outskirts, but the views from the castle side remain untouched.

Orientation

Across Bezručova from the bus station, head uphill (west) on Kapitan Jaroše, which climbs up to the old town (look for the green signs saying 'zámek', which means castle). Continue on ulice 5.května and through the arch beneath the clock tower to reach náměstí Míru, the main square. Svatováclavská, first street on your left, leads to Mělník chateau and the church of SS Peter & Paul.

Information

KB (náměstí Míru 26) Has an ATM and exchange desk.
Tourist information centre (☎ 315 627 503; infocentrum@melnik.cz; náměstí Míru 11; ☑ 9am-5pm May-Sep, Mon-Fri only Oct-Apr) Sells maps and historical guides, and can help with accommodation.

Sights

The town's main attraction is the Renaissance **Mělník chateau** (zámek Mělník; ☎ 315 622 121; adult/concession 70/50Kč; ☑ castle 10am-6pm, wine cellar 10am-5pm), acquired by the Lobkovic family in 1739 and opened to the public in 1990. You can wander through the former living quarters, which are crowded with baroque furniture and 17th- and 18th-century paintings; additional rooms have changing exhibits of modern works and a fabulous collection of 17th-century maps detailing Europe's great cities. A separate tour descends to the 14th-century wine cellars where you can taste the chateau's own wines; a shop in the courtyard sells the chateau's own label.

Next door to the chateau is the 15th-century Gothic **church of SS Peter & Paul** (kostel sv Petra a Pavla), with baroque furnishings and tower. Remnants of its Romanesque predecessor have been incorporated into the rear of the building. The old crypt is now an **ossuary** (adult/child 25/15Kč; ☑ 9.30am-12.30pm & 1.15-4pm Tue-Fri, 10am-12.30pm & 1.15-4pm Sat & Sun), packed with the bones of some 10,000 people dug up to make room for 16th-century plague victims, and arranged in macabre patterns.

The compact old town huddles around **náměstí Míru**, a square lined with pastel-tinted Renaissance and baroque façades, and overlooked by the **Prague gate** (Pražská brána), a medieval gate tower. The ho-hum **Mělník regional museum** (☎ 315 630 922; www.muzeum-melnik.cz; náměstí Míru 54; adult/concession 25/15Kč; ☑ 9am-noon & 1-5pm Tue-Sun) has displays on viticulture, folk architecture and children's toys. The prize for most eccentric exhibit goes to the collection of historical perambulators from 1890 to 1969.

Both Husova and Svatováclavská streets lead southwest from the square to a **terrace** with superb views across the central Bohemian countryside. The steep slopes below the terrace are planted with vines – supposedly descendants of the first vines to be introduced to Bohemia, by Charles IV, back in the 14th century. Off to the left is the junction of the Labe and Vltava rivers; the channel directly in front of you is an early 20th-century ship canal.

Sleeping

Autocamp Mělník (☎ 315 623 856; www.campmelnik.cz; Klášterní 720; car/tent/adult/child 35/85/70/45Kč; **P**) This camping ground is 1km north of the old town and offers basic chalets (from 1260Kč for a double) as well as tent pitches.

Penzión v podzámčí (☎ 315 622 889; www.penzionvpodzamci.cz; Seiferta 167; s/d incl breakfast 650/1300Kč) This reasonably central place (three blocks from náměstí Míru, to the left as you face the chateau) has modest, modern rooms above a Bohemia crystal shop.

Hotel U Rytířů (☎ 315 621 440; www.urytiru.cz; Svatováclavská 17; d 1900-2500Kč) Conveniently located right next to the castle, this opulent little place has plush, spacious, apartment-style rooms with all mod cons. There's also a garden restaurant with mains from 100Kč to 250Kč.

Eating & Drinking

Restaurace sv Václav (☎ 315 622 126; Svatováclavská 22; mains 90-180Kč; ☑ 11am-11pm) Dark wood décor, cigar humidors, red leather seats and an outdoor terrace that's a lunchtime sun-trap conspire to make this one of Mělník's most appealing restaurants.

Kavárna ve Věži (☎ 315 621 954; ulice 5.května; ☑ 8am-10pm Mon-Thu, 8am-11pm Fri, 2-11pm Sat, 2-10pm Sun) Set in the medieval tower of the Prague gate, this atmospheric café and art gallery spreads across three floors linked by creaking wooden stairs. Enjoy the service of an ingenious dumb waiter: write your order on the note pad, ding the bell, and the tray goes down, returning a few moments later with your order. Choose from a wide range of freshly ground coffees and exotic teas, local wines, beer and *medovina* (mead).

The best local white and red wines are both called Ludmila, after the saint and grandmother of St Wenceslas. The best places to taste (and buy) them include the chateau and the **Moravenka Vinoteka** (☎ 315 625 614; Palackého 136), just off náměstí Míru.

Getting There & Away

Mělník is 30km north of Prague. On weekdays buses run to Mělník (38Kč, 40 minutes)

CENTRAL BOHEMIA

every 15 to 30 minutes from stop No 10 in the bus station outside Praha-Holešovice train station; there are less frequent services on weekends (hourly or thereabouts).

AROUND MĚLNÍK
Kokořínsko

The region to the northeast of Mělník is known as the Kokořínsko Protected Landscape Area (CHKO Kokořínsko). It's a fascinating place to explore, with a scenic maze of minor roads, footpaths and cycle trails winding among wooded hills, water meadows and sandstone crags and gorges. Picturesque villages such as Konrádov, Jestřebice, Nosalov and Nedvězí are dotted with pretty 18th- and 19th-century timber cottages, neatly painted in brown and white and sporting traditional fretwork eaves, while the crags are riddled with unusual rock formations, both natural and manmade.

The main sight is the dramatic **Kokořín castle** (hrad Kokořín; ☎ 315 695 064; adult/concession 40/20Kč; ☉ 9am-4pm Tue-Sun May-Sep, 9am-3pm Sat & Sun Apr & Oct), rising in fairy-tale fashion above the forest a kilometre northeast of the village of Kokořín. There are *pension*s and restaurants in Kokořínský Důl, in the valley below the castle, and in the village of Ráj, 4.5km to the northwest.

If you want to explore the back roads and hiking trails, get hold of VKÚ's 1:50,000 map *Mělnicko a Kokořínsko* (sheet No 16). For further information, contact the tourist information centre in Mělník (p155).

Veltrusy

This prim symmetrical chateau 15km southwest of Mělník was built in the early 18th century as a summer retreat for the aristocratic Chotek family. As the Choteks collaborated with the Nazis in WWII, the Czechoslovak government expelled them and seized the chateau for the state. Sadly, the chateau was badly damaged in the 2002 floods, and at the time of research was still not fully open to the public.

However, you can wander through the extensive landscaped grounds, whose beautiful woods are dotted with little follies, including an old mill, artificial ruins and an Egyptian pavilion, complete with a sphinx.

It's not worth a trip from Prague in itself, but makes a good add-on to a day in Mělník (if you have a car).

PŘEROV NAD LABEM

The **Labe river region ethnographic museum** (Polabské národopisné muzeum; ☎ 325 565 272; adult/concession 50/30Kč; ☉ 9am-5pm Tue-Sun May-Oct, last admission 4pm) is the oldest open-air museum of traditional architecture in Bohemia, established in 1895. Its focus is a house, Staročeská chalupa (Old Bohemian cottage), which is from nearby Přerov village and is decorated in herringbone timber cladding and carved ornaments. Other buildings have been brought in piecemeal from around the region – more than a dozen houses, as well as belfries, pigsties and decorated beehives. Staff tend the gardens and raise bees using traditional methods. An English-language brochure is available for 20Kč extra.

The village of Přerov nad Labem is 30km east of Prague, near Čelákovice. Infrequent buses run via Mochov to and from Prague's Černý Most (22Kč, 30 minutes, every one to two hours).

KUTNÁ HORA
pop 21,000

Now dwarfed by 21st-century Prague, Kutná Hora once marched in step with the capital and, with a little help from fate, might even have stolen its crown. Enriched by the silver ore that ran in veins through the surrounding hills, the medieval city was once the financial heart and soul of Bohemia, becoming the seat of Wenceslas II's royal mint in 1308 and the royal residence of Wenceslas IV a century later. The silver *groschen* that were minted here at that time represented the hard currency of Central Europe. But while boom-time Kutná Hora was Prague's undisputed understudy, the town receded from history when the silver mines began to splutter and run dry in the 16th century, a demise hastened by the Thirty Years' War and capped by a devastating fire in 1770. While Prague continued to expand, its sister city sank below the political horizon.

Which is not to say everyone has forgotten about it. Kutná Hora has risen from the ashes of obscurity to become an A-list tourist attraction – it was added to Unesco's World Heritage List in 1996 – luring visitors with a smorgasbord of historic sights and more than a touch of nostalgic whimsy. Standing on the ramparts surrounding the mighty cathedral of St Barbara, looking out across rooftops eerily reminiscent of Prague's Malá Strana, it's all too easy to indulge in a spot of melancholic what-might-have-been.

Orientation

The old town centre is compact enough to explore on foot. Most attractions lie between the central square, Palackého náměstí, and the cathedral of St Barbara in the southwestern corner of town.

The bus station is 500m north of the town centre. Although there's a train station (called Kutná Hora-město) just east of the old town, trains from Prague stop only at Kutná Hora-hlavní nádraží in the suburb of Sedlec, 3km to the northeast.

Information

ČSOB (Husova 108; ☽ 8.30-11.30am & 12.30-5pm Mon & Wed, to 4pm Tue, Thu & Fri) Has an exchange desk and ATM.

Hospital (okresní nemocnice; ☎ 327 503 111; Kouřimská) Located about 1km west of the main square.

Knihkupectví U Stříbrného Groše (Palackého náměstí 91; ☽ 8am-5pm Mon-Fri, 11am-5pm Sat) Has a good selection of hiking maps and town plans.

Post office (Husova 149) Located near the ČSOB.

Tourist information office (informační centrum; ☎ 327 512 378; www.kh.cz; Palackého náměstí 377; ☽ 9am-6pm Apr-Oct; 9am-5pm Mon-Fri, 10am-4pm Sat & Sun Nov-Mar) Arranges accommodation, tours and guides. Also has internet access (1Kč per minute, 15Kč minimum) and rents bicycles.

Sights & Activities

CATHEDRAL OF ST BARBARA

The miners' guilds of Kutná Hora trumped Prague in the cathedral department: their Gothic **cathedral of St Barbara** (chram sv Barbora; ☎ 776 363 938; adult/concession 30/15Kč; ☽ 9am-5.30pm Tue-Sun May-Sep, 10-11.30am & 1-4pm Apr & Oct, 10-11.30am & 2-3.30pm Nov-Mar), dedicated to the patron saint of miners, is one of the finest Gothic churches in Europe and is listed as a Unesco World Heritage Site.

Rivalling Prague's St Vitus cathedral (p89) in size and magnificence, its soaring nave culminates in elegant, six-petalled ribbed vaulting. Work was started in 1380, interrupted during the Hussite Wars and abandoned in 1558 when the silver began to run out. It was finally completed in neo-Gothic style at the end of the 19th century. Inside, eight ambulatory chapels surround the main altar, some with vivid frescoes – including mining scenes – dating from the 15th century. The lofty ceiling vault is covered in a tangle of ribs, stars and floral patterns, and the coats of arms of the miners' guilds and local nobility.

The northwest chapel has an eye-popping mural of the *Vision of St Ignatius*, founder of the Jesuit order.

Take a walk around the outside of the cathedral, too; the terrace at the east end enjoys the finest view in town. At its eastern end is the inconspicuous **Corpus Christi chapel** (kaple Božího těla; adult/concession 20/10Kč; ☽ 9am-6pm Apr-Sep, 10am-5pm Mar & Oct, 10am-4pm Nov-Feb), built in the 14th century. From the viewpoint on its roof you can look across the valley to a rock face in the woods where you will see the giant, carved face of Jaroslav Vrchlický (1853–1912), a famous Czech writer.

Tickets for cathedral and chapel are available from a small information office at the end of Barborská.

CZECH SILVER MUSEUM

The Little castle (Hrádek), originally part of the town's fortifications, was rebuilt in the 15th century as the residence of Jan Smíšek, administrator of the royal mines, who grew rich from silver that he mined illegally right underneath the building. It now houses the excellent **Czech silver museum** (České muzeum stříbra; ☎ 327 512 159; adult/concession 60/30Kč; ☽ 10am-6pm Jul & Aug; 9am-6pm May, Jun & Sep; 9am-5pm Apr & Oct; closed Mon) with exhibits celebrating the mines that made Kutná Hora wealthy, including a huge wooden device once used to lift loads weighing as much as 1000kg from the 200m-deep shafts. You can even don a miner's helmet and lamp and join a 45-minute guided tour (adult/child 110/70Kč) through 500m of **medieval mine shafts** beneath the town. During the summer months it is best to book the underground tour in advance.

ITALIAN COURT

The **Italian court** (Vlašský dvůr; ☎ 327 512 873; Havlíčkovo náměstí 552; adult/concession 80/50Kč; ☽ 9am-6pm Apr-Sep, 10am-5pm Mar & Oct, 10am-4pm Nov-Feb) is the former royal mint; it took its name from the Italian craftsmen (brought in by Wenceslas II to kick-start the business) who began stamping silver coins here in 1300.

The oldest remaining part, the (now bricked-up) niches in the courtyard, were minters' workshops. The original treasury rooms now hold an exhibit on coins and minting. The guided tour (with English text) is worth taking for a look at the few historical rooms open to the public, notably a 15th-century Audience hall with two impressive 19th-century murals,

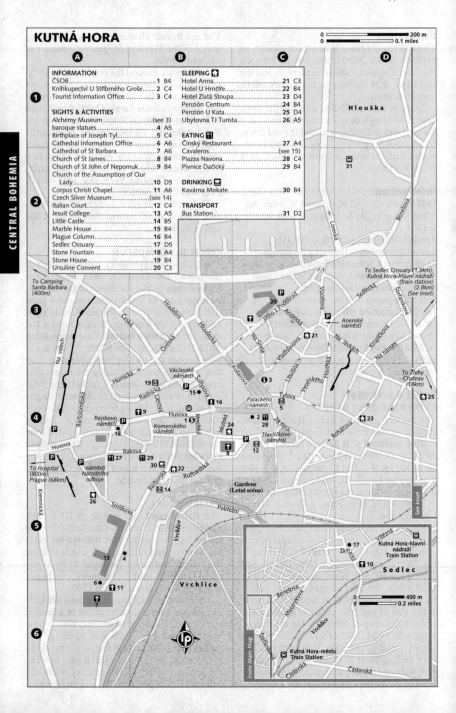

KUTNÁ HORA

0 ━━━━━ 200 m
0 ━━━━━ 0.1 miles

INFORMATION
ČSOB...1 B4
Knihkupectví U Stříbrného Groše....2 C4
Tourist Information Office................3 C4

SIGHTS & ACTIVITIES
Alchemy Museum.........................(see 3)
baroque statues..............................4 A5
Birthplace of Joseph Tyl.................5 C4
Cathedral Information Office...........6 A6
Cathedral of St Barbara..................7 A6
Church of St James..........................8 B4
Church of St John of Nepomuk........9 B4
Church of the Assumption of Our
Lady...10 D5
Corpus Christi Chapel....................11 A6
Czech Silver Museum..................(see 14)
Italian Court.................................12 C4
Jesuit College...............................13 B4
Little Castle..................................14 B5
Marble House................................15 B4
Plague Column..............................16 B4
Sedlec Ossuary.............................17 D5
Stone Fountain.............................18 A4
Stone House..................................19 B4
Ursuline Convent..........................20 C3

SLEEPING
Hotel Anna....................................21 C3
Hotel U Hrnčíře.............................22 B4
Hotel Zlatá Stoupa........................23 D4
Penzión Centrum..........................24 B4
Penzión U Kata.............................25 D4
Ubytovna TJ Turista......................26 A5

EATING
Čínský Restaurant.........................27 A4
Cavaleros...................................(see 15)
Piazza Navona..............................28 C4
Pivnice Dačický............................29 B4

DRINKING
Kavárna Mokate............................30 B4

TRANSPORT
Bus Station...................................31 D2

To Camping
Santa Barbara
(400m)

Hlouška

To Sedlec Ossuary (1.9km);
Kutná Hora-hlavní nádraží
(train station)
(2.8km)
(See inset)

To Žleby
Chateau
(18km)

Václavské
náměstí

Palackého
náměstí

Anenské
náměstí

Husova

Komenského
náměstí

Havlíčkovo
náměstí

To Hospital
(800m);
Prague (68km)

náměstí
Národního
odboje

Gardens
(Letní scéna)

Rejskovo
náměstí

Vrchlice

Kutná Hora-hlavní
nádraží
Train Station

Sedlec

Kutná Hora-město
Train Station

0 ━━━━━ 400 m
0 ━━━━━ 0.2 miles

Joins Main Map

one depicting the election of Vladislav Jagiello as king of Bohemia in 1471 (the angry man in white is Matthias Corvinus, the loser), and the other showing the Decree of Kutná Hora being proclaimed by Wenceslas IV and Jan Hus in 1409.

About all that remains of Wenceslas IV's chapel of SS Wenceslas & Vladislav (kaple sv Václava a Vladislava) is the oriel window, which is best seen from the courtyard, although the 1904 Art Nouveau interior renovation is very striking.

The **galérie Félixe Jeneweina**, just inside the courtyard, has changing art exhibits (same opening hours as the Italian court).

SEDLEC OSSUARY

If you arrive in Kutná Hora by train, a natural first stop is the remarkable **Sedlec ossuary** (Kostnice; ☎ 327 561 143; Zámecká 127; adult/concession 45/30Kč; ☉ 8am-6pm Apr-Sep, 9am-noon & 1-5pm Oct, to 4pm Nov-Mar), just a 10-minute walk south from the main train station.

Sedlec's medieval boom-time was ignited when a 13th-century abbot came back from Jerusalem with a pocketful of earth and sprinkled it on the local monastery's graveyard. The Cistercian monastery, Bohemia's earliest, had been around since 1142, but when the plague struck demand for grave plots skyrocketed. With tens of thousands already buried here, the bones began to pile up and the small 14th-century All Saints' chapel (kaple Všech svatých) was soon pressed into service as an ossuary.

When the Schwarzenberg family purchased Sedlec monastery in 1870 they allowed a local woodcarver named František Rint to get creative with the bones that had been piled in the crypt for centuries. But this was no piddling little heap of bones; it was the remains of no fewer than 40,000 people. The result was spectacular: garlands of skulls and femurs are strung from the vaulted ceiling like Addams Family Christmas decorations, while in the centre dangles a vast chandelier containing at least one of each bone in the human body. Four giant pyramids of stacked bones squat in each of the corner chapels, and crosses, chalices and monstrances of bone adorn the altar. There's a Schwarzenberg coat of arms made from bones, and Rint even signed his name in bones at the foot of the stairs.

A few minutes' walk east of the ossuary, on the main road, is the monastery's **church of**

the Assumption of Our Lady (kostel Nanebevzetí Panny Marie), which was renovated at the beginning of the 18th century by Giovanni Santini in his 'baroque-Gothic' style, unique to Bohemia. Part of Kutná Hora's Unesco World Heritage List, the church was still closed for renovations at time of research.

The ossuary is 2.5km northeast of Kutná Hora's old town and can be reached by local bus (see p161), or a 30-minute walk along Maysarykova and Vítězna streets.

Walking Tour

Begin in Kutná Hora's main square, Palackého náměstí, which is unremarkable except for the **Alchemy museum** (☎ 327 511 259; Palackého náměstí 377; adult/concession 40/25Kč; ☉ 10am-5pm Apr-Oct, 10am-4pm Nov-Mar), complete with basement laboratory, Gothic chapel and mad-scientist curator (enter via the tourist information office).

From the southeast corner of the square, go along 28.řijna and then bear right across the square to reach the **Italian court** (p157). Head west towards the colossal **church of St James** (kostel sv Jakuba), begun in 1330 but only completed a century later. Pass south of the church and you'll find **Ruthardská**, a venerable and photogenic lane running alongside the old town walls. It's named after Rožina Ruthard who, according to local legend, was sealed alive in a closet by her medieval burgher father.

At the far end of the lane is the **Little castle** (Hrádek), which houses the **Czech silver museum** (p157). Turn left along Barborská, past the monolithic façade of the former **Jesuit college** (1700), the biggest in the Czech Republic after Prague's Klementinum (p102). On the left side of the street is a row of 13 **baroque statues** of saints, an arrangement inspired by the statues on Prague's Charles bridge. All are related to the Jesuits and/or the town; check out the second one – the woman holding a chalice, with a stone tower at her side, is St Barbara, the patron saint of miners and therefore of Kutná Hora.

After visiting the **cathedral of St Barbara** (p157), return past the Jesuit college and turn left through náměstí Národního odboje and left again on Husova to see remnants of the **old city walls**. Return along Husova, via Rejskovo náměstí with its 1495 Gothic **Stone fountain** (Kamenná kašna), to the baroque **church of St John of Nepomuk** (kostel sv Jana Nepomuckého; adult/

concession 30/15Kč; ✆ 10am-5pm Apr & Jun-Oct, 9am-5pm May) with its frescoed ceiling depicting the legend of Bohemia's patron saint.

Turn left on Lierova to Radnická. The Gothic confection at No 183 is the **Stone house** (Kamenný dům; ☎ 327 512 821; adult/concession 40/20Kč; ✆ 9am-6pm Tue-Sun May, Jun & Sep, 10am-6pm Jul & Aug, 9am-5pm Apr & Oct), a burgher's house dating from 1490, now home to a museum with exhibits on mining, burgher culture and 17th- to 19th-century life.

East and then south is Šultysova, once part of the town's medieval marketplace, lined with handsome townhouses, in particular the **Marble house** (dům U Mramorů) at No 173. At the bottom of the street is a 1715 **plague column**.

Cross Palackého náměstí and walk down Tylova to No 507, the **birthplace of Josef Tyl** (Tyluv dům; ☎ 327 511 504; adult/concession 10/5Kč; ✆ 10am-6pm Tue-Sat Apr-Oct), the 19th-century playwright who wrote *Kde domov můj?* (Where Is My Home?), which became part of the Czech national anthem.

Cross the square again to Kollárova and turn right on Jiřího z Poděbrad. Two blocks down is the former **Ursuline convent** (klášter Voršilek), with a 1743 chapel by Kilian Dientzenhofer.

Sleeping

Camping Santa Barbara (☎ 327 512 051; santabarbara .cam@worldonline.cz; Česká ulice; tent per person 70Kč; P) The nearest camp site is northwest of town off Česká, near the *hřbitov* (cemetery).

Ubytovna TJ Turista (☎ 327 512 960; náměstí Národního odboje 56; dm 160Kč; P) This attractive, central hostel has four-bed dorms. It gets very busy and reception opens erratically – book ahead.

Penzión U Kata (☎ 327 515 096; www.ukata.cz; Uhelná 596; s/d from 450/600Kč; P) This quiet, back-street *pension* offers basic but comfortable rooms, all with private bathrooms.

Hotel U Hrnčíře (☎ 327 512 113; hotel.hrncir@tiscali.cz; Barborská 24; d 750-2000Kč) This beautifully ornate pink townhouse has five stylish double rooms (rate depends on season and facilities) and a delightful garden terrace out back.

Hotel Anna (☎ 327 516 315; hotel.anna@seznam .cz; Vladislavova 372; s/d 730/1150Kč; P) This pleasant, family hotel offers comfortable, modern rooms with shower, TV and breakfast in a lovely old building with an atmospheric stone-vaulted cellar restaurant.

Penzión Centrum (☎ 327 514 218; www.centrum .penzion.cz; Jakubská 57; d/tr 1000/1400Kč; P) Tucked away in a quiet, flower-bedecked courtyard off the main drag, this place offers snug rooms and a sunny garden.

Hotel Zlatá Stoupa (☎ 327 511 540; zlatastoupa@iol .cz; Tylova 426; s/d from 1220/1980Kč; P) If you feel like spoiling yourself, the most luxurious place in town is the elegantly furnished 'Golden Mount', set on a quiet back street with secure parking. You've got to like a hotel whose minibars contains full-size bottles of wine.

Eating & Drinking

Pivnice Dačický (☎ 327 512 248; Rakova 8; mains 60-100Kč; ✆ 11am-midnight) Get some froth on your moustache at this old-fashioned, wood-panelled Bohemian beer hall, where you can dine on dumplings and choose from five different draught beers, including Hoegaarden.

Čínský Restaurant (☎ 327 514 151; náměstí Národního odboje 48; mains 90-200Kč; ✆ 11am-10pm Tue-Sat, 11am-2.30pm Sun) Set in a plush old house with a garden out back, the imaginatively named 'Chinese' is a little heavy on the MSG but still manages a tasty chicken *kung-po*.

Piazza Navona (☎ 327 512 588; Palackého náměstí 90; mains 100-130Kč; ✆ 9am-midnight May-Sep, 9am-8pm Oct-Apr) Fill up on pizza at this homely Italian café-bar, plastered with Ferrari flags and Inter Milan pennants. Tables spill onto the main square in summer.

Cavaleros (☎ 327 513 810; Šultysova 173; mains 100-200Kč; ✆ 11am-11pm Mon-Sat, 11am-1pm Sun) This lively (but smoky) Mexican restaurant in the Marble house may not win a golden sombrero for authenticity, but it's not bad for Central Bohemia – the salsa is fresh and the *chimichangas* are tasty.

Kavárna Mokate (Barborská 37; ✆ 8am-10pm Mon-Fri, 10am-10pm Sat, 10am-8pm Sun) This cosy little café, with ancient earthenware floor tiles, timber beams, mismatched furniture and oriental rugs dishes up a wide range of freshly ground coffees and exotic teas, as well as iced tea and coffee in summer.

Getting There & Away

Kutná Hora is 65km southeast of Prague. There are direct trains from Prague's Hlavní nádraží (main train station) to Kutná Hora-hlavní nádraží (98Kč, 55 minutes, seven daily). Each has a good connection by local train (10Kč, eight minutes) to Kutná Hora-město station, adjacent to the old town.

There are about six direct buses a day, on weekdays only, from stop No 2 at Prague's

Florenc bus station to Kutná Hora (58Kc, 1¼ hours).

Getting Around

On weekdays local bus 1 runs between the town centre and the main train station (Kutná Hora-hlavní nádraží) every 30 minutes; get off at the Sedlec-Tabak stop (beside a big church) for Sedlec ossuary. On weekends, the route is served by bus 7 (every one to two hours). Buy your ticket (9Kč) from the driver. A taxi from the station into town costs around 80Kč.

AROUND KUTNÁ HORA
Žleby Chateau

Dating from around 1289, the first castle to stand here was flattened by the Hussites during the wars of the early 15th century. Žleby has since worn a variety of architectural faces, acquiring its latest romanticist look between 1849 and 1868 at the behest of its then owner, Karel Vincent Auersperg. Typically chocolate box in appearance, modern-day Žleby sports all the required fairy-tale accoutrements, from pastel décor to gleaming spires.

The Auerspergs lived here until 1945, when they fled to Austria, leaving everything behind. **Žleby chateau** (☎ 327 398 121; ⊗ 9am-5pm Tue-Sun Jul & Aug, 9am-4pm Tue-Sun Sep, 8am-4pm Tue-Sun May & Jun, 9am-3pm Sat & Sun Apr & Oct) is therefore in

immaculate – and authentic – shape, offering a glimpse of how the other half lived in Czechoslovakia in the early 20th century.

Inside it's all armour and mounted firearms, wood panelling and leather wallpaper, rococo flourishes and a treasure trove of old furniture. Highlights include the Knights' hall, with a huge baroque cupboard and rows of Czech and German glass; the Duchess study, with a replica Rubens on the ceiling and a fantastic door of inlaid wood; and the kitchen, fitted out with the 19th-century's most up-to-date equipment.

There are two tours: Tour 1 (adult/concession 80/40Kč, or 120/60Kč with an English-speaking guide) takes in the romanticist interior, including the Knights' hall, Duchess study and the library, while Tour 2 (100/50Kč, or 160/80Kč with an English-speaking guide) visits the kitchens, the chapel and the Great tower, with sweeping views of the surrounding area.

GETTING THERE & AWAY

The chateau is accessible from Kutná Hora by bus (40Kč, 45 minutes to 1½ hours). There are only two morning services, on weekdays only, changing at Čáslav. Get off at Žleby náměstí, the square at the foot of the chateau. Check return times, as the last bus returns around 4.45pm.

CENTRAL BOHEMIA

South Bohemia

For many travellers, the lakes, forests and fields of South Bohemia whiz by in a cinematic scroll from the window of a bus from Prague to Český Krumlov. And while the region's pampered main attraction will steal your heart, be ready to share your devotion with busloads of other suitors. Stroll the medieval maze of Český Krumlov, but also seek out tranquillity and history elsewhere in South Bohemia.

High in the forests of the Šumava mountains, hiking and mountain biking tracks link comfortable *pensions* and alpine lodges where hush comes as standard. Near the Austrian border, the melancholy serenity of Slavonice almost demands you whisper. And when things get too relaxed, head to the whisper-free beer halls of České Budějovice. Don't expect tranquillity though, but remember it's not good to drink on your own anyway.

After a few beers with the locals, bring history to life in the chateaux dotting every corner of the region, from the delicate lakeside confection at Červená Lhota, to the imposing architectural diversity of Jindřichův Hradec. Enduring traces of Austrian and German culture linger, blending with the legacy of earlier eras. Get pleasantly lost amidst the narrow lanes radiating from the photogenic main square of Tábor, the imposing bastion of the unyielding Hussites, or take a leisurely boat cruise to discover the spectacular twin castles of Zvíkov and Orlik.

All the while, give yourself a round of applause and a glass of Budvar lager for not settling for that hurried day trip from Český Krumlov. This spectacular and idiosyncratic region demands much more of your attention.

HIGHLIGHTS

- Climb the castle tower in **Český Krumlov** (p172) for stunning views of Central Europe's prettiest town
- Bring history to life in the former Hussite bastion of **Tábor** (p190)
- Immerse yourself in the hushed Renaissance perfection of **Slavonice** (p198)
- Overcome castle overkill by getting active in the stunning landscapes of the **Šumava** (p178) mountains
- Imbibe the original Budweiser beer in **České Budějovice** (p164), an energetic blue-collar brewery town

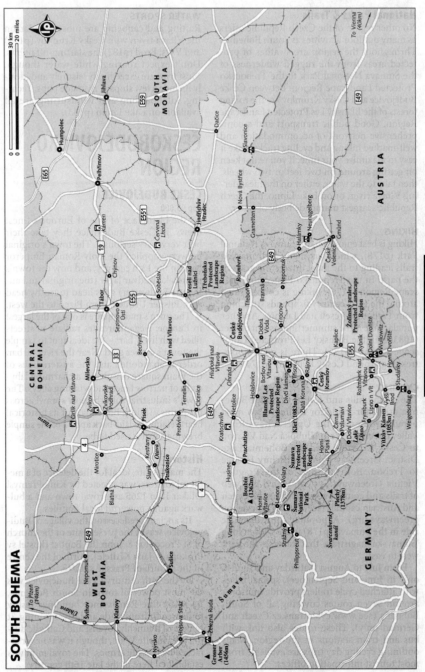

SOUTH BOHEMIA

National Parks & Trails

No other region of the Czech Republic offers as many outdoor activities as South Bohemia. Throughout the region are swathes of protected areas from the rugged wilderness of the Šumava National Park to the Třeboňsko Protected Landscape Region. Between České Budějovice and Český Krumlov are the rolling forests of the Blanský Les Protected Landscape Region. Good public transport and a comprehensive network of accommodation and well-marked hiking and cycling tracks make it easy to maximise your time. If you're not keen on getting around on two feet or two wheels, then take to the water, either on the meandering Vltava river, or on Lake Lipno, the Czech Republic's largest manmade body of water.

HIKING

Hiking is best enjoyed in the Šumava National Park (p178), which has many well-marked trails leading to the most interesting areas of the park. In the Třeboňsko Protected Landscape Region (p176), hiking is concentrated around the 15th-century fishponds stretching from Třebon to Veselí nad Lužnicí. Another popular hike is the summertime ascent of Kleť (1083m) in the Blanský Les Protected Landscape Region (p175). There is good horse-trekking around Český Krumlov (p174).

CYCLING

The rolling hills and forests of South Bohemia are tailor-made for cycling. Two most popular routes are the Upper Vltava River Valley Greenway from Hluboká Nad Vltavou to Český Krumlov, and the Bohemia Lake District Greenway from Jindřichův Hradec to Třebon. Both are part of the Prague–Vienna Greenways System, which is a web of trails and country roads joining the Czech and Austrian capitals (see www.praguevienna greenways.org). A popular long distance ride in the Šumava (p178) is the 240km long 'Šumavská magistrála' that traverses the park west to east.

From July to August (Saturday and Sunday only in June and September), special buses with attached cycle trailers provide transport around seven routes covering all of South Bohemia (see www.cyklotrans.cz Czech and German only). These routes also link with bus and train stations in the region. Maps outlining cycling day trips are available from most tourist information offices.

WATER SPORTS

Rafting and canoeing are most popular on the Vltava river, with Český Krumlov (p173) and Vyšší Brod (p182) the starting-off points. Don't expect roaring white-water though. Most trips are exceedingly leisurely and ideally include a few stops at riverside pubs. Yachting, kiteboarding and windsurfing are all available on Lake Lipno (p183).

ČESKOBUDĚJOVICKO REGION

ČESKÉ BUDĚJOVICE

pop 95,000

As the birthplace of one of Europe's finest brews, in České Budějovice they take their beer very, very seriously. The town's original brewery supplied the Holy Roman Emperor back in the 13th century, and now the town's namesake Budvar lager (the original and authentic Budweiser) goes head to frothy head with Pilsner Urquell, from Plzeň to the west.

The town's main square is one of the largest in Europe; elegant arcades radiate to streets filled with lively bars – the ideal spot to sample the town's amber gold. Near the river, urban order is abandoned and the austere lines of the main square dissolve in a charming labyrinth of narrow lanes and winding alleys. The town's industrial suburbs now sprawl across the plains of South Bohemia, but its historical heart retains the laid-back appeal of the simple brewing town it used to be.

History

The marshy site, ideal for the defence of a medieval fortress, was selected by King Přemysl Otakar II in 1265 as a royal town and a bulwark against powerful local families.

Its ancient predecessor, the village of Budivojovice, was at the present site of the church of St Procopius & John the Baptist (kostel sv Prokopa sv Jana Křtitele), north of the centre in the suburb of Pražské sídliště.

By the 14th century České Budějovice was the most powerful town in South Bohemia. Its many fine Renaissance buildings testify to its wealth from trade and silver mining. It remained staunchly royalist and Catholic during the Hussite Wars, though it was never attacked by Hussite armies. The royal mint was established here in the late 16th century.

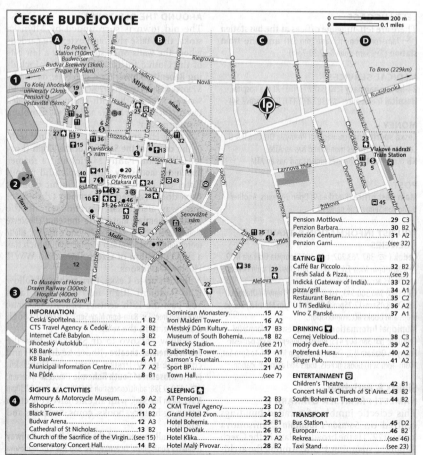

ČESKÉ BUDĚJOVICE

INFORMATION	
Česká Spořitelna.................................1	B2
CTS Travel Agency & Čedok...............2	B2
Internet Café Babylon.......................3	B2
Jihočeský Autoklub............................4	C2
KB Bank...5	D2
KB Bank...6	A1
Municipal Information Centre...........7	A2
Na Půdě..8	B1

SIGHTS & ACTIVITIES	
Armoury & Motorcycle Museum...........9	A2
Bishopric...10	A2
Black Tower.....................................11	B2
Budvar Arena...................................12	A3
Cathedral of St Nicholas..................13	B2
Church of the Sacrifice of the Virgin...(see 15)	
Conservatory Concert Hall...............14	B2
Dominican Monastery......................15	A2
Iron Maiden Tower...........................16	A2
Mestský Dům Kultury.......................17	B3
Museum of South Bohemia..............18	B2
Plavecký Stadion.........................(see 21)	
Rabenštejn Tower............................19	A1
Samson's Fountain...........................20	B2
Sport BP...21	A2
Town Hall....................................(see 7)	

SLEEPING	
AT Pension......................................22	B3
CKM Travel Agency.........................23	D2
Grand Hotel Zvon............................24	B2
Hotel Bohemia................................25	B1
Hotel Dvořak...................................26	B2
Hotel Klika.......................................27	A2
Hotel Malý Pivovar.........................28	B2
Pension Mottlová.............................29	C3
Penzion Barbara..............................30	B2
Penzion Centrum.............................31	A2
Penzion Garni.............................(see 32)	

EATING	
Caffé Bar Piccolo.............................32	B2
Fresh Salad & Pizza.....................(see 9)	
Indická (Gateway of India)............33	D2
pizza/grill..34	A2
Restaurant Beran.............................35	C2
U Tří Sedláku...................................36	A2
Víno Z Panské.................................37	A1

DRINKING	
Cernej Velbloud...............................38	C3
modrý dveře.....................................39	A2
Potrefená Husa................................40	A2
Singer Pub.......................................41	A2

ENTERTAINMENT	
Children's Theatre............................42	B1
Concert Hall & Church of St Anne...43	B2
South Bohemian Theatre.................44	B2

TRANSPORT	
Bus Station......................................45	D2
Europcar..46	B2
Rekrea..(see 46)	
Taxi Stand..................................(see 23)	

Prosperity continued until the Thirty Years' War, when a disastrous fire (in 1641) destroyed half the town. The silver also began to run out and the royal mint was closed.

České Budějovice only began to recover with the establishment of a major school in 1762 and a bishopric in 1785. Industry arrived when the first railway train on the continent travelled from here to Linz, Austria, in 1832.

After WWI the southern part of South Bohemia was given to Czechoslovakia, although more than half its population was German. Though Germans and Czechs had coexisted peacefully for centuries, after WWII all Germans were expelled from České Budějovice in 1945.

Orientation

From the adjacent bus and train stations, it's 1km along Lannova třída to the town centre. Parking is cheaper outside the old town.

Information
EMERGENCY

Jihočeský autoklub (☎ 386 356 566; Žižkova třída 13) Offers motoring assistance.

Police station (☎ 974 221 111; Pražská 5) Has a section for foreigners.

INTERNET ACCESS

Both charge 60Kč per hour:
Internet Café Babylon (5th fl, náměstí Přemysla Otakara II 30; ☷ 10am-10pm Mon-Sat, 1-9pm Sun)
Na Půdě (Krajinská 28; ☷ 8am-10pm)

LEFT LUGGAGE

There are left-luggage offices at the **bus station** (☒ 7am-7pm Mon-Fri, 7am-2pm Sat) and the **train station** (☒ 5am-noon & 12.30-7pm).

MEDICAL SERVICES

24-hour pharmacy (☎ 387 873 103) At the hospital.
Hospital (nemocnice; ☎ 387 871 111; B. Němcové 54)

MONEY

Česká spořitelna (cnr náměstí Přemysla Otakara II & U Černé věže') Changes money and has an ATM.
KB (Krajinská 19) Changes money and has an ATM.

POST

Main post office (Pražská 69) Open 24 hours. Another branch on Senovážné náměstí.

TOURIST INFORMATION & TRAVEL AGENCIES

Čedok (☎ 387 763 202; náměstí Přemysla Otakara II 39; ☒ 9am-6pm Mon-Fri, to noon Sat) Bus and train tickets and books accommodation.
CTS (☎ 386 360 543; 1st fl, náměstí Přemysla Otakara II 38; ☒ 8.45am-12.15pm & 12.45-4.30pm Mon-Fri) Stocks maps and books accommodation.
Municipal Information Centre (Městské Informarční Centrum; ☎ 386 801 413; www.c-budejovice.cz; náměstí Přemysla Otakara II 2; ☒ 8.30am-6pm Mon-Fri, to 5pm Sat, 10am-4pm Sun) Books tickets, tours and accommodation.

Sights & Activities

NÁMĚSTÍ PŘEMYSLA OTAKARA II

This eclectic jumble of arcaded buildings centred on **Samson's fountain** (Samsonova kašna; 1727) is the broadest plaza in the Czech Republic, spanning 133m. Among the architectural treats is the 1555 Renaissance **town hall** (radnice), which received a baroque face-lift in 1731 from AE Martinelli. The allegorical figures on the balustrade – Justice, Wisdom, Courage and Prudence – are matched by an exotic quartet of bronze gargoyles.

Off the square on U Černé věže is the dominating, 72m Gothic-Renaissance **Black tower** (Černé věž; ☎ 386 352 508; adult/concession 25/15Kč; ☒ 10am-6pm Tue-Sun Apr-Oct), built in 1553. Climb its 225 steps (yes, we counted them) for fine views. The tower's two bells – the Marta (1723) and Budvar (1995; a gift from the brewery) – are rung daily at noon.

Beside the tower is the **cathedral of St Nicholas** (katedrála sv Mikuláše), built as a church in the 13th century, rebuilt in 1649 and made a cathedral in 1784.

AROUND THE OLD TOWN

The old town is surrounded by Mlýnská stoka, the Malše river and extensive gardens where the walls once stood. Only a few bits of the Gothic fortifications remain, including **Rabenštejn tower** (Rabenštejnská věž; cnr Hradební & Panská; adult/concession 40/20Kč; ☒ 10am-6pm Mon-Fri, 9am-noon Sat), and the 15th-century **Iron Maiden tower** (Železná pana; Zátkovo nábřeží), a crumbling former prison.

Along Hroznová, on Piaristické náměstí, is the **church of the Sacrifice of the Virgin** (kostel Obětování Panny Marie) and a former **Dominican monastery** with a splendid pulpit. Enter the church from the Gothic cloister. Next door is a medieval **armoury** (zbrojnice) that was also a salt warehouse; and the **South Bohemian Motorcycle museum** (Jihočeské Motocyclové; ☎ 723 247 104; Piaristické náměstí; adult/concession 40/20Kč; ☒ 10am-6pm Tue-Sun), which has a fine collection of Czech Jawas and WWII Harley-Davidsons.

Return up to Česká, turn right and follow it to Radniční. Right into Biskupská takes you past the 18th-century **bishopric** (biskupství; admission free; ☒ 8am-6pm May-Sep). Enter through a small gate in the wall.

Follow Zátkovo to dr Stejskala. Pass the **South Bohemian theatre** (Jihočeské divadlo) and continue to JV Jirsíka. Right into Dukelská, is the **museum of South Bohemia** (Jihočeské muzeum; ☎ 387 929 328; adult/concession 50/20Kč; ☒ 9am-12.30pm & 1-5.30pm Tue-Sun), with an extensive collection covering history, books, coins, weapons and wildlife.

A small **museum of the Horse-Drawn Railway** (Památky koněspřežní železnice; ☎ 386 354 820; Mánesova 10; ☒ 9am-12.30pm & 1-5pm Tue-Sun) is south of the centre, near the Koh-i-noor factory – only for horsey types and/or railway buffs.

BUDVAR BREWERY

Touring the modern **Budvar brewery** (pivovar; ☎ 387 705 341; www.budweiser.cz; cnr Pražská & K Světlé; adult/concession 100/50Kč; ☒ 9am-4pm) with all its sights, smells and science is less interesting than product sampling in the city's beer halls. Nevertheless, a pilgrimage to the home of Budvar, 3km north of the city (take bus 2), is still mandatory. Book the 60-minute tour in advance by phoning the brewery, or through the tourist information office. Ask for the English language tour.

Afterwards put your feet up in the attached **Budvar beer hall** (☒ 10am-10pm).

SOUTH BOHEMIA

Sleeping

Accommodation can get tight in July and August, so book in advance. Prices fluctuate seasonally – these are high (summer) season rates. In the low season discounts can be as much as 25%.

BUDGET
Hostels

The **municipal information centre** (Městské Informarční Centrum; ☎ 386 801 413; www.c-bude jovice.cz; náměstí Přemysla Otakara II 2; ☷ 8.30am-6pm Mon-Fri, to 5pm Sat, 10am-4pm Sun) and **CKM Travel Agency** (☎ 387 424 505; Lannova třída 63; ☷ 9am-5pm Mon-Fri), near the train station, can arrange accommodation in dormitories from 150Kč per person. All the listed tourist offices can book private rooms for about 300Kč.

Pension U výstaviště (☎ 387 240 148; trpakdl@email .cz; U výzstaviště 17; r per person 270Kč; ⓟ) The closest thing to a travellers hostel, this student accommodation block is 30 minutes west of the city centre on bus 1 (board outside the bus station). Go to the stop (U parku), and the *pension* is 100m along Čajkovského, on the right.

Kolej jihočeské univerzity (☎ 387 774 201; Studentská 13-19; d 440Kč; ☷ Jul-Sep; ⓟ) Another student block, 2km west of the centre.

Pension Mottlová (☎ 386 357 135; Alešova 5; s/d 350/700Kč) In a quiet street you'll get a warm welcome from both the hosts and their cocker spaniel. Shared bathrooms only.

Camping

Stromovka Autocamp (☎ 387 203 597; tent/3-bed bungalow 60/600Kč; ☷ Apr-Oct; ⓟ) Just past Dlouhá Louka Autocamp, this has so-so bungalows and ample tent space. Queues for the showers can be long.

Motel Dlouhá Louka Autocamp (☎ 387 203 601; www.dlouhalouka.cz; Stromovka 8; tent/s/d 65/600/1000Kč; ⓟ) This motel and camp site is 2km southwest of town (take bus 6 from in front of Městský dům kultury). Camp from May to September, or take a rather uninspiring motel room year-round.

MIDRANGE

Small private *pension*s are often a better deal than hotels.

AT Pension (☎ 603 441 069; www.atpension.cz; Dukelská 15; s/d incl breakfast 550/900Kč; ⓟ) Don't hold your breath for stunning (or even late-20th-century) décor, but this convenient spot is mighty friendly with mighty big breakfasts.

Penzión Centrum (☎ 387 311 801; www.penzion centrum.cz; Biskupská 130/3; s/d incl breakfast 900/1200Kč) Huge rooms with satellite TV, queen-size beds with crisp white linen, and thoroughly professional staff all make this a top reader-recommended spot near the main square.

Hotel Bohemia (☎ 386 354 500; www.bohemiacb.cz; Hradebni 20; s/d incl breakfast 1490/1790Kč; ⓟ) Carved wooden doors open to a restful interior in two old burghers' houses in a quiet street. The restaurant comes recommended by the tourist information office.

Other recommendations:

Penzion Barbara (☎ 736 426 472; www.penzion barbara.cz; Siroká 15; s/d 500/1000Kč) A newish spot with light and bright rooms above a cosy kavárna. Look for the letters 'BB' on top of the building.

Penzion Garni (☎ 386 353 475; www.budweb.cz /penzion-garni; Na Mlýnské stoce 7; s/d incl breakfast 800/950Kč; ⓟ) Located on quiet Mill Race Lane, the Garni shares a building with Caffé Piccolo, a terrific spot for espresso and hot chocolate.

TOP END

Hotel Klika (☎ 387 318 171; www.hotelklika.cz; Hroznová 25; s/d incl breakfast 1630/2300Kč) A riverside location sometimes let down by off-hand service, but the modern rooms are light and airy, and anywhere that integrates 14th-century walls into their design is OK by us.

Hotel Malý Pivovar (☎ 386 360 471; www.maly pivovar.cz; Karla IV 8-10; s/d incl breakfast 2300/3300Kč; ⓟ ✗ 🐾) With a cabinet of sports trophies and sculptured leather sofas, the lobby resembles a gentleman's club. However the elegant rooms will please both the men and the ladies, and it's just a short stroll to the cosy Budvarka beer hall downstairs.

Hotel Dvořak (☎ 386 253 140; dvorakcb@genea 2000.cz; náměstí Přemysla Otakara II 36; s/d incl breakfast 2400/2900Kč; ✗ 🐾) Don't be fooled by the elegant façade: the Dvořak's rooms are modern and clean but lacking in character. The friendly staff and good-value last-minute specials (up to 40% off) still make this a worthwhile standby.

Grand Hotel Zvon (☎ 387 311 384; www.hotel.zvon .cz; náměstí Přemysla Otakara II 28; s/d 2500/3000Kč; ✗ 🐾) 'Since 1533' says the sign but we're sure the city's top hotel has been renovated since then. The ritzy façade across three main square buildings is let down by the standard rooms, but the executive rooms (add a whopping 80% to listed prices) would be classy in any town.

Eating

CAFÉS

Fresh Salad & Pizza (Hroznová 21; pizza 100Kč & salads 60Kč) Have a healthy lunch at this spot near the Motorcycle museum. Add extra horsepower to your jerk chicken or couscous and salmon salads with one of eight different dressings.

Caffé Bar Piccolo (Na Mlýnské stoce 9; ☉ 7.30am-7pm Mon-Thu, 7.30am-10pm Fri & Sat) Down by the old Mill Race this friendly spot serves up bracing coffee and decadent hot chocolate.

RESTAURANTS

Try the local carp from nearby Třeboň.

pizza/grill (Panská 17; pizzas 100Kč; ☉ closed Sun) Just maybe where the phrase 'hole-in-the-wall' came from, pizza/grill fits a wood-fired oven, a vintage espresso machine, and seating for five diners into a tiny space. Grab takeaway *pivo* 'n' pizza and dine *al fresco*.

U Tří Sedláku (☎ 387 222 303; Hroznová 488; mains 100-160Kč) Locals celebrate that nothing much has changed at U Tří Sedláku since it opened in 1897. Tasty meaty dishes go with the Pilsner Urquell constantly being shuffled to busy tables.

Indická (Gateway of India) (☎ 386 359 355; 1st fl, Chelčického 11; mains 100-150Kč; ☉ closed Sun) From Chennai to České comes respite for travellers wanting something different. Request spicy because they're used to dealing with timid Czech palates.

Víno z Panské (☎ 387 318 511; Panská 14; mains 110-170Kč; ☉ closed Sun) If you're feeling all *pivo*'d out, there's a good selection of wines in this relaxed restaurant in the old town's Gothic section. The best wines are only available by the bottle so bring some friends.

Restaurant Beran (☎ 386 359 559; Žižkova 3; mains 100-250Kč) Follow the cast-iron goat's head above the door, into the eclectic interior with a 2m-tall model of the Leaning Tower of Pisa. Beran is very popular with locals who jam-pack this cellar bar/restaurant for Czech, Italian and Mexican food.

Drinking

PUBS

Singer Pub (Česká 55) With Czech and Irish beers, and potent cocktails, don't be surprised if you get the urge to rustle up something on the Singer sewing machines on every table. If not, challenge the regulars to a game of *foosball* with a soundtrack of nicely noisy rock.

Potrefená Husa (Česká 66) CB's bright young things come out to play at this spot owned by Prague's Staropramen brewery. With tasty bar snacks, Belgian beers, and a summer terrace overlooking the water, the burghers of Budvar might be a tad concerned at the enemy in their midst.

CLUBS

Černej velbloud (☎ 728 725 419; www.velbloud.info; U tří lvů 4; ☉ 10am-midnight Mon-Fri, 3pm-midnight Sat & Sun) One half is a cruisy *kavárna* with occasional live music and eclectic snacks, and the other half a camel-bedecked (*velbloud* means 'camel') unpretentious venue with lots of interesting sounds. In any week you'll hear anything from old-school ska to drum 'n' bass.

modrý dveře (☎ 386 359 958; Biskupská 1; ☉ 10am-midnight) By day, modrý dveře is a welcoming bar/café with vintage pictures of US singer and Rat Pack member, Frank Sinatra. At dusk the lights dim for regular jazz piano gigs on Wednesdays (from 7pm) and live blues and jazz on Thursdays (from 8pm). Tell them Frank sent you.

Entertainment

DRAMA, CLASSICAL MUSIC & CINEMA

South Bohemian theatre (Jihočeské divadlo; ☎ 386 356 643; www.jihoceskedivadlo.cz; dr Stejskala 23) The city's main theatre presents plays (usually in Czech), operas and concerts.

Children's theatre (Malé divadlo; ☎ 386 352 508; Hradební 18) Puppets and pantomime.

Chamber Philharmonic Orchestra of South Bohemia (☎ 386 353 561; www.music-cb.cz; Kněžská 6) Performances take place in the church of St Anne.

Conservatory (konzervatoř; ☎ 386 110 410; Kanovnická 22) This Stalinist shoebox hosts classical music performances.

Cinestar (☎ 385 799 999; www.cinestar.cz in Czech; Obchidní Centrum Čtyři Dvory) One kilometre west of the centre, this multiplex shows Hollywood's latest (90Kč).

SPORT

Budvar Arena (☎ 386 107 111; www.hokejcb.cz; FA Gerstnera; ☉ Sep-Apr) Ice hockey matches are staged here. Contact the tourist information office for details.

Plavecký Stadion (☎ 387 315 784; ☉ 10am-8pm) This sports hall has swimming pools and saunas open to the public.

SOUTH BOHEMIA

Getting There & Away

BUS

From České Budějovice, direct buses (☎ 386 354 444) go to Prague Roztyly (142Kč, three hours), Jihlava (90Kč, 2½ hours), Tábor (56Kč, one hour) and Český Krumlov (28Kč, 50 minutes).

TRAIN

There are fast, direct trains (☎ 387 854 361) to Plzeň (162Kč, two hours), Tábor (88Kč, one hour), Prague (204Kč, 2½ hours) and Jihlava (162Kč, 2½ hours).

Twice a day there are trains to and from Linz, Austria (2¼ hours, 125km). Three times daily trains go to Linz with a change at the border stations (Horní Dvořiště and Summerau).

Trains between Prague and Vienna connect at České Velenice, 50km southeast of České Budějovice. Two daily trains run to and from Vienna (Franz-Josefsbahnhof) with a change in Gmünd.

Getting Around

The city is well connected by bus (8Kč). The main **taxi stand** (☎ 800 141 516; Lannova 1) is by the train station.

To rent a car, see **Čedok** or **Europcar/Rekrea** (☎ 387 312 290; Široká 12; ⏱ 9am-4.30pm Mon-Fri).

Bikes (230Kč per day), rafts (650Kč per day) and canoes (180Kč per day) can be hired at **Sport BP** (☎ 387 318 439; Sokolovsky ostrov 1; ⏱ 9am-noon & 1-6pm Mon-Fri, to 11.30am Sat). Expect to pay a 1500Kč deposit.

SHOCart GeoClub's *Českobudějovicko* (1:75,000) map shows local cycle routes.

AROUND ČESKÉ BUDĚJOVICE

Trocnov

The birthplace of Hussite hero Jan Žižka is 12km southeast of České Budějovice and has a small **museum** (☎ 387 995 235; www.pamatnikjz.cz; adult/concession 30/15Kč; ⏱ 9am-5pm Tue-Sun May-Sep) dedicated to him. From České Budějovice there are at least six daily buses (15Kč, 28 minutes).

Holašovice

South Bohemia is well known for its ornate, 19th-century 'folk baroque' country houses and barns. Some of the best examples are in the tiny village of **Holašovice** (www.holasovice.cz, in Czech), a Unesco World Heritage Site 15km west of České Budějovice.

Traditionally, holidays and festivals were celebrated in the large square complete with a pond and chapel, and each spring maypoles are still erected in many villages to celebrate the end of winter. There are four buses daily from České Budějovice (15Kč, 30 minutes).

Kratochvíle

This attractive Renaissance **chateau** (☎ 388 324 380; tours in Czech/English 60/120Kč; ⏱ 9am-5pm Tue-Sun Jun-Aug, to 4.15pm May & Sep, 9am-4pm Sat & Sun Apr & Oct) was completed in 1589 for the Rožmberk family and is decorated inside with stucco reliefs and murals based on classical mythology. Kratochvíle is also home to an interesting **museum of Animated Film**, with examples from notable Czech producers like Jiří Trnka and Hermína Týrlová.

Take a bus to Netolice from České Budějovice (28Kč, 40 minutes) or Prachatice (20Kč, 25 minutes); walk the remaining 1.5km.

SOUTH BOHEMIA

JAN ŽIŽKA

Hussite Count Jan Žižka was born in Trocnov, just outside České Budějovice, in 1376. He spent his youth at King Wenceslas IV's court and fought as a mercenary in Poland, but returned to the Czech kingdom at the beginning of the Reformation and became the leader of the Taborites (p190). His military genius was responsible for all of the Hussite victories, from the 1420 Battle of Žižkov onwards. After losing both eyes in two separate battles, Žižka eventually died of the plague in 1424.

Žižka's army was highly organised and was the first to use a system of wagons with mounted artillery – the earliest tanks in history. These vehicles allowed him to choose where to draw up position, taking the initiative away from the crusaders and making them fight where he wanted. The technique proved almost invincible.

The Hussites successfully saw off their enemies for a decade following Žižka's death, but were defeated by a combined army of the rival Hussite faction of the Utraquists and the Holy Roman Empire in 1434. Surprisingly, Žižka's invention was not incorporated into other armies until Sweden's King Gustavus II Adolphus adopted it two centuries later.

HLUBOKÁ NAD VLTAVOU

pop 4800

Crowned with a stunning chateau, this little village draws visitors from across the country. Most tourists depart after seeing the castle, making Hluboká a pleasant place to stay if accommodation is tight in České Budějovice.

Information

Česká spořitelna (Masarykovo 38) changes money and has an ATM.

The **tourist information centre** (☎ 387 966 164; www.hluboka.cz; Masarykovo 35; ☼ 9am-6pm) publishes a useful map and has internet access for 1Kč per minute.

Sights

A crow pecking the eyes from a Turk's head, the grisly crest of the Schwarzenberg family, may be the recurrent motif in the décor of the **Hluboká chateau** (☎ 387 843 911; www.zamekhluboka .cz in Czech; ☼ 9am-6pm Jul & Aug, 9am-5pm Tue-Sun May-Jun, 9am-4.30pm Apr, Sep & Oct) but this grisly image is totally at odds with the building's overt romanticism.

Built by the Přemysl rulers in the latter half of the 13th century, Hluboká was taken from the Protestant Malovec family in 1662 for supporting an anti-Hapsburg rebellion, and sold to the Bavarian Schwarzenbergs. Two centuries later, they gave the chateau the English-Tudor, Gothic-style face it wears today, modelling its exterior on Britain's Windsor Castle. Crowned with crenellations and surrounded by a dainty garden, Hluboká is too prissy for some, but this remains the second-most visited chateau in Bohemia after Karlštejn, and for good reason.

There are two tours through the chateau: the **main tour** (adult/concession 80/40Kč, in a foreign language 150/80Kč) passes through the Schwarzenberg's ceremonial chambers, including the private apartments of Duchess Leonora, the ornate reception rooms and the grandiose large dining room with space for 72 guests. A dash through the armoury provides a contrast. The **second tour** (adult/concession 80/50Kč, in a foreign language 150/80Kč) delves into the chateau's unique kitchen, where the families' favourite recipes are still on show.

Unless the chateau is crowded, tours do not run between 12.30pm and 1pm and the last tour commences an hour before closing time. The chateau grounds are open year-round, free of charge.

The exquisite **South Bohemian Aleš gallery** (Alšova jihočeská galérie; ☎ 387 967 041; www.aig.cz; adult/concession 40/20Kč; ☼ 9am-noon & 1-6pm May-Sep, to 4pm Oct-Apr) is to the right of the castle gate, in a former riding school (jízdárna). On display is a fabulous permanent collection of Czech religious art from the 14th to 16th centuries, plus 17th-century Dutch masters and changing exhibits of modern art.

Sleeping & Eating

The tourist information centre can recommend private rooms. Also watch for 'Zimmer frei' or 'privát' signs along Masarykovo.

Autokemping Křivonovska (☎ 387 965 285; tent/bungalow per person 65/220Kč; ☼ May-15 Sep; P) Three kilometres north of Hluboká at Křivonovska, this place includes bungalows.

Pension Kalivoda (☎ 387 965 608; www.kalivoda .info; Nádražní 528; s/d incl breakfast 600/800Kč; P ☐) The friendly Kalivoda is just across the river in the suburb of Zámostí.

Hotel Štekl (☎ 387 967 491; www.bohemiagold.cz; s/d incl breakfast from 3500/3900Kč; P ✗ ☐) Originally part of the castle, the Štekl was converted in 1997 into an opulent hotel where it's now easy to feel like a lord or a lady.

Pizzerie Ionia (☎ 387 963 109; Masarykova 33; pizza 90Kč) Opposite the tourist office, Ionia is generous with their pizza toppings and the amount of red, green and white paint they've splashed on to create a suitably Italian ambience.

Getting There & Away

Buses run from České Budějovice to Hluboká's main square every 30 to 60 minutes (16Kč, 20 minutes).

AROUND HLUBOKÁ

The baroque **Ohrada chateau** (☎ 387 865 340; www .nzm.cz; adult/concession 40/20Kč; ☼ 9am-5.30pm Jul-Aug, 9am-4.30pm Tue-Sun May & Sep, 9am-2pm Tue-Fri to 3.30pm Sat & Sun Apr & Oct) is 2km southwest of Hluboká. A former Schwarzenberg hunting lodge, it's now a museum of hunting and forestry featuring wildlife, hunting trophies and odd furniture made from antlers. A small **zoo** is attached.

Public transport is irregular, but the castle is a pleasant walk from Hluboká.

ČESKÝ KRUMLOV

pop 14,000

Crowned by a spectacular castle, and centred on an elegant old town square, Český Krumlov is a pocket-sized Prague. Renaissance and

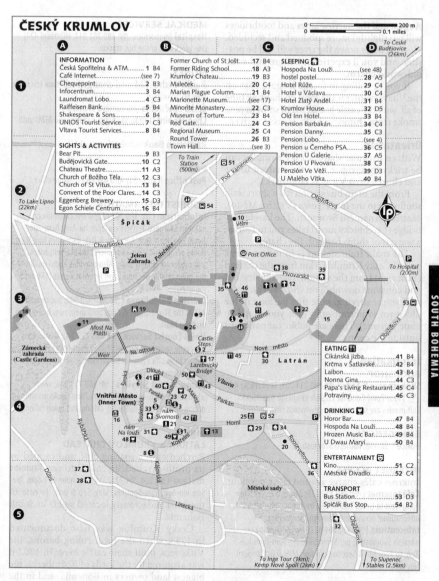

ČESKÝ KRUMLOV

0 ___ 200 m
0 ___ 0.1 miles

INFORMATION
Česká Spořitelna & ATM........ **1** B4
Café Internet........................(see 7)
Chequepoint............................ **2** B3
Infocentrum............................ **3** B4
Laundromat Lobo.................... **4** C3
Raiffeisen Bank....................... **5** B4
Shakespeare & Sons................ **6** B4
UNIOS Tourist Service............ **7** C3
Vltava Tourist Services............ **8** B4

SIGHTS & ACTIVITIES
Bear Pit...................................**9** B3
Budějovická Gate...................**10** C2
Chateau Theatre.....................**11** A3
Church of Božího Těla............**12** C3
Church of St Vitus..................**13** B4
Convent of the Poor Clares.....**14** C3
Eggenberg Brewery.................**15** D3
Egon Schiele Centrum.............**16** B4

Former Church of St Jošt........**17** B4
Former Riding School.............**18** A3
Krumlov Chateau....................**19** B3
Maleček...................................**20** C4
Marian Plague Column............**21** B4
Marionette Museum...........(see 17)
Minorite Monastery.................**22** C3
Museum of Torture..................**23** B4
Red Gate.................................**24** C3
Regional Museum....................**25** C3
Round Tower...........................**26** B3
Town Hall............................(see 3)

SLEEPING
Hospoda Na Louži..............(see 48)
hostel postel...........................**28** A5
Hotel Růže..............................**29** C4
Hotel u Václava......................**30** C4
Hotel Zlatý Anděl....................**31** B4
Krumlov House........................**32** D5
Old Inn Hotel..........................**33** B4
Pension Barbakán....................**34** C4
Pension Danny........................**35** C3
Pension Lobo......................(see 4)
Pension u Černého PSA..........**36** C5
Pension U Galerie...................**37** A5
Pension U Pivovaru.................**38** C3
Penzión Ve Věži......................**39** D3
U Malého Vítka.......................**40** B4

EATING
Cikánská jízba.........................**41** B4
Krčma v Šatlavské..................**42** B4
Laibon....................................**43** B4
Nonna Gina............................**44** C3
Papa's Living Restaurant........**45** C4
Potraviny................................**46** C3

DRINKING
Horor Bar...............................**47** B4
Hospoda Na Louži..................**48** B4
Hrozen Music Bar....................**49** B4
U Dwau Maryí.........................**50** B4

ENTERTAINMENT
Kino.......................................**51** C2
Městské Divadlo.....................**52** C4

TRANSPORT
Bus Station.............................**53** D3
Spičák Bus Stop......................**54** B2

To České Budějovice (26km)

To Train Station (500m)

To Lake Lipno (22km)

Špičák

Chvalšinská

Jelení Zahrada

Pod kamenem

Obižďková

Post Office

Pivovarská

Latrán

Klášterní

To Hospital (200m)

Most Na Plášti

Zámecká zahrada (Castle Gardens)

Weir

Na ostrově

Castle Steps

Nové město

Latrán

SOUTH BOHEMIA

Vnitřní Město (Inner Town)

Dlouhá

Soukenická

Panská

Radniční

Masná

Lazebnický Bridge

Vltava

Parkán

nám Svornosti

Horní

nám Na louži

Kostelní

Roosveltova

Rybářská

Dlní

Kájovská

Linecká

Městské sady

To Inge Tour (1km); Kemp Nové Spolí (2km)

To Slupenec Stables (2.5km)

baroque buildings enclose the meandering arc of the Vltava river, housing riverside cafés and bars. Following architectural neglect during the communist era, the undeniable fairy-tale beauty of Český Krumlov is radiant again, with thoughtful restoration transforming the heritage buildings lining the narrow lanes into cosy restaurants and classy boutique hotels.

After earning a spot on Unesco's World Heritage List in 1992, Český Krumlov has become the Czech Republic's second busiest tourist town after Prague. Visit in summer and it may feel like a theme park, with street performers punctuating every corner, and tour buses overwhelming the car parks. But come a few months either side of July and

August and the narrow lanes and footbridges will be (slightly) more subdued and secluded. Floating lazily down the river will still be possible, and you'll experience a more authentic old-world charm.

If you're willing to forego languid days on the Vltava, winter is the most enchanting time of all, with the castle blanketed in snow as pine smoke from chimneys wafts across the river.

Orientation

With an irregular shape, Český Krumlov can be tricky to navigate. Use the chateau tower and church of St Vitus as landmarks.

From the main bus station it's a short walk southwest to the Inner Town (Vnitřní Město), centred on náměstí Svornosti. The Lazebnický bridge (Lazebnický most) takes you to Latrán, a warren of shops beneath the chateau.

The main train station is in the northern part of Český Krumlov, 1km from the chateau (turn right from the station, take the first left and continue downhill on třída Míru).

If you're driving, note that parking in the old town is permit-only (ask your hotel to issue you one). There are public car parks just outside the centre.

Information

BOOKSHOP

Shakespeare & Sons (☎ 380 711 203; Soukenická 44; ⏰ 11am-7pm) Good for English-language paperbacks. Cult movies are screened in a downstairs cinema (p175).

EMERGENCY

Police (☎ 158; náměstí Svornosti 1)

INTERNET ACCESS

Internet cafés charge around 60Kč per hour.
Café Internet (☎ 380 712 219; Zámek 57; ⏰ 9am-9pm) Next to Unios Tourist Service (right); also offers international phone calls through the internet.
Infocentrum (☎ 380 704 622; www.ckrumlov.cz; náměstí Svornosti 1; per 5 min 5Kč; ⏰ 9am-8pm Jul-Aug, to 7pm Jun & Sep, to 6pm Apr, May & Oct; to 5pm Nov-Mar)

LAUNDRY

Laundromat Lobo (☎ 380 713 153; Latrán 73; 140Kč per load; ⏰ 8am-8pm) Self-serve washing machines and dryers.

LEFT LUGGAGE

Unios Tourist Service (☎ 380 725 110; www.unios.cz; castle courtyard Zámek 57; ⏰ 9am-6pm) Stores baggage for 5Kč per hour per item.

MEDICAL SERVICES

Hospital (nemocnice; ☎ 380 761 911; Hřbitovní 424) One block east of the bus station.

MONEY

Banks with ATM and change facilities include the following:
Česká Spořitelna (cnr náměstí Svornosti)
Chequepoint (Latrán 5) Changes money (no ATM) until late.
Raiffeisen Bank (náměstí Svornosti 15)

POST

Post office (Latrán 81) Also has an exchange office.

TOURIST INFORMATION

Infocentrum (☎ 380 704 622; www.ckrumlov.cz; náměstí Svornosti 1; ⏰ 9am-8pm Jul-Aug, 8am-7pm Jun & Sep, 8am-6pm Apr, May & Oct; 8am-5pm Nov-Mar) Books accommodation and concert tickets, sells maps, and organises guided tours. Also provides audio guides to the town (100Kč per hour) and internet access (5Kč per 5 minutes).
Oldřiška Baloušková (☎ 737 920 901; Soukenická 44) At the Shakespeare & Sons bookshop; runs interesting walking tours.
Unios Tourist Service (☎ 380 725 110; www.unios .cz; castle courtyard Zámek 57; ⏰ 9am-6pm) This private information office provides a similar range of services to Infocentrum.
Vltava Tourist Services (☎ 380 711 988; www .ckvltava.cz; Kájovská 62; ⏰ 9am-7pm) Books accommodation and arranges canoeing, rafting and horse riding.

Sights

LATRÁN & KRUMLOV CHATEAU

Perched atop a soaring cliff, and capped by its proto-psychedelic round tower, **Krumlov chateau** (☎ 380 704 721; ⏰ 9am-noon & 1-6pm Tue-Sun Jun-Aug, 9am-5pm Apr, May, Sep & Oct), is one of the most audaciously located sights in South Bohemia.

Český Krumlov was first documented in 1253, when the local ruling barons, the Vítkovecs, built their castle here. In 1302 it was acquired by the lords of Rožmberks, the biggest land owners in Bohemia, and in the late 16th century Vilém Rožmberk ordered a Renaissance-style makeover. When their line expired it was handed to the Eggenbergs in 1622. The Schwarzenbergs took the castle over in 1719, and owned it until 1945.

Approaching from the south, cross the wooden **Lazebnický bridge** (Lazebnický most) and climb to the courtyard via the **Chateau** steps (Zámecké schody). A more traditional approach is from the north via the **Budějovická gate** (Budějovická brána; 1598); pass the post office and go through the Red gate (Červená brána) into the chateau's first courtyard.

Below the entrance bridge are two brown (and pretty unhappy) bears, traditional residents since the 16th century. Through a passageway is the second courtyard, with the ticket office. Here you can climb the multi-hued **round tower** (válcová věž; adult/concession 30/20Kč; ☺ 9am-5.30pm Tue-Sun Jun-Aug, 9am-4.30pm Apr & Oct, 9.30am-3.30pm Apr & Oct), painted in 1590 by Bartholomew Beránek. Another passageway leads into courtyards three and four, their walls covered in trompe l'oeil painting.

There are three tours: **Tour I** (adult/concession 90/45Kč, in a foreign language 150/75Kč) takes in the opulent Renaissance rooms, including the chapel, baroque suite, picture gallery and masquerade hall, while **Tour II** (adult/concession 70/40Kč, in a foreign language 140/70Kč) covers the Schwarzenberg portrait gallery and more sedate 19th-century interiors.

Just across the bridge behind the chateau is the rococo **Chateau theatre** (Zámecké divadlo), which can only be seen on **Tour III** (adult/concession 100/50Kč, in a foreign language 170/90Kč; ☺ 10-11am & 1-4pm Tue-Sun May-Oct). This amazing theatre is one of the only two left in the world that still has all its original decorated stage set and working wooden machinery. Behind the theatre, a ramp to the right leads up to the former Riding school (Zámecká jízdárna), now a restaurant. Above the school are the serene chateau **gardens** (☺ 8am-7pm Jun-Aug, 8am-6pm May & Sep, 8am-5pm Apr & Oct; admission free).

Back down the hill off Latrán is the **Minorite monastery** and **convent of the Poor Clares** (Minoritský klášter), with pretty gardens providing an escape from the tourist hordes. At the time of writing the monastery and convent were closed for refurbishment. Check with Infocentrum for the current status.

The former armoury is now the **Eggenberg Brewery** (☎ 380 711 225; www.eggenberg.cz; Latrán 27; tours with/without tasting 130/100Kč), built in 1630, and the source of the town's freshest (and cheapest) beer. Book tours at Infocentrum or Unios (see Tourist Information, opposite).

INNER TOWN

South from the chateau along Latrán you pass the former **church of St Jošt** (kostel sv Jošta) on the way to Lazebnický bridge, from where the

Inner Town opens up. The church houses a small **Marionette museum** (Latrán 6; adult/concession 80/40Kč; ☺ 10am-5pm mid-Mar–Oct). Turn right into Parkán to Na ostrově, a tiny island with views across the river to the chateau.

Below the square, in a former brewery, is **Egon Schiele Centrum** (☎ 380 704 011; www.schiele artcentrum.org; Široká 70-72; adult/concession 180/105Kč; ☺ 10am-6pm). Established in 1993, this excellent private gallery has a respectable retrospective of Viennese painter Egon Schiele (1890–1918), who lived briefly in Krumlov in 1911, and raised the ire of townsfolk by hiring young girls as nude models. For this and other sins he was eventually driven out. It also houses temporary exhibitions of other A-list artists.

Continue on Široká and Na louži, and turn left to náměstí Svornosti, with its 16th-century **town hall** and **Marian plague column** (Mariánský sloupek), from 1716. Several buildings feature valuable stucco and painted decorations. See the hotel at No 13 and the house at No 14. Near Infocentrum you will also find the **museum of Torture** (cnr náměstí Svornosti & Radniční; adult/concession 80/40Kč; ☺ 9am-8pm) displaying ghoulish implements, and a heavy metal 'iron maiden' in the foyer.

Back at the square, follow Horní uphill and past Kostelní to the 14th-century **church of St Vitus** (kostel sv Víta). Continue on Horní past the 1588 **Jesuit college** (Jesuitská kolej), now housing the plush Hotel Růže.

Opposite is the **Regional museum** (Regionální muzeum v Českém Krumlově; ☎ 380 711 674; www.muzeum .ckrumlov.cz; Horní 152; adult/concession 50/25Kč; ☺ 10am-6pm Jul-Aug, 10am-5pm May-Jun & Sep, 9am-4pm Tue-Fri, 1-4pm Sat & Sun, Mar-Apr & Oct-Dec) featuring folk art from the Šumava region, archaeology, history, fine arts, furnishings and weapons. The highlight is a room-sized model of Český Krumlov c 1800.

Activities

During summer rent a variety of craft for lazy hours on the **Vltava** – canoes, kayaks – even inner tubes. Companies usually offer one-way transport to towns upriver, where you can begin your river journey back to Český Krumlov; around seven hours from Vyšší Brod, five hours from Rožmberk, or three from Branná. En route take things leisurely at riverside beer gardens and camp sites. You can also head north from Český Krumlov to Zlatá' Koruna (five hours) and Boršov nad

Vltavou (nine hours). Prices average around 950Kč per day for an open canoe (two persons) and 1350Kč per day for a raft (three to four people). Shorter, less expensive trips are also available. Reliable companies include **Vltava Tourist Services** (p172) and **Maleček** (☎ 380 712 508; www.malecek.cz; Rooseveltova 28). Maleček also runs more sedate river trips through Český Krumlov on wooden rafts seating up to 36 people (280Kč, 45 minutes).

Slupenec Stables (☎ 380 711 052; www.jk-slupenec.cz; Slupenec 1; ☼ 9am-6pm Tue-Sun) hires horses for trips and lessons (one/11 hours 250/2000Kč). The stables are 2.5km south of town. Book through Infocentrum (p172). Longer expeditions can be arranged for groups of at least four.

Hire bikes for 320Kč per day from Unios Tourist Service and Vltava Tourist Services (see Tourist Information, p172).

Festivals & Events

Infocentrum sells tickets to major festivals, including the **Chamber Music Festival** in late June/early July, the **International Music Festival** (www.czechmusicfestival.com) during August and the **Jazz at Summer's End Festival** (www.jazz-krumlov.cz) in September. The **Pětilisté Růže Festival** (Five-Petalled Rose Festival) in mid-June features street performances, parades and medieval games (expect a small admission fee).

Sleeping

There are thousands of beds, but accommodation is tight in summer. Winter rates drop by up to 40%.

BUDGET

Expect to pay from 450Kč per person for a private room, often with breakfast included. Inquire at the tourist information offices.

Kemp Nové Spolí (☎ 380 728 305; tent per person 65Kč; ☼ Jun-Aug; Ⓟ) On the right (east) bank of the Vltava, about 2.5km south of town, this rustic camp site gets super-busy.

hostel postel (☎ 380 715 631; www.hostelpostel.cz; Rybářská 35; dm/d 250/600Kč; 🖳) Situated near good bars in Rybářská, hostel postel has a sunny courtyard with shady umbrellas to wake you up s...l...o...w...l...y after a big night.

Krumlov House (☎ 380 711 935; www.krumlovhostel.com; Rooseveltova 68; dm/d 300/650Kč; 🖳) Perched above the river, Krumlov House is friendly and comfortable, and has plenty of books, DVDs, and local information to feed your inner backpacker. Lots of day trips are on offer.

MIDRANGE

Pension U Pivovaru (☎ 775 963 868; pensionupivovaru@ seznam.cz; Pivovarska 181; s/d 800/1300Kč; Ⓟ) In a quiet lane near the town's brewery, the owners also rent bikes and canoes.

Pension Lobo (☎ 380 713 153; www.pensionlobo.cz; Latrán 73; d incl breakfast 1100Kč) Pension Lobo offers more than just spotless and central rooms. See them also for the convenient Laundromat Lobo (p172).

Pension U Černého PSA (☎ 380 712 366; www.pension -cerny-pes.cz; Rooseveltova 36; d incl breakfast 1200Kč; Ⓟ) The name means 'Place of the Black Dog', and the black labrador in the photo outside just begs you to stay. Follow your heart and make the dog happy at this friendly spot with retro '70s furniture.

Hospoda Na Louži (☎ 380 711 280; www.nalouzi.cz; Kájovská 66; d incl breakfast from 1350Kč) The outside dates from 1459, and the interior is early 20th century. In a new century there are now 11 cosy rooms above a great pub (opposite).

U Malého Vítka (☎ 380 711 925; www.vitekhotel .cz; Radniční 27; d incl breakfast from 1450Kč; Ⓟ) Right in the old town stay in comfortable, quirky rooms named after traditional Czech fairytale characters.

Pension Barbakán (☎ 380 717 017; www.barbakan.cz; Horní 26; d incl breakfast from 1700Kč; Ⓟ 🖳) Originally the town's gunpowder arsenal, Barbakán now creates fireworks of its own with super-comfy rooms featuring polished wooden floors. Its excellent restaurant sits spectacularly above the river.

Hotel Zlatý Anděl (☎ 380 712 310; www.hotelzlatyandel .cz; náměstí Svornosti 10; s/d incl breakfast 1700/2000Kč; Ⓟ ✗ 🎜) The Zlatý Anděl's façade may be the slimmest on the main square, but good value and spacious rooms are concealed within.

Other recommendations:

Pension Danny (☎ 380 712 710; www.pensiondanny .cz; Latrán 72; d incl breakfast from 990Kč) Exposed beams plus restored brickwork equals simple charm.

Pension U Galerie (☎ 337 711 829; Rybářská 40; d incl breakfast 1000Kč) Readers have praised the U Galerie's 'good prices and good kitchen'. We agree.

Penzión Ve Věži (☎ 380 711 742; www.ckrumlov .cz/pensionvevezi; Pivovarská 28; d incl breakfast 1200Kč; Ⓟ) Spartan rooms, but where else can you sleep in a Gothic tower with a brewery over the road?

TOP END

Hotel u Václava (☎ 380 715 094; www.uvaclava.cz; Nové Město 25; d 2500Kč; Ⓟ) Four-poster beds create a romantic atmosphere that's perfect for that first (or second) honeymoon or spontaneous holiday fling. Not recommended for single travellers, but you won't go wrong with a loved one.

Hotel Růže (☎ 380 772 100; www.hotelruze.cz; Horní 154; s/d incl breakfast 4200/5800Kč; P ✕ ✕ ⌨ ♨) CK's flashest hotel fills the old Jesuit college and is popular with tour groups who welcome its medieval bling. We're not sure about the mannequins in the lobby. Have they escaped from the nearby wax museum?

Eating

Laibon (☎ 728 676 654; Parkán 105; mains 80-160Kč) Candles and vaulted ceilings create a nicely 'boho' ambience in Bohemia's best vegetarian teahouse. Start with Middle Eastern and Indian flavours, and finish with fluffy blueberry dumplings.

Krčma v Šatlavské (☎ 380 713 344; Horní 157; mains 100-150Kč) Nirvana for meat-lovers is this barbecue cellar serving sizzling platters in a medieval labyrinth illuminated by candles and the flickering flames of open grills. Wash it all down with wine served in earthenware goblets. Book ahead.

Cikánská jizba (☎ 380 717 585; Dlouhá 31; mains 100-200Kč; ✆ 3pm-midnight Mon-Sat) Known locally as the Gypsy Room, this is the best spot in town to try the flavours of the Roma with pumping live music at weekends.

Nonna Gina (☎ 380 717 187; Klášterini ul 52; pizza 110Kč) The authentically Italian Massaro family conjure up authentic Italian flavours.

Papa's Living Restaurant (☎ 380 711 585; Latrán 13; mains 120-270Kč) Try the hearty steak 'n' ribs in this riverside ode to the Mediterranean with good food and a silly name.

Potraviny (supermarket; Latrán 55) Picnic anyone?

Drinking
PUBS

Hospoda Na Louži (☎ 380 711 280; Kájovská 66; mains 120-180Kč) Nothing has changed in this wood-panelled *pivo* parlour for almost a century. Locals pack Hospoda Na Louži for tasty dark beer from the Eggenberg brewery and huge meals.

U Dwau Maryí (☎ 380 717 228; Parkán 104; mains 80-175Kč) Dive into the authentic medieval interior and emerge onto a sunny riverside terrace. Inside or outside, the food and drink go down easily in this enjoyably raucous tavern.

CLUBS

Hrozen Music Bar (náměstí Svornosti 7; ✆ 9pm-3am Wed-Thu, 9pm-6am Fri & Sat) If you're into intense beats and foam parties, you'll probably love this Eurobrash kind of place.

Horor Bar (☎ 728 682 724; Masná 22; ✆ 6pm-late) Occasional live gigs surface in this kitschy labyrinth celebrating the (un)dead.

Entertainment
THEATRE & CINEMA

Městské divadlo (☎ 380 711 775; www.divadlo.ckrumlov .cz; Horní 2) The town theatre holds regular performances.

Kino (☎ 380 711 892; Špičák 134) The latest Hollywood fare (80Kč).

Shakespeare & Sons (☎ 380 711 203; Soukenická 44) Cult and art-house films downstairs from a bookshop (p172).

Getting There & Away

Seven buses (140Kč, three hours) and one direct train (224Kč, 3¾ hours) run to/from Prague daily. Buses run all day to/from České Budějovice (28Kč, 50 minutes) and seven times a day to/from Rožmberk nad Vltavou (24Kč, 40 minutes). Eight trains a day run to České Budějovice (46Kč, one hour), with connections to Prague.

AROUND ČESKÝ KRUMLOV
Blanský Les

The **Blanský Les** Protected Landscape Region is good hiking territory, particularly near the summit of the **Kleť** (1083m); in winter it is a ski resort. A **chairlift** (adult/concession 60/30Kč; ✆ 9am-5pm Jul-Aug, Wed-Sat May-Jun, Sat & Sun Sep-Feb) climbs to the summit from the car park above Krasetín, 2km from Holubov, where the Český Krumlov-České Budějovice train stops.

Kleť can also be reached on foot via a green-marked trail from near Český Krumlov's main train station. Other trails are marked on SHOCart's GeoClub *Českobudějovicko* (1:75,000) map.

Zlatá Koruna
pop 550

Above the Vltava is the wee village of Zlatá Koruna and a well-preserved Gothic **monastery** (Cisterciácký klášter; adult/concession 85/40Kč; ✆ 9am-noon & 1-5pm Tue-Sun Apr-Oct), founded in 1263 by Přemysl Otakar II to demonstrate his power in the region.

SOUTH BOHEMIA

Originally called the Saintly Crown of Thorns, the monastery was renamed the Gold Crown (Zlatá Koruna). The walled complex also houses a **museum of South Bohemian Literature** (Památník písemnictví jižních Čech). The complex can be visited on regular guided tours (minimum five people; last tour 4.15pm).

INFORMATION

Infocentrum (☎ 380 743 275; www.sweb.cz/zlatakoruna; ☺ 9am-1pm & 2-5pm Jul & Aug closed Wed) provides maps and helps with accommodation. It is in the Obecní Urad, just before the monastery.

SLEEPING & EATING

There are private rooms here and in the adjacent village of Rájov, a 1.5km downhill walk south.

Zlatá Koruna Kemping (☎ 777 729 444; www.kemp -koruna.cz; tent per person 70Kč; ☺ May-Sep) This slightly rundown camp site is across the bridge at the bottom of town.

Pension Koruna (☎ 380 743 194; Zlatá Koruna 26; s/d incl breakfast 400/800Kč) Attached to a restaurant, this inn-style place has comfy rooms.

GETTING THERE & AWAY

Regular buses run to/from Český Krumlov (13Kč, 15 minutes).

Around Zlatá Koruna

Dívčí kámen, a ruined castle above the Vltava, was founded by the Rožmberks in 1349 but abandoned in 1541. It's a robust 7km walk on a red-marked trail by the river, north from Zlatá Koruna.

TŘEBOŇ

pop 8900

Most of the live carp sold on Christmas Eve throughout the Czech Republic come from the centuries-old fish ponds around the spa town of Třeboň. With a fine main square, a pretty chateau, and a good local brewery, the town deserves to be more on the tourist circuit.

Orientation

Old Třeboň is entered through its venerable gates to the main square, Masarykovo náměstí.

The main train station is 1.5km northwest of the old town. There's also a smaller station on the same line, Třeboň Lázně, 800m

northeast. The bus station is 1km due west, off Svobody.

Information

The **tourist information office** (Informační středisko; ☎ 384 721 169; www.trebon-mesto.cz; Masarykovo náměstí 103; ☺ 9am-6pm Mon-Fri, 9am-noon Sat & Sun Jun-Aug, 8am-5pm Mon-Fri Apr-May) helps with accommodation and has internet access.

Česká spořitelna (Masarykovo náměstí 100) changes money and has an ATM. The **post office** (Seifertova 588) is west of the main square.

Sights

AROUND MASARYKOVO NÁMĚSTÍ

The main attractions are the Renaissance and baroque houses on the square and within the town walls, which date from 1527. Don't miss the **town hall** on the square, and **St Giles church** (kostel sv Jiljí) and the **Augustine monastery** (Augustinský klášter) on Husova. The **brewery** (pivovar; Trcnovské náměstí) has been home to Regent beer, one of Bohemia's oldest beers, since 1379. The brewery is closed to the public, but it does have a raucous *pivnice* (beer hall) for sampling its five different brews.

TŘEBOŇ CHATEAU

The **chateau** (zámek; ☎ 384 721 193; ☺ 9am-5.15pm Tue-Sun Jun-Aug, to 4pm Apr-May & Sep-Oct; adult/concession 80/40Kč to 140/70Kč) includes a **museum** with a small collection of furniture and weapons. There are three tour routes to choose from. Enter through a gate (opposite Březanova) from Masarykovo náměstí or via the courtyard off Rožmberská.

SCHWARZENBERG MAUSOLEUM

Many Schwarzenbergs are buried in this 1877, neo-Gothic **mausoleum** (Švarcenberská hrobka; adult/concession 30/20Kč, in English 60/30Kč; ☺ same as chateau) in Park U hrobky, on the other side of the pond from Třeboň.

TŘEBOŇSKO PROTECTED LANDSCAPE REGION

A good **forest walk** through the Třeboňsko Protected Landscape Region begins at **Masarykovo náměstí**. Following the blue-marked trail northeast to **Na kopečku** (1.5km, 30 minutes). From Na kopečku, keep on the blue-marked trail to **Hodějov Pond** (7.5km, 2½ hours). A yellow trail then runs west to **Smítka**, (2km, 45 minutes) where it joins a red trail heading north to **Klec** and a primitive camp site (6km, two hours).

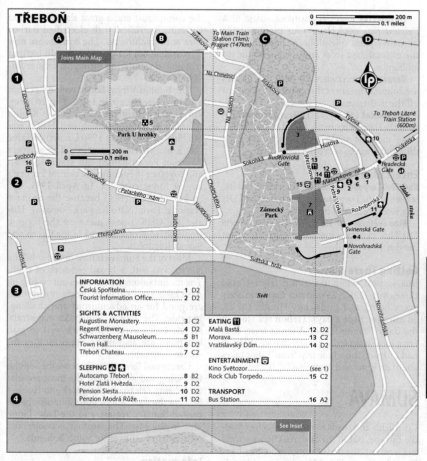

TŘEBOŇ

SOUTH BOHEMIA

From there, for a further 13km (four hours), the red trail runs north, past more fishponds, forests and small villages to **Veselí nad Lužnicí**, a major railway junction. Camping is allowed only in official camp sites throughout the protected landscape region. This route can also be ridden on your mountain bike.

Sleeping

Autocamp Třeboň (☎ 384 722 586; www.autocamp -trebon.cz; tent/bungalow per person 100/165Kč; ☼ May-Sep; P) This pleasant site is south near the Schwarzenberg Mausoleum.

Pension Siesta (☎ 384 724 831; penzionsiesta@tiscali .cz; Hradební 26; s/d incl breakfast 500/1000Kč) Cute turrets and a balcony make this spot on the canal a little bit unique.

Penzion Modrá Růže (☎ 384 722 167; www.modra-ruze .cz; Rožmberská 39; s/d incl breakfast 600/1200Kč) With super-helpful owners providing loads of local information, this *pension* on a quiet lane is one of Třeboň's best.

Hotel Zlatá Hvězda (☎ 384 757 111; www.zhvezda .cz; Masarykovo náměstí 107; s/d incl breakfast 1860/2520Kč) Třeboň's smartest offering has flash rooms, a spa centre, and a bowling alley; all in a 430-year-old building.

Eating

Malá Bastá (☎ 384 722 563; Masarykovo náměstí 87; mains 80-160Kč) Carp is cooked at least 10 different ways at this main-square suntrap. Don't forget to try the 'carp chips' with a glass of local beer.

Vratislavský dům (cnr Masarykovo náměstí 97 & Březanova; pizza 100Kč) Have your pizza outside in main square splendour, or head inside to the mismatched sofas and a vaguely student ambience.

Morava (Březanova; mains 100-180Kč) The dishes are robustly meaty at this courtyard spot just off the main square.

Bílý koníček (☎ 384 721 213; Masarykovo náměstí 97; mains 120-220Kč) Perennially popular, the 'White Pony' may just outdo Malá Bašta for the most different ways to serve the local carp.

Entertainment

Rock Club Torpedo (Zámek 110; ☯ to midnight Mon-Thu, to 2am Fri & Sat), Torpedo features bands and DJs in a sweaty chateau basement.

Kino Světozor (☎ 384 722 850; Masarykovo náměstí 103) This central cinema screens the latest movies…eventually.

Getting There & Away

Bus is best when travelling from České Budějovice (22Kč, 25 minutes, approximately every hour) and Jindřichův Hradec (32Kč, 30 minutes, nine a day). Třeboň is a stop on the daily Prague–Tábor–Vienna train line. On a local train from Tábor, change at Veselí nad Lužnicí; the whole trip from Tábor takes about an hour and costs 76Kč.

ŠUMAVA

Cornfields and roads may cover much of Middle Europe, but in the Šumava (Böhmerwald in German), the dense woodland harks back to wilder times. This 125km sweep of largely unpopulated wilderness on the Austrian and German border remains one of the region's rural treasures, with pockets like the Boubín Virgin Forest still regarded as pristine.

Including some of the country's grandest peaks, the humpbacked mountains (highest summit: Plechý, 1378m) of Šumava are now home to returning populations of deer, lynx and owl. They are also the source of the mighty Vltava, the river that rolls beneath Prague's Charles bridge 250km north. Cut through with waterways and peppered with lakes and sweeping slopes, Šumava offers plenty of outdoor attractions for the active traveller.

It hasn't always been this way. Ironically, while Šumava now personifies fresh air and freedom, it was a closed border zone during

the communist era: a great slab of the Iron Curtain, interlaced with electrified barbed wire and watchtowers. The barriers are now dismantled, but for Czechs a certain intrigue remains in wandering through a former forbidden zone.

The Boubín Virgin Forest region has been a nature reserve since 1858. The 1630-sq-km Šumava Protected Landscape Region (Chráněná krajinná oblast, or CHKO) was established in 1963. In 1990 Unesco declared this a biospheric reservation. The adjacent Bavarian Forest gained this status in 1981, and together they comprise central Europe's largest forest complex. In April 1991, 685 sq km of the CHKO became the Šumava National Park (Národní park Šumava). This and the CHKO now make up the biggest, single, state-protected area in the Czech and Slovak Republics.

Most of the Šumava is now open for hiking (turistická) with a broad network of trails. The mountainous terrain rules out cycling on most hiking trails, though the many dirt roads are good for an adventurous and challenging ride. The 240km 'Šumavská magistrála' bicycle trail traverses the park west to east, but there are also many opportunities for shorter journeys.

Czechs and Bavarians appreciate the Šumava for skiing and ski touring, the most popular areas being Železná Ruda, Špičák and Hojsova Stráž in the west, Zadov and Churáňov in the central Sumava region, and the Lake Lipno area in the east. The weather is cooler and wetter than in the rest of South Bohemia.

Information

For information online, www.sumava.com and www.npsumava.cz are your best English-language options.

Maps

The best hiking map is Klub českých turistů's *Šumava* (1:50,000), which includes marked trails. SHOCart's *Šumava Trojmezí velká cykloturistická* (1:75,000) map is must for cyclists.

Getting There & Away

There are several train routes into the Šumava, such as from Plzeň and Klatovy in West Bohemia, Strakonice or České Budějovice. Another rail option is from the German side on Prague-bound trains.

Getting Around

From June to September a fleet of ecologically friendly **'Green Buses'** run on four routes to link towns, villages and trailheads (see www .npsumava.cz in Czech). These services can also transport bicycles. Regular bus and train services are relatively infrequent.

NATIONAL PARK WALKS

Of the many trails we list three here, it's simple to devise your own walk with the help of the maps. A very long but interesting walk is along the length of the national park, from Nová Pec, at the northern tip of Lake Lipno, to Nýrsko, southwest of Klatovy.

The national park must be entered by the trails, with camping only at designated sites. Fires can only be lit at those camp sites. The colour-coded trails are well marked with distance and walking-time information. If you pass a trail intersection and don't see a marker within about 300m, return to the intersection and try again. Also note that some of the reserve is totally off-limits: watch for 'Vystup zakázán' (do not enter) signs.

Bear Trail

The **Bear Trail** (Medvědí stezka) passes **Bear Rock** (Medvědí kámen), where the last bear in Bohemia was killed in 1856. This is the oldest walking trail in the Šumava. It starts at the Ovesná train stop and ends at a train stop in Černý Kříž (Black Cross), 14km later. Some sections are hard, such as along the rocky formations of the Jelení vrchy and up to the 1049m summit of Perník (avoid this section in bad weather).

The trail continues past Deer Lake (Jelení jezírko), Jelení village, the Schwarzenberg Canal, Bear Rock (Medvědí kámen memorial; engraved with 'Bären Stein', and about 50m off the trail), and along Hučivý stream into Černý Kříž.

The Ovesná train stop is best reached by train from either Volary (28Kč, 25 minutes, three daily) or Horní Planá (16Kč, 15 minutes, three daily). From Černý Kříž you can return by train to Ovesná (15Kč, 15 minutes, three daily), and from there return to either Volary or Horní Planá.

Povydří Trail

One of the Šumava's best trails is along the Vydra river, especially in the area called Povydří, between Čeňkova Pila and Antýgl.

Vydra means 'otter', and the river got its name from the many otters that used to live in it. Today, only a few otters live high up in the mountains.

Starting at Čeňkova Pila, the trail goes along the Vydra to Modrava, taking you past Turnerova hut (chata), Antýgl, the right side of the Vchnickotetovský Canal, Rokyta and finally to Modrava. This is an easy and scenic 14km trail. It's also possible to start further down the river at Rejštejn.

Eight buses a day run from Sušice to Čeňkova Pila (34Kč, 45 minutes) and four buses return from Modrava to Sušice (48Kč, 1½ hours). Both Modrava and Čeňkova Pila are stops on the 'Green Bus' that runs from June to September.

Boubín Virgin Forest

The 46-hectare **Boubín Virgin Forest** (Boubínský prales), surrounds the peak of Boubín (1362m) and was one of the world's first nature reserves, founded in 1858. Beech, spruce and pine predominate and some trees are estimated to be over 400 years old. The forest itself is largely out of bounds to visitors.

If you're driving, the easiest approach is via the car park at Kaplice. From here it's an easy 2.5km to U pralesa lake, on a green and then blue trail. To reach Boubín, stay on the blue trail along the boundary of Boubínský prales. After 6km you reach Křížova Smrč, and from there it's 1.5km to the top of Boubín. Without a car you need get off at the zastávka Zátoň train stop and walk an additional 2km to the trailhead at Kaplice.

A longer (17.5km) and more enjoyable walk takes in all the above but continues on the blue trail southwest from the summit of Boubín past Johnův kámen to Kubova Huť. Give yourself at least five hours from Kaplice to Kubova Huť.

Sleeping

There is plenty of accommodation in the region, but private rooms are often the best bet – houses will often have 'Zimmer frei' signs in the window. There's little to see in the region's towns, so you won't be missing anything by staying in the wilds.

Lenora's pensions are hard to find from the train station (head 10 minutes downhill to the main road).

Between Lenora and Vimperk, Kubova Huť is a ski resort in winter and is literally

SOUTH BOHEMIA

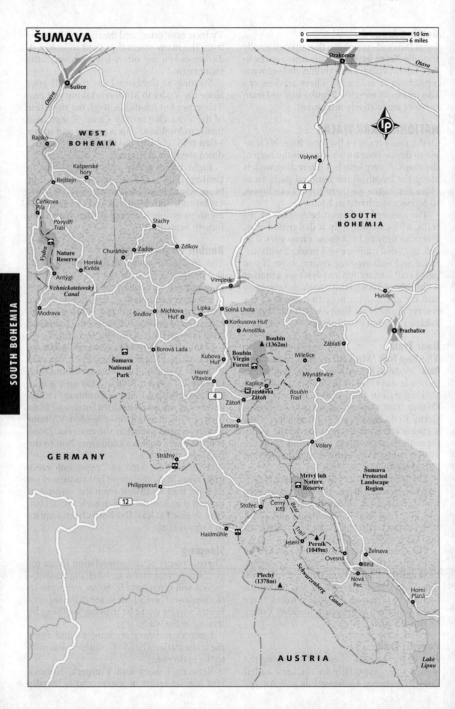

ŠUMAVA

0 ___ 10 km
0 ___ 6 miles

teeming with resorts, *pension*s and private rooms. Further to the west the settlements are smaller and more rustic.

Pension Kuboňová (☎ 728 082 132; http://penzion ukubonu.wz.cz; Soumarská 408; s/d incl breakfast 400/800Kč; P) In Volary, Pension Kuboňová has comfy rooms in a brighter part of town. It's on the road out of Volary to Lenora.

Pension Lenora (☎ 388 438 813; s/d incl breakfast 540/900Kč) Friendly and comfortable, this is the best of them in Lenora.

Amber Hotel Kuba (☎ 388 436 319; www.legner.cz; s/d incl breakfast 950/1400Kč; P) This comfy three-star spot in Kubova Huť also has cheaper 'turist' rooms with shared bathrooms (single/double 400/700Kč).

Hotel Klostermannova Chata (☎ 376 599 067; www.klostermannovachata.cz d incl breakfast 1400Kč; P) In Modrava splurge at this stunning alpine lodge originally built by the Czechoslovak Tourist Club in 1924 and recently refurbished.

Autocamp Antýgl (☎ 376 599 331; May-Oct). This is the only option in Antýgl.

Pension Bystřina (☎ 388 599 221) This *pension* is in Čeňkova Pila, along with a basic camp site.

Pension Kizek (☎ 388 582 527; s/d incl breakfast 500/900Kč) Try this *pension* in Rejštejn.

Sport Hotel Pekárna (☎ 376 526 869; www.hotel-pekarna.de; TG Masaryka 129; s/d incl breakfast 600/900Kč) Located in Sušice, a pleasant gateway town.

Getting There & Away

Up to eight trains a day run between Volary and Strakonice (98Kč, two hours), stopping at Lenora and two other stations – zastávka Zátoň and Horní Vltavice, both of which are about 10km from their respective towns (Kubova Huť and Vimperk). From Volary you can get direct trains to Horní Planá (40Kč, 35 minutes) and Český Krumlov (88Kč, 1¾ hours).

On weekdays there are six runs on the very scenic, 29km Vimperk to Lenora route (40Kč, 50 minutes), via Kubova Huť and Horní Vltavice. Between Sušice and Modrava a bus runs once or twice a day.

BORDER CROSSINGS

There are border crossings to Germany south of Vimperk. A 24-hour vehicle and pedestrian crossing at Strážný, to Philippsreuth, can be reached by local bus from Horní Vltavice. Another at Stožec, to Haidmühle, is for pedestrians and cyclists only and is open from 9am to 9pm.

ROŽMBERK NAD VLTAVOU

pop 350

Perched on the slimmest of ridges above a hairpin bend in the Vltava river, Rožmberk is one of South Bohemia's loveliest castles, and surprisingly quiet for somewhere so near tourist magnet Český Krumlov. Most visitors are thirsty canoeists who drop in for a refreshing beer on their way from Vyšší Brod, but with a couple of romantic riverside hotels with charming outdoor restaurants, it's a low-key alternative to staying in crowded Český Krumlov.

The so-called **Upper castle**, built in the mid-13th century, was destroyed by fire in 1522; the only reminder today is the crumbling **Jakobín tower** in the trees above. The 1330s **Lower castle** (☎ 380 749 838; www.hrad-rozmberk.cz; adult/concession 75/50Kč, in English 140/80Kč; 9am-4.30pm Tue-Sun Jun-Aug, to 3.15pm May & Sep, 9am-3.15pm Sat & Sun Apr & Oct) was rebuilt in the Renaissance style in the 1550s. It's said to be haunted by a ghost called the White Lady (Bílá paní), the long-suffering wife of one of the Rožmberks.

After the Battle of the White Mountain the castle came into the hands of the Buquoy family. All the paintings, sculpture, porcelain, furniture, weapons and some particularly nasty torture instruments are all from their era. The treat of the tour is the banquet hall, covered in 16th-century Italian frescoes. One fresco, behind a grille, is encrusted with jewels confiscated during the Thirty Years' War.

Sleeping & Eating

The village below has some private rooms (look for signs with '*privát*' or '*ubytování*') starting from 400Kč per person.

Kemp Rožmberk (☎ 380 749 816; tent 65Kč; May-Sep; P) North of the castle, across the river from the Český Krumlov road, this pleasant camp site has the perfect riverside setting.

Penzion Adler (☎ 380 749 844; s/d incl breakfast 380/760Kč) Tucked in a quiet lane behind the Penzion Romantik, the Adler has a sunny patio and basic but comfortable rooms. The restaurant is popular with locals.

Hotel u Martina (☎ 380 749 745; www.hotelumartina .cz; s/d 500/800Kč; P) Look for the white horse above the entrance of this riverside hotel right on the main square next to the Hotel Růže. In summer there are DIY barbecues on the outside terrace.

Penzion Romantik (☎ 380 749 906; www.penzion romantik.cz; s/d incl breakfast 690/1180Kč; P) The rooms are wonderfully clean and crisp at this spot with river views 200m before the main square on the Český Krumlov road.

Hotel Studenec (☎ 380 749 818; www.hotel-studenec .com; s/d incl breakfast 750/1380Kč; **P**) There's stunning views and a majestic display of stags heads, but vegetarians might feel queasy at the menagerie of stuffed animals in the restaurant. Canoes and bikes can be hired.

Hotel Růže (☎ 380 749 715; www.hotelruze.rozmberk .cz; s/d incl breakfast 800/1250Kč; **P**) Nice and comfortable, the Hotel Růže has a charming outdoor terrace with old-style lamps. Romantic castle views are included at no extra cost.

There is a supermarket on the main square.

Getting There & Away

Seven buses a day come from Český Krumlov (24Kč, 35 minutes) continuing on to Vyšší Brod.

VYŠŠÍ BROD

pop 2650

Vyšší Brod is another popular riverside stop for canoeists, and plenty of Austrian tourists travel the 8km from the border to visit the Cistercian monastery. The town is an easy 24km from Český Krumlov.

Information

Infocentrum (☎ 380 746 627; náměstí 104; ☽ 9am-1pm & 1.30-5.30pm) organises accommodation, sells maps and has internet access for 1Kč per minute.

Sights

CISTERCIAN MONASTERY

This fortified **monastery** (cisterciácký klášter; ☎ 380 746 674; cist.klaster@vyssibrod.cz; adult/concession 70/50Kč, in English 130/100Kč; ☽ 9.30-11.30am & 1.15-4.15pm Tue-Sat, 1.15-4.15pm Sun Apr-Sep) was founded by Vok Rožmberk in 1259, but not completed until the late 14th century. It withstood two Hussite assaults in the 15th century. Later owners were the Eggenbergs and the Schwarzenbergs. It was closed by the communists in 1950 and its monks imprisoned. After a period of neglect repairs began in 1990.

It has one of Bohemia's finest Gothic buildings, the **Chapter house** (Kapitulní síň), completed in 1285, its roof supported by a single pillar. A highlight is its 70,000-volume **library**, founded with the monastery. The large library hall is entered by a secret door through a bookcase in the small library hall. Note the gold leaf, rococo ceiling.

In the monastery grounds, there is also a **postal museum** (poštovní muzeum; adult/concession 25/10Kč; ☽ 9am-noon & 1-5pm Tue-Sun Apr-Oct), for fans of the days before email.

Activities

If you're interested in paddling down the Vltava, **Inge Tour** (☎ 380 746 139; www.ingetour.cz; Miru 379) operates out of the **Inge Penzión**, right below the monastery, and hires out canoes and rafts for the one-way trip to Rožmberk and Český Krumlov. Prices average about 950Kč per day for an open canoe (two persons) and 1350Kč per day for a raft (three to four people).

Sleeping & Eating

Pod hrází (☎ 380 746 427; tent/bungalow per person 65/220Kč; ☽ May-Sep; **P**) This camp site is between the monastery and the river.

Café/Penzión Alpská Růže (☎ 380 746 315; villa@volny.cz; náměstí 73; s/d incl breakfast 500/1000Kč) Aromas from delicious cakes waft from this arty café/pension dubbed the 'Rhododendron'. Don't worry if you eat too much because the rooms are very comfortable.

Inge Penzion (☎ 380 746 482; www.pensioninge.cz Miru 379; s/d incl breakfast 620/1000Kč; **P**) On a bend in the river under the Cistercian monastery, this spot gets busy with thirsty canoeists who stop for a beer, and stay for the comfy rooms and popular restaurant. Camping is available in the garden for 100Kč per person.

Hotel Panský dům (☎ 380 746 669; www.hotelpansky dum.cz; Miru 82; s/d incl breakfast 650/1300Kč) Check out the interesting sepia photographs from the days of the Hapsburgs in the lobby, but rest assured the rooms are now smart and modern. Look for the green building just off the main square.

Getting There & Away

The town is on a rail spur on the well-serviced České Budějovice–Austria line. There are at least 11 trains a day from Rybník (20 minutes), and it's about 1¼ hours from there to České Budějovice (45Kč).

Frymburk-bound buses run approximately seven times a day from Český Krumlov via Rožmberk nad Vltavou to Vyšší Brod (32Kč, 50 minutes to an hour).

BORDER CROSSINGS

Two 24-hour vehicle and pedestrian crossings to Austria are near Vyšší Brod: Studánky to Weigetschlag, and Dolní Dvořiště to Wullowitz.

LAKE LIPNO
pop 5000

Visitors come from miles around to splash in Lake Lipno, but there's not much here except the Czech Republic's largest artificial body of water, and loads of summertime ice-cream stalls. Adjoining a dam 8km west of Vyšší Brod, this huge watery expanse is a worthwhile, if touristy, stop-off. Recent developments include lakeside apartments, a yacht marina and mini-golf. During summer expect to hear lots of German and Austrian accents thrilled by a good exchange rate.

Orientation

The largest town along the lake is Horní Planá, a major centre with accommodation, shops and transport. The smaller towns of Frymburk and Černá v Pošumaví can also be used as bases to explore the area.

Information

KIC Infocentrum (☎ 380 738 008; www.horniplana.cz; náměstí 8; ☒ 7.30am-6pm May-Aug, to 4pm Oct-Apr), in Horní Planá, sells hiking and cycling maps, and arranges accommodation. It also has internet access (2Kč per minute) and rents bikes.

Activities

Boats, windsurfers, kiteboards, bikes and skis (in winter) are available from rental outfits across the area. Speak to KIC Infocentrum (see above) about the best deals.

Sleeping & Eating

Along the lakefront, especially the eastern shore, there are many camp sites and *pensions*, but few hotels. Without a booking in July or August, your only hope is a camp site, most of which open from May to September. Prices plummet outside the summer season.

HORNÍ PLANÁ

There are plenty of hotels on the main square, but they are a hike from the lake itself.

Autocamping U pláže (☎ 337 738 374; www.hotel -plaz.cz; tent/bungalow per person 60/370Kč; ℗) Just minutes from the ferry terminal and the beach, the camp site at Horní Planá is conveniently located.

Hotel Na Pláži (☎ 337 738 374; www.hotel-plaz.cz; s/d incl breakfast 540/980Kč; ℗) Three hundred metres down the road is the camp site's sister hotel. It's pretty swish for the area but the rooms

are a tad clinical. More relaxed is the beach volleyball, crazy golf and pedal boats for hire on the hotel's sandy 'beach'.

ČERNÁ V POŠUMAVÍ

The lakeside here is crowded with camp sites.

Autokemping Jihočeského Autoklubu (☎ 380 744 125; tent/bungalow per person 70/200Kč; ℗) This camp site gets seriously busy, and is a lively and social place.

Hotel Swing (☎ 380 744 294; www.hotelswing.cz; s/d incl breakfast 600/1000Kč; ℗ ☒) Down on the lake gets noisy in summer and this spot is more relaxed. The architecture is a little dour, but there is a swimming pool if you're feeling too lazy to walk 250m to the lake. Hotel Swing is well signposted from the main road.

FRYMBURK

The most pleasant place to stay, Frymburk is a bustling market town with a leafy main square.

Camping Frymburk (☎ 380 735 284; www.camping frymburk.cz; tent 90Kč; ☒ May-Oct) North of town, this also has two-, three- and four-bed huts (500/550/600Kč).

Maxant (☎ 380 735 229; www.hotelmaxant.cz; s/d incl breakfast 1020/1630Kč; ℗) The marionettes in the lobby are a little spooky, but there's nothing else scary about this welcoming place on the main square. Relax in the comfortable rooms or in the solarium and massage area.

Hotel Vltava (☎ 380 735 418; www.hotel-vltava.com; s/d incl breakfast 1500/3000Kč; ℗ ☒ ☒ ☒) Also on the main square, this new place has lifted the game in Frymburk with classy rooms, a solarium and a heated swimming pool.

Getting There & Away

Five buses a day run from Horní Planá through Černá v Pošumaví and Frymburk to Lipno nad Vltavou (28Kč, 40 minutes). Many continue to Český Krumlov (34Kč, 1¼ hours).

Up to five trains a day travel from České Budějovice (88Kč, two hours) to Volary. From Volary, trains go to Prachatice (40Kč, 40 minutes) and beyond eight times a day.

Getting Around

Apart from local buses, regular ferries (adult/concession 10/5Kč) cross the lake from Horní Planá, Dolní Vltavice and Frymburk.

In July and August **Lipno Line** (☎ 380 736 276; www.lipno-line.com; Přístav 71) runs **sightseeing cruises**

SOUTH BOHEMIA

on the lake from both Lipno nad Vltavou and Frymburk. The two-hour cruises (adult/concession 235/130Kč) depart daily at 1.30pm, and shorter 80-minute cruises (adult/concession 195/95Kč) depart daily at 9.30am, 11am and 3.30pm. From July to August a three-hour music cruise (adult/concession 420/195Kč) departs at 6pm on Fridays from Lipno nad Vltavou. Bookings are recommended.

PRACHATICE
pop 11,800

A grim arc of Stalinist concrete shoeboxes does its best to overwhelm the well-preserved and evocative centre of Prachatice, but thankfully a largely intact 14th-century defensive wall has kept ancient enemies and modern architectural contamination at bay. And when you tire of the Renaissance splendour and a cosmopolitan selection of local restaurants, there's plenty to do in the surrounding hills and woodlands of the Šumava region.

History

The town of Prachatice was founded in the 13th century as a trading post along the important Golden Trail (Zlatá stezka), bringing salt from Bavaria in return for Czech grain.

Hussites under General Jan Žižka conquered Prachatice in 1420; as a reward for its later return to the royalist fold in 1436, King Sigismund made it a royal town.

After a fire in 1507, Prachatice, by then in the hands of the Rožmberks, was rebuilt; most of the Renaissance structures to be seen today come from that time.

Petr Vok, the last of the Rožmberks, sold it to Rudolf II in 1601, but the town sided with the Protestants during the rebellion of the Czech nobles, and in 1620 it was heavily damaged by one of Rudolf II's generals, Buquoy.

During the rule of later aristocratic families, Prachatice stagnated, though one result of the neglect was the survival of the town walls.

Orientation

The main train station is at the end of Nádražní, the continuation of Zvolenská, a 500m-walk east of the old town. The main bus station is a bit closer, on the corner of Nádražní and Nebahovská.

Part of the old town is pedestrianised – there is a car park at the northern end of Velké náměstí.

Information

Club 111 (☎ 388 315 888; Křišťanova 111; ☽ 10am-midnight) is a sports bar with internet access.

ČSOB (Nádražní 67) has an exchange desk and an ATM.

The **hospital** (nemocnice; ☎ 388 600 111; Nebahovská) is 500m east of the centre.

Infocentrum (☎ 388 312 563; www.prachatice.cz; Velké náměstí 1; ☽ 9am-6pm Mon-Fri, 10am-noon & 1-5pm Sat & Sun Jun-Sep, limited hr out of season) can also organise accommodation.

The **post office** (cnr Pivovarská & Malé náměstí) is just north of the old town.

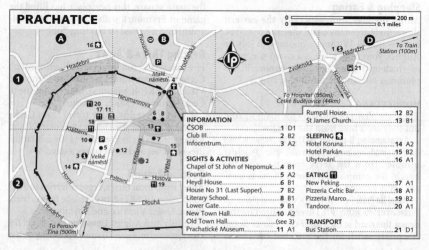

PRACHATICE

INFORMATION	
ČSOB	1 D1
Club III	2 B2
Infocentrum	3 A2

SIGHTS & ACTIVITIES	
Chapel of St John of Nepomuk	4 B1
Fountain	5 A2
Heydl House	6 B1
House No 31 (Last Supper)	7 B2
Literary School	8 B1
Lower Gate	9 B1
New Town Hall	10 A2
Old Town Hall	(see 3)
Prachatické Museum	11 A1

Rumpál House	12 B2
St James Church	13 B1

SLEEPING	
Hotel Koruna	14 A2
Hotel Parkán	15 B2
Ubytování	16 A1

EATING	
New Peking	17 A1
Pizzeria Celtic Bar	18 A1
Pizzeria Marco	19 B2
Tandoor	20 A1

TRANSPORT	
Bus Station	21 D1

To Train Station (100m)

To Hospital (550m); České Budějovice (44km)

To Pension Tina (500m)

Sight & Activities

Coming from the bus or train station, along Zvolenská and Malé náměstí, you are faced with the 14th-century **town walls**, which were beefed up in 1620. On the left is the **chapel of St John of Nepomuk** (kaple sv Jana Nepomuckého).

Enter the old town and historic Velké náměstí through the **Lower gate** (Písecká brána). Through the gate, on the left behind the heavily decorated **Heydl house** (Heydlův dům), at No 30, is the 16th-century **Literary school** (Literátská škola), where Jan Hus is said to have studied.

In front of you is the 14th-century **St James church** (sv Jakuba kostel), with a little park behind it. The house on the south side, at No 31, bears a sgraffito depicting the Last Supper.

At Velké náměstí 41 is **Rumpál house** (Rumpálův dům), a former brewery covered with Renaissance battle scenes. Opposite are the **Old town hall** (Stará radnice; 1571) and the neo-Renaissance **New town hall** (Nová radnice; 1903), both covered in sgraffito.

The **Prachatické museum** (☎ 388 311 419; Velké náměstí 13; adult/concession 40/15Kč; ✆ 9am-5pm Tue-Sun Jul-Aug, 9am-4pm Tue-Fri Apr-Jun, 10am-4pm Sat & Sun Sep-Dec) was built as a palace in 1572 by the Rožmberks and still has the town's finest façade, plus a collection of weapons and old postcards.

Festivals & Events

Prachatice goes fairly wild during the mid-June **Gold Trail Festival** (Slavnosti zlaté stezky), with medieval costumes, fencing tournaments and fireworks. An annual **Folk Music Festival** is held on the last Saturday in February.

Sleeping & Eating

Infocentrum can help with private rooms (from 350Kč per person).

Ubytování (☎ 602 474 270; Starokasárenská 192; dm per person 225Kč) Here's the ideal dorm – cheap, clean and (relatively) central.

Hotel Koruna (☎ 388 310 177; www.pthotel.cz; Velké náměstí 48; s/d incl breakfast 650/950Kč) Tucked nicely down a quiet alley just off the main square, the Koruna has a striking Renaissance façade and a popular cellar restaurant. The rooms don't live up to the beautiful façade, but they are clean and comfortable.

Hotel Parkán (☎ 388 311 868; www.hotelparkan .cz; Věžní 51; s/d incl breakfast 690/990Kč; ✖ ❄) Built around Prachatice's original 14th-century

town walls, this is the flashest place in town and has a sunny deck that looks out on the town's park.

Pizzeria Marco (☎ 388 316 950; Husova 106; mains 100-130Kč; ✆ 11am-10pm Mon-Thu, to midnight Fri & Sat, 4pm-midnight Sun) The public library is just across the road. It could also take you a while to read through the substantial menu of tasty Italian favourites.

Tandoor (☎ 388 310 618; Horní 165; mains 100-130Kč; ✆ 11.15am-3pm & 5.30-9pm Mon-Thu, to 11pm Fri-Sun) Hidden away in a town in South Bohemia is a very good North Indian restaurant. Look for the statues of Hindu gods with little flashing lights in the window.

Other recommendations:

Pension Tina (☎ 388 319 318; Pod Lázněmi 318; s/d 400/700Kč) Friendly and homely in a chalet style house.

Pizzeria Celtic Bar (☎ 388 310 048; Velké náměstí; mains 70-80Kč; ✆ to 5am Fri & Sat) Guinness and cheap pizza at night and gelati on the square during the day. How very Celtic.

New Peking (☎ 721 631 964; Velké náměstí 10; mains 100Kč; ✆ 10.30am-10.30pm) Is the food at the New Peking as good as old Peking? Probably not, but it's passable Chinese.

Getting There & Away

There are 12 buses a day to Prague (120Kč, 2½ hours), 15 to České Budějovice (40Kč, one hour) and departures all day to Husinec (13Kč, 10 minutes) and Vimperk (24Kč, 40 minutes).

Prachatice is on a minor train line from Volary to Čicenice (40Kč, 45 minutes, 11 trains a day), where it joins the České Budějovice–Plzeň main line.

HUSINEC

pop 1350

The small village of Husinec, 5km north of the town of Prachatice, is known for the **Jan Hus house** (Jana Husav dům), where the reformist preacher Jan Hus is said to have been born around 1371, and its small **museum** (☎ 388 331 284; adult/concession 20/10Kč; ✆ 9am-noon & 1-4pm Tue-Sun May-Sep). In early July this is the scene of a **Jan Hus commemoration**, with a remembrance ceremony, cultural events and exhibitions. The main square, Prokopovo náměstí, has a large **statue of Hus** that was erected in 1958.

Penzión u Blanice (☎ 388 331 062; Komenského 38; s/d 450/800Kč) Conveniently near the bus station, this is a reasonable option for stopovers.

SOUTH BOHEMIA

VIMPERK
pop 8000

This is a pleasant town with a castle majestically perched on a hill – but not much else. The **castle**, founded at the end of the 13th century but incinerated after a lightning strike in 1857, is still extremely dilapidated, but the views make a climb up the **Vlček tower** (Vlčkova věž; admission 5Kč) worthwhile. There's also a small **museum** (adult/concession 20/10Kč; 9am-noon & 1-4pm Tue-Sun May-Oct), with some so-so glass (Vimperk is a centre for glass manufacturing) exhibits. Bohemia's first calendar was printed here in 1484, but you get the feeling that not much has happened since.

The town grew around the castle, prospering from trade along the so-called Golden trail (Zlatá stezka) between Bavaria and Bohemia. Some Gothic and Renaissance houses remain in the square, along with the Gothic **Black tower** (Černá věž). A small **museum** about the Golden trail (adult/concession 20/10Kč; by appointment) is in the same building as the tourist information office.

Orientation & Information

The train and bus stations are 3km from the castle and old town; turn left onto the highway and continue downhill. Buses to town are frequent in the morning, less so in the afternoon.

The **tourist information office** (městské informační středisko; 388 411 894; www.mesto.vimperk.cz; náměstí Svobody 8; 9am-5pm Mon-Fri, 9am-4pm Sat & Sun May-Sep, 9am-4pm Mon-Fri Oct-Apr) is on the main square.

Sleeping & Eating

Autocamp Vodnik (388 415 656; www.autokemp vodnik.cz; Jiraskova 278; tent/bungalow 80/170Kč; Jun-Aug; P) This camp site, 2km from the train station (follow signs to Zdíknov), is the closest to the centre.

Terasa Hotel (388 411 212; www.hotelterasa.cz; Pasovská 34; s/d incl breakfast 690/1380Kč; P) Just off the main road to Strakonice, the huge rooms in this grand old dame have recently been refurbished. Friendly staff and a popular downstairs restaurant make this Vimperk's best bet.

Amber Hotel Anna (388 412 050; www.legner.cz; Kaplířova 168; s/d incl breakfast 1600/2200Kč; P) Loads of marble in the lobby but slightly impersonal staff make this spot the poshest place in town.

Restaurace Lotte (388 514 034; Rožmberská 4; mains 100-200Kč; 10am-10pm Mon-Thu, to midnight Fri & Sat, to 9pm Sun) Concealed on the first floor down a sleepy shopping arcade is this bright and buzzy spot with huge steaks and a big local following.

Getting There & Away

Buses are less frequent but faster than trains to Strakonice (30Kč, 40 minutes), Prachatice (28Kč, 35 minutes), České Budějovice (72Kč, 2¼ hours) and Prague (110Kč, three hours).

Vimperk is an hour from either end of the Strakonice–Volary train line, with eight trains a day (46Kč) through beautiful mountain and forest scenery.

ŽELEZNÁ RUDA & AROUND

The name of this popular Šumava ski resort means 'Iron Ore', which hints at its 16th-century mining origins. The main thing to do now, however, is walk.

Orientation

The train station for the village of Železná Ruda is 2km from the German border, at an elevation of about 750m.

Along the road to Nýrsko, a green-marked trail (4km in all) climbs north to Špičák, a ski area in a saddle (Špičácké sedlo) at about 1000m. About 7km beyond this, at 900m, is another village and ski area, Hojsova Stráž.

Activities

About 2.5km from the village towards the saddle is a year-round **chairlift** to a lookout tower at the summit of **Pancíř** (1214m). Alternatively, you can hike up to it from the saddle on a red-marked trail.

From Špičák you can also climb to the Šumava's two largest glacial lakes. The 18-hectare **Black lake** (Černé jezero) is 4.5km to the northwest on a yellow-marked road. Smaller **Devil's lake** (Čertovo jezero) is 2.5km southwest of the saddle, by trail only. Both lakes are on a red-marked trail that continues northwest along the border for 25km.

Sleeping

There are plain camp sites 1km northeast of Železná Ruda on the road to Čachrov, and at Brčálník, about midway between Špičácké sedlo and Hojsova Stráž.

There are plenty of hotels, although private rooms are better value (watch for signs).

Getting There & Away

Železná Ruda is easiest to reach by train from Plzeň (120Kč, 2½ hours, about 10 direct trains a day) or Klatovy (64Kč, one hour, 12 a day). About half of these continue across the border to Bayerisch Eisenstein; the border is open 24 hours.

PÍSECKO REGION

PÍSEK

pop 30,000

At the heart of Písecko, a traditional gold-panning area, Písek is named for the Czech word for the sand (*písek*) from which the gold was panned. In typical Czech style, the town's elegant old town is surrounded by an expanding ring of industry. Unlike other Bohemian towns however, sympathetic modern development is occurring side-by-side with the historic heart. Cross Bohemia's oldest bridge to the western side of the Otava river, and a funky new neighbourhood is adding a new chapter to the town's interesting history that is displayed in Písek's fine museum.

History

The town and castle, plus a church and monastery, were founded in 1243 by Přemysl Otakar II. The town prospered from its position on the Golden Trail trading route, and Charles IV established salt and grain storage houses here. Písek backed the Hussites, but was taken and virtually emptied by Hapsburg forces early in the Thirty Years' War. It was re-energised with the logging trade in the late 18th century.

The poet Frána Šrámek (1877–1952), who has inspired a number of directors to make films in the town, lived here.

Orientation

The train and bus stations are near each other, 1km south of the city centre. To get to the centre walk up Nádražní, turn right at Budovcova, left at Chelčíkeho, cross Alšovo náměstí, and take Jungmannova to the main square, Velké náměstí.

Information

Infocentrum (☎ 382 213 592; www.icpisek.cz; Heydukova 97; ☺ 9am-6pm May-Sep, 9am-5pm Mon-Fri Oct-Apr) is just off Velké náměstí. It has internet access (1Kč per minute) and in summer provides walking tours of the town (adult/concession 100/50Kč).

KB (Velké náměstí) has an exchange and ATM.

Sights

The 13th-century castle was never rebuilt after a 1510 fire. Only the original right wing remains today, hidden inside a courtyard just off the main square. Nowadays, it houses the superb **Prácheňské historické muzeum** (☎ 382 211 111; Velké náměstí 114; adult/concession 30/10Kč; ☺ 9am-6pm Tue-Sun Mar-Sep, to 5pm Oct-Feb), with first-rate displays on the Nazi and communist eras.

Next door is the baroque **town hall**, which replaced the castle's left wing. **Putim gate** (Putimská brána) is the only section left from the castle's original fortifications.

There are some finely decorated Renaissance and baroque houses on Velké náměstí and Jungmannova. Mikuláš Aleš (see Around Blatna, p189) designed the sgraffito decoration of the **Hotel Otava**. Most enjoyable is a walk along the Otava near the stone **Kamenný bridge**, which dates from the second half of the 13th century and is the oldest in Bohemia (even predating Prague's Charles' bridge).

Across the bridge on the western side of the river is a new development including shops and apartments that locals have taken to calling it **Portyč**, a reference to its resemblance to Portici near Naples. Wishful thinking maybe, but the area comes as a pleasant (and modern) surprise when you're beginning to become blasé about the heritage glories of so many Bohemian old towns.

Festivals & Events

The Písecko region's preoccupation with gold-panning is celebrated in early August with a **panning championship** that is held anywhere between Slaník, a few kilometres east of Strakonice, and Kestřany, near Písek. In early June there is also the **Písek Historical Festival**.

Sleeping

Municipal Ubytovna (☎ 382 214 644; Dr M Horákové 1748; dm per person 150Kč; P) Just over 1km east of the main square, down Budá and left into Harantova, this hostel is cheap and clean.

Pension u Kloudů (☎ 382 210 802; Nerudova 66; s/d 500/850Kč) The downstairs bar is busy, but the rooms are quiet and comfortable.

Hotel Bílá Růže (☎ 382 214 931; www.hotelbilaruze.cz; Šrámkova 169; s/d incl breakfast 1000/1250Kč; P) Undergoing refurbishment at the time of writing, the

'White Rose' is blooming again to provide a more traditional alternative to the minimalist stylings of the newly opened Biograf.

City Hotel (☎ 382 215 634; www.cityhotel.cz; Alšovo náměstí 35; s/d incl breakfast 1000/1250Kč) With rooms even more chintzy than the Bílá Růže, the City is your best bet for a good old-fashioned night's sleep in this comfortable heritage hotel on a quiet square.

Biograf (☎ 380 425 510; www.hotelbiograf.cz; Gregorova 124; s/d incl breakfast 1100/1550Kč; 🖳) Write your own life story at this flash new boutique hotel in a refurbished cinema on the edge of the old town.

Eating

Restaurace U Přemysla Otakara II (☎ 382 212 132; Velké náměstí 114; mains 80-170Kč) Sure it's a beer hall, but with less smoke, tasty Bohemian food, and a more diverse clientele, it's a cut above most others.

U Zlatého Býka (☎ 382 221 286; Kocínova 1; mains 90-220Kč) Písek's best steaks and brochettes are served up in the trendy interior, or out on the sunny terrace. Head south off Velké náměstí down Frán Štrámka.

Pizzeria San Marco (☎ 382 224 389; Velké náměstí 18; pizza 100Kč) Písek's hipper citizens crowd this popular terrace eatery for good thin-crust pizza and then linger over nice strong coffee.

Julius Meinl supermarket (cnr Velké náměstí & Jungmannova) For self-caterers.

Getting There & Away

Regular direct trains run to Plzeň (140Kč, two hours), České Budějovice (64Kč, 1¼ hours) and Tábor (76Kč, 1½ hours). Other services change at Ražice or Protivín.

Buses also run to České Budějovice (48Kč, 50 minutes), Prague (84Kč, 1½ hours) and Orlik (32Kč, 40 minutes).

STRAKONICE

pop 23,800

Filling the locals with pride is Strakonice's reputation as a centre for bagpipes (*dudy* in Czech), and the industrial town now turns out a diverse quattro of Turkish fez hats, handguns, CZ Motorcyles and the aforementioned musical instruments (try combining all four in one twisted image). We're not sure which of them made General Patton base himself in the town when the US army liberated parts of Bohemia in 1945.

Orientation & Information

The train and bus stations are about 1km southeast of the city centre.

Česká spořitelna (Velké náměstí 55) changes money and has an ATM.

Ciao (☎ 383 323 400; Zámek 1; ⏰ 8am-6pm Mon-Fri) doubles as the tourist information office.

Sights

In the remains of the derelict **castle** (Strakonický hrad; admission free; ⏰ 9am-5pm Tue-Sun Jul-Aug, 8am-4pm May, Jun, Sep & Oct) is the **regional museum** (muzeum Středního Pootaví Strakonice; adult/concession 30/20Kč; ⏰ same as castle) with exhibits on gold panning and local industry, including a collection of *dudy*. There is also a **tower** (adult/concession 10/5Kč) to climb. In the southern area of the castle is the two-aisled **St Procopius church**. The adjoining four-winged **Gothic monastery** dates from the 13th century and includes an important collection of paintings from the early 14th century.

Of Velké náměstí's sgraffitoed buildings, the finest is the former **town hall** by Mikuláš Aleš; others are the **municipal headquarters** (městký úřad) and **Investiční banka**.

Festivals & Events

In mid-August the castle hosts an **International Bagpipe Festival** (Mezinárodní dudácký festival; www.dudackyfestival.cz). The festival occurs every two years and was last held in 2006.

Sleeping & Eating

Autokemping Podskalí (☎ 383 322 024; tent/3-bed hut 70/450Kč; ⏰ Apr-Sep; 🅿) This is a long walk west out of town and past the castle, along the Otava. You can also catch buses 380160 and 380130 from the station or near the castle.

Hotel Bílá Růže (☎ 383 321 946; www.hotelruzest.cz Palackého náměstí 80; d 1000Kč) There are lots of 'White Roses' (Bílá Růže), on the exterior façade and in the lobby, but they're looking a little wilted now. The rooms are plain, and this elegant building is just crying out for refurbishment. Downstairs is a passable Chinese restaurant (mains 80Kč).

Amber Hotel Bavor (☎ 383 321 300; www.legner.cz; Na Ohradě 31; s/d incl breakfast 1450/2000Kč; 🅿 ♿) Located in what could be described as an ugly shoebox of a building, the Amber Hotel Bavor nonetheless has clean and modern (1980s) rooms. When we visited, a conference for vacuum cleaner salespeople was being held. Yep, it's that kind of place.

Restaurace Kalích and **U Madly** (☎ 383 321 306; Velké náměstí 80; mains 100-160Kč; ⏰ 11am-midnight Mon-Thu, 11.30am-2am Fri, 2pm-2am Sat) Both spots are opposite the **municipal headquarters** (městký úřad). Kalích is a huge medieval restaurant, and U Madly a relaxed bar with a wide range of beers.

For a taste of Strakonice's own Nektar or Dudák beers head to **U zborova** (Bavorova 20).

Pekast (cnr Palackého náměstí & SV Markéty) For pastries, cakes and baguettes.

Getting There & Away

There are regular direct trains to Plzeň (98Kč, one hour), Blatná (40Kč, 44 minutes), Písek (34Kč, 33 minutes) and České Budějovice (76Kč, 50 minutes). Buses are a bit cheaper on the same routings and are the best bet for Prague (96Kč, two hours).

BLATNÁ

pop 6700

Blatná's name comes from the district's *blata* (fens) that were drained and made into ponds. If you're in the area it is worth seeing the 13th-century castle General Patton occupied in 1945. Before 1989 the town's liberation by the US Army on 5 May 1945 was not celebrated, but now locals are making up for lost time.

The **tourist information office** (informační centrum; ☎ 383 420 389; JP Koubka 7; ⏰ 9am-5.30pm Mon-Fri, 9am-1pm Sat, 2-5pm Sun) can help with accommodation and internet access.

Sights

The 13th-century **castle** (Vodní hrad; ☎ 383 422 934; adult/concession 80/60Kč, in English 150/80Kč; ⏰ 10am-4pm Tue-Sun Jun-Sep, 10am-4pm Sat & Sun Apr, May & Oct) was rebuilt several times before a major makeover in the mid-19th century. A 50-minute tour takes in the **Hunting room** (Lovecký sál), with furniture made from stag horns. The castle is connected by a bridge to the large **English garden** (anglický park), ideal for picnics.

The **cathedral of the Virgin** (chrám Panny Marie), across from the castle on náměstí Míru, is one of Bohemia's most valuable, late-Gothic structures.

Sleeping & Eating

The tourist information office can suggest private rooms.

Penzion Foto-Art (☎ 603 231 456; TG Masaryka 270; s/d 800/1400Kč) The super clean and comfy rooms above this camera shop are decorated with

owner Pavel's photographs. They're really rather good.

Pizzeria Casa Verde (☎ 775 168 775; náměstí míru 107; pizza 100Kč; ⏰ 11am-10pm Mon-Thu, to 11pm Fri & Sat) It's actually in a yellow building, but we'll forgive them because the pizza is so good.

Getting There & Away

Regular buses link Blatná and Strakonice (40Kč, 45 minutes). To/from Plzeň, change at Nepomuk. There are infrequent buses to Prague (76Kč, 1½ hours).

AROUND BLATNÁ

About 11km east of Blatná is **Mirotice**, the birthplace of Mikuláš Aleš (1852–1913). Aleš was the foremost artist of Bohemia's so-called 'National Theatre generation', which focused on folk themes from Czech history. His designs decorate houses in Písek, Plzeň and Strakonice; and the house where he was born is now a small **museum** (adult/concession 25/10Kč; ⏰ 10am-4pm Tue-Sun Apr-Oct) dedicated to him. The museum is down Mikoláše Aleše, which runs from the southern corner of the main square.

The village is just west of the Písek-Březnice road, with several buses a day travelling the 20km to Písek (15Kč, 30 minutes).

ORLÍK NAD VLTAVOU

Though still one of the finest castles in the republic, Orlík has been vigorously renovated to the point of sterility; in summer it's also oppressively crowded. (The nearby Zvíkov castle offers a more authentic experience; see p190.) Orlík's main asset is its setting – on a cliff-lined bay encircled by trees. The castle was once high above the Vltava, but the Orlík dam has filled the valley almost to the castle's lower walls.

The town of Orlík is 500m north of the castle.

Orlík Castle

The original, early-Gothic **castle** (☎ 382 275 101; adult/concession 70/30Kč, in English 140/70Kč; ⏰ 9am-6pm Tue-Sun Jun-Aug, to 5pm May & Sep, to 4pm Apr & Oct) dates from the 13th century. After fires in 1514 and 1802, it was rebuilt and extended. The last Czech owner, Krištof ze Švamberka, lost the castle after the Battle of the White Mountain, when it fell into Austrian hands; the Schwarzenbergs held it from 1719 until 1945, when it was seized by the state.

SOUTH BOHEMIA

In 1992 it was returned to the Schwarzen-bergs, and the one-hour castle tour is mainly about them. The highlight is a magnificently carved wooden ceiling that took four years to complete. In the thickly wooded gardens is the **Schwarzenberg mausoleum** (Švarcenberská hrobka). A number of hiking trails start from here.

From late June to August **Quarter** (☎ 382 275 333; www.lodnidopravaquarter.cz) runs five boats a day (less often in May and September), to the dam (adult/concession 100/50Kč, one hour) and Zvíkov castle (adult/concession 80/40Kč, 50 minutes). Tickets can be bought from the boats, which depart from just below the castle. The castle cash desk has timetables.

Small boats also offer short cruises of the lake.

Sleeping & Eating

Restaurace U Cvrků (☎ 382 275 124; s/d 200/400Kč) This inn in the centre of the village has robust food and basic rooms.

Restaurace U Toryka (☎ 382 275 181; mains 100-140Kč) Near the castle, this place serves the tourist crowd, so its tasty meals are a tad overpriced.

Getting There & Away

By bus from Prague you'll need to change at Písek (1½ hours, 80Kč). From Písek it's another 50 minutes to Orlík (32Kč).

ZVÍKOV CASTLE

pop 250

This small Gothic **castle** (☎ 382 285 676; adult/concession 50/30Kč; ☺ 9am-noon & 1-5pm Tue-Sun Jun-Aug, to 4pm May & Sep, 9.30am-noon & 12.30-3.30pm Sat & Sun Apr & Oct), built by the Přemysl princes in the 13th century, commands a better position than Orlík. The castle sits high above the lake, at the point where the Otava and Vltava rivers enter it. During the rebellion of the Czech Estates in 1618, a garrison of 140 men successfully defended the castle against 4000 Hapsburg troops. Unlike many Bohemian castles, it retains a medieval look.

A self-guided tour takes in furniture, weapons and a frescoed ballroom, plus a chapel with an altar featuring the Deposition of Christ and Veneration of the Three Kings (Oplakávání Krista a Klanění Tří králů), all in one painting.

From personal experience we do not recommend driving a Skoda Fabia across the castle's narrow stone bridge. You'll soon discover there's nowhere to turn around on the other side.

Sleeping & Eating

Without a car, it is difficult to see both Zvíkov and Orlík castles without staying the night. At the village of Zvíkovské Podhradí, a walk of just over 1km south from Zvíkov castle, there are private rooms available.

Pivovar Zvíkov (☎ 382 285 660; www.pivovar-zvikov .cz; d with breakfast 1240Kč; ℗) On the road from the village to the castle, this new place combines tidy rooms with a micro-brewery and spacious restaurant.

Getting There & Away

Up to seven buses a day cover the 19km from Písek to Zvíkovské Podhradí (20Kč). Alternatively, it is a fine 14km walk on a marked trail beside the lake between the castles of Zvíkov and Orlík, or you can take a boat (see Orlík castle, p189). Cyclists have to use the minor road further inland.

NORTHEASTERN REGION

Infused in this quiet, predominantly rural corner of South Bohemia are some of the darkest times in European history. As the hub of the Hussite movement, lead by Jan Žižka and Prokop Holý, the area was central to the Protestant sect's struggle with the Catholic authorities, which eventually escalated into the Thirty Years' War and engulfed Central Europe.

Today the languid landscape of rolling cornfields and quiet village squares conceals the ideological battles, and only the former Hussite bastion of Tábor hints at a military past punctuated by blood and religion.

The area's highlights include its spiritual heart, Tábor, the serene Renaissance perfection of Slavonice and the lakeside castle at Jindřichův Hradec.

TÁBOR

pop 36,000

Perched on a steep hillside falling to dense woodland on three sides, the natural defences of Tábor's old town are as daunting today as they were when the Hussites established their

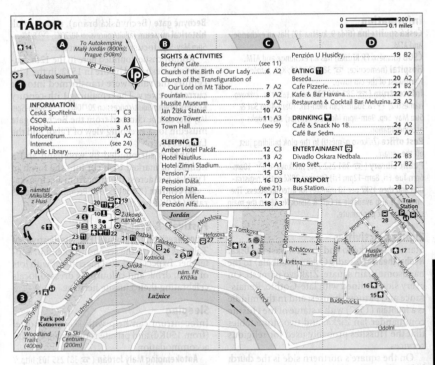

TÁBOR

0 .... 200 m
0 .... 0.1 miles

INFORMATION
Česká Spořitelna..................1 C3
ČSOB..................................2 B3
Hospital..............................3 A1
Infocentrum........................4 A2
Internet..........................(see 24)
Public Library.....................5 C2

SIGHTS & ACTIVITIES
Bechyně Gate...................(see 11)
Church of the Birth of Our Lady 6 A2
Church of the Transfiguration of
   Our Lord on Mt Tábor...........7 A2
Fountain.............................8 A2
Hussite Museum.................9 A2
Jan Žižka Statue................10 A2
Kotnov Tower....................11 A3
Town Hall........................(see 9)

SLEEPING
Amber Hotel Palcát............12 C3
Hotel Nautilus..................13 A2
Hotel Zimni Stadium...........14 A1
Pension 7.........................15 D3
Pension Dáša.....................16 D3
Pension Jana..................(see 21)
Pension Milena..................17 D3
Penzión Alfa.....................18 A3

Penzión U Husičky..............19 B2

EATING
Beseda..............................20 A2
Cafe Pizzerie.....................21 B2
Kafe & Bar Havana...............22 A2
Restaurant & Cocktail Bar Meluzina.23 A2

DRINKING
Café & Snack No 18.............24 A2
Café Bar Sedm....................25 A2

ENTERTAINMENT
Divadlo Oskara Nedbala.........26 B3
Kino Svět..........................27 B2

TRANSPORT
Bus Station........................28 D2

bastion here six centuries ago. Enriched by a robust diet of ideology and warfare, the radical Protestant sect further enhanced the location's innate defensive qualities by constructing their town as a maze of narrow lanes and protruding houses.

Rather than 15th-century Catholic warriors, today it is an army of tourists challenged by the wildly winding alleys and lanes, to finally re-emerge on one of Bohemia's most beautiful and idiosyncratic town squares.

Evident all around the old town, the nonconformist streak initiated by the town's original inhabitants is maintained in a collection of funky and youthful bars, cafés and *pensions*.

History

Archaeological evidence suggests that Tábor was a Celt settlement in around 100 BC. A castle and town called Hradiště were established by Přemysl Otakar II in the 13th century, only to be burned down in 1277 by the Víteks. In the 14th century the lords of Sezimové z Ústí built a castle here, of which all that remains is the single Kotnov tower.

God's Warriors, the Hussites, founded Tábor proper in 1420 as a military bastion in defiance of Catholic Europe. The town was organised according to the biblical precept that 'nothing is mine and nothing is yours, because the community is owned equally by everyone'. New arrivals threw all their worldly possessions into large casks at the marketplace and joined in communal work. This extreme nonconformity helped to give the word 'Bohemian' the connotations we associate with it today. Planned as a bulwark against Catholics in České Budějovice and further south, Tábor is a warren of narrow streets with protruding houses that were intended to weaken an enemy attack. After the Taborites' defeat at the Battle of Lipany in 1434, the town's significance declined.

Orientation

The old town is 500m west from the train and bus stations, through Husův park and along 9. května. The latter runs to náměstí FR Křižíka, from where Palackého and Pražská lead through the old town to Žižkovo náměstí.

SOUTH BOHEMIA

Information

Česká spořitelna (třída 9. května 10) Has an exchange and ATM.

ČSOB (náměstí FR Křižíka) Has an exchange and ATM.

Hospital (nemocnice; ☎ 381 608 111; Kpt. Jaroše) Northwest of the old town.

Infocentrum (☎ 381 486 230; www.tabor.cz; Žižkovo náměstí 2; ⊗ 8.30am-7pm Mon-Fri, 10am-4pm Sat & Sun May-Sep, 9am-4pm Mon-Fri Oct-Apr) Also books accommodation.

Post office (Žižkovo náměstí) In the pink building just off the square.

Public Library (☎ 381 252 750; Jiřskova 4; ⊗ 10am-6pm Tue-Fri, 8am-12pm Fri) Charges 20Kč initial registration and then 15Kč per 10 minutes for internet access. The internet is also available at Café & Snack No 18 on the main square for 1Kč per minute.

Sights & Activities

Start on Palackého and go west past the **Oskar Nedbal theatre** (divadlo Oskara Nedbala) to the handsome main square, Žižkovo náměstí. On every side it's lined with late-Gothic, Renaissance and baroque houses; and in the middle is a **fountain** (1567) with a statue of the Hussite commander Jan Žižka, and two stone tables that the Hussites probably used for religious services.

On the square's northern side is the **church of the Transfiguration of Our Lord on Mt Tábor** (kostel Proměnění Páně na hoře Tábor), built between 1440 and 1512 and known for its vaulting and the neo-Gothic altar) its **tower** (adult/concession 20/15Kč; ⊗ 10am-5pm May-Aug, Sat & Sun only Sep & Oct, weather dependent) is open for a sweeping view of Tábor.

The other imposing building on Žižkovo náměstí is the early-Renaissance **town hall** (1521), now the **Hussite museum** (Husitské muzeum; ☎ 381 252 245; adult/concession 60/30Kč; ⊗ 8.30am-5pm Apr-Oct, Mon-Fri only Nov-Mar), with a copy of a peasant wagon mounted with cannons – the ingenious prototype tank invented by Jan Žižka.

Also here is the entrance to a 650m stretch of **underground passages** (podzemní chodby; adult/concession 40/20Kč; ⊗ same as museum), which is open for visits only when a group of five people forms. The passages, constructed in the 15th century as refuges during fires or times of war, were also used to store food and to mature beer.

The archipelago at Žižkovo náměstí 22, beside the town hall, leads into Mariánská and then Klokotská, which runs southwest to

Bechyně gate (Bechyňská brána), now a small **historical museum** (adult/concession 40/20Kč; ⊗ 8.30am-5pm May-Sep) focusing on peasant life.

Kotnov castle, founded here in the 12th century, was destroyed by fire in 1532; in the 17th century the ruins were transformed into the current brewery. The remaining 15th-century **Kotnov tower** (adult/concession 20/10Kč; ⊗ 8.30am-5pm May-Sep) can be climbed from the Bechyně gate museum for a sweeping view of Tábor and the Lužnice river.

Tábor is surrounded by woodland and a number of marked **trails** cut into the forest of Tynska, just across the river from Bechyňská.

Ski Centrum (☎ 381 251 369; Bechyňská 398) rents rafts (450Kč per day).

Festivals & Events

Tabor Meetings, the annual Hussite Festival of Tábor is held on the second weekend in September. Expect medieval merriment with lots of food, drink and colourfully dressed locals celebrating their Hussite heritage.

Sleeping

Infocentrum can help with seasonal hostel (from 150Kč) and private room (from 250Kč) accommodation.

Autokemping Malý Jordán (☎ 381 235 103; http://web.quick.cz/atc-mj; tent/bungalow per person 60/150Kč; ⊗ May-Sep; **P**) This camp site is 1km north of the town near Lake Jordán. Catch bus 20 or 21 from the main train station.

Pension Milena (☎ 381 254 755; milena.sport@volny .cz; Husův náměstí 529; s/d 300/400Kč) This welcoming hostel-style place can supply breakfast, or you can make your own mess in the 'ezy-kleen' Formica-encased shared kitchen.

Penzión Alfa (☎ 381 256 165; www.pensionalfa.zde .cz; Klokotská; s/d/tr 500/800/1200Kč) This popular spot occupies a cosy corner just metres from the main square. Upstairs the rooms are snug but spacious, and downstairs you can get your Geronimojo back at the funky Native American-themed café. If that doesn't work, try the groovily hip massage place across the lane.

Pension Jana (☎ 381 254 667; www.bedandbreak fast.euweb.cz; Kostinická 161; s/d/tr 600/1000/1250Kč; **P**) Expect a warm welcome and spacious attic rooms at the friendly spot tucked down a quiet lane.

Pension 7 (☎ 381 252 039; Bílkova 783; s/d incl breakfast 650/900Kč) Functional but friendly place with shared bathrooms.

Penzión u Husičky (☎ 381 256 419; Tržní 274; s/d incl breakfast 700/900Kč) There are inviting fragrances coming from the health food store downstairs, and the large modern rooms and giant breakfasts don't disappoint either. You'll need to get there by 5pm before the owner closes up his great smelling shop.

Pension Dáša (☎ 381 256 253; www.travelguide.cz /pensiondasa; Bílkova 735; s/d incl breakfast 700/990Kč; P) Work off the *pivo* in the sauna and gym at this friendly and convenient *pension*.

Hotel Nautilus (☎ 380 900 900; www.hotelnautilus.cz; Žižkovo náměstí 20; s/d 1950/2200 to 2500Kč; P 🔀) Tabor's first and only boutique hotel is pure class from the effortlessly cool bar to the crisply minimalist rooms, and surprisingly affordable for such international ambience right on the main square.

Eating & Drinking

Kafe & Bar Havana (☎ 381 253 383; Žižkovo náměstí 17; mains 60-200Kč) Is this place Czech-Mex or Czé Guevara? Either way the combination of Czech and Mexican food and good honest cocktails makes for main square fun.

Café & Snack No 18 (Žižkovo náměstí 18; snacks 70Kč) Taborites drop by after work and stay for the lively atmosphere and tasty nibbles. We came for a single beer and stayed for the cocktails and weirdly familiar-sounding Czech indie pop.

Café Pizzerie (☎ 381 254 048; Kostnická 159; pizza 70-115Kč) Grab a spot on the tiny outside terrace and enjoy good Italian food.

Beseda (☎ 381 254 180; Žižkovo náměstí 17; mains 100-200Kč; ☯ to 3pm Sat, closed Sun) Rough and ready – and that's just the mob beside you. Beseda is popular with locals for the great value daily specials on robust Czech favourites. There's Bernard and Budvar on tap and you might even get lucky with live music at night.

Entertainment

Divadlo Oskara Nedbala (☎ 381 254 701; www.divadlo tabor.cz in Czech; Palackého) Tábor's theatre is closed in summer, but during the rest of the year you can see everything from jazz and classical music to Czech theatre.

Kino Svět (☎ 381 252 200; náměstí FR Křižíka 129) See Hollywood favourites at Tabor's cinema (80Kč), and chat about them afterwards at the café next door.

Getting There & Away

Bus (☎ 381 253 898) is generally the best way in and out of Tábor. Direct services include:

Prague (80Kč, 1½ hours), České Budějovice (60Kč, one hour), Jihlava (68Kč, 1½ hours) and Brno (150Kč, three hours). Most services to Plzeň are via Prague or České Budějovice, but there is one direct service a day (120Kč, 2½ hours). For Telč, you will have to change in Jihlava.

Trains (☎ 381 484 111) also make the run to Prague (144Kč, 1½ hours), but they are generally more expensive and less convenient.

AROUND TÁBOR
Chýnov Cave

At the **Chýnov Cave** (Chýnovská jeskyně; ☎ 361 809 034; adult/concession 50/25Kč; ☯ 9am-4.30pm Tue-Sun Jul-Aug, to 3.30pm May, Jun, Sep & Aug) a narrow passage descends 37m to the colourful stalagmites formed by slowly dripping, mineral-laden water. Re-opened in 2006 with dramatic new lighting, the cave is a 3km walk on a blue-marked trail northeast from the train station at Chýnov, which is four stops east of Tábor on the Pelhřimov line.

Soběslav
pop 7300

During the Hussite Wars Soběslav, 18km south of Tábor, was Oldřich Rožmberk's main defensive stronghold against the Hussite armies.

The main attractions of this small town are its two double-naved Gothic churches: **St Vitus church** (kostel sv Víta) and the **church of our Lady** (kostel Panny Marie). The latter is notable for its tower, built in 1487, and an elaborate vaulted ceiling in the crypt.

BECHYNĚ
pop 5700

A quiet spa town, largely off the beaten track, Bechyně has been revitalised in recent years with the renovation of its beautiful castle. Standing over the precipice of the Smutná creek (there are vertiginous views coming into town over the bridge from Tábor), the chateau backs onto an impressive square featuring a few worthwhile sights of its own. The town is one of the oldest settlements in Bohemia with archaeological evidence of settlement 3000 years ago.

Orientation & Information

The adjacent bus and train stations are 500m southwest from the castle and the main square, náměstí TG Masaryka.

Avanti Travel (☎ 381 213 822; www.avantitravel
.cz; náměstí TG Masaryka; ⏰ 8am-7pm May-14 Sep; 10am-
noon & 2-5pm Mon-Fri 15 Sep-Apr) is on the northeast
side of the town square. Friendly owners
John Davey from England, and his Czech
wife Ilona, provide interesting walking tours
and also act as the local tourist information
office.

Sights & Activities
CASTLE
The **castle** (☎ 381 213 143; www.zamekbechyne.cz adult/
concession 90/50Kč, in English 150Kč; ⏰ 10am-5pm Tue-Sun
18 May-Sep) is one of many founded by Přemysl
Otakar II and later owned by a parade of noble
families, including the Rožmberks.

After years of dereliction, it was recently
returned to its original owner and, following
hefty reconstruction, now looks in fabulously
fine fettle.

You can visit large portions of the interior,
including its impressive weapons collection,

Black Kitchen (the historic kitchen complete with all the old cooking paraphernalia)
and portrait galleries as part of a 50-minute
tour.

In the castle grounds, you can also visit the
Vladimír Preclík museum (muzeum Vladimíra Preclíka;
adult/concession 50/30Kč; ⏰ same as castle), which offers an interesting insight into the life of this
famous Czech writer/sculptor. The attractive
grounds are perfect for a picnic and host an
annual **summer cultural programme**.

The **Franciscan monastery** (Klršterini; adult/conces-
sion 100/80Kč) high above the river is now a ceramics school but visits can be arranged from
May to September through Avanti Travel.

MUSEUMS & CHURCHES
In the 15th century Bechyně grew famous
for its ceramics. The large **South Bohemian Aleš
gallery** (Alšova Jihočeská galerie; adult/concession 30/15Kč;
⏰ 9am-noon & 1-5pm Tue-Sun May-Sep) is in a former
brewery just off náměstí TG Masaryka.

THE HUSSITES
When Jan Hus was burned for heresy at Constance in 1415, the consequences were far greater
than the Catholic authorities could have foreseen. His death caused a religious revolt among the
Czechs, who had seen Hus' adoption of the Czech mass as a step towards religious and national
self-determination. Hus himself had not intended such drastic revolution, focusing on a translation of the Latin rite, and the giving of bread and wine to all the congregation instead of to the
clergy alone. But for many the time was ripe for church reform.

Hus was born around 1372 in Husinec, South Bohemia. From a poor background, he managed
to become a lecturer at Charles University in Prague and in 1402 was ordained a preacher. He
dreamt of a return to the original doctrines of the church – tolerance, humility, simplicity – but
such a message had political overtones for a church that treated forgiveness as an opportunity
to make money.

Tried on a trumped-up charge of heresy at Constance, in present-day Germany, Hus was burned
at the stake on 6 July 1415. The trial was doubly unjust, in that Hus had been given safe conduct
by the Holy Roman Emperor Sigismund.

In Bohemia many nobles offered to guarantee protection to those who practised religion
according to Hus' teachings, and Hussite committees became widespread. The movement split
over its relationship with the secular authorities, with the moderate Utraquists siding in 1434
with the Catholic Sigismund.

The more radical Taborites, seeing themselves as God's warriors, fought the Catholics in every
way. As the military base for the Hussites, Tábor – named after the biblical Mt Tabor – was successfully defended by a mainly peasant army under Jan Žižka (see p169) and Prokop Holý.

The movement also attracted supporters from other Protestant sects in Europe. Many con-
verged on Tábor and many of the groups joined against the crusading armies of the Holy Roman
Empire.

Hussite ideals were never extinguished in Bohemia. Although the Utraquists became the dominant force after defeating (with the help of Sigismund's Catholic forces) the Taborites at the Battle
of Lipany in 1434, the peace guaranteed religious freedom for the movement. It took almost 200
years before Protestantism was suppressed in the Czech Lands by the Catholic Hapsburg rulers
following the Battle of the White Mountain.

The small **Firefighting museum** (Hasičské muzeum; adult/concession 30/15Kč; 9am-noon & 1-5pm Tue-Sun Jul-Sep), in a sturdy corner building on the main square, displays several wonderful old fire engines. Outside of summer access is possible for groups of five people or more. Ask at Avanti Travel.

At the time of writing a new **museum of Tourism** (adult/concession 40/20Kč; 9am-5pm Jul-Sep) was opening in the Old Synagogue on the main square.

The nearby **Franciscan church**, with fine vaulting and a dazzling clock tower, is open for services only.

Sleeping & Eating

See Avanti Travel for cheap private rooms. Also ask them about the three apartments (1000 to 1250Kč; May to September) they rent in a restored building just off the main square.

Penzión & Vinarna u Pichlů (☎ 381 211 022; d incl breakfast 650Kč) Here's everything you need when you're in Bechyně, with snug rooms above a Gothic restaurant and a spot right on the main square.

Hotel Panska (☎ 381 212 550; www.hotel-bechyne .cz; s/d incl breakfast 1190/1490Kč; P ☒ ☒ ☐) Bechyně's premium accommodation is a tad expensive, but in summer the sunny deck is the place to be.

Getting There & Away

Ten trains a day come from Tábor (40Kč, 47 minutes). In 1903 the Tábor to Bechyně line opened as the Austro-Hungarian Empire's first electrified line and on Saturdays in July and August you can join special excursions on the original train. Buses are faster to Tábor (24Kč, 40 minutes) and České Budějovice (51Kč, 52 minutes).

KÁMEN
pop 125

The Czech word for rock (*kámen*) lends itself to the great boulder that Kámen castle sits on. Founded in the 13th century, the castle was renovated in the 17th century in early-baroque style.

Apart from a few historical displays, the castle's main attraction is a **Motorcycle museum** (muzeum Motocyklo; adult/concession 40/20Kč; 9am-noon & 1-5pm Tue-Sun May-Sep, to 4pm Sat & Sun Apr & Oct), featuring Czech motorbikes from 1899 to the 1960s, including late-model Jawas and ČZs, in their time among the best in the world.

Getting There & Away

Up to five daily buses run to/from Tábor (28Kč, 30 minutes).

PELHŘIMOV
pop 17,000

Slow-moving and pretty, this industrial town has a fine catalogue of Renaissance and baroque houses. Stop by if you're in the area, or if you're into weird world records, otherwise it's not really worth a special trip.

Orientation & Information

The train station is 1.5km south of the old town; to reach it turn left onto Nádražní, follow it past the bus station (keep sharp left) and take Poděbradova left up to the main square.

The **tourist information office** (☎ 565 326 924; www.pelhrimovsko.cz; Masarykovo náměstí 1; 9am-5pm Jun-Sep, to 9.30am Sat & closed Sun Oct-May) is helpful and has internet access for 1Kč per minute. Nearby **Česká spořitelna** has an ATM.

Sights

Most Renaissance houses on and around the square were rebuilt in baroque style after a devastating fire in 1766. One at Masarykovo náměstí 13 was given a striking cubist face by Pavel Janák in 1913.

Also on the square is the ho-hum **Pelhřimov museum** (muzeum vysočiny Pelhřimov; ☎ 565 323 184; adult/concession 30/15Kč; 9am-noon & 12.30-5pm Tue-Sun Apr-Sep, Tue-Fri Oct-Mar). In the courtyard behind the museum a statue of St Václav guards the entrance to a tiny castle, completed in 1554 for the Lords of Říčany, which now houses an extension of the Pelhřimov museum (same opening times and prices).

If you're developing castle fatigue, the **museum of records and curiosities** (muzeum rekordů a kuriozit; ☎ 565 321 327; www.dobryden.cz; Jihalvaskí brřna; adult/concession 40/20Kč; 9am-5pm Apr-Sep) is where you can see a wooden bicycle, a giant ski jacket, and loads of impressive stunts with beer. The guy who runs the museum claims he doesn't like the taste of beer. A Czech man who doesn't partake of *pivo*? Now that's a record. Every year on the second weekend of June the town hosts the annual Festival of Records where Czech gonzos do whatever it takes to set loopy world records.

Just north of the castle is the **church of St Bartholomew** (kostel sv Bartoloměj), with its 61m **lookout tower** (vyhlídkova věž; adult/concession 15/10Kč; same as museum).

Sleeping & Eating

See the information office for a list of accommodation.

Hotel Slavie (☎ 565 321 540; www.hotelslavie.web
.tiscali.cz; Masarykovo náměstí 29; s/d incl breakfast 600/800Kč;
P) With comfortable rooms on the main
square, a sunny downstairs restaurant serving the local Poutník beer, and a first-floor
pizzeria, what more do you need?

Penzion Lucerna (☎ 565 333 333; www.penzionlucerna
.cz; Solní 853; d incl breakfast 900Kč; **P** 🖳) Spacious rooms around a paved courtyard are
Pelhřimov's best value accommodation, and
there is a also a good restaurant and wine bar.

Cukrarna u Radnice (Masarykovo náměstí; sandwiches
11Kč, baguettes 22Kč; 🕑 7am-6pm Mon-Thu, 8am-5pm Sat,
10am-5pm Sun) Grab a coffee and a tasty chicken
schnitzel baguette and watch the world go
slowly by on the main square.

Getting There & Away

Buses run reasonably frequently to Jihlava
(28Kč, 40 minutes). Long-distance buses run
to Prague (81Kč, two hours, up to five a day)
and Brno (105Kč, two hours, up to six a day).
Pelhřimov is on the Jihlava–Tábor train line,
an hour from Tábor (80Kč, 10 trains a day)
and 1¼ hours from Jihlava (72Kč).

JINDŘICHŮV HRADEC

pop 22,600

Back in the Middle Ages quiet Jindřichův
Hradec was one of Bohemia's most important
towns, with wealth drawn from its position
on a trading route to Austria. Reconstruction
from fires in 1435, 1773 and 1801 has created
a broad collage of architecture from the 15th
to the 19th centuries. At its centre is a well-
preserved old town square, and a stunning
lakeside chateau. If you're feeling all castled
out, focus on the new National museum of
Photography, or get wound up by the world's
largest mechanised nativity scene.

Orientation & Information

The adjacent bus and train stations are 1km
from the city centre; to reach the main square
walk south down Nádražní, turn left past a
church onto Klášterská and continue south
down Panská to the main square, náměstí
Míru.

The **tourist information office** (informační středisko;
☎ 384 363 546; www.jh.cz; Panská 136; 🕑 8am-7pm Mon-
Fri, to noon Sat & Sun Jul-Aug, 8am-5pm Mon-Fri, to noon Sat
Sep-Jun) also arranges accommodation.

MyFun NetK@fè (☎ 607 845 155; náměstí Míru) at the
southwest end of the main square has internet
access for 1Kč per minute. There is a wi-fi
hotspot at the **Hotel Concertina.**

ČSOB (náměstí Míru) has exchange and ATM
facilities.

Sights

CHATEAU

Jindřichův Hradec is the Czech Republic's
third-largest **chateau** (☎ 331 321 279; zamekjindrichu
vhradec@elsynet.cz; 🕑 9am-4.15pm Tue-Sun Jun-Aug, 10am-
noon & 1-4.15pm May & Sep, 10am-3.15pm Apr & Oct), covering 3.5 hectares and boasting a hotchpotch
of treasures. A lavish 16th-century monument
to the Renaissance at first glance, the chateau
is in fact a medley of architectural styles, spanning the ages from its foundation at the hands
of Jindřich Vitek in the early 13th century,
right through to the present day.

The jewel of the Renaissance chateau is the
Rondel, an unusual Italianate garden pavilion
decorated with gilded stucco and colourful frescoes, designed in 1591 by Baldassare
Maggi. The highlight of the older, Gothic part
of the castle is the **Ceremonial hall**, where original, 14th-century frescoes illustrate scenes
from the life of St George.

There are three **routes** (one route adult/concession 65/35Kč, in a foreign language 140/70Kč, all three routes
170/80Kč, in a foreign language 400/180Kč) through the
castle. **Route A** takes in Adam's Building, the
Renaissance interiors, Napoleon's bed from
Vienna and the piano played by Mozart; **Route
B** covers the medieval, Gothic interiors; and
Route C explores the 18th- and 19th-century
interiors as well as the Rondel.

AROUND THE OLD TOWN

Sections of the old **town walls** still remain. To
the west is the gate, **Nežárecká brána** (1466). The
main square (náměstí Míru) has several late-
Gothic, Renaissance and baroque houses, the
most notable being the sgraffitoed **Langrův dům**
(náměstí Míru 139) and its vaulted archway.

The **church of the Assumption of Our Lady** (kostel Nanebevzetí Panny Marie), behind the
town hall, has a good cycle of 17th-century
frescoes and photogenic views from its **tower**
(adult/concession 10/5Kč; 🕑 10am-noon & 1-4pm). The
church of St John the Baptist (kostel sv Jana Křtitele;
admission 10Kč; 🕑 9am-noon & 12.30-4.30pm Jun-Aug) is
the oldest church in town and is noteworthy
for some 600-year-old frescoes, including one
of St Louis of Toulouse.

SOUTH BOHEMIA

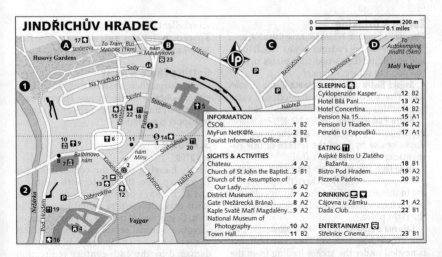

JINDŘICHŮV HRADEC

INFORMATION
ČSOB..............................1 B2
MyFun NetK@fé................2 B2
Tourist Information Office.......3 B1

SIGHTS & ACTIVITIES
Chateau...........................4 A2
Church of St John the Baptist...5 B1
Church of the Assumption of
  Our Lady.......................6 A2
District Museum..................7 A2
Gate (Nežárecká Brána).........8 A2
Kaple Svaté Maří Magdalény...9 A2
National Museum of
  Photography..................10 A2
Town Hall.......................11 B2

SLEEPING
Cyklopenzión Kasper............12 B2
Hotel Bílá Paní.................13 A2
Hotel Concertina................14 B2
Pension Na 15...................15 A1
Pension U Tkadlen...............16 A2
Penzión U Papoušků.............17 A1

EATING
Asijské Bistro U Zlatého
  Bažanta.......................18 B1
Bistro Pod Hradem..............19 A2
Pizzeria Padrino................20 B2

DRINKING
Cájovna u Zámku................21 A2
Dada Club......................22 B1

ENTERTAINMENT
Střelnice Cinema................23 B1

NATIONAL MUSEUM OF PHOTOGRAPHY
Recently opened in the sgraffito and frescoed splendour of the Jesuit college is the **National museum of Photography** (☎ 384 362 459; Kostelní 20/1; www.nmf.cz in Czech; adult/concession 60/30Kč; ☒ 10am-5pm Tue-Sun). The permanent and temporary exhibitions focus mainly on Czech photographers, but even if you're not a shutterbug junkie it's worth visiting to appreciate the sympathetic restoration the building has undergone.

DISTRICT MUSEUM
The Jesuit seminary opposite the Jesuit college houses the **District museum** (muzeum Jindřichohradecka; ☎ 384 363 660; adult/concession 40/20Kč; ☒ 8.30am-noon & 12.30-5pm Jun-Sep, Tue-Sun Apr, May & Oct). The foremost attraction is an extraordinary, **mechanical Nativity scene** completed by one Tomáš Krýza in 1756, after 60 years of labour. The scene comprises over 1000 handcrafted figurines and fills an entire room.

Sleeping
BUDGET
Autokemping Jindřiš (☎ 384 326 758; www.cbox.cz /behoun; Jindřiš 15; tent 60Kč) In the village of Jindřiš, this is 5km east from town on a narrow gauge train from the main station.

  Penzión U tkadlen (☎ 384 321 348; www.utkadlen .wz.cz; Pod hradem 7/IV; per person 300Kč) Restful, rustic and right on the canal, this traditional *pension* has two and three-bed rooms and also offers discounts to members of Hostelling International.

MIDRANGE
The tourist information office books private rooms for about 230Kč per person.

  Cyklopenzión Kasper (☎ 384 361 474; www.cyklopen zion.cz; náměstí Míru; s/d 630/1260Kč) Cycle (or walk) on in to this comfortable and cosy spot just off the main square. Just mind the particularly robust cobblestones, OK?

  Pension Na 15 (☎ 384 363 021; www.15polednik.cz; Kostelní 76; s/d incl breakfast 700/1250Kč; ☒) Antique wrought-iron furniture and terracotta tiles provide a relaxing heritage ambience. Downstairs there's a cosy vaulted restaurant and a café looking out onto a quiet square.

  Hotel Bílá paní (☎ 384 363 329; www.hotelbilapani .cz; Dobrovského 5; s/d incl breakfast 700/1150Kč) There are frescoes and creeping ivy outside, and the comfy-as interior is retro-furnished like your grandparents' house. And yes, that's a good thing.

  Penzión u Papoušků (☎ 384 362 235; papousek@esnet .cz; Na Příkopě 188/11; d incl breakfast 1000Kč). Daubed in a startling shade of duck-egg blue, this quiet place has nicely furnished rooms, some with exposed beams, and an Italo-Czech eatery downstairs. However we're not sure what 'Mould Steak' is.

TOP END
Hotel Concertina (☎ 384 362 320; www.concertina.cz; náměstí Míru 141/1; s/d incl breakfast 1480/2180Kč; ☒ ☒ ☒) With loads of different national flags outside, they're obviously very welcoming. This four-star chain hotel is the snazziest in town, and even offers wi-fi for the laptop traveller.

Eating & Drinking

Pizzeria Padrino (☎ 777 660 870; náměstí Míru 158; mains 100Kč; ⊗ to 8pm Sun) Padrino means 'Godfather', and you'll find their wood-fired pizzas an offer too good to refuse. *Capisce?*

Asijské Bistro u Zlatého Bažanta (Panská 97; mains 60Kč) The Vietnamese spring rolls are extra good at this pick-and-point Asian buffet.

Bistro Pod Hradem (☎ 384 362 203; Pod hradem; mains 90-160Kč; ⊗ from 4pm) Watch the swans and ducks cruise by from the terrace of this romantic spot right on the canal.

Dada Club (☎ 331 361 368; Kostelní 73/1) Regular photographic exhibitions keep things happening in this arty bar. Find the brightly coloured iron letters spelling D-A-D-A and you're in the right place.

Cájovna u Zrmku (☎ 728 74 470; Dobrovského 1; tea from 30Kč; ⊗ 2-10pm, Tue-Sun) This cosy teahouse is nestled under the arches leading from the main square to the chateau.

Entertainment

Střelnice cinema (☎ 384 351 405; náměstí Masarykovo; 80Kč) This is a central cinema that shows films nightly.

Classical music concerts are held across town. Ask tourist information for the latest programme.

Getting There & Away

Reasonably regular buses make the run to Telč (40Kč, one hour), Tábor (44Kč, one hour), Slavonice (40Kč, 1¼ hours), České Budějovice (42Kč, 1¼ hours), Brno (135Kč, three hours) and Prague (109Kč, four hours).

Jindřichův Hradec is on the train line between České Budějovice (88Kč, one hour) and Jihlava (88Kč, 1¼ hours). Useful services also run to Tábor (76Kč, one hour) and Prague, via Veselí (184Kč, three hours).

ČERVENÁ LHOTA

This romantic, faded pink **chateau** (☎ 384 384 228; www.cervenalhota.com; adult/concession 60/30Kč, in English 100/50Kč; ⊗ 9.30am-5.15pm Tue-Sun Jun-Aug, to 4pm May & Sep, 9am-4pm Sat & Sun Apr & Oct) sits on an outcrop in the middle of a lake. It got its name ('Red Lhota') in 1641 due to its innovative, bright-red roof tiles. The 14th-century Gothic fortress was rebuilt into a Renaissance castle that was later adapted in baroque style. In the second half of the 18th century the jovially-named German composer Karl Ditters von Dittersdorf lived here. Červená Lhota makes

an excellent day trip from Jindřichův Hradec. Tours of the interior run every hour or so (last tour 45 minutes before closing).

Getting There & Away

On weekdays there are four daily buses from either Soběslav or Jindřichův Hradec, each about half an hour away (22Kč). Weekend transport is sporadic.

SLAVONICE

pop 2700

Barely hanging onto the coat-tails of the Czech Republic, (the border with Austria is just 1km away), Slavonice is a perfect little town that any country would be proud to own. Comprised of two delicate town squares, Slavonice's initial century of prosperity was shattered by the Thirty Years' War, further damaged by the 18th-century redirection of the main road from Prague to Vienna, and finally crushed by the expulsion of German-speaking townspeople in 1945. In the grimmest days of the Cold War, the town was stranded agonisingly close to the West, on the edge of the forbidden zone with Austria. Ironically the economic degradation of the centuries, and more recent social isolation, has ensured the survival of some of Bohemia's most pristine examples of Renaissance architecture. And once the Austrian day-trippers have left, Slavonice resurrects its beautiful and compellingly moody atmosphere like nowhere else.

Orientation

From the train station it's 400m northeast along Nádražní to Slavonice's old town. The bus station is 200m north of the main square, náměstí Míru.

The **tourist office** (☎ 384 493 320; www.i.slavonice -mesto.cz; náměstí Míru 480; ⊗ 9am-6pm Jun-Sep, 10am-4pm Mon-Fri Oct-May) also has internet access for 1Kč per minute. You can access the free wi-fi hotspot at the Besídka restaurant with your own laptop.

Sights

The town's architectural treasures are around náměstí Míru, Horní náměstí and Boženy Němcové. The **sgraffito at Horní náměstí 88** depicts the Hapsburgs and figures from Greek mythology. The 1599 **town hall** stands out, as does the Gothic **church of the Assumption of Our Lady** (kostel Nanebevzetí Panny Marie), surrounded by 14th- to early-16th-century houses on náměstí Míru. As ever, you can climb the church **tower** (Navštivte věž; adult/concession 15/10Kč; ☺ 9am-6pm Jun-Aug, Sat & Sun only May & Sep) for fine vistas. Once you are finished up high, venture into the 13th-century **underground tunnels** running under the square (náměstí Míru 480; ☺ 9am-6pm Jul-Aug).

Also on the square is a small **museum** (městské muzeum; adult/concession 15/10Kč; ☺ 9am-noon & 1-5pm Tue-Sun May-Sep) with some artefacts from the medieval village of Pfaffenschlag.

Sleeping & Eating

Apartment Součkova (☎ 384 493 432; souc@centrum.cz; náměstí Míru 468; per person 250Kč) Two doors up from Arkáda (look out for the 'Penzión' banner). Ring the 'Součkovi' buzzer for some of the cheapest beds in town.

Hotel Arkáda (☎ 384 408 408; www.hotelarkada.cz; náměstí Míru 466; s/d 620/980Kč) Ask for one of the pleasant rooms on the top floor with airy skylights and exposed beams. Just watch out for the pelt of a huge wild boar as you ascend the stairs though.

Hotel u Růže (☎ 384 493 004; www.dumuruze.cz; náměstí Míru 452; s/d 1900//2300Kč; P ⊠ 🐾 🔁 🖳) Slavonice's best hotel combines a sauna and

swimming pool, with wi-fi access and a nicely sophisticated art gallery downstairs. And the rooms upstairs are pretty good too.

Besídka (☎ 384 493 293; Horní náměstí 522; mains 110Kč; ☺ 10am-11pm Mon-Thu, 10am-1am Fri, 9am-1am Sat, 9am-11pm Sun) The buzziest restaurant in town has superb pizza, relaxed breakfasts, free wi-fi and a funky Art Deco bike stand out the front.

La Petite Mort (náměstí Míru 526; coffee 30Kč; ☺ 9am-9pm) At the foot of the church of the Assumption of Our Lady, this hip, hole-in-the-wall café delivers consistently with top-notch coffee and is another good spot for a leisurely breakfast.

Getting There & Away

Slavonice is at the end of a minor train line that goes through Telč in South Moravia (40Kč, one hour) to Kostelec u Jihlavy. The bus from Prague takes 3½ hours to Dačice (130Kč), where you must change for Slavonice (30 minutes).

BORDER CROSSING

Just over 1km south of Slavonice is a vehicle and pedestrian border crossing, to Fratres in Austria (6am to 10pm daily).

West Bohemia

The famous effervescent liquids of West Bohemia are a balance of virtue and vice, good and (not so) evil, and provide a relaxing distraction from the tourist commotion of Prague.

Virtue is on tap at the elegant spa towns, where visitors can immerse themselves physically and emotionally in the waters bubbling under the classy streets of Karlovy Vary, Mariánské Lázně and Františkovy Lázně. And if you're looking for that extra smidgen of spiritual guidance, it could well come from a sip of Becherovka liqueur, the so-called '13th spring of Karlovy Vary' and the real reason many visitors leave with a spring in their step.

Balance is provided by the healthy and hearty vice of West Bohemia's liquid gold and true *aqua vitae*, Pilsner Urquell, the world's first (and finest) lager. There's no better spot for your first Pilsner Urquell than the bustling student pubs of brewery town Plzeň, or in the underground caverns of the town's famous brewery.

Once you've investigated your own balance of virtue and vice, there's lots more to discover. Active types can explore the rustic woodlands of the Šumava region bordering Germany and comprising the biggest national park in the Czech Republic. The rugged borderlands include the Chodsko region, home of the Chods, the traditional protectors of the border.

And a few days in beautifully sleepy villages like Loket and Domažlice will give you a glimpse into hushed West Bohemian life, well away from the thoroughly enjoyable distractions of bubbling springs and foaming beer.

HIGHLIGHTS

- Boost your cultural credibility at one of the elegant summertime music festivals in **Mariánské Lázně** (p209)

- Savour the subdued Euroglam ambience of spa town **Karlovy Vary** (p211)

- Meet the locals in the lively pubs of **Plzeň** (p223), home of one of the world's best beers

- Wander lazily around the captivating town of **Loket nad Ohří** (p217) and its impressive Gothic castle

- Discover the unique culture of the Chods in the delightfully sleepy town of **Domažlice** (p227)

★ Karlovy Vary
★
Loket nad Ohří

★ Mariánské Lázně

★ Plzeň

★ Domažlice

WEST BOHEMIA

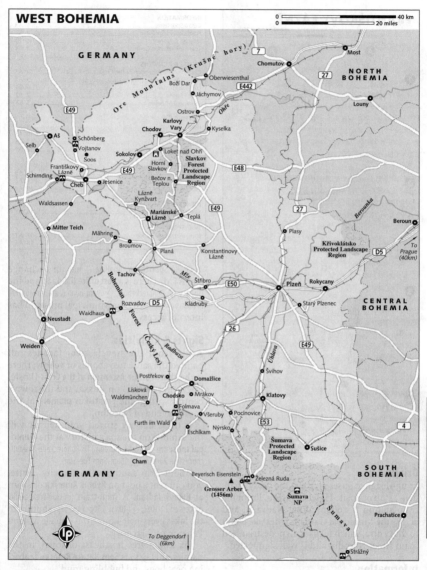

0 — 40 km
0 — 20 miles

GERMANY

Ore Mountains (Krušné hory)

Most

Chomutov

7

27

NORTH BOHEMIA

Oberwiesenthal

E442

Boží Dar

Jáchymov

Louny

Ostrov

Ohře

E49

Karlovy Vary

Kyselka

Chodov

Aš

Schönberg

Selb

Vojtanov

Soos

Sokolov

Loket nad Ohří

Slavkov Forest Protected Landscape Region

E48

Františkovy Lázně

Horní Slavkov

Schirnding

Cheb

Jesenice

Bečov n. Teplou

Waldsassen

Lázně Kynžvart

Mariánské Lázně

Teplá

E49

Mitter Teich

Máhring

Plasy

Beroun

Broumov

Planá

Konstantinovy Lázně

Bohemian Forest

Tachov

Mže

Stříbro

E50

Plzeň

Rokycany

CENTRAL BOHEMIA

Rozvadov

D5

Kladruby

Starý Plzenec

Neustadt

Waidhaus

26

Weiden

Radbuza

Český Les

E49

Postřekov

Švihov

Domažlice

Líšková

Waldmünchen

Chodsko

Mráкov

Klatovy

Folmava

Všeruby

Pocínovice

Furth im Wald

Eschlkam

Nýrsko

E53

Šumava Protected Landscape Region

Sušice

4

Cham

GERMANY

SOUTH BOHEMIA

Beyerisch Eisenstein

Železná Ruda

Grosser Arber (1456m)

Šumava NP

Prachatice

Úhlava

27

Berounka

Křivoklátsko Protected Landscape Region

D5

To Prague (40km)

Šumava

To Deggendorf (6km)

Strážný

WEST BOHEMIA

FRANTIŠKOVY LÁZNĚ
pop 5400

With a buttery veneer of yellow paint, and wide avenues with spa patients and tourists walking unbearably slowly, Františkovy Lázně is the archetypal spa town. Well-tended parkland with statues and springs is the only concession to reality in this spa-town 'theme park'.

Beethoven and Goethe were among Františkovy Lázně's most famous guests, but with the spa best known for the treatment of female infertility, they were more likely drawn by a lively café society. Today, the sidewalk cafés are relaxingly soporific, and late-night action is sound asleep in this Bohemian version of *The Truman Show*.

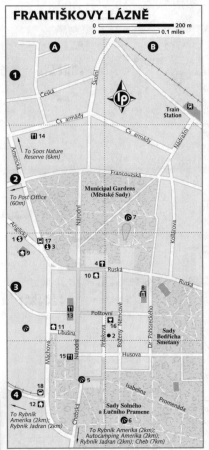

FRANTIŠKOVY LÁZNĚ

Česká Spořitelna (Anglická 7) has an exchange and ATM. There is a **post office** (Lidická 8), and the **library** (Dr Pohoreckého 8; ☾ 9am-noon & 2-4pm Mon-Fri, to noon only on Tue) by the Municipal museum has internet access.

Sights & Activities

Aside from the neoclassical façades, all painted the same two shades of yellow, there is the **church of the Ascension of the Cross** (kostel Povýšení sv Kříže) on Ruská, and the town's central spring, the **Františkův pramen**, at the southern end of Národní.

If these haven't stirred you, neither will the exhibits on the spa's history at the **Municipal museum** (Městské muzeum; Dr Pohoreckého 8; adult/concession 20/8Kč; ☾ 10am-5pm Tue-Sun).

About 2km southwest of the city centre, you can rent a boat on **Rybník Amerika** or swim at **Rybník Jadran**. A **mini-train** (mikrovláček; adult/concession 20/10Kč; ☾ 10am-4.30pm Apr-Sep) shuttles to the lakes every half-hour from outside Milano Penzión on Máchova.

Six kilometres northeast of town, in the hamlet of Hájek, is **Soos Nature Reserve** featuring peat bogs and bubbling mud.

Orientation

Long-distance buses arrive at the 'Sady' (gardens) stop opposite Hotel Centrum. From the train station it's 600m along Nádražní and across the Municipal Gardens (Městské Sady) to the centre, which focuses on pedestrianised main street Národní and is well signposted.

Information

The **Town Information Centre** (Městské Informační Centrum; ☎ 354 543 162; www.frantiskovy-lazne.cz; Americká 2; ☾ 6am-6pm Mon-Fri, 8am-2pm Sat & Sun) provides maps and accommodation advice.

For spa treatments and accommodation, contact **Františkovy Lázně AS** (☎ 354 201 104; www.franzensbad.cz; Jiráskova 3; per person from 1400Kč; ☾ 9am-5pm Mon-Fri, to noon Sat).

Sleeping

The Town Information Centre can help with private rooms. Accommodation here is seasonal. Prices shown are peak season – they *may* fall by up to 20% out of season.

Autocamping Amerika (☎ 354 542 518; tent 70Kč; ☾ May-Sep; **P**) Beside Rybník Amerika, this camp site has double/quad bungalows (340/700Kč) and a restaurant.

Milano Penzión and Kavarna (☎ 604 602 080; Máchova 8; s/d 400/650Kč; **P**) An enthusiastic English-speaking owner offers snug, modern rooms over his café.

Hotel Savoy (☎ 354 203 000; www.franzensbad .cz; Ruská 4; s/d incl breakfast 1000/1600Kč; **P**) You're in spa country now, Toto, with recuperating guests in smocks and slippers shuffling through a sleepy reception, and a whole raft of treatments available.

Hotel Centrum (☎ 354 543 156; www.spahotel centrum.cz; Anglická; s/d incl breakfast 1020/1620Kč; **P**) Away from the promenading hordes, the best rooms at this crisply modern spot overlook a park.

Hotel Tři Lilie (☎ 354 208 900; www.franzensbad .cz; Máchova; s/d incl breakfast 1700/2500Kč; **P** ✕ ✿) Quality rooms, attentive staff and the occasional B-list celeb come as standard at this luxury place that's more vibrant and friendly than other places around town.

Eating & Drinking

Vídeňska Kavárna (☎ 602 460 921; Národní 1; snacks 60Kč, mains to 500Kč) The 'Viennese Café' offers more than just coffee 'n' cake. If you can't make your mind up over the huge list of ice cream, come back after dark when the café morphs into a formal eatery.

Café Slovan (☎ 354 542 841; Národní 5; mains 100Kč) Ignore the frumpy retro décor and enjoy the old-fashioned prices at this café-meets-wine-bar that's the main drag's best value.

Saloon Bažina (☎ 603 236 410; Americká 95/10; mains 130Kč) Break away from your spa-town health kick with a slab of beef at this rustic 'saloon' serving Tex-Mex tucker with live country music.

Selská Jizba (☎ 602 460 921; Poštovní; meals 70-120Kč) No-nonsense and full of loyal locals, this has good, honest Bohemian food and cheaper drinks to counteract the high-priced primness of surrounding eateries.

Getting There & Away

Buses are more direct and more frequent than trains. A daily bus comes direct from Prague via Karlovy Vary (150Kč, 3½ hours), and three a day come from Plzeň (112Kč, two hours). For long-distance options and international connections, go via Cheb, with buses to Františkovy Lázně every 30 minutes (12Kč, 15 minutes).

CHEB

pop 33,500

Cheb (pronounced 'kheb'), another pretty Bohemian old town ringed by grimy industry, conceals a recent history that is fundamental to 20th-century Europe. In 1897 Cheb gave birth to German National Socialism, which later evolved into the Nazi party. Hitler visited here in 1938, just before German troops seized control of the surrounding Sudetenland. Payback came with the 1945 expulsion of Cheb's German population of 30,000. Now, significant Vietnamese, Slovak and Roma populations reflect Central Europe's evolving demography in this town that sits astride the traditional, historical and cultural fault line between Germany and the Czech Republic.

At the city's heart, winding alleys peel away from the raffish town square, and a unique red-brick fortress provides a refreshing antidote to the contrived façades of the nearby spa towns. But leave the quaint centre and Cheb's double life is reinforced, with prostitutes working sullen streets tarnished by years of heavy industry.

Orientation

From the adjacent bus and train stations it's 1km west, then northwest, along Svobody to the old town's sloping, triangular main square, náměstí krále Jiřího z Poděbrad (King George of Poděbrady square).

Information

Infocentrum (☎ 354 440 302; www.mestocheb.cz; náměstí krále Jiřího z Poděbrad 33; ☉ 9am-5pm Mon-Fri, 10-2pm Sat, 10am-1.30pm Sun May-Sep) sells maps, books theatre and concert tickets and provides guides; internet access is 1Kč per minute.

Česká Spořitelna (náměstí krále Jiřího z Poděbrad) has an ATM and exchange desk. There's a second branch at Májová 36.

The **post office** (Slikova 15) is just south of the main square.

Sights

NÁMĚSTÍ KRÁLE JIŘÍHO Z PODĚBRAD

The main square has a selection of architectural treats. The best is the teetering tangle of 16th-century former Jewish merchants' houses called **špalíček** ('the Block'). Another late-Gothic refugee is **Schirnding house** (Schirndingovský dům; náměstí Krále Jiřího z Poděbrad 508), with its crow-step gables.

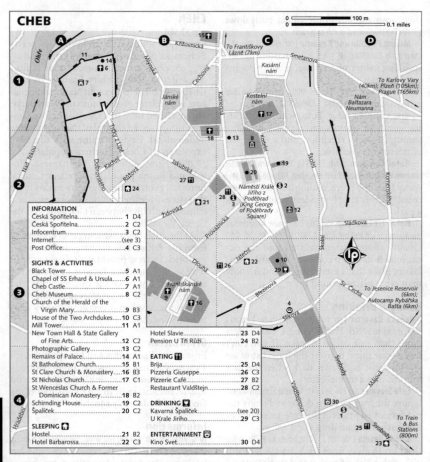

CHEB

The 18th-century baroque **New town hall** (Nová radnice; adult/concession 80/40Kč, free 1st Thu of the month; 9am-noon & 12.30-5pm Tue-Sun) incorporates the **State gallery of fine arts** (Státní galerie výtvarného umění; admission incl in town hall fee) with changing exhibits of modern Czech art. Note the **house of the two archdukes** (dům U dvou arcivévodů; náměstí Krále Jiřího z Poděbrad 26/471) at the top of the square was once the town's oldest inn and is now a **music shop** (9am-5pm Mon-Fri, 9am-noon Sat) and **restaurant** (noon-1am).

North on Kamenná is **St Wenceslas church** (kostel sv Václava), which once operated as a **Dominican monastery**, and a small **photographic gallery** (Galerie Fotografie; Kamenná 2; admission free; 10am-6pm Tue-Fri, to 5pm Sat) with a diverse selection of prints by contemporary Czech shutterbugs.

CHEB MUSEUM

Wallenstein (see opposite) met a sticky end while staying at the pink Renaissance **Pachelbel house** (Pachelblův dům; náměstí Krále Jiřího z Poděbrad 492) at the northern end of the square. It's now the **Cheb museum** (Chebské muzeum; 354 422 386; adult/concession 50/25Kč; 9am-12.30pm & 1-5pm Tue-Sun).

The highlight is a gallery of 20th-century paintings of the town, which graphically illustrate Cheb's decline. There's a mock-up of the bedroom where Wallenstein was run through, a moment re-enacted in many illustrations.

ST NICHOLAS CHURCH

Baroque **St Nicholas church** (kostel sv Mikuláš) is of interest for its age (13th century), its Romanesque basilica plan and its sheer size.

FRANTIŠKÁNSKÉ NÁMĚSTÍ

On the eastern side of the square, beyond Dlouhá, is the former **St Clare church** (kostel sv Klára) and monastery, a fine piece of high baroque by Kristof Dientzenhofer. Opposite is the Gothic **church of the Herald of the Virgin Mary** (kostel Zvěstování Panny Marie).

CHEB CASTLE

The red-brick **fortress** (hrad; www.chebskyhrad.cz, Czech & German only; adult/concession 30/15Kč; ☺ 9am-noon & 1-6pm Tue-Sun Jun-Aug, to 5pm May & Sep, to 4pm Apr & Oct), mostly ruined except for its towers, is a must-see for its extraordinary chapel and because it's the biggest Romanesque castle in Bohemia. No tours are available but an English text is.

Only the northeastern corner walls are still standing, with multiple-arched windows hinting at its former elegance. Westward are the foundations of a later building, where four officers loyal to Wallenstein (see below) were killed just before his demise.

Don't miss the boxy little **chapel of SS Erhard & Ursula** (kaple sv Erharda a Uršuly). In the early-Gothic lower storey (probably once a crypt), four individually carved granite pillars support a vaulted ceiling. Upstairs is a sublime version of the same thing, with delicate, late-Gothic marble columns, again each carved differently. The upstairs room once had its own entrance from the castle.

Above the moat bridge, the dusty, thick-walled **Black tower** (Černá věž) offers views of the river, old-town rooftops and distant apartment blocks from its 18.5m height. In an adjacent building is an interesting **archaeological exhibit** on Chebsko (the Cheb region), unfortunately without English captions.

To appreciate the scale of the fortifications, take the steep path leading down to Křížovnická, past the round, late-Gothic **Mill tower** (Mlýnská věž) and the stretch of town walls.

Sleeping

Autocamp Rybářska Bašta (☎ 354 431 951; berdy chp@quick.cz; tent/bungalow per person 60/220Kč; ☺ May-Sep; [P]) Around 6km east of the city centre at Dřenice, this well-equipped camp site is by the popular Jesenice reservoir (vodní nádrž Jesenice).

Pension U Tří Růží (☎ 354 423 384; http://penzion utriruzi.wz.cz; Růžový Kopeček 395/9; s/d 450/800Kč)

WALLENSTEIN

In an era characterised by violence and greed, Albrecht von Wallenstein (Valdštejn, 1583–1634) was more powerful and avaricious than all his contemporaries. The most infamous warlord of the Thirty Years' War, he acquired wealth by marrying a rich widow who fortuitously died soon after. Leveraging her estates in Moravia, Wallenstein forged a relationship with Prince Ferdinand, the Hapsburg heir.

Following the Battle of White Mountain in 1620, Wallenstein negotiated a crafty deal with Ferdinand, now Holy Roman Emperor. The grasping Wallenstein donated to Ferdinand the services of his private army of up to 100,000 men in exchange for the absolute right to plunder the lands they conquered. By 1625 Wallenstein was incredibly wealthy and owned a quarter of all Bohemia. Ferdinand was quick to harness Wallenstein's talent for war, and in the following years the Czech 'military entrepreneur' achieved many battlefield victories on behalf of Ferdinand in Germany. A whole raft of titles followed, including Duke of Friedland and Governor of Prague.

In 1630 the increasingly ambitious Wallenstein was relieved of his military duties when Ferdinand suspected him of planning to overthrow the Holy Roman Empire. Wallenstein retired to his duchy of Friedland in Jičín (p258). A year later the emperor had to seek Wallenstein's assistance again, when Bohemia was invaded by the Saxons. By 1633 Wallenstein had again retired from fighting Ferdinand's battles, angry at the emperor's Edict of Resolution, which transferred many Protestant assets to the Catholics. Although a staunch Catholic, Wallenstein saw the edict as interfering in the lands he owned and controlled.

Rumours surfaced that Wallenstein was preparing to join forces with the Saxon and French enemies, and on 18 February 1634 he was charged with treason. Most of his massive army defected to the emperor's cause, while Wallenstein fled to Cheb with a supposedly loyal retinue of a few hundred soldiers. On 25 February 1634, a group of his own Scottish and Irish mercenaries, actually loyal to Ferdinand, slaughtered Wallenstein in his bedchamber.

The décor is old-school frumpy but the welcome is friendly at this *pension* in a quiet square near the castle.

Hotel Barbarossa (☎ 354 423 446; www.hotel -barbarossa.cz; Jateční 7; s/d incl breakfast 1050/1350Kč; P) Restful jazz in reception, and flash bathrooms, make this hotel Cheb's top spot.

Also recommended:

Hostel (☎ 603 344 140; Židovská 7; per person 150Kč; ☺ 8am-noon & 4-8pm) No-frills cheap beds with strict hours of reception.

Hotel Slavie (☎ 354 433 216; www.hotel-slavie.cz; třída Svobody 75; s/d incl breakfast 850/1450Kč; P ☐) Simple and spartan, but clean and convenient.

Eating & Drinking

Pizzerie Café (☎ 354 436 143; Jakubská 1; pizza 70Kč) This pizzeria is around half the price of Pizzeria Giuseppe, but the pizzas are just as good at this 'back streets of Naples' kind of place.

Restaurant Valdštejn (☎ 354 442 561; náměstí krále Jiřího z Poděbrad; mains 75-150Kč) The steak 'n' schnitzel specialties pack 'em in at this tourist-friendly main-square eatery.

Pizzeria Giuseppe (☎ 354 438 200; Jateční 18; pizza 120Kč) Bright colours light up this cosy *trattoria* while the punters enjoy the golden glow of tasty Italian specialties.

U Krale Jiriho (cnr náměstí krále Jiřího z Poděbrad & Březinova; mains 75-100Kč) The flash façade of the house of the two archdukes conceals the more rustic and raucous interior of this popular beer hall.

Also recommended:

Brija (třída Svobody 28; snacks 20Kč; ☺ 7am-5.30pm Mon-Fri, 8am-12.30pm Sat) Mini food court with salads and crepes.

Kavarna Špalíček (náměstí krále Jiřího z Poděbrad; coffee 30Kč) A cosy spot for coffee in the oddly angled špalíček.

Entertainment

Most of Cheb's so-called night clubs are really brothels or strip joints. A night at the movies in **Kino Svet** (☎ 354 437 722; Májová 29) should be safe.

Getting There & Away

There are direct buses from Prague (150Kč, three hours, four daily), Karlovy Vary (56Kč, one hour, seven daily) and Mariánské Lázně (40Kč, 30 minutes, 12 daily). Regional buses run between Cheb and Františkovy Lázně (12Kč, 15 minutes) every hour.

Express trains from Prague (250Kč, three hours) are less frequent but faster than the bus. For shorter trips – for example, from Plzeň, Františkovy Lázně or Karlovy Vary – there are several fast trains a day but they're pricier than ordinary trains and the bus.

Cheb is a convenient point for international train connections.

MARIÁNSKÉ LÁZNĚ
pop 14,100

Any place that can bring a smile to Mr Melancholy himself, Franz Kafka, must have something going for it. At the height of Mariánské Lázně's (formerly Marienbad) popularity, Kafka was joined in West Bohemia's prettiest spa town by luminaries such as Goethe, Thomas Edison, Britain's King Edward VII and his Hapsburg contemporary, Franz-Josef I. Up to 20,000 visitors came each year for treatment amidst the neoclassical and Art Nouveau elegance sprinkled generously throughout this niche in the Slavkov forest. Walking in the crisp, fresh mountain air was as important as partaking of the precious, pure waters, and a maze of lazy trails still transects the rolling forest.

After being isolated by the Cold War from 1948, the town re-emerged in 1989, and nearly two decades later Mariánské Lázně is resurrecting its reputation. Today it's an equal-opportunity and thoroughly inclusive spa town, so don't come expecting the glitz and glamour of yesteryear. But with a robust array of good restaurants and cosy bars and a full retinue of spa services on offer, Mariánské Lázně is a top spot to explore the balance between virtue and vice.

Orientation

Mariánské Lázně stretches for 4km along Hlavní třída. From the adjacent bus and train stations at the southern, 'business' end of town, it's 2km on trolleybus 5 to the spa area's main bus stop (opposite Hotel Excelsior).

The spa area is a network of paths, parks and 39 therapeutic springs, centred on the photogenic Colonnade (Kolonáda) and surrounded by streets of plush hotels and mansions. Mírové náměstí has a summer *kavárna* (café) and an open-air stage. The spa is at the southern edge of the Slavkov Forest (Slavkovský les) Protected Landscape Region.

Parking is largely confined to pricey car parks – there's a multistorey near Hotel Europa (24Kč per hour from 8am to 7pm; 11Kč per hour after 7pm).

MARIÁNSKÉ LÁZNĚ

0   500 m
0   0.3 miles

INFORMATION
ČSOB Bank.............................. 1 B2
Infocentrum........................... 2 B2
KB Bank................................. 3 B3
Marienbad Spa Hotels Information
   Office.............................. 4 C2
Post Office.............................. 5 B3

SIGHTS & ACTIVITIES
Ambrožův Spring..................... 6 C2
Anglican Chapel...................... 7 B2
Chopin Haus........................... 8 B2
Church of the Assumption of the Virgin
   Mary................................ 9 C2
Colonnade (Kolonáda)............ 10 C2
Cross Spring.......................... 11 C2
Ferdinandův Spring................ 12 C5
Forest Spring......................... 13 B1
Goethovo Náměstí.................. 14 C2
Hotel Panoráma..................... 15 C3
Karolínin Spring..................... 16 C2
Mariin Spring........................ 17 C2
Monument to the US Army...... 18 C2
Motorcycle Race Track............ 19 B6
Municipal Museum.................. 20 C2
New Baths............................. 21 C2
Prelátův Spring...................... 22 D6
Public Pool............................ 23 B4
Rudolfův Spring..................... 24 C5
Ruin of Cervená karkulka Café.. 25 D5
St Vladimir Church................. 26 B3
Singing Fountain.................... 27 C2
Town Library......................... 28 B4
Watchtower........................... 29 C3

SLEEPING
Hotel Bohemia....................... 30 B2
Hotel Europa......................... 31 B2
Hotel Koliba.......................... 32 D2
Hotel Kossuth........................ 33 B2
Hotel Paris............................ 34 C2
Hotel Richard......................... 35 B3
Olympia Hotel........................ 36 B2
Pension Edinburgh................(see 46)
Penzion Oradour.................... 37 B2
Provence Apartments.............. 38 B2

EATING
China Restaurant.................... 39 B3
Filip 1.................................. 40 B3
Lil....................................... 41 C3
Pueblo Mexicano.................... 42 B5
U Zlaté Koule........................ 43 C2

DRINKING
Irish Pub.............................. 44 B3
New York Restaurant.............. 45 B4
Scottish Pub Highlanders........ 46 B4

ENTERTAINMENT
Kino Slava............................ 47 B4
NV Gogol Theatre................... 48 B2

SHOPPING
Kolonada Oplatky................... 49 C2

TRANSPORT
Bus Station........................... 50 A6
Cable Car.............................. 51 D3
Main Bus Stop in Spa Area....... 52 B3

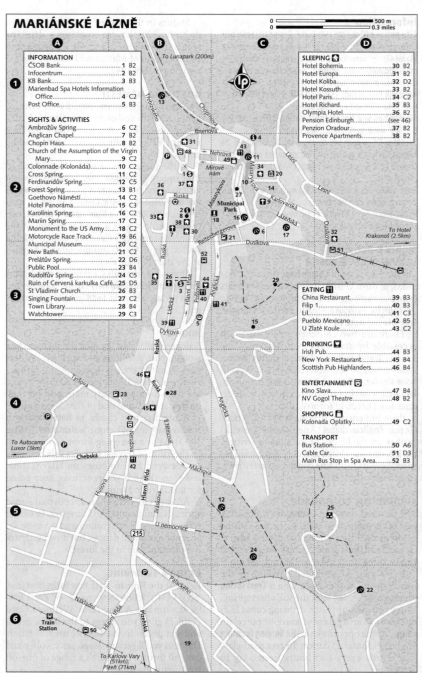

WEST BOHEMIA

Information

City police office (☎ 158; Ruská) Behind the town hall.

Infocentrum (☎ 354 622 474; www.marianskelazne.cz; Hlavní 47; ⊗ 9am-noon & 1-6pm) Sells theatre tickets, maps and guidebooks, organises guides, books accommodation and provides internet access at 1Kč per minute.

KB bank (Hlavní třída 132) and **ČSOB** (Hlavní třída 81) Both have ATMs and exchange desks.

Marienbad Spa Hotels Information Office (☎ 354 655 501; www.marienbad.cz; Masarykova 22; ⊗ 9am-5pm Mon-Fri, to noon Sat) Manages and books eight of the biggest spa hotels and has information on spa packages (around €100 per person per night). Check the website for special offers.

Post office (Poštovní) South of the main bus stop (200m).

Town Library (Městská Knihovna; ☎ 354 622 115; Hlavní 370/3; ⊗ 9-11am & 1-6pm Mon-Fri) Charges 1Kč per minute for internet access.

Sights & Activities

HLAVNÍ TŘÍDA & RUSKÁ

On the 2nd floor of **Chopin haus** (dům F Chopina), in dům U Bílé labutě, is a little **museum** (www.chopinfestival.cz; Hlavní 47; adult/concession 20/10Kč; ⊗ 2-5pm Tue, Thu & Sun Apr-Sep) to Frédéric Chopin, who stayed here in 1836.

There are two churches on Ruská (both accessible by stairways from Hlavní). The 1901 red-and-yellow **St Vladimír church** (kostel sv Vladimíra; Ruská 347-9; admission 20Kč; ⊗ 8.30am-noon & 1-5pm May-Oct, 9.30-11am & 2-4pm Nov-Apr) is a plush, Byzantine-style Orthodox church with an amazing porcelain iconostasis.

Prim but equally striking is the 1879 neo-Gothic **Anglican chapel** (Anglikánský kostelík) further up the block. At the time of writing, the interior was closed and only being used for special events including concerts and festivals. Check with Infocentrum.

AROUND THE COLONNADE

The restored cast-iron **Colonnade** (Kolonáda), east of the municipal park, is the spa's visual centrepiece. From a little bandstand inside, classical and brass-band concerts are presented two or three times a day in the high season.

In its own whitewashed pavilion by the northern end of the Colonnade is **Cross spring** (Křížový pramen; ⊗ 6am-6pm), the spa's first spring, where you can buy plastic drinking cups (3Kč) or choose from a galaxy of souvenir porcelain mugs. At the opposite end, the **Singing fountain** (Zpívající fontána) dances to recorded classical music every two hours from May to September.

Statues in the pristine municipal park (no dogs, no bicycles, no smoking – drinking seems to be allowed) include a **monument** to the liberation of Mariánské Lázně by the US army on 6 May 1945.

GOETHOVO NÁMĚSTÍ

This manicured square, edged with extravagant late-19th- and early-20th-century buildings, probably looks much as it did when King Edward VII et al patronised the surrounding hotels.

At the site of a house where Goethe stayed (the square is named after him) on his last visit to Mariánské Lázně is a ho-hum **Municipal museum** (Městské muzeum; Goethovo náměstí 11; adult/concession 60/30Kč; ⊗ 9.30am-5.30pm Tue-Sun), although it does give a good overview of the town's history (with Czech captions). Ask the staff to put on the 30-minute video in English at the start of your visit.

Opposite is the bulky, octagonal **church of the Assumption of the Virgin Mary** (kostel Nanebevzetí Panny Marie) built in 1848 in 'neo-Byzantine' style.

HIKING

A dozen trails wind through the surrounding woods, past pavilions and springs. Wilderness it isn't (there are signs showing cardiac, energy-use data!), but pleasant it is. The routes are shown on some city maps and on map boards at the south end of the Colonnade.

A popular trail climbs to **Hotel Panoráma**, round past an old stone **watchtower** (climb 100 steps to a sweeping forest view) and on to the ruin of **Červená karkulka Café**. Mortals can descend here to buses on Hlavní (total less than 4km). If you're serious, keep going for a 7km round trip.

An easier loop trail heads north past Forest spring (Lesní pramen) to Lunapark. In earlier times this was a fairground and a venue for afternoon teas and dances, but now Lunapark is a pleasant café in the forest.

BATHS & SWIMMING

Relax at the Roman-style **New baths** (Nové lázně; ☎ 354 644 111; Reitenbergerova 53; ⊗ 2-8pm Mon-Fri, 9am-8pm Sat). A one-hour Wellness Card (250Kč) gives you access to the baths, sauna and spa pools. Invest 1290Kč on a Wellness Day and you'll get a massage, juice, coffee and cake all thrown in. There's a range of one-off treatments available.

You can swim in the **public pool** (plavecký stadión; ☎ 354 623 579; Tyršova 617; adult/concession 60/25Kč; 🕑 11am-9pm Mon-Sat), southwest of the city centre.

Walking Tour

From the bus stop on Poštovní, cross north into the municipal park, past the **memorial to the American liberation (1)** of Mariánské Lázně in WWII. On the far side is the centrepiece of the spa, the **Colonnade (2)**, along with the popular **Singing fountain (3)**.

East beyond the Colonnade is Goethovo náměstí, with several venerable hotels, the octagonal **church of the Assumption of the Virgin Mary (4)** and the **Municipal museum (5)**. Detour east on Karlovarská and south on Dusíkova to the folksy Hotel Koliba & Restaurace, from where a **cable car (6)** climbs to Hotel Krakonoš every 10 minutes from 9am to 4.15pm during May to September (adult/concession 35/20Kč). Southward, for 1.5km, the woods are laced with hiking trails.

Walk west along Reitenbergerova, past the **New baths (7)** offering spa services to walk-in guests. Cross Hlavní, head south past the Hotel Excelsior and climb the steps to the Orthodox **St Vladimír church (8)**. Some 200m north on Ruská is an **Anglican chapel (9)**. Return down to Hlavní via another set of steps.

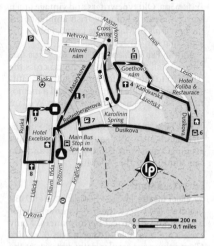

Festivals & Events

The town has a lively summertime cultural life, including the opening of the spa season in May, a week-long **Frédéric Chopin Music Festival**

(☎ 354 622 617; www.chopinfestival.cz) in mid-August, the **Mozart Festival** in October, and frequent outdoor concerts.

Sleeping

Mariánské Lázně has many hotels, but prices tend to be high (similar to Prague) and seasonal. The prices quoted are high-season summer rates (expect discounts of up to 30% during low season).

Infocentrum books private rooms from around 400Kč per person and arranges hotels.

Most hotels charge extra for overnight parking.

BUDGET

Autocamp Luxor (☎ 354 623 504; www.luxor.karlovasko .cz; tent/bungalow per person 70/230Kč; 🕑 mid-Apr–Sep; Ⓟ) Autocamp Luxor is located in Velká Hleďsebe (2km west along Chebská, then 1km south). Catch trolleybus 6 from the town centre to Velká Hleďsebe.

Penzion Oradour (☎ 354 624 304; www.penzion oradour.wz.cz; Hlavní 43; s/d incl breakfast 355/710Kč; Ⓟ) A super central location, clean rooms and a huge breakfast make this the best budget option in an expensive town.

MIDRANGE

Pension Edinburgh (☎ 354 620 804; www.pension edinburgh.com; Ruská 56; s/d from 600/840Kč, apt 1740Kč; Ⓟ) Five refurbished rooms and one apartment are tucked away upstairs from a Scottish pub. In keeping with the Celtic theme, each room has a well-stocked minibar...and dressing gowns.

Hotel Europa (☎ 354 622 063; www.kosev.cz; Třebízského 2; d without/with bathroom incl breakfast 910/1500Kč; Ⓟ) With a location that's rubbing (well-massaged) shoulders with the flash hotels, the Europa combines friendly staff, OK rooms and a full range of treatments for that more affordable spa experience.

Provence Apartments (☎ 608 161 415; www.apartma -marienbad.com; Hlavní 51; d 1800Kč; Ⓟ) Spacious self-catering apartments around a quiet courtyard bring a touch of the south of France to the west of Bohemia. Massage and physiotherapy sessions are available.

Hotel Paris (☎ 354 628 894; hotelparis@seznam .cz; Goethovo náměstí 15/3; s/d incl breakfast 1450/2100Kč; Ⓟ) High on the hill overlooking Goethovo náměstí, this is your chance to stay in the same ritzy area as King Edward VII, but at slightly less regal prices.

OPLATKY

To quote Monty Python, 'Do you get wafers with it?' The answer is a resounding 'yes' according to locals, who prescribe the following method of taking your spring water: have a sip from your *lázeňský pohárek* (spa cup), then dull the sulphurous taste with a big, round, sweet wafer called *oplatky*. *Oplatky* are sold for 5Kč each at a few spa hotels and speciality shops, or you can pick them up at **Kolonada Oplatky** (cnr Nehrova & Masarykova). Steer clear of the fancy chocolate or hazelnut flavours, though; they're never as crunchily fresh and warm as the standard flavour.

Also recommended:

Hotel Kossuth (☎ 354 622 861; www.kosev.cz; Ruská 77; d without/with bathroom incl breakfast 970/1400Kč) Great location high on Ruská, but so-so rooms.

Hotel Koliba (☎ 354 625 169; www.hotel-koliba.cz; Dusíkova 592; s/d incl breakfast 1220/1760Kč; **P**) Tucked away amidst the pines is this Swiss-style chalet with alpine hush.

TOP END

Olympia Hotel (☎ 354 931 111; www.olympiamarienbad.cz; Ruská 88/861; s/d incl breakfast 1900/3800Kč; **P** **⊠** **⊠** **⊠**) With a slick but friendly edge, the newly opened Olympia offers great top-end value with comfortable rooms, youthful staff, and a Greek-themed bar and restaurant in the lobby – just what you always wanted, right?

Hotel Bohemia (☎ 354 610 111; www.orea.cz/bohemia; Hlavní 100; s/d incl breakfast 2550/3640Kč; **P** **⊠** **⊠**) Even with its façade transplanted from the French Riviera, a ritzy self-opening front door and very comfortable rooms, we can't excuse the snobby staff at reception on our visit. Flash? Yes. Friendly? Could try harder.

Hotel Richard (☎ 354 696 111; www.hotelrichard .com; Ruská 487/28; s/d incl breakfast 2690/3690Kč; **P** **⊠** **⊠** **⊠**) Named after composer Richard Wagner, but the rooms and décor are thankfully more stylish and low-key than his overwrought music.

Eating

Eating grandly is all part of 'the cure' and Mariánské Lázně is full of elegant, high-priced restaurants.

Pueblo Mexicano (☎ 354 620 318; Chebská; mains 90-200Kč; ☽ 5pm-5am) About as authentic as a fake Mayan pyramid (yes, they do have one), but mucho east-of-the-German-border fun when the tequila and fajitas begin to flow. And who needs Chopin or Mozart when there's live country music every Thursday from 8pm?

Lil (☎ 354 603 339; Anglická 36; mains 250Kč; ☽ 11.30am-2am) Experience old-school Marienbad dining in this elegant villa sitting amidst a grove of shady pines. There's an extensive wine list, and cheek-to-cheek dancing on a Sunday to complete the illusion of days gone by.

U Zlaté Koule (☎ 354 624 455; Nehrova 26; mains 300Kč; ☽ 11am-11pm) A stunning cocktail of five-star class and cosy informality, this swish eatery features creaking wooden beams, sparkling glassware and antiques. The game-rich menu effortlessly whips up the 'wow' factor.

Also recommended:

Filip 1 (☎ 354 626 161; Poštovni 96; mains 100-150Kč) Czech food without the tourist mark-up but with a strong recommendation from the folks at Infocentrum.

China Restaurant (☎ 354 626 819; Lidická 125; mains 120Kč) Befitting spa country, this velvet-bedecked Asian eatery is a cut above your average noodle bar.

Drinking

Irish Pub (☎ 354 620 828; Poštovni 96; Guinness 65Kč; ☽ from 5pm) Old typewriters and vintage green bicycles create a suitably Irish ambience for the best *craic* in Mariánské Lázně. Follow the signs that say 'Irish Pub'.

Scottish Pub Highlanders (Ruská 56; ☽ from 4pm) Lovers of all things Scottish should cross the Irish Sea to this pub for more Celtic shenanigans amidst single malt heaven and a memorial to Mel Gibson (sorry, we mean William Wallace).

New York (☎ 354 623 033; Hlavní třída 233; ☽ to 2am) Jazz bands play this snug club venue most evenings from 8pm. Close your eyes and you can almost hear the 'A-Train'.

Entertainment

NV Gogol theatre (divadlo NV Gogola; ☎ 354 622 036; Třebízského 106) Check the programme here for musical and theatrical performances. Many events are also held at **Chopin haus** (Hlavní třída 47) and there are regular daily concerts at the **Colonnade** from May to September. Ask at Infocentrum (p208).

Kino Slava (☎ 354 622 347; Nerudova 437) For the latest Hollywood blockbusters.

Getting There & Away

Half a dozen fast trains a day run from Prague (224Kč, three hours) all via Plzeň (98Kč, 1 hours), and more from Cheb (40Kč, 30 minutes). Buses from Prague (136Kč, three hours), Plzeň (74Kč, 1¼ hours) and Cheb (40Kč, 25 minutes) are less frequent (up to five a day) and take as long as the train. The train journey from Karlovy Vary (76Kč, 1¾ hours) is slow but scenic.

AROUND MARIÁNSKÉ LÁZNĚ
Teplá Monastery
pop 3100

Founded in 1193, the **Premonstratensian monastery** (Premonstrátský klášter; ☎ 354 392 264; www .klastertepla.cz, Czech & German only; tour in Czech/English 60/120Kč; ⏰ 9am-4pm Mon-Sat, 11am-4.30pm Sun May-Oct, 11am-3pm Nov-Apr, closed Jan) at Teplá was one of the richest landowners in Bohemia in the 16th century. Among its holdings was Mariánské Lázně itself.

Though a bit run-down now (it served as an army barracks during the communist years), it boasts a sturdy Romanesque-Gothic church that has survived almost intact from 1232, and the second-largest library in the country, with around 80,000 books.

Organ and chamber concerts are held here in summer, and on 14 July there is an annual procession by former political prisoners incarcerated by the Nazis and communists.

Klášterní Hospice (The Cloister Inn; ☎ 354 392 264; www.hotelklastertepla.cz; s/d incl breakfast 950/1650Kč; ⓟ) Part of the monastery itself, this hotel has swish rooms that are anything but monastic.

GETTING THERE & AWAY

There are eight trains a day to/from Mariánské Lázně (28Kč, 30 minutes). By car, take the Karlovy Vary road for 7km and turn east.

KARLOVY VARY
pop 52,000

If you've been hiding a designer dog or an ostentatious pair of sunglasses in your luggage, then Karlovy Vary (Karlsbad in German) is your chance to give them both an airing. This fashionable town is the closest the Czech Republic has to a glam resort, but Karlovy Vary is still glam with a small 'g'. Well-heeled hypochondriacs from Germany, Austria, Russia and, increasingly, Arab nations make the pilgrimage to try to enjoy courses of 'lymphatic drainage' and 'hydrocolonotherapy' –

all activities that should be outlawed under several international agreements.

If you're really keen to discover the dubious pleasures of a steam inhalation session or a sulphur bath, you'll need to make a prior appointment. If not, there's good hiking in the surrounding hills, and a busy arts and entertainment programme. Sample the tepid mineral-rich water on offer, or just have a drink at the riverside cafés. In our opinion, a beer or a coffee is a better option than the sulphurous gunk everyone else is sipping on.

History

Today it may look like a monument to order and good sense, but according to legend, Karlovy Vary's springs were chanced upon. They were discovered by a dog that fell into the first of the town's springs while hunting with Emperor Charles IV. The loss of the dog was negligible compared with the profits to be made from the warm springs, and in 1358 Charles had a hunting lodge built near the largest, and granted the town status as 'Charles Spa'.

The town soon became a magnet for European aristocrats, who flocked to the growing watering hole hoping to purge themselves of the digestive disorders that were fashionable at the time. Russian tsar Peter the Great, Frederick I of Prussia and Empress Maria Theresa all made a splash in the early years.

Its popularity was further enhanced when Dr David Becher invented Becherovka, a potent herb liqueur, while analysing the composition of the town's waters in about 1790. This gave people the opportunity to get sozzled and healthier simultaneously. Unsurprisingly, Becherovka remains the mainstay of Karlovy Vary's souvenir industry today.

Attracting a growing population of aristocrats with plenty of money and plenty of time to kill between treatments, Karlovy Vary soon became a centre for the arts. The playwright Johann Schiller honeymooned here, and Goethe returned 13 times. Visiting composers included Bach, Beethoven, Brahms, Wagner, Tchaikovsky, Schumann, Liszt and Grieg. Dvořák's symphony *From the New World* premiered here in 1884, and the Dvořák Autumn Festival is held each September.

As the money and famous faces poured in, the buildings went up and the 'neo'-style and Art Nouveau structures that graced the skyline in the late 19th and early 20th centuries remain in fabulous condition today.

Now the celebrities are more B-list, attending the Karlovy Vary International Film Festival in July while wondering how their invitation to Cannes got lost in the mail.

Orientation

The business end of town is centred on Dr Bechera, while the spa sprawls for 3km up the Teplá valley, in the northern corner of the Slavkov forest (Slavkovský les).

Trains from Cheb, Plzeň and Prague, and most international connections, arrive at the upper station (horní nádraží), also called main station (hlavní nádraží), 400m from the other side of the Ohře. Those from Mariánské Lázně and the south use the lower station (dolní nádraží), on the spa side of the Ohře.

Long-distance buses and international buses to Germany use stands by the lower train station. The main junction for city and regional buses is on Varšavská.

MAPS

Infocentrum sells a useful Karlovy Vary map (30Kč), as well as one incorporating the surrounding area. Both are published by Paret.

Information

BOOKSHOPS

Nava (TG Masaryka 12) This bookshop sells regional maps.

EMERGENCY

Tourist Police (☎ 974 366 803; Závodu míru 16, Stará Role) Reached on bus 3 from Tržnice bus station.

INTERNET ACCESS

Moonstorm Internet (TG Masaryka 31; ⏱ 9am-9pm) Charges 12Kč per 15 minutes for internet access.
Kino Panasonic (☎ 353 233 933; www.kinopanasonic .cz; Vítězná 48) Free wi-fi at this art-house cinema's café.

INTERNET RESOURCES

The town's website, www.karlovyvary.cz, is a good resource with many useful contacts.

MEDIA

Promenáda (www.promenada.cz; 20Kč) is a monthly multilingual booklet full of information on spa history, cultural events, shopping and transport.

MEDICAL SERVICES

Aesculap (☎ 353 222 870; náměstí Dr M Horákové 8) Pharmacy near Dolní nádraží.

Nemocnice Karlovy Vary (☎ 353 115 111; Bezručova 19) The town hospital.

MONEY

Česká Spořitelna (TG Masaryka 14) Has an exchange counter and ATM.

POST

Main post office (TG Masaryka 1)

TOURIST INFORMATION

Infocentrum (☎ 353 232 838; www.karlovyvary.cz; Západni; ⏱ 9am-5pm Mon-Fri, 10am-4pm Sat & Sun) In Dolni nádraží. Stocks maps, books accommodation and gives transport advice. A **second branch** (☎ 353 224 097; Lázeňska 1) in the centre stays open for two additional hours each day.

TRAVEL AGENCIES

Čedok (☎ 353 227 837; Dr Bechera 21-23) Caters to most travel needs.

Sights & Activities

AROUND THE COLONNADES

The spa proper starts at **Poštovní bridge**, where late-19th- and early-20th-century mansions face off the blockish communist-era (1976) **Hotel Thermal** sanatorium across the river.

The 13th spring is the most famous but there are 15 springs housed in or near five colonnades (kolonády) along the Teplá. The first is the whitewashed and wrought-iron **Park spring colonnade** (Sadová kolonáda).

Further on is the biggest and most popular, the neo-Renaissance **Mill colonnade** (Mlýnská kolonáda; 1881), with five different springs, rooftop statues depicting the months of the year and a small bandstand (see also Entertainment, p216). **Petra Restaurant**, opposite, is the spot (but not the original building) where Peter the Great allegedly stayed in 1711.

Straight up Lázeňská is a gorgeous Art Nouveau building called **dům Zawojski** (1901). Nearby you can do some very upmarket window shopping along Lázeňská and Tržiště, including at the **Moser glasswork shop** (Tržiště 7). The Moser company opened its first shop in Karlovy Vary in 1857 and by 1893 had established a glassworks in the town. Less than a decade later Moser became the official supplier to the Imperial Court of Franz Josef I, who obviously put in a good word with his friend, King Edward VII, as Moser also became the official supplier of glass to British royalty in 1907. (See also Moser museum of Glass, p214.)

KARLOVY VARY

0 —————— 500 m
0 —————— 0.3 miles

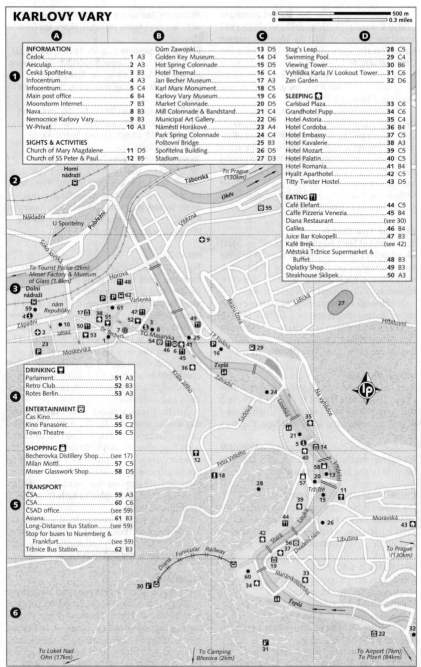

INFORMATION
Čedok...............................1 A3
Aesculap...........................2 A3
Česká Spořitelna..................3 B3
Infocentrum......................4 A3
Infocentrum......................5 C4
Main post office.................6 B4
Moonstorm Internet.............7 B3
Nava................................8 B3
Nemocnice Karlovy Vary........9 B3
W-Privat..........................10 A3

SIGHTS & ACTIVITIES
Church of Mary Magdalene.....11 D5
Church of SS Peter & Paul......12 B5

Dům Zawojski......................13 D5
Golden Key Museum.............14 D4
Hot Spring Colonnade..........15 D5
Hotel Thermal....................16 C4
Jan Becher Museum.............17 A3
Karl Marx Monument............18 C5
Karlovy Vary Museum...........19 C6
Market Colonnade...............20 D5
Mill Colonnade & Bandstand....21 C4
Municipal Art Gallery.............22 D6
Náměstí Horákové................23 A4
Park Spring Colonnade 24 C4
Poštovní Bridge...................25 B3
Spořitelna Building...............26 D3
Stadium............................27 D3

Stag's Leap........................28 C5
Swimming Pool...................29 C4
Viewing Tower....................30 B6
Vyhlídka Karla IV Lookout Tower....31 C6
Zen Garden........................32 D6

SLEEPING 🏠
Carlsbad Plaza...................33 C6
Grandhotel Pupp.................34 C6
Hotel Astoria.....................35 C4
Hotel Cordoba....................36 B4
Hotel Embassy...................37 C5
Hotel Kavalerie...................38 A3
Hotel Mozart.....................39 C5
Hotel Palatin......................40 C5
Hotel Romania....................41 B4
Hyalit Aparthotel................42 B3
Titty Twister Hostel..............43 D5

EATING 🍴
Café Elefant......................44 C5
Caffe Pizzeria Venezia..........45 B4
Diana Restaurant.................(see 30)
Galilea.............................46 B4
Juice Bar Kokopelli..............47 B3
Kafé Brejk........................(see 42)
Městská Tržnice Supermarket &
Buffet...........................48 B3
Oplatky Shop.....................49 B3
Steakhouse Sklipek..............50 A3

DRINKING 🍷
Parlament.........................51 A3
Retro Club........................52 B3
Rotes Berlin......................53 A3

ENTERTAINMENT 🎭
Čas Kino..........................54 B3
Kino Panasonic...................55 C2
Town Theatre.....................56 C5

SHOPPING 🛍
Becherovka Distillery Shop......(see 17)
Milan Mottl.......................57 C5
Moser Glasswork Shop..........58 D5

TRANSPORT
ČSA................................59 A3
ČSA................................60 C6
ČSAD office.......................(see 59)
Asiana.............................61 B3
Long-Distance Bus Station......(see 59)
Stop for buses to Nuremberg &
Frankfurt........................(see 59)
Tržnice Bus Station..............62 B3

WEST BOHEMIA

Across the road is the **Market colonnade** (Tržní kolonáda) with its delicate, white 1883 woodwork; one of its two springs, **pramen Karla IV**, is the spa's oldest. Behind this is the **Castle colonnade** (Zámecká kolonáda) and a castle tower, the **Zámecká věž**, erected in place of Charles IV's hunting lodge after it was destroyed by fire in 1604.

The steam billowing from the direction of the river comes from the incongruous, modern, 1975 building around the **Hot spring colonnade** (Vřídelní kolonáda). Inside is the spa's biggest, hottest spring, **pramen Vřídlo** (Sprudel to Germans), belching 15m into the air. People lounge in the geyser room for the vapours, or sample the waters from a line of progressively cooler taps in the next room.

EAST OF THE TEPLÁ

The **church of Mary Magdalene** (kostel sv Maří Magdaléná; 1737) is across the river. Whatever your thoughts on the excesses of baroque architecture, it's hard not to fall for this confection by Kilian Ignaz Dientzenhofer.

Southward on Moravská is a striking cluster of mansions, from neo-Gothic (No 4, where Dvořák stayed in 1879) to Art Nouveau (**Spořitelna building**, Divadelní náměstí). Across the square is the 1886 **Town theatre** (p216).

UPPER VALLEY

Back on the western side you can have coffee at the classic **Café Elefant** (p216) or peek into the concert hall and two-storey-high dining rooms of the gigantic **Grandhotel Pupp**, the spa's first hotel.

About 500m past the Pupp is the **Municipal Art Gallery**, and a little further still, you can unwind in the **Zen Japanese garden**.

CHURCH OF SS PETER & PAUL

On Krále Jiřího is the incongruous but deluxe Orthodox **church of SS Peter & Paul** (kostel sv Petra a Pavla), with five polished onion domes and vaguely Art Nouveau exterior murals.

MUSEUMS & GALLERIES

There's an art gallery and four relatively interesting museums in town:

Municipal Art Gallery (Galerie Umění; ☎ 353 224 387; Goethova stezka 6; adult/concession 30/20Kč; ☹ 9.30am-noon & 1-5pm Tue-Sun) Features a modest collection of 20th-century Czech art.

Karlovy Vary museum (Krajské muzeum Karlovy Vary; ☎ 353 226 252; Nová Louka 23; adult/concession 30/15Kč; ☹ 9am-noon & 1-5pm Wed-Sun) Has exhibits on Karlovy Vary's history and natural history, and Czech glasswork.

Golden key museum (muzeum Zlatý klíč; ☎ 353 223 888; Lázeňská 3; adult/concession 20/10Kč; ☹ 9am-noon & 1-5pm Wed-Sun) Has a low-key display of old-time Karlovy Vary and paintings of the spa by Viennese artist Wilhelm Gause.

Jan Becher museum (☎ 353 170 156; www.becherovka.cz; TG Masaryka 57; adult/concession 100/50Kč; ☹ 9am-5pm) Deals with all things Becherovka, the town's famed herbal liqueur.

Moser museum of Glass (Sklářské muzeum Moser; ☎ 353 449 455; www.moser.cz; Kpt Jaroše 19; admission free; ☹ 8am-5.30pm Mon-Fri, to 3pm Sat) Offers a history of local glass-making and visits to the glassworks.

Moser factory glassworks (admission adult/concession 90/45Kč; ☹ 9am-1pm Mon-Fri). Book visits in advance through Moser museum of Glass.

HIKING

For light relief, follow one of the steep trails from the Teplá into fragrant woods filled with statues and decaying pavilions. One of the most popular trails ascends 1.5km from the Grandhotel Pupp to a hilltop **viewing tower** (vyhlídka vez; admission free; ☹ 9.15am-5.45pm), with the garden **Diana Restaurant** (☎ 353 222 872). The woods on the way to the lookout are peppered with monuments, including one to that crusty old bourgeois, Karl Marx, who visited Karlsbad (Karlovy Vary) three times between 1874 and 1876.

Alternatively, you can ride a **funicular railway** (lanovka; single/return 36/60Kč; ☹ 9am-6pm) from behind Grandhotel Pupp. The trip to Diana takes five minutes. **Stag's leap** (Jelení skok), the promontory where Charles IV's dog made its famous discovery, is 500m northeast from an intermediate stop on the funicular. Another lookout tower is on **vyhlídka Karla IV**, south of Grandhotel Pupp.

If you're feeling energetic, it's 17km on a blue-marked trail, via the Diana lookout, along the Ohře to the romantic castle and village of **Loket nad Ohří** (p217).

SWIMMING

For a quick dip, the **swimming pool** (admission per hr 40Kč; ☹ 8am-8.30pm Mon-Sat, 9am-9.30pm Sun, closed every 3rd Mon) at Hotel Thermal offers simple swimming, or there's a range of spa treatments. There's also a **sauna** (☹ 10am-9.30pm), solarium and fitness club here. Head up the left-hand staircase at the rear of the hotel.

WEST BOHEMIA

Walking Tour

Starting from the post office at the eastern end of TG Masaryka, turn right and follow Zahradní southeast along the southern bank of the Teplá river. Just after the river curves, leave Zahradní and follow the footpath into the **Dvořák gardens (1)**. At the garden's eastern end is the delicate wrought-iron filigree of the **Park spring colonnade (2)**. Continue east to Lázeňská. On your right is **Spa No 3 (3)**, a popular spa for drinking. Tacky souvenir spa cups *(becher)* are available from a stall near the spring.

Further along Lázeňska is the **Mill colonnade (4)**, Karlovy Vary's most impressive, neo-Renaissance colonnade with four different springs, each progressively hotter. Continue round the next bend in the river to the **Market colonnade (5)** on Tržiště. From the Market colonnade head towards the billowing steam emanating from the ugly concrete **Hot spring colonnade (6)** dominating the middle of the river. Inside is the spectacular pramen Vřídlo. Buy a few *oplatky* (spa wafers), grab a seat and take in the action.

Exit the Hot spring colonnade on the opposite (eastern) side of the river. After the brutal Stalinist architecture of the Hot spring colonnade, the baroque **church of Mary Magdalene (7)** is a welcome contrast. Continue southward (with the river on your right) to the Art Nouveau **Spořitelna building (8)** on Divadelní náměští. At the southwest end of the square is Karlovy Vary's **Town theatre (9)**. Cross the river again to Stará Louka on the western bank, which is brimming with the town's flashest boutiques; a good spot to relax and recharge with coffee and cake is the elegant **Café Elefant (10)**.

Festivals & Events

The **Karlovy Vary Film Festival** (www.kviff.com) in July always features the year's top films as well as attracting plenty of (B-list) stars. It's rather behind the pace of the likes of Cannes, Venice and Berlin but is well worth the trip. The next generation of film-makers strut their stuff at the **International Student Film Festival** (www.freshfilmfestival.net; ☼ late Aug).

Other cultural events are the **Jazz Festival** in May and the **Dvořák Autumn Festival** in September.

Sleeping

Accommodation costs are similar to Prague, especially in the peak film festival month of July. Budget accommodation is at a premium. Book ahead in summer. Prices quoted are for high season (May to September, plus Christmas and New Year). During low season, discounts of up to 40% are available. Expect to pay an additional 'spa tax' (15Kč per bed per night).

Čedok (☎ 353 222 994; Dr Bechera 21; ☼ 9am-6pm Mon-Fri, 9am-noon Sat) and **W-Privat** (☎ 353 227 768; nám Republiky 5; ☼ 8.30am-5pm Mon-Fri, 9.30am-1pm Sat) can book private rooms from 400Kč per person, but you may need to stay for three or more nights. Infocentrum (p212) can find hostel, *pension* and hotel rooms.

BUDGET

Camping Březova (☎ 353 222 665; www.brezovy-haj.cz; tent/bungalow per person 90/150Kč; ☼ Apr-Oct; **P** 🖳) Beside a river valley, this camp site is 3km south of town. Catch the Březova bus from Tržnice bus station to the village of Březova.

Titty Twister Hostel (☎ 353 239 071; www.hosteltt .cz; Moravská 44; per person from 390Kč) In a town where cheap sleeps aren't exactly bubbling over, this little hostel with a silly name rises to the top. Accommodation is in apartments with two, four or six beds, and all have separate kitchens.

MIDRANGE

Hotel Kavalerie (☎ 353 229 613; www.kavalerie.cz; TG Masaryka 43; s/d incl breakfast from 950/1225Kč) Friendly staff abound in this cosy spot above a café near the bus and train stations and away from the high restaurant prices of the spa district.

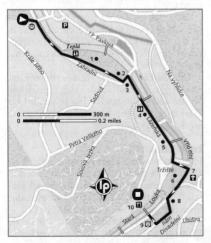

Hotel Romania (☎ 353 222 822; www.romania.cz; Zahradni 49; s/d incl breakfast 1000/1750Kč; **P**) Don't be put off by the ugly monolith of the Hotel Thermal dominating the views from this good-value reader-recommended hotel. Just squint a little, because the spacious rooms are very tidy and the English-speaking staff very helpful.

Hotel Astoria (☎ 353 335 111; www.astoria-spa.cz; Vřídelní 92; s/d incl breakfast from €40/80; ✖ ☎) A snazzy riverside location opposite the Mill colonnade completes this classy option with a full range of treatments. The leafy lobby relaxes you as soon as you walk in.

Hyalit Aparthotel (☎ 353 229 638; www.hyalit.cz; Stará Luka 62; d from 1900Kč; **P**) With stylish décor and kitchens, these five apartments are recommended for self-caterers. Children under 15 stay free.

Also recommended:

Hotel Mozart (☎ 353 236 072; www.hotel-mozart.cz; Stará Luka 18; s/d incl breakfast €50/75) Not quite a full-blown symphony inside, but the romantic exterior will definitely pull at your heart strings.

Hotel Palatin (☎ 353 304 111; www.energotour.com; Lázeňská 10; s/d incl breakfast 1600/2200Kč) Crisp, clean and on a good street for shopping.

Hotel Cordoba (☎ 353 200 255; www.hotel-cordoba.com; Zahradní 37; d incl breakfast 1800Kč) A worthwhile backup.

TOP END

Hotel Embassy (☎ 353 221 161; www.embassy.cz; Nová Louka 21; s/d incl breakfast 2190/2980Kč; **P** ▣) This riverside place is very proud that both Michael Douglas and Sir Ben Kingsley have dropped in at the Embassy Pub downstairs. Upstairs the rooms are cosy and comfortable, matching the charming exterior.

Carlsbad Plaza (☎ 353 225 501; www.carlsbadplaza.cz; Mariánskolázeňská 23; s/d €120/170; **P** ✖ ✖ ▣ ☎) Seriously stylish, this new hotel has raised the bar in spa town with soothingly modern treatment facilities, classy rooms and a smoothly Zen Asian restaurant. Who's top dog now, Grandhotel Pupp?

Eating

Food prices, especially around the colonnades, will seem high unless you've arrived from Prague. And check your bill: 'mistakes' happen.

You can buy *oplatky* (see p210) at the Městská tržnice supermarket by the bus stop on Varšavská, or at many locations across town.

Caffe Pizzeria Venezia (☎ 353 229 721; Zahradní 43; pizza 120Kč) After a few espressos blur your eyes through your designer sunnies, see if you can spot any gondoliers from this pretty-in-pink spot looking out on the Teplá river.

Galilea (☎ 353 221 183; TG Masaryka 3A, Pasáž Alfa; mains 130-180Kč) Hookah pipes are optional at this authentic Middle Eastern spot with creamy dips and Arabic bread. Downstairs grab a felafel kebab (65Kč) and relax by the river. Both the restaurant and kebab shop have good vegetarian options.

Steakhouse Sklipek (☎ 353 229 197; Zeyerova 1; steaks 180Kč) With red checked tablecloths and rustic wood furniture this place looks like a hang-out for Tony Soprano and his mates. The huge meaty meals are big enough to feed your entire mob too.

Also recommended:

Juice Bar Kokopelli (☎ 353 236 254; Bulharská 9; juice & smoothies 20-37Kč; ☯ 10am-7pm) For fruit smoothies that are probably healthier than sulphur-laden spa water.

Café Elefant (☎ 353 223 406; Stará Louka 30; coffee 45Kč) Classy old-school spot for coffee and calorie-rich cake.

Kafé Brejk (Stará Louka 62; coffee 35Kč, baguettes 50Kč; ☯ 9am-5pm) Trendy new-school spot for takeaway coffees and healthy design-your-own sandwiches and baguettes.

Drinking

Parlament (☎ 353 586 155; Zeyerova 5; ☯ closed Sun) With outdoor tables on the bustling TG Masaryka pedestrian mall, this is a favoured drinking place for locals. And the food's pretty good too.

Retro Club (TG Masaryka 18; ☯ 10am-midnight, to 3am Fri & Sat) Here's the most accurate name in all the Czech Republic, with regular nights celebrating the unique musical decade that was the 1980s.

Rotes Berlin (☎ 353 233 792; www.rotesberlin.com; Jaltská 7; ☯ to 3am) Outside this club is promised 'music and propaganda'. Inside you'll hear everything from hip-hop and world music to nicely thrashy indie rock.

Entertainment

Town theatre (Městské divadlo v Karlových Varech; ☎ 353 224 302; www.divadlokarlovy.cz; Divadelní náměstí 2) Drama, comedy and musicals are all featured. Tickets (100Kč to 500Kč) are available from the theatre or Infocentrum (p212).

Karlovy Vary Symphony Orchestra (☎ 353 228 707; www.kso.cz; IP Pavlova 14) The town's orchestra stages a regular programme of concerts. See its website or *Promenáda* for details. From mid-May to mid-September, **concerts** are also held in the **Mill colonnade** (p212) from Tuesday to Sunday.

Čas Kino (☎ 353 223 272; TG Masaryka 3) Cinema-lovers can get their flick fix here.

Kino Panasonic (☎ 353 233 933; www.kinopanasonic .cz; Vítězná 48) A compact art-house cinema with a good café and free wi-fi access.

Shopping

Becherovka distillery shop (☎ 353 170 156; TG Masaryka 57; ⊙ 9am-5pm) This shop is next to the Jan Becher museum (p214) and is the place to stock up on the goodies from the 13th spring – you'll find the Becherovka cheaper here than in souvenir shops.

Moser glasswork shop (☎ 353 235 303; Tržiště 7; ⊙ 9am-5pm Mon-Sat). If you can't make it to the factory (p214) on the Cheb road in the western outskirts, this is the spot to pick up the glasses for your Becherovka, among other things.

For more contemporary styles head to **Milan Mottl** (☎ 353 222 011; Tržiště 29; ⊙ 9am-5pm Mon-Sat). This innovative company was established in 1993 and specialises in handcrafted leadless crystal. There are many other excellent shops on **Tržiště** worth getting lost in.

Karlovy Vary porcelain is also famous, and not just those funny spa cups. The top local name is Pirkenhammer.

Getting There & Away

AIR

ČSA (☎ 239 007 007; www.csa.cz; Mírové náměstí 2) flies to Moscow four times a week (12,600Kč) from **Karlovy Vary International Airport** (KLV; ☎ 353 360 611; www.airport-k-vary.cz), 7km from the town.

Bus 8 runs to and from the airport from Tržnice bus station. The cost is 10Kč with an additional charge of 10Kč for luggage.

BUS & TRAIN

Regular **ČSAD** (☎ 353 913 550; Terminal Dolní Nádraží) buses run to Prague (150Kč, two hours) and are faster than **trains** (☎ 353 913 559), which take four hours (275Kč).

Asiana (☎ 353 360 411; Varšavká 11/1141; ⊙ 9am-5pm Mon-Fri) runs buses to Prague Florenc (140Kč) and Prague's Ruzyně Airport (190Kč) every hour. There is another office at **Terminal Dolní Nádraží** (☎ 353 633 283; ⊙ 7am-6pm).

A seat reservation *(místenka)* is recommended for Prague (book a day or two in advance) and for international connections (book at least a week in advance).

There are also departures to Nuremberg and Frankfurt once a week (you need to book this as it does not stop in Karlovy Vary if there are no bookings), and Amsterdam once a week, from the lower train station.

Getting Around

Local buses run at 20- to 30-minute intervals; routes are posted at the stop on Varšavská. Bus tickets (10Kč) are sold in kiosks and from machines at major stops. Transfer tickets (15Kč) can be re-used within 40 minutes but are only available from the driver.

Bus 11 runs hourly from Karlovy Vary horní nádraží train station to the Tržnice bus station at the market, then over the hills to Divadlo náměstí and the Vřídelní colonnade. Bus 2 runs between Tržnice and Grandhotel Pupp (Spa No 1) every half-hour or so from 6am to 11pm daily.

TAXIS & PARKING

A 24-hour taxi service is **Willy Taxi** (☎ 800 100 154).

A large, partially underground car park is next to Hotel Thermal sanatorium on IP Pavlova (50/100Kč for two/24 hours).

LOKET NAD OHŘE

pop 3200

Surrounded by a wickedly serpentine loop in the river Ohře, the almost unbearably picturesque village of Loket may as well be on an island. According to the local tourist office it was 'JW Goethe's favourite town' and, after a lazily subdued stroll around the gorgeous main square and castle, it may be yours as well.

Loket's German name is Elbogen (German for 'elbow', after the extreme bend in the river) and it's been famous by that name since 1815 for the manufacture of porcelain, as have the neighbouring towns of Horní Slavkov (Schlackenwald) and Chodov (Chodan). Shops in town have a fine selection of the local craftsmanship.

Orientation & Information

The bus from Karlovy Vary provides a cinematic look at the town, almost completely circling it on approach.

WEST BOHEMIA

The local tourist information office, **Infocentrum** (☎ 352 684 123; www.loket.cz; TG Masaryka 12; ⏲ 10am-12.30pm & 1-5pm), is by the bridge. Internet access is 10Kč per 15 minutes.

Česká Spořitelna (TG Masaryka 101) has an exchange counter and an ATM.

At the end of July, the **Loket Summer Cultural Festival** (www.loketfestival.info) features opera performances in the open-air theatre below the castle walls (contact Infocentrum for details).

Sights & Activities
CASTLE
The beautiful **castle** (hrad Loket; ☎ 352 684 104; adult/concession with English guide 90/60Kč, with English text 80/45Kč; ⏲ 9am-4.30pm May-Oct, to 3.30pm Nov-Apr) was built on the site of an earlier Romanesque fort, of which the only surviving bits are the tall square tower and fragments of a rotunda and palace. Its present late-Gothic look dates from the late 14th century. From 1788 to 1947 it was used as the town prison. The town, not the state, did the impressive restoration work in the 1970s.

A tour isn't necessary, and the English text on the castle's history has little on the exhibits inside; several cutaway sections from archaeological work on the castle and two rooms full of luscious ceramics are barely enough to whet the appetite. Check out the postcard views of the village and forest from the tower.

OTHER SIGHTS
The narrow, curving square, TG Masaryka, has its fair share of handsome Gothic façades. But one of the most eye-catching buildings is the recently renovated neo-Gothic **Hostinec Bílý kůň** (White Horse Inn), where Goethe stayed.

In the early-baroque **town hall** (radnice), you can visit the town's vaguely interesting (for bibliophiles) **bookbinding museum** (adult/concession 35/20Kč; ⏲ 10am-1pm & 2-6pm). Ceramics junkies can also get a fix wandering around the town's **ceramics showrooms**, including a shop selling Loket's own Epiag brand.

Two old gate towers, Černá věž and Robičská věž, are still standing. Join in the Czech fascination with lookout towers and climb the **Black gate tower** (Černá věž; TG Masaryka; admission 15Kč; ⏲ 10am-5pm Jul & Aug, Fri-Sun only May, Jun & Sep), which houses a small art gallery and wine shop and offers some tip-top photo opportunities. Outside the gate towers is the tiny baroque **St Anne chapel** (kaple sv Anny), now empty.

The red-and-white 18th-century **church of St Wenceslas** (kostel sv Václava) is on your way to the castle.

RAFTING
Rafting Ohře (☎ 606 902 310; www.putzer.cz) offers canoeing and rafting trips on the Ohře river, beginning in Loket. Especially beautiful is the stretch between Sokolov and Kadaň. Trip duration varies from two hours to eight hours. Prices for canoes (two people) range from 500Kč to 750Kč and rafts (four to six people) from 1200Kč to 2400Kč. Bookings can be made through Infocentrum.

Sleeping
Lazy River Hostel (☎ 352 685 204; www.lazyriverhostel.com; Kostelni 72; per person 250Kč) Tucked in under the castle, this friendly, laid-back budget spot is also worth considering as a base for visiting flasher-than-flash Karlovy Vary. Book ahead because there are only nine beds.

Pension Hála (☎ 352 684 440; TG Masaryka 115; per person incl breakfast 400Kč) On the square, Pension Hála is slightly less flash than Pension Ulrika, but just as comfy *and* 100Kč less.

Pension Ulrika (☎ 352 684 103; Zámecká 19/1; per person incl breakfast 500Kč) Four newly renovated rooms with wooden floors and cheerily rustic furniture look out on the main square.

Hotel Bílý Kůň (☎ 352 685 002; www.hotel-horse.cz; TG Masaryka 8; s/d incl breakfast 1190/1690Kč) A favourite of that incurable romantic, Goethe, but the renovated and comfortable rooms lack the 19th-century charm he would remember. Eat and drink to his memory on the summer terrace overlooking the river.

Eating
Pizzeria na Růžka (☎ 606 433 282; cnr TG Masaryka & Kostelni; pizza 110Kč) Add sunflower paintings to a cosy wood-fired oven and you've got more indisputable proof that you're never far from a good pizza anywhere in the Czech Republic.

U Šejk (☎ 353 221 401; TG Masaryka 115; mains 140Kč) Once called U Fausta and now called U Šejk, this spot is yet another U Biquitous 'Good Soldier' theme restaurant – always a reliable choice for hearty Czech food.

Getting There & Away
Buses link Loket with Karlovy Vary's lower train station (20Kč, 25 minutes). There are seven departures per day on weekdays, fewer on weekends.

You can hike from Karlovy Vary on a very fine 17km trail (marked blue) beside the Ohře (p214).

PLZEŇ
pop 163,000

After the quaintly contrived elegance of the West Bohemian spa towns, the rugged blue-collar energy of Plzeň comes as a welcome relief. The capital of West Bohemia has authentic industrial credibility as the home of the Skoda Engineering Works and as the original source of Pilsner beer. Workers the world over are especially pleased with that last fact.

As the country's fourth-largest city, Plzeň's gritty suburbs sprawl across the surrounding hills, but at its heart lies a spectacular old town square wrapped in a halo of tree-lined gardens.

A lively student population ensures the town's pubs provide many opportunities to sample Plzeň's heritage as the original fountain of eternal golden froth. A varied programme of music and arts allows you to feed your soul as well as quench your thirst, and excellent museums cover everything from Pilsner to Patton.

Plzeň may not have the immediate and elegant extravagance of nearby Karlovy Vary or Mariánské Lázně, and it takes hold rather more slowly. But after a day of imbibing the city's raffish charm (and its most famous liquid export), you won't be missing the crowded bus parks, the pushy tour groups or the surface gloss of the spa towns at all.

History
Founded as West Bohemia's administrative capital in 1295 by Přemysl King Václav II, the fortified, solidly Catholic Plzeň grew quickly, becoming Bohemia's third-largest town, after Prague and Kutná Hora, by the 14th century.

Among other things, Václav II granted to some 260 Plzeň burghers the exclusive right to brew beer. By the time of the Thirty Years' War there were 26 separate basement breweries, each with its own beer hall – though many of the products were not particularly drinkable. In 1842 the crafty brewers pooled their experience, installed 'modern' technology and founded a single municipal brewery, with spectacular results. Their golden beer, labelled Plzeňský Prazdroj (*prazdroj* is old

Czech for 'the original source'; Pilsner Urquell in German), is now one of the world's best – and most imitated – beers.

At the same time, Plzeň began to industrialise. The Škoda Engineering Works was founded in 1869 and prospered as a manufacturer of armaments. Since WWII it has been known mainly for the ubiquitous Škoda car, as well as locomotives and industrial machinery. In the midst of post-1989 euphoria, Volkswagen offered Škoda a staggering US$1 billion development loan, and the German car manufacturer now has a majority share in the company.

Orientation
Plzeň sits near the confluence of four sizable rivers, two of which, the Mže and the Radbuza, flow past the old town centre.

The central bus station (centrální autobusové nádraží) is west of the town centre, 1km along Husova to the main square, náměstí Republiky. The main train station (hlavní nádraží) is the same distance on the other side of town; turn right under the tracks and left (west) onto Americká, then cross the Radbuza; the second, third and fourth right turns will take you to náměstí Republiky.

Information
CULTURAL CENTRES
American Center Plzeň (☎ 377 237 722; www .americancenter.cz; Dominikánská 9; ⏰ 9am-10pm) Mainly a business resource centre, with a restaurant/bar and CNN news.

INTERNET ACCESS
American Center Plzeň (☎ 377 237 722; www .americancenter.cz; Dominikánská 9; per hr 60Kč; ⏰ 9am-10pm) Also see above.
Internet Kavarna (☎ 377 222 146; 1st fl, Tylova 6; per hr 40Kč; ⏰ 8am-10pm Mon-Thu, 8am-7.30pm Fri, noon-8pm Sat & Sun)
City Information Centre (Městské Informační Středisko; ☎ 378 035 330; www.plzen-city.cz; náměstí Republiky 41; per min 1Kč; ⏰ 9am-7pm) Also see p220.

MONEY
Česká Spořitelna (náměstí Republiky) By the Archdeacon's house; has an ATM and exchange counter.
ČSOB (cnr Sady 5 kvetna & Františkánská) Just south of the main square.

POST
Main post office (Solní) West of the main square.

TOURIST INFORMATION

City Information Centre (Městské Informační Středisko; ☎ 378 035 330; www.plzen-city.cz; náměstí Republiky 41; ☺ 9am-7pm) Reserves accommodation, organises guides, sells maps and changes money. There is **another branch** (☎ 972 524 313; ☺ 9am-5pm) at the main railway station.

TRAVEL AGENCIES

CKM (☎ 377 236 393; ckmplzen@tiscali.cz; Dominikánská 1; ☺ 8am-6pm Mon-Thu, to 5pm Fri) Books international travel and cheap accommodation.

Sights & Activities

NÁMĚSTÍ REPUBLIKY

Plzeň's main square, náměstí Republiky, is the hub of the city's lively and attractive old town. It's notable for the gigantic Gothic **St Bartholomew church** (kostel sv Bartoloměje; adult/concession 20/10Kč; ☺ 10am-6pm Wed-Sat Apr-Sep, Wed-Fri Oct-Dec), which towers over the surrounding façades from the centre of the square. Look inside at the delicate marble 'Pilsen Madonna' (dating from c 1390) on the main altar, or climb 301 steps to the top of the **tower** (adult/concession 30/10Kč; ☺ 10am-6pm weather permitting) for serious views.

Plzeň is less plastered with baroque façades than many Bohemian towns. The best Renaissance structures in the old centre are in and around the square. Check out **Chotešov house** (náměstí Republiky 106/13) and, around the corner, the delightful old **Gerlach house**.

One of the most charming buildings in Bohemia is Plzeň's **Old town hall** (Staroměstská radnice; admission free; ☺ 8am-6pm). The bottom four floors, built in 1558, are pure Italian Renaissance. A few years later the top floor, tower, multiple gables and little brass flags were added; all it needs is a liveried ensemble doing trumpet fanfares from the roof. The sgraffito on the front dates from the 16th century. There is also a model of the old city centre here. In front is a 1681 **plague column**.

The 1710 **Archdeacon's house** (Arciděkanství; náměstí Republiky 234/35) by Jakub Auguston, who was a local boy, is on the western side of the square.

The southern half of the square becomes a lively **craft market** eight times a year, mainly around public holidays. Check at the helpful City Information Centre for exact dates.

UNDERGROUND PLZEŇ

The extraordinary **museum of Plzeň's historical underground** (Plzeňské historické podzemí; ☎ 377 225 214; Perlová 4; adult/concession 45/25Kč; ☺ 9am-5pm Tue-Sun Jul-Sep, Wed-Sun Apr-Jun, Oct & Nov) is a web of passages under the town. The earliest were probably dug in the 14th century, perhaps for beer production or defence; the latest date from the 19th century. Of an estimated 11km excavated in the 1970s and '80s, some 500m is open to the public.

Plzeň's wealthier set used to have wells in their cellars. Overuse led to severe water shortages until a municipal water system was established in the 15th century. When wells dried up they were often filled with rubbish and buried; these have yielded an amazing trove of artefacts. The tunnels are dotted with exhibits of wooden water pumps, mining tools, pewter, pottery and, to the surprise of some historians, Czech glass dating back to the 14th century.

A good English text is available, but bring extra clothing (it's a chilly 10°C); a torch (flashlight) will let you peer into the eeriest corners. The last tour is at 4.20pm.

ASSUMPTION CHURCH & FRANCISCAN MONASTERY

South of the square on Františkánská is the **Assumption church** (kostel Nanebevzetí Panny Marie); when entering you pass an unusual crucifix with a clean-shaven Christ nailed to the cross by only one hand and one foot.

In the former **Franciscan monastery** (klášter Františkánů) next door is the **Diocese museum** (Diecésní muzeum; Františkánská 11; adult/concession 30/20Kč; ☺ 10am-6pm Tue-Sun Apr-Sep) with tours of a fine collection of church statues. The real reason to visit is to see the little **St Barbara chapel** (kaple sv Barbory) on the cloister's eastern side; structurally unaltered since it was built in the 13th century, it bears the remains of decorative frescoes added as early as the 15th century.

AROUND NÁMĚSTÍ REPUBLIKY

The streets of Nový Plzeň's original 'chessboard' layout are good for browsing.

At least three buildings (on Solní and náměstí Republiky) bear bright **murals by Mikuláš Aleš**, a central figure of the so-called 'National Theatre generation' of the Czech National Revival.

At the end of Pražská is a stone **water tower** (vodárenská věž) dating from 1530 and part of the first town water system (this tower supplied fountains in the square until the

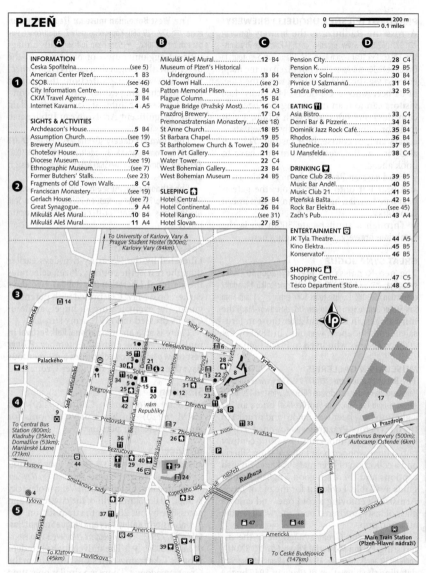

PLZEŇ

INFORMATION	Mikuláš Aleš Mural............................**12** B4	Pension City.......................................**28** C4
Česka Spořitelna.............................(see 5)	Museum of Plzeň's Historical	Pension K...**29** B5
American Center Plzeň.......................**1** B3	Underground...............................**13** B4	Penzion v Solní.................................**30** B4
ČSOB...(see 46)	Old Town Hall...............................(see 2)	Pivnice U Salzmannů.......................**31** B4
City Information Centre.......................**2** B4	Patton Memorial Pilsen....................**14** A3	Sandra Pension.................................**32** B5
CKM Travel Agency.............................**3** B4	Plague Column..................................**15** B4	
Internet Kavarna................................**4** A5	Prague Bridge (Pražský Most)........**16** C4	**EATING** 🍴
	Prazdroj Brewery..............................**17** D4	Asia Bistro...**33** C4
SIGHTS & ACTIVITIES	Premonastratensian Monastery.....(see 18)	Denní Bar & Pizzerie........................**34** B4
Archdeacon's House............................**5** B4	St Anne Church.................................**18** B5	Dominik Jazz Rock Café...................**35** B4
Assumption Church..........................(see 19)	St Barbara Chapel.............................**19** B5	Rhodos...**36** B4
Brewery Museum.................................**6** C3	St Bartholomew Church & Tower....**20** B4	Slunečnice...**37** B5
Chotešov House..................................**7** B4	Town Art Gallery...............................**21** B4	U Mansfelda......................................**38** C4
Diocese Museum...............................(see 19)	Water Tower......................................**22** C4	
Ethnographic Museum.......................(see 7)	West Bohemian Gallery.....................**23** B4	**DRINKING** 🍷
Former Butchers' Stalls....................(see 23)	West Bohemian Museum **24** B5	Dance Club 28...................................**39** B5
Fragments of Old Town Walls............**8** C4		Music Bar Anděl................................**40** B5
Franciscan Monastery......................(see 19)	**SLEEPING** 🛏	Music Club 21....................................**41** B4
Gerlach House...................................(see 7)	Hotel Central....................................**25** B4	Plzeňská Bašta..................................**42** B4
Great Synagogue.................................**9** A4	Hotel Continental.............................**26** B4	Rock Bar Elektra.............................(see 45)
Mikuláš Aleš Mural............................**10** B4	Hotel Rango...................................(see 31)	Zach's Pub..**43** A4
Mikuláš Aleš Mural............................**11** A4	Hotel Slovan......................................**27** B5	
		ENTERTAINMENT 🎭
		JK Tyla Theatre.................................**44** A5
		Kino Elektra.......................................**45** B5
		Konservatoř.......................................**46** B5
		SHOPPING 🛍
		Shopping Centre...............................**47** C5
		Tesco Department Store...................**48** C5

beginning of the 20th century). Opposite is a former arcade of medieval **butchers' stalls** (masné krámy), which is now part of the **West Bohemian gallery** (☎ 377 223 759; Pražská 13; adult/concession 20/10Kč; 🕙 10am-6pm Tue-Fri) with its changing exhibits of modern Czech art.

Heading out where a town gate used to be, you cross **Prague bridge** (Pražský most) over

the former site of a moat. Turning left brings you to some weedy, reconstructed **fragments of the old town walls**.

South of the square on Smetany is the very baroque **St Anne church** (kostel sv Anny), another work by Jakub Auguston. The former **Premonstratensian monastery** next door is now part of a State Science Library.

WEST BOHEMIA

PRAZDROJ (PILSNER URQUELL) BREWERY

Across the Radbuza is the **brewery** (pivovar; ☎ 377 062 888; www. prazdroj.cz.cz; U Prazdroje 7; admission 120Kč; ⏰ 10am-9pm Mon-Sat, 10am-8pm Sun, tours in English at 12.30pm & 2pm) that put Plzeň on the map, entered via the gate that has graced the label of its beer since 6 October 1842. Individual visitors can join an interesting (for beer aficionados) one-hour tour with a film, a visit to the brewing rooms and chilly fermentation cellars and, of course, beer tasting. You can also visit at the weekend, but you have to book ahead.

Head east on Pražská, then cross the river and bear left onto U Prazdroje; the gate is near a pedestrian bridge, 750m from náměstí Republiky.

Through a similar gate 500m on is the **Gambrinus brewery**. Sorry, no tours here.

GREAT SYNAGOGUE

The neo-Renaissance **Great synagogue** (Velká synagóga; ☎ 377 223 346; Sady Pětatřicátníků 11; adult/concession 45/30Kč, English tours 50Kč extra; ⏰ 11am-6pm Sun-Fri Apr-Sep, to 5pm Jun, to 4pm Oct, closed Nov-Mar), the third-largest in the world after those in Jerusalem and Budapest, was built in 1892 by the 2000 or so Jews who lived in Plzeň then.

MUSEUMS & GALLERIES

The **Brewery museum** (☎ 377 235 574; www.prazdroj.cz; Veleslavínova 6; adult/concession 80/50Kč, with text 120/60Kč; ⏰ 9am-6pm Tue-Sun, 9am-5pm Oct-Mar) offers an insight into how beer was made (and drunk) in the days before Prazdroj was founded. Highlights include a mock-up of a 19th-century pub, a huge wooden beer tankard from Siberia and a collection of beer mats. All have English captions and there's a good English written guide available. Look out for the pic of Louis Armstrong enjoying a cold one, and enjoy a glass of tasty unfiltered beer afterwards in the attached pub.

North of the Great synagogue is the interesting **Patton Memorial Pilsen** (☎ 377 320 414; Podřežni 10; adult/concession 45/25Kč; ⏰ 9am-5pm Tue-Sun) detailing the liberation of Plzeň in 1945 by the American army under General George Patton. Especially poignant are the handwritten memories of former American soldiers who have returned to Plzeň in a new century, and the museum's response to the communist-era revisionist fabrications that claimed Soviet troops, not Americans, were responsible for the city's liberation.

The **West Bohemian museum** (Západočeské muzeum; ☎ 377 329 380; Kopeckého sady 2; adult/concession per exhibit 20/10Kč; ⏰ 9am-5pm Tue-Sun) fills a magnificent agglomeration of buildings. In the basement the original armoury *(zbrojnice)* features a weapons collection; the ground floor has changing exhibits while the second floor houses an exhibit of glass and porcelain in the magnificent Art Nouveau Jubilee hall (Jubilejní sál).

The **Town Art Gallery** (Galerie Města Plzně; ☎ 378 035 310; Dominikánská 3; adult/concession 20/10Kč; ⏰ 10am-noon & 1-6pm Tue-Sun) hosts art and design exhibitions.

The **Ethnographic museum** (☎ 377 324 028; náměstí Republiky 106/13; adult/concession 20/10Kč; ⏰ 9am-5pm Tue-Sun) has a small collection of moderate interest.

Festivals & Events

Liberated by the US army two days earlier than the rest of the country, Plzeň celebrates the national **Liberation Day Holiday** two days earlier, on 6 May. Celebrated with perennial gusto, the event features a huge parade of Czechs dressed in WWII army surplus.

There is also an **International Folk Festival** in mid-June. At the end of September, **Pilsner Fest** (www.pilsnerfest.cz) celebrates a momentous day: the first brewing of Pilsner Urquell.

Sleeping

The City Information Centre (p220) and CKM (p220) can book private rooms for around 350Kč per person.

BUDGET

Autocamp Ostende (☎ 377 520 194; www.cbox.cz/atc -ostende; tent/bungalow per person 80/200Kč; ⏰ May-Sep; Ⓟ) Autocamp Ostende is on Velký Bolevecký rybník, a lake 6km north of the city centre and accessible by bus 20 near the train station.

University of Karloy Vary and Prague Student Hostel (☎ 377 259 381; www.webpark.cz/bolevecka; Bolevecká 34; s/d 250/500Kč; Ⓟ) The university has student rooms. Take tram 4 two stops north from the Great synagogue. There is a similar operation at the Bolevecká 30 (☎ 377 259 814). Both get busy so try to phone ahead.

MIDRANGE

Hotel Slovan (☎ 377 227 256; http://hotelsslovan.pilsen .cz; Smetanovy sady 1; s/d without bathroom 530/810Kč, s/d with bathroom 1450/2100Kč, all incl breakfast; Ⓟ) The Slovan's old-world glamour is now a tad faded and the rooms are functional, but it's a good central and historic option. In WWII the hotel was the US Army Officers' Club, and it's just a matter of time before it is redeveloped to luxury status. Stay there while you can still afford it.

Pivnice U Salzmannů (☎ 377 235 855; www.usalzmannu .cz; Pražská 8; s 550-1350Kč, d 750-1500Kč) Right above one of Plzeň's most historic pubs is a range of rooms from budget to midrange. Your big decision: do you go for a cheaper room and then have more to spend downstairs on the beer and hearty food?

Penzion v Solní (☎ 377 236 652; www.volny.cz/pension solni; Solní 8; s/d 600/1020Kč) The best deal in town is at this compact and friendly spot sandwiched between a deli and a clothes shop. With only three rooms, it's essential to book ahead.

Pension City (☎ 377 326 069; fax 377 222 976; Sady 5 kvetna 52; s/d incl breakfast 1000/1390Kč; (P)) On a quiet street near the river, the City has comfortable rooms and friendly, English-speaking staff armed with lots of local information.

Also recommended:

Pension K (☎ 337 329 683; pensionk@volny.cz; Bezručova 13; s/d with breakfast 890/1350Kč) Slightly dowdy but clean rooms in a central street with restaurants and music clubs.

Sandra Pension (☎ 377 325 358; sandra.101@seznam .cz; Kopeckého sady 15; s/d with breakfast 990/1260Kč; (P)) Three clean rooms above a parkside restaurant; good English spoken.

TOP END

Hotel Continental (☎ 377 235 292; www.hotelcontinental .cz; Zbrojnicka 8; s/d without bathroom 860/1460Kč, s/d with bathroom 1580/2150Kč, all incl breakfast) The Continental has survived being hit by an Allied bomb in WWII and playing host to Gerard Depardieu and John Malkovich – we're not sure what's worse. Before the war, Ingrid Bergman and Marlene Dietrich also stayed here, and the hotel still retains its Art Deco glamour. There are also flasher rooms called 'luxury parlors' (2450Kč to 4500Kč).

Hotel Rango (☎ 377 221 188; www.rango.cz; Pražská 10; s/d 1450/2150Kč) The 11 rooms at this spot near the main square are tasteful enough to almost push the Rango into 'boutique hotel' status. Downstairs there's a good restaurant.

Also recommended:

Hotel Central (☎ 377 226 757; www.central-hotel .cz; náměstí Republiky 33; s/d incl breakfast 1700/2390Kč; (P) (🖳)) Business-oriented hotel with internet connections in all rooms, and a wi-fi hotspot.

Eating

Denní Bar & Pizzerie (☎ 377 237 965; Solní 9; pizza 75Kč) Come for the interesting photographs of old Plzeň and stay for the tasty food in this snug little place.

U Mansfelda (☎ 377 333 844; cnr Dřevěna & Křížíkovy sady; mains 90-140Kč) In a city of raucous pubs, this spot is a classier option with a summer terrace, an upstairs wine bar and interesting takes on Czech cuisine such as wild boar *gulaš* (spicy meat and potato soup).

Dominik Jazz Rock Café (☎ 377 323 226; Dominikánská 3; mains 100Kč; (🕙) 9am-11pm Mon-Thu, 9am-1am Fri, 3pm-midnight Sat, 3pm-10pm Sun) Get lost in the nooks and crannies of this vast student hang-out, or take on Plzeň's best at pool or *foosball* (table soccer). There are cool beats all day, every day, and good-value salads and sandwiches at lunchtime. After dark it gets enjoyably raucous.

Rhodos (☎ 736 677 344; Bezručova 20; mains 130Kč) More 'Alan the Very Good' than Alexander the Great, this spot serves up Greek fare in leafy surroundings with a sunny skylight. The 'assemble yourself' *gyros* with pita bread are good value and we recommend you finish with a slice of naughtily sweet *baklava*.

Also recommended:

Slunečnice (Jungmanova 10; baguettes 50Kč; (🕙) 7.30am-6pm) For fresh, tasty baguettes and sandwiches on the go.

Asia Bistro (Pražská 31; mains from 70Kč; (🕙) 11am-11pm) Mr Han from Hanoi cooks up tasty Vietnamese fare including good spring rolls.

Drinking

Plzen is a both a brewery town and a big student town, so there are plenty of good places to kick back with your beverage of choice.

PUBS

Zach's Pub (☎ 377 223 176; Palackého náměstí 2; (🕙) 1-9pm Mon-Thu, 1pm-2am Fri, 5pm-2am Sat, to midnight Sun) Head to Zach's for live music, filling and tasty pub food and a suitably student atmosphere.

Plzeňská Bašta (☎ 377 237 262; Riegrova 5; (🕙) 11am-1am) Wooden beams and cosy booths make this a nicely rustic spot for your first (and just maybe your best) Pilsner Urquell.

CLUBS

Music Bar Anděl (☎ 377 323 226; Bezručova 7; (🕙) 10am-3am) By day a coolly hip café, the Anděl is transformed after dark into a rocking live-music venue featuring the best of touring Czech bands and occasional international acts.

For pre-recorded beats until the early hours try:

Dance Club 28 (☎ 608 701 470; Prokopova 28)
Music Club 21 (☎ 377 220 860; Prokopova 21)

Entertainment

THEATRE & MUSIC

JK Tyla Theatre (☎ 378 038 001; Prokopova 14) Plzeň's main theatre stages regular performances.

Konzervatoř (Conservatory; ☎ 377 226 325; Kopeckého sady 10) The majority of classical concerts are held here.

Kino Elektra (☎ 377 270 243; Americká 24) Film buffs can catch a flick before heading to the attached Rock Bar Elektra for late-night drinks and tunes.

Getting There & Away

There are plenty of direct buses (80Kč, 1½ hours) and trains (140Kč, 1¾ hours) daily to/ from Prague.

To and from Karlovy Vary, buses are quicker (76Kč, 1¾ hours) and more frequent (about eight a day) than the train (no direct services).

For České Budějovice, the train (162Kč, 1¾ hours) is usually quicker but more expensive than the bus (110Kč, 2½ hours).

Getting Around

You can buy tickets (12Kč) for the buses, trolleybuses and trams from kiosks and *tabák* (tobacco) shops, or from machines at major stops. There are also day passes available (40Kč per day).

AROUND PLZEŇ

Kladruby

pop 750

A Benedictine abbey was founded here in 1115 by Prince Vladislav I. Following repeated plundering during the Thirty Years' War, the Counter-Reformation abbots undertook a major face-lift of the buildings by two of the most prominent Bohemian artists of the time, Giovanni Santini and Kilian Ignatz Dientzenhofer.

The main attraction is the **abbey church of the Holy Virgin** rebuilt between 1712 and 1726 by Santini in an extraordinary 'baroque Gothic' style seen nowhere outside Bohemia. (An earlier Santini work in this style is the abbey church at Sedlec, near Kutná Hora;

see p159.) Bohemia abounds in fine but often repetitive architecture; here is something very different.

The church has the original floor plan of a Romanesque basilica and is the longest in Bohemia (85m). The church itself – Santini's design, from the fantastically complex vaulting right down to the pews – is an improbable marriage of baroque flamboyance and Gothic severity that would verge on tongue-in-cheek if it weren't so beautiful. At the front, to the left, is the **tomb of Vladislav I**, one of the few Přemysl rulers not buried either at Prague castle or Zbraslav.

The standard tour includes the cloisters, with several dozen allegorical sculptures from the workshop of the celebrated baroque sculptor Matthias Bernard Braun. Of the monastery buildings themselves (not on the tour), the west wing is the **Old prelature** (abbot's residence), now a church library. The baroque east wing is the so-called **New convent** built to a design by Dientzenhofer between 1729 and 1739 and now beautifully renovated.

The **abbey** (☎ 374 631 773; www.klasterkladruby .cz; adult/concession 40/30Kč; ⏲ 9am-5pm Tue-Sun Jun-Aug, 9am-4pm Tue-Sun May & Sep, Sat & Sun Apr & Oct) hosts hourly group tours in Czech (foreign text available for 60Kč extra). There are two circuits: Tour I (one hour) includes the monastery and church; Tour II (45 minutes) takes in the chateau. In summer, occasional classical concerts are held in the abbey's grounds. See the website for details.

GETTING THERE & AWAY

Kladruby village is about 35km west of Plzeň, just south of Stříbro. Getting there as a day trip from Plzeň involves taking one of the frequent trains to Stříbro (46Kč, 45 minutes) and then catching a local bus the last 6km to Kladruby (10Kč, 12 minutes).

From Kladruby's main square, walk (in the direction of the parish church) 1.5km to the monastery.

KLATOVY & AROUND

pop 22,900

Fine views of the Šumava mountains herald Klatovy's place as the gateway to this pristine, romantic region. A sleepy Renaissance square provides more than enough for a few hours of meandering, but the town, which was founded in 1262, is really just a stopover en route to bigger (and more beautiful) things.

Orientation & Information

The main train station and the bus station are about 1.5km northwest of the central square, náměstí Míru. Take bus 1 or 2 from either one.

Informanči Centrum (☎ 376 347 240; www.klatovy .cz/icklatovy; náměstí Míru 63; ⏲ 9am-noon & 1-5pm May-Sep, Mon-Fri only Oct-Apr), beside the Old town hall, has information on Klatovy and the Šumava area.

KB (cnr náměstí Míru & Křížová) changes money and has an ATM.

The **main post office** (Domažlická) is west of the centre.

Internet Café (Václavská 19; ⏲ noon-4pm & 6-10pm Mon-Fri, 2-10pm Sat & Sun) is where you can get online.

Sights & Activities

BLACK TOWER & AROUND

The **Black tower** (Černá věž; adult/concession 20/10Kč; ⏲ 9am-noon & 1-5pm Tue-Sun May-Sep, to 4pm Apr & Oct) at the hub of the old town was completed in 1557 and given its present roof in 1872 after the old one blew off in a storm. It has also burnt down three times.

Next door is the late-16th-century **Old town hall**. The handsome neo-Renaissance façade was added in 1925 by architect Josef Fanta.

JESUIT CHURCH & CATACOMBS

Opposite the Black tower is the sober-faced **church of the Immaculate Conception & St Ignatius**, worth a visit for its extraordinary trompe l'oeil frescoes. Towering over the tiny main altar is a painting of the immense altar and domes the Jesuits possibly wished they could have had.

Across Balbínova is the **former Jesuit hostel**. After the Jesuits were forced out of Bohemia, the two-block-long building was subdivided into a school, brewery and army barracks. It's now a shopping mall.

Klatovy's most ghoulish attraction lies beneath the Jesuit church. In the **catacombs** (☎ 376 347 240; adult/concession 50/25Kč; ⏲ 9am-noon & 1-5pm May-Sep, Sat & Sun only Oct-Apr) more than 200 corpses, including Jesuit monks and many local luminaries, were buried from 1676 to 1783. Over the centuries a clever system of natural air-conditioning preserved the corpses, although many were desecrated by grave-robbers. The

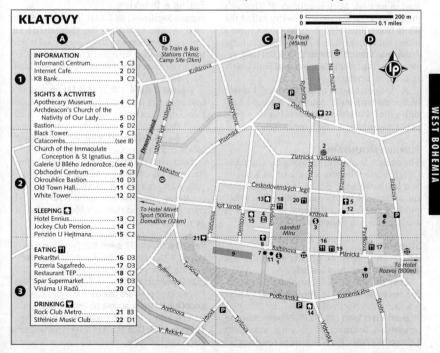

KLATOVY

INFORMATION	
Informanči Centrum	1 C3
Internet Cafe	2 D2
KB Bank	3 C2

SIGHTS & ACTIVITIES	
Apothecary Museum	4 C2
Archdeacon's Church of the Nativity of Our Lady	5 D2
Bastion	6 D2
Black Tower	7 C3
Catacombs	(see 8)
Church of the Immaculate Conception & St Ignatius	8 C3
Galerie U Bílého Jednorožce	(see 4)
Obchodní Centrum	9 C3
Okrouhlice Bastion	10 D3
Old Town Hall	11 C3
White Tower	12 D2

SLEEPING	
Hotel Ennius	13 C2
Jockey Club Pension	14 C3
Penzión U Hejtmana	15 C2

EATING	
Pekařstvi	16 D3
Pizzeria Sagafredo	17 D3
Restaurant TEP	18 C2
Spar Supermarket	19 D3
Vinárna U Radů	20 C2

DRINKING	
Rock Club Metro	21 B3
Střelnice Music Club	22 D1

arrival of tourists in recent decades has further upset this delicate balance of humidity and dignity, and now only 30 cadavers remain in the catacombs; many others have been reburied in the local graveyard. Despite the escalation in decay caused by tourists, the catacombs are Klatovy's most popular attraction. Ironically, their very popularity may eventually become their ruination.

APOTHECARY MUSEUM

A few doors down, on the western side of náměstí Míru, is the **White unicorn apothecary** (U bílého jednorožce) with its lavish original rococo furnishings from the 17th and 18th centuries. It was a working pharmacy until the 1960s and is now a **museum** (☎ 376 313 109; adult/concession 40/20Kč; ☣ 9am-noon & 1-5pm May-Oct) offering guided tours. Book ahead if there are fewer than five in your group.

Next door is an art gallery, **Galerie U bílého jednorožce** (☎ 376 312 049; náměstí Míru 149; adult/concession 25/15Kč; ☣ 10am-noon & 1-5pm Tue-Sun), with mostly modern exhibits.

WHITE TOWER & ARCHDEACON'S CHURCH

East of náměstí Míru is another of Klatovy's great towers, a Renaissance belfry called the **White tower** (Bílá věž). Nearby is the town's oldest church, the early-Gothic (16th century) **Archdeacon's church of the Nativity of Our Lady**, restored to its present state by Josef Fanta early in the 20th century.

A block east is one of the surviving **bastions** of the **old town walls**. Another, a round bastion called **Okrouhlice bastion**, is beside a path between Balbínova and Komenského.

ŠUMAVA MOUNTAINS

The ancient Šumava range along the German–Czech border begins southeast of Klatovy and boasts some of Bohemia's most pristine mountains. It forms one of the Czech Republic's most recent national parks and lies mainly in South Bohemia (p178).

Sleeping

There are plenty of private rooms – ask Informanči Centrum for help.

Camp site (☎ 376 310 779; pour@tsklatovy.cz; Dr Sedlaka; tent per person 65Kč; ☣ May-Sep; P ☒) There is a camp site north of town.

Hotel Mivet Sport (☎ 376 310 910; www.sumavanet .cz/hotelsport; Domažlická 609; per person without/with bathroom 300/350Kč; P) Noisy quads and triples come attached to a smoky beer hall. It's a 1.2km walk from the town centre (west on Domažlická, north on Nerudova), or catch bus 2 to the Zimní Stadion stop. The accommodation is tucked away on the left-hand side of the Zimní Stadion.

Penzión U Hejtmana (☎ 376 317 918; www.uhejtmana .klatovynet.cz; kpt Jaroše 145; s/d 340/590Kč) Don't expect flash but do expect good value and central rooms with private bathrooms.

Jockey Club Pension (☎ 376 313 060; www.sweb .cz/jockeyclub/; cnr Videňská & Podbránská; s/d incl breakfast 570/840Kč; P) Downstairs in the restaurant there are more horse photos than you can crack a whip at, but Mr Ed is obviously not allowed upstairs because the rooms are groomed to be super clean.

Also recommended:

Hotel Rozvoj (☎ 376 311 609; www.klatovynet .cz/rozvoj; Prochazkova 110/5; s/d 450/650Kč) A basic cheapie just out of the centre that's a good bet for self-drive travellers.

Hotel Ennius (☎ 376 320 567; www.sweb.cz/ennius; Randova 111; s/d incl breakfast 800/1200Kč) Up a notch, cosy and welcoming.

Eating & Drinking

Pizzeria Sagafredo (☎ 771 101 764; Pavlíkova 6; pizza 100Kč; ☣ 10am-midnight Sun-Thu, 10am-2am Fri & Sat) The combination of classy leather seats and modern wooden furniture completes a nicely restored space. Expect fun times with cocktails after dark.

Vinárna U Radů (☎ 376 314 594; cnr Pražská & Československých legií; mains 100-130Kč) The faded publicity shots in the window (still!) remain since the previous Lonely Planet update, and the robust Czech food remains popular with locals and passing German tourists.

Restaurant TEP (☎ 376 311 958; cnr Randova & náměstí Míru; mains 100-160Kč) On level one there's a cosy pub, with a more flash eatery and velvet-lined booths on level two. The menu is surprisingly cosmopolitan and includes Mexican and Argentinean flavours.

Also recommended:

Pekařstvi (Plánicka 70; donuts 8Kč; ☣ 6.30am-5pm Mon-Fri, 7-11am Sat) Fresh donuts and takeaway coffee complete the tasty essentials at this bakery.

Spar Supermarket (Plánicka 67; ☣ 6.30am-6pm Mon-Fri, 7am-1pm Sat) For self-caterers.

Rock Club Metro (Vančurova 57; ☣ 5pm-1am) Hosts live bands as a good background to good drinking.

Střelnice Music Club (Pražská 122; ☣ 5pm-1am) Same deal as Rock Club Metro.

Getting There & Away

In general, the bus is the most convenient way to get here from Prague (110Kč, three hours), running about twice a day; Plzeň (48Kč, one hour) five times; and Domažlice (38Kč, 45 minutes) five times. If you're going to carry on south to Železná Ruda on the German border, trains are better, with four fast ones daily.

Getting Around

Informanči Centrum rents out mountain bikes for 200/300Kč per half/full day.

CHODSKO REGION

Chodsko (pronounced 'khodsko') is the Bohemian border region where the Bohemian forest (Český les) and Šumava ranges splice together. The Chods, a sturdy, independent people traditionally from 11 villages situated in an arc from Postřekov to Pocínovice, were first entrusted with patrolling the Bavarian border by King John of Luxembourg in 1325, in return for formal exemption from feudal servitude.

After the Thirty Years' War the Hapsburgs reneged, handing over the region to favoured courtiers and generals. When these courtiers and generals refused to honour the old agreements, the Chods took up arms, briefly and disastrously.

The Chod way of life, which is neither Bohemian nor Germanic, survives in unique customs and speech, although only on special occasions are you likely to hear the Chod *dudy* (bagpipes) or catch sight of Chod women's long, printed dresses. The most likely place is in the upper Chod region around the village of Mrákov. One such occasion is the annual summer Chod Festival (Chodské slavnosti) held in Domažlice on the Friday and weekend around 14 August, St Lawrence's (sv Vavřinec) Day.

DOMAŽLICE

pop 10,800

Depending on the day of the week, the energy levels in little Domažlice ebb and flow considerably. Come for market day on a Wednesday and the main square is awash with stalls and shoppers. On other days it reverts to the 10th-century customs settlement it once was, and

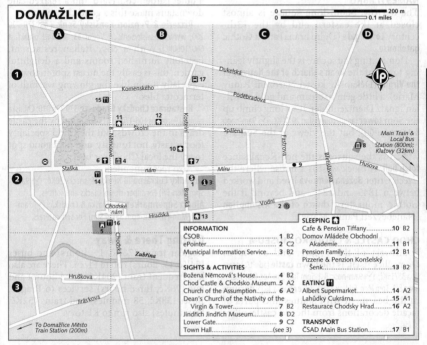

DOMAŽLICE

0 ____ 200 m
0 ____ 0.1 miles

INFORMATION	
ČSOB	1 B2
ePointer	2 C2
Municipal Information Service	3 B2

SIGHTS & ACTIVITIES	
Božena Němcová's House	4 B2
Chod Castle & Chodsko Museum	5 A2
Church of the Assumption	6 A2
Dean's Church of the Nativity of the Virgin & Tower	7 B2
Jindřich Jindřich Museum	8 D2
Lower Gate	9 C2
Town Hall	(see 3)

SLEEPING	
Cafe & Pension Tiffany	10 B2
Domov Mládeže Obchodní Akademie	11 B1
Pension Family	12 B1
Pizzerie & Penzion Konšelský Šenk	13 B2

EATING	
Albert Supermarket	14 A2
Lahůdky Cukrárna	15 A1
Restaurace Chodsky Hrad	16 A2

TRANSPORT	
ČSAD Main Bus Station	17 B1

WEST BOHEMIA

you get the impression that no-one would notice if the already leaning 13th-century church tower were to topple over.

Orientation & Information

From the joint train and local bus station it's about 1km on Masarykova and Husova to the main square, náměstí Míru. A few trains, such as those from Planá, also stop at Domažlice město station, which is 500m from the centre via Jiráskova and Chodská. The ČSAD bus station is on the corner of Poděbradova and Prokopa Velikého.

The **Municipal Information Service** (Městská Informační Centrum; ☎ 379 725 852; www.mesto-domazlice .cz; náměstí Míru 51; ☉ 7.30am-5pm Mon-Fri, 9am-noon Sat Jun-Sep, to 4pm Mon-Fri Sep-May) is in the town hall and can also advise on accommodation.

ČSOB, next door, changes money and has an ATM.

The **post office** (Staška) is just west of the main square.

There is internet access at **ePointer** (Vodní 90; ☉ 9am-9pm).

Sights & Activities

NÁMĚSTÍ MÍRU

The narrow, 500m-long square is almost closed at the eastern end by the 13th-century **Lower gate** (Dolní brána) and a Gothic **gatehouse**.

Dominating the square is the slightly leaning tower of the **Dean's church of the Nativity of the Virgin** (Děkanský kostel Narození Panny Marie), a little gem in cream and gold by Kilian Ignatz Dientzenhofer. It's a long climb up the 56m **tower** (adult/concession 20/10Kč; ☉ 9am-noon & 1-5pm Apr-Oct), but the views of the Šumava are fine.

Across the square is the neo-Renaissance **town hall**. A block west is a house where the Czech writer **Božena Němcová** lived and worked between 1845 and 1847, and beyond it the Gothic monastery **church of the Assumption** (Nanebevzetí Panny Marie).

CHOD CASTLE & CHODSKO MUSEUM

Southwest of the square, and as old as Domažlice itself, is the town **castle** (adult/concession 35/15Kč; ☉ 9am-noon & 1-5pm Tue-Sun Apr-Oct, 10am-noon & 1-3pm Mon-Fri Nov-Mar). There is a lapidarium in the basement with statues and parts of façade decorations from the old castle; other

rooms have rich exhibits of local folklore including bagpipes and dresses.

JINDŘICH JINDŘICH MUSEUM

You can get a good look at some aspects of the Chod lifestyle – such as handicrafts, clothing, a typical home – at a little **museum** (Husova; adult/ concession 20/10Kč; ☉ 10am-noon & 1-5pm 15 Apr-15 Oct) based on the collections of a composer named Jindřich Jindřich, who lived here in the 1960s. It's just outside the Lower gate.

Sleeping & Eating

Domov Mládeže Obchodní Akademie (☎ 379 722 386; B Němcové 116; dm per person 160Kč) Basic dorm beds are on offer here, but phone ahead as reception isn't always staffed.

Café & Pension Tiffany (☎ 379 725 591; www.tiffany .wz.cz; Kostelní 102; s/d incl breakfast 570/1140Kč) Spacious, eclectic rooms complement a funky downstairs café run by English-speaking Otto. Bring along any interesting banknotes you have to decorate the walls around the bar.

Pension Family (☎ 379 725 962; pavla.michl@volny .cz; Školní 107; s/d 580/980Kč; ☉ café 8am-7pm Mon-Thu, 8am-11pm Fri & Sat, 8am-6pm Sun) Pleasant rooms, a quiet garden courtyard and a relaxed café downstairs make this a good choice.

Pizzerie & Penzion Konšlský Šenk (☎ 379 720 200; www.konselskysenk.cz; Vodní 33; s/d incl breakfast 660/1060Kč) With a cosy Italian restaurant, tastefully furnished rooms and a delightful garden, this is easily the nicest spot in town – especially if you like the glowing warmth of terracotta tiles.

Restaurace Chodsky Hrad (☎ 379 776 010; Chodské náměstí 96; mains 100-170Kč) Its location by the castle drags in the crowds, but the Chod speciality food is tasty, not touristy, and it's a good spot to try the local Chodovar beer.

Also recommended:

Lahůdky Cukrárna (B Němcové; snacks 20Kč; ☉ 9am-5pm Mon-Fri) For super-cheap snacks and coffees.

Albert Supermarket (cnr Staška & Chodská; ☉ 7am-7pm Mon-Fri, 7am-4pm Sat & Sun) For self-caterers.

Getting There & Away

Regular trains (76Kč, 1½ hours) and buses (54Kč, 1½ hours) run to Plzeň. There are also less frequent train (204Kč, three hours) and bus (96Kč, three hours) services to Prague. Buses (38Kč, 58 minutes) and trains (52Kč, 50 minutes) also run to Klatovy.

North Bohemia

Overtly, North Bohemia highlights the most tragic excesses of the region's experience of a turbulent 20th century, but scratch its grimy and harsh surface and there's plenty of offer for the inquiring traveller keen on discovery.

At first, the country's gritty industrial heart seems tortured and sullen. Freeways fringed by electricity pylons and billowing smokestacks crisscross a strangely compelling lunar landscape stripped by acid rain. But get off the main roads and its rugged edge is retained, and transformed into the dazzling landscapes and sublime hiking opportunities of the Sandstone Rocks of Labe. Travel quietly by boat through the primeval river gorges of the region and industrial pollution will be the last thing on your mind.

As a sobering antidote to the genteel overkill of perfect town squares and poetic chateaux elsewhere in the country, North Bohemia's most grimly fascinating town is the imposing fortress of Terezín. Built from local sandstone in the 18th century, the Napoleonic bastion was transformed into a concentration camp by the Nazis in another tragic century, and now contains the compelling museum of the Ghetto. Nearby pretty Litoměřice provides an emotional release to Terezín's harrowing but essential travellers' experience.

The region's industrial damage is now being reversed. Even the strategic river city of Děčín, once choked with coal smoke, is regenerating with a green tinge to match the reinvigorated forests surrounding it. All across the region air quality has greatly improved since the end of communism and the Czech Republic's entry into the European Union in 2004.

HIGHLIGHTS

- Negotiate the primeval river canyons and bizarre rock formations of the **Sandstone Rocks of Labe** (p240)

- Confront history's darkest depths in the imposing fortress of **Terezín** (p231), a former Nazi concentration camp

- Ascend the imposing 'Long Ride' to the brooding castle in **Děčín** (p237)

- Descend to the ancient wine cellars under the sleepy streets of **Litoměřice** (p235)

- Admire the exquisite rococo splendour of **Ploskovice chateau** (p236)

★ Sandstone Rocks of Labe
★ Děčín
★ Ploskovice Chateau
Litoměřice ★
★ Terezín

NORTH BOHEMIA

NORTH BOHEMIA

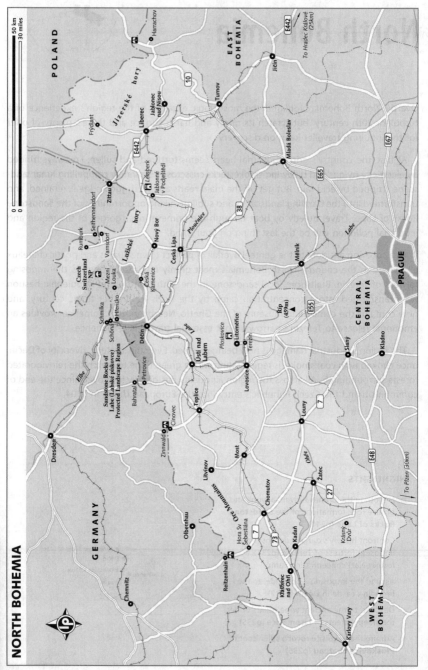

TEREZÍN

pop 2960

After the beauty of many Czech towns, the imposing fortress of Terezín is a moving reminder of tragic aspects of Central Europe's past. The massive bastion of stone and earth was built in 1780 by Emperor Joseph II to keep the Prussians at bay, and could accommodate up to 11,000 soldiers. The fortress was never used in wartime, instead it was turned into a prison in the mid-19th century. Gavrilo Princip, the Serb nationalist who assassinated Archduke Franz Ferdinand in 1914 to ignite WWI, died in the prison in 1918.

In 1940, the Gestapo established a prison in the lesser fortress. The following year, all townspeople were evicted from the Main Fortress to accommodate a transit camp for European Jews. In total more than 140,000 Jews passed through Terezín; 33,000 died victims of the camp's degrading conditions, and 88,000 were sent to Auschwitz. Less than 17,500 remained alive when the Red Army liberated the camp on 9 May 1945. Many survivors died of typhus even after liberation. Between April and September 1942 conditions were the most appalling. The population increased from 12,698 to 58,491, leaving each prisoner only 1.65 sq m of space. During this period, the number of deaths increased by 15 times.

Ironically, Terezín played a terrible role in deceiving the world of the ultimate goals of the Nazi's 'Final Solution'. Official visitors were immersed in a tragic charade, with Terezín being presented as a Jewish 'refuge', complete with banks, shops, schools and cultural events – even a self-administering Jewish 'government'. As late as April 1945, Red Cross visitors returned with positive reports.

Today Terezín is a melancholic town; the wide, empty streets seem more inhabited by the ghosts of recent history than contemporary townspeople. It's a compelling and moving lesson in the harsh realities of modern history, and an essential day trip from Prague.

Orientation

Public buses stop at náměstí Československé armády, the central square area of the town within the main fortress. The lesser fortress is an 800m-walk east across the Ohře river.

Information

All the information you need can be picked up from the museum.

Česká Spořitelna (náměstí Československé armády) Has an ATM and exchange desk.
Post office Near the northern side of náměstí Československé armády.

Sights

Tickets can be purchased at the museum of the Ghetto (below) – or from each of the other venues – and cost 180/140Kč (adult/concession) for combination entry to the museum of the Ghetto, Magdeburg barracks, the Crematorium and the lesser fortress, or 160/130Kč (adult/concession) for the museum of the Ghetto and Magdeburg barracks only. The museum has good multilingual self-guide pamphlets, a large selection of books for sale, and guides for hire (some of them ghetto survivors). When you pay your admission, put your name down to watch two videos on Terezín's history at the end of your visit.

MAIN FORTRESS

From the ground, the sheer scale of the walls and moats that surround the main fortress (hlavní pevnost) is impossible to fathom – mainly because the town is concealed inside them. When you first arrive by bus or car, you may think the central square looks no different to many other small town centres. Look at the aerial photograph in the museum of the Ghetto on Komenského, or wander past the walls en route to the lesser fortress, however, and a very different picture begins to emerge.

At the heart of the main fortress is the squared-off, boxy town of Terezín. There's little to look at except the chunky, 19th-century **church of the Resurrection**, the arcaded **commandant's office**, the neoclassical administrative buildings on the square and the surrounding grid of houses with their awful secrets.

South of the square are the anonymous **remains of a railway siding**, built by prisoners, on which loads of further prisoners arrived – and departed. Two **water gates** (for access to the river) remain.

The main attraction is the compelling **museum of the Ghetto** (muzeum ghetta; ☎ 416 782 576; www.pamatnik-terezin.cz; Komenského; ⏰ 9am-6pm Apr-Oct, 9am-5.30pm Nov-Mar), which has two branches. The main museum, on Komenského by the highway, explores the rise of Nazism and life in the Terezín ghetto, using the discarded bric-a-brac of the time to evocative effect. Erected in the 19th century to house the local school, the building was later used by the Nazis to

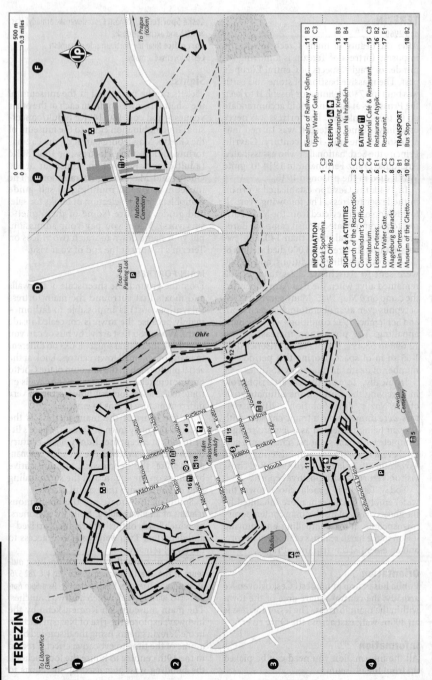

NORTH BOHEMIA

TEREZÍN

INFORMATION
Ceská Spořitelna....................1 C3
Post Office.............................2 B2

SIGHTS & ACTIVITIES
Church of the Resurrection.....3 C2
Commandant's Office..............4 C2
Crematorium...........................5 C4
Lesser Fortress........................6 E1
Lower Water Gate...................7 C2
Magdeburg Barracks................8 C3
Main Fortress..........................9 B1
Museum of the Ghetto...........10 B2
Remains of Railway Siding......11 B3
Upper Water Gate..................12 C3

SLEEPING
Autocamping Kréta.................13 B3
Pension Na hradbách..............14 B4

EATING
Memorial Café & Restaurant...15 C3
Restaurace Atypik...................16 B2
Restaurant.............................17 E1

TRANSPORT
Bus Stop................................18 B2

THE SECRET MAGAZINE OF THE BOYS OF TEREZÍN

Terezín was designated as a camp for prosperous and well-educated Jewish families from Germany, Austria and Czechoslovakia, and this tragic focus ensured a rich cultural life within the walls of the fortress. Cultural activities were encouraged by the Nazis to maintain a veneer of normality, but other clandestine activities were also organised by the artists, musicians and writers imprisoned in the camp. The artist Friedl Dicker-Brandeis ran art classes for children who contributed drawings and poetry to *Vedem* ('In the Lead') magazine. More than 100 boys helped produce *Vedem* from 1942 to 1944, but only 15 survived; the others were deported to Auschwitz in 1944. Concealed manuscripts were discovered after the war, and a selection of illustrations and articles were republished in the 1994 book, *We Are Children Just the Same: Vedem, the Secret Magazine of the Boys of Terezín*.

---

accommodate the camp's 10- to 15-year-old boys. The children's haunting artwork still decorates the walls.

A newer branch is in the former **Magdeburg barracks** (Magdeburská kasárna; cnr Tyršova & Vodárenská; 9am-6pm Apr-Oct, 9am-5.30pm Nov-Mar) that served as the seat of the Jewish 'government'. There is a reconstructed prisoners' dormitory and exhibits on the extraordinarily rich cultural life – music, theatre, fine arts and literature – that somehow flourished against this backdrop of fear. Most poignant are the copies of *Vedem* magazine (see boxed text, above).

Both museums are closed Christmas Eve to Boxing Day and New Year's Day.

There is also the **Crematorium** (Kramatorium; 9am-6pm Apr-Oct, 9am-4pm Nov-Mar) in the Jewish Cemetery just off Bohušovická brána about 1km south from the main square in Terezín. There is another small exhibit here.

LESSER FORTRESS
You can take a self-guided tour of the **lesser fortress** (malá pevnost; 8am-6pm May-Sep, to 4.30pm Oct-Apr) through the prison barracks, isolation cells, workshops and morgues, past execution grounds and former mass graves. It would be hard to invent a more menacing location. As you wander through the seemingly endless tunnels beneath the walls you can fully appreciate the fort's huge dimensions. The Nazis' mocking concentration-camp slogan, *Arbeit Macht Frei* (work makes you free) hangs above a gate. In front of the fortress is a National Cemetery, founded in 1945 for those exhumed from mass graves.

Sleeping & Eating
Only committed history buffs will want to stay in Terezín, with Litoměřice just minutes away.

Autocamping Kréta (☎ 416 782 473; http://autocamp .kreta.sweb.cz; sites per tent 70Kč, huts 150Kč; Jun-Sep) This camping ground is by the stadium west of the main fortress.

Pension Na hradbách (☎ 723 287 738; www.sweb .cz/nahradbach; Bohušovická brána 335; s/d incl breakfast 750/1500Kč) Just outside the western walls of the main fortress, this tidy spot exudes a cheery ambience despite the location.

Restaurace Atypik (☎ 416 782 780; Máchova 91; mains 70-120Kč) Atypik by name, but typical by nature, this busy place offers all the Czech favourites.

Memorial Café & Restaurant (☎ 416 783 082; náměstí Československé armády; meals 120-200Kč) This former coffee and cake place has been overhauled to become a full-blown restaurant, and is popular with tour groups.

There are incongruous fast-food stalls at the tour-bus car park, and a **restaurant** (meals 45-80Kč) in the German officers' mess in the lesser fortress. There is also a restaurant at Pension Na hradbách.

Getting There & Away
Hourly buses leave from Prague's Florenc bus station (61Kč, one hour).

Buses leave Terezín from the northeastern corner of náměstí Československé armády and run to/from Litoměřice station (3km away) roughly hourly (8Kč, 10 minutes). The last bus leaves Terezín at 7.30pm.

LITOMĚŘICE
pop 23,900

Visiting Terezín demands an emotional release, and Litoměřice is the perfect balance with its pretty square etched in pastel shades and the baroque structures of local 18th-century architect Ottavio Broggio. The horrors of Terezín are only a few kilometres south, but Litoměřice's town square seems like another world.

The history of the town has not always been so benign. The once boldly Hussite town was levelled in the Thirty Years' War, and in 1945 the predominantly German-speaking populace was forcibly expelled. Unlike Terezín, which feels anchored by its tragic past, Litoměřice is a vivacious combo of old-school architecture and a youthful 21st-century outlook; belying its establishment as an ecclesiastical centre almost a millennium ago in 1057. The town's lively cafés and restaurants showcase vibrant after-hours action, and there's even a bar, Music Club Viva (p236), in the old town bastion – somewhere most Czech towns would fill with a stuffy museum.

Orientation

Litoměřice sits at the confluence of the Labe and Ohře rivers. From the train station or adjacent bus station, the old centre begins across the road to the west, past the well-preserved 14th-century walls. Walk down Dlouhá to the central square, Mírové náměstí.

Information

Internet Club Centrum (☎ 416 736 060; 1st fl, Mírové náměstí 125; per min 1Kč) A lively internet café with comfy old sofas.

Jonas Knihkupectví (jonas@kna.cz; Mírové náměstí) This bookshop sells maps.

KB bank (Mírové náměstí 37) Has an ATM and exchange desk.

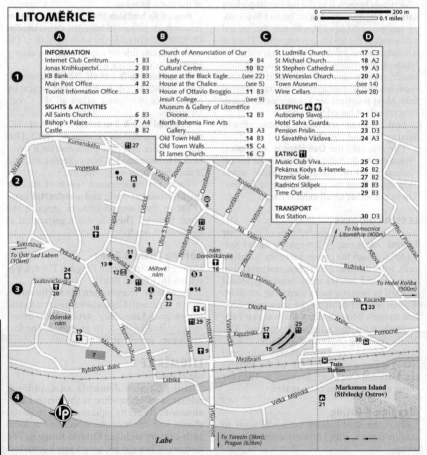

LITOMĚŘICE

0 —— 200 m
0 —— 0.1 miles

INFORMATION
Internet Club Centrum...............1 B3
Jonas Knihkupectví....................2 B3
KB Bank....................................3 B3
Main Post Office........................4 B2
Tourist Information Office.........5 B3

SIGHTS & ACTIVITIES
All Saints Church.......................6 B3
Bishop's Palace.........................7 A4
Castle..8 B2
Church of Annunciation of Our
 Lady.....................................9 B4
Cultural Centre.......................10 B2
House at the Black Eagle.......(see 22)
House at the Chalice..............(see 5)
House of Ottavio Broggio........11 B3
Jesuit College........................(see 9)
Museum & Gallery of Litoměřice
 Diocese...............................12 B3
North Bohemia Fine Arts
 Gallery.................................13 A3
Old Town Hall.........................14 B3
Old Town Walls.......................15 C4
St James Church.....................16 C3
St Ludmilla Church..................17 C3
St Michael Church...................18 A2
St Stephen Cathedral..............19 A3
St Wenceslas Church...............20 A3
Town Museum......................(see 14)
Wine Cellars.........................(see 28)

SLEEPING
Autocamp Slavoj.....................21 D4
Hotel Salva Guarda..................22 B3
Pension Prislin.........................23 B3
U Savatého Václava.................24 A3

EATING
Music Club Viva.......................25 C3
Pekárna Kodys & Hamele.......26 B2
Pizzeria Sole............................27 B2
Radniční Sklípek......................28 B3
Time Out..................................29 B3

TRANSPORT
Bus Station..............................30 D3

Main post office (cnr Osvobození & Na Valech) Two blocks north of Mírové náměstí.

Nemocnice Litoměřice (☎ 416 723 111; Žitenická) This hospital is 1km northeast of the centre.

Tourist information office (městské informační centrum; ☎ 416 732 440; www.litomerice.cz in Czech & German; Mírové náměstí 15/7; ⏰ 8am-6pm Mon-Sat, 8am-4pm Sun May-Sep, 8am-4pm Mon-Fri, to 11am Sat Oct-Apr) This office is in the town hall and can help with accommodation. From May to September it runs sightseeing tours for 60Kč per person. In April and October tours run Monday to Friday only.

Sights

MÍROVÉ NÁMĚSTÍ

Dominating this attractive square is the Gothic tower of **All Saints church** (kostel Všech svatých), which was built in the 13th century and 'Broggio-ised' in 1718.

Beside it, with multiple gables, pointy arches and a copper-topped tower, is the handsome Gothic **Old town hall** (Stará radnice), with a small **town museum** (Okresní Vlastivědné Muzeum Litoměřice; adult/concession 20/10Kč; ⏰ 10am-5pm Tue-Sun) inside.

A visit to the **wine cellars** (historické sklepy) can be arranged through the Radniční sklípek restaurant (p236). As well as providing storage for wine, the cellars were used as a place of refuge when the town was under siege.

Most striking is the 1560 Renaissance **house at the Black Eagle** (dům U Černého orla; Mírové náměstí 12), which is covered in sgraffito biblical scenes and houses the Hotel Salva Guarda (p236). A few doors down is the present town hall, in the 1539 **house at the Chalice** (dům U Kalicha; Mírové náměstí 15/7), with a massive Hussite chalice on the roof. This building also houses the tourist information office. The slice of baroque whimsy is the **house of Ottavio Broggio**.

Interesting art is exhibited in the **museum and gallery of Litoměřice Diocese** (muzeum a galerie litoměřické diocéze; ☎ 416 732 382; Mírové náměstí 16; adult/concession 20/10Kč; ⏰ 9am-noon & 1-6pm Tue-Sun Apr-Sep, to 5pm Oct-Mar). The collection runs through several beautiful old burghers' houses and includes modern art as well as works from St Stephen cathedral.

AROUND THE SQUARE

Another Broggio original, built for the Jesuits, is south of the square: the pink-and-white **church of Annunciation of Our Lady** (kostel Zvěstování Panny Marie). Nearby is the **Jesuit College** (Jezuitská).

West of the square is another house with a Broggio make-over, now home to the **North Bohemia fine arts gallery** (Severočeská galerie výtvarného umění; ☎ 416 732 382; www.galerie-ltm.cz; Michalská 7; adult/concession 32/16Kč; ⏰ 9am-noon & 1-6pm Tue-Sun Apr-Sep, to 5pm Oct-Mar). Work from the 14th to 20th centuries is displayed, and its pride and joy is a set of panels on the life of the Virgin from the *Litoměřice Altarpiece*, one of Bohemia's most famous works of Renaissance art, by the anonymous 'Master of Litoměřice' (whose work also graces Prague's St Vitus cathedral).

Other Litoměřice monastery churches of the Counter-Reformation include the remains of the **St Michael church** (kostel sv Michala), west of the fine arts gallery, the **St James church** (kostel sv Jakuba; náměstí Dominikánské), which is northeast of the square, and **St Ludmilla church** (kostel sv Ludmily), southeast of the centre.

CATHEDRAL HILL

Southwest of Mírové náměstí is Dómské náměstí, site of an ancient Slavic fortress and, despite its forlorn appearance, the town's historical heart.

On the way (along Dómská from the fine arts gallery), don't miss Broggio's finest work, the tiny **St Wenceslas church** (kostel sv Václava; 1716), a short detour to the west along Svatovaclavská.

At the top of Cathedral hill (dómský pahorek) is the town's oldest church, the huge **St Stephen cathedral** (katedrála sv Štěpána), built in the 11th century and rebuilt in the 17th. Spacious and Romanesque in shape, a tall arch reaches out to an 1880s belfry. Behind it is the renovated former **Bishop's palace**.

CASTLE

The town's heavily reconstructed 14th-century **castle** is north of Mírové náměstí, up Lidická, and has been closed for several years. Never a very interesting building to begin with, it now adjoins an ugly **cultural centre** (dům kultury).

Sleeping

The tourist information office can help with private rooms from around 350Kč per person.

Autocamp Slavoj (☎ 416 734 481; kemp.litomerice@ post.cz; sites per tent 70Kč, bungalow 200Kč; ⏰ May-Sep; Ⓟ ⓓ) South of the train station, this Slavoj is on Marksmen Island (Střelecký ostrov).

Hotel Koliba (☎ 416 732 861; http://koliba.wz.cz; Českolipská; s/d 450/700Kč) About 1km east of the centre (look for the Hennlich office), this place has clean budget rooms, a sauna and solarium, and room to pitch a tent.

U Svatého Václava (☎ 416 737 500; www.upfront .cz/penzion; Svatovaclavská 12; s/d incl breakfast 600/1000Kč) Nestled beside St Wenceslas church, this haven has well-equipped rooms, a choice of cooked breakfasts, and owners whose English is much better than they think.

Pension Prislin (☎ 416 735 833; Na Kocandě 12; s/d incl breakfast 700/1200Kč; P) On a busy road near the train station, Pension Prislin cunningly conceals a quiet garden with views of the river.

Hotel Salva Guarda (☎ 416 732 506; www.salva -guarda.cz; Mírové náměstí 12; s/d 990/1450Kč; P ⛓) With interesting old maps in reception, it's a shame they keep the lights so low. However the spotless rooms are well-lit in this classy hotel that's housed in a building dating from 1566.

Eating & Drinking

Pekárna Kodys & Hamele (Novobranská 18) This friendly bakery does sweet and savoury nibbles, with an emphasis on the very sweet.

Pizzeria Sole (☎ 416 737 150; Na Valech 56; pizza 75Kč) The sun's always out at this no-frills Italian café with cheap pizzas and good value combos of soup, pasta and dessert.

Radniční sklípek (☎ 416 731 142; Mírové náměstí 21; mains 80-170Kč) Keep your head down in this labyrinth of underground cellars. It should be easy because you'll be tucking into great value grills and beers. The wine list is also very good.

Music Club Viva (☎ 606 437 783; Mezibrani; mains 90-220Kč) Big shared tables ensure the conversation flows as naturally as the drinks in this hip spot in the old town bastion. You'll find all your favourites on the walls from Bob Marley to Sinatra and Elvis.

Time Out (☎ 603 470 165; Jezuitská 1; mains 70-180Kč) Sports on the telly, crowds at the bar, and it's only Wednesday night. On weekends this spot gets seriously busy with late night frolics.

Getting There & Away

There are bus connections between Litoměřice and Terezín (only 3km away) roughly hourly (8Kč, 10 minutes).

Buses from Prague's Florenc station (61Kč; 1¼ hours) to Ústí nad Labem stop here hourly.

By train it's a tedious trip via a branch line from Lovosice.

PLOSKOVICE

pop 344

Ottavio Broggio may have left a panoply of churches behind him, but his secular works are less prevalent. Ploskovice chateau is a notable exception and a worthwhile diversion for those demanding a thorough understanding of the architect's work. It has more personality than his churches in Litoměřice, especially after the crazily rococo interior renovations by painter Josef Navrátil, part of an 1850s extreme make-over ordered by Emperor Ferdinand V.

Sights & Activities

The guided tour of the **chateau** (☎ 416 749 092; adult/concession 50/30Kč; ⏱ 9am-6pm Tue-Sun Jul-Aug, to 5pm May, Jun & Sep, to 4pm Apr & Oct) takes in about 10 rooms used by the emperor and empress (the tour's in Czech, but an English text is available). Highlights include the emperor's ostentatious bedroom, complete with unusual bidet, and the stunning main hall at the rear, with murals by Václav Vavřinec Reiner representing the four corners of the world. Most of the chateau's other murals are by the immodest Josef Navrátil. On the ceiling of the empress' study he painted himself beside her favourite sculptor, Benvenuto Cellini.

At the rear is a manicured garden, complete with rampaging peacocks.

Getting There & Away

Irregular buses link Litoměřice and Ploskovice (15Kč, 20 minutes). Take a bus bound for Třebušín, but check return times with the driver as times may not be posted in Ploskovice.

TEPLICE

pop 52,000

Once the spa town of Teplice was as famous as Karlovy Vary, Mariánské Lázně and Františkovy Lázně in West Bohemia, and Beethoven, Chopin, Goethe and Liszt were all regular visitors. Since its 19th-century heyday, the town has been blighted by industrial pollution and an ugly communist architectural make-over. Elegant slices of the town's halcyon past remain, but you'll need to search them out amid the brutal and boxy structures that now frame Teplice.

While lacking the glamour of its West Bohemian cousins, the town's spa services are well regarded, especially for the treatment of vascular conditions like hypertension, and the alleviation of locomotive disorders including chronic arthritis. The **Teplice** (www.teplice .cz) website links to tourism and accommodation information, and specialist information on spa services is available on **Lázně Teplice V Čechách** (www.lazneteplice.cz).

Accommodation is in a range of heritage hotels owned by Lazne Teplice. Prices for 'treatment' programmes begin at €64 per person per day, while 'relaxation' programmes, including full board, start at €51 per person per day. Hotel accommodation without sampling the spa services is significantly cheaper (double including breakfast €37 to €42).

Getting There & Away
Trains to Teplice depart from Prague's hlavní nádraží and Masarykovo six times a day (162Kč, 2¼ hours). There's two trains a day from Litoměřice (64Kč, two hours), and trains head north from Teplice to Děčín 12 times a day (52Kč, 1¼ hours). Buses link Teplice with Děčín (44Kč, 45 minutes, two daily), Litoměřice (44Kč, one hour, one daily) and Holešovice train station in Prague (140Kč, 1½ hours, four daily).

DĚČÍN
pop 51,900
With a dramatic location astride the Labe river, the port city of Děčín deserves its improving reputation, as it emerges from a cocoon of industrial soot to become a bustling stop on the EU trade bandwagon from Germany. Originally settled by the Slavic Děčané tribe in the 9th century, the 14th-century emergence of Děčín's old town took place high above the river. The Labe is the town's lifeblood, and occasionally still shows the locals who's boss, most recently flooding in 2002 and 2006. With a brooding, and recently restored, castle, and a renewed dedication to preserving the city's historical heart, Děčín is worth a look before continuing to the grime-free vistas of the nearby Sandstone Rocks of Labe.

Orientation
The town has two distinct centres – Děčín, on the east bank of the Labe, and Podmokly on the west, at the foot of Shepherd's Wall (Pastýřská

stěna). The Děčín side has the town's few historical attractions, while Podmokly has the train and bus stations.

Information
Club 52 (cnr Thomayerova & Teplická, Podmokly; per min 1Kč) Internet connection.
ČSOB Podmokly (cnr Zbrojnická & Československých legií) Děčín (cnr Řetězová & Radniční) Both branches have ATMs.
Dezka (☎ 412 532 111; Prokopa Holého 8; ◷ 9am-5pm Mon-Fri) This office in Podmokly acts as the local tourist office.
Information centre (☎ 412 518 905; www.mudecin .cz; ◷ 9am-6pm Jul-Aug, 9am-5pm Mar-Jun & Sep-Dec, 9am-5pm Thu-Sun Jan-Feb) Across the river there is an information centre at the entrance to the chateau.
Post office Podmokly (cnr Podmokelská & Poštovní) Děčín (náměstí Svobody)

Sights
OLD TOWN & CHATEAUX
A compact section of old-town Děčín has been preserved at the eastern foot of the castle. The centrepiece is the **church of the Ascending Holy Cross** (kostel povýšení sv Kříže), with its high-domed, Romanesque exterior and its frescoed, baroque interior. From here a walled avenue, the **Long Ride** (Dlouhá jízda), climbs to the castle, with a separate, covered walkway along one side.

Děčín's one real historical attraction is its huge, brooding **chateau** (zámek Děčín; ☎ 412 518 905; www.zamekdecin.cz; adult/concession 48/36Kč, foreign language text 12Kč; ◷ 9am-6pm Jul-Aug, 9am-5pm Mar-Jun & Sep-Dec, 9am-5pm Thu-Sun Jan-Feb) founded in 1305 by the Přemysl King Václav III. Baroque accents were added to its original Renaissance bones, and restoration work has recently commenced. At the time of writing, the castle was partially open to visitors, a highlight being the luxurious private apartment of former owner Count Thun-Hohenstein. Ask at the information centre if any additional sections of the castle have opened.

The castle passed into the hands of the Czechoslovak state in 1932, before becoming a garrison for German, and then Soviet troops. The newly independent Russian army left in 1991, but the Long Ride, with its high grey walls, retains an intimidating Stalinist air. Attached is the **Regional museum of Děčín** (Oblastní muzeum v Děčín; adult/concession 30/15Kč; ◷ 9am-noon & 1-5pm Tue-Sun), which showcases local history.

Stroll through the beautiful **Rose gardens** (Růžová zahrada; adult/concession 12/6Kč; ◷ 9am-8pm

May-Aug, to 6pm Apr, Sep & Oct) beside the castle; accessible from the Long Ride, or via a footpath from the church of the Ascending Holy Cross to a rear entrance.

STONE BRIDGE

This melancholy **stone footbridge** over the Ploučnice river, features a slowly crumbling, baroque group of sculptures by Jan Brokoff (whose work also decorates Charles bridge in Prague). The footbridge is south of the castle, surrounded by weeds and traffic flyovers on U starého mostu.

SHEPHERD'S WALL

On the Podmokly side, walk up Žižkova to this cliff, with a startling bird's-eye view over the castle and Děčín side. A small **zoo** (☎ 412 531 164; adult/concession 60/40Kč; ☼ 8am-6pm Apr-Sep, 8am-4pm Oct-Mar) is behind the chateau at the top.

REGIONAL MUSEUM

In an 18th-century palace, in the north of Podmokly, is the interesting **Regional museum** (Okresní muzeum; Československé mládeže 1; adult/concession 30/15Kč; ☼ 9am-noon & 1-5pm Tue-Sun). The best displays focus on the castle (including its earlier versions and various royal and aristocratic owners) and shipping on the Labe. Who'd have guessed that until 1886, some Labe boats pulled themselves along a 720km chain between Mělník (Central Bohemia) and Hamburg?

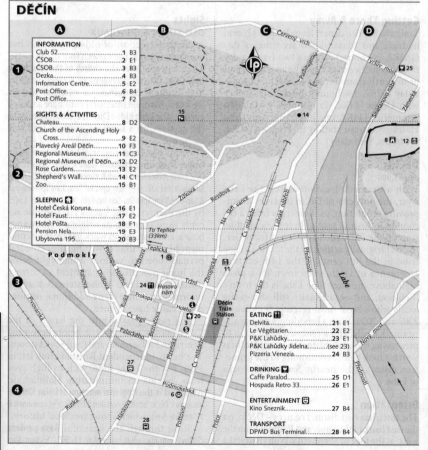

DĚČÍN

INFORMATION
Club 52	.....1 B3
ČSOB	.....2 E1
ČSOB	.....3 B3
Dezka	.....4 B3
Information Centre	.....5 E2
Post Office	.....6 B4
Post Office	.....7 F2

SIGHTS & ACTIVITIES
Chateau	.....8 D2
Church of the Ascending Holy Cross	.....9 E2
Plavecký Areál Děčín	.....10 F3
Regional Museum	.....11 C3
Regional Museum of Děčín	.....12 D2
Rose Gardens	.....13 E2
Shepherd's Wall	.....14 C1
Zoo	.....15 B1

SLEEPING
Hotel Česká Koruna	.....16 E1
Hotel Faust	.....17 E2
Hotel Pošta	.....18 F1
Pension Nela	.....19 E3
Ubytovna 195	.....20 B3

EATING
Delvita	.....21 E1
Le Végétarien	.....22 E2
P&K Lahůdky	.....23 E1
P&K Lahůdky Jídelna	.....(see 23)
Pizzeria Venezia	.....24 B3

DRINKING
Caffe Paralod	.....25 D1
Hospada Retro 33	.....26 E1

ENTERTAINMENT
Kino Sneznik	.....27 B4

TRANSPORT
DPMD Bus Terminal	.....28 B4

Activities

Plavecký Areál Děčín (☎ 412 704 211; Oblouková 1400; adult/concession 55/35Kč; ☺ 10am-8pm) This flash swimming area has saunas and a bar.

Sleeping

Dezka (p237) can book private rooms from around 300Kč per person.

Ubytovna 195 (☎ 412 518 835, Zbrojnická 18; per person 195Kč) This no-name spot is opposite the train station. Note that reception is only open from 7pm to midnight.

Hotel Pošta (☎ 412 511 544; www.hotelposta.cz; Masarykovo náměstí 9; s/d from 550/1350Kč, apt 2900Kč) From the town square the building looks small, but good design accommodates 100 people from single rooms to a six-person apartment.

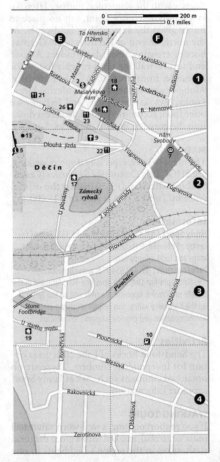

Hotel Faust (☎ 412 518 859; www.hotel.cz/faust; U Plovárny 43; s/d incl breakfast 700/1250Kč; Ⓟ) At these prices you won't have to sell your soul, although the 1970s furniture was definitely bought from the devil's-own garage sale. Enjoy the lakeside setting with vistas of white swans…and a nearby freeway.

Pension Nela (☎ 412 512 612; www.volny.cz/nela .dc; U starého mostu 4; s/d incl breakfast 800/1000Kč; Ⓟ) Near both the old (stone) bridge and the new (blue) bridge, this welcoming spot somehow manages to fit a spacious garden – with a pond and umbrellas, no less – into a bizarre location amidst the strands of a spaghettilike junction.

Hotel Česká koruna (☎ 412 516 104; www.hotel ceskakoruna.cz; Masarykovo náměstí 6; s/d incl breakfast 900/1180Kč; Ⓟ ♿) Děčín's best spot celebrates with an authoritative brace of European flags. The promise is fulfilled with slick service, thoroughly deserving three stars.

Eating

Le Végétarien (☎ 776 249 505; Nároží 5; mains 70-90Kč; Ⓥ) In modern surroundings just outside the Long Ride, tasty vegetarian soups, risottos and curries are all on offer.

Pizzeria Venezia (☎ 607 766 280; Husovo náměstí 5; pizza 100Kč; ☺ Mon-Sat) Yes, this spot recommended by a reader does have a kitschy chef's statue out of the front, and while it's smaller than most others, it's no reflection on the quality of its tasty food.

P&K Lahůdky (☎ 412 541 367; Masarykovo náměstí; snacks 40Kč; ☺ 7am-6pm Mon-Fri; 8-11am Sat) This deli serves stand-up snacks, while its sister outfit, **P&K Lahůdky Jidelna** (mains 50Kč; ☺ 10am-3pm Mon-Fri), around the back, delivers super-cheap meals in sit-down surrounds.

The **Delvita** (Tyršova) supermarket provides for self-caterers.

Drinking

Hospoda Retro 33 (☎ 412 510 400; Radniční 10) This fills up with diners during the day and gets even busier with drinkers come nightfall. Kind of retro and kind of Irish, it all hangs together in a welcoming and very Czech kind of way.

Caffe Paralod (☎ 412 519 866; Tyršova 347; cocktails 70Kč, coffee 25Kč) A boat-style bar perched above the river, Caffe Paralod is a great place for a daytime espresso, or something considerably stronger once the sun has passed the yard arm.

NORTH BOHEMIA

Entertainment
Kino Sneznik (☎ 412 531 431; www.kass.cz in Czech; Podmokelská 1070/24; tickets 75Kč) Near the bus station, this cinema shows English-language films.

Getting There & Away
Dopravní Podnik Města Děčína (DPMD; ☎ 412 531 400) runs most of the long-distance buses out of the main bus terminal (which sits on an unnamed road through a park). It has seven buses a day to/from Prague's Florenc station (85Kč, 1¾ hours). There are also four buses a day to Hřensko (18Kč, 30 minutes), for the Sandstone Rocks of Labe.

Trains (☎ 412 503 481) take a little longer to get to Prague (162Kč, two hours), but also run to cities elsewhere in Europe, including Dresden via Bad Schandau or Schöna (130Kč).

Getting Around
Most municipal bus lines run between the train station (Podmokly) and Masarykovo náměstí (Děčín). Bus tickets are available from automated machines on the bus (9Kč).

SANDSTONE ROCKS OF LABE
North of Děčín, the road snakes for 12km through the Labe valley to Hřensko on the German border. At Hřensko the entire North Bohemian watershed empties into Germany through a slim notch in the rolling hills. In exchange Germany provides a stream of tourists lured by the tacky Vietnamese-owned souvenir stalls lining the roads, selling cheap DVDs, bogus football shirts, and a mind-bending array of concrete gnomes, and other dodgy garden 'art'. Hřensko itself is one of the country's most kitsch tourist spots, so take the short walk from the centre to ensure an enticing glimpse of the staggering landscapes that are secreted beyond the river valley.

The **Sandstone Rocks of Labe** (Labské pískovce) Protected Landscape Region, is one of Bohemia's characteristic 'rock towns', and occupies a 5km by 35km strip along the border. Called 'Czech Switzerland' (Český Švýcarsko) by Czechs and 'Saxon Switzerland' (Sächsische Schweiz) by Germans, the meadows and chalets do look vaguely Swiss, but the steep gorges and dramatic sandstone formations are anything but. The region was named when Anton Graff and Adrian Zingg, two Swiss Romantic artists living in Dresden, moved here after being bewitched by the area's

potential for painting. Ironically Hřensko is the lowest point in Bohemia (116m above sea level). Don't expect vertiginous alpine vistas.

The part east of the road to Hřensko and beyond became the **Czech Switzerland National Park** (Národní park České Švýcarsko) in January 2000, and offers leisurely walking through spectacular, natural landscapes, and relaxed boat rides that negotiate the deep gorge of the Kamenice river. The most popular (and crowded) attraction is a huge, natural, stone bridge called the **Pravčická brána** (Pravčická gate).

Orientation
Wedged picturesquely at the Labe's rocky confluence with the Kamenice, touristy Hřensko is a handy reference point, but no place to linger given the surrounding landscapes. At the northern end of Hřensko is the German border crossing towards Dresden. A road and several walking trails roughly follow the Kamenice from Hřensko to Česká Kamenice. Along or near it, the villages of Mezná, Mezní Louka, Vysoká Lípa, Janov and Jetřichovice offer food, accommodation and access down into the gorge or up into the rocks.

MAPS
The maps to have, especially if you're walking, are SHOCart's *Českosaské Švýcarsko* (Czech-Saxon Switzerland) 1:50,000 or the official *Národní Parky České Švýcarsko* 1:25,000.

Information
Hudy Sport (☎ 412 554 086; Hřensko 131) East of the centre of Hřensko, this outlet offers camping equipment, maps and local information.
Infocentrum (☎ 412 554 286; www.hrensko.cz; ⏰ 9am-6pm Apr-Oct, 9am-4pm Nov-Mar) Situated in the middle of Hřensko, opposite the river and on the turn-off up the Kamenice valley, this helpful office can arrange accommodation and provide transport information.

Activities
The Sandstone Rocks of Labe are a great option for independent climbers. There are no organised climbs as such. Ask at Hudy Sport for more information.

WALKING TOURS
If you're short on time, a well-worn **nature trail** (naučná stezka), marked with a green diagonal slash, takes in the region's highlights in one

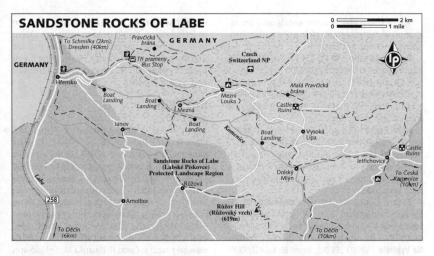

SANDSTONE ROCKS OF LABE

long day. From Hřensko it runs beside the road for 3km to a bus stop at Tři prameny, 2km up to the **Pravčická brána** natural bridge and 6km back to the road at Mezní Louka. From there it plunges 2.5km into the **Kamenice gorge** (right) below Mezná and returns to Hřensko – part of the way by boat. A variation that skips the gorge is the yellow-marked trail from Mezná back to Tři prameny.

A 'grand tour' of the area is a red-marked, high trail that follows the nature trail from Hřensko to Mezní Louka (6km by road; the trail itself may be longer as it doesn't follow a straight line) and then continues to Jetřichovice (15km), with options to spend the night at Mezní Louka or Vysoká Lípa. Additional attractions en route include a smaller stone bridge, the **Malá Pravčická brána**, and **castle ruins** north of Vysoká Lípa and also just east of Jetřichovice.

A shorter alternative follows a blue-marked trail from Mezní Louka down into the Kamenice gorge at Dolský Mlýn, and a yellow trail back out to Jetřichovice.

Pravčická Brána

With postcard views south to the 619m cone of **Růžov hill** (Růžovský vrch), this 30m-high natural **stone arch** (www.pbrana.cz; adult/concession 50/30Kč; ☯ 10am-6pm Apr-Oct, 10am-4pm Sat & Sun Nov-Mar) is Europe's highest. Nestled improbably in a rocky nook beneath the arch is the Falcon's Nest, a rustic chateau that now houses a national park museum and restaurant. If you don't want to walk all the way there, get off a Hřensko–Vysoká Lípa bus at Tři prameny and walk up for 2km.

Kamenice Gorge

Break your hike with a placid float along the dammed-up stretches of the Kamenice river above and below Mezná. Whatever the weather up above, it's mossy, damp, cool and very Jurassic at the bottom of this spectacular canyon.

If you're only interested in the boat trip, you still have to walk: 2km from Hřensko to the lower end; a very steep, sharp 1.5km below Mezná to the middle two boat landings; or 3km down a blue trail from Mezní Louka to the upper end. From the upper end you could also continue southeast to Vysoká Lípa or Jetřichovice.

There are two sections – **Edmundova soutěska** (Edmund's gorge; ☯ 9am-6pm daily May-Aug, Sat & Sun Apr, Sep & Oct) and **Divoká soutěska** (Savage gorge; ☯ 9am-5pm daily May-Aug, Sat & Sun Apr, Sep & Oct) – that have been dammed; here you continue by punt, poled along by a ferryman through a canyon barely 5m wide and 50m to 150m deep. There's a charge for each ferry trip (adult/concession 60/30Kč).

Sleeping

You'll hardly go 2km along the road without seeing *Zimmer frei* (room for rent) signs. Some villages also have camp sites, fairly cheap *pensions* and pricier hotels. In Hřensko, accommodation can be difficult to find in summer; booking ahead is recommended.

NORTH BOHEMIA

All of these places serve meals and are either plush hotels or inn-style pubs with rooms above a restaurant-bar.

Pension Lugano (☎ 412 554 146; fax 412 554 156; Hřensko; s/d incl breakfast 600/1200Kč) Tucked into a bend in the river is this bright and sunny spot. A nicely rustic restaurant downstairs serves a terrific breakfast that will see you through the longest of hiking days.

Hotel Praha (☎ 412 554 066; www.hotel-hrensko.cz; Hřensko 37; s/d incl breakfast 1550/2400Kč; P) Hřensko's best hotel is a proud Tudoresque confection at the quieter end of town with extremely comfortable rooms and a sunny outdoor terrace restaurant.

Mezní Louka has **Hotel Mezní Louka** (☎ 412 554 220; s/d incl breakfast 1050Kč; P) and **Camp Mezná Louka** (☎ 412 554 084; sites per person 60Kč; bungalow 450Kč; P). In nearby Mezná there is **Penzión Na Vyhlídle** (☎ 412 554 065; Mezná 80; s/d 450/900Kč; P) with basic rooms and a sunny terrace overlooking the forest. The restaurant here is exceptionally cosy.

Further on in the Saxon village of Vysoká Lípa stay at **Restaurace a minipension U nás** (☎ 412 555 004; Vysoká Lípa; s/d incl breakfast 600/1000Kč; P) with a bustling dining room decorated with souvenirs from the owners' worldwide travels.

If you've got your own transport, the pretty villages of Janov and Jetřichovice are picturesque bases to explore the region. In Janov **Pension Pastis** (☎ 142 554 037; www.pastis.cz; Janov 22; s/d incl breakfast 550/1100Kč; P) has an excellent restaurant, and the nicest spot in Jetřichovice is **Pension Dřevák** (☎ 412 555 015; www.cztour.cz/drevak; s/d incl breakfast 700/1050Kč; P).

Getting There & Away

Buses run from Děčín to Hřensko (14Kč, 20 minutes) and from Děčín via Česká Kamenice to Jetřichovice, Vysoká Lípa or Janov every two or three hours. The last bus from Hřensko to Děčín leaves at 6.30pm.

BORDER CROSSING

Buses run from Schöna, on the German side to Dresden (one hour). Some trains between Děčín and Dresden stop at Schöna, on the German side of the river, opposite Hřensko. From the train station, a ferry shuttles to and from Hřensko (12Kč) on demand.

Getting Around

Buses run between Hřensko and Mezná (via Mezní Louka) six times a day (14Kč, 15 min-

utes). There are no direct buses from Hřensko to Jetřichovice, You'll need to transit in Děčín by bus or have your own transport. If you are driving, note there is a hefty 5000Kč fine if you park anywhere on the road between Hřensko and Mezní Louka.

NOVÝ BOR
pop 12,000

Further east is the heartland of Bohemia's glass-making industry. In Nový Boř, the **Glass museum** (Sklářské museum; ☎ 487 726 196; www.novy -bor.cz/sklarske_muzeum in Czech; náměstí Míru 105; adult/ concession 40/20Kč; ⏰ 9am-noon & 1-4pm Tue-Sun) was founded in 1893. The examples of Bohemian artistry date from the 17th century, and there is also a replica glassworks. Entry to the museum includes the 'Masters of the Glass Crafts' exhibition above the **tourist office** (☎ 487 726 815; www.novy-bor.cz in Czech; TG Masaryka 46; ⏰ 9am-4pm Mon-Fri Apr-Oct), which presents the winning contemporary work from an annual glassmaking competition initiated in 1994. Most of the factories have attached shops where prices are lower than in Prague and other tourist centres. Visit the **Slavia Glassworks** (☎ 48 712 915; Kollárova 313) for handmade art glass, or ask at the tourist office about visiting glass factories in the area. In the last week of June the town hosts an annual **glass-making festival**.

Sleeping & Eating

The tourist office staff can organise cheap rooms in Nový Bor.

Parkhotel (☎ 487 723 157; www.parkhotel.clnet.cz; Žižkova 269; s/d incl breakfast 800/1500Kč) This refurbished hotel has a good restaurant and arranges visits to glass factories.

Getting There & Away

One bus a day (38Kč, 40 minutes) and two trains a day (76Kč, 1½ hours) trundle from Děčín to Nový Bor. Instead, head to the junction town of Česká Lípa where there are 10 buses a day covering the 8km north to Nový Bor (16Kč, 15 minutes).

JABLONNÉ V PODJEŠTĚDÍ & LEMBERK CHATEAU
pop 3800

The chateau of Lemberk (or Löwenberg; 'Lion Mountain'), on the outskirts of Jablonné v Podještědí, was founded in 1240 by Havel Markvartic, head of a North Bohemian feudal aristocratic family. Its best-known resident was Havel's frail Moravian wife, Zdislava, who was made a saint in 1995 for her exemplary life.

Later owners turned the castle into a comfortable Gothic and then Renaissance chateau. It owes its present baroque face to Albrecht von Wallenstein (see p205), the Hapsburg general who grew rich on confiscated Hussite property, and the family of one of his officers who contrived to keep the castle after Wallenstein's murder.

The last private owners, the Auerspergs (who also owned Žleby chateau in Central Bohemia), lent the castle to the German army during WWII.

Though out of the way as a trip from Prague, it's worth visiting en route to/from Děčín or Český ráj in East Bohemia.

Orientation & Information

The chateau is in the hamlet of Lvová on the outskirts of Jablonné v Podještědí, midway between Česká Lípa and Liberec. It's a 500m climb up through scented woods from the Lvová stop on the Česká Lípa–Liberec train.

Alternatively, get off the bus or train at Jablonné, make for the domes of St Lawrence church a few hundred metres up the hill and then walk 3.5km northeast on a green-marked trail to the chateau.

There is a **tourist information office** (informační centrum; ☎ 487 762 441; náměstí Míru; ☯ 7.30am-11.30am & noon-4pm Mon-Fri) offering private rooms and local information near the church in Jablonné.

Sights

ST LAWRENCE CHURCH & MUMMIES

St Lawrence church (kostel sv Vavřince; náměstí Míru), completed in 1722, is apparently where Zdislava is buried. Beneath the building is a **crypt** with mummified corpses dating from the 17th and 18th centuries, amazingly well preserved

thanks to a clever ventilation system. At the time of writing the crypt was not open to visitors; check with the tourist information office.

LEMBERK CHATEAU

A 45-minute, Czech-language tour (foreign guide available for 50Kč extra) of the **chateau** (zámek Lemberk; www.szlemberk.xf.cz; adult/concession 50/30Kč; ☯ 9am-4pm Tue-Sun May-Sep, 9am-3pm Sat & Sun Apr & Oct) takes in the open-hearth kitchen, chapel, rooms full of furniture and church furnishings, and an upstairs hall with a ceiling featuring 70 panels (dating from 1608) depicting German proverbs and Aesop's fables. Other rooms showcase Zdislava's life.

A few rooms are used for changing exhibitions. Definitely check these out, as you may get to see the most interesting parts of the chateau, a little upstairs baroque chapel beside the castle tower – and possibly the tower too. Outside the gate are several well preserved North Bohemian half-timbered houses.

Sleeping & Eating

The tourist office staff can organise cheap rooms in Jablonné.

U Salvátora (☎ 775 027 044; www.pensionusalvatora .cz; náměstí Míru 162; s/d incl breakfast 400/800Kč; mains 80-120Kč) With a prime spot on the main square in Jablonné, U Salvátora offers salvation with a cosy restaurant and the best rooms in town.

Getting There & Away

Jablonné is on long-distance bus routes linking Karlovy Vary (in West Bohemia), Děčín, Liberec and the Krkonoše resorts in East Bohemia. One bus a day (except Sunday) makes the three-hour trip from Prague's Florenc station (86Kč). All buses stop at the train station.

Trains are limited, with occasional links to Liberec, Cheb and Děčín.

East Bohemia

Contrast is the key to East Bohemia. The Polabí, the fertile area of plains radiating from the Labe river, is one the flattest parts of the Czech Republic, but just 50km north on the border with Poland, the Krkonoše (Giant) Mountains escalate to the 1602m summit of Sněžka, the country's highest mountain. And while 1602m is minor league compared to the nearby Alps, there are enough alpine (with a small 'a') attractions to keep skiers, hikers and climbers active across all seasons. Come in winter and you'll be treated to very affordable skiing action, while in summer the resort of Špindlerův Mlýn transforms itself into an adventure sports hub.

Urban contrast is manifest in the busy provincial capital, Hradec Králové, with architectural design and the Labe river vigorously dividing the fascinating old and new towns. To the south is Pardubice, its beautifully preserved Renaissance square surrounded by an indus-trial halo that produced one of the 20th century's most notorious catalysts for destruction. Nearby the Renaissance splendour of the chateau at Litomyšl has achieved Unesco World Heritage recognition. Off the beaten track, hidden historical gems dominate quiet villages. The castles at Častolovice and nearby Opočno are exceptionally well restored, while the baroque sculptures of Matthias Bernard Braun overlook the sleepy town of Kuks.

Natural contrast shines in Adršpach-Teplice and Český ráj with their eccentric and bizarre landscapes carved across the millennia from sandstone. In Adršpach-Teplice your climbing or hiking will traverse hidden river valleys, while in Český ráj craggy castle ruins form part of the idiosyncratic vistas.

HIGHLIGHTS

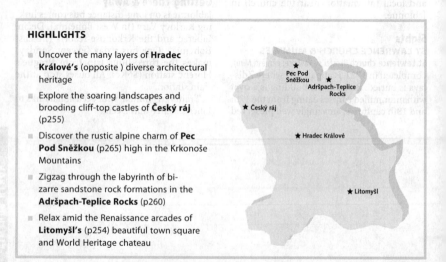

- Uncover the many layers of **Hradec Králové's** (opposite) diverse architectural heritage

- Explore the soaring landscapes and brooding cliff-top castles of **Český ráj** (p255)

- Discover the rustic alpine charm of **Pec Pod Sněžkou** (p265) high in the Krkonoše Mountains

- Zigzag through the labyrinth of bi-zarre sandstone rock formations in the **Adršpach-Teplice Rocks** (p260)

- Relax amid the Renaissance arcades of **Litomyšl's** (p254) beautiful town square and World Heritage chateau

★ Pec Pod Sněžkou
★ Adršpach-Teplice Rocks
★ Český ráj
★ Hradec Králové
★ Litomyšl

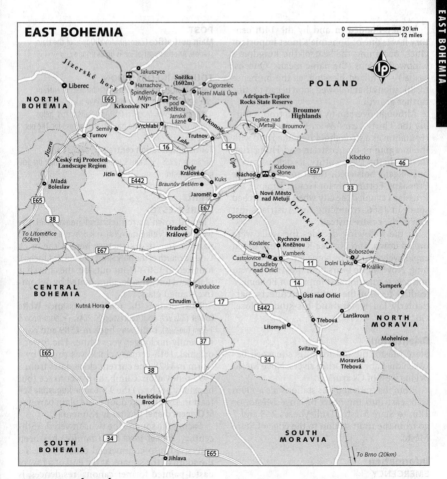

EAST BOHEMIA

HRADEC KRÁLOVÉ

pop 95,000

Outwardly Hradec Králové might seem like the Czech Republic's most schizophrenic city, with the contrasting architectural styles of different eras slicing the East Bohemian capital in two. On the eastern bank in Staré Město, the old town frames the appropriately named Big square (Velké náměsti) with an elegant sweep of arcades and façades encompassing Gothic, Renaissance and baroque styles. To the northeast, Little square (Malé námesti) continues the same architectural theme. West of the river, the new town, Nové Mešto, is a sprawl of grandiose Art Nouveau and functionalist buildings that are a fascinating, if slightly brutal, contrast to the flounce and frills of the old town. Seemingly kept apart by both design and the Labe river, Hradec Králové's unity is secured by the vibrancy of its bars and restaurants, and a fine selection of galleries and museums that cast a non-judgemental eye over all the city's different histories.

History

Two rivers and a hill: the ideal foundations for a fortified town. And it didn't take long for the local warlords to notice. By the 9th century, a stronghold had been constructed at the confluence of the Labe and Orlice rivers and within 300 years the fledgling city had become the administrative centre of East Bohemia.

Money flooded in and by the 14th century it was one of Bohemia's most important cities, becoming the seat of the kingdom's widowed queens (the name means 'Queens' castle') – a mixed blessing, as the immense fortifications that followed soon began to stifle further growth.

Although overrun by Swedish troops during the Thirty Years' War, Hradec Králové's reputation as a stronghold remained and with the merging of the Austrian and Hungarian thrones in the 19th century, its defences were once again bolstered, this time against the Prussians. Fortunately for Hradec Králové, the Prussians avoided the city when they marched south in 1866, trouncing the Austrians just east of the centre instead.

In the following decades the walls were pulled down, and Hradec Králové expanded explosively, guided by some far-sighted planning. Nové Město bears both the Art Nouveau and severe functionalist imprint of Bohemia's leading turn-of-the-century architects, particularly Jan Kotěra and his student Josef Gočár.

Orientation

Staré Město, the old town, is squashed between the Labe and Orlice rivers. Nové Město begins west of Čs armády.

From the train and bus stations it's a 400m walk east into the heart of Nové Město, or 1km to Staré Město. Trolleybuses 2, 3 and 7 go from the train station to the edge of Staré Město.

Information
EMERGENCY
Foreigners' police office (☎ 158; Riegrovo nám) By the train station.

INTERNET ACCESS
Tourist Information centre (☎ 495 580 492; Velké nám; per hr 45Kč; ☽ 8am-4.30pm May-Sep, Mon-Fri Oct-Apr)
Roxy Bar (Masarykovo nám; per min 1Kč; ☽ 10am-3am Tue-Sat, 2pm-3am Mon-Sun)

MEDICAL SERVICES
Hospital (nemocnice; ☎ 495 831 111; Sokolská) Located 500m south of the old town.

MONEY
Česká Spořitelna (cnr Čs armády & Palackého) Has an exchange desk and ATM.

POST
Main post office (Zamenhofova) Opposite the train station. Another post office is on Čs armády.

TOURIST INFORMATION
Tourist information centre (Informační centrum; ☎ 495 580 492; www.ic-hk.cz; Velké nám; ☽ 8am-4.30pm May-Sep, Mon-Fri Oct-Apr) Sells maps, helps with accommodation and has internet access for 1Kč per minute.
Tourist information centre (☎ 495 534 482; Gočárova 1225; ☽ 8am-5.30pm Mon-Fri) Another branch in Nové Město.

Sights
STARÉ MĚSTO
The old town's architectural heart is at the west end of Velké nám (also known as Žižkovo nám). The oldest structure here is the brick Gothic **church of the Holy Spirit** (kostel sv Ducha), founded in 1307. Dour outside, the church is plain and lofty inside, illuminated by decorative stained glass.

Next door is the 68m Renaissance **White tower** (Bílá věž; adult/concession 20/10Kč; ☽ 9am-noon & 1-5pm Tue-Sun), built way back in 1589 and consequently no longer very white. The tower's original, 16th-century clock was ruined by a storm in 1828; the current clock dates from a 1993 renovation. Climb the tower to see (but hopefully not hear) the 9.8-tonne **Augustine Bell** (cast in 1506). Next door is the plain baroque **St Clement chapel** (kostel sv Klimenta).

Facing the square, the twin-towered, 15th-century, **former town hall** (radnice) has been converted into commercial office space. To the south of the square, at the end of a row of pastel-painted former canons' residences, is the skeleton of the **municipal brewery**, which was closed for restoration at the time of writing.

Sturdy arcades line the north side of the square; opposite is the Jesuits' **church of the Assumption of the Virgin** (kostel Nanebevzetí Panny Marie), light and pretty despite its baroque baggage. This and the adjacent **Jesuit College** and **Bishop's Palace** date from the 17th century, when a bishopric was established in Hradec Králové. Tucked beside the church is a Josef Gočár modern addition, a staircase down to Komenského ulice.

A highlight of Hradec Králové is the regional **Gallery of modern art** (Galérie moderního umění; Velké nám 139-140; adult/concession 30/15Kč; ☽ 9am-noon & 1-6pm Tue-Sun). Housed in a handsome Art Nouveau building (designed by Osvald Polívka) is a superb collection of late-19th- and 20th-century Czech painting and sculpture, as well as changing modern exhibitions.

NOVÉ MĚSTO – EAST OF THE RIVER

Nové Město begins from Čs armády, although the strip east of the Labe is more neglected than the clean-cut neighbourhoods west of the river.

Where Palackého meets the river is the **East Bohemia regional museum** (Krajský muzeum vychodních Čech; ☎ 495 512 462; www.muzeumhk.cz in Czech & German; Eliščino nábřeží 465; adult/concession 30/15Kč; ☿ 9am-noon & 1-5pm Tue-Sun), a graceful, Art Nouveau building of red brick, designed by Kotěra, with seated giants on either side of the door. Inside are old photos, clockworks, mammoth bones and a fascinating scale model of Hradec Králové dating from 1865, showing the fortress that bound the town for four centuries.

Down at the confluence of the two rivers is **Jiráskovy sady**, a wooded park which features a 16th-century **wooden church** brought from Ukraine in 1935.

NOVÉ MĚSTO – WEST OF THE RIVER

Gočár's showpiece square, boxy Masarykovo nám, is overtly tidy and thoroughly functional, and best shows his wider vision for the city. Nowadays it's linked by a pedestrianised mall to the livelier Baťkovo nám.

To the south are several brick school buildings designed by Gočár between 1925 and 1928. The most interesting is the **State Grammar School** (Státní gymnázium), with a severe façade like a textbook. Dominating a nearby corner is another arresting Gočár work, the wedge-shaped Protestant **Ambrosian chapel** (Ambrožů sbor). The outside looks overly austere but inside a lovely courtyard presents a softer countenance.

On Nám 28.října, search out the functionalist **church of the Blessed Heart of Our Lord** (kostel Božího Srdce Páně), with a dramatic arched space inside.

Sleeping

The tourist office books private rooms from around 300Kč per person. The nearest **camping ground** (☎ 495 482 677; Stříbrný rybník) is 5km east of the centre (take bus 17).

BUDGET

Ubytovna ZVU (☎ 495 511 175; www.hotelovydum.cz; Heyrovského 4; dm/s/d 210/290/580Kč) This hostel has

dorms and private rooms and is popular with workers from local construction sites. Book ahead.

Penzion Amátka (☎ 495 514 935; www.sweb.cz /amatka, in Czech; Malé námesti 120; s/d 300/600Kč) Basic rooms with shared bathrooms, but a good location in the old town's quieter, smaller square.

MIDRANGE

Penzion Nové Adalbertinum (☎ 495 063 111; www .adalbertinum.diecezehk.cz; Velké nám 32; s/d incl breakfast 860/1320Kč; **P**) Comfortable rooms with modern furniture fill this 17th-century Jesuit college on the main square. Breakfast starts at 6.30am if you're seized by any monk-like urges.

Pension U sv Lukáše (☎ 495 518 616; www.usvate holukase.com; Úzká 208; s/d incl breakfast 1000/1400Kč) This stately townhouse near the main square conceals charming old-world rooms and a very good restaurant.

Pod Věží Penzion (☎ 495 514 932; www.pod-vezi.cz; Velké nám 165; s/d incl breakfast 1190/1575Kč; **P** **❒** **⅋**) Comfy rooms, a fitness centre and in-room internet are all cunningly integrated in this slender building beside the even more slender White tower.

Also recommended:

Hotel Stadión (☎ 495 514 664; hotel-hradec-kralove -stadion@quick.cz; Komenského 1214; s/d incl breakfast 780/850Kč; **P**) Clean and basic digs beside the ice hockey stadium.

U Česke Koruny (☎ 495 540 490; www.uceskekoruny .com; Tomkova 180; d from 1350Kč; **P** **❒**) This funky restored building has a snug tavern downstairs. All the rooms are different colours, but they're all very comfortable.

TOP END

Hotel U královny Elišky (☎ 495 518 052; www.euroa gentur.cz; Malé námesti 117; s/d incl breakfast 2400/2800Kč; **P** ✕ ❄ ⅋) Hradec Kralové's best rooms are in this renovated townhouse in quieter Malé námesti. There are weekend discounts of up to 20%, and a fitness centre, sauna and pool.

Eating

different:drinks-food-sound (☎ 495 511 380; Velké nám 22; snacks 50Kč; meals 80-120Kč; ☿ 7.30am-midnight Mon-Thu, 7.30am-1am Fri, 9am-1am Sat, 9am-11pm Sun) Expect tasty breakfasts, snacks and huge meals at this new eatery with brightly cinematic décor and Hradec Králové hipsters at the bar. Have a ciabatta sandwich and a latte while you hitch your laptop to their wi-fi network.

HRADEC KRÁLOVÉ

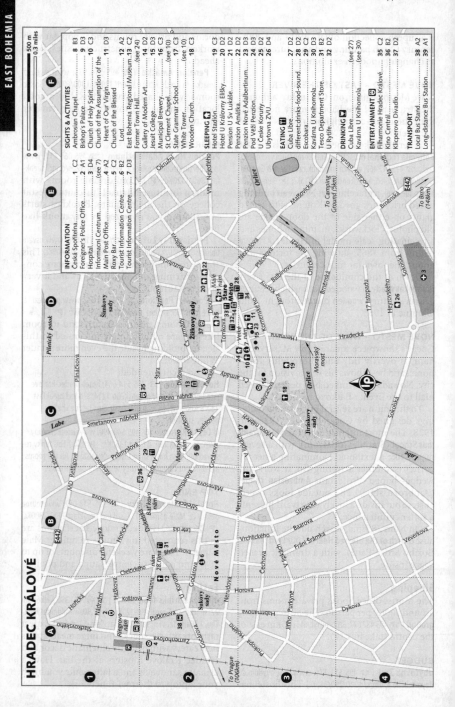

U Rytíře (☎ 603 464 389; Velké nám 144; mains 160-220Kč) The tasty Czech grills at 'The Knight', a popular spot on the main square, would go down well even without the funky young wait staff and medieval ambience.

Escobara (☎ 608 140 741; Karla IV 611; mains 170Kč) The curvy 1980s armchairs could be from a drug lord's super yacht, and you'll want to linger in them for the tasty pastas, grills and cocktails. There's a buzzy terrace for people watching in the summer.

Also recommended:

Tesco Department Store (Dukelská) Self-catering central.

Drinking

Kavárna U Knihomola (☎ 495 516 089; Velké nám 26; mains 90-180Kč; ⏰ 7am-11pm Mon-Thu, 7am-2am Fri, 10am-2am Sat, 10am-11pm Sun) Steaks, salads, coffee and cocktails fuel the city's bright young things in this lively bar-restaurant that's a popular haunt all day everyday. The site was one of the city's first bookshops (the name means 'At the Bookworm') and a cool literary ambience is still extant.

Cuba Libre (Malé námesti 14-15; ⏰ 8am-10pm Mon-Fri; 4-10pm Sat) This funky bar–art gallery is named after just one of the cocktails on offer; at least the owners didn't call it Screaming Orgasm or Dirty Banana.

Entertainment

Filharmonie Hradec Králové (☎ 495 211 375; www.fhk.cz; Eliščino nábřeží 777) The city orchestra stages regular classical concerts.

Klicperovo divadlo (☎ 495 514 590; Dlouhá 98) Theatre (usually Czech) is on the programme here.

Kino Centrál (☎ 495 213 613; Karla IV 774) For Czech and foreign films.

Getting There & Away

Direct **buses** (☎ 495 521 742) link Hradec Králové with Prague (78Kč, 1½ hours) and Brno (130Kč, 2½ hours), with departures all day.

There are about 12 **trains** (☎ 495 537 555) a day to Prague (140Kč, 1½ hours), three to Brno (204Kč, 2½ hours) and dozens to Pardubice (34Kč, 30 minutes).

PARDUBICE

pop 92,000

Like a sweet, gooey centre in a chewy piece of nougat, Pardubice's drop-dead-gorgeous Renaissance square is surrounded by the harsh realities of a sprawling industrial city. And just to reinforce the incongruity of the juxtaposition, the city with (arguably) the country's most exquisite town square is also the home of the infamous Semtex plastic explosive that fuelled countless terrorist aspirations. Unlike neighbouring Hradec Králové, where the old town feels robust enough to counter the architectural muscle surrounding it, Pardubice's delicate heart and recently renovated chateau and gardens feel slightly fragile and under pressure from the encompassing greyness. Luckily the proud people of Pardubice protect what's left of their Renaissance heritage. With several elegant old town hotels and many lively bars and restaurants lining the main square, it's a breeze to tune out the city's harsher elements.

History

Founded around 1340, Pardubice caught the noble eye of the Moravian Pernštejn family when they took ownership of the whole region in 1491. After giving it a bit of a makeover, the new landlords moved into the town's castle soon after. Over the next century, with the help of Italian artisans and the unexpected assistance of two devastating fires, the Pernštejns built Pardubice a glossy new Renaissance face. Though only a fraction of the their legacy still stands today (thanks to the work of a Swedish siege army in the Thirty Years' War), the town centre remains achingly pretty.

Orientation

Míru, the artery of 'new' Pardubice, is an 800m walk east along Palackého from the bus and train stations (or take any bus or trolleybus for 15Kč). On the east side of Nám Republiky is a Gothic gate tower into the old centre, Pernštýnské nám.

Information

Česká spořitelna (Nám Republiky) Has an ATM and exchange desk.

ČSOB (Míru) Has an ATM opposite the main post office.

Internet People (Bratranců Veverků 316; per hr 42Kč; ⏰ 11am-9pm) One flight downstairs from ČSOB.

Main post office (Míru)

Tourist information office (☎ 466 613 223; www.ipardubice.cz; Míru 61; ⏰ 9am-6pm) Has maps and accommodation information.

Sights & Activities

NÁMĚSTÍ REPUBLIKY

This modern square is home to three of Pardubice's oldest and most interesting buildings.

The most arresting, with its picturesque gablets and needle-thin tower, is **St Bartholomew church** (kostel sv Bartoloměj), dating originally from the 13th century. Its present form dates from about 1515, when it was rebuilt after being razed by the Hussites.

At the other end of the square is the fine Art Nouveau **Municipal theatre** (Městské divadlo). On the eastern side, brandishing flags and pointy gables, is the 16th-century **Green tower** (Zelená brána; adult/concession 15/10Kč; 9am-noon & 1-5pm May-Sep, Sat & Sun only Oct), which you can climb for views over the town's two faces.

PERNŠTÝNSKÉ NÁMĚSTÍ

This cobbled square is one of Bohemia's most handsome, completely enclosed by bright Renaissance buildings, including a genial, neo-Renaissance **town hall**. The square's most notable façade is the 18th-century, snow-white, stucco relief of Jonah being swallowed by the whale, on the house called **dům U Jonáše** (466 510 003; adult/concession 40/20Kč; 10am-6pm Tue-Sun), which contains a small gallery often showing surprisingly interesting and nicely avant-garde work.

Walk through the narrow alleys to the north and east of the square, beneath bulky stone arches supporting heavily sloping, virtually arthritic Renaissance buildings. Among the most venerable is the **house at Pernštýnská 11**, more or less unchanged since the 16th century.

PARDUBICE CASTLE

The **castle** (zámek; adult/concession 60/30Kč; 10am-6pm Tue-Sun), filled with courting peacocks, is accessible from Zámecká, north of Pernštýnské nám. Inside is the renovated **palace**, featuring some exquisite Renaissance murals of Moses receiving the Ten Commandments. Opposite, in two smaller wings, are a superb gallery and a museum, both included in the entrance fee. The **East Bohemian gallery** (Východočeská galérie) has a permanent collection of 19th- and 20th-century Czech art, including unexpected modern sculptures around the grounds. A rather immodest exhibit on the role of the Pernštejns in Czech history is featured in the **East Bohemian museum** (Východočeská muzeum) as well as vintage postcards and coins from the days before Lonely Planet and credit cards.

PARDUBICE

0 — 200 m
0 — 0.1 miles

To Hradec Králové (17km); Prague (105km)

Labe

To Camp Site (600m)

Chrudimka (Labská)

Tyršovy sady

Sukova Třída

Masarykovo nám

Kostelní sv Anežky

Zámecká

Pernštýnské nám

Na Hrádku

nám Republiky

U divadla

To Bus & Train Stations (600m)

Nerudova

Smilova

Hronovická

Nádražní

Arnošta z Pardubic

Hlaváčova

THE GREAT PARDUBICE STEEPLECHASE

Renowned as the world's toughest horse-race after the Grand National at Aintree, the Velká Pardubická (Great Pardubice Steeplechase) was established in 1874 by Count Octavian Kinsky. Equine tradition flows deep in the Kinsky family's veins, beginning in 1723 when the Bohemian cavalry commissioned the aristocratic family to breed horses from the athletic herds running wild on their estates since the 15th century. In 1883, just nine years after the first running of the Velká Pardubická, another Kinsky (Count Karel) won the Grand National with a Czech-bred horse. The Velká Pardubická was suspended during WWII and the 1946 return of the race drew a record 60,000 spectators. Auspiciously the 100th race in 1990 was the first running of the race since the end of communism. Each year in early October, huge crowds gather to watch the 6900m race that is a torrid event for both jockeys and horses. It's not uncommon for horses to be destroyed after breaking a leg, and each year animal rights activists protest the running of the race. The Velká Pardubická race is now an international affair and horses from as far away as France, Slovakia, Italy and Ireland line up for a crack at the winner's purse of 2,250,000Kč (around US$100,000 at the time of writing).

Sleeping

The tourist information office books private rooms, and there is a camping ground north of the river opposite the castle. Prices are generally on the high side.

Arnošt (☎ 466 613 668; www.hotel-arnost.cz; Arnošta z Pardubic 676; s/d from 570/600Kč, apartments 1440Kč; P 🖳) A makeover's given this former hostel a new spring in its step with a range of spacious rooms including family apartments. All rooms have kitchen facilities, and the Arnošt is easily the best value in town.

Hotel Sport (☎ 466 512 221; www.hotelsport.cz; Sukova Třída 1735; s/d incl breakfast 830/970Kč; P) Near the stadium, this 1970s spot is as boxy and safe as an ice-hockey goalie and a very reliable back up.

Hotel 100 (Sto) (☎ 466 511 179; fax 466 501 825; Kostelní Sv Anežky; 100; s/d incl breakfast 1000/1300Kč; P) A comfortable and confident patina of age surrounds this restored burgher's house in the absolute heart of the old town. That just makes it all the more charming.

Penzion Atrium (☎ 466 615 146; www.penzionatrium .cz; Smilova 343; s/d incl breakfast 1000/1300Kč; P ✗) Clean and classy rooms sit atop a buzzy café, with a quiet garden out the back and a convenient location in Pardubice's more modern precinct.

Hotel U anděla (☎ 466 535 656; www.hotelzlandel .pardubicko.com; Zámecká 25; s/d incl breakfast 1100/1300Kč; P) Tuck yourself away in the stylish rooms in this traditional inn en route to the castle.

Eating

U Čtyr Prstu (☎ 466 516 709; Pernštýnské nám; dishes 60-160Kč) Interrupt your stroll around Pernštýnské nám with coffee and cake at this cosy *kavárna*

(café). You never know when you'll get the chance to recharge in such Renaissance splendour again.

U černého orla (☎ 466 511 611; Pernštýnské nám; mains 80-140Kč) The tasty Czech favourites are priced very reasonably given the prime location right on Pernštýnské nám. There's another huge outside terrace to watch the world go by in old world charm.

Pizzeria Galera (☎ 466 530 083; Pernštýnské nám; pizza 120Kč) Old town crowds spill out onto the sunny alfresco terrace at Pizzeria Galera like your thin-crust pizza spills over the edge of your plate. The pizzas are simply huge. You have been warned.

Also recommended:

Albert supermarket (Míru 2672) For self-catering.

Drinking

U Hrbaty Kozy (☎ 466 611 734; Sladkovského 507; ☼ 3pm-midnight Mon-Fri, 5pm-midnight Sat) Follow your thirst to this tiny watering hole. Look for the 'Sex Shop Pamela' sign, walk through the empty garage, and go down the stairs on your right to good times with a slight Irish accent. And don't worry, Pamela's nowhere to be seen.

Velvet (☎ 466 535 773; Míru 109) There's more subterranean shenanigans at Velvet, this time with specialty beers and a self-contained bowling alley. Adjourn to the bustling summer terrace at street level if you don't like drinking underground.

Getting There & Away

Pardubice is 30 minutes from Hradec Králové by bus (23Kč) or train (34Kč). Buses go about

SEMTEX

Invented in 1966 by Stanislav Brebera, who was only paid a couple of hundred dollars for his efforts, Semtex plastic explosive was manufactured by Pardubice's Explosia factory for more than 30 years. Widely used by commercial miners, the original Semtex was odourless, highly versatile and devastatingly efficient (a mere 250g could down an airliner), making it an attractive proposition for terrorists. Nearly 700 tonnes, enough for 1.5 million of the bombs that brought down the Pan-Am jet over Lockerbie in 1988, was exported to Libya in the 1970s. More recently, Semtex was also the basis of the 'shoe bomb' which British al-Qaeda acolyte Richard Reid used in an attempt to blow up an American Airlines flight from Paris to Miami in December 2001. In the post-9/11 environment production has fallen dramatically and now only 10 tonnes is exported each year, all produced at a new factory in Brno in South Moravia. Exports are now under strict government control, and all new supplies contain an identifying metal code and carry a distinctive vapour signature to aid detection. The name Semtex is now also known in the Czech Republic as a taurine-based energy drink (see www.semtexculture.cz).

every half hour, trains go hourly. Tickets are available from machines in the station.

There are over a dozen direct trains daily from Pardubice to Olomouc (184Kč, two hours).

A visit is feasible as a day trip from Prague, best by fast train (130Kč, 1¼ hours, approximately every hour). Buses take an hour longer but are a bit cheaper.

OPOČNO

Plots, schemes and intrigue put an interesting spin on this beautiful castle, which looms over the village of Opočno, 25km northeast of Hradec Králové.

There was a Přemysl fortress at Opočno by the 11th century, but after a later owner, Jan Městecký, abandoned the Hussite cause, it was trashed by disciples of the Hussite military hero Jan Žižka.

In the 16th century the fortress was converted by the Trčkas, one of Bohemia's richest families, into the neo-Romanesque chateau you see today. The last of the line, Adam Erdmann Trčka, was killed in 1634 in the course of a plot to assassinate Ferdinand II. The emperor then sold the chateau to the Italian Colloredo family, who lived in it right up until 1945.

In 1813, King Friedrich Wilhelm II of Prussia, Austrian Chancellor Metternich and Russian Tsar Alexander II met here in the course of forming their 'Holy Alliance' against Napoleon.

Orientation & Information

The joint train and bus stations are 1.5km west from the castle: follow Nádražní to Kupkovo nám then veer right on Zámecká. The chateau is a 400m climb from Opočno's renovated central square.

Sights

The prettified, pastel **chateau** (9-11.30am & 12.30-6pm Tue-Sun Jul & Aug, until 5pm May, Jun & Sep, until 4pm Sat & Sun only Apr-Oct, last tour 1¼ hr before closing) is impressive partly because it still looks lived-in. The owner at the start of the 20th century, Josef II Colloredo-Mannsfeld, filled one end of the castle with his hunting trophies and artefacts from Africa and the Americas. Tours (in Czech) cost 40/20Kč (adult/concession), or 60/30Kč including a diversion into the armoury. It's worth spending the extra 25 minutes in the armoury to see an entire heavy metal video's worth of suits of armour. You might be surprised how small folks were in the old days.

All that remains of the older fortress is one cylindrical tower. The baroque houses around the chateau are worth a peek, as is the surrounding **Zámecký park** (7am-8pm).

Sleeping & Eating

Penzión Podloubí (☎ 443 641 885; www.podloubi.zde .cz; s/d 800/1200Kč; P) On the square opposite the castle entrance, this place has tidy rooms and a good restaurant.

U Slunce (off Kupkovo náměstí) On the road to the chateau, this is a bustling beer hall that's a top spot for lunch. Next door there is internet access at 1Kč per minute.

Getting There & Away

Buses run from Hradec Králové every hour or so (32Kč, 40 minutes). From Prague there are three buses a day (96Kč, 2¾ hours).

ČASTOLOVICE & AROUND

The 13th-century stronghold of Častolovice, 31km southeast of Hradec Králové, was renovated as a Renaissance chateau at the end of the 16th century; it passed into the hands of the Šternberk (Sternberg) family in 1694, and then into the hands of the state at the end of WWII. The Šternberks reclaimed it in the 1990s (see boxed text p325), repairing the communist-era pillage and opening some of its 150 rooms to visitors. Current owner Diana Phipps Sternberg is a renowned interior decorator, and after emigrating to Britain in 1948 aged 12, returned to the Czech Republic in 1990 to assist Václav Havel's wife Olga in the post-communist makeover of Prague castle.

Highlights of the **chateau** (www.zamek-casto lovice.cz; adult/concession 90/45Kč; 9am-6pm Tue-Sun May-Sep) tour include a vast Knights' Hall with biblical scenes on the ceiling, the family's fine collection of 17th- to 19th-century furniture and portraits of every one of the Czech kings. The chateau is surrounded by a sedate, English-style park. The last tour (in Czech) is an hour before closing and an English text is available.

The chateau makes an easy excursion from Hradec Králové, or you could make a long day trip full of chateaux and castles, including those at **Kostelec** and **Doudleby nad Orlicí** (respectively about 2km and 7km beyond Častolovice on Hwy 11), and at **Rychnov nad Kněžnou** (a few kilometres on to Vamberk and 5km north on Hwy 14). In fact there are some 30 castles and chateaux, from Romanesque to Renaissance, in a 50 sq km area around Hradec Králové.

Getting There & Away

Buses run about hourly from Hradec Králové (38Kč, 35 minutes). All the castles (except Rychnov) are on the railway line from Hradec Králové.

At least two buses a day go to Častolovice from Prague Florenc (96Kč, 2½ hours). There are also a few direct trains (184Kč, 2¼ hours).

KUKS

Few of the region's sights are as ghoulish as **Kuks** (499 692 161; www.kuks.cz in Czech; adult/concession 50/30Kč, in English 100/60Kč; 9am-noon & 1-5pm Tue-Sun May-Aug, until 4pm Sep, until 4pm Sat & Sun Apr & Oct), the spooky carcass of a fine baroque building on the banks of the Labe river. While the present structure would hold its own as

a devilish lair in a horror movie, Kuks was originally constructed in the early 18th century as an immodest monument to art patron Franz Anton von Sporck's bulging bank balance. Having discovered a mineral spring on his land, 30km north of Hradec Králové, Sporck set out to impress his neighbours with the ultimate 'water feature', erecting a deluxe spa complex, complete with baths, infirmary, chapel, racecourse, theatre, gardens, guesthouses and a chateau. The concerts, salons, hunts and lavish parties at this upper-class 'resort' briefly made it a rival to the West Bohemian spa towns.

The party ended in 1740, two years after Sporck's death, when a massive flood washed away many of the buildings and destroyed the spring. All that remains today are the **chapel** and **infirmary**, a big staircase leading nowhere, and a fine collection of **statues** depicting the 12 virtues and 12 vices by Matthias Bernard Braun (1684–1738), one of Bohemia's masters of baroque sculpture. Challenge yourself to work out what each statue represents before resorting to the English translations. Another highlight is a wonderfully restored **18th-century pharmacy**. Above the door of the pharmacy is (allegedly) the horn of a unicorn. That's funny. We could have sworn it was from a narwhal.

All the sights are included in the 45-minute guided tour but you'll need the English text to get the most out of it. Definitely consider stopping if you're in the area, otherwise give it a miss.

Braunův Betlém

About 3km west of Kuks is **'Braun's Bethlehem'**, an alfresco gallery with several extraordinary religious sculptures – hermits, saints and biblical scenes, some with little grottoes behind them – all but one by Braun, hewn directly from the rock outcrops scattered through the woods. This is all that remains of another Sporck project, which once had fountains and chapels as well.

Getting There & Away

Buses come from Hradec Králové (32Kč, 30 minutes) about hourly, stopping at Kuks village, across the Labe from the infirmary. South of the infirmary is a whistle stop on the railway line.

To get to Braunův Betlém, walk west on a red-marked path from Kuks village or on a yellow path from the infirmary. By car, drive 3km west from Kuks village to Žíreč, turn left, cross the railway and climb for 2km to a car park on the far side of the woods; it's an 800m walk from there.

LITOMYŠL

pop 10,200

Founded in the 13th century as an important stop on the Trstenice trading route linking Bohemia and Moravia, Litomyšl is best known for its stunning 16th-century Renaissance chateau, and as the birthplace of Czech composer Bedřich Smetana, who was born here in 1824. More recently the town hosted the 1994 summit of seven Central European leaders including Václav Havel, and Poland's Lech Walesa. If you're into Eastern religions or crazily energetic art then a simple house in a side street should not be missed.

Orientation

Litomyšl straddles the Loučná River, with the old town curving around its northeastern edge, and the modern city, including the train and bus stations on the opposite bank. To get to the town's main square, Smetanovo nám, from the bus station, walk northeast across the river on Mařákova, and then turn left into Šmilovského. From the train station, cross the river and walk southeast on Bernardka, and then left into Ropkova. From either the bus station or train station it takes less than five minutes to walk to Smetanovo nám.

Information

Česká spořitelna (cnr Smetanovo nám & Špitálská) Has an ATM and exchange desk.

Post office (cnr Smetanovo nám & Jiraskova ulice) At the northern end of the main square.

Tourist information office (☎ 420 612 161; www .litomysl.cz/ic; Smetanovo nám 72; ⊙ 9am-7pm Mon-Fri & 9am-3pm Sat & Sun Apr-Sep, 8.30am-6pm Mon-Fri & 9am-2pm Sat Oct-Mar) Books accommodation and provides transport information and internet access (1Kč per minute).

Sights

Smetanovo náměstí, the town's main square, is a slender procession of arcades and burghers' houses with baroque and Neoclassical façades. At No 110 is the 16th-century **Knight's House** (U rytířů) festooned with vigorously detailed carvings of knights and merchants and now housing an art gallery. Northeast of the main

square is the **chateau** (zámek; ☎ 464 615 067; www .litomysl.cz/zamek; ⊙ 9am-noon & 1-5pm Tue-Sun May-Aug, 9am-noon & 1-4pm Tue-Sun Sep, 9am-noon & 1-4pm Sat & Sun Apr & Oct), built by the Pernštejns in the 16th century and added to Unesco's World Heritage List in 1999. Additional baroque features were grafted onto the original Renaissance sgraffito arcade style in the 18th century. The 50-minute **Tour 1** (adult/concession 80/40Kč) takes in the ostentatious state rooms and the **18th-century theatre** where local boy Smetana made his piano debut, and **Tour 2** (adult/concession 80/40Kč), also 50 minutes, includes the chateau's **chapel** and the banqueting rooms. If you don't want a guided tour, visit the pretty castle **gardens** (admission free; ⊙ 5am-10pm Mon-Sat, 8am-8pm Sun). Bedřich Smetana was born in the former **castle brewery** (adult/concession 20/10Kcv; ⊙ same as castle), in the grounds, and the building now hosts a modest **museum** about the life of the composer of the nationalist epic *Má vlast* (My Country).

Southeast of the castle, in a nondescript bungalow in a quiet residential lane, is the wondrous **Portmoneum** (Terézy Novákové 75; adult/concession 30/20Kč; ⊙ 9am-noon & 1-5pm Tue-Sun May-Oct) where the walls, ceilings and furniture are covered in the hyper-real paintings of the idiosyncratic Josef Váchal. Váchal completed the paintings from 1920 to 1924 for the owner of the house, Josef Portman, and the proto-psychedelic images blend Christian iconography and Hindu inscriptions with a deliciously ghoulish bent. It's all wonderfully weird like some forgotten album cover from an obscure 1960s rock band.

Sleeping

Restaurace & Penzion Pod Klášterem (☎ 461 615 901; www.podklasterem.cz; B Němcové 158; d/apt incl breakfast 1040K/1440Kč; P) Sunny rooms and a spacious apartment are tucked away in a quiet garden underneath the castle ramparts. The restaurant translates Moravian tastes with Italian flair.

Pension Petra (☎ 461 613 061; www.pension-petra .cz; B Němcové 166; d incl breakfast 1000Kč; P ⊠ 🖳) In a newly restored heritage building, lots of potted plants and a strict nonsmoking policy earns this place two green thumbs up.

Hotel Zlatá Hvězda (☎ 461 614 834; www.zlatah vezda.cz; Smetanovo nám 84; s/d incl breakfast 1200/1800Kč; P ⊠ 🖳) Litomyšl's poshest hotel began life as a 14th-century brewery. In the foyer there are signed photographs of all the Central European bigwigs who stayed there in 1994. No doubt they liked a drink or two as well.

Eating & Drinking

Pizzeria Bella Napoli (☎ 461 612 767; Smetanovo nám 91; ✽ 11am-2pm & 5-11pm Mon-Fri) Try not to be lured in by the garlicky aromas wafting across the main square.

Pekarsti (Smetanovo nám 73; ✽ 7am-6pm Mon-Fri, 8am-noon Sat) Tasty baked goodies with the tourist information office on one side and a fruit shop on the other.

Buddy Bar (☎ 461 616 789; Smetanovo nám 73; ✽ 2pm-2am Mon-Fri, 6pm-2am Sat, 6pm-midnight Sun) This nautically themed bar rocks to well after midnight most nights. Don't go overboard though.

Getting There & Away

Buses are the best way to get to Litomyšl as the train station lies on a quiet secondary line. From Hradec Králové, there are around 20 buses a day (54Kč, one hour). Heading east to Moravia, regular buses run to Olomouc (90Kč, two hours, eight daily), and Brno (80Kč, 1½ hours, 12 daily). If you insist on arriving by train you'll need to change at Choceň, (34Kč, one hour).

ČESKÝ RÁJ

Spectacular landscapes dotted with the ruins of audaciously located castles make this maze of sandstone 'rock towns' and basalt volcanic fingers a rugged contrast to the prettified backdrops found elsewhere in Bohemia. Walking trails weave through the bizarre landscape as Český ráj ascends gently to morph into the foothills of the Krkonoše mountains. During the Czech National Revival, poets, sculptors and painters were inspired by the compelling panoramas, and today the collages of weirdly shaped sandstone and basalt attracts hikers and climbers. Summer (June to August) gets exceptionally busy so try and do the smart thing and visit in spring (April to May) or autumn (September to October).

The towns of Turnov and Jičín are the most convenient bases for exploring Český ráj. With a grand 17th-century square and some good restaurants Jičín is the more interesting and appealing. The towns are linked by road and rail and there's a lot to see and do in their respective old town centres.

A small part (92 sq km) was designated the Bohemian Paradise Protected Landscape Region in 1955, though 'Český ráj' is used loosely for a much wider area.

Information

The tourist offices in Jičín and Turnov stock maps and can book accommodation. Also check out www.cesky-raj.info for more local info.

SHOCart has a large-scale map of *Jizerské Hory a Český ráj* (1:100,000, sheet No 203) as well as the more detailed *Český ráj Mladobole-slavsko* (1:50,000, sheet No 21). The best map for cyclists is SHOCart Active's *Český ráj – Veľ ká Cykloturistická* (1:50,000, sheet No 112). The best map for the Prachovské skalý formations is Geodézie ČS' *Plán města Jičín – Prachovské skalý* (1:7000), which looks like a cheap leaflet (but isn't). There's also a 1:10,000 map of *Prachovské skály* (Prachov Rocks) by Kartografie Praha.

Walks

A good, short option is to take a bus from Jičín to the Prachovské skály rock formations, where there are easily enough walking trails to occupy a morning or afternoon.

Option two is to take a train from Jičín or Turnov to Hrubá skála and see Trosky castle, the Hruboskálské skalní město rock formations and Valdštejn castle (13km total) before returning on a train via Turnov Město.

The most direct (red) trail from Jičín to Turnov is about 32km, possible in one long day for fit hikers. If you've got the gear, it's worth planning a leisurely two or three day expedition, camping en route.

Bikes can be hired for around 300/1200Kč per day/week.

Climbing

The sandstone formations at Prachovské skály are renowned through Europe for rock climbing. Your best source of local information is Hudy Sport in Jičín (p258) which hires all necessary gear including harnesses, karabiners, ropes and helmets. It can also provide information including weather reports, location recommendations and local climbing regulations. Ask for David Hanak who has climbed all across the Czech Republic. If he's not at the shop, there is almost always someone else who speaks good English that will be able to help.

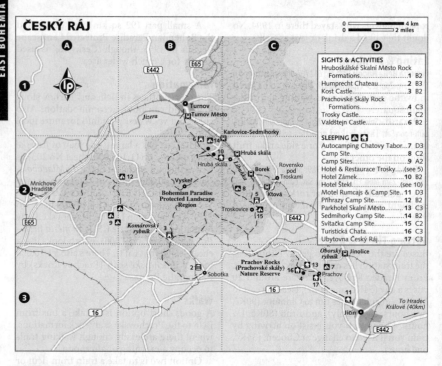

ČESKÝ RÁJ

SIGHTS & ACTIVITIES
Hruboskálské Skalní Město Rock
Formations............................1 B2
Humprecht Chateau..................2 B3
Kost Castle...............................3 B2
Prachovské Skály Rock
Formations............................4 C3
Trosky Castle............................5 C2
Valdštejn Castle........................6 B2

SLEEPING
Autocamping Chatovy Tabor.......7 D3
Camp Site.................................8 C2
Camp Sites...............................9 A2
Hotel & Restaurace Trosky.....(see 5)
Hotel Zámek...........................10 B2
Hotel Štekl..........................(see 10)
Motel Rumcajs & Camp Site...11 D3
Přihrazy Camp Site..................12 B2
Parkhotel Skalní Město...........13 C3
Sedmihorky Camp Site............14 B2
Svítačka Camp Site.................15 C2
Turistická Chata......................16 C3
Ubytovna Český Ráj................17 C3

Getting There & Away

During the day, trains run from Hradec Králové to Jičín (76Kč, one hour) and Turnov (110Kč, two hours) every hour or two. Buses also make the run from Hradec Králové to Jičín (50Kč, one hour) and Turnov (70Kč, 1¾ hours). From Prague it's an easy 1½ hours to Jičín (84Kč).

A local train chugs between Turnov and Jičín (40Kč, 45 minutes) about every two hours, and local buses service all the villages that aren't near the railway line.

Getting Around

From Turnov, a tourist bus travels six routes through Český ráj. Routings are available from tourist information offices or are published in the annual Český ráj newspaper (12Kč), which is available at tourist information offices.

PRACHOVSKÉ SKÁLY

This is the biggest skalní město (rock town) – a labyrinth of sandstone pinnacles, caves and passages – in Český ráj. The rocks are accessible (admission 30Kč) via colour-coded hik-

ing trails from two points on the minor road beyond Motel Rumcajs: Ubytovna Český ráj (red trail) and the Turistická chata (green, yellow and red trails). All three trails meet up. A full loop on the green trail is about 5km (up to two hours) and covers the main sights.

Sleeping & Eating

Accommodation here is overrun in summer, when you're better off booking ahead from Jičín.

Autocamping Chatovy Tabor (☎ 493 591 929; tent per person 60Kč; ⌚ Jun-Sep) This camp site is just southwest of Jinolice.

Ubytovna Český ráj (☎ 493 524 626; per person 150Kč; P) Hostel veterans will feel right at home in this simple place.

Turistická chata (☎ 493 524 641; per person 220Kč; ⌚ mid-Apr–Sep; P) More substantial, this place has chocolate-box charm and a popular restaurant.

Parkhotel Skalní město (☎ 493 525 011; www.skalni mesto.cz; s/d incl breakfast 800/1360Kč; P) Pleasantly upmarket (but not too much), this place has well-tended lawns and comfortable rooms.

Getting There & Away

From Turnov, there is a tourist bus which runs six routes through Český ráj. Routes are available from tourist information offices or are published in the annual *Český ráj* newspaper (12Kč), available at tourist information offices.

From Jičín, local buses also run right past these places about every two hours; stops are labelled 'Holín (Prachov skalní město)' to the Parkhotel or 'Holín (Turistická chata)' to the Turisticka chata. Or you could walk it, a relatively easy 8km hike from Rumcajs Motel at Jičín.

HRUBÁ SKÁLA & AROUND

Another 'rock town', Hruboskálské skalní město is a dull uphill hike from the Hrubá skála train station; turn right across the tracks and follow the blue trail 3km to the Hotel Štekl car park. From here, take the red trail southeast to **Trosky castle** (6.5km) or northwest to **Hruboskálské skalní město** (1.5km) and Valdštejn castle (another 1.5km).

Valdštejn castle (www.hrad-valdstejn.cz; adult/concession 30/10Kč; 9am- 4.30pm Tue-Sun May-Sep, until 4pm Sat & Sun Apr & Oct), dating from the 13th century, was used variously by Hussite rebels, bandits and Albrecht of Wallenstein (Valdštejn; see p205) and has now been renovated.

Sleeping

Sedmihorky camp site (481 391 162; www.campsedmihorky.cz; tent per person 100Kč; P) A 1.5km hike from the Karlovice-Sedmihorky train stop, this pretty spot has a pond with a little beach. Open all year round.

Guarding the trail heads are two year-round hotels:

Hotel Zámek (481 389 681; www.hrubaskala.cz, in Czech; s/d incl breakfast 700/820Kč; P) Here's your chance to stay in a romantic cliff-top castle. And if you're doing that you may as well stay in one of their 'luxury' rooms (s/d 1420/1960Kč).

Hotel Štekl (481 389 684; www.hotel-stekl.cz; s/d incl breakfast 680/900Kč; P) In the style of an Italian villa, the Štekl is a reliable backup just minutes from the trail.

Getting There & Away

From Turnov there is a tourist bus which runs six routes through Český ráj. Routings are available from tourist information offices or are published in the annual *Český ráj* newspaper (12Kč), available at tourist information offices.

By train, the most convenient access to Hruboskálské skalní město is from the stations at Hrubá skála or Turnov Město (red trail; 5.5km). Express trains do not stop at either station, but at least 10 daily local trains serve Turnov–Jičín and Turnov–Hradec Králové (via Jičín).

KOST CASTLE

Lying 15km west of Jičín, **Kost castle** (493 571 144; www.kinsky-dal-borgo.cz; adult/concession 150/70Kč; 9am-6pm Jul & Aug, 9am-4.30pm Tue-Sun May, Jun & Sep, 9am-3.30pm Sat & Sun Apr & Oct) is on a minor road a few kilometres from the village of Sobotka. Dramatically situated atop a crag overlooking a tranquil pond, Kost is one of the best preserved Gothic castles in Bohemia. A four-person apartment can be booked through the castle's website (June to September 2000Kč, and October to March 1500Kč).

Kost castle can also be reached via a 6.5km hike on a red trail from Sobotka, or a 10km red or green trail from Hruba skála.

TROSKY CASTLE

Like a pair of extinguished cigar butts, the crooked towers of **Trosky castle** (www.trosky.cz, in Czech & German; adult/concession 40/25Kč; 8.30am-6pm Tue-Sun May-Aug, until 4pm Tue-Sun Sep, until 4pm Sat-Sun Apr & Oct) teeter on twin basalt towers, setting the scene for one of the most dramatic ruins in the country. Built around 1380 by Honoratus of Vartenburg, the strategically placed castle has changed hands frequently over the centuries; in addition to its many lawful owners was a gang of 15th-century robbers who terrorised the countryside for several years.

The higher tower is called Panna (the Maiden) and the other is Bába (the Granny). Panna and some lower walls were restored in the early 1990s and the views, from 514m above sea level, are awesome whether you are looking up at the castle from the main road, or down across the plains from the towers themselves.

At the foot of the towers is the sprawling **Hotel & Restaurace Trosky** (481 382 290; www.hoteltrosky.cz; s/d 405/810Kč; P). Alternatively, follow the green trail 1km south to the very basic **Svitačka camp site** (per person 60Kč).

Getting There & Away

The odd bus from Turnov stops below the hotel, from where it's 500m up to the castle. Better alternatives for walkers are local trains (not express) to Ktová plus a 2km hike up the green trail, or to Borek plus a 4km walk up a blue trail. It's also possible to walk from Hruboskálské skalní město.

JIČÍN

With a pretty main square, leading to a bustling main drag, Jičín is the best base for exploring Český ráj. The Hapsburg warlord Wallenstein (Valdštejn; see p205) was a big fan and made it the centre of his personal duchy of Friedland, transforming the old castle into his flash abode from 1625 to 1633, and even building a mint to make the town's own coins.

Orientation

Husova, the pedestrianised main street, is a block north of the bus station, or 700m north of the train station. Head west along it towards Žižkovo nám and continue beneath the red-topped gate tower into the main square, Valdštejnovo nám. Both of the squares and much of Husova have been pedestrianised.

Information

The useful **tourist information centre** (městské informačni centrum; ☎ 493 534 390; www.jicin.org; Valdštejnovo nám; ☿ 9am-5pm Mon-Sat, 9am-6pm Sun Jun-Sep, 9am-5pm Mon-Fri, 9am-1pm Sat Oct-May) sells hiking maps, books accommodation and has transport schedules. It also rents bikes for 275/1100Kč per day/week.

Hudy Sport (☎ 493 535 985; jicin@hudy.cz; Husova 59; ☿ 8.30am-5.30pm Mon-Fri, 8.30am-noon Sat) An outdoor activities shop that provides information about local rock climbing. Climbing gear is also available for hire.

Jičín Café Internet (1st fl, Husova 1058; per min 1Kč; ☿ 10am-9pm) East of the main square.

KB (Valdštejnovo nám) Adjacent to the tourist information centre. Has an ATM and exchange counter.

Post office (Šafaříkova 142) East of the main square.

Sights

You can enjoy a bird's-eye view of town from the Gothic **Valdická gate** (Valdštejnovo nám; adult/concession 15/10Kč; ☿ 9am-5pm Jun-Aug, 2-5pm Tue-Sun Apr, May & Sep). You enter the square past the unsteepled Jesuit **St James church** (kostel sv Jakuba), which has a Renaissance façade and a baroque interior.

The square and its Renaissance façades are dominated by the chateau built by Wallenstein's Italian architects. A rather uninspiring

regional museum (okresní muzeum; ☎ 493 532 204; www.mujicin.cz; adult/concession 60/30Kč; ☿ 9am-5pm Tue-Sun) fills eight halls of the chateau, with archaeology, local history and art exhibits.

A block west of the square is the big, crumbling Gothic **St Ignatius church** (kostel sv Ignác).

Sleeping

Motel Rumcajs (☎ 493 531 400; Koněvova 331; tent/hut per person 60/280Kč; motel room s/d 260/435Kč; ℗) About 1.5km northwest on the Sobotka road, this camp site also has a restaurant, bungalows and motel rooms.

Penzion Lucie (☎ 493 531 192; www.penzion-lucie .cz; Fugnerova 197; s/d incl breakfast 600/900Kč, apt 1500Kč; ℗ 🐾) Another new(ish) opening is this spic-and-span *pension* on a quiet street just off Husova. Downstairs is a sleekly modern restaurant with not a stuffed animal in sight, and there's even a swimming pool in the back garden.

Hotel Rieger (☎ 493 533 752; http://hotelrieger.top web.cz; Nám Komenského 34; s/d incl breakfast 990/1290Kč; ℗) This newly opened partner hotel to the Hotel Jičín has cosy rooms and a funky bar-pizzeria downstairs. You even get to experience the country's best breakfast buffet in the dining room at the Hotel Jičín.

Hotel Jičín (☎ 493 544 250; www.hoteljicin.cz; Havlíčkova 21; s/d incl breakfast 1100/1450Kč; ℗) With a high-profile corner address, Jičín's best hotel doesn't disappoint with comfortable rooms and delicious breakfasts.

Eating & Drinking

Divá Bara (☎ 493 524 887; Husova 39; mains 100-200Kč) The trendy bricks and stainless steel décor combine with sports on the big screen and steaks on the big plates. Jičín's younger crowd laps it up. We can personally recommend Divá Bara as a top spot to watch the ice-hockey playoffs.

Harmonie (☎ 771 651 916; Chelčikého 39; salads 80-160Kč) Specialising in salads, this light and bright wine bar provides a healthy balance to the meaty Bohemian dishes served elsewhere in town.

Osmička (☎ 606 113 388; Chelčikého 8; ☿ 9am-midnight, to 2am Sat, from 1pm Sun) Jičín's trendies line up for coffee, cake and cocktails in a surprisingly sophisticated, wee spot.

Also recommended:

Asia Dragon (cnr Palackého & Židovská; mains 60Kč) For cheap, Asian eats.

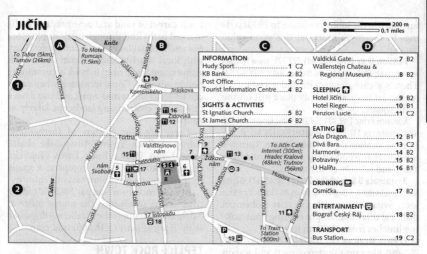

JIČÍN

INFORMATION					
Hudy Sport	1 C2		Valdická Gate	7 B2
KB Bank	2 B2		Wallenstejn Chateau &	
Post Office	3 C2		Regional Museum	8 B2
Tourist Information Centre	4 B2			
			SLEEPING	
SIGHTS & ACTIVITIES			Hotel Jičín	9 B2
St Ignatius Church	5 B2		Hotel Rieger	10 B1
St James Church	6 B2		Penzion Lucie	11 C2
			EATING	
			Asia Dragon	12 B1
			Divá Bara	13 C2
			Harmonie	14 B2
			Potraviny	15 B2
			U Halířu	16 B1
			DRINKING	
			Osmička	17 B2
			ENTERTAINMENT	
			Biograf Český Ráj	18 B2
			TRANSPORT	
			Bus Station	19 C2

U Halířu (cnr Palackého & Na Příkpech) Takeaway bakery treats.

Potraviny (Valdštejnovo nám 77) Self-catering on the western side of the main square.

Entertainment

Biograf Český ráj (☎ 493 532 823; 17 listopadu 47; tickets 80Kč) English-language (eventually) films make the rounds at this cinema.

Getting There & Away

To get to Jičín from Prague it's best to go by bus (84Kč, 1½ hours). To access the Adršpach-Teplice Rocks there is one bus daily from Jičín to Trutnov (63Kč, one hour) and an extra four Monday to Friday.

TURNOV

Turnov has plenty of cheap lodgings and is a convenient, if dull, Český ráj gateway. A reason for visiting is the town's heritage as the centre of garnet (granát) mining in East Bohemia.

Orientation

The town square is Nám Českého ráje. The train station is about 1km west, across the river on Nádražní. Regional buses (to/from Jičín, for example) stop at the big bus station by the river; Prague and other long-distance buses deposit you by the train station.

Information

ČSOB (Nám Českého ráje) Has an exchange desk.

Information centre (☎ 481 366 256; info@turnov.cz; Nám Českého ráje; ⏲ 8am-6pm Mon-Fri, until 4pm Sat,

until 2pm Sun Jul & Aug, until 5pm Mon-Fri, until noon Sat Sep-Jun) Stocks hiking maps and books local and regional accommodation. It also has a couple of internet terminals (1Kč per minute).

KB (Palackého 192) Has an ATM.

Main post office (Skálova) Just off the main square.

Sights

In the major tourist areas of the Czech Republic you'll see Granát Turnov stores selling jewellery that uses Bohemian garnets. This cooperative is the only company authorised to extract garnets from two remaining mines in Bohemia, and it supplies other retailers in the Czech Republic. Be aware, however, that some garnets for sale are actually from Germany or Poland, so ask for a certificate of authenticity to ensure you're buying authentic Bohemian garnets. In Turnov you can visit the **Gallery Granát** (☎ 481 325 989; www. granat.cz; Nám Českého ráje 137; admission free; ⏲ 9am-5pm Tue-Fri, to noon Sat) for examples of jewellery incorporating the semiprecious stone dating back to the 18th century. In town are four Granát Turnov stores, and you can secure good discounts at the factory shop on nám Českého. Turnov is also a good place to buy unset stones if you have a favourite jewellery designer back home.

Sleeping & Eating

The information centre can help with private rooms and other cheap places.

Hotel Alfa (☎ 481 320 078; www.sweb.cz/alfahotel; Palackého 211; s/d incl breakfast 350/700Kč) The 1960s furniture in the lobby graduates to 1970s stylings in the so-so rooms at this good-value backup.

Pension U sv Jana (☎ 481 323 325; www.svatyjan .euroregin.cz; Hluboká 142; s/d incl breakfast 700/1000Kč) There's a café downstairs and a restaurant on the 1st floor at this tidy place just off the main square.

Korunní Princ (☎ 481 324 212; www.korunniprinc.cz; Nám Českého ráje 137; s/d incl breakfast 920/1240Kč; **P**) In a prime location on the main square, Turnov's top hotel has a good Italian restaurant downstairs and reliably comfy rooms.

Restaurace U Belgického Dvora (☎ 481 321 357; cnr Nám Českého ráje & A Dvořákova; mains 70-130Kč) Try the local Svijany beer with the tasty Bohemian dishes at this popular spot offering nonsmoking lunches from 11.30am to 1pm.

El Paso Mexican (☎ 604 284 147; Markova; mains 90-160Kč) Elvis on the stereo, cacti and wagon wheels add up to relatively authentic eating south of the (Polish) border.

Pizzeria Korunní Princ (☎ 481 324 212; Nám Českého ráje 137; pizza 100Kč) Quirky bric-a-brac and tasty food lifts the Korunní Princ to *numéro uno* in Turnov's pizza stakes.

Getting There & Away

There are direct trains to/from Prague (130Kč, two hours) and around 10 buses (88Kč, 1¾ hours).

From Turnov, there is also a tourist bus which runs six routes through Český ráj. Routings are available from tourist information offices or are published in the annual *Český ráj* newspaper (12Kč), available at tourist information offices.

ADRŠPACH-TEPLICE ROCKS

The 'rock towns' of Český ráj may be more well-known, but the country's most rugged and dramatic formations are the Adršpach-Teplice Rocks (Adršpašsko-Teplické skály), hidden away in the Broumov highlands (Broumovská vrchovina), a protrusion of East Bohemia that juts into Poland.

Situated tantalising close to the main road, within minutes you can hike into concealed natural cloisters, ringed by spectacular sandstone rocks with imaginative monikers like 'Giant's Armchair' and 'Sugar Cone', amid

a soft carpet of sand and pine needles. Well-marked paths lead through luscious pine forests and spectacular valleys. Summer gets busy with local tourists and German and Polish visitors, and you'll need to book accommodation in advance. Come in winter, when snow can linger as late as mid-April, and you'll have this crazily entertaining landscape largely to yourself.

There are two clusters of formations: Adršpach Rock Town (Adršpašské skalní město) and Teplice Rock Town (Teplické skalní město). They now comprise a single state nature reserve, 15km east of Trutnov.

At each 'rock town' you pay 50/20Kč (adult/concession) admission. The tourist office at Adršpach can supply the excellent *Adršpašské skály Teplické skály* (1:16,000) trail map.

TEPLICE ROCK TOWN

About 200m west of the Teplice nad Metují-Skály train station is a car park and the Hotel Orlík. From here a blue-marked trail climbs the valley of the **Skalní potok** (Rocky stream), making a 7km loop through some of the more impressive formations.

About 1km along, those not subject to vertigo or shortness of breath can detour by stairs and ladders to the **Střmen castle ruins**. This and neighbouring formations were the site of a 13th-century wooden castle, destroyed in 1447 when the Hussites hiding in it were defeated.

Two scenic trails continue along the valley floor to Teplice Rock Town. Here you can follow walkways through narrow rock clefts, to the cool, ferny **Sibiř gorge** (Siberia gorge).

From the blue loop trail's west end, follow the green then another blue trail 4km to a yellow trail, which meanders 3km north up **Wolf gorge** (Vlčí rokle) to connect with Adršpach. A yellow trail that starts just before Střmen and continues 4km north up Wolf Gorge is much shorter.

Sleeping & Eating

Hotel Orlík (☎ 491 581 025; www.orlik.hotel-cz.com; s/d incl breakfast 500/1000Kč; **P**) Very popular, especially at the weekends, the Orlik is a good place to recharge and relax. The bar is a popular social hub for locals

Pension Skály (☎ 491 581 174; www.adrspach-skaly .cz; Střmenské Podhradí 132; s/d incl breakfast 500/1000Kč; **P** **X**) This new *pension* has a cosy restaurant and bar and even cosier rooms for post-hike relaxation.

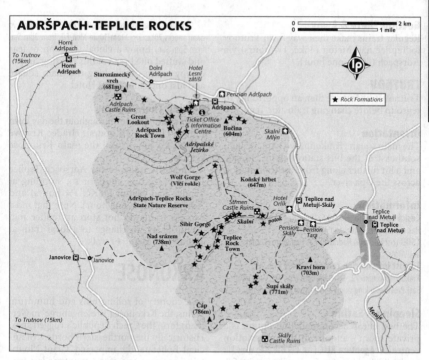

ADRŠPACH-TEPLICE ROCKS

Pension Tara (☎ 491 581 122; s/d 500/1000Kč; **P**)
With alpine looks, well-kept lawns and a rustic bridge, this traditional place has a quieter and wilder riverside setting.

Skalní Mlýn (☎ 491 586 961; www.skalni-mlyn.cz; s/d incl breakfast 580/1060Kč, apt 2160Kč; **P**) In a quiet setting between Teplice nad Metují-Skály and Adršpach, the rustic rooms and friendly dogs make this restored river mill a special place to stay if you have your own transport. There's also a four-bed log cabin available from July to October (600Kč per person) and the excellent restaurant is recommended all year round.

ADRŠPACH ROCK TOWN

These rock formations are easiest to reach from Adršpach train station.

The green trail makes a 2.5km loop past the Czech Republic's tallest sandstone towers, a duet of rushing waterfalls and **Adršpašské jezírko**, a tiny lake concealed in a compact canyon.

The green trail also takes in the **Great lookout** (Velké panorama), where you can admire the rolling sea of pinnacles escalating above the pines before threading through the **Mouse hole** (Myší dírá), a barely shoulder-width vertical fissure.

You can make a good cross-country hike south on the yellow trail (via Wolf Gorge) to the Teplice nad Metují-Skály train station.

There is a small **information office** (☎ 491 586 012; www.skalyadrspach.cz; ☒ 8.30am-6pm Apr-Oct) by the Adršpach train station.

Sleeping & Eating
Both these places offer good discounts for stays of more than one night.

Penzion Adršpach (☎ 491 586 102; www.adrspach -skaly.cz; s/d incl breakfast 500/1000Kč; **P**) Situated 300m from Adršpach on the road to Teplice, this modern place discreetly overcomes a lack of old world charm with comfortable rooms, an excellent restaurant and a friendly Border collie.

Hotel Lesní zátiší (☎ 491 586 202; s/d incl breakfast 550/1100Kč; **P**) The rock trail conveniently begins just outside, but the good-sized rooms are in some need of sprucing up. However, the restaurant's a busy hikers' hub come lunchtime and you just can't beat the location.

EAST BOHEMIA

Getting There & Away

Regular trains make their way from Trutnov to Teplice nad Metují (46kč, 1¼ hours) via Adršpach (40Kč, one hour).

TRUTNOV

Trutnov is little more than an opportunity to regroup before changing trains for Teplice.

Orientation

The main square, Krakonošovo nám, is 500m southeast of the bus station along Horská, and a bit further along from the train station across the Úpa river.

Information

Česká Spořitelna (Horská 5) Opposite the bus station. Has exchange counters and ATMs.

ČSOB (cnr Horská & Nádražní) Has exchange counters and ATMs.

Tourist information centre (☎ 499 818 245; Krakonošovo nám 72; ☺ 9am-6pm Mon-Fri, 9am-noon Sat) Provides hiking maps and a list of private rooms.

Sleeping & Eating

The best cheap accommodation option is a private room – inquire at the information centre or **Agentura KLÍČ** (☎ 499 818 308; www.klictravel.cz; Halíčkova 7; ☺ 9am-5pm Mon-Thu, 9am-3pm Fri). Otherwise, hotels are quite expensive. Rates increase around 15% during the ski season.

Hotel Krakanos (☎ 499 819 190; www.hotel-krakanos.cz; Barvířská 41; s/d 650/1000Kč; **P**) Newly renovated, this heritage hotel has friendly staff and comfortable rooms. The beer garden is Trutnov's best place to try the local Krakanos beer.

Penzion Pohada (☎ 499 815 025; www.penzionpohoda.com; Horská 7; s/d 1000/1400Kč, apt 1600/2000Kč) Another recent renovation, the Pohada has bright wood-floored rooms and spacious, family-friendly apartments on a quiet pedestrian mall.

Hotel Adam (☎ 499 811 955; Halíčkova 7; s/d incl breakfast 1050/1550Kč) A nicely baroque foyer sets the scene and the rooms don't disappoint in this friendly place that offers weekend discounts of up to 30%.

Pizzeria Santa Maria (Na vrchu; pizza 85Kč) Checked tablecloths and summery colours produce a touch of the Med in this gateway to the mountains.

Restaurant Grill (☎ 499 810 470; Krakonošovo nám 72; mains 80-170Kč) Big coffees and even bigger ice creams go down well on the summer terrace. In less perfect weather there's warm as toast open grills for meaty platters.

Cajovna u Zeleneho' (☎ 603 779 234; Krakonošovo nám; snacks 70Kč; ☺ 11am-10pm Mon-Fri, from 2pm Sat, from 5pm Sun) Enjoy a global selection of teas and stuffed pita bread at this relaxing hippy-drippy haven overlooking the main square and just opposite Grand Hotel.

Getting There & Away

Buses run to Trutnov throughout the day from Prague (131Kč, 2¾ hours), Hradec Králové (50Kč, 1¼ hours) and the main Krkonoše centres.

There are trains to the Adršpach-Teplice Rocks every two hours or so, stopping at Teplice nad Metují (46Kč, 1¼ hours) and Adršpach (40Kč, one hour). Note that most express trains do not stop at Teplice nad Metují-Skály, so change to a local train at Teplice nad Metují or walk.

KRKONOŠE

In a country of rolling hills and humdrum plains, the Krkonoše ('Riesengebirge' in German) form the Czech Republic's rugged apex. Historically the northeastern borders of ancient Bohemia, the imposing 'Giant Mountains' are now one of the country's last true wilderness areas. Looming above the Polish frontier, and swathed in spruce forests amid undulating valleys, this rugged hinterland is surprisingly easy to get to and enjoy.

With a growing reputation for more affordable winter sports than other parts of Europe, the mountains are now studded with resorts and easily reached by good roads and bus services. Even the 1602m summit of Sněžka, the Czech Republic's highest peak, can be accessed via a leisurely chairlift. In the area's resorts there's everything from the bustling, wannabe atmosphere of Špindlerův Mlýn to the more rustic simplicity of Pec pod Sněžkou.

And if sitting in a chairlift is too passive, there's superb hiking away from the towns and villages. Once the snow melts, the region's vistas can be shrouded in a cape of mist and drizzle, but it's worth persevering to discover the hidden valleys amid the dense woods and lofty summits.

Orientation

Most 'villages' in the park are functional resorts with innumerable places to sleep and

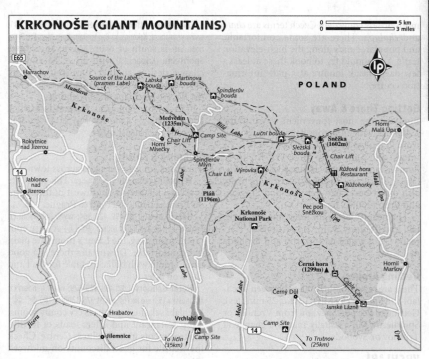

KRKONOŠE (GIANT MOUNTAINS)

eat. The main centres are Harrachov for skiing and Špindlerův Mlýn and Pec pod Sněžkou for walking.

Vrchlabí is sometimes referred to as the park's 'gateway', but in fact the bigger resort centres inside the park have better information, a wider range of accommodation and restaurants, and it's easy to reach many of them directly from Prague and Hradec Králové.

Information

National park information centres in the main towns have brochures, maps and accommodation advice. For up-to-date trail and weather information, go to the nearest Mountain Rescue Service (Horská služba) in Špindlerův Mlýn or Pec pod Sněžkou.

Kartografie Praha has a *Krkonoše* (1:50,000) map with details of the main centres and colour-coded hiking trails. There is also a two-part, 1:25,000 map.

Activities

There are walking trails galore, including the red-marked **Czech-Polish friendship trail** (Cesta česko-polského přátelství) along the border ridge. Couch potatoes, and travellers with children, can get up into the high country year-round via chairlifts at Pec pod Sněžkou (to the summit of Sněžka) and Špindlerův Mlýn, and via a cable car at Janské Lázně.

Link roads, some with limited (or no) public motor access, are a treat for cycling enthusiasts. And of course there's skiing in winter. It's possible to rent ski equipment at Harrachov, Vrchlabí, Špindlerův Mlýn and Pec pod Sněžkou. In high season a day's ski pass costs from 550Kč to 750Kč.

Sleeping

There are literally hundreds of hotels and chalets in the park. The hotels tend to be full year-round, but in the summer many chalets at lower elevations are used for *pension* or private accommodation. For two people, figure on about 800Kč and up, with breakfast, but prices can skyrocket in ski season – quoted prices are for the cheaper summer season.

The local word for a mountain hut, chalet or hotel is *bouda* ('b' on maps), a term originally used for shepherds' huts. Other more-or-less equivalent Czech terms are *chata* and *chalupa*. There are some comfortable, and popular, *boudy* along the high-elevation trails. You should try to book these at least a few days ahead; inquire at a park information centre.

Getting There & Away

Buses are the most convenient way into the Krkonoše, with numerous daily direct services from Prague to Pec pod Sněžkou (155Kč, 3½ hours) and Špindlerův Mlýn (137Kč, three hours), and others via Hradec Králové, Vrchlabí and Trutnov. In the ski season there are also direct buses between Pec pod Sněžkou and Brno (230Kč, five hours).

The nearest fast-train junctions are Vrchlabí and Trutnov, with connections to Harrachov, Rokytnice nad Jizerou and Svoboda nad Úpou.

Getting Around

There are regular hourly buses between Vrchlabí and Špindlerův Mlýn (21Kč, 25 minutes). Getting to Pec pod Sněžkou from Vrchlabí or Špindlerův Mlýn usually means a change at Trutnov or Svoboda.

VRCHLABÍ

Although billed as the gateway to the peaks, Vrchlabí actually feels a long way from the wilds. Despite an unsightly suburban sprawl, it's an okay place to get organised and you will probably have to make a transport connection here at some point.

Orientation & Information

The town straggles inconveniently along the Labe for several kilometres. From the adjacent bus and train stations it's 1.5km north (cross the river and take the second right on Slovanská, which becomes Krkonošská) to the town centre at Nám Masaryka. Nám Míru, overlooked by a church tower, is a further 200m north.

WARNING

Despite the relatively modest elevations, it's usually windy and extremely cold year-round at the higher elevations. Even in summer, mountain fog creates a hypothermia risk (see p467 for details). Don't go up without the appropriate gear.

The **town information centre** (☎ 499 451 111; www.vrchlabi.cz; Krkonošská 8; ☉ 9am-6pm Mon-Fri, 9am-noon Sat) is south of Nám Masaryka; a **Česká Spořitelna** (Krkonošská) with an ATM and exchange desk is another 30m south. A **park information centre** (☎ 499 421 474; Nám Míru; ☉ 9am-4pm Mon-Sat) has maps and brochures.

Check your email at **Internet Café** (1st fl, Krkonošská 182; ☉ 10am-11pm Mon-Sat, 1-11pm Sun), opposite the tourist office.

Sleeping & Eating

There are *Zimmer frei* signs across town.

Vejsplachy camp site (☉ Jun-Sep) This camp site is several kilometres southwest of the centre on Pražská třída, the road to Prague.

Hotel Labut (☎ 499 421 964; www.hotellabut.cz; Krkonošská 188; s/d 870/1160Kč; P ☐) A cosy spot on the main drag, the Labut's rooms are plain but comfortable. Downstairs there is a good games room with billiards, table football and chess on offer.

Hotel Gendorf (☎ 499 429 629; www.gendorf.cz; Krkonošská 153; s/d incl breakfast 975/1300Kč; P ☒ ☒) Vrchlabí's flashest spot has very comfy rooms, a top restaurant and offers loads of fortifying treatments in its Wellness Centre. Check the website for good discounts on midweek rates.

Klasika (☎ 499 421 260; Nám Masaryka; pizza 90Kč, s/d 500/1000Kč) This atmospheric Italian spot has a huge terrace for beer and wood-fired pizza, and will arrange good-value rooms for when you need a lie down after eating and drinking too much.

Getting There & Away

Vrchlabí is connected by regular buses to Prague (118Kč, 2½ hours) and Hradec Králové (68Kč, 1½ hours). Buses run frequently all day to Špindlerův Mlýn (21Kč, 25 minutes) and (usually indirectly) to Pec pod Sněžkou (41Kč, one hour).

ŠPINDLERŮV MLÝN

With the highest hotel density of just about anywhere in the country, Špindlerův Mlýn has more in common with a theme park than a functioning town. Views tend to be of high-rise hotels rather than mountain peaks, but there are countless accommodation options and come winter this becomes the largest recreation centre in the region: forget about the vistas and get out on the slopes. Traditionally the resort has been only about winter activities, but a range of outdoor fun not needing snow is now growing in popularity.

Orientation & Information

From the bus stop, the **Mountain Rescue Service** (Horská služba; ☎ 499 433 230; Svatopetrska) is 500m east, after a right turn at the post office.

There are dozens of information offices. **Infocentrum** (☎ 499 433 148; www.spindleruv-mlyn.cz; Predni Labska 47; ⏰ 8am-7pm) is 200m north of the bus stop and can help with accommodation. A second, private **Information Centre** (☎ 499 433 407; www.spindl.com; Svatopetrska 297; ⏰ 9am-6pm) is just before the mountain-rescue office and has internet access. Both can advise on skiing, cycling and other activities.

Sights & Activities

A **chairlift** runs northwest to the top of Medvědín (1235m) for 100/130Kč one way/return, and another runs south up Pláň (1196m).

You can hike up to the **Labe headwaters** on a blue-marked trail heading north and northwest. At the top of a nasty 200m ascent at the end of the valley is the Labská bouda chalet; the **source of the Labe** (*pramen Labe* on maps) is about 800m further on, along the red trail. Return to Špindlerův Mlýn on the red trail south via Horní Mísečky, or on a green trail east via Martinova bouda, making a round-trip of five or six hours.

In summer you can ride a **bobsled** (☎ 499 433 430; www.bobovka.cz; adult/concession 80/60Kč; ⏰ 10am-8pm Mon-Thu, 10am-10pm Fri-Sun) down the hills above town. **Yellow Point Adventure** (☎ 499 433 505; www.yellow-point.cz; Svatopetrská 278) can arrange everything from abseiling and climbing, to paragliding and all-terrain scootering.

Sleeping & Eating

There are dozens of hotels and *pension*s in and around town – shop around or ask at the information centre.

Autokemp (☎ 499 523 534; tesspindl@quick.cz; tent per person 70Kč; ⏰ year-round; **P**) About 1.5km up the valley road from the bus stop, this camp site is owned by the Krkonoše National Park.

Pension Pohada (☎ 499 523 539; www.pension -pohoda.cz; Svatý Petr 231; s/d incl breakfast 550/1100Kč; **P** 🖥) Run by a friendly family, this *pension* has a spa and sauna. Window boxes and a pine-bedecked restaurant provide just the right amount of alpine appeal after a big day on the slopes.

Penzion Erika (☎ 499 523 247; www.penzionerika.cz; Špindlerův Mlýn 223; s/d 580/1060Kč; **P**) Drag yourself out of your super-comfy rooms to the cosy brick-lined bar and restaurant downstairs at this tidy spot surrounded by nice gardens; not overly alpine but a good choice for a summer, spring or autumn visit.

Eating out is pretty much confined to the hotels and *pension*s, but **Pavilon** (Predni Labska 47), in the same building as Infocentrum, does a decent pizza.

Getting There & Away

There are at least a dozen buses a day to and from Vrchlabí (21Kč, 25 minutes) and Prague (137Kč, three hours).

Getting Around

A bus runs from the Špindlerův Mlýn bus stop up the Labe valley to Špindlerův bouda on the main Krkonoše ridge (1100m). See tourist information for the latest timetable.

PEC POD SNĚŽKOU

Known to its friends as plain old 'Pec', this has some of the best skiing in the Czech Republic and an enviable location beneath the country's highest peak. It's not the Alps, but then you're not paying Alpine prices. In contrast to the Disneyland atmosphere of Špindlerův Mlýn, Pec retains an old-fashioned charm, with many heritage wooden buildings lining its main drag. Get past the communist-era architectural horror show that is the Hotel Horizont, and it's a great alternative to Špindlerův Mlýn.

Orientation & Information

Veselý Výlet (Jolly Jaunt; ☎ 499 736 130; www.veselyvylet .cz; ⏰ 9am-5.30pm), near the bus stop, is a little gallery with excursion ideas, accommodation advice and internet access (1½Kč per minute). It also publishes an excellent free brochure full of regional lore and relevant excursions. A further 30m downhill from the bus stop, there is an information board with a phone that links directly through to various accommodation options. Online see www.skipec .com and www.pecpodsnezkou.cz for more information.

The **national park information centre** (☎ 499 896 213; tespec@quick.cz; ⏰ 8am-4.30pm) is 200m up the hill on the unnamed main street at No 172. A further 400m along is the **Mountain Rescue Service** (Horská služba; ☎ 499 896 233).

There is a KB ATM opposite the Enzian Grill in Pec's main drag.

Sights & Activities

CLIMBING SNĚŽKA

In the 19th century you could get carried up Sněžka (Snow Peak) for six gold coins and 40 Kreutzers. Today, unless you take the chairlift, it is a three-hour climb or a five-hour round-trip. From near the Hotel Horizont, climb the green-marked Čertový schody (Devil's staircase) trail northwest to a chalet at Výrovka, then north up the red ridge trail to Luční bouda chalet.

A blue trail crosses a marshy area east to Slezská bouda on the Polish border, from where you make your assault on the treeless summit of Sněžka. The peak is bang on the border (Poles call it Śnieżka). You must share your triumph, and the grand views, with Czech and Polish guards and an army of tourists who have come up the easy way by chairlift from both sides.

From Sněžka, take the yellow ridge trail south to chalets at Růžohorky, and then descend along a steep green trail back to Pec.

If you can't handle the climb, walk 300m back from the bus stop and about 1.5km up the valley of the Úpa to the chairlift *(lanovka)*, and ride right to the top. The two-stage trip (300Kč return) takes half an hour each way. There's a restaurant halfway up, at Růžová hora.

Sleeping

The hillsides above Pec are thick with chalets, many open to tourists in summer.

Penzion Sněžka (☎ 603 336 764; penzion .snezka@tiscali.cz; s/d incl breakfast 390/780Kč) The cosy rooms atop this pub have globe table lamps so you can plan your next trip. To get there, head 250m downhill from the bus stop and turn left.

Penzion Nikola (☎ 499 736 151; www.nikolapec.cz; s/d incl breakfast 550/1100Kč; P) Overlooking the park information office, Nikola has alpine charm, with carved wood décor and snug rooms.

Eating & Drinking

As in Špindlerův Mlýn, most of Pec's eateries are in the hotels and *pensions*, but the following two are stand-alone options, and all the better for it.

Rag-Time Bar (U Zeleneho Potoka 213) It's official. We've found the Czech Republic's cosiest bar. Grab some ski-buddies and share a 2.5L *mojito* (600Kč) amid antique skis and retro sports shirts. Come for happy hour (7pm to 8pm), and then return after dinner at the Enzian Grill.

Enzian Grill (☎ 499 736 357; U Zeleneho Potoka 209; mains 150-250Kč) With meaty grills, loads of different beers, and a top-notch wine list this spot is surprisingly cosmopolitan given its mountain location. Winter is exceptionally cosy inside, and in summer the lively terrace is the place to be seen in Pec.

Getting There & Away

There are regular buses to Pec from Trutnov (25Kč, 30 minutes), Hradec Králové (78Kč, two hours) and Prague (153Kč, 3½ hours).

North Moravia

To lazily pay heed to the reputation endured by North Moravia, you'd assume (wrongly) that the region is a shabby grab bag of industry and mining, all isolated by the tyranny of distance from the interest and influence of faraway Prague. And while some areas do retain a distinct grittiness, there's simply too much of interest to give the region the travellers' cold shoulder.

The glorious cityscape of Olomouc (possibly Central Europe's most underrated), hosts an urbane population inspired by a lively influx of students. Thanks to a profound lack of tourists, Olomouc provides the truest sense of what Prague would be like without the crowds: in a word, fabulous. Contrasting with the city's lively present and future is a fascinating and ancient ecclesiastical history that is unmissable.

In the looming northern steel town of Ostrava a proud industrial heritage is being reborn with the energy of the 21st century. On the weekend crowds gather in one of the country's biggest party scenes, which can get a tad crazy – who says Moravians are reserved? There's more celebration of industry at the fascinating Tatra museum in Kopřivnice.

Outside of the cosmopolitan 'double-O' axis of Ostrava and Olomouc, the rugged Jeseníky Mountains (Nízký Jeseník) bordering Poland contain pretty spa towns and some fine opportunities for hiking, cycling and cross-country skiing. The terrain is lower in the Beskydy mountains bordering Slovakia, but there's nothing second-fiddle about the traditional architecture and interesting Wallachian culture surrounding Štramberk and Rožnov pod Radhoštěm.

HIGHLIGHTS

- Admire the stunning **Holy Trinity column** (p271) in Olomouc, the country's most underrated city

- Catch the quirky midday display of Olomouc's proletarian **astronomical clock** (p269)

- Discover the rustic past amid the traditional wooden buildings of **Štramberk** (p280) and Rožnov pod Radhoštěm's **Wallachian open-air museum** (p289)

- Party hard in the raucous bars and clubs of Ostrava's notorious **Stodolní ulice** (p279)

- Relax and recharge in the delightfully wooded spa town of **Jeseník Lázně** (p275)

★ Jeseník Lázně

Ostrava Stodolní ulice ★

Olomouc Holy Trinity Column & astronomical clock ★

★ Štramberk

★ Wallachian Open-air Museum Radhoštěm

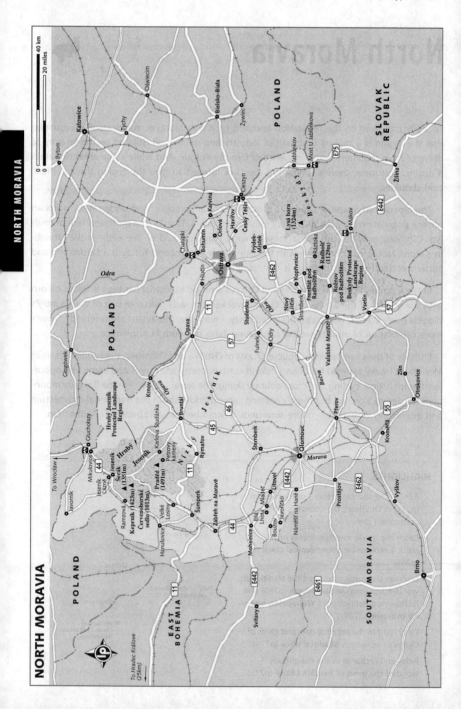

OLOMOUC

pop 105,000

As countless tourists embrace the overt charms of Prague and Český Krumlov, Olomouc (*Olla*-moats) exudes a subdued appeal, emerging as the travellers' equivalent of a special restaurant that is your own little secret. An old town square rivalling that in Prague for scale and beauty, combines with the youthful vivacity of a modern student town amid the graceful campus of the country's second oldest university. Some of Moravia's most impressive religious structures play host to a thrilling history, and a youthful population looks to the future with a quiet confidence. And, with tourist numbers at a mere trickle, Olomouc is one of the Czech Republic's best-value cities.

History

Legend has it that Olomouc was founded by Julius Caesar. It later became a major seat of administrative power when Moravia and Bohemia were united in the 11th century, then a bishopric in 1063. Olomouc has the bearing of a capital city, and was the Moravian capital from the 12th century until it was occupied and looted by Swedish troops between 1642 and 1650. It has been the seat of the metropolitan archbishop of Moravia since 1777. Industrialisation passed it by until well into the 20th century.

Orientation

The main train station (*hlavní nádraží*) is 2km east of the old town, over the Morava river and its tributary the Bystřice (take tram 1, 2, 5 or 6 heading west). The bus station is 1km further east (take tram 4 or 5).

The old town is around the two linked squares of Horní (Upper) and Dolní (Lower) náměstí. The eastern part of the old town, with the Přemysl palace and the university, lies along narrow Ostružinická and třída 1.máje.

Information

BOOKSHOPS

Tycho (☎ 585 225 095; Ostružnická 3) A good source of maps.

EMERGENCY

Foreigners' police (Cizinecká policie; ☎ 585 223 333; Smetanova 14) In the police building, near the train station.

INTERNET ACCESS

Both of these options provide internet and Skype at 1Kč per minute.

ISIC Net (třída 1 Máge 12; ⊗ 8am-10pm Mon-Fri, 10am-10am Sat & Sun) 50% discount for student card-holders.

Internet U Martina (Ostružnická 29; ⊗ 9am-midnight)

MEDICAL SERVICES

Hospital (Nemocnice; ☎ 585 851 111; Pavlova 6) South of the centre, on tram routes 1, 4 and 6.

MONEY

Česká spořitelna (Horní nám 17) ATM and exchange counter.

KB (třída Svobody) ATM and exchange counter.

ČSOB (Dolní nám 28-9)

POST

Main post office (Nám Republiky) There is another branch on Horní nám.

TOURIST INFORMATION

Beristo is a free bi-monthly events guide available in bars and clubs. It's in Czech, but the club and cinema listings are useful. *DDD* magazine is similar and available from bookshops for 10Kč.

Main tourist information office (Olomoucká informační služba; www.olomouc-tourism.cz) town hall (☎ 585 513 385; Horní nám; ⊗ 9am-7pm); train station (☎ 585 785 620; ⊗ 8am-4pm Mon-Fri) Sells maps and makes accommodation bookings. Both branches sell the Olomouc Card (3/5 days 160/340Kč), which includes free entry to sights and discounts at hotels. If you're only staying a few days, you may not get value from the card.

TRAVEL AGENCIES

Čedok (☎ 582 228 831; Nám Národních Hrdinů 4; ⊗ 9am-6pm Mon-Fri, 9am-noon Sat) Books train, plane and bus tickets and helps with accommodation.

CKM (☎ 585 222 148; www.ckmolomouc.cz; Denisova 4; ⊗ 9am-5.30pm Mon-Fri) Books travel tickets, sells ISIC and HI cards, and advises on budget accommodation.

Sights & Activities

HORNÍ NÁMĚSTÍ & AROUND

The splendid, polymorphous **town hall** (*radnice*) in the middle of the square was built in 1378, though its present architectural style and needlelike **tower** (věž; admission 15Kč; ⊗ tours 11am & 3pm Mar-Oct) date from 1607. Note the **oriel window** of the 15th-century chapel on the south side and don't miss the **astronomical clock** on the north side, remodelled in communist

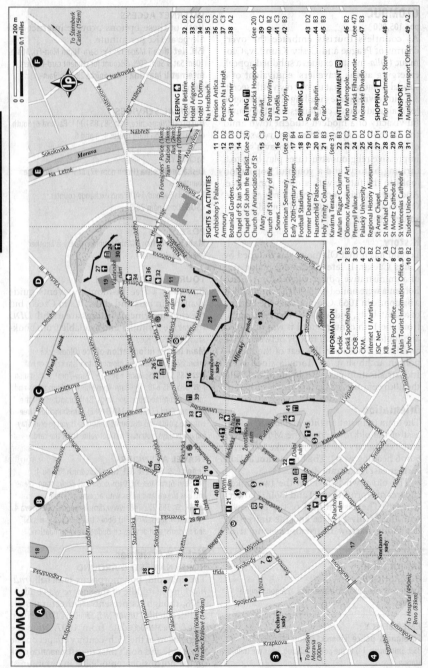

OLOMOUC

NORTH MORAVIA

To Šternberk Castle (15km)

INFORMATION

Čedok	1	A2
Česká Spořitelna	2	B3
ČSOB	3	C3
ČKM	4	C2
Internet U Martina	5	B2
ISIC Net	6	D2
KB	7	A3
Main Post Office	8	C2
Main Tourist Information Office	9	B3
Tycho	10	B2

SIGHTS & ACTIVITIES

Archbishop's Palace	11	D2
Armoury	12	D2
Botanical Gardens	13	D3
Chapel of St Jan Sarkander	14	C2
Chapel of St John the Baptist	(see 24)	
Church of Annunciation of St		
Mary	15	C3
Church of St Mary of the		
Snows	16	C2
Dominican Seminary	17	B4
Early 20th-century Houses	18	B1
Football Stadium	19	D1
Former Deanery	20	B3
Hauenschild Palace	21	B3
Holy Trinity Column	22	B3
Kavárna Terasa	(see 31)	
Marian Plague Column	23	B2
Olomouc Museum of Art	24	C2
Přemysl Palace	25	D1
Palacký University	26	C2
Regional History Museum	27	D1
St Anne Chapel	28	C3
St Michael Church	29	C2
St Moritz Cathedral	30	D1
St Wenceslas Cathedral	31	D2

SLEEPING

Hostel Betánie	32	D2
Hotel Arigone	33	C2
Hotel U Dómu	34	D2
Na Hradbach	35	C2
Pension Antica	36	D2
Penzion Na Hradě	37	C3
Poet's Corner	38	A2

EATING

Hanácká Hospoda	(see 20)	
Konvikt	39	C2
Sana Potraviny	40	B2
U Anděla	41	C2
U Netopýra	42	B3

DRINKING

9a	43	D2
Bar Rasputin	44	B3
Crack	45	B3

ENTERTAINMENT

Kino Metropole	46	B2
Moravská Filharmonie	(see 47)	
Moravské Divadlo	47	B3

SHOPPING

Prior Department Store	48	B2

TRANSPORT

Municipal Transport Office	49	A2

style so that each hour is announced by ideologically pure workers instead of pious saints. The best display is at midday.

Across the square, **Holy Trinity column** (Sousoší Nejsvětější trojice) is impossible to miss. A baroque mélange of gold and grey, its monumental form is reminiscent of the Buddhist shrine of Borobudur in Indonesia. Built between 1716 and 1754 to a design by V Render, a local sculptor, it is supposedly the biggest single baroque sculpture in Central Europe. On most days a delightful nun will explain to you the meaning of the interior sculptures in a variety of languages. In 2000, the column was awarded an inscription on Unesco's World Heritage list.

Surrounded by a jaw-dropping roll call of historic façades, the square also contains two of the city's six baroque fountains. The **Hercules fountain** (Herkulova kašna) dates from 1688 and features the muscular Greek hero standing astride a pit of writhing serpents. To the east of the town hall, the **Caesar fountain** (Caeserova kašna) was built in 1724 and is Olomouc's biggest. During the communist era the Roman emperor straddling his horse was crowned with a single red star; proof that the Nazis were not the only totalitarian regime to co-opt the essence of ancient Rome.

Olomouc's tradition of building fountains was continued in 2002 when a seventh fountain was erected in Horní nám featuring turtles and a rampant dolphin. A few rascally locals claim that rubbing the head of the turtle nearest the Holy Trinity column will bring you good luck. Try it and see.

Down Opletalova is Olomouc's original parish church, the vast **St Moritz cathedral** (chrám sv Mořice). Thoroughly Gothic, it was built between 1412 and 1540. The western tower is a remnant of its 13th-century predecessor. The cathedral's amazing island of peace is shattered every September with an International Organ Festival (the cathedral's own organ is Moravia's mightiest).

DOLNÍ NÁMĚSTÍ & AROUND

The 1661 **church of Annunciation of St Mary** (kostel Zvěstování Panny Marie) stands out with its beautifully sober interior. Its antithesis is the opulent 16th-century Renaissance confection, the **Hauenschild palace** (not open to the public). The square also sports its own **Marian plague column** (Mariánský morový sloup), and baroque **fountains** dedicated to Neptune and Jupiter.

Picturesque lanes thread northeast from Dolní nám to Žerotínovo nám, named after the Žerotíns, a landowning family who set Velké Losiny's gruesome 17th-century witch trials in motion (see p276). Here you'll find the green-domed landmark of **St Michael church** (kostel sv Michala), with its robust baroque interior. Among the furnishings is a rare painting of a pregnant Virgin Mary. Wrapped around the entire block is an active **Dominican seminary** (Dominikánský klášter).

Nearby is the tiny round **chapel of St Jan Sarkander** (kaple sv Jana Sarkandra; ⏰ 10am-noon & 1-5pm), named after a local priest who died under torture in 1620 for refusing to divulge false confessions. It's built on the site of the jail where he died, part of which is preserved in the cellar.

NÁMĚSTÍ REPUBLIKY & AROUND

The original Jesuit college complex, founded in 1573, stretches along Universitní and into Nám Republiky. It includes the baroque **church of St Mary of the Snows** (kostel Panny Marie Sněžné), which is full of fine frescoes.

Across the road is the **Olomouc museum of art** (Olomoucký muzeum umění; ☎ 585 514 111; Denisova 47; adult/concession 20/10Kč, Wed free; ⏰ 10am-6pm Tue-Sun), an excellent gallery with changing displays of 20th-century Czech paintings and sculpture, plus shows of contemporary artists. Upstairs is the musical theatre (p273) which still hosts regular performances.

Next door in a former convent, is the **Regional History museum** (Vlastivědné muzeum; ☎ 585 515 111; www.vmo.cz; nám Republiky 5; adult/concession 40/20Kč, Wed free; ⏰ 9am-6pm Tue-Sun Apr-Sep, 10am-5pm Wed-Sun Oct-Mar) with historical, geographical and zoological displays.

Escape the mad traffic on třída 1.máje and head up Křížovského, past the 17th-century canons' residences that now house part of **Palacký University** (Universita Palackého). The *kavárna* (café) at the student union is good for a coffee break.

Around the corner in Biskupské nám is the **Archbishop's palace** (Arcibiskupský palác), completed in 1685, which is not so much interesting as merely huge. The monolith on the south side of the square is a former **armoury** (1711).

PŘEMYSL PALACE & ST WENCESLAS CATHEDRAL

In the peaceful, pocket-sized Václavské nám, in the northeast corner of the old centre are the most venerable of Olomouc's historical buildings.

Originally a Romanesque basilica, consecrated in 1131, the **St Wenceslas cathedral** (dóm sv Václava) was rebuilt several times before being thoroughly 'neo-Gothicised' inside and out in the 1880s.

Pride of place goes to the remnants of the early 12th-century **Přemysl palace** (Přemyslovský palác; adult/concession 20/10Kč; ☷ 10am-6pm Tue-Sun Apr-Sep), originally built for Bishop Jindřich Zdík. A detailed English text walks you through a cloister with 15th- and 16th-century frescoes on the original walls up to the archaeological centrepiece, the bishops' rooms with their Romanesque walls and windows (rediscovered in 1867), and artistry unequalled elsewhere in the Czech Republic, even in Prague castle. Downstairs, surviving 16th-century frescoes in the **chapel of St John the Baptist** (kaple sv Jana Křtitele), completed in 1262, include angels with instruments of torture (a sign of ecclesiastical approval?).

To the left of the palace is the **St Anne chapel** (kaple sv Anny), and beyond that are the long, yellow walls of the **former deanery** where Wenceslas III, the last of the Přemysl line, was mysteriously assassinated in 1306. This building is now part of Palacký University.

OTHER ATTRACTIONS

In the southwest of town on Vídeňská are four wonderfully fanciful **early 20th-century houses**. Similar houses are dotted nearby on the edge of **Smetanovy sady**, one of the large parks that enclose the historical centre to the west and east.

A staircase at the rear of St Michael church on the southern end of Universitini leads through the walls of the old town to **Bezručovy sady**, a pretty park wrapped around the meandering Mlýnský potok. The **botanical gardens** (botanická zahrada; adult/concession 30/20Kč; ☷ 9.30am-5pm) are across the river further to the east.

Sleeping

The tourist information office and CKM can help you with advice on private and hotel rooms.

BUDGET

Poet's Corner (☎ 777 570 730; www.hostelolomouc.com; 3rd fl, Sokolská 1; dm/tw 300/800Kč) Aussie owner Greg is a wealth of local information at this exceptionally friendly and well-run hostel – even if he thinks the dark chocolate pie from Café 87 is better than their white chocolate pie. Bicycles can be hired for 100Kč per day.

Hostel Betánie (☎ 585 233 860; hostel.olomouc@charita .cz; Wurmova 5; s/d 350/450Kč; ℗) Near the university this church-run hostel has a funky café and clean rooms with shared facilities. With a slightly monastic air, it's not a party place, but is friendly and welcoming.

MIDRANGE

Pension Moravia (☎ 585 416 403; www.pension-moravia .com; s/d 500/800Kč; ℗ ▯) A 10-minute walk from the town centre, this *pension* provides good value in a quiet residential street without the potential parking hassles of the old town. If you arrive by public transport, catch bus 19 from the railway station to the Dvořákova stop.

FIVE THINGS THAT WILL GROW ON YOU

After living in Olomouc for a few years, Australian Greg Chandler appreciates the idiosyncrasies of life in the Czech Republic.

■ 'I love the felt slippers worn over your shoes to protect the floors of the museum. They reduce noise and also add a little physical adventure to your visit.'

■ 'Even big, tough guys in leather jackets are happy to stroll around with little cones of strawberry ice-cream – all year round.'

■ 'The ticket system in bars and restaurants shows the owners trust you, and saves you fighting your way to the bar every time you want a drink.'

■ 'When the water truck sprays the streets on a hot day, everyone has to scatter – grandmothers with shopping, babies in prams and tourists gazing skywards.'

■ 'Over-attentive museum stewards (usually women) always like to be in the same room as you. If you show a special interest in the exhibits, you'll have a friend for life.'

Na Hradbach (☎ 585 233 243; nahradbach@quick .cz; Hrnčířská 3; s/d 600/800Kč) On one of Olomouc's prettiest streets sits probably the best value *pension*, with two of the town's finest restaurants across the lane. We strongly recommend booking ahead.

Pension Antica (☎ 731 560 264; www.pension.an tica.cz; Wurmova 1; s/d incl breakfast from 800/1600Kč to 1200/2000Kč; **P**) Warning: if you're travelling by yourself, don't read this. If you're looking for a romantic stay in a quietly romantic city, read on. With antique furniture, crisp white duvets and oriental rugs covering polished wood floors, there's every chance you won't leave these stunning apartments long enough to enjoy the easy-going Renaissance charm of Olomouc.

Hotel u Dómu (☎ 585 220 502; hotel_u_domu@email .cz; Dómská 4; s/d incl breakfast 1200/1600Kč; **P**) In a quiet street amid the age-old shadows of St Wenceslas cathedral, this boutique-style hotel has comfortable rooms and authentically charming décor.

Penzion Na Hradě (☎ 585 203 231; www.penzion nahrade.cz; Michalská 4; s/d 1590/1690; **P** **✗**) Tucked away in the robust silhouette of St Michael church, this new designer *pension* has sleek, cool rooms and professional service creating a contemporary ambience in the heart of the old town.

Hotel Arigone (☎ 585 232 350; www.ariogne.web .tiscali.cz; Universitní 20; s/d incl breakfast 1690/1900Kč) Wooden beams, parquet floors and skylights combine in a charming lane in the closest place Olomouc has to a romantic, boutique hotel. A few picturesque doors down they also run a cosy wine bar.

Eating

Café 87 (Denisova 87; chocolate pie 30Kč, coffee 25 Kč; ☽ 7.30am-8pm) Locals flock to this arty, sunny café beside the Olomouc Museum of Art for great coffee and their special recipe chocolate pie. You be the judge – dark chocolate or white chocolate? Across Olomouc the debate continues.

Hanácacká Hospoda (☎ 582 237 186; Dolní nám 38; mains 70-100Kč) Just when you're finally getting to grips with a Czech menu, this incredibly popular spot lists everything in the local Haná dialect. It's worth persevering though because the Moravian meals are robust, tasty and supreme value.

U Netopýra (☎ 776 735 534; Lafayettova 6; pizza 80Kč) Use sonar at 'the place of the bat' to find a spot in the labyrinth of nooks and crannies, then switch to your sense of taste to appreciate the good thin crust pizza and well-priced beer.

Konvikt (☎ 585 631 486; Universitini 3; mains 130-200Kč; ☽ 9am-midnight Mon-Fri, 10am-11pm Sat & Sun) Here you have two choices: dine in the spacious restaurant and sunny terrace on the walls of the old town, or head inside to the Konvikt Bar for more raucous student-fuelled fun.

U Anděla (☎ 585 228 755; Hrnčířská 10; mains 130-395Kč) After you order, wander round and look at the fascinating memorabilia displayed in every nook and cranny. Don't be too long though because the service is prompt and the Moravian food very good.

Sana Potraviny (Horní nám 9) This is the main-square supermarket.

Drinking

9a (Nábřeží Premyslovcú 9; ☽ noon-midnight Mon-Fri, noon-3pm Sat & Sun) Light and dark wood and bricks combine in a spot that's a cut above other, grungier, student bars. Try your hand (and feet) on the climbing wall.

Crack (☎ 585 208 428; Mlýnská 4) The eclectic seating arrangement in this bar includes old sofas, church pews and old theatre seats. It's not particularly Irish, but it is reliably warm and comfy.

Bar Rasputin (Mlýnská) This place is hard to find behind the Crack, but worth seeking out for the slightly louche Russian ambience.

Entertainment

Moravské Divadlo (☎ 585 223 531; www.moravskedi vadlo.cz, in Czech; Horní nám 22) The town theatre puts on plenty of shows.

Moravská Filharmonie (☎ 585 206 520; www.mfo.cz, in Czech; Horní nám 23) The local orchestra presents regular concerts.

Kino Metropole (☎ 585 222 466; Sokolská 25) This is one of many cinemas in Olomouc.

Musical theatre (Hudebné divadlo; ☎ 585 223 565; www.divadlohudby.cz, Czech only) This theatre still operates today and is upstairs from the Olomouc museum of art (p271).

Getting There & Away

From Ostrava to Olomouc there are regular buses (120Kč, two hours) and fast trains (130Kč, 1½ hours). From Brno there are about 15 buses (60Kč, 1¼ hours) and five direct fast trains (120Kč, 1½ hours) each day. The fast train connections from Prague (294Kč, 3¼ hours) depart from Praha hlavní nádraží.

First-class SuperCity Pendolino trains run from Praha-Holešovice (500Kč, 2¼ hours) to Olomouc and from here on to Ostrava (340Sk, one hour).

From Bratislava in Slovakia you'll need to change at Brno.

Getting Around

Bus tickets cost 6/12Kč and last for 40/60 minutes. You can buy them from *tabák* (kiosk) and newsstands or from the yellow machines at some stops.

A 24-hour transport pass *(denní jízdenka)* is available for 26Kč from the **municipal transport office** (DPMO; cnr Legionářská & Palackého; ☼ 6am-6pm Mon-Fri, 7am-1pm Sat) and from the main bus station.

AROUND OLOMOUC
Šternberk Castle

Fifteen kilometres north of Olomouc, **Šternberk castle** (hrad Šternberk; www.sternberk.cz; adult/concession 60/30Kč; ☼ 9am-4pm Tue-Sun May-Sep, 9am-3pm Sat & Sun Apr & Oct, 10am-2pm Sat & Sun Nov-Dec) was founded in the late 13th century by the Šternberk family. It received a Renaissance face-lift in about 1480, and its Romantic look from Duke Jan II of Liechtenstein in 1886.

Now open to the public, Šternberk castle's historical interiors range from Gothic to baroque.

The castle is 300m up the hill from Šternberk's main square, Hlavní náměstí. The real landmark here is the **parish church of the Annunciation of Our Lord** (farní kostel Zvěstování Páně) on the way up to the castle. In contrast to its bombastic baroque façade, the interior is spacious, sparsely furnished and topped with fine murals.

GETTING THERE & AWAY

You can get to/from Olomouc by bus (15Kč, 20 minutes) or train (22Kč, 20 minutes).

Bouzov Castle

The impressive pile of **Bouzov castle** (☎ 585 346 201; www.hrad-bouzov.cz, in Czech; ☼ 9am-4pm Tue-Sun May-Sep, 9am-3pm Sat & Sun Apr & Oct) was the seat of the Grand Masters of the Order of Teutonic Knights from 1799 to 1939. The oldest parts date from the 14th century, but it was renovated in neo-Gothic style between 1895 and 1910. The order was abolished in 1939 and the castle was occupied and looted by the Nazis during WWII.

The restored apartments include the Grand Master's Bedroom and office, the Hunter's Hall and the huge basement kitchens kitted out with the latest labour-saving devices of the early 20th century. The magnificent Knights' Hall has elaborate woodcarvings and a barrel-vaulted wooden ceiling decorated with the sun and the stars. The sculptures of St George and a jousting knight symbolise the spiritual and material aspects of the order.

Choose from the 30-minute 'classic' tour (adult/concession 80/40Kč), which takes in the main sights, or one of two longer (up to two hours) tours (adult/concession 140/70Kč). Tours are in Czech so ask for an English text.

GETTING THERE & AWAY

There are two buses daily Monday to Friday from Olomouc to Bouzov (48Kč, one hour, 10 minutes), but only one bus returning in the opposite direction.

Javoříčko Caves

From Bouzov castle it's a 5km walk south on a blue-marked trail, (or you can take the occasional local bus), to Javoříčko and the impressive local underground attraction, the **Javoříčko caves** (Javoříčské jeskyně; adult/concession 60/30Kč; ☼ 9am-3pm Tue-Sun Apr-Oct).

You can either stay the night (there are basic hotels in Šternberk and near the caves) or continue northeast on a scenic red-marked trail for 8km to Bílá Lhota. Another 4km on are the smaller **Mladeč caves** (Mladečské jeskyně) at Mladeč, and a further 5km on is Litovel.

JESENÍKY MOUNTAINS

The twin ranges that make up the Jeseníky Mountains (Nízký Jeseník) also mark the boundaries of one of the Czech Republic's forgotten spaces. The rugged Hrubý Jeseník rise in the northwest corner of the region to Moravia's highest summit, Praděd (1491m). On a clear day (and with a good pair of binoculars) you can see both the Krkonoše of East Bohemia and the Tatras of Central Slovakia from its peak.

The surrounding Hrubý Jeseník Protected Landscape Region (Chráněná krajinná oblast Hrubý Jeseník) is home to deer and wild boar.

The Hrubý Jeseník have been developed for winter skiing and ski touring, but there are also plenty of walking opportunities. A town of particular historical interest is Velké Losiny, the site of blood-chilling witch trials during the 17th century. Both Velké Losiny and Jeseník Lázně on the other side of the mountains are Moravian spa centres.

HRUBÝ JESENÍK

Šumperk, Velké Losiny, Ramzová and Jeseník are all convenient bases. The **information centre** (informační centrum; ☎ 584 498 155; www.jeseniky.net; Masarykovo nám 167; ⌚ 9am-5pm Mon-Sat Jun-Aug, 9am-5pm Mon-Fri Sep-May) in Jeseník can help with transport, accommodation and activities information. The map to have is Kartografie Praha's *Jeseníky – turistická mapa* (No 19).

Sights & Activities

This is a great area for cross-country skiing and walking, and trails abound. From **Červenohorské sedlo**, a 1013m pass on the Šumperk–Jeseník road that frequent buses pass by all day, there's a 10km trek southeast on a seriously strenuous red-marked trail to **Praděd** and on to **Petrovy kameny** (Peter's stones). Praděd has a 162m transmitter tower with a restaurant in it.

Alternatively, from Červenohorské sedlo take the red ridge-trail west to **Šerák** (1351m) via Červená hora and Keprník (1423m). There, a year-round **cable car** descends to Ramzová (or you can walk down on the red trail), which has buses and local trains back to Šumperk. This is an easy overnight trip, with *boudy* (huts) at Červenohorské sedlo and on Šerák.

When you're finished walking, head to **Jeseník Lázně** perched haughtily above the market town of Jeseník. Jeseník Lázně was established as a Moravian alternative to the Bohemian spa scene in the 19th century by local farmer Vincent Priessnitz. Today the pretty spa town cascades down a pine-studded slope and is a low-key contrast to the glamour (albeit with a small 'g') of Bohemian spa centres such as Karlovy Vary and Mariánské Lázně. Priessnitz established cold water 'hydrotherapy' in Jeseník Lázně, and the interesting **muzeum Vincent Priessnitz** (☎ 584 411 633; Priessnitzova 175; adult/concession 20/10Kč; ⌚ 12.30-5pm Tue-Fri, 10am-5pm Sat & Sun) details the occasionally bizarre procedures in an eye-opening series of 19th-century lithographs. Pretty **walks** traverse the surrounding slopes, which are dotted with memorials from grateful spa patients.

More contemporary are the soothing healing sessions that use salt crystals from the Dead Sea and the Himalayas at the **Solvita salt cave** (☎ 584 452 579; www.solvita.cz; Pressnitzova 12/299; per person 130Kč; ⌚ 9am-7pm Mon-Fri, 10am-5pm Sat & Sun). Deckchairs and soothing new-age beats are mandatory.

Sleeping

There's private rooms and *pensions* in every town and village. Šumperk, Velké Losiny, Ramzová and Jeseník have plenty of accommodation possibilities. High-country camping is restricted, but there are lots of mountain chalets. The following listings are in spectacular locations.

Sporthotel Kursovní (☎ 583 779 003; www.praded-sporthotel.cz; s/d incl breakfast 440/800Kč; Ⓟ) Just east of the summit of Praděd, this has similar rooms to Horský Hotel Červenohorské sedlo, but in a more remote setting.

Pension Slezský Dům (☎ 584 413 704; www.slezskydum.cz; Lipovská 630; s/d incl breakfast 490/980Kč; Ⓟ) The loft rooms are especially cosy in this chalet-style place in Jeseník.

Horský Hotel Červenohorské sedlo (☎ 583 295 101; www.hotel-cervenohorskesedlo.cz, in Czech; s/d incl breakfast 500/100Kč; Ⓟ) At the top of the pass on the Šumperk–Jeseník road, enjoy the great views and a good massage after a long walk in the surrounding mountains.

Priessnitz Spa Health Resort (☎ 584 491 266; www.priessnitz.cz; Priessnitzova 12; s/d 600/1200Kč) In Jeseník Lázně, this resort has four different spa hotels in various parts of town. Including accommodation, treatments begin at 1200Kč per day.

Getting There & Away

There are two buses a day from Olomouc to Šumperk (50Kč, 1¼ hours) and half a dozen from Ostrava (110Kč, three hours). At least two run daily from Brno to Šumperk (100Kč, 2¾ hours), with one going on to Ramzová (45Kč, 3¾ hours).

From Olomouc there are six daily fast trains to Šumperk (76Kč, one hour) and many slower ones, most continuing to Ramzová. Five daily express trains run from Prague to Šumperk (260Kč, four hours) with local connections from there.

Getting Around

There are only five daily buses (fewer on the weekend) running between Šumperk and

THE BOBLÍG INQUISITION

During the 17th and 18th centuries North Moravia was swept by a wave of religious hysteria that makes the Salem witch hunts, happening in the USA at the same time, look like a Sunday outing.

In 1678 the Žerotíns hired František Boblíg to undertake the role of inquisitor to eradicate what they perceived to be ungodly and superstitious practices.

The inquisitor fulfilled his commission with zeal. Over the course of 15 years he accused scores of people, mostly women, of witchcraft; many of whom met a grizzly end at the stake. When nobles in Šumperk grew critical of the amount of property that Boblíg and his 'judges' were confiscating, he accused them of devilish sympathies as well.

Almost 15 years after they had started, the Žerotíns were persuaded by King Leopold I to take steps to end the persecutions, and the murderous Boblíg was forced to retire. He died of natural causes at an advanced age and was never held to account for the purges.

Jeseník, via Velké Losiny and Červenohorské sedlo. Direct train connections are not much better, with only four daily trains between Šumperk and Jeseník, via Ramzová, taking two hours. The indirect trains on this line are more frequent but require at least one change, usually at Hanušovice. Regular buses travel the 2km from Jeseník to Lázně Jeseník (15Kč, 10 minutes).

VELKÉ LOSINY

Today a minor spa town, from 1496 to 1802 Velké Losiny was the seat of the powerful Žerotín family. A factory (with a small museum) established here by the family still produces handmade paper.

Sights

The striking, U-shaped lakeside **Žerotín chateau** (zámek; adult/concession 40/20Kč, English text 40Kč; ⏰ 9am-noon & 1-5pm Tue-Sun May-Aug, 9am-noon & 1-4pm Tue-Sun Sep, 9am-noon & 1-4pm Sat & Sun Apr & Oct) is one of Moravia's best preserved Renaissance properties. The group tour in Czech (there's an English text) takes in empire furniture and a 16th-century tiled stove, as well as portraits of the Žerotíns and paintings collected by them. It avoids the actual room – the grotesquely named Hall of Justice – where the infamous witch trials took place (see above), and goes into little detail about them.

Getting There & Away

For information on getting to Šumperk, see p275. From there, Velké Losiny is a 15-minute train ride, with about eight departures a day. The chateau is about 1km southwest on a green-marked path from the train station.

OSTRAVA

pop 310,000

The Czech Republic's third-largest city is one of the country's most dynamic urban centres, arguably evolving even more quickly than faraway Prague. Inextricably linked with the gargantuan Vitkovice steelworks, which closed in 1998 after 170 years dominating Ostrava's smoggy smokestack skyline, the city is now reinventing its industrial heritage to become a centre of high-tech and service industries. Its proud industrial past is not forgotten, and Vitkovice has been nominated for a place on Unesco's World Heritage List (see p278).

The environmental damage resulting from decades of heavy industry is now receding and Ostrava's modern cityscape is peppered with parks, ironically making it one of the greenest cities in the country. After decades of suffocating under the aching monotony of heavy industry, a more enterprising and energetic Ostrava is emerging, and nowhere is the city's renewed verve more evident than in its booming bar and nightclub scene.

Orientation

Ostrava is BIG, but only the central part on the west bank of the river is of interest to travellers.

Most trains use the main station, Ostrava hlavní nádraží, from where it's 2.5km south on Nádražní to the centre (take tram 2 or 8). The small Ostrava-střed train station and the main bus station are about 1km southwest of the centre; catch tram 1, 2 or 14 going north on Vítkovická in front of the bus station.

Information

BOOKSHOPS

Knihkupectví Librex (☎ 596 117 676; Smetanovo nám; ☽ 9am-7pm) Five floors of books, a café and internet access, including wi-fi.

EMERGENCY

Foreigners' police office (Úřadovna cizinecké policie; ☎ 596 141 111; Ostrčilova 4) Two hundred metres north of the new town hall.

INTERNET ACCESS

@Internet Café (☎ 596 113 456; Škroupova 10; ☽ 9am-10pm Sun-Thu, 9am-3am Fri & Sat)

MEDICAL SERVICES

Hospital (nemocnice; ☎ 596 191 111; Hornopolní) Five hundred metres west of the town centre.

MONEY

There are banks across town.

ČSOB (Nádražní 10) Has an ATM and exchange counter.

POST

Main post office (Dvořákova) Three blocks northeast of Nádražní. There's also a 24-hour branch at Wattova 1046.

TOURIST INFORMATION

Stodolní Noviny is a free monthly magazine listing nightlife.

Municipal information centre (Městské informační centrum, MIC; www.ostravainfo.cz) Main office (☎ 596 123 913; Nádražní 7/686; ☽ 8am-6pm Mon-Fri, 9am-2pm Sat); Ostrava hlavní nádraží (☎ 596 136 218; ☽ 7am-8.30pm Mon-Fri, 7am-3pm Sat, 1pm-8.30pm Sun); new town hall (☎ 599 443 096; ☽ 9am-5pm) This helpful information centre also books accommodation.

Sights

In this metropolitan monument to modernity, the oldest public building is the **former town hall** (stará radnice) on Masarykovo nám. Inside is the small **Ostrava museum** (Ostravské muzeum; ☎ 596 123 760; adult/concession 30/20Kč; ☽ 9am-5pm Mon-Fri, 9am-1pm Sat, 1-5pm Sun Oct-May, 9am-5pm Mon-Fri, 9am-1pm Sat Jun-Sep) with exhibitions on regional natural history and archaeology, including the 20,000-year-old tiny statue of Petřkovická Venus.

Nearby on Pivovarská is one of Ostrava's newest public buildings, the **puppet theatre** (divadlo loutek, ☎ 596 114 884; Pivovarská 5), which sports five giant sculpted puppets around the

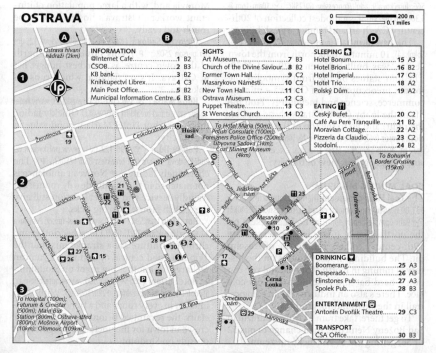

OSTRAVA

INFORMATION	
@Internet Cafe	1 B2
ČSOB	2 B3
KB bank	3 B2
Knihkupectví Librex	4 C3
Main Post Office	5 B2
Municipal Information Centre	6 B3

SIGHTS	
Art Museum	7 B3
Church of the Divine Saviour	8 B2
Former Town Hall	9 C2
Masarykovo Náměstí	10 C2
New Town Hall	11 C3
Ostrava Museum	12 C3
Puppet Theatre	13 C3
St Wenceslas Church	14 D2

SLEEPING	
Hotel Bonum	15 A3
Hotel Brioni	16 B2
Hotel Imperial	17 C3
Hotel Trio	18 A2
Polský Dům	19 A2

EATING	
Český Bufet	20 C2
Café Au Pere Tranquille	21 B2
Moravian Cottage	22 A2
Pizzeria da Claudio	23 C2
Stodolní	24 B2

DRINKING	
Boomerang	25 A3
Desperado	26 A3
Flinstones Pub	27 A3
Spolek Pub	28 B3

ENTERTAINMENT	
Antonín Dvořák Theatre	29 C3

TRANSPORT	
ČSA Office	30 B3

To Ostrava hlavní nádraží (2km)

To Hotel Maria (50m); Polish Consulate (100m); Foreigners Police Office (200m); Libyona Sadová (1km); Coal Mining Museum (4km)

To Bohumin Border Crossing (15km)

To Hospital (100m); Futurum & Cinestar (500m); Main Bus Station (800m); Ostrava-střed (800m); Mošnov Airport (10km); Olomouc (109km)

NORTH MORAVIA

OSTRAVA'S BID FOR WORLD HERITAGE STATUS

Most sites inscribed to Unesco's World Heritage List are centuries old but the efforts of a few proud residents of Ostrava seem set to break the mould. Recognising the city's unique industrial history, in 2001 Ostrava's Heritage Council joined with the Ministry of Culture in Prague to successfully lobby Unesco to accept the city's looming steelworks on the 'Tentative' list for World Heritage recognition. In the words of Unesco, 'Ostrava's industrial complexes are unique in the international context since they comprise, in a single locality, coal mines, coking plants and blast furnaces.' High praise indeed and when a decision is reached in 2010, the foreboding steeltown skyscapes of Ostrava may be protected along with similar sites such as the mining landscape of Cornwall and West Devon, and Sewell mining town in Chile; all inscribed to World Heritage status in 2006.

---

entrance – Punch, the King, the Queen, the Angel and the Devil – all looking remarkably like pieces from the world's largest chess set.

To the east on Kostelní nám is the elegant **St Wenceslas church** (kostel sv Václav). The late-Gothic building has a baroque façade on Romanesque foundations. Two blocks eastwards from Nádražní, on Československých legií, is a neo-Renaissance basilica, the parish **church of the Divine Saviour** (chrám Božského Spasitele), dating from 1889.

Ostrava's **art museum** (dům umění; ☎ 596 112 566; Jurečkova 9; adult/concession 60/25Kč; ⊗ 10am-1pm & 1.30-6pm Tue-Sat) has a modest collection of 20th-century Czech art and temporary exhibitions.

The **new town hall** (nové radnice; ☎ 596 283 096; Sokolská), 10 minutes' walk north from the town centre, was built between 1929 and 1930. The four statues on the front symbolise the former preoccupations of Ostrava – mining, commerce, science and metallurgy. Find the lift in the lobby (up the stairs ahead and on the right) and go to the top of the 85.6m-tall **clock tower** (věž; adult/concession 20/10Kč; ⊗ 10am-7pm Apr-Oct, 10am-5pm Nov-Mar) for an excellent, and surprisingly green, view of the city.

COAL MINING MUSEUM

The **Coal Mining museum** (Hornické muzeum; ☎ 596 131 803; www.muzeumokd.cz; adult/concession 80/40Kč; ⊗ 9am-6pm, last entry 4pm), at Pod Landekem on the north edge of town, is a preserved late 19th-century colliery on the site of Anselm pit. The buildings house exhibits on the history of mining in North Moravia, and you can don a hard hat and descend to the old coal face. There's also an industrial archaeological trail in the surrounding grounds.

To get there, take tram 12 from Nádražní to Sad Boženy Němcové, then change to bus 52 or 56, getting out at Hornické muzeum.

Festivals

Colours of Ostrava (www.colours.cz; admission 650Kč) This is an annual four-day music festival held mid- to late July. The best of Czech bands and DJs are represented and there is a significant focus on world music. Past headliners have included Robert Plant and Salif Keita.

Sleeping

The tourist information office books hotels and private rooms. Accommodation prices are high compared to other parts of North Moravia and, with a large population of itinerant workers, Ostrava's hostels tend to be rough and ready.

Ubyovna Sadová (☎ 596 118 369; Sadová 12; dm per person 250Kč; P) This hostel, 1.5km north of the town centre, is your best budget bet in Ostrava. It's on Sadová, which runs off Sokolská.

Hotel Maria (☎ 596 110 676; Přívozská 23; www.hotel-maria.cz; s/d incl breakfast 780/980Kč) Quickly fading three stars, but Hotel Maria is good value in the big city.

Polský Dům (☎ 596 122 001; www.polskydum.cz; Poděbradova 53; s/d incl breakfast 850/1250Kč; P) The charmingly fading Art Nouveau ambience is not matched in the slightly dowdy rooms, but friendly service and a quiet location still give the 'Polish House' two big ticks.

Hotel Trio (☎ 596 111 427; www.hotel-trio.cz; Pobialova 10; s/d incl breakfast 970/1340Kč) Floral bedclothes and chrome furniture are a strange mix, but the Trio is a good central option where you can recharge for another big night on Stodolní.

Hotel Brioni (☎ 599 500 500; www.hotelbrioni.cz; Stodolní 8; s/d incl breakfast 1280/1600Kč) With wi-fi internet in every room and a trendy bar downstairs, the revamped Brioni targets a younger crowd in town for the nocturnal delights right outside on Stodolní.

Hotel Bonum (☎ 596 114 050; www.t-bonum.cz; Masná 6; s/d incl breakfast 1380/1980Kč) On a quieter side street, the Bonum blends comfortable attic rooms with an Egyptian restaurant featuring a mini-Sphinx – somehow it all hangs together nicely.

Hotel Imperial (☎ 599 099 099; www.imperial.cz; Tyršova 6; s/d incl breakfast 2000/300Kč; P ⊗ ⊠ ⊠ ⅋) One hundred years of heritage is hard to spot as Ostrava's flashest hotel has morphed into a very comfortable, if slightly prim, spot with all amenities and a business focus.

Eating

In Ostrava eating often plays second fiddle to drinking and dancing, but if you look hard enough there are a few gems.

Café Au Pere Tranquille (☎ 595 136 715; Musorgského 839/8; crepes 100Kč; ⏱ 7am-11pm Mon-Fri, 10am-11pm Sat, 2pm-11pm Sun) Healthy sweet and savoury crepes and salads are served at this French-style bistro just off Stodolní. It's popular for breakfasts too, proving there's more to Stodolní than nightlife.

Pizzeria da Claudio (☎ 603 708 138; Masarykovo nám 13; pizza 100Kč) The service can be a bit slack (the result of a big night out on Stodolní we're picking), but it's worth waiting for the wood-fired pizza with generous toppings.

Moravian Cottage (Moravská Chalupa; ☎ 596 234 937; Musorgského 9; mains 110-220Kč; ⏱ Mon-Sat) Locals pack this spot for home-style Moravian cooking and a good selection of Moravian wine.

Also recommended:

Český Bufet (cnr Zámecká & Masarykovo nám; ⏱ 7am-6.30pm Mon-Fri, 7am-1pm Sat) For cheap and cheerful buffet eats.

Stodolní (snacks 70Kč; ⏱ from 7pm Fri & Sat) Tasty barbecued chicken sandwiches and sausages from kerbside vendors.

Drinking

Head to Stodolní where you'll find more than 60 pubs and clubs. A few locals reckon that the street's lost its grungy indie heritage, but it's now more popular than ever. The trend is towards dance-oriented clubs and bars with a shrinking range of identikit beats. Friday and Saturday nights are almost uncomfortably hectic. Try the following places for something a bit different.

Desperado (☎ 596 121 365; cnr Stodolní 31) The original bar on Stodolní is still one of the best. Lots of Mexican iconography and 30 different tequilas draw a wider age range

than the bass-thumping shoeboxes elsewhere on the strip.

Flintstones Pub (☎ 602 150 652; Stodolní 20; ⏱ 5pm-4am Wed-Sat) When a bar is named after a classic 1960s cartoon it would be foolish to expect too much in the way of sophistication. The décor is a rustic approximation of Fred Flintstone's own abode, and the atmosphere is played strictly for laughs – you're guaranteed loads of fun, and a bona fide yabba dabba doozy.

Boomerang (☎ 608 707 717; Stodolní 22; ⏱ 10pm-4am Wed-Sat) This club features an eclectic mix of live music and DJs.

Spolek Pub (cnr Nádražní & Jurečkova) More traditional and relaxed than the heaving masses on Stodolní, the Spolek's relaxed garden bar is essential during spring and summer.

Entertainment

Cinestar (☎ 595 699 999; Novinářská) This multiplex cinema is in the Futurum shopping centre, west of the town centre.

Antonín Dvořák theatre (☎ 595 151 111; Smetanovo nám 1) The newly constructed Antonín Dvořák Theatre hosts opera, ballet and plays.

Getting There & Away

ČSA (☎ 596 123 164; www.csa.cz; Jurečkova 20) has daily flights between Prague and **Ostrava Mošnov Airport** (OSR; ☎ 597 471 136; www.airport-ostrava.cz) from 2350Kč return.

Trains (train station info ☎ 972 762 555) are the easiest way to get between Ostrava and the other big cities. Regular fast trains run to Prague (484Kč, 4½ hours), Brno (204Kč, 2¾ hours) and Olomouc (130Kč, 1¼ hours).

SuperCity Pendolino trains (www.scpendolino.cz), a 1st class–only service launched in 2005, runs to Ostrava from Praha-Holešovice (600Kč, 3½ hours) through Olomouc (340Sk, one hour).

Buses (bus station info ☎ 596 633 751) to these destinations take marginally longer but are also around half the price.

It's 15km from central Ostrava to the Polish border crossing at Bohumín, linking to Katowice. Buses (15Kč, 25 minutes) and trains (16Kč, 10 minutes) make the run.

At Ostrava hlavní nádraží you can also catch one of dozens of fast trains passing each day from Prague and Brno to the border.

There are also fast trains and buses from Ostrava to the border crossing at Český Těšín (40Kč, one hour), continuing to Kraków.

Getting Around

Mošnov airport is 10km southwest of the centre. Bus 33 runs infrequently to the airport (25 minutes) daily.

The same tickets are used for all of Ostrava's buses, trolleybuses and trams. Buy them in the main train station, at MIC, newsagents and from the orange machines at some stops. They cost 8Kč for 15 minutes, 12Kč for 45 minutes and 32Kč for 24 hours.

WESTERN BESKYDY

Nomadic sheep-farmers, the Vlachs, moved into this region in the 15th century giving their name to Wallachia (Valašsko in Czech), the area they came to occupy. By the 18th century the Vlachs had largely been absorbed into the Hapsburg Empire, but they retained their rural traditions, including the carved timber architecture best seen in the *skansens* of Rožnov pod Radhoštěm.

The Beskydy hills themselves, peaking with Lysá hora (1324m), are popular for walking and winter sports. The map to have is the *Kartografie Praha's Beskydy No 42* (1:100,000) trail map.

ŠTRAMBERK

With gabled wooden cottages cascading down the slopes of Bílá hora (White mountain), the tiny village of Štramberk is a pristine slice of Wallachia. The aromas of wood smoke and pine infuse the air, and the ruined clifftop castle delivers fine views across the surrounding valleys. With a pretty main square and a fine restored Municipal Brewery, Štramberk gets especially busy on summer weekends, so try for a mid-week appointment with one of the country's most enchanting villages.

Information

The **Municipal information centre** (Městské informační centrum; ☎ 556 812 085; www.stramberk.cz; ☼ 9am-noon & 12.30-5pm Tue-Sun Apr-Sep, 9am-noon & 12.30-4pm Tue-Sun Oct-Mar) is in the Zdeňka Buriana Museum just below the main square and has internet access for 1Kč per minute.

Sights

The path up Bílá hora from north of the village square passes through a stone gate inscribed 'Cuius Regio – Eius Religio – 1111' (whose place – his place). On the slopes are the remains of

the Gothic **castle walls**, and at the peak you can climb 166 steps to the top of the **tower** (Trúba; adult/concession 20/10Kč; ☼ 9am-5pm Tue-Sun Apr-Nov, 9am-5pm Sat & Sun Dec-Mar) for vertiginous views.

On the village square is **muzeum Štramberk** (☎ 556 701 156; adult/concession 20/10Kč; ☼ 9am-noon & 1-5pm Tue-Sun) which has exhibits of local archaeology, folk furniture and art. South of the square is the interesting **muzeum Zdeňka Buriana** (☎ 556 852 240; adult/concession 20/10Kč; ☼ 9am-noon & 12.30-5pm Tue-Sun Apr-Sep, 9am-noon & 12.30-4pm Tue-Sun Oct-Mar), which commemorates the locally born painter, who chose Stone Age people as his subjects.

On the southern edge of the square, Štramberk's **Municipal Brewery** (Městský Pivovar; ☎ 556 813 710; www.truba.cz) has recently reopened after more than 150 years. You can visit the stone cellars and try their light and dark unfiltered Truba beers on the terrace overlooking the square. The brewery also has an excellent restaurant with bar snacks and full meals.

Further south is the entrance to the **national gardens of Kotouč** (národní sad na Kotoučí). It was here, in the **Šipka cave** (jeskyně Šipka), that archaeologist KJ Maška found the jawbone of a Neanderthal child in 1880. The discovery became the inspiration for Zdeněk Burian's paintings.

Sleeping & Eating

Penzión Stará Skola (☎ 556 852 697; www.penzionstaraskola.cz; s/d incl breakfast 460/920Kč; P) By the church on the square, the rooms in Štramberk's old school house are comfortable, but the real attraction is the spacious garden around the back.

Hotel Šipka (☎ 556 852 181; www.hotelsipka.cz; s/d incl breakfast 750/1280Kč; P) The dark wooden furniture is a little glum, but you can't beat the top location (also enjoyed by the restaurant) overlooking the square.

Penzion Jaroňkova Pekárana (☎ 556 808 843; jaronek@smira-print.cz; Náměsti 7; apartments from 1800Kč; P ▣) In a former bakery beside the brewery are two relaxed apartments above a vaulted wine cellar. Brekkie is freshly baked croissants and coffee. Bring along a loved one for the romantic ambience.

While you're in town, try *Štramberské uši* (Štramberk ears) – conical ginger biscuits with honey and spices, usually served with cream. According to legend, the ears originally belonged to unfortunate Tatar prisoners-of-war.

(Continued on page 289)

282

Pravčická brána, Sandstone Rocks of Labe (p240), North Bohemia

RICHARD NEBE

Previous Page: David Černý's *Miminka,* TV tower (p117), Prague
RICHARD NEBESKÝ

Plzeň (p219), West Bohemia

Sedlec ossuary (p159), Kutná Hora,
Central Bohemia

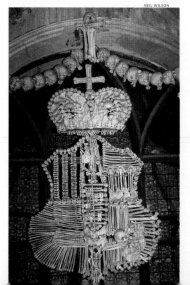

RICHARD NEBESKÝ

Sgraffitoed façade, Slavonice (p198),
South Bohemia

RICHARD NEBESKÝ

Konopiště chateau (p152), Central Bohemia

Gold Trail Festival (p185), Prachatice, South Bohemia

RICHARD NEBESKÝ

ALISTAIR DOVE/ALAMY

Cave, Moravian karst (p306), South Moravia

Opposite: Adršpach-Teplice Rocks (p260), Broumov highlands, East Bohemia
NEIL WILSON

Horní náměstí, Olomouc (p269), North Moravia

MICHAELA DUSIKOVA/PROFIMEDIA INTERNATIONAL S.R.O./ALAMY

Suchá Belá gorge, Slovenský raj National Park (p420), East Slovakia

Orava castle (p386), Orava valley, Central Slovakia

RICHARD NEBESKÝ

Jasná run (p392), Demänova valley, Low Tatras, Central Slovakia

Next Page: New bridge
(p347) over the Danube river,
Bratislava
JENNY JONES

Open-air Museum of Folk Architecture (p429), Bardejovské Kúpele, East Slovakia

RICHARD NEBESKÝ

(Continued from page 280)

Getting There & Away

Nový Jičín is a stop for most Olomouc–Ostrava buses, and from there local buses run twice a day to Štramberk (15Kč, 20 minutes). However, the most enjoyable way to get here is on foot through the hills – 8km on a red-marked trail from Nový Jičín train station, or across the river from Nový Jičín horní nádraží station.

KOPŘIVNICE

A short bus ride from Štramberk lies the industrial town of Kopřivnice, famed for its transport museum. Today it's mostly known as the home of the vehicle manufacturer Tatra, which produces large trucks.

The popular **Tatra Technical museum** (Technické muzeum Tatra; ☎ 656 821 415; www.tatra.infomorava.cz; Záhummení 369; adult/concession 70/40Kč; ☯ 9am-5pm Tue-Sun May-Sep, 9am-4pm Oct-Apr) is housed in purpose-built premises – you can't miss the red locomotive outside. For fans of old cars, trucks and trains, the Tatra factory has a dazzling display of its prized vehicles, including a replica of its first car, the 'Präsident' (1897). The company originally specialised in passenger cars and trucks, but during the later days of communist rule most production shifted to trucks and over-the-top Cold War limousines for use by diplomats. Don't miss the fan propelled V855 air sledge, or the Tatra 87 that Czech adventurers Hanzelka and Zikmund drove 63,000km through 48 countries from 1947 to 1950 (all without a Lonely Planet guidebook). Excellent video kiosks provide words and pictures in several languages.

There are regular buses to Štramberk (10Kč, 10 minutes).

ROŽNOV POD RADHOŠTĚM

Rožnov pod Radhoštěm (Rožnov-under-Radhoš) first became renowned for its *skansen*, or open-air museum, in 1925, when traditional wooden architecture was brought piece by piece from around the Beskydy region. When rebuilt in a spacious riverside park the exhibits caused an immediate stir, and decades later their presence has transformed Rožnov into a bustling resort town

The tourist and accommodation crush is amplified by a heavy schedule of contrived 'folk events', which change the face of the quiet provincial town during summer weekends. Stay overnight though, and arrive at the *skansen* after an early breakfast and you'll have largely unimpeded viewing.

More modern Wallachian culture, albeit with a Southern US accent, is on display around July 4 every year when Texans of Czech descent roll into Rožnov for a weeklong Independence Day jamboree, complete with barbecues, a rodeo and belly loads of Radegast beer. Don't even think about finding a hotel room at that time. Folk festivals such as the Easter Traditions or the folk song and dance festival (held on the first weekend of July) are quieter. See www.vmp.cz for full details of annual events at the *skansen*.

Orientation

From the adjacent train and bus stations it's a 400m walk east across the river to the main square, Masarykovo náměstí. The *skansen* is about another 800m east on Palackého.

Information

The extremely helpful **Wallachian kingdom information centre** (Informační centrum Valašského království; ☎ 571 655 196; www.roznov.cz, in Czech; Palackého 484; ☯ 8.30am-6pm May-Sep, 9am-3pm Mon-Fri Oct-Apr) provides information about local attractions, transport and accommodation. Ask them about scoring a Wallachian Kingdom passport (see p291).

Česká spořitelna (cnr Masarykovo nám & Lázeňská) and **ČSOB** (Nerudova 2201) both have ATMs and exchange counters. You can access the internet at **Planet Internet** (☎ 571 629 217; Na Zahřadach; ☯ Mon-Fri 9am-9pm, 11am-9pm Sat & Sun). Go around the back and up the stairs.

Sights & Activities

WALLACHIAN OPEN-AIR MUSEUM

Made up of three separate *skansens*, the **Wallachian open-air museum** (Valašské muzeum v přírodě; ☎ 571 757 111; www.vmp.cz) is an impressive effort to keep a grip on the region's architectural and cultural past. Multilingual maps and inventories of the buildings are available at the entrances.

The biggest and best of the three *skansens* is the **Wallachian village** (Valašská dědina; adult/concession 60/30Kč; ☯ 9am-5pm May-Aug, 10am-5pm Sep), which climbs right up the hillside to a ridge boasting exceptional views. It's a good attempt at reconstructing an entire shepherds' village, right down to the orchards and livestock, which are still raised using traditional methods.

NORTH MORAVIA

The **Wooden hamlet** (Dřevěné městečko; adult/concession 50/25Kč; 9am-5pm Apr-Sep, 9am-5pm Tue-Sun Jan & Oct, 9am-4pm Sat-Sun Dec) is the most fun, with its Wallachian-style *hospoda* (pub) where you can actually get a beer and a good Moravian meal. Other highlights are a pretty church from the village of Větřkovice and a collection of wooden beehives decorated with smirking faces. It is closed from 3 November to 5 December and during Christmas and New Year.

The **Mill valley** (Mlýnská dolina; adult/concession 50/25Kč; 9am-5pm May-Aug, 10am-5pm Sep) is a fascinating collection of water-driven mills with a working smithy and miller.

A **combined ticket** (adult/concession 120/60Kč) for all three attractions is also available.

WALKING UP RADHOŠŤ

It's 5.5km on a red-marked trail from the Wooden hamlet museum past Rožnov camp site and up to Černá hora (885m), then 2.5km up the ridge to fine views from Radhošť (1129m).

From there it's 3.5km on a blue trail to a saddle below Tanečnice peak. On the way you pass a little wooden church and a stone statue of a pre-Christian mountain spirit called Radegast (after whom the local beer is named). From Tanečnice a year-round chairlift descends to Ráztoka, where you can catch a bus back to Rožnov pod Radhoštěm (15 minutes).

Sleeping

Camping Rožnov (571 648 001; www.camproznov.cz; tent/bungalow per person 105/275Kč;) This attractive family site is 1km east of the museum.

Domov Mládeže Při Szeš (571 651 248; Zemědělská 500; per person 260Kč;) In a grey tower behind the train station, this dormitory is about the cheapest place in town. Good luck finding the receptionist though.

Horský Hotel Radegast (556 835 130; www.hotelradegast.cz; per person incl breakfast 370Kč) Near Radhošť, this chalet is best for those wanting to wake up breathing crisp mountain air.

Penzion & Restaurant El Greco (571 657 572; www.elgreco.cz; Hradištko 285; d incl breakfast 990Kč; apt incl breakfast 1980Kč;) There's nothing vaguely Greek about the comfortable rooms at this new place, but the *souvlaki* on the menu will stop you getting the lawyers involved for misleading advertising. It's a brisk 1km walk from

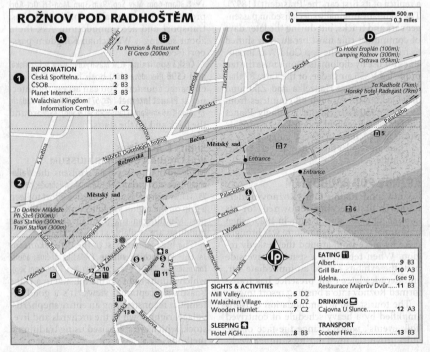

ROŽNOV POD RADHOŠTĚM

500 m
0.3 miles

INFORMATION
Česká Spořitelna..................1 B3
ČSOB...................................2 B3
Planet Internet.....................3 B3
Walachian Kingdom
  Information Centre..........4 C2

To Penzion & Restaurant
El Greco (200m)

To Hotel Eroplán (100m);
Camping Rožnov (300m);
Ostrava (55km);

To Radhošť (7km);
Horský hotel Radegast (7km)

Městský sad

Entrance

Entrance

To Domov Mládeže
Při Szeš (300m);
Bus Station (300m);
Train Station (300m)

Městský sad

SIGHTS & ACTIVITIES
Mill Valley...........................5 D2
Walachian Village................6 D2
Wooden Hamlet..................7 C2

SLEEPING
Hotel AGH..........................8 B3

EATING
Albert..................................9 B3
Grill Bar..............................10 A3
Jídelna..........................(see 9)
Restaurace Majerův Dvůr....11 B3

DRINKING
Cajovna U Slunce...............12 A3

TRANSPORT
Scooter Hire.......................13 B3

DISCOVERING THE 'KINGDOM OF WALLACHIA'

The innovative and friendly tourist information office in Roznov is seriously keen to increase the number of travellers to their interesting region. The kingdom has its own air force flying the official coat of arms with a rampant chicken (OK, it's one ageing Cessna), and can issue you a Wallachian Kingdom passport in seven different languages. The Wallachian flag (featuring a taller-than-tall black hat and two axes) has been flown atop the Himalayas, at Machu Picchu and even at the Panama Canal. The Kingdom of Wallachia has consular representation from Scotland to India and New Zealand, and in 1999 an entrant flying the Wallachian flag won the truck section of the Granada–Dakar rally. They've even minted their own money featuring a rock singing Queen Mother with folk music roots. Unfortunately the money is the only currency in the world backed by straw.

town north across the river to Bezručova, and then turn right Hradišťko.

Hotel AGH (☎ 571 625 666; www.hotel-agh.cz; Čechova 142; s/d from 1200/1440Kč) Just off the main square the newest and snazziest hotel in town is also the most central, and with at least five bars and restaurants you won't get bored or hungry.

Hotel Eroplán (☎ 571 648 014; www.eroplan.cz; Horní Paseky 451; s/d incl breakfast 1390/1590Kč; bungalows with shared bathroom 1200Kc/v; P X ⬚ ▣) Take your pick between the flash rooms with all mod cons (year-round) or rustic bungalows that can accommodate up to six people (June to September only).

Eating & Drinking

There aren't too many places in town, and most are closed by 9pm.

Grill Bar (☎ 571 654 766; 2nd fl, Masarykovo nám 186; mains 75-160Kč) This reliable place dishes up tasty grilled platters in contemporary surrounds overlooking the square.

Cajovna U Slunce (☎ 608 717 488; Nádražni 187; tea & coffee 40Kč; snacks 50Kč; ⏱ 11am-10pm Mon-Sat, 2-8pm Sun) Silk and rattan, pita and couscous, and more than 100 different teas and coffees create a gauzy New Age ambience (but not in an annoying Shirley MacLaine kind of way).

Also recommended:

Restaurace Majerův Dvůr (☎ 608 828 988; Nerudova 141; mains 80Kč; ⏱ 11am-7pm Mon-Sat) Czech specialities in a garden setting.

Albert (Masarykovo nám) Supermarket on the main square.

Jídelna (Masarykovo nám; ⏱ 7.30am-5pm Mon-Fri, 7.30am-noon Sat) Sandwiches and self-serve meals above the supermarket.

Getting There & Away

Buses are usually the easiest way to get here. There are reasonably regular direct buses from Brno (156Kč, three hours) and Olomouc (82Kč, 1 hours). To get here by train requires at least one change at Valašské Meziříčí, 13km away, which is on the Prague–Košice main railway line. The train takes 2½ hours to Brno (130Kč).

Getting Around

You can hire **scooters** (půjčovna skůtrů; ☎ 571 620 315; Bayerova 52; per day 500Kč; ⏱ 9am-5pm Mon-Fri) from a computer shop just off the main square.

ČESKÝ TĚŠÍN

An international border was laid through the middle of this town at the end of WWI using the natural division of the Olše river: to the west is Český Těšín in the Czech Republic, and to the east is Cieszyn in Poland. Most of the original town, and all the interesting historical sights, ended up on the Polish side (refer to Lonely Planet's *Poland* guidebook). The only reason to be here is if you have arrived from, or are off to, Poland.

The river is the border, with separate 24-hour crossings for each direction: Hlavní most (Hlavní bridge) is for entering the Czech Republic, Střelniční most for leaving. From the railway tracks on the Czech side, each bridge is about 500m along a street of the same name. Český Těšín's bus station is west of the tracks, via a pedestrian underpass on Hlavní or an automobile underpass on Viaduktova.

The **regional information centre** (regionální informační centrum; ☎ 558 711 866; itesin@grendel.cz; Hlavní 15; ⏱ 8am-5pm) has plenty of information on the region. Contact the tourist information office in Polish Cieszyn on ☎ 00 48 33 852 3050. **ČSOB** (Nádražní 4) has an exchange counter and ATM, as does the post office beside the train station.

NORTH MORAVIA

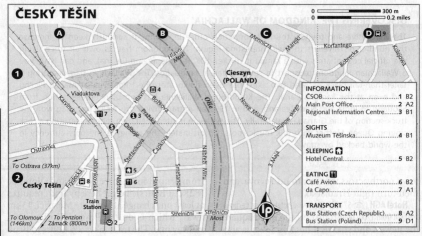

ČESKÝ TĚŠÍN

INFORMATION	
ČSOB...1	B2
Main Post Office............................2	A2
Regional Information Centre.........3	B1
SIGHTS	
Muzeum Těšínska.........................4	B1
SLEEPING	
Hotel Central................................5	B2
EATING	
Café Avion....................................6	B2
da Capo...7	A1
TRANSPORT	
Bus Station (Czech Republic).......8	A2
Bus Station (Poland)....................9	D1

Muzeum Těšínska (☎ 558 710 087; Hlavní 3; adult/concession 10/5Kč; ☉ 9am-5pm Tue-Fri, 9am-1pm Sat, 1-5pm Sun) has exhibits on the history and ethnography of the region.

Sleeping & Eating

Hotel Central (☎ 558 713 113; www.hotel-central.cz; Nádražní 10; s/d incl breakfast 650/1300Kč; ☐) Loads of character, a handy location opposite the railway station, plus the Cascada Mexican restaurant downstairs make this the best place in town.

Penzion Zámačk (☎ 558 746 015; www.sweb.cz/pensionzamecek; Jablunkovská 852; s/d 800/1200Kč) The best rooms are tucked away in the attic amid the turrets of this delightful character building. Walk south from the railway station for 800m.

Café Avion (Nádražní 12; coffee 30Kč; ☉ 9am-7pm Sun-Fri, 9am-9pm Sat) This trendy café opposite the railway station has miraculously been transplanted from London or Melbourne to this remote Czech border town.

Da Capo (☎ 558 712 212; cnr Sokola Tumy & Vladuktova; pizza 90Kč) Good pizza and seafood are on offer at this corner restaurant that would not be out of place in Naples.

Getting There & Away

There are seven fast trains a day to Prague (484Kč, 5½ hours), and seven to Košice (4½ hours) via Žilina (one hour) and Poprad (three hours).

Local trains run to Ostrava (60Kč, one hour) all day.

Buses also leave 12 times a day for Ostrava (40Kč, one hour), where you can change for Olomouc and other destinations. On the Polish side, there is an express bus every hour or two to Katowice, plus several per day for Kraków.

South Moravia

You get the feeling South Moravia would be perfectly happy declaring its independence from the Czech Republic. So strong and confident is the region's ability and desire to keep its culture alive that metamorphosis into a separate buffer state between Bohemia and Slovakia would be a powerful way to reinforce a potent sense of identity.

The most overt demonstration of this robust identity comes during the summer festival season, when communities from Telč to Moravské Slovácko dress up in traditional garb and sing and dance their way to a profoundly authentic display of 'living history' – all the while mellowed by wine from the local vineyards on the southern border with Austria. Since 1989, Moravian wine has been improving with every vintage, and as a drawcard for travellers, wine tourism now competes with the alluring World Heritage chateaux at nearby Lednice and Valtice. Further west, the untainted Renaissance perfection of Telč is equally spectacular and also demands your attention.

Nature steps up to the mark with the incredible cave systems of the Moravian karst (Moravský kras) and the vertiginous clifftop locations of the chateaux at Pernštejn and Vranov, two of the Czech Republic's most spectacular castles.

Finally, there's Brno, the cosmopolitan heart of the region, where communist-era Trabants jostle with post-EU Audis amid an elegant display of galleries, museums and theatres. And after the theatre, expect the busy chatter in the bars and cafés to be not about distant Prague, but more often about what really matters in Moravia.

HIGHLIGHTS

- Experience big-city life, Czech style, without Prague's tourist commotion, in cultured and bustling **Brno** (p295)

- Explore the fascinating Jewish heritage of picturesque **Mikulov** (p321)

- Be surprised by the fascinating functionalist architecture of **Zlín** (p329)

- Soak up the unblemished Renaissance perfection of the gorgeous town square in **Telč** (p313)

- Lose yourself in the cinematic canvases of Mucha's sublime *Slav Epic* in quiet **Moravský Krumlov** (p310)

SOUTH MORAVIA

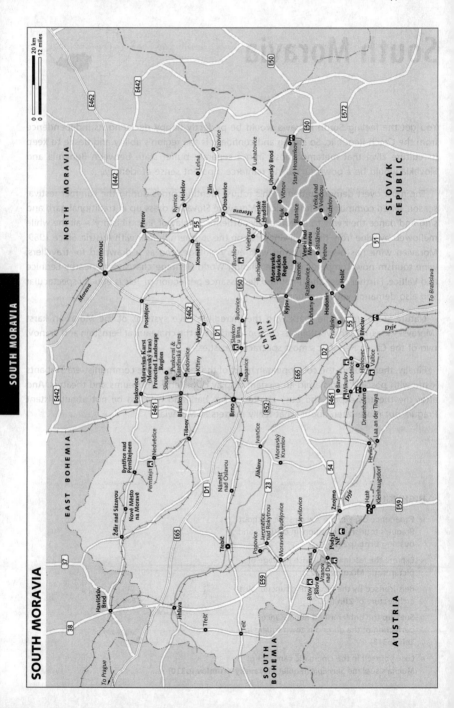

BRNO

pop 385,000

With flashy Prague being the city at the top of many travellers' must-do list, Brno, just 210km to the west, could be forgiven for developing a slight inferiority complex. But in reality the people of Brno are perfectly OK with their city's lot as the Czech Republic's second city.

Despite having a population of less than 400,000, Brno behaves like the cosmopolitan capital it is (ie of Moravia), and stately boulevards and parks give it an almost Parisian air. This vaguely Gallic ambience is further enhanced by a population with contagious enthusiasm for caffeine, chat and culture, which they energetically bring to life in the city's cafés and bars.

Brno has an after-dark reputation for keeping its top button firmly done up, but spend a few hours in a local pub and you'll soon see that traditional Moravian reserve melt away. Maybe it's because they don't have to share their old town with legions of tourists.

And even if Brno's historical hub is small change compared with the architectural overachievement that is Prague, the city can stand alone with an array of excellent galleries and museums, a brooding castle fortress and a robust confidence in the relevance and importance of surrounding Moravia, comfortably away from the sometimes myopic focus of the national capital.

History

The present-day suburb of Líšeň was a Slav fort, Staré Zámky, at the time of the Great Moravian Empire. Around AD 1000 a settlement was founded on the Svratka river, where the suburb of Staré Brno now stands.

In the 11th century the Přemysl princesses built a castle on Petrov hill. By the middle of the 13th century the town around it had acquired a defensive wall. At this time another castle was built on Špilberk hill. During the reign of John of Luxembourg, Brno became an important centre of arts and trade. In the late 1300s it became Moravia's capital for the first time. Most of Brno's monasteries date from that time.

This predominantly Catholic town sided with King Sigismund in the Hussite Wars; the Hussites twice tried to take it but failed. In the mid-15th century Brno sided with an enemy of the Czechs, Matthias Corvinus (Matyáš Korvín). Later in the 16th century Brno turned Protestant and joined the unsuccessful anti-

Hapsburg rebellion by the Czech Estates. In the ensuing Thirty Years' War, the town was able to defend itself against the Swedes from 1643 to 1645.

Botanist Gregor Mendel (1822–84) established the modern science of heredity through his studies of peas and bees at the Augustinian monastery in Brno.

After the Brno–Vienna railway was completed in 1839, Brno developed into a major industrial centre. As the most important town in the Czechoslovak state after Prague, it acquired a university and, in the 1920s, some major exhibition buildings. Brno is one of Europe's leading venues for trade fairs.

Orientation

The town is dominated by Špilberk castle, on the hill of the same name; vying for attention are the spires of the cathedral of SS Peter & Paul on Petrov hill.

Brno's main train station *(hlavní nádraží)* is just south of the town centre. Opposite the station is the beginning of Masarykova, a main pedestrian thoroughfare that leads north to triangular náměstí Svobody, the centre of town. The bus station *(autobusové nádraží)* is 800m south of the train station, via the Galerie Vankovka (Map p298) shopping centre and Tesco department store.

Brno's Tuřany airport is 7.5km southeast of the train station.

MAPS

SHOCart's GeoClub 1:15,000 *Brno plán města* is recommended.

Information

BOOKSHOPS

Geokart (Map p298; ☎ 542 216 561; Vachova 8) Stocks maps and travel guides.
Knihkupectví Literární Kavárna (Map p298; ☎ 542 217 954; náměstí Svobody 13) Has English-language titles.

CULTURAL CENTRES

British Council (Map p298; ☎ 545 210 174; www .britishcouncil.cz; Solniční 12) UK newspapers are available.

EMERGENCY

Tourist Police Station (Map p298; ☎ 974 626 100; Bartošová 1)

INTERNET ACCESS

Internet Centrum (Map p298; 1st fl, Masarykova 22-24; per hr 45Kč; ☯ 8am-midnight)

Laundromat@Bar Pod Balony (Map p298; ☎ 736 277 570; Hybešova 45; per hr 50Kč; ☼ 10am-1pm Mon-Fri, 2pm-1am Sat, 2-11pm Sun)

LAUNDRY
Laundromat@Bar Pod Balony (Map p298; ☎ 736 277 570; Hybešova 45; ☼ 10am-1pm Mon-Fri, 2pm-1am Sat, 2-11pm Sun) Self-service washers and dryers, a bar and internet access. Charges 70Kč per load.

LEFT LUGGAGE
Train station (Map p298; per day 26Kč, ☼ closed 11pm-4am) Located on the ground floor.
Bus station (Map p297; ☼ 5.15am-10.15pm Mon-Fri, from 6am Sat & Sun)

MEDIA
Metropolis A free fortnightly events magazine (in Czech) featuring cinema, theatre and club listings.

MEDICAL SERVICES
Lékárna Koliště (Map p298; ☎ 545 424 811; Koliště 47) Twenty-four-hour pharmacy.
Úrazová hospital (nemocnice; Map p298; ☎ 545 538 111; Ponávka 6)

MONEY
KB bank (Map p298; cnr Kozí & Kobližná); branch (Map p298; náměstí Svobody 21) Exchange and ATM services.

POST
Post office Main (Map p298; Poštovská 3/5; 1 block east of the main square); branch (Map p298; Nádražní; by the train station; ☼ 24hr)

TOURIST INFORMATION
Tourist Information Office (Kulturní a Informační Centrum – KIC; Map p298; ☎ 542 211 090; www.ticbrno .cz; Old town hall, Radnická 8; ☼ 8am-6pm Mon-Fri, 9am-5.30pm Sat & Sun Apr-Sep; to 5pm Sat, to 3pm Sun Oct-Mar); branch (Map p298; opposite the train station; ☎ 542 221 450; Nádrazvní 6; ☼ 9am-6pm Mon-Fri) Sells maps and books accommodation.

TRAVEL AGENCIES
Čedok (Map p298; ☎ 542 321 267; Nádražní 10/12)
České dráhy (Map p298; ☎ 542 221 507) In the main train station; also sells bus tickets to Western Europe.
GTS International (Map p298; ☎ 542 221 996; gts .brno@gtsint.cz; Vachova 4) This youth travel agency sells international air, bus and train tickets.

Dangers & Annoyances
Several cases of pickpocketing are reported daily. There's an area just east of the centre – surrounded by the streets Cejl, Francouzská, Příkop and Ponávka – that can be dangerous, especially at night.

Sights & Activities
CITY CENTRE
From the main train station, Masarykova leads to Kapucínské náměstí. At No 5 is the **church of the Holy Cross** (kostel sv Kříže, Map p298) and the adjoining and gruesomely compelling **Capuchin monastery** (Kapucínský klášter).

The monastery's ghoulish attraction is a dry, well-ventilated **crypt** (krypta; adult/concession 40/20Kč, English text additional 40Kč; ☼ 9am-noon & 2-4.30pm Tue-Sat, 11-11.45am & 2-4.30pm Sun, closed Dec & Jan) with the natural ability to turn dead bodies into mummies.

Up to 150 cadavers were deposited here prior to 1784, and the desiccated corpses include 18th-century monks, abbots and local notables, from a nameless 12-year-old ministrant to hard-working chimney sweeper Barnabas Orelli, still wearing his boots. In a glass-topped coffin in a separate room is Baron von Trenck – soldier, adventurer, gambler and womaniser – who bequeathed loads of cash to the monastery. At least he got his own room!

Cabbage Market & Surrounding Area
Opposite the monastery a lane leads into the sloping square of **Zelný trh** (Cabbage market, Map p298), the heart of the old town and where live carp were sold from the baroque **Parnassus fountain** (1695) at Christmas. The fountain is a symbolic cave encrusted with allegorical figures. Hercules restrains three-headed Cerberus, watchdog of the underworld, and the three female figures represent the ancient empires of Babylon (crown), Persia (cornucopia) and Greece (quiver of arrows). The triumphant woman on top (arrogantly) symbolises Europe. The square has been the best place in town to buy fruit and vegies since the 13th century, and smart shoppers still flock to it. However, the fountain's grotesque design remains an acquired taste.

On the southeast (uphill) side of the square is the former **Ditrichstein palace** (Ditrichštejnský palác), which now houses the **Moravian museum** (Moravské zemské muzeum; Map p298 ☎ 542 321 205; Zelný trh 8; adult/concession 36/18Kč; ☼ 9am-5pm Tue-Sat). Exhibits straddle the intellectual gulf between extinct life and the medieval village.

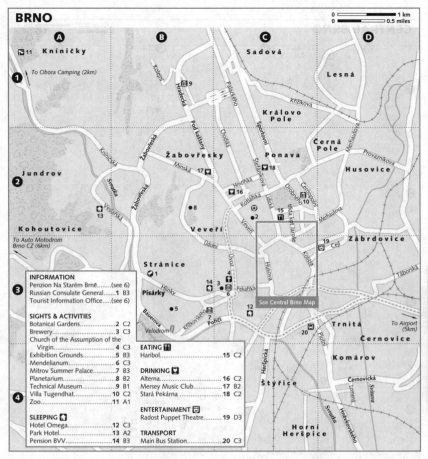

BRNO

0 ————————— 1 km
0 ————————— 0.5 miles

INFORMATION
Penzion Na Starém Brně........(see 6)
Russian Consulate General.......1 B3
Tourist Information Office.....(see 6)

SIGHTS & ACTIVITIES
Botanical Gardens...................2 C2
Brewery.................................3 C3
Church of the Assumption of the
  Virgin...............................4 C3
Exhibition Grounds.................5 B3
Mendelianum........................6 C3
Mitrov Summer Palace............7 B3
Planetarium..........................8 B2
Technical Museum..................9 B1
Villa Tugendhat...................10 C2
Zoo....................................11 A1

SLEEPING
Hotel Omega........................12 C3
Park Hotel...........................13 A2
Pension BVV.........................14 B3

EATING
Haribol................................15 C2

DRINKING
Alterna...............................16 C2
Mersey Music Club.................17 B2
Stará Pekárna.......................18 C2

ENTERTAINMENT
Radost Puppet Theatre..........19 D3

TRANSPORT
Main Bus Station...................20 C3

See Central Brno Map

SOUTH MORAVIA

In a courtyard on the right of the Moravian museum is the **Biskupský yard museum** (Map p298; ☎ 542 321 205; Muzejní 1; adult/concession 30/15Kč; ☼ 9am-5pm Tue-Sat), with the largest freshwater aquarium in the country, plenty on Moravian wildlife, lots of model mushrooms and a sleepy section on the history of money. How's that for a diverse series of exhibitions?

In 1767 Mozart, aged 11, performed at the **Reduta theatre** (Reduta divadlo; Map p298; Zelný trh 4) on the square's eastern side. Following sparkling restoration, the theatre reopened in 2005.

Petrov Hill & Cathedral of SS Peter & Paul

From the top of Zelný trh, Petrská climbs Petrov hill, site of the gargantuan cathedral of SS Peter & Paul (katedrála sv Petra a Pavla,

Map p298). Ascend its **tower** (věž; adult/concession 35/30Kč; ☼ 10am-5pm Tue-Sun) for great views of Brno, or descend into its forlorn **crypt** (krypta; adult/concession 15/10Kč; ☼ same as tower).

The 14th-century cathedral was originally built on the site of a pagan temple to Venus and has been reconstructed many times since. The highly decorated 11m-high main altar with figures of SS Peter and Paul was carved by Viennese sculptor Josef Leimer in 1891. The Renaissance **Bishop's palace** (Biskupská palác, closed to the public) adjoins the cathedral. To the left is the pleasant **Denisovy Sady** park, which sweeps in a verdant arc around Petrov hill.

Old Town Hall & Around

From the downhill end of Biskupská, Starobrněnská turns right to the **former site of**

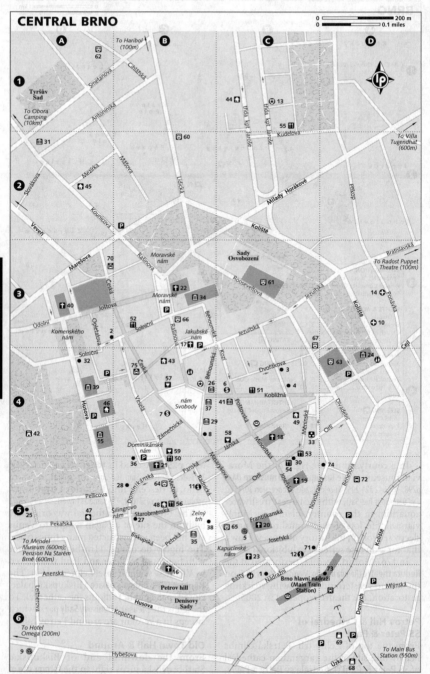

CENTRAL BRNO

the brewery (Map p298), now reinstalled to the delight of local drinkers in bigger and better premises at the **current site of the brewery** (Map p297) near Mendlovo náměstí.

From Starobrněnská, Mečova runs left to abut the back wall of the **Old town hall** (Stará radnice; Map p298; 9am-5pm). At Mečova 5, about 5m up the wall, is what looks like the **face of a man**. The well-lubricated urban legend goes that a Brno councillor who plotted with the Hussites to surrender the town in 1424 was overheard by Borro, Emperor Sigismund's court clown, while a prisoner of the Hussites. Borro escaped and told the story, and the councillor was sealed alive in the wall.

The original, early-13th-century building, which became the town hall in 1343, has been incorporated into today's structure. A peculiar sight by the entrance on Radnická is a Gothic portal with a crooked middle turret, made by Anton Pilgram in 1510. According to legend, he was not paid the agreed amount by the council and, in revenge, left the turret (above the statue of Righteousness) crooked.

The town hall **tower** (adult/concession 20/10Kč; 9am-5pm), raised by 5m during repairs in 1905 so as not to disappear among the newly built houses around it, offers magnificent views. For another 30Kč you can also see the town hall's interior, including the **Crystal hall**, **Fresco hall** and **Treasury**.

The building is full of oddities. Hanging from the ceiling at the entrance is the corpse of a legendary **Brno dragon** that terrorised the city's waterways. It is, in fact, an Amazon River crocodile, donated by Archprince Matyáš in 1608. Note also the **Brno wheel**, made by an enterprising cartwright from Lednice. In 1636 he bet a mate he could fell a tree, build a wheel and roll it 50km to Brno – all before dusk. He was successful, and the hastily made and quickly rolled wheel has been on display ever since. Unfortunately, someone started the dodgy rumour that the cartwright had received diabolic assistance, and he died penniless when his customers went elsewhere.

Minorite Monastery & Around

To the east of the main shopping street, Masarykova, is a brace of churches. The **church of St Mary Magdalene** (kostel sv Máří Magdalény, Map p298) on Františkánská stands on the former site of a synagogue, and on Josefská is the **church of St Joseph** (kostel sv Josefa, Map p298), first consecrated in 1674.

Further north on Masarykova, Orlí leads to the **Měnín gate** (Měnínská brána, Map p298) built around 1600 and now housing a small **archaeological museum** (542 214 946; Měnínská 7; adult/concession 25/15Kč; 9am-6pm Tue-Sun May-Sep, to 5pm Oct-Apr).

AHEAD OF THEIR TIME

The bells of the cathedral of SS Peter & Paul disconcertingly ring noon an hour early, at 11am. Legend has it that when the Swedish laid siege to the city in 1645, their commander, General Torstenson, who had been frustrated by Brno's defences for more than a week, decided to launch a final attack, with one caveat: if his troops could not prevail by noon, he would throw in his hand.

By 11am the Swedes were making headway, but the cathedral's tower-keeper had the inspired idea to ring noon early. The bells struck 12, the Swedes withdrew and the city was saved.

On nearby Minoritská (off Orlí) is the **church of St John** (kostel sv Janů, Map p298) and the Minorite monastery founded in 1230. (The Minorites are the only order in Moravia still in their original quarters.)

Náměstí Svobody & Around

Heading north, Masarykova leads to Brno's elegant and spacious main square, náměstí Svobody, the city's bustling central hub. On the eastern side of the square is the **house of the four mamlases** (dům U čtyř mamlasů; Map p298; náměstí Svobody 10). The façade is supported by a quartet of extremely muscled but clearly moronic 'Atlas' figures, each struggling to hold up the building and their loincloths at the same time. Created by Germano Wanderley in 1928, the building has provoked a longstanding and robust debate over whether the statues aptly reflect the elegant face of the Moravian capital.

Náměstí Svobody dates from the early 13th century, when it was called Dolní trh (Lower market). Its **plague column** dates from 1680. On the corner of the square and Kobližná is the **palác Říkovský z Dobrčic** (Map p298), also known as the house at the red ox (dům U rudého vola). At Kobližná 4, the **Schrattenbachův palác** (Map p298) has a niche containing a 1637 statue of the Madonna.

Showcasing Moravia's obsession with tradition, the **Ethnographic museum** (Etnografické muzeum; Map p298; ☎ 542 422 361; Kobližná 1; adult/concession 30/15Kč; ☼ 9am-5pm Tue-Sat) gives a comprehensive insight into the region's traditional culture from the 18th to 20th centuries.

North of the square, Běhounská leads to Jakubské náměstí and the monumentally austere 15th-century **church of St James** (kostel sv Jakuba, Map p298). It has a baroque pulpit with reliefs of Christ dating from 1525. Also here is the baroque tomb of the French Protestant Raduit de Souches, who died leading the defence of Brno in 1645. The church's biggest drawcard is a small stone figure known by its local nickname of 'Nehaňba' ('The Shameless'). Look up at the first-floor window on the south side of the tower at the west end of the church; at its top is the tiny stone figure of a man baring his buttocks in the general direction of the cathedral (you really need binoculars or a telephoto lens to see him clearly). Local legend claims this was a disgruntled mason's parting shot to his rivals working on Petrov hill.

Dominikánské Náměstí & Around

From náměstí Svobody, Zámečnická leads west to Dominikánské náměstí, a humble square dominated by the **church of St Michael** (kostel sv Michala, Map p298), which has an interesting, ornate main altar (1759) by Josef Winterhalter and a massive pair of cupola-topped towers.

Also facing the square is the 16th-century **New town hall** (Nová radnice) with its impressive frescoes.

Church of St Thomas & Around

The church of St Thomas (kostel sv Tomáše, Map p298), with a soaring nave in the purest Gothic style, abuts a 14th-century **Augustinian monastery** that today houses a branch of the **Moravian gallery** (below).

Along Joštova, past the neo-Renaissance **assembly** (zemská sněmovna), stands the Evangelical Comenius church (kostel JA Komenského), better known as the **Red church** (Červený kostel, Map p298) for its red-brick exterior; it was built between 1862 and 1867 to a design by H Ferstel. On the corner of Husova and Komenského náměstí is the **Meeting house** (Besední dům, Map p298), one of the best works of 19th-century Danish architect Theofil Hansen and now home to the Brno State Philharmonic Orchestra. The name of the building comes from its role as a social rendezvous point for locals, a tradition still being maintained in the 21st century with the assistance of text messaging.

Moravian Gallery

If proof were needed that the people of Brno were pathological art-lovers, the fact that there are *three* branches of the Moravian gallery (Moravská galerie) is surely it. Entry to all three galleries is free on the first Friday of the month.

Adjoining the church of St Thomas, **Místodržitelský palace** (Map p298; ☎ 532 169 130; Moravské náměstí 1A; adult/concession 50/25Kč; ☒ 10am-6pm Wed-Sun, 10am-7pm Thu) hosts a variety of changing exhibitions.

The second branch, the **Applied Arts museum** (Map p298; Uměleckoprůmyslové muzeum; ☎ 532 169 130; Husova 14; adult/concession 50/25Kč; ☒ 10am-6pm Wed-Sun, 10am-7pm Thu), focuses on the evolution of arts and crafts from the Middle Ages to Art Nouveau and also holds regular, temporary exhibitions.

Up the road, the third branch is inside **Pražákův palace** (Map p298; ☎ 532 169 111; Husova 18; adult/concession 80/40Kč; ☒ 10am-6pm Wed-Sun, 10am-7pm Thu); it focuses on the Czech modernist movement and 20th-century art.

ŠPILBERK CASTLE

Špilberk castle (Map p298) may lack fairy-tale good looks, but it has been a crowning feature of the city's skyline for centuries. Founded in the early 1200s, the castle was lived in by the Czech kings before being transformed into a military fortress in the 18th century. In this form the castle became 'home' to enemies of the Austro–Hungarian Empire. A multinational band of rebels was incarcerated in the so-called Prison of the Nations. The prison closed in 1853 but was reopened by the occupying Nazis in WWII. Baron von Trenck (see Capuchin monastery, p296) died here in 1749.

Some of Špilberk's casemates (*kasematy*), the dark corridors beneath the bastions, are now a **museum of prison life** (☎ 542 123 614; adult/concession 60/30Kč; ☒ 9am-6pm Jul & Aug, closed Mon Oct-Jun, to 5pm Oct-Apr). The last entry to the museum is 45 minutes before closing time.

The castle itself houses the **Brno city museum** (muzeum města Brna; Map p298; ☎ 542 123 611; www.spilberk .cz; adult/concession 100/50Kč; ☒ 9am-5pm Tue-Sun Oct & Apr, 10am-5pm Wed-Sun Nov & Mar), which hosts permanent exhibitions on the history of construction, Brno's monuments and architecture, plus a fine arts gallery. Especially interesting is the section on the castle's past as a prison and the exquisite and colourful **Brno Law Book and Bibles** made for Arnošt of Pardubic (Arnost of Pardubice), who was appointed the first Archbishop of Prague in 1364. (In the early days of Prague's Charles University, his support was

vital when he ordered all monks to study there, thus raising the educational standards of the institution.)

There is also an exquisite **baroque pharmacy** (adult/concession 20/10Kč; ☒ 9am-6pm Tue-Sun May-Sep) dating from the mid-18th century. For great views climb the **lookout tower** (adult/concession 20/10Kč) and admire the rather impressive **chime** (in the second courtyard), which musically sees in the hour from 10am to 6pm. Discounted **combination tickets** (adult/concession 120/60Kč) for the *kasematy*, lookout tower and exhibitions are also available.

The castle is approachable only on foot, up the hill through the quiet gardens.

Below the hill, on the corner of Pellicova, there is a 1914 **cubist house** (Map p298) by František Uherka. From Šilingrovo náměstí, Dominikánská runs north to a **former Dominican monastery** (Dominikánský klášter, Map p298).

OUTSIDE THE OLD TOWN
Near Špilberk Castle

Over Špilberk hill from the old town, on the corner of Úvoz and Pekařská, is the **church of the Assumption of the Virgin** (kostel Nanebevzetí Panny Marie, Map p298), Brno's finest late-Gothic building. Inside is the oldest painting on wood in the Czech Republic, the 13th-century *black Madonna* (černá Madona).

Around the corner at Mendlovo náměstí, in part of the **abbey of St Thomas**, the **Mendelianum** (Map p297; ☎ 543 424 043; www.mendel-museum.org; Mendlovo náměstí 1; adult/concession 80/40Kč; ☒ 10am-6pm May-Oct, 10am-4pm Wed-Sun Nov-Apr) is a museum devoted to the father of modern genetics, botanist Gregor Johann Mendel (1822–84), who opened up new realms of possibility in this area with his pioneering work on the humble garden pea. He was a former abbot of St Thomas. Mendel's work went largely unnoticed until after his death, when it was discovered that he had identified the principle of inheritance that governs how characteristics are passed on through the generations. A tour of the abbey costs 60Kč extra.

Take tram 1 from the train station to Mendlovo náměstí, and the museum is through a gate into a garden, second door on your right.

North of the Centre

A short walk from the old town is the small **Leoš Janáček memorial museum** (památník Leoše Janáčka; Map p298; ☎ 542 212 811; Smetanova 14; adult/concession 20/10Kč; ☒ 1-4pm Wed, 9am-noon & 1-4pm Thu & Fri) dedicated to the composer. Janáček was born in Hukvaldy (North Moravia) but lived in Brno from childhood until his death in 1928. Janáček is the least known of the 'big three' Czech composers, the others being Smetana and Dvořák. All were exponents of 'musical nationalism', incorporating folk music into their pieces.

Further north, on adjacent Veveří (to the west), are the **Botanical gardens** (Botanická zahrada; Map p297; ☎ 541 129 397; ⚇ 9am-5pm Mon-Fri, to 3pm Sat & Sun); from the city centre take tram 3 or 13.

Villa Tugendhat (Map p297; ☎ 545 212 118; www .tugendhat-villa.cz; Černopolni 45; adult/concession 120/60Kč; ⚇ 10am-6pm Wed-Sun), a modern functionalist building in the suburb of Černá Pole, is the work of well-known German architect Ludwig Mies van der Rohe (1886–1969) and a shrine for students of modern architecture. Hired by rich newlyweds to build them a home, Mies turned it into one of the first open-plan houses. In 2001 it was added to Unesco's list of World Cultural and Natural Heritage Sites. Don't miss the huge glass windows that disappear into the floor to flood the house with birdsong. Forward bookings are mandatory, so phone ahead. Take tram 3, 5 or 11 from Moravské náměstí up Milady Horákové to Černopolní, then walk 300m north.

Exhibition Grounds & Around

The Exhibition Grounds (Výstaviště, Map p297) in the suburb of Pisárky (take tram 1 from the train station) were opened in 1928. They are now a year-round trade fair venue. In addition to the **palace of Industry** (Průmyslový palác) other interesting buildings include the **Congress hall** (Kongresová hala) and Bauhaus-style **New house** (Nový dům).

In the space between Rybářská and Křížkovského is the quaint **Mitrov summer palace** (letohrádek Mitrovských; Veletržní 19).

Other Museums & Galleries

Contemporary art exhibitions are held at the **city art gallery** (dům umění; Map p298; ☎ 542 211 808; www.dumb.cz; Malinovského náměstí 2; adult/ concession 50/25Kč; ⚇ 10am-6pm Tue-Sun). It's free on Wednesday.

Walking Tour

Begin at the **church of St James** (1; p300) in Jabubské náměstí and make sure you spy the odd little statue near a south-facing window in the church tower. It will give you something to ponder as you're walking. From Jabubské

náměstí, head south along Rašinova to **náměstí Svobody** (2; p300), Brno's epic main square. At the northern end of the square is the town's **plague column** (3; p300), and on the eastern side on the corner with Kobližná is the **palác Říkovský z Dobrčic** (4; p300) dating from the 1730s. Across the road on Kobližná, the **Ethnographic museum** (5; p300) is worth seeing. Return to náměstí Svobody, and further down the square's eastern side is the compelling **house of the four mamlases** (6; p300), now contrasting with the modern façades of nearby shopping arcades. Follow náměstí Svobody as it squeezes southwards into Masarykova, a bustling pedestrian mall. Turn right into Panská and then left into Radnická. On your right on Radnická is the **Old town hall** (7; p299). In the entrance hall are oddities, including the Brno wheel and the Brno dragon, and a weirdly angled front spire. Opposite, climb the tower for good views of the old town. Follow Radnická south to the sloping expanse of **Zelný trh** (8; p296) and maybe buy some fresh fruit to sustain you for the walk up **Petrov hill** (9; p297). To get there climb Petrská at the southwest (uphill) end of the square. Atop Petrov hill is the **cathedral of**

SS Peter & Paul (**10**; p297), with excellent views from the cathedral's tower or from the **Denisovy Sady** (**11**; p297) gardens to the south. From the gardens follow Dominikánská back down the hill. Turn right into Starobrněnská and then left into Mečova. On your right, about 5m up the rear wall of the Old town hall is the **face of a man** (**12**; p299), allegedly a former councillor who plotted to overthrow the city in 1424. Follow Mečova north to **Dominikánské náměstí** (**13**; p300) where you can have designer tea and coffee at Čhajovna (p304) or something stronger at the funky Livingstone bar (p304), and carry on pondering the statue at the church of St James.

Brno for Children

There is a **planetarium** (Map p297; ☎ 541 321 287; www.hvezdarna.cz) at Kraví hora 2 (tram 4), and a **zoo** (Zoologická zahrada; Map p297; ☎ 546 432 311; www.zoobrno.cz; ☯ 9am-6pm) at Bystrc-Mniší hora (tram 1, 3 or 11).

Brno's new **Technical museum** (Technické muzeum vs Brně; Map p297; ☎ 541 421 411; www.technicalmuseum.cz; Purkyňova 105; adult/concession 50/25Kč; ☯ 9am-5pm Tue-Sun) is worth a half day of anyone's time. Highlights are cool retro Tesla televisions and stereos, and the wonderful 'Orchestrion', a huge wind-up forerunner to the jukebox with mini drums and cymbals crashing in perfect unison. Don't miss the **Panoptikon** on the first floor; this huge wooden stereoscope allows up to 20 viewers to look at 3-D images from antique glass slides that are changed on a regular basis. Catch tram 13 to Králove Pole.

Radost puppet theatre (Radost divadlo; Map p297; ☎ 545 321 273; www.divadlo-radost.cz; Bratislavská 32) is a fabulous theatre that puts on kids shows during the day, with occasional evening shows for adults. Either way, it's all great fun.

Festivals & Events

The **Auto Motodrom Brno CZ** (☎ 546 216 406; www.automotodrombrno.cz; Ostravačice) holds events for revheads throughout the year, culminating in August's **Moto Grand Prix** (www.motograndprix.com; admission from 700Kč). Tickets are available from the circuit and **Tourist Information Office** (Map p298; ☎ 542 211 090; www.ticbrno.cz; Radnická 8). Brno is packed out at this time and hotel prices can double. The racing circuit is just off the D1 road to Prague, 10km west of Brno. It's well signposted.

In early June, Brno celebrates **Brno Days** for four days with shows, exhibitions and fireworks.

Sleeping

In February, April, August, September and October, Brno hosts numerous major international trade fairs, and hotel rates increase by 40% to 100%. Book ahead.

BUDGET

The Tourist Information Office (p296) can help with accommodation in private rooms from around 400Kč.

Hostels

The Tourist Information Office (p296) and Čedok and GTS International travel agencies (p296) can help with accommodation in student dormitories during July and August.

Traveller's Hostel (Map p297; ☎ 542 213 573; www.travellers.cz; Jánská 22; dm incl breakfast 290Kč; ☯ Jul & Aug) Gregor Mendel first presented his genetic research in this stately building in 1865. Every summer the rooms are filled by backpackers in a super-central and friendly spot close to good nightlife and not far from the railway station.

Camping

Obora Camping (☎ 546 223 334; www.autocampobora.cz; tent per person 80Kč, dm 200Kč; ☯ May-Sep; **P**) This camp site is at the Brněnská přehrada (Brno dam), northwest of the city centre. Get there from the main train station on tram 1 to the zoo, then change to bus 103. The camp ground is at the seventh stop.

MIDRANGE

Penzion Na Starém Brně (Map p297; ☎ 543 247 872; www.pension-brno.com; Mendlovo nám 1a; s/d incl breakfast 850/1050Kč) An atmospheric Augustinian monastery conceals five compact rooms that come reader-recommended. And with an attached wine bar offering the best of Moravian vintages, there's no reason to be too pious.

Pension BVV (Map p297; ☎ 543 213 426; www.bvv.cz/ft; Hlinky 28A; s/d incl breakfast 890/1180Kč) Situated within close proximity of the Mendlovo námesti transport interchange, this three-star spot has robust breakfasts, comfy rooms and the lure of the Starbrno brewery just down the road.

Hotel Omega (Map p297; ☎ 543 213 876; www.hotelomega.cz; Křídlovická 19b; s/d incl breakfast 890/1350Kč; **P**) In a quiet neighbourhood a brisk 1km walk from the centre, this tourist information favourite has sunny, spacious rooms decorated in cool pastels and with modern pine furniture. There's a squash court if you still have energy after a day's sightseeing.

Hotel Amphone (Map p298; ☎ 545 428 310; www .amphone.cz; třída kpt Jaroše 29; s/d incl breakfast 990/1490Kč; P) On an elegant tree-lined street, the friendly Amphone has bright and airy rooms around a garden filled with birdsong. Attached is Sabaidy (right), a spicily authentic Lao restaurant.

Hotel & Pivnice Pegas (Map p298; ☎ 542 210 104; www.hotelpegas.cz; Jakubská 4; s/d 1000/1550Kč) With a buzzy microbrewery downstairs offering four different beers, you won't have far to go to your room. And despite the hops-fuelled mayhem in the bar, the rooms are quiet, if a tad dowdy.

Hotel Pod Špilberkem (Map p298; ☎ 543 235 003; www.hotelpodspilberkem.cz; Pekařská 10; s/d incl breakfast 1100/1450Kč; P) Tucked away beneath the castle, this spot has quiet rooms around a central courtyard and complimentary off-street parking. Recommended for self-drive travellers.

Hotel Continental (Map p298; ☎ 541 519 111; www .continentalbrno.cz; Kounicova 6; s/d incl breakfast 1450/1900Kč; P ✕ ▯) The sweeping retro staircase and curvy leather chairs in reception are straight from Dr Evil's lair, and upstairs the rooms are businesslike with spacious bathrooms.

TOP END

Park Hotel (Map p297; ☎ 543 236 350; www.parkhotel .cz; Veslařská 250; s/d incl breakfast from 1596/2100Kč; ✕ ▯ ☎) This 19th-century mansion in parkland above the Svrakta river has 20 individually decorated rooms.

Hotel International (Map p298; ☎ 542 122 111; www.hotelinternational.cz; Husova 16; s/d incl breakfast 3000/3390Kč; ✕ ✕ ▯ ☎) Look forward to all mod cons, including a fitness centre, at this reliable business offering from Best Western.

Hotel Royal Ricc (Map p298; ☎ 542 219 262; www .romantichotels.cz; Starobrněnská 10; s/d incl breakfast 3500/3900Kč; ✕ ✕ ▯) An utterly captivating mix of traditional and modern, this intimate hotel with 29 rooms would be right at home in Paris or Venice. Bring along your loved one and fulfil the promise of the hotel's website address.

Eating

Čhajovna (Map p298; Dominikánské náměstí 6/7; tea 30Kč) Relax with more than 40 types of tea and cruisy world music. If you're feeling really chilled, linger for one of the yoga sessions upstairs.

Rebio (Map p298; ☎ 542 211 110; Orli 16; mains 60-90Kč; ✆ 8am-8pm Mon-Fri, 10am-3pm Sat; V) Who says vegetarian food can't taste great? The décor of warm, natural wood complements a menu of healthy risottos, vegetarian pies and

a soothing selection of tasty desserts in this very popular self-service spot.

Spolek (Map p298; ☎ 542 213 002; Orli 22; mains 70-100Kč; ✆ 10am-10pm Mon-Sat) You'll get friendly, unpretentious service at this coolly 'bohemian' (yes, we're in Moravia) haven with interesting salads and soups and a concise but diverse wine list. Photojournalism on the walls is complemented by a funky mezzanine bookshop.

Sabaidy (Map p298; ☎ 545 428 310; třída kpt Jaroše 29; mains 100-220Kč; ✆ 5pm-11pm Mon-Fri) The spicily authentic tastes of Laos are served in this atmospheric restaurant attached to the Hotel Amphone. With décor incorporating Buddhist statues, and a very talented Laotian chef, it's a case of 'Ommm…' and 'Mmmm…'

Špaliček (Map p298; ☎ 542 215 526; Zelný trh 12; mains 140-300Kč) Brno's oldest (and just maybe its 'meatiest') restaurant sits on the edge of the Cabbage market. Ignore the irony and dig into the huge Moravian meals partnered with something from the good local wine list.

U Staryho Billa (Map p298; ☎ 545 244 453; Kudelova 7; mains 160Kč) 'Old Bill's' serves up rip-roaring steaks and Tex-Mex tastes in an eclectic space bedecked with cow skulls, Confederate flags and outlaw country music. Each day begins with happy hour from 2.30pm to 5.30pm and the chance to try wines from 15 countries.

Also recommended:

Pizza okNo (Map p298; Solniční 8; pizza slice 15Kč) For hole-in-the-wall and eat-on-the-run pizza.

Bambus (Map p298; Kobližná 13; mains from 70Kč) For hole-in-the-wall and eat-on-the-run Asian food.

Haribol (Map p297; Lužanecká 4; mains 70Kč; ✆ 11am-4pm Mon-Fri) Wholesome vege feasts at this friendly Hare Krishna–run place.

Drinking

PUBS

Pivnice Pegas (Map p298; Jakubská 4) *Pivo* melts that old Moravian reserve (the locals become pleasantly noisy and animated) in a cosy spot enshrined in moody lighting and dark wood panelling. Try refreshing wheat beer with a slice of lemon.

Livingstone (Map p298; Dominikánské náměstí 5; ✆ to 1am) Become an explorer yourself to find this eclectic and raucous spot tucked away under an archway. Think funky world discoverer meets Irish pub and you're part way there. There's an adventure travel agency on hand if you get all inspired. It fills up late.

Černohorský Sklep (Map p298; náměstí Svobody 5; ✆ closed Sun) The busy, busy, busy waiters at the Black Mountain Brewery's Brno tavern can be a little surly, but you'll forgive them once you taste the Black Hill aperitif beer or the Kvasar brew flavoured with honey.

BARS & CLUBS
Brno has a vibrant music scene. The free guide *Metropolis* has invaluable listings. Also check the numerous flyers around town. At the time of writing the following clubs were popular:

Mersey Music Club (Map p297; ☎ 541 240 623; www .mersey.cz; Minská 15; ☺ 9pm to late) Nicely noisy beats provided by local and international DJs.

Stará Pekárna (Map p297; ☎ 541 210 040; www .starapekarna.cz; Štefánikova 8; ☺ to 1am) Old and new music with blues, world beats and drum 'n' bass. Catch tram 1, 6 or 7 to Pionýrská.

Also recommended:

Alterna (Map p297; ☎ 541 212 091; Kounicova 48, blok B; ☺ to 2am) For rock, punk and occasional jazz.

Klub 7 (Map p298; Jánská 9) Sweaty underground club popular with the younger crowd.

Entertainment
CINEMAS
As a centre for the arts, Brno has plenty of cinemas. They include:

Kino Art (Map p298; ☎ 541 213 542; www.kinoartbrno .cz; Cihlářská 19) For art-house films. From June to August cult movies are screened at an outdoor cinema in Špilberk castle.

Palace Cinemas (Map p298; ☎ 543 560 111; www .palacecinemas.cz; Mečova 2) In the Velký Spalicek shopping centre; shows all the latest Hollywood releases.

Scala (Map p298; ☎ 542 211 659; Moravské náměstí 3) Shows a mix of mainstream and art-house films.

CLASSICAL MUSIC & THEATRE
Except in midsummer when the artists are on holiday, Brno's theatres offer excellent performances. In Brno you are expected to dress up a bit. The **Theatre Booking Office** (Národní Divadlo v Brně Prodej Vstupnek; Map p298; ☎ 542 158 252; www .ndbrno.cz; Dvořákova 11; ☺ 8am-5.30pm Mon-Fri, to noon Sat), behind Mahen's theatre, sells tickets for the Mahen's, Janáček and Reduta theatres.

Following are some major venues:

Janáček theatre (Janáčkovo divadlo; Map p298; Sady osvobození) Shows opera and ballet.

Mahen's theatre (Mahenovo divadlo; Map p298; Divadelni) For classical drama (usually in Czech) and operettas.

City theatre (Městské divadlo; Map p298; ☎ 545 321 269; www.mdb.cz; Lidická 16) Hosts Broadway-style musicals and a selection of more sedate plays.

Brno State Philharmonic Orchestra (Map p298; ☎ 542 214 255; www.sfb.cz; Komenského náměstí 8) Holds regular concerts in the Meeting house.

Reduta theatre (Reduta divadlo; Map p298; Zelný trh 4) Newly restored, with an emphasis on Mozart (he played there in 1767).

Getting There & Away
AIR
Brno Tuřany airport (code BRQ; ☎ 545 521 302; www .airport-brno.cz) is 7.5km southeast of the train station, along Křenová (which becomes Olomoucká). Bus 76 runs from the train station and bus station to the airport (13Kč). A taxi will cost around 300Kč.

ČSA (Map p298; ☎ 542 211 414; www.csa.cz; Nádražní 4) has scheduled flights to Prague.

Ryan Air (www.ryanair.com) has daily flights from London, and **Cirrus Air** (www.cirrus-world.de) flies daily to/from Munich.

BUS
Two main companies, **Tourbus** (Map p298; ☎ 543 163 493; www.tourbus.cz) and **Student Agency** (Map p298; ☎ 542 424 242; www.studentagency.cz), battle it out on the competitive route between Prague and Brno (130Kč, 2½ hours). Buses to Prague leave from Benešova, north of the train station and opposite the Grand Hotel. Tourbus also runs to many European destinations, including Vienna (200Kč), Dresden (770Kč) and Aachen (1760Kč). Note that only buses to Prague leave from Benešova. Local buses and international buses leave from the **main bus station** (Map p297), 800m south of the train station.

For short trips, buses are faster and more efficient than trains, especially to Telč (88Kč, two hours), Trenčín (125Kč, three hours), Znojmo (60Kč, one hour), Strážnice (via Hodonín, 73Kč, 1¾ hours) and Kroměříž (58Kč, 1¼ hours).

TRAIN
Brno's **train station** (Map p298; ☎ 541 171 111), a major rail hub, has frequent express-train connections to Prague (294Kč, 3½ hours). See p456 for information on international train travel. There are direct trains to destinations within Moravia such as Břeclav (76Kč, 40 minutes), Jihlava (130Kč, two hours), Třebíč (88Kč, 1½ hours), Žďár nad Sázavou (110Kč, one hour), Blansko (34Kč, 20 minutes), Přerov (110Kč, 1¼ hours), Ostrava (204Kč, 2½ hours) and Veselí nad Moravoun (110Kč, 1¾ hours). You can reserve couchettes or sleepers at ČD Centrum, to the right of the station's entrance.

SOUTH MORAVIA

Getting Around

DPMB (Map p298; ☎ 543 174 317; www.dpmb.cz; Novobranská 18; ☿ 6am-6pm Mon-Fri, 8am-3.30pm Sat) sells tickets and monthly passes for public transport. Tickets valid for 40/60 minutes cost 13/19Kč and allow unlimited transfers; 24-hour tickets are 50Kč. There's also a 10-minute, no-transfer ticket (8Kč). You can also buy tickets from *tabák* (tobacco) shops or from the orange ticket machines at some tram stops.

From April to October environmentally friendly **riverboats** (www.dpmb.cz; adult/concession 80/45Kč) run between 11 stops on the Brno water reservoir. Ask at DPMB for more information.

City Taxis (☎ 542 321 321) can be called for bookings in advance.

Avis (Map p298; ☎ 542 122 670; www.avis.cz; Husova 16) car rental has an office at the Hotel International (p304).

AROUND BRNO

MORAVIAN KARST

The Moravian karst (Moravský kras) is a beautiful, heavily wooded, hilly area north of Brno, carved with canyons and honeycombed with some 400 caves.

Karst formations result from the seepage of faintly acidic rainwater through limestone, which slowly dissolves it and, over millions of years, creates hollows and fissures. In caves, the slow dripping of this water produces extraordinary stalagmites and stalactites.

To hire **climbing gear** and source local information, see **Hudy Sport** (Map p298; ☎ 542 221 144; Orlí 20) in Brno.

Getting There & Away

Unless you have a car, the simplest way to the Moravian karst is by train from Brno to Blansko, and by bus from there. Check with the Tourist Information Office (p296) in Brno for the latest on guided tours from there.

Blansko

pop 21,000

Functional Blansko is little more than a jumping-off point. The only thing of interest in town is a small **museum** (☎ 516 417 221; Zámek 1; adult/concession 40/20Kč; ☿ 9am-5pm Tue-Sun Apr-Oct, Tue-Fri Nov-Mar) in a cute chateau up the hill and across the road from the tourist office.

ORIENTATION & INFORMATION

The main square, náměstí Svobody, is 1km northeast of the train station, which is directly across the Svitava river from the bus station.

The **Tourist Information Office** (Blanenská Informační Kancelář; ☎ 516 410 470; www.blansko.cz; Rožmitálova 6; ☿ 9am-6pm Mon-Fri, 9am-noon Sat) sells maps and advance tickets to the Punkevní and Kateřinská caves, fields transport questions and can help with accommodation. It also has internet access (per hour 40Kč) and bike hire (per hour 20Kč).

ČSOB, with an exchange desk and ATM, is next door.

SLEEPING

The Tourist Information Office (above) can book cheap private rooms from 300Kč per person.

Hotel Panorma (☎ 516 418 111; www.hotelpanorma .cz; Husova 1; s/d incl breakfast 890/1280Kč; **P**) A boxy, chocolate-brown exterior conceals modern rooms, and sauna and massage facilities to revive you at day's end. It's 2km from the centre, in Češkovice.

Hotel Macocha (☎ 516 419 661; www.hotel-macocha .cz; Svitavská 35; s/d incl breakfast 900/1200Kč; **P**) Big and bold, this new place has spacious rooms, functional IKEA-style furniture and a popular restaurant downstairs.

GETTING THERE & AWAY

There are 33 trains a day to/from Brno (34Kč, 25 minutes). Buses direct from Brno are less frequent.

Skalní Mlýn & the Caves

Skalní Mlýn is the administrative centre for the two most popular caves, Punkevní and Kateřinská. At the far end of the Skalní Mlýn car park are two offices: the first sells train (*vlak*, on wheels) and gondola (*lanovka*) tickets to reach Punkevní cave and Macocha abyss (it's possible simply to walk); the second, called **Ústřední Informační Služba** (Central Information Service; ☎ 516 413 575; www.cavemk.cz), sells the entrance tickets to Punkevní and Kateřinská.

Arrive early in summer, as tickets sell out. Consider buying Punkevní or Kateřinská tickets in advance from Blansko's Tourist Information Office (above).

PUNKEVNÍ CAVE & MACOCHA ABYSS

The first part of the tour through **Punkevní cave** (Punkevní jeskyně; ☎ 516 418 602; www.cavemk.cz; adult/

concession 100/50Kč; ⊗ 10am-3.50pm Mon, 8.20am-3.50pm Tue-Sun Apr-Sep, to 5pm Jul & Aug, 8.40am-2pm Tue-Sun Oct-Mar) involves a 750m walk through caverns draped with stalactites and stalagmites before you emerge, blinking, at the bottom of Macocha abyss. You then board a small, electric-powered boat for a cruise along the underground Punkva river back to the entrance. On weekends and in July and August, tickets for tours can sell out up to a week in advance, so book ahead. The tour is wheelchair accessible.

Just beyond the cave's entrance, a **cable car** (60/50Kč return) will whisk you to the upper rim of spectacular Macocha abyss, a dizzying 140m-deep sinkhole. If that seems too lazy, you can hike to the top on a blue-marked trail (2km).

KATEŘINSKÁ CAVE
Kateřinská cave (Kateřinská jeskyně; ☎ 516 413 161; adult/concession 40/20Kč; ⊗ 8.20am-4pm Apr-Sep, to 2pm Oct, 10am, noon & 2pm Feb & Mar) is only 300m from the Skalní Mlýn car park yet is much less crowded. The 30-minute tour covers two massive chambers, one of which hosts music concerts on summer weekends.

OTHER CAVES
The least visited cave is **Balcarka jeskyně** (☎ 516 444 330; adult/concession 50/30Kč; ⊗ 7.30am-3.30pm Tue-Fri, 8.30am-3.15pm Sat & Sun Apr-Sep, 7.30am-3.30pm Tue-Fri, 8.30am-2.30pm Sat & Sun Oct, 9am, 11am & 1pm Feb & Mar), a 2km walk from Skalní Mlýn (or there are a few buses from Blansko). On the way to Balcarka jeskyně is a turn-off to the upper rim of Macocha abyss.

The fourth cave, **Sloupsko-Šošůvské jeskyně** (☎ 516 435 335; adult/concession 70/30Kč; short tour 50/20Kč; ⊗ 8am-3.30pm Apr-Sep, 8.30am-1.30pm Oct, 10am, noon & 1pm Feb & Mar), is near the village of Sloup and is also the deepest, at 1670m. There are two tours: 1½ hours and one hour.

SLEEPING & EATING
Chata Macocha (☎ 516 444 250; www.smk.cz; dm 260Kč; P) This summer-only hostel with dorm beds is near Macocha abyss.

Hotel Skalní Mlýn (☎ 516 418 113; www.smk.cz; s/d incl breakfast 980/1320Kč; P) Opposite the ticket offices, this is the perfect place to warm up after a trip into the depths of the earth. The restaurant is also good.

GETTING THERE & AWAY
Take a train (33 trains a day) to Blansko, then walk over to the adjacent bus station. From

May to September there are five regular **ČSAD** (☎ 516 418 610) buses between Blansko (stand 6) and Skalní Mlýn (12Kč; 10 minutes; 7.40am, 9.35am, 11.40am, 3.10pm, 4.50pm). Note that only the first three will get you there in time for the cave tours. The buses return directly (7.55am, 9.50am, noon, 3.25pm, 5pm).

Off season, buses run to Skalní Mlýn at 7.40am, 3.10pm and 4.50pm only, returning at 7.55am, 3.25pm and 5pm.

On foot it's 5.3km from Blansko's train station to Skalní Mlýn's car park. To get there turn right across the bridge onto the highway, left at Hotel Morava, and follow the signs to Hotel Skalní Mlýn.

PROSTĚJOV
pop 47,100

Prostějov dates back to a castle built here in 1213. Seeing the few sites takes a couple of hours.

Orientation & Information
From the adjoining train and bus stations, head straight up Svatoplukova for 800m to the main square, náměstí TG Masaryka.

Next to the town hall on the main square is the **Tourist Information Office** (Informační a Turistická Kancelář; ☎ 582 329 722; www.mestopv.cz; náměstí TG Masaryka 12; ⊗ 8am-4pm Mon-Fri).

Sights
The remains of the pretty **castle** (zámek; Pernštýnské náměstí 8) are 200m north of the main square; it was closed for restoration at time of writing.

The **town museum** (muzeum Prostějovska; ☎ 582 344 990; náměstí TG Masaryka; adult/concession 20/10Kč; ⊗ 9.30am-noon & 1-5pm Tue-Sun), in the **Old town hall** (Stará radnice), features shoes, local history and traditional handicrafts.

František Bílek (1872–1941) painted the Stations of the Cross in the **cathedral of the Ascension of the Holy Cross** (chrám Povýšení sv Kříže; Filipcovo náměstí). There are also some striking buildings such as the Art Nouveau **Národní dům** (Vojáčkovo náměstí), which now houses the **town theatre** (☎ 582 333 390), and the 1910 **villa** (náměstí Padlých hrdinů) of architect E Králík. Both are a short walk northeast of the central square.

Sleeping & Eating
Grand Hotel (☎ 582 332 311; www.grandhotel.cz; Palackého 3/5; s/d incl breakfast 1350/2110Kč; P ✗) The plushest place in town has slick rooms and a good restaurant.

Also recommended:

Hotel Romže (☎ 582 365 493; www.hotelromze.wz.cz; Olomoucká 275; dm/d 150/400Kč; **P**) Cheap dorms and basic rooms.

Hotel Avion (☎ 582 334 561; www.avion.prostejov .cz; náměstí E Husserla; s/d incl breakfast 550/950Kč; **P**) Also has rooms without bathroom (s/d 350/600Kč).

Getting There & Away

Trains link Prostějov with Brno (98Kč, two hours) and Olomouc (28Kč, 30 minutes). Buses are also frequent to Brno (55Kč, 1½ hours) and Olomouc (30Kč, 25 minutes).

VYŠKOV

Vyškov, on the Haná river, is worth a visit only if you have a *serious* interest in folk museums. The **tourist office** (informační centrum; ☎ 517 301 312; www.vyskov-mesto.cz; Masarykovo náměstí 1; ☼ 8.30am-5pm Mon-Fri) is on the pretty main square.

The oldest building in town is the Gothic **Archbishop's chateau** (Arcibiskupský zámek), which now houses a **museum** (muzeum Vyškovska; ☎ 517 348 040; http://muzeum.vyskov.cz; adult/concession 20/5Kč; ☼ 8am-4pm Mon-Fri, 10am-noon & 2-4pm Sat & Sun) that features an interesting section on the folk traditions of the Haná region, including a beehive made from a tree trunk and a mock-up room from a peasant house. It's behind the town hall and through the car park.

Chalupa U městské brány (☎ 517 341 907; www .penzionchalupa.cz; Masarykovo náměstí 21; s/d incl breakfast 650/980Kč), on the main square, has snug rooms and an excellent restaurant with wood beams and an open fire.

The oddly named **Brett's Hole Irish Pub** (Nádražní 21; ☼ noon-midnight Mon-Fri, 4pm-midnight Sat & Sun) beside the entrance to the chateau has a sterling range of beer and whiskey.

Getting There & Away

Trains run to/from Brno (64Kč, 40 minutes). Buses travel to Prostějov, Kroměříž and Blansko.

SLAVKOV U BRNA & AROUND
pop 6000

Slavkov (Austerlitz) and its surrounds were almost as significant players in the Napoleonic Wars as the little Frenchman himself. As the setting for the pivotal Battle of the Three Emperors in 1805, it was here that Napoleon defeated the combined (and superior) forces of Austrian Emperor Ferdinand I and Russian Tsar Alexander I. For more information see opposite.

Orientation & Information

From Slavkov's train station, turn left onto the highway, go past the bus station and continue straight up Palackého náměstí to the **chateau**. The **Tourist Information Office** (Informační Regionální Centrum; ☎ 544 220 988; info@austerlitz@infos.cz; Palackého náměstí 1; ☼ 9am-5pm Mon-Fri, 10am-4pm Sat & Sun), under the ramp going up to the castle, can help with accommodation.

Sights

Napoleon stayed for several days at **Slavkov chateau** (zámek Slavkov; ☎ 544 221 204; www.zamek-slavkov .cz; ☼ 9am-6pm Jul & Aug, 9am-5pm Tue-Sun May, Jun & Sep, to 4pm Tue-Sun Apr, Oct & Nov), where the treaty with Austria was signed. Built around 1700 to a design by Martinelli, the chateau was enlarged in the mid-18th century and its rooms are adorned with stucco decorations and ceiling murals.

You can take a **tour** (adult/concession 60/40Kč, in English 105/85Kč) of the chateau, or experience the **'Virtual Battle'** (adult/concession 70/50Kč). Promising '3-D virtual reality' but delivering a slightly enhanced PowerPoint presentation, it does give you a good handle on the surrounding terrain on which the battle was fought. From December to March, visits are by reservation only (prices 200% more).

Complete the Austerlitz circuit with a trip to **Pracký kopec**, a hill 12km east of Slavkov, where the Battle of the Three Emperors was actually decided. At the site is the **Cairn of peace** (Mohyla míru; adult/concession 75/35Kč; ☼ 9am-6pm Jul & Aug, to 5pm May, Jun & Sep, 9am-5pm Tue-Sun Apr, 9am-3.30pm Tue-Sun Oct-Mar) honouring those who fell, with a small **museum** with handy touch-screen information kiosks about the battle.

Unfortunately, Pracký kopec is difficult to reach by public transport and hard to find. You can get a bus from Brno's bus station to Prace (10 buses a day; ask to get off at the Náves stop), from where it's a 1.6km walk south to the top of the hill. On weekends you'll need to catch one of the more frequent Brno–Slavkov trains (14km, 10 trains a day), getting off at Ponětovice and walking the 3.5km southeast through Prace.

Sleeping & Eating

Hotel Soult (☎ 544 227 148; hotel-soult@volny.cz; Nádražní 909; s/d incl breakfast 500/950Kč) Opposite the train station, this is a reasonable backup if Hotel Sokolský dům is full.

Hotel Sokolský dům (☎ 544 221 103; www.hotelsokol skydum.cz; Palackého náměstí 75; s/d incl breakfast 600/1000Kč;

BATTLE OF AUSTERLITZ

The battle took place 10km west of Slavkov, around the village of Šlapanice, on 2 December 1805 – the anniversary of Napoleon's coronation as emperor. A day before the battle, Napoleon evacuated the Pracký plateau (Pracký kopec; opposite), hoping the allies would occupy the site. Allied troops advanced on the French through the fog-filled lowlands the next morning, their plan being to attack the French right flank and cut off supply lines from Vienna. But under the cover of fog Napoleon regrouped, and when the fog lifted, counter-attacked, recapturing the plateau. By the afternoon the allies were defeated, suffering losses five times higher than the French. Austria signed a peace treaty and the Russian troops returned home. The Battle of Austerlitz led to the disintegration of the anti-Napoleon coalition and to a new European political map. It is re-enacted annually in December.

P) The most popular choice in town serves up decent Czech specialties in its restaurant below.

Hostinec U černého lva (Palackého náměstí; mains 70Kč) Meaty mains are the order of the day at 'Black Ivan's'.

Getting There & Away

Slavkov is 21km east of Brno and easily reached by bus (24Kč, 40 minutes) and train (40Kč, 45 minutes).

PERNŠTEJN

If you've overdosed on effete Renaissance chateaux, here's the antidote: a medieval castle, with a capital 'C', that has discarded gilt edges and carved stonework for hard rock and heavy metal. Dating from the late 13th century, this beautifully preserved Gothic **fortress** (☎ 566 566 101; hrad.pernstejn@iol.cz; ☼ 9am-5pm Tue-Sun Jul & Aug, to 4pm May, Jun & Sep, 9am-3pm Sat & Sun Apr & Oct) high above the small town of Nedvědice is one of the Czech Republic's most evocative medieval monuments – a link to a time that has otherwise largely crumbled away. From the 1450s to the 1550s it was enlarged and rebuilt in several stages as the residence of the leading Moravian noble family of Pernštejn, but the beautiful bare bones of the original castle still shine through.

Among the highlights are the small towers, which were part of the original and solid-looking fortifications, and a smorgasbord of renovated rooms, attics, nooks and crannies. A number of tours are on offer: **Tour A** (adult/concession 65/40Kč; 1hr) takes in the main halls of the castle, **Tour B** (150/100Kč; 1½ hrs) covers the 19th-century living areas, **Tour C** (150/100Kč; 1½ hrs) explores the cellars and attics, and **Tour D** (100Kč) shows off the chapel and Cork tower. All tours are conducted in Czech and only Tour A has English text.

Sleeping

In Nedvědice there are private rooms; look out for 'Zimmer frei' signs.

Pod hradem (☎ 566 622 462; www.pensionsholemar.cz; s/d 400/800Kč; P) This pretty pension has a great location at the bottom of the road leading up to the castle, but the owners can be tough to track down.

Pension Barborska (☎ 566 566 317; www.pension baborka.cz; s/d incl breakfast 500/750Kč; P) Twin fir trees mark the entrance to this friendly place opposite the village pond.

Getting There & Away

There are regular daily trains from Brno to Nedvědice (48Kč, one hour), with a change to a local train at Tišnov.

Without a car the surest way to Pernštejn from Nedvědice is a 2km walk northwest. There are only three daily buses to Pernštejn on weekdays and one on weekends.

TIŠNOV

pop 8300

En route from Brno to Pernštejn is the cross-shaped **Porta Coeli Cistercian convent** (founded 1233) in the Tišnov suburb of Předklášteří. The church's beautifully carved Romanesque/ Gothic portal dates from the early 13th century. The convent also houses a small **museum** (muzeum Brněnska; ☎ 549 412 293; adult/concession 20/15Kč; ☼ 9am-noon & 1-5pm Tue-Sun). Tours of the convent cost an extra 35Kč and keep the same hours as the museum (last tour 4pm). The convent is on the west side of town, across the Svratka river.

NÁMĚŠŤ NAD OSLAVOU

pop 5200

Náměšť is known for its 13th-century **chateau** (☎ 568 620 319; www.zamek-namest.cz; adult/concession 50/30Kč, in English 100Kč; ☼ 9am-6pm Tue-Sun Jul & Aug,

SOUTH MORAVIA

9am-5pm May, Jun & Sep, 9am-4pm Sat & Sun Apr & Oct). Its present Renaissance face is largely the work of architect Leonardo Garvi. Highlights include 24 Renaissance and baroque tapestries and a library adorned with murals.

There are several cheap accommodation options – contact the **Tourist Information Office** (☎ 568 620 493; mks-namest@iol.cz; Masarykovo náměstí 100). **Zámecký pension** (☎ 568 620 319; holy@zamek -namest.cz; d incl breakfast 900Kč), attached to the chateau, has a variety of so-so doubles.

Getting There & Away

Náměšť is 26km west of Brno and is easy to reach by bus (36Kč, 45 minutes). The bus station is 300m east from the main square, and the train station is northeast a few minutes further on.

Regular trains also run to/from Brno (64Kč, one hour) and Třebíč (28Kč, 25 minutes).

MORAVSKÝ KRUMLOV
pop 6000

Despite its idyllic location in the valley of the Rokytná river, Moravský Krumlov would be just another entry on a train timetable if it weren't for Alfons Mucha, who was born in the nearby village of Ivančice in 1860. This little village is now home to the artist's *Slav Epic*, arguably the finest work of the nation's finest painter. There isn't much else to see, but these 20 canvasses inject more colour into the nation's history than all the books yet written about it.

Mucha Gallery

The **gallery** (☎ 515 322 789; adult/concession 60/30Kč; ⊗ 9am-noon & 1-4pm Tue-Sun Apr-Oct) is housed in a slightly moth-eaten Renaissance chateau 300m off the main square. Inspired by Slav history, Mucha's **Slav Epic** *(Slovanská epopej)* is unlike the Art Nouveau style of the artist's Paris posters, yet it retains the same mythic, heavily romanticised quality. The huge canvases (the biggest are 8m by 6m) are wonderfully cinematic and verge on science fantasy, with wild-eyed priests, medieval pageantry and battlefield carnage all under brooding northern skies.

Mucha worked abroad for several years but returned to his newly independent homeland in 1918 and designed some of its banknotes and stamps. No building other than this chateau could be found to accommodate the huge *Slav Epic* paintings, which Mucha worked on between 1912 and 1930. In 2006, approval was given to move the collection to a purpose-built gallery, scheduled to open in 2010, in Prague's Stromovka Park.

Getting There & Away

Moravský Krumlov is best visited as a day trip from Brno by bus. From Brno six buses a day (two on weekends) stop on Moravský Krumlov's main square (36Kč, one hour). The train station is about 2km from náměstí TG Masaryka, though local buses aren't so good about meeting the 11 daily trains that come through from Brno (46Kč, one hour).

JIHLAVSKO REGION

Rolling hills studded with compact stands of forest mark the border between Bohemia and Moravia. The region runs south to Austria from the pleasant city of Jihlava and includes the picturesque town of Telč and the fascinating Jewish heritage of Třebíč. Cycling is a good way to travel the short distances from town to town across the undulating hills.

JIHLAVA
pop 50,100

Jihlavasko's 'Big Smoke' is a tad incongruous amid the pastoral landscapes of this predominantly rural region, but Jihlava sports a fine historical centre to counter an encompassing ring of industrial suburbs. The town square is one of the country's largest (36,650 sq m) but is unfortunately filled by one of the country's biggest, ugliest department stores. Fortunately a pretty selection of Renaissance façades and pleasantly crumbling town walls help to offset the past architectural follies of dodgy communist councils. The zoo's pretty good, too.

Orientation

There are two train stations. The main station (Jihlava hlavní nádraží; for trains to and from Brno, Třebíč and Prague) is 2km north of the centre; take trolleybus A, B or B1 to the main square, náměstí Masarykovo.

The Jihlava město station (for trains to Tábor and České Budějovice) and the **bus station** (cnr Tolstého & Jiráskova) are each a five-minute walk north of the old town.

Information

Česká Spořitelna (cnr náměstí Masarykovo & Křížová) Has an exchange and ATM.

Knihkupectvi Cajovna (☎ 567 312 873; náměstí Masa-rykovo 21; ✆ 9am-10pm) Bookshop with internet access.
Main post office (cnr náměstí Masarykovo & Komen-ského) On the main square.
Tourist Information Office (Turistické Informační Centrum; ☎ 567 308 034; www.jihlava.cz; náměstí Masraykovo 19; ✆ 8am-5pm Mon-Fri, to noon Sat) Arranges accommodation. In July and August it also opens on Sunday from 1pm to 5pm.

Sights

The Gothic **church of St James** (kostel sv Jakuba), on Jakubské náměstí, has a gilded Renaissance baptismal font, a baroque chapel and the requisite **lookout tower** (adult/concession 10/5Kč; ✆ 10am-1pm & 2-6pm Tue-Sun Jun-Aug, Sat & Sun May & Sep). In the 13th-century **church of the Assumption of the Virgin Mary** (kostel Nanebevzetí Panny Marie), to the west on Minorítská, are some Gothic frescoes and the oldest picture of the town, a 16th-century work showing the defeat of Zikmund Křižanovský z Rokštejna by the local residents in 1402.

In the baroque **church of St Ignatius** (kostel sv Ignáce; 1689), on náměstí Masarykovo, are an emaciated Christ, some Tepper frescoes on the vaulted ceiling, and a fine main altar. To the left of the church is the entrance to the **catacombs** (historické katakomby; náměstí Masarykovo 64; adult/concession 40/20Kč; ✆ 9am-5pm Jun-Aug, 10am-4pm Apr-May & Sep-Oct). Tours are held on the hour except 1pm (minimum four people).

The **Highlands museum** (muzeum Vysočiny; ☎ 567 301 680; náměstí Masarykovo 58; adult/child 30/15Kč; ✆ 9am-5pm Tue-Sun) is housed in a late-Gothic villa and includes fine Gothic, Renaissance and baroque interiors and a display of folk arts and handicrafts.

The **Vysočina gallery** (Oblastní galerie Vysočiny; adult/concession 30/15Kč; ✆ 9am-5pm Mon-Fri, 10am-4pm Sat & Sun) displays Czech art and sculpture from the 1930s to '60s in two locations: Komenského 10 and náměstí Masarykovo 24. Both have the same opening times and admission charges.

At the end of Matky Boží you can see what remains of the **old town walls**, including the impressive clock tower and the **Holy Mother gate** with an archway through to Hradebni.

Off the southern end of the square, the **museum of the Young Gustav Mahler** (expozice Mladý Gustav Mahler) was closed at the time of writing. Check with the Tourist Information Office (above) to see if it has reopened.

A real highlight is Jihlava's **zoo** (☎ 567 573 730; www.zoojihlava.cz; Březinovy sady 10; adult/concession 60/30Kč; ✆ 8am-6pm May-Sep, 9am-5pm Apr & Oct, 9am-4pm Nov-Mar), 400m from the main square. More than 400 animals – notably Sumatran tigers, snow leopards and a dozen species of monkey – are kept in open-air compounds. There's even a replica African village with thoroughly authentic African animals.

Sleeping

The Tourist Information Office (left) can arrange private accommodation from around 250Kč per person.

Ubytovna u Zimniho Stadionu (☎ 606 190 021; mileska@seznam.cz; Jiráskova 6; dm 120Kč; Ⓟ) Jiráskova has plenty of cheap hostels (check out No 32 and 69 as well).

Penzion Horacka Rychta (☎ 567 302 721; Komen-ského 11; s/d incl breakfast 990/1120Kč) Tidy, central rooms sit above a snack bar with comfy old sofas and tasty comfort food.

Hotel Grand (☎ 567 303 541; www.grandjihlav.cz; Husova 1; s/d incl breakfast 1140/1690Kč; Ⓟ) The lobby looks like a lounge singer's lounge, but thankfully the rooms are less cheaply ostentatious. There are also less expensive digs with shared bathrooms (s/d 590/790Kč).

Penzion U Svatého Jakuba (☎ 567 579 411; penzionjakub@ji.cz; Jakubské náměstí 103/4; s/d incl breakfast 1265/1930Kč; Ⓟ 🖳) Warm colours inside and out are the go at this comfortable place tucked in a quiet square beneath the church of St James.

Eating

Knihkupectvi Cajovna (☎ 567 312 873; náměstí Masarykovo 21; snacks 60Kč) Deliciously hip, this incense-laden, Indian-style teahouse meets funky bookshop is the kind of place you wish your home town had.

Pizza in Piazza (☎ 567 301 940; náměstí Masarykovo 3; pizza 100Kč) Down a quiet lane off the main square, this perennially popular spot is as bright and multicoloured as its tasty pizza toppings.

Amazonia (☎ 567 300 280; Husova 26; mains 100-200Kč) Worship the sun gods adorning the walls at this Latin American place. Tapas and mojitos make it relatively authentic and the prices are not a sacrifice.

Also recommended:
U Vévody Albrechta (☎ 567 308 074; 1st fl, náměstí Masarykovo 40; mains 90-200Kč) Czech pub décor and hearty local fare.

Drinking

PUBS
Pivovarská Restaurace (☎ 567 564 163; Vrchlického 2). Try the local Ježek ('Hedgehog') beer here;

SOUTH MORAVIA

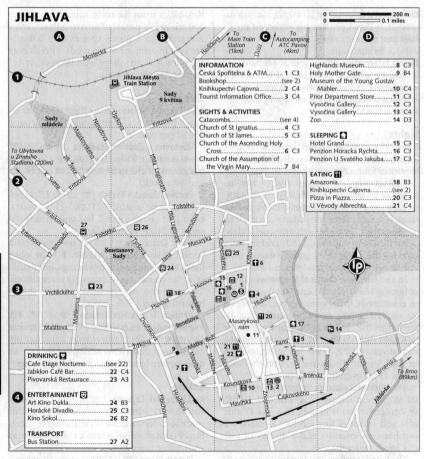

JIHLAVA

0 — 200 m
0 — 0.1 miles

INFORMATION
Česká Spořitelna & ATM........ 1 C3
Bookshop..............................(see 2)
Knihkupectvi Cajovna............2 C4
Tourist Information Office.......3 C4

SIGHTS & ACTIVITIES
Catacombs............................(see 4)
Church of St Ignatius..............4 C3
Church of St James..................5 C3
Church of the Ascending Holy
   Cross..................................6 C3
Church of the Assumption of
   the Virgin Mary...................7 B4

Highlands Museum.................8 C3
Holy Mother Gate...................9 B4
Museum of the Young Gustav
   Mahler..............................10 C4
Prior Department Store..........11 C3
Vysočina Gallery....................12 C3
Vysočina Gallery....................13 C4
Zoo.....................................14 D3

SLEEPING
Hotel Grand..........................15 C3
Penzion Horacka Rychta.......16 C3
Penzion U Svatého Jakuba.....17 C3

EATING
Amazonia..............................18 B3
Knihkupectvi Cajovna............(see 2)
Pizza in Piazza.......................20 C3
U Vévody Albrechta...............21 C4

DRINKING
Cafe Etage Nocturno............(see 22)
Jabklon Café Bar...................22 C4
Pivovarská Restaurace...........23 A3

ENTERTAINMENT
Art Kino Dukla.......................24 B3
Horácké Divadlo.....................25 C3
Kino Sokol.............................26 B2

TRANSPORT
Bus Station............................27 A2

there are nine brews available. Try them all and you could be curling up in a ball just like the brewery's spiky namesake.

CLUBS
Café Etage Nocturno (☎ 721 639 984; 2nd fl, náměstí Masarykovo 39; ☽ 6pm-2am) Booze plus fish tanks, wicker chairs and trendy exposed air vents equals a perennially popular 'soul and funky night bar' (their words, not ours).

Jabklon Café Bar (☎ 608 811 884) This bar, on the next floor down, has live music some nights.

Entertainment
Horácké divadlo (☎ 567 321 717; Komenského 22) Jihlava's swish modern theatre has a regular programme of events.

Kino Sokol (☎ 567 300 801; Tyršova 12) Cinema-goers can see the latest releases here.

Art Kino Dukla (☎ 602 193 918; Jana Masaryka 20) The place to try for art-house flicks.

Getting There & Away
Direct train services run to/from Jihlava and Brno (130Kč, two hours), Třebíč (64Kč, one hour), Prague (204Kč, 2½ hours) and České Budějovice (162Kč, 2½ hours).

Express bus services, which are often quicker and always much cheaper (about half the price), run to/from Jihlava and Brno (65Kč, 1½ hours), Prague (100Kč, two hours), Tabor (68Kč, 1½ hours), Telč (32Kč, 30 minutes) and Žďár nad Sázavou (37Kč, 1½ hours).

ŽĎÁR NAD SÁZAVOU

pop 23,900

Žďár is a bland industrial town with two hot attractions: the Cistercian monastery and the church of St John of Nepomuk, both by architect Giovanni Santini. If it weren't for them, it wouldn't be worth getting off the bus.

Orientation & Information

The monastery is 3km north of the adjacent train and bus stations. The central square, náměstí Republiky, is 1km northwest of the stations; follow Nádražní. Local buses pass the monastery from the stations, hourly on weekdays and less frequently on weekends.

Santini Tour (☎ 566 625 808; santini@santini-tour.cz; náměstí Republiky; ☽ 9am-noon & 1-5pm Mon-Fri, to noon Sat), in the Old town hall, is central and can help with accommodation. The official **tourist office** (☎ 566 629 152; www.zamekzdar.cz; ☽ 9am-5pm Tue-Sun Apr-Sep, to 4pm Oct-Mar) is in the monastery grounds.

Cistercian Monastery

Founded in 1252, the **Cistercian monastery** (klášter Cisterciáků; ☽ 9am-5pm Tue-Sun Apr-Sep, 8am-4pm Tue-Sun Oct-Mar) was burned down by the Hussites in 1422. Reconstruction began in 1638, and Giovanni Santini started work here in 1706, though he never completed the project. In it he attempted to combine the medieval with the baroque in a distinctive dark-and-light style. His **church of the Assumption of the Virgin Mary** (kostel Nanebevzetí Panny Marie) contains an altar by Řehoř Thény. The former monastery stables are now a **museum** (adult/concession 70/35Kč) devoted to Santini and an excellent and unique exhibit of historical pianos. You can buy individual tickets to the monastery (100/50Kč) and the church of St John of Nepomuk (50/30Kč), or a combined ticket (140/70Kč) that also includes the piano museum.

The superb **book museum** (muzeum knihy; adult/concession 30/15Kč; ☽ 9am-5pm Tue-Sun Apr-Sep, 8am-4pm Tue-Sun Oct-Mar) on the evolution of writing, calligraphy and printing is also in another part of the monastery.

Church of St John of Nepomuk

A little closer to town, on a hill called Zelená hora (Green mountain), is this peculiar but brilliant Santini church (1727) in the shape of a five-pointed star. It's on Unesco's list of World Cultural Heritage Sites.

According to legend, John of Nepomuk's tongue was cut out for his not revealing royal confessions, and he was thrown off Prague's Charles bridge to his death. Five stars are said to have appeared above the spot where he drowned. Thus the church of St John of Nepomuk (kostel sv Jana Nepomuckého) is chock-full of tongue motifs and circles of five stars.

See the Cistercian monastery (left) for opening times and prices.

Sleeping

Hotel U labutě (☎ 566 622 949; www.oxygen.cz/u-labute; náměstí Republiky 70; s/d incl breakfast 500/700Kč) and **Hotel Fit** (☎ 566 623 508; www.hotelfit.unas.cz/; Horní 30; d incl breakfast 600Kč) offer passable, central rooms.

Getting There & Away

Žďár is on the Brno (110Kč, 1½ hours) to Prague (204Kč, 2½ hours) main line, with about 10 express connections and a few other slower trains a day. There are up to six daily buses to Jihlava (47Kč, 1½ hours).

TELČ

pop 5700

Yesterday's travel secret may now be a burgeoning tourism hot spot, but that's OK because Telč's appeal is too special to be dissipated by a few tour buses. Surrounded on three sides by medieval fish ponds, the pristine town square is precisely separated from the modern part of town. Strolling across the narrow bridges under the imposing gates is like time-travelling to the heart of the Renaissance.

Inside, the square does not disappoint with a grand array of façades, covered arcades and walkways and the beautiful Water chateau. Park yourself with a good book and a glass of Moravian wine at one of the cafés on the square and you'll remember all over again just why you like to travel.

The best time to visit is late July/early August when the town explodes into life during the **Prázdniny v Telči folk music festival** (www.prazdninyvtelci.ji.cz). An eclectic selection of local and international performers is usually on offer.

In 1992 Telč's unadulterated 16th-century splendour was recognised with a spot on Unesco's list of World Heritage Sites.

History

Telč was founded in the 14th century by the feudal lords of Hradec as a fortified settlement, with a castle separated from the town by

SOUTH MORAVIA

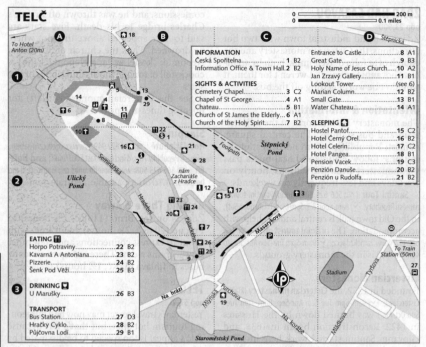

TELČ

INFORMATION
Česká Spořitelna	**1** B2
Information Office & Town Hall	**2** B2

SIGHTS & ACTIVITIES
Cemetery Chapel	**3** C2
Chapel of St George	**4** A1
Chateau	**5** B1
Church of St James the Elderly	**6** A1
Church of the Holy Spirit	**7** B2
Entrance to Castle	**8** A1
Great Gate	**9** B3
Holy Name of Jesus Church	**10** A2
Jan Zrzavý Gallery	**11** B1
Lookout Tower	(see 6)
Marian Column	**12** B2
Small Gate	**13** B1
Water Chateau	**14** A1

SLEEPING
Hostel Pantof	**15** C2
Hotel Černý Orel	**16** B2
Hotel Celerin	**17** C2
Hotel Pangea	**18** B1
Pension Vacek	**19** C3
Penzión Danuše	**20** B2
Penzión u Rudolfa	**21** B2

EATING
Horpo Potraviny	**22** B2
Kavarná A Antoniana	**23** B2
Pizzerie	**24** B2
Šenk Pod Věží	**25** B3

DRINKING
U Marušky	**26** B3

TRANSPORT
Bus Station	**27** D3
Hračky Cyklo	**28** B2
Půjčovna Lodí	**29** B1

a strong wall. The artificial ponds on each side of Telč provided security and a sure supply of fish. After a fire in 1530, Lord Zachariáš, then governor of Moravia, ordered the town and castle to be rebuilt in the Renaissance style by Italian masons.

After the death of Zachariáš in 1589, building activity ceased and the complex you see today is largely as it was then. The main square is unmarred by modern constructions, and the **fire hall** (náměstí Zachariáše z Hradce 28) is evidence of local concern to keep it that way.

Orientation

The old centre of Telč, including náměstí Zachariáše z Hradce and the chateau, is nearly surrounded by two ponds. The train and bus stations (one street apart) are 800m southeast of the town centre.

Information

Česká Spořitelna (náměstí Zachariáše z Hradce 21) Has an exchange and ATM.
Post office (Staňkova) A block from the train station.
Tourist Information Office (Informační Středisko; ☎ 567 112 407; www.telc-etc.cz; ☼ 8am-5pm Mon-Fri, 10am-4pm Sat & Sun May-Sep, 8am-5pm Mon-Fri Oct-Apr) Located inside the town hall. It can book accommodation and also provides internet access at 1Kč per minute.

Sights
CHATEAU

The glacé cherry on a very pretty cake, Telč's Renaissance chateau, part of which is known as the Water chateau, guards the north end of the peninsula, looking more like it's there to ward off a downturn in the tourist industry than protect against invaders. Rebuilt from the original Gothic structure by Antonio Vlach (from 1553 to 1556) and Baldassare Maggi (from 1566 to 1568), the surviving structure remains in remarkably fine fettle, with immaculately tended lawns and beautifully kept interiors.

In the ornate **chapel of St George** (kaple sv Jiří), opposite the ticket office, are the remains of the castle's founder, Zachariáš z Hradce.

There are two tours through the **chateau** (zámek; ☎ 567 243 821; ☼ 9am-noon & 1-5pm Tue-Sun May-Aug, to 4pm Apr, Sep & Oct). **Route A** (adult/concession 80/40Kč, in English 160Kč, 1hr) takes you through the

Renaissance halls, and **Route B** (adult/concession 70/35Kč, in English 140Kč, 45 min) through the castle apartment rooms. Also worth visiting is the local **historical museum** (muzeum vysočiny Jihlava; ☎ 567 243 918; enter from the chateau courtyard; adult/concession 20/10Kč; ☉ same as chateau), with its scale model of Telč in 1895, or the small **Jan Zrzavý gallery** (galérie Jana Zrzavého; ☎ 567 243 649; adult/concession 30/15Kč; ☉ same as chateau).

OTHER ATTRACTIONS

Telč's stunning town square is bordered on three sides by Renaissance houses built on the ruins of their Gothic predecessors after the 1530 fire. Though it's from another era, the baroque **Marian column** (1717) in the square doesn't detract from the town's overall character and is a popular early evening meeting point.

Dominating the town centre are the Gothic towers of the **church of St James the Elderly** (kostel sv Jakuba Staršího), which has a **lookout tower** (věž; adult/concession 20/15Kč; ☉ 10-11.30am & 1-6pm Tue-Sun Jun-Aug, 1-5pm Sat & Sun May & Sep). Also watching over the square is the baroque **Holy Name of Jesus church** (kostel Jména Ježíšova) completed in 1667 as part of a Jesuit college.

North of the square is a narrow lane leading to the old town's **Small gate** (Malá brána), through which is a large English-style park surrounding the duck ponds (once the town's defensive moat).

South along Palackého, towards the **Great gate** (Velká brána), is the imposing Romanesque **church of the Holy Spirit** (kostel sv Ducha; early 13th century). Outside the Great gate you can walk along parts of Telč's remaining bastions.

Sleeping

Accommodation can be hard to get and therefore expensive during the annual Prázdniny v Telči folk music festival in late July/early August. Book ahead.

BUDGET

Penzión u Rudolfa (☎ 567 243 094; www.volny.cz/libuse.javurkova; náměstí Zachariáše z Hradce 58; s/d 300/600Kč) A pretty merchant's house on the main square conceals a friendly home with shared kitchen facilities.

Hostel Pantof (☎ 776 887 466; www.pantof.cz; náměstí Zachariáše z Hradce 42; dm 300Kč, d 800Kč; ☉ Jul & Aug; ℗) A friendly and relaxed atmosphere and rooms overlooking one of the country's prettiest squares add up to one of the Czech Republic's best hostels.

Penzión Vacek (☎ 567 213 099; www.penzionvacek.cz; Mlýnská 104; s/d incl breakfast 400/800Kč) Bed-and-breakfast service at (almost) hostel prices are standard at this homey spot.

MIDRANGE

Penzión Danuše (☎ 567 213 945; www.telc-etc.cz/cz/privat/danuse; Hradebni 25; s/d 450/900Kč, 4-bed apt 2000Kč) Discreet wrought-iron balconies and wooden window boxes give this place a touch of class on a quiet corner just off the main square.

Hotel Celerin (☎ 567 243 477; www.hotel-celerin.cz; náměstí Zachariáše z Hradce 1/43; s incl breakfast 800-1100Kč, d incl breakfast 1300-1600Kč; ☒ ☒ ☒) Variety is king in the Celerin's 12 comfortable rooms, with décor ranging from cosy wood to white wedding chintz. Take a look first.

Hotel Pangea (☎ 567 213 122; www.pangea.cz; Na Baště 450; s/d incl breakfast 1200/1600Kč; ℗ ☒ ☒ ☒ ☒ ☒) Huge buffet breakfasts and loads of facilities make this slightly functional spot very good value. Outside of July and August, rates fall by up to 30%.

TOP END

Hotel Anton (☎ 567 223 315; www.hotel-anton.cz; Slavatovská 92; s/d incl breakfast 1350/1800Kč; ℗ ☒) Designer furniture, private balconies and a great restaurant downstairs combine in Telč's best accommodation. No wonder this newly opened hotel has been recommended by Lonely Planet readers.

Hotel Černý Orel (☎ 567 243 222; www.cernyorel.cz; náměstí Zachariáše z Hradce 7; s/d incl breakfast 1350/1800Kč; ☒ ☒ ☒) Its self-appointed 'four-star' status is stretching things, but if you're into slightly faded old-world glamour right on the main square, look no further than the 'Black Eagle'.

Eating

Kavárná A Antoniana (☎ 603 519 903; náměstí Zachariáše z Hradce 23; cake 25Kč; ☉ 8am-2am) With interesting documentary-style photographs of (not so) old Moravia, and dangerously strong coffee, this café is a handy modern refuge from the gorgeous Renaissance overkill outside.

Šenk Pod Věži (☎ 603 526 999; Palackého 116; mains 100-180Kč; ☉ 11am-3pm & 6-9pm Mon-Sat, 11am-4pm Sun) Sizzling grills, tasty pizza and occasional live music are the big drawcards at this cosy and traditional restaurant tucked under the tower.

Also recommended:

Pizzerie (☎ 567 223 246; náměstí Zachariáše z Hradce 32; pizza 110Kč) Right on the main square and right on the money for tasty pizza.

Horpo Potraviny (náměstí Zachariáše z Hradce 65) Your friendly local supermarket.

Drinking

U Marušky (☎ 605 870 854; Palackého) Telč's hipper young citizens crowd this buzzy bar for cool jazz, a funky selection of old radios, and a wider-than-usual selection of beer and wine.

Getting There & Away

Frequent buses go from Telč to Jihlava (32Kč, 30 minutes) and Znojmo (70Kč, two hours). Buses from České Budějovice (90Kč, two hours) to Brno (90Kč, two hours) stop at Telč about five times a day. Seven buses a day run to Prague (120Kč, 2½ hours).

Trains from Telč are fairly useless but do go to Slavonice (40Kč, one hour).

Getting Around

Hračky Cyklo (náměstí Zachariáše z Hradce 23; per day 100Kč; ☻ 8am-5pm Mon-Fri, 9am-noon Sat) rents out bikes.

From July to August you can rent rowboats from **Půjčovna Lodí** (beside the East gate; per 30 min 25Kč; ☻ 10am-6.30pm)

TŘEBÍČ

Pop 39,000

Pollution has scoured the sheen from this industrial city's old centre. Its Jewish ghetto – one of the best preserved in the country – is worth a brief stopover, though.

Orientation & Information

The train station is 1km south of the main square, Karlovo náměstí. The bus station is at Komenského náměstí, 500m west of the main square.

The **tourist office** (informační a turistické centrum; ☎ 568 847 070; www.kvistrebic.cz; Karlovo náměstí 53; ☻ 9am-5pm Jun-Sep, to 1pm Sat, closed Sun Nov-Apr) can book accommodation. There are other tourist offices at **St Procopius' Basilica** (☎ 777 746 982; ☻ 9am-4.30pm Tue-Fri, 1-5pm Sat-Mon) and the **Rear (New) synagogue** (☎ 568 823 005; ☻ 10am-5pm).

ČSOB (Karlovo náměstí 21) changes money and has an ATM.

Sights

The castle and former Benedictine monastery (klášter Benediktínů) around which the town originally grew was founded in 1101 and re-built shoddily as a **chateau** (zámek; ☎ 568 840 518; www.zamek-trebic.cz; adult/concession 40/20Kč; ☻ 8am-5pm Jul & Aug, 8am-noon & 1-5pm Tue-Sun Apr-Oct, to 4pm Nov-Mar) at the end of the 17th century. Inside, a **museum** (muzeum Vysočiny Třebíc) has a small collection of Nativity scenes and pipes.

Also in the complex is the World Heritage-listed **St Procopius' Basilica** (Bazilika sv Prokopa; ☎ 568 824 692; adult/concession 40/20Kč; ☻ 9am-5pm Tue-Thu, to 3pm Fri, 1-5pm Sat & Mon, 1-6pm Sun Jun-Aug) with its attractive chancel and carved north portal (portal Paradisi).

East of the monastery is the former **Jewish ghetto**. The 1639 **Front (Old) synagogue** (Přední (Stará) synagóga; Tiché náměstí) now belongs to the Hussite Church; the **Rear (New) synagogue** (Zadní (Nová) synagóga; ☎ 568 823 005; Subakova 1/44; adult/concession 40/25Kč; ☻ 10am-noon & 1-5pm) has beautifully restored frescoes. The 17th-century **Jewish cemetery** (Židovský hřbitov; admission free; ☻ 8am-6pm) on Hrádek, 600m north of the Old synagogue, is the largest in the country with more than 11,000 graves, the oldest dating to 1641. Třebíč's Jewish quarter is a Unesco World Heritage Site.

Sleeping & Eating

Autokemping Poušov (☎ 568 850 641; tent/cottage per person 60/110Kč; ☻ May-Sep; (P)) Situated 2km west of town, this camp site also has cottages.

Grand Hotel (☎ 568 848 560; www.grand-hotel.cz; Karlovo náměstí 5; s/d incl breakfast 1220/1400Kč; (P)) Situated above a rough-and-ready shopping arcade, the hotel's brightly redecorated rooms with new wooden floors are actually more comfortable than you'd expect.

Also recommended:

Penzión u Synagogy (☎ 568 821 665; Subakova 3; s/d incl breakfast 490/790Kč; (P)) Near the Rear (New) synagogue.

Restaurant Neptun (☎ 776 350 850; Tiché náměstí 3; mains 60-80Kč) Pasta, seafood and steak are served with an eclectic twist near the Front (Old) synagogue.

Getting There & Away

Třebíč is on a main line between Brno (88Kč, 1¾ hours) and Jihlava (64Kč, one hour), with about 14 trains a day. There are also buses to Brno (56Kč, 1¼ hours), Jihlava (37Kč, 1¼ hours) and Telč (34Kč, 40 minutes).

JAROMĚŘICE NAD ROKYTNOU

pop 4000

The unassuming small town of Jaroměřice is home to one of Europe's largest baroque chateaux – a typical example of Counter-Reformation architecture in the style fancied by the new nobility, in this case Johann von Questenberg. The visitors come in droves.

A tour of the red-and-white striped **castle** (☎ 568 440 237; www.zamek-jaromerice.cz; adult/concession 60/30Kč, foreign language additional 10%; ⏰ 9am-noon & 1-6pm Tue-Sun Jul & Aug, to 5pm May, Jun & Oct, 9am-noon & 1-4pm Sat & Sun Apr & Oct) includes the **Hall of the forefathers** (Sál předků), with its inlaid wooden ceiling, and the stucco-decorated **Dance hall** (Taneční sál).

In the castle grounds the 18th-century baroque **St Margaret church** (kostel sv Markéty) boasts a large cupola with a busy fresco by Karel Töpper. The interior can only be seen during services or if you manage to find the caretaker (správce).

In the large French-and-English-style gardens is a **theatre** where the first Czech opera, O původu Jaroměřic (The Origin of Jaroměřice) by František Míča, premiered in 1730.

In August the chateau hosts the annual **Peter Dvorský international music festival** (mezinárodní hudební festival Petra Dvorského; http://jaromerice .box.cz)

Sleeping

Opera Hotel (☎ 568 440 230; Komenského náměstí 996; s/d incl breakfast 450/700Kč) This is one of the few options in town but offers spacious rooms with shower and TV.

Getting There & Away

Jaroměřice, 14km south of Třebíč, is best reached by bus. There are up to five buses a day from Brno (68Kč, 1¾ hours) and 12 from Třebíč (16Kč, 20 minutes).

The train station is 2km away in the village of Popovice.

SOUTH MORAVIAN BORDERLANDS

Running in a swathe along the Austrian border, much of this low-lying rural and light industrial area was owned by the Liechtenstein family from the Middle Ages to 1945. Forced to leave during the mass German expulsions after WWII, they retreated to their tiny alpine principality sandwiched between Switzerland and Austria, leaving behind a diverse legacy of castles, estates and churches. Since the passing of restitute (restitution law) in 1990, the Liechtenstein family has been striving for compensation from the Czech government (see p325). The highlight of the

area previously owned by the Liechtensteins includes the gorgeous chateaux at Lednice and Valtice.

Another legacy of the earlier German-speaking inhabitants of the region are the prosperous towns and villages that now form the heart of the Moravian wine industry. Mikulov, Valtice and Znojmo have many wine salons where you can sample the rapidly improving local vintages. Southeast Moravia's rolling hills are also ideal for cycling, especially in the Unesco World Heritage area surrounding Lednice and Valtice. Further east there's excellent hiking and mountain biking in the Podyjí National Park, which surrounds the Dyje river as it meanders from Vranov to Znojmo.

ZNOJMO
pop 38,000

Perched high above the Dyje river, Znojmo conceals one of Moravia's more interesting old towns amid its industrial sprawl. Villagelike alleys link intimate plazas with bustling main squares, and hilltop lookout points provide vistas across the valley. Blur your eyes a little and the atmosphere is almost Italian. With a decent tally of grand religious buildings, and beautiful Romanesque frescoes, Znojmo deserves to be more than just a signpost on the main road from Austria.

Orientation

The bus and train stations are 800m from the main square, Masarykovo náměstí. From the bus station go up Tovární, turn left at náměstí Republiky, then right onto Vídeňská. From the train station, walk up 17 listopadu and, at the roundabout (Mariánské náměstí), veer left onto Pontassievská.

Information

The **Tourist Information Office** (Turistické Informační Centrum; ☎ 515 222 552; www.znojmo.cz; Obroková 10; ⏰ 8am-6pm Mon-Fri, 9am-5pm Sat, closed Sat afternoon Oct-April) also books accommodation. A second office, next door in the **Town hall tower** (Radniční věž; ☎ 515 216 297; Obroková 12; ⏰ 9am-1pm & 2-6pm Mon-Fri, to 5pm Sat & Sun, closed Sat afternoon Oct-April), books theatre tickets.

Česká Spořitelna (Masarykovo náměstí 2) Exchanges money and has ATMs.

Na Věcnosti (☎ 515 221 814; www.navecnosti.cz; Velka Mikulášská 11). Internet access (including wi-fi) at this groovy club.

Post office (Horní náměstí) North of the centre.

Raiffeisenbank (Obroková 15) Exchanges money and has ATMs.

Sights
MASARYKOVO NÁMĚSTÍ & AROUND
The **South Moravian museum** (Jihomoravské muzeum; ☎ 515 226 529; www.znojmuz.cz; adult/concession 20/10Kč; Masarykovo náměstí 11; ☺ 9am-7pm Tue-Sat) is on the main square, inside the House of Art (dům umění). The collection includes Czech religious icons, sculpture and temporary art exhibitions. There's another branch (below) at Václavské náměstí.

In the southern part of the square are the **church of St John the Baptist** (kostel sv Jana Křtitele) and the **Capuchin monastery** (Kapucínský klášter).

North of the square, on Obroková, looms the handsome and scalable **Town hall tower** (Radniční věž; adult/concession 20/10Kč; ☺ 9am-1pm & 2-6pm Mon-Fri, to 5pm Sat & Sun), 66m tall and one of Moravia's best examples of late-Gothic architecture (c 1448).

Enter Kramářská from Obroková and go through the arch to the old chicken market (Slepičí třída); at No 2 is the entrance to the **Znojmo catacombs** (Znojemské podzemí; ☎ 515 221 342; adult/concession 50/30Kč; ☺ 9am-5pm Jul & Aug, to 4pm May, Jun & Sep, 10am-4pm Mon-Sat Apr, 10am-4pm Sat Oct). In the 14th century the town's cellars were linked by some 27km of these tunnels, which were used for both storage and defence.

East of Kramářská is the 13th-century **church of the Holy Cross** (kostel sv Kříže), part of an active Dominican monastery. The early-Gothic church received a baroque face-lift in the 1780s.

OTHER SQUARES
North of Horní náměstí, via Divišovo náměstí, is Jezuitské náměstí and the Jesuit **church of St Michael** (kostel sv Michala), a 'baroquefied' Romanesque church at the highest point of the old town.

From here Veselá leads south to Václavské náměstí, where a right turn into Přemyslovců takes you to a former Minorite monastery, now a branch of the **South Moravian museum** (Jihomoravské muzeum; ☎ 515 224 961; Václavské náměstí 6; adult/concession 20/10Kč; ☺ 10am-5pm Tue-Sun May-Aug, 9am-6pm Mon-Fri Oct-Apr) with exhibits of crafts and trades, geology, archaeology and oriental weapons.

ROTUNDA OF OUR LADY & ST CATHERINE
The 11th-century **rotunda of Our Lady & St Catherine** (rotunda Panny Marie a sv Kateřiny; ☎ 515 222 311; admission 90Kč; ☺ 10.15am-4.15pm Sat & Sun Jun-Sep) is one of the republic's oldest Romanesque structures and contains a beautiful series of 12th-century frescoes showing the life of Christ. Formerly used as a pigsty and a beer hall, the rotunda is now strictly protected. Visits are restricted to a maximum of 15 minutes and the structure is closed during bad weather. Nearby, the remains of **Znojmo castle** (☎ 515 222 311; adult/concession 40/20Kč; ☺ 10am-6pm Tue-Sun Jun-Sep, Sat & Sun May) are along a scenic path that follows the old city walls from the dead-end street of Přemyslovců. On weekends you can get here from Václavské náměstí down Hradní, through the **brewery** (pivovar; closed to the public). Both sites are visited as part of a tour, with the last tour of the castle at 5pm.

CHURCH OF ST NICHOLAS
From Hradní take Velká Františkánská to Klácelova and turn right into náměstí Mikulášské. Ahead is the church of St Nicholas (kostel sv Mikuláše), once Romanesque but rebuilt as the present monumental Gothic structure.

In a side chapel near the entrance is the so-called *bread Madonna*. According to legend, during the Thirty Years' War a box beneath this image was always found to be full of food, no matter how much was removed. Beside the church is the Orthodox **St Wenceslas chapel** (kaple sv Václava).

Sleeping
The Tourist Information Office (p317) books private rooms from 300Kč per person. Count on an additional 15Kč tourist tax from May to September.

BUDGET
Cyclopenzión U Mikuláše (☎ 607 555 202; paty@club34 .cz; Mikulášské náměstí 8; s/d from 200/400Kč) In a serene location, this has basic beds above the cheerful Café U Rolanda.

Pension Kaplanka (☎ 515 242 905; www.kaplanka .cz; U branky 6; s/d without bathroom from 200/400Kč; ⓅⓁⓇ) This whitewashed heritage place has a variety of rooms from so-so to respectable midrange (prices and bathroom facilities increase accordingly). Sample the local vino in the garden as you look across the Dyje river valley and you could almost be in Tuscany.

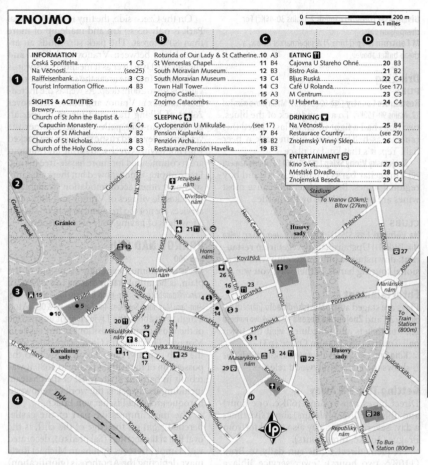

ZNOJMO

INFORMATION
Česká Spořitelna..........................1 C3
Na Věčnosti..............................(see25)
Raiffeisenbank............................3 C3
Tourist Information Office.........4 B3

SIGHTS & ACTIVITIES
Brewery..5 A3
Church of St John the Baptist &
　Capuchin Monastery..............6 C4
Church of St Michael....................7 B2
Church of St Nicholas...................8 B3
Church of the Holy Cross.............9 C3

Rotunda of Our Lady & St Catherine..10 A3
St Wenceslas Chapel...................11 B4
South Moravian Museum............12 B3
South Moravian Museum 13 C4
Town Hall Tower..........................14 C3
Znojmo Castle..............................15 A3
Znojmo Catacombs.....................16 C3

SLEEPING
Cyclopenzión U Mikuláše............(see 17)
Pension Kaplanka.......................17 B4
Penzión Archa.............................18 B2
Restaurace/Penzión Havelka......19 B3

EATING
Čajovna U Stareho Ohné.............20 B3
Bistro Asia...................................21 B2
Bljus Ruská..................................22 C4
Café U Rolanda.........................(see 17)
M Centrum..................................23 C3
U Huberta....................................24 C4

DRINKING
Na Věčnosti................................25 B4
Restaurace Country..................(see 29)
Znojemský Vinný Sklep..............26 C3

ENTERTAINMENT
Kino Svet......................................27 D3
Městské Divadlo..........................28 D4
Znojemská Beseda......................29 C4

MIDRANGE

Restaurace/Penzión Havelka (☎ 515 220 138; http://havelka.euweb.cz; Mikulášské náměstí 3; d incl breakfast 750Kč) In the shadow of a church, this immaculate *pension* opts for soda-white, holier-than-thou décor and a Madonna in the garden.

Penzión Archa (☎ 515 225 062; www.pensionarcha.cz; Vlkova 4; d incl breakfast 840Kč) The building is from the 17th century, the awning considerably newer, but the comfy rooms are good enough for the new millennium.

Eating

Café U Rolanda (☎ 607 555 202; Mikulášské náměstí 8; breakfast 60Kč) The curvy wooden chairs and terracotta tiles give this place a vaguely Gallic ambience, and it's perfect for *le petit déjeuner* (breakfast) if you're staying in one of the nearby *pensions*.

U Huberta (☎ 515 221 102; Dolní Česká; mains 80-140Kč) Dark and broody, this place features old-school hunting lodge chic. Old-school hunting types crowd in for cheap Czech food and Hostan beer brewed just up the road.

Bljus Ruská (☎ 515 260 782; Dolní Česká; mains 100-200Kč; ⏲ 11am-4pm Mon-Fri, closed Sat & Sun) Locals with short memories cram this lunch spot for tasty *borscht* (beetroot soup) and other Russian goodies. Pass the salt (mine), comrade.

Also recommended:

Čajovna U Stareho Ohné (☎ 605 803 702; Staré Město 1; ⏲ 3-10pm Mon-Sat) Just may be the country's best teahouse, with tasty snacks.

Bistro Asia (Divišovo náměstí 2; mains 30-45Kč) For cheap Asian eats.

M Centrum (Slepiči třída 7) A supermarket below, a cheap buffet above.

Drinking
PUBS
Restaurace Country (☎ 602 549 759; Masarykovo náměstí 22; mains 90-150Kč) To a soundtrack of the blues, two dogs had a fight when we last visited this raucous-as-hell but loads-of-fun steak 'n' beer hall. Yep, it's that kind of place.

   Znojemský Vinný Sklep (☎ 515 261 872; Horní náměstí 20) This cellar bar is the place to try and buy regional wines. Bring a friend because most wines are only available by the bottle.

CLUBS
Na Věčnosti (☎ 515 221 814; www.navecnosti.cz; Velka Mikulášská 11) Upstairs a tasty vegetarian restaurant, downstairs a pub meets club with occasional touring bands. Either way, you win.

Entertainment
Plays are staged at the **Městské divadlo** (náměstí Republiky 20) and **Znojemská Beseda** (Masarykovo náměstí 22). For tickets and schedules, visit the town hall Tourist Information Office (p317).

   Kino Svet (☎ 515 224 034; www.illusiion.cz; Havlíčkova 7) shows the latest Hollywood releases.

Getting There & Away
Direct buses run to Brno (60Kč, one hour) and Jihlava (60Kč, 1¾ hours) about five times a day. Several buses a day also travel to/from Prague (162Kč, three hours).

   Frequent direct trains run daily to Brno (110Kč, two hours); fewer service Jihlava (120Kč, two hours).

PODYJÍ NATIONAL PARK
Officially opened in 1991, **Podyjí National Park** (www.nppodyji.cz) is one of the Czech Republic's more recent and most spectacular protected areas.

   Bordering the park on the southern bank of the Dyje river (Thaya in German) is the Thayatal National Park in Austria, which was inaugurated in 2001.

   During the Cold War, the area was a restricted border zone, and the flora and fauna of the region is still remarkably undisturbed. Some hiking trails are trans-border, providing the opportunity to hike in both Austria and the Czech Republic.

On the Czech side, the tiny Podyjí National Park is only 63 sq km and made up of more than 80% forest. The park surrounds an artificial lake between Vranov and Bitov and encases the Dyje river as it meanders eastwards to Znojmo. In some areas the spectacular river valley is up to 200m deep. As well as the incredible chateaux at Vranov and Bitov, there's over 76km of hiking trails and plenty of specialist mountain-bike paths. In the summer the verdant valleys and rustic riverside are packed with holidaying Czechs, so spring and autumn are recommended for more hassle-free hiking. Free camping is not allowed but there are camp sites and other accommodation available in the lakeside villages of Vranov and Bitov. Bus services are not too frequent, so plan on staying a few days or having your own transport.

VRANOV NAD DYJÍ
pop 900
West of Znojmo, seemingly rising out of the plain, is beautiful **Vranov chateau** (☎ 515 296 215; vranov@pambr.cz; ☉ 9am-noon & 1-6pm Tue-Sun Jul & Aug, 9am-5pm May, Jun & Sep, 9am-4pm Sat & Sun Apr & Oct). Atop a high crag above the Dyje river, it enjoys one of the most dramatic positions of any castle in Moravia. The chateau's Gothic core dates from the 14th century, but when it came into the possession of the Althan family in 1680 it was rebuilt in baroque style. Most of the chateau, including its chapel, is the work of renowned baroque architect Fischer von Erlach.

   The most impressive part of the castle, perched right on the edge of the cliff, is the oval **Hall of the ancestors** (Sál předků), decorated with famous frescoes by Johann Michael Rottmayr depicting the Apotheosis (glorification) of the Althan family, and statues representing the Althan ancestors.

   The guided **tour** (adult/concession 75/40Kč, in a foreign language 150/115Kč) of the castle takes you through many ornate apartments dating from the 18th-century when Spanish princess Maria Anna Pignatelli lived here. There is a royal bath that looks like a modern hot tub, and two elegant ceramic stoves in the Pignatelli bedroom. One of the rooms was used for Freemasonry – a very fashionable pursuit for 18th-century aristocrats – and is decorated with Masonic symbols, including the set square and compasses, the pyramid and the Star of David.

   The chateau can be reached across a bridge, about 1km uphill from the quiet town. Shorter tours are available through the chateau's

SOUTH MORAVIA

gardens (adult/concession 50/30Kč) and the chapel (adult/concession 25/15Kč).

Sleeping & Eating

The **tourist office** (☎ 515 296 285; infocentrum@ouvranov .cz; Náměstí 47; ♡ 9am-5pm Mon-Fri, 9am-3pm Sat & Sun Jul & Aug, Mon-Fri Sep-Jun) can help with private rooms and hostel beds.

Penzión Jelena (☎ 515 296 116; www.vranov.com; Zámecká 250; d 900Kč; P ♿) Sparkling rooms come standard in this newly refurbished place. There are also more expensive family apartments (from 1250Kč).

Zámecký Hotel (☎ 515 296 101; www.zameckyhotel .cz; s/d incl breakfast 800/1150Kč; P ♿) This four-star and immaculate place has a pleasant terrace restaurant overlooking the river.

Getting There & Away

There are up to nine daily bus connections from Znojmo, 20km away. Three daily buses run the 26km to and from Bítov.

BÍTOV

pop 400

The best thing about Bítov is the getting there. Surrounded by thickly wooded hills and set above the pea-green Dyje river, Bítov enjoys a truly photogenic setting. The original 11th-century **castle** (☎ 515 294 622; bitov@brno.npu.cz; ♡ 9am-noon & 1-6pm Tue-Sun Jul & Aug, to 5pm May, Jun & Sep, to 4pm Sat & Sun Apr & Oct) was rebuilt in early-Gothic style and extended during the 15th to 17th centuries. There are two tours. The first (adult/concession 70/50Kč) takes in the palace, while the second (95/70Kč) lingers over the armoury. Tours in English cost twice as much.

The castle is 3km northwest of Bítov village, and unless you have your own wheels, you must walk (follow the road north from the main square, past Hotel Bítov). If you're driving from Znojmo, don't be fooled by the derelict ruins of **Kornštejn castle**, a few kilometres southwest of Bítov village; continue past them to Bítov.

Sleeping

Autokemping Bítov Horka (☎ 602 712 720; tent/dm per person 70/140Kč; ♡ Jun-Sep; P) Beside the castle near the lake, this pretty spot also has dormitory accommodation.

Pension U Tesařů (☎ 515 294 616; http://utesaru .hyperlinx.cz; s/d incl breakfast 450/700Kč; P) This pretty place in the centre of the village has a popular restaurant and tidy rooms.

Getting There & Away

Buses are infrequent from Znojmo and Jihlava. The best connection is from the train station at Šumná, which is serviced by 13 trains from Znojmo and two from Jihlava.

ČÍŽOV

pop 300

In Čížov you can see the last remnants of the **Iron Curtain** dividing the former Czechoslovakia and Austria, with a preserved section of the imposing barbed-wire fence complete with a guard tower. There is also a small **visitor centre** (♡ 9am-5pm Jun-Aug, Sat & Sun Apr, May, Sep & Oct) for the Podyjí National Park. Two buses per day run from Znojmo to Čížov (58Kč, 1½ hours). There are no direct buses from Vranov or Bítov.

MIKULOV

pop 7800

Sitting atop a rocky hillside rising from the surrounding plains, Mikulov will be in sight well before you get there. However, 30 minutes of visual expectation doesn't dull the reality of arrival.

Topped with an imposing chateau and studded with a legacy of baroque and Renaissance façades, Mikulov thoroughly deserves its growing popularity amid the burgeoning Moravian wine country. And once you've experienced enough pretty Renaissance architecture, the legacy of Mikulov's once-thriving Jewish community is a compelling alternative.

Orientation

To get into town from the train station, turn right onto 28 října, left onto Nádražní, and right onto Hraničářu to Piaristů. The bus station is a bit closer to town, on the corner of Piaristů and 28 října.

Information

Česká Spořitelna (Náměstí 19) Has an exchange desk and ATM.

Post office (Česká 7) Northeast of the main square.

Tourist Information Office (Turistické Informační Centrum; ☎ 519 510 855; www.mikulov.cz; Náměstí 30; ♡ 8am-6pm Mon-Fri, 9am-6pm Sat & Sun Jun-Sep, 8.30am-noon & 1-5pm Mon-Fri Oct-May) Organises tours (including specialist outings for wine buffs) and accommodation.

Town library (Brněnská 15; ♡ 9am-6pm Mon-Fri) Has internet access on the first floor.

MIKULOV

INFORMATION
Česká Spořitelna.............................1 A6
Library...2 A5
Tourist Information Office.............3 B5

SIGHTS & ACTIVITIES
Chateau...4 A5
Dietrichstein Burial Vault..............5 B5
Goat Hill..................................(see 7)
Jewish Cemetery.............................6 B4
Lookout Tower................................7 B4
Synagogue......................................8 A5
Top Bicycle.....................................9 B5
Town Hall......................................10 B5
Vinařské Centrum.........................11 B5

SLEEPING
Fajká Penzion...............................12 A6
Hotel Templ..................................13 A6
Pension Moravia Centrum............14 B5
Pension Prima...............................15 A6

EATING
Café Paris................................(see 15)
Party Servis...................................16 B5
Petit Café.......................................17 B5
Restaurace Alfa.............................18 B5

DRINKING
U Devatero Řemesel...............(see 15)

ENTERTAINMENT
Kino Hvezda Mikulov....................19 B5

To Tanzberg Winery (4km); Brno (50km)

To Bus Station (500m); Train Station (800m)

Sights & Activities

CHATEAU

A fortified Slav settlement once stood here, but the present walls and towers are part of a 13th-century castle. The heavy baroque renovations were the work of the Dietrichstein family, who owned it from 1575 to 1945. The **chateau** (☎ 519 510 255; adult/concession 60/30Kč; 9am-5pm Tue-Sun May-Sep, to 4pm Apr & Oct) was burned down by the Germans in February 1945 and has been painstakingly restored.

The **chateau museum** (included in chateau entry price) includes exhibits on folk traditions and wine-making. In the cellar is the largest wine barrel in central Europe, made by Kryštof Secht of Brno in 1643. The barrel has a capacity of 101,000L, though it's now suffering from dry rot.

OTHER ATTRACTIONS

The 15th-century **synagogue** (synagóga; ☎ 519 510 255; Husova 11; adult/concession 20/10Kč; 1-5pm Tue-Sun 15 May-30 Sep) has background on the local Jewish quarter. The **Jewish cemetery** (Židovský hřbitov; adult/concession 20/10Kč; 9am-5pm Mon-Fri Jul & Aug), founded in the 15th century, is off Brněnská. There are tours every half-hour.

An 'instructive trail' now runs through the Jewish quarter, with information plaques in English. You can pick it up at the end of Husova near Alfonse Muchy. Above the Jewish quarter is **Goat hill** (Kozí hrádek) topped with a 15th-century **lookout tower** (9am-6pm Apr-Sep).

The town's main square, simply called Náměstí, has many houses of interest, including the **town hall** at No 1 and the sgraffitoed **Restaurace Alfa** (see Eating & Drinking, opposite) at No 27. At No 5 is the **Dietrichstein burial vault** (Dietrichštejnská hrobka; adult/concession 35/15Kč; 9am-5pm Tue-Sun Apr-Oct) with guided tours available.

There's some good **hiking** to be had in the nearby **Pavlovské hills** (Pavlovské vrchy), while wine lovers can visit **Tanzberg's Bavory winery** (Vinařství Bavory; ☎ 519 500 040; www.tanzberg.cz) 4km north of Mikulov (on the Brno road) in the village of Bavory (organise your visit in advance). A pleasant way to visit smaller, local vineyards across the rolling countryside is by bicycle on the **Mikulov Wine Trail**. The Tourist Information Office (p321) can recommend a one-day ride that also takes in the nearby chateaux at Valtice and Lednice. Bicycles and additional cycle touring information are available from **Top Bicycle** (☎ 519 513 745; www.topbicycle .com; Náměstí 24/27).

In town visit **Vinařské Centrum** (☎ 519 510 368; Náměstí 11; ☺ 8am-10pm Apr-Oct, 9am-8pm Nov-Mar), which has an excellent range of local wines available in small tasting glasses (10-20Kč), or whole bottles when you've finally made up your mind up.

Sleeping

Pension Prima (☎ 519 511 793; www.pensionprima.cz; Piaristů 9; s/d 400/600Kč; **P**) Comfy but plain rooms with kitchen facilities are available above an atmospheric, traditional-style pub.

Pension Moravia Centrum (☎ 519 511 644; www .moravia.penzion.com; Poštovní 1; d 700Kč) The location's a tad dull, but a bright exterior and spotless rooms ensure a good night's sleep.

Fajká Penzion (☎ 732 833 147; www.fajka-mikulov.cz; Alfonse Muchy 18; s/d 400/800Kč) Bright, newly decorated rooms sit above a cosy wine bar.

Hotel Templ (☎ 519 510 692; www.templ.cz; Husova 50; s/d incl breakfast 1300/1500Kč; ☒ ☒) Newly opened in a restored chapel, Mikulov's ritziest accommodation features discreetly furnished rooms and a supremely stylish restaurant.

Eating & Drinking

Party Servis (Náměstí 20; breakfast 50Kč) Have breakfast of coffee, pastries and fresher-than-fresh open sandwiches at the outdoor tables.

Petit Café (Náměstí 27; crepes 50-70Kč) Tasty crepes and coffee are dished up in a hidden courtyard. Later at night have a beer or a glass of wine.

Café Paris (Piaristů 10; pizza 90-110Kč; ☺ 9.30am-9.30pm Mon-Fri, 11am-midnight Sat & Sun) A top spot for pizza, with a steady stream of loyal locals grabbing takeaway – always a good sign.

Restaurace Alfa (☎ 519 510 877; Náměstí 27; mains 120-240Kč) Game dishes are the specialty of the house in this slightly stuffy spot housed in a beautiful sgraffito building on the main square.

U Devatero Řemesel (Piaristů 9) Just next door to Café Paris, escape this cosy pub's smoky interior by sitting in the airy beer garden.

Entertainment

Kino Hvezda Mikulov (Česká) The local cinema shows films on Friday and Saturday. Check with the Tourist Information Office (p321) for details.

Getting There & Away

There are eight daily trains from Znojmo (64Kč, one hour) and Břeclav (34Kč, 30 minutes) that have direct connections from Brno and Bratislava. Buses are faster from Lednice (29Kč, 30 minutes) and Brno (52Kč, 1¼ hours).

VALTICE

pop 3600

Valtice lies between Břeclav and Mikulov in the heart of Moravia's prime wine region. The town's chateau was one of the main residences of the Liechtenstein family, who owned it for five-and-a-half centuries. This powerful aristocratic family had almost 100 estates in Moravia, many of which were confiscated from the Protestant Czech Estates when they lost the Battle of the White Mountain in 1620. In the 20th century much of the Liechtensteins' land was appropriated and they are now seeking compensation, according to the law of *restituce* (restitution; see p325), from the Czech government.

The area that encompasses both Valtice and Lednice was declared a Unesco World Heritage Site in 1997; the Lednice–Valtice Cultural Landscape (Lednicko–valtický areál) is the most architecturally valuable region in the country.

Orientation & Information

The train station is on the northern edge of town, on the road to Lednice. Buses stop on the main road, where it meets náměstí Svobody. The **Tourist Information Office** (Turistické Informační Centrum; ☎ 519 352 978; www.radnice-valtice .cz; náměstí Svobody 4; ☺ 8.30am-12.30pm & 1-5pm Apr-Sep, 7am-3.30pm Mon-Fri Oct-Mar) is on the main square below the chateau.

Sights

The 12th-century **castle** (☎ 519 352 680; adult/ concession 70/50Kč; ☺ 9am-noon & 1-5pm Tue-Sun May-Aug, to 4pm Apr, Sep & Oct), on náměstí Svobody, has had face-lifts over the years and is now recognised as one of the country's finest baroque structures, with work by JB Fischer von Erlach and Italian architect Domenico Martinelli.

The chateau tour (in Czech with English text) lingers over all the belongings and furnishings left behind when the Liechtensteins fled from the advancing Soviet army in 1945. Of interest are the walls themselves, plastered with 7.5kg of gold. **National Salon of Czech Republic Wines** (☎ 519 352 072; www.salonvin.cz; ☺ 9.30am-5pm), in the chateau, is the place to buy and try local wines.

In front of the chateau is the **church of the Assumption of the Virgin Mary** (kostel Nanebevzetí Panny Marie) with a Rubens painting behind the main altar.

Next to the Tourist Information Office is an interesting (for agriculturalists) **agricultural museum** (Národní Zemědělské muzeum v Praze; adult/concession 20/10Kč; ⏰ 9am-5pm Tue-Sun Apr-Oct).

Festivals & Events

In July each year, Valtice holds a **Baroque Music Festival** (Zámecké barokní léto; www.radnice-valtice.cz) in many parts of the chateau, complete with a party and fireworks.

Sleeping & Eating

Hotel Hubertus (☎ 519 352 537; www.hotelhubertus.cz; s/d incl breakfast 1050/1300Kč) This place inside the castle is a bit 1950s frumpy, but you can't beat the location or the wine-tasting in its cellar.

Restaurant & Cajovna Avalon (☎ 603 867 469; Příční 46; mains 90-160Kč) Interesting dishes with a vegetarian skew feature in this nicely hippy spot just off the main square.

Also recommended:

Penzión Prinz (☎ 519 352 869; www.valtice.cz/prinz; náměstí Svobody; s/d incl breakfast 700/1200Kč; Ⓟ 🐾) Colourful, comfortable and cosy.

Lahudky V&V (náměstí Svobody; ⏰ 5.30am-5.30pm Mon-Fri, 7am-noon Sat) Deli-style next door, with everything for a picnic in the castle gardens.

Getting There & Away

Regular trains go to Mikulov (22Kč, 15 minutes) and Břeclav (22Kč, 15 minutes) with connections to Brno and Zlín. From Mikulov the train continues to Znojmo. There are up to seven buses a day to Lednice (13Kč, 15 minutes).

LEDNICE

pop 2400

It's frigid by name (*lednice* means icebox in Czech), but this little town warms up in summer when crowds flock here to see one of the country's most popular chateaux.

Information

Information Centre (Informační Centrum; ☎ 519 340 986; www.lednice.cz; Zámecké náměstí 68; ⏰ 9-11am & noon-3pm Mon-Fri, 10am-3pm Sat & Sun Apr-Oct) On the main square.

Sights

Lednice's drawcard is its ostentatious 1856 neo-Gothic **chateau** (☎ 519 340 128; lednice@brno .npu.cz; ⏰ 9am-noon & 1-5pm Tue-Sun May-Aug, to 5pm Sep, to 4pm Sat & Sun Apr & Oct) by J Wingelmüller. The Liechtensteins held it from 1582 to 1945 but now the chateau is pretty much in the hands

of the visitors queuing up to take one of the tours. There are two to choose from: **Tour 1** (adult/concession 80/40Kč, 45 min) takes you through a selection of the major rooms while **Tour 2** (100/50Kč, 45 min) concentrates on the Liechtenstein apartments. There is a 50Kč supplement for tours in a foreign language.

To the right is a **greenhouse** (skleník; adult/concession 50/25Kč) with a collection of exotic flora. The chateau's extensive **gardens** (⏰ 5am-11pm May-Sep, 6am-8pm Oct-Apr), complete with lakes and the odd pavilion, are excellent for long summer walks. A highlight is the Turkish-style **minaret** (adult/concession 15/10Kč).

Pleasure boats (☎ 519 340 619; www.1plavebni.cz; ⏰ 9.30am-5pm Jul & Aug, Tue-Sun May, Jun & Sep, Sat & Sun Apr & Oct) cruise between the chateau and minaret (adult/concession 60/30Kč) and between the minaret and Janův castle (opposite; 80/40Kč).

Sleeping & Eating

The Information Centre (left) can help with bookings for private rooms and hostel beds (from 200Kč per person).

Penzion Lednice (☎ 519 340 986; ubytovani@lednice .cz; Mikulovská 120; s/d 280/560Kč; Ⓟ) On the road to Mikulov, this is a low-key, good-value spot.

Penzion Myslivna (☎ 519 340 220; www.myslivna -lednice.cz; Nádražní 675; s/d 400/800Kč, apt 1650Kč; Ⓟ) Along with comfy, clean rooms this spot offers billiards, bowling and beer. Visiting the chateau may just have to wait.

Pension Onyx (☎ 519 340 068; www.onyx-made.cz; Nejdecká 176; s/d 420/660Kč; Ⓟ) Near car park 1, this features a heaving restaurant, spit roasts and tidy rooms.

Kavárna U Markýzy (Valtická 252; coffee 25Kč, cake 35Kč; ⏰ 11am-5pm Tue-Sun, 1-5pm Sat) Ice creams, cakes and coffee.

Pizzerie Na Knihovné (☎ 519 340 751; Mikulovská 74; pizza 80-120Kč; Ⓟ) Tasty grills and pizza are served up in the town's old library, right on the main square.

There's a supermarket on the main square.

Getting There & Away

The train station is in the southern part of town, on the road to Valtice, but buses to Breclav (13Kč, 20 minutes) and Valtice (13Kč, 15 minutes) are more convenient.

AROUND LEDNICE

The flat region around Lednice is fairly easy to explore on foot or bicycle. See **Peňáček** (☎ 776 625 817; Břeclavská 366; per day 100Kč) for bike rental. Using

SHOCart's hiking map, *Turistická mapa – Břeclavsko, Pálava* (1:50,000), or cycling map, *Cykloturistická mapa – Pálava, Lednicko-valtický areál* (1:75,000), you can spend an interesting day or two exploring the smaller, scattered Liechtenstein chateaux, temples and pavilions around Lednice and beyond.

Just over 2km east of Lednice, on a green- or yellow-marked trail through forests and meadows, or by pleasure boat (opposite), is the rarely visited but picturesque **Janův castle** (Janův hrad; adult/concession 30/15Kč; ☺ 9am-5pm Tue-Sun May-Sep, Sat & Sun Apr & Oct).

Most of the other buildings can be visited on a red-marked trail south from Lednice. Past the Apollo camping ground, south of Mlýnský rybník, are the **Apollo temple** (Apollónův chrám; 1817) and **Nový dvůr stables** (1890).

Further on, a yellow trail digresses to **Hlohovec** and **Hraniční chateau** (Hraniční zámek; 1816). On a rise in the southern part of Hlohovec village there are several **wine cellars**, where you can try the local product.

From Hlohovec take the yellow trail joining the dead-straight Valtice–Lednice road to return to Lednice.

MORAVSKÉ SLOVÁCKO REGION

Moravia is at its most colourful when celebrating its traditional folk culture, and the Moravské Slovácko region is its spiritual heart. Every summer locals don traditional costume to celebrate the region's festival season, and any traditional Moravian reserve melts in a frenzy of music, dance and merry mayhem, creating one of the most intense expressions of regional identity seen anywhere in Europe.

Culturally, the inhabitants of the region, which straddles the gap between the Chřiby hills (southeast of Brno) and the White Carpathians (across the border in West Slovakia), are neither Moravian nor Slovak, but something in between, and draw on influences and traditions from both sides of the physical divide.

The region's unique flavour arises not only from a mild climate (which favours production of the republic's best wine) but also from the character of the people, who have an innate predisposition to the arts. Be it in the clothes that are worn, the wine that is drunk, the songs that are sung or the houses that are built, the communities of Moravské Slovácko appear to add a little bit of art to every facet of daily life.

Folk dress heavily decorated with embroidery and lace includes a head covering and dress for women, hat, shirt (and sometimes a waistcoat) and trousers for men, and boots or leather thongs for both genders. These often differ according to the age of the wearer.

Some of the houses in many villages are still painted in traditional white with a blue band around the bottom, many embellished with painted flowers or birds. Good souvenirs include the famous local pottery, often decorated with floral and other designs, as well as embroidery and woodcarvings.

Wine Cellars

The region's distinctive *vinné sklepy* (wine cellars) are generally open for tastings from

SOUTH MORAVIA

RESTITUCE

Following the demise of the communist era in 1989, the new government passed the law of *restituce* (restitution) which demanded that all property seized by the communists after 1948 be returned to its original owners. While this legislation has seen the return of significant estates to some aristocratic families (eg the return of Častolovice chateau to the Šternberks; see p253), the powerful Liechtenstein family continues to lobby the Czech government for compensation for estates appropriated by the state in 1918 and 1945. Unfortunately for the Liechtensteins, the law of restitution only applies to a very specific time frame, ie 25 February 1948 to 1 January 1990 – essentially the communist era. In addition, claimants must be Czech citizens. The land in debate amounts to 1600 sq km – 10 times the area of the titular Alpine principality the Liechtensteins retreated to in 1945. Reinforcing how seriously the Liechtensteins regard these demands, the case was heard by the International Court of Justice (ICJ) in the Hague in 2005. Unfortunately the ICJ refused to make a ruling on the case. Meanwhile, in other news, the Prince of Liechtenstein is reported to be the world's fifth-wealthiest head of state, with an estimated fortune of four billion dollars.

mid-May to late September. In places such as Petrov (3km southwest of Strážnice), where they are called *plže* instead of *vinné sklepy*, they are partially underground; in Vlčnov they are more like huts *(vinařské búdy)*.

In some villages, wine cellars virtually constitute a separate village, such as at Raštíkovice or Prušánky. Normally they are within the village boundaries. Many wine cellars have seating for eager tasters, but take your own containers if you're keen to buy.

Unfortunately, buses around these villages (except to Petrov) are erratic.

Festivals & Events

The best time to see folk dress and to hear the local music is during a regional festival. The following are some major ones:

Hluk – Dolňácké Festival First weekend in July, every four years (next in 2009).

Kyjov – Kyjovsko Summer Festival On a weekend in mid-August, every four years (next in 2007).

Strážnice – International Folk Festival Last weekend in June.

Velká nad Veličkou – Horňácko Festival Folk music and dance, on a weekend in the second half of July.

Vlčnov – Ride of the Kings Last weekend in May.

More details are given under Strážnice (right) and Blatnice and Vlčnov (opposite).

STRÁŽNICE

pop 6000

Strážnice comes into its own during the annual International Folk Festival (right), one of the best attended in the region. Outside the festival whirlwind, the town is also home to an excellent *skansen* (open-air village museum) but has little else of interest. It is best visited as a day trip from Uherské Hradiště.

Orientation

The train and bus stations are near the main square, Předměstí; walk straight out of the train station, turn right onto the main road and follow it for 200m before turning left.

Information

Irra travel agency (☎ 518 332 184; Předměstí 388; ⏱ 8am-5pm Mon-Fri) doubles as the tourist information office.

Česká Spořitelna, with exchange desk and ATM, is nearby.

The town's website, www.straznice-mesto .cz, has plenty of information in English.

Sights & Activities

Only two of the Renaissance town gates are left from the town's defensive wall. The originally Gothic castle (1261–64), which was rebuilt as a neo-Renaissance **chateau** in the mid-19th century, is today a **museum** (☎ 518 332 132; adult/concession 40/20Kč; ⏱ 9am-5pm Tue-Sun Jul & Aug, to 4pm May, Jun, Sep & Oct) that includes good displays on the folk culture of the Slovácko region. From Předměstí, walk north on kostelní, turn right and cross náměstí Svobody to Rybářská, then go left up Bzenecka.

Across the road and slightly closer to town is the **skansen** (☎ 518 332 173; www.nulk.cz; Bzenecká 671; adult/concession 50/25Kč; ⏱ 9am-5pm Tue-Sun Jul & Aug, to 4pm May, Jun, Sep & Oct) with its large collection of Slovácko buildings from the last century, including smithies, wineries and colourfully decorated beehives. Most houses are furnished.

Půjčovna Lodí Strážnice (☎ 603 371 350; www.batuv kanal.net/) hires out canoes (100Kč per hour) and organises boat tours (adult/concession 90/45Kč). It's by the bridge on Rybářská, en route to the chateau.

Festivals & Events

The Strážnice three-day **International Folk Festival**, held on the last weekend in June, was the first such festival held in the Czech Republic, back in 1945. It gave a major boost to the preservation of traditional culture.

Most of the festivities go on in the chateau's park, including open-air stage performances and impromptu jams, and food stalls with plenty of booze. The entry fee into the park is 130Kč per day or 300Kč for three days. One of the highlights is a procession from the town's main square to the chateau's garden.

Sleeping & Eating

Autokempink Strážnice (☎ 518 332 037; www.camp -straznice.cz; Bzenecká 1533; tent/hut per person 55/145Kč; ⏱ May-Oct; P ☎) Near the chateau, this also has rooms, bungalows and a buffet; book ahead around festival time.

Turistická Ubytovna (☎ 518 334 501; Bzenecká; dm 150Kč; P) Signposted across the sports field next to the *skansen*, this has basic beds in basic surroundings.

Strážnice-Flag (☎ 518 332 444; www.hotelflag.cz; Předměstí 3; s/d 900/1180Kč) It's a bit of a shoebox but the rooms offer typical three-star comfort.

Restaurace Na rynku (náměstí Svobody; mains 60-90Kč)
Near the village centre, this offers no-fuss,
pub-style Czech fare.

Getting There & Away

Direct buses connect Strážnice with Veselí
nad Moravou (12Kč, 15 minutes), Hodonín
(24Kč, 25 minutes), Uherské Hradiště (27Kč,
45 minutes) and, twice a day, Brno (58Kč,
two hours).

Trains are pricier but also run to Veselí
nad Moravou (16Kč, 15 minutes), Hodonín
(28Kč, 30 minutes) and Uherské Hradiště
(34Kč, 45 minutes).

KUŽELOV

Kuželov's Dutch-style **windmill** (admission 25Kč;
9am-noon & 1-5pm Sat & Sun Apr-Oct) dates from
1842 and is one of only a handful to survive in
Moravia (there were 700 in the 19th century).
The caretaker will show you how it works and
take you through a little museum full of old
furnishings, clothing and utensils.

Buses are scarce, with irregular connections to/from Strážnice (19km) and Veselí
nad Moravou (28km).

BLATNICE

Blatnice is 5km west of Veselí nad Moravou
and is known for the **St Anthony pilgrimage**,
which is held on the weekend nearest the
period 13 to 16 September. The colourful
pilgrimage takes place around the **chapel of St
Anthony** (kaple sv Antonína), built in the 17th
century. Many of the pilgrims are dressed in
traditional dress, and the songs and music are
traditional as well.

VLČNOV

There is little to see in Vlčnov – apart from
some decorated houses and the village's 40
or so *búdy* (wine cellars) – unless you're
here for the annual **Ride of the Kings** (Jízda Králů;
http://jizdakralu.vlcnov.cz) folk festival (p328).

The closest accommodation is in Uherské
Hradiště (15km away), to which there are
several daily buses (many more are added
during festival time). Entrance to the festival
costs 100/50Kč for adult/concession.

UHERSKÉ HRADIŠTĚ

pop 26,200
Most mid-size towns would be content with
one pretty main square, but Uherské Hradiště
fits two into its well-preserved historical

centre. Both have a lively selection of bars
and restaurants.

Outside the old town, Uherské Hradiště
gets increasingly gritty. However, good hotels and a pair of interesting museums make
it a good base to explore the surrounding
region.

Orientation

Uherské Hradiště train station is southwest
of the city centre, on the corner of Nádražní
and Spojovací, but it's only on a rail link between two main lines. Břeclav–Přerov trains,
including from Hodonín and Rohatec, stop
in the northern suburb of Staré Město. Brno–
Slovakia trains, including those from Kyjov,
stop in the southern suburb of Kunovice.

The bus station is at Velehradská třída, near
the Centrum department store. To get to the
main square, Masarykovo náměstí, walk west
along Obránců míru as far as Velehradská
and turn left along Krátká and Šromova to
the square.

Information

Česká Pojišťovna (Masarykovo náměstí 34) Has an
exchange desk and ATM during office hours.
Post office (Masarykovo náměstí)
Tourist Information Office (Městské Informační
Centrum; ☎ 572 525 525; www.mic.uh.cz; Masarykovo
náměstí 21; 8am-noon & 12.30-6pm Mon-Sun) Books
accommodation and provides internet access (40Kč per
hour).

Sights

PAMÁTNÍK VELKÉ MORAVY

The archaeological site **Památník Velké Moravy**
(Great Moravia Monument; ☎ 572 543 382; Jezuitská 1885;
adult/concession 20/10Kč; 9am-noon & 12.30-5pm Apr-
Nov) is believed to be a major centre of the
9th-century Great Moravian Empire. Many
of the artefacts found here, such as jewellery, weapons and ice skates made from bone,
have been collected in the museum. You can
also see foundations dating back to the 8th
century.

It's in Staré Město, 2km north of the city
centre. To get there from the main square
walk east on Havlíčkova to the highway (Velehradská třída), turn left and cross the Morava
river, continue along Hradištská, turn right
into Velkomoravská and take the second left
at Jezuitská. Alternatively, take bus 4 from the
bus station on Obránců míru; it stops near
this corner, two stops past the bridge.

THE RIDE OF THE KINGS

Dating back to the old European festival of Whitsuntide, the Ride of the Kings (Jízda Králů) festival in Vlčnov is a celebration of spring and a young man's rite of passage.

The king, who must be chaste, is always a 10- to 12-year-old boy. His helpers can be up to 18 years old. To prevent him speaking or smiling, he holds a rose in his teeth throughout the ceremony. He and two helpers dress in women's clothing, symbolising the escape of Hungarian king Mathias Korvin after losing a battle with Czech king George of Podebrady. Mathias evaded capture by dressing as a woman, and the rose is a symbol of his silence during his successful escape. The horses are decorated with ribbons and paper flowers and there's folk dancing and singing. Starting from the home of the king, the ride winds through the village. His helpers call out old verses in the king's honour and ask for gifts for him; the crowd stuffs money in the helpers' boots.

In Vlčnov this two-day festival happens on the last weekend in May, with the 'ride of the kings' on the Sunday. The ride also takes place in nearby Kunovice and Hluk, where it happens only every four years, and is celebrated with a Haná spin in Doloplazy and Kojetin near Olomouc in North Moravia.

SLOVÁCKÉ MUSEUM

In addition to its excellent collection of traditional folk dress, the **Slovácké museum** (☎ 572 551 370; Smetanovy sady 179; adult/concession 20/10Kč; ☉ 9am-noon & 12.30-5pm) has unusual 'folk art': an exhibit of 17th- to 19th-century shooting targets (from the days of local civil defence militias) featuring politicians, musicians, mythological characters, animals and birds. It's in Smetanovy park (Smetanovy sady) behind the cinema, at the intersection of Havličkova and the highway.

The **Gallery of Slovácké museum** (Galerie Slováckého muzea; ☎ 572 552 425; Otakarova 103; adult/concession 20/10Kč; ☉ 9am-noon & 12.30-5pm Tue-Sun), just north of the main square, is a branch of the museum exhibiting local art.

Sleeping

Hotel Quadro Club (☎ 542 540 554; www.hotel-quadro.com; Maršála Malinoveského 360; s/d 600/800Kč) A snazzy new spot on the main road into town but an easy walk to the two town squares.

Hotel Grand (☎ 572 551 511; www.granduh.cz; Palackého náměstí; s/d 850/1240Kč; ☐) At the lower end of the Best Western comfort scale, but still good value.

Hotel Slunce (☎ 572 432 640; www.synothotels.com; Masarykovo náměstí 150; s/d incl breakfast 1700/2600Kč; P ✗ ⊠ ☐ ☐) Care has been taken to showcase the building's original (from 1578) Renaissance features, but not at the expense of modern and comfortable rooms.

Eating & Drinking

Ziné Kavarna & Gallerie (☎ 739 020 847; Havličkova; mains 80Kč; ☉ 8am-10pm Mon-Thu, to midnight Fri & Sat, from 1pm Sun) Interesting breakfasts, salads and pizza shine in this modern space that moonlights as a gallery for local artists.

Corso (☎ 672 552 180; Masarykovo náměstí 147; ☉ to 1am) After dark this humble café transforms into the after-hours haunt of Uherské Hradiště's VIPs.

Getting There & Away

Trains to/from Hodonín (52Kč, 45 minutes) stop at the Staré Město station, while those to and from Kyjov (52Kč, 50 minutes) use the Kunovice station (see also Orientation, p327).

There are regular buses to Buchlovice (16Kč, 25 minutes) and Zlín (36Kč, 45 minutes) and less frequent services to Brno (70Kč, 1½ hours).

Getting Around

City bus 1 links Staré Město and Kunovice train stations, via the city centre, while bus 4 connects Uherské Hradiště and Staré Město train stations.

BUCHLOVICE

pop 2500

The baroque **Buchlovice chateau** (☎ 575 595 112; www.zamek-buchlovice.cz; adult/concession 70/30Kč; ☉ 9am-noon & 12.30-6pm Jul & Aug, to 5pm Tue-Sun May, Jun & Sep, to 3pm Sat & Sun Apr & Oct) was built in the 1700s, probably to a design by Martinelli, with ornate stucco decorations. On display are the furnishings left behind by the Berchtold family, who fled the advancing Soviet forces in 1945. En route to the chateau you pass through a **garden** (adult/concession 20/10Kč) of preening peacocks.

Sleeping & Eating

The **tourist office** (☎ 572 595 996; tic@buchlovice.cz; Svobody 6; ⏰ 9am-4.30pm Tue-Sun) can help with cheap accommodation.

Hotel Buchlovice (☎ 572 596 021; www.hotelbuchlovice.cz; Svobody 426; s/d 1050/1250Kč; ⓟ) This central place has smart rooms and an excellent terrace restaurant.

Getting There & Away

Infrequent buses stop here en route from Uherské Hradiště (16Kč, 25 minutes) to Kunovice.

BUCHLOV CASTLE

In the Chřiby hills, **Buchlov castle** (☎ 572 595 161; www.zamek-buchlovice.cz; adult/concession 70/35Kč; ⏰ 9am-5pm Jul & Aug, to 4pm Tue-Sun May, Jun & Sep, to 3pm Sat & Sun Apr & Oct) was built in the 13th century and, although it's been enlarged, it hasn't been restyled since its founding. Its last owners, the Berchtold family, turned it into a museum during the 19th century.

This simple place has none of the overwrought decoration of the baroque style. Rooms are sparsely furnished but interesting. As in most medieval castles, there are plenty of weapons and instruments of torture on display.

Hotel Buchlov Park (☎ 572 577 925; www.buchlovpark.cz; s/d incl breakfast 1350/2250Kč; ⓟ 🐾), which is right next to the castle, organises horse-riding trips (200Kč per hour).

Getting There & Away

The castle turn-off is on the Brno highway, 4km west of Buchlovice. On foot or by bike it's uphill all the way. Four daily buses between Uherské Hradiště and Kunovice stop at the castle turn-off, from where it's a pleasant 2km walk through the forest.

VELEHRAD

pop 1300

Not far from Uherské Hradiště, at Velehrad, is the **Cistercian monastery** (klášter Cisterciáků; ☎ 572 571 130; admission free; ⏰ 7am-6pm). It was long considered (though mistakenly) to have been the archiepiscopal seat of St Methodius, who may have died in the area in 885. Pilgrims have been flocking to the shrine for centuries, including Pope John Paul II in 1990.

Under the monastery's church is a **lapidarium** (adult/concession 30/15Kč; ⏰ 9am-4.30pm Tue-Sun Apr-Oct) with the remains of the original basilica.

On the road from Uherské Hradiště sits the **Archeoskanzen** (☎ 572 571 180; www.archeoskanzen.cz, in Czech; ⏰ 9am-5pm May-Sep, to 4pm Tue-Sun Apr & Oct; adult/concession 50/20Kč), a replica Great Moravian village complete with animal pens, a defensive palisade and a restaurant.

There are regular buses during weekdays (fewer on weekends) from Uherské Hradiště (12Kč, 20 minutes).

ZLÍNSKO REGION

ZLÍN

pop 78,500

After the prettified architectural excesses found elsewhere in the country, the robust and uniform structure of Zlín is a welcome contrast. Developed as a planned community by philanthropist shoe millionaire Tomáš Baťa (pronounced 'Batya'), Zlín is a fascinating legacy of one man's vision. Factories, offices, shopping centres and houses all use lookalike red bricks and a functionalist template, to provide 'a total environment' to house, feed and entertain the workers at Baťa's massive factory. Wide avenues and planned gardens produce a singular ambience, giving Zlín an expansive and unnervingly modern appearance in contrast with the saccharine historical centres of other towns.

Zlín also has a tradition of film-making. The town's studios began making films to promote Baťa shoes, and more than 2000 films have been made in the last half-century. At opposite ends of the 'entertainment' spectrum, Zlín is the birthplace of playwright Tom Stoppard (born Thomas Straussler in 1937, when his father worked at the Baťa factory) and Ivana Trump, socialite former wife of New York property tycoon Donald Trump.

Orientation

The train station (Železniční stanice) stands just off Gahurova, south of the river. The bus station is about 100m closer to the centre. The town centres on functional náměstí Míru.

Information

ČSOB (náměstí Práce) Has ATMs and exchange desks.
KB (cnr Dlouhá & třída Tomáše Bati) Has ATMs and exchange desks.
Tourist Information Office (Městské Informační a Turistické Středisko; ☎ 577 630 270; www.mestozlin.cz; náměstí Míru 12; ⏰ 8am-5.30pm Mon-Fri, to noon Sat) Arranges accommodation and has internet access (1Kč per minute).

Sights

The Zlín chateau houses the **museum of South-East Moravia** (muzeum jihovýchodní Moravy; ☎ 577 004 611; Soudní 1; adult/concession 20/10Kč; ☼ 9am-noon & 1-5pm Tue-Sun), which has displays of local film studios, folk music instruments and utensils from the Slovácko and Haná regions. Upstairs is a branch of the **State Gallery** (Galerie Výtvarného Umění ve Zliné; adult/concession 20/10Kč; ☼ same as museum), with permanent displays of 20th-century Czech art and sculpture.

The interesting **Shoe museum** (Obuvnické muzeum; ☎ 577 522 225; třída Tomáše Bati 1970; adult/concession with English text 30/20Kč; ☼ 10am-noon, 1-5pm Tue-Sun, Sat & Sun Nov-Mar) has more various footwear than Imelda Marcos could dream of, including basketball player Shaquille O'Neal's 41cm-long Timberland boots and some effortlessly cool 1960s loafers. In a corner of the museum is Tomáš Baťa's amazing office which doubled as a lift, allowing him to move up and down in the Baťa HQ. Don't miss the video showing retro Baťa TV advertising.

A few 20th-century buildings are also worth a look. František Gahura's **House of Art** (dům umění; ☎ 577 218 317; náměstí TG Masaryka 2570; adult/concession 15/5Kč; ☼ 9am-5pm Tue-Sun) hosts another branch of the State Gallery featuring works by Mucha, among others. It's also home to the Zlín Philharmonic Orchestra.

Another curiosity is the gargantuan **Grand cinema** (Velké kino; ☎ 577 432 936; www.velkekino.cz; náměstí Práce 2511) built in the 1960s and capable of seating 2000.

Sleeping & Eating

For private rooms (from around 250Kč per person) talk to the Tourist Information Office (p329).

Hostel Duo Zlín (☎ 577 433 112; www.hotelduozlin.cz; Rŭmy 1391; s/d 350/550Kč) is a cheaper hostel that shares a building with the refurbished business-oriented **Park Hotel Zlín** (☎ 577 056 111; www.parkhotelzlin.cz; s/d incl breakfast 1250/1740Kč).

Hotel Garni Zlín (☎ 577 210 458; www.hotelgarnizlin.cz; nám TG Masaryka 1335; s/d 1000/1200Kč; ☒) A quiet business hotel with spick-and-span rooms, the Garni has excellent weekend discounts and a cosy Portuguese wine cellar.

Hotel Moskva (☎ 577 561 111; www.moskva-zlin.cz; náměstí Práce 2512; s/d incl breakfast 1000/1500Kč; ☐ ☐) Dominating the town with its gargantuan functionalist façade, the Moskva has an enjoyably retro selection of more than 100 rooms, and 10 bars and restaurants (some equally old school).

Záložno (náměstí Míru; mains 80-140Kč) This place is at the eastern edge of the main square and provides good views from its popular terrace restaurant.

Café Archa (☎ 577 211 083; třída Tomáše Bati 190; mains 100Kč; ☼ 8am-10pm) This is an elegantly cool and versatile spot that's good for breakfast, lunch, dinner or end-of-day cocktails.

Getting There & Away

To go anywhere by train usually requires a change at Otrokovice; the 127km to Brno (162Kč) takes three hours. Buses are faster; there regular links to Uherské Hradiště (30Kč,

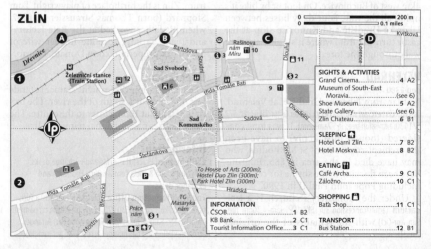

ZLÍN

0 ――― 200 m
0 ――― 0.1 miles

SIGHTS & ACTIVITIES	
Grand Cinema	**4** A2
Museum of South-East Moravia	(see 6)
Shoe Museum	**5** A2
State Gallery	(see 6)
Zlín Chateau	**6** B1

SLEEPING 🛏	
Hotel Garni Zlín	**7** B2
Hotel Moskva	**8** B2

EATING 🍴	
Café Archa	**9** C1
Záložno	**10** C1

SHOPPING 🛍	
Baťa Shop	**11** C1

INFORMATION	
ČSOB	**1** B2
KB Bank	**2** C1
Tourist Information Office	**3** C1

TRANSPORT	
Bus Station	**12** B1

SOUTH MORAVIA

THE PEOPLE'S SHOE

Before its present incarnation, humble Zlín was one village among many – an unassuming dot on the map. Its present form, a herringbone pattern of streets radiating from the main thoroughfare, dates from 1894 when Tomáš Baťa, the omnipresent shoe manufacturer, began to expand his enterprise (Baťa had made a fortune from the sale of boots to the Austrian army in WWI). The town grew quickly and between 1910 and 1930 its population trebled to 36,000.

Baťa (and later his son) grew the company into a sizable multinational and by the early 1930s it had become the world's leading footwear exporter, designing, producing and marketing shoes in 30 countries by 1938.

Tomáš Baťa was killed in a plane accident in 1932, but the company remains largely a family affair. From humble beginnings it now has 4600 stores, 40 factories and 40,000 employees and operates in more than 50 countries. Every day more than one million customers are served in a Baťa store.

You can invest in your own pair of local shoes at the **Baťa shop** (Dlouhá 130) in Zlín.

40 minutes), Olomouc (68Kč, 1½ hours) and Kroměříž (38Kč, 55 minutes).

VIZOVICE
pop 4500

As the home of the Jelínek distillery, this small town 15km east of Zlín is the source of some of the country's finest *slivovitz* (plum brandy).

The rather ordinary **Vizovice chateau** (zámek Vizovice; ☎ 577 452 762; http://zamek-viz.hyperlink.cz; adult/concession 40/20Kč; ☼ 9am-noon & 1-5pm Tue-Sun May-Aug, to 4pm Sat & Sun Apr, Sep & Oct), 100m off the main square, does have some good exhibits on traditional trades and crafts.

There are regular daily train and bus connections to/from Zlín.

LEŠNÁ
The attractions of tiny Lešná, 8km north of Zlín, include a romantic-style chateau and a better-than-average zoo.

Lešná chateau (zámek Lešná; ☎ 577 914 180; adult/concession 50/35Kč; ☼ 9am-4pm Tue-Fri, to 5pm Sat & Sun May-Sep, to 3.30pm Sat & Sun Oct, to 5pm Sat & Sun Apr) is an overdecorated concoction of towers and shutters.

The surrounding **zoo** (www.zoolesna.cz; adult/concession 75/55Kč; ☼ 9am-6pm Tue-Sun Apr-Sep, to 4pm Oct-Mar) is in an English-style park, with 2500 animals largely free to roam in fairly spacious enclosures.

There are hourly buses from Zlín (20Kč, 30 minutes); fewer at weekends.

LUHAČOVICE
pop 5400

With the notable absence of the sickly yellow *Kaisergelb* paint that festoons the spas of West Bohemia, Luhačovice also lacks the primness that blights Mariánské Lázně' and Karlovy Vary. Instead the town has an everyday no-fuss feel and is all the better for it. Architecturally it's a bit of a mishmash with rustic half-timbered houses abutting a few Soviet-style blocks, but with the serene woodland setting and friendly, unpretentious locals, it's a pleasantly low-key Moravian alternative to the spa town excesses in the west.

Orientation & Information
Luhačovice snakes along Šťavnice creek and the main road that runs parallel to it. The train and bus stations are at the southwest end of town; walk out of the stations, turn left onto Masarykova and continue past the police station.

Luha (☎ 577 133 980; www.mesto.luhacovice.cz; Masarykova 950; ☼ 8am-4pm Mon-Fri) arranges accommodation and has a good selection of maps. It also opens weekends in July and August.

There is a **KB** (Masarykova 950) ATM outside the Elektra Restaurant.

Sights & Activities
Luhačovice has some fine examples of rustic architecture incorporating Wallachian farmhouse motifs. Among the town's more interesting Tudoresque houses are **Jestřábí dům** and **Vodoléčebný ústav** on L Janáčka, and **Jurkovičův dům** on Dr P Blaha. Designed by Slovak architect Dušan Jurkovič, Jurkovičův dům blends rustic Slovak folk traditions with the whimsy of Art Nouveau and has recently reopened as a luxury spa hotel.

The spa follows the creek, lined with trees, spa hotels and fountains. Perhaps the most visited spas are **Ottovka**, in the gazebo by the

SOUTH MORAVIA

tennis courts, and **Aloiska** behind the Palace Sanatorium.

Many spa hotels offer specialised treatments: paraffin packs, four-chamber baths, you name it. The average 'cure' lasts about a week; contact the spa's main office, **Lázně Luhačovice** (☎ 577 682 111; www.lazneluhacovice.cz; Lázeňské náměstí 436).

The **Luhačovice museum** (muzeum v Luhačovicích; ☎ 577 132 883; adult/concession 15/10Kč; ☺ 9am-noon & 1-5pm Tue-Sun Apr-Oct, to 4pm Nov-Mar), next to the tennis courts, has a small collection of painted Easter eggs *(kraslice)*, ceramics, embroidery and other folk art.

Sleeping

There is plenty of accommodation in all ranges, including private rooms from 250Kč per person. Luha (p331) can help with these.

Autokemping Luhačovice (☎ 577 133 318; tent/ chalet per person 70/140Kč; ☺ May-Sep; Ⓟ) This pretty camp site with chalets is at the Údolní dam (Údolní přehrada), 3km north of town along the stream. Get there on bus 7.

Penzion Stella (☎ 577 132 339; http://penzionstella .luhacovice.cz; Solné 1010; s/d incl breakfast 685/1020Kč; Ⓟ) The welcome is super friendly and the rooms spacious in this new place with great views. There's every chance the owner will join you for a sundowner beer and his homemade *slivovitz* (plum brandy). Be warned – it's very strong.

Pension Růža (☎ 577 134 202; www.penzionruza .cz; U Šťávnice 256; d incl breakfast 1100Kč) Housed in a traditional villa down a quiet side street, this has smart rooms and a welcoming bar.

Also recommended:

Hotel Zálesí (☎ 577 134 060; hotely@zalesi.cz; Zatloukalova 70; s/d incl breakfast 800/1300Kč) Bright and modern with a solarium and massage facilities.

Eating

As in all Czech spa towns, *oplatky* (sweet wafers) are a popular snack.

The spa hotels have some of the town's smartest eateries.

Divadelní kavárna (Masarykova 950; snacks 60Kč; ☺ to 6pm) A pleasant café beside the town theatre.

Restaurace Elektra (☎ 577 134 335; Masarykova 950; mains 130Kč) While the rest of Luhačovice is spa town quiet, this grill and pizza place is busy and cosmopolitan well into the night.

Also recommended:

Lotos (☎ 572 132 720; Masarykova 151; mains 80-120Kč; ☺ 11am-8pm) Vaguely Greek and vaguely Italian, the fish dishes and pizza are good in this slice of southern Europe in southern Moravia.

Getting There & Away

Buses are easier and quicker than trains from most destinations, with up to 11 a day from Zlín (30Kč, 40 minutes) and eight from Uherský Brod (24Kč, 20 minutes).

KROMĚŘÍŽ

pop 29,100

Everywhere you go you'll find towns compared to Athens, Venice or Paris, and in this quiet corner of Moravia, this pretty little town fits the bill perfectly.

Known locally as Hanácké Athény (the Athens of Haná), Kroměříž was the home base of the powerful bishops of Olomouc from the 12th to 19th century. Religious wrangling has now made way for tourism in this pleasantly provincial town, and the bishops' flash baroque chateau and spacious gardens are well worth a trip.

History

German colonists began arriving in the 13th century, when the town was fortified.

The town was practically destroyed by the Swedes in the Thirty Years' War, but in 1664 the bishops undertook their major baroque construction effort. The castle was rebuilt by Italian architects Tencalla and Lucchese to a commission by Charles II of Liechtenstein-Kastlekorn, a bishop.

In the mid-18th century, Kroměříž and the chateau were damaged during an occupation by the Prussian army, and later from a fire.

Orientation

If you're arriving at the train or bus stations, get onto Hulínská and cross the river. The interesting bits of town are centred on the chateau and Velké náměstí.

Information

The **Tourist Information Office** (Informační Centrum; ☎ 573 221 473; www.mesto-kromeriz.cz; Velké náměstí 50; ☺ 8.30am-5pm Mon-Fri, 9am-1pm Sat & Sun) organises accommodation, rents out bikes (200Kč per day), has a left-luggage office and changes money.

Česká Spořitelna (Velké náměstí 43) and **ČSOB** (Riegrovo náměstí 182) both have exchange offices and ATMs.

The main post office is on the corner of Oskol and Denkova. There's a second branch in the train station. You can access the internet at **dc Internet Café** (☎ 737 883 400; Velké náměstí 39; ⊗ 10am-7pm Mon-Fri, from 1pm Sat & Sun).

Lékárna v Kovářské (☎ 573 337 425; Kovářská 18) is a central pharmacy.

Sights

ARCHBISHOPS' CHATEAU

North of Velké náměstí is the **Archbishops' chateau** (Arcibiskupský zámek; ☎ 573 502 011; www.azz .cz; adult/concession with guide 180/1000Kč; ⊗ 9am-5pm Tue-Sun May-Sep, Sat Apr, Sun & holidays Oct) with its 84m baroque tower. It takes 1½ hours to tour the interior, which features rococo ceilings and murals by Franz Anton Maulpertsch and Josef Stern. The **Manský hall** (Manský sál) has Maulpertsch's skilful ceiling paintings. The best-known room is the **Assembly hall** (Sněmovní sál), where scenes for the film *Amadeus* were shot. It costs extra to tour the **tower** (adult/concession 40/20Kč) and **Sala terena** (adult/concession 20/10Kč).

You can also visit the **Chateau gallery** (Zámecká obrazárna; adult/concession 100/50Kč), which has a

valuable collection of 16th and 17th century paintings. Pride of place goes to Titian's *Flaying of Marsyas*.

Behind the chateau is **Podzámecká garden** (Podzámecká zahrada; ⊗ 6.30am-8pm), designed in the 17th century by Lucchese and one of the largest in the country, with 64 hectares of greenery.

Nearby, the **Bishop's mint** (Biskupskou mincovnu; Na Sladovnách; adult/concession 15/10Kč; ⊗ 9am-5pm Tue-Sun May-Sep, Sat & Sun Oct-Apr) is worth a peek if you're interested in making (in the less interesting sense) money.

AROUND THE OLD TOWN

Leaving the chateau through Sněmovní náměstí, on the right is the **Mill gate** (Mlýnská brána).

On Pilařova is the **Collegiate cathedral of St Maurice** (Kolegiátní chrám sv Mořice), a seminary built around 1260 and one of the oldest surviving structures in Kroměříž.

Continue on Pilařova to the baroque **church of St John the Baptist** (kostel sv Jana Křtitele), built 1737–68, which features frescoes by JJ Etgens and Stern.

SOUTH MORAVIA

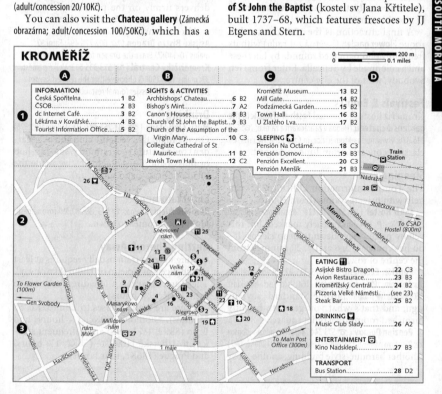

KROMĚŘÍŽ

0 ———————— 200 m
0 ———————— 0.1 miles

INFORMATION
Česká Spořitelna.................1 B2
ČSOB..................................2 B3
dc Internet Café..................3 B2
Lékárna v Kovářské..............4 B3
Tourist Information Office......5 B2

SIGHTS & ACTIVITIES
Archbishops' Chateau..........6 B2
Bishop's Mint.......................7 A2
Canon's Houses...................8 B3
Church of St John the Baptist..9 B3
Church of the Assumption of the
    Virgin Mary....................10 C3
Collegiate Cathedral of St
    Maurice..........................11 B2
Jewish Town Hall.................12 C2

Kroměříž Museum..............13 B2
Mill Gate............................14 B2
Podzámecká Garden...........15 B2
Town Hall............................16 B3
U Zlatého Lva......................17 B2

SLEEPING
Pensión Na Octárné.............18 C3
Penzión Domov...................19 B3
Penzión Excellent................20 C3
Penzión Menšík...................21 B3

EATING
Asijské Bistro Dragon...........22 C3
Avion Restaurace.................23 B3
Kroměřížský Centrál.............24 B2
Pizzeria Velké Náměsti.......(see 23)
Steak Bar............................25 B2

DRINKING
Music Club Slady.................26 A2

ENTERTAINMENT
Kino Nadsklepí....................27 B3

TRANSPORT
Bus Station..........................28 D2

From Masarykovo náměstí, a walk along Jánská back towards Velké náměstí passes a group of colourful **Canon's houses** (Kanovnické domy) on the left. In the square, on the corner with Kovářská, is the 16th-century Renaissance **town hall**.

On Velké náměstí, the **Kroměříž museum** (muzeum Kroměřížska; ☎ 573 338 388; Velké náměstí 38; adult/concession for all exhibitions 60/30Kč, Max Švabinský only 35/20Kč) has a permanent collection of the works of Max Švabinský (born in Kroměříž in 1873), a specialist in colourful nudes and the designer of many of Czechoslovakia's early postage stamps.

At No 30 is the town's oldest pharmacy *(lékárna)*, **U Zlatého lva**, which was established in 1675. The cobblestone square also has a decorative **fountain** and **plague column**.

From Velké náměstí, take Vodní and continue along Farní past the **church of the Assumption of the Virgin Mary** (kostel Nanebevzetí Panny Marie). On the left is Moravcova, where halfway along is a reminder of the town's Jewish history, the old **Jewish town hall** (Židovská radnice).

A final attraction is the 17th-century baroque **Flower garden** (Květná zahrada) with its frequently photographed rotunda by Lucchese and a colonnade by Tencalla. Enter from Gen Svobody, west of the city centre.

Festivals & Events
Kroměříž hosts the annual **Festival of Music in the gardens & chateau** (Hudba v zahrádkách a zámku; ☎ 573 315 376; www.hudba-kromeriz.cz, in Czech), a series of classical concerts, from June to August.

Sleeping
The Tourist Information Office (p332) can help with private rooms (from 300Kč).

ČSAD Hostel (☎ 517 316 111; Skopalíkova 2385; s/d 215/430Kč; **P**) It isn't clearly marked, but this yellow place offers decent cheap sleeps. It's on bus routes 1, 2, 6 and 7, 20 minutes from the centre of town.

Penzión Excellent (☎ 573 333 023; www.excellent .tunker.com; Riegrovo náměstí 164; s/d incl breakfast 660/990Kč; **P** 🖳) 'Europe Standard' says its sign, and that's what you get with brightly furnished rooms on a quiet square.

Penzión Domov (☎ 573 344 744; www.penziondomov .cz; Riegrovo náměstí 157; s/d incl breakfast 900/1200Kč; **P**) Another baroque-style building, another cosy

pension with slightly ageing rooms – a good backup, if a tad overpriced.

Pensión Na Octárné (☎ 573 515 555; www.octarna .cz; Tovačovského 318; d incl breakfast 1800Kč; **P** 🖳) A restored Franciscan monastery is now a classy guesthouse with a quiet courtyard shaded by market umbrellas. Downstairs is a stylish candlelit wine cellar.

Also recommended:
Penzión Menšík (☎ 602 569 863; Velké náměstí 107; d 650Kč) Main square location with suburban prices.

Eating
Avion Restaurace (☎ 573 339 446; Velké náměstí 111; mains 55Kč) No frills and no-fuss buffet meals are standard fare at this popular self-service restaurant.

Pizzeria Velké Náměstí (☎ 573 343 460; Velké náměstí 109; pizza 70-90Kč) Grab an espresso at the stand-up bar, or take your time with a more leisurely pizza while overlooking the main square.

Steak Bar (☎ 573 333 388; Ztracená 65; mains 100-1600Kč) This rustic spot with a sunny terrace delivers firmly on the promise of its name with robust, meaty Moravian platters.

Also recommended:
Asijské Bistro Dragon (☎ 602 778 497; Farní 97; mains 70-140Kč) Enter the Dragon for Asian favourites.
Kroměřížský Centrál (☎ 573 335 513; Velké náměstí 37; mains 100-250Kč) Choose either the relaxed *kavárna* (bar-cafe) or the classier formal restaurant.

Drinking
Music Club Slady (☎ 731 267 423; Na Sladovnách 1576) On any night this versatile club and beer garden could feature rock, country, ska, hip-hop or brass-band music (actually, we made the bit about brass-band music up).

Entertainment
Kino Nadsklepí (cinema; ☎ 573 339 280; Miličovo náměstí) Hollywood comes to town.

Getting There & Away
Getting here by train usually requires at least one change – at Kojetín or Hulín (8km away). There are, however, a few direct services to Brno (98Kč, 1¼ hours).

There are regular buses to Zlín (32Kč, 55 minutes), Olomouc (60Kč, 1¾ hours) and Brno (58Kč, 1¼ hours) and infrequent services to Uherské Hradiště (50Kč, 1¼ hours) and Prague (186Kč, four hours).

SOUTH MORAVIA

Slovakia

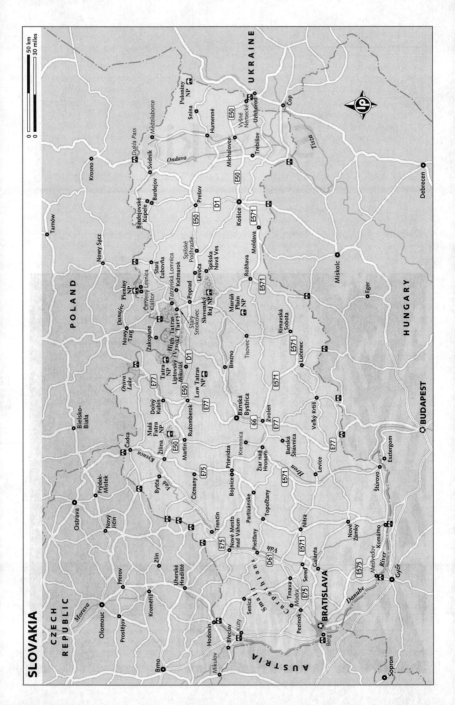

Bratislava

If you focus on the compact historic centre, you'll see cobblestoned roads, pedestrian plazas, pastel 18th-century rococo buildings and street cafés galore. Expand your gaze and you can't miss the institutional housing blocks and bizarre communist construction beyond. An age-old castle shares the skyline with a 1970s UFO-like bridge. And that's Bratislava: a mix of new, old and older. All of which is worth a look.

As post-EU-membership investment pours in, the whir of construction equipment in all quarters signals that Slovakia's capital is growing. The city has a buzz to it: beautiful people wearing black flock to the newest chichi eatery as soon as it opens. Weekend nights it'd be odd if you didn't see a gang or two of non-Slovak-speaking blokes wandering around the streets of the old town. There's something a bit reckless about the development, though. Zoning laws are largely ignored, and an odd mix of antireform-minded parties took control of the parliament in June 2006.

Who knows what the town will be like in a few years, but for now the old centre is supremely strollable. Amble around the mazelike pedestrian alleys, stopping for a coffee – or an adult beverage or two – in cafés along the way. Hike up to the city castle (or head out to the suburbs to see Devín castle). You may want to pop into a museum if it's raining, but otherwise the best thing to do is just to take in the different views, even as it all changes before your eyes.

HIGHLIGHTS

- While away the hours at one of the many **street cafés** (p350) in the 'rabbit warren' old town
- Have your picture taken with **The Watcher** (p352) statue near Hlavné nám
- Cruise along the Danube from Bratislava to below the clifftop ruins of **Devín castle** (p353)
- Climb up to **Bratislava castle** (p343) to contrast old-town architecture with the communist-era New bridge and Petržalka

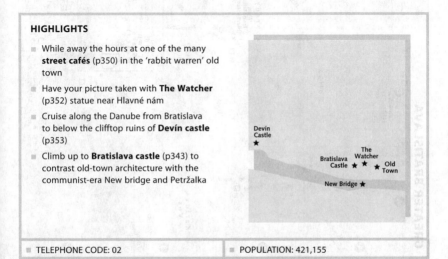

Devín
Castle
★

The
Watcher
Bratislava ★ ★
Castle ★ Old
Town

New Bridge ★

■ TELEPHONE CODE: 02 ■ POPULATION: 421,155

GREATER BRATISLAVA

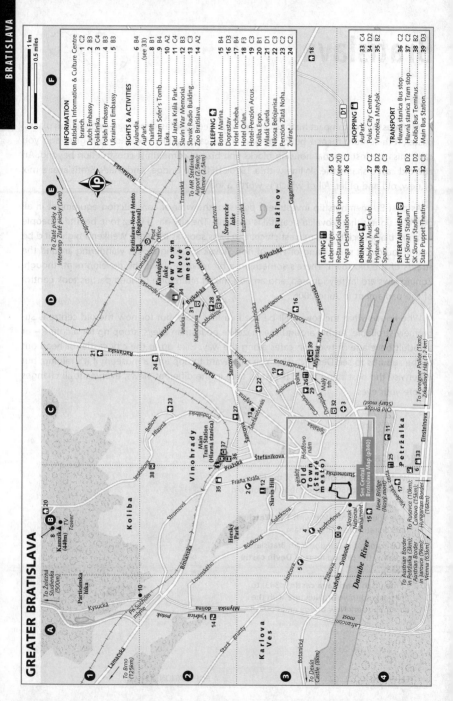

INFORMATION
Bratislava Information & Culture Centre branch..................	1 C2
Dutch Embassy..................	2 B3
Poliklinika..................	3 C4
Polish Embassy..................	4 B3
Ukrainian Embassy..................	5 B3

SIGHTS & ACTIVITIES
Aulandia..................	6 B4
AuPark..................	(see 33)
Chairlift..................	8 B1
Chatam Sofer's Tomb..................	9 B4
Luka..................	10 A2
Sad Janka Kráľa Park..................	11 C4
Slavín War Memorial..................	12 B3
Slovak Radio Building..................	13 C3
Zoo Bratislava..................	14 A2

SLEEPING
Botel Marina..................	15 B4
Dopraštav..................	16 D3
Hotel Incheba..................	17 B4
Hotel Orlan..................	18 F3
Hotel-Penzión Arcus..................	19 C3
Koliba Expo..................	20 B1
Mladá Garda..................	21 D1
Nikosa Belojanisa..................	22 C3
Penzión Zlatá Noha..................	23 C2
Zvárač..................	24 C2

EATING
Leberfinger..................	25 C4
Reštaurácia Koliba Expo..................	(see 20)
Vega Destination..................	26 C3

DRINKING
Babylon Music Club..................	27 C2
Hystéria Pub..................	28 D2
Sparx..................	29 C3

ENTERTAINMENT
HC Slovan Stadium..................	30 D2
SK Slovan Stadium..................	31 D2
State Puppet Theatre..................	32 C3

SHOPPING
AuPark..................	33 C4
Polus City Centre..................	34 D2
Vinotéka Matýšak..................	35 B2

TRANSPORT
Hlavná stanica Bus stop..................	36 C2
Hlavná stanica Tram stop..................	37 C2
Koliba Bus Terminus..................	38 B2
Main Bus Station..................	39 D3

HISTORY

It's hard to believe the capital of Slovakia hasn't been Slovak for very long. Officially, 'Bratislava' came into existence only in 1919; for 700 years preceding that it was known as Pressburg (in Austrian German) or Pozsony (in Hungarian) and the population had a very international flair.

The site of the city has been inhabited, more or less, for the past 4000 years. In the 2nd century AD it was the Romans, in the 5th century the first Slavs arrived, and by the 10th century the Magyars (Hungarians) had taken over (and would stay until WWI).

In 1465 King Matthias Corvinus founded the first university in the Hungarian Kingdom, the Academia Istrpolitana, in Bratislava. Then came the invading Turks, and the Hungarian capital was hurriedly moved from Budapest to Bratislava in 1536. Wealthy burghers and Viennese aristocrats built grand palaces, many of which still stand today. Musical life flourished; frequent visitors included Haydn, Mozart, Beethoven and, later, Liszt. Although the Austrian Hapsburgs finally retook Budapest in 1686, Hungarian royalty continued to be crowned in Bratislava's St Martin's Cathedral until 1830.

It was in the 19th century that Slovak national awareness began to grow; one of its leading literary figures, Ľudovít Štúr, lived and published in this city. In 1848 Ferdinand V signed his name to one of Štúr's demands: the abolition of serfdom.

Despite, or perhaps because of, a subsequent policy of Hungarianisation in schools and government, Slovak intellectuals cultivated ties with the Czechs, and after WWI the city, with its Slovak name Bratislava, became part of the new Czechoslovakia.

Bratislava's dress rehearsal as a national capital came in March 1939, when leaders set up Slovakia as a fascist puppet state and a German ally. It was not, however, a populist move and in August 1944 Slovak partisans instigated the ill-fated Slovenské Národné Povstanie (Slovak National Uprising; SNP), a source of ongoing national pride (and innumerable street names).

In the 1970s Bratislava was ruthlessly modernised. The New bridge (Nový most) overpass was built over the bulldozed remains of the city's old Jewish quarter, and Petržalka's vast tower blocks began to replace the villages on the south side of the Danube.

Bratislava once again became a capital city in 1993 with the creation of the independent Slovak Republic, and the old town got a new coat of paint.

Good thing EU membership came when it did in May 2004, because buildings were already starting to show wear.

Money is once again pumping into the city, though, and new facilities will be going up over the next few years in preparation for Bratislava's hosting of the ice hockey World Cup in 2011.

BRATISLAVA IN...

Two Days

Start the morning by wandering along the ramparts of **Bratislava castle** (p343). Enter through the **Historical Museum** (p343) to climb the crown tower *(korunná veža)* for the highest views of the old town. On your way back down to town, stop at the **Museum of Jewish Culture** (p343) before having lunch at **Prašná Bašta** (p350). Spend the afternoon strolling through the old town, stopping to drink at as many café terraces as you dare. If you schedule it right, you could catch an opera at the **Slovak National Theatre** (p351) or a band at the **Café Štúdio Club** (p351). The following day, take a trip out of town to explore **Devín castle** (p353).

Four Days

Expand the two-day itinerary, spending two days instead of one wandering about the old town and sights such as **St Martin's Cathedral** (p343), the **Slovak National Gallery** (p344) and the **Blue Church** (p344). Then on the third day head out to Devín. On day four you could either head up to the hilltop park at **Koliba** (p345) for some hiking, a chairlift ride, and some traditional Slovak food, or you might consider a day trip into the **Small Carpathians** (p356) where there are wineries and Červený Kameň castle to explore.

ORIENTATION

Bratislava's old town (staré mesto) lies on the north bank of the Danube. The pedestrian zone, where you'll probably spend most of your time, starts south of Hodžovo nám. Note that throughout the Slovakia chapters of this book we have used *nám*, the common abbreviation of *námestie* (square). The pedestrian zone is bounded by the castle and the UFO-like New bridge in the west, Tesco and Šafárikovo nám to the east, and the Danube river to the south. The large plaza, Hviezdoslavovo nám is a convenient reference point, with the Slovak National Theatre on its east end.

To the north of the old town is Koliba, a hillside residential district with megamillion mansions and a leafy park at the top. The new

town (nové mesto), with its high-rise blocks and sports stadiums, stretches 9km east to the airport. Petržalka is the massive housing estate south of the Danube.

Bratislava's main train station, Hlavná stanica, is 1km north of the old town. Tram 13 runs from the station to Nám L Štúra, just south of Hviezdoslavovo nám, and bus 93 stops at Hodžovo nám. The main bus station (autobusová stanica) is 1.5km east of the historical centre. Bus 206 shuttles between there and the main train station, stopping at Hodžovo nám in between.

Maps

The best map is VKÚ's 1:15,000 *Bratislava* (130Sk), complete with street index, tram

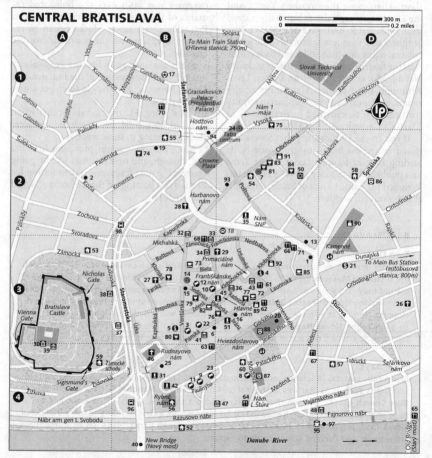

and bus routes, 1:5000-scale plan of the city centre and 1:50,000-scale map of the surrounding region.

INFORMATION
Bookshops
Artforum (Map p340; ☎ 5441 1898; Kozia 20) Great Slovakia-oriented English-language section, art books and literature.

Interpress Slovakia (Map p340; Sedlárska 2; ☽ 9am-10pm Mon-Sat, 2-10pm Sun) Foreign newspapers, and Bratislava periodicals in English.

Knihy Slovenský spisovateľ (Map p340; ☎ 5443 3760; Laurinská 2) Useful maps, hiking guides and picture books.

Next Apache (Map p340; Panenská 28; ☽ 9am-10pm Mon-Fri, 10am-10pm Sat & Sun) Loads of used English books and a comfy café.

Cultural Centres
British Council (Map p340; ☎ 5443 1074; Panská 17; ☽ 10am-7pm Mon-Fri, 10am-5pm Sat) Library and café open to public.

Emergency
Emergency (☎ 112)
Main police station (Map p340; ☎ 159; Gunduličova 10)

Foreigner Police (Map p338; ☎ 0961036855; Hrobákova 44; ☽ 7.30am-noon & 1-3pm Mon, 7.30am-noon & 1-6pm Wed, 7.30am-noon Fri)

Internet Access
An hour online costs anything from the price of a drink to 120Sk, but 60Sk is a pretty common rate. There are many small i-cafés scattered around the old town. Free wi-fi access is available on Primaciálne, Hviezdoslavovo, Hlavné and Františkánske squares. There are also free internet kiosks near the old town hall, the Primate's Palace and in the Bratislava Culture & Information Centre. An increasing number of restaurants, cafés and bars – such as Slovak Pub and Jazz Café – are offering free wi-fi as well.

Café Online (Map p340; ☎ 5464 2277; Obchodná 48; ☽ 9am-midnight) Really a bar that happens to have internet terminals.

Internet Centrum (Map p340; Michalská 2; ☎ 0903693577; ☽ 9am-4am) Six of the eight computers have webcam and Skype access.

Wifi Café (Map p340; Ground fl, Tatracentrum, Hodžovo nám; ☽ 8am-10pm Mon-Fri, 10am-10pm Sat, 11am-10pm Sun) Use the flat-screen terminals gratis at this smoke-free café, as long as you have a beverage. Wi-fi too, obviously.

Internet Resources

Bratislava (www.bratislava.sk) City-sponsored site with loads of tourist info.

Enjoy Bratislava (www.enjoybratislava.sk) City guide with monthly updates.

Slovak Spectator (www.slovakspectator.sk) Online version of the English-language weekly, with current affairs and event listings.

What's On Slovakia (www.whatsonslovakia.com) Entertainment listings for Bratislava and beyond.

Laundry

Bratislava does not have a laundrette, no kidding. Arrangements can be made with most lodgings to do your washing, even if it's not offered as an official service.

Left Luggage

In left-luggage offices, lunch breaks are generally taken from 12.30pm to 1pm, dinner from 6pm to 6.30pm. Items up to 15kg/over 15kg cost 30/45Sk per day.

Bus station (Mlynské nivy; Map p338; ⏱ 5.30am-10pm Mon-Fri, 6am-6pm Sat & Sun)

Main train station (Hlavná stanica; Map p338; ⏱ 6.30am-11pm)

Media

In Bratislava, Fun Radio (94.3 FM) is the popular pop-music station. BBC Worldservice is 93.8 FM.

Kam v Bratislave (Where in Bratislava; www.kam domesta.sk in Slovak; free) Monthly Slovak-language schedule for exhibits, operas and clubs; easy enough to decipher.

Slovak Spectator (www.slovakspectator.sk; 35Sk) Weekly English-language newspaper.

What's On Slovakia (www.whatsonslovakia.com; 40Sk) Monthly English-language magazine listing cultural events, live music and cinema schedules.

Medical Services

24-hour Pharmacy (Map p340; ☎ 5443 2952; Nám SNP 20)

Poliklinika (Map p338; ☎ 5296 2461; Bezručova 5) Twenty-four-hour emergency services, including dental.

Money

In Bratislava there's an excess of banks and ATMs in the old town, with several convenient branches located on Poštová and around Kamenné nám.

Most banks will cash travellers cheques and exchange foreign currency. There are also ATMs and exchange booths in the train and bus stations, and at the airport.

Tatra Banka (Map p340; Dunajská 4) English-speaking staff.

Post

Main post office (Map p340; Nám SNP 34-35) Address mail c/o Poste restante, 81000 Bratislava 1.

Telephone

Most pay phones these days require a local *telefónna karta* (phonecard), which can be purchased at newsstands. Many also sell international telephone cards, such as those from **EZ Phone** (www.ezcard.sk; 150/300/500Sk), with rates to the UK and US starting at per minute 2Sk. Both local and international phonecards can look a lot like the mobile phone credit cards also hung in the newsstand windows; watch what you're pointing at.

Toilets

Have coins handy; public toilets generally cost between 2Sk and 5Sk.

Tourist Information

Bratislava Culture & Information Centre (BKIS; ☎ 5249 5906; www.bkis.sk) centre (Map p340; Klobučnícka 2; ⏱ 8.30am-6pm Mon-Fri, 9am-3pm Sat); main train station (Map p338; Hlavná stanica; ⏱ 8am-7.30pm Mon-Fri, 8am-5pm Sat Jun-Sep & 8am-4.30pm Mon-Fri, 9am-2pm Sat Oct-May); airport (Map p338; MR Štefánika airport; ⏱ 8am-7.30pm Mon-Fri, 10am-6pm Sat) The official central tourist point is a little sterile, and the staff can seem uninterested, but keep pressing and they'll help you.

Bratislava Tourist Service (BTS; Map p340; ☎ 5464 1271; www.bratislava-info.sk; Ventúrska 9; ⏱ 10am-8pm) A tiny office, but it has a younger, more helpful staff than the BKIS and lots of maps and knick-knacks.

DANGERS & ANNOYANCES

Bratislava is relatively free of violent crime compared to Western capitals. To avoid annoyances, be as cautious as you'd normally be at home. Pickpocketing scams usually include some sort of distraction followed by someone coming up behind you to grab the goods. Car theft, not of the car but of the things inside, is all too common. Do not leave any valuables in view on car seats, even in a locked car – unless you're trying to get rid of them.

SIGHTS

Bratislava is more about the overall experience than about seeing spectacular, singular attractions. Ambling around the old town streets is probably how you'll spend most of your time. The main sights are gathered near the castle, on Hlavné nám and along the Danube. Bratislava's pedestrian core is small and easily covered in a day. Don't forget to put some of the many cafés, bars and restaurants onto your itinerary. To be honest, more than a few of the museums are quite boring (we've only listed the best), but the observation towers are worth the views. To explore further a field you'll need public transport. Many buses leave from Hodžovo nám or under the New bridge.

Bratislava Castle & Around

Lording over the west side of the old town, **Bratislava castle** (Bratislavský hrad; Map p340; grounds admission free; 9am-8pm Apr-Sep, to 6pm Oct-Mar) dominates the hill above the Danube. The winding ramparts and grounds provide a great vantage point for comparing ancient and communist Bratislava, the barrel-tile roofs of the old town versus the vast concrete housing estates of Petržalka. There are a couple of cafés and craft shops on the grounds.

The castle looks a bit like a four-poster bed, a shape that was well established by the 15th century. During the Turkish occupation of Budapest, this was the seat of Hungarian royalty. A fire devastated the fortress in 1811 and most of what you see today is a reconstruction from the 1950s (bland white interiors and all). The saving grace of the castle's ho-hum **Historical Museum** (Map p340; 5441 1441; www.snm .sk; adult/student 100/40Sk; 9am-6pm Tue-Sun) is you can climb up the crown tower (korunná veža). In good weather you can see Austria (3km southwest) and Hungary (16km south).

At the time of writing, the tiny **treasury** (klenotnica) was closed for reconstruction with no certain reopening date. When it does reopen, the highlight will still be the unbelievable 25,000-year-old Venus of Moravany, a miniature fertility statue of a headless, naked woman that is carved from a mammoth tusk. Far more interesting than the **museum of Music** (Hudobné múzeum; Map p340; 5441 3349; adult/student 40/20Sk; 9am-5pm Tue-Sun) is the chance to walk down into the bastion in the castle wall.

(To see a more historically complete castle, take a bus or boat out to **Devín castle**, p353, 9km outside the centre.)

A series of old homes wind down the castle hill along Židovská in what remains of the former Jewish quarter. The reputedly skinni-

est house in Central Europe contains a little **Museum of clocks** (Múzeum hodín; Map p340; 5441 1940; Židovská 1; adult/student 40/20Sk; 10am-5pm Tue-Sun). Inside the **Museum of Jewish culture** (Múzeum Židovskej kultúry; Map p340; 5441 8507; www .chatamsofer.com; Židovská 17; adult/student 200/100Sk; 11am-5pm Sun-Fri) there are moving exhibits about Slovakia's Jewish community that was decimated during WWII, the buildings were demolished in the 1960s and on Judaism in general. The staff can help arrange a visit to rabbi **Chatam Sofer's tomb** (Map p338; www.chatamsofer.com; Žižkova; donations accepted; by appointment only) near the tram tunnel under castle hill.

Cross under the Staromestská highway to the pedestrian old town and there's a small **Holocaust Memorial** (Map p340) near where the old synagogue once stood. A relatively modest interior in the Gothic 14th-century **St Martin's Cathedral** (Dóm sv Martina; Map p340; admission 60Sk; 9-11am & 1-5pm Mon-Sat, 1-5pm Sun) belies the elaborate history of the place. Here 11 Hungarian Hapsburg ruling monarchs were crowned from 1563 to 1830 (10 kings and one queen). The steeple is topped by a golden crown in place of a cross. Inside look for a 1734 statue of St Martin cutting off the corner of his cloak for a beggar; it was created by Georg Raphael Donner, Austria's best-known baroque sculptor. The cathedral is constantly under threat of damage as bridge traffic is shaking it to the core.

CHATAM SOFER

Born Moshe Schreiber in Frankfurt, Chatam Sofer (1762–1839) moved to Bratislava in 1806 to accept a position as a rabbi. Here he founded a yeshiva, a school for rabbis, and in the course of his life trained more than 150 (including his two sons). The school became one of the best known in Europe, and operated up until the first years of WWII when it had to be moved to Israel. Rabbi Sofer was a staunch defender of traditional Judaism and was against reform practices. His tomb became a place of pilgrimage, especially for Orthodox Jews from all over Europe. During the Nazi occupation the cemetery was buried under rubble, but his tomb has a new memorial entrance and is now Slovakia's most important Jewish site.

Along the Danube & Hviezdoslavovo Nám

Plans to make the Danube riverfront more of an attraction are in the works, but for now it's just a large, pleasant, tree-lined place to walk. Waterfront and centre is the **Slovak National Gallery** (Map p340; ☎ 5443 4587; www.sng.sk; Rázusovo nábrežie 2; adult/student 80/40Sk; ✆ 10am-5pm Tue-Sun), which houses the nation's biggest art collection. An 18th-century palace and a Stalinist-modernist building make interesting cohosts for the eclectic showing, which ranges from Gothic to graphic art.

The 1st floor exhibits of the **Slovak National Museum** (Map p340; ☎ 5934 9122; www.snm.sk; Vajanského nábrežie 2; adult/student 60/20Sk; ✆ 9am-5pm Tue-Sun) provide a superb overview of the folk cultures and customs of Slovakia's regions; skip the tired natural history stuff upstairs.

The narrow, tree-lined **Hviezdoslavovo nám** traces a filled-in moat outside the old town walls. It's named after Pavol Orságh Hviezdoslav. Presiding over the square is the neobaroque **Slovak National Theatre** (p351), the city's premier opera and ballet venue, completed in 1886. Unfortunately, the only way to see the lush interior of the theatre is to attend a performance. At the western end of Hviezdoslavovo nám is an 18th-century **plague column** on Rybné nám (Fish Sq), all that remains of the city's old fish market (yet another victim of the New bridge).

South of Hviezdoslavovo nám on Mostová is the beautiful neobaroque **Reduta Palace** (p351) completed in 1914 as a dancehall. It's home to the city symphony orchestra and open only during performances, but you can get an idea of the extensive gilding from the foyer on your way to the ticket office.

Historic Centre

The historic, pedestrian centre of the old town has some beautiful baroque palaces, built after the Hungarians moved their capital here. Once the centre and main market of the old town, **Hlavné nám** still fills up with craft stalls during the Easter and Christmas markets. Built in 1572, **Roland's Fountain** (Map p340), at the centre of the square, may have originally been a fire hydrant.

Flanking one side of the square is the **old town hall** (1421) containing the **Municipal Museum** (Map p340; ☎ 5920 5130; Hlavné nám; adult/student 50/20Sk; ✆ 10am-5pm Tue-Fri, 11am-6pm Sat & Sun). Buzz past the tedious archaeological cases and look for the stairs down to the torture chambers in the cellar; they come complete with illustrated murals.

One of Slovakia's finest neoclassical buildings, the **Primate's Palace** (Primaciálny Palác; Map p340; adult/student 40Sk/free; ✆ 10am-5pm Tue-Sun) is topped with a 150kg cast-iron bishop's hat. Napoleon and the Austrian emperor Franz I signed the Treaty of Pressburg on 26 December 1805 here in the Hall of Mirrors. The 17th-century English tapestries on display in the 2nd-floor gallery were found hidden under wallpaper during a 1903 reconstruction.

The town's only surviving tower gate, **Michael tower** (Michalská veža; Map p340; ☎ 5443 3044;

ST ELIZABETH OF HUNGARY

Born in Bratislava castle in 1207, Elizabeth was the daughter of King Andrew II. She got engaged at the ripe old age of four to a Germanic prince of Thuringia, where she was shipped off to. She and Ludwig didn't actually marry until she was 14, he was 21. While Ludwig was away on business, the bubonic plague and a flood hit their land. Elizabeth took control and started handing out supplies to the poor, including court robes from her castle home in Wartburg.

But her sainthood rises from a time after her husband was killed in a crusade. Legend has it that her in-laws weren't too fond of her charitable inclinations and so she hid under her aprons the bread she took out to peasants. When confronted, she lied and said the bread was roses. When she was forced to show the contents of her aprons, roses miraculously appeared. She was driven from her castle and went to the town of Malburg, where she helped build hospitals and devoted herself full time to the Franciscan order. She died at age 24. Shortly after her death, miracles of healing began to be associated with her grave and the canonisation was initiated.

A mosaic depicting the revelation of the roses hangs at the entrance to the Church of St Elizabeth, more commonly known as the **Blue church** (Modrý kostol; Map p340); Bezručova 2; admission free; ✆ 7am-7pm). The cool sky-blue-and-white church (1911) is an Art-Nouveau fantasy. On Saturdays it acts as a wedding machine – rather appropriate as it does look like an elaborate cake.

Michalská 24; adult/student 40/20Sk; ☺ 10am-5pm Tue-Fri, 11am-6pm Sat & Sun), has a 14th-century base, a 16th-century top and an 18th-century steeple. Go inside to climb up and see the view across the rooftops. There's also a small display of antique swords, armour and guns.

Milan Dobeš Museum (Map p340; ☎ 5443 2305; www .milandobes.sk; Zámočnícka 13; ☺ 10am-6pm Tue-Sun) is a cool little contemporary museum that hosts international exhibits. The **City Gallery of Bratislava** (☎ 5443 1556; www.gmb.sk; ☺ 11am-6pm Tue-Sun) has two palatial show spaces: **Mirbach Palace** (Map p340; Františkánske nám 11; adult/student 60/30Sk), built in 1770, is a beautifully restored rococo building housing older baroque art; and **Pálffy Palace** (☎ 5443 3627; Panská 19; adult/student 20/10Sk; ☺ 10am-6pm Tue-Sun), a pre-1715 house built on the site of a 13th-century structure, contains a mix of 19th- and 20th-century Slovak art.

Scattered about the pedestrian centre are numerous churches, the oldest of which is the **Franciscan Church of the Annunciation** (Kostol Zvestovania-Františkáni; Map p340; Františkánske nám). Consecrated in 1297, it was later 'baroquified' by the Jesuits. It's normally open only for services. The **Church of the Clarissine Order** (Kostol Klarisiek; Map p340; Klariská 3) has an ornate 14th-century Gothic tower. No longer active, it is sometimes used as a concert hall. Nearby Kapitulská is one of the oldest and quietest streets in the city. The baroque **Church of the Holy Trinity** (Kostol Trinitárov; Map p340; Župné nám 11; admission free; ☺ 7am-7pm) is worth a look for the trompe l'oeil dome painted on the ceiling.

Nám SNP & Around

The central feature of the vast Nám SNP is a bronze **Monument of the Slovak National Uprising**, honouring the antifascist uprising for which the square is named. In November 1989 huge crowds assembled here in the days leading up to the fall of the communist regime, and it was also here that Slovaks gathered before the Velvet Divorce from the Czech Republic.

Two blocks northeast of Nám SNP is the city's only operating **synagogue** (Map p340; Heydukova 11-13; ☺ closed to the public).

Slavín Hill

On Slavín Hill, northwest of the old town, stand a cemetery and garden with fine views over the city. Towering over them is the **Slavín War Memorial** (Map p338), an enormous pillar erected in 1960 in memory of the 6000 Soviet soldiers who died pushing the Nazis out of West Slovakia.

To get there, take trolleybus 208 west from Hodžovo nám to the end of the line on Šulekova (20 minutes), and climb for 1km up Timravina and Mišíkova.

ACTIVITIES
Hiking

To get out of the city and into the forest, take trolleybus 203 northeast from Hodžovo nám to the end of the line at **Koliba** (Map p338), then walk up the road for about 20 minutes to the **TV tower** at Kamzík (440m). Maps posted at the trail head outline the many hiking possibilities in the forest surrounds and there are a couple of hotels with restaurants in the park. A **chairlift** (lanovka; Map p338; ☎ 4425 9188; adult/student return 90/60Sk; ☺ 10am-4pm Oct-May) makes the 15-minute journey down to the picnic areas and playgrounds of **Železná studienka**. You might like to hike down and hitch a ride back up.

Cycling

Though cycling is very popular with locals, the dearth of bike-hire agents makes it tough for visitors. **Luka** (Map p338; ☎ 0907683112; Pri Suchom mlyne 84) is the only agency that hires bikes (800Sk per day). A good, but steep, route from the Luka office northeast of the centre is to continue north on Kysucká to the picnic and park area of Železná studienka, where there's a chairlift (see Hiking, above). The adventurous can transport themselves and the bike up via the chairlift and ride back down the mountain cycle path. Flatter routes include along the Danube to Devín castle (8km).

Swimming

Zlaté piesky (Golden sands; Map p338; Senecká cesta; adult/student 40/20Sk; ☺ 9am-6pm) is a lake resort 7km northeast of the old town. It's where locals escape the summer heat. You can hire rowing boats and sailboards in summer. Take tram 4 from Kamenné nám, near the Tesco department store, to the terminus (20 minutes) and walk east for a couple of blocks; the lake will be on your right.

Bratislava itself doesn't have any thermal waters, but there is a swimming/spa waterpark complex of sorts on top of the **AuPark** (Map p338; ☎ 6826 6111; Einsteinova) shopping centre. **Aulandia** (Map p338; ☎ 6820 1031; www.aulandia.sk; Einsteinova 18; all day adult/under 12yr 550/400Sk; ☺ 10am-10pm) has family-friendly pools and water slides, as well as a more adult spa zone where skimpy terry-cloth wraps (and hitting on strangers) are required.

Take bus 80, 83 or 93 from Zochova across the New bridge one stop to AuPark.

Rafting
You can go white-water rafting on manmade rapids in a Danube channel with Action Land (see p354).

WALKING TOUR
The following is a walk through history. A 5th-century Slav fort – called Brezalauspurc – grew into an important citadel of the Great Moravian Empire at the site of today's **Bratislava castle** (**1**; p343), so we start our trip through time here. Peer down onto the east terrace and you can see the outlines of a Great Moravian basilica foundation from the 9th century. One of the oldest parts of the castle itself is the crown tower (1245) accessible through the **Historical Museum** (**2**; p343).

Descend into the old town down Zámocké Schody, part of the former Jewish quarter. Most of Bratislava's Jewish residents (10% of the city's pre-WWII population) were deported to concentration camps. Cross under the New bridge to get into the pedestrian centre and you are at **St Martin's Cathedral** (**3**; p343), where Maria Theresa of Austria was crowned in 1740.

Skirt around the church and head north on Ventúrska, at No 3 is the **Academia Istrpolitana** (**4**; closed to the public) building. Founded in 1465 as the first university in the Kingdom of Hungary, it lasted only until King Mathias Corvinus' death in 1490. The building is now the Academy of Music & Drama.

In 1762 six-year-old Wolfgang Amadeus Mozart performed at a Pálffy family residence generally known today as **Mozart house** (**5**; Mozartov dom; Ventúrska 10; closed to the public). Up the street at **Leopold de Pauli Palace** (**6**; Ventúrska 13; closed to the public) now a university building, nine-year-old Franz Liszt gave one of his early recitals in 1820.

Further north is the 1756 **Palace of the Royal Chamber** (**7**; Michalská 1; closed to the public). Now a university library, it was formerly the seat of the Hungarian parliament, or diet, from 1802 to 1848. At the last meeting held there, town deputy Ľudovít Štúr spoke for Slovak rights and the elimination of serfdom.

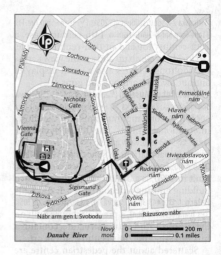

At the head of Michalská is the city's only remaining gate, **Michael Tower** (**8**; p344). From here the watchman called out the hour. It's rumoured that the bubonic plague entered through this gate in 1711.

Turn right and in a few steps you are at **Nám SNP** (**9**), the square where on 31 December 1992, more than 200,000 people gathered towards midnight to celebrate not only the New Year, but a new nation – an independent Slovakia. For more, see the boxed text, p32.

BRATISLAVA FOR CHILDREN
Bratislava isn't overly populated with playgrounds, or restaurants with children's menus for that matter, but there are a couple of places to keep the little ones entertained. **Bibiana** (Map p340; ☎ 5443 1308; www.bibiana.sk; Panská 41; admission free; 10am-6pm Tue-Sun) calls itself an 'International House of Art for Children'. There's an art gallery aimed at little ones and it sponsors frequent puppet and musical performances and craft classes. The fun **State Puppet Theatre** (Štátne Bábkové Divadlo; Map p338; ☎ 5292 3668; www .babkovedivadlo.sk; Dunajská 36) also puts on shows, pretty much daily at 10am, and sometimes again at 2pm.

Zoo Bratislava (Map p338; ☎ 6542 0985; www.zoobrati slava.sk; Mlynská dolina 1; adult/under 15yr 100/60Sk; 9am-6pm Apr-Oct, 11am-3pm Nov-Mar) covers 96 hectares. Take bus 30 or 37 from under the New bridge to the Slávičie údolie stop (five to 10 minutes). Closer to the centre, across the Danube from the old town, is **Sad Janka Kráľa Park** (Map p338) with paths and a few sorry amusement rides.

Nearby restaurant Leberfinger (p350) has indoor and outdoor playgrounds and a kid-sized menu.

QUIRKY COMMUNIST BRATISLAVA

Forty-five years of communist rule was bound to leave a mark. An obsession with modern functionalism resulted in many odd, sometimes depressing, structures.

The **New bridge** (Nový most; Map p340; ☎ 6252 0300; www.u-f-o.sk; Viedenská cesta; observation deck 100Sk; ☉ 10am-11pm), or the UFO (pronounced *ew-fo*) bridge, in Bratislava is a modernist marvel from 1972. After a three-year renovation, the UFO-on-a-stick reopened in 2006. There's an overhyped nightclub aloft, in addition to the prerequisite overpriced restaurant and viewing platform.

And, no, you're not seeing things – there *is* an upside-down pyramid in the new town; that's the **Slovak radio building** (Slovenský rozhlas; Map p338; cnr Mýtna & Štefanovičova).

The entire **Petržalka** (Map p338) concrete-jungle housing estate is a good example of the communist egalitarian ethics of old. These ugly buildings all look identical. (We couldn't find any studies reporting how many people go to the wrong flat after a drink or two…)

On Slavín Hill, northwest of the old town, the **Slavín War Memorial** (Map p338) is one of the few remaining testaments to socialist realism as an art. A soldier holds a romantically waving flag atop an obelisk.

If you're still nostalgic for the good old days, down a brewsky or two with Stalin, Lenin and the boys (or at least their statues) at the **KGB bar** (p351).

TOURS

BTS (p342) and BKIS (p342) both lead two-hour daily **walking tours** (450Sk; ☉ 2pm) of the historical centre departing from their respective offices. The former also has themed walks, including one that follows the coronation route of Hungarian royalty.

A 45-minute Bratislava return-trip **boat tour** (adult/under 15yr 105/65Sk; ☉ 11am & 3.30pm May-Aug), run by **Slovak Shipping & Ports** (Slovenská plavba a prístavy; Map p340; ☎ 5293 2226; www.lod.sk; Fajnorovo nábrežie 2), takes you past the city's five bridges. The tour must have 30 passengers to depart, so book ahead.

FESTIVALS & EVENTS

Bratislava's best events are arts related:
Cultural Summer Festival (Kultúrne leto; ☎ 5441 3063; www.bkis.sk) Brings a smorgasbord of operas, plays and performances to the streets and venues around town from June to September.
Bratislava Jazz Days (Bratislavských jazzových dní; ☎ 5293 1572; www.bjd.sk) Swings for three days in September.
Bratislava Music Festival (Bratislavské hudobné slávnosti; ☎ 5443 4546; www.bhsfestival.sk in Slovak) Classical music takes centre stage at this event running from late September to mid-October.
Christmas market Usually begins 26 November on Hlavné nám. Craft and food vendors fill the square and there are weekend evening performances beneath the twinkly lights.

SLEEPING

Bratislava's lodging is no longer dirt-cheap, but there is a full range of places to stay – from 600Sk backpacker hostels to high-end hotels, where prices can be as much as in Prague or

---

GAY & LESBIAN BRATISLAVA

Bratislava has the biggest gay and lesbian scene in Slovakia, but that's not saying much. Websites of interest include www.gay.sk and www.gayinfo.sk, which both have listings in Bratislava.

Ganymedes (☎ 5022 8704; www.ganymedes.info in Slovak; PO Box 4, 830 00 Bratislava) is the local gay-rights organisation. The lesbian organisation is **Museion** (☎ 0905804456; www.lesba.sk in Slovak; PO Box 47, 840 02 Bratislava).

For up-to-the-minute gay and lesbian info, you'd probably do just as well asking around at the café **U Anjelov** (p350). Another mixed gay/lesbian/straight hang-out is **Café Antik** (Map p340; ☎ 5443 0260; Rybárska brána 2; ☉ 8am-midnight Sun-Thu, until 1am Fri & Sat).

The gay dance club in town is **Apollon Club** (Map p340; ☎ 0915480031; www.apollon-gay-club.sk; Panenská 24; ☉ 6pm-3am Mon-Thu & Sun, 6pm-5am Fri & Sat), with two bars and three stages. Thursdays are for boys only. **Spider Club** (Map p340; ☎ 0903758096; Jedlíkova 9; ☉ 6pm-2am Mon-Thu & Sun, 6pm-4am Fri & Sat) is a bar during the week and a disco on the weekend. **Barbados** (Vysoká 20; ☉ 11am-midnight Sun-Thu, until 1am Fri & Sat) is a popular little gay bar.

Budapest (and not always with comparable quality). Good midrange guesthouses aren't in abundance and rooms at these book up fast year-round. Breakfast is either included in the price at hotels and *penzión*s, or can be added for 100Sk to 200Sk; ask before you agree to take the room.

Budgetwise, your best bet is to visit in summer when student dormitories open to travellers. With a few exceptions, these and other budget digs tend to require public transport to get to the centre. BKIS can help with somewhat unreasonably priced private rooms (1100Sk per person) and a complete list of student dorms.

Central Bratislava

BUDGET

Patio Hostel (Map p340; ☎ 5292 5797; www.patiohostel .com; Špitálska 35; dm 450-550Sk, d per person 860-900Sk; P ☒ ☐) Clean and fresh and like a university dorm – that is if you were allowed to paint the concrete-block walls with bright colours and stylised graffiti at university. Each floor in this 100-bed hostel has a kitchenette, and there's a courtyard patio in addition to the computer room and basement rec room. The latter has TV and *foosball* (table football).

Downtown Backpackers (Map p340; ☎ 5464 1191; www.backpackers.sk; Panenská 31; dm 500-600Sk, d per person 1000Sk; ☒ ☐) If you'd rather have lively conversation and laid-back Bohemian charm than a lock on your door, you've found your place. Some of the eight- and 10-bed dorm rooms act as a corridor to one another. The communal lounge room has a bar.

MIDRANGE

Private apartments (generally €60 to €90), mostly in the old town, can be booked with the owner through www.bratislavahotels.com.

City Hostel (Map p340; ☎ 5263 6041; www.cityhostel .sk; Obchodná 38; s/d 1050/1650Sk; ☒ ☐) Small, modern singles, doubles and triples really resemble a basic hotel more than a hostel. Each has its own facilities, but TV costs extra. You could always watch the flat screen in the mod reception area. No breakfast available.

Pension Castle Club (Map p340; ☎ 5464 1472; www .stayslovakia.sk; Zámocké schody 4; s/d with shared bathroom €60/75, q €120; ☒) It's quite the uphill hike to this town house B&B near the castle. The few basic rooms book up fast. An attic quad (more stairs!) has en suite bathroom, high-speed internet connection and two double beds.

Penzión Chez David (Map p340; ☎ 5441 3824; www .chezdavid.sk; Zámocká 13; s €64-74, d €78-88; P ☒) A cool-blue colour scheme, great old photos of synagogues on the walls, and a primo location. You'll hardly even notice the building's boxy functionalism (although the rooms are small).

Several boat hotels line up along the Danube shore:

Botel Gracia (Map p340; ☎ 5443 2132; www.botel -gracia.sk; Rázusovo nábrežie; s/d 2045/2790Sk; P) It isn't the most updated but it's the closest to the old-town centre.

Botel Marina (Map p338; ☎ 5464 1804; www.botel marina.sk; Nábrežie arm gen L Svobodu; s/d 2250/2900Sk; P ☒ ☒) This is the most stylishly nautical (white, navy and red trim, cherry-wood cabin panelling and brass lamps) but is 1.5km east along the river from the old town.

TOP END

Hotel Danube (Map p340; ☎ 5934 0000; www.hoteldanube .com; Rybné nám 1; s €189-225, d €209-250; P ☒ ☒ ☐ ☒) A business behemoth, the Danube has serious services and can-do staff. Oh, and the riverfront location is nice. Weekend rates and online packages can bring the price way down.

Radisson Carlton (Map p340; ☎ 5939 0500; www.radis sonsas.com; Hviezdoslavovo nám; r €240; P ☒ ☒ ☐ ☒) The Carlton cruises like a big luxury liner on one of Bratislava's main squares, across from the Slovak National Theatre. The traditional rooms (think Louis-the-something reproductions) seem to fit the 1837 building better than the hypermodern ones done in black and red.

AUTHOR'S CHOICE

Hotel Marrol's (Map p340; ☎ 5778 4600; www.hotelmarrols.sk; Tobrucká 4; s 7000Sk, d 7300-9600Sk; P ☒ ☒ ☐ ☒) Black-and-white movie stills, sleek leather chairs, sumptuous fabrics: Hotel Marrol's is straight off the silver screen, c 1940. It's hard to imagine more retro refinement being packed into one cultural-landmark town house. White-gloved doormen greet returning guests by name and usher them into the parlour that serves as reception. Downstairs the Jasmine spa has a neoclassical look created with columns and trompe l'oeil. Only one word of warning: avoid the small 'ladies chamber' singles unless you like flowers – they're on the walls, covering the bedspread, in the bath salts…

Greater Bratislava

BUDGET

Intercamp Zlaté piesky (Map p338; ☎ 4425 7373; www
.intercamp.sk; Senecká cesta 2; sites person/tent 100/70Sk)
Bratislava's camping ground sits astride Zlaté
piesky lake. Here you can rent water bikes,
play minigolf and lie on the beach. Bungalows
(1050Sk for two) have bathrooms; chalets
(500Sk) share tent-site facilities.

Zvárač (Map p338; ☎ 4924 6000; www.vuz.sk; Pionierska
17; s/d with shared bathroom 700/1100Sk) This perfectly
functional four-storey worker's hostel isn't
much on looks, but it's clean enough. Two
double rooms with twin beds share a bathroom. The receptionist has a handy refrigera-
tor stocked with beer (36Sk) and champagne
(150Sk). Take tram 3 seven stops from the
main train station.

Doprastav (Map p338; ☎ 5557 4313; www.doprastav
.sk; Košická 52; dm 280-360Sk; s/d 700/1100Sk) Another
worker's lodging, men and women's hostel
sections are separate here. You can also opt for
more upscale 'hotel' rooms with bathrooms.
Being near a shopping complex (grocery store,
restaurant, bakery) has its advantages. Take
trolleybus 201 from the main train station
nine stops to Miletičova.

Student dorms (open to travellers July and
August only):

Mladá Garda (Map p338; ☎ 4425 3065; www.mlada
garda.info; Račianska 103; s/d 360/520Sk) A little noisy
because of trams; take tram 3 from the main train station.

Nikosa Belojanisa (Map p338; ☎ 5249 7169; eliska
.tissova@stuba.sk; Wilsonova 6; s 300-500Sk, d 600-1000Sk)
Located a 1.5km walk from the main train and bus stations.

MIDRANGE

Hotel Orlan (Map p338; ☎ 4363 3704; www.hotel-orlan.sk;
Strojnícka 99, Rusinov; s/d 1190/1500Sk; P ☐ ☒) More
home than hotel, this pale green guesthouse
is quite the suburban slice. Each simple but
cheery room is slightly different (a sunset-
coloured wall with gerbera-daisy art, for example). The attached restaurant has good
Hungarian and Slovak food at low prices
(80Sk for a lunch menu). Take trolleybus
201 from the main train station 14 stops to
Ondrejova.

Penzión Zlatá Noha (Map p338; ☎ 5477 4922; www
.zlata-noha.sk; Bellova 2, Koliba hill; without breakfast s 1350Sk,
d 1700-1900Sk; P ☒ ☐) Tranquillity and family-
run attention make up for the steep driveway
at this homy modern *penzión* above town. The
owners even rent out horses. If you want to
use the wi-fi, ask for a room near the recep-

tion. Take bus 203 from Hodžovo nám and
get off at the fifth stop, Jeséniova.

Hotel-Penzión Arcus (Map p338; ☎ 5557 2522; www
.hotelarcus.sk; Moskovská 5; s 1400-1800Sk, d 2600Sk; P ☒)
This friendly, popular hotel near the main bus
station is only 15 minutes' walk from the old
town. Although updated in 2001, the various
rooms (some with balcony, some with courtyard views) still seem a little outmoded.

TOP END

Koliba Expo (Map p338; ☎ 5920 0620; www.koliba-expo.sk;
Kamzíkov vrch; r 3000Sk, ste 4000-5500Sk; P ☐) Perch
among the trees in the peaceful, forested park
above the city. Local flower and bird motifs
decorate honey-coloured wood beds; a sheer
canopy drapes over a dark four-poster, complemented by dusty-rose walls. Think folk art
at its most romantic. A grill restaurant and
large terrace are part of the package.

EATING

The old town certainly isn't lacking in dining options. Foreign restaurant names and
cuisines are dead giveaways that prices are
going to be higher than in the rest of Slovakia. Compared to Western Europe, however,
prices still aren't bad. The poshest places are in
and around Hviezdoslavovo nám and Hlavné
nám. With a university campus at one end, it's
no wonder that Obchodná (shopping street)
has a string of small, reasonable eateries selling Chinese dishes, pizza and sandwiches).

Central Bratislava

BUDGET

Old Market (Stara Tržnica; Map p340; Nám SNP 25; ⌚ 7am-
9pm Mon-Fri, 7am-6pm Sat, 1-6pm Sun) The landmark
Old Market has been restored and once again
welcomes vendors. Fresh fruit and veggie
stands are in the centre and fast-food store-
fronts line the perimeter. Upstairs there's a
bar-restaurant and a cafeteria.

U Jakubu (Map p340; ☎ 5441 7951; Nám SNP 24; mains
59-65Sk; ⌚ 8am-6pm Mon-Fri) Point and pay: all the
Slovak standards are laid out for you behind
the glass at this large self-service restaurant. A
soup-and-main menu costs as little as 80Sk.

Divesta diétna jedáleň (Map p340; Laurinská 8; mains
60-80Sk; ⌚ 11am-3pm Mon-Fri) People have been
queuing up for the veggie tucker at this central
buffet every day for more than 10 years; the
staff must be doing something right.

Samoobsluha reštaurácie, jedáleň and
bufet, all self-service cafeterias, cater to office

BRATISLAVA

workers and are great places to eat during the day (they close early). The downtown **Tesco** (Map p340; Kammené nám) has a supermarket in the basement and a cafeteria on the 2nd floor, tucked behind the garden department. Food stands surround the department store.

MIDRANGE

Pizza Mizza (Map p340; ☎ 5296 5034; Tobrucká 5; mains 99-160Sk) The city's best slice. This modern, multistorey pizzeria is extremely popular, especially with expats, so you may want to book ahead. English is spoken here.

Prašná Bašta (Map p340; ☎ 5443 4957; Zámočnícka 11; mains 105-215Sk) Good, reasonable Slovak food with even a few vegetarian options such as risotto with mixed vegetables and cheese. The round-vaulted interior oozes old Bratislava charm. Hopefully the courtyard terrace (under construction at this writing) will reopen soon.

Mýtny domček (Map p340; ☎ 0911433763; Starý most; mains 109-209Sk) Pictures of old Bratislava decorate the walls of the restaurant in the former toll house on the Old bridge. All the typical grilled and fried meats are on the menu, but there are also meal-sized salads with chicken or tuna.

U Remeselníka (Map p340; ☎ 5273 1357; Obchodná 64; mains 109-209Sk) This tiny folk-craft-centre café may be the best place in town to have traditional home-style dishes. Little old ladies meet here for a lunch of a *halušky* for two, a trio of dumplings with sheep's cheese and bacon, with *kolbasa* (sausage) and cabbage.

Archa (Map p340; ☎ 5443 0865; Uršulínska 6; mains 180-320Sk) Chicken sautéed with avocado? This is Slovak cuisine gone international. The interior is designed to look like a ship (an ark), and there are a few tables outside.

TOP END

Traja Mušketieri (Map p340; ☎ 5443 0019; Sládkovičova 7; mains 350-600Sk) This stylised, up-market version of a medieval tavern comes complete with a poetic menu ('Treacherous Lady de Winter' is a skewered chicken stuffed with Parma ham). The staff excel at courteous service. Reservations recommended.

Of the many spiffy global-food alternatives in the old town, **Kogo** (Map p340; ☎ 5464 5094; Hviezdoslavovo nám 21; mains 260-650Sk), for Italian seafood, is among the newest; and **Malecón** (Map p340; ☎ 0910274583; Nám L Štúra 4; mains 269-459Sk) has the most-praised Latino fare (and mojitos).

Greater Bratislava

Vega Destination (Map p338; ☎ 3352 6994; Malý trh 2; mains 120-180Sk; ✗) Space-age décor complements the artistic presentation of the mostly vegetarian meals here. Dishes include tofu sautéed with a redcurrant sauce, pastas and risotto. There are even a few choices with meat.

Reštaurácia Koliba Expo (Map p338; ☎ 5920 0610; Kamzíkov vrch; mains 180-300Sk) Typically a *koliba* is a rustic restaurant, but an overhaul in 2006 overelegantised the interior (brocade chairs and candlelight). Never mind, you can eat on the wooden deck outside among the trees of the city park on Koliba hill.

Leberfinger (Map p338; ☎ 6231 7590; Viedenská cesta 257; mains 209-359Sk) Murals of historic Bratislava enliven this house across the river from the old town. Napoleon is supposed to have stopped here. Veal goulash, grilled fish and stuffed aubergine may seem upscale, but the restaurant is entirely family-friendly (kids' menu and playgrounds).

DRINKING

Bratislava doesn't have a concentrated entertainment district, but there are plenty of places in the old town pedestrian centre to poke your head into. From mid-April to October, street cafés sprout up on every corner – any one will do for a drink.

The college-age crowd heads to the bars on Obchodná; in fact, the whole street acts as a gathering place. There are a few atmospheric, artsy cellar bars along the north side of Hviezdoslavovo (you'll see them through the window grates at your feet).

Cafés

Čokoládovňa (Map p340; ☎ 5433 3945; Michalská 6; ☽ 9am-9pm) This tiny 'chocolate café' has cocktails, coffees and desserts made with the dark ambrosia.

Roland Café (Map p340; ☎ 5443 1372; Hlavné nám 5; ☽ 9am-1am) It seems like Roland café has been on the main square forever. This institution has a full menu as well as alcoholic beverages, and coffee and cakes.

Čajovňa Pohoda (Map p340; ☎ 5443 3103; Laurinská 3; ☽ 9am-10pm Mon-Fri, from 10am Sat & 11am Sun; ✗) Exotic teas, and more potent brews, are on offer in this nonsmoking tearoom.

U Anjelov (Map p340; ☎ 5443 2724; Laurinská 19; ☽ 9am-midnight Mon-Thu, until 1.30am Fri, 1pm-1.30am Sat, 1pm-midnight Sun) Bratislava's gay café serves creative mixed drinks, sometimes garnished with a candied marshmallow, while Frank Sinatra croons overhead.

Bars & Pubs

KGB (Map p340; ☎ 5273 1279; Obchodná 52; ☯ 10am-2am Mon-Fri, 4pm-3am Sat, 4pm-midnight Sun) Drink a dark and smoky toast to a statue of Stalin under a Soviet flag at KGB bar.

Downtown (Map p340; ☎ 5443 4317; Klariská 8; ☯ 10am-midnight Sun-Thu, 11am-3am Fri & Sat) Lime green is the refreshing colour of this urban cocktail lounge. About a million liquors line the bar wall.

Slovak Pub (Map p340; ☎ 5441 0706; Obchodná 62; ☯ 10am-midnight Mon-Thu, 10am-1am Fri & Sat, noon-midnight Sun) We'd be remiss if we didn't mention the number one English-advertised hang-out. The historic theme rooms are appropriately pubby, and it's popular with local college students (cheap food and beer) as well as foreign travellers.

Dubliner (Map p340; ☎ 5441 0706; Sedlárska 6; ☯ 11am-3am Mon-Sat, until 1am Sun) If you want to meet other English speakers, head to this Irish sports pub. If you don't, you may want to avoid it.

Clubs

Admission into clubs ranges from zip to upwards of 100Sk.

Café Štúdio Club (Map p340; ☎ 5443 1796; cnr Laurinská & Radničná; ☯ 10am-1am Mon-Wed, until 3am Thu & Fri, 4pm-3am Sat) Bop to the oldies, or chill out to jazz; most nights there's live music of some sort. A 1950s vibe prevails.

Jazz Café (Map p340; ☎ 5443 4661; Ventúrska 5; ☯ 10am-2am) Live jazz from Thursday to Saturday nights in a packed cellar pub. Get here before 8pm if you want a table.

Hysteria Pub (Map p338; ☎ 0910447744; Odbojárov 9; ☯ 10am-1am Mon-Thu; until 5am Fri & Sat, 11am-midnight Sun) Comical murals depict inebriated cowboys downing tequila at this fun-loving restaurant-bar-disco. It's multigenerationally popular.

Sparx (Map p338; ☎ 0903403097; Cintorínska 32; ☯ 11am-midnight Mon-Wed, until 1am Thu, until 3am Fri & Sat) This cavernous bar (once a big beer hall) has live music Thursdays and becomes a disco at the weekend.

Babylon Music Club (Map p338; ☎ 0915769230; Karpatská 2; ☯ 5pm-2am Sun-Thu, until 4am Fri & Sat) Live music acts range from hip-hop to reggae to ska to local folk-rock.

ENTERTAINMENT

Here you'll find opera, ballet and theatre as well as traditional folk performances, all at much lower prices than across the border in Vienna. See p342 for entertainment publications with listings.

Performances & Concerts

Opera and ballet are performed at the ornate **Slovak National Theatre** (Slovenské Národné Divadlo; Map p340; www.snd.sk; Hviezdoslavovo nám). Get tickets in advance at the **booking office** (pokladňa; Map p340; ☎ 5443 3764; cnr Jesenského & Komenského; ☯ 8am-5.30pm Mon-Fri, 9am-1pm Sat) behind. A new theatre has been under construction since 1988.

Reduta Palace (Map p340; cnr Nám L Štúra & Medená; ☯ ticket office 1-7pm Mon, Tue, Thu & Fri, 8am-2pm Wed) houses a theatre where you can see the state orchestra, the **Slovak Philharmonic** (Slovenská Filharmónia; ☎ 5920 8233; www.filharmonia.sk).

Folk-dance and music ensembles such as **Sľuk** (☎ 6285 9125; www.sluk.sk) and **Lúčnica** (☎ 5292 0068; www.lucnica.sk) perform at various venues around town. Groups such as **Muzička** (☎ 0905213638; www.muzicka.sk) play traditional folk music for dances at local culture-centre clubs, for instance **Zrkadlový Háj** (☎ 6383 6776; www.kzp.sk in Slovak; Rovniankova 3, Petržalka).

Sport

New ice-hockey and football stadiums are in the works. At least until 2008, Bratislava's hallowed ice-hockey team, HC Slovan, plays at the **HC Slovan stadium** (Map p338; ☎ 4445 6500; www.hcslovan.sk in Slovak; Odbojárov 3) northeast of the old town. Nearby, the home-town football team, SK Slovan, kicks at **SK Slovan stadium** (Map p338; ☎ 4437 3083; Junácka 2). You can buy tickets for both online at www.ticketportal.sk.

Cinema

Charlie Centrum (Map p340; ☎ 5296 8994; Špitálska 4) is a cinema that occasionally shows Czech and Slovak classics; next door is an associated night club.

SHOPPING

Bratislava is not a major shopping city, but there are several crystal, craft and jewellery stores selling garnets in and around Hlavné nám.

Nie je sklo ako sklo (Map p340; ☎ 5441 1296; Laurinská 6) sells gorgeous modern-art glass in sleek shapes and vibrant colours. Upstairs is a showroom for Rona, one of Slovakia's most popular glassmakers.

LOOKING FOR A MAN AT WORK

What's the most photographed sight in Bratislava? The castle? The New bridge? Nope, it's a bronze statue called **The Watcher** (Čumil; Map p340). He peeps out of an imaginary manhole at the intersection of Panská and Rybárska brána, below a 'Men at Work' sign. And he's not alone. There are other quirky statues scattered all around the old town. See if you can find them: **The Frenchman**, a replica of one of Napoleon's soldiers who passed through in 1809, leans on a park bench; **The Photographer** stalks his subject paparazzi-style around a corner; **Schöner Náci**, a 20th-century dandy, tips his top hat to the square he stands on; and a **soldier** stands guard in front of a water fountain. Look up for other questionable characters, such as a timepiece-toting monk and a rather naked imp, decorating building façades.

Úľuv (Map p340; ☎ 5273 1351; www.uluv.sk; Obchodná 64) Serious art-buying folk head to this big craft-cooperative, where there are two stores and a courtyard filled with artisans' studios.

Vinotéka sv Urbana (Map p340; ☎ 5433 2573; Klobučnícka 4) has a virtual library of *vino* for sample and sale, so if you're not going to the Small Carpathians this is a good place to buy regional wine.

Vinotéka Matyšak (Map p338; ☎ 2063 4001; www.vinomatysak.sk; Pražská 15) has an ancient cellar with room for 45,000 bottles. A large selection is available for tasting at the store, and there's a restaurant and hotel associated with this vintner.

Tesco Department Store (Map p340; Kamenné nám) It may not soothe your socially conscious soul, but this big downtown store has just about everything you could need – crystal, wine, *slivovitz* (a clear plum liquor that's a lot like firewater), jewellery, maps, groceries – at prices that undercut other stores.

The city's biggest shopping malls are **Polus City Centre** (Map p338; ☎ 4910 2031; Vajnorská), northeast of the city, and **AuPark** (Map p338; ☎ 6826 6111; Einsteinova), south across the Danube.

GETTING THERE & AWAY

For details on going beyond the Czech and Slovak Republics by air, hydrofoil (you can take one to Budapest and Austria), bus or train, see p452.

Air

Bratislava's **MR Štefánika Airport** (BTS; Map p338; ☎ 3303 3353; www.airportbratislava.sk) is 7km northeast of the centre. **Sky Europe** (☎ 4850 4850; www.skyeurope.com) has two to three daily flights to Košice (50 minutes, three daily) for as little as 190Sk (plus 300Sk in taxes) if you book ahead. **Czech Airlines** (ČSA; ☎ 5296 1042; www.czechairlines.com) flies to Prague three times per day.

Bus

The **main bus station** (autobusová stanica, AS; Map p338; ☎ reservations 5556 7349; www.eurolines.sk) is 1.5km east of the old town. Locals call it Mlynské Nivy, after the street it's on. Buses leaving from here head to towns across Slovakia, including Žilina (203Sk, three hours, seven daily), Poprad (345Sk, seven hours, four daily), Košice (441Sk, eight hours, nine daily) and Bardejov (491Sk, nine to 11 hours, three daily).

Eurolines (☎ 5556 7349; www.eurolines.sk) buses go from Bratislava to Prague's Florenc station (410Sk, 4½ hours, seven daily), Brno (200Sk, two hours, eight daily) and other Czech cities.

For schedules, check out http://cp.zoznam.sk/ConnForm.asp; click on the British flag for the English-language version.

Car & Motorcycle

Numerous international-chain rental agencies have offices at the airport. The local **Alimex** (Map p338; ☎ 5564 1641; www.alimex.sk) charges from 699Sk per day (if you're willing to drive with advertising on your car). **Avis** (Map p340; ☎ 5341 6111; www.avis.sk; Rybné nám 1) has a desk in the Hotel Danube, but prices are high (from 1200Sk per day).

Two 24-hour border crossings to Austria are at Petržalka and Jarovce.

Train

The **main train station** (Hlavná stanica; Map p338; www.zsr.sk) is about 1km north of the centre. At least 11 express trains per day connect Bratislava to Košice (518Sk, 6½ hours), most via Trenčín (180Sk, two hours), Žilina (268Sk, three hours) and Poprad (420Sk, five hours). Intercity (IC) trains (four daily) are slightly faster and require seat reservations.

All express trains to Prague (755Sk, 4½ hours, six daily) pass through Brno (305Sk, 1½ hours).

Walking into Austria

The Austrian border is about 4km beyond the New bridge along Viedenská cesta. Take bus 81 southbound across the bridge from Hodžovo nám and get off at the next stop after high-rise Hotel Incheba. Walk 2km to the border.

GETTING AROUND
To/From the Airport

Bus 61 links the airport with the main train station (18Sk; 20 minutes).

Taking a taxi from the airport is more expensive than taking one in town; and, as everywhere, drivers are able to set their meters at different rates. There seems to be an unofficial English-language surcharge. Before you get in the cab, show the driver the address and ask '*Kolko to bude?*' ('How much will it be?') or motion them to write down a price on your notepad. To the centre it really shouldn't cost much more than 500Sk, but we've heard of travellers who've been charged as much as 1800Sk. You may not succeed in haggling the price down beforehand, but at least maybe the driver won't try to cheat you as badly.

Boat

Slovak Shipping & Ports (Slovenská plavba a prístavy; Map p340; ☎ 5293 2226; www.lod.sk; Fajnorovo nábrežie 2; adult/student return 150/95Sk; ☼ 10am & 2.30pm Tue-Sun May-Aug) runs a ferry from Bratislava to Devín castle (right). Boats depart at 1.30pm and 6pm from the hydrofoil terminal (Map p340) in Bratislava. The trip takes 90 minutes upriver but only 30 minutes back down from Devín.

Car & Motorcycle

Headaches for drivers include pedestrian areas around the old town, numerous (and poorly marked) one-way streets, limited parking and sharp-eyed traffic police. Parking in the city centre is fairly restricted, so consider paying around 50Sk an hour at a private car park. Those car parks with free spaces are listed at www.parkovanieba.sk. Better yet, park at your hotel and walk.

Public Transport

Dopravný Podnik Bratislava (DPB; ☎ 5950 5950; www.dpb.sk) runs an extensive tram, bus and trolley-bus network. You can buy tickets (14/18/22Sk for 10/30/60 minutes) at newsstands, and some big stops have ticket-vending machines; validate on board. *Turistické cestovné lístky*

(tourist passes) cost 90/170/270/310Sk for one/two/three/seven days and are sold at the **DPB Office** (☼ 9am-5.30pm Mon-Fri). There's one below Hodžovo nám and another at Obchodná 14. To search for routes and schedules, go to www.imhd.sk.

Bratislava Culture & Information Centres sell the **Bratislava City Card** (1/2/3 days, 200/300/370Sk), which covers you for city transport and provides discounted museum admissions among other benefits.

Trams and buses run from 5am to 11.30pm, but there are a few night-service lines (numbered in the 500s); schedules are posted at stops. Be aware that politeness is the norm on public transport in Bratislava – give up your seat for the elderly and mothers with young children or expect to be glared at.

Taxi

Bratislava's taxis have meters, but drivers can set them to run at different rates. Cheating is becoming less common; going anywhere in the old town should cost more than 300Sk. Call **Transtel Taxi** (☎ 16 301) or **Super Taxi** (☎ 16 616).

AROUND BRATISLAVA

Most of West Slovakia (p355) can be considered a day trip from Bratislava, especially the Small Carpathian mountains. The sights listed in this section are accessible by Bratislava city buses.

DEVÍN CASTLE

One of the best sights in town is actually 9km west of the city centre. The first walled buildings at **Devín castle** (☎ 6573 0105; Muranská; adult/student 80/30Sk; ☼ 10am-5pm Tue-Fri, until 6pm Sat & Sun mid-Apr–Oct) date from Roman times, remnants of which you can still see. As ownership passed from Prince Rastislav and the Great Moravian Empire in the 9th century to the Hungarian Kingdom, more buildings and defences were added. It was Napoleon's army, rather than the Turks, that breached the defences and blew the place up in 1809. Extensive excavations and some reconstruction have taken place in recent years.

Climb up the hill and you pass vestiges of various historical periods: a 15th-century guardhouse, a 16th-century gate, and reconstructed foundations of a 9th-century church. Just across the castle moat is a partially reconstructed 16th-century palace, with an extensive exhibit of artefacts on the lower level. At the western end of the complex is a restored 13th-century citadel.

The precipitous turret mounted atop a spirelike rock is known as the Virgin Tower. Legend has it that the lord of Devín castle fell in love with a noble lady who shared his sentiment, and he brought her to the castle. When her uncle took to arms to get her back, she leapt to her death from this perch rather than live without love (yeah, right).

Frequent festivals are held on the castle grounds; check with Bratislava's information offices. There are several food stands and a hotel at the base of the castle hill.

On weekdays and summer weekends, local bus 29 departs from Bratislava about every half-hour from the New bridge bus stop; the terminus is at the castle's car park (20 minutes). Better yet, take the ferry (p353).

ČUNOVO

Danubiana Meulensteen Art Museum (☎ 6252 8501; www.danubiana.info; Vodné dielo, Čunovo; adult/child 60/30Sk; ☷ 10am-8pm May-Sep, 10am-6pm Oct-Apr), 15km south of Bratislava, is a temple to modern art. It opened in 2000 on a spit of land jutting into the Danube, as part of a millennial celebration. The red, blue and silver construction houses some of the more cutting-edge art in Slovakia, and the exhibitions constantly change. The museum is surrounded by a landscaped park, also used as exhibition space, and has a great little outdoor café.

Less cerebral fun is also available in Čunovo. **Action Land** (☎ 6252 8077; www.actionland.sk; Areál VS Čunovo; 1 ride €5, 2hr pass €35; ☷ 4.30-7.30pm Tue-Fri, 2-7.30pm Sat & 10am-3pm Sun Apr-Oct) has white-water rafting on a dammed channel in the Danube. Action Land provides the equipment and training; you provide the adrenaline.

Unfortunately it's not easy to get to Čunovo without a car. Take bus 91 from under the New bridge to the terminus (35 minutes) in front of the Čunovo city office. Cross Hriančiarska and walk east on Rača. You have to turn north (left) for a block on Na hrádzi before turning east (right) again onto the road through the forest that leads to the peninsula in the Danube (about 3km for both).

RUSOVCE

This small suburb 10km south of Bratislava contains the excavations of an ancient Roman fort. A garrison was long known to be stationed here from the 1st to the 4th centuries, but it wasn't until 1965 that the **Antic Gerulata** (☎ 6285 9332; Gerulatská 69, Rusovce; adult/student 40/20Sk; ☷ 10am-5pm Tue-Sun May-Sep) was found.

Take bus 91 or 191 from the New bridge bus stop to the Miú Rusovce bus stop (15 minutes) and walk towards the church. The archaeological site is at the end of the road.

West Slovakia

All of West Slovakia might be considered a day trip from Bratislava. It's a region of therapeutic and rejuvenating spas, romantic and ruined castles, vineyard-covered hills and lowland plains. Here the vast Danubian basin meets the Small Carpathian hills, and cliffs rise above the Váh river valley. The region's towns, many of which are mentioned in the earliest Slovak chronicles, are a mix of old and new. Architectural gems cuddle up next to communist-era monstrosities, as in the spa town of Piešťany.

Perhaps most striking, though, are the ancient fortifications rising high on lonely ridges or dominating towns, such as in Trenčín, a vivid reminder of West Slovakia's strategic importance. The region was once the Hungarian Empire's last stand against the invading Turks as they pushed north to occupy Budapest for 150 years (and barely missed taking nearby Vienna). It's a rare clifftop in the region that doesn't have some sort of castle ruins perched aloft, and in the southern reaches of the region, Hungarian is still heard on the streets at least as often as Slovak. West Slovakia is today, as it has long been, the place of clashing cultures.

HIGHLIGHTS

- Be wrapped naked in mud in the neoclassical spa town of **Piešťany** (p360)

- Hike up to the meticulously restored **Trenčín castle** (p363)

- Take a leisurely tour of the wine country of the **Small Carpathians** (p356), but make sure to bring a designated driver

- Brush up on your falconry skills at **Červený Kameň castle** (p357)

★ Trenčín Castle

Červený Kameň Castle ★

★ Piešťany

★ Small Carpathians

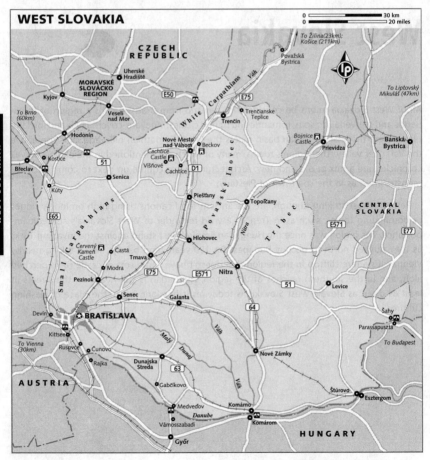

WEST SLOVAKIA

Getting There & Away

A convenient train line runs northeast from Bratislava through Trnava, Piešťany and Trenčín on its way towards Košice.

For travel to Nitra and Komárno, buses are a better deal, as trains are either slower or involve tedious connections.

The E75, Slovakia's longest stretch of motorway, runs from Bratislava to Považská Bystrica via Piešťany and Trenčín. Construction continues with the goal of making the motorway connect all the way through eastern Slovakia to the Ukraine.

To get between Trnava and Nitra, take Hwy 51.

Most other roads are small but in good condition.

SMALL CARPATHIANS

Rolling hills stretch for 100km northeast from Bratislava. The undulating Small Carpathians (Malé Karpaty) are not especially mountain-like, but the woodlands are pleasant for hiking, and the soil is ripe. Vineyards extend right down to the outskirts of Bratislava. Also in the region is the fine Červený Kameň castle, and Modra, a small town where in addition to wine the nation's most colourful and well-known ceramics are made.

Modra

☎ 033 / pop 8660

A sleepy little town, Modra makes a pleasant stop on a wine-tasting tour. Frankovka Modra grapes produced in the area form a ruby-red, low-acid wine with hints of cinnamon. Modra not only produces Slovakia's best red wines but is also celebrated for its ceramics. *Modransky keramic* is glazed majolica pottery decorated with flowers and folk-art motifs; yellow and blue are the dominant accent colours on a white field.

Modra is also the town where the Slovak nationalist Ľudovít Štúr (1815–56) spent his later years, and there's a small museum dedicated to him.

ORIENTATION & INFORMATION

The town centres on the main street, Štúrova, which runs past the bus stop before changing its name to Dukelská. The **Small Carpathian Tourist Information Office** (☎ 647 4302; www.tik.sk, www.modra.sk; Štúrova 84; ⊙ 9.30am-4.30pm Mon-Fri) sells maps and can help with winery visits. There's an ATM a few doors down.

SIGHTS & ACTIVITIES

Choose from among the several *vináreň* (wine bar–restaurants) and wine shops (where you can also taste) in and around Modra's main street. Even restaurants have lengthy lists of local wine sold by the decilitre (usually priced from 15Sk to 30Sk). Shop at **Pavúk** (☎ 647 5039; Štúrova 92; ⊙ 10am-8pm Mon-Sat), or settle in for more leisurely consideration at the small, associated café. **Vináreň u Ludvika** (☎ 0915408350; Dukelska 2; mains 140-245Sk) is everything a Slovak wine restaurant should be: it's in a 300-year-old cellar with cobblestone fireplace and fur-covered wooden benches. Twenty-seven regional wines are available. Both the café at Pavúk and Vináreň u Ludvika serve food.

Watch artisans hand-painting vases and jugs and then buy your own at the ceramics factory **Slovenská ľudová majolika** (☎ 647 2942; Dolná 138; www.majolika.sk; admission free; ⊙ 8.30am-4.30pm Mon-Fri). Weekend tours are available by arrangement.

Keep pressing the buzzer if the little **Ľudovít Štúr Museum** (Štúrova 50; adult/student 20/10Sk; ⊙ 9am-4pm Tue-Fri, 9am-3pm Sat) appears to be closed. Here, in what used to be the town hall, you'll find the writing desk of Ľudovít Štúr, 19th-century nationalist, linguist and poet.

SLEEPING

Modra, 24km northeast of Bratislava, can easily be done as a day trip, but if you're stuck overnight, **Penzión Club MKM** (☎ 647 5313; Štúrova 25; r 680-1200Sk; P ⊠) is in a pleasant old neo-classical building. Updated add-ons include a fitness room, *foosball* (table football) and a bowling lane.

GETTING THERE & AWAY

Buses leave for Modra several times every hour from Bratislava's main station (40Sk, 45 minutes). There are frequent bus connections to and from Trnava on weekdays, but only three on weekends (47Sk, one hour).

Around Modra
ČERVENÝ KAMEŇ

Wandering up the forest path to **Červený Kameň** (Red Stone; ☎ 649 5132; www.snm.sk; grounds admission free; ⊙ 9am-5pm May-Aug, 9am-4pm Mar-Apr & Sep-Oct, 9.30am-3.30pm Nov-Feb) you get the feeling the Pálffy family might have felt lonely being so isolated from the village, high above the trees. But, then again, they did have a *castle* to fill with people. Queen Constance, wife of Czech king Přemysl, Otakar I, first built Červený Kameň in about 1230 in woodlands roughly 5km north of Modra. In the late 16th century the Pálffys dismantled the castle bit by bit to

---

THE WINE WAY

The **Small Carpathian Wine Way** (Malokarpatská viná cesta; www.mvc.sk) promotes vintners and events. Pick up a *Malokarpatská viná cesta* map (1:75,000) at the tourist office in Modra; it lists local wineries and castles, and shows colour-coded walking trails. The area around **Pezinok** (☎ 641 2550; www.pezinok.sk; tourist office, Radničné nám 9; ⊙ 9am-5pm Mon-Fri) is known for light whites; Modra is famous for its dry reds. You can take a bus between Bratislava and Pezinok (25Sk, 30 minutes, at least half-hourly) and on from Pezinok to Modra (10Sk, 12 minutes, every 15 minutes).

On one weekend in mid-November most of the winemakers from Bratislava to Trnava participate in **Open Cellar Day** (Deň otvorený pivníc; ☎ 643 3489; www.mvc.sk; ⊙ 1-7pm). For 800Sk you get a map, a wine glass and a pass entitling you to tastings at dozens of wineries along the 40km route. Unfortunately, there's no tour bus to shuttle you between them. You can take buses between the big towns, or negotiate to hire a driver in Bratislava.

remake it into a deluxe fortified palace. They went on remodelling it until they fled Czechoslovakia in 1945. The castle suffered some damage in WWII and was subsequently confiscated by the government. Restoration began in 1947 and today it is mostly complete.

Walk up from the car park past the **falconry yard** (adult/concession 65/35Sk; ☉ shows 12.15pm, 2.15pm, 4.15pm) and you have free access to climb around the outer walls or have a coffee in the inner courtyard café. To see the inside of the palace and cellar, you have to join a tour (adult/student 130/70Sk). Most of the rooms are set up as if the Pálffy family had just stepped out. The gigantic cellar is 78m long by 9m high (and is available for parties). Here you can see where the iron oxide has stained the rock red, giving the castle its name.

Just outside the gate, **Taverna pod bastou** (☎ 690 5869; mains 120-170Sk) serves a full menu and has a fine terrace.

GETTING THERE & AROUND
The easiest way to travel the 5km north of Modra is by car. During the week buses depart every few minutes from Bratislava (53Sk, one hour) via Modra (14Sk, ¼ hour) to Častá village (get off at the Zakladina stop); on weekends only three buses make the trip. From Zakladina, Červený Kameň is 1km west (30 minutes' walk up) on the green-marked trail.

TRNAVA
☎ 033 / pop 69,140
History is what attracts most people to Trnava. Slovakia's oldest town was the first to get a royal charter as a free borough (from Hungarian king Béla IV in 1238), and has a good part of the medieval town walls still intact. Trnava was once the seat of Hungarian Catholicism, and there are a few churches (and two synagogues) worth seeing. The old town centre is pleasant enough, but the most ancient elements were hidden when the town was remodelled in baroque style during the 1700s. The baroque is mostly what's reflected today. Sadly, some of the historic buildings are crumbling, and industrialisation and communist style have affected the town.

History
Lying on the Prague–Budapest and Vienna–Kraków trade routes, Trnava was already one of Hungary's biggest and wealthiest towns by the 13th century. After the 1526 Turkish vic-

tory at Mohács, the archbishops of Esztergom transferred their seat here, and beefed up the town walls. One after another, Catholic Orders moved in with churches, monasteries and schools. The Jesuit university, founded in 1635, was the only university in Hungary at the time (the University church of St John the Baptist is still the town's star attraction). But all good things must end and in 1777 Empress Maria Theresa had the entire university moved to Budapest, and in 1820 the archbishops went back to Esztergom. (An archbishop wasn't again seated in Trnava until 1987.)

The town's other claim to historical fame is that Anton Bernolák, codifier of the standardised Slovak language, founded the Slovak Learned Society (Slovenské učené tovarišstvo) here in 1792. The soon-to-be Czechoslovak city industrialised early (the first steam train in Slovakia left here in 1872) and thoroughly. Manufacturing is still the city's mainstay, led by Peugeot-Citröen, which built a manufacturing plant on the outskirts in 2003.

Orientation
The bus and train stations are south of the old town centre, the heart of which is Trojičné nám. Pedestrian Hlavná runs into the square. You could easily see all of Trnava's attractions in a half-day trip from Bratislava.

Information
City Police (☎ 551 1555; Trhová 3)
Heso Com (Hviezdoslavova 13; per hr 30Sk; ☉ 10am-midnight) Internet access.
Hospital (☎ 553 6103; Andreja Žarnova 11)
Main post office (Trojičné nám 4)
Trnava Information Service (TINS; ☎ 551 1022; www.trnava.sk; Trojičné nám 1; ☉ 9am-6pm Mon-Sat May-Sep, 9am-5pm Mon-Fri Oct-Apr) In the Municipal Tower.
Všeobecná úverová banka (VÚB; Hlavná 31) This bank has an ATM.

Sights
UNIVERSITY DISTRICT
In the baroque neighbourhood around the old university is one of Slovakia's finest churches, the huge **University church of St John the Baptist** (Univerzitný kostol sv Jána Krstiteľa; Univerzitné nám), designed by Pietro Spezzo and built by Italian and Viennese artisans between 1629 and 1637. Though severe-looking on the outside, it's all lush baroque and rococo inside, with a beautiful altar reaching to the ceiling.

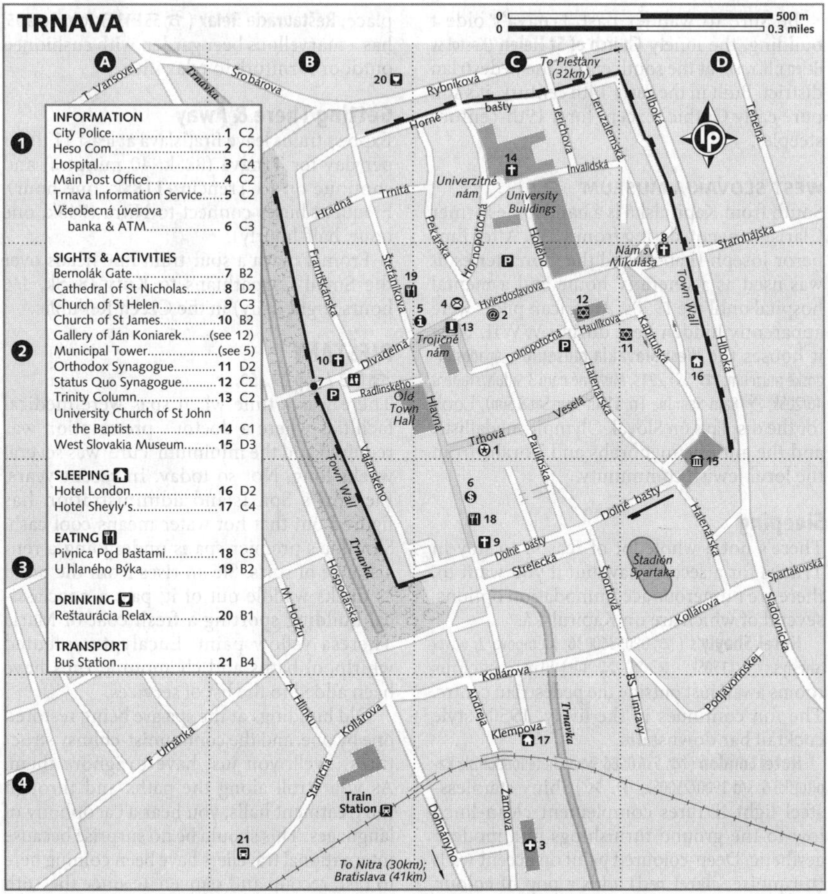

Named after the patron saint of merchants, the **Cathedral of St Nicholas** (Dóm sv Mikuláša; nám Mikuláša) was founded as a Gothic parish church in about 1380, and promoted to the status of a cathedral when the archbishops arrived from Esztergom. It was given a baroque face-lift in the 17th century and a new interior in the 18th century.

Southwest from St Nicholas is all that remains of Trnava's 19th-century Jewish heritage. The **Status Quo Synagogue** houses the **Gallery of Ján Koniarek** (☎ 551 4657; www.gjk.sk; Halenárska 2; adult/student 30/15Sk; 🕑 9am-noon & 1-5pm Mon-Fri, 1-6pm Sat & Sun). The small but impressive collection here mixes modern art with Jewish artefacts. The ruins of the **Orthodox Synagogue** (Havlíka) are in sad, sad shape.

AROUND TROJIČNÉ NÁM

Restored brick town walls, first built between the 13th and 16th centuries, stretch almost completely around the historical centre. In the west wall is the **Bernolák gate** (Bernolákova brána), the only surviving tower. Through the gate and past the Franciscans' 1640 **Church of St James** (Kostol sv Jakuba; ☎ 551 1211; Františkánska; adult/student 30/15Sk; 🕑 1-4pm Mon & Fri, 9-11am & 1-4pm Tue-Thu, 9-11am Sat) is the main square, Trojičné nám. It's dominated by a Renaissance **Municipal tower** (Mestská veža; Trojičné nám 1; adult/student 30/15Sk; 🕑 10am-6.30pm Jun-Sep), built in 1574 but with a baroque top, which provides views of the city. The 17th-century **Trinity Column** in the square, removed by the communists in 1948, was replaced in 1989 by popular demand.

Be sure to wander past Trnava's oldest building, the lonely **Church of St Helen** (Kostol sv Helena; Hlavná), at the south end of the pedestrian district. Built in the early 14th century, it's still pure early Gothic (except for a 19th-century steeple).

WEST SLOVAKIA MUSEUM
South from Kapitulská is a handsome former Clarist convent, dating from 1239. After Emperor Joseph II abolished the monasteries, it was used as a veterans' home and a mental hospital until the 1950s. American pilots were apparently hidden here during WWII. Now it houses the **West Slovakia museum** (Západoslovenské múzeum; ☎ 551 2913; Múzejné nám 3; adult/student 40/20Sk; ⏱ 8am-5pm Tue-Fri, 11am-5pm Sat & Sun). Look for the displays on Slovak Olympic medallists, and the antique menorahs and Torahs from the local Jewish community.

Sleeping
There's not a whole lot of reason to stay in Trnava for a second day, but if you want to, there are numerous accommodation options, several of which are on Kapitulská.

Hotel Sheyly's (☎ 0905360036; Klempova 2; www.sheylys.sk; r 1150Sk; P X ⚉ ▯) Hip, spacious rooms await just outside the pedestrian centre. The fun continues in the lively, 1950s-style cocktail bar downstairs.

Hotel London (☎ 534 0586; www.hotellondon.sk; Kapitulská 5; s/d 1900/2500Sk; P X) Shiny stainless-steel light fixtures complement clean-lined low-to-the-ground furnishings in a modern aesthetic. Deep-coloured paint on accent walls (turquoise, claret red) adds a pop of colour. Even the little bar is sophisticated.

Eating & Drinking
Most places in town offer a two-course lunch menu for about 100Sk.

Pivnica pod baštami (☎ 551 4049; Hlavná 45; mains 65-120Sk; ⏱ closed Sun) Sautéed, grilled or stuffed, chicken seems to be the house meat of choice, but there are a few pasta and veggie options. Dine on the covered terrace or down in the brick-vaulted *pivnice* (cellar).

U hlaného Býka (☎ 551 4452; Štefánikova 3; mains 89-350Sk) Pub food, pizza...and steak. In a nation that loves meat, a good steak is surprisingly hard to find. Not so here at 'the Bull'.

For drinks, Hotel Sheyly's 1950s dinerlike bar, with its occasional live concerts and range of 150-plus cocktails, is quite the happenin'

place; **Reštaurácia Relax** (☎ 551 1323; Rybníková 15) has a marvellous beer garden with cushioned outdoor furniture to relax into.

Getting There & Away
Express trains leave Bratislava at least 11 times per day for Trnava (82Sk, 40 minutes) and continue on to Trenčín (118Sk, one hour). Frequent buses connect to Nitra (74Sk, one hour, half-hourly).

From Trnava a spur train line heads over the Small Carpathians to Kúty (84Sk, 1½ hours, eight daily) in the Czech Republic.

PIEŠŤANY
☎ 033 / pop 29,950
There was a time when spas were medical facilities where a doctor's prescription was required and the minimum 'cure' was several weeks long. Not so today. In recent years, Piešťany's Spa Island administration has figured out that hot water means cool cash. Slovakia's premier spa is undergoing a renaissance of sorts. Steam rises from the pond as ducks waddle out of it, past a neoclassical building sporting a fresh coat of Maria Theresa yellow paint. Eucalyptus-scented whirlpool baths and chamomile rubs have been added to the list of services.

Old buildings at the spa are being restored one by one, and the communist-clumsy structures...well, you just have to ignore them. As you stroll along the paths and through the treatment halls, you hear a cacophony of languages. This should be no surprise because international travellers have been coming here to rest, recoup and rejuvenate since the 16th century. As other patrons pass by and you smell a faint whiff of rotten eggs, remember that the sulphur in the water has healing properties.

Orientation
The town itself is centred on the pedestrian streets around Winterova, flanked to the north by the city park. Bathing facilities, pools and spa hotels are to the east on Spa Island (Kúpeľný ostrov). The train and bus stations sit side by side 2km northwest of the town centre.

Information
The **Piešťany Information Office** (☎ 771 9622; www.pic.piestany.sk; Pribinova 2; ⏱ 9am-6pm Mon-Fri, 9am-2pm Sat, 2-6pm Sun) can help with information

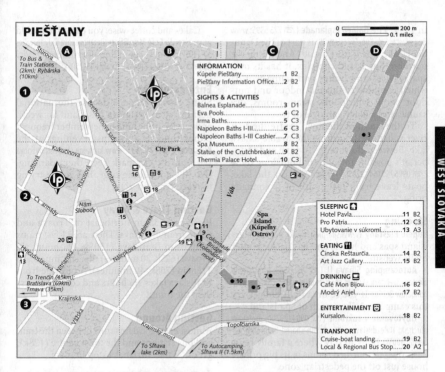

PIEŠŤANY

0 ——— 200 m
0 ——— 0.1 miles

INFORMATION
Kúpele Piešťany.....................1 B2
Piešťany Information Office.....2 B2

SIGHTS & ACTIVITIES
Balnea Esplanade....................3 D1
Eva Pools...............................4 C2
Irma Baths.............................5 C3
Napoleon Baths I-III................6 C3
Napoleon Baths I-III Cashier....7 C3
Spa Museum..........................8 B2
Statue of the Crutchbreaker.....9 C3
Thermia Palace Hotel.............10 C3

SLEEPING
Hotel Pavla............................11 B2
Pro Patria..............................12 C3
Ubytovanie v súkromí.............13 A3

EATING
Čínska Reštaurčia...................14 B2
Art Jazz Gallery......................15 B2

DRINKING
Café Mon Bijou......................16 B2
Modrý Anjel...........................17 B2

ENTERTAINMENT
Kursalon................................18 B2

TRANSPORT
Cruise-boat landing................19 B2
Local & Regional Bus Stop.....20 A2

WEST SLOVAKIA

about the town and non–Spa Island accommodations and events. The office stays open until 8pm weekdays from May to September. There's one slow computer with internet access (50Sk per hour) in the corner. For information on week-long spa treatment plans, inquire at the **Kúpele Piešťany** (☎ 775 2198; www .spa-piestany.sk; Winterova 29; ☼ 7am-5pm Mon-Fri) spa office; for day services go directly to the Spa Island cashier (see below). Banks and services are on Winterova.

Sights & Activities
The town, although it has a few modest Art Nouveau buildings, is pretty nondescript. Numerous trails crisscross the large city park, which is home to a small **Spa museum** (Balneologické múzeum; ☎ 772 2875; www.balneomuzeum.sk; Beethovenova sady; adult/student 30/15Sk; ☼ 9am-noon & 1-5pm Tue-Sun) with ethnographic and spa history displays.

Functionalist **Colonnade bridge** (Kolonádový most), designed and built in 1932, serves as a platform for Thermae Piešťany's (trademarked) symbol, the **statue of the crutchbreaker**. Into the bridge's glass walls are etched pastoral

scenes by 20th-century Slovak artist Martin Benka, which were saved by residents before the Nazis blew it up (it was reconstructed in 1956). Once across the bridge you are on **Spa Island** (Kúpeľný ostrov). At the time of writing, the island's two Art-Nouveau jewels, **Thermia Palace Hotel** and **Irma baths** (both built 1912) were under construction, but they should be fully restored and reopened by mid-2007.

Straight ahead from Irma baths, the 1821 neoclassical buildings **Napoleon baths I-III** (Napoleónske kúpele I-III) are home to mud pools, mineral pools, massage rooms and a salt cave. You can sign up for services at the **cashier** (kasa; www.spa-piestany.sk; Napoleon 1; ☼ 7.30am-7pm). A 45-minute mud wrap is the most expensive treatment at 800Sk; a 20-minute massage costs about 440Sk; and a 20-minute soak in the thermal 'mirror' pool is 400Sk. An immersion mud bath requires a medical exam. Some of the treatments are in the nearby hotels.

You don't need a reservation to swim in the warm mineral waters of the **Eva Pools** (Kúpalisko Eva; adult/child 150/50Sk; ☼ 9am-6pm May-Sep, 2-5pm Mon-Fri, 1-6pm Sat & Sun Oct-Apr). The 25m indoor pool and 50m outdoor pool were both built

in 1934. The **Balnea Esplanade** (☎ 775 5395; www
.spa-piestany.sk; Kúpeľný ostrov 29) is part of the Danu-
bia Health Spa Resort brand. Anchoring the
northern Spa Island complex, it has its own
spa services and 'water and sauna world',
which contains connected indoor and outdoor pools, whirlpools, steam rooms, dry
saunas and a fancy gargoyle or two.

To the south of the town centre the Váh
river is dammed, forming the sizable Sĺňava
lake. Between the months of June and October, it's possible to enjoy an hour-long **cruise**
(☎ 0905250164; 120Sk; ☼ 9am-5pm) on the lake;
boats leave from just south of Colonnade
bridge.

Sleeping

Kúpele Piešťany (www.spa-piestany.sk) administers
island spas and hotels and has package rates
on its website.

Autocamping Sĺňava II (☎ 762 3563; http://camp
piestany.webpark.sk; sites per person/tent 80/80Sk, 4-person
bungalow 860Sk) If you're on a tight budget, try
this camp site 1.5km south of Spa Island.

Ubytovanie v súkromí (☎ 0904129700; grofova@
nurch.sk; Hviezdoslavova 25; r with shared bathroom per
person 400Sk) Book to stay where a family rents
basic one- to four-bed rooms in its big private
house just off the pedestrian zone.

Pro Patria (☎ 775 6262; www.spaPiestany.com;
Kúpeľný ostrov; r €39; **P**) Completed in 1916 during WWI, the Pro Patria opened just in time
to serve as a hospital for 500 soldiers. Today
the pink spa hotel has 101 pastel-and-white
rooms upstairs, and mud treatments and mineral pools on ground level.

Hotel Pavla (☎ 7734 222; Sad Andreja Kmeťa 76;
www.hotelpavla.com; r €115-145; **P** ⊠ 🖭 🖳) This
is where modern elegance meets 1920s design.
Upscale touches in this restored hotel, opened
in 2005, include high-end linen, brushed-
nickel fixtures and a rooftop hot tub.

Eating & Drinking

Čínska Reštaurčia (☎ 772 5122; Alexander Centrum; mains
88-200Sk) The Chinese mother-daughter team
here serves great food. Set menus at lunch
cost around 100Sk.

Art Jazz Gallery (☎ 7625 559; Winterova 29; mains
90-250Sk; ☼ to 1am Fri & Sat) Jazz bands sometimes
play in this rambling, eclectic café. The food is
an improvisation on Slovak themes: *palacinky*
(crepes) filled with salmon mousse instead of
sweets, and *halušky* (dumplings) with spinach
instead of bacon, for example.

Cake- and coffee-wise, you can go old world
at parkside **Café Mon Bijou** (Beethovenova sady 16; cakes
30-110Sk), or new age at the supermodern **Modrý
Anjel** (Sad Andreja Kmeťa 28; cakes 45-150Sk; ⊠).

Entertainment

Some Slovak citizens do use the national
health system to stay on the island for weeks
and weeks; from June to September frequent
oldies concerts and gypsy evenings at the
Kursalon (☎ 775 7531; www.kursalon.sk; Beethovenova
sady 5) in the city park keep them dancing.
(No, it's not cutting edge, but you're trying
to relax, remember?)

Getting There & Away

Piešťany is 35km northeast of Trnava and
66km from Bratislava. There are 11 fast trains
daily from Bratislava (130Sk, 1¼ hour) via
Trnava (62Sk, 30 minutes) that continue on to
Trenčín (76Sk, 40 minutes). A bus ride from
Bratislava takes 1½ hours and costs 30Sk less
than the train.

Getting Around

Almost every local bus runs between the train
and bus stations and the town centre (12Sk);
get off at the Nitrianska stop in town.

ČACHTICE & BECKOV CASTLES

In the 17th century a mad Hungarian countess
named Alžbeta Báthory (known as Bloody Liz
to her mates) tortured and murdered more
than 600 peasant women at **Čachtice castle**
(Čachtický hrad), where she was eventually
imprisoned. Legend has it that she bathed in
her victims' blood to keep her skin young, but
that's largely been dismissed by scholars. A
fire destroyed the castle in 1708 and the ruins
aren't much to look at today, but atop the
castle hill you have great views of the adjacent
regional nature reserve, and can experience an
eerie, lonely feeling.

There are no roads leading directly to the
freely accessible site. The castle is a 25-minute
trail hike from the small village of Višnové,
where there's a pub. To get to Višňové from
Bratislava, take the train to Nové Mesto nad
Váhom (146Sk, 1½ hours, 109km, 12 daily),
then switch to a train for Višňové (12Sk, 15
minutes, four daily, six on weekends). From
Trenčín to Nové Mesto nad Váhom (52Sk, 25
minutes), there are 11 trains daily. It's tricky
to coordinate, so check return schedules carefully at www.zsr.sk.

Another one of Alžbeta's horrific castle playgrounds, **Beckov** (☎ 777 7125; Beckov village; adult/student 60/30Sk; ❂ 9am-6pm Tue-Sun May-Sep) is 5km north of Nové Mesto nad Váhom. Like Čachtice, this 12th-century castle was destroyed by fire in the 1700s, but more of it survived and it was partially reconstructed in 1996. Though still largely in ruins, you can tour the furnished palace and chapel.

Again, it's challenging to get here without a car. You can take the train to Nové Mesto nad Váhom and from there, on weekdays only, 12 buses run to Beckov village (14Sk, 20 minutes). Hike the 10 minutes up to the castle from the village.

TRENČÍN
☎ 032 / pop 56,850
What's not to like about a place with a mighty clifftop castle, pretty Renaissance buildings and a lively university population?

Here you could easily spend a couple of days touring the Roman fortress, day-tripping out to Beckov castle (opposite) or the spa town Trenčianske Teplice (p366), or revelling in night-time. There are several small museums in town, including an excellent contemporary Czech and Slovak art museum.

For centuries Trenčín castle has guarded the southwestern gateway to Slovakia, where the Váh river valley begins to narrow between the White Carpathians (Bílé Karpaty) and the Strážov hills. Roman legionnaires established the outpost of Laugaricio here in the 2nd century; a rock inscription dated AD 179 proves it. This was the northernmost Roman camp in Eastern Europe.

The castle that now towers above the town was first mentioned in 1069 in a Viennese chronicle. In the 13th century the castle's master, Matúš Čák, held sway over much of Slovakia, and in 1412 Trenčín obtained the rights of a free royal city. The present castle dates from the 15th century, and although both castle and town were destroyed by fire in 1790, much has been restored.

Modern Trenčín is an important centre for the Slovak textile industry and a bustling little community.

Orientation
From the adjacent bus and train stations, walk west through the city park MR Štefánika and underneath the highway past the Hotel Tatra, left uphill on Mierové nám.

To the east, through an ancient town gate, Mierové meets Štúrovo nám, also a pedestrian plaza. The entire centre is easily walkable.

Information
Cultural Information Centre (☎ 161 86; www .trencin.sk; City Office, Sládkovičova; ❂ 8am-6pm May-Sep, 8am-5pm Mon-Fri Oct-Apr) Helpful, well-informed staff.
Dom Knihy (Hviedoslavova 13; ❂ 9am-5pm Mon-Fri) Bookstore with a good selection of hiking maps and travel books.
Main post office (Mierové nám 21)
Mike Studio (Mierové nám 25; per min 1Sk; ❂ 9am-10pm Mon-Sat, 10am-10pm Sun) Just internet, no café.
Police Station (☎ 159; Štúrovo nám 10)
Všeobecná úverová banka (VÚB; ☎ 741 7111; Mierové nám 37)

Sights
TRENČÍN CASTLE
Dominating a rocky crag above the old town, **Trenčín castle** (Trenčiansky hrad; ☎ 743 5657; adult/student 80/40Sk; ❂ 9am-5.30pm May-Oct, to 3.30pm Nov-Apr) is difficult to miss – especially at night when it's lit with green and purple spotlights. You have a hike to get here, but from the ramparts you're rewarded with sweeping views of the Váh river plain. Much of the series of fortifications and palaces you'll see is a reconstruction.

The **Well of Love**, purportedly dug by a man trying to win his lover back from servitude in the castle, was probably dug by Hapsburg soldiers.

To go inside the upper castle's three palaces, which are filled with decorative and fine artwork and weaponry, you have to join one of the frequent tours (in Slovak only; call two days ahead to arrange an English-speaking guide).

The oldest remaining structures are parts of a Slavic rotunda (9th or 10th century), beneath the **Barbara Palace**, and the **Mathias Tower** (11th century), with an observation gallery.

There are events almost daily in summer, including concerts and **historical performances** (www.trencin.sk).

The best time to tour is on an evening when torch-lit, two-hour **medieval night tours** (adult/student 100/50Sk; ❂ 9pm, various evenings) take you past knights and knaves sword-fighting, minstrels performing, and the staging of other scenes from the period.

WEST SLOVAKIA

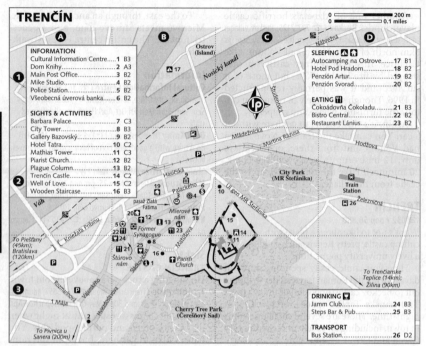

TRENČÍN

0 ———————— 200 m
0 ———————— 0.1 miles

INFORMATION
Cultural Information Centre.....1 B3
Dom Knihy.................................2 A3
Main Post Office.......................3 B2
Mike Studio..............................4 B2
Police Station..........................5 B2
Všeobecná úverová banka......6 B2

SIGHTS & ACTIVITIES
Barbara Palace..........................7 C3
City Tower...................................8 B3
Gallery Bazovský.......................9 B2
Hotel Tatra..............................10 C2
Mathias Tower.........................11 C3
Piarist Church.........................12 C3
Plague Column........................13 B2
Trenčín Castle.........................14 C2
Well of Love............................15 C2
Wooden Staircase..................16 B3

SLEEPING
Autocamping na Ostrove.......17 B1
Hotel Pod Hradom..................18 B2
Penzión Artur..........................19 B2
Penzión Svorad.......................20 B2

EATING
Čokoádovňa Čokoladu............21 B3
Bistro Central..........................22 B2
Restaurant Lánius...................23 B2

DRINKING
Jamm Club...............................24 B3
Steps Bar & Pub......................25 B3

TRANSPORT
Bus Station..............................26 D2

Ostrov (Island)

Nábrežná

Nosický kanál

Študentská

Mládežnická

Martina Rázusa

Hodžova

City Park (MR Štefánika)

Train Station

Železničná

Ul gen MR Štefánika

Hasičská

Palackého

pasaž Zlatá Fatima

Mierové nám

Matúšova

Sládkovičova

Štúrovo nám

Parish Church

Váh

Knieža'ca Pribinu

Rozmarínová

Vajanského

Hviezdoslavova

1.Mája

To Piešťany (45km); Bratislava (120km)

To Pivnica u Sanera (200m)

Cherry Tree Park (Čerešňový Sad)

To Trenčianske Teplice (14km); Žilina (90km)

MIEROVÉ NÁM & AROUND

The famous Roman inscription of AD 179 is on the cliff behind the **Hotel Tatra** (☎ 650 6111; www.hotel-tatra.sk; Ulica gen MR Štefánika 2) and can only be seen through a viewing window on the hotel's staircase. Ask at the reception for permission to see it. The translation reads: 'To the victory of the emperor and the army which, numbering 855 soldiers, resided at Laugaricio. By order of Maximianus, legate of the 2nd auxiliary legion'.

Temporary exhibits at the **Gallery Bazovský** (☎ 743 6858; http://gmab.scot.sk in Slovak; Palackého 27; adult/student 40/10Sk; ⏰ 9am-5pm Tue-Sun) are a great representation of contemporary Czech and Slovak artists. The permanent collection includes works by local abstract painter Miloš Bazovský (1899–1968).

The pleasant Mierové nám, lined with Renaissance burghers' houses, is dominated at its west end by the **Piarist church** (Piaristický kostol), built in baroque style in 1657. In the centre of the square is a **plague column** that dates from 1712.

You can climb the **City tower** (Mestská brána; ☎ 650 4317; Sládkovičova; adult/student 30/15Sk; ⏰ 10am-

8pm Jun-Sep) above the old town's only remaining gate. South of the tower, a 16th-century covered **wooden staircase** (Kryté schody) climbs to a bright-yellow 14th-century **Parish church** (Farský kostol) that has a simple outline bearing Gothic, Renaissance and baroque traces. The adjacent small cemetery chapel is probably the only purely Gothic building in town. From here you can ascend to the castle gate.

Sleeping

Trenčín has many more *penzións* (guesthouses) than we can list; ask at the tourist office if the ones listed here are full.

Autocamping na Ostrove (☎ 743 4013; http://web .viapvt.sk/autocamping.tn; sites per car/tent 50/70Sk, per person in hut 200Sk; ⏰ May-15 Sep) This decent camping ground on an island in the Váh river is within walking distance of the city centre. Two- to five-bed *chaty* (huts) are for rent, in addition to field space for tents.

Penzión Svorad (☎ 743 0322; www.svorad-trencin .sk; Palackého 4; s 450-800Sk, d 700-1200Sk; ✗) Frayed curtains, peeling linoleum – but oh, the castle views! It's clear this utilitarian dorm was part of an old grammar school; the staff are still quite rule oriented. Absolutely no smoking (or you'll be kicked out).

Penzión Artur (☎ 748 1029; www.arturtn.sk; Palackého 23; s/d/tr 1200/1500/2000Sk) A wine restaurant and street café add to the appeal of this colourful old-town inn. Rooms are modern modular, nothing special.

Hotel Pod Hradom (☎ 744 2507; www.podhradom.sk in Slovak; Matúšova 12; r 2300-2950Sk) On a wee winding street en route to the castle, this pretty little lodging has a primo location and patio. Many of the rooms have sloped ceilings and skylights, some have a *maželska postel* (literally 'marriage bed'; one queen mattress instead of two twins), a rarity in Slovakia.

Eating

A couple of pizza places on Mierové and Štúrovo vie for your favour; they're really much the same.

Restaurant Lánius (☎ 744 1978; Mierové nám 20; mains 90-190Sk) The rustic setup – creaking beams, a wood fireplace – matches the hearty Slovak fare. Pass by the dining room at the front; the one up the stairs at the rear of the courtyard is more fun.

Pivnica u Sanera (J Braneckého 15; breakfast 35-68Sk, mains 95-165Sk; ☺ 8.30am-10pm) Specialities from different Slovak regions add flavour to the cellar-restaurant menu: the Liptov schnitzel is topped with onions and bacon.

For a snack, you can grab a takeaway kebab wrapped in *langoš* (fried bread) from **Bistro Central** (Štúrovo nám 10; mains 42-86Sk; ☺ 9am-7pm Mon-Thu, 9am-4pm Fri, 7pm-4am Sat), or if you crave

something sweeter go to **Čokoládovňa Čokoladu** (Chocolate Café Chocolate; ☎ 0903480318; Štúrovo nám 7; cakes 30-110Sk; ☺ 9am-8pm Mon-Sat, 1-8pm Sun).

Drinking

The pedestrian squares have several good cafés and bars.

Steps Pub & Bar (☎ 744 6252; Sládkovičova 4-6; ☺ 10.30am-1am Sun-Thu, till 4am Fri & Sat) The ground-floor pub has imported beer on tap. Upstairs, the bar attracts a beautiful, college-age crowd.

Jamm Club (Štúrovo nám 5; ☺ noon-1am Mon-Thu, till 3am Fri, 2pm-3am Sat, 2pm-1am Sun) Red-and-black painted walls make this cellar-club seem extra dark, if that's possible. Live jazz and blues alternate with '70s and '80s disco nights.

Festivals & Events

Eight stages, circus tents, camping grounds, a dance tent, hundreds of WCs: **Bazant Pohoda Festival** (www.pohodafestival.sk) is the largest music festival in Slovakia. Bands come from 15 countries, including Ireland, the US and France to play here. Jazz, pop-rock, classical, electronica, even breakdance is represented over one frenetic weekend in July (1099Sk for a two-day ticket).

Getting There & Away

The train is the quickest and most cost-efficient way to get here. Eleven fast trains on the main line from Bratislava (180Sk, two hours, daily) stop in Trenčín before continuing on to Žilina (180Sk, 1½ hours) and Košice

---

CASTLE HUNTING

Look up at the cliffs as you travel along almost any valley in Slovakia and you'll start to notice the stony manmade shapes rising out of the rocks. Castles and ruins abound in this country. Some of the most well known and accessible are listed in this book; a few of these have been restored, but there are dozens more that are still in ruins.

The castle system in Slovakia began in the 12th century when the Turks first threatened Hungary (of which Slovakia was a part). Defences were bulked up after the Turks later took control of Budapest, in the 16th and 17th centuries. As the danger from invaders abated, and fire caused damage, the stony beasts were abandoned, left to rot in skeletal form. And there they lie today.

So, get yourself a national map, pick one of the ruin symbols and start hiking. There's almost always a marked trail to take you where you want to go. The reward for a hearty climb might be only an ancient hearth, or the outlines of rooms in ruin, but there are always great views from these defensive sites.

Several sources can help in your quest, including *111 Castles*, by Vladimír Bárta, and the VKÚ map and booklet *Hrady, zámky, kaštiele*, which has explanatory English text. The green hiking maps from VKÚ are always good. Also check out www.castles.sk. Write and tell us which ones you've conquered and which you liked the best – happy hunting!

(420Sk, four hours). Intermediate stops include Nové Mesto nad Váhom (52Sk, 25 minutes), Piešťany (76Sk, 40 minutes) and Trnava (118Sk, one hour).

TRENČIANSKE TEPLICE

☎ 032 / pop 5000

This sedate spa town in the Teplička valley, 14km northeast of Trenčín, has some 19th-century buildings and lots of trees, but few of the spa's services are available unless you're part of the Slovak health system and have a doctor's referral. The *Trenčín-Trenčianske Teplice* (1:10,000) map lists trails for hiking the surrounding hills.

The train station is near the post office on Šrobárova, which runs north and parallel to the main road, Kúpeľná. There's no information office in town, so stop by the Cultural Information Centre in Trenčín before you come. At the end of June the town hosts **Art Film** (www.artfilm.sk), a small independent film festival.

The opulent 1888 Turkish-style **bath house** (hammam; Kúpeľňa), opposite the Pax sanatorium, is now part of the men's changing room for the spa. The **thermal swimming pool** (termálny bazen; ☎ 651 4728; adult/child 100/50Sk; ⏰ entry at 9am, 10am, 11am, 12.30pm & 1.30pm) is open to the public only on Sundays and on a first-come, first-served basis at the given hours.

Art Film Restaurant (TG Masaryka; mains 70-130Sk) has meals named after film stars.

A train ride between Trenčín and Trenčianske Teplice requires a switch to a narrow-gauge rail in Trenčianska Tepla and can take up to an hour; it's much easier to take the bus (14Sk, 15 minutes, hourly).

NITRA

☎ 037 / pop 87,570

The first Christian church in the Czech and Slovak Republics, if not all of Central and Eastern Europe, was founded here. Nothing remains today of that original structure (or if it does, it hasn't been uncovered yet), but Nitra is still known for its churches. The largest town in West Slovakia is a fairly quiet place neatly split between the upper town, with its fortified houses of worship and cobblestone streets, and the lower town. Further out, modern, industrialised Nitra has developed.

History

The Celts inhabited this site centuries before Nitra became a principal seat of the Veľká

Moravia (Great Moravian Empire) in the 800s. Atheistic, but crafty, Prince Pribina built the first Christian church in Slovak Lands, c 830. In 1302 religion took over completely: the Nitra bishops assumed feudal hegemony of the region, which lasted for almost five centuries.

The Ottoman Turks took southern Hungary in 1526 at the Battle of Mohács and pushed north occupying more and more territory until southwestern Slovakia was on the front lines of the Turkish Wars. Nitra was hit in sporadic attacks, fighting was especially tough during the Fifteen Years War (1591–1606). During the 19th century, industrialisation set in. Recently, most of Nitra's money has been pumped into the sprawling Agricultural University and the surrounding Agrokomplex Exhibition Halls, the largest series of convention centres in Slovakia.

Orientation

Beneath what remains of the castle fortifications is the former clerical enclave called the upper town (Horné mesto). Southward are the remnants of the lower town (Dolné mesto), centred on the grandiose Svätoplukovo nám. The lower town's axes – Štefánikova and Štúrova – cross beside the big district market. The bus and train stations are 500m southwest of the lower town centre.

Information

I Net (Štefánikova 46; per hr 60Sk; ⏰ 9am-10pm Mon-Sat, noon-8pm Sun)

Information Centre NISYS (☎ 741 0906; www.nisys .sk, www.nitra.sk; Štefánikova 1; ⏰ 8am-6pm Mon-Fri, 8am-noon Sat) The usual info, plus guide service and sightseeing tours.

Kníhkupectvo pod Vŕškom (☎ 652 6546; Kupecká 7) Excellent bookstore.

Main post office (Svätoplukovo nám)

Tesco Department Store (Štefánikova 48) ATM, grocery store, café, everything.

Všeobecná úverová banka (VÚB; Štefánikova 44) Exchange office and ATM.

Sights & Activities

NITRA CASTLE

Actually, castle may be a bit of an overstatement. There's no palace as such, just a series of five baroque bastions and walls enclosing an ecclesiastical complex. Three small but beautiful churches inside are collectively known as **St Emeram Cathedral** (Katedrálny Biskupský

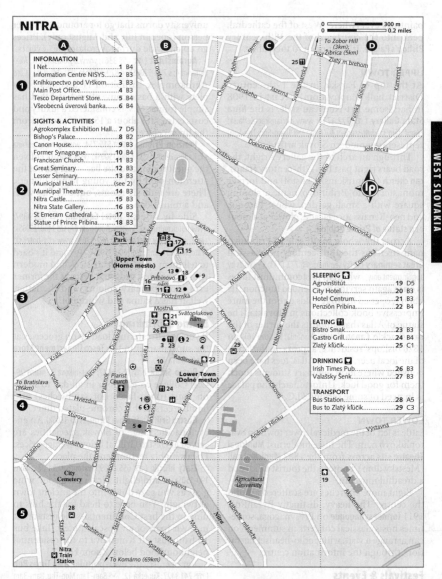

NITRA

0 —————— 300 m
0 —————— 0.2 miles

INFORMATION
I Net...1 B4
Information Centre NISYS.......2 B3
Knihkupectvo pod Vŕškom....3 B3
Main Post Office.......................4 B3
Tesco Department Store...........5 B4
Všeobecná úverová banka.......6 B4

SIGHTS & ACTIVITIES
Agrokomplex Exhibition Hall....7 D5
Bishop's Palace.........................8 B2
Canon House.............................9 B3
Former Synagogue...................10 B4
Franciscan Church....................11 B3
Great Seminary........................12 B3
Lesser Seminary........................13 B3
Municipal Hall......................(see 2)
Municipal Theatre...................14 B3
Nitra Castle.............................15 B3
Nitra State Gallery..................16 B3
St Emeram Cathedral...............17 B2
Statue of Prince Pribina..........18 B3

SLEEPING
Agroinštitút..............................19 D5
City Hotel................................20 B3
Hotel Centrum.........................21 B3
Penzión Pribina.......................22 B4

EATING
Bistro Smak.............................23 B3
Gastro Grill.............................24 B4
Zlatý kľúčik.............................25 C1

DRINKING
Irish Times Pub........................26 B3
Valašský Šenk.........................27 B3

TRANSPORT
Bus Station...............................28 A5
Bus to Zlatý kľúčik....................29 C3

Chram sv Emerama; ☎ 772 1724; admission free; ☉ 9am-noon & 2-4pm Oct-Apr, 9am-noon & 2-6pm May-Sep) The oldest of these is **St Emeram Church** (Kostola sv Emeráma), a tiny 11th-century Roman-esque rotunda, to the right of the anteroom. Try your luck; it's not always open. Some sources say parts of Prince Pribina's original church were incorporated into the rotunda.

At the rear of the anteroom and up the stairs is the 1642 **Lower church** (Dolný kostol), a dark, vaguely lopsided room with a remarkable marble relief of Christ being taken down from the cross. Up more stairs you'll find the **Upper church** (Horný kostol), completed in 1355 but filled now with baroque gilt and red marble, a massive organ gallery, and frescoes and paintings everywhere. West of the cathedral, peek into the courtyard of the 18th-century **Bishop's Palace**. It's not open to the public.

UPPER TOWN

At the top of Farská, in the 19th-century District hall (Župný dom), recast in 1908 in handsome Art-Nouveau style, is the **Nitra State Gallery** (☎ 772 1754; www.nitrianskagaleria.sk; Župné nám 3; adult/student 40/20Sk; ⓨ 10am-5pm Tue-Sun) representing modern Slovak artists.

Through an arch to the gallery's right, the road bears right past the 17th-century **Franciscan church** (Františkánsky kostol) and former monastery into Pribinovo nám, a sloping square with a small garden, whose baroque and neo-Renaissance façades glower at a modern **statue of Prince Pribina**.

Across the whole south side of Pribinovo nám stretches the 18th-century neoclassical **Great seminary** (Velký seminár; ☎ 772 1743; ⓨ visits by appointment only), which in postcommunist times is once again serving its intended function. Its library, opened in 1877, holds one of the more impressive book collections in Slovakia. The statue of Atlas that supports the corner of the ramshackle **Canon House** (Kanónia; Samova 16), an 1820 bishops' residence, appears on the labels of the local beer, Corgon. Atlas' toes have been polished where local seminary students touch them for good luck. Unfortunately the palace is in need of some serious TLC.

LOWER TOWN

Little is left of the medieval lower town on Svätoplukovo nám. The huge modernist **Municipal Theatre** sits across from the 1882 **Municipal hall** (Mestský dom), home to the tourist office and a dreadful museum.

Eight more churches are scattered around the centre. The heavy, distinctly Byzantine, 1911 **former synagogue** on Prí synagoga, sometimes hosts classical concerts in summer. You can arrange a visit, with audio-headset narration, through the information centre.

Festivals & Events

The **Agrokomplex Exhibition Hall** (www.agrokomplex .sk) hosts exhibitions throughout the year, the biggest of which is its international trade fair at the end of August.

Sleeping

Nitra has no private rooms, but the information centre has a comprehensive list of university dorms that go for around 300Sk per person (open in July and August only). Prices go up citywide during Agrokomplex events.

Agroinštitút (☎ 653 3361; www.agroinstitut.sk; Akademická 4; s 700-1200Sk, d 820-1300Sk; P ⊠ ▣) The Agrokomplex Exhibition Hall comes complete with a basic convention hotel that has simple rooms. (TV is considered a luxury and costs extra.) It's about a 15-minute walk from the town centre.

Penzión Pribina (☎ 6515 754; www.penzionpribina .sk; Radlinského 15; s/d 1100/1500Sk; P) Plants enliven the guest rooms and the bar – just part of the attention paid by the young family owners. There are only six rooms, but each has wi-fi and a minifridge.

Side by side sit **Hotel Centrum** (☎ 655 4397; www.hotelcentrum.sk; Svätoplukovo nám 1A; s/d 1400/2500Sk; P) and **City Hotel** (☎ 652 1203; www.city-hotel.sk; Svätoplukovo nám 1; s/d 1600/2500Sk; P), and it's hard to tell them apart. Both are sleek and modern with all the latest gadgetry. Perhaps the former uses more primary colours, and the latter, well, it has a sauna and whirlpool.

Eating & Drinking

If you're self-catering, load up on groceries at the supermarket in the **Tesco Department Store** (Štefánikova 48).

Bistro Smak (☎ 652 6047; Štefánikova 2; mains 29-49Sk) College co-eds pour in all day to snack on *toast* (open-faced hot sandwiches) and hamburgers in this chrome-plated diner.

Gastro Grill (Štefánikova 33; mains 80-160Sk) An encyclopaedic range of Slovak specialities are served at Gastro Grill, at below-average prices. Locals highly recommend the place.

Zlatý klúčik (☎ 655 0289; Svatourbanská 27; mains 190-350Sk) Candlelight flickers off your wine glass as you gaze down into the ancient town at twilight. You have to head for the hills to dine in the best Continental-style restaurant in town (part of an upscale hotel). Take bus 10 from just off Kmeťkova to the residential neighbourhood below Zobor Hill.

For beer, try the ever-popular **Irish Times Pub** (☎ 741 3427; Kupecká 12; ⓨ 8am-1am Mon-Thu, 8am-3am Fri & Sat, 11am-midnight Sun) or the macho sports bar **Valašsky Šenk** (Mostná 35; ⓨ 2pm-4am Mon-Fri, 5pm-4am Sat, 5pm-1am Sun).

Getting There & Away

Buses bound for Nitra depart from Bratislava at least every half hour (117Sk, 1½ hours). Train travel to Nitra from most cities involves multiple transfers; there is a direct train to/from Prievidza (98Sk, two hours, six daily) near Bojnice castle.

KOMÁRNO
☎ 035 / pop 36,731

The cultural centre of the Hungarian minority in Slovakia lies at the confluence of the Danube and Waag rivers on their way into Hungary. Wander across the bridge and you are in Hungary. Roughly two-thirds of the local population speak Hungarian and all the signs are bilingual. During the last weekend of April and the first week of May the Komárno Days festival celebrates Hungarian and Slovak song and dance with wine and food on the square.

Other than the odd building that might be of interest and the chance to eat Hungarian food, the real reason to come here is simply to pass through. Domestic train fares on either side of the border are usually cheaper than international (about €14 to €28 Bratislava–Budapest direct, €6-10 for the total trip through Komárno).

The adjacent train and bus stations are 15 minutes on foot north of the town centre, 20 minutes from the international border crossing. The **Tourist Information Office** (☎ 773 003; www.komarno.sk; Župná 5; ☑ 9am-5pm Mon-Fri) is on the town's main pedestrian street, Župná, near several banks, such as **Všeobecná úverová banka**.

More than 20 architectural styles – from Icelandic to Irish – are represented in **Europe Place** (Nádvorí Európy), a millennial monument finished in 2000. The buildings in this square contain some shops and cafés, but mostly offices and apartments. There are several small museums around town, including **Zichy Palace** (☎ 773 0055; Nám gen Klapku 9; adult/student 30/15Sk; ☑ 10am-5pm Tue-Sat), which has displays on local Hungarian writer Jókai Mór and interesting 19th- and 20th-century photos of the town. The crumbling 16th-century **Old fortress** (Stará pevnosť; ☎ 0907178906), on the east end of the town peninsula, is open only for group tours.

If you have to stay overnight, utilitarian **Hotel Európa** (☎ 773 1349; www.hoteleuropa.sk; Nám Štefánika 1; s/d 980/1560Sk; ℗) is convenient, en route from the bus and train stations and the international bridge. **Hostinec u čierneho**

psa (Black dog pub; Nám MR Štefánika 13; mains 80-160Sk; ☑ 10am-11pm Mon-Thu, 10am-midnight Fri, 11am-10pm Sat), known as Fekete kutyak vendeglö in Hungarian, serves Slovak and Hungarian staples and cold *pivo* (beer); ask for *sör* in Hungarian.

It costs nothing to walk across the 1892 bridge linking Slovakia with Hungary. Seven buses (128Sk, 1¾ hours) and trains (126Sk, 2¼ hours) per day run between Bratislava and Komárno. Up to five buses per day run between Nitra and Komárno (91Sk, 1¾ hours). Up to 18 local trains per day leave from the Komárom train station on the Hungarian side (two hours, 1004Ft) for Budapest.

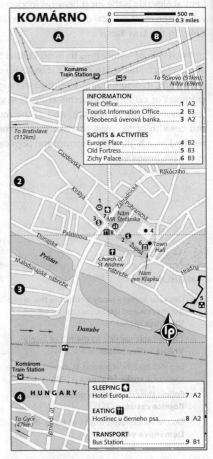

KOMÁRNO
0 — 500 m
0 — 0.3 miles

INFORMATION
Post Office.........................1 A2
Tourist Information Office.........2 B3
Všeobecná úverová banka.........3 A2

SIGHTS & ACTIVITIES
Europe Place......................4 B2
Old Fortress......................5 B3
Zichy Palace......................6 B3

SLEEPING 🏠
Hotel Európa......................7 A2

EATING 🍴
Hostinec u čierneho psa...........8 A2

TRANSPORT
Bus Station.......................9 B1

Central Slovakia

Here among the forested hills and stony mountains lies the consciousness of a nature-oriented nation. And no wonder, the landscapes of Central Slovakia are as accessible as they are stunning. Stand on the high plain beyond Liptovský Mikuláš and on a clear day you can see no fewer than five mountain ranges: the Western Tatras, the smaller but no less impressive Low Tatras, the very accessible Malá and Veľká Fatras, and in the distance, the mighty High Tatras. The ranges are blanketed with trees – at more than 50% coverage, Central Slovakia is the most heavily wooded part of either republic – and carved with deep valleys, the most magical of which are the Vrátna valley in the Malá Fatra and the Demänova valley in the Low Tatras.

A rich vein of history runs through Central Slovakia. In the 19th century, literary organisations in Martin helped to create a standardised language and national awareness. Below the mountains, mining brought wealth to the region and Banská Štiavnica contains wonderful examples of centuries-old architecture. Folk villages, such as Čičmany and Vlkolínec, represent another kind of treasure. And of the multitude of castles scattered along the length and breadth of Slovakia, the two most complete and ornate are here: Orava, impossibly perched on a high, rocky outcrop; and Bojnice, more like a fairy-tale than Walt Disney could ever have imagined.

HIGHLIGHTS

- Get your camera ready to capture the photogenic plastered log houses in the village of **Vlkolínec** (p390)

- Take a cable car ride to the top of lovely **Vrátna valley** (p382)

- Dig into historical mining at museums in the town of **Banská Štiavnica** (p374)

- Follow the crowd to the ghost festival at **Bojnice castle** (p379)

- Ski the much-loved slopes of Jasna, in the **Demänova valley** (p391)

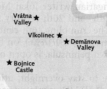

Vrátna Valley ★

Vlkolínec ★

★ Demänova Valley

★ Bojnice Castle

★ Banská Štiavnica

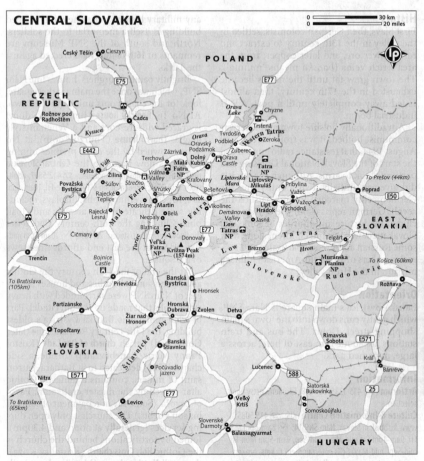

CENTRAL SLOVAKIA

0 30 km
0 20 miles

CENTRAL SLOVAKIA

Getting There & Away

Slovakia's main train line, connecting Bratislava and Košice, cuts across the top third of Central Slovakia, allowing fast connections to Žilina and Martin. Because of the steep valleys and limited train runs, it's best to take the bus if you're going straight to the region's more central towns and cities. Though the train journey from Košice to Banská Bystrica, along the southern border of the Low Tatras, is quite rewarding.

Getting Around

Much of Central Slovakia is hilly and often mountainous. Therefore, the bus or car may be your only option for transport to the region's more inviting areas, especially

for north–south travel. Roads are generally good, and a lot of fun, what with all the steep gradients and windy sections.

BANSKÁ BYSTRICA

☎ 048 / pop 81,704

In the valley where the Low Tatras, Veľká Fatra and Slovenské rudohorie mountains meet sits Banská Bystrica. Slovaks know it best as the cradle of the Slovak National Uprising (Slovenské národné povstanie; SNP) against the Nazis and their Slovak puppet state. The SNP Museum here is probably the best museum in the country.

Banská Bystrica's small but handsome old town centre includes the remnants of a 15th-century citadel.

History

First Slavs, then German colonists, settled in the valley in the 13th century to extract and refine silver ore, and later copper, from the area's rich veins (*banská* means 'mining'). The town grew fat until the mines became exhausted in the 17th century, then almost faded away completely until a post-WWII industrial boom.

A traditionally bolshie town and interwar communist hotbed, it was from here, on 29 August 1944, that resistance radio announced the start of the Slovak National Uprising and partisans took to arms. Although the fascists did give way initially, two months later the German army marched in and crushed the revolt. German reprisals for the uprising included the torture and murder of some 900 Slovak men, women and children, along with some Russian and French partisans, and several members of an Anglo-American military mission in the Hron valley.

Orientation

Banská Bystrica's main square is Nám SNP, which gently runs down into the town's main shopping street, Dolná. The bus and train stations are about 1km east of here, across a large, unnamed park.

Information

Artforum (☎ 415 1335; Dolná 8) Excellent, artsy book selection.

Culture & Information Centre (KIS; ☎ 415 5085; www.kisbb.sk in Slovak; Nám SNP 14; ☼ 8am-6pm Mon-Fri, 9am-1pm Sat mid-May–mid-Sep, 9am-5pm Mon-Fri mid-Sep–mid-May) Sells entertainment tickets, brokers private rooms, arranges walking tours.

Game Over (☎ 415 1511; Nám SNP 15; per hr 50Sk; ☼ 9.30am-10pm Mon-Fri, 2-10pm Sat & Sun) Twenty-plus computers with internet access.

Police station (9 Mája)

Post office (☎ 415 4780; Horná 1)

Všeobecná úverová banka (VÚB; Nám Slobody 1)

Sights

A Soviet-memorial oddity on the outside, on the inside **SNP Museum** (☎ 412 3259; www .muzeumsnp.sk; Kapitulská 23; adult/child 50/20Sk; ☼ 9am-6pm Tue-Sun May-Sep, 9am-4pm Tue-Sun Oct-Apr) is the most technologically advanced museum in the country. Flat-screened TVs and interactive displays bring to life not only the Slovak National Uprising, but Slovakia's involvement in the two world wars. This is a must-see for

any military history buff. The oddly shaped building is itself a memorial to the soldiers. North and south of the SNP Museum are remnants of **16th-century walls** erected against the Turks.

Brightly painted burghers' houses line Nám SNP, which was once the main market square; look for the chain roofs unique to the town. At No 16, **Benický house** (Beniczkého dom) is graced with frescoes and a Venetian-style loggia. **Thurzo house** (Thurzov dom), at No 4, once owned by the city's premier mining family, is now home to the **Central Slovakia museum** (Stredoslovenské múzeum; ☎ 412 5897; adult/student 30/15Sk; ☼ 8am-noon & 1-4pm Tue-Fri, 10am-5pm Sun), which has ethnographic displays, including some delicate bronze armlets and cloak pins. Climbing the 16th-century **Clock tower** (Hodinova veža; adult/student 20/10Sk; ☼ 10am-8pm mid-May–mid-Sep) at the east end affords fine views of the square.

At the end of the 15th century the Gothic and Renaissance churches and houses northeast of Nám SNP were surrounded with heavy stone walls that made up the old citadel. Part of what remains is Banská Bystrica's oldest building, the 13th-century Romanesque (later Gothicised) parish **church of Our Lady** (Kostol Panny Márie Nanebevzatej). Inside, a side chapel (1500) dedicated to St Barbara, patron saint of miners, contains a fantastic Gothic altar carved by the master craftsman, Pavol of Levoča. (Some say in repayment of some of his son's debts.) The church is only open during services (generally at noon and 4.30pm). Joined by fortifications behind the church is the Gothic **Holy Cross church** (Kostol sv Kríža), the small **Matthias house** (Matejov dom) built for the Hungarian King Matthias Corvinus, plus three bastions, a peaceful cemetery and bits of the original walls.

Sleeping

The Culture & Information Centre has a list of student dormitories (about 300Sk) open to travellers in summer.

ATC Tajov (☎ 419 7320; Tajov; person/tent 90/50Sk; ☼ year-round) The nearest camp site, 7km west of town, has a lovely rural setting among pine trees. There are 20 tent sites and 16 bungalows (per person 200Sk).

Penzión Kúria (☎ 412 3255; www.kuria.sk; Bakossova 4; s/d 800/1200Sk; P) The atmospheric, old-world feel means this *pension* is often booked by groups.

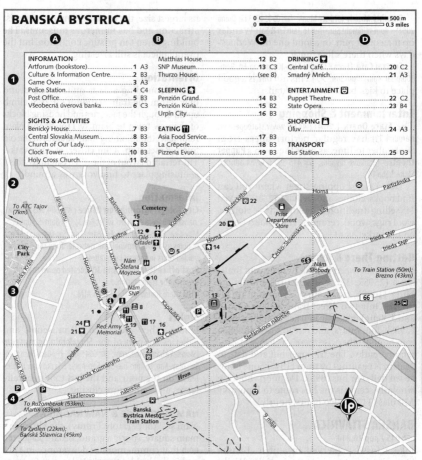

BANSKÁ BYSTRICA

INFORMATION		
Artforum (bookstore)	1	A3
Culture & Information Centre	2	B3
Game Over	3	A3
Police Station	4	C4
Post Office	5	B3
Všeobecná úverová banka	6	C3

SIGHTS & ACTIVITIES		
Benický House	7	B3
Central Slovakia Museum	8	B3
Church of Our Lady	9	B3
Clock Tower	10	B3
Holy Cross Church	11	B2
Matthias House	12	B2
SNP Museum	13	C3
Thurzo House	(see 8)	

SLEEPING		
Penzión Grand	14	B3
Penzión Kúria	15	B3
Urpín City	16	B3

EATING		
Asia Food Service	17	B3
La Crêperie	18	B3
Pizzeria Evuo	19	B3

DRINKING		
Central Café	20	C2
Smadný Mních	21	A3

ENTERTAINMENT		
Puppet Theatre	22	C2
State Opera	23	B4

SHOPPING		
Úľuv	24	A3

TRANSPORT		
Bus Station	25	D3

CENTRAL SLOVAKIA

Penzión Grand (☎ 415 5173; www.penziongrand.sk; Horná 32; s/d 800/1200Sk; P) Younger cousin to Kúria, this *pension* is lighter on the outside but still has the gorgeous, rustic dark wood panelling in the rooms.

Urpín City (☎ 472 3511; www.urpincity.sk; Cikkerova 5; s/d 1950/2950Sk; P) This is the ultimate in *urpín* (urban) minimalism. The wi-fi enabled lounge, restaurant, bar and bedrooms all have a sleek, Zenlike appeal, with low-lying beds and wheat grass as decoration. Apartments are available on a nightly or long-term basis.

Eating & Drinking
Nám SNP has several attractive outdoor cafés to choose from, for Slovak specialities, head to the folk knick-knack–filled restaurant at Penzión Kúria.

Asia Food Service (☎ 415 3358; Národná 9; mains 55-110Sk; 11am-10.30pm Mon-Fri, 4-10pm Sat) Chinese staples are served from the counter front. There are a few steely bar tables and counters to chow down at in this tiny modern eatery.

La Crêperie (Passage Arkade; mains 60-100Sk; 9am-10pm) Think of some doughy delight you can stuff – crepes, dumplings, potato pancakes – and you can get it here, both sweet and savoury. The café also has internet access.

Pizzeria Evuo (☎ 415 2752; Nám SNP 8; pizzas 100-150Sk) Just the aroma from this pizzeria is fattening, and the pizza tastes even better than it smells. The entrance is on Národná.

Smadný Mních (Thirsty Monk; ☎ 0905421317; Dolná 20; ☺ 4pm-midnight Sun-Thu, to 1am Fri & Sat) Wander up for a quiet pint, or a loud one on Wednesdays when there's live music.

Central Café (Horná 37; ☺ 7am-10pm Mon-Fri, 9am-10pm Sat, 4pm-10pm Sun; ☒) This hip bar is a good place to kick back with a cocktail.

Entertainment & Shopping

The **State Opera** (☎ 412 4418; www.stateopera.sk; Národná 11) has regular performances from September to June, as does the town's **Puppet theatre** (Bábkové divadlo; ☎ 415 3023; www.bdnr.sk; Skutečkého 14).

Dolná is a shopping street where you can find books, clothes and an **Úľuv** (☎ 4841 241; Dolná 14) selling traditional handicrafts – clothes, wool rugs, wood, ceramics, embroidery – with an upmarket slant.

Getting There & Away

Buses run between Banská Bystrica and Bratislava (250Sk, 3½ to 4½ hours), mostly via Nitra (160Sk, two hours), every one to 1½ hours. Only two direct trains a day (6.15am and 3.30pm) make the journey from Bratislava (292Sk, four hours) and one to Košice (292Sk, four hours), otherwise there's a change at Zvolen or Vrútky. The trip over hill and dale to Martin is beautiful by train (104Sk, one hour, seven daily) or bus (89Sk, 1¼ hours, hourly); similarly scenic is the bus route to Liptovský Mikuláš (117Sk, two hours, hourly).

BANSKÁ ŠTIAVNICA

☎ 045 / pop 10,814

Like a fossil preserved in amber, Banská Štiavnica is a town frozen in time. Walking up and down among the steep hillsides crowded with town buildings, churches, alleys and stairways, you can't help but get a sense of another era (unless you're distracted by the exertion of climbing through town). Look across the deep valley from the old castle to the new and contemplate whether the view alone wasn't worth the effort.

Banská Štiavnica began as a medieval mining centre, exploiting some of Europe's richest gold and silver veins. Already a showcase town in the 13th century, in its 18th-century heyday it became Hungary's second-largest town. But then the mines began to dry up, and the town slipped out of the flow of time. In 1972 Banská Štiavnica was added to the Unesco World Heritage List. Today, at half its largest size, the town is primarily a tourist attraction and has numerous museums. The buildings aren't in pristine condition, but the overall effect is still arresting.

Orientation

The surrounding area is quite wooded and hilly. From the train station it's a 2km climb uphill through the factories and housing blocks of the new town to Nám sv Trojice and Nám Radničné, the adjoining main squares in the old town. Buses stop 500m closer, at Križovatka. The terraced layout of the town can make this a confusing place to find your way around.

Information

City Tourist Information Office (☎ 694 9653; www .banskastiavnica.sk; Nám sv Trojice 3; ☺ 8am-5.30pm May-Sep, 8am-4pm Mon-Fri, 8am-2pm Sat Oct-Apr) Also doubles as a two-terminal internet café. They can arrange guided tours in several languages.

Post office (Kammerhofská 30) Located down the hill towards the train station.

VÚB (Nám Radničné 15) Has an ATM.

Sights

Unless otherwise stated, all museums and galleries are part of the **Slovak mining museum** (Slovenské banské múzeum; ☎ 694 9422; ☺ 8am-5pm Mon-Sun May-Aug, to 4pm Tue-Sun Sep-Apr). Museum tours leave on the hour and the last tour generally leaves an hour before closing.

NÁM SV TROJICE & NÁM RADNIČNÉ

Nám sv Trojice (Holy Trinity), the old town's main square, sports a grand, ornate **plague column** that commemorates deliverance in 1711 and is flanked by the old palaces of German and Hungarian merchants and mine owners. Behind the bold sgraffito at No 12 is the **Jozef Kollár gallery** (adult/student 40/20Sk), which exhibits 13th-century Gothic to modern art, with emphasis on local Slovak painter Jozef Kollár. At No 6 is the **Mineral museum** (adult/student 40/20Sk), with more than 400 minerals from around the world and a historical mine mock-up.

At the bottom of the square, opposite the pastel-yellow house with mining motifs, the Gothic parish **Church of St Catherine** (Kostol sv Kateríny) still has some original murals and statues among the baroque furnishings. A little further southwest is the **town hall** (radnica) with a backwards clock, and across Nám Radničné a richly decorated 18th-century **Evangelical church** (Evanjelický kostol). Miners'

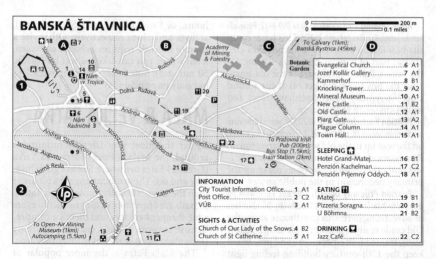

BANSKÁ ŠTIAVNICA

0   200 m
0   0.1 miles

Evangelical Church	6	A1
Jozef Kollár Gallery	7	A1
Kammerhof	8	B1
Knocking Tower	9	A2
Mineral Museum	10	A1
New Castle	11	B2
Old Castle	12	A1
Piarg Gate	13	A2
Plague Column	14	A1
Town Hall	15	A1

SLEEPING
Hotel Grand-Matej	16	B1
Penzión Kachelman	17	C2
Penzión Príjemný Oddych	18	A1

EATING
Matej	19	B1
Pizzeria Soragna	20	B1
U Böhmna	21	B2

DRINKING
Jazz Café	22	C2

INFORMATION
City Tourist Information Office	1	A1
Post Office	2	C2
VÚB	3	A1

SIGHTS & ACTIVITIES
Church of Our Lady of the Snows	4	B2
Church of St Catherine	5	A1

houses line the back alleys behind the main buildings.

Uphill from the town square is Banská Štiavnica's ancient heart, the **Old castle** (Starý zámok; adult/student 60/30Sk). Between 1546 and 1559 an older Romanesque church was walled in, revamped and fortified to protect the municipal riches from the Turks, who never conquered the town. It houses baroque sculpture and historical town exhibits.

NEW CASTLE & AROUND
At No 7, on the way up on Andreja Sládkovičova to the castle, you pass a tearoom in the 1681 **knocking tower** (klopačka) – a sort of town alarm clock used to signal the miners' shifts and special events.

Five years after the Old castle was finished, the burghers evidently decided they needed more protection on the hill opposite, thus the strikingly simple **New castle** (Nový zámok; Novozámocká; adult/student 50/20Sk), a whitewashed block with four corner towers. It contains a 'Museum of the History of the Struggle against the Turks on the Territory of Slovakia' and has fine views over the town.

To the east of the castle is the **Church of Our Lady of the Snows** (Kostol Panny Márie Snežnej) and the 15th-century **Piarg gate** (Piargska brána) that was one of six portals in the walls dividing the inner and outer town.

OTHER ATTRACTIONS
A former mining camp 1.25km south of the city centre is set up as the **Open-air Mining mu-**seum (Banské múzeum v prírode; JK Hella 12; adult/student 80/30Sk). Take a trip down the mine, and check out the machinery, workshops and a wooden miners' church.

Kammerhof (Kammerhofská 2; adult/student 40/20Sk) is yet another museum devoted to mining, this time dealing with its technical history. The working models of mining machines are its most intriguing displays.

About 1km northeast of the old town is the 1751 **Calvary** (Kalvária). Here baroque chapels with wood carvings illustrate the Stations of the Cross (14 images of the last stages of Jesus Christ's life before his crucifixion). The largest red-and-white chapel is visible for miles around and the site has understandably great vistas.

Festivals & Events
The annual three-day festival of **Salamander** starts on the Friday evening closest to 12 September. The townspeople dress up in miners' clothing and medieval garb and perform songs and dances. Events include a market, a beer day and arm-wrestling contests. The origins of the festival can be traced back to the 19th-century mining academy student ceremonies. This is one of Slovakia's best local festivals and is worth staying for the weekend.

Sleeping
The info office keeps a big list of private rooms and penzión; many line Kammerhofská and Andreja Sládkovičova.

Autocamping (☎ 0904668340 or 699 4112; Počúvad-lianske jazero 43; sites per tent 200Sk) This basic camp sits beside one of several artificial lakes created as part of a water-pumping scheme for the mines, 5.5km southwest of the old town. Take the bus to Levice, get off at the second stop (Štiavnické Bane, Rychnava rázc) and walk 1km south to the camp.

Penzión Kachelman (☎ 692 2319; www.kachelman .sk; Kammerhofská 18; r 990Sk; P) Front and centre on the way up to the old town is a large, square Renaissance building-turned-30-bed inn. Antlers and other hunting trophies make up the primary decoration in the public spaces.

Penzión Príjemný Oddych (☎ 692 1301; www.pri jemnyoddych.sk; Starozámocká 3; r 1100Sk; P ✗) No lies in advertising here; this guesthouse above the Old castle really is *príjemný* (pleasing). Yellow walls, framed folk embroidery and pine wood keep the 17th-century building feeling light and fresh. In addition to the restaurant, there's a garden playground and a sauna for guests.

Hotel Grand-Matej (☎ 692 1232; www.grandmatej.sk; Kammerhofská 8; s/d 950/1790Sk; P) With flags flying and window boxes in bloom, the Grand-Matej has an air of formality; it is indeed the grandest option in town. It rents bicycles for 300Sk a day.

Eating & Drinking

Pizzeria Soragna (☎ 691 2001; Akademická 9; pizzas 90-120Sk) A favourite among the pizza choices. A large terrace doubles seating capacity (from 30 to 76), but it's often still packed in summer.

Matej (☎ 691 2051; Akademická 4; mains 100-150Sk) Not the grand hotel, but the little Matej restaurant across from it is the best option for Slovak food in town. Dine on the green, shaded terrace.

U Böhmna (☎ 0903525022; Strieborná 7; mains 100-250Sk) Spoon into some really good homemade soups like the *kapustnica* (cabbage and sausage). Wild game is also on the menu.

For something a bit stronger, try the **Pražovná Irish Pub** (☎ 692 0076; Kammerhofská 12; ☽ 11am-midnight Mon-Thu, to 1am Fri & Sat), which attracts a rowdy, bra-bearing young crowd, and the quieter **Jazz Café** (Kammerhofská 12; ☽ 11am-midnight Mon-Thu, to 1am Fri & Sat).

There's also a grocery store at the bus stop.

Getting There & Away

Banská Štiavnica is not the easiest place to get to without your own transport. Only one bus daily departs from Bratislava (230Sk, 3½ hours) or Banská Bystrica (74Sk, 1¼ hours), at 1pm and 11am respectively. Otherwise a train or bus ride requires a change at Zvolen, from where you can take a direct bus (47Sk, 50 minutes); nine buses depart on weekdays but only one on Sunday.

MALÁ & VEĽKÁ FATRA

By far the most user-friendly mountains around, the Malá (Lesser) Fatra and Veľká (Greater) Fatra are where Slovaks go to hike, bike and ski. These mountains are a bit lower than the internationally known High Tatras, so trails are open more of the year. Services are a bit cheaper here too, and there's a comprehensive network of trails, chairlifts and *chaty* (mountain huts) scattered throughout.

The Malá Fatra is the more popular of the two mountain groups (despite the name, its peaks rise higher than those of the Veľká Fatra). The Váh river slices the Malá Fatra into two parts – the rounded Lúčanská Fatra west of Martin and the craggy Krivánská Fatra to the northeast. Most of the Krivánská Fatra is now the Malá Fatra National Park, centred on what many claim to be the most beautiful valley in Slovakia, Vrátna.

Žilina to the north, and folk culture–rich Martin between the ranges are the largest towns.

ŽILINA

☎ 041 / pop 85,268

A Slavic tribe in the 6th century was the first to recognise Žilina's advantageous location at the intersection of several important trade routes on the Váh river. Today travellers see it as a base for exploring the Malá Fatra National Park (p380), area fortresses and folk villages. Even Martin can be a day trip. In town, besides the old palacelike castle on the outskirts, there aren't a lot of sights, but the place has a lively young vibe and good, reasonable restaurants, because of the university population.

Žilina grew around a fortress in the middle ages. An influential compendium of principles on civic rights and obligations, written here in 1370, might be the oldest existing text in the Slovak language.

The town was occupied by the Hussites from 1429 to 1434 and, after being ravaged by the Thirty Years' War, faded away until the railway brought industrialisation in the late 19th century. Today both the country's main motorway and the main Bratislava–Kosice train line pass through here.

Orientation

Žilina is 64km northeast of Trenčín. From the train station the shopping street Národná leads into the old market square, Hlinkovo nám. Marble stairs and narrow Farská climb from here into the old town, centred on Mariánské nám. From the south end of the bus station, follow Jána Milca northwest to Národná.

Information

CK Selinan (☎ 562 0789; www.zilina.sk; Burianova medzierka 4; 8am-5pm Mon-Fri) Ample information about Žilina and the Malá Fatra, including hiking maps.

Internet Caffe (☎ 0903522226; Bottova 12; per min 1.5Sk; 10am-10pm Mon-Fri, 2-10pm Sat & Sun) Full bar adjacent.

Left luggage office (per item per day 30Sk; 6.30am-11pm) At train station.

Ľudová banka (Národná 28) ATM and exchange.

Post office (Hviezdoslava)

Sights

North across the Váh river, the **Budatín castle** (Budatínsky zámok; ☎ 562 0033; Topoľová 1; adult/student 50/30Sk; 9am-5.15pm Tue-Sun Jul & Aug, to 4pm Apr-Jun, Sep & Oct) dates from at least the 13th century, when its Romanesque central tower was built. The Renaissance palace was part of a face-lift in 1551. (The last restoration was in 1920.) Inside, the **Považské museum** includes an unusual tinkers' trade exhibition with naive art figures of metal and wire, as well as displays on period furniture, church art and early history. Take bus 21 from the train station; otherwise it's a 20-minute walk from Hviezdoslava.

The old town square of Mariánské nám is completely surrounded by arcaded burghers' houses, which are intruded upon by the Jesuits' baroque **St Paul's church** (kostol sv Pavla), built in 1743. The fountain and open-air cafés make this a fine place to pause over coffee and cake.

Považská gallery (☎ 562 6931; www.pgu.sk; Štefánikova 2; adult/student 30/10Sk; 9am-5pm Tue-Fri, 10am-5pm Sat & Sun), on the southern side of the wide open Hlinkovo nám, displays thought-provoking contemporary art and has a suitably dark, smoky café attached.

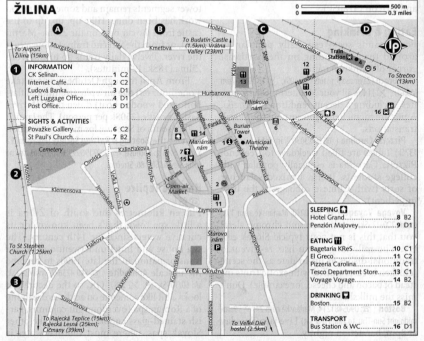

ŽILINA

St Stephen Church (Kostol sv Štefana; ☎ 0903116624; Závodská cesta; ◷ services 10am Sun or by appointment) is one of the earliest Romanesque churches; the most ancient parts, including some frescoes rediscovered in the 1950s, date from around 1250. It's 1.25km southwest of the centre.

Sleeping

The information office has a list of private rooms for rent (about 300Sk per person) and student dorms that take summer travellers.

Velký Diel (☎ 500 5249; kadorova@dm.utc.sk; Žilinská univerzita, Vysokoškolákov 20; dm 300-500Sk; ✗) A student dorm open to travellers during July and August, Veľký Diel is worth contacting year-round in case it has a vacancy. Take tram 1 from the bus or train station.

Penzión Majovey (☎ 562 4152, fax 5625 239; Jána Milca 3; s/d 1000/1750Sk; breakfast 100Sk) The deep coral colour outside is more interesting than the stark white inside, but the bathrooms are huge and the tiled floors keep things cool.

Hotel Grand (☎ 562 6809; www.hotelgrand.sk; Sládkovičova 1; s/d 1590/2630Sk; Ⓟ) The floor-to-ceiling windows brighten up the bland rooms in this 90-year-old hotel off the main square. Go deluxe and ask for one with a whirlpool tub and air-con (3180Sk).

Eating & Drinking

Food stands seem especially popular all around town, including on the northeast corner of Hlinkovo nám.

El Greco (Zaymusa 8; mains 90-160Sk; ◷ 10.30am-7pm Mon-Fri; ✗) Has all your Mediterranean favourites, including a decent rendition of *tzatziki*. A picture menu helps you sort out the Slovak translations.

Pizzeria Carolina (☎ 500 3030; Národná 5; pizzas 98-137Sk) Tables are filled weekdays to weekend; Pizzeria Carolina is especially popular with college students. It has a mixed salad bar of sorts (with Chinese cabbage as the base ingredient).

Voyage Voyage (☎ 564 0230; Mariánske nám 191; mains 100-175Sk) Sleek neon and chrome alerts you that this is not your typical Slovak eatery. The mile-long menu lists re-invented traditional dishes as up-to-date as the scene (chicken breasts stuffed with exotic fruits instead of bacon and cheese, for example). Don't miss the milkshakes.

Boston (☎ 0905481214; Mariánské nám 24; ◷ 9am-midnight Sun-Thu, to 2am Fri & Sat) Live jazz Tuesday at 8pm; bar action nightly.

Self-caterers head to the **Tesco Department Store** (Hlinkovo nám), but the **Bagetaria KReS** (cnr Národná & Jána Milca; sandwiches 30-60Sk, hot dishes 60-80Sk; ◷ 8am-7pm Mon-Sat) is almost as cheap.

Getting There & Away

The main train line goes from Bratislava (268Sk, 2¾ hours, 12 daily), through Trenčín (180Sk, one hour, 20 daily) to Žilina, and on to Poprad (200Sk, two hours, 17 daily) and Košice (316Sk, three hours, 10 daily). Buses are quicker and more useful for smaller, regional destinations.

Airport Žilina (ILZ; ☎ 552 3288; www.letisko.sk), 15km west of the centre, has one daily flight: six days a week, Sunday through Friday, to and from Prague. Buses to the airport go from bus station stand No 1.

AROUND ŽILINA

Rising dramatically on a rocky outcropping, **Strečno castle** (☎ 041-569 7400; adult/student 50/30Sk; ◷ 9am-5pm May-Sep, to 4pm Oct) stands guard over the Váh river, 13km east of Žilina on the road to Martin. The fortress, built in the 14th century by warlord Matúš Čák, has been in ruins for three centuries, but sizeable wall and tower segments remain and some restoration work has been done. Hike up, up, up to the castle from the car park on the Žilina–Martin road, or from the Strečno train station across the river. Twelve daily trains go to and from Žilina (18Sk, 12 minutes).

From April through October you can take a one-hour **raft ride** on a *plte* (traditional flat-bottomed wooden boat) down the Váh river past the castle (250Sk per person). The launch is 7km south of Strečno; for more information contact the **Boating & Rafting Society** (Prvá pltnícka a raftingová spoločnosť; ☎ 0907196999; http://plte.strecno .sk in Slovak; SNP 86, Strečno).

Rajecké Teplice
☎ 041

Fifteen kilometres due south of Žilina is a little spa town that's been known for its curative waters since the 14th century. The spa house and hotel underwent a complete transformation in the late 1990s to become the upscale **Aphrodite** (☎ 549 4256-7; www.spa.sk; s/d 60/109Sk; Ⓟ ✗ ⊠). OK, so the decoration looks a bit like someone on acid was dreaming of a Roman spa (overdone gilt columns, garish stained-glass cupola…) But unlike other Slovak spas, where most thermal water is reserved for individual services, here they have different temperature public pools (200Sk for two hours, free for hotel guests) meandering among the marble and palm trees. 'Sauna World' (300Sk for two hours) includes entry to steamy eucalyptus rooms, salt and herbal saunas, as well as regular wet and dry steam rooms.

Private accommodation and restaurants cluster around the small village lake. The **Tourist Information Office** (☎ 549 4366; Osloboditeľov 90; www.rajeckapohoda.sk; ⏰ 8.30-11.30am & 12.30-6pm) has a welcoming little store and a comprehensive website. From Žilina, trains (18Sk, 33 minutes) and buses (22Sk, 30 minutes) zoom in at least nine times a day.

Rajecká Lesná
☎ 041

Further up the hill, the tiny village of Rajecká Lesná is insignificant except for the **Slovak Bethlehem** (Slovenský betlehem; admission by donation; ⏰ 9am-noon & 1-6pm), a 10m wood-carved tableau of the Nativity interweaves with tiny animated figures illustrating Slovak rural life. Local carver Jozef Pekara began the project in the early 1980s. The tableau is next to the church – follow signs from the bus stop. Up to 10 daily buses from Žilina (36Sk, 39 minutes) stop here on the way to Čičmany (14Sk, 10 minutes), but few go midday.

Čičmany
☎ 041

Famed for a 200-year-old custom of painting its wooden cottages in patterns based on traditional embroidery motifs, **Čičmany** (www .cicmany.viapvt.sk) is a photographer's dream. The ubiquitous white graphic patterns on dark log houses are a striking example of living folk art. Varnishing the logs brown or black is part of a centuries-old preservation process. The white stripes and squiggles that repetitively cover every spare inch are purely decorative. Blooms in the spring flower boxes add a festive splash of colour to photos, but then again, the white snow in this mountain village is quite the contrast.

Most of the decorated log buildings are still homes, but one, **Radenov dom** (Čičmany 42; adult/student 40/20SK; ⏰ 8am-6pm Tue-Sun) is a branch of the Považie museum. Old furnishings, embroidered snow-white folk dresses, and local handiwork for sale are inside. Embroidered linens were originally part of elaborate

dowries that accompanied a new bride. So important was this skill that an embroidery needle was put in a baby girl's bath to ensure she would become skilled at the art. Across the road is a reconstructed two-family house (included in the museum entry) traditionally outfitted.

You can rent out a couple of the *drevenica* (wood cottage). One has been turned into the **Penzión Katka** (☎ 549 2132; penzionkatka@stonline .sk; r without bathroom per person 290-370Sk), near the museum.

At least five buses from Žilina (47Sk, one hour) stop at Čičmany on their way to Prievidza (51Sk, one hour), near Bojnice castle. Another five turn immediately around and head back to Žilina. Get off the bus as soon as you see the first of the log buildings and walk up. Day trippers take note, there may be a lapse of several hours between buses – especially around midday and on weekends.

BOJNICE
☎ 046

Could Walt Disney have built Bojnice castle, or maybe crazy King Ludwig? No? Well, the Pálffy family, owners from the 1600s to 1945, must have had a well-developed imagination. The elaborate crenulations and cylindrical towers are straight out of a fairy tale, and at festival time the costumed guides spin some fanciful tales. Slovakia's pre-eminent romanticised castle is the main attraction in the village of Bojnice, above Prievidza.

Orientation & Information

The nearest train and bus stations are 2.5km east of Bojnice in the town of Prievidza. Local buses from Prievidza stop at Bojnice's main square, Hurbanovo nám, just below the castle.

The **Tourist Information Office** (☎ 540 3251; tik .bojnice@stonline.sk; Hurbanovo nám 19; ⏰ 8am-7pm) is approximately 200m east of the castle. There are a couple of ATMs on the main square and a **post office** on Sládkovičova.

Sights

The ornate exterior is your first clue that **Bojnice castle** (Bojnický zámok; ☎ 543 0633; www.bojnice castle.sk; adult/student 130/50Sk; ⏰ 9am-5pm Tue-Sun May, Jun & Sep; 9am-5pm Jul & Aug; 10am-3pm Tue-Sun Oct-Apr) is not the original 12th-century Gothic structure. It's an early 20th-century reconstruction modelled on the romantic style. Nevertheless, a few remains of the original Gothic and

Renaissance parts of the castle survive within the present structure.

The castle has the usual exhibits of furniture, paintings, statues, weapons, glass and porcelain in lavishly decorated rooms. Highlights include the Bojnice Altar, the only surviving complete work of Italian painter Nardo di Cione, the Golden Hall, with its gilded ceiling and a small cave system, some 26m below the courtyard, complete with its own well.

The time to visit is during one of the many festivals and night-time tours, the biggest of which is the **International Festival of Spirits and Ghosts** (adult/student 200/70Sk) for a week in May, which attracts as many as 3000 a day. Costumed guides re-enact legends and put on performances throughout the castle grounds. The place also gets decked out for Christmas, Valentine's Day and medieval events, among others; check the website for schedules. Queues get very long on weekends and holidays, so arrive early.

Sleeping & Eating

Numerous small guesthouses line the streets around the castle and most have restaurants. This is a tourist town after all.

Camping Bojnice (☎ 541 3845; person/tent/car/bungalow 140/100/100/1080Sk; ❤ mid-May–mid-Sep) Pine trees rise above the camp site 2km west of Bojnice on the bus route to Nitrianske rudno; A-frame huts (700Sk for three) are completely shaded. There's a small buffet on site.

> ### YOU SAY CASTLE, I SAY POTATO
>
> In Slovak, as in German, there are two words for the English equivalent of 'castle' – a cause for much confusion when translating. A *hrad*, like the German *burg*, was a highly fortified medieval residence; a *zámok*, like the German *schloss*, was primarily a palace-like structure with less defensive intent. The latter are often translated in English as *châteaux*, which isn't quite accurate as in Slovakia these buildings rarely resemble their French counterparts. In Slovakia they call both 'castle' and just know that one is fancier than the other. A *kaštieľ*, on the other hand, is a manor house or mansion, and a *palác*, a palace – usually in town. At least that's straightforward enough.

Hotel Lipa (☎ 543 0308; www.hotel-lipa-bojnice.sk; Sládkovičova 20; s/d 900/1300Sk; **P**) Peach walls set off simply elegant carved-wood beds at Hotel Lipa. The playground on the hillside terrace is full of laughing children in summer.

Penzión Bojnice (☎ 540 2141; www.penzionbojnice .sk; Prievidzská 39; s/d 700/1000Sk; **P**) Odd how some pastel paint and flowers can liven up a concrete box. The modern rooms are fresh too, and the accommodating staff will make you dinner upon request.

There are several eateries and cafés on Hurbanovo nám, including **Pálfyho Pizzeria** (☎ 543 1888; Hurbanovo nám 5; pizzas 110-150Sk), with large pizzas and views of the castle.

Getting There & Away

There is one direct bus a day from Bratislava (354Sk, 3¾ hours, 6.15am) to Bojnice. Nearby Prievidza has more connections from Bratislava (208Sk, 3¼ hours, 10 daily), as well as Žilina (89Sk, 1¼ hours, 10 daily) and Banská Bystrica (119Sk, 1½ hours, 15 daily). Local bus 3 takes you to the castle.

The only place of interest you can get to easily by train from Prievidza is Nitra (98Sk, 2½ hours, 11 daily).

MALÁ FATRA NATIONAL PARK
☎ 041
Precipitous peaks top the pine-clad slopes and sentinel-like formations stand watch at the rocky gorge entrance. The beautiful Vrátna valley is the focus of the 198-sq-km Malá Fatra National Park. The area contains some of the most accessible high-altitude walking in Slovakia, Veľký Kriváň (1709m) being the tallest peak, and services galore.

Terchová
The long village of Terchová is known for more than just being the lower entrance to the Vrátna valley (though it is a good base to gather info and maps). It was the birthplace of one of Slovakia's favourite folk heroes, Juraj Jánošík (p382), in 1688.

The **Tourist Information Centre Terchová** (☎ 569 5307; www.ztt.sk; Sv Cyrila a Metoda 96; ❤ 9am-6pm) has hiking, cycling and ski trail maps, souvenirs, and internet access for 100Sk per hour. Next door is an ATM.

Above the village of Terchová is an immense aluminium **statue of Juraj Jánošík**, and west of the village bus stop next to the *Obecný úrad* (village office) is a little branch of **Považke**

CENTRAL SLOVAKIA

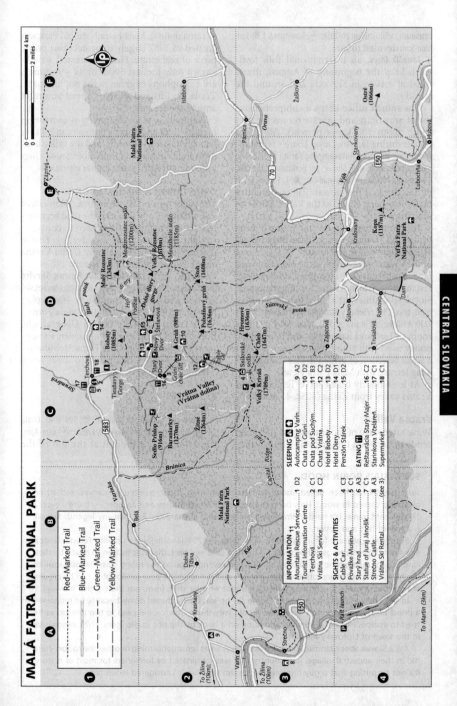

MALÁ FATRA NATIONAL PARK

Legend

- - - - Red-Marked Trail
- - - - Blue-Marked Trail
- - - - Green-Marked Trail
- - - - Yellow-Marked Trail

0   4 km
0   2 miles

CENTRAL SLOVAKIA

INFORMATION
Mountain Rescue Service	1 D2
Tourist Information Centre	
Terchová	2 C1
Vrátna Ski Service	3 C2

SIGHTS & ACTIVITIES
Cable Car	4 C3
Považke Museum	5 C1
Starý hrad	6 A3
Statue of Juraj Jánošík	7 C1
Strečno Castle	8 A3
Vrátna Ski Rental	(see 3)

SLEEPING
Autocamping Varín	9 A2
Chata na Grúni	10 D2
Chata pod Suchým	11 B3
Chata Vrátna	12 C2
Hotel Boboty	13 C2
Hotel Diery	14 D1
Penzión Starek	15 D2

EATING
Reštaurácia Starý Majer	16 C2
Starinkova Vceláreň	17 C1
Supermarket	18 C1

museum (adult/student 20/10Sk; ☺ 9am-1pm & 1.30-3pm Mon-Sun) devoted to him.

Jánošík Days, an international folk festival held at the beginning of August, draws musical acts from Slovakia and around the world.

The tourist office keeps a comprehensive list of area *chaty* and private rooms for rent (both about 300Sk per person). All prices double during Jánošík Days. There's no camping in the park, so **Autocamping Varín** (☎ 562 1478; Varín; www.selikan.sk in Slovak; per person/tent 75/75Sk, 4-person hut 1000Sk; ☺ May–mid-Oct; ☒), 15km west of Terchová, is the closest. Žilina–Terchová buses pass here; get off at the Varín, Konhora rázc stop.

It's more interesting to stay in the Vrátna valley, but if you're stuck, **Hotel Diery** (☎ 569 5322; www.hotel-diery.sk; s/d 850/1200Sk; ℗), 1km east of the Vrátna valley road, is the old-fashioned favourite because of its log-lined *koliba* (rustic restaurant with an open fire, serving traditional Slovak specialities). It's at the base of a hiking trail, too. The friendly **Starinkova Včeláreň** (☎ 599 3130; A Hlinku 246; snacks 20-50Sk, mains 100-150Sk) tea-room in Terchová has scones and homemade honey to go with your brew. You can also get a small selection of grilled dishes to enjoy on a big terrace with Malá Fatra views.

At least hourly buses serve Terchová and Vrátna valley from Žilina (40Sk, 45 minutes).

Vrátna Valley

Wave after wave of mountains rise to a crescendo in the peaks that encircle Vrátna valley (Vrátna dolina). Malá Fatra National Park was created in 1987 largely to protect this prime piece of real estate. Heavily forested – rock-strewn only the last 500m or so – summers are a symphony of green in the popular park. Trails, ski lifts and a cable car put you right among the scenery.

Naturally, a place this pretty is overrun in high summer and winter, but you can hike far enough to lose the crowds, and the valley is almost empty in May and September. Snow hangs around until April at the higher elevations.

ORIENTATION & INFORMATION

The valley turn-off is at Terchová, 25km east of Žilina. South from Terchová the road branches left to the hamlet of Štefanová; continue straight and Starý Dvor is midvalley. You've reached the top of the valley at Chata Vrátna about 5km from the highway turn-off.

Check with the **Mountain Rescue Service** (Horská služba; ☎ 569 5232, Štefanová; http://his.hzs.sk/) for trail and weather conditions. If you plan to hike, get the VKÚ's 1:50,000 *Malá Fatra – Vrátna* map (sheet No 110) or Geografische Boekhandel Jacob van Wijngaarden's *Knapsacked Travel in The Malá Fatra Mountains*.

For trail and lodging info online, www .vratna.sk is the best.

ACTIVITIES
Hiking

A **cable car** (kabínkova lanovka; ☎ 599 3049; Chata Vrátna; adult/student one way 250/170Sk; ☺ 8am-4pm) runs from above the hut at the top of the

---

SLOVAKIA'S ROBIN HOOD

Juraj Jánošík has been talked about, written about, sung about, painted on canvas, etched on glass and carved in wood. He's been the subject of three movies and an opera – there's even a Jánošík card game. It's hard to imagine a bigger national character. But, like any legend, Jánošík is a mix of fact and fiction.

Born into a peasant family in Terchová in 1688, in 1703 Jánošík joined up with Ferenc Rákóczi II to fight the Habsburgs. While away his mother died and his father was beaten to death by their landlord for taking time off to bury her. Vowing revenge against the ruling class, Jánošík took to the hills and spent years robbing from the rich and giving to the poor (although it can be argued that he didn't make much of a distinction about who he stole from, nor did he give it away).

In 1713 he was captured in a pub. (Some say he was finally chased down because he murdered a priest he stole from.) Story goes that an old lady threw down some peas to trip him up as he tried to escape. He was sentenced and hung on a hook by the ribs to die (gory, eh?) somewhere in the town of Liptovský Mikuláš.

Ask a Slovak about Jánošík and you'll likely hear what sensational thing or other the robber-hero did in their ancestral village. In a country that was dominated by foreigners for most of history, it's not surprising that a guy fighting the system (maybe) is considered legendary.

valley to **Snilovské sedlo** (1524m) below two peaks, **Chleb** (1647m) and **Veľký Kriváň** (1709m). It's about a half-hour climb to either summit and both are on the red, 43km-long **Capital Ridge trail** (Hlávný hrebeň) that stretches the length of the range. From Chleb you could walk north to **Poludňový grúň** (1636m), then head northwest, passing Chata na Grúni and ending at Starý Dvor, where there's a bus stop, restaurants and services. From the cable car that would be about a four-hour journey. Or continue on from Poludňový grúň to **Medziholie sedlo** (1185m) and descend to Štefanová village (six hours from the cable car).

One of the most beautiful, and most demanding, hikes is the trail from Štefanová (at about 620m) east to Medziholie sedlo, and then up over **Veľký Rozsutec** (1610m), with some steep sections that have ladders and chains. (Note: the trail is closed from 1 October to 30 June.) An easier return trail leads east to **Medzirozsutec sedlo** (1200m) then down through the **Dolné diery gorge** and back to Štefanová, crossing a stream several times. It's a 5½ hour loop.

For those with more time you could do the ridge in three days, starting at Zázriva bus stop, stopping the first night at Chata na Grúni (seven hours) and the second at Chata pod Suchým (eight hours), passing the freely accessible ruins of **Starý hrad** (old castle) before ending at Strečno (p378).

About as easy at it gets is the 1½ hour interpretative nature trail between Štefanová village and Hotel Diery in Terchová.

Skiing

The Vrátna valley is one of the more popular winter destinations in Slovakia. The ski centre encompasses a total of 14 ski tows, a winter-only chairlift, a year-round cable car and almost 13km of prepared ski runs, open December to April. A day-pass costs 680Sk for adults and 480Sk for children under 15. Buy your ticket from the **Vrátna Ski Service** (Lyžiarska stredisko Vrátna; ☎ 569 5055; www.vratna.sk) in Starý Dvor; look for the big car park and the *kasa* (cashier) on the left side midway up the valley. Next door there's a shack with **ski rental** (per pair 300Sk; ☉ 8am-4pm), and the biggest ski area is just above.

Sleeping

There's no free camping allowed in the park; the closest is Autocamping Varín (opposite). The Tourist Information Centre Terchová has

lists of private rooms for rent (from 300Sk per person) on its website (www.ztt.sk), as does www.vratna.com.

Chata Vrátna (☎ 569 5739; www.vratna.sk/chata vratna/; dm 220Sk, d with shared bathroom 760Sk; P) Muddy hikers, giggling children and fragrant wood smoke fill this well-worn, chalet-style outfit at the top of Vrátna valley.

Penzión Stárek (☎ 569 5359; www.penzionstarek .sk; Štefanová 124; r per person 400-540Sk; ✕) A warm and welcoming eight room log cabin. You'll often find the owner's family gathered at the restaurant's outdoor picnic tables.

Hotel Boboty (☎ 569 5228; www.hotelboboty.sk; Nový Dvor; s 800Sk, d 900-1900Sk; P ✕ 🖳 🖳) Skyscraping windows in the dining room create tremendous vistas of forests and mountains beyond, in a clean-line contemporary style. Expect services galore, including sauna, massage, billiards, a free ski shuttle and some in-room internet connections. From the bus stop at Nový Dvor walk five minutes north in the direction of Štefanová.

Up on the mountain trails, there are several hikers lodges. On the western end of the Capital Ridge trail is the 40-bed **Chata pod Suchým** (☎ 569 7394; s/d 200/400Sk). In the valley below Poludňový grúň, near the upper terminus of the Paseky chairlift, **Chata na Grúni** (☎ 569 5324; www.chatanagruni.sk; per person 270Sk) has four- to six-bed rooms with shared facilities and a self-service restaurant.

Eating

The food situation in the park is pretty bleak; most Slovaks bring their own. There are takeaway stands at Starý Dvor and there's a **supermarket** (*potraviny*) at the valley turn-off in Terchová. Farm implements decorate the walls at **Reštaurácia Starý Majer** (☎ 569 5419; mains 100-200Sk; ☉ 10am-9pm), whose hearty *halušky* (*gnocchi*-like dumplings, usually served with sheep's cheese and bacon) top the menu.

Pretty much every lodging has some sort of restaurant. The pizza at **Penzión Stárek** is pretty darn good (80Sk to 120Sk).

Getting There & Around

Plenty of buses serve Terchová from Žilina; several on weekdays and weekends continue on from Terchová to valley stops including Vrátna Štefanová (40Sk, 50 minutes), Vrátna Starý Dvor (47Sk, 55 minutes) and Vrátna výtah (50Sk, one hour), at the top of the valley near Chata Vrátna.

In the winter there's a free ski shuttle between the valley resort areas. Ask about bicycle rental at the Tourist Information Centre Terchová; places that rent come and go.

MARTIN

☎ 043 / pop 59,490

Museums, museums, museums. If you have an interest in folk arts and architecture, linguistic and national history, or in Slovak fine art and photography, then Martin has something to offer for you. The industrial ugliness of the town seems in direct contrast to its significance in Slovak national identity. Martin sits in the broad Turiec valley separating the Malá and Veľká Fatra ranges. Unless you're going hiking in the area's hills, you might want to make this a day trip from Žilina. But whatever you do, stay long enough to try the other thing Martin is famous for, the dark, delicious Martiner beer.

History

In 1861 Turčiansky Svätý Martin, a minor town, was pushed into the history books when a meeting of intellectuals here issued the so-called Martin Memorandum, urging the establishment of a Slovak-language administrative district within Hungary.

This drew only silence from the authorities at the time. Two years later a private cultural and educational foundation called Matica Slovenská (the kernel of Slovakia) was launched. The foundation promoted Slovak-language schools, museums, musical societies, publishing etc. During subsequent years of Hungarian cultural domination, Martin became the epicentre of simmering Slovak aspirations. On 30 October 1918 the Martin Declaration, in which the Slovaks formally opted to federate with the Czechs, was issued here. Though Bratislava became the capital of Slovakia, the town of Martin remained its sentimental centre. Today the town is still known for its strong nationalist slant.

Orientation

Most long-distance trains stop at the Vrútky station, in a modern industrial suburb to the north. From there bus 10 and 12 go the 7km south to the long-distance bus station in what remains of 'old' Martin. The small train station opposite is used mostly for regional connections. The main square, Nám SNP, is three blocks east.

In addition to the bus station, you can catch local buses is by the open-air market south of Nám SNP. The *skanzen* (open-air village museum) is 3km southeast of the centre (about 100Sk by taxi).

Information

There are plenty of ATMs scattered around Nám SNP.

Netcafé (☎ 439 3195; Divadelná 7; per hr 30Sk; ⏰ 10.30am-7.30pm Mon-Sat) In the courtyard.

Post office (cnr Pavla Mudroňa & Andreja Kmeťa)

Tourist Information Office Martin ☎ 423 8776; www.tikmartin.sk; Štefánika 9A) Loads of information are available on the 2nd floor of a funky glass-walled millennial monument midsquare. Pick up area hiking and biking maps here.

Sights

Traditional plaster and log buildings from all over the region have been moved to the **Museum of the Slovak Village** (Múzeum Slovenské Dediny; ☎ 423 9491; adult/student 50/30Sk; ⏰ 9am-6pm Mon-Sun May-Aug, to 5pm Sep & Oct, 10am-2.30pm Tue-Fri Nov-Apr). The country's biggest *skanzen* comes complete with a working *krčma* (tavern). Colourful costumed models and decorations that change with the season add interest to the traditional furnishings. Weekend programmes often include folk music. From the Vrútky train station take bus 10 or 11, or from the open-air market bus stop take southbound bus 10, 11, 20 or 41 to the end of the line at the Ľadoveň housing estate. The museum is a further 1km hike up through the woods. It's only a 100Sk taxi ride from town.

Thought-provoking photography exhibits change regularly at the nationally run **Ethnographic museum** (☎ 413 1011; Maláhora 2; adult/student 50/25Sk; ⏰ 9am-4.30pm Tue-Sun). The encyclopaedic collection of Slovak folk costumes here is regarded as one of the most complete in Europe, though the display is a bit static.

The Matica Slovenská began in the building that is now the **Slovak National Literary museum** (☎ 413 4152; Osloboditeľov 11; adult/student 30/15Sk; ⏰ 8am-4pm Tue-Sun). Today the Matica is housed in modern headquarters on Mudroňova, in the hills east of the city centre. Slovak artists and other cultural heroes rest in the modest **National cemetery** (Národný cintorín).

The former home and studio of Slovakia's best-known 20th-century painter is now the namesake **Martin Benka museum** (☎ 413 3190; Kuzmányho 34; adult/student 30/15Sk; ⏰ 8am-4pm Tue-Fri,

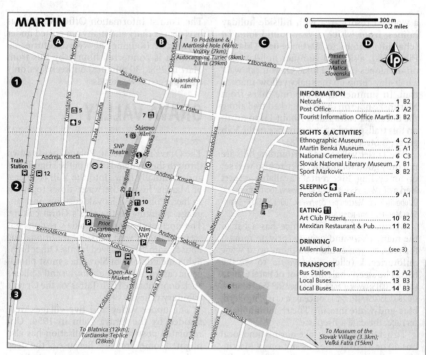

MARTIN

0 ——————— 300 m
0 ——————— 0.2 miles

INFORMATION		
Netcafé	**1**	B2
Post Office	**2**	A2
Tourist Information Office Martin	**3**	B2

SIGHTS & ACTIVITIES		
Ethnographic Museum	**4**	C2
Martin Benka Museum	**5**	A1
National Cemetery	**6**	C3
Slovak National Literary Museum	**7**	B1
Sport Markovič	**8**	B2

SLEEPING 🏠		
Penzión Čierná Pani	**9**	A1

EATING 🍴		
Art Club Pizzeria	**10**	B2
Mexičan Restaurant & Pub	**11**	B2

DRINKING		
Millennium Bar	(see 3)	

TRANSPORT		
Bus Station	**12**	A2
Local Buses	**13**	B3
Local Buses	**14**	B3

CENTRAL SLOVAKIA

9am-5pm Sat & Sun). The gallery brims with his happy, soft-focus paintings of rural life.

Sleeping & Eating

Seeing the museums as a day trip from Žilina, or from Lúčanská Fatra (right), are both viable alternatives to sleeping in a lacklustre town.

Autocamping Turiec (☎ 428 4215; www.autocamp ingturiec.sk; Kolónia Hviezda 92; per person in tent 130Sk, per person in bungalow 180-350SK) Pleasant A-frame cottages sleep five, small cabins sleep two, and there's a field for tents. From the bus station take northbound bus 23 to the end of the line. Hike 1km west of the highway at Vrútky.

Penzión Čierná Pani (☎ 413 1523; www.penzion -cierna-pani.sk in Slovak; Kuzmányho 24; s/d 650/1100Sk) It's hard to miss this bright yellowish orange *pensión* as you go down the street. The furniture is kind of cheap, but then so are the room rates. Price includes the sauna. Book ahead.

Mexičan Restaurant & Pub (☎ 090341695; Oslobodíteľov 3; mains 120-180Sk; ⏱ 10am-11pm Mon-Thu, 10am-3am Fri, noon-3am Sat & 2-11pm Sun) Hey *muchacho*, the burritos and fajitas are surprisingly good here (though jalepeños are scarce). This is a good place to socialise on weekends.

The pedestrian zone has several places to eat or drink, including the **Art Club Pizzeria** (Oslobodíteľov 8; pizzas 80-150Sk) and the ultramodern **Millennium Bar** (Štefánika 9; ⏱ 11am-midnight Sun-Thu, 11am-1am Fri & Sat) in the all-glass building constructed midsquare to celebrate the year 2000.

Getting There & Away

One daily express trains from Bratislava (316Sk, 3½ hours) and seven from Žilina (36Sk, 30 minutes), but at least 10 a day stop from each at Vrútky, 7km north of the town. Local trains go south to Banská Bystrica (84Sk, 1½ hours). There are six daily direct bus connections from Bratislava (272Sk, 4½ to five hours), and 10 to Žilina (44Sk, 30 minutes).

AROUND MARTIN

☎ 043

Lúčanská Fatra

The western, non-national park half of the Malá Fatra range, the Lúčanská Fatra, gets its name from its dominant peak, Veľká lúka (1476m), northwest of Martin. The hills are traversed by popular trails. **Podstráne** is a wooded resort area with hillside holiday homes, from which a year-round *lanovka* (chairlift) climbs to **Martinské hole** (Martin Pinnacles), a ski and summer holiday area on the slopes of Veľká lúka. Or you can walk a half-day climb up the snaky yellow-marked trail. In summer there are fine hikes from Martinské hole on the red-marked trail along the Lúčanská Fatra ridge. About 11km north on this trail, guarding the entrance to the Váh gorge, is Strečno castle (p378).

The Turiec valley and surrounding hills are not only good for hiking, they're also well set up for cycling. Bike rental's available at **Sport Markovič** (Map p385; ☎ 422 3000; www.sportmarkovic.sk; Osloboditeľov 6, Martin; per day/week 300/1200Sk; ☺ 9am-5pm Mon-Fri, 9am-noon Sat).

Martin's information office has a list of the many *chaty* and *privaty* (private rooms) for rent, or you could look them up at www .infoturiec.sk (click '*ubytovanie*' to see the list). The steep chaletlike roof of **Hotel Grandis** (☎ 422 0015; www.grandis.sk; Hrdinov SNP 350, Podstráne; s/d 2800/3300Sk; ☐ ☒) conceals a crisp, modern, blue-and-white interior. The restaurant has a terrace, the café a fireplace.

To get to Podstráne, take northbound local bus 40 or 41 from the bus station in Martin, about 4km to the end of the line. The chairlift is 800m from the bus.

Veľká Fatra National Park

There are numerous marked trails in the 403-sq-km **Veľká Fatra National Park** (www.sopsr .sk/velkafatra), down from the ridge line into the river valley south of Martin. If you're planning on walking in the area, be sure to buy the detailed hiking and cycling VKÚ map No 121 (1:50,000; 80Sk).

Long and short loop trails start at the picturesque village of **Blatnica**, 15km south in the Turiec valley. A fine, long day hike follows the Gaderská valley at the foot of the 1574m Krížna peak, with an option to return down the valley of Blatnica past a 13th-century castle. The ridges between these two valleys contain several nature reserves. The town itself contains the small **Karol Plicka museum** (☎ 494 8142; Prónayovská kúria, Blatnica; adult/student 30/15Sk; ☺ 10.30am-1.30pm Tue-Sat), dedicated to the nationally famous photographer who lived from 1894 to 1987.

Autocamping Blatnica (☎ 494 4207; per person/tent 40/60Sk, per person d 200Sk), 2km south of the centre, has a big field for 100 tents and hostel rooms.

The Tourist Information Office Martin has lists of area *chaty* and many are posted under *ubytovanie* (lodging) at www.infoturiec.sk. Blatnica is connected hourly by bus from Martin (25Sk, 30 minutes) on weekdays, only a couple go on weekends.

ORAVA VALLEY

☎ 043

The Orava river rises in Poland, twists down through the highlands west of the High Tatras and eventually flows into the Váh river east of Martin. Just as the water flows together, so have Polish and Slovak customs and language, resulting in the area's Goral culture. The northernmost of Slovakia's regions has scenic villages, with ranks of traditional log houses, some with carved fronts. Other highlights include one of Slovakia's most photogenic castles, a first-rate *skanzen* and a hiker's back door into the High Tatras via the Orava's tributary valleys.

The upper valley and five villages were flooded by the Orava Dam in 1954. Unregulated postwar industrialisation has also blighted some stretches. Because of the steep valleys, regional transport can be tedious. About 6km north of Trstená on Hwy 59 is a border crossing to Chyzne in Poland, on the road to Kraków.

ORAVA CASTLE

The classic 1922 vampire film *Nosferatu* featured the pointed towers of **Orava castle** (Oravský hrad; ☎ 582 0240; www.oravamuzeum.sk; adult/student 140/80Sk; ☺ 8.30am-5.30pm Jun-Aug, 8.30am-5pm May, Sep & Oct; by appointment Jan-Mar), which rise from the impossibly narrow blade of rock. The little town of Oravský Podzámok is quite overshadowed by this imposing structure. The castle is visible from the train station, across the river.

The oldest parts of one of the most complete castles in Slovakia date from at least 1267, with later additions by many royal and aristocratic owners. Today's look is largely the result of a reconstruction after the 1800 fire.

Ask if an English-speaking guide is available to take you on the compulsory tour. The museum is full of weapons, folk art and period furniture. It's said that looking in one of the mirrors can make you beautiful, and another one, ugly – make sure to ask your guide to point out the difference.

During special summer programmes fairy-tale characters re-enact their legends as you tour, you can visit the castle at night, or opt to be lead by vampires (in late August). Sword fights and medieval marketplace hawkers are standard.

Below the castle in the village there's a small grocery and a pizza place/beer hall. **Penzión Toliar** (☎ 589 3124; www.penzion-rosnicka.sk; r per person 400Sk; P) is a fine grey-and-white rococo inn at the foot of the castle. Concerned owners spruce up the lodging and the restaurant before every tourist season. On the road to Dolný Kubin, 1.5km south of the castle, **Penzión Racibor** (☎ 582 3353; www.racibor.sk; Raciborie 382; r 600Sk; P ✗) is a newish log lodge with a fire ring out back for barbecues, and a sauna for cooking indoors.

Trains bound for Oravský Podzámok require a change in Kraľovany (36Sk, one hour, 10 daily), 27km north. Žilina is a 40-minute onward train ride (48Sk, 18 daily) from there, and Liptovský Mikuláš (56Sk, 20 daily) is 45 minutes.

PODBIEL

A photogenic little village well known for its *drevenica* (log cottages), Podbiel is on your way to and from almost anywhere in Orava. A small museum dedicated to folk customs is open only sporadically. From here you can take a two-hour **raft trip** (☎ 532 0451; per person 250Sk) down river to Oravský Podzámok beneath the castle. Traditional *plte* are poled along by guides dressed up in Goral folk costume. (Want a shorter trip? One-hour trips leave from Horná Lehota.) Look for the beehives on the side of the road as you go along. This area is known for its honey.

Podbiel is on the train line north of Oravský Podzámok (18Sk, 30 minutes, 10 daily).

ZUBEREC

The village of Zuberec, 13km up the Studený valley from Podbiel, is a pretty little gateway to the Western Tatras, with its fair share of traditional architecture at the nearby *skanzen*. The **Tourist Information Office Zuberec** (☎ 532 0777; www.zuberec.sk; Hlavná 289; ☽ 8am-5pm Mon-Sat Jun & Sep; 8am-6pm Jul & Aug) can provide you with hiking maps and books. There's a little pastry shop café and the three-terminal **Internet Čitaren** (Hrady 307; ☽ 2-10pm).

Orava Village Museum (Múzeum Oravskej Dediny; ☎ 539 5149; adult/student 50/30Sk; ☽ 8am-5pm daily Jul & Aug, 8am-5pm Mon-Sat Jun & Sep, 8am-3.30pm Tue-Sat Oct-May), 3km east of the village, has a more traditional layout than many *skanzens*. Its 50 or so log buildings are huddled close to the stream, as was typical in mountain villages. Since it's one of the few open year-round, here you can experience first-hand the harshness of a snowy winter. The oldest and most impressive building is an early 15th-century wooden church. Ask for the explanatory pamphlet in English.

The street from the village toward the *skanzen* is lined with *privaty* and *Zimmer frei* (free rooms) signs. By all means stop by the open fire at **Koliba Josu** (☎ 539 5915; www.kolibajosu.sk; 469 Zuberec; mains 70-120Sk; P ✗); Slovak home cooking doesn't get any better. To start, try the fried potato pancake topped with *bryndža* (sheep's cheese) and crackling, or maybe the goulash soup made with lamb. Blueberry dumplings for dessert are a rare treat. The large log cabin has double rooms upstairs and cabins out back. Rooms per person cost 290Sk. It's 2km south on the road to Liptovský Mikuláš.

Zuberec is not on a train line and bus connections are sporadic. Two buses a day connect to Liptovský Mikuláš (47Sk, one hour). Counter to the usual pattern, more buses go to Podbiel (18Sk, 20 minutes) on weekends (daily on weekdays, 11 on weekends), from where you can switch to a train heading to Oravský Podzámok.

Centru Športu (☎ 539 5294; Zuberec 449) rents mountain bikes for a song at 120Sk per day.

WESTERN TATRAS

One way to escape the eager crowds in the High Tatras is to explore the western end of the range, called the **Western Tatras** (Západné Tatry; www.tatry.bsk.sk in Slovak). You have to be a go-getter though; transport's thin, facilities limited and the trails demanding. VKÚ map No 112 (1:50,000; 100Sk) has both hiking and cycling trails clearly marked. For weather and mountain conditions contact the local **Mountain Rescue Service** (☎ 539 5218; ☽ 8am-3pm) in Zveroka, 8km east of Zuberec. Trails from these points quickly lead into some of the highest mountains in Central Europe; don't attempt any long-distance treks here unless you have experience with high-altitude walking and climbing.

CHEESY BITS

Spend a few days in Central Slovakia and you'll realise just how important sheep's cheese is to the local economy. You can buy it at roadside stands, at stands near the ski slopes, and from display refrigerators in restaurants. A variety of different shapes and sizes is available: *ostiopok* is a semihard ball shape, *korbački* (little whips) are braided ropelike strands, and then there's *bryndža,* the cheese at the heart of Slovak tradition. The soft, spreadable cheese is first mentioned by chronicles in the 15th century. It's thought that Vlach (Wallachian) shepherds may have introduced the process into Slovakia after wandering out of Romania.

The first *bryndža* factory was built in 1787 and prior to EU admission farmers and producers fought hard for their right not to pasteurise. Samples were sent off to French and German labs and *bryndža* was pronounced a viable EU product – hoorah! You can try it on top of *halušky* (gnocchi-like dumplings) and *pirohy* (moon-shaped dumplings, like Polish *pierogies*), mixed with butter and paprika as an appetiser spread, in *demikat* soup, and on top of fried potato pancakes. If you haven't had enough, look for *žinčina,* a traditional sheep's whey drink. Nowhere is it as fresh as in the rolling hills of Central Slovakia.

From the trailhead at **Chata Zverovka** (☎ 539 5327; www.chatazverovka.sk; Zverovka; dm/d 270/680Sk) there's a good day's hike to **Roháčska plesá** (1719m), where a small plateau hides three alpine lakes and a picturesque waterfall.

A very popular camp site, **ATC Oravice** (☎ 539 4114; www.oravice.sk/atc/slovak.htm; per person/tent 50/80Sk) is 15km north of Zverovka.

Buses run from Zuberec to both Zverovka (14Sk, 15 minutes, daily on weekdays, six on weekends) and Oravice (22Sk, 30 minutes, three daily).

LOW TATRAS

☎ 044

For many, the Low Tatras (Nízke Tatry) are synonymous with Jasná, Slovakia's best-known ski resort, in Demänova valley.

The 80km east–west ridge, framed between the valleys of the upper Váh river and the smaller Hron river, is most dramatic where it pushes above the tree line, and excellent hiking trails and ski runs crisscross the territory.

Since 1978 much of the mountains have been part of the 810-sq-km Low Tatras National Park, though the lower eastern half is the wildest, with significant numbers of brown bears, wildcats and other wildlife.

Historically, the administrative district that encompassed this area was called Liptov, and residents still refer to it as such. A national landmark village, a *skanzen* and the nation's biggest folk festival preserve the indigenous culture of the region.

As you travel look for roadside stands selling fresh cheese. Oh, and don't miss the thermal waters.

The website www.liptov.sk has thorough accommodation listings for the region.

LIPTOVSKÝ MIKULÁŠ

pop 32,930

As a base for heading off into the Low Tatras and exploring nearby villages, Liptovský Mikuláš is useful enough, and the sight of peaks rising on all sides of the valley is quite striking. Still, who wants to be in a city when the mountains and nature are so close?

Other than being the place where Juraj Jánošík (the 'Slovak Robin Hood'; p382) was executed, the town today is known for being near the mammoth thermal water park, Tatralandia.

Orientation

The mighty Váh river doesn't look so big here, pooling into a 24-sq-km reservoir called Liptovská Mara, the 'Liptov Sea', which starts 2km west of town and has public access 6km west, near Tatralandia.

The bus and train stations are located 500m north of the small main square, Nám Osloboditeľov.

Information

City Information Centre (☎ 552 2418; www.icm .mikulas.sk; Nám Mieru 1; ☺ 8am-6pm Mon-Fri, 8am-noon Sat, 11am-4pm Sun mid-Jun–mid-Sep; 9am-5pm Mon-Fri, 8am-noon Sat mid-Sep–mid-Jun) Well prepared for the onslaught of tourists in summer and winter – hit 'em with any question you have about the region.

Liptour (☎ 551 4141; www.liptour.sk; Nám mieru 1) Can book accommodation in Demänova valley.

Post office (Hodžova)

Z@vináč Internet Café (Pišúta 19; per hr 60Sk; ☽ 10am-10pm Mon-Sat, 2-10pm Sun) Internet and email.

Sights & Activities
JANKO KRÁĽ MUSEUM

The leading poet of Slovak romanticism is honoured at the **Janko Kráľ museum** (☎ 552 2554; Nám Osloboditeľov 30; adult/student 30/15Sk; ☽ 10am-5pm mid-Jun–mid-Sep; 9am-4pm Mon-Fri, 10am-5pm Sun mid-Sep–mid-Jun), which also houses a reconstruction of **Mikuláš torture chamber** (Mikulášska mučiareň; adult/student 10/5Sk), the town dungeon where Juraj Jánošík was 'interrogated'.

AQUA PARK TATRALANDIA

The first water park in Slovakia, **Aqua Park Tatralandia** (☎ 547 4536; adult/student 450/280Sk; ☽ 9am-9pm Jun-Sep, 10am-9pm Apr-May & Oct-late Dec; 10am-10pm late Dec-Mar), just keeps getting bigger and bigger: six thermal pools (four open year-round), two regular swimming pools, slides and rides galore; an indoor spa with grottos and saunas; and outdoor sports, like a summer rope course and winter snow-tubing run. Western World, the newest attraction, is a rodeo theme show. There are cabins to rent and a train-shaped shuttle bus that runs to the park from the station in town (20Sk, hourly, 9am to 8pm). Tatralandia is quite the spectacle. The car park plateau has the most beautiful valley view of five mountain ranges (sigh).

Dip in the same thermal waters, with less hoopla, at the Bešeňová Thermal Park (p390), 18km west of Liptovský Mikuláš. The **Liptovská Mara** reservoir was the town's original aquatic playground. Head to the ATC Liptovský Trnovec camping ground, where there's boat hire and a popular beach.

Mutton Sport Services (☎ 0907 481311; www.mutton .sk; Ul 1 mája 25) can arrange canoe trips on the Váh river as well as adventure sports, like paragliding in the Low Tatras.

Sleeping

ATC Liptovský Trnovec (☎ 559 8458; www.atctrnovec .sk; Liptovský Trnovec; per person/tent 110/60Sk, 4-person bungalow 2200Sk; P ☒) Families fill up the 1000-person capacity of this lakeside camping ground, attracted by the swimming pool, beach, fishing, boat rental, playgrounds, miniature golf course...

Like sports? Play while you stay at **Penzión Bowling** (☎ 562 0625; www.penzionbowling.sk; Starohorského 3; P), with three lanes in the lobby/bar, and at **Penzión Squash** (☎ 562 0053; www.squash-liptov .sk; Starohorského 1; P), with a glass-walled court as you enter. Both are modern (wi-fi and all).

Eating & Drinking

The main square has many eateries.

Reštaurácia pod Šibenicou (☎ 554 1130; Palučanská 5; mains 100-170Sk) Located across the river, this place is a local fave.

Salaš Žiarska Dolina (☎ 558 6318; www.salasziar .sk; Žiarska dolina; mains 60-120Sk) If you have a car, drive the 10km for the real deal; this 'sheep

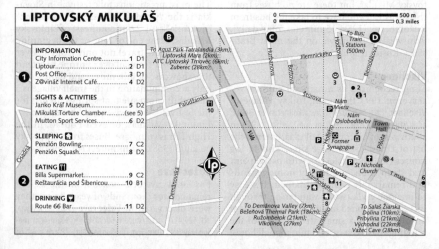

LIPTOVSKÝ MIKULÁŠ

INFORMATION	
City Information Centre	1 D1
Liptour	2 D1
Post Office	3 D1
Z@vináč Internet Café	4 D2

SIGHTS & ACTIVITIES	
Janko Kráľ Museum	5 D2
Mikuláš Torture Chamber	(see 5)
Mutton Sport Services	6 D2

SLEEPING	
Penzión Bowling	7 C2
Penzión Squash	8 D2

EATING	
Billa Supermarket	9 C2
Reštaurácia pod Šibenicou	10 B1

DRINKING	
Route 66 Bar	11 D2

To Aqua Park Tatralandia (3km); Liptovská Mara (2km); ATC Liptovský Trnovec (6km); Zuberec (28km)

To Bus; Train Stations (500m)

To Demänova Valley (7km); Bešeňová Thermal Park (18km); Ružomberok (21km); Vlkolínec (27km)

To Salaš Žiarska Dolina (10km); Pribylina (21km); Východná (22km); Važec Cave (28km)

0 — 500 m
0 — 0.3 miles

CENTRAL SLOVAKIA

dairy' restaurant has the freshest *bryndža* soup (called *demikat*) and *halušky* around. Rooms upstairs (per person 300Sk) are simple and filled with the valley's peace.

The huge **Billa supermarket** (Garbiarska ul) is hard to miss; it's right near the large **Route 66 Bar** (☎ 562 3017; Billa shopping centre; ☒ 9am-midnight Mon-Thu, 10am-2am Fri & Sat, 11am-midnight Sun; ☒).

Getting There & Away

Liptovský Mikuláš is on the main train line between Bratislava (364Sk, four hours) and Košice (220Sk, two hours), and is served by fast trains every hour or two. The Poprad (94Sk) and Žilina (83Sk) stops are both about an hour away; get off at Kraľovany (76Sk, 45 minutes) to switch if you want to go to Oravský Podzámok. Bus connections are tedious, only two a day go to Zuberec (47Sk, one hour).

AROUND LIPTOVSKÝ MIKULÁŠ
Bešeňová

In an effort to compete with the force of man that is Tatralandia water park, **Bešeňová Thermal Park** (☎ 439 2429; www.besenova.com; adult/student 260/170Sk; ☒ 10am-9pm Sun-Thu, to 10pm Fri & Sat) spruced up, adding a hotel (double rooms for 2200Sk) and an indoor slide in 2006. The pools are still more natural (yes, the curative mineral water is supposed to be brown) and the prices lower. Evening bathing in the winter is quite the thing.

The village has numerous private accommodation. It's just 18km west of Liptovský Mikuláš, but there are no buses from there. Instead you have to take the bus from Ružomberok (12Sk, 15 minutes, nine daily), 9km west of Bešeňová, on the main Bratislava–Košice train line.

Vlkolínec

Long recognised as a national cultural reserve, in 1993 the small, folksy village of **Vlkolínec** (☎ 432 1023; www.vlkolinec.sk in Slovak; adult/student 30/20Sk; ☒ 9am-3pm), about 27km southwest of Liptovský Mikuláš, entered the list of Unesco's heritage sites. The 45 log houses (mostly plastered), with pastel paint and steep roofs, are highly homogeneous and remarkably well maintained. It's easy to imagine a *vlk* (wolf) wandering through this steeply wooded mountainside settlement arranged along a small stream. One of the buildings has been turned into a small house

museum, but this is still a living village – if just barely. Of the 35 remaining residents, only three are male (12 are school-age children).

Walking along the streets you're endowed with a sense of the remote mountain life, but you can go deeper by staying overnight. Several of the usually two-room *drevenica* are for rent (from 250Sk per person). They all have kitchens, but you need to bring in your own food; there's no store near the village. Check out **No 9006** (☎ 903470051; http://vlkolinec .szm.sk), owned by the gatekeeper's son.

Driving or hiking the 6km uphill from Ružomberok is the only way to get here. Buses to Ružomberok from Liptovský Mikuláš (40Sk, 36 minutes) go about every half hour, while trains (56Sk, 18 minutes) are less frequent.

Pribylina

About 21km northeast of Liptovský Mikuláš, just past Pribylina village, is a small *skanzen*, the **Museum of Liptov Village** (Múzeum Liptovskej Dediny; ☎ 529 3163; adult/student 60/30Sk; ☒ 9am-6.30pm Jul & Aug; 9am-4.30pm mid-May–Jun, Sep & Oct; 9am-3.30pm Nov–mid-May). Most of the plastered log buildings are from the Liptovská Mara area and were relocated here just before the dam was completed and the valley flooded.

Two buses a day (nine on weekends) make the trip from Liptovský Mikuláš (47Sk, 45 minutes).

Východná

The most prestigious folk festival in Slovakia is the **Východná Folk Festival** (www.liptov.sk /vychodna in Slovak), 22km southeast of Liptovský Mikuláš, at the end of June or the beginning of July. People travel not only from all over Slovakia, but from all over Europe to attend this showcase of folk music and dance. The only accommodation in the small village is a makeshift camp site that springs up just for the festival – otherwise you'll have to make Liptovský Mikuláš, or even Poprad, in the High Tatras your base. Buses from Liptovský Mikuláš (36Sk, 27 minutes) run hourly.

Važec Cave

Fossilised cave bear bones from the ice age remained for thousands of years before they were discovered in **Važec cave** (Važeská jaskyňa; ☎ 529 4171; adult/student 60/30Sk; ☒ 10am-4pm Tue-Sun May-Nov, 10am-3pm Tue-Sun Feb-Apr) 28km east of

Liptovský Mikuláš. Tours leave every hour on the hour, and up to 11 buses (42Sk, 40 minutes) travel between Liptovský Mikuláš and Važec daily.

DEMÄNOVA VALLEY

The village of Jasná at the head of the Demänova valley (Demänovská dolina) is the republic's premier ski resort, and undiscovered it's not. Bright ski suit–clad tourists clunking around in winter snow boots from January to April are replaced come summer with hordes of backpack-toting hikers. In between, the pretty, forested valley under the crest of the Low Tatras can be remarkably peaceful. Nonstop development (despite national park status) means you'll find ample upmarket accommodation (and prices), and easy access by footpath or chairlift to windswept walks and downhill glides. The region's two most interesting caves are also in the valley.

Orientation

The valley begins near the village of Pavčina Lehota, 7km south of Liptovský Mikuláš. Strung along the valley is a diffuse collection of chalets, hotels and chairlifts. The first ski village is 7km uphill in Záradky, 1km further is Jasná (1200m). Accommodation strings all the way up the valley; there is a *chata* (mountain hut) or two to sleep at on the trails.

Information

Hotel Tri Studničky Email access available for 60Sk per hour.

Mountain Rescue Service (☎ 559 1678) Up the slope from Jasná, contact this service for trail and weather information. The best map for hiking and cycling routes, is VKÚ's *Nízke Tatry* map No 1 (1:25,000; 100Sk). *The Low Tatras* book (240Sk), part of the Knapsacked Walking series, has detailed descriptions of 50 hiking trails in English. Online check out www.jasna.sk.

Post office Located in or around the Grand Hotel, there's a small info booth, ATM and various sport rental places.

Slovakotour Agency (☎ 554 9026; slovakotour@nextra.sk; 🕙 7.30am-6.30pm Jan-Apr, 7.30am-5pm May-Oct, 8.30am-3.30pm Nov & Dec) Can help with accommodation, hiking maps and can arrange an assortment of outdoor activities.

Sights & Activities

Záradky is adrenaline central, with bungee jumping, go-karts and a rope course available. Most big hotels in the valley rent mountain bikes (about 300Sk per day). Outfitters like

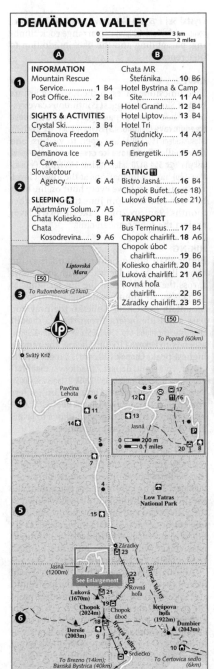

DEMÄNOVA VALLEY

INFORMATION	
Mountain Rescue Service	1 B4
Post Office	2 B4

SIGHTS & ACTIVITIES	
Crystal Ski	3 B4
Demänova Freedom Cave	4 A5
Demänova Ice Cave	5 A4
Slovakotour Agency	6 A4

SLEEPING	
Apartmány Solum	7 A5
Chata Koliesko	8 B4
Chata Kosodrevina	9 A6

Chata MR Štefánika	10 B6
Hotel Bystrina & Camp Site	11 A4
Hotel Grand	12 B4
Hotel Liptov	13 B4
Hotel Tri Studničky	14 A4
Penzión Energetik	15 A5

EATING	
Bistro Jasná	16 B4
Chopok Bufet	(see 18)
Luková Bufet	(see 21)

TRANSPORT	
Bus Terminus	17 B4
Chopok chairlift	18 A6
Chopok úboč chairlift	19 B6
Koliesko chairlift	20 B4
Luková chairlift	21 A6
Rovná hoľa chairlift	22 B6
Záradky chairlift	23 B5

Crystal Ski (☎ 559 1460; www.crystalski.sk; Hotel Grand complex; ⊗ 9am-4.30pm) can arrange rock climbing, paragliding and the like, in addition to bike rental.

CAVES

Two limestone caves in the lower valley are part of Slovakia's biggest continuous cave system. About 2km of passages in the **Demänova freedom cave** (Demänovská jaskyňa slobody; ☎ 559 1673; adult/student 150/130Sk) are open to visitors, and the smaller **Demänova ice cave** (Demänovská ľadová jaskyňa; ☎ 554 8170; adult/student 140/120Sk; ⊗ mid-May–Sep) has ice formations at the lowest level. Daily cave tours leave every hour on the hour between 9am and 4pm June to August; other months, 9am to 2pm. Take an extra layer against the subterranean chill.

HIKING

Better than going below ground is rising above it, on fine ridge walks with long views across the Tatras. From the bus terminus at Jasná it's a 20-minute walk up (south) to the mountain hut Chata Koliesko (halfway you pass a hillside *bufet*). From there a **chairlift** (adult/student round-trip 150/120Sk; ⊗ 8.30am-3.30pm) ascends to **Luková** (1670m) below the range's highest peak, **Chopok** (2024m). To get a little closer, you could depart Záradky via **chairlift** (1 stage round-trip adult/student 150/120Sk, 2 stages 250/200Sk; ⊗ 8.30am-4.30pm) to **Rovná hola** (1483m), where you change to go on to **Chopok úboč** (1829m). From there a trail returns via Luková to Jasná. Take extra layers even in summer.

Chopok is typically packed with people; you can escape the crowds by following the rocky, red ridge trail along the crest, west for 35 minutes to **Dereše** (2003m), or east two hours to **Ďumbier** (2043m), from where you could take the green trail through Široka valley down to the valley road and bus stops below Záradky. Or, continue west past Ďumbier and in six hours you reach **Čertovica sedlo**, a mountain pass village with services on a north–south road. (There are *chaty* en route.)

Alternatively, from Chopok you could mount the crest and hike down the *juh* (south) side 1½ hours to the Chata Kosodrevina in the less-developed Bystrá valley. From there a **chairlift** (adult/student 130/100Sk; ⊗ 8.30am-4.30pm Jun-Sep), or another 1½-hour walk, lands you in Srdiečko, a village with several hotels and the occasional bus out, via Brezno, to Banská Bystrica.

SKIING

Jasná is the best downhill skiing area in both republics. It's possible to ski both the *sever* (north) and the *juh* sides of Chopok mountain. With 24 runs (eight with snow-making capacity, three lighted), there's a good range for all levels. Equipment rental stores and stands (open 8.30am to 4.30pm) are near the car park at the base of each ski area. Skis or snowboard equipment go for about 400Sk per day. During peak season, lift passes for an adult/student are 690/490Sk per day and 3990/2660Sk per week. Crystal Ski (left) can arrange snowmobile rides and snow windsurfing. There's an ice rink and skate rental behind the Hotel Liptov and snow rafting in Záradky.

Sleeping

There are accommodation options everywhere you look in Jasná. The odds of finding a room without a booking are pretty good in summer but nil in winter. A multitier system, slightly different at every hotel, makes quoting rates tricky. Prices are at the highest during Christmas and Easter. The next tier, about 30% less, is January to March for most hotels. Here we quote mid–high season (June to September), generally 20% less than the high-season prices. Low season (April and May, October to Christmas) rooms can be up to 50% off the highest room price.

Slovakotour (p391) and Liptour (p389) can help with private accommodation in the valley, at prices starting at 300Sk per person. Also check out the private listings on www.liptov.sk (called 'bed and breakfast').

AUTHOR'S CHOICE

Hotel Tri Studničky (☎ 547 8000; www.tri studnicky.sk; s/d 1725/2200Sk; Ⓟ ✗ ✗ 🖳 🕱) Massive logs hold up the glass-and-stone front entrance, a roaring fire blazes in the stone hearth inside. Furnishings are mid-century mod with low-slung lines and earthy hues. A copper wall in the restaurant sets off all the wood and stone to good effect. A few feet behind the hotel runs a picturesque stream with a wooden bridge and path beyond. Upstairs, the plaid bedspreads are appropriately woodsy, just not as upscale as the fabulous public room appointments. You really can't do better in the valley.

LOWER VALLEY

Hotel Bystrina & Camp Site (☎ 554 8163; www
.hotelbystrina.sk; s/d 875/1100Sk, per person/tent 100/80Sk;
P) The plain and simple doubles are some
of the cheapest around. There's an 8-hectare
camping ground that is quite shady around
the edges at the base of the valley. Two restaurants are on site.

Penzión Energetik (☎ 547 6911; www.slovrekrea.sk
in Slovak; r/ste 900/1300Sk) One of the many accommodation options with the log lodge look, this
one has a sauna, sun bed and hydromassage
shower. Some of the rooms are wheelchair-
friendly, quite a rarity.

Apartmány Solum (☎ 562 3853; www.solum.sk;
4-person apt 2400Sk; **P** **X**) What a modern marvel: new and stylish one-bedroom apartments
have a small kitchen and pull-out couch in the
seating area. Downstairs, the communal living
room has leather couches to lounge around
the fireplace beside the billiard table. Offers
wi-fi and bike rental.

JASNÁ

Hotel Liptov (☎ 559 1506; www.hotelliptov.sk; s/d
750/1000Sk, without bathroom 350/800Sk; **P**) Small
shared bathrooms are the bargain of the hill
(200m from the ski slopes). Adjacent to the
sport-oriented hotel is an archery park, a
paintball course and an ice skating rink (in
season). Ski and sport rental.

Hotel Grand (☎ 559 9141; www.grandjasna.sk; s/d
1950/2600Sk; **P** **X** **X** **□** **⊛**) One hundred and
twenty rooms fan out in two wings from
a central hub that looks a bit like a shopping centre. There's even a small information
centre next to the ski rental place. Bike rental,
one chairlift ticket, pool and sauna are all
included in the room rate. A wi-fi hotspot
and baby-sitting are available.

MOUNTAIN HUTS

Chaty (mountain huts) can be anything from
a basic roof over your head to a *horský hotel*
(mountain hotel). All have food service of
some sort.

Chata MR Štefánika (☎ 619 5120; www.chatamrs
.sk in Slovak; dm 270Sk) You're at the top of the
world in this hiker's hut near Ďumbier peak.
Breakfast is included and full board (200Sk)
is an option. Six-bed rooms.

Chata Kosodrevina (☎ 0905516519; www.chata
kosodrevina.sk in Slovak; d/tr/q per person 350/300/250Sk)
Over the hill and through the woods, dorm-
like Chata Kosodrevina is on the south side
of Chopok mountain. Sleeping-bag space will
set you back just 150Sk.

Chata Koliesko (☎ 559 1674; www.liptov.sk/koliesko/;
s/d 850/1700Sk; **P**) A short hike up from Jasná, at
the base of the chairlift, Koliesko could hardly
be in a better spot or feel more like an alpine
lodge. The kitschy-in-a-good-way restaurant
(mains 160Sk to 350Sk) has a fireplace and
the requisite skiing trophies.

Eating

Stand-alone restaurants are an endangered species here, but most lodgings have decent, handy
restaurants. The ones in Hotel Tri Studničky
(fancy) and Chata Koliesko (casual) are good.
There are small buffets at the Luková and
Chopok chairlift terminals. There's a *krčma*
and food stands at Záradky and near the car
park south of the ice cave. Small **Bistro Jasná**
(☎ 559 1554; mains 95-150Sk; ☯ 8am-7pm), above the
main Jasná car park, serves standard stuff.

Getting There & Away

Almost hourly buses run between Liptovský
Mikuláš (with valley stops along the way) to
Jasná (23Sk, 40 minutes).

High Tatras

When you first see the alpine, snow-strewn High Tatras jutting out of the valley floor north of Poprad, you may do a double take. This isn't Switzerland after all. But Gerlachovský štít (2654m) is the highest peak in the entire Carpathian range, and the Tatras tower over most of Eastern Europe. Photo opportunities at higher elevations can get you fantasising about a career at *National Geographic* – pristine snowfields, ultramarine mountain lakes, crashing waterfalls. Sadly, a massive windstorm roared through in late 2004, uprooting much of the dense pine forest at mid-elevation, especially near the resort towns of Starý Smokovec and Tatranská Lomnica. Huge swaths will look barren – war ravaged even – for years to come. Tree trunks have been cleared and shipped off for building, leaving fields full of massive upturned stumps and clumps of dirt, but this hasn't stopped the crowds from showing up.

Some five million people a year come to walk, climb, cycle or ski here. A 600km network of hiking trails, chairlifts and cable cars reach all the alpine valleys and some peaks, with *chaty* (mountain huts) to stop at along the way. In high summer and winter seasons, trails are densely crowded. You'll need to climb further than in Slovakia's other mountains to have some of it to yourself, but the rewards are breathtaking.

HIGHLIGHTS

- Have a shot of vodka at the *bufet* (cafeteria) atop the 2634m summit of **Lomnický štít** (p403), just don't tell anyone you took the cable car up

- Hike from Hrebienok past the Obrov waterfalls and reward yourself with a night at the alpine chalet **Zamkovského chata** (p401)

- Ski by day, by night stay in an atmospheric old log house in **Ždiar** (p405), part of the Belá Tatras.

- Enjoy a hot wine and spit-fired chicken; food for the hiker's soul at **Zbojnícka Koliba** (p404)

- Soak away your aches at the thermal pools of the environmentally aware **Aqua City** (p399) in Poprad

★ Ždiar

★ Lomnický štít

Zbojnícka Koliba ★
★ Zamkovského chata

★ Aqua City

■ TELEPHONE CODE: 052

HIGH TATRAS

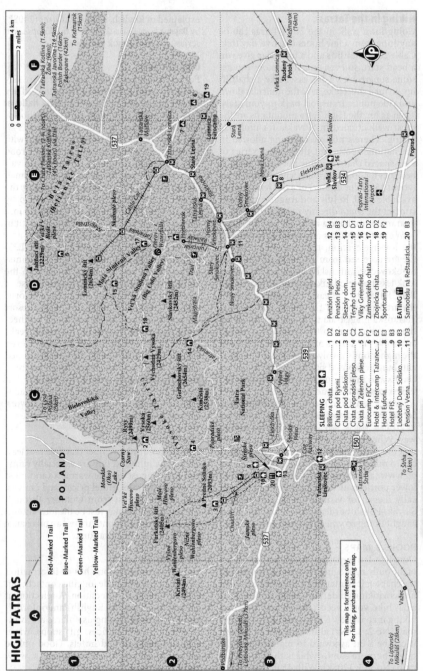

Legend
Red-Marked Trail
Blue-Marked Trail
Green-Marked Trail
Yellow-Marked Trail

0   4 km
0   2 miles

To Tatranská Kotlina (1.5km);
Zdiar (6km);
Tatranská Javorina (14.5km);
Polish Border (16km);
Zakopane (42km)

To Chata Plesnivec (2 ¾ hours);
Zelezná Kotlina
(4¾ hours) via Zdiar

Biela Tatra
(Belianske Tatry)

To Lysá
Poľana (20km)

POLAND

To Poprad
To Kežmarok (16km)

To Kežmarok (15km)

To Pribylina (20km);
Liptovský Mikuláš (37km)

To Podbanské

To Štrba (1km)

To Liptovský
Mikuláš (28km)

To Važec

Peaks / places:
Jahňací štít (2229m)
Lomnický štít (2634m)
Slavkovský štít (2452m)
Vichodná Vysoká (2429m)
Gerlachovský štít (2654m)
Končistá (2538m)
Rysy (2499m)
Vysoká (2560m)
Krivaň (2493m)
Ľadové pleso (2627m)
Furkotský štít (2406m)
Predné Solisko (2093m)

Poprad-Tatry
International
Airport

Tatra
National Park

This map is for reference only.
For hiking, purchase a hiking map.

HIGH TATRAS

Hiking in the Tatras

Going for a walk in the High Tatras can be anything from a few hours to a five-day trek. Cable cars, chairlifts and a funicular give you a head start, so even couch potatoes can get some superb views. It's easy: take a chairlift up, go for a short hike, take the funicular down and ride public transport back to your start. Then again, the High Tatra mountains are the most well situated in Slovakia for multiday hiking. There's no free camping allowed in the national park, but there are a series of well-spaced *chaty* that line the upper trails. A bed goes for 300Sk to 500Sk a night, and meals (about 150Sk for dinner) or a full restaurant is available at all. In July and August especially, contact the *chata* directly to book ahead and guarantee you have a bed.

We've listed hikes and *chaty* according to the lower-elevation, trailhead resort towns they're accessed from – Štrbské Pleso, Starý Smokovec or Tatranská Lomnica. Don't overlook less traversed hiking possibilities in the Belá Tatras, to the east. The main artery of the trail network is the 65km, red-marked Tatranská magistrála trail, which runs along the southern flank of the High Tatras, and is accessible via dozens of branch trails. Some of the higher trails involve steep scrambling and climbing in exposed situations with the aid of chains and metal rungs – not recommended unless you have a head for heights.

Trail advice from the park's **Mountain Rescue Service** (Horská Záchranná Služba; ☎ 4422 820, emergency 18 300; ths@tanap.sk; Starý Smokovec 23) goes a long way. When planning your trip, keep in mind that the higher trails are closed from November to mid-June (a list of closings is available on www.tanap.org), and avalanches may close lower portions as well. Note that it is technically illegal for visitors to walk across the Slovak–Polish border in the mountains – if caught doing so you could be fined.

BOOKS & MAPS

Our High Tatras map has trails, *chaty* and some of the outlying lodging mentioned throughout the chapter. It is intended for orientation only, not as a hiking guide. For anything more than a day hike, you'll need a decent map. The best hiking map is the VKÚ *Vysoké Tatry* 1:25,000 map (No 2; 120Sk) although, due to its size, it can be a bit awkward to manoeuvre. You might be more comfortable with the 1:50,000 map (No 113; 120Sk). With 45 detailed hikes explained in English, *The High Tatras* (240Sk) by **Dajama** (www.dajama.sk), part of the *Knapsacked* series, is a good book to have.

Orientation

For all their majesty, the High Tatras are surprisingly compact at only 55km long. They form part of the 795-sq-km **Tatra National Park** (Tatranský národný park), Czechoslovakia's first national park, founded in 1949. The High Tatras are geologically young, with sharp, frost-shattered summits and broad valleys carved by glaciers. Three dozen valleys contain over 100 *plesy*, or tarns (small glacial lakes). The pine forest, skirting the range below 1600m, has been damaged by windstorms. Some 25 peaks measure more than 2500m, with the 2634m Lomnický štít in second place after Gerlachovský štít.

The main east–west regional highway (E50) passes through Poprad, the park's administrative centre and the main gateway to the Tatras. An upper road following the base of the mountains links all the village resorts. Starý Smokovec (990m) is the biggest resort town, with the most facilities and connections, and a clear view of the mountain peaks without a pine forest to look through. Eleven kilometres to the west is the overdeveloped Štrbské Pleso (1350m), which still has trees, and 5km to the east is the more peaceful, but barren Tatranská Lomnica (850m). Poprad is linked to all the resorts by road, bus network and electric train.

Climate & When to Go

There's snow by November that lingers at least until May. June and July are especially rainy. July and August are the warmest (and most crowded) months. Hotel prices, and crowds, are at their lowest from October through April. September may just be the ideal month to visit, but in any month there's an off chance of snow at higher elevations.

Information

Each of the main resorts has an information office; they can provide lodging contacts, but do not book accommodation. A selection of guidebooks (some in English) and information booklets of varying usefulness are available from tourist offices, gift shops, travel agencies and top-end hotels. Good online sources of info include www.tanap.sk, www.tatry.sk and www.tatry.net.

BETTER TO BE SAFE

Around 15 to 20 people die every year in the High Tatras, due mainly to extremely capricious weather conditions – it can change from warm, brilliant sunshine to snow, rain, hail or wind within a few minutes. Beware of sudden thunderstorms on ridges and peaks where there's no protection. Stay off the ridge tops if they're in cloud. Check the weather forecast at the Mountain Rescue Service before setting out for overnight trips. Take their advice seriously. The emergency assistance of the Mountain Rescue Service is not free; you will pay to be rescued.

It's a good idea to carry your own water and some food, even if you have a *chata* booking with meals; you'll burn up a lot of energy and will need snacks along the way. Wear hiking boots and layered clothing; the highest elevations are cool year-round. Carry a whistle for emergencies; six blasts is an internationally recognised distress call.

The rules: stay on the trails, don't pick the flowers, take your rubbish with you and don't cut wood or build open fires.

Sleeping

Frequent, cheap transport means you can stay almost anywhere. Lodging rates are high in the three main resorts, if you're looking for bargains you have to go down hill. In villages like Nová Lesná, Stará Lesná, Tatranská Štrba and Veľký Slavkov you'll find plenty of signs advertising private rooms. Most are near train stops. To make sure you have a place, it's best to book private rooms (from 300Sk per person) via the internet (www.tatry.sk and www.tanap.sk/homes.html have listings). Though no free camping is allowed, there are a couple of organised camping grounds near Tatranská Lomnica.

Rates given below are for the high winter (December to March) and summer (June to August) season. In spring and autumn prices dip by at least 20%.

Getting There & Away

Few buses go directly to the Tatra resort towns from far afield, for most you will need to switch in Poprad. Trainwise, you can change in Poprad from the main Bratislava–Kosice line to take the electric train to mountain resorts, or you could switch at Tatranská Štrba, and take the *ozubnicová železnica* (cog railway) up to Štrbské Pleso.

Poprad airport has a few London-bound flights each week. See the individual town sections for more information about getting there and away.

BORDER CROSSINGS

The closest border crossing between Slovakia and Poland is at Lysá Poľana near Tatranská Javorina, 30km from Tatranská Lomnica via Ždiar by bus. Buses depart from Poprad and

Tatranská Lomnica. From the Polish side of the border crossing there are regular public buses and private minibuses to Zakopane (26km).

Getting Around

BICYCLE

Places renting mountain bikes are mentioned throughout the chapter.

BUS

Local buses run between the resorts every 20 minutes and tend to be quicker than the train – they have fewer stops. From Starý Smokovec it takes 10 minutes to Tatranska Lomnica (10Sk) and 30 minutes to Štrbské Pleso (28Sk). Schedules are posted on major bus stops.

Buses from Poprad travel to Starý Smokovec (18Sk, 20 minutes, every half hour), Tatranská Lomnica (25Sk, 35 minutes, hourly) and Štrbské Pleso (45Sk, 50 minutes, every 45 minutes).

TRAIN

The **Tatra Electric Train Service** (Tatranská elekrická železnica, TEZ) links most of the towns and villages in the Tatras at least hourly (schedules at www.zsr.sk). There are so many stops that it's likely one is near your lodging. A 20Sk ticket covers a 6km to 14km ride. It's easier to buy a one-/three-/seven-day pass for 100/200/360Sk. If there's no ticket window at your stop, buy one from the conductor. Validate it on board.

One line runs from Poprad via Starý Smokovec (30 minutes) to Štrbské Pleso (one hour). Another line connects Starý Smokovec to Tatranská Lomnica (15 minutes), so you have to change to travel from Štrbské Pleso to Tatranská Lomnica. A third route from Tatranská

Lomnica through Studený potok (15 minutes) loops round to Poprad (25 minutes).

A cog railway connects Tatranská Štrba (on the main Žilina–Poprad railway line) with Štrbské Pleso (30Sk, 15 minutes, hourly).

POPRAD

pop 55,404

Views of the High Tatras' jagged peaks accost you at every turn in Poprad. This valley town, just 13km south of Starý Smokovec, is the major transport hub for mountain-bound nature lovers. You could also use this big little city as a base for seeing not only the mountains but also the surrounding Spiš Region (p412).

Poprad was originally a 13th-century Spiš town. Little of the Germanic influence remains on the main square, but you'll see broad gables and carved timber in Spišská Sobota, a neighbouring suburb. Much of the city is highly industrialised and there's no real reason to make a special trip, but if you're passing through…

Orientation

From the bus and train stations (and the electric train terminal above the main station) it's 1km southeast to the main square, Nám sv Egídia, which is lined with shops and eateries. Poprad-Tatry airport, the highest in Europe, is about 5km west of town.

Information

City Information Centre (☎ 772 1700; www .poprad.sk; Nám sv Egídia 15; 🕙 8am-6pm Mon-Fri, 9am-noon Sat Jul-Aug; 8.30am-5pm Mon-Fri, 9am-noon Sat Sep-Jun) Tatra and town info, including private room accommodation.

Ľudová banka (Prior, Nám sv Egídia 124) ATM and exchange.

Post office (Mnoheľova 11)

Sinet (Nám sv Egídia 28; per hr 50Sk; 🕙 9am-9pm Mon-Sat, from 1pm Sun) Internet café.

T-Ski Travel (☎ 788 2911; www.slovakiatravel.sk; Hviezdoslavova; 🕙 9am-4.30pm Mon-Fri) High Tatras accommodation booking and sports store, near the bus and train stations.

Sights

The Gothic **Church of St Egidius** (Nám sv Egídia; adult/student 20/10Sk; 🕙 9.30am-noon & 1-4pm Mon-Fri, or by appointment), in the middle of the square, sports Spiš-style gablets on the roofline. The

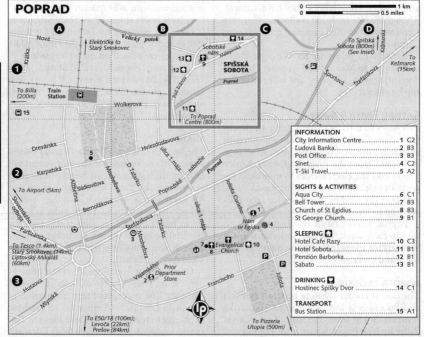

POPRAD

Bell Tower (adult/student 10/5Sk; 🕑 8am-noon, 1-4.30pm Tue-Sun) has views over the town towards the magnificent High Tatras.

The colourful Renaissance merchants' and artisans' houses lining the central square of **Spišská Sobota**, 3km northeast of the main square, are quite charming (and contain the town's best places to stay). Look for the altar made by Master Pavol of Levoča in 1516, inside the Gothic **St George Church** (Kostol sv Juraj; adult/student 30/15Sk; 🕑 9am-5pm Sun-Fri, 9am-2pm Sat). To get here walk northeast on Štefánikova and turn north on Kežmarská, or take bus 2 or 3 from the station.

Aqua City (☎ 785 1222; www.aquacitypoprad.sk; Športová 1397; 🕑 9am-9pm), Poprad's urban water park, tries hard to be environmentally friendly. The water, heat and most of the electricity come from geothermal sources on site, and 15% of the park's profits goes back to the town (as will electricity some day). Prices for the different sauna, swim and slide zones differ; access to the thermal pools and slides is 450/250Sk per day for adults/students.

Sleeping

The City Information Centre has a big list of private rooms (about 300Sk per person) around town and T-Ski Travel can book rooms in the Tatras.

Hotel Cafe Razy (☎ 776 4101; www.hotelcaferazy.sk; Nám sv Egídia 58; s/d 900/1600Sk; 🖳) The unadorned bedrooms in this renovated old town hotel, with wood beds and floors, are really pretty sane. Perhaps it's the hotel's Irish pub patrons that have inspired the name CRazy?

Penzión Barborka (☎ 776 2545; www.penzionbarborka .sk; Pod bránou 4, Spišská Sobota; r 800Sk) Dark wood trim sets off the white plaster of this rustic old house. Inside, oak panelling and a homey mishmash of furnishings, along with a publike restaurant, make this a comfortable choice.

Also in Spišská Sobota:

Sabato (☎ 776 9580; www.sabato.sk; Sobotské nám 1730/6; r 1400-3800Sk) Medieval luxury: me thinketh I be in the wrong century, me lord.

Hotel Sobota (☎ 466 3121; www.hotelsobota.sk; Kežmarská 15, Spišská Sobota; s/d 1750/2200Sk; 🅿 ⊠ ⊠ 🖳) New hotel with an old slate-and-timber aesthetic.

Eating & Drinking

Numerous restaurants, bars and cafés line Nám sv Egídia.

Pizzeria Utopia (☎ 773 2222; Dostojevského 23; pizzas 100-200Sk) Head south across the E18 for everybody's favourite pizza and pasta. Eclectic bric-a-brac decorate the rambling houselike restaurant.

Hostinec Spišky Dvor (☎ 0903706929; Sobotské nám 58; 🕑 9am-10pm Sun-Thu, until midnight Fri & Sat) Your friendly Spišská Sobota neighbourhood pub has a billiard table and wine bottles melted into art.

There's a large **Billa** (cnr Wolkerova & Slovenského) grocery store 200m west of the bus station, and just outside town on the E50 motorway to Žilina is a 24-hour Tesco Hypermart (Teplická cesta) with a supermarket and all kinds of camping essentials.

Getting There & Away

Sky Europe (NE; ☎ 02-4850 4850 reservations; www.sky europe.com) flies between London Stansted and the **Poprad-Tatry International Airport** (TAT; ☎ 776 3875; www.airport-poprad.sk; Na Letisko 100) on Wednesday and Saturday. Bus 12 takes you the 5km from the airport to Poprad city centre. **ČSA** (OK; ☎ 678 2490; www.czechairlines.com) runs a two-hour bus service from Poprad-Tatry airport to Košice, in conjunction with flights to Prague (billed as one ticket, from 5042Sk).

For longer land distances in the region, trains are your best bet. Up to 11 fast trains a day run to Bratislava (420Sk, five hours) and Košice (154Sk, 1½ hours). Night trains connect Poprad with Brno (679Sk, 7½ hours) and Prague (1180Sk, nine hours), plus 174Sk for a sleeper supplement.

On Thursday and Saturday mornings (currently at 6am) a bus goes directly to Zakopane (300Sk, 2¼ hours). Otherwise, you can take a bus from Poprad to Tatranská Javorina, Lysá Poľana stop (58Sk, 1¼ hours, four daily), near the Polish border. Walk across to the buses waiting to take you to Zakopane.

For more on getting to mountain resorts, see p397.

ŠTRBSKÉ PLESO

A 20-hectare, alpine *pleso* (lake), the second biggest in the park, defines the High Tatras' westernmost resort. Hotel after hotel lines the banks, and though the place is overdeveloped (and in the high seasons, over-run), Štrbské Pleso retains a natural beauty because it was spared by the 2004 storm. Pine trees still snuggle up to the shoreline and the reflective waters, crowding out some of the ugliness.

North of the lake are a number of runs that make up the park's most popular ski area, and a year-round chairlift takes you up to trails.

Orientation & Information

The red-marked Tatranská magistrála trail that travels the length of the Tatras winds around the southern end of the lake here at 1346m. To pick it up in the easterly direction, walk north from the station and after 500m bear right towards the Helios sanatorium; the trail is on the left, just past a small stream. Most of the town is arranged around the large lake, Štrbské Pleso, northeast of which is the ski area in the Areál FIS. Southwest is the smaller Nové Štrbské Pleso. None of the buildings have proper street addresses; they can be located by finding one of these three areas.

The staff at the **Tatra National Park Info Centrum** (☎ 449 2391; www.tanap.sk; Štrbské Pleso; ☼ 9am-4pm) are quite knowledgeable about trails, including closures. There's an ATM across the parking lot, by the Hotel Panorama. Two computers in the lobby of **Hotel FIS** (☎ 449 2221; Areál FIS; per hr 100Sk; ☼ 24hr) are available for internet rental.

Activities

A relatively easy (and crowded) walk from Štrbské Pleso is up the magistrála to and even more idyllic pond, **Popradské pleso** (1494m), which takes one to 1½ hours one way. From there a more demanding two-hour blue trail takes you to **Velké Hincovo pleso** (1946m), the biggest and deepest of the park's tarns. From Popradské pleso you could also continue east on a challenging zigzaggy section of the Tatranská magistrála about 3½ hours to **Sliezsky dom** hiker's hut and about five hours to **Hrebienok** (1285m), where a funicular goes down to Starý Smokovec.

There is also a year-round **chairlift** (☎ 449 2343; www.parksnow.sk; adult/student return 200/140Sk; ☼ 8am-3.30pm) from the ski area north of Štrbské Pleso to the **Solisko** mountainside terminus (1830m) near a chata, from here it's a steep one-hour walk north along the red trail to the 2093m summit of **Predné Solisko**.

You can hire skis, snowboards, even mountain bikes (all about 300Sk a day) from **Crystal Ski** (☎ 449 2834; www.crystalski.sk; Areál FIS; ☼ 8.30am-4.30pm). When there's snow, there's usually a guy (in the field on the side of the road) hawking rides on a **snowmobile** (snižký scooter; 10 min 600Sk) to the chairlift and Areál FIS.

Sleeping

Penzión Ingrid (☎ 0905108088; www.ingrid.sk; Tatranská Štrba 1121; apt per person 400-800Sk; P ✗) This tidy new accommodation opened 500m from the cog railway stop, 3km south of Štrbské Pleso in late 2005. Apartments each have a two-burner cooktop, a small fridge and an electric kettle.

Penzión Pleso (☎ 449 2160; Nové Štrbské Pleso 11; www.penzionpleso.sk; r per person 650Sk, ste per person 800Sk; P) The contemporary inside of this refurbishment-in-progress is well ahead of the outside. Choose suite 11 because of the mountain views from full-length corner windows. Breakfast is 90Sk.

Old-fashioned **Liečebný Dom Solisko** (☎ 478 0722; www.solisko.sk; Štrbské Pleso 27; s/d 2350/3900Sk; P ⛷) and modern, off-kilter A-shaped **Hotel Patria** (☎ 449 2591; www.hotelpatria.sk; Štrbské Pleso 48; s/d 2400/3260Sk; P ⛷) are both lakeside.

MOUNTAIN HUTS

Chata pod Soliskom (1800m; ☎ 0905652036; www .chatasolisko.sk) Nine beds, nice terrace, no hiking required (it's next to the chairlift).

Chata Popradské pleso (1500m; ☎ 449 2177; www .popradskepleso.sk) Sizeable chalet with restaurant and 132 beds in two- and eight-bed rooms. The attic floor sleeps 25 in sleeping bags.

Chata pod Rysmi (2250m; ☎ 0903181051, 4422 314; ☼ 15 Jun-Oct) Highest and smallest of them all. Sleep mattress to mattress under the eaves. Board available.

Sliezsky dom (1670m; ☎ 442 5261; www.sliezskydom .sk) Doubles and four-bed dorms (131 rooms) in a 1971 concrete block with restaurant and cafeteria.

Eating

All the hotels and *pensions* have restaurants.

Samoobslužná Reštaurácia (☎ 478 1011; Hotel Toliar, Štrbské Pleso 21; mains 40-70Sk; ☼ 7am-10pm) This self-service cafeteria serves one-pot meals (goulash, chicken stir-fry) and some vegetarian options.

Janova Koliba (☎ 449 2422; Areál FIS; mains 60-250Sk) Sure, the rustic restaurant by the ski slopes is a little kitsch, but sharing an evening of beer and folk music with German-speaking tourists can be lively.

SMOKOVCE RESORTS

At the turn of the 20th century, fancy-hat ladies and topcoat gentlemen strolled past grand alpine hotels and churches with half-timber decoration. Some of that grandeur remains in restored old buildings in the Smokovce Resorts – the collective name we use for Old (Starý), New (Nový), Upper (Horný) and Lower (Dolný) Smokovec. The villages run together but have separate electric train stops. It will take years for the trees around the resorts to grow back after storm damage, but in the meantime, some hotel rooms have much clearer views of the peaks above. Is that a silver lining?

Information

Junior Sport (Starý Smokovec 29; per day 38Sk; ⏰ 10am-6pm Mon-Thu, 9am-6pm Fri-Sun) Left luggage storage in sport store above train station.

Slovenská Sporiteľňa (Cesta Slobody 24, Starý Smokovec) Bank on the main road, has an ATM and exchange.

T-Ski Travel (☎ 442 3200; www.slovakiatravel.sk; Starý Smokovec 46; ⏰ 9am-4pm Mon-Thu, to 5pm Fri-Sun) Books lodging, including some huts, and arranges ski and sport programmes. It's in the funicular station.

Tatra Information Office (TIK; ☎ 442 3440; www .tatry.sk; Dom služieb 24, Starý Smokovec; ⏰ 8am-8pm Mon-Fri, to 1pm Sat) Regular area info.

U Michalka Café (Starý Smokovec 4; per hr 80Sk; ⏰ 11am-10pm) One internet terminal.

Activities

HIKING

From Starý Smokovec a **funicular railway** (pozemná lanovka; ☎ 446 7618; www.tldtatry.sk; adult/student return 100/60Sk; ⏰ 7.30am-7pm), or a 55-minute hike on the green trail, takes you up to **Hrebienok** (1280m). From here you have a great view of the Veľká Studená valley and a couple of hiking options. You could follow the magistrála trail west to the Sliezsky dom (two hours), and down a small green segment to the yellow-marked trail back to Starý Smokovec (two hours).

Head northeast from Hrebienok on the red magistrála trail (or past the **Bilíkova chata** on the steeper, streamside green trail) for about one to 1½ hours to the **Obrov waterfalls** (Obrovsky vodopad). If you're fit, a recommended option is a blue-trail turn-off before the falls and the four-to-five-hour climb up Veľká Studená Valley to a hot meal and warm bed at the **Zbojnícka chata**; make sure to prebook.

From the Obrov waterfalls you could instead continue west on the red magistrála to **Zamkovského chata** (past more waterfalls) and on to Skalnaté pleso (1½ hours), where there's a cable car down to Tatranská Lomnica. Or at Zamkovského chata turn up a green trail into the Malá Studená valley. Two hours will see you at the **Téryho chata**, which is beside a lake at about 2010m. You could stay there and the next day continue on the green trail over a 2373m pass and down the long Bielovodská valley five hours down to Tatranská Javorina in the **Belá Tatras** (p404) near the Polish border, where there are buses back to Tatra resort towns.

MOUNTAIN CLIMBING & BIKING

You can reach the top of **Slavkovský štít** (2452m) via the blue trail from Starý Smokovec (seven hours return), but to scale the peaks without marked hiking trails (Gerlachovský štít included) you must hire a mountain guide (members of recognised climbing clubs who've checked in with the mountain service are excluded). In addition to guide service, the **Mountain Guides Society Office** (☎ 442 2066; www.tatraguide .sk; Starý Smokovec 38; ⏰ 10am-6pm Mon-Fri, noon-6pm Sat & Sun Jun-Sep, 10am-6pm Mon-Fri Oct-May) has climbing classes and climbing and biking tours.

FROM WEST TO EAST ACROSS THE TATRAS

So you want to hike across the High Tatras? The Tatranská magistrála is going your way. It has some definite elevation changes, but it starts off easy. From Podbanské, you walk along a valley edge past Jamské pleso (3¼ hours) before skirting the parking lots of resort town Štrbské Pleso (one hour), where you can stop, or press on to **Chata Popradské pleso** (opposite) for the night (total 5½ hours). One of the most difficult sections is right after Popradské pleso, where you crest a ridge. A five-hour day hike lands you at **Zamkovského chata** (p402) for the night. The third day you pass the cable cars at Skalnaté pleso bound for a night at **Chata pri Zelenom plese** (p404); a five-hour day, with a steep section at the end. You're only 30 minutes from the end of the trail at Veľké Biele. Instead of backtracking, take the green trail 3½ hours down to Tatranská Kotlina (p405) where you can catch a bus onward.

Buses go to Podbanské from Starý Smokovec (40Sk, 38 minutes) three times a day in summer. Make sure you check in with the Mountain Rescue Service (p396) for trail conditions before setting out on any multiday hike.

HIGH TATRAS

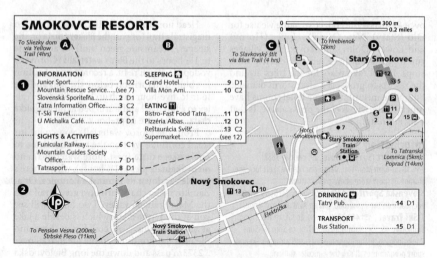

Rent mountain bikes (and skis and snowboards, each about 300Sk a day) from **Tatrasport** (☎ 442 5241; www.tatry.net/tatrasport; Starý Smokovec; ⏰ 8am-noon & 1-6pm) above the bus station parking lot.

Sleeping
Pension Vesna (☎ 442 2774; vesna@stonline.sk; Nový Smokovec 69; r per person 600Sk; P) Both family-oriented and friendly. Most of the seven rooms at this guesthouse have three beds and a separate living area. Vesna's below Nový Smokovec train stop, behind the sanatorium.

Hotel Euforia (☎ 478 3061; www.hoteleuforia.sk; Nová Lesná 399; s/d 1150/1550Sk; P) With blonde wood and cobalt-blue rugs, Euforia is fresher and brighter – newer, frankly – than most of what's up the hill. A big terrace closes off in winter. It's 3km south of Starý Smokovec, near the Nová Lesná train stop.

Grand Hotel (☎ 487 0000; www.grandhotel.sk; Starý Smokovec 38; s/d 2300/3900Sk; P X) More than 100 years of history are tied up in this full-service property that's front and centre in Old Smokovec. The basement pool, sauna, Jacuzzi complex is quite refreshing.

Other mid-elevation options:
Vilky Greenfield (Map p395; ☎ 422 4600; www .greenfield.sk; Velký Slavkov; 4-/6-person bungalow 1330/1930Sk; P) Red two-bedroom cottages sleep six in bedrooms, 10 with couches. It's 7km south of Starý Smokovec on the back road to Poprad.
Villa Mon Ami (☎ 478 0940; www.monami.sk; Nový Smokovec 31; r 1800-2200Sk; P) Scrolled ironwork beds and chandeliers; very romantic.

Atrium Hotel (Map p395; ☎ 542 2422; www.atrium hotel.sk; Nový Smokovec 42; s/d 1975/2575Sk; P) Super modern cylindrical hotel. High-speed connections.

MOUNTAIN HUTS
Bilíkova chata (Map p395; 1220m; ☎ 442 2439, fax 4422 267) Hotel-like chalet with restaurant and one-, two- and three-bed rooms with shared bathrooms.
Zbojnícka chata (Map p395; 1960m; ☎ 0903638000; www.zbojnickachata.sk) Sixteen beds, dorm style, restaurant (breakfast included).
Zamkovského chata (Map p395; 1475m; ☎ 442 2636; www.zamka.sk) Alpine chalet with 24 beds in four-bed rooms; board available.
Téryho chata (Map p395; 2015m; ☎ 442 5245) Twenty-four beds in bunks, and a restaurant.

Eating & Drinking
All the hotels, and some of the guesthouses, have restaurants; the *salaš* (rustic restaurant specialising in traditional shepherd dishes) at Vilky Greenfield is quite popular locally.

The big hotels usually have discos or bars, but Atrium Hotel goes one better with both an upscale wine bar and a fun-loving bowling bar (two lanes for rent).

Pizzéria Albas (☎ 442 3460; Albas shopping centre, Starý Smokovec; pizzas 100-170Sk) Everyone under 30 you talk to seems to recommend this big, antiseptic pizzeria. It's the pizza, not the place.

Reštaurácia Svišť (☎ 442 2545; Nový Smokovec 30; 120-200Sk) Dine on the pleasant log terrace. All the typical pork options are available, but they also have tofu and a children's menu.

Tatry Pub (☎ 442 2448; Starý Smokovec; ☺ 1-11pm Mon-Thu, 11am-midnight Fri-Sun) The official watering hole of the Mountain Guide Club provides a convivial atmosphere.

For cheap eats, there's a convenient **supermarket** (potraviny; Albas shopping centre), below the pizzeria, and **Bistro-Fast Food Tatra** (Starý Smokovec; mains 30-100Sk; ☺ 8am-7pm) northwest of the bus station, near Hotel Smokovec.

Getting There & Away

There's one direct bus from Bratislava (5.40am) to Starý Smokovec (434Sk, six hours), and one (5.05am) from Trenčín (326Sk, five hours).

For more on getting between mountain villages and to Poprad, see p397.

TATRANSKÁ LOMNICA

A lazy stream runs through the easternmost of the High Tatras' three main resorts, and that's about the pace of life here. It's quieter, smaller and a bit removed from its resort counterparts. Several of the c 1900 buildings are disintegrating. (Anyone have money to invest?) Unfortunately, the massive windstorm devastated the landscape here too. The east view doesn't green up again until you get to the Belá Tatras. The real attraction here, apart from relative peace, is the cable car up to Lomnický štít, the second-highest peak in the range.

Information

Bookshop (☺ 9am-5pm Mon-Fri, 9am-noon Sat) Next to an ATM, this well-stocked bookshop has hiking maps, guidebooks and gifts.

Tatra Information Office (TIK; ☎ 446 8118; Cesta Slobody; ☺ 10am-6pm Mon-Fri, 9am-1pm Sat) On the main street diagonally opposite Penzión Encian.

Townson Travel (☎ 478 2731; Tatranská Lomnica 94; per hr 80Sk; ☺ 9am-5pm Mon-Fri) Has one computer with internet access, as does the Grandhotel Praha.

Activities

An extremely popular **cable car** (kabínková lanovka; www.tldtatry.sk; adult/student return 390/270Sk; ☺ 8.30am-7pm Jul-Aug, to 3.30pm Sep-Jun) links Tatranská Lomnica with the bustling lake and winter sports area of Skalnaté pleso (1751m). From there, another **cable car** (adult/student return 550/350Sk; ☺ 8.30am-7pm Jul-Aug, to 3.30pm Sep-Jun) goes on to the precipitous 2634m summit of **Lomnický štít**. Queues are long during peak season, and tickets may sell out, so get there early to reserve a time. The narrow summit

ridge (site of a meteorology research station) can be crowded. One way to beat the queues is to walk up to Skalnaté pleso (2½ hours).

There is also an ordinary **chairlift** (sedačkova lanová drahá; adult/student one way 150/110Sk; ☺ 9am-5pm Jul & Aug, 9am-3.30pm Sep-Jun) from Skalnaté pleso to **Lomnické sedlo**, a 2190m saddle below the summit. Pack warm clothing – it's very cold, even in midsummer.

It's a rollercoaster, it's a summer bobsled. No, it's **Tatrabob** (☎ 446 7951; Tatranská Lomnica 29; per ride 50Sk; ☺ 9am-10pm Jul & Aug, 9am-7pm Sep-Jun). Located in town, individual riders get hauled up on a track and are then let go to control their own undulating descent.

HIKING

An easy (and popular), all-day walk starts with an early cable-car ascent to Skalnaté pleso. From here the red magistrála trail reveals grand views on its way west to Hrebienok (three hours), where you can catch the funicular railway down to Starý Smokovec and the electric train back to Tatranská Lomnica. An alternative is to walk down from Hrebienok to Tatranská Lomnica on a blue trail (five hours) through the Veľká Studená valley.

Go north three hours from Skalnaté pleso and you're at **Chata pri Zelenom plese**, on your way into the Belá Tatras and **Chata Plesinec** (p405), 2¾ hours further. You could stop overnight at one then continue over the mountains down to Tatranská Kotlina buses.

SKIING

Expert-level ski runs are at higher altitudes up by Skalnaté Pleso and Lomnické sedlo. They are accessed by cable car and chairlift. More moderate is the **Jamy** ski area (east of the village), with a rope pull and night skiing. Lift tickets for the whole area cost 690/480Sk per day for adults/children six-12, six days is 2900/2030Sk. Students aged 12-26 get a 20% discount, kids under six are free. You can rent skis (and mountain bikes) at **WR Sport** (☎ 446 3440; Hotel Slalom, Tatranská Lomnica 94; ☺ 8am-6pm) for about 400Sk a day.

Sleeping

Eurocamp FICC (Map p395; ☎ 446 7741; www.eurocamp-ficc.sk; per person/tent 110/80Sk, 2-/3-/4-bed bungalows 1200/1400/1600Sk; P ☻) Row upon row of caravans line up at this 1500-capacity ground. On site are two restaurants, a bar, billiards, a supermarket, a swimming pool and sauna,

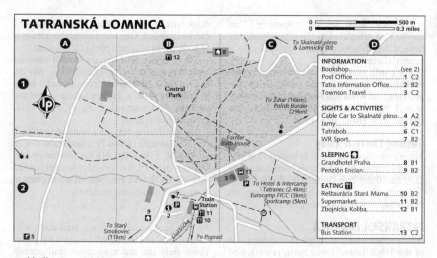

TATRANSKÁ LOMNICA

0 —————— 500 m
0 —————— 0.3 miles

To Skalnaté pleso
& Lomnický štít

Central
Park

To Ždiar (16km);
Polish Border
(29km)

Former
Bath House

6

Train
Station

3 @ 13

To Hotel & Intercamp
Tatranec (2.4km);
Eurocamp FICC (3km);
Sportcamp (5km)

1

To Starý
Smokovec
(11km)

9

7

2

11

10

Električna

5

To Poprad

INFORMATION
Bookshop...........................(see 2)
Post Office...............................1 C2
Tatra Information Office........2 B2
Townson Travel......................3 C2

SIGHTS & ACTIVITIES
Cable Car to Skalnaté pleso...4 A2
Jamy...5 A2
Tatrabob..................................6 C1
WR Sport..................................7 B2

SLEEPING
Grandhotel Praha...................8 B1
Penzión Encian........................9 B2

EATING
Reštaurácia Stará Mama......10 B2
Supermarket..........................11 B2
Zbojnícka Koliba...................12 B1

TRANSPORT
Bus Station............................13 C2

and ball courts. It's five minutes northeast of the Lomnica-Eurocamp train station on the line to Studený potok.

Športcamp (Map p395; ☎ 446 7288; http://sportcamp .host.sk in Slovak; per person/tent 100/100Sk; P) Two kilometres south past Eurocamp FICC is a less hyper, 100-site camping ground with tennis and volleyball courts.

Hotel & Intercamp Tatranec (Map p395; ☎ 446 7092; www.hoteltatranec.com; per person/tent 100/80Sk, r 800Sk; P) Six-person cabins with shared facilities (450Sk) and a motel surround the large field for tents. There's a *koliba* (rustic restaurant with open fire) on site.

Penzión Encian (☎ 446 7520; penzion.encian@sinet.sk; s/d 1000/1500Sk; P) You couldn't ask for better hosts than Zdenka and Štefan Unák. They've warmed up the small restaurant with a fire in the hearth and old skiing memorabilia on display. Eave-top room 13 has a great view of Lomnický štít.

Grandhotel Praha (☎ 446 7941; www.grandhotel praha.sk; s/d 2900/3900Sk; P ☒ ☐ ☒) Remember a time when train travel to mountain-hotel destinations was elegant? OK, so we're all too young, but the 1899 Grandhotel isn't. Rooms are appropriately classic, and there's a new spa.

MOUNTAIN HUTS

Three hours northeast from Skalnaté pleso is **Chata pri Zelenom plese** (Map p395; 1540m; ☎ 446 7420; www.zelenepleso.sk), a large, lakeside hikers lodge with four- to 12-bed rooms. You could also hike west from Skalnaté and be within a couple hours reach of the huts above Starý Smokovec (p402).

Eating

Reštaurácia Stará Mama (☎ 446 7216; shopping centre Sintra; mains 65-172Sk) Substantial soups and homemade dumplings are the reason hikers frequent this rustic fave, but the menu is actually quite extensive.

Zbojnícka Koliba (Tatranská Lomnica; mains 150-350Sk) Musicians play gypsy songs on the cimbalom while your chicken roasts over the open fire. Sit back, order some *bryndža* (sheep's cheese) to spread on bread, have some hot spiced wine and wait. The chicken takes an hour to cook. This *koliba* is on the road up to the Grandhotel Praha.

There's a supermarket *(potraviny)* just east of the train station, where there are also several food stands.

Getting There & Away

From Tatranská Lomnica buses leave for Kežmarok (22Sk, 30 minutes) at least every 1½ hours, and for Tatranská Javorina (30Sk, 45 minutes), at least five times daily. From the latter the Polish border crossing at Lysá Poľana is 2km north. Walk to the Polish side, where there are regular public buses and private minibuses to Zakopane (26km).

BELÁ TATRAS

Go east in the High Tatras and you start to hear a Polish accent. The traditional Goral folk culture is still going strong in the small northeastern arm of the High Tatras. The Belá Tatras (Belianské Tatry) are only 64 sq km. This part of the Tatras was off-limits until 1993 (protecting nature or state secrets?) Limestone prevails here, and there is a large cave system at Tatranská Kotlina. The local culture is evident in the wooden cottages in Ždiar.

Tatranská Kotlina

Over 1km of the **Belianska Cave** (☎ 446 7375; www .ssj.sk in Slovak; adult/student 150/130Sk) is open to the public, with hourly tours from 9am to 4pm Tuesday to Sunday, from mid-May to August, and every 1½ hours from 9.30am to 2pm the rest of the year.

From the south end of Tatranská Kotlina it's a two-hour hike up the green trail to **Chata Plesinec** (1290m; ☎ 0905256722; dm 350Sk). Another two hours takes you past the alpine meadow, **Rakúska poľana**, and limestone formations before you get to **Veľké biele pleso** (Big White Lake) at 1613m. Forty minutes further and you're at **Chata pri Zelenom plese** (opposite), where you can stay overnight, or continue three hours to the cable car, which will take you down to Tatranská Lomnica from Skalnaté pleso.

Ždiar

Decorated timber cottages line the long and narrow **Ždiar** (www.zdiar.sk), the only substantial settlement predating the High Tatra resorts (inhabited since the 16th century). Goral traditions have both been bolstered and eroded by alpine tourism. Several sections of the village are historical reservations, including the **Ždiar house museum** (Ždiarsky dom; ☎ 449 8142; adult/student 20/10Sk; ⏰ 10am-4pm Mon-Fri, 10am-2pm Sat & Sun May-Sep, 10am-3pm Mon-Fri Oct-Apr). Inside you can see the colourful local costumes and furnishings.

Cross over the main road from the museum and a green trail skirts the river through Monkova Valley (880m) for a half hour before climbing over **Širkové sedlo** (1826m) to get to **Kopské sedlo** (1750m) in about three hours. At this point you've pretty much crossed out of the Belá Tatras and Chata pri Zelenom plese (opposite) is an hour away.

The northern part of the village is a big ski area with seven tow lines and 10 moderate to easy runs, as well as cross-country paths at **Strednica** (www.strednica.sk; ski pass adult/child per day 350/250Sk). Ski rental is available at the base (about 250Sk a day). **Penzión Strachan** (☎ 449 8189; Ždiar 530; ⏰ rental hours 8am-8pm) rents bikes (200Sk a day) in summer and sledges (100Sk a day) in winter.

The town museum has a small restaurant, as does Penzión Strachan (mains at both are 80Sk to 160Sk). There are *bufets* by the ski hills and a few small grocery stores in town. The Goral *krčma* (pub), near the museum, is part of **Penzión Ždiar** (☎ 449 8138; www.penzionzdiar.sk; Ždiar 460; s/d 500/700Sk; 🅿). At the far north end of town, **Penzión Vasko** (☎ 449 8133; www.pensionvasko .sk; Ždiar 631; s/d 400/800Sk; 🅿) is a new wood-and-stone lodge near the ski area.

Getting There & Away

There are four buses daily to Ždiar from Poprad (53Sk, one hour) via Starý Smokovec (40Sk, 45 minutes), Tatranská Lomnica (31Sk, 35 minutes) and Tatranská Kotlina (10Sk, 10 minutes). Four daily buses travel from Ždiar to the Polish border at Lysá Poľana (22Sk, 25 minutes), 2km north of Tatranská Javorina. More buses go on weekends and during July and August. From there you can walk across the border. On Thursday and Saturday, two morning buses go directly to Zakopane (196Sk, 1½ hours).

HIGH TATRAS

East Slovakia

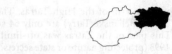

Wooden churches, sprawling castle ruins, crashing waterfalls – just beyond the High Tatras lies the most intriguing, and least accessible, region in Slovakia. Its isolation has for centuries preserved many folk customs, as well as protected a rich architectural heritage and natural beauty. Here you can step back into the 15th century in Spiš, or explore one of four national parks. Visit the wooden churches, or a *skanzen* (open-air village museum) in the borderlands and Sariš areas to experience the traditional culture.

If you're craving city life, the east has that too. Košice, the country's second-largest city, is a grand mix of old and new, with a lively bar and café scene and a towering Gothic cathedral. Among all this eastern beauty is spread a fair share of industrial ugliness, but in general the region still has a rural tranquillity and sense of remove worth discovering.

Much of the Spiš region is within easy day-trip distance from the resort towns of the High Tatras.

HIGHLIGHTS

- View the striking Renaissance square in Unesco-listed **Bardejov** (p427)
- Climb a ladder alongside a waterfall at **Slovenský raj National Park** (p420)
- Hike to **Spiš castle** (p418), the largest castle in Slovakia
- See Slovakia's greatest Gothic altar at the Church of St James in **Levoča** (p416)
- Take a break in the pleasant town square beneath the Tatras in **Kežmarok** (p412)
- Float gently down the river between the towering cliffs of **Dunajec gorge** (p414)
- Go deep into the earth in the caves of the **Slovak Karst** (p424)

★ Dunajec Gorge   ★ Bardejov

★ Kežmarok

Levoča ★   ★ Spiš Castle

★ Slovenský raj
National Park

★ Slovak Karst

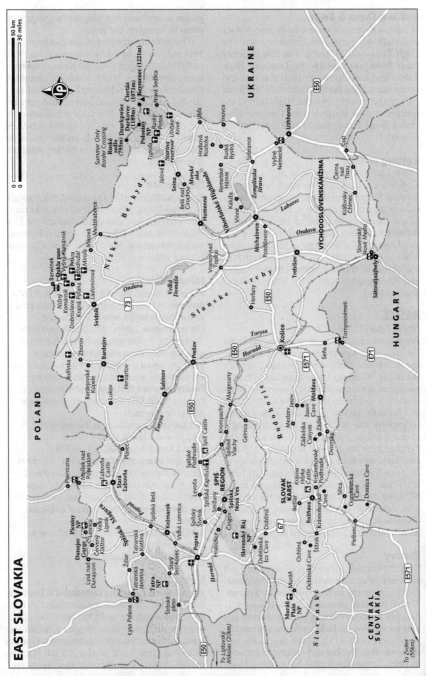

Getting There & Away

If time is short, it's easiest to fly into Košice and start exploring East Slovakia – and the High Tatras – from there. The E50 highway from Bratislava dissects the Low and High Tatras and has motorway sections. Bus and train connections running across the northern part of the country (via the High Tatras) are quicker and, in general, more frequent than connections across the southern part of the country.

Getting Around

Train and bus services west of Prešov and Košice are reliable and reasonably frequent. East of Prešov and Košice regular public-transport links become scarce and most places can only be reached by (sometimes infrequent) buses. Car rental in Košice is a good option. The majority of roads are rural lanes in good condition. The only stretch of motorway in the east runs between Košice and Prešov, but construction is underway to augment this.

KOŠICE

☎ 055 / pop 235,000

People just naturally seem to congregate along the long town square where café terraces line the streets and monumental architecture fills the centre. Buildings range from 12th-century Gothic to 20th-century Art Nouveau. Crane your neck to admire the massive Cathedral of St Elizabeth, before you head underground to explore the ancient city's archaeology. Come evening, gather with the locals on the benches near the musical fountain, stop in a café for a drink or attend a performance at the State Theatre. Slovakia's second city has a real sense of cohesion and community in the old town, which is missing from the capital. The industrial outskirts and vast residential districts built during the communist era do leave something to be desired though.

History

Košice received its city coat of arms in 1369 and became an eastern stronghold and manu-facturing centre in the Hungarian Empire. Transylvanian prince Ferenc Rákóczi II had his headquarters in Košice during the Hungarian War of Independence against the Hapsburgs (1703–11), which failed. He was shipped off to Turkey and reburied here only in 1905. To this day Košice has a strong Hun-garian accent and the Magyar language can often be heard on the street.

The town became part of Czechoslovakia in 1918 but was occupied by Hungary from 1938 to 1945. On 5 April 1945 the Košice Govern-ment Program – which made communist dictatorship in Czechoslovakia a virtual cer-tainty – was announced here. Subsequently, the communists built a large steelworks on the outskirts of the city. You can't miss US Steel's influence today – from the stacks at the steelworks to the new ice hockey stadium it sponsored.

Orientation

Košice is 20km north of Hungary, 90km south of Poland and 80km west of the Ukraine. The adjacent bus and train stations are less than 200m east of the main square, Hlavná, which broadens into Nám Slobody and Hlavné nám.

Information

Plane, train and bus stations all have ATMs.

Artforum (☎ 623 2677; Mlynská 6) Coffee-table pictori-als and fiction in English, some by Slovak authors.

City Information Centre (☎ 625 8888; www.kosice .sk; Hlavná 59; ☾ 9am-6pm Mon-Fri, 9am-1pm Sat) The large, busy official tourist office has books and maps galore, and internet terminals for 30Sk per hour. It also runs info stands at the airport and train stations (same hours).

Faculty hospital L Pasteura (Fakultná nemocnica L Pasteura; ☎ 615 3111; Rastislavova 43) One kilometre south of the main square.

Left Luggage (train station; per day/item 40Sk; ☾ 3.30-noon & 1pm-12.30am)

Ľudová Banka (Mlynská 29) Bank and ATM.

Municipal Information Centre Košice (MIC; ☎ 16 168; www.mickosice.sk) Tesco Department Store (Hlavná 111; ☾ 8am-8pm Mon-Fri, 8am-4.30pm Sat); Dargov Department Store (Hlavná 2; ☾ 8am-7pm) Small, personal info stands, with vibrant staff and tons of knick-knacks for sale.

Net Club (Hlavná 9; per hr 50Sk; ☾ 9am-10pm) Fast internet connections.

Police (☎ 622 4289; Pribinova 6)

Sights

The dark and brooding **Cathedral of St Elizabeth** (Dóm sv Alžbety; ☎ 0908667093; adult/student 70/35Sk; ☾ 1-5pm Mon, 9am-5pm Tue-Fri, 9am-1pm Sat) wins the prize for sight most likely to grace your Košice postcard home. Europe's easternmost Gothic cathedral (first built in about 1380 but re-modelled many times) dominates the square.

KOŠICE

0 ————— 200 m
0 ————— 0.1 miles

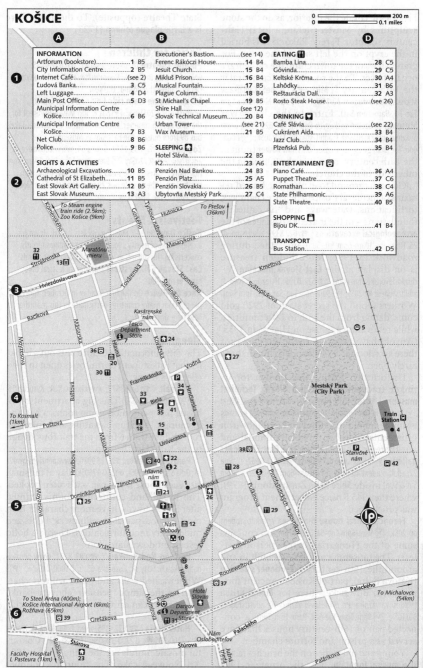

INFORMATION
Artforum (bookstore)..................**1** B5
City Information Centre.............**2** B5
Internet Café..........................(see 2)
Ľudová Banka..........................**3** C5
Left Luggage.............................**4** D4
Main Post Office.......................**5** D3
Municipal Information Centre
   Košice....................................**6** B6
Municipal Information Centre
   Košice....................................**7** B3
Net Club...................................**8** B6
Police.......................................**9** B6

SIGHTS & ACTIVITIES
Archaeological Excavations.......**10** B5
Cathedral of St Elizabeth...........**11** B5
East Slovak Art Gallery..............**12** B5
East Slovak Museum..................**13** A3

Executioner's Bastion.............(see 14)
Ferenc Rákóczi House...............**14** B4
Jesuit Church............................**15** B4
Mikluš Prison............................**16** B4
Musical Fountain.......................**17** B5
Plague Column..........................**18** B4
St Michael's Chapel...................**19** B5
Shire Hall...............................(see 12)
Slovak Technical Museum.........**20** B4
Urban Tower..........................(see 21)
Wax Museum............................**21** B5

SLEEPING
Hotel Slávia.............................**22** B5
K2..**23** A6
Penzión Nad Bankou.................**24** B3
Penzión Platz...........................**25** A5
Penzión Slovakia......................**26** B5
Ubytovňa Mestský Park............**27** C4

EATING
Bamba Lina...............................**28** C5
Góvinda...................................**29** C5
Keltské Krčma...........................**30** A4
Lahôdky...................................**31** B6
Reštaurácia Dalí.......................**32** A3
Rosto Steak House..................(see 26)

DRINKING
Café Slávia............................(see 22)
Cukráreň Aida..........................**33** B4
Jazz Club.................................**34** B4
Plzeňská Pub............................**35** B4

ENTERTAINMENT
Piano Café...............................**36** A4
Puppet Theatre.........................**37** C6
Romathan.................................**38** C4
State Philharmonic....................**39** A6
State Theatre...........................**40** B5

SHOPPING
Bijou DK..................................**41** B4

TRANSPORT
Bus Station...............................**42** D5

EAST SLOVAKIA

Frescoes decorate the interior, as do the stone sculptures by Master Štefan, a local 15th-century sculptor. Ferenc Rákóczi II is buried in the crypt on the left side of the nave. For grand views of the town climb the cathedral's ornate tower. To the south of the cathedral is the 14th-century **St Michael's Chapel** (Kaplinka sv Michala; adult/student 30/15Sk; 1-5pm Mon, 9am-5pm Tue-Fri, 9am-1pm Sat). Entry to the cheesy **Wax Museum** (Múzeum voskových figurín; ☎ 623 2534; www.waxmuseum.sk; Hlavná 3; adult/student 120/80Sk; noon-4pm Tue-Sun) gets you inside **Urban Tower** (built in the 14th century, rebuilt in the 20th), on the other side of the church.

Go underground to explore the buried remains of medieval Košice – defence chambers, fortifications, waterways and the cathedral foundations – in the mazelike passages of the **archaeological excavations** (☎ 622 8393; adult/student 25/10Sk; 10am-6pm Tue-Sun), unearthed during roadwork in 1996. More hidden treasure is on display at the **East Slovak museum** (Východoslovenské múzeum; ☎ 622 0309; Hviezdoslavovo 3; adult/student 40/20Sk; 9am-5pm Tue-Sat, 9am-1pm Sun). Workers found the secret stash of 2920 gold coins, dating from the 15th to 18th centuries, while renovating a house on Hlavná in 1935. (Anyone have a shovel?) In the museum yard there's a relocated 1741 wooden church that's rarely open.

Historically, Košice was known for its tinker tradesmen, and the **Slovak Technical museum** (☎ 622 4035; Hlavná 88; adult/student 40/20Sk; 8am-5pm Tue-Fri, 9am-2pm Sat, noon-5pm Sun) shows examples of old machines and wrought-iron ornamental work. A mix of traditional and out-there art characterises the **East Slovak Art gallery** (Východoslovenská galéria; ☎ 622 6667; Hlavná 27; adult/student 40/20Sk; 10am-6pm Tue-Fri, 2-5.30pm Sat & Sun) inside **Shire hall** (Župný dom; 1779), where the 1945 Košice Government Program was proclaimed.

Ferenc Rákóczi House (Hrnčiarska 7; adult/student 40/20Sk; 9am-5pm Tue-Sat, 9am-1pm Sun) contains some of the Hungarian heroes personal effects. The museum complex was built in and around the 15th-century **Executioner's bastion** (Katova bašta), part of Košice's ancient fortifications. Buy tickets here for **Mikluš prison** (Miklušova väznica; Pri Miklušovej väznici 10; adult/student 30/10Sk; 9am-5pm Tue-Sat, 9am-1pm Sun), a connected pair of 16th-century houses that once served as a prison and torture chamber.

Young and old gather on the benches facing the **musical fountain**, near the ornate, c 1900 State Theatre (opposite). To the north there is a large **plague column** (1723).

Košice for Children

Puppet Theatre (Bábkové divadlo; ☎ 622 0455; www.bdke.sk; in Slovak; Rooseweltova 38) Holds daytime performances throughout the year.

Steam engine train ride (☎ 622 5925; Črmel; adult/student 20/10Sk; Sat & Sun May-Aug) Great for the kids during summer. Located north of the centre. Take bus 89 from outside the East Slovak Museum.

Zoo Košice (☎ 633 1517; Široka 31; www.zookosice.sk; adult/student 40/20Sk; 9am-7pm May-Oct, 10am-3pm Nov-Apr) Located in the small village of Kavečany, 9km north. To get there, take bus 29 from near the East Slovak museum to the final stop.

Festivals & Events

Košice Days On 1–7 May the city lets its hair down for a celebration of its city's founding that involves nightly concerts on the square, as well as food and beer stands.

East Slovak Folk Festival This annual festival takes place in mid-June.

Race for Peace On the first Sunday in October, sports people from many countries participate in this marathon, held here since 1924.

Sleeping

The City Information Centre puts out a booklet that lists student dormitories open to travellers in summer.

Kosmalt (☎ 642 3572; www.kosmalt.sk; Kysucká 16; s/d 590/630Sk; P) This big apartment-block hostel has a common game room, a bar and restaurant, antique elevators and tolerable rooms. Take tram 6 from the train/bus station to the Kino Družba stop.

Penzión Slovakia (☎ 728 9820; www.penzionslovakia.sk; Orlia 6; s 950-1150Sk, d 1350-1750Sk) Stay at the small city guesthouse if you can – it's often booked. The broadband-connected rooms, named after Slovak towns, have more character than most – wood-panelled ceilings, skylights and midcentury mod furnishings. There's a boffo restaurant downstairs, too.

Penzión Nad Bankou (☎ 683 8221; www.penzionnadbankou.holiday.sk; Kováčska 63; s/d 1000/1400Sk; P) Whitewashed walls and pine furniture characterise the simple *pension* 'above a bank'. The owners can arrange a light airplane ride for 1950Sk.

Hotel Slávia (☎ 622 4395; www.hotelslavia.sk; Hlavná 63; s 2100-3050Sk, d 2700-3900Sk; P) Colourful mosaic murals are the icing on this 1902 Art Nouveau cake. The flourish continues inside with serpentine, flower-shaped lights and candy-coloured pastel walls in the rooms. Don't skip the pastry-and-coffee tradition at the grand 1st-floor café.

Other options:

Ubytovňa Mestský Park (☎ 633 3904; www.ubytovna -ke.sk; Mestský Park 13; dm 220Sk) Workers' hostel, mostly male guests.

K2 (☎ 625 5948; Štúrova 32; s/d without bathroom 350/700Sk) Bed-only singles and doubles that fill fast.

Penzión Platz (☎ 622 3450; www.platz.sk; Dominikánske nám 23; r 1500-1800Sk) It's a modular veneer world behind the pretty plaster façade.

Eating

Though this city isn't far behind the capital in population, don't expect exotic food options; most menus have a generic international mix.

Lahôdky (Hlavná 2; mains 20-80Sk; ☺ 7am-7pm Mon-Fri, 9am-5pm Sat, 9am-3pm Sun) The ground-floor cafeteria at the Dargov Department Store serves hot dishes – sausages, stuffed cabbage rolls – as well as sandwiches and salads. There's a supermarket too.

Góvinda (☎ 620 0428; Puškinova 8; mains 80-120Sk; ☺ noon-7pm Mon-Sat) Enjoy divine vegetarian Indian food at a small eatery run by Hare Krishnas. At midday there's usually a symboltapping chant parade.

Bamba Lina (☎ 622 0180; Mlynská 22; pizzas 110-160Sk; ☺ 11am-1am Mon-Thu, 11am-3am Fri, 6pm-3am Sat, 5pm-midnight Sun) The young and the hip fill the modern, loftlike dining room at all hours. They have a pretty good selection of veggie pizzas, including broccoli.

Keltské Krčma (Celtic Pub; ☎ 622 5328; Hlavná 80; mains 160-300Sk; ☺ 10am-11.30pm Mon-Thu, to 1am Fri & Sat, 3pm-11.30pm Sun) Vaulted ceilings, ancientlooking masks and wood booths do create a Celtic sort of vibe that is conducive to leisurely eating or drinking. The eclectic menu includes Slovak pork in an apricot sauce, English roast beef and Mexican enchiladas.

Still hungry?

Reštaurácia Dalí (☎ 625 1908; Strojárenska 21; mains 200-400Sk) Timepieces hang from the ceiling where upscale Slovak dishes are served.

Rosto Steak House (☎ 728 9820; Penzión Slovakia; Orliá 6; mains 100-250Sk) Tasty grilled meats with various dipping sauces.

Drinking

Plzeňská Pub (☎ 622 0402; Hlavná 92; ☺ noon-midnight Mon-Thu, to 1am Fri-Sun) Czech beer on tap and roast pork and dumplings in the kitchen (mains from 120Sk to 250Sk). Imbibe to your heart's content out back in the beer garden.

Drink your coffee or cocktail in turn-of-the-20th-century style at **Café Slaviá** (☎ 623 3190; Hotel Slaviá, Hlavná 63; ☺ 7am-11pm) or indulge in a creamy cake with your java down the street at locally revered **Cukráreň Aida** (☎ 625 6649; Hlavná 81; ☺ 8am-10pm). Snacks cost 30Sk to 100Sk. Ice cream for breakfast, yum.

Entertainment

The free monthly publication *Kam do mesta* has comprehensive entertainment and restaurant listings in Slovak and is relatively easy to decipher.

The City Information Centre sells some tickets for the opera and dance performances at the **State Theatre** (Štátne Divadlo Košice; ☎ 622 1231; www.sdke.sk; Hlavná 58; ☺ box office 9am-5.30pm Mon-Fri, 10am-1pm Sat). The city's orchestra, the **State Philharmonic** (Štátna Filharmónia Košice; ☎ 622 4514; www.sfk .sk; Moyzesova 66), has extra performances in May during the spring music festival. Though staged rarely, a performance by **Romathan** (☎ 622 4980; www.romathan.sk; Štefánikova 4), the country's only Roma theatre group, is a mix of song, dance and exuberance worth seeing.

A dance music DJ spins most nights in the cellars of the **Jazz Club** (☎ 622 4237; Kováčska 39; ☺ 11am-midnight Mon-Thu, 11am-2am Fri, 4pm-2am Sat, 4am-midnight Sun) and at the **Piano Café** (☎ 0915517339; Hlavná 92; ☺ 10-midnight Mon-Thu, 10am-1am Fri, 3pm-1am Sat, 3pm-midnight Sun), but each occasionally has live jazz. The latter also has an enclosed courtyard where a pianist plays while diners chow down on pizza.

In February 2006, the town's revered ice hockey team HC Košice got a new home: **Steel Aréna** (www.steelarena.sk; Nerudova 12) will co-host the 2011 hockey world cup with Bratislava. Buy tickets at the Municipal Information Centre Košice or at www.ticketportal.sk.

Shopping

Wander onto Hrnčiarska for some truly unique shopping. Along this traditional craftsman alley there's a potter's shop, an ironworks master, a semiprecious gem specialist, a baker and an herbalist store. The leather-maker is just around the corner at Kováčska 19.

Bijou DK (☎ 6259 859; Biela 7; ☺ 10am-8pm Mon-Fri) Buy hand-painted art you can wear (scarfs), drink from (wine glasses) and sparkle in (jewellery).

EAST SLOVAKIA

Getting There & Away

AIR

Košice International Airport (KSC; ☎ 622 1093; www
.airportkosice.sk) is about 6km southeast of the
centre. **Sky Europe** (☎ reservations 02-485 04850; www
.skyeurope.com) has two or three daily flights to
and from Bratislava (one hour) that can cost
as little as 500Sk one way (with tax), if you
book ahead. **Czech Airlines** (ČSA; ☎ 678 2490; www
.czechairlines.com) has three daily flights to and
from Prague. For more on getting to Košice
from beyond the Czech & Slovak Republics,
see p453.

BUS

Buses wind their way to and from Levoča
(117Sk, 2½ hours, two daily), Bardejov (98Sk,
1¾ hours, eight daily), and Poprad (134Sk,
2½ hours, four daily). Buses also travel to
Uzhhorod in the Ukraine (140Sk, 2½ hours)
at least once daily (twice from Tuesday to
Sunday) and to Nowy Targ in Poland (180Sk,
four hours) on Thursday and Saturday. A
bus goes from Košice to Miskolc (120Sk, two
hours) in Hungary on Wednesday, Friday
and Saturday. For longer distances the train
is usually best, having comparable prices and
shorter connection times.

CAR

Big international chain rental agencies **Hertz**
(☎ 789 6041; www.hertz.sk) and **Europcar** (☎ 683 2132;
www.europcar.sk) are represented at the airport,
but **Alimex** (☎ 729 0100; www.alimex.sk) is cheaper,
especially if you're willing to drive around
with adverts painted on the car (as little as
699Sk per day with unlimited kilometres).

TRAIN

Frequent express trains run to and from Poprad (154Sk, 1¼ hours, up to 10 daily) and
Žilina (316Sk, 2¾ hours, 14 daily). If you're
commuting all the way to and from Bratislava
it can take six to seven hours on a fast train
(518Sk); an Intercity or Eurocity train (IC or
EC, five hours, four daily) is a better bet. It's
the same price, except you need a seat reservation, which is 20Sk to 40Sk extra. For domestic
schedules visit www.zsr.sk.

A sleeper train leaves Košice every morning
for Kiev in the Ukraine (913Sk, 22½ hours),
stopping at Čop (193Sk, 2½ hours), 14km
from Uzhhorod. Two daily trains (one overnight) head for Prague (1140Sk, 11 hours),
two for Budapest in Hungary (967Sk, four

hours) and three to Kraków in Poland (844Sk,
6½ hours).

Getting Around

Transport tickets (one zone 12Sk) are good for
buses and trams in most of the city centre; buy
them from newsstands and public transport
kiosks, then validate on board. Bus 23, which
runs between the airport and the train station,
requires a two-zone ticket (19Sk).

SPIŠ REGION

A singular blend of Slovak and German culture, and a whole lotta Gothic art, are the
defining characteristics of a Spiš town. In
the 13th century Hungarian King Bela IV
invited Germanic-Saxon craftsmen and mining experts to settle this area (which had been
depopulated by wars) and to protect against
further invasion. What developed was an administrative area with a distinct Germano-
Slavic style architecture with elaborate roofline
ornamentation evident in all the towns. Also
look for landmarks like the Church of St James
in Levoča. The region's most arresting sight is
the stoic ruin of Spiš castle.

Not all the region's beauty is manmade
though. Steep waterfall-filled ravines call out
to be climbed at Slovenský raj National Park
and you can float through the 500m-high
cliffs of Dunajec river gorge in Pieniny National Park.

Though rich in history, the Spiš region
has pockets of abject poverty and some of
the area's large Roma population lives in
shanty-town settlements in below-standard
conditions.

KEŽMAROK

☎ 052 / pop 12,740

Snuggled beneath the brooding peaks of the
High Tatras, Kežmarok may not seem dramatic, but it's a truly pleasant place, with
numerous architecturally distinct churches, a
pocket-sized old town with resident castle…
All those ice-cream shops and sidewalk cafés
alone make it worth a day trip from the Tatra
resort towns, but you might want to use this
as a base to explore further north.

Kežmarok was granted free royal town
status in 1380 and was the second most important Spiš town after Levoča, from medieval times until the 19th century. Native son

Imre Thököly was a contemporary of Ferenc Rákóczi who, like him, revolted against the Hapsburg takeover of Hungary and died in exile in Turkey. Things have slowed since and the relative quiet is part of the attraction.

Orientation & Information

Kežmarok is 14km from Tatranská Lomnica and 16km from Poprad. The bus and train stations are located about 500m northwest of the town centre.

Alter Ego (☎ 452 5432; Hlavné nám 3) Has one of the best bookstore map selections in the country.

Internet Netca (Hlavné nám 62; per hr 35Sk; ☼ 10am-9pm) Email available.

Kežmarok Information Agency (☎ 452 4047; www .kezmarok.net; Hlavné nám 46; ☼ 8am-noon & 1-5pm Mon-Fri, 9am-2pm Sat, 9am-2pm Sun Jun-Sep) Stocks heaps of brochures and souvenirs. The staff can help with info about the eastern Tatras, too.

Všeobecná úverová banka (VÚB; Hviezdoslavova 5) Has an ATM and exchange.

Sights

The massive pea-green-and-red **New Evangelical church** (Nový Evanjelický kostel; ☎ 452 2242; cnr Toporcerova & Hviezdoslavova; admission 30Sk; ☼ 10am-noon & 2-4pm Mon-Sat May-Sep) is a pseudo-Moorish fortress of a 20th-century church. Inside is Imre Thököly's mausoleum. Next door is the plastered old **Wooden Evangelical church** (Drevený Evanjelický kostol; ☎ 452 2242; admission 30Sk; ☼ 10am-noon & 2-4pm Mon-Sat May-Sep), built without a nail in 1718. The cross-shaped interior of carved and painted wood is beautiful.

On the site of one of the Germanic settlers' original churches is the late–15th-century **Basilica of the Holy Cross** (Bazilika Svätého Kríža; ☎ 452 2220; Nám požiarnikov; admission 10Sk; ☼ 9am-5pm Mon-Fri Jun-Sep), whose wooden altars are said to have been carved by students of Master Pavol of Levoča (Majster Pavol z Levoča). The finely sgraffitoed, Renaissance belfry to the south was erected in 1591.

The whitewashed **castle** (hrad; ☎ 452 2618; Hradné nám 45; adult/student 60/30Sk; ☼ 9am-noon & 1-5pm Tue-Sun May-Sep; on the hour 8am-3pm Mon-Fri Oct-Apr) houses a museum with archaeology, town history and period furniture exhibits. Constructed in the 15th century, it was later surrounded with massive bastions set off by delicate Spiš-style battlements. A few remaining bits of the

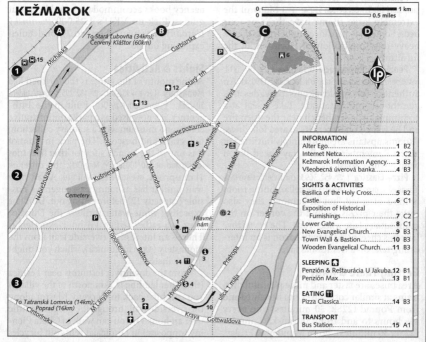

KEŽMAROK

0 _____ 1 km
0 _____ 0.5 miles

INFORMATION	
Alter Ego	1 B2
Internet Netca	2 C2
Kežmarok Information Agency	3 B3
Všeobecná úverová banka	4 B3

SIGHTS & ACTIVITIES	
Basilica of the Holy Cross	5 B2
Castle	6 C1
Exposition of Historical Furnishings	7 C2
Lower Gate	8 C1
New Evangelical Church	9 B3
Town Wall & Bastion	10 B3
Wooden Evangelical Church	11 B3

SLEEPING ⌂	
Penzión & Reštaurácia U Jakuba	12 B1
Penzión Max	13 B1

EATING ⊞	
Pizza Classica	14 B3

TRANSPORT	
Bus Station	15 A1

EAST SLOVAKIA

original town walls linger, including the **lower gate** (nižná brána).The Szimary house, lived in until 1973 by a baroness, now shelters the **Exposition of Historical Furnishings** (Expozícia bytovej kultúry; ☎ 452 2906; Hlavné nám 55; adult/student 30/15Sk; 🕙 9am-noon & 1-5pm Tue-Sun May-Aug, 8am-noon & 1-4pm Mon-Fri Sep-Apr). At the southern corner of the old town, along Priekopa, are fragments of a reconstructed 14th-century **town wall** and **bastion**.

Festivals & Events

On the second weekend of July, the **European Folk Craft Market** (Európske ľudové remeslo; www.kezmarok .net) attracts artisans from across the country. There's oodles of fine craft work, live music, food, drink and general merriment to enjoy.

Sleeping & Eating

The Kežmarok Information Agency has a list of private rooms (250Sk per person) for rent, some of which are also posted on its website. There are no fewer than six *cukráreň* (pastry cafés) serving cakes and ice cream in the pedestrian area.

Penzión Max (☎ 452 6324; www.maxpenzion.kezmarok .net; Starý trh 9; r per person 550Sk; (P)) Many of the extremely large rooms have three or four beds. Somebody here loved upholstery: there's heavy-duty multicoloured fabric on all the furniture.

Penzión & Reštaurácia U Jakuba (☎ 452 6314; www.penzionujakuba.sk; Starý trh 39; d 880-1190Sk) An authentic, folksy Slovakness pervades this guesthouse and restaurant. Take a seat at a communal wooden bench near the open fire and be waited on by servers in area folk dress. (Rooms upstairs are more simply outfitted in pine.) Remember to call a day ahead if you want a whole roast pig.

Pizza Classica (☎ 452 3693; cnr Hviezdoslavova & Hlavné nám; pizzas 90-170Sk) The cellar dining room is kind of small, but in summer they also serve their pizzas around the corner on the main square (see waiter run). The *bryndzové* (sheep's cheese) pizza with bacon is an interesting take on a traditional fave.

Getting There & Away

Area buses are faster and more plentiful than trains at similar cost. Buses run hourly to and from Poprad (22Sk, 30 minutes) and every 1½ hours to and from Tatranská Lomnica (22Sk, 30 minutes). From Monday to Friday, there are three buses a day to Červený Kláštor (58Sk, 1½ hours) and four to and from Levoča (40Sk, 50 minutes). Unless you take the one weekday bus from Košice (2½ hours, 138Sk) at 2.55pm, to get here you have to switch at Poprad.

PIENINY NATIONAL PARK
☎ 052

The main reason people come to the tiny, 21-sq-km Pieniny National Park (Pieninský národný park; Pienap), is for a chance to float on a raft through **Dunajec gorge**. The park was created in 1967, in combination with a similar park near Szczawnica in Poland to protect the 9km gorge near the village of Červený Kláštor and its eponymous monastery. A bit further downstream, Lesnica is the terminus for rafting trips in Slovakia. Past 500m-tall cliffs, the gentle waters of the Dunajec carry tourists in a *plte* (shallow, flat-bottomed wood rafts), complete with a pole-wielding, costumed guide.

A small **Information Centre** (☎ 482 2122; www .pieniny.sk; 🕙 9am-5pm May-Oct) is about 2km west of the monastery. **CK Pieniny Klub** (☎ 439 7303; www.sl.sinet.sk/pieniny; Lesnica 62,Červený Kláštor) travel agency books accommodation and hires out guides. Pick up VKÚ's 1:25,000 *Pieninský Národný Park* map (sheet No 7) for detailed exploring on foot.

Sights & Activities

At the mouth of the gorge is the fortified **Red Monastery** (Červený Kláštor; ☎ 482 2955; adult/student 50/25Sk; 🕙 9am-5pm May-Oct). Built in the 14th-century, it's now used as a park administrative centre and museum with a statuary collection, folk crafts and frescoes. The park in front of it is one of the launch sites for **river float trips** (adult/student 250/100Sk; 🕙 May-Oct), the other is 1km upriver, west of the village. A raft may wait until it has as many passengers as possible (capacity 12) before setting out. Don't be expecting white-water thrills – the Dunajec river is a rather sedate 1½ hour experience. There's an interesting riverside trail from the monastery (4km to Lesnica), which you might opt for instead.

From the downriver terminus near Lesnica (the water landing is 1km north of the village) you can hike back to Červený Kláštor along the riverside trail through the gorge in a little over an hour. Or you can walk to Chata Pieniny (opposite) in Lesnica; it rents out bicycles

EAST SLOVAKIA

RAFTING IN POLAND

The Dunajec river divides Slovakia and Poland, though once on the river it's something like an international free-for-all. The Poles offer much longer trips, including a two-day, 50km voyage from Katy to Krościenko. Depending on your stamina and visa status, it may be worthwhile crossing over into Poland to do your rafting from there. There's a pedestrian-only **border crossing** (9am-9pm Apr-Sep, 9am-5pm Oct-Mar) from Lesnica to the Polish town of Szczawnica. From there frequent daily buses go to Nowy Targ (38km) where you switch to a bus going to the main rafting centre at Katy. By car, you can cross the Slovak–Polish border at Lysá nad Dunajcom (6km west of Červený Kláštor).

---

one way (100Sk per day) for the riverside trail. Ride back to the monastery where you return the bikes. The lodge also runs a shuttle bus to Červený Kláštor (50Sk, 20km by road).

Festivals & Events

Brightly attired dancers perform at the annual **Zamaguria Folk Festival** (Zamagurský folklórny slávnosti) near the monastery in the middle of June. Each September the **International Pieniny Canoe Slalom** (Medzinárodný pieninský slalom) is held on the river here.

Sleeping & Eating

CK Pieniny Klub travel agency handles private rooms (some are posted on their website) for about 250Sk per person. Also look for private signs on the main road in Červený Kláštor. Food stalls stand between the monastery and the river launch.

Chata Pieniny (439 7530; www.chatapieniny.sk; Lesnica; dm 280Sk) Cheap and cheerful Chata Pieniny is an old log lodge with two- to six-bed rooms at the raft terminus. There's a restaurant, minimarket and bike rental.

Dunajec Recreational (Rekreačné zariadenie; 439 7105; www.dunajec.sk; s/d without bathroom 300/600Sk; 2 persons in hut 580Sk, per person/tent 60/50Sk; P) One kilometre south of the monastery, toward Veľký Lipník, this complex has five huts for rent (sleeping six), a restaurant, a bar, bike rental, a camping ground and sports courts.

Penzión Holica (439 7114; Lesnica 156; r/apt 700/1000Sk) Spotless, if bare, rooms here are worth seeking out, 1km south of the village. This *penzión* and small restaurant are quite popular with groups.

Hotel Pltník (482 2525; Červený Kláštor; www.hotel pltnik.sk; s/d 720/870Sk, per person/tent 60/50Sk; P) The not-so-youthful hotel has small rooms with wood-panelled ceilings and not much else. It runs a camping ground in the big riverfront field adjacent.

Getting There & Away

Getting here is a challenge unless you have a car. Buses run to Červený Kláštor from Kežmarok (58Sk, 1½ hours, three daily) and to and from Poprad (89Sk, 1¾ hours, three daily Monday to Saturday, one Sunday). From Košice (152Sk, 3½ hours) there's one direct afternoon bus, otherwise you have to change in Stará Ľubovňa (40Sk, 35 minutes, six daily).

STARÁ ĽUBOVŇA

052 / pop 16,200

Skip the nondescript town; head to the castle overlooking the Poprad river, and the *skanzen* below. From the adjacent bus and train stations, walk up to the main road and turn left, follow the 2.5km red-marked trail to the castle. If you turn east instead and go 1km, you'll get to Nám sv Mikuláša, the main town square, with the **City Information Centre** (432 1713; www.staralubovna.sk; Nám sv Mikuláša 12; 9-11.30am & 1-5pm Mon-Fri, 10am-2pm Sat) and a couple of banks with ATMs.

Sights & Activities

Striking **Ľubovňa castle** (Ľubovniansky hrad; 432 2030; adult/student 60/30Sk; 9am-6pm May-Sep, 10am-3pm Mon-Sat Oct-Apr) lies half in ruins, half in reconstruction, but the mix of Gothic, baroque and Renaissance styles makes for an interesting self-guided tour. The sky-clad location of its top tower (think lots of climbing) provides views across the valley to the Spišska Magura mountains, as well as the Roma shanty town on the edge of Stará Ľubovňa. Different parts of the palace contain exhibits on the castle history, weaponry and period furniture. Every June, a **medieval encampment** gathers below the gates to re-enact an ancient battle; just one of many summer weekend festivals.

The few plastered wooden houses and a church in the **skanzen** (adult/student 30/15Sk;

(🕑 9am-6pm May-Sep, 10am-3pm Oct) reflect a blend of the styles typical of the Spišská Magura region – Slovak, Polish, Rusyn and German.

Sleeping & Eating

Ubytovací hostinec Peters (☎ 432 4891; Pod hradom; s/d 200/400Sk; **P**) If you're stuck on the way up to the castle, this place has basic rooms and a restaurant.

Salaš U Franka (☎ 436 9292; Popradská 34; mains 100-150Sk) This sprawling, rustic eatery lies 3km south on the road toward Poprad. It serves a fresh variety of dumpling dishes topped with *bryndža* (sheep's cheese) and bacon, cabbage, onions or *kielbasa*. Occasional folk nights include live bands.

Getting There & Away

Buses connect with Červený Kláštor (40Sk, 35 minutes, six daily), Bardejov (78Sk, 1½ hours, seven daily) and Kežmarok (44Sk, 45 minutes). There are up to 11 trains a day between Stará Ľubovňa, Kežmarok (36Sk, 50 minutes) and Plaveč (24Sk, 20 minutes), where you change trains if you're bound for Poland. Five daily buses run to and from Košice (143Sk, 2½ hours).

Getting Around

Up to eight town buses travel to and from the castle and the train and bus stations (12Sk) Monday to Friday, but services are rare on weekends.

LEVOČA

☎ 053 / pop 14,400

Medieval walls stand stolid and defensive, protecting the age-old centre from onslaught. Levoča is one of the few Slovak cities to have its ancient old town defences largely intact. The pride of Slovakia's religious art collection, an 18m-high altar carved by renowned artist Master Pavol of Levoča, resides within the centre square's Church of St James. Surrounding the church is a panoply of ancient houses with mostly Renaissance façades.

History

Like other Spiš towns, Levoča was settled and enriched by a wave of Saxon artisans in the 13th century. It prospered from trade in gold and woodcarving for centuries. Much of its present Renaissance personality comes from a building boom after a huge fire in the 16th century.

Levoča's fortunes collapsed in the 17th century after an area anti-Hapsburg uprising failed. Again on the temporarily losing side, a Slovak army garrison from Levoča joined in the short-lived, antifascist Slovak National Uprising in 1944. German troops occupied the town until its liberation by the Soviets in February 1945.

Orientation

Levoča is on the E50 motorway between Poprad (28km) and Košice (94km). The centre is 1km north of the train and bus stations. Most buses also stop at Nám Štefana Kluberta, a few blocks east of the main square, Nám Majstra Pavla.

Information

Levonet Internet Café (Nám Majstra Pavla 38; per hr 80Sk; 🕑 10am-midnight)

Post office (Nám Majstra Pavla 42)

Tourist Information Office (☎ 451 3763; www .levoca.sk; Nám Majstra Pavla 58; 🕑 9am-5pm Mon-Sat, 10am-2pm Sun May-Oct; 9am-4.30pm Mon-Fri Nov-Apr) Ask for the free photocopied map staff hide under the counter.

Všeobecná úverová banka (VÚB; Nám Majstra Pavla 28)

Sights

The Gothic spindles-and-spires **Church of St James** (Chrám sv Jakuba; ☎ 451 2347; www.chramsvjakuba .sk; adult/student 50/30Sk; 🕑 tours 11.30am, 1pm, 2pm, 3pm & 4pm Tue-Sat Sep-Jun, 11am-5pm Mon, 9am-5pm Tue-Sat Jul & Aug) is basically a museum of medieval religious art and rare furnishings, though everyone comes to see the splendid three-sided wooden altar (1517) created by Master Pavol of Levoča. At more than 18m high, and 6m wide, it's said to be the world's largest. Exquisite 3-D representations of the Last Supper and the Madonna and Child decorate the structure. (Think Mary looks familiar? Her face appears on the 100Sk banknote.) The **church ticket office** (kasa; 🕑 11am-5pm) is inside the **Municipal Weights House** (Budova mestských váh). Off season, if there are fewer than five people at a tour time, the keeper may not open up.

The originally Gothic **town hall** (*radnica*) and tower got a Renaissance face-lift in 1551, creating what is now one of Levoča's most beautiful buildings. Inside is the **Spiš museum** (☎ 451 2449; www.snm.sk; adult/student 50/20Sk; 🕑 9am-5pm), which displays folk dresses and town artefacts in wood-panelled chambers. South of the town hall is the **Cage of Shame** (Klietka hanby), where naughty boys and girls were publicly punished.

The pedestrian centre is chock-a-block with Gothic and Renaissance eye candy. The finest is the **Thurzov house** (Thurzov dom; 1532) at No 7, with its characteristic frenetic Spiš Renaissance roofline. At No 20, **Master Pavol House** (Dom Majstra Pavla; ☎ 451 3496; adult/student 40/20Sk; ☺ 9am-5pm), run by the Spiš museum, is devoted to the town's famous sculptor son.

From town you can see the **Church of Mariánska hora**, on a hill 2km north.

Festivals & Events

On the first weekend in July up to a quarter of a million pilgrims converge on the Church of Mariánska hora for a **Marian Pilgrimage** (Marian púť). Mass is celebrated hourly from 6pm on Saturday, but the one to wait for is at 10am on Sunday.

Sleeping & Eating

Oáza (☎ 451 4511; www.ubytovanieoaza.sk; Nová 65; per person 300Sk) The two-bed rooms with shared bathrooms, and the four-bed en-suite rooms with kitchen, are just what the budget doctor ordered. There's a big garden with a lawn, vegetable garden a chicken coup. The super-personable owner speaks several languages.

Penzión U Leva (☎ 450 2311; www.uleva.sk; Nám Majstra Pavla 24; s/d/apt 1100/2000/2400Sk; Ⓟ) A new elevator is a welcome addition to these two town-square buildings turned modern, reader-recommended lodging. Apartments have kitchens.

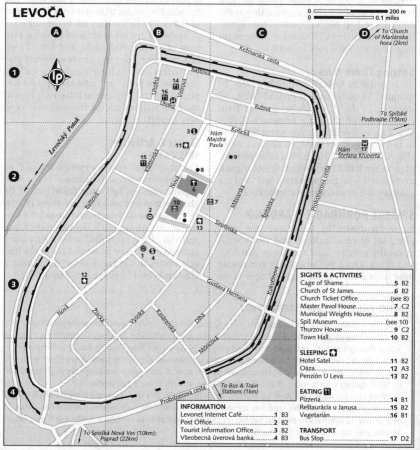

LEVOČA

0 — 200 m
0 — 0.1 miles

SIGHTS & ACTIVITIES	
Cage of Shame	5 B2
Church of St James	6 B2
Church Ticket Office	(see 8)
Master Pavol House	7 C2
Municipal Weights House	8 B2
Spiš Museum	(see 10)
Thurzov House	9 C2
Town Hall	10 B2

SLEEPING 🛏	
Hotel Satel	11 B2
Oáza	12 A3
Penzión U Leva	13 B2

EATING 🍴	
Pizzeria	14 B1
Reštaurácia u Janusa	15 B2
Vegetarián	16 B1

INFORMATION	
Levonet Internet Café	1 B3
Post Office	2 B2
Tourist Information Office	3 B2
Všeobecná úverová banka	4 B3

TRANSPORT	
Bus Stop	17 D2

To Church of Mariánska hora (2km)

To Spišské Podhradie (15km)

To Bus & Train Stations (1km)

To Spišská Nová Ves (10km); Poprad (22km)

EAST SLOVAKIA

Hotel Satel (☎ 451 2943; www.hotelsatel.com; Nám Majstra Pavla 55; s/d 1765/2730Sk; **P**) Float into the swish luxury of the town's top hotel. You can tell the building dates back to the 14th century by the rooms' arched, vaulted ceilings and the atrium arcade. However, its amenities are modern, and it has wi-fi and a massage service.

Vegetarián (☎ 451 4576; Uhoľná 137; mains 45-90Sk; ⏰ 10am-3.15pm Mon-Fri) Wholesome smells and a no-fuss menu make this basic veggie haunt a hit. Casseroles and tofu dishes are on the rotating list of dishes.

Reštaurácia u Janusa (☎ 451 4592; Kláštorská 22; mains 70-120Sk) Choose from all the fried pork favourites at the locals' pick for Slovak food. Tables fill up quick at lunchtime.

Pizzeria (☎ 0905396528; Vetrová 4; pizzas 100-160Sk) For such a smoky, nameless place, they really don't serve bad pizza. Upstairs, two apartments with kitchens (1000Sk) and one small single room (500Sk) are for rent.

Getting There & Away
Buses travel to Spišské Podhradie (22Sk, 20 minutes, 11 daily) and to Poprad (40Sk, 30 minutes, 21 daily), which has onward train connections on the main Bratislava–Košice line. Two to five buses a day wend their way to and from Košice (128Sk, two hours). Buses also run to Spišská Nová Ves (18Sk, 20 minutes, every half hour), which is not a great town, but it is on the main train line (and is a gateway to Slovenský raj National Park).

SPIŠSKÉ PODHRADIE & AROUND
From far down the motorway you catch glimpses of eerie outlines and stony walls crowning a ridge. 'Can it really be that big?' you think. Once you're upon it you realise how truly daunting the sight of Spiš castle

must have been for ancient enemies. Sitting hilltop 200m above a broad valley floor the 4 hectare spread still inspires awe today – and it's in ruins.

In the 12th century a settlement, Spišské Podhradie, appeared below the neighbouring castle. It developed into an artisans' town in the 13th century when, to the west, Spišská Kapitula (Spiš Chapter) developed. The village itself isn't the attraction, it's the Unesco-listed castle that's one of Slovakia's true wonders.

Orientation & Information
Spišské Podhradie is 15km east of Levoča, off the main E50 highway between Košice and Poprad. Most long-distance buses stop in the main square, Marianské nám, where there's a post office, an ATM and a bus stop. The Spišské Podhradie train station is 1.5km east of the centre, below the path to the castle.

Spišská Kapitula is on another ridge 1km west of Spišské Podhradie, and has its own bus stop. For a day trip arrive early and give yourself at least 4½ hours (including walking time) to see both the castle and Spišská Kapitula. You may be able to leave your bags at the train station (ask the stationmaster very, very nicely).

Sights & Activities
SPIŠ CASTLE
You may think you're experiencing *déjà vu* the first time you catch a glimpse of the photogenic ruins of **Spiš castle** (Spišský hrad; ☎ 454 1336; www.spisskyhrad.com in Slovak; adult/student 100/60Sk; ⏰ 9am-6pm May-Oct, by appointment Nov-Apr); the castle appears on so much Slovak promotional material (showing the field below it alternately covered in snow or flowers). One of the biggest castles in Central Europe, it has been a Unesco World Heritage site since 1993.

WHO THE HECK IS MASTER PAVOL?

Why, he's from Levoča, of course, just ask anyone. But the nation's premier medieval artist is a bit more elusive than that. He *was* a sculptor and carver who did amazing Gothic things with wood during the 15th and early 16th centuries – OK we've got that. And he had a woodcarving workshop in Levoča, where he married a wealthy woman and sat on the town council. But where was he born? When did he die? No one can say for sure. A damaging fire swept through Levoča in 1550, taking with it most of the town's archives and Mr Pavol's last name.

What else do we know? Well, he worked an awful lot. To this day there are intricate altars and engaging statues he and his students carved scattered across the Spiš region. Rumour has it that one of the 12 apostles in the *Last Supper* on the St James altar in Levoča is really a self-portrait. Maybe you can figure out who he is.

References to the castle first appear in a 1209 chronicle, and the central residential tower, at the highest elevation, is thought to date from that time (there are great views from the top). Defenders repulsed the Tatars in 1241, and the rulers and noble family owners kept adding on to the place during the 15th and 16th centuries. By 1780 when a fire hit, much of the military threat had abated and it was largely deserted. Few structures remain whole today, but there's a cistern, a chapel and a rectangular Romanesque palace, which holds the museum. Descend to the dungeon to see the meaty bits – it's incredible the torture devices the human mind can think up.

Throughout summer the castle hosts medieval festivals, which consist mainly of music and mock battles. To get to the castle, cross the tracks near the train station and follow the yellow markers up the steep trail. By car, the easiest approach to the castle is via the main highway from the east (Prešov) side.

SPIŠSKÁ KAPITULA

Another national treasure is a short distance away. The partially active Spišská Kapitula (Spiš Chapter) is an ecclesiastical complex built in the 13th century, completely encircled by a 16th-century wall. Charming Gothic houses line the single street running between the two medieval gates. Buy tickets and pick up a guide from the **Information Office** (☎ 0907388411; adult/student 20/10Sk; 🕒 11.15am-2.45pm). At the upper end is the magnificent Romanesque **St Martin's Cathedral** (Katedrál sv Martin; 1273) with twin towers and an ancient Gothic sanctuary. Inside are several trifold painted Gothic altars from the 15th century that are impressive. On either side of the cathedral are the **seminary** (seminára) and the Renaissance **bishop's palace** (biskupský palác; 1652).

Sleeping & Eating

Penzión Podzámok (☎ 454 1755; www.penzionpodzamok .sk; Podzámková 28, Spišské Podhradie; s/d without bathroom 300/650Sk; Ⓟ 🛏) Three family houses cobbled together make a 42-bed guesthouse (meals available) with a unobstructed castle view from the garden. It's at the end of the street east of the bridge, between Marianské nám and the train station.

Spišský Salaš (☎ 454 1202; www.spisskysalas.sk; Levočská cesta 11; s/d 420/800Sk; Ⓟ) What rustic fun! Dig into lamb stew at the folksy restaurant (or have grilled chicken by the outdoor fire)

and then settle into a simple wood-panelled room for the night. This log-cabin complex is on the road to Spišské Podhradie, 3km west of Spiš Chapter.

Kolping House (☎ 0905790097; www.hotelkolping .sk; Spišská Kapitula 15; s/d 1100/1600Sk; Ⓟ 🛏) A romantic little outfit actually inside the walls of Spišská Kapitula. Antiques and reproductions fill the rooms and restaurant.

Getting There & Away

A railway line connects Spišské Podhradie to Spišské Vlachy (12Sk, 10 minutes, eight daily), a station on the main line from Poprad to Košice. Relatively frequent buses run to and from Levoča (22Sk, 20 minutes, 11 daily) and Poprad (55Sk, 50 minutes, eight daily). If you're travelling to Spišská Kapitula by bus from Levoča, get off before the main town at Spišské Podhradie, Kapitula.

SPIŠSKÁ NOVÁ VES

☎ 053 / pop 39,200

You may have to stop at this unfortunate town on the Hornád river before going to nearby Slovenský raj National Park; there are few markets within the park's boundaries and to get to most of the park villages requires a transport change here. No need to linger though.

The bus and train stations are northwest of the centre; walk south on Odborárov and turn left on Dulianska, which morphs into the main square Radničné nám, bounded by Letná and Zimná (Summer and Winter).

There's an ATM at the train station and at banks on the main square. Help at the **Tourist Information Centre** (Map p421; ☎ 442 8292; Letná 49; 🕒 8am-5pm Mon-Fri, 9.30am-1.30pm Sat Jun-Sep, 8am-4.30pm Mon-Fri Oct-May) is hit or miss. Connect to the wider world at **Internet Klub** (Map p421; ☎ 441 4402; Letná 4; per hr 50Sk; 🕒 9am-9pm).

Opposite the bus station is a massive Billa supermarket (Map p421), which is the best thing about the place. If you're waiting for the tourist office to open after a break, you could eat at **Café Nostalgia** (Map p421; Letná 49; mains 95-250Sk). The '50s memorabilia goes with the names of the dishes (like James Dean chicken salad).

Spišská Nová Ves lies on a main line served by 11 daily express trains between Bratislava (450Sk, 5¼ hours) and Košice (104Sk, one hour), with a stop at Poprad (56Sk, 20 minutes). There's a frequent bus service to and from Levoča (18Sk, 20 minutes, every half hour). For onward destinations near Slovenský raj National Park (see p422) connections aren't the best (you may want to consider springing for a car in Košice).

SLOVENSKÝ RAJ NATIONAL PARK

Rumbling waterfalls, steep gorges, sheer rock faces, thick forests and hilltop meadows: **Slovenský raj** (Slovak paradise; www.slovenskyraj.sk; admission 20Sk) is a national park for the passionately outdoorsy. The park is 90% covered in dense pine and deciduous forest, and has several rare species found only within its borders, including 17 butterfly types and 20 wildflower varieties. Easier trails exist, but the one-way ladder- and chain-assist ascents are the most dramatic. You cling to a metal rung headed straight up a precipice while an icy waterfall splashes and sprays a metre away. And that's after you've scrambled horizontally across a log ladder to cross the same stream down below. Pure exhilaration. Poprad is the gateway to Slovenský raj National Park as well as the Tatras.

Orientation

Slovenský raj National Park starts just 9km south of Poprad. Most public transport access to the park is through Spišská Nová Ves, which is 23km southeast of Poprad, at the eastern end of the Low Tatras. The main trailhead villages on the northern edge of the national park are Čingov, 5km west of Spišská Nová Ves, and Podlesok, 2km southwest of Hrabušice. There are lodgings in park villages but for full town services, you'll have to go into Spišská Nová Ves or Hrabušice. Dedinky, at the south end of the park, is a regular lakeside village with a pub, *potraviny* (supermarket) and houses.

Information

Before you go trekking buy VKÚ's 1:25,000 *Slovenský raj* hiking map (No 4), available at many tourist offices and bookshops countrywide. This can be complemented by the 40 walks found in *The Slovak Paradise* (No 2) book, part of the Knapsacked Travel series.

For the best trail and weather information, and help in booking a *chata* along the way, contact the park's **Mountain Rescue Service** (Horská služba; ☎ 053-449 1182; Čingov; ☒ 8am-6pm). There's a small **Tourist information Office** (☎ 053-429 9854; Hlavná, Hrabušice ☒ 8am-6pm Jul & Aug, 8am-4pm Mon-Fri

Sep-Jun) in Hrabušice, not far from the **Ascona Café** (Hlavná 99; per hr 25Sk; ☒ 1pm-midnight Sun-Thu, to 3am Fri & Sat), which has internet. Helpful park websites include www.slovenskyraj.sk and www.slovenskyraj.org.

Sights & Activities

Most campgrounds and hotels have bike rentals, including the Hotel Flora and Park Hotel in Čingov, and skis are available for rent at the base of the hill at Dedinky. Mlynky, 3km east of Dedinky, is the area's ski central with five T-bar lifts. Equipment rental (about 250Sk a day) is available from the **Hotel Mlynky** (☎ 053-449 3523; www.hotelmlynky.sk; Mlynky-Biele Vody 252).

HIKING

The 326km of trails through the park's rugged gorges include some fun and challenging sections equipped with 'technical aids' (ladders, chain handrails, and metal steps). These stretches are one way (marked with arrows on maps), and slippery when wet, so plan ahead. Note that fines of up to 5000Sk are payable on the spot for going the wrong way, littering, lighting a fire or picking plants within the park.

The shortest hike that includes a one-way *roklina* (gorge) ascent is the one-hour **Zejmarská gorge** hike on the blue trail. It starts at Biele Vody (25 minutes northeast of Dedinky on the red trail). To get back, follow the green trail down to Dedinky (40 minutes), or there's a **chairlift** (adult/child 30/15Sk; 9am-5pm) between Geravy and Dedinky that, if it's working, goes on the hour.

From Čingov a yellow trail heads to the ever-popular lookout point, **Tomášovský výhľad** (667m), and on to **Letanovský mlyn** and the **Hornád river**. From here, head west again along the Hornád to **Kláštorská gorge**, south up a one-way technically aided section to **Kláštorisko chata**, where there's a restaurant, small cabins and a great meadow for picnics. Follow the green trail back along the ridge towards Čingov. Allow at least six hours for the circuit, lunch at Kláštorisko chata included. To hike from Čingov to Dedinky takes about eight hours; head west to Biely potok and follow the green trail by the stream to the photogenic lake at Klauzy, continuing on a ridge trail that eventually leads down to Dedinky.

From Podlesok an excellent day's hike heads up the **Suchá Belá gorge** (with several steep ladders, the tallest 30m). At the top of

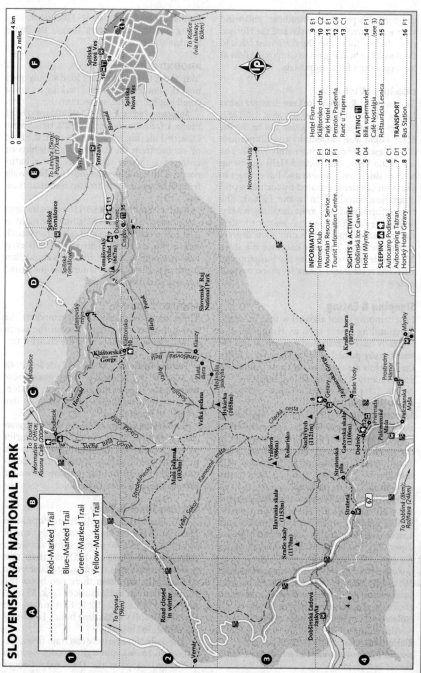

the gorge it's possible to head east and wind your way down to Kláštorisko and the Hornád river, before following the river west back to Podlesok (or heading on to Čingov). Allow at least six hours for a round-trip.

DOBŠINSKÁ ICE CAVE

The unusual **Dobšinská Ice Cave** (Dobšinská Ľadová Jaskyňa; ☎ 058-788 1470; adult/student 150/130Sk; ☼ 9am-4pm Tue-Sun Jun-Aug, 9.30am-2pm Tue-Sun May & Sep) is 6km west of Dedinky and 12km south of Podlesok (via a summer-only road). The ice in the Veľká sieň (Grand Hall) can be up to 20m thick, and smooth and flat enough to skate on (as demonstrated by former world champion Karol Divín in the 1950s). The frozen formations are most dazzling in May, before they start to melt (no matter the date the ambient temperature is only a few degrees above freezing). The cave entrance is a steep 20-minute hike south from the bus stop and adjacent restaurant. Tours leave every hour or less.

Sleeping & Eating

Free camping is not allowed within the park. Surrounding towns such as Hrabušice and Smižany have private and *pension* rooms for rent (many posted at www.slovenskyraj.sk); those below are closer to the trails. Almost all area restaurants are inside lodgings.

AROUND ČINGOV

Autocamping Tatran (☎ 053-429 7105; www.durkovec .sk; per person/tent/dm 80/60/220Sk, 2-person hut without bathroom 190Sk; P ⚿) Tents crowd together in the pasture surrounded by tiny huts, a big dormitory and multiroom rental houses with satellite TV (2500Sk). Take a 2.2km tramp west of the Čingov bus stop.

Hotel Flora (☎ 053-4491129;www.hotelfloraslovenskyraj .sk; s/d 750/1200Sk; P ⚿) The lobby and worthwhile restaurant are mountain-fabulous, with a stone fireplace, leather chairs and big windows. Pity the rooms didn't come along for the renovation ride.

Park Hotel (☎ 053-442 2022; www.parkhotel.vitex .sk/; s/d 950/1200Sk; P) All rooms have a balcony or a terrace. Pool tables, volleyball and tennis courts, and a sauna up the fun factor. Nicely isolated 1.2km before Čingov village.

Also in the area:

Kláštorisko chata (☎ 053-449 3307; cabins per person 250Sk) Small mountain huts and restaurant located midtrail. Book ahead.

Reštaurácia Lesnica (☎ 053-449 1518; Penzión Lesnica; mains 90-200Sk) Residents' favourite; kids like the ice-cream sundaes.

AROUND PODLESOK

May to September there are food stands open near the Podlesok trailhead parking lot and a small but full-service restaurant.

Autocamp Podlesok (☎ 053-429 9165; slovrajbela@ stonline.sk; Podlesok; per person/tent 60/60Sk, huts per person 230Sk; P) Big, big, big. Pitch a tent in the field or choose from the A-frames, small huts or cottages with two to 12 beds and a bathroom. The camping ground is a 2km walk from Hrabušice; there are two restaurants on site.

Ranč u Trapera (☎ 0911987231; www.rancutrapera .skg.sk; Podlesok 16; r per person 450Sk) Stay the night in a large log cabin dream and take a horseback ride in the morning. This ranch B&B even has front porch rocking chairs. It's about 2km south of Podlesok (on the summer-only road toward Dedinky).

AROUND DEDINKY

The pub and the *potraviny* (supermarket), the two staples of any village, are on the north side of the lake, near where the chairlift terminates.

Penzión Pastierňa (☎ 058-798 1175; Dedinky 42; s/d 300/600Sk; P) A small wooden guesthouse waits at the edge of the village, near the forest and green trailhead. There are only five rooms, so book ahead.

Horský Hotel Geravy (☎ 058-798 1179; www.geravy .com; Geravy; dm 250Sk) At the top of the chairlift above Dedinky sits this mountain hotel with pub and picnic tables. Bunkroom accommodation is basic but the meadow views are unbeatable. Full board available.

Getting There & Away

A few buses run directly from Poprad to Dedinky (53Sk 1¼ hours, three daily) and to Hrabušice (25Sk, 40 minutes, five on weekdays, one on weekends). Other than that Spišská Nová Ves is the main transfer point to Slovenský raj. From there two buses (no trains) a day run to Hrabušice (22Sk, 35 minutes), two to Čingov (10Sk, 12 minutes) and three to Dedinky (53Sk, one hour). Few buses are scheduled midday.

The daily Horehoronec fast train from Bratislava (6.16am), through Banská Bystrica (10.04am), stops at the Dobšinská Ľadová

Jaskyňa (420Sk, 5¾ hours), Dedinky (420Sk, five hours 50 minutes) and Mlynky (420Sk, six hours). In reverse it leaves Košice at 2.50pm stopping at Dedinky (146Sk, two hours) etc. Otherwise, to get between Dedinky and Košice requires a switch at Margecany (84Sk, 1½ hours, six daily).

Getting Around

Getting around is not so easy really, unless you hike or drive. One bus a day goes each way between Čingov and Hrabušice (10Sk, 45 minutes), Hrabušice and Dedinky (18Sk, one hour), and Dedinky and Čingov (25Sk, two hours).

SLOVAK KARST

☎ 058

Boat along the river Styx, traipse through a fairytale castle and admire an aragonite flower. Do all this and more, among the fanciful underworld formations of the Slovak Karst (Slovenský kras).

This region of limestone canyons and caves lies at the eastern end of Slovenské rudohorie (the Slovak Ore Mountains), a major range that reaches the border with Hungary. Its most spectacular landscapes are within the 440-sq-km Slovak Karst National Park, promoted to a Unesco World Heritage site in 1995. Five of the subterranean domains are open to the public.

Above ground the area has the dramatic Krásna Hôrka Castle and ornate Betliar Palace. In this region all roads lead to the administrative capital, Rožňava, and transport is infrequent. This makes it hard to see more than one sight in a day without a car.

ROŽŇAVA

pop 19,260

Scattered outside the region's central city are some interesting monuments and natural wonders. Rožňava is a good base for exploring the Slovak Karst National Park, as well as the area's castles.

This former mining town, 20km north of the border, has an understandably big Hungarian-speaking minority. It was the region's main gold, silver and iron ore centre until the 17th century. Nám Baníkov, the town centre, is 2.5km north of the train station via Šafaríkova and the bus station is one

block southeast of the centre, on Zeleného stromu. The staff at the **Tourist Information Centre** (☎ 732 8101; www.roznava.sk; Nám Baníkov 32; ☺ 8am-4pm Mon-Fri, 8am-noon Sat) willingly help you sort out the bus schedules to various caves.

Stuck in town? Nám Baníkov's buildings include the 1654 **watch tower** (stražná veža; adult/student 30/15Sk; ☺ 10-11.30am & 1-5.30pm Mon-Fri, 10am-3.30pm Sat, noon-3.30pm Sun Jun-Aug; at 10am, 11am, 1pm & 2pm Mon-Fri Sep-May) and the **Cathedral of the Assumption of the Virgin Mary** (Katedrála Nanebovzatia panny Márie; adult/student 30/15Sk), with a Renaissance altar depicting miners at work.

Restaurant-Penzión Alfa (☎ 788 0701; Nám Baníkov 33; r per person 600Sk) opened on a busy street corner in late 2005. It has a stonework restaurant (part Slovak, part Italian menu) and comfy rooms with pine beds. **Hotel Čierny orol** (☎ 732 8186; www.ciernyorol.sk; Nám Baníkov 17; s/d 700/1100Sk; P) is the main town hotel, restaurant, beer cellar – everything. It is right next to the visitor centre.

Five fast trains a day connect Rožňava with Košice (118Sk, one hour), and there are more frequent milk runs. One daily bus connects to and from Poprad (100Sk, two hours) and three to and from Dedinky (53Sk, one hour) in Slovenský raj.

AROUND ROŽŇAVA
Betliar

The attraction of this town 4km north of Rožňava is grand **Betliar Manor House** (Kaštieľ Betliar; ☎ 798 3118; adult/student 100/50Sk; ☺ 8am-4.30pm Tue-Sun May-Oct, 9.30am-2pm Tue-Sun Nov-Apr). Built in the 18th century for the Andrássy family, it's stuffed with elegant furnishings, relics collected in Africa and Asia, and a library of 20,000 books. That really was the life. A stately garden encloses the estate.

The former family stables now contain the **Penzión pri kaštelí Betliar** (☎ 788 2002; www.kastielbetliar.sk; Kaštieľna 16; s/d 600/900Sk; P) and its first-rate restaurant serving delectable Hungarian and Slovak dishes (mains 80Sk to 150Sk) and desserts. Rooms aren't fancy, but they are new.

There are near-hourly buses through Betliar from Rožňava (10Sk, 10 minutes).

Krásnohorské Podhradie

Eight kilometres east of Rožňava, on a hill above the village of Krásnohorské Podhradie, **Krásna Hôrka Castle** (Hrad Krásna Hôrka; ☎ 732 4769;

adult/student 100/70Sk; 8am-4.30pm Tue-Sun May-Oct, by appointment 9.30am-3.30pm Tue-Sun Nov-Apr) was built in 1320. In the 16th century the Andrássy family bought it, 'Renaissanced' it and reinforced it. Most buildings burned in 1817, but in the early part of the 20th century, Count Dionysius Andrássy restored it and turned it into a family museum.

The green, shady **Camping pod hradom** (058-732 5457; person/tent130/40Sk) is just beyond the village on the way to the castle.

Seven to 11 buses serve Krásnohorské Podhradie from Rožňava (10Sk, 10 minutes). The closest train station is 1km south, at Lípovník; slow trains (osobný vlak, Os) between Rožňava (12Sk, 10 minutes) and Košice (84Sk, 1¼ hours) stop there. The castle, visible from everywhere, is a 3km walk east, up from the village.

CAVES OF THE SLOVAK KARST

Slovak Karst National Park (Národný park Slovenský Kras) encompasses more than 34,000 hectares and contains many of the 47 known jaskyňa (caves) in the region. It connects to a similar park on the Hungarian side of the border. In 1995 Unesco put 12 of the caves in both parks on the World Heritage list (including Dobšinska Ice Cave, p422). Below are the five in or near the park that are open to the public. Public transport in the district is a bit rare, especially on weekends. None of the caves are set up for the mobility-impaired. The Tourist Information Office in Rožňava can help with transport details. Tours take 35 to 45 minutes.

Many of the delicate aragonite formations in the **Ochtinská Cave** (Ochtinská Aragonitová Jaskyňa; 488 1051; adult/student 120/100Sk; tours 9am-4pm hourly Tue-Sun Jun-Aug; 9.30am, 11am, 12.30pm & 2pm Tue-Sun Apr, May, Sep & Oct) are 14,000 years old. The inside-out stalactites grow from thin limestone tubes that water passes through, leaving deposits at the growing end. The minerals form into white and orange twists and spikes, shapes resembling flowers and sea anemones. A tour takes about 35 minutes.

Perhaps the most accessible, **Gombasecká Cave** (Gombasecká Jaskyňa; 788 2020; adult/student 70/60Sk; tours 9am-4pm hourly Tue-Sun Jun-Aug, 10am, 11am, 2pm & 3pm Tue-Sun Apr, May, Sep & Oct) is only 10km south of Rožňava. Thin, strawlike stalactites up to 3m long are what this cave is known for, but the mineral-dyed orange walls are also striking. Overall, this

35-minute tour requires the least physical exertion of the Slovak Karst cave tours, though there are some stairs. Buses connect to Rožňava (13Sk, eight daily) from Tuesday to Friday only.

Domica Cave (Jaskyňa Domica; 788 2010; adult/student 80/40Sk, with boat trip 150/130Sk; tours 9am-4pm hourly Tue-Sun Jun-Aug; 9.30am, 11am, 12.30pm & 2pm Tue-Sun Apr, May, Sep & Oct) is the biggest, best-known and most beautiful cave, full of colour, and with some stalactites as thick as tree trunks. Almost 2km of the 5km length can be seen by boat along the underground river Styx. (With a boat ride the tour takes 85 minutes, without, half that.) The cave is part of a 22km-long system, most of which is in Hungary (where it's called Baradla). Domica is 28km south of Rožňava, via Plešivec. Buses depart up to 10 times a day from Tuesday to Friday (36Sk, 45 minutes) and three times on weekends. You can hike to Domica from Gombasek (15km) on a yellow and then a red trail via Silica.

Two less visited caves are **Krásnohorská Cave** (Krásnohorská Jaskyňa; 788 2020; group admission 230Sk; tours by appointment), containing a mighty tall stalagmite (32.6m), and **Jasov Cave** (Jasovská Jaskyňa; 055-466 4165; adult/student 60/30Sk; tours 9am-4pm hourly Tue-Sun Jun-Aug, 10am-3pm Tue-Sun Apr, May, Sep & Oct), which has been open to visitors since 1846. It bears some graffiti apparently left by Hussites in the 15th century. The first cave is 6.5km southeast and the second 40km northeast of Rožňava.

Woods surround the **Hotel Hrádok** (486 0110; r 700-900Sk;), 2km before the Ochtinská cave entrance. This holiday house has tennis courts and volley ball courts, a swimming pool, bike rental and a restaurant. From Tuesday to Friday five buses (32Sk) run the 22km from Rožňava west of the cave. Buses drop to two on weekends.

MURÁN PLAIN NATIONAL PARK

Thirty-five kilometres west-northwest of Rožňava is **Murán Plain National Park** (Národný park Muranska planina; www.muranska-planina.net, in Slovak), a limestone massif dotted with wildflowers and meadows. Truth is, there's a reason not so many people come here. It's out of the way, difficult to get around by public transport, and does not have as many facilities as the nation's other parks. Murán is the main village (and a trailhead), five buses a day arrive from Rožňava (74Sk, 1¼ hours).

ŠARIŠ REGION

Each region of Slovakia has its own particular folk tradition, with a distinct singing style, folk costume, dances and the like. The Šariš region, of which Prešov is the economic centre, has protected and perpetuated its culture more than most. Locals even have their own dialect, derived from a shepherding lifestyle, that is mutually unintelligible to Bratislavans. Bardejov is the region's star with a Unesco-quality town square, a neighbouring spa town and area wooden churches.

PREŠOV

☎ 051 / pop 91,700

If one of the local folk ensembles is performing, by all means go see it. Prešov is a city proud of its culture. Unlike other towns, here you can readily buy folk crafts and music at reasonable prices. The local museum does an excellent job illuminating colourful local shepherd traditions. Though this is basically an industrial city, the historical buildings on the main square have been nicely restored (most were heavily damaged during WWII).

History

Archaeologists say there was a Slav settlement here by the late 8th century. Hungarian colonists arrived in the 11th century and in 1687, 24 Protestants were executed here for their support of Hungarian Imre Thököly and his anti-Hapsburg uprising. Prešov (Eperejes in Hungarian), instead of joining the Czechoslovak nation, tried to proclaim itself a socialist state (the Slovak Republic of Councils) tied to Hungary. The Czechoslovak army took the city and shooed the Hungarian troops out. Today, Prešov is the third-largest city in Slovakia.

Orientation

Hlavná, Prešov's main street (literally), is a 20-minute walk north up busy Masarykova from the adjacent bus and train stations (or you can take trolleybus 1 or 4 north for two stops).

Information

A couple of banks with ATMs line up along Hlavná, and both the bus and train stations have ATMs.

I-Netcafé (Nám Legionárov 1; per hr 42Sk; ☉ 8am-8pm Mon-Fri, 8am-3pm Sat, 9am-1pm Sun) On the upper floor of the Tesco Department Store.

Post office (Masarykova 2)

Prešov Information Service (PIS; ☎ 773 1113; www.presov.sk; Hlavná 67; ☉ 9am-6pm Mon-Fri, 9am-1pm Sat) Maps, books, souvenirs.

Sights

The 16th-century Rákóczi Palace contains the **Regional museum** (Krajské múzeum; ☎ 759 8220; Hlavná 86; adult/student 30/10Sk; ☉ 9am-5pm Mon-Fri, 1-6pm Sun). Seek out the ethnographic displays hidden up an interior staircase to see playful displays of the felt-wearing, axe-wielding, romanticised life of a *bača* (head shepherd).

Assembled at the **Šariš gallery** (☎ 772 5423; Hlavná 51; adult/student 20/10Sk; ☉ 9am-5pm Mon-Fri, 2-6pm Sun) is a collection of 20th-century Slovak art that includes painters from the Rusyn culture (p434) of east Slovakia.

It was at the 17th-century **town hall** (radnica; Hlavná 73) that the short-lived, socialist Slovak Republic of Councils – backed by the Hungarian Red Army – was proclaimed a nation of sorts in 1919. Accessible through the building's arcade is a cellar **Wine Museum** (Múzeum vín; ☎ 773 3108; Floriánova; adult/student 20/10Sk; ☉ 8am-noon & 12:30-6pm Mon-Fri, 8am-noon Sat) that looks suspiciously like a wine shop, but the sampling's fun.

Master Pavol of Levoča's workshop created some of the sculpture in the Gothic Roman Catholic **Parish church of St Nicholas** (Farsky kostol sv Mikuláše), first remodelled in 1515. Peek inside the ornate Greek Catholic **Church of St John the Baptist** (Kostol sv Jána Krstiteľa) to see the handsome iconostasis.

Five kilometres north of Prešov you can hike up to the few remaining ruins of what was Slovakia's largest fortification, **Šariš castle** (Šarišiský hrad). Built in the 13th century, it lasted only until the 17th century when a Polish king burnt it down. Follow the yellow trail 1½ hours from the village of Veľký Šariš.

Sleeping

Turistická ubytovňa (☎ 772 0628; www.pis.sk/turisticka ubytovna; Vajanského 65; s/d 350/600Sk; **P**) Bare-bones basic – a bed (though we'd hardly call that a mattress), table, and chair. There is a kitchen for guests though.

Penzión Adam (☎ 758 1789; www.penzionadam.sk; Jarková 16; s/d 1300/1500Sk; **P**) Something about this *penzión* feels especially sunny and bright. Maybe it's the superhigh ceilings, orange bed spreads and modern furniture, or golden

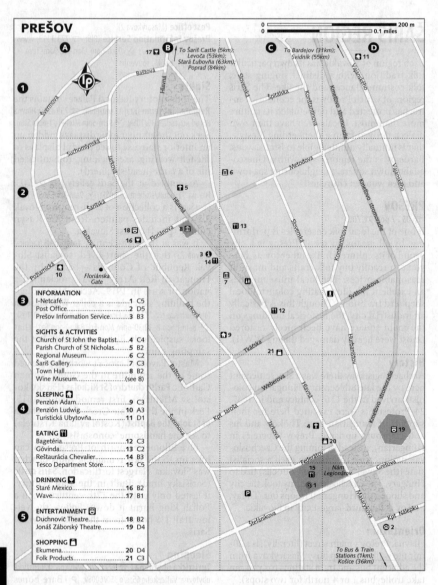

PREŠOV

exterior. Or maybe it's just that it's so new (opened mid-2006). Top-notch staff.

Penzión Ludwig (☎ 0908254211; www.penzionludwig .sk; Požiarnická 2; s/d 1900/2200Sk; P) Sloping eves and half-timber beams add to the old-world feel of this elegant inn. Duck in to your room, sit down on the brocade and carved-wood settee, and connect your laptop to the internet.

Dining downstairs is under panelled ceilings and glittering chandeliers.

Eating & Drinking

National law says you have to have nonsmoking sections in restaurants; guess local eateries must be classed as pubs because there are few with nonsmoking sections.

Góvinda (☎ 0911309108; Hlavná 70; mains 80-150Sk; ⏰ 11am-7pm Mon-Fri) This is one of three Indian vegetarian self-service restaurants run by Hare Krishnas in Slovakia.

Reštaurácia Chevalier (☎ 758 1590; Hlavná 69; mains 100-250Sk) Drink from stone goblets in a vaulted cellar and imagine Prešov in the middle ages. Slovak specialities here are well executed.

For fast cheap eats, stop at the **Bagetéria** (Hlavná 36; sandwiches 30-75Sk; ⏰ 6am-10pm Mon-Fri, 8am Sat & Sun), or in warm weather, at one of several cafés that put up covered platforms on the main square. The Tesco Department Store has a grocery.

Staré Mexico (☎ 0915308285; Jarková 63; ⏰ 10am-midnight Sun-Thu, 10am-1am Fri & Sat) pub has occasional live bands, or you can get funky at the gallery-internet café-disco **Wave** (Hlavná 1; ⏰ 10am-midnight Mon-Thu, 10am-1am Fri, 4pm-1am Sat, 4pm-midnight Sun), with various live sets Fridays and DJs throughout the week.

Entertainment

There are several folk ensembles in town, including **Šarišan** (www.sarisan.sk), that play traditional songs and dances at various venues. The **Duchnovič Theatre** (☎ 772 3261; www.divadload.sk; Jarková 77) is a Rusyn minority playhouse where the folk ensemble Puľs performs.

Jonáš Záborský Theatre (☎ 772 4622; www.djz.sk; in Slovak; Nám Legionárov 6) presents classical concerts and plays from September through May.

Shopping

The usual Ulúv store is on the main square, but it's better to stop at the excellent **Folk Products** (☎ 773 2694; www.oliviasimports.com; Hlavná 21; ⏰ 11am-7pm) for handmade wood-carving, embroidery, lacework, as well as *fujary* (metre-plus horns made out of wood) and *valašky* (shepherds' staffs that resemble a decorative axe). Down the block you can buy hand-painted icons at **Ekumena** (☎ 772 0477; Hlavná 1).

Getting There & Away

Prešov is 36km north of Košice and 21 daily trains (38Sk, 45 minutes) connect the two. No matter where you're coming from, you'll have to transfer in Prešov for Bardejov (56Sk, 1¼ hours, five daily). Buses with a dozen or more departures a day connect to and from Košice (47Sk, 35 minutes), Bardejov (58Sk, 50 minutes), Svidník (78Sk, 1½ hours), Levoča (89Sk, 1½ hours), Poprad (124Sk, 1¾ hours) and Stará Ľubovňa (89Sk, 1¾ hours).

BARDEJOV

☎ 054 / pop 33,400

It may as well be the 15th century, this old town centre has been so enthusiastically preserved. All steep roofs and flat fronts, the Gothic-Renaissance burghers' houses on the main square seem strikingly homogeneous at first. Look closer and you notice an ethereal sgraffito decoration or a pastel hue and plaster detail that sets each apart – get your camera ready. Unesco must have been impressed too, they put Bardejov on the World Heritage list in 2000. The quiet square is the main drawcard today, but there's also an excellent icon museum that sheds light on this region's eastern-facing religion.

Nearby in Bardejovské Kúpele (p429) you can take the cure at a hotspring spa and explore an open-air village museum. The wooden churches in the area reflect the Carpatho-Rusyn heritage shared with neighbouring parts of the Ukraine and Poland.

History

Bardejov received its royal charter in 1376 and grew rich on trade with Poland and Russia. In the 17th century many of the Gothic town square buildings were made over in Renaissance style (porticos and arcades added), and some had rococo elements (ornamental plasterwork) tacked on in the 18th century. The Thirty Years' War, an anti-Hapsburg revolt and the plague ended the town's development but saved the fine centre square. None of the original 80 buildings has been lost, and only four houses have been added since the 1600s. Restoration is an ongoing process, so expect to see a building under scaffolding at all times.

Orientation

Radničné nám, the town's main square, is about 400m southwest of the bus and train station. The old town walls hide the centre from the main road between Prešov and Svidník. If walking from the stations enter through the gate off Slovenská at Baštová.

Information

ČSOB (Radničné nám 7) Bank and ATM.
Golem Internet Café (Radničné nám 25; per hr 25Sk; ⏰ 9am-11pm Mon-Fri, 1-11pm Sat & Sun)
Post office (Dlhý rad 14)
Tourist Information Centre (☎ 474 4003; www.e-bardejov.sk; Radničné nám 21; ⏰ 9am-5.30pm Mon-Fri year-round, also 11.30am-3.30pm Sat & Sun May-Sep) Info, souvenirs and guide service.

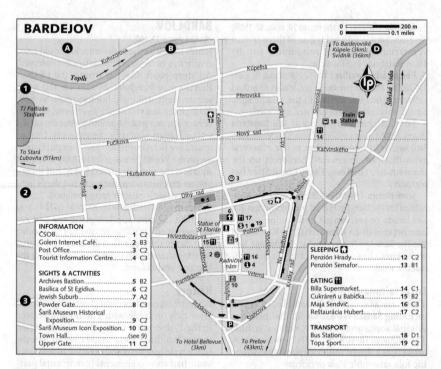

BARDEJOV

0 — 200 m
0 — 0.1 miles

To Bardejovské Kúpele (3km); Svidník (36km)

To Stará Ľubovňa (51km)

TJ Partizán Stadium

To Hotel Bellevue (3km)

To Prešov (43km);

Sights

There are two branches of the **Šariš museum** (Sariške múzeum; ☎ 472 4966; www.muzeumbardejov.sk; adult/student 40/20Sk; ⏳ 8am-noon & 12.30-4pm Tue-Sun) on the square. At the **Icon Exposition** (Expozícia ikony; Radničné nám 27) you can see more than 160 dazzling icons from the 16th to 19th centuries. Originally, the stylised portraits of Christ Pantocrator, the Mother of God and a whole flock of saints decorated Greek Catholic and Orthodox churches east of here. The other branch, the 1509 **town hall** (radnica; Radničné nám 48), centre square, houses the **Historical Exposition** (Historická expozícia). The building is a unique piece of early Renaissance architecture: note the bay staircase, the carved stone portals and the wooden inlay ceiling in the Meeting Room. The rooms contain local paintings, coins and weaponry.

A fine example of late Gothic architecture inside and out, the 15th-century **Basilica of St Egídius** (Bazilika Sv Egídia; adult/student 30/20Sk, tower 40/20Sk; ⏳ 10am-3pm Mon-Fri, to 2pm Sat) is packed with no less than 11 winged Gothic altarpieces built from 1460 to 1510. West of the square the 18th-century **Jewish suburb** (Židovské

suburbium; Mylnská 6-7) has a synagogue in need of restoration and a small Jewish cemetery.

Remnants of the town's ancient defences include the restored **Upper gate** (Dolná brána), on Baštová, the **Powder gate** (Prašná brána) to the south and the chunky, 14th-century **Archives bastion** (Archívna bašta) to the northwest, now occupied by a bar.

Festivals & Events

Friday evenings in July there are often concerts on the square as part of the **Bardejov Musical Summer** (Bardejovské Hudobné Leto). The nearby *skanzen* in Bardejovské Kúpele (opposite) has events all summer long.

Sleeping & Eating

Penzión Hrady (☎ 0903211865; www.penzionivana.sk; Stöcklova 8; s/d/tr 495/750/880Sk; P) Need your hair cut? There's a salon across the hall, and an eatery downstairs, in this busy, old-town building. The wood veneer rooms are nothing special.

Penzión Semafor (☎ 0905830984; www.penzion semafor.sk; Kellerova 13; s/d 700/900Sk, ste 800-1100Sk; P) If the large, bright doubles are good, the 'apartments' (larger rooms) are even better. All share a communal kitchen in this family-run guesthouse recommended by our readers.

Hotel Bellevue (☎ 472 8404; www.bellevuehotel.sk; Mihalov 2503; s/d 1900/2600Sk; P ⊠ ⊠ ⊠ ⊠) As swank as Bardejov gets: stay high on the hill above the old town, with great views from the glass-enclosed pool, sleep atop classic but modern cherry-wood beds and eat at a darn good full-service restaurant. Bellevue is 3km south of the centre; take bus 8 from the train station.

Reštaurácia Hubert (☎ 0908982738; Radničné nám 4; mains 100-169Sk; ☺ 10am-10pm Mon-Fri, 11am-3pm Sat & Sun) Game dishes and other meaty fare top the list in this cellar restaurant. There are a few animal-protein-free pastas available too.

Cukráreň U Babička (Radničné nám 49; cakes 30-100Sk) On the main square, in a Renaissance arcade, Babička serves pastries and cakes like your Slovak grandma used to make.

Maja Sendvič (☎ 091941064; Radničné nám 15; sandwiches 40-50Sk; ☺ 8am-8pm Mon-Thu, 8am-midnight Fri, 3-11pm Sat & Sun) Sells baguette sandwiches to go.

Billa supermarket (Slovenská) A bit further afield, the supermarket is next to the bus station.

Looking for an adult beverage? Several cafés, pubs – and a pizzeria with cold beer – front the main square. A few more drinkeries are along Stöcklova near Penzión Hrady.

Getting There & Around

Local trains run regularly between Bardejov and Prešov (56Sk, 1¼ hours, nine daily). But the bus is faster if you want to go to and from Košice (100Sk, 1¾ hours, eight daily) or Poprad (135Sk, 2½ hours, 12 daily). From Bratislava, three daily buses make the nine- to 10-hour journey (590Sk) direct.

Topa Sport (☎ 474 4282; Poštová 1; ☺ 9am-5pm Mon-Fri, 9am-noon Sat) rents bicycles for 120/450Sk per day/week.

BARDEJOVSKÉ KÚPELE

At least six species of evergreen shade the paths of pedestrian-only Bardejovské Kúpele, 3km north of Bardejov. And then there's the abundant shrubbery, flowers and other kinds of trees. This could be an arboretum instead of a leafy little spa town. Couples meander about with birdsong as the only noise pollution and relaxing their only goal. Several of the 19th- century rooming houses still exist, but they are mixed in among 1970s-modern

institutional structures to surreal effect. In addition to spa treatment facilities, lodging and shops, among the trees is one of Slovakia's best village museums (skanzen). A good time to visit is mid-July, for the annual two-day **Rusyn-Šariš Folk Festival**, but the museum often has programmes on summer weekends.

Orientation & Information

The bus station and parking lot (no cars allowed in the main town area) are at the base of a slope on the town's southeast end. It's all uphill from there. The Spa House and the skanzen are toward the top of town.

Herkules (☎ 474 4744; www.herkules.sk; Kino Žriedo; 8am-4.30pm Mon-Sat) is the local travel agent/tourist information office. Staff can arrange a week-long spa stay with treatments and food.

Sights & Activities

To experience the local waters, make an appointment for a mineral bath at the **Spa house** (Kúpelné dom; ☎ 477 4255; www.kupele-bj.sk; spa services 150-300Sk; 8am-noon & 1-5pm Mon-Sat), on the east side at the top of the main path. Or maybe you'd like a whirlpool soak, or a Scottish shower (where they line you up against a tile wall and squirt you with what looks like a water canon in the name of massaging).

The main cure people come for can be sipped at the **colonnade** (kolonáda; admission free; ☺ 6-8am, 10.30am-1pm & 4.30-6.30pm). Each of the eight springs that feed the water taps has different mineral properties. A huge wall chart details which spring treats what ailment; brush up on your periodic table before trying to decipher it and stick close to a bathroom after imbibing.

To the west of the colonnade is the **Museum of Folk Architecture** (Múzeum Ľudovej Architektúry; ☎ 472 2070; adult/student 40/20Sk; ☺ 9am-5pm Tue-Sun May-Sep, to 3pm Oct-Apr). The onion-domed dark wooden church from Zboj is among the 25 area buildings moved to this skanzen, composed of sparsely furnished log and plaster cabins, barns and smithy workshops, beehives and haylofts. Peer into the simple dwellings and see how some rural folk still live. In 2005 the church from Mikulašova (1730) was completely reconstructed here (thus the light wood) and put in use for Sunday liturgy.

Sleeping & Eating

The majority of spa guests are still those with medical prescriptions for three- to six-week

EAST SLOVAKIA

WOODEN CHURCHES AROUND BARDEJOV

At the crossroads of Eastern and Western Christianity developed a particular form of sacral architecture – the *dreveny kostol* (wooden church). The simple, yet somehow sublime outward appearance belies the rich interiors packed with religious images. At the front you have the iconostasis, or icon screen, lined with the venerated representations of Christ and the saints. The most precious icons have been moved to the Šariš museum (p428) in Bardejov and replicas put in their place.

Some of the churches are still used for services but most remain locked during the week. The caretaker, upon seeing a stranger in the small village, may wander up and offer to open it. If not, politely asking the nearest older person – smile, point at the church, make a key gesture – seems to lead to finding someone who can let you in. (At least a 20Sk donation to the key guy and one to the church is appropriate.)

The most easily accessible wooden churches around Bardejov:

- Two Greek Catholic churches from the area are now in the open-air musem in Bardejovské Kúpele, 3km north of Bardejov. Both have striking iconostasis, the latter is newly reconstructed and in use on museum grounds.

- The small three-dome Greek Catholic church (1763) in Jedlinka, with a baroque interior, was built in honour of the Mother of God, of whom there is a highly prized icon. It's 14km north of Bardejov, and frequent buses between Svidník and Bardejov stop here.

- The Roman Catholic exception to the rule resides in Hervartov. This St Francis of Assisi is the oldest wooden church in Slovakia (built around 1500, reconstructed in 1990). The interior of the nave is from 1665, and is richly decorated with frescoes. It's 9km southwest of Bardejov; at least three buses daily travel between the village and Bardejov.

For more information buy the full-colour English language booklet *Wooden Churches near Bardejov* from the Bardejov tourist office. *Carpathian Wooden Pearls* is a map of 27 wooden churches (also online) put out by the **Prešov Diocese** (www.grkatpo.sk/drevenecerk/). There are also clusters of wooden churches in villages near Svidník and Snina in the Eastern Borderlands.

stays (nice, huh?). Their programme includes buffet meals, so restaurants around town aren't great. Several of the lodgings take individual travellers, and you can opt for full board. The Herkules tourist office arranges private rooms (across the path from an ice-cream shop).

Alžbeta (☎ 477 4470; www.kupele-bj.sk; r €20-27) This Victorian lady sits at the top of the hill next to the Spa House. She's a bit old fashioned – with dark wood and small spaces – but that's what makes you able to imagine the time when empresses stayed here. There's a salt-cave treatment room on the ground floor.

Afrodita (☎ 472 7148; mastery@slovanet.sk; r 750Sk; ☒) The town's pizzeria rents out two flats above the restaurant, one with high-speed internet connection. It doesn't make a bad slice o' pizza either (pizzas 90Sk to 115Sk).

Salaš Lesná (☎ 474 2433; mains 55-90Sk; ☷ 8.30am-11pm) Has all the Slovak specialities at their folksy best. Dig into your fresh *halušky* (small, *gnocchi*-like dumplings usually topped with sheep's cheese and bacon bits) while admir-

ing the hand-carved chairs and rustic décor. Lesná is 1km south of Bardejovké Kúpele on the main road from Bardejov.

Getting There & Away

If you like you can walk the 3km north from Bardejov, with the last 1.5km meandering through wooded countryside. Bardejovské Kúpele is connected at least hourly to the Bardejov bus station (18Sk) via city bus 1, 2, 7, 8, 10 and 12. The last bus back is at around 7.30pm.

EASTERN BORDERLANDS

Shingled onion domes rise above the dark wooden churches as Old Church Slavonic chants float from within; you know that there's something different about this part of the country. The borderlands are home to a large Rusyn minority (see the boxed text, p434) that also has members in neighbouring Ukraine and Poland. In fact, many of the village signs are written twice, once in the Cyrillic alphabet. Life here is generally quiet, rural, industrial and poor. The wooden churches spread throughout the region are the attraction, but they are located in tiny villages with few services. A hearty hiker could reach a few from Snina in a day.

At the far eastern edge of the country, Poloniny National Park is a striking expanse of hilly forest largely untouched by man. The surprise of the district is the Andy Warhol museum in Medzilaborce, near where his family came from.

Unless you have lots of time to explore the borderlands, it's best to rent a car in Košice; buses here are infrequent and train service all but nonexistent.

MICHALOVCE
☎ 056 / pop 39,842
A sterile little town centre, with one heck of a socialist-realist 'happy peasant' statue at its heart, provides little reason to stop. In a few shops on the square you can buy the well-known rustic brown-glazed pottery, decorated with graphic patterns and folk symbols, that's produced south of here in towns like Pozdišovce. Otherwise you can connect to the Ukraine from this eastern outpost.

Bus is the best way to get here from Košice (89Sk, 1½ hours, at least 10 daily). An hourly bus service connects to Humenné (44Sk, 30 minutes). Up to four buses a day make the one-hour drive to Uzhhorod in the Ukraine (296Sk).

HUMENNÉ
☎ 057 / pop 35,008
This peaceful town on the Laborec river has a French-style baroque chateau, which began as a Gothic castle turned museum and a *skanzen*. Everything is on the main square, Nám Slobody, where you'll also find banks and the **Internet Klub** (Nám Slobody 4; per hr 40Sk; 10am-7pm Mon-Fri). The adjacent bus and train stations are 500m due west of the vast, pedestrian-friendly square; the **Information Office** (☎ 788 1051; 8am-noon & 1-6pm) is in the train station.

The local palace now contains the **Vihorlatské museum** (☎ 775 2240; adult/student 35/10Sk; 9am-6pm Mon-Fri, 2-6pm Sat & Sun May-Oct), with exhibits on archaeology, local history and feudal housing. Uphill from there is the associated **skanzen** (adult/student 30/15Sk; 9am-6pm May-Oct), with about 10 Rusyn rural wooden houses from around the region, dating from the 19th and early 20th centuries. Pride of place goes to a wooden church built in 1754. Summer festivals enliven the place with folk song and dance.

The up-to-date suites at **Penzión Albina** (☎ 775 6303; Nám Slobody 61; r 1900Sk; P) are very close to the museums. The restaurant is quite popular at lunchtime. You can have a meat fest with four of your best friends at the cavernous beer hall/grill restaurant **Yes** (☎ 0903655770; Nám Slobody; mains 100-150Sk; 9am-11pm Mon-Thu, 9am-2am Fri & Sat, 2-11pm Sun); for 480Sk you get ribs, wings, sausage and bacon for four.

Humenné is on a rail spur line from Michalovce (52Sk, 30 minutes, 10 daily) and Medzilaborce (56Sk, 1¼ hours, 11 daily). Buses are better for other destinations: Košice (128Sk, two hours, five daily), Prešov (100Sk, 1½ hours, five daily), Svidník (100Sk, two hours, four daily).

SNINA
☎ 057 / pop 21,382
Plonked between the Vihorlatské Highlands and Poloniny National Park is this nondescript refinery town that is valuable as a base for exploring the area's wooden churches (see the boxed text, p432). The dynamite little **CKU** (☎ 768 5735; unitur@stonline.sk; Strojárska 102; 9-11am & noon-5pm Mon-Sat Jun-Sep, closed Sat Oct-May) travel agency/tourist office is a real revelation. They have tons of literature about the churches, including *Icon Cyclotour* booklets that have a map and colour photos of area churches, and one family member or other of the staff knows all the lodging owners personally. Don't forget to pick up the VKÚ map *Bukovské Vrchy* (1:50,000, No 118, 90Sk) for hiking. Hotel Kamei rents bikes.

The modern town centre is a bit run down, but inside one of the blocky buildings the **Caravella** (☎ 758 1071; www.caravella.s-n.sk; dm/apt 300/1000Sk; pizzas 75-115Sk) pizzeria and *penzión* has been recently renovated (rooms redone in 2006). Apartments have colourful paint on the wall and Ikea-like furnishings. Outside of town, in the woods, 3km east of the centre, is the holiday-oriented **Hotel Kamei** (☎ 768 2187; www.kamei.sk; s/d 1100/1600Sk; P ☎). A five-minute walk from here leads to two local lakes for swimming (free to guests) and

EAST SLOVAKIA

WOODEN CHURCHES AROUND SNINA

Near the Ukrainian border are some beautiful examples of the traditional wooden churches reflective of the local Rusyn culture. By car, bike or foot is the only way to get around, as buses between villages are sporadic at best, and most don't run on weekends. Churches are locked except for services; ask around for someone who can let you in.

The first wooden church is 3km east of Snina in the village of **Jalová**. This tiny 1792 church was completely rebuilt by traditional methods in 2004. High on a hill, **Topoľa**, 13km east of Snina, is more impressive. The 18th-century iconostasis and 1819 Old Church Slovanic liturgy book are still inside the church.

From Topoľa, instead of following the road, you can hike over the hill via the blue trail (2½ hours) to **Ruský Potok**, 24km east of Snina. The church itself dates from the 1740s, but the rare liturgy books date from 1626 and 1654. Note the richly carved woodwork. A further 1½-hour hike east on the blue trail brings you to **Uličske Krivé** (1718), 35km east of Snina. The structure is quite large, as wooden churches go, with correspondingly elaborate iconography inside. Look for the Jesus Pantocrator icon (with his two right fingers held up in blessing), which was painted in the 1500s.

The end of this particular road is 7.5km further at **Nová Sedlica**. The church has been moved to the village museum in Humenné (p431), but this town – the furthest east in Slovakia – is the point for leaping into **Poloniny National Park** (below).

If you have your own transport, don't stop here: look for the church symbol and words *drevený kostol* (wooden church) marked on regional maps, then explore on. You'll find many more wooden churches throughout the area.

fishing, and the hotel rents bikes and skis. Full board at the restaurant is 550Sk.

Trains (32Sk, 40 minutes, 10 daily) and buses (31Sk, 40 minutes, four daily) run between Snina and Humenné.

POLONINY NATIONAL PARK

Bordering both Poland and Ukraine is the 29,805-hectare Poloniny National Park (Poloniny národný park), a wild area 90% forested with beech and fir-oak trees, and home to the likes of wolves, lynxes and wildcats. You can walk for ages without seeing another person or anything man-made. Even the undulating drive, over steep hills, past forest vistas, is refreshing.

The park engulfs the village of Nová Sedlica. A popular day walk begins here and makes a beeline for the highest point in the park, Kremenec (1221m), which marks the converging borders of Slovakia, Poland and Ukraine (four hours on the red trail). An elevation change–free hour and a half follows a ridge west along the Polish border to Čiertáz (1½ hours), where you can turn south on the green trail to get back to Nová Sedlica (2½ hours). Or continue on past Čiertáz and Dzurkpwiec Durkovec (1189m) before dropping down to the Ruské sedlo (795m). From here it's possible to cross into Poland (a summer-only border crossing) to a small camping ground and *chata*. There's no wild camping in the park, but you can stay at the comfy **Penzión Kremence** (☎ 769 4156; www.kremenec.sk; r per person 350Sk) in Nová Sedlica, amid the village houses on the highest street. The friendly family will serve you meals too.

There are five buses Monday to Friday from Snina to Nová Sedlica (66Sk, 1¼ hours), one on Saturday. You have to switch in Snina to get here from anywhere else.

MEDZILABORCE

☎ 057 / pop 6650

It is a bit surreal to see a large Campbell's soup can in a small village in the far northeast corner of Slovakia. The town has exactly one claim to fame: the **Andy Warhol Family Museum of Modern Art** (☎ 748 0072; Andyho Warhola; adult/student 100/50Sk; 10am-4pm Mon-Fri, noon-4pm Sat & Sun). Though the artist Andy Warhol (1928–87) was born in Pittsburgh, USA as Andrej Varchola, his parents came from the village of Miková, 8km northwest of Medzilaborce. Warhol never acknowledged his roots, even though he could speak Rusyn. The museum was founded after his death by his US and Slovak relatives, especially his brother John.

Inside are family memorabilia and many Warhol originals, including *Red Lenin*,

Campbell Soup II, Hammer & Sickle and *Mao Tse Tung*. There are also paintings by his nephew James Warhol and older brother Paul Warhola. Paul, a chicken farmer living near Pittsburgh, took up painting at the age of 61; his *Heinz Ketchup Bottle* painting sold for $US10,000. To get there from the train station, turn left onto Andyho Warhola and keep going straight for 800m – look for the Campbell's soup cans out front.

Opposite the museum is **Penzión Andy** (☎ 732 1640; www.penzionandy.sk; Andy Warhola 121; 3-person r 1800Sk; **P**), with large apartments and a decent restaurant adorned with Warhol prints.

Medzilaborce is up a rail spur line from Humenné (56Sk, 1¼ hours, up to 10 daily). Almost all buses from Prešov and Košice require a change at Humenné (89Sk; 1½ hours, up to six daily). One morning bus a day connects to Svidník (66Sk, 1¼ hours).

SVIDNÍK
☎ 054 / pop 12,534

Get up close and personal with Rusyn culture. This eastern outpost has some first-rate Rusyn ethnographic sights and events, including a huge hillside *skanzen* accessed through the Rusyn museum in town, and an annual festival celebrated since 1956. This area was also significant in WWII; military history buffs enjoy the roadside tanks that stand as battlefield monuments and the Military Museum. The town itself was all but destroyed in both world wars and the town square today is unfortunately functional looking; the area is industrial.

The best alternative to staying the night in the dismal town with great sights is to sleep in Bardejov (35km away) and take a day trip.

History
Svidník evolved from Vyšný and Nižný (Upper and Lower) Svidník, which had as much as an 80% Rusyn population according to the 1930 census. German and Soviet forces clashed here in November 1944. The Germans knew that if the Soviets breached German defences around the Dukla Pass they could easily advance across the plains to the south, so some of the most ferocious fighting of WWII took place in and around Svidník. Communist Slovakia outlawed the Greek Catholic faith and declared the Rusyn minority Ukrainian (and thus Orthodox). Still, around 15% of the population once again claims Rusyn as their ethnic identity. For more see the boxed text, p434.

Orientation & Information
The bus station is 200m east of centre, just off Centrálna, the main pedestrian square. The sights are spread out along Bardejovská.

City Information Centre (☎ 752 0461; Sovietskych hrdinov 38; 🕒 9am-4.30pm Mon-Fri) Pretty unhelpful.

Všeobecná úverová banka (VÚB; Centrálna) Has an exchange desk and an ATM.

Sights
The **Museum of Ukrainian-Rusyn culture** (Múzeum Ukrajinsko-Rusínskej kultúry; ☎ 752 2271; www.muk.sk; Centrálna 258; adult/student 60/30Sk; 🕒 8.30am-4pm Tue-Fri, 10am-4pm Sat & Sun) offers a good look at

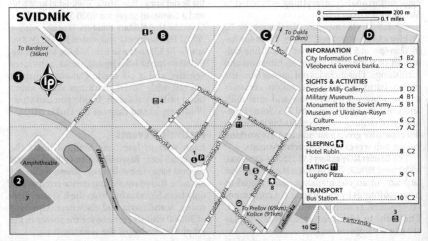

SVIDNÍK

0 — 200 m
0 — 0.1 miles

To Bardejov (36km)

To Dukla (20km)

L. Štúra

Duchnovičova

Festivalová

Cd. armády

Bardejovská

Pionierska

Sovietskych hrdinov

Kutuzovova

Komenského

Centrálna

Poštová

Ondava

Amphitheatre

Dr. Goldbergera

Stropkovská

To Prešov (65km); Košice (91km)

Ľudmírna

Partizánska

EAST SLOVAKIA

THE RUSYNS & RELIGION

Scholars disagree about when the east Slavic people arrived in the Carpathian mountains, but their connection to Eastern Christianity is clear. If you had asked a Rusyn what ethnicity he was before WWI, he would likely have told you he was Greek Catholic. This hybrid faith originated in the Carpathian region that is now part in eastern Slovakia, part in the Ukraine and part in Poland. In 1596 and 1646 the Union of Uzhhorod and the Union of Brest brought the local Orthodox churches back in union with Rome (Christianity had split into east/west Byzantine/Roman around 1054). Many of the traditions of Orthodoxy were maintained – plain-chant liturgies, onion dome architecture, icon veneration, married priests – but the leader of the church is the pope, and the theology Catholic. Most of the wooden churches you see in the region were originally Greek Catholic, also called Uniate and Byzantine Catholic, until history intervened.

During WWI the many Rusyns who had emigrated to find work in the coalfields of the Eastern US took part in negotiations that resulted in the Pittsburgh Agreement recommending that Podkarpatska Rus (Subcarpathian Ruthenia) become a part of a newly created Czechoslovakia. This lasted until after WWII, when the territory was mostly annexed to the USSR, with little pieces left in Slovakia and Poland. (On a side note: an independent governorship existed in Podkarpatska Rus for several months in 1939. Once Hitler fully controlled the Czech Lands, the governor declared his territory a nation – the Carpatho-Ukraine. Hungarian troops rolled in the next day and nixed that.)

The Rusyns that were left in Czechoslovakia under communism were declared 'Ukrainian' and some Greek Catholic churches turned over to Orthodoxy, if they were allowed to continue at all. (In the Ukraine, Greek Catholic churches were confiscated wholesale.) Post–Velvet Revolution, many of the Greek Catholic properties were returned to the church and there is once again a bishop sitting in Prešov.

Thanks in part to the vocal émigré population, the Rusyn language was codified in 1996 and Rusyns have become a recognised minority in Slovakia. Svidník is probably the closest there is to a Rusyn cultural centre, with a dedicated museum, a *skanzen*, an art gallery and a festival. Prešov (p425) has a theatre and a Rusyn dance troupe, as well as a Greek Catholic cathedral and several churches. Step into any wooden church in the eastern borderlands, or admire the icons at the Bardejov Icon Exposition (p428) and you're witnessing a part of a uniquely Carpathian culture.

---

traditional Rusyn culture and history. The best bits are the folk dresses and painted Easter eggs; unfortunately, everything is labelled in Slovak and Rusyn only.

Operated by the museum, the **skanzen** (☎ 752 2952; Festivalová; adult/student 60/30Sk; ◷ 8.30am-6pm Tue-Fri, 10am-6pm Sat & Sun May–mid-Oct) has a fine collection of traditional Rusyn architecture and furnishings. This includes old houses from the region, barns, a school, fire station, ceramics and weaving workshops, saw and grist mills and wooden church built in 1776. Some time-honoured farming and sheep-raising is done on the expansive green grounds, and the working village pub serves welcome refreshments.

The **Dezider Milly gallery** (☎ 752 1684; Partizánska; adult/student 30/10Sk; ◷ 8.30am-4pm Mon-Fri, 10am-4pm Sat & Sun), in an old mansion, was created to house paintings by its namesake, a contemporary painter, as well as by other Rusyn artists. The 16th- to 19th-century icons on display are equally impressive.

Opposite the *skanzen*, on the other side of Bardejovská, stands a 37m-tall **Monument to the Soviet army** (Pamätník Sovietskej armády) and a common grave for 9000 Soviet soldiers. Outside the **Military museum** (Vojenské múzeum; ☎ 752 1397; Bardejovská; adult/student 30/15Sk; ◷ 8am-4pm Tue-Fri, 8.30am-5pm Sat & Sun Jul & Aug; 8am-4pm Tue-Fri, 9.45am-2pm Sat & Sun Sep-Jun), tanks, armoured vehicles and a US-made Dakota transport aircraft with Soviet markings stand about like a military *skanzen*. Inside you can study photographs and maps of the Dukla battle.

Festivals & Events

Each year in late June Svidník hosts the weekend-long **Rusyn-Ukrainian Cultural Festival** (Slavnosti kultúry Rusínov-Ukrajincov Slovenska; www.muk .sk), with Rusyn music and dance troupes not only from Slovakia but from the Ukraine, Germany, Scandinavia and elsewhere. Upwards of 30,000 visitors come to see the shows in the amphitheatre below the *skanzen*.

Sleeping & Eating

Hotel Rubín (☎ 752 4210; hotelrubin@stonline.sk; Centrálna 274; s/d 500/900Sk; P) The somewhat dingy Hotel Rubín is on the main square, across from the Ukrainian-Rusyn museum. Rooms are modern enough and there's a restaurant and nightclub.

Eating options are generally grim – you can dine on pizza and calzone at **Lugano Pizza** (☎ 752 3990; Sovietskych hrdinov 467; pizzas 90-150Sk), or there are a couple of places along Centrálna.

Getting There & Away

You can bus to and from Bardejov (53Sk, 50 minutes, 15 on weekdays, four weekends), Prešov (89Sk, 1½ hours, nine daily), Košice (128Sk, two hours, three daily) and Dukla (32Sk, 40 minutes, four daily).

AROUND SVIDNÍK

The road north of Svidník leads to Dukla Pass on the Polish border, where there is a huge war memorial. This area is an open-air collection of WWII weaponry – mainly Soviet, some German – left where it was abandoned in the battle for the pass. The many onion-domed wooden Rusyn churches in the area are a bit more uplifting. A car is really useful here.

Sights & Activities

The **Valley of Death** (Údolí smrti) lies along the first major road to the left after heading north from Svidník on the road to Ladomirová; at the crossroads is a monument made of a Soviet T-34 tank crushing a German Panzer. This road leads to the village of **Dobroslava** and its 1932 wooden church with three large onion domes. Along the road are preserved Soviet tanks, seemingly frozen in the act of advancing across the fields.

Ladomirová, the first village on the main road northeast of Svidník, has a handsome, onion-domed church built in 1742. Take the southeast turn-off at Krajná Poľana to reach

a second church at **Bodružal** (1648) and, on a brief detour almost to the Polish border, the three-domed church at **Príkra**, built in 1777. A few kilometres south of Bodružal is a photogenic three-domed church at **Miroľa** (1770).

Back on the Svidník–Dukla road, in **Nižný Komárnik**, is one of the region's newer wooden churches (1938), with bright-yellow doors, bits of stained glass and unusually broad domed towers.

The last village with a church before the Dukla Pass is **Vyšný Komárnik**. A few hundred metres before the Vyšný Komárnik turn-off, on the left (west) side of the highway, is a marker for a 30-minute loop trail past foxholes and anti-aircraft guns.

The **Dukla Pass** (Dukliansky priesmyk), about 20km from Svidník, is the lowest point in the Laborec range, and is named after the Polish town of Dukla on the other side. Czechoslovak units fighting with the Soviets crossed here and liberated Vyšný Komárnik on 6 October 1944. The battle for the pass lasted from 8 September to 27 November 1944, during which 85,000 Soviet soldiers and 6500 Czechoslovaks died or were wounded.

About 1km south of the 24-hour border crossing to Poland is a 49m stone **war memorial** (admission free; ⊙ 8.30am-5pm Tue-Fri, 9.30am-6pm Sat & Sun mid-Apr–mid-Oct), on the spot where the Czechoslovak General Svoboda had his observation post. The surrounding area is littered with rusting machine guns, mortars and other weapons that act as monument and museum.

Getting There & Away

There are two buses a day Monday to Friday to Dobroslava from Svidník (18Sk, 15 minutes). Buses run to the wooden churches along the main Svidník–Dukla road at fairly regular intervals on weekdays, but to reach the others you'll need a car. Four buses a day connect Svidník with Dukla (32Sk, 40 minutes).

Directory

CONTENTS

ACCOMMODATION

From camp sites with big fields and bungalows to family-run *pensiony/penzióny* (guesthouses), from rustic mountain huts to five-star hotels with white-gloved bellmen: lodging in the two republics runs the gamut. It may be a communist hold over, but most towns have at least one hotel, and even in villages there's someone willing to rent a room. You can usually get a list of all accommodation (private rooms, student dorms, *pensions* and hotels) in the area from the local tourist office, and it may be at least partially posted on the town/tourist office website.

The listings in the sleeping sections of this book fall under three broad categories: budget (under 600Kč/1000Sk), midrange (600Kč/1000Sk to 2000Kč/2700Sk) and top

end (more than 2000Kč/2700Sk). As you would expect, accommodation in the capitals is more expensive, particularly in Prague: budget (under 2000Kč), midrange (2000-4000Kč), top end (greater than 4000Kč). Accommodation in West Bohemian spa towns, such as Karlovy Vary, and in Slovak's second city, Košice, tends to cost more as well.

Unless otherwise noted, we quote rates for the high season (usually April or May through September or October). Major ski areas like the Krkonoše and Tatras mountains have a winter price peak from January through March or April that exceeds the summer peak, with prices over the Easter and Christmas/New Year holidays being the highest. Lodging establishments in resort areas drop their rates dramatically during spring and autumn. Some hotels quote their rates in euros and, when this occurs, we've done the same.

Breakfast may be included in the rate; if not, it can usually be added for 80Kč/Sk to 200Kč/Sk. Guarded parking can cost anything from 100Kč/100Sk to 450Kč/300Sk per day. In Slovakia an accommodation tax of 30Sk per person is always tacked on to the bill. High-speed internet access, where available (big cities), is usually complimentary, but a few places charge around 300Kč/Sk a day.

Nonsmoking rooms are not always an option nation-wide; the further east you go, the less likely you'll find dedicated, smoke-free rooms.

Prices in this book are quoted in the currency the establishment uses. Most base their rates on the crown, but a few are tied to the euro, especially top-end hotels.

BOOK ACCOMMODATION ONLINE

For more accommodation reviews and recommendations by Lonely Planet authors, check out the online booking service at www.lonelyplanet.com. You'll find the true, insider lowdown on the best places to stay. Reviews are thorough and independent. Best of all, you can book online.

The following websites might be of help:

Bookings.sk (www.bookings.sk) Slovakia-wide accommodation reservations.

Czech Hotels (www.czechhotels.cz) Hotels in the Czech Republic.

Limba (www.limba.sk) Private *chaty* you can rent across Slovakia.

Travel.cz (www.travel.cz) Prague and Czech Republic accommodation booking service.

Travel Guide (www.travelguide.cz, www.travelguide.sk) Comprehensive online accommodation listings, with booking facilities.

Ubytujsa (www.ubytujsa.sk) Good number of private accommodation, guesthouses and huts in Slovakia.

Apartments

If you're planning to stay a while, it might be worth considering renting an apartment. *Prague Post's* and *Slovak Spectator's* classified sections are good sources of information for long-term rentals, as is www.praguehome.com. Apartments with kitchens in Prague start at around 14,000Kč per month. For shorter term rentals you'll pay prices comparable to hotel rooms (€60 to €150 a night in Bratislava).

Short-term internet resources:

Interhome (www.interhome.us) Lists apartments and homes by week/weekend in Czech and Slovak Republics (there is a booking fee).

Apartments.cz (www.apartments.cz) Studios to three-bedrooms in Prague's centre.

Bratislava Hotels (www.bratislavahotels.com) Apartments in Bratislava's old town and beyond.

Camping

Camping grounds vary greatly across both countries; generally there are spaces for caravans and most have basic bungalows, huts or cabins for rent. Often tents are pitched randomly in a big open field in the centre and the cabins are arranged around the edge, near the tree line.

Facilities may be basic and run down, or you might find bars, discos, minigolf and boat rentals in a lakeside location. Most have some food service. Unless otherwise noted in this book, all camping grounds are open from May to October only.

Typical prices include a per-person rate, which is generally from around 50Kč/80Sk to 120Kč/100Sk plus charges per tent (50Kč/60Sk to 100Kč/100Sk). A car will cost about 70Kč/90Sk extra. Huts or bungalows are usually 120Kč/150Sk to 260Kč/250Sk per bed, more if they have bathrooms.

Camp CZ (www.camp.cz is) an excellent online source for Czech camping. In conjunction with the **Slovak Camping and Caravaning Club** (www.caravaning.sk), VKÚ maps puts out the *Mapa Autokempingov*, listing camping grounds throughout Slovakia.

Hostels

A hostel can be anything from a bunk bed in room of 12 to a double with shower, the common factor being that you pay by the bed (if you want a double to yourself, you have to pay for two beds). Outside the capitals there aren't a lot of backpacker-style hostels *(hostel)* with nifty internet connections, game rooms and kitchens. Mostly what you'll find are basic tourist or worker hostels *(ubytovna/ubytovná)* where sleeping may be dorm style, or you may get a tiny room with shared facilities.

In July and August, student dormitories open to all travellers and provide the cheapest lodging (about 300Kč/Sk to 500Kč/Sk per person). Only a few of these have places to eat or kitchens on the premises. Most do not have curfews.

Hotels

Prague has some truly stylish top-end sleeps that are comparable to Western Europe standards and prices. Bratislava lags behind a bit; no five-star ratings there, though Hotel Marrol's (p348) comes awfully close. The main difference between midrange hotels and *pensions* are the facilities. A hotel will almost always have a restaurant and a bar, and may have business services, a fitness centre and pool.

Single-bed rooms are regularly available, and single occupancy of a double room is normally two-thirds the cost of full occupancy. If sleeping near your partner is important to you, check if the place has a room with a *manželská postel* (literally 'marriage bed', a bed with one continuous queen mattress) as doubles are often designed with two twin beds for conventioneers. Even when the twin beds are pushed together, you have a gap. *Apartmány* are more expensive and they are usually suites, not apartments, as few have kitchens.

Mountain Huts

In hilly or mountainous natural areas you have yet another lodging option. *Chata/chaty* (singular/plural) are mountain huts (also called *bouda* or *chalupa* in Czech), which can be anything from shack to chalet. In national parks these huts sit along high-altitude trails, creating sleeping network for hikers. They may be rustic log or communist concrete, dorm- or hotel-style, but some sort of food is usually available at all of them. Off trail, near villages (usually at lower elevations), a *chata* is as likely to be a log cottage for rent to holiday travellers as it is a rustic mountain guesthouse. Prices are quite reasonable, no matter the type (200Kč/250Sk to 300Kč/500Sk per person); the clean air and nature are thrown in for free.

Pensions

Pension or *penzión* equates to the similar word in English, and most of these are family-run guesthouses that have breakfast rooms, if not a small restaurant. Some larger hotels have co-opted the word to sound homey, but, in general, *pension*s have more character and are smaller than hotels. Depending on the quality of the appointments and the proximity to a town centre, you may pay just as much at one of these as at a hotel. With midrange prices, *pension*s are more often than not the best choice, especially if you want to avoid institutional high-rise lodging.

Private Rooms

Keep your eye out for signs on homes advertising *Zimmer frei* (German for 'room available') or *privat* (private room). Renting rooms in private homes is common near the more popular tourist destinations. Touts swarm around the capitals' main train stations, some of them honest amateurs with good deals to offer – but check the map and the transport, as some places are way out in the 'burbs. You may have to share the bathroom with the

family, but, more and more, these places are being run like tiny *pension*s.

The local tourist office will usually have a list of private accommodation and you can find some on town and tourist websites. Where there's a particular street or neighbourhood with a lot of good options, we've listed them in the destination sections. Rooms generally go for around 300Kč/250Sk to 450Kč/500Sk per person; add another 30% to 50% when you're staying in Prague and Bratislava. Most private accommodation offers discounts for longer stays but put their prices up for Easter, Christmas and some European holidays.

BUSINESS HOURS

Most shops open from 9am to 5pm or 6pm Monday to Friday, and until noon or 1pm on Saturday. The small, local *potraviny* (supermarket) opens earlier (at 6:30am or 7am) but otherwise has normal shop hours. Big chain department and grocery stores (like Billa and Tesco) stay open until 9pm weekdays and 7pm weekends if they are in an old town centre; a *hypermarket* on the outskirts of big cities may be open 24 hours.

Restaurant and café hours are from around 10:30am to 10:30pm daily; where they deviate from these times by more than an hour, we've noted this throughout the book. Bars and nightclubs are a bit trickier. As a general rule, bars and pubs are open from around noon until midnight or 1am, but stay open later on Friday and Saturday. Clubs may not open until 4pm, and on weekends may stay open until 4am. Those in smaller cities sometimes only open on weekends.

Banks and post offices are generally open from 8.30am to 4.30pm weekdays. Exchange offices in Prague are open later. Note that many places, including some tourist and left luggage offices in small towns, close for a lunch break between noon and 1pm.

CHILDREN

Czechs and Slovaks are generally family oriented, but most restaurants do not specifically cater to children and you'll rarely find one with a kids' playground and high chairs. Some list a children's menu *(dětský jídelníček/detský jedálny lístok)*, but when they don't they may be able to provide smaller portions for a lower price. While the attitude towards children is welcoming, breast feeding and nappy changing in public is pushing the limit.

Everything you would find in Western countries, such as disposable nappies and baby food, is widely available throughout the larger towns. Day-care centres are practically nonexistent, but some of the top-end hotels have baby-sitting services. Generally speaking, only the top-end hotels can provide cots and other child-oriented equipment. International and more reliable car-rental agencies hire out child safety seats.

At present, there are no organisations specifically catering to children's travel needs in either republic. A useful source of information when travelling with children is Lonely Planet's *Travel with Children,* by Cathy Lanigan.

Sights & Activities

Especially in the big cities there are plenty of activities for children – museums, zoos and the ever-popular puppet theatres *(loutkové divadla/bábkové divadlo).*

Among the possibilities for children in Prague (p120), check out the Toy Museum and the large playground on Petřín Hill. In Brno there's a planetarium (p302); Bratislava has a cool zoo (p346) and Košice a steam train ride (p410). All four cities also have puppet theatres with matinees.

Little ones under six gain free entry into sights and travel free on public transport; children between six and 14, as well as students with an ISIC card, will receive a discount.

CLIMATE CHARTS

The damp continental climate of most of the Czech Republic and Slovakia is characterised by warm, showery summers and cold, snowy winters. Spring and autumn feature generally changeable conditions with rain always possible. Although the Czech Republic enjoys marginally milder weather than Slovakia, variations between them are small compared with those between the low elevations and the mountains.

The following climate charts show average temperatures and rainfall in the larger cities, but these can vary wildly from year to year. For instance, in spring 2006, both countries experienced minor flooding (minor compared with the flood in 2002 anyway).

See When to Go (p14) for more information on seasons.

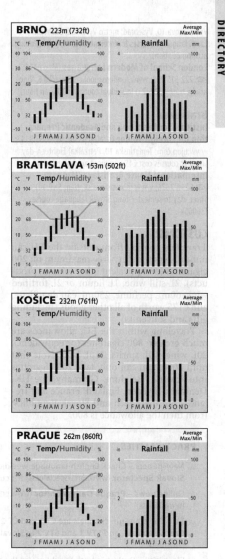

COURSES

If you're interested in learning a few tongue twisters in Czech or Slovak, a language course is the way to go. The larger cities have language schools; some of the better establishments are listed here.

Prague

Institute for Language & Preparatory Studies
(ÚJOP; Map p112; ☎ 224 990 411; www.ujop.cuni.cz;

DIRECTORY

Vratislavova 10, Vyšehrad; metro Vyšehrad) Six-week Czech language courses for foreigners (€585, not including accommodation).
London School of Modern Languages (Map p116; ☎ 222 515 018; www.londonschool.cz; Budečká 6, Vinohrady; tram 4, 22, 23) Individual courses (610Kč an hour).

Bratislava
Institute for Language and Academic Preparation for Foreign Students (Map p338; ☎ 6353 3147; www.ujop.com; Tematínska 10, Petržalka) Eighteen-day summer courses cost €450 (without accommodation).
International House Bratislava (Map p340; ☎ 5296 2675; www.ihbratislava.sk; Nám SNP 14) Three-day to semester-long Slovak language courses (3600Sk).

CUSTOMS
Travellers coming from outside the EU can import/export a duty-free maximum of: 200 cigarettes (or equivalent other tobacco products), 2L still wine, 1L liquor *or* 2L fortified wine, 60mL perfume, 250mL eau de toilette, and €175 worth of all other goods (including gifts and souvenirs).

Travelling within the EU, allowances are much greater: 800 cigarettes (or equivalent), 20L wine, 10L spirits, 110L beer. Note that until 2008, you can only take 200 cigarettes into Austria, Belgium, Germany, the UK, Denmark, Sweden, Finland, France and Ireland from the Czech and Slovak Republics; from then the allowance is 800.

Pets can be brought into the republics with a rabies vaccination certificate and an examination certificate made out within three days of departure.

Antiques technically need a certificate declaring that they are not an 'article of national cultural heritage', which are prohibited from export. The dealer you buy them from should be able to help.

In the Czech Republic you can import or export unlimited amounts of Czech and foreign currency, but amounts exceeding 500,000Kč must be declared. Slovakia allows the import or export of up to 150,000Sk of local or foreign currency.

With accession to the EU, customs checking at EU border points has become rather lax. The only place you are likely to encounter delays is entering Slovakia from the Ukraine – thorough searches for contraband cigarettes take ages.

DANGERS & ANNOYANCES
Prague has some typical big-city problems (for more information, see p86), but outside these, serious crime directed at travellers is fairly remote. One the other hand, pickpocketing and the theft of valuables from car seats (even in locked cars) does happen. Be aware of your surroundings in crowds and don't leave anything in view. Also, secure your belongings on overnight trains; the thieves that roam the cars while you sleep may be an urban myth, by why chance it?

PRACTICALITIES

■ Newspapers – Check English-language weeklies **Prague Post** (www.thepraguepost.com) and **Slovak Spectator** (www.slovakspectator.sk) for current affairs and event listings.

■ Online news – **Prague Daily Monitor** (www.praguemonitor.com), **News Agency of Slovakia** (www.task.sk).

■ TV – The state-run channels are ČT 1 and ČT 2 (analogue), ČT24 and ČT4 sports (digital) in the Czech Republic, and STV 1 and STV 2 in Slovakia. Foreign programs are dubbed rather than subtitled.

■ Electricity – Outlets in both republics use the two small round holes common throughout central Europe (220V AC, 50Hz).

■ Toilets – Carry small change (anything from 2Kč/Sk to 5Kč/Sk) for public toilets. Men's are marked *muži* or *páni,* women's *ženy* or *dámy.*

■ Laundry – Brno and Prague have self-service laundrettes (there are none in Bratislava). Outside these, even laundry service outlets *(prádelna/čistiareň)* are rare.

■ Weights and measures – The metric system is used throughout the republics; a comma is used in place of a decimal point, and full stops are used in place of a comma in numbers in the thousands, millions etc.

Local police investigators aren't known for being the world's most helpful, and you might find it useful to contact your embassy for assistance navigating the police report if you have something stolen.

Scams

There are a number of troublesome scams or annoyances, not all specific to this region, to watch out for. Naturally enough, the prime trouble spots for pickpocketing are where people gather in crowds. Classic pickpocket set ups involve someone creating a distraction (kids surrounding and hassling you, a man pushing the wrong way on a door from the outside so you can't exit a shop) while accomplices delve into your bags and pockets. Another favourite situation for a pickpocket is boarding a crowded tram or metro train, then stepping off with your goods right as the door closes.

Another scam involves a 'lost tourist' asking for directions (usually in halting English). Once you're talking, two people claiming to be plain-clothes policemen (who are actually the 'tourist's' friends) come up and accuse you of changing money illegally. They will demand to see your wallet and passport, but if you hand them over they will just run off. If in doubt, insist on accompanying them to a police station. (Note: ticket inspectors on public transport are notoriously low-key, and occasionally look a little thug-like. If you have the wrong ticket, or have travelled longer than the allotted time, they have the right to demand the fine on the spot. This is not a scam.)

Finally, in this plastic world, it pays to let your credit cards and banks know where to reach you. We've heard of the occasional credit card number stolen without the card being missing (it was either bought from a vendor who swiped it or from a fake reader placed in an ATM machine). Most cards have fraud protection, but if it happens to you, filing a police report can help prove you're in the Czech Republic, not in Bangladesh or wherever the money was charged.

DISABLED TRAVELLERS

The reality is that facilities for disabled people are only slowly coming to the Czech and Slovak Republics, with Prague being by far the most well equipped. The handy *Wheeling the Czech Republic* booklet, available from **Czech Tourism** (Map p116; ☎ 221 580 111; www.czechtourism .com; Vinohradská 46, Vinohrady; ⏰ 8:30am-noon & 1-4pm) is worth getting hold of. It has information on arriving in the Czech Republic and lists wheelchair-friendly hotels and tourist attractions across the country. They will send a copy to you if you email them. The **Prague Wheelchair Users Organisation** (Map p98; Pražská organizace vozíčkářů; ☎ 224 827 210; www.pov.cz, in Czech; Benediktská 6, Staré Město) is a good source of information and publishes a handy guide and CD-ROM called *Accessible Prague*. In Prague, even the monthly what's-on booklet *Přehled* (in Czech) indicates venues with wheelchair access. The www.czecot.com website has a page 'for disabled' where you can search for accessible restaurants and hotels. **Czech Blind United** (Sjednocená organizace nevidomých a slabozrakých v ČR; ☎ 221 462 146; www.braillnet.cz; Krakovská 21, Nové Město) represents the vision-impaired.

In Prague several bus routes and metro stations are wheelchair accessible; a list is available online from **Prague Public Transport** (DDP; www.dp-praha.cz). **Czech Railways** (ČD; www.cd.cz) claims that all of the larger stations in the Czech Republic have ramps and lifts for assisting wheelchairs onto the train, but the harsh reality is that the service is poor.

Unfortunately Slovakia's capital is quite a bit behind its neighbour. The main organisation fighting to improve the situation is the **Slovak Union for the Disabled** (Slovenský zväz telesne postihnutých; Map p338; ☎ 02-6381 4478; www .sztp.sk; Ševčenkova 19, Bratislava), where English is spoken. Most top-end hotels in Bratislava have wheelchair ramps. Slovakia's trains often have a wheelchair access carriage; it's just a pity that the train stations aren't as user-friendly. To get to most platforms you have to go down stairs, under the track, and back up a set of stairs.

DISCOUNT CARDS
Hostel Card

Hostels in the Czech and Slovak Republics do not require you to have a **Hostelling International** (HI; www.hihostels.com) or affiliate card. That said, the HI card entitles you to 20% to 30% discounts at some hostels and junior hotels. Apply for your HI card at home.

Seniors Cards

While seniors over 65 visiting the Czech Republic receive discounts at museums, transport ticket reductions are for residents only.

In Slovakia, it never hurts to ask if a museum offers a discount, but it's mainly applicable for resident retirees. To get discounts of 40% on the Slovak railways, buy a Senior Card (199Sk), which is good for a year, at any train station.

Student & Youth Cards

ISIC (www.isiccard.com) and Euro26 (www.euro26.org) cards will get you discounts at most museums, galleries, theatres and at some hotels. You may even get a discount on air tickets. It's possible to buy a Euro26 card in both countries.

EMBASSIES & CONSULATES

It's important to understand what your home country's embassy can and can't do to help if you get into trouble. Generally speaking, they won't be much help in emergencies if the trouble you're in is even remotely your own fault and they will expect you to travel with insurance. If your money and documents are stolen, your embassy can assist you to get a new passport, however, a loan for onward travel is out of the question. Consular service hours (usually weekdays 9am to noon) at embassies in the Czech and Slovak Republics are limited.

Czech Republic
CZECH EMBASSIES & CONSULATES

The **Czech Ministry of Foreign Affairs** (www.mfa.cz) website contains a full list of embassies and consulates around the world.

Australia (☎ 02-6290 1386; www.mfa.cz/canberra; 8 Culgoa Circuit, O'Malley, Canberra, ACT 2606)

Austria (☎ 01-8995 81 11; www.mfa.cz/vienna; Penzingerstrasse 11-13, 1140 Vienna)

Canada (☎ 613-562 3875; www.mfa.cz/ottawa; 251 Cooper Street, Ottawa, Ontario, K2P 0G2)

France (☎ 01-727 6130; www.mfa.cz/paris; 15 Ave Charles Floquet, Paris 75007)

Germany (☎ 030-226 380; www.mfa.cz/berlin; Wilhelmstrasse 44, 10117 Berlin)

Hungary (☎ 01-4625 011; www.mfa.cz/budapest; Rózsa utca 61, 1064 Budapest VI)

Ireland (☎ 01-668 1135; www.mfa.cz/dublin; 57 Northumberland Rd, Ballsbridge, Dublin 4)

Netherlands (☎ 070-313 00 31; www.mfa.cz/hague; Paleisstraat 4, 2514 JA Den Haag)

New Zealand (☎ 09-353 9766; Auckland@honorary .mzv.cz; BMW Mini Centre, 11-15 Great South Rd, PO Box 7748, Auckland)

Poland (☎ 022-525 1850; www.mfa.cz/warsaw; Koszykowa 18, 00-555 Warsaw)

Slovakia (☎ 02-5920 3305; www.mfa.cz/bratislava; Hviezdoslavovo nám 8, 810 00 Bratislava 1)

UK (☎ 020-7243 1115; www.mfa.cz/london; 26 Kensington Palace Gardens, London W8 4QY)

USA (☎ 202-274 9100; www.mfa.cz/washington; 3900 Spring of Freedom St NW, Washington, D.C. 20008)

EMBASSIES & CONSULATES IN THE CZECH REPUBLIC

The following are in Prague unless otherwise noted.

Australia (☎ 296 578 350; www.embassy.gov.au /cz.html; 6th fl, Klimentská 10, Nové Město) Honorary consulate for emergency assistance only (eg a stolen passport). The nearest Australian embassy is in Vienna.

Austria (Map p115; ☎ 257 090 511; www.austria.cz, in German & Czech; Viktora Huga 10, Smíchov)

Canada (☎ 272 101 800; www.canada.cz; Muchova 6, Bubeneč)

France (☎ 251 171 711; www.france.cz, in French & Czech; Velkopřerovské náměstí 2, Malá Strana)

Germany (Map p92; ☎ 257 113 111; www.deutsch land.cz, in German & Czech; Vlašská 19, Malá Strana)

Ireland (Map p92; ☎ 257 530 061; pragueembassy@dfa .ie; Tržiště 13, Malá Strana)

Netherlands (☎ 233 015 200; www.netherlands embassy.cz; Gotthardská 6/27, Bubeneč)

New Zealand (☎ 222 514 672; egermayer@nzconsul .cz; Dykova 19, Vinohrady) Honorary consulate providing emergency assistance only (eg stolen passport). The nearest New Zealand embassy is in Berlin.

Poland Prague (Map p92; ☎ 257 099 500; www .prague.polemb.net; Valdštejnská 8, Malá Strana); Ostrava (☎ 596 118 074; Blahoslavova 4; ⏱ 8.30am-noon Mon-Fri) Issues same-day visas.

Slovakia (☎ 233 113 051; www.slovakemb.cz, in Slovak; Pod Hradbami 1, Dejvice)

UK (Map p92; ☎ 257 402 111; www.britain.cz; Thunovská 14, Malá Strana)

USA (Map p92; ☎ 257 022 000; www.usembassy .cz; Tržiště 15, Malá Strana)

Slovakia
SLOVAK EMBASSIES & CONSULATES

For a comprehensive embassy list, check out the **Slovak Ministry of Foreign Affairs** (www.mfa .sk) website.

Australia (☎ 02 6290 1516; www.slovakemb-aust.org; 47 Culgoa Circuit, O'Malley, Canberra, ACT 2606)

Austria (☎ 01-318 905 5200; www.vienna.mfa.sk; Armbrustergasse 24, 1-1190 Wien)

Canada (☎ 613-749 4442; www.ottawa.mfa.sk 50 Rideau Terrace, Ottawa, Ontario K1M 2A1)

Czech Republic (☎ 233 113 051; www.praha.mfa.sk; Pod Hradbami 1, 16000 Praha 6)

France (☎ 01-44 14 56 00; www.amb-slovaquie.fr; 125 Rue de Ranelagh, 75016 Paris)

Germany (☎ 030-8892 6 200; www.botschaft-slowakei .de; Fredrichstrasse 60, Berlin 10707)

Hungary (☎ 01-460 9010; www.budapest.mfa.sk; Stéfania út 22-24, H-1143 Budapest XIV)

Ireland (☎ 01-660 0012; www.dublin.mfa.sk; 20 Clyde Rd, Ballsbridge, Dublin 4)

Netherlands (☎ 070-416 7777; www.hague.mfa.sk; Parkweg 1; 2585 JG Den Haag)

UK (☎ 020-7313 6470; www.slovakembassy.co.uk; 25 Kensington Palace Gardens, London W8 4QY)

USA (☎ 202-237 1054; www.slovakembassy-us.org; 3523 International Court NW, Washington, D.C. 20008)

EMBASSIES & CONSULATES IN SLOVAKIA

Australia and New Zealand do not have embassies in Slovakia; the nearest are in Vienna and Berlin respectively. The following are all in Bratislava:

Austria (Map p340; ☎ 02-5443 1443; www.embas syaustria.sk; Ventúrska 10)

Canada (Map p340; ☎ 02-5920 4031; brtsv@international.gc.ca; Mostová 2)

Czech Republic (Map p340; ☎ 02-5920 3303; www .mzv.cz/bratislava/; Hviezdoslavovo nám 8)

France (Map p340; ☎ 02-5934 7111; www.france .sk; Hlavné nám 7)

Germany (Map p340; ☎ 02-5920 4400; www .pressburg.diplo.de; Hviezdoslavovo nám 10)

Hungary (Map p340; ☎ 02-5920 5200; www .hungemb.sk; Sedlárska 3)

Ireland (Map p340; ☎ 02-5443 5715; bratislava@iveagh.irlgov.ie; Carlton Savoy Building, Mostová 2)

Netherlands (Map p338; ☎ 02-5262 5081; www .holandskoweb.com; Fraňa Kráľa 5)

Poland (Map p338; ☎ 02-5441 3174; www .polskevelvyslanectvo.sk; Hummelova 4)

UK (Map p340; ☎ 02-5998 2000; www.british embassy.sk; Panská 16)

Ukraine (Map p338; ☎ 02-5920 2810; www .ukrembassy.sk; Radvanská 35)

USA (Map p340; ☎ 02-54 43 33 38; www.us embassy.sk; Hviezdoslavovo nám 5)

FESTIVALS & EVENTS

The vast array of festivals and celebrations in the Czech and Slovak Republics is quite impressive and ranges from international music festivals to village folk fairs. On the Czech side, the Moravské Slovácko region (p326), in South Moravia, is a hot spot for local folk festivals. **Czech Tourism** (www.czechtourism.com) has a top events list on its website and the **Folklore**

Association of the Czech Republic (www.fos.cz) is another good source of information.

Slovakia is even more folk-oriented than its larger neighbour and just about every little village and *skanzen* (open-air village museum) seems to have a folk music and dance festival during the summer months (June through August). Look online at the **Slovak Tourist Board** (www.slovakiatourism.sk) for a comprehensive list of cultural and sporting events held throughout the year.

Larger cities in both countries sponsor seasonal music and cultural festivals that bring out special operas and concerts over the course of a month or two.

April

Burning of the Witches (Pálení čarodějnic; 30 April) Essentially the Czech version of German *Walpurgisnacht*, a pre-Christian festival for warding off evil influence, especially witches. Bonfires are lit all over the country (including on Petřín hill in Prague), old brooms are put to the torch and people party on through the night.

Easter Monday (Velikonoce/Veľkánoc) Not the most pleasant of events for women. If you're in a village, you may see young girls being swatted with braided willow switches (more so in the Czech Republic) or being doused with buckets of water (more Slovak) in a perpetuation of an old pagan springtime rejuvenation ritual. Women are supposed to reciprocate by giving the guys decorated eggs, go figure.

May

Prague Spring (Pražské Jaro; www.festival.cz) Prague's biggest festival begins on 12 May and the classical music continues until 2 June. Operas and concerts sell out, so book ahead.

Ride of the Kings (Jízda Králů; http://jizdakralu.vlcnov .cz) One of the Czech nation's more colourful local festivals, during which a young 'king' and helpers dress in women's clothes and ride through the streets on ribbon-bedecked horses in a re-enactment of a medieval escape. Vlčnov, in South Moravia, thus celebrates the last weekend in May.

June

Rusyn-Ukrainian Cultural Festival (Slavnosti kultúry Rusínov-Ukrajincov Slovenska; www.muk.sk) Rusyn (an east Slavic minority) music and dance troupes from Slovakia, the Ukraine, Germany, Scandinavia and elsewhere perform one weekend in late June. Upwards of 30,000 visitors come to see the show in Svidník, in east Slovakia.

July

Východná Folk Festival (Folklórny Festival Východná; www.obec-vychodna.sk, in Slovak; Východná) In late June or early July folk dancers and musicians from across the nation and Europe gather at the biggest international folk festival in Slovakia, in the Low Tatras.

European Folk Craft Market (Európske ľudové remeslo; www.kezmarok.net) On the second weekend of July, national and international artisans gather in Kežmarok, Slovakia, to demonstrate and sell their wares.

August
Moto Grand Prix (www.automotodrombrno.cz) Brno's Auto Motodrom buzzes with excitement as international motorcycle racing stars line up in late August.

September
Bratislava Jazz Days (Bratislavských jazzových dní; www.bjd.sk) One long weekend each September really swings in Bratislava. International jazz musicians sit in on a session or two.

December
Christmas market (November 26) A few weeks before Christmas, booths selling handmade crafts and other gifts pop up on the main pedestrian square in towns across the republics. Hot spiced wine and occasional concerts are also on tap.
Mikuláš (St Nicholas; 5 December) On Nicholas's saint day, he comes to leave treats for children. In the Czech Republic he comes in person and has to contend with the Devil (both dressed-up parents, uncles or neighbours) who may leave coal or potatoes instead of chocolate and fruit. In Slovakia, St Nick is a bit more stealthy – he just leaves chocolate (or sticks) in children's shoes overnight. That explains all the chocolate Santas being sold on the streets.

FOOD
A full rundown on local cuisine, drinks and where to eat can be found in the Food & Drink chapter (p66). Restaurants in the larger centres have been broken down under various district headings into three budget categories: budget (mains less than 150Kč/Sk), midrange (mains averaging 150Kč/Sk to 300Kč/Sk) and top end (anything greater than 300Kč/Sk). Though smaller sections are undivided, they are still listed by price.

GAY & LESBIAN TRAVELLERS
Czech Republic
Homosexuality has long been legal in the Czech Republic (the age of consent is 16), and in July 2006 same sex partnerships became lawful as well. For a while it looked as if it wouldn't happen: President Klaus vetoed the authorising bill, but parliament overturned that decision. Same-sex partnerships are now granted many legal rights regarding financial and health matters, but they are still not allowed to adopt children. **Gay Iniciativa** (Gay Initiative; ☎ 224 223 811; www.gay.iniciativa.cz, in Czech; Senovážné náměstí 2, Nové Město) is a national gay and lesbian advocacy organisation that has information on area resources

Bimonthly gay magazine **Amigo** (www.amigo .cz) is a combination of personal ads, and a guide to gay and lesbian bars and accommodation in the Czech Republic (with a few listings for Slovakia thrown in). Other useful websites include www.gay.cz and prague .gayguide.net.

Prague, of course, has the biggest scene in either republic, for more information see Gay & Lesbian Prague (see p123).

Slovakia
In Slovakia, too, homosexuality has been legal since the 1960s (the age of consent is 16). But the Catholic Church has a much larger influence in conservative Slovakia than in the Czech Republic. Partnership bills have consistently been shot down in parliament, but in June 2006 right-of-centre parties lost the parliamentary elections. Though there are members in the prime minister's cabinet who are pushing for a law legalising same-sex unions, conservative coalition partners are unlikely to go along with it.

The gay and lesbian public presence in Slovakia is noticeably small. Though there's no gay bashing to speak of, neither is there much support. The largest gay rights organisation is **Ganymedes** (☎ 5022 8704; www.ganymedes.info in Slovak; PO Box 4, 830 00 Bratislava) and lesbian-specific, **Museion** (☎ 0905804456; www.lesba.sk; PO Box 47, 840 02 Bratislava). Helpful websites listing gay bars, hotels and cruising areas countrywide include www.gay.sk and www.gayinfo.sk.

HOLIDAYS
The following are public holidays in the Czech and Slovak Republics, when banks, offices, and many shops and grocery stores close. Some restaurants, museums and tourist attractions stay open, but public transport is greatly reduced. Getting around the countries by bus on these days is especially difficult.

School holidays fall in the months of July and August, over the Christmas period and during Easter. Like elsewhere, families take advantage of these times so expect accommodation and transport facilities to be full.

Czech Republic

New Year's Day (Nový rok) 1 January; also anniversary of the founding of the Czech Republic.

Easter Monday (Pondělí velikonoční) March or April

Labour Day (Svátek práce) 1 May

Den osvobození (Liberation Day) 8 May

Den Cyrila a Metoděje (SS Cyril & Methodius Day) 5 July

Jan Hus Day (Den Jana Husa) 6 July

Czech Statehood Day (Den éeské státnosti) 28 September

Independence Day (Den vzniku Československa) 28 October

Freedom & Democracy Day (Den boje za svobodu a demokracii) 17 November

Christmas (Vánoce) 24-26 December

Slovakia

New Year's Day (Nový rok) 1 January; also the anniversary of the founding of the Slovak Republic.

Three Kings Day (Tři králové) 6 January

Easter Friday & Monday (Veľké Nocy) March or April

Labour Day (Sviatok práce) 1 May

Victory Over Fascism Day (Deň ví ťazstva nad fašizmom) 8 May

SS Cyril & Methodius Day (Sv Cyril a Metod) 5 July

Slovak National Uprising Day (Slovenské národné povstanie) 29 August

Constitution Day (Deň Ústavy Slovenskej republiky) 1 September

St Mary's Day (Sedembolestná Panna Maria) 15 September

All Saints Day (Sviatok Všetkých svätých) 1 November

Christmas (Vianoce) 24-26 December

INSURANCE

Travel insurance policies covering travel changes, theft, loss and medical problems are many, and each has its own caveat, so check the small print. For example, some policies specifically exclude 'dangerous activities' (eg motorcycling, rock climbing, canoeing and even hiking), or require you to return to your home country every 31 days.

You can get quotes on international travel insurance at www.lonelyplanet.com/travel _services.

For more information on health insurance, see Health (p465); for information on insurance for rental vehicles, see Transport (p459).

INTERNET ACCESS

Like almost every country in Europe, the republics are quite internet savvy. You'll find plenty of internet cafés in the major cities and at least one in most towns. Villages can sometimes prove to be a problem. Places with internet access are listed throughout this book. Connection speeds and the number of terminals vary from one café to the next, but most are on high-speed lines and some have web cams for video calling. In bigger cities, prices can be as low as 50Kč/60Sk per hour and as high as 75Kč/120Sk. In smaller centres expect to pay from around 30Kč/Sk to 60Kč/Sk. In some cafés you can use your own laptop on their wi-fi system for the cost of a beverage.

THE CZECH CALENDAR

While most Western European languages name the months of the year according to their old Latin names, Czech uses far more poetic names taken from nature. Even natives are often uncertain of the derivations. Here's the best we could do:

leden (January) From *led* (ice); the month of frost and ice.

únor (February) From *nořit* (to sink); possibly to do with the breaking and sinking of ice on the rivers.

březen (March) From *bříza* (birch tree); the month of birches.

duben (April) From *dub* (oak tree); the month of budding oaks.

květen (May) From *květ* (flower); the month of blooming flowers.

červen (June) From *červ* (worm); the month when worms (which were once used to make a red dye) were collected. The word *červen* also means 'red'.

červenec (July) As for June.

srpen (August) From *srp* (sickle); the month of harvest.

září (September) Either from *za říje* (before the rutting season) or from *zářít* (to shine, glow), a reference to sunny autumn evenings.

říjen (October) From *říje* (the rut); the month when rutting deer are heard roaring in the woods and hills.

listopad (November) From *list* (leaf) and *pád* (fall); the month of falling leaves.

prosinec (December) From an old Czech word meaning 'grey'.

DIRECTORY

If you've brought your notebook or palmtop computer with you, remember that the power supply voltage in the Czech and Slovak Republics may be different from that at home. You'll also need a European plug adaptor; often it's easiest to buy these before you leave home.

Many hotel rooms (almost all those at top-end prices) in the capitals and second cities have either wi-fi or broadband access through Ethernet ports. It can be handy to bring your own Ethernet cable, as not all places provide them in-room (or they're too short). Telephone jacks are usually USA standard (RJ-11). If you're dialling up, you may want to invest in a line tester to bring with you. That way you can tell if a dangerous electrical current that could potentially damage your modem is travelling over a hotel's digital telephone line.

International ISPs (internet service providers) such as **AOL** (www.aol.com), **CompuServe** (www.compuserve.com) and **AT&T** (www.attbusiness.net) have dial-in nodes throughout the Czech and Slovak Republics; download a list of the dial-in numbers before you leave home. Major ISPs in the Czech Republic include **Czech On Line** (www.col.cz) and **T-Com** (www.telecom.sk). Free web-based email services include **Google Mail** (Gmail; www.gmail.com) and **Yahoo** (www.yahoo.com).

Prague (p84) and Bratislava (p341) have numerous free wi-fi zones in cafés, bars and on public squares, and the number of venues increases daily.

For websites about the Czech and Slovak Republics see Getting Started (p16).

LEGAL MATTERS

Penalties for possession of drugs are harsh and it's unlikely that your embassy can do much to help you if you are caught. In the Czech Republic in 1999 it became illegal to possess 'more than a small amount' of drugs. Unfortunately the law does not define 'a small amount' or specify which drugs, giving the police a free hand to nick anyone in possession of any amount of any drug. Slovakia's situation is quite similar; you can be sentenced for up to five years for possession of a small amount of marijuana. It's simply not worth the risk to import, export or possess any illegal substances.

If you find yourself under arrest in either republic for any reason whatsoever, you are entitled to call your embassy. Note that it is

---

LEGAL AGE

- Drinking alcohol – 18
- Driving – 18
- Heterosexual/homosexual sex – 16
- Marriage – 18
- Smoking – 16
- Voting – 18

---

technically illegal not to carry some form of identification (normally your passport). If you can't prove your identity, police have the right to detain you for up to 48 hours.

Drink-driving is strictly illegal; both republics have a zero blood-alcohol limit for drivers – zero, nulla, none. Random police breathalyser stops are common. You could be sentenced to two years in jail if convicted in Slovakia and one in the Czech Republic. The fine for littering (paid on the spot) can be as much as 1000Kč/Sk. In Prague, there's a 1000Kč fine for smoking at bus and tram stops, even if they're in the open air.

MAPS

Maps of the Czech and Slovak Republics are available in any good bookshop throughout the republics; outside the region it's best to try international publisher **Freytag & Berndt** (www.freytagberndt.com), which has good maps of both countries.

Some of the best Czech country and city maps are those by **Kartografie Praha** (www.kartografie.cz). Particularly good are the *Česká republika automapa* (1:500,000 to 1:750,000) and *Česká republika atlas* (1:150,000 to 1:700,000) series. Freytag & Berndt's multilingual *Czech Republic Road Map* (1:500,000) has route distances, sights of interest, mountain-shading and other geographical info.

VKÚ (www.vku.sk), a Slovak publisher, produces the best maps of Slovakia and her cities by far, as well as some for the Czech Republic. There is the *Automapa Slovenská republika* (1:250,000 to 1:1,000,000) or the more detailed *Autoatlas Slovenská* (1:150,000 to 1:500,000). It also produces *Vreckový Autoatlas Česká & Slovenská republika* (1:1,000,000), a pocket atlas of both republics. They also create excellent hiking (green) and skiing (blue) trail maps, as well as castle-oriented maps with descriptive booklets.

Good online maps for the Czech Republic can be found at www.supernavigator.cz and for Slovakia at www.kompas.sk. For more information on city maps, see the destination chapters.

MONEY

The Czech and Slovak Republics have separate currencies, the Koruna česká (Czech crown; Kč) and the Slovenská koruna (Slovak crown; Sk). US dollars and euros are the most sensible foreign currencies to pack. This book's inside cover has a handy exchange rate table, and the Getting Started chapter has a general rundown on costs (p16). The euro will not be introduced until 2009 at the earliest.

The Koruna česká is divided into 100 haléřů, or heller (h). Notes come in 20Kč, 50Kč, 100Kč, 200Kč, 500Kč, 1000Kč and 5000Kč denominations. Coins are 1Kč, 2Kč, 5Kč, 10Kč, 20Kč and 50Kč, and 50h. Always have a few 2Kč and 5Kč coins for use in public toilets and transport ticket machines.

The Slovenská koruna equals 100 halierú, or heller (h). Notes come in 20Sk, 50Sk, 100Sk, 200Sk, 500Sk, 1000Sk and 5000Sk denominations. Coins are 1Sk, 2Sk, 5Sk, 10Sk and 50h.

ATMs

By far the best way to carry money around is not to. ATMs *(bankomat)*, which accept debit and credit cards (Visa, MasterCard, Plus, Cirrus, Eurocard and EC), can be found almost everywhere in the Czech and Slovak Republics, even in smaller towns, and you generally get the market rate of exchange. Look for ATMs at transport depots, and banks on a town's pedestrian square.

Banks

In both nations banks are plentiful. Almost all branches have both an ATM and an exchange desk. **Komerční banka** (KB; www.kb.cz), **Česká spořitelna** (www.csas.cz) and **Živnostenská banka** (www1.zivnobanka.cz) are the main players in the Czech Republic. **Všeobecná úverová banka** (VÚB; www.vub.sk), **Slovenská sporiteľňa** (www.slsp.sk) and **Tatra Banka** (www.tatrabanka.sk) are in Slovakia, and **Československá obchodní banka** (ČSOB; www.csob.cz, www.csob.sk) operates in both. Branch locations and phone numbers are listed on their websites. Currency exchange commissions vary by location, but around 2% for cash and travellers cheques is standard.

Credit Cards

American Express, MasterCard and Visa are widely accepted at top-end and midrange hotels, restaurants and shops in big cities; Discover and Diners Club less so. In smaller establishments and towns, American Express may not be accepted. The farther east and the smaller the town you go to in Slovakia, the less likely proprietors are to accept credit cards of any kind.

Credit cards can often be used for cash advances at ATMs if you have set up a pin ahead of time, but will likely incur a higher transaction fee than a debit card.

International Transfers

Wire money from home through **Western Union** (www.westernunion.com); you will be paid in crowns on the receiving end and there will be a hefty fee for the sender (around €30). Numerous pick-up locations in both countries include local banks and Tesco Department Stores.

Moneychangers

Private exchange offices *(směnárna/ zmenareň)* are quite often conveniently located and have long hours, but that's about as far as the advantage goes. Some have great rates of exchange but charge high commissions (up to 10% in Prague) or an 'undisclosed' handling fee, while others charge zero commission but have a dismal rate of exchange. Better to use banks, if time allows, or ATMs, otherwise be sure to check all rates and fees twice. Hotels typically charge 5% commission.

You'll have no problem exchanging US dollars, British pounds and euros, but it's harder to change Polish zlotys and Hungarian forints, and you can only buy or sell Ukrainian hryvnias in Hungary.

Travellers Cheques

Travellers cheques are accepted at most banks and are relatively easy to replace if lost. Eurocheques are also widely accepted with a cheque guarantee card.

American Express (www.americanexpress.com) cashes its travellers cheques without charging commission. There's an office in Prague (p85) but not the Slovak Republic (the closest is 60km away in Vienna).

Travelex (www.travelex) also has an office in Prague.

POST
Postal Rates

The two republics' postal services, **Česká pošta** (www.cpost.cz) and **Slovenská pošta** (www.slposta.sk), are fairly efficient and not too expensive. In both republics it's safest to mail international parcels from main post offices in large cities. However, anything you can't afford to lose should go by registered Express Mail Service (EMS).

Mail to Europe (automatically airmail) is 10Kč/12Sk for postcards and letters up to 20g; to anywhere else it costs 12Kč/16Sk. EMS is fast and secure and is available in both countries; prices start at 600Kč/600Sk. A 2kg parcel by airmail costs around 400Kč/650Sk to Europe and 560Kč/570Sk to elsewhere. Only larger post offices will let you send parcels of books or printed matter up to 15kg.

Remember to always ask for a receipt (*potvrzení/potvrdenie*) when mailing anything larger than a letter by airmail or a more expensive mail service to ensure that it is actually sent via the correct service.

If you are sending anything that looks like an antique you will probably be directed to the nearest customs clearance post office (*Pošta celnice/Poštovní colnica*).

Sending & Receiving Mail

You can buy stamps in post offices and from street vendors and newsagents. Letters go in the orange boxes outside post offices and around town.

Most larger post offices have a separate window for poste restante mail (*uložené zásilky/poste restante*), though the most reliable services are at the main post offices in Prague and Bratislava. You must present your passport to claim mail. Check under your given name too.

SHOPPING

Prague, like any cosmopolitan megacapital, abounds in shopping opportunities from high-end fashion to low-end souvenirs, but there are a few items the two republics are known for. Bohemian crystal has been attracting attention for centuries: back in the 1700s, it was already being sold in 12 European capitals. The traditional stuff is weighty (24% lead) and intricately cut – the more engraved lines and stars, the more expensive. But Czech glassmakers have also embraced the medium as modern art. Vibrant and funky colours and

shapes enliven art glass. The quintessential Czech crystal company, Moser, bridges the gap with heavy, but simply elegant designs, sometimes in translucent colours. Prague clearly has the highest concentration of stores, and Moser is made in Karlovy Vary (p211), but most towns in the Czech Republic have at least one crystal shop.

Also indigenous is the *česky granát* (Czech garnet), a semi-precious stone that is usually deep red. It's mined near the East Bohemian town of Turnov, and **Granát Turnov** (www.granat -cz.com) is the only company authorised to mine and set Czech garnets. Either buy from one of the official factory stores (there's one in Prague; see p140), or make sure you get a certificate of authenticity when buying from another shop. Designs are usually characterised by numerous smaller stones arranged in clusters in necklaces, rings, bracelets, earrings and pins. Again, there are jewellery stores in most old town centres in the Czech Republic.

Though Slovakia does have its own crystal-making tradition and items found in stores across the country can be much less expensive than the Czech equivalents, it's the folk crafts and ceramics here that are especially unique. Modra (p356), outside Bratislava, is the ceramic centre, turning out bright patterns in yellows and blues. Dishes, plaques and figurines often have village themes. Folk arts – woodcarving, ceramics, embroidery, painted eggs – are available at **Úľuv** (www.uluv .sk) co-operative stores across the country, and at crafts fairs during holidays.

SOLO TRAVELLERS

There's no stigma attached to travelling solo in either country. Many hostels, *pensions* and hotels have a couple of single rooms available; they generally cost a little more than half the price of a double room.

A growing number of young people speak a smattering of English and are happy to give it a whirl, though outside the larger cities it can prove hard to meet locals. That's not to say that it won't happen, but you'll probably have to make the first move, so to speak.

Prague is easily the best city to meet other travellers and expats; they're everywhere. Jáma (p136) is a well-known meeting point, as are the more popular Irish bars around town. Some hostels have their own bars so you may not even have to leave the building to start up a conversation. In Bratislava, the Dubliner (p351) and the Slovak Pub (p351) are the English speaker hang-outs.

TELEPHONE

If you have your computer and microphone or webcam with you, **Skype** (www.skype.com) telephony service is an excellent alterative to phoning. With this service you set up a call from computer to computer for free. Skype Out allows you to call from your computer to land lines back home for as low as US$.02 per minute. Some internet cafés are Skype equipped.

Czech Republic

The Czech Republic's country code is ☎ 420. All numbers consist of nine digits; you have to dial all nine for any call, local or long distance. There are no area codes. For directory inquiries dial ☎ 1180; international directory inquiries call ☎ 1181. To make direct-dial international calls from within the Czech Republic, dial ☎ 00, the country code and the phone number.

MOBILE PHONES

The Czech Republic is no different to the rest of Europe – everyone seems to have a mobile phone. The country uses GSM 900, which is compatible with the rest of Europe and Australasia, but not with the North American GSM 1900 (though some North Americans have GSM 1900/900 phones that do work). Before you leave home check rates and procedures with your provider. Some companies require that international roaming be activated before use: prices can be exorbitant and special dialling instructions may be needed.

If you plan to spend some time here, and your phone is unlocked, consider purchasing a pay-as-you-go SIM card, which will get you a local number. (Note: you won't be able to use your existing number.) The main players in the market are **T-Mobile** (www.t-mobile.cz), **Vodaphone** (www.vodaphone.cz) and **EuroTel** (www.eurotel.cz). Cards sell for anywhere between 300Kč and 2000Kč and credit can be added as you go. Check with your home provider to make sure your phone will work before leaving. It can be quite confusing to figure it out in-country.

PUBLIC PHONES & PHONECARDS

Blue coin telephones accept only 2Kč, 5Kč, 10Kč and 20Kč coins, but they are being replaced by telephones that take *telecard* (phonecards). Prepaid phone cards are sold at post offices, newsagents, newsstands, petrol stations and supermarkets, and come in 150Kč to 1000Kč denominations. Czech Telecom cards are for calling within the country while companies such as **Smartcall** (www.smartcall .cz) are for international calls. Prices can be as low as 2Kč per minute off-peak to the US, UK and Australia.

Slovakia

Slovakia's country code is ☎ 421. When dialling a long-distance number from another city in Slovakia, you must dial both digits of the area code (for instance ☎ 02 for Bratislava). If you are calling long distance from outside Slovakia, you drop the zero. Local calls do not require any area code: you need only dial the local seven-digit (eight for Bratislava) number. Many businesses use mobile phones, which have numbers that generally begin with 09. In the country you need to dial all 10 numbers. If you are calling a Slovak cell phone from outside the country, again, drop the zero.

For domestic directory inquiries dial ☎ 1181; for international directory inquiries call ☎ 12149. To make direct-dial international calls dial ☎ 00, the country code and the number.

MOBILE PHONES

Like the Czech Republic, Slovakia uses GSM 900, and the same rules apply when using your phone. It's also possible to buy pay-as-you-go SIM cards here. Slovakia's main service providers, **Orange** (www.orange.sk) and **T-Mobile** (www .t-mobile.sk), have rechargeable SIM cards for sale, ranging from 400Sk to 1000Sk. You cannot use your home number with either service.

PUBLIC PHONES & PHONECARDS

Most pay phones these days require a *telefónna karta* for domestic calls, available in denominations of 175/350Sk. Purchase them at newsstands, tobacco shops, some post and tourist offices, and at petrol stations. International phone cards, like **EZ Phone** (www .ezcard.sk) are also sold there. They are the best way to call home from any phone. Rates start at just 2Sk per minute to the UK and US (3Sk to Australia). Cards are often posted in kiosk windows next to cell phone credit cards, which they look an awful lot like. Be careful what you're pointing at.

TIME

Like the rest of Continental Europe, the Czech and Slovak Republics are both on Central European Time (ie GMT/UTC plus one hour). Clocks are moved one hour forward to daylight-saving time (DST) on the last weekend in March, then back again on the last weekend in October.

Czechs quote time on a 24-hour clock. So do most Slovaks, but occasionally when speaking they may use the 12-hour clock and add *ráno* (morning) or *večer* (evening) after the number if the time of day isn't clear.

TOURIST INFORMATION
Local Tourist Offices
CZECH REPUBLIC

Czech Tourism (Map p116; ☎ 221 580 111; www.czech tourism.com; Vinohradská 46, Vinohrady; ☼ 8:30am-noon & 1-4pm) handles tourist information regarding sights, museums, festivals etc for the entire Czech Republic. Its network of municipal information centres (*městské informační centrum* or *středisko*) covers all the major tourist areas throughout the Czech Republic and is easily the best source of information.

SLOVAKIA

Getting information on Slovakia as a whole can be challenging in person. The **Slovak Tourist Board** (Slovenská agentúra pre cestovný ruch; ☎ 048-413 614 648; www.slovakiatourism.sk; PO Box 35, 974 05 Banská Bystrica) does not have an office open to the public but it does host an excellent website and produce slick booklets and brochures that you can write away to obtain. A few of the brochures are available at town info centres.

Most city information centres in Slovakia are independently run members of the **Association of Information Centres of Slovakia** (Asosiácia Informačných Centier Slovenska, AICES; www.aices.sk). You'll find a complete list of offices on their website.

Tourist Offices Abroad
CZECH TOURISM

Twenty Czech Tourism offices exist across the globe: we've provided a sampling below. A full list can be found online at www.czech tourism.com.

Austria (☎ 01-533 21 93; info-at@czechtourism.com; Herrengasse 17, 1010 Vienna)
Canada (☎ 416-363 9928; info-ca@czechtourism.com; Czech Airlines Office, Suite 1510, Simpson Tower, 401 Bay St, Toronto, Ontario M5H2YA)

France (☎ 01 53 73 00 32; info-fr@czechtourism.com; Rue Bonaparte 18, Paris)
Germany (☎ 030-204 47 70; info1-de@czechtourism .com; Friedrich Strasse 206, 10 178 Berlin)
Netherlands (☎ 020-575 30 14; info-nl@czechtourism .com; Strawinskylaan 517, 1077 XX Amsterdam)
UK (☎ 020-7631 0427; info-uk@czechtourism.com; 13 Harley St, London W1G 9QG)
USA (☎ 212-288 0830; info-usa@czechtourism.com; 1109 Madison Ave, New York, NY 10028)

SLOVAK TOURIST BOARD

Austria (☎ 01-513 95 69; sacr-wien@aon.at; Prinz Eugen Strasse 70, 1040 Vienna)
Czech Republic (☎ 224 946 082; sacrpraha@seznam .cz; Jilska 16, 110 00 Prague 1)
Germany (☎ 030-25 94 26 41; sacr-berlin@botschaft -slowakei.de; Zimmerstrasse 27, 10969 Berlin)
Netherlands (☎ 020-575 2181; info@slowaaks -verkeersbureau.nl; WTC Amsterdam, Strawinskylaan 623, 1077 XX Amsterdam)
Poland (☎ 022-827 00 09; sacr@poczta.onet.pl; ul. Krakowskie Przedmiescie 13 pok.17, 00-071 Warszawa)

VISAS

Both the Czech Republic and Slovakia joined the EU in 2004 and are working to get their visa regulations in line so they can join the Schengen group (possibly in 2007). Until this happens, Czech and Slovak visas are not good for entering other EU countries and visa versa. EU citizens do not need a visa for either republic and can enter with a national ID card.

Without a visa, nationals of the US, Australia, New Zealand and Canada (as well as many others) can visit both the Czech Republic and Slovakia for up to 90 days each. Citizens of South Africa and the Ukraine are among those that require a visa (free to €50). A full list of countries with visa waivers for the Czech Republic is available in the travel and living abroad section of the Ministry of Foreign Affairs' website (www.mfa.cz); for Slovakia check out www.mzv.sk, under the Ministry and the Travel tabs. Visas are not issued at airports or border crossings.

If you want to extend your visa, the easiest way to do so is to day trip to a neighbouring country that has an embassy for the country you want an extension for. The nightmare bureaucratic method is to contact the **Foreigners' Police & Passport Office** Prague (Úřadovna cizinecká policiea pasové služby; Olšanská 2, Žižkov; Map p118; ☎ 974 820 238; ☼ 7.30- 11.30am, noon-4.30pm & 5-7pm Mon-Thu);

Bratislava (Úradovňa cudzineckej polície a pasovej služby; Map p338; ☎ 0961-036 855; Hrobákova 44, Petržalka).

EU visitors who want to stay longer than 90 days need to check in with a different **Foreigners Police Station** (Map pp82-3; ☎ 974 820 925; Sdružení 1, Pankrac; ⏱ 7.30-11.30am & 12.15pm-3pm Mon, Tue & Thu, 8am-12.15pm & 1-5pm Wed) in Prague, and the same one previously noted in Bratislava.

Technically, visitors must have the equivalent of US$50 for each day they plan to spend in country and be able to prove they have medical insurance.

WOMEN TRAVELLERS

Prague is a major metropolitan area and, as such, has some areas to be avoided as well as a burgeoning sex industry; see Dangers & Annoyances (p86) for specifics. In general solo women travellers are as safe as they are in other cities elsewhere in Europe.

However, even Slovak women walking into a *hostinec* or *krčma* (local pub) would get a strange look, especially if they are alone. These hard-drinking workers' temples tend to be male territory, but there are plenty of touristy pubs (usually called *pub*), cafés and wine bars (*vinárny/vináreň*).

There are few services for women such as help lines, and refuge- or rape-crisis centres; one good contact throughout the Czech Republic is **White Circle of Safety** (Bílý kruh bezpečí; ☎ 257 317 110; www.bkb.cz; Duškova 20, Smíchov), which provides help and counselling to victims of crime and violence. In Slovakia you can contact **Victim Support Services** (☎ 0805-011 1321; ⏱ 10am-2pm & 4-8pm Mon-Fri, 6pm-10pm Sat).

Attitude-wise the republics are still a bit behind the times. Even mainstream advertising has no qualms about using the occasional naked breast to sell products. Women often work full time and take care of all the domestic duties, however, state financial support for maternity leave is good (six months on 90% of salary).

WORK

If you are looking to do a little volunteer work while you travel, **Volunteer Abroad** (www.volunteerabroad.com) is a good clearing house organisation that lists opportunities in both the Czech and Slovak Republics. **EURES** (http://europa/eures/) helps EU citizens link up with jobs in other EU nations and has Czech and Slovak advisors.

Czech Republic

Competition for job opportunities for foreigners in Prague is tough. By far the biggest demand is for teaching English, but you need a Teaching English as a Foreign Language (TEFL) certificate. Contact **TEFL Worldwide** (☎ 603 486 830; www.teflworldwideprague.com) about certification for teaching English; they help with job placement across the nation after completion of the certificate.

You might also try for hospitality jobs in expat-run bars and restaurants. There are a few foreign-firm computing, real estate and management or financial jobs, but these jobs are usually easier to get from home. The classified ads in the **Prague Post** (www.praguepost.com) are a good starting point; you can also check out the following websites: www.expat.cz, www.sigmar.cz, www.jobmaster.cz and www.jobs.cz.

Citizen of EU nations do not need a work permit. For others, normally your employer will organise a work visa for you; after you have one, you will need to obtain a residency permit from the Foreigner's Police. If you need to arrange it yourself, you must apply for one at a Czech embassy or consulate outside the Czech Republic. For more information go to the Travel and Living Abroad section of the Ministry of Foreign Affair's website (www.mfa.cz).

Slovakia

As in the Czech Republic, the largest numbers of jobs available are in teaching English (TEFL certificate required), but pay rates are lower and you may have to cobble together a couple of gigs to receive a full salary. Other opportunities for non-Slovak speakers exist in working for a foreign company – in which case it is much easier to find the job from home.

The **Slovak Spectator** (www.slovakspectator.sk) classified section is the first place to look. They publish an annual *Career and Employment Guide* that has a lot of useful information on subjects such as visas, work conditions, firms and studying in Slovakia. You can order it online.

EU citizens do not need a work permit but they do have to report in with the Foreigner's Police (see Visas, left). All other nationals should technically have a work and residency permit before coming to Slovakia to settle, however, applying for one over the border at the Slovak Embassy in Vienna is not a long trip.

Transport

CONTENTS

GETTING THERE & AWAY

In the past few years low-cost carrier flights to the Czech and Slovak Republics have multiplied like *králiky* (rabbits). But it's also easy to get to the republics by land from Continental Europe via the extensive train, bus and road networks.

You can enter the Czech Republic across the borders with Germany, Austria and Poland; and Slovakia from Austria, Hungary, Poland and the Ukraine. That's not to mention the many crossing points between the two nations.

Additionally, you can arrive in Bratislava by boat from Vienna (a viable alternative airport hub) and Budapest.

This section deals only with travel to/from the republics; travel between the two countries is dealt with in Getting Around (p457).

Look for domestic travel information in the individual city sections.

ENTERING THE COUNTRY

Your passport must be valid for at least six months after your intended departure date when you enter the Czech and Slovak Republics.

AIR

Most international flights arrive in Prague and Bratislava. You can get to Bratislava from destinations throughout Europe and to Prague, well, where can't you get to Prague from? A few international flights go directly to Brno, Karlovy Vary, Košice and Tatry-Poprad airports.

The high season for air travel to the Czech and Slovak Republics is roughly from May to September, and during the Easter and Christmas/New Year holidays.

Airports & Airlines
CZECH REPUBLIC

Prague-Ruzyně Airport (PRG; ☎ 220 113 314; www.csl .cz) receives flights from around the world on all the carriers listed in this section and then some. **ČSA** (OK; ☎ in Prague 239 007 007, in Bratislava 02-5296 1042, in Košice 052-6782 490; www.czechairlines.com), the national carrier of the Czech Republic, flies to destinations such as New York, Montreal, Mexico City, Seoul and Sri Lanka, in addition to European cities such as London, Paris and Madrid.

From **Brno Tuřany Airport** (BRQ; ☎ 545 521 302; www.airport-brno.cz) you can fly to London on Ryanair, and to Munich and London on Cirrus Airlines. ČSA runs four flights a week to Moscow from **Karlovy Vary International Airport** (KLV; ☎ 353 360 611; www.airport-k-vary.cz).

Main airlines flying to/from the Czech Republic:
Aer Lingus (EI; ☎ 224 815 373; www.aerlingus.ie)
Aeroflot (SU; ☎ 227 020 020; www.aeroflot.ru)

THINGS CHANGE...

The information in this chapter is particularly vulnerable to change. Check directly with the airline or a travel agent to make sure you understand how a fare (and ticket you may buy) works and be aware of the security requirements for international travel. Shop carefully. The details given in this chapter should be regarded as pointers and are not a substitute for your own careful, up-to-date research.

CLIMATE CHANGE & TRAVEL

Climate change is a serious threat to the ecosystems that humans rely upon, and air travel is the fastest-growing contributor to the problem. Lonely Planet regards travel, overall, as a global benefit, but believes we all have a responsibility to limit our personal impact on global warming.

Flying & Climate Change

Pretty much every form of motor transport generates CO_2 (the main cause of human-induced climate change) but planes are far and away the worst offenders, not just because of the sheer distances they allow us to travel, but because they release greenhouse gases high into the atmosphere. The statistics are frightening: two people taking a return flight between Europe and the US will contribute as much to climate change as an average household's gas and electricity consumption over a whole year.

Carbon Offset Schemes

Climatecare.org and other websites use 'carbon calculators' that allow travellers to offset the greenhouse gases they are responsible for with contributions to energy-saving projects and other climate-friendly initiatives in the developing world – including projects in India, Honduras, Kazakhstan and Uganda.

Lonely Planet, together with Rough Guides and other concerned partners in the travel industry, supports the carbon offset scheme run by climatecare.org. Lonely Planet offsets all of its staff and author travel.

For more information check out our website: www.lonelyplanet.com.

TRANSPORT

Air France (AF; ☎ 221 662 662; www.airfrance.com/cz)
Alitalia (AZ; ☎ 224 194 150; www.alitalia.com)
Austrian Airlines (OS; ☎ 227 231 231; www.aua.com)
British Airways (BA; ☎ 239 000 299; www.british airways.com)
Cirrus Airlines (C9; ☎ 542 213 525; www.cirrus-world.de)
Croatia Airlines (OU; ☎ 222 222 235; www.croatia airlines.hr)
Czech Airlines (OK; ☎ 239 007 007; www.csa.cz)
easyJet (EZY; www.easyjet.com)
El Al (LY; ☎ 224 226 624; www.elal.co.il)
FlyGlobespan (B4; ☎ 220 113 171; www.fly globespan.com)
Germanwings (4U; www.germanwings.com)
JAT Airways (JU; ☎ 224 942 654; www.jat.com)
KLM (KL; ☎ 233 090 933; www.klm.com)
LOT (LO; ☎ 222 317 524; www.lot.com)
Lufthansa (LH; ☎ 224 422 911; www.lufthansa.com)
Malev (MA; ☎ 220 113 090; www.malev.com)
Ryanair (FR; www.ryanair.com)
SAS (SK; ☎ 220 116 031; www.scandinavian.net)
SkyEurope (NE; ☎ 900 141 516; www.skyeurope.com)
Smart Wings (QS; ☎ 900 166 565; www.smartwings.net)
SN Brussels Airlines (SN; ☎ 220 116 352; www.flysn.com)
Turkish Airlines (TK; ☎ 234 708 708; www.turkish airlines.com)

SLOVAK REPUBLIC

Twenty-two European destinations are served from Bratislava's **MR Štefánika Airport** (BTS; ☎ 02-

3303 3353; www.airportbratislava.sk) on the carriers listed below. SkyEurope is the major airline based in Slovakia. For long-haul direct flights to/from Australia and the Americas, you'll need to fly into **Vienna International Airport** (Wien Schwechat airport; VIE; ☎ 1-7007-22233; www.viennaairport .com), 60km west in Austria. A regular one-hour bus ride connects the two airports.

Austrian Airlines flies direct from Vienna to **Košice International Airport** (KSC; ☎ 052-6221 093; www.airportkosice.sk). Once a week SkyEurope flies between London Stansted and **Poprad-Tatry International Airport** (TAT; ☎ 052-7763 875; www .airport-poprad.sk; Na Letisko 100) beneath the High Tatra mountains.

Airlines flying to and from the Slovak Republic:
Aeroflot (SU; ☎ 02-4342 6896; www.aeroflot.com)
Air Slovakia (GM; ☎ 02-4342 2744; www.airslovakia.sk)
Austrian Airlines (OS; ☎ 02-4940 2100; www.aua.com)
ČSA (OK; ☎ 02-5296 1042; www.czechairlines.com)
easyJet (EZ; www.easyjet.com)
Ryanair (FR; www.ryanair.com)
SkyEurope (NE; ☎ 02-4850 485; www.skyeurope.com)
Slovak Airlines (6Q; ☎ 02-4870 4870; www.slovak airlines.sk)

Tickets

No-frills airlines like easyJet, Germanwings, Ryanair, Smart Wings and SkyEurope often have supercheap specials, but if you leave booking flights until the last minute, you'll pay much more. Not all low-cost carriers have local Czech or Slovak contact numbers and some, like Smart Wings, add a surcharge for booking over the phone instead of on the internet.

You can compare several regular carrier prices by searching through www.lonely planet.com/travel_services.

From Australia & New Zealand

From Australia or New Zealand you'll have to transit through London, Paris, Frankfurt or another major European capital to get to Prague, Bratislava or Vienna. For Australian branches of **STA Travel** (☎ 1300 733 035; www .statravel.com.au), call or visit their website. **Flight Centre** (☎ 133 133; www.flightcentre.com.au) has offices throughout Australia. For online bookings, try www.travel.com.au.

In New Zealand, both **Flight Centre** (☎ 0800 243 544; www.flightcentre.co.nz) and **STA Travel** (☎ 0508 782 872; www.statravel.co.nz) have branches throughout the country. The site www.travel.co.nz is also recommended for online bookings.

From Continental Europe

Prague is incredibly well-connected with other European cities by air. ČSA, flies to all the biggies – Paris, Budapest, Madrid, Frankfurt etc – but also connects with smaller cities such as Marseille, Bologna and Cologne. That's not to mention its many Eastern European destinations such as Kiev, Riga and Belgrade. Furthermore, the choice is no longer just between ČSA and competing national destination airlines; SkyEurope, Germanwings, Smart Wings and the like connect Prague with many secondary airports at a lower cost.

Many of the airlines serving Bratislava are no-frills, and competition is fierce – it seems like new connections are added every month. Between SkyEurope, Ryanair and Slovak Airlines, most major European cities are covered (Amsterdam, Paris, Barcelona, Rome, Brussels, Moscow, Stuttgart…). SkyEurope's Eastern European destinations include beachside Split and Zadar in Croatia, and Bourgas in Bulgaria.

Recommended travel agencies include the following:

France
Anyway (☎ 0892 893 892; www.anyway.fr)
Lastminute (☎ 0892 705 000; www.lastminute.fr)

Nouvelles Frontières (☎ 0825 000 747; www .nouvelles-frontieres.fr)
OTU Voyages (www.otu.fr; ☎ 0155 823 232) Specialises in student and youth travel.

Germany
Expedia (www.expedia.de)
Just Travel (☎ 089 747 3330; www.justtravel.de)
Lastminute (☎ 01805 284 366; www.lastminute.de)
STA Travel (☎ 01805 456 422; www.statravel.de) For travellers under the age of 26.

Italy
CTS Viaggi (☎ 06 462 0431; www.cts.it) Specialising in student and youth travel.

The Netherlands
Airfair (☎ 020 620 5121; www.airfair.nl)

From the UK

National and no-frills carriers connect London's various airports, as well as cities like Manchester and Edinburgh, with Prague and Bratislava daily. EasyJet serves the Midlands and Slovak Airlines occasionally flies from Birmingham to Bratislava (then on to Amitar, India).

Discount air travel is big business in London. Advertisements for many travel agencies appear in the travel pages of the weekend broadsheet newspapers, in *Time Out*, *The Evening Standard* and in the free online magazine *TNT* (www.tntmagazine.com).

Recommended travel agencies include the following:
Bridge the World (☎ 0870 444 7474; www.b-t-w .co.uk)
Flightbookers (☎ 0870 814 4001; www.ebookers.com)
Flight Centre (☎ 0870 890 8099; flightcentre.co.uk)
North-South Travel (☎ 01245 608 291; www.north southtravel.co.uk) Donates part of their profit to projects in the developing world.
Quest Travel (☎ 0870 442 3542; www.questtravel .com)
STA Travel (☎ 0870 160 0599; www.statravel.co.uk) For travellers under age 26.
Trailfinders (www.trailfinders.co.uk)
Travel Bag (☎ 0870 890 1456; www.travelbag.co.uk)

From the USA & Canada

ČSA has direct flights from New York, Montreal and Toronto to Prague. No direct flights depart North America for Bratislava, but Austrian Airlines flies from Toronto, New York and Washington DC direct to Vienna.

AIR FARES

The following are low-price samples for round-trip flights (including tax), booked three weeks in advance:

From	To	Cost
Prague	Bratislava	4264Kč/5003Sk
Prague	Košice	4264Kč/4000Sk
Prague	Brno	2320Kč
Prague	Ostrava	2320Kč
Bratislava	Košice	1484Sk
Žilina	Prague	4945Sk
Poprad	Prague	5042Sk (via Košice)

Discount travel agents in the US are known as consolidators (although you won't see a sign on the door saying 'Consolidator'). Some good deals can be found in the Sunday travel sections of big city newspapers and there are numerous online agencies.

Recommended agents include:

Cheap Tickets (www.cheaptickets.com)
Expedia (www.expedia.com)
Orbitz (www.orbitz.com)
STA Travel (☎ 800 781 4040; www.statravel.com) Has offices throughout the US for travellers under age 26.
Travel CUTS (☎ 866 246 9762; www.travelcuts.com) Canada's national student travel agency.
Travelocity (www.travelocity.com for USA, www.travelocity.ca for Canada)

LAND
Border Crossings

As long as all your paperwork and insurance card is in order, you should have no problems crossing into the Czech or Slovak Republics. You may encounter delays travelling to or from the Ukraine, but that's about it. See also customs (p440) and visa (p450) requirements.

Both of the country maps (p78 and p336) show major, 24-hour international border crossings for cars, buses and motorcycles. Note that these may change in 2007; at the time of writing both the republics were working to get their laws in line with the EU Schengen agreement (in which internal borders between EU states can be removed).

BICYCLE & WALKING

There are a few border crossings between Germany and the Czech Republic, and Slovakia and Poland, that are limited to pedestrians

and cyclists in both countries. Some are only open during the summer months. For more information, see the relevant destination chapters.

Crossing from eastern Slovakia to the Ukraine by foot is a definite no-no and by bicycle it's frowned upon, but you can easily walk over the bridge from Komárno in southern Slovakia to Komárom in Hungary, or cycle from Bratislava into Austria.

Bus

Travelling by bus may not be the most comfortable way to cross Europe, but it is the cheapest. Youth and senior discounts are available on almost all fares and passes.

It's easiest to book ahead with **Eurolines** (www.eurolines.com), a consortium of 32 coach companies with offices all over Europe. Fifteen and 30-day passes (€279/359 respectively) are cheaper outside of the summer season.

There are direct connections to Prague and Bratislava from dozens of major European cities.

A sampling of services to Prague include from London (£43, 22 hours, daily), Berlin (€34, six hours, three daily) and Budapest (€41, seven hours, daily); and to Bratislava, from London (€100, 23 hours, five weekly), Frankfurt (€58, 12 hours, three weekly) and Vienna (€6, one hour, hourly).

Capital Express (☎ in Prague 220 870 368; www.capitalexpress.cz) has daily bus services between London and Prague via Plzeň.

Tourbus (☎ 543 163 493; www.tourbus.cz) travels between Brno and continental European destinations in addition to London.

Both companies sometimes have more competitive prices than those listed here.

Car & Motorcycle

The Czech Republic recognises British and EU driving licenses; all other nationalities require an International Driving Permit.

All foreign national driving licenses with photo ID are valid in Slovakia.

In both countries drivers must also have their passport, vehicle registration papers and the 'green card' that shows they carry at least third-party liability insurance (see your domestic insurer about this).

If the car isn't yours, avoid potential headaches by carrying a notarised letter from the owner saying they give their permission for you to drive it.

TRANSPORT

In your car you will need to carry a first-aid kit and a red-and-white warning triangle. You must display a nationality sticker on the rear.

For information about road rules and fuel, see Getting Around (p459).

The E65 is the major motorway connecting the two republics, from Prague through Brno to Bratislava; to the south it joins to the E60, which heads to Budapest. The E50 connects Germany to Prague through West Bohemia. Driving in from Vienna to Slovakia, you'd be on the E58. The E75 goes east from Bratislava and on to Košice and will eventually be a motorway all the way to the Ukraine (they're working on it, they're working on it...).

Hitching

Hitching is never entirely safe anywhere in the world and we don't recommend it. Travellers who decide to hitch should understand that they are taking a small but potentially serious risk. Those who choose to hitch will be safer if they travel in pairs and let someone know where they are planning to go.

If you are set on hitching across Europe, a worthwhile website to check is www.hitchhikers.org. It provides information on drivers looking for passengers for trips across the continent. Most drivers ask a minimal fee from those catching a lift.

Train

The Czech Republic is pretty well connected to the rest of the European train network; Slovakia is only slightly less so. Most long distance trains have both 1st- and 2nd-class carriages, and sometimes a sleeper wagon (which requires a supplement). It's advisable to reserve a sleeper ahead of time year-round and, during summer, booking your international train ticket in advance wouldn't hurt. Place reservations are usually required for Intercity (IC) and Eurocity (EC) trains.

The **Thomas Cook European Timetable** (www.thomascookpublishing.com) is the trainophile's bible, giving a complete listing of train schedules. Fares quoted here are based on average second-class rates at the time of research.

Most international trains arrive at Prague's main station, **Praha hlavní nádraží** (☎ 972 241 152; Wilsonova 8); a few go to **Praha-Holešovice** (☎ 972 224 633; Partyzánská 24) or **Praha-Smíchov** (☎ 972 226 150; Nádražní 1, Smíchov).

Direct connections from Prague include Budapest (1243Kč, seven hours), Vienna (841Kč, 4½ hours, five daily), Warsaw (1143Kč, 8½ to 10 hours, two daily) and Berlin (1347Kč, five hours, eight daily). One nightly train goes

---

YOU'RE GOING WHERE?

Although staff at the train station international ticket counters (*mezinárodní jízdenky* or *medzinárodný lístok*) may speak at least some English, those selling domestic tickets may not. Writing down what you want and handing it to the clerk helps avoid confusion (this works for bus tickets, too).

Write it down like this in Czech/Slovak:

- *od:* (from) departure station, eg PRAHA
- *do:* (to) destination station
- *čas:* (time) departure time using 24-hour clock
- *datum:* (date) day/month in Roman numerals
- *třídá/trieda:* (class) 1 or 2
- *osoby:* (people) number of passengers
- *jednosměrný/jednosmerna* (one way) or *zpáteční/spiatočný* (return)
- *místenka/miestenka:* (reservation) write this word to get an assigned seat number

One-way domestic train tickets for distances of more than 50km are valid for 24 hours from time of purchase, but for distances under 50km only until 6am the next day. Note that unscheduled domestic return tickets are only valid for 48 hours from time of purchase – if you plan to be away for more than two days, buy two singles.

RAIL PASSES

If you plan to travel widely in Europe, the following special tickets and rail passes may be better value for travelling in and out of the Czech and Slovak Republics, but not within them. You can purchase rail passes from travel agents at home or from sites like www.raileurope.com.

InterRail Pass

Available to anyone who has lived in Europe for at least six months, the **InterRail Pass** (www .interrail.com) gives travellers unlimited, second-class travel for up to one month on most of the state railways of Western and Central Europe (except in their own country). The one-zone pass (Zone D) for travel in the Czech and Slovak Republics, Hungary, Poland, Boznia and Herzogovina, and Croatia costs about £215 for 16 days (£145 for those under 26). An all-zone pass, valid for a month, is £405 (£285 for those under 26).

European East Pass

The European East Pass is only available in the USA and provides unlimited travel in the Czech and Slovak Republics, Austria, Hungary and Poland for any five days within a month. Tickets for 1st-/2nd-class travel cost US$244/172. Each extra day costs an additional US$29/23.

from Prague to Kraków (1164Kč, 8½ hours) and one to Frankfurt (2380Kč, 8½ hours).

From Brno you can go straight to Vienna (537Kč, two hours, four daily), Budapest (939Kč, four hours, three daily) and Berlin (1748č, 7½ hours, eight daily). Four times a day there are trains to Linz, Austria from České Budějovice (431Kč, 2½ hours).

International trains generally arrive at or depart from Bratislava's main station, **Hlavná stanica** (www.zsr.sk). Direct day trains run between Bratislava and Vienna (297Sk, one hour, up to 30 daily) and Budapest (486Sk, three hours, seven daily). Night departures link Bratislava with Moscow (2738Sk, 32½ hours, one daily) and Warsaw (1410Sk, 10½ hours, one daily).

One train a day passes through Košice on its way from Budapest (967Sk, 4½ hours) to Kiev (1913Sk, 21 hours).

WARNING

The overnight international trains to/from the Czech Republic have become notorious for bold thefts from sleeping passengers – keep a grip on your bags.

RIVER

Floating down the Danube River is a cruisy way to get between Bratislava and Vienna (€21 one way, 1½ hours) or Budapest (€69 one way, four hours). From mid-April to September, **Slovak Shipping and Ports** (Slovenská plavba a prístavy; ☎ 5293 2226; www.lod.sk) runs at least one hydro-

foil to Vienna and one to Budapest daily from the **hydrofoil terminal** (Fajnorovo nábrežie 2). From June to October the **Twin City Liner** (☎ 0903 610 716; www.twincityliner.com) operates three boats a day between the Bratislava **propeller terminal** (Rázusovo nábrežie), in front of Hotel Devin, and Vienna.

GETTING AROUND

The Czech Republic has one of the most dense rail networks in Europe. Slovakia's is less extensive due to its mountainous landscape. The bus network in the republics is excellent, but only slightly cheaper than trains. The general rule of thumb is if you're travelling between larger cities take a train; to villages, take a bus.

The roads are in good condition, and there are over 1000km of European-style motorways within the two countries so far, with more being added. Main thoroughfares that pass through small villages make the going slow but scenic.

An excellent online source of bus and train information are the national databases, with links to city bus networks: for the Czech Republic try www.idos.cz; for Slovakia, http:// cp.zoznam.sk/ConnForm.asp?tt=c&cl=E5.

Bus and train connections noted in this section are direct services only. Prices are for one-way journeys and for 2nd-class seats on trains.

TRANSPORT

Border Crossings between the Republics

At this writing, the Czech–Slovak borders function like any other border in Europe. This may change if they both comply with the Schengen agreement in 2007. There are currently 15 official border crossings. The most often-used border is on the D2 motorway between Kúty and Břclav, however, this is the only crossing which cannot be used by pedestrians.

AIR

Air travel possibilities have expanded in the past few years. In addition to the airports that receive flights from abroad (see p452), **Ostrava Mošnov Airport** (OSR; ☎ 597 471 136; www .airport-ostrava.cz), in the Czech Republic, and **Airport Žilina** (ILZ; ☎ 5523 288; www.letisko.sk), in Slovakia, operate within the two republics. **ČSA** (OK; ☎ in Prague 239 007 007, in Bratislava 02-5296 1042, in Košice 052-6782 490; www.czechairlines.com) is the major inter-republic airline. **SkyEurope** (NE; ☎ in Prague 900 141 516, in Bratislava 02-4850 485; www.sky europe.com) flies to Košice from Bratislava.

BICYCLE

For general information on cycling in the Czech and Slovak Republics, see the relevant section in Outdoor Activities (p61).

Hire

The Czech and Slovak Republics are only slowly cottoning on to the fact that a buck can be made from renting bikes. Prices range from 100Sk to 800Sk per day.

Many of the bigger cities have a bike-rental place or two (Bratislava has one), but they are more common in the popular tourist spots and mountainous regions (Krkonoše in the Czech Republic, High and Low Tatras and the Mála Fatra in Slovakia) – check with the upmarket hotels there.

Czech Railway rents bikes in several natural areas; log on to www.cd.cz/static/eng/bike hireservice.htm for locations.

Individual rental places are noted throughout the destination chapters.

Purchase

If you're planning to spend some time cycling around the republics and you can't be bothered dragging your bike with you, buying one when you arrive is an option. A new mountain bike costs from 11,000Kč/13,000Sk to 16,000Kč/19,000Sk and almost every town has a sports shop selling bikes.

BOAT

On the whole, most Czech and Slovak rivers are too shallow for passenger transport. In the summer there are a few near-town options.

In the Czech Republic boats ply the Vltava between Prague and Troja (p121), and in Slovakia there are trips along the Danube between Bratislava and Devín (p353).

BUS

Buses are popular and there are comprehensive networks in both republics. Stations are normally within walking distance of town centres, and often adjacent to the train station. During the week there are generally frequent services but this peters out to only a handful on weekends (or none at all). Mountainous locations may only be accessible by bus.

ČSAD (Česká automobilová doprava) is the state bus company in the Czech Republic, and SAD (Slovenská autobusová doprava) in Slovakia. To find schedules online the national timetables are best; try www.idos.cz for the Czech Republic and http://cp.zoznam .sk/ConnForm.asp?tt=c&cl=E5 for Slovakia. From Prague, two private bus companies, **Tourbus** (☎ 543 163 493; www.tourbus.cz) and **Student Agency** (☎ 542 424 242; www.studentagency.cz), battle it out on the competitive route between Prague and Brno.

BUS TIMETABLES

The timetables will drive you cross-eyed, peppered with symbols showing the days buses go and don't go. Remembering that *ne* indicates negative, as in *nejede/neide* or *nepremáva* (doesn't go, doesn't operate) helps. A circled number one to seven indicates the day of the week (Monday to Sunday). Below are some of the most common symbols, but be ready for local variations.

R	reservation available
✗	workdays (Monday to Friday)
†	holidays
b	workdays and Saturdays
a	Saturdays and holidays only
r	not on 24 & 31 December
I	bus doesn't stop here

Sample prices and average times:

From	To	Cost	Duration
Prague	Bratislava	288Kč	4¾hr
Prague	Košice	550Kč	10½hr
Prague	Brno	130Kč	2½hr
Brno	Bratislava	110Kč	2hr
Brno	Košice	410Kč	8hr
Bratislava	Košice	441Sk	7hr

Reservations

Travel agencies don't book internal coaches, though some may have timetable information. Short-haul tickets are sold on the bus, long-distance tickets are usually bought at the station. If you're travelling on a weekend on one of the more popular routes, it's not a bad idea to book ahead.

At stations with offices, handing the clerk a scrap of paper with your destination (see You're Going Where When?, p456) is a lot more fun than wrestling with the timetables. Big stations like Florenc in Prague have charts with all the route numbers for each major destination and all the departure times for each route number, plus timetables for every route. To figure out when the next bus leaves at smaller stations without an office, you'll probably have to look at timetables posted at several different numbered platforms.

CAR & MOTORCYCLE

The Czech and Slovak Republics are covered by a network of generally good roads. The main motorways are the D1 (or E50/E65) between Prague, Brno and Olomouc, the D2 (or E65) between Brno and Bratislava, and the D5 (or E50) linking Prague and Plzeň. The D1 (or E75), between Bratislava and Žilina, will eventually connect to Uzhhorod, Ukraine via Košice.

The major motorways require a toll sticker (for two weeks/one year 200/900Kč in the Czech Republic, 150/800Sk in Slovakia), which can be purchased at most border crossings, some petrol stations and from the automobile organisations in both countries. (Rental cars come with them.) Fines of up to 5000Kč/Sk are payable if you're caught without a sticker.

Motorways and city centres have heavy traffic. Country highways tend to have light traffic, but follow old routes through villages and small towns, with sudden sharp bends

and reduced speed limits. Excessive speeding and drivers passing on blind corners are problems in both countries, so it's best to drive defensively.

Automobile Associations

The Czech Republic has two automobile associations: the **Ústřední AutoMotoKlub** (ÚAMK; ☎ 1230; www.uamk.cz) and **Autoklub Bohemia Assistance** (ABA; ☎ 1240; www.aba.cz). Slovakia's automobile association is the **Autoklub Slovakia Assistance** (ASA) (ASA; ☎ 18124; www.autoklub.sk).

Bringing Your Own Vehicle

You'll experience no major hassles bringing your own vehicle into either republic. Cars with foreign license plates can be a target for thieves (as in any country) and no one should leave valuables in view. That said, the number of car thefts in the republics is no higher than in Western Europe. For information on the documents required to take your car into the republics see Getting There & Away (p455).

Fuel

Petrol or gasoline (benzín) is not hard to find (natural is 95 octane, super is 98 octane). Diesel (nafta) is also available at many stations. Unleaded petrol costs about 40Kč/44Sk per litre. LPG (autoplyn) is available in every major town, but at very few outlets and rarely at petrol stations. You're not allowed to take more than 10L of fuel in or out of the country in a spare container.

Hire

Normally you have to be 21 years of age to hire a vehicle and sometimes 25. Apart from that, renting a car is relatively easy. It's possible to arrange a pick-up in one republic and drop off in another, but there is usually a hefty fee involved.

Prague and Bratislava have numerous local and international rental agencies at the airport and in town. Major international companies, such as **Europcar** (www.europcar.com), **Sixt** (www.sixt.com), **Hertz** (www.hertz.com) and **Avis** (www.avis.com), are well represented at airports around the two countries. For specific contact details, see the relevant sections in the destination chapters.

Insurance

Third-party insurance is required in both countries. If you arrive at the border in an uninsured car, you will have to pay for

TRANSPORT

DRIVING DISTANCES

From	To	Distance
Prague	Bratislava	350km
Prague	Košice	670km
Prague	Brno	200km
Prague	Ostrava	380km
Bratislava	Brno	130km
Bratislava	Košice	400km
Bratislava	Poprad	350km

insurance (about 4300Kč/5400Sk) on the spot. If you are hiring a car, be sure to check your liability in case of an accident. Rather than risk paying out thousands of dollars if you do have an accident, you can take out your own comprehensive insurance on the car, or (the usual option) pay an additional daily amount to the rental company for an 'insurance excess reduction' policy.

The police should be contacted immediately in the case of an accident when repairs are required or if there is an injury. It's essential to get a police report if you plan to make an insurance claim.

Parking

Most city centres have restricted parking within marked zones at parking meters, and parking rules are similar to those in the rest of Europe. They are controlled either by parking meters or parking cards, which can be bought in kiosks, shops, hotels or, in small towns, from the man wandering around the cars with a satchel on his stomach. Carry plenty of small change as most parking meters don't take bank notes. In larger cities, street parking is at a premium and finding a space can prove impossible (parking on footpaths is not uncommon). It's often best to head for the nearest car park (or your hotel) and then use the extensive public transport.

Road Rules

Road rules in both republics are basically the same as throughout the rest of continental Europe: drive on the right-hand side of the road; always wear a seatbelt; children under 12 must ride in the back; mobile telephones can only be used with a hands-free set; and pedestrians have the right of way at zebra crossings (although this is hardly ever observed). In the Czech Republic vehicles must have their

headlights turned on 24 hours a day. Don't drink even a sip of alcohol and drive: regulations stipulate only a zero blood-alcohol level is allowed, random breathalyser stops are common and penalties are severe (up to a year in jail in the Czech Republic and two in Slovakia). The legal driving age is 18.

The speed limit within built-up areas is 50km/h in the Czech Republic and 60km/h in Slovakia. On major roads the limit is 90km/h and on motorways it is 130km/h for both countries. The official speed limit at the countries' many railway crossings is 30km/h, but you are better off stopping and looking, since many well-used crossings have no barriers and some don't even have flashing lights.

Riders of motorcycles greater than 50cc must wear helmets and goggles, and their passengers must also wear helmets. The motorcycle's headlight must be on at all times (on low beam). The maximum speed for motorcycles, even on major highways, is 90km/h.

Fines for speeding and minor offences are between 500Kč/Sk and 5000Kč/Sk, levied on the spot. If you don't get a docket or receipt *(paragon* or *doklad),* you may be getting overcharged – so politely insist on a receipt. If that does not work try to bargain the fine down.

Pay particular attention to trams: it's best to give them the right-of-way in every situation as you'll come off second best if one happens to bump into you.

Road Signs

Standard European signs are in common use throughout both republics. Some that may be unfamiliar to Britons and non-European visitors are:

- Blue disk with red border and crossed red slashes – no stopping
- Blue disk with red border and red slash – no parking
- Red disk with horizontal white line – no entry
- White disk with red border – no vehicles allowed
- White triangle (point down) with red border – give way to crossing or merging traffic.

In cities and towns, keep a sharp eye out for *pěší zóna* signs, indicating pedestrian-only areas, many of which look just like normal streets.

HITCHING

As stated earlier, hitching is never entirely safe anywhere in the world, and we don't recommend it. Travellers who decide to hitch should understand that they are taking a small but potentially serious risk.

That said, many Czechs and Slovaks, women included, do hitch and do pick up hitchhikers, especially from one small village to the next.

LOCAL TRANSPORT

Public transport in towns and cities normally consists of a comprehensive bus network, which is sometimes complemented by trams and trolley-buses (electric buses). They are well used by locals, so you'll often find more services in the morning and early evening.

Bus, Tram & Trolley-Bus

On the whole, services are frequent and reliable. Typical hours of operation are from 5am to 11pm or midnight. Prague, Brno and Bratislava also have limited night bus services.

Depending on the town, a ride is 20Kč/18Sk or less, with discounts available for kids aged from 10 to 16 years and the elderly. In Prague, Brno and Bratislava you can also buy multiday and monthly passes for unlimited travel. Tickets are sold at public transport offices, newsstands, tobacco kiosks and from machines at major stops. In most places a single ticket is valid for all forms of transport.

You validate your ticket by punching it in a little machine on board (or in Prague's metro station lobbies). It's an honour system, but inspectors pop up fairly often and are keen to levy instant fines on anyone without a valid ticket.

Metro

Prague is the only city with a metro, and that consists of three lines. For more information, see p144.

Taxi

Most towns have at least a few taxis for hire. Prague and Bratislava have cracked down on crooked taxi drivers, though it is still possible that you will be charged a slightly higher rate than the locals – call it an English-speaking surcharge. Thankfully more courteous and fair drivers are becoming the norm. It's cheaper to call a taxi (or have someone call for you) than to hail one on the street.

TRAIN

ČD (České dráhy, Czech Railways; www.cd.cz) is the state rail company in the Czech Republic and its Slovakian equivalent is **ŽSR** (Železnica Slovenskej republiky, Railways of the Slovak Republic; www.zsr.sk). Trains go almost anywhere you want to in the Czech Republic, and you only have to resort to buses or private transport in far eastern Slovakia.

If you wish to transport your car, it is possible but only on the route between Prague and Poprad. Canoes can be transported in special carriages while bicycles are transported in the normal cargo carriages.

Classes

The fastest trains are international EC/IC (EuroCity/InterCity), Czech domestic SC (SuperCity) and slightly slower fast/express *(rychlík/rýchlik)* services, which are shown in shaded columns and bold print in timetables. On the two railway maps (p462 and p463), all of these fall under Express Trains. Slowest of all is the local train *(osobní vlak/osobný vlak)*.

In October 2005, supermodern SC Pendolino trains went into service from Praha-Holešovice to Ostrava (600Sk, 3½ hours). These fancy cars are 1st class only; check 'em out at www.scpendolino.cz. (Prices are reduced in summer.)

TRAIN TIMETABLE SYMBOLS

🎫 after the name of the station = tickets issued on train only
✗ in the train column = dining car included
🛏 in the train column = train includes sleeping cars or couchettes
R in the train column = for indicated cars, reservation is possible
Ⓡ in the train column = train with obligatory seat reservation
🛏 in the train column = train carries only sleeping cars and couchettes
♿ in the train column = there is a coach for wheelchairs
in front of time descriptions = request train to stop only
🚲 the notes have information on transport of bicycles
↯ train travels on another line
| train doesn't stop at this station
① Mon ② Tue ③ Wed ④ Thu ⑤ Fri ⑥ Sat ⑦ Sun
✗ workdays only (normally Mon-Fri)
† holidays (except 24 Dec, 1 & 8 May, 5 Jul) and 2 Jan only

TRANSPORT

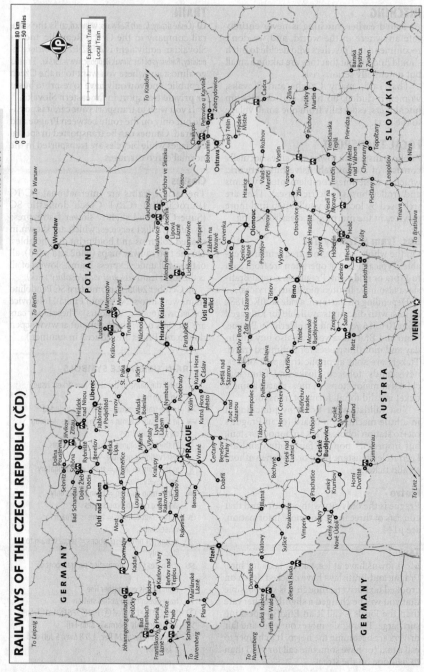

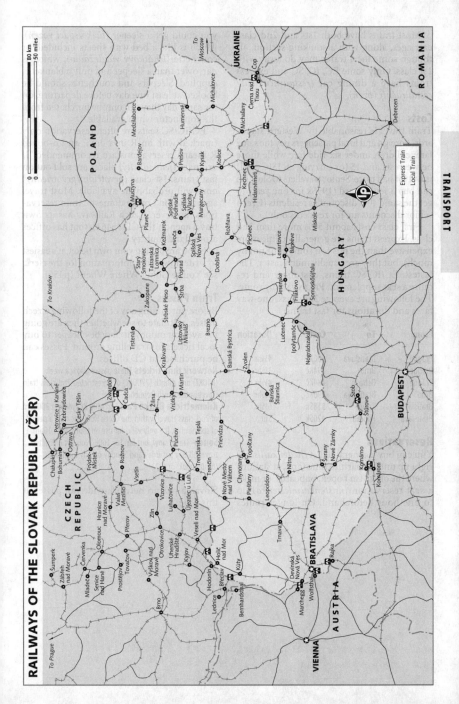

RAILWAYS OF THE SLOVAK REPUBLIC (ŽSR)

Most trains have both 1st- and 2nd-class carriages, along with a smoking section, although some local trains may do away with 1st class. Only some EC, IC, SC and express trains have a dining car *(restaurační vůz/ restauráčnij vozeň)*.

Costs

Train travel is reasonable by Western standards. Foreign and local passengers pay the same fare: children under six ride free while those between six and 15 (or carrying an ISIC card) travel for half price. Senior travellers to Slovakia can buy a senior card (199Sk for one year) to get the same 40% discount as residents (Czech senior discounts are for residents only).

First class costs about 50% more than 2nd class. Express trains are generally a little more expensive than the bus (on some runs not by much), but they are usually much faster. The fastest, EC/IC/SC trains, cost more and require a seat supplement. Prices vary by route. The following are average 2nd-class, one-way fares and durations for fast trains:

From	To	Cost	Duration
Prague	Bratislava	500Kč	4¼hr
Prague	Brno	294Kč	3½hr
Prague	Ostrava	484Kč	4½hr
Brno	Bratislava	196Kč	1½hr
Bratislava	Košice	518Sk	6½hr
Bratislava	Poprad	420Sk	5hr

Reservations

You can buy a general ticket *(jízdenka/lístok)* right up until departure time (and, at stations where the office isn't open, onboard), or make a seat reservation *(místenka/miestenka)* up to one hour beforehand. On longer routes you could get a sleeper *(lůžko/spací vozeň)*, which is like a bed with sheets included, or couchette *(lehátkový vůz/ležadlo)*, which is narrower than a sleeper and only a blanket is supplied. Sleepers and couchettes should be booked at least one day before departure; on the same day they can only be purchased from the conductor when available.

EC/IC/SC seats are often reservation only (marked with an R in a box); an un-boxed R means reservations are recommended. If ordinary *(jednoduchý)* places are sold out on fast trains, 1st-class *(prvotřídní/prvotriedny)* ones will probably be available. Most travel agencies won't make domestic train reservations, however, Czech Railways has its own travel agency, the ČD (p461), that has offices around the country.

If you are buying your own ticket, it's easiest to write down your information for the clerk; see You're Going Where When? (p456).

Train Passes

Before purchasing any of the following Czech passes, calculate to see whether they are going to save you money; it may be cheaper to buy local tickets for travelling around. Passes can be purchased at ČD offices.

Network time tickets These passes allow a week (810Kč) or a month (2700Kč) of unrestricted 2nd-class train travel in the Czech Republic.

Kilometricka Banka Pass For 1400 Kč, you get 2000km of 2nd-class travel within the Czech Republic over a period of six months. It's only valid for use on trains after 10am.

Sone+ Travel slow, but far. For 160Kč you get unlimited travel all day Saturday and Sunday on any local train *(osobní vlak, or Os)*.

Slovakia has no network-wide rail passes at this time.

Health

CONTENTS

Travel health depends on your predeparture preparations, your daily health care while travelling and how you handle any medical problem that does develop. Healthwise, the Czech and Slovak Republics are not going to worry you, and the worst you'll get is a stomach upset or dehydration from too much beer the night before.

BEFORE YOU GO

Prevention is the key to staying healthy while abroad. A little planning before departure, particularly for pre-existing illnesses will save trouble later: see your dentist before a long trip; carry a spare pair of contact lenses and glasses, and take your optical prescription with you. Bring medications in their original containers and make sure they're clearly labelled. A signed and dated letter from your physician describing your medical conditions and medications, including generic names, is also a good idea. If carrying syringes or needles, be sure to have a physician's letter documenting their medical necessity.

INSURANCE

The European Health Insurance Card (EHIC) entitles EU citizens to the same health-care benefits as local citizens receive from their national health care; therefore, most medical care in the Czech and Slovak Republics will be free, but transporting you to your home country, should you fall ill, will not be covered. Citizens from other countries should find out if their personal insurance policy covers them abroad. Doctors expect cash if you do not have a national or European health-insurance card; make sure your insurance plan will reimburse your expenses. Everyone entering the Czech and Slovak Republics is required to have medical coverage, and technically police could ask for proof. We hate to say never, but this rarely happens. For more on temporary, travel-related insurance, see p445.

RECOMMENDED VACCINATIONS

The World Health Organization (WHO) recommends that travellers should be covered for diphtheria, tetanus, measles, mumps, rubella and polio, as well as hepatitis B, regardless of their destination. Since most vaccines don't produce immunity until at least two weeks after they're given, visit a physician at least six weeks before departure.

ONLINE RESOURCES

The WHO's publication *International Travel and Health* is revised annually and is available online at www.who.int/ith/. Other useful websites:

www.ageconcern.org.uk Travel advice for the elderly.
www.fitfortravel.scot.nhs.uk General travel advice for the layperson.
www.mariestopes.org.uk Information on women's health and contraception.
www.mdtravelhealth.com Travel-health recommendations for every country; updated daily.

FURTHER READING

'Health Advice for Travellers' (currently called the 'T6' leaflet) is a leaflet that is updated annually by the Department of Health in the UK and is available free in UK post offices. As well as some general information, it outlines legally required and recommended vaccines for different countries, reciprocal health agreements and includes an EHIC application form.

Lonely Planet's *Travel with Children* includes advice on travel health for young children. Other recommended references include

Traveller's Health by Dr Richard Dawood and *The Traveller's Good Health Guide* by Ted Lankester.

IN TRANSIT

Deep-vein thrombosis (DVT) is a blood clot that may form in the legs during flights, chiefly because of prolonged immobility. The longer the flight, the greater the risk. The chief symptom of DVT is swelling or pain of the foot, ankle, or calf, usually but not always on just one side. When a blood clot travels to the lungs, it may cause chest pain and breathing difficulties. Travellers with any of these symptoms should immediately seek medical attention.

To prevent the development of DVT on long flights, you should walk about the cabin, contract the leg muscles while sitting, drink plenty of fluids and avoid alcohol and tobacco.

IN THE CZECH & SLOVAK REPUBLICS

AVAILABILITY & COST OF HEALTH CARE

Medical care in Prague, Brno and Bratislava is generally quite good and the chances of finding an English-speaking doctor are high. Embassies, consulates and four- and five-star hotels can usually recommend doctors or clinics. (Note: few doctors outside major cities speak English.) Every sizable town has a *polyklinika* (medical centre), though few have seen many foreigners. Medical training, equipment and standards of hygiene (and funds for training doctors) are adequate for routine, walk-in problems.

Services for EU citizens with an EHIC are free, but for everybody else contract prices apply (a doctor's visit costs about €45).

Almost every town has a state-run pharmacy *(lékárna/lekáreň)*. It's a good place to buy aspirin, vitamin C and over-the-counter ointments, but you need a Slovak or Czech doctor's prescription (in the respective countries) to get anything more serious.

INFECTIOUS DISEASES
Bird Flu
Bird flu landed in the Czech and Slovak Republics in February and March 2006, respectively. In all four diagnosed cases, the dead birds carrying the virus were swans. They were found north of Bratislava and in South Bohemia. A ban on transport of poultry and free-range poultry farming has been put into effect.

To date, 100 people internationally have died from a mutation of the bird flu, the nearest being in Turkey. Doctors say that in order for the virus to be transmitted to humans, it's likely the victim would already have to have the human flu virus. Both the Czech and Slovak Republics have vaccines and emergency plans in case the danger spreads. There is no need to panic, but do use common sense – avoid poultry farms, wash your hands if you are around wild birds, and for heaven's sake, don't go near any dead swans.

Rabies
Spread through bites or licks on broken skin from an infected animal, rabies is always fatal if left untreated. Animal handlers should be vaccinated, as should those travelling to remote areas where a reliable source of postbite vaccine is not available within 24 hours. Three injections are needed over a month. If you have not been vaccinated, you will need a course of five injections starting 24 hours, or as soon as possible, after the injury. If you have been vaccinated, you will need fewer injections and have more time to seek medical help.

Tick-Borne Encephalitis
If you are going to spend any time camping or walking through the wonderful woodlands of the Czech and Slovak Republics, you should be aware of tick-borne encephalitis (TBE). This serious brain-affecting virus is mainly contracted from the bite of minute ticks that you probably won't even notice (50% of patients don't, according to the US Centers for Disease Control).

Preventative measures include covering up, tucking your pants into your socks, wearing light-coloured clothing (so you can see the ticks more clearly) and inspecting yourself for the little beggars after a walk in the forest. Vaccination is advised for anyone travelling for extended periods or camping in high-risk wooded areas. Two doses of vaccine will give a year's protection, three doses (spread out over four to 12 weeks) give up to three years' protection.

If you do find a tick, remove it with tweezers by squeezing as close to your skin as possible. Try to get it all in one swift motion, and pull straight out instead of twisting. Remove any remaining parts with a sterilised pin. Symptoms usually occur one to four weeks after a bite; those infected develop flulike symptoms that progress to meningitis or encephalitis.

Typhoid & Hepatitis A

Both typhoid and hepatitis A are spread through contaminated food (particularly shellfish) and water. Typhoid can cause septicaemia; hepatitis A causes liver inflammation and jaundice. Neither is usually fatal but recovery can be prolonged. Typhoid vaccine (Typhim Vi, Typherix) will give protection for three years. In some countries, the oral vaccine Vivotif is also available. Hepatitis A vaccine (Avaxim, VAQTA, Havrix) is given as an injection. A single dose will give protection for up to a year; a booster after a year gives 10 years' protection. Hepatitis A and typhoid vaccines can also be given together as a single-dose vaccine (Hepatyrix, Viatim).

TRAVELLER'S DIARRHOEA

To prevent diarrhoea, avoid drinking tap water unless it has been boiled, filtered or chemically disinfected (with iodine tablets), and steer clear of ice. Eat fresh fruits or vegetables only if they have been cooked or peeled; be wary of dairy products that might contain unpasteurised milk. Eat food that is hot right through and avoid buffet-style meals. If a restaurant is full of locals, the food is probably safe.

If you develop diarrhoea, be sure to drink plenty of fluids, preferably an oral rehydration solution, eg Dioralyte. A few loose stools don't require treatment, but if you have more than four or five stools a day you should start taking an antibiotic (usually a quinoline drug) and an antidiarrhoeal agent (such as loperamide). If diarrhoea is bloody, persists for more than 72 hours or is accompanied by fever, shaking, chills or severe abdominal pain, you should seek medical attention.

ENVIRONMENTAL HAZARDS
Heat Exhaustion & Heatstroke

Heat exhaustion occurs following excessive fluid loss with inadequate replacement of fluids and salt. Symptoms include headache, dizziness and tiredness. Dehydration is already happening by the time you feel thirsty – aim to drink sufficient water to produce pale, diluted urine. To treat heat exhaustion, replace fluids with water and/or fruit juice and cool the body with cold water and fans. Treat salt loss with salty fluids such as soup or Bovril, or add a little table salt to foods.

Heatstroke is much more serious, resulting in irrational and hyperactive behaviour and eventually loss of consciousness and death. Rapid cooling by spraying the body with water and fanning is ideal. Emergency fluid and electrolyte replacement by intravenous drip is recommended.

Hypothermia

Proper preparation will reduce the risks of getting hypothermia. Even on a hot day in the mountains, the weather can change rapidly. Carry waterproof garments, warm layers and inform others of your route.

Acute hypothermia follows a sudden drop of body temperature over a short time. Chronic hypothermia is caused by a gradual loss of temperature over hours.

Hypothermia starts with shivering, loss of judgment and clumsiness. If not rewarmed, the sufferer deteriorates into apathy, confusion and coma. Prevent further heat loss by seeking shelter and warm, dry clothing, drinking hot sweet drinks and sharing body warmth.

Frostbite is caused by freezing and results in subsequent damage to the body's extremities. Its effect varies according to wind chill, temperature and length of exposure. Frostbite starts as frost-nip (white numb areas of skin), from which complete recovery is expected with rewarming. As frostbite develops, the skin blisters and then becomes black. The loss of damaged tissue eventually occurs. Wearing adequate clothing, staying dry, keeping well hydrated and ensuring adequate calorie intake best prevent frostbite. Treatment involves rapid rewarming, avoiding refreezing, and rubbing the affected areas.

Insect Bites & Stings

Ticks, which are common in forests, scrublands and long grass, can carry encephalitis (see opposite).

Mosquitoes are found in most parts of Europe. They may not carry malaria but can cause irritation and infected bites. Use a DEET-based insect repellent.

Bees and wasps cause real problems only to those with a severe allergy (anaphylaxis). If you have a severe allergy to bee or wasp stings, carry an 'epipen' or similar adrenaline injection.

HEALTH

Bedbugs lead to very itchy, lumpy bites. Spraying the mattress with crawling-insect killer, after changing bedding, will get rid of them.

Scabies are tiny mites that live in the skin, particularly between the fingers. They cause an intensely itchy rash. Scabies are easily treated with lotion from a pharmacy; other members of the household also need treatment to avoid spreading scabies between asymptomatic carriers.

Snake Bites

The only poisonous snake in either republic is the *zmije* (viper), for which an antivenin is widely available. The *zmije* is unlikely to be deadly unless you are allergic to the venom. It's recognisable by a wavy black line that stretches the length of its grey back. Avoid getting bitten by wearing boots, socks and long trousers while hiking, and do not stick your hand into holes or cracks. Half of those travellers bitten by venomous snakes are not actually injected with poison (envenomed). If bitten, do not panic. Immobilise the bitten limb with a splint (eg a stick) and apply a bandage over the site with firm pressure, similar to a bandage over a sprain. Do not apply a tourniquet, or cut or suck the bite. Get the victim to medical help as soon as possible so that antivenin can be given if necessary.

Water

Tap water may not be safe to drink so it is best to use bottled water, boil water for 10 minutes, or use water purification tablets or a filter. Don't drink water from rivers or lakes as it may contain bacteria or viruses that can cause diarrhoea or vomiting.

TRAVELLING WITH CHILDREN

All travellers with children should know how to treat minor ailments and when to seek medical treatment. Make sure the children are up to date with routine vaccinations, and discuss possible travel vaccines with a physician well before departure as some vaccines are not suitable for children under a year old.

Remember to avoid contaminated food and water. If your child is vomiting or has diarrhoea, make sure you replace lost fluid and salts. It may be helpful to take rehydration powders with you for reconstituting with boiled water.

Encourage children to avoid and mistrust any dogs or other mammals because of the risk of rabies and other diseases. Any bite, scratch or lick from a warm-blooded, furry animal should be cleaned immediately and thoroughly. If there is any possibility that the animal is infected with rabies, seek immediate medical assistance.

WOMEN'S HEALTH

Emotional stress, exhaustion and travelling through different time zones can all contribute to an upset in the menstrual pattern. If using oral contraceptives, some antibiotics, diarrhoea and vomiting can stop the pill from working and lead to the risk of pregnancy – take condoms with you just in case. Time zones, gastrointestinal upsets and antibiotics do not affect injectable contraception.

Travelling during pregnancy is usually possible but there are important things to consider. Always undergo a medical check-up before planning your trip. The most risky times for travel are during the first 12 weeks of pregnancy and after 30 weeks.

SEXUAL HEALTH

The **International Planned Parent Federation** (www.ippf.org) can advise about the availability of contraception in different countries. If emergency contraception is needed in the Czech and Slovak Republics, head to the nearest hospital or health-care centre.

Condoms are readily available throughout both republics. When buying condoms, look for the European CE mark, which means they have been rigorously tested, and then keep them in a cool dry place, otherwise they may crack and perish.

Language

CONTENTS

Outside the tourist areas of Prague, Brno and Bratislava, most Czechs and Slovaks speak no English, though many older people speak German. Russian was compulsory in school under communism, so most can speak it, but prefer not to.

The Czech and Slovak languages, along with Polish and Lusatian, belong to the West Slavonic group of Indo-European languages. Czech is the mother tongue of about 10 million people; Slovak of about five million. The two languages are very closely related, and mutually understandable.

English speakers need to learn some new linguistic tricks in order to speak Czech or Slovak. The Czech tongue-twister *strč prst zkrz krk* (stick your finger through your neck) will give you an idea of what you're up against; another one is the word *řeřicha* (nasturtium).

Common Czech and Slovak terms used throughout this book are listed in the Glossary (p476). For useful Czech and Slovak words and phrases you'll need when eating out or buying food, see p72. For a more comprehensive guide to Czech, pick up a copy of Lonely Planet's *Czech Phrasebook*. Alternatively, both Czech and Slovak are covered in Lonely Planet's *Eastern Europe Phrasebook*. If you're keen on the idea of studying either language in-country, see 'Courses' (p439).

CZECH & SLOVAK PRONUNCIATION

The following table shows the symbols we've used to represent the sounds of Czech and Slovak for the pronunciation guides included in this language guide and in the Food & Drink chapter.

Vowel Sounds

Letter	Symbol	English Equivalent
á	a	father
aj	ai	aisle
é	air	hair
ó	aw	law
e/ä	e	bet
í/ý	ee	see
ej	ey	hey
i/y	i	bit
o	o	pot
ou	oh	oh
ú	oo	zoo
au	ow	how
oj	oy	toy
u	u	put
a	uh	run
ô	wo	quote

Consonant Sounds

Czech	Symbol	English Equivalent
č	ch	cheat
ch	kh	loch
ď/dž	dy	during
dz	dz	adds
ľ	ly	million
ň	ny	canyon
r	r	run (rolled in Czech)
ř	rzh	rolled r followed by zh
š	sh	shot
c	ts	hats
ť	ty	tutor
j	y	yes
ž	zh	pleasure
'		a slight y sound

Word Stress

In Czech and Slovak, stress always falls on the first syllable of a word, but it's quite light.

CZECH & SLOVAK WORDS & PHRASES

While you'll notice that many words in Czech and Slovak are pronounced and spelt the same way, in the following list of words and phrases we've included both languages; the Czech is listed first, the Slovak second. Elsewhere in this book, words separated by a slash are Czech/Slovak translations respectively; where only one word is given, it's the same in both languages.

ACCOMMODATION

Where's a ...?

Kde je ...?	gde/kdye ye ...
camping ground	
táboříště	ta-bo-rzhish-tye
táborisko	ta-bo-ris-ko
guesthouse	
penzion	pen-zi-on
penzión	pen-zi-awn
hotel	
hotel	ho-tel
youth hostel	
mládežnická ubytovna	mla-dezh-nyits-ka u-bi-tov-nuh
nocľaháreň pre mládež	nots-lyuh-ha-ren' pre mla-dyezh

Can you recommend somewhere ...?

Můžete mi doporučit něco ...?	
moo-zhe-te mi do-po-ru-chit nye-tso ...	
Môžete odporučiť niečo ...?	
mwo-zhe-tye od-po-ru-chit' ni-ye-cho ...	
cheap	
levného	lev-nair-ho
lacné	luhts-nair
good	
dobrého	dob-rair-ho
dobré	dob-rair
nearby	
nejbližšího	ney-blizh-shee-ho
nablízku	nuh-bleez-ku

I have a reservation.

| Mám rezervaci. | mam re-zer-vuh-tsi |
| Mám rezerváciu. | mam re-zer-va-tsi-yu |

Do you have a double-bed room?

| Máte pokoj s manželskou postelí? | ma-te po-koy s muhn-zhels-koh pos-te-lee |
| Máte izbu s manželskou postelou? | ma-tye iz-bu s muhn-zhels-koh pos-tye-lyoh |

Can I see it?

| Mohu se na něj podívat? | mo-hu se na nyey po-dyee-vuht |
| Môžem to vidieť? | mwo-zhem to vi-di-yet' |

Do you have a ... room?

Máte ... pokoj?	ma-te ... po-koy
Máte ... izbu?	ma-tye ... iz-bu
single	
jednolůžkový	yed-no-loozh-ko-vee
jednoposteľový	yed-no-pos-tye-lyo-vee

two-bed	
dvoulůžkový	dvoh-loozh-ko-vee
dvojposteľový	dvoy-pos-tye-lyo-voo

How much is it per ...?

Kolik to stojí ...?	ko-lik to sto-yee ...
Koľko to stojí ...?	koľ-ko to sto-yee ...
night	
na noc	nuh nots
person	
za/na osobu	zuh/nuh o-so-bu

CONVERSATION & ESSENTIALS

Hello/Hi.

| Ahoj/Čau. | uh-hoy/chow |
| Dobrý deň/Ahoj. | do-bree dyen'/uh-hoy |

Good night.

| Dobrou noc. | do-broh nots |
| Dobrú noc. | do-broo nots |

Goodbye/Bye.

| Na shledanou/Ahoj. | nuh-skhle-duh-noh/uh-hoy |
| Do videnia/Ahoj. | do vi-dye-ni-yuh/uh-hoy |

Yes.

| Ano. | uh-no |
| Áno. | a-no |

No.

| Ne. | ne |
| Nie. | ni-ye |

Please.

| Prosím. | pro-seem |

Thank you (very much).

| (Mnohokrát) Děkuji. | (mno-ho-krat) dye-ku-yi |
| Ďakujem (veľmi pekne). | dyuh-ku-yem (veľ-mi pek-nye) |

You're welcome.

| Prosím. | pro-seem |

Excuse me.

| Promiňte. | pro-min'-te |
| Prepáčte. | pre-pach-tye |

Sorry.

| Promiňte. | pro-min'-te |
| Prepáčte. | pre-pach-tye |

Mr/Mrs

| pan/paní | puhn/puh-nyee |
| pán/pani | pan/puh-nyi |

Miss

| slečna | slech-nuh |

How are you?

Jak se máte? (pol)	yuhk se ma-te
Jak se máš? (inf)	yuhk se mash
Ako sa máte? (pol)	uh-ko suh ma-tye
Ako sa máš? (inf)	uh-ko suh mash

SIGNS	
Vchod	Entrance
Východ	Exit
Otevřeno/Otvorené	Open
Zavřeno/Zatvorené	Closed
Informace/Informácie	Information
Zakázáno/Zakázané	Prohibited
Policejní Stanice/	Police Station
Policajná Stanica	
Záchody/WC/Toalety	Toilets
Páni (also **Muži** in Czech)	Men
Dámy (also **Ženy** in Czech)	Women

What's your name?

Jak se jmenujete? (pol)	yuhk se yme·nu·ye·te
Jak se jmenujete? (inf)	yuhk se yme·nu·yesh
Ako sa voláte? (pol)	uh·ko suh vo·la·tye
Ako sa voláš? (inf)	uh·ko suh vo·lash

My name is ...

Jmenuji se ...	yme·nu·yi se ...
Volám sa ...	vo·lam suh ...

I'm pleased to meet you.

Těší mě.	tye·shee mye
Teší ma.	tye·shee muh

Where are you from?

Odkud jste?	ot·kud yste
Odkiaľ ste?	od·kyuhľ stye

I'm from ...

Jsem z ...	ysem s ...
Som z ...	som z ...

DIRECTIONS

Where is ...?

Kde je ...?	gde ye .../kdye ye ...

Can you show me (on the map)?

Můžete mi to ukázat	moo·zhe·te mi to u·ka·zuht
(na mapě)?	(nuh muh·pye)
Môžete mi ukázať	mwo·zhe·tye mi u·ka·zuhť
(na mape)?	(nuh muh·pe)

What's the address?

Jaká je adresa?	yuh·ka ye uh·dre·suh
Aká je adresa?	uh·ka ye uh·dre·suh

How far is it?

Jak je to daleko?	yuhk ye to duh·le·ko
Ako je to ďaleko?	uh·ko ye to dyuh·le·ko

It's straight ahead.

Je to přímo.	ye to przhee·mo.
Je to rovno.	ye to rov·no

Turn ...

Odbočte ...	od·boch·te ...
Zabočte ...	zuh·boch·tye ...
at the corner	
za roh/na rohu	zuh rawh/nuh ro·hu

at the traffic lights

u semaforu	u se·muh·fo·ru
na svetelnej križovatke	nuh sve·tyel·ney kri·zho·vuht·ke

left/right

do leva/prava	do le·vuh/pruh·vuh
doľava/doprava	do·lyuh·vuh/do·pruh·vuh

north	sever	se·ver
south	jih/juh	yih/yooh
east	východ	vee·khod
west	západ	za·puhd

castle	hrad/zámok	hruhd/za·mok
cathedral	katedrála	kuh·te·dra·luh
museum	muzeum/múzeum	mu·ze·um
old city	staré město	stuh·rair myes·to
palace	palác	puh·lats
ruins	zříceniny/	zrzhee·tse·nyi·ni/
	zrúcaniny	zroo·tsuh·nyi·ni

HEALTH

Where's the nearest ...?

Kde je nejbližší ...?	
gde ye ney·blizh·shee ...	
Kde je najbližší/najbližšia ...? (m/f)	
kdye ye nai·blizh·shee/nai·blizh·shyuh ...	
dentist	
zubař (m)	zu·buhrzh
doctor	
lékař/doktor (m)	lair·kuhrzh/dok·tor
hospital	
nemocnice	ne·mots·nyi·tse
nemocnica (f)	ne·mots·nyi·tsuh
(night) pharmacist	
(non-stop) lékárník	(non·stop) lair·kar·nyeek
(pohotovostná) lekáreň (f)	(po·ho·to·vost·na) le·ka·ren'

I'm sick.

Jsem nemocný/nemocná. (m/f)	
ysem ne·mots·nee/ne·mots·na	
Som chorý/chorá. (m/f)	
som kho·ree/kho·ra	

I need a doctor (who speaks English).

Potřebuji (anglickomluvícího) doktora.	
pot·rzhe·bu·yi (uhn·glits·kom·lu·vee·tsee·ho) dok·to·ruh	
Potrebujem lekára, (ktorý hovorí po anglicky).	
po·tre·bu·yem le·ka·ruh (kto·ree ho·vo·ree po uhng·lits·ki)	

I have (a) ...

Mám ...	mam ...
asthma	
astma/astmu	uhst·muh/uhst·mu
diarrhoea	
průjem/hnačku	proo·yem/hnuhch·ku
fever	
horečka/horúčku	ho·rech·kuh

EMERGENCIES

Help!
Pomoc!
po·mots
Go away!
Běžte pryč!/Choďte preč!
byezh·te prich/*khod'*·tye prech
Could you help me, please?
Můžete prosím pomoci?
moo·zhe·te *pro*·seem po·mo·tsi
Môžete mi prosím pomôcť?
mwo·zhe·tye mi *pro*·seem po·mwotst'
I'm lost.
Zabloudil/Zabloudila jsem. (m/f)
zuh·bloh·dyil/zuh·bloh·dyi·luh ysem
Stratil/Stratila som sa. (m/f)
struh·tyil/struh·tyi·luh som suh

Call ... !
Zavolejte ...!   zuh·vo·ley·te ...
Zavolajte ...!   zuh·vo·lai·tye ...
  a doctor
  lékaře/lekára   lair·kuh·rzhe/le·ka·ruh
  an ambulance
  sanitku/záchranku   suh·nit·ku/zakh·ruhn·ku
  the police
  policii/políciu   po·li·tsi·yi/po·lee·tsi·yu

It hurts here.
Tady to bolí.   tuh·di to *bo*·lee
Tu ma to bolí.   tu muh to *bo*·lee
I have a headache.
Mám bolesti hlavy.   mam *bo*·les·tyi *hluh*·vi
Bolí ma hlava.   *bo*·lee muh *hluh*·vuh
I have nausea.
Mám nevolnost.   mam *ne*·vol·nost
Je mi nazvracanie.   ye mi *nuhz*·vruh·tsuh·ni·ye
I have a sore throat.
Mám bolest v krku.   mam *bo*·lest f *kr*·ku
Bolí ma hrdlo.   *bo*·lee muh *hrd*·lo

I'm allergic to ...
Jsem alergický/alergická na ... (m/f)
ysem uh·ler·gits·kee/uh·ler·gits·ka nuh ...
Som alergický/alergická na ... (m/f)
som uh·ler·gits·kee/uh·ler·gits·ka nuh ...
  antibiotics
  antibiotika/antibiotiká   uhn·ti·bi·o·ti·ka
  penicillin
  penicilin   pe·ni·tsi·lin

condoms
prezervativy   pre·zer·vuh·ti·vi
kondómy   kon·daw·mi

contraceptives
antikoncepce   uhn·ti·kon·tsep·tse
antikoncepcia   uhn·ti·kon·tsep·tsi·yuh
painkillers
prášky proti bolesti   prash·ki pro·tyi *bo*·les·tyi
analgetiká   uh·nuhl·ge·ti·ka

LANGUAGE DIFFICULTIES

Do you speak English?
Mluvíte anglicky?   mlu·vee·te uhn·glits·ki
Hovoríte po anglicky? ho·vo·ree·tye po uhng·lits·ki
Do you understand?
Rozumíte?   ro·zu·mee·te
Rozumiete?   ro·zu·mye·tye
I understand.
Rozumím.   ro·zu·meem
Rozumiem.   ro·zu·myem
I don't understand.
Nerozumím.   ne·ro·zu·meem
Nerozumiem.   nye·ro·zu·myem
How do you pronounce this?
Jak se toto vyslovuje? yuhk se *toh*·to vis·lo·vu·ye
Ako sa toto vyslovuje? uh·ko suh *to*·to *vi*·slo·vu·ye
What does ... mean?
Co znamená ...?   tso znuh·me·na ...
Čo znamená ...?   cho znuh·me·na ...

Could you please write it down?
Prosím, můžete to napsat?
pro·seem moo·zhe·te to *nuhp*·suht
Môžete prosím to napísať?
mwo·zhe·tye pro·seem to *nuh*·pee·suht'

NUMBERS

0	*nula*	nu·luh
1	*jeden* (m)	ye·den
	jedna (f)	yed·na
	jedno (n)	yed·no
2	*dva* (m)	dvuh
	dvě (Czech n/f)	dvye
	dve (Slovak n/f)	dve
3	*tři/tri*	trzhi/tri
4	*čtyři/štyri*	chti·rzhi/shti·ri
5	*pět/päť*	pyet/pet'
6	*šest/šesť*	shest/shest'
7	*sedm/sedem*	se·dm/se·dyem
8	*osm/osem*	o·sm/o·sem
9	*devět/deväť*	de·vyet/dye·vet'
10	*deset/desať*	de·set/dye·suht'
11	*jedenáct/jedenásť*	ye·de·natst/ye·de·nast'
12	*dvanáct/dvanásť*	dvuh·natst/dvuh·nast'
13	*třináct/trinásť*	trzhi·natst/tri·nast'
14	*čtrnáct/štrnásť*	chtr·natst/shtr·nast'

15	patnáct/pätnásť	puht·natst/pet·nast'
16	šestnáct/šestnásť	shest·natst/shes·nast'
17	sedmnáct/sedemnásť	se·dm·natst/se·dyem·nast'
18	osmnáct/osemnásť	o·sm·natst/o·sem·nast'
19	devatenáct/devätnásť	de·vuh·te·natst/dye·vet·nast'
20	dvacet/dvadsať	dvuh·tset/dvuh·tsuht'
21	dvacet jedna	dvuh·tset yed·nuh
	dvadsaťjeden	dvuh·tsuht'·ye·den
22	dvacet dva	dvuh·tset dvuh
	dvadsaťdva	dvuh·tsuht'·dvuh
30	třicet/tridsať	trzhi·tset/tri·tsuht'
40	čtyřicet/štyridsať	chti·rzhi·tset/shti·ri·tsuht'
50	padesát/päťdesiat	puh·de·sat/pe·dye·syuht
60	šedesát/šesťdesiat	she·de·sat/shes·dye·syuht
70	sedmdesát	se·dm·de·sat
	sedemdesiat	se·dyem·dye·syuht
80	osmdesát	o·sm·de·sat
	osemdesiat	o·sem·dye·syuht
90	devadesát	de·vuh·de·sat
	deväťdesiat	dye·ve·dye·syuht
100	sto	sto
1000	tisíc	tyi·seets

SHOPPING & SERVICES

Where's a/an/the ...?
Kde je ...?　　　　gde ye ...

ATM
bankomat　　　　buhn·ko·muht
nejaký bankomat　　nye·yuh·kee buhn·ko·muht

bank
banka　　　　buhn·kuh

city centre
centrum　　　　tsen·trum
mestské centrum　　mes·kair tsen·trum

foreign exchange office
směnárna　　　　smye·nar·nuh
nejaká zmenáreň　　nye·yuh·ka zme·na·ren'

grocery store
smíšené zboží　　　smee·she·nair zbo·zhee
potraviny　　　　po·truh·vi·ni

market
trh/(also *tržnice* in Czech)　trh/(tr·zhnyi·tse)

newsagency
tabák　　　　tuh·bak
predajňa novín　　pre·dai·nyuh no·veen

police station
policejní stanice　　po·li·tsey·nyee stuh·nyi·tse
policajná stanica　　po·li·tsai·na stuh·nyi·tsuh

post office
pošta　　　　posh·tuh

public toilet
veřejný záchod　　ve·rzhey·nee za·khod
verejný záchod　　ve·rey·nee za·khod

supermarket
samoobsluha　　suh·mo·op·slu·huh

tourist office
turistickáinformační　tu·ris·tits·ka in·for·muhch·nyee
kancelář　　　　kuhn·tse·larzh
turistická kancelária　tu·ris·tits·ka kuhn·tse·la·ri·yuh

I'd like to buy a phonecard.
Chtěl/Chtěla bych koupit telefonní kartu. (m/f)
　ktyel/khtye·luh bikh koh·pit te·le·fo·nyee kuhr·tu
Chcel/Chcela by som si kúpiť telefónnu kartu. (m/f)
　khtsel/khtse·luh bi som si koo·pit' te·le·faw·nu kuhr·tu

Where's the local Internet café?
Kde je místní internetová kavárna?
　gde ye meest·nyee in·ter·ne·to·va kuh·var·nuh
Kde je miestne internet café?
　kdye ye myes·ne in·ter·net kuh·fair

I'd like ...
Chtěl/Chtěla bych ... (m/f)
　khtyel/khtye·luh bikh ...
Chcel/Chcela by som ... (m/f)
　khtsel/khtse·luh bi som ...

　to change a travellers cheque
　proměnit cestovní šek　pro·mye·nyit tses·tov·nyee shek
　zameniť cestovný šek　zuh·me·nyit' tses·tov·nee shek
　to change money
　vyměnit peníze　　vi·mye·nyit pe·nyee·ze
　zameniť peniaze　　zuh·me·nyit' pe·ni·yuh·ze
　to check my email
　zkontrolovat můj email　skon·tro·lo·vuht mooy ee·meyl
　si skontrolovať email　si skon·tro·lo·vuht' ee·meyl
　to get internet access
　přístup na internet　przhees·tup nuh in·ter·net
　sa pripojiť na internet　suh pri·po·yit' nuh in·ter·net
　a mobile/cell phone for hire
　si půjčit mobil　　si pooy·chit mo·bil
　si prenajať mobilný　si pre·nuh·yuht' mo·bil·nee
　　telefón　　　　te·le·fawn
　a SIM card for your network
　SIM kartu pro vaší síť　sim kuhr·tu pro vuh·shee seet'
　SIM kartu pre vašu sieť　sim kuhr·tu pre vuh·shu syet'

Where can I buy ...?
Kde si mohu koupit ...?　gde si mo·hu koh·pit ...
Kde si môžem kúpiť ...?　kdye si mwo·zhem koo·pit' ...
I'm looking for ...
Hledám ...　　　　hle·dam ...
Hľadám ...　　　　hlyuh·dam ...
How much is it?
Kolik to stojí?　　ko·lik to sto·yee
Koľko to stojí?　　koľ·ko to sto·yee
Can you write down the price?
Můžete mi napsat cenu?　moo·zhe·te mi nuhp·suht tse·nu
Môžete napísať cenu?　mwo·zhe·tye nuh·pee·suht' tse·nu
That's too expensive.
To je moc drahé.　　to ye mots druh·hair
To je príliš drahé.　to ye pree·lish druh·hair

What time does it open/close?

V kolik hodin otevírají/zavírají?
f *ko*·lik *ho*·dyin *o*·te·vee·ruh·yee/*zuh*·vee·ruh·yee
O kolkej otvárajú/zatvárajú?
o *kol'*·key ot·va·ruh·yoo/*zuht*·va·ruh·yoo

Do you accept ...?

Mohu platit ...?   *mo*·hu *pluh*·tyit ...
Prijmate ...?   *pree*·muh·tye ...
  credit cards
kreditními kartami   kre·dit·nyee·mi *kuhr*·tuh·mi
kreditné karty   kre·dit·nair *kuhr*·ti
  travellers cheques
cestovními šeky   tses·tov·nyee·mi *she*·ki
cestovné šeky   tses·tov·nair *she*·ki

TIME & DATES

What time is it?

Kolik/Kolko je hodin?   ko·lik/*kol'*·ko ye *ho*·dyin
It's (one) o'clock.
Je (jedna) hodina.   ye *yed*·nuh *ho*·dyi·nuh
It's (10) o'clock.
Je (deset) hodin.   ye (*de*·set) *ho*·dyin
Sú (desat) hodiny.   soo (*dye*·suht') *ho*·dyi·ni
At what time?
V kolik hodin?   f *ko*·lik *ho*·dyin
O kolkej ...?   o *kol'*·key ...

Monday	*pondělí/pondelok*	pon·*dye*·lee/pon·*dye*·lok
Tuesday	*úterý/utorok*	oo·te·ree/u·to·rok
Wednesday	*středa/streda*	strzhe·duh/*stre*·duh
Thursday	*čtvrtek/štvrtok*	chtvr·tek/*shtvr*·tok
Friday	*pátek/piatok*	pa·tek/*pyuh*·tok
Saturday	*sobota*	*so*·bo·tuh
Sunday	*neděle/nedeľa*	ne·dye·le/*nye*·dye·lyuh

January	*leden/január*	le·den/*yuh*·nu·ar
February	*únor/február*	oo·nor/*feb*·ru·ar
March	*březen/marec*	brzhe·zen/*muh*·rets
April	*duben/apríl*	du·ben/*uhp*·reel
May	*květen/máj*	kvye·ten/mai
June	*červen/jún*	cher·ven/yoon
July	*červenec/júl*	cher·ve·nets/yool
August	*srpen/august*	sr·pen/*ow*·gust
September	*září/september*	za·rzhee/*sep*·tem·ber
October	*říjen/október*	rzhee·yen/*ok*·taw·ber
November	*listopad/november*	li·sto·puht/*no*·vem·ber
December	*prosinec/december*	pro·si·nets/*de*·tsem·ber

TRANSPORT

One ... ticket to (...), please.

... do (...), prosím.   *... do (...) pro*·seem
Jeden ... lístok do (...),   ye·den *... lees*·tok do (...)
prosím.   *pro*·seem

one-way
Jednosměrnou jízdenku   yed·no·smyer·noh *yeez*·den·ku
jednosmerný   yed·no·smer·nee
return
Zpáteční jízdenku   zpa·tech·nyee *yeez*·den·ku
spiatočný   spyuh·toch·nee

How much is it?

Kolik to stojí?   ko·lik to *sto*·yee
Kolko to stojí?   kol'·ko to *sto*·yee

How long does the trip take?

Jak dlouho trvá cesta?   yuhk *dloh*·ho *tr*·va tses·tuh
Koľko trvá cesta?   kol'·ko *tr*·va tses·tuh

Where can I find a luggage locker?

Kde mohu najít zavazadlová schránka?
gde *mo*·hu *nuh*·yeet zuh·vuh·zuhd·lo·va skhran·kuh
Chcel/Chcela by som skrinku na batožinu. (m/f)
khtsel/*khtse*·luh bi som *skrin*·ku nuh *buh*·to·zhi·nu

Is this the ... to (...)?

Jede tento/tato ... do (...)? (m/f)
ye·de *ten*·to/*tuh*·to ... do (...)
Je toto ... do (...)?
ye *to*·to ... do (...)
  bus
autobus (m)   *ow*·to·bus
  train
vlak (m)   vluhk

When's the ... bus?

V kolik jede ... autobus?   f *ko*·lik ye·de ... *ow*·to·bus
Kedy príde ... autobus?   ke·di pree·dye ... *ow*·to·bus
  first
první/prvý   prv·nyee/*pr*·vee
  last
poslední/posledný   po·sled·nyee/*po*·sled·nee
  next
příští/nasledujúci   przhe·shtyee/*nuh*·sle·du·yoo·tsi

What time does the bus/train leave?

V kolik hodin odjíždí autobus/vlak?
f *ko*·lik *ho*·dyin od·yeezh·dyee *ow*·to·bus/vluhk
O kolkej odchádza autobus/vlak?
o *kol'*·key od·kha·dzuh *ow*·to·bus/vluhk

What time does the bus/train arrive?

V kolik hodin přijíždí autobus/vlak?
f *ko*·lik *ho*·dyin przhee·yeezh·dyee *ow*·to·bus/vluhk
O kolkej prichádza autobus/vlak?
o *kol'*·key pri·kha·dzuh *ow*·to·bus/vluhk

Please tell me when we get to ...

Prosím vás řekněte mi kdy budeme v ...
pro·seem vas rzhek·nye·te mi kdi *bu*·de·me f ...
Môžete ma prosím upozorniť keď budeme na ...
mwo·zhe·tye muh pro·seem u·po·zor·nyit' ked'
bu·dye·me nuh ...

Is this taxi available?

Je tento taxík volný?
ye *ten*·to tuhk·seek *vol*·nee
Je tento taxík volný?
ye *ten*·to tuhk·seek *vol'*·nee

How much is it to ...?

Kolik stojí jízdenka do ...?
ko·lik *sto*·yee *yeez*·den·kuh do ...
Kolko to bude stáť do ...?
kol'·ko to bu·dye staťʼ do ...

Please put the meter on.

Prosím zapněte taxametr.
pro·seem *zuhp*·nye·te *tuhk*·suh·me·tr
Zapnite taxameter, prosím.
zuhp·nyi·te *tuhk*·suh·me·ter pro·seem

Please take me to (this address).

Prosím odvezte mě na (tuto adresu).
pro·seem od·ves·te mye na (*tu*·to *uh*·dre·su)
Zavezte ma (na túto adresu), prosím.
zuh·vez·tye muh (nuh *too*·to *uh*·dre·su) pro·seem

Private Transport

I'd like to hire a ...

Chtěl/Chtěla bych si půjčit ... (m/f)
khtyel/*khtye*·luh bikh si *pooy*·chit ...
Chcel/Chcela by som si prenajať ... (m/f)
khtsel/*khtse*·luh bi som si *pre*·nuh·yuhť ...

bicycle

kolo/bicykel
ko·lo/*bi*·tsi·kel

car

auto
ow·to

motorbike

motorku
mo·tor·ku

oil

olej
o·ley

petrol

benzin
ben·zin

tyre

pneumatika
pne·u·muh·ti·kuh

Is this the road to ...?

Vede tato silnice do ...?
ve·de tuh·to *sil*·ni·tse do ...
Je toto cesta na ...?
ye *to*·to tses·tuh nuh ...

I need a mechanic.

Potřebujimechanika.
pot·rzhe·bu·yi *me*·khuh·ni·kuh
Potrebujem auto-
po·tre·bu·yem ow·to·
mechanika.
me·khuh·ni·kuh

I've run out of petrol.

Došel mi benzin.
do·shel mi *ben*·zin
Minul sa mi benzín.
mi·nul suh mi *ben*·zeen

I have a flat tyre.

Mám defekt.
mam *de*·fekt
Dostal/Dostala som
dos·tuhl/*dos*·tuh·luh som
defekt. (m/f)
de·fekt

Glossary

You may encounter the following terms and abbreviations in your travels throughout the Czech and Slovak Republics. Where relevant, the Czech/Slovak terms are separated by a slash (/). See also the Language (p469) and Food & Drink (p72) chapters.

atd – etc

bankomat – ATM
Becherovka – potent herb liqueur
benzín – petrol/gasoline
bez poplatku – free of charge
bouda (s), **boudy** (pl) – mountain hut
boží muka/božie muky – wayside column or shrine

čajovna – tearoom
ČD – Czech Railways
Čedok – Czech travel agency
celnice/colnica – customs
čeština – the Czech language
chalupa/chata (s), **chaty** (pl) – mountain hut
CHKO (chráněná krajinná oblast/ chránená krajinná oblasť) – Protected Landscape Region
chrám/dóm – cathedral
cintorin (Slovak) – cemetery
čistírna/čistiareň – dry-cleaner
cizinci/cudzinci – foreigners
ČSA – Czech Airlines
ČSAD – Czech Bus Lines
ČTK – Czech Press Agency
cukrárna/cukráreň – cake shop

dámy – sign on women's toilet
dolina – valley, dale
dům kultury/dom kultúry – house of culture, for concerts and music practice
dům umění/dom umenia – house of art, for exhibitions and workshops

h. (hod) – hours
hlavní nádraží/hlavná stanica – main train station
hora – mountain
hospoda or **hostinec** – pub
hrad – castle
hřbitov (Czech) – cemetery
HZDS (Hnutie a demokratické slovensko) – Movement for Democratic Slovakia

impuls (s), **impulsů** (pl) – 'beep' or time interval used for determining telephone charges

jeskyně/jaskyňa – cave
jezero/jazero – lake
jídelní lístek/jedálny lístok – menu
jízdenka – ticket
JZD – state farm (during communist rule)

kaple/kaplnka – chapel
kavárna/kavarieň – café
Kč (koruna česká) – Czech crown
KDH (Kresťansko demokratické hnutie) – Christian Democratic Movement
kino – cinema
knihkupectví/kníhkupectvo – bookshop
koloniál – mixed-goods shop
kostel/kostol – church
koupaliště/kúpalisko – swimming pool
kreditní karta – credit card
KSČM (Komunistická strana Čech a Moravy) – Czech & Moravian Communist Party

lekárna/lekáreň – pharmacy
les – forest
lístek/lístok – ticket

maso uzeniny/mäso – meat, smoked meat and sausages
město/mesto – town
místenka/miestenka – reservation
mlékárna/mliekáreň – dairy
most – bridge
muži – sign on men's toilet

n.l (př.n.l)/n.l (pr.n.l) – AD (BC)
nábřeží (nabř)/nábrežie (nábr) – embankment
nádraží/stanica – station
nafta – diesel fuel
náměstí/námestie (nám) – square
natural – unleaded petrol/gasoline
nemocnice/nemocnica – hospital

ODS (Občanská demokratická strana) – Civic Democratic Party
OF (Občanské fórum) – Civic Forum
OSN – UN
ostrov – island
otevřeno/otvorené – open
ovoce – fruit

páni – sign on men's toilet
paragon – receipt or docket
parkovište/parkovisko – car park
pekárna/pekáreň – bakery
penzión – guesthouse
pěší zóna/pešia zona – pedestrian zone
pivnice/piváreň – (small) beer hall
pivo – beer
pivovar – brewery
platební karta/platobná karta – ATM cash card
pleso (Slovak) – mountain lake or tarn
počítač – computer
po-pa/po-pi – Monday to Friday
potok – stream
potraviny – grocery or food shop
prádelna/práčovňa – laundry
přestup/prestup – transfer or connection

radnice/radnica – town hall
řeka/rieka – river
reservovaný – reserved
rokle/roklina – gorge
Roma – a tribe of people who migrated from India to Europe in the 10th century
rybník – fish pond

SAD – Slovak Bus Lines
sady – park
samoobsluha – self-service (usually with reference to an eatery)
samoobslužná prádelna – self-service laundry
Satur – Slovak travel agency
SDĽ (Strana demokratické ľavice) – Democratic Left Party
sedlo – saddle (in mountains)
sem – pull (sign on door)
sgraffito – mural technique whereby the top layer of plaster is scraped away or incised to reveal the layer beneath
Sk (Slovenská koruna) – Slovak crown
skansen/skanzen – open-air museum of traditional architecture
slovenčina – the Slovak language
SNP (Slovenské národné povstanie) – Slovak National Uprising

so-ne – Saturday and Sunday
svatý/svätý (sv) – saint

tam – push (sign on door)
tel. č – telephone number
telecard or telefonní karta/ telefónna karta – telephone card
toalet – toilet
toaletní papír – toilet paper
tramvaj/electrička – tram
třída/trieda – avenue

ubytovna/ubytovňa – dormitory accommodation
účet volaného – collect or reverse-charges call
údolí/údolie – valley
ulice – street
uložené zásilky/poste restante – poste restante
úschovna/úschovňa – left-luggage office

V. Brit. – UK
vesnice/dedina – village
věž/veža – tower
vinárna/vináreň – wine bar
vlak – train
vrchy – hills
vstup – entrance
vstup zakázaný – no entry
výstup – exit

WC – toilet

záchod – toilet
zahrada – gardens, park
zakázán – prohibited
zámek/zámok – castle
zastávka – bus, tram or train stop
zavřeno/zatvorené – closed
zelenina – vegetables
železniční zastávka/železničná stanica – railway stop
ženy – sign on women's toilet
Zimmer frei – room free (for rent)
ŽSR (Železnica Slovenskej republiky) – Railways of the Slovak Republic

Behind the Scenes

THIS BOOK

The 1st edition of Lonely Planet's *Czech & Slovak Republics* was written by John King and Richard Nebeský. John King, Richard Nebeský and Scott McNeely updated the 2nd edition. Neil Wilson and Richard Nebeský updated the 3rd edition. Neal Bedford, Jane Rawson and Matt Warren updated the 4th edition. The 5th edition was commissioned in Lonely Planet's London office and produced by the following:

Commissioning Editor Janine Eberle
Coordinating Editor Liani Solari
Coordinating Cartographer Csanad Csutoros
Coordinating Layout Designer Carlos Solarte
Managing Editor Melanie Dankel
Managing Cartographer Mark Griffiths
Assisting Editors Stephanie Ong, Susan Paterson, Lauren Rollheiser, Simone Egger, Louise Stirling, Monique Choy, Helen Yeates, Kate Whitfield, Yvonne Byron
Assisting Cartographers Anita Banh, Barbara Benson, Joanne Luke, Valentina Kremenchutskaya
Cover Designer Karina Dea
Indexer Justin Flynn
Project Managers Craig Kilburn, John Shippick
Language Content Coordinator Quentin Frayne

Thanks to Imogen Bannister, Fiona Buchan, David Burnett, Helen Christinis, Sally Darmody, Jennifer Garrett, Mark Germanchis, Carol Jackson, Laura Jane, Rebecca Lalor, Chris Lee Ack, Chris Love, Katie Lynch, Trent Paton, Stephanie Pearson, Averil Robertson, Jessica Rose, Suzannah Shwer, Nicholas Stebbing, Glenn van der Knijff, Celia Wood

THANKS

LISA DUNFORD

Dearest Saša, what would I have done without you and the whole Petris family (Fero, Šimon, Sara, and Mum and Dad Augustin)? Thank you doesn't seem to cover it. To Magda Latalova and son Martin: you've been helping me since the day I moved to Slovakia; you're always in my thoughts. To my coauthors, Neil and Brett: it was great working with you guys; sorry I missed the beerfest in Prague. Thanks to the random strangers who tolerated my Slovak and put me on the right bus. The Lonely Planet editors – Janine Eberle and Imogen Bannister especially – provided loads of support and, as always, it's the copy editors, cartographers and imaging staff who make this all look so good; I'm grateful. Catherine, you and the kula kept me sane during write-up – thanks. Finally, Billy: you're a better travelling companion than I could have dreamed of (icau).

NEIL WILSON

Mockrat děkuji to tourist office staff in Prague and Central Bohemia, to Richard Nebeský and Tomaš Harabís for their insights into Czech society, and to coauthors Lisa and Brett. And a big thank you to Carol and Brendan for helping out with the eating, drinking and shopping research in Prague.

BRETT ATKINSON

A first round of thank-you *pivo* to my coauthors, Lisa and Neil. Your professionalism and support made my job much easier. The next round is on me, Neil – Auckland or Edinburgh? Thanks to

---

THE LONELY PLANET STORY

The story begins with a classic travel adventure: Tony and Maureen Wheeler's 1972 journey across Europe and Asia to Australia. There was no useful information about the overland trail then, so Tony and Maureen published the first Lonely Planet guidebook to meet a growing need.

From a kitchen table, Lonely Planet has grown to become the largest independent travel publisher in the world, with offices in Melbourne (Australia), Oakland (USA) and London (UK). Today Lonely Planet guidebooks cover the globe. There is an ever-growing list of books and information in a variety of media. Some things haven't changed. The main aim is still to make it possible for adventurous travellers to get out there – to explore and better understand the world.

At Lonely Planet we believe travellers can make a positive contribution to the countries they visit – if they respect their host communities and spend their money wisely. Every year 5% of company profit is donated to charities around the world.

Tomáš and Kateřina for overwhelming me with Wallachian hospitality (long may the chicken fly, and see you in Enzed, guys). In LPville, thanks to Judith Bamber and Janine Eberle for giving me this opportunity. Hi and thanks to Greg and the crew in Olomouc, to Oldřiška in Český Krumlov, and to David in Jičín. *Dobrý den* and *děkuji* to all the tourism offices around the Czech Republic that provided me with information, often meeting me halfway with the challenges of language. Back in New Zealand, thanks to Mum and Dad for their unconditional support and love, and special thanks to Carol, my partner in travel adventures and life. Long may the adventures continue...

OUR READERS

Many thanks to the travellers who used the last edition and wrote to us with helpful hints, useful advice and interesting anecdotes:

A Richard Amis, Madhu Anhes **B** Dennis Baca, Steve Balog, Andrea Barbati, Craig Battersby, Vladimir Belohlavek, Judy Benschop, Petr Bohac, Michelle Brazier, Tomas Brisuda, Patricia Broser, Anna Byk **C** Shaun Casey, Ryan Chaplin, John Chapman, Merle Cooke, Columba Cryan, Michael Cwach **D** Billy Dalto, Kate Darwent, Sharon DeQuine, Julieanne & Stephen Dimitrios, Ian Donchi, Andrew Dral, Richard Drapes **E** Catherine Eagles, Juergen Esders, Tim Eyre **F** Deirdre Feddes, Lars Floter, Philip Francis **G** Peter Garvey, Maurice George, David Gillam, Paul Gleeson, Ralf Gmell, Denise Gomez, Peter Goodson, Pauline Graafmans, Eric Grist **H** Christine Hall, Geoff Hall, G Halpin, Wendy Hamilton, Jan Haverals, Steven Herbert, Robin Hill, Pavel Hrica, Jan Hruza **I** Hiroshi Ikeda, Juliet Izatt **J** Jana Jahodarova, Laurence Jean, Alex Johnstone, Tomas Jurdak **K** Martina Kamenikova, Andrew Knight, Iris Kolkman, Jaro Kormanak, Jan Kotuc **L** Ruud Lampf, Frantisek Lengal, Angelika Lichnerova, Nicholas Little **M** John Macaulay, John Martin, Linda Martinsson, Mirek Marut, John Mason, Robert Mason, Neil & Helen Matthews, Ross McAlpine, Ellen McCutcheon, JS McLintock, Nick Miller, Paul Mollatt, Steve Moore, Rich Morgan, Don Munro, Joanne Murphy, Beth Mylius

SEND US YOUR FEEDBACK

We love to hear from travellers – your comments keep us on our toes and help make our books better. Our well-travelled team reads every word on what you loved or loathed about this book. Although we cannot reply individually to postal submissions, we always guarantee that your feedback goes straight to the appropriate authors, in time for the next edition. Each person who sends us information is thanked in the next edition – and the most useful submissions are rewarded with a free book.

To send us your updates – and find out about Lonely Planet events, newsletters and travel news – visit our award-winning website: **www.lonelyplanet.com/contact**.

Note: we may edit, reproduce and incorporate your comments in Lonely Planet products such as guidebooks, websites and digital products, so let us know if you don't want your comments reproduced or your name acknowledged. For a copy of our privacy policy visit www.lonelyplanet.com/privacy.

N Robin & Carol Nance, Emma Newton, Carrie Ng, Mic Nov **O** Roald Oosterhoff **P** Scott Parker, Mike Payne, Carl Pickerill, Karen Playfair, Frank Prins **R** Deryl Rennie, Gavin Riggs, Melanie Robertson, Achalavira Rose, Paul Rosenberg, Armin Rosencranz, Glenn Rounding **S** Olli Salonen, Michael Sankot, Nikola Sardelis, Levente Sarnoczay, Gabriele Schindl, Shareen Song, Alexey Statsenko, Reni Stoll, Bill & Ann Stoughton, John Streets, Jenna Stroud **T** Janice Tedstone, David Turner, Gillian Twigg **V** Family van de Vlag, Geert Verhoeven, Femke Vermue, Jozef Vikarsky, Kevan Vogler, Robert Vrlak **W** Richard & Sasti Watson, Peter Weller, Mavis Whitfield, Mike Whitfield, Liz Wightwick, Ruth Willmott, John Woods, Holger Wortmann, Alishia Wurgler **X** Debbie Xenophou **Y** Pete Yates **Z** Sarah Zarrow, Pavel Zvolanek.

Index

488   Index (C)

000 Map pages
000 Photograph pages

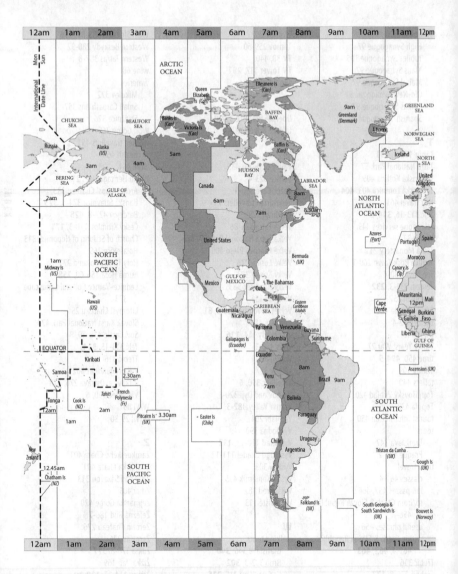

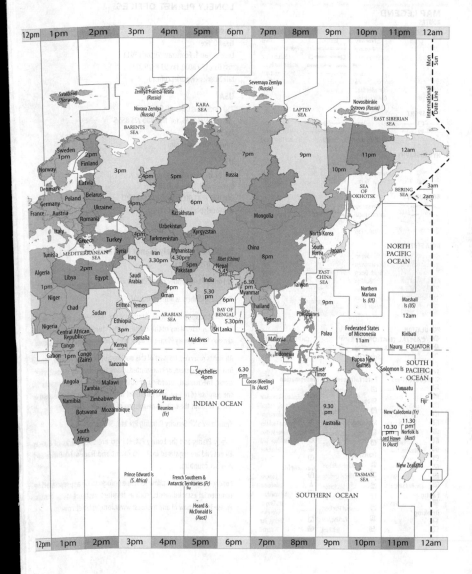

MAP LEGEND

ROUTES

Tollway	Mall/Steps
Freeway	Tunnel
Primary	Pedestrian Overpass
Secondary	Walking Tour
Tertiary	Walking Tour Detour
Lane	Walking Trail
Under Construction	Walking Path
Unsealed Road	Track
One-Way Street	

TRANSPORT

Ferry	Tram
Rail	Cable Car, Funicular
Rail (Underground)	Rail (Fast Track)

HYDROGRAPHY

River, Creek	Canal
Intermittent River	Water
Swamp	Lake (Dry)

BOUNDARIES

International	Regional, Suburb
State, Provincial	Ancient Wall
Disputed	Cliff
Marine Park	

AREA FEATURES

Airport	Land
Area of Interest	Mall
Beach, Desert	Market
Building	Park
Campus	Reservation
Cemetery, Christian	Rocks
Cemetery, Other	Sports
Forest	Urban

POPULATION

CAPITAL (NATIONAL)	CAPITAL (STATE)
Large City	Medium City
Small City	Town, Village

SYMBOLS

Sights/Activities
- Beach
- Buddhist
- Canoeing, Kayaking
- Castle, Fortress
- Christian
- Jewish
- Monument
- Museum, Gallery
- Pool
- Ruin
- Skiing
- Zoo, Bird Sanctuary

Eating
- Eating

Drinking
- Drinking
- Café

Entertainment
- Entertainment

Shopping
- Shopping

Sleeping
- Sleeping
- Camping

Transport
- Airport, Airfield
- Border Crossing
- Bus Station
- Cycling, Bicycle Path
- General Transport
- Parking Area
- Taxi Rank

Information
- Bank, ATM
- Embassy/Consulate
- Hospital, Medical
- Information
- Internet Facilities
- Police Station
- Post Office, GPO
- Telephone
- Toilets

Geographic
- Lookout
- Mountain
- National Park
- Pass, Canyon
- River Flow
- Shelter, Hut
- Waterfall

LONELY PLANET OFFICES

Australia
Head Office
Locked Bag 1, Footscray, Victoria 3011
☎ 03 8379 8000, fax 03 8379 8111
talk2us@lonelyplanet.com.au

USA
150 Linden St, Oakland, CA 94607
☎ 510 893 8555, toll free 800 275 8555
fax 510 893 8572
info@lonelyplanet.com

UK
72–82 Rosebery Ave,
Clerkenwell, London EC1R 4RW
☎ 020 7841 9000, fax 020 7841 9001
go@lonelyplanet.co.uk

Published by Lonely Planet Publications Pty Ltd
ABN 36 005 607 983

© Lonely Planet Publications Pty Ltd 2007

© photographers as indicated 2007

Cover photographs: Prague, Staromestske Namesti (street), Guido Cozzi/Atlantide. Many of the images in this guide are available for licensing from Lonely Planet Images: www.lonelyplanetimages.com.